The CASTLE DIARIES

1964–1976

The
CASTLE DIARIES
1964–1976

Barbara Castle

PAPERMAC

First published by George Weidenfeld and Nicolson Ltd as *The Castle Diaries 1974–76* in 1980 and *The Castle Diaries 1964–70* in 1984

This edition first published 1990 by
PAPERMAC
a division of Macmillan Publishers Limited
4 Little Essex Street London WC2R 3LF
and Basingstoke

Associated companies in Auckland, Delhi, Dublin, Gaborone, Hamburg, Harare, Hong Kong, Johannesburg, Kuala Lumpur, Lagos, Manzini, Melbourne, Mexico City, Nairobi, New York, Singapore and Tokyo

ISBN 0-333-49949-2

A CIP catalogue record for this book is available from the British Library

Typeset by Wyvern Typesetting Ltd, Bristol

Printed in Hong Kong

Contents

To Ted, as always

Introduction: 1964

In October 1964 I was swept into the Cabinet from the back benches as Britain's first Minister of Overseas Development. Labour had been out of office for thirteen years. The fine reforming momentum of the 1945 Labour Government had fizzled away in 1951 as the tired leaders, who had borne the brunt of the wartime coalition, ran out of ideas. The Tory governments that followed it concentrated – apparently successfully – on sweeping away controls and encouraging the short-term material satisfactions of the consumer society, which culminated in Harold Macmillan's electoral victory in 1959 on the slogan 'You've never had it so good.' The gradual post-war recovery had played into the Tories' hands, making the austerity measures of 1945–51 less necessary, so that Macmillan was able to claim that a large number of people were enjoying a new affluence with a little car in the garage and a washing machine in the kitchen. It seemed as though the Tory hold on the electorate would never be broken.

By 1963, however, the Conservative Government, too, began to run out of steam. Its consumer society had neither brought social justice nor solved Britain's basic industrial weakness, which was relentlessly revealed in our failure to export enough manufactured goods to pay our way. Macmillan's insouciance seemed increasingly inappropriate and a number of unhappy developments, including the Profumo scandal and his own illness, contributed to his downfall. His successor, Sir Alec Douglas-Home, a county landowner with no pretensions to intellectual brilliance, played into the hands of Harold Wilson who had been elected leader of the Labour Party on Hugh Gaitskell's death in 1963. Wilson, the bright grammar-school boy from a modest family who had risen to the top by his own brains, skilfully judged the uneasy national mood, deriding the Tory establishment for producing a member of the effete aristocracy as its Prime Minister. In a scintillating speech to the Labour Party conference of 1963 he interpreted socialism as the essential vehicle for exploiting the 'white-hot technological revolution' with which Britain had to come to terms. In the general election of October 1964 Douglas-Home conceded defeat and I found myself, along with a number of Wilson's former Bevanite allies, in the Cabinet.

At first I was swamped with the pressure of mastering my departmental work. Then, as the economic problems piled in on the Government, I decided in January 1965 that I must keep a detailed diary. I had kept a diary only intermittently during my parliamentary life since 1945, finding the chore of keeping up a regular account of events too demanding. But this was different. I was at the very heart of government watching the evolution of Labour policy and helping to make history. From that time onwards I kept a regular record of what happened in Cabinet and in the Labour movement, generally typing it on my little portable late at night or at weekends when my Cabinet boxes had been cleared and my husband had gone to bed.

I had at first no intention of publishing my diaries, having a vague idea that some historian might find them of value after my death. But two things changed my view. The first was Dick Crossman's bold decision to publish his Cabinet diaries for 1964–70 as soon as possible after he left office. To this end he enlisted the help of Michael Foot as his literary executor. Although Dick had always been very frank with his Cabinet colleagues about his intentions, the revelation of impending publication after the 1974 election led the Labour Government to seek an injunction in the High Court preventing it. It was left to Michael Foot to battle the case through, since Dick died in April of that year. He succeeded in beating off the injunction with the help of a remarkably liberal judgment by Lord Justice Widgery who found that publication was not against the public interest. I was initially shocked by Dick's breach of collective responsibility, of which I was a rather prim supporter, but then I discovered that his belief in open government was justified. The heavens did not fall. Cabinet colleagues were not inhibited by fear that what they said might appear in print. I began to toy with the idea that my diaries, too, might be published without political catastrophe for the Labour Party.

Indeed, my own belief was growing that secrecy is the curse of government. As I sat round the Cabinet table I often thought that people outside would be less alienated if they knew of the problems with which some twenty men and women were struggling to deal to the best of their ability. As a former socialist Prime Minister of France, Mr Mendès-France, put it, 'To govern is to choose', and there can be honest differences about the choice. If democracy is to function effectively, people must be given the facts with which to share in it. Government propaganda is no substitute.

I signed a contract with George Weidenfeld to publish my diaries, although I did not allow them to appear until after the general election of 1979. We decided to start with my second period in government (1974–76) since Dick's diaries had not covered that. This first volume appeared in 1981 and the second one, covering 1964–70, was published in 1984. This may have been confusing for some readers and I am glad that Macmillan are now making it possible to read the whole story as it unfolds, as this gives a comprehensive view of the fifteen years preceding Mrs Thatcher's victory.

To combine the two volumes in one book has inevitably meant abridging them. I am indebted to Peter James for his skilful selection of the necessary cuts, and the care that he took in ensuring that his omissions did not damage the political validity of the diaries. I have added some refinements. I am also grateful to my secretary, Joan Woodman, for her efficient typing of the Introduction, the link passage – 'The Heath Years' – and the Epilogue, which I have updated. The original volumes reproduced the diaries almost in their entirety, though some pruning of detail had to be done even so, particularly of the 1964–70 period when six years of office had to be compressed into one book – but the cuts were made with the knowledge of my publishers. As an additional guarantee that I have not falsified any of the facts I have arranged to leave the full original typescript of the diaries to Bradford University on the understanding that the public can have access to it. I chose Bradford because the city had a great influence on me in my formative years at Bradford Girls Grammar School. I am indebted to the University for making me an Honorary Doctor of Technology in 1966.

Some people objected to the publication of my diaries – as they did to Dick's – as a breach of confidence between colleagues, but as the years have passed I have become even more convinced that Dick and I were right. Society and the world economy have been changing rapidly since the Fifties and have altered the context in which socialist ideas must be expressed. An examination of what Labour tried to do in government, how far it succeeded and where it failed, is vital to the rethinking that socialist parties throughout the world are having to do. In 1959, when the Tories won power for the third time, I commented that 'only the facts can help us now'. This is even more true today.

The outlook was not propitious as Labour scraped back to power in October 1964. Two problems threatened to swamp the new Government. Peril No. 1 was the Government's minute majority. Despite the *élan* with which Harold Wilson had conducted the election campaign, outclassing a fumbling Douglas-Home, the outcome had been balanced on a knife-edge to the very end, and the result (Labour 317, Conservative 303, Liberal 9, the retiring Speaker 1) gave Labour, even with a Conservative Speaker, an overall majority of only five. From the word go the Government had to act in the knowledge that its life could be very limited.

Peril No. 2 was the balance of payments deficit, which had been mounting up under Reginald Maudling, the Conservative Chancellor, for the previous two years. Maudling was an expansionist, but his 'dash for growth' had not been accompanied by measures to strengthen Britain's industrial base. Labour had itself fought the election on expansionist policies and had talked of 'mobilizing the resources of technology under a national plan' to cure Britain's economic backwardness, but the first urgent problem it had to face was how to deal with a deficit which at nearly £800 million was twice what it had anticipated and which threatened to absorb all our reserves. The immediate decision that had to be taken, therefore, was either to devalue or to deflate. The choice was effectively made on the day after the election by three people: the Prime Minister, Jim Callaghan – the Chancellor – and George Brown – head of a new Department of Economic Affairs (DEA). While other Ministers were assiduously linking up with their Permanent Secretaries, the three met at No. 10 on Saturday, 17 October to 'open the books', and decided that a Labour government must not be associated once again with devaluation as it had been in 1949. They therefore agreed that the parity of sterling must be defended at all costs. This decision put the Government in a straitjacket for the next three years until the decision to devalue the pound by 14.3 per cent in November 1967. But even then Harold Wilson and Jim Callaghan refused to float the pound and the new parity had to be defended by the same policies.

Like other members of the Cabinet I had meekly accepted the economic propositions that were put to us at our first Cabinet: defend the pound with the help of a 15 per cent surcharge on all imports except food, tobacco and basic raw materials; subsidize exports through a tax rebate scheme; enter into consultations with unions and employers on a prices and incomes policy and 'review' public expenditure. The latter exercise was not made easier by the

Tory Government's announcement, during its last months, of a lavish five-year programme of public expenditure which its economic performance could not have sustained. It had also postponed a number of price increases in nationalized industries, notably postal charges, with which Tony Wedgwood Benn, the new Postmaster-General and not in the Cabinet, had to deal. At the same time it had launched a number of costly 'prestige projects', such as Concorde, which we were determined to review.

We were not dispirited. There seemed plenty to hearten us: Harold Wilson had created a number of new Ministries to carry out our Manifesto aims: the DEA to offset the deflationary bias of the Treasury, a Ministry of Technology to stimulate the modernization of industry; my own Ministry of Overseas Development, with the Cabinet seat as a guarantee that overseas aid was no longer to be regarded as a charitable donation from rich to poor, but as an essential motor of world development. Some appointments seemed inspired: Dick Crossman at Housing and Local Government; Frank Cousins, General Secretary of the Transport and General Workers Union (TGWU) who had been given leave of absence from the union to go to Technology; Fred Peart, a prominent anti-marketeer, at Agriculture, where he would be able to do battle against the Common Agricultural Policy of the European Economic Community (EEC). There were also some imaginative appointments among non-Cabinet Ministers, notably Jennie Lee,[1] who was put in charge of the Arts, and Hugh Foot,[2] who, as Lord Caradon, became not only Permanent Representative at the UN, but Minister of State at the Foreign Office – another break with tradition.

We were also heartened by the contents of the Queen's Speech, which embodied many of our Manifesto commitments: a new redundancy payments scheme to encourage mobility of labour in response to the new technology; the setting up of regional economic planning councils to spread industrial development more widely; an immediate increase in pensions and other benefits with the promise of a long-term review; the abolition of prescription charges; a big housing programme; the repeal of the Conservative Rent Act of 1957, which had decontrolled private rents; the setting up of a land commission to acquire land more cheaply for public purposes; leasehold enfranchisement – of particular interest to Welsh MPs; the taking of the steel industry into 'public ownership and control'; law reform and the appointment of an Ombudsman.

But it also contained one fateful phrase: 'At home my Government's first concern will be to maintain the strength of sterling.' This meant that the Government was at the mercy of financial interests. The first impact of this was felt immediately after Jim Callaghan's Budget statement on 11 November:

[1] Widow of Aneurin Bevan and a Labour MP since 1929. She was a member of the National Executive of the Labour Party. She became Parliamentary Secretary at the Ministry of Works in 1964, in charge of the Arts, and later moved to Education, where she became Minister of State in 1967. She took a life peerage in 1970.

[2] One of the four famous sons of Isaac Foot, former Liberal MP for Bodmin: Dingle, Hugh, John and Michael, of whom Dingle, Hugh and Michael joined the Labour Party. Sir Hugh had made a name for himself as a progressive colonial administrator, but Dingle, MP for Ipswich and Solicitor-General, was more instinctively radical while Michael had been a scourge of Labour governments ever since he entered the House in 1945. Having lost Devonport in 1950 he concentrated on journalism for ten years, editing *Tribune* for seven years. He had returned to the House in 1960 for Ebbw Vale, inheriting not only Aneurin Bevan's seat but his mantle of left-wing rebelliousness.

within days of his speech, sterling was under intense pressure. Yet it was certainly not a spendthrift Budget. The proposed increase in pensions and other benefits, announced for the following March, and the abolition of prescription charges were to be covered by an increase of 6*d* ($2\frac{1}{2}$ new pence) in the standard rate of income tax. Any inflationary effects of the import surcharge were to be offset by an immediate increase of 6*d* a gallon on the petrol tax. Nonetheless speculators, encouraged by the Opposition and the press, decided that the Government had been 'profligate'. Its crime was not that it was squandering money, but that it was redistributing it. Lord Cromer, Governor of the Bank of England, moved in to demand savage cuts in public expenditure, particularly in the social services. Harold Wilson has described how he refused to accept that a democratically elected government could not be allowed to carry out Labour policies. Yet the Government was forced relentlessly into deflationary policies to create 'confidence'.

Few members of the Cabinet were privy to the crucial discussions going on behind the scenes, such as the meeting of the inner cabal of Ministers at Chequers during the weekend of 21–22 November. It was at this meeting that the decision to raise the bank rate by 2 per cent was taken – a deflationary step which did nothing to staunch the outflow of sterling until Lord Cromer was prevailed upon to raise a loan of $3,000 million (£1,040 million) from the central banks to supplement the £354 million standby credit from the International Monetary Fund (IMF) that Jim Callaghan had negotiated.

It was at this meeting, too, that the main lines of our defence policy were worked out in preparation for Harold Wilson's visit to Washington. It was clear that our limited resources were seriously overstretched by the world-wide commitments that successive British governments had undertaken, notably in Europe, the Far East and the Persian Gulf. Many of us believed that, if our inflated defence budget was to be reduced, we must withdraw from some of them, but Harold Wilson, and Denis Healey at Defence, resisted this strongly, as did the Americans. In his visit to Washington Wilson developed a personal rapport with President Johnson which came to bedevil the Government's policy on Vietnam.

Two other international issues were already beginning to absorb our time. The first was Rhodesia where the Prime Minister, Ian Smith, was threatening a unilateral declaration of independence (UDI) on the basis of the country's racialist constitution, granted to the colony in 1961 against Labour opposition. Ian Smith had powerful friends among the right-wing lobby of Conservative MPs, but even Sir Alec Douglas-Home conceded that independence could only be granted on the basis of majority rule and if it was acceptable to the African majority. On taking office, Harold Wilson's immediate reaction was to try to start talks with Smith. This led to tortuous negotiations over the next five years during which he was obsessed with the need to reach a consensus with the Conservatives over Rhodesia if at all possible.

The second issue was South Africa. In opposition Labour had vehemently opposed the sale of arms to the apartheid regime and one of the Cabinet's first problems was what to do about the contracts the Conservative Government had negotiated. Since these were mainly for naval vessels Cabinet agreed that they should go ahead, though the export of sporting weapons and ammunition was immediately prohibited. The order for Buccaneer aircraft was more difficult. Eventually Cabinet agreed to permit the export of the sixteen Buccaneers already contracted for, and their spare parts, together worth £25 million to our beleaguered economy, but to refuse the further sixteen in which South Africa was interested. But there were already mutterings by some Ministers that we could not afford such expensive principles.

At the DEA George Brown was working out his planning machinery. He announced the strengthening of the National Economic Development Council (NEDC) and set up Regional Economic Planning Councils, which were, however, purely advisory. His greatest success had been to win the support of the TUC and employers' organizations for a joint Statement of Intent with the Government on prices and incomes policy. In it, management and unions pledged to support the growth of national output and to co-operate with the Government in introducing machinery 'to keep under review the general movement of prices and of money incomes of all kind'. This led to the setting up of the Prices and Incomes Board in 1965 under the chairmanship of Aubrey Jones, a former Conservative Minister.

I was busy in my Ministry taking over responsibility for the aid programme from the five Departments among which it had been distributed: the Foreign Office, the Commonwealth Relations Office, the Colonial Office, the Board of Trade and the Department of Technical Co-operation, to say nothing of the Treasury, which had always had an intrusive finger in the pie. I had informed Parliament on 10 October that I was to be responsible for aid in all its forms, capital aid as well as technical, and had enjoyed R. A. Butler's shocked reaction to my assertion that in future the purpose of our aid was not to secure political or trade advantages, but to 'maximize development'. With the help of Thomas Balogh, Fellow of Balliol and Reader in Economics at Oxford University, recruited by Harold Wilson as Economic Adviser to the Cabinet, I had built up an Economic Planning Department in the Ministry under Dudley Seers, whom I had brought over from Addis Ababa where he was serving as Director of the Economic Development Division of the United Nations Economic Commission for Africa. I had worked with Tommy Balogh on development questions when Labour was in opposition, and in office I found his advice invaluable. In my new appointments, many of which he inspired, I had many tussles with my Permanent Secretary, Andrew Cohen, who found some of them alarmingly radical but who gradually adapted himself to the new approach and served me loyally. I planned a series of visits to our overseas development offices and had already visited India and Pakistan.

In the meantime Labour MPs had become restless at the trend of the Government's economic policy. They had been alarmed by Jim Callaghan's Budget speech, praising the Victorian virtues of paying our way and not borrowing, which held out little hope of an expansionist policy. There was trouble over our administrative inability to get the pensions increase into payment before Christmas, which the introduction of a Christmas bonus did little to alleviate, and public opinion was outraged when the Government accepted the Lawrence report increasing MPs' salaries from 16 October. The contrast seemed cynical and the public was not mollified by the fact that there had been an all-party agreement before the election to accept the report or by

Cabinet's decision that Ministers would only take half of their own recommended increase and then not until April the following year. Matters were made worse by Harold Wilson's manœuvres to get two of his intended Ministers into Parliament – Patrick Gordon Walker, who had lost his seat in the General Election and whom he wanted to make Foreign Secretary, and Frank Cousins, who had never been in Parliament. Two respected Labour MPs for the relatively safe Labour seats of Leyton and Nuneaton were persuaded to go to the Lords to make way for them. The result was disastrous. After a bitter campaign and a low poll Gordon Walker lost Leyton by 205 votes. Frank Cousins did better at Nuneaton, but the Labour majority there was halved. It was against this troubled background that I decided to start keeping a diary.

1965

Tuesday, 26 January. A crucial Cabinet, the first after the Leyton by-election result. The only official item on the agenda was Sir Winston Churchill – the discussion about his funeral arrangements was soon dealt with. And then, for the first time since we became a Government, Sir Burke Trend and the other Cabinet secretaries were asked to leave the room.[1] It was a council of war. Harold was relaxed as usual, but he did suggest that we must consider our whole strategy in the light of Leyton and Nuneaton. He admitted that the results were both probably due to the mistaken attempts to impose on them Ministers who were not yet MPs: this was particularly so in the case of Leyton.

Frank Cousins opened the ensuing discussion by saying that the main problem at Nuneaton had been the delay in paying old age pensions increases compared with the immediate implementation of MPs' salaries, along with queries about the future of the aircraft industry, and the increase in mortgage rates; the latter was merely part of a widespread concern about the rise in the cost of living. He thought we had been far too high-minded as a government and it was time that we became more political. This view was echoed by a number of others. I suggested the trouble was that we had not been able to get a clear message across. What was it we were trying to say to the people? Were we offering them blood, sweat and tears? With hope for better things in, say, two years time? If this was so, this didn't tally with our policy on MPs' salaries or Cabinet ones either. You couldn't make that kind of appeal while making things much more comfortable for yourself. Alternatively, were we merely saying that things were a bit difficult but it was on the whole business as usual? On the question of the cost of living, too, our message had been confused. If our first aim was to keep down prices, how could we justify the petrol tax in the November Budget? This was a side glance at Jim Callaghan, reflecting the anxiety that a number of us felt at his decision to put a tax on petrol and thus put prices up all along the line.

In spite of this, Jim Callaghan then supported me. He said he agreed the message had been wrong but he for one was all in favour of blood, sweat and tears. George Brown jumped in at this point with a now typically pragmatic and fighting speech. He said vigorously that we had been guilty of too much morality and not enough politics. (Lord Longford nearly swooned at this. He said limply that he hoped he had misheard the First Secretary, but George waved him airily aside.) Here we were with a majority of three which could be undermined at any moment by one of our Members falling under a bus. We

[1] Sir Burke Trend, Secretary of the Cabinet, was a power behind the throne. Pleasant and unassuming he had quickly captured Harold's confidence. He was to remain Secretary till 1973, becoming a life peer in 1974.

should now conduct ourselves in every exercise as though a spring Election was inevitable.

Summing up a long discussion, Harold said that the first conclusion was that the country did not want an early Election, that we needed to be a little more political, and that as far as some of our pledges were concerned we were temporarily having to move away from them.

The meeting broke up without any demoralization and in a fighting mood ready for the next stage.

Wednesday, 27 January. Arriving home late at night I had a phone call from Wedgie who asked me in anxious tones if my phone was scrambled. When I said it wasn't we proceeded to talk in hieroglyphics. His main concern was that his proposals for increasing postal charges had suddenly been turned down and he wanted to know what the hell we were at in the Cabinet. He pointed out that he could never get the Post Office financially on its feet on a long-term basis without putting up charges, which the Tories ought to have done months ago. I indicated to him that the real question was when the next General Election would be. If it was in a matter of months, and obviously it might have to be in advance of the Budget, then we would be absolutely ridiculous to do the Tories' dirty work for them. Putting up postal charges would help them to win the Election, then they would inherit the benefit. Tony was somewhat depressed but nonetheless impressed by the argument and he said if that was the basis on which the discussion was going to take place, it ought to be made quite clear.

Thursday, 28 January. Another Cabinet meeting, this time an official one. The major item was the discussion of the long-term financial estimates. Jim Callaghan had put forward a paper outlining the basis on which we ought to proceed over the next five years from a budgetary point of view.

George Brown followed him with his usual rousing lead. 'For a Labour Government there must be a different approach on defence.' We could not, he said, refuse our people the rising standard of life they elected us to provide. He admitted that cutting hardware was very difficult politically because it meant creating redundancies in the aircraft industry. All right then, we must cut commitments and he hoped there would not be any more of this talk about a Labour Government not dodging our responsibilities 'East of Suez'. We ought to go back to square one and make a realistic review of our defence policy.

We all then took it in turns to put in our spoke for our own Departments. Dick Crossman made a big plea for housing development and I made a passionate speech rejecting the Chancellor's assumption that expenditure on overseas aid put a special burden on our balance of payments. 'You are trying to accuse me of special sin,' I said, 'You only commit budgetary sin. I am supposed to commit balance of payments sin as well.' But my economists did not accept the Treasury's estimate that 50 per cent of expenditure on aid created a burden of foreign exchange; we estimated that the figure was much lower than that and we wanted a joint exercise on this matter with the Treasury. I must say I got a more sympathetic reception than I anticipated and I was warmly supported by Tony Greenwood and by Michael Stewart. Summing up,

Harold pointed out that there could be no sacred cows in this business. We had inherited paper commitments by our predecessors which would pre-empt all the growth in the national income for the next five years. But we did not have to be committed to their priorities. These would have to be re-examined in July and everyone seemed to agree with him that it was the road programme that would have to give way to our other estimates. We all agreed that the discussion had been invaluable.

At last it was the turn of Wedgie, who had been waiting for two hours to raise with us the question of an increase in the postal charges. He had, he said, inherited a deficit. There was a slight profit on telecommunications, but the postal services were badly in the red. He wanted to increase the postage stamp to 4*d* and put up the parcel charges too. This, of course, had been agreed a short while ago. He wanted to know why there was now a reconsideration of this policy. George Brown soon made it clear again where he stood, namely that we must resist any more price increases, however rational the case that could be made for them. Why should we pull the Tories' chestnuts out of the fire for them when there might be an early General Election and all we would get for our pains would be a Tory victory with them dodging the unpopular decisions which we had taken in advance?

The Cabinet soon divided along the lines of for or against financial rectitude. Once again Jim Callaghan took a high-minded line. He reiterated all the growing burdens on the Exchequer and the need for us to take a tough line on financial policy and he was backed in this by Douglas Houghton.[1] But some of us were impatient of it by this time. I suddenly exploded by saying we were trying to do too much at once. We were trying to put all the country's finances right at a moment when we were engaged on fundamental realignments in economic and social policy. 'The Tories have got on all right without financial rectitude for fifteen years,' I declared, at which Harold buried his head in his hands in silent laughter while Wedgie Benn recoiled in horror. But I was backed up by the Chief Whip[2] who said he thought there was a death wish in the Cabinet. To increase postal charges now would be political suicide, as well as ruining the incomes policy. In the end politics won, and it was decided to postpone the increase in the letter rate, on the argument that the Postmaster-General was engaged on an efficiency audit and we ought to wait and see what the outcome of it was. By this time it was 1.30 pm. One of the longest Cabinets since the Government had been returned to power.

Tuesday, 2 February. A noisy debate on the Tory censure motion. The Tories are obviously out for blood but nonetheless both Harold and George Brown stood up to them.

[1] Labour MP for Sowerby since 1949 and an expert on pensions. As Chancellor of the Duchy of Lancaster he had been made the representative in Cabinet of the two social service Ministers, Margaret Herbison, Minister of Pensions and National Insurance, and Kenneth Robinson, Minister of Health. He was also given other trouble-shooting jobs, such as presiding over the farm price review negotiations.

[2] Edward Short, Labour MP for Newcastle-upon-Tyne Central since 1951, had been an Opposition Whip. He had been appointed Parliamentary Secretary to the Treasury with the duties of Government Chief Whip, in which capacity he attended Cabinet. In 1966 he became Postmaster-General and joined the Cabinet in 1968 as Secretary of State for Education and Science.

Earlier in the office I had the unpleasant job of telling Andrew Cohen that I wasn't prepared to send a career diplomat as aid attaché to Washington. I insisted on having an economist and wanted him to try and get Caustin. He was very sullen at this and said as he went to the door, 'I am afraid I must say I am very unhappy indeed about this decision.' I know he has been telling everyone what a joy it is to walk into the room of the Minister not knowing whether or not you were going to get your own way, but he does make it difficult when one stands up to him. The business of being boss in one's own Ministry isn't easy.

Thursday, 4 February. The *Guardian* carried a front-page story by Hella Pick deploring Harold's decision not to visit the UN after all and maintaining that this was because we were knuckling in to the Americans over Article 19.[1] She even suggested that this was the reason for our delay in holding up the announcement of our increased contribution to the Special Fund and Technical Assistance Board [TAB] of the UN. I was livid when I read it. It is now three weeks since I cabled from India that we oughtn't to hold up the announcement of our increase any longer. I told Andrew to clear it with the Treasury urgently. Yet we are still waiting. Inter-departmental haggling holds up more effective action. When I arrived in the office I sent Andrew an imperious Minute attaching the newspaper cutting and asking him to clear this increase with the Treasury today so that an announcement could be made over the weekend. He came in to see me with his usual hang-dog face and said that the Chief Secretary was still considering my figure. He doubted whether we could get an announcement out so soon. However, a few hours later I received a message that the Chief Secretary had agreed to my sum and Rednall accompanied it with a grin saying Sir Andrew asked me to say you were right once more.[2]

At the Party meeting this morning the UN point was taken up with Harold by David Kerr, the Labour MP for Wandsworth Central. Harold assured him we would take an initiative to break the deadlock as soon as it was clear that this point had been reached. Personally I think the Americans are wrong in their interpretation of Article 19 and it's a pity we haven't taken an independent initiative much earlier.

Friday, 5 February. Another Cabinet meeting. Harold had obviously been influenced by the Party meeting. He said that it had apparently not been appreciated that we have been trying to save the General Assembly. We should now urgently consider what new initiative we should take. George Brown

[1] The Soviet Union, its Eastern Bloc allies and France had been refusing to contribute to the UN's peace-keeping operations in the Congo and the Middle East which they said were illegal because they had been launched by the General Assembly and not the Security Council. The United States was insisting that under Article 19 of the charter those members who were in arrears had forfeited their voting rights and had said it would withhold its own support from certain UN agencies. The UN, therefore, was in both a financial crisis and a constitutional one. It was to be saved from collapse by the launching in June of a voluntary fund to which Britain contributed $10 million in addition to the earlier increases in her donations to the Special Fund and technical assistance programme. In August the United States was to climb down on the constitutional point and abandon its insistence on the application of Article 19.

[2] John Rednall, my Principal Private Secretary.

reported on the progress of his prices and incomes machinery.[1] He pointed out that it had taken the Swedes twenty years to get their machinery accepted.

Over the weekend the Party's morale was lifted by the by-election results, particularly Salisbury which had a 1 per cent swing to us.[2] Clearly, Leyton was not representative, but the serious Sundays were full of criticisms that the Government was beginning to waddle almost as much as the Tories had. Tony Howard let go on this theme in the *Sunday Times*.

Thursday, 11 February. Harold opened Cabinet by referring to Vietnam. He said he had just had two hours' talk with the President of the United States and he had explained our attitude to him. We stand ready to take action for a settlement at any time action is appropriate. But for any of us to take overt action at this stage would just be to secure the reverse of what we wanted to achieve. There might come a time when the Americans would welcome an initiative from us but that was not yet.

The next item was a request by Dick Crossman for permission to increase this year's housing programme by 12,000 houses from last year's out-turn of 144,000 in the public sector, on condition that all the additional 12,000 houses were built by industrialized methods. Jim Callaghan responded vigorously. He pointed out that one after another members of the Cabinet were coming along demanding increases in social services on the grounds that they otherwise would not do any better than the Tories had done: 'It is no use my colleagues complaining that I am only allowing them to do as much as the Tories were going to do because the Tories never had any intention of carrying their programmes out,' he maintained. He added, 'If you are going on like that, we are sliding into catastrophe.' Every item of additional social service expenditure was noted by the bankers who had lent us money. They did not hesitate to write in to him. The governor of one Commonwealth bank had done so when we announced that local authorities would be able to borrow from the Public Works Loans Board instead of at the higher market rate.

To this Harold Wilson retorted mildly that we must not give the impression that we could not have a Labour Government in this country and that the last Election was a farce.

At a quarter to one we turned exhausted to the proofs of the Defence White Paper. I hadn't even read it. Frank Cousins was the only one who raised a murmur. He protested that he had received his documents last night and had not had adequate time to study such a detailed defence policy. Harold

[1] George Brown had lost no time in following up the Statement of Intent and had won the support of both employers and unions to the setting up of a National Board for Prices and Incomes, colloquially known as the PIB. On 11 February he was to publish the agreed details in a White Paper, 'Machinery of Prices and Incomes Policy' (Cmnd 2577). The NEDC, a tripartite body on which management and unions sat with the Government, was to keep under review the general movement of prices and 'money incomes of all kinds', while the PIB was to investigate particular cases of price and income behaviour and recommend changes in pay structures where necessary. It was to consist of an independent chairman, a number of independent members, a businessman and a trade unionist. Co-operation with its investigations and findings was to be voluntary, but the White Paper added in paragraph 18 that the Government might reluctantly have to resort to 'other methods' if the voluntary method failed.

[2] Three by-elections had taken place on 4 February in the Conservative-held constituencies of Altrincham and Sale, East Grinstead, and Salisbury. In each case the Conservative majority was reduced and in Salisbury Labour's proportion of the poll increased by 3 per cent while the Conservatives' proportion fell by 0.1 per cent.

apologized for this. He said the White Paper was only an interim statement. A review of all our commitments was now going on on a very thorough basis. In defence of his document, Denis Healey pointed out that the policy showed a cut of £55m on the detailed programme which had been put in front of him when he became a Minister. For the first time in many years, the increase in the defence budget was smaller than the increase in the Gross National Product [GNP].

Friday, 12 February. David Ennals[1] talked to me about the back-bench anxieties on foreign policy.[2] He said he had not signed the Motion on Vietnam but was taking a deputation to the Prime Minister to ask for a British initiative.

Monday, 15 February. The newspapers were full of a speech by Lord Cromer, giving a warning about the increase in public expenditure. This was being taken as proof of a battle raging between Jim Callaghan and George Brown on deflation versus expansion. I saw J. Callaghan in the cafeteria at lunch and asked him what he proposed to do about it. He merely grinned and didn't look too displeased at Lord Cromer's effort. This seemed to confirm press suggestions that Cromer was acting as Jim's mouthpiece. However, he did add that he must seek the right moment to deal with Cromer and it hadn't arrived yet.

Later I ran into Bill Grieg, formerly of the *Daily Mirror*, now PRO to George Brown. He said he was enjoying life but how different things looked when one was 'on the other side'! I said I thought George was doing a grand job and he agreed, but said he was worried about his health: 'He is so tense all the time. He is working himself to death. He gets up at 6 am and is in his office by eight. He stays there till 8 pm and then takes a couple of Cabinet boxes home with him. In a taxi the other day *en route* to the TV studios he was in a terrible state. I didn't think he was going to be able to go through with it. He did of course, but he is under a terrible strain.' Another thing which had shaken him was his discovery of the great power of the civil service. He, too, has discovered that a minister may give instructions but there is no guarantee that they will not get lost in the wash.

Sunday, 21 February. Dinner at Michael Foot's for an informal discussion of general strategy. Dick Crossman complained that we never got a chance to think of wider issues. Nonetheless, he was himself rather irritable and preoccupied and slipped away early. Frank Cousins reduced me and the rest of us to despair by his muddle-headedness. He would keep mixing up the words deflation and devaluation. Mike Foot was magnificent and backed me up in my statement that we must be prepared to face the political consequences of defying the bankers and risking a run on the pound. On the whole we agreed that it was better to reject the deflationary Budget and risk devaluation if necessary. We were also strengthened in the belief that we must ask for an

[1] MP for Dover, whom I had appointed my Parliamentary Private Secretary.

[2] Forty-seven Labour MPs, headed by Sydney Silverman, left-wing MP for Nelson and Colne, had signed an Early Day Motion calling on the Government to take the initiative to bring about a cease-fire and political settlement in Vietnam.

earlier control of the Budget proposals instead of these being produced to the Cabinet on the eve of Budget Day.

Monday, 22 February. Our first opportunity came at the Cabinet the next day. Harold opened with a solemn statement about Tony Howard's article in the *Sunday Times*.[1] He said the paper had thrown down a challenge to the Government by the creation of a Whitehall correspondent. 'We can't recognize any such Whitehall animal. I have instructed Ministers not to see this journalist. In spite of this two Ministers at least did. In the last resort this attempt to identify the attitude of civil servants is bound to be damaging to the Government. We shall be plunged right into the middle of the American system. I am asking every Minister to instruct their civil servants that they are not to give this man any facilities they do not give to every other journalist. This is a very dangerous man doing a very dangerous job.' This discussion gave me the opportunity to ask whether we should be given the chance to discuss our general budget strategy before the Chancellor brought his actual Budget proposals before us on the eve of Budget Day. Dick Crossman backed me up and said that it was very confusing to read the press reports. It made some of us feel there were a lot of discussions going on which we knew nothing about. After hedging a bit, Harold said that no doubt the Chancellor had noted what we said. This new joint initiative by Dick and me was one useful outcome of Sunday night's discussion.

Thursday, 25 February. At the Cabinet, Michael Stewart surprised us by saying that on 20 February he had made an approach to the Russians as co-chairman of the Geneva conference suggesting that we and they should start probing the attitude of the other countries concerned to see if there was a possible basis for a calling of a successful conference. So far there had been no reply and, if the Russians did not answer soon, we might have to consider announcing publicly an independent initiative. He told us that he had done this with the knowledge and approval of the Americans. Harold agreed we could not remain silent much longer. So it looks as though back-bench pressure has had its effect.

The main item was Dick Crossman's request to be allowed to build 12,000 houses more this year by industrial systems. Various people examined what effect Dick's proposals would have on our general resources. The discussion went on and on for an hour and a half, with one speaker after another repeating the arguments. I groaned to Tony Crosland[2] that this was the most talkative

[1] Appointed by the *Sunday Times* to be a new type of journalistic animal – a Whitehall correspondent who would reveal the inner battles in the Labour Government, not only between individual Ministers but between individual civil servants – Anthony Howard had been working hard to justify his assignment. His latest article, 'A clash has been arranged', purported to reveal the struggle for power at both ministerial and official level between the Treasury and the new DEA. The 'Whitehall correspondent' did not survive very long.

[2] Tony Crosland, Labour MP since 1950, for South Gloucestershire and later for Grimsby, had been appointed Minister of State for Economic Affairs on the formation of the Government, but had been quickly promoted in January 1965 to become Secretary of State for Education and Science in the Cabinet. With a brilliant academic mind, he had made a big impact on middle-of-the-road Labour opinion with his book, *The Future of Socialism*, published in 1956. Though I liked and admired him, I was critical of his failure to carry analysis into action, and we often sparred in Cabinet.

Cabinet in political history. And he said he agreed. He had never expected that the Cabinet would be like this. Finally, Harold brought it to a head by saying that we had to take a basic decision of principle. So we agreed to let Dick go ahead and sent him and the Chancellor away to work out a licensing policy.

Thursday, 4 March. Before Cabinet I had a word with Michael Stewart about the story on which the *Sun* had led this morning saying that Wilson was backing the American raids on North Vietnam. Michael said it was completely untrue. When I told him that the writer had got it from a Foreign Office briefing he said he would look into it. In Cabinet he said there had been no progress over Vietnam as we had received no reply from the Russians to our overture of 20 February.

The other items on the agenda had at first sight appeared trivial but we managed to spend three-quarters of an hour discussing the creation of new premises at Chelsea for the National Army Museum. I doodled through the endless discussion. Tony Crosland complained to me, 'There are twenty Ministers debating this. If only there had been as much heat generated over Vietnam.' I retorted acidly, 'The Parkinson's Law of words operates in this Cabinet. Words expand to fill the time available for them. The length of these Cabinet meetings is purely dictated by the PM's engagements.' He grinned agreement.

Friday, 5 March. At the Overseas Policy Committee Arthur Bottomley and Gerald Gardiner reported on their visit to Rhodesia.[1] They were very gloomy about the future.

After the meeting, Harold kept some of us back to discuss the message he had from Kenneth Kaunda urging us to do everything possible to support Julius Nyerere. He wanted us to examine again the question of aid for the Tanzania/Zambia railway and Harold asked me to have another look at this.[2] I told him my experts had already evaluated it and decided it was not an economic proposition. But Harold insisted that political considerations should now dominate, particularly in view of the possibility of UDI. I suggested I might go and have a look on the spot in Tanzania to see whether there were other ways in which more effective help might be given, and Harold thought this was a good idea.

Thursday, 11 March. At Cabinet Michael Stewart's report on the overseas situation was more perfunctory than ever. On Vietnam, he had nothing to say and I was in despair till Harold took up the theme himself. He repeated that this was not a propitious moment for an initiative. There had been no reply from

[1] As part of his unremitting efforts to avoid a Unilateral Declaration of Independence by Ian Smith, Harold Wilson had sent Arthur Bottomley, Secretary of State for Commonwealth Relations, and Gerald Gardiner, the Lord Chancellor, to Rhodesia to sound out the mood of the Smith regime. Arthur Bottomley was to share my increasing disquiet at Harold Wilson's obsession with the need to placate Smith.

[2] Dr Julius Nyerere, President of Tanzania, and Dr Kenneth Kaunda, President of Zambia, were determined to build a 1,320 mile-long railway from the copperbelt in Zambia to the Tanzanian coast in order to make Zambia independent of the Rhodesian railway system in her copper exports. My experts advised that the scheme could not be considered a top development priority, but we had offered to contribute to a survey of its feasibility. The railway was later built with Chinese help.

the Russians to our overtures but he hoped they would get more out of Gromyko[1] during his visit next week.

Tuesday, 16 March. Lunch with Dingle Foot: he told me hair-raising news about South Africa. His brother Hugh had been called to a Cabinet meeting on Friday last to discuss the fact that the Afro-Asians were going to call for a Security Council endorsement of sanctions against SA. Apparently, the committee decided we should have to veto this, the first time we shall have ever used our veto and on SA too! Hugh apparently was pretty upset. I agreed with Dingle that this would be disastrous and promised to raise it in Cabinet.

Thursday, 18 March. I went along to the Cabinet determined to have a showdown about one or two things. To begin with, I wanted to ask when we were going to have the special discussion on the economic decisions which would govern the Budget. I had had a word with Harold about this when he gave us a birthday drink after Cabinet last week. I reminded him of the promise he had made to me and Dick and asked whether I should put the item down on the agenda. 'No,' he said, 'leave it to me.' He said that 'discussions among one or two of us are going very well. We shall have to have surtax increases but no great deflationary moves.' He promised a report to Cabinet. I noted his admission of the existence of the inner Cabinet. But there is still no sign of his report. I also wanted to have a showdown on a whole range of foreign policy.

Before leaving home I phoned Dingle to say I couldn't find anything among my Cabinet committee papers about Hugh's summons on South Africa. How then could I raise it in Cabinet? I didn't want to get Hugh into trouble. Dingle suggested I had a word with Michael Stewart first and he didn't mind my saying I had learned about it from him. However, traffic was bad and I only arrived as the Cabinet was starting. Giving his usual weekly report, Michael had already opened on Vietnam. Talks with Gromyko had shown that the Russians were prepared to issue a joint statement but only one entirely denunciatory of the United States for helping the aggressors. Michael said he would be seeing the US Secretary of State Dean Rusk in the US next week and would discuss with him the next move we might make. Harold said he thought that the States would now be willing for us to take a unilateral initiative. Once again, it had all got to be left to him and Michael. I chipped in to ask whether we could not have a special meeting of the Cabinet to discuss the whole position of our foreign policy. Every day we read accounts in the press of this or that development in our policy of which most of us in the Cabinet knew nothing. Was it true, for instance, that we were now making overtures to the Common Market Six? Most of us simply did not know. Harold agreed immediately. He had been thinking for a long time that we ought to have a long discussion in Cabinet on foreign affairs but it would have to be after Michael's visit to Washington on

[1] Andrei Gromyko, Foreign Minister of the Soviet Union, was jointly responsible with the British Foreign Secretary for monitoring the Geneva Agreement on Vietnam reached at the Geneva Conference of 1954 which had ended the war between France and the Viet Minh. The conference, of which the British and Soviet Foreign Ministers were co-chairmen, had led to the partitioning of Vietnam between North and South and the setting-up of an International Control Commission to police the cease-fire. It was a prime aim of Harold Wilson's policy on Vietnam to get the Geneva Conference recalled so that Britain and the Soviet Union could mediate in the conflict between North and South.

Sunday. Nobody backed me up from the left wing, though Fred Peart and others murmured noises of approval.

We then moved on to iron and steel nationalization. Harold asked the civil servants to leave so we could have a political discussion first. He said we ought to face certain facts. There was some evidence of a growing view in the Party that we ought not to risk a defeat on steel. Mannie Shinwell had been to see him to convey some of these views.[1] Personally, Harold believed that, if we once started giving in to pressure groups, our authority as a Government was finished. To be truthful, the country was not very excited about steel, but it was in the programme and whatever the risks we should go through with it. The problem was one of parliamentary time because we faced a long Finance Bill. His suggestion was therefore that we should issue a White Paper at Easter stating categorically our intention to nationalize steel this session. If we were defeated on the White Paper we need not resign but could go to the Commons on a vote of confidence the next day and thereafter review the situation: either an early election or drop steel. If, however, we were not defeated we would know we could force people to show their hands and could go forward to introduce the Bill in the summer. We could carry it through this session if we were prepared to sit possibly as late as December. Everyone thought this idea was very ingenious. There was also unanimity that we could not drop steel. George Brown said that we had no dignity as a Government if we did. Callaghan said, 'As my Cabinet colleagues know, I am passionately in favour of the Steel Bill, but I must warn them that the Finance Bill will be a long one.' I warned that, if we were not careful, the idea would get abroad that the White Paper was just a device and it would not be taken as fatal if we were defeated. This might give our Woodrow Wyatts and Desmond Donnellys the chance to have the best of both worlds.[2] The others agreed this was a danger and Harold said he would stress that we would take the White Paper vote as one of confidence.

Monday, 22 March. I went along to the Cabinet offices at ten o'clock for a meeting of the Home Policy Sub-Committee of the Cabinet. The purpose was to examine a paper by the Minister of Transport on the extension of the powers of British Railways to manufacture different items in railway workshops. I was interested because of the Prime Minister's proposal that we should examine the use of surplus capacity in railway workshops for the aid programme. Tom Fraser's paper was completely negative. He argued that the railway workshops could only manufacture the old-type steam locomotives and not the modern diesels or electrified equipment. George Brown weighed in to express his astonishment. The people in Derby, he said, expected the restrictions on the nationalized industries to be removed. Everybody backed George up. Frank Cousins protested that the Tory Minister of Transport had used almost the

[1] Emmanuel Shinwell, MP for Easington, was Chairman of the Parliamentary Labour Party from October 1964 until his resignation in 1967. He had held various posts in previous Labour Governments, notably as Minister of Fuel (1945–47) and Minister of Defence (1950–51).

[2] Woodrow Wyatt and Desmond Donnelly were Labour MPs who, starting on the Left, had moved steadily to the Right and were opposing our plans for the outright nationalization of the major companies in the steel industry. Wyatt was to press proposals for more limited public ownership. See footnote to page 17.

same words when the transport unions had protested against the restrictions placed by the Tory Government on the manufacturing capacity of nationalized industries. He argued that the workshops had been well fitted to join in the diesel field if they had only been allowed to do so. I agreed but said the argument was whether we should go in for the modernization of the workshops in a big way. The National Coal Board had all the freedom and facilities it required to go into ancillary manufacture but hadn't done so. A Labour Government must make up its mind whether it wanted to encourage the nationalized industries to expand their activities. Fraser was completely outnumbered and it was agreed that we should announce immediately our intention to introduce legislation in due course to remove the restrictions from the nationalized industries. I must say, Tom Fraser, like many another Minister, has been only too ready to accept the inherited arguments of the civil service. Once again, George Brown has shown great political vigour, which would surprise the left wing.

Wednesday, 24 March. There was a very small attendance on the political side at the National Executive Committee [NEC]. Neither Harold Wilson nor George Brown were there. Under any other business, Johnnie Boyd[1] raised the appointment of Aubrey Jones. He said it had caused a good deal of anxiety and would be attacked at union conferences. He was sorry George Brown wasn't there to give them an explanation. Danny McGarvey backed him up. Bill Simpson said he was not against the national incomes policy but he would have liked more explanation of what was going on. Walter Padley and Ray Gunter made soothing noises in reply and said that George would be asked specially to be present next time to deal with it.

Thursday, 25 March. Cabinet: Harold welcomed Michael Stewart back from Washington with the remark that he had had an extremely successful mission in very difficult circumstances. On the face of it, none of us could see much success, but I was relieved when Michael proceeded to spell out a coherent policy on Vietnam, even if one did not agree with it. He said he was satisfied that the sole object of the US was to stop infiltration from North Vietnam. He

[1] John Boyd of the Amalgamated Engineering Union was one of the twelve members of the trade union section of the Labour Party National Executive Committee. The other members were Frank Donlon of the National Union of Railwaymen [NUR], Joe Gormley of the Mineworkers [NUM], Albert Hilton of the Agricultural Workers [NUAW], Jack Jones of the TGWU, Danny McGarvey of the Boilermakers, Wesley Perrins of the General and Municipal Workers [NUGMW], Bill Simpson of the Foundry Workers, and Stan Taylor of the Woodworkers [ASW]; Ray Gunter of the Transport Salaried Staffs Association was current chairman of the Party, and Walter Padley of the Shopworkers [USDAW] vice-chairman. Dai Davies of the Iron and Steel Workers [BISARTA] was acting treasurer. The constituency parties were represented by seven members, currently, in order of votes, Tony Wedgwood Benn, Jim Callaghan, myself, Dick Crossman, Tom Driberg, Tony Greenwood and Ian Mikardo. In addition there were five women members elected by the whole Party conference and therefore largely by trade union votes. They were Alice Bacon, Bessie Braddock, Peggy Herbison, Jennie Lee, and Eirene White, all MPs, as were the members of the constituency section. The elections took place annually at Party conference, and there were great manœuvrings for votes. Finally, Arthur Skeffington (junior Minister at the Ministry for Land and Natural Resources) represented the Socialist, Co-operative and Professional Organizations, while Harold Wilson and George Brown were members *ex-officio* as Leader and Deputy Leader of the Parliamentary Party.

had repudiated Maxwell Taylor's statement about escalation and found that it had been quoted out of context.[1]

Harold followed this up by saying the situation had improved during the past week. The talks with Gromyko had been abortive. Gromyko maintained that America must cease its aggression as a pre-condition of talks. America insisted that North Vietnam must ditto. We had suggested to the Russians that these two conditions cancelled each other out, but Gromyko would have none of this so there would be no initiative from the Russians. This meant 'we are the only people working for peace'. The Foreign Secretary's rebuke about the gas with his reference to the declaration of independence had been very firm.

We then passed on to George Brown's White Paper on national incomes and prices policy.[2] George emphasized that the aim was not only to restrain. One of the prime purposes was to identify the small people who lacked bargaining power and see that they got some priority. He admitted there were thorny problems to be settled long-term. In the meantime, the incomes policy was a starting-point.

Monday, 29 March. Meeting of the Economic Policy Committee of the Cabinet [EPC] to discuss Douglas Jay's[3] proposal that we should except certain imports from developing countries from the imports surcharge. Of course I backed him up enthusiastically. In the end, Douglas and I were massively beaten down. After the meeting I had a quick word with Tony and Arthur about South Africa and asked them to support my suggestion that we should under no circumstances use our veto in the Security Council on this issue. They agreed. They both derided the idea that Caradon was against our using the veto and insisted that he himself had suggested it was unavoidable. I am not surprised.

[1] On 22 March General Maxwell Taylor, US ambassador in Saigon, had alarmed critics of American policy in Vietnam by declaring in an interview with *La Stampa* that 'there are no limits set to the escalation' of the war. Alarm was heightened by the fact that the US had been intensifying its air attacks on North Vietnam and that General Taylor and the Chiefs of Staff were pressing for the despatch of a US expeditionary force. Opposition to American involvement was growing, not only in the Labour Party but among Democratic members of Congress, who were shocked by the Defence Department's admission that the US was using napalm bombs and 'a type of tear gas' against civilians in Vietnam. A Motion calling on the Labour Government to 'dissociate Great Britain from these actions and views', was tabled in the House of Commons and signed by 100 Labour and Liberal Members.

[2] George Brown had successfully completed the third stage of his voluntary policy by agreeing with employers and unions the criteria which should govern increases in prices and incomes. These were published on 8 April in a White Paper, 'Prices and Incomes Policy' (Cmnd 2639). Assuming an average annual growth in output of 3½ per cent per head in the period up to 1970 the White Paper set a 'norm' for increases in income of 3–3½ per cent while insisting that 'price increases should be avoided where possible' and 'prices should be reduced where circumstances permit'. Some exceptions to these rules were to be allowed, but on the incomes side two situations warranting exceptional treatment were set out in terms that were to cause fierce arguments in particular cases: 1) 'general recognition that existing wage and salary levels are too low to maintain a reasonable standard of living' and 2) 'widespread recognition that the pay of a certain group of workers has fallen seriously out of line'. The White Paper also provided that excessive increases in profits or in the charges made by the self-employed could be referred to the PIB under the prices provisions. On 30 April the General Council of the TUC reported back to a conference of trade union executives on what it had agreed and the report was adopted by 6,649,000 votes to 1,811,000. One of the delegates speaking against the policy was Jim Mortimer of the Draughtsmen's and Allied Technicians Association [DATA].

[3] Labour MP for North Battersea since 1946 and President of the Board of Trade. Though instinctively right-wing on most issues, he became an ally of the Left in his passionate opposition to Britain's entry into the EEC.

Lunch in the cafeteria at the House. Frank Cousins came over to me looking very depressed. He said he was beginning to think that it was time he said goodbye to the Cabinet. Too many matters were being decided by a little inner clique. Why on earth did Harold insist on surrounding himself by right-wingers at the key points? I told him that our chance would come tomorrow to raise all our anxieties about foreign policy. We had no right to complain about Harold unless we insisted on our own rights as members of the Cabinet. He shrugged this off and I felt again the danger of his tendency to be negative. He wandered off rather disconsolately with the final note that we oughtn't to have to press for these things. 'If we're not in the centre of this Government, there is no point in our being in it at all.'

Tuesday, 30 March. Despite a streaming cold, I had to turn up to the long-awaited special Cabinet meeting on foreign policy which I had requested. Frank jumped in to ask if we could deal with Vietnam first. Michael went over the old ground. What our own supporters really wanted was for us to try and get a settlement. The Communists insisted that the basis for this was that America should withdraw completely from South Vietnam but he did not think that the great bulk of our supporters wanted an unconditional withdrawal of this kind. I asked what was our long-term policy. Could there be stability as long as Vietnam was divided? Unless Vietnam was unified would not the Americans have to occupy South Vietnam indefinitely? Did it necessarily follow that Ho Chi Minh was a Communist stooge? To this Harold replied that we could not decide on the long-term solution at this stage. The first thing was to get talks started. The trouble was that no one had got a line out to Hanoi. That was why he was sending Patrick Gordon Walker on his tour.

No one else contributed anything so we passed on to the Atlantic Nuclear Force. Here again, Michael's paper would have gone through uncontested but I insisted on raising some points. Was it not a fact that our policy was based on two aims: first, to get rid of our independent nuclear deterrent, and secondly to stop the proliferation of nuclear weapons in a way which would not alienate the Russians? Was it not a fact that Gromyko had turned down the ANF? Michael agreed this was so but insisted that he might change. Harold maintained that by our proposals the Russians would get much more than through the MLF because one of our conditions was that the Germans would be prevented from acquiring nuclear weapons, whereas the treaty only prohibited them from manufacturing them. Since no one else chipped in, we moved on to the paper on the Middle East.

Here, at last, Tony Greenwood piped up. He said that he hoped we did not visualize any permanent retention of the Aden base as this was linked up with his political negotiations. This let loose a flood of comment.

Harold promised that we would continue the discussion at another Cabinet. I hope so because we never reached Southern Africa.

After Questions on the bench Harold beckoned me to his side and said he was sorry he had not kept his promise to hold a special meeting on the economic basis of the Budget, but in fact the discussions had been going very well. It won't be too bad a Budget, he said. They were all agreed except for Nicky

Kaldor, who had issued an ultimatum calling for more deflation.[1] He quoted Tommy approvingly: 'The trouble with Nicky is that he is a theoretical economist.'

Monday, 5 April. A pre-Budget Cabinet meeting to hear what Jim had in store for us.[2] On the whole his proposals were well received.

Tuesday, 13 April. Cabinet: better news about Vietnam. The Russians had proposed that we should join with them in initiating a conference on Cambodia. Michael thought we should respond to this but Harold should discuss it first during his visit to the US.

Had to go over to No. 10 for a late meeting of Overseas and Defence Policy [OPD] Committee before Harold's departure for Washington. I was called in for Item 2 on the Mekong River.[3] Since George was late, Harold decided to call this first, but as soon as I got into the room George arrived so we switched back to Item 1. This meant I was trapped for one and half hours while George conducted a one-man filibuster against Healey's proposals to call up 175 Ever Readies to fill deficiencies in our Aden complement.[4] George was in a strange state – I wouldn't have said intoxicated (though Ted told me he was roaring tight in the House later that night) so much as auto-intoxicated. He got himself into a fine state saying he thought it was incredible we should consider calling up reserves for anything but an emergency, which this clearly was not. Tony supported him in his usual tentative way. I didn't like this first small re-introduction of conscription myself, but couldn't say anything because this wasn't my item. Harold doggedly backed Healey up, but George went on and on, even wildly hinting he might have to resign. Eventually Harold's patience wore him down to grumbling defeat. We then disposed of the Mekong River project in a couple of minutes. I had a brief on the economic implications of our participation, but Harold wasn't interested. He just wanted to 'respond' to Johnson's initiative.

[1] Nicholas Kaldor, Fellow of King's College, Cambridge and Reader in Economics (later Professor of Economics) at the University, had been brought into the Treasury as Special Advisor to the Chancellor. He became particularly famous – or infamous – as the author of the Selective Employment Tax [SET] which Jim Callaghan introduced in his Budget of May 1966. Designed to squeeze labour out of the service industries and into manufacturing SET was a tax on employment accompanied by a rebate, or 'premium', for manufacturing employers, but not for service ones. It was highly unpopular. With Kaldor's fellow Hungarian economist, Thomas Balogh, installed in No. 10, the press made great play with the influence of the 'terrible twins' on the Government.

[2] His Budget had two main aims: strengthening the balance of payments and tax reform. The unpleasant things in it – increased duties on tobacco, drink and road vehicles – were offset in the Party's eyes by measures to introduce a capital gains tax, corporation tax, restrictions on overseas investment outside the sterling area, tighter control of tax avoidance and a new tax-free redundancy payments scheme. He also announced the cancellation of TSR2 at a saving of £35 million in the coming year. The Budget infuriated the Opposition who fought it all the way.

[3] On 7 April President Johnson had offered American economic assistance to South-East Asia and as part of this was backing ambitious power projects on the Mekong River which had been launched by the four riparian countries – Cambodia, Laos, Thailand and South Vietnam. Britain offered technical assistance.

[4] The Regular Army had been on extensive overseas tours dealing with emergencies in the Middle East and Far East, and it was proposed to call up some of the Territorial Army Emergency Reserve (the 'Ever Readies') to reinforce our troops in Aden. Fred Mulley, Minister of State for the Army, announced the decision to the House on 14 April.

Tuesday, 20 April. Left for Tanzania, despite warnings by my ear specialist that I should not fly, because of my sinus trouble.

The purpose of my visit to Tanzania and Zambia was not only to discuss development projects, particularly the Tan–Zam railway, but to mend the Labour Government's fences with these two countries which had been damaged by the Government's prevarications over Rhodesia. Julius Nyerere and Kenneth Kaunda were old friends from my Movement for Colonial Freedom days and I managed to assuage some of their anxieties. I took with me Chris Hall, a bright young journalist from the Sun *who shared my ideals and whom, on my husband's recommendation, I had brought into the Department to strengthen the press side, and in Tanzania he secured a scoop. While I was touring villages in the bush he arranged for me to be photographed outside one of the huts holding an African baby in my arms. To our surprise this was given a prominent show in the* Daily Express *over the caption 'A cuddle in the sun', a welcome human touch at a time when the aid programme was under attack in certain quarters as a luxury we could not afford. One less welcome result of the flying I had to do was that my sinus trouble became worse and I had to have an operation when I returned.*

Thursday, 6 May. I left my bed in University College Hospital with tubes in my nose to go to vote on the Steel White Paper. I faced a battery of flash bulbs at the exit.[1] At the House I waited in the car for them to verify that I had been checked through the division lobby. They came back triumphantly to say that we had won by four votes. I was jubilant until I learned that G.B. had enticed Woodrow and Donnelly into the lobby with us by a vague promise to 'listen' to their proposals, and I went back to the hospital with a heavy heart.

Friday, 7 May. All hell let loose in the press about steel with everyone speculating as to what Brown's offer meant.[2] The day produced revelations from Donnelly that Brown had been in negotiation with him and Wyatt for several days. This is the worst blow yet for the Government.

Tuesday, 11 May. The Cabinet room was empty of officials when we met at 11.30 and Harold said he thought it was right for us to have a private discussion on the effects on our legislative programme of the steel incident. He wanted to begin by making a personal explanation. He was satisfied that George's intentions had been the most honourable. It was true that he, Harold, had had a discussion with Woodrow about the steel industry, but at no stage was there any suggestion of bargaining. When he arrived on the front bench for the steel debate George told him roughly what he intended to say and it struck him it was completely innocent. There was never in G.'s mind or anyone else's any suggestion of compromise to bring Woodrow and Donnelly into the lobby. The

[1] My operation at UCH was to be resurrected against me in 1974 during my battle with consultants as Secretary of State for Social Services. See p. 474.

[2] During the steel debate Woodrow Wyatt had been urging a compromise under which the Government would take a 51 per cent holding in thirteen of the major companies. Winding up George Brown had made a direct appeal to Wyatt, saying the Government was prepared to listen to the industry. Challenged by Wyatt as to whether the Government was prepared to listen to proposals for control 'on something less than 100 per cent', George Brown had replied, ' "Listen" is the word. "Listen", certainly.'

most important thing for us was not to indulge in recriminations about the past but to decide our future policy.

George followed him with a long explanation which in my view didn't put the matter particularly right. On the merits George argued that he had always believed we should put the case for steel more positively and show its relevance to our economic problems. It was right for us to be willing to listen to the views of the steel industry, though he personally had never thought anything would come of it. He ended by expressing the hope that the Party would underwrite his attitude, namely that we should be willing to 'listen' though we were determined to go ahead with public ownership.

Thursday, 13 May. After discussion of parliamentary business at Cabinet, we agreed that the odds were strongly against our getting steel this session. Harold hinted darkly that our fate might hang on the life of one of our back benchers. We must prepare the ground for an October election if driven to it. He had clearly been looking facts in the face more realistically. We agreed that steel and land should be introduced concurrently – perhaps even debated – before the summer recess. The House should then adjourn in the normal way, but our intention would be to prorogue in the autumn and put these two at the head of the legislation of the new session, along with house finance if possible. This would leave us room for manoeuvre if forced to the country. I agreed with this, having been told by my own lads in Blackburn that they wished we would postpone steel and get some social reforms through instead.

Wednesday, 26 May. An OPD meeting chiefly to discuss the Trucial States.[1] George Thomson has just done a tour of them during which our political Residents in the Persian Gulf have sold him the line that we must pour in [£1m] more aid to keep Nasser out.

I intervened to say that we ought to explore the possibility of organizing consortia for wider areas in the Middle East, including the UAR which – from a development point of view – was a better candidate for aid than any other Middle East country. H. said we must give the £1m but authorized me to examine the possibilities of wider consortia during my coming visit to our Middle East Development Division [MEDD] in Beirut.

Monday, 31 May. An unpleasant meeting of the Cabinet Sub-Committee on Commonwealth Economic Relationships to discuss trade possibilities. It was soon clear that George was high. He was offensively truculent about everyone's ideas and hectored the Aviation and Defence representatives for their lack of sales drive in Commonwealth countries. H. seemed tired and a bit disorganized. The meeting dragged on to its undignified end. Whether anything will come of the rather ragged ideas for stimulating Commonwealth trade must await the Commonwealth Prime Ministers' conference. Later Harold had

[1] The seven Trucial Coast Sheikdoms were important for their strategic position in the Persian Gulf and for oil. Though they were self-governing, Britain was responsible for their defence and external relations. The Foreign Office, always suspicious of President Nasser of the United Arab Republic [UAR] for his non-aligned views and his contact with the Soviet Union, tried to keep them isolated from his influence and that of the Arab League. George Thomson, as Minister of State at the Foreign Office, had been sent to assess the situation.

a word with me in the chamber. I asked him if George was tight. 'As a coot,' he replied grimly. I asked if we couldn't get rid of him before he got us into real trouble. H. said the main worry was when he was on television. People who had voted for George as leader were now coming and asking him to sack him. 'If I did he'd only make cause with Wyatt and Donnelly to destroy us.'

Thursday, 3 June. When we entered the Cabinet room, Harold had his breakfast tray in front of him. Apologizing, he said he had been busy on talks with the Chancellor since the early hours and had an urgent matter he wanted to report to us. We were in a 'rut, groove, corner': no room for manœuvre: and the time had come to break out. If we did not lower bank rate now, we should probably never have another chance. We had taken physical steps to control credit, though there was still a loophole through the hire purchase activities of the finance houses. If we were to close that, we could cut bank rate to 6 per cent. With credit controls in operation, bank rate was largely a psychological weapon to create confidence. But there were signs that a continuing crisis level for bank rate actually destroyed confidence by implying we had no faith in sterling ourselves. They (he, the Chancellor and the First Secretary) had therefore discussed the idea with the Governor of the Bank of England, who was in favour of a cut and thought he could sell it abroad as part of a package deal, including hire purchase restrictions. But the court must be informed as soon as possible so that they could agree at their meeting at 11.30 am. It had to be done today or never, following the announcement of the improvement in our gold and dollar reserves. If the whole thing went wrong, we should be in a mess. He did not underestimate the risk. But there was a sporting chance that it would enable us to break out, politically as well as economically. He personally strongly recommended it to Cabinet. Jim Callaghan backed him, telling us frankly that his Treasury advisers were opposed. But he was heartened by the support of the Governor who, after all, had a professional interest in keeping sterling strong. The HP restrictions would not be popular, but they would not bite seriously and they could always be relaxed, or purchase tax reduced, if unemployment began to appear.

George Brown came out against. Tony Crosland was very hostile. This would not only appear a gimmick but was intended as one. Wasn't one of the aims of high bank rate to attract foreign funds and wasn't this still necessary? Denis Healey tended to support George. But after a rushed discussion it was clear most were in favour. I said it was difficult to decide without the answers to questions there was no time to ask. H. kept chipping in, fighting for his own point of view for once. By 11.25 it was agreed and a message rushed to the bank.

At 3.30 I abandoned my Departmental engagements to go into the House for Jim's statement on bank rate. It was surprisingly well received. A few hours later I ran into Harold who was as chirpy as a bird. He pulled me back to say sterling had strengthened and money was pouring in. 'You see, you can never tell.' City politics, obviously, are as unpredictable as ours.

Tuesday, 8 June to Friday, 11 June. Visited MEDD and was greatly impressed by the calibre of our people in it. *Not* impressed by the calibre of our ambassadors in either Beirut or Amman. Had long discussion with the MEDD boys about the Trucial States. They are appalled by the proposed extra £1m – a waste when there are so many other worthwhile development projects in the Middle East we can't afford to finance.

The struggle to hold the value of sterling remained intense. In May the adverse trade balance rose to £56 million compared with an average of £17 million for the first four months of the year. Imports were up and exports slightly down. As a result sales of sterling were renewed and pressure on our reserves intensified. On Vietnam Labour anger at America's increased intervention was mounting and Harold Wilson decided the time had come to launch a peace initiative. At the Commonwealth Prime Ministers' conference, which opened on 17 June, he secured agreement to the sending of a Commonwealth peace mission under his chairmanship to make contact with the Governments principally concerned. Its other members were to be President Nkrumah of Ghana, Sir Abubaker Tafawa Balewa, Prime Minister of Nigeria and Dr Eric Williams, Prime Minister of Trinidad and Tobago. China immediately rejected the proposal, deriding the British Labour Government as the 'errand boy of the United States'. Moscow and Hanoi also refused to co-operate and the idea was finally abandoned.

Tuesday 15 June. Went to Cabinet determined to have a showdown about Vietnam. Opinion is mounting against the Americans as Johnson puts in thousands more ground troops and abandons all pretence that the Americans are there merely to 'advise'. However, Harold forestalled me by opening with a reference to mysterious negotiations of which he had high hopes. If they came off, the *coup* would be pretty big. He and the Foreign Secretary were in the middle of a very delicate operation and he asked us not to press for more details at this stage. I merely contented myself with asking whether Vietnam would be discussed at the Commonwealth PMs' conference. After trying to hedge for a moment, he replied, 'Undoubtedly.'

This hint of progress cheered us up for the next item: the very disappointing trade returns. Harold said we should not play it too tragically. The bunching of imports for the surcharge cut showed how right we had been to impose it in the first place. The slight but disturbing downturn of exports (coupled with the rise in imports of manufactures) revealed the deep industrial malaise the Tories had left behind and which could only be cured on the long term. Steps had been taken to defend sterling. He was setting up a committee of non-spending ministers to review public expenditure and to decide on the rival merits of the claims our various Departments had put in. My worry is that there is not a single overseas minister on it: I shall have to get them all together to back me in my demands for aid.

Tom Fraser then presented a limp statement on the Geddes Report on carriers' licensing and told us that Hinton has come out against any return to the integration of transport on 1945 lines.[1] Apparently he thinks that co-operation is best achieved by friendly discussions between the managements of

[1] In 1963 Ernest Marples, then Minister of Transport, had set up a committee under Lord Geddes to examine the operation and effects of the system of carriers' licences. The report, which was published on 22 June 1965, rejected all restrictions on the number of lorries and on the work for which they might be used.

rail and road![1] Ted Short was muttering to me about how hopeless Tom was. The PLP Transport Group apparently is getting restless. 'He can't make a decision,' I whispered back. 'I'll never know why Harold appointed him.' But Harold is in no position to put through Cabinet reshuffles which might be taken as a sign of demoralization at this tricky time. His remedy is to try to impose action on weak Ministers. He now said the time had come for some decisions to be taken and he proposed to set up a committee of Ministers, serviced by officials, to produce a policy.

Went into the chamber for the PM's Questions. Harold had some from Zilly on Vietnam and took the opportunity of hinting at his negotiations.[2] Said he hoped to make a statement soon. He whispered to me that he was on to something really big, if it came off. I asked, 'Something on the lines of the compromise Shastri has been discussing with Lester Pearson in Canada?'[3] 'Much bigger than that.' It is amazing how cheerful we all keep. I simply can't get depressed, despite the hazards. The interest of my job just carries me along. Harold remains unbelievably buoyant. Once again he knocked his questioners for six.

Over a coffee at the Welsh table I sounded out the boys about the Beatles' MBES.[4] The reaction was wholly unfavourable, the word 'gimmick' being prominent. This ploy of Harold's seems to have boomeranged. It is on a par with some of his assessments of individuals, both for ministerial office and for other jobs. He seems to have a streak of vulgarity which is also part of his strength.

Wednesday, 16 June. While waiting to go into OPD meeting, had a chat with Gerald Gardiner and asked him what he thought of politics. He said he was struck by how hard we all worked: he could barely keep pace, even by cutting out social engagements. But the whole system was astonishingly inefficient on the parliamentary side – so much time-wasting. But he said that he was enjoying it nonetheless.

In the afternoon I won a great victory over the terms of aid: I am to announce interest-free loans on Monday.[5] Slowly but surely one manages to influence

[1] Shortly after the Labour Government took over, Dr Beeching, chairman of the British Railways Board [BRB] and author of the controversial report on 'The Re-shaping of British Railways', had informed the Government of his desire to return to ICI. There had been some discussion in Cabinet as to whether he might be used to draw up a transport co-ordination plan in the hope that he would do a similar hatchet job on the road haulage side, but the railway unions' suspicions of him were too great. On 5 February, therefore, Tom Fraser had announced that he had appointed Lord Hinton of Bankside, until recently chairman of the Central Electricity Generating Board, as his Special Advisor on Transport Planning to recommend ways of co-ordinating road and rail transport. Dr Beeching left BRB on 21 April and was succeeded as chairman by Stanley Raymond, one of the two vice-chairmen.

[2] Konni Zilliacus, Labour MP for Gorton, Manchester, and an expert on foreign affairs.

[3] Shri Lal Bahadur and Lester (Mike) Pearson were Prime Ministers of India and Canada respectively.

[4] In the Queen's Birthday Honours List all four members of the Beatles pop group had been awarded the MBE, at Harold Wilson's personal recommendation. Not all Labour Members disagreed with him. Eric Heffer, Labour MP for Liverpool Walton, had tabled a Motion in the House strongly appreciating the award because of 'the great good and happiness that the Beatles have brought to millions throughout the world'.

[5] The burden of interest and debt repayment on the poorer developing countries had been a matter of concern to the experts on development aid, including the World Bank. I was therefore delighted when I persuaded the Treasury to allow the Ministry of Overseas Development to make interest-free loans to selected developing countries whose low income per head made it impossible for them to service their debt even on favourable terms.

policy. With any luck I shall gradually build up ODM till it plays a decisive influence in foreign affairs.

Thursday, 17 June. Harold, coming in to answer his PQs, slipped in next to me on the bench. He was as excited as a schoolboy: said he had worked out his peace initiative on Vietnam, sounded out a number of Commonwealth PMs and was just off to put it to them. If all went well, he hoped to be able to interrupt parliamentary business at about 6 pm to make his statement. It was 'very big'.

At 6 pm I was hanging about in my room, afraid to go and change [for Harold's Commonwealth reception at No. 10]. No ring from the bobby to tell me the PM had gone into the chamber. At 7 pm I went downstairs to reconnoitre. Bert Bowden,[1] dolled up for dinner, told me there was no sign of the PM so he couldn't have got it through. Bathed hurriedly for the Lord Chancellor's dinner and returned to my room half-dressed to be told by Ted [Castle] that the Whips had rung to say we must all be on the front bench by 7.50. Just made it in a somewhat dishevelled state to learn that the Speaker had ruled he could not interrupt business for a statement.

What to do now? We hung around waiting for orders. Message: the statement would be at 10 pm. Dashed to Lancaster House where Gerald said the dinner had been put back half an hour anyway. At 9.45 our front bench people made a dash back to the House. In the chamber, another set-back: the Highlands Bill was still going strong and we dare not interrupt it because it would have meant giving it another day. So over to No. 10 for the PM's reception. In the heat of the crowded room I began to reel with fatigue. Talked to the Kenya Foreign Minister, Murumbi. He was very disgruntled by Harold's initiative, said he had rushed the conference too much. Anyway, it was quite wrong that Harold should be chairman of the mission: he was too committed to the American line. 'We expected better things of the Labour Government.' At 11 pm back to the House once again through the rain and the waiting crowds. But we still had to wait while normal business was concluded. I was disappointed by the nature of Harold's 'very big' achievement. There was no statement of principles to suggest the basis of a solution. The whole thing struck me as a gesture rather than conviction. But when at last Harold was called I fell sound asleep on the front bench and missed the great moment after all!

Friday, 18 June. The papers have given a glowing reception to Harold's initiative, but rumbles of discontent from some of the Commonwealth delegates are growing. Julius Nyerere has come out categorically against it as 'putting China in the dock'. (Apparently he asked Harold at yesterday's session how he could record his disagreement and Harold had said, 'You can't,' so he has been getting his own back.) Ted and I were due for dinner with some of the PMs at Chequers: our first visit there. It said black tie so I put on my best long. We drove through a lovely summer evening through the Bucks countryside to the great park. To my embarrassment I found myself walking into a cosy domestic atmosphere with Mary in a modest short dress, a crocheted stole round her shoulders. (Why 'black tie' I shall never know.) Mike

[1] Herbert Bowden, Lord President of the Council and Leader of the House of Commons.

Pearson's wife saved me by also appearing in a long, though humbler than mine. Obote, Kwame Nkrumah and Dr Williams were the other guests.

Monday, 21 June. Busy all morning preparing my statement on interest free loans. There was some pressure from Dorneywood and Chequers to get me to postpone it, and my chaps and I agreed it was safer to have it in the bag.[1]

After my statement, held my first lobby conference as Minister.[2] It seemed to go quite well.

Wednesday, 23 June. Went to Marlborough House to open discussion on aid: the first woman ever to do so at a Commonwealth conference. I was struck by the good-humoured atmosphere. The representatives (particularly the Africans) are ready to burst into laughter and jokes at the slightest opportunity. I was also struck by the disconnection between one speech and the next: there was no attempt to follow up the points I made, even where I threw them out for discussion, though my reference to interest-free loans was well received.

Thursday, 24 June. In the afternoon Arthur and I resumed the discussions on the rail link. Kenneth Kaunda clearly wants to go ahead with the joint survey and bid for a consortium, but Julius has gone off on a sideline of his own. He admitted that in Peking he had asked for Chinese aid and it had been granted. A Chinese survey team had already arrived in Tanzania. How could he send it away when there wasn't any Western offer to build his railway? I suggested that a parallel survey of the whole route should also be carried out by Max Stamp[3] and Kenneth seemed to welcome this. He is obviously worried by Julius's aberrations.

Tuesday, 29 June. A reception at No. 10 for Ministers. Marcia[4] was in a militant mood about the plotting which she insisted the Right was still carrying on against Harold. I said I couldn't understand why he didn't realize his own strength. He had deliberately chosen to surround himself with people who were not exactly reliably loyal. She was vehement in agreement, couldn't understand in particular why he had put Michael Stewart at the FO. 'Doesn't he see that this is his most dangerous rival? I keep telling him, but he won't listen.'

Sunday, 4 July. One of the bleakest days in my political life. Had Andrew Cohen and Martin Lynch of the Department over to the cottage to tighten up my brief for the Public Expenditure Scrutiny Committe [PESC] which met all day. My careful preparation of an opening submission went for nothing: Jim didn't want to hear it. Instead they jumped into hostile cross-examination. I

[1] Dorneywood House in Bucks had been presented to the nation in 1943 and was used by Foreign and Commonwealth Secretaries as a country retreat and for entertaining foreign visitors.

[2] The lobby are a formidable body of journalists specially accredited to work at Westminister. They have the privilege of access to the Members' lobby where they can talk to MPs and Ministers on 'lobby terms', *i.e.* they may use any information they obtain but must not divulge its source.

[3] An economic consultant who had carried out various missions for ODM.

[4] Marcia Williams had been Harold Wilson's personal secretary while he was in Opposition and he had brought her into No. 10 as confidante as much as secretary. She had a strong political influence on him, and published her very strong views about the civil service in her book *Inside No. 10*, in 1972.

have never been in a more unfriendly crowd. George Brown on my right and Frank Cousins on my left joined in attacking our figures. In vain I pointed out that our basic allocation would mean a cut-back on present policies. They obviously couldn't care less about the Party's commitment to 1 per cent of GNP. They dismissed aid as irrelevant. I crawled home exhausted and dispirited. Andrew's worst fears have been realized.

Wednesday, 7 July. Another shock. Having spent the previous two days mobilizing the overseas Departments against the threat to our aid programme, I went along to my ministerial Development Committee [DVO] to put through the White Paper [WP] on the work of my Department on which my chaps had worked day, night and weekends for six weeks. Although they had thrashed out details at official level and I had been forced to swallow many unpalatable alterations to meet the restrictionist views of Treasury and DEA, I was faced with refusal by both of them to agree to publication before the summer recess. Jack Diamond[1] complained it was too 'expansionist' and said it had better be put off, vaguely, till the autumn when, apparently, our creditors would be less frightened by it. This aroused even Eirene White[2] into vigorous support, but in vain. All we could get was the reluctant agreement of Treasury and DEA to continue negotiations on detail at official level, though they would not hold out any hope that they would change their minds.

Thursday, 8 July. At Cabinet we had a protracted discussion on the Immigration White Paper.[3] I fought for at least some cut in alien immigration and for the restoration of Category C, so that some unskilled chaps could come in instead of our picking all the skilled workers for ourselves. This 'one-way technical assistance' was nauseating.

After Cabinet, I flew to Geneva for a 24-hour visit to ECOSOC [the Economic and Social Council of the UN]. Had a pleasant dinner party with the delegates and heard Adlai deliver his last public speech: beautiful prose but not much content.[4] My own more modest but factual speech seems to have gone down well.

Tuesday, 13 July. Attended my first state banquet at night for President Frei of Chile. The setting was pure Ruritania: gold plate, knee-breeched gentlemen advancing in an organized phalanx to serve the courses, roses everywhere,

[1] Labour MP for Gloucester and Chief Secretary to the Treasury. He was made a life peer in 1970.

[2] Labour MP for East Flint and a member of the NEC of the Labour Party. She had been made Under-Secretary of State for the Colonies in 1964 and was promoted Minister of State at the Foreign Office in 1966, moving to the same post in the Welsh Office in 1967.

[3] As the Smethwick by-election had shown, immigration had become a very hot issue in parts of the country where the immigrants were concentrated, and in some areas the local authorities were complaining they could not deal with the housing and education problems involved. The Government had earlier tightened up on evasions of the 1962 Commonwealth Immigrants Act and introduced the Race Relations Act to deal with racial discrimination. On 2 August it announced a big cut-back on entry permits in a White Paper 'Immigration from the Commonwealth' (Cmnd 2739). Work vouchers were to be cut from 20,800 a year to 8,500 and would only be given to applicants in Category A (those with a specific job to come to) and category B (those with special qualifications, such as nurses, teachers, doctors). Category C for the unskilled was to be abolished.

[4] Adlai Stevenson, US Ambassador to the United Nations, had been the Democratic candidate in the US presidential elections of 1952 and 1956. He collapsed and died in a London street on 14 July, six days after making the speech I had listened to.

minstrels in the gallery, and the dining-room dominated by a huge canopied throne. The food was simple, but excellent, including the best green pea soup I have ever tasted. Frei, a charming, modest man, made a gallant shot at speaking in English. Afterwards, just as I was wondering when I could slip back to the House for the death penalty votes, Lady Euston, one of the ladies-in-waiting, came to say that she knew I had to get away so would I come and talk to the Queen right away. I left the throng to go into an inner drawing-room where Mrs Speaker and a few other ladies were standing around. The Queen was chatting on the sofa to Mary Wilson, so Lady Euston asked me if I would talk to the Duchess of Gloucester for a moment – a poor, nervous, bemused thing. Then I was called over to sit next to the Queen, giving my usual half-bow because I won't curtsey. The Queen talked to me very sensibly about my visit to Africa, saying she didn't think Julius Nyerere had seemed his usual self at the Commonwealth conference. Then a flunkey came and whispered in her ear and she excused herself, saying laughingly that 'poor Charles' was doing his O-levels the next day and just wanted a bit of reassurance. As I stood up Princess Margaret came over to talk to me, looking *outreé* in a very with-it gown and hair-do. Her manner was positively brash. She said, 'You've got to go back and vote or something,' and when I said yes, against the death penalty, she said, 'Ooh, you mustn't miss that. I care very much about that.'

The Queen came back and we three stood chatting for quite a while. The Queen was very relaxed. I like her enormously. She chatted on about Charles and said he was nervous, but she thought he'd get on all right. Weren't these exams awful? Turning to Margaret, she said, 'You and I would never have got into university.' I said I was sure they would: it wasn't as formidable as it seemed. I told her how beautiful her dress was – a ravishing, gossamery thing – quite the loveliest I had ever seen, and she thanked me with obvious pleasure. Margaret then pointed to the Order which was perched on the Queen's right breast and chipped, 'That's rather prominent, darling. Well, it does rather stick out.' The Queen laughed and said, 'It's all right for the men; they can wear it in their lapel, but I have to pin it on somewhere.' Then Margaret murmured, 'I suppose we ought to permeate,' so we all moved into the outer drawing-room where a select coterie of men were waiting. Angus Ogilvy came up to gossip with me in a most friendly way. After a few moments I made my excuses and said goodnight. In the state-room Tony Greenwood was looking positively jealous and Ted said, 'You've been monopolizing the Queen.' At last I managed to slip away, having enjoyed myself far more than I thought I would.

Tuesday, 20 July. Got up at 4.30 am to mug up my briefs in preparation for my trial in Cabinet. We plunged into overseas aid right away. I spelt out in detail the consequences of keeping me to my 'basic' of £216m in 1966–67 and £230m in 1969–70. Jim Callaghan said it was all very sad but where was the money coming from: which domestic Minister would take a cut? At the end all Harold succeeded in doing was to avoid Cabinet reaching a conclusion, saying we had got to wait for the outcome of the social services review.

One achievement in Cabinet, however, I was able to chalk up. When we came to my White Paper the lobbying I had done stood me in good stead, Frank

Soskice in particular weighing in on my behalf. My bright idea (that we must produce the WP at the same time as the Immigration WP in order to take the bad taste of the latter out of our people's mouths) obviously had an effect. Jim Callaghan resisted with all he'd got, even trying to get his disagreement recorded in the Cabinet minutes, but fortunately for me George Brown had left. In the end I won and emerged emotionally wrung out.

Wednesday, 21 July to Friday, 23 July. Off to Paris for the ministerial meeting of the DAC [Development Assistance Committee of OECD]. While I was there we heard of Sir Alec's resignation from the Tory leadership.[1] I refused to comment to the press and was very glad I had when, late at night, I got a message from the PM asking Ministers not to comment. The weekend was darkened by a speech from the PM warning of coming cuts in public expenditure.

Monday, 26 July. Had a row with Andrew because, in my absence, our officials had agreed to still more watering-down of the White Paper. I insisted on some of the cuts being restored before it was rushed to the printers.

Had dinner with Ted and Tommy and Penny Balogh. Tommy said the FO had received glowing accounts of my DAC visit. How ironical! As I settled down to another late night at the House, the duty officer at ODM phoned to say that the Cabinet paper which should have arrived at 8 pm was still being drafted and when was I going home, as the PM wanted all Ministers to read it tonight. When I left at just before midnight it still wasn't ready so I asked for it to be delivered at 5.45 am. I am learning to manage on five hours' sleep – and often less – per night.

Pressure on sterling had continued and, despite drawings on the borrowing facilities that had been made available to us by the US and West Germany, our reserves had fallen by £24 million during June and another £50 million in July. Better trade figures in June, with the adverse trade balance falling from £56 million to £33 million, brought only temporary relief. In fact, despite all the traumas, we had been doing nearly twice as well as our predecessors, with the monthly trade deficit averaging £26 million in the first half of 1965 compared with £46 million in 1964. Nonetheless confidence remained extremely volatile and with Harold Wilson and Jim Callaghan determined to reject devaluation at all costs, they were at the mercy of the relentless pressures brought to bear on them by the Governor of the Bank of England and the US Treasury.

On 27 July Jim Callaghan astounded his Cabinet colleagues, and later the House, by announcing sweeping new deflationary measures which he had worked out with Harold Wilson and George Brown. Faced with a fait accompli, *Cabinet had no choice but to accept, though a number of our treasured Election policies were dropped. The measures included a standstill on the expansion of the building programmes for housing, hospitals and schools; a cut in local authority spending, particularly on mortgage advances with a*

[1] On 28 July he was succeeded by Edward Heath, MP for Bexley since 1950, who had been rising steadily in the Conservative hierarchy. He had been Government Chief Whip in 1955, Minister of Labour in 1959 and in 1960 had been made Lord Privy Seal with Foreign Office responsibilities, including the attempt to get Britain into the EEC. From 1963 till 1964 he had been Secretary of State for Industry and Trade. On the fall of the Labour Government in 1970 he was to become Prime Minister.

ban on the forward purchase of land; a tightening of hire-purchase provisions and restrictions on private investment. Our proposals for an income guarantee scheme, for the abolition of prescription charges and for specially favourable interest rates for new owner-occupiers, were to be postponed indefinitely. Next year's defence programme was to be cut by 'about £100 million'. Export credit guarantees were to be improved.

Tuesday, 27 July. The crucial Cabinet. I was so dizzy with fatigue after my early rising that I failed to notice it started at 10 am and had a frantic dash even to arrive seven minutes late. Harold was in the middle of the explanation of the statement: a standstill for non-essential projects, the 'containment' of housing and health policies, the dropping of mortgage rebates and the income guarantee; some exchange controls and financial tightening up on imports. Harold played it cool; Jim followed to explain that in the past few days we had lost one tenth of our reserves (which in any case were only £900m). If we did not do something drastic immediately, they might well run out by the end of the week.

To my delight Crosland jumped in right away to say that, though at this stage this action might be inevitable, we ought to recognize where it was leading us: straight into stagnation and Tory policies. There was no guarantee these steps would do the trick and the Chancellor might have to come back for another dose before very long. This should be regarded, therefore, merely as a holding operation while import controls and really savage cuts in defence spending were prepared. (Harold murmured that all these things were under discussion.) Frank Cousins was bitterly critical and demanded the same two things. Dick said the constant nibbling at the problem was all wrong. I said that it was now clear that those who had urged last autumn that we ought to have devalued immediately or we should find ourselves in a trap had been right. There was still an alternative which I favoured: to devalue now by refusing to adopt Tory remedies. Failing that, I was not prepared to accept the statement unless we were given a guarantee that immediate preparations would be made for import controls and further cuts in defence. Crosland nodded and I passed him a note: 'Wouldn't you prefer devaluation, even now?' 'Of course,' he whispered, 'but I promised Jim not to press this.' Others rejected this suggestion, and George Brown said that the statement represented an agreed compromise view.

A long discussion followed. In the end it was only Frank who said categorically that he opposed the statement. I asked whether the PM would now keep his promise to have a Chequers weekend of the whole Cabinet to discuss general strategy – both political and economic – as some of us were constantly finding ourselves confronted with situations which arose from economic decisions on which we had not been consulted. Harold agreed he would try to do this. Shortly after, Frank rose and said, 'Well, if you'll excuse me, Prime Minister, I'm going to leave.' For a shocked moment we thought he was going to resign, but it appeared that it was merely that he was top for PQs [Parliamentary Questions]!

When I left at 1.15 pm for an FBI [Federation of British Industry] lunch they were still at it,[1] and Jim was trying to pass the job of making the statement on to

[1] The FBI merged with the National Association of British Manufacturers and the British Employers' Federation in 1965 to form the Confederation of British Industry [CBI].

the PM. He was being very temperamental about it, even trying to suggest that the statement had been wrung out of him against his will. I backed George Brown in saying it was his job. After all, Jim has had a pretty free rein with his financial policies and I didn't see why he should dodge this one. In the event he carried off the statement in the House quite effectively. Our people took the statement in numbed silence, but morale that night in the tea-room was pretty low.

Thursday, 29 July. Up at 6.30 am again to refresh my memory on the aid arguments for Cabinet. To my surprise, when we got there Jim opened by saying he had been going very carefully into my figures, understood my difficulties and, as the result of some elaborate calculations, suggested my basic for 1966–67 should be increased to £225m on the understanding that all contingencies were included. George Brown and Frank Cousins registered outraged astonishment. Where was the extra to come from? Jim hinted from the contingency figure. I explained that his calculations still did not take certain things into account. Nonetheless I passed him a note: 'I really *am* grateful. Stand firm.' Harold jumped at the opportunity to back him up. Crosland protested we had already spent two hours on overseas aid, now another hour. On education a mere five minutes. Higher education had been slashed already for aid. And he muttered under his breath, 'They'll only waste it.' (How my colleagues must hate Harold for putting ODM in the Cabinet!) Then Jack Diamond piped up, trying to be helpful, 'I think we should take into account that the aid figures are cash figures. The rest are at constant prices.' More astonishment, even Frank Cousins pointing out that this would mean aid would be taking a savage cut. I insisted that I had assumed I was on the same basis as everyone else. Harold seized the opportunity to say I ought to go away and sort the whole thing out with the Chief Secretary. When George scowled at this he added hastily, 'And then with the Public Expenditure Committee.' Another reprieve, but my prospects of going on holiday get more and more remote.

Opening for us on a censure debate on our 'broken pledges', Harold made one of the speeches of his life and left the Tories so numb no one got up to speak and the vote almost had to be put immediately! Our boys came out of the chamber with their tails up. Morale has mounted visibly.

Friday, 30 July. An exhausting two hours with my officials and the Chief Secretary, trying to agree on what the Chancellor's concession meant for the aid programme. Jack was grimly stubborn: it must be a 'hump' of £225m for 1966–67 turning into a plateau for the rest of the period, *i.e.* an average per cent of GNP equivalent to the present one – or nothing. I fought all the way and got him to agree that £225m would be the out-turn figure, not the commitments one. He tried all his accountant's arguments to prove that aid estimates should be on a cash basis, not a constant prices one like the rest, and I retorted with development arguments. Here again I got him to agree that, if we accepted the cash basis for 1966–67, the succeeding programmes should be reviewed in the light of price increases. Since there is certainly no sympathy for our point of view in Cabinet, I realized this was the best we could do. Crawled home for the weekend completely fagged out.

Tuesday, 3 August. Got up at 6 am to read the National Economic Plan before Cabinet.[1] The discussion on it was pretty perfunctory till I waded in with the criticisms Dudley Seers had sent me: it lacked historical context, was too parochial, failed to integrate social purposes with economic ones, and was professionally pretty bad planning anyway. Crosland rejected my criticisms indignantly. George took them more calmly, even admitting there was some substance in my complaint we had said nothing about world trends, *e.g.* in trade. Tempers are getting very frayed as this exacting term draws to its close. At one stage Crosland protested that the standstill had wrecked his long-term target. It was not merely a standstill but a postponement all down the line. When Jim denied this, Dick backed Crosland up, saying he had spent the past six days arguing with Treasury officials about the terms of a circular he was trying to get out. (My sympathies went out to him.) Jim snapped back, 'If you all go on like this, I shall resign. I warn you, I'm not prepared to take much more.' Fred Peart said mildly, 'We all need a holiday.'

Went to the House to make my statement on the White Paper.[2] The Tories tried to sneer so I hit back. For the first time I felt I could really dominate the House from the dispatch box.

Wednesday, 4 August. The White Paper has been very well received, except by the *Daily Telegraph*. Good leaders in *The Times* and *Guardian*. Only Cabinet tomorrow, then I can go and join Ted on that postponed holiday, navvying to get Hell Corner Farm into shape.[3]

Thursday, 5 August. Last Cabinet before the delayed holiday. I was desperate to get away. Harold had a proposal to relax the fifty-year rule about the publication of Cabinet documents into a thirty-year one: said it would be good for our 'liberal image'. Dick supported vigorously, quoting the outrageously one-sided nature of the present position whereby former Cabinet ministers, with the approval of the PM, can scoop the pool lucratively with their memoirs at any time, *e.g.* Lord Avon. I discovered that an official secret is what we say it is. Ex-Cabinet ministers *are* bound by the Official Secrets Act but a current PM is free to decide what 'secrets' to reveal at any time. With typical Establishment caution the Foreign Secretary wanted forty years, supported by Jim Callaghan, but the liberal image won, backed by supporting noises from Crosland and me.

[1] It was published on 16 September as Cmnd 2764. Though setting a target of 25 per cent expansion over the next five years, it once again gave priority to the correction of the balance of payments deficit while admitting this would make the achievement of the 3.8 per cent annual growth target for the next two or three years more difficult. The plan was criticized as being a catalogue of optimistic predictions rather than a co-ordinated plan and as relying too much on the industry-by-industry discussions in the 'little Neddies' set up under the NEDC.

[2] 'Overseas Development: The Work of the New Ministry' (Cmnd 2736). 'Aid', we wrote, 'is a means of promoting long-term economic development. . . . Aid is not a means of winning the friendship of individual countries, though we are glad to give aid to our friends.' We intended, therefore, to channel more of our aid gradually through international organizations and in our bilateral aid to provide visiting teams from our Economic Planning staff to help draw up development plans. The Treasury had not allowed us to include any figures of aid expenditure.

[3] We had recently bought Hell Corner Farm [HCF], a rambling old cottage in the Chiltern hills, with a large neglected garden and orchards. There was a great deal of work to be done on it both inside and outside and Ted and I intended to spend our August holiday clearing the garden and painting the inside. My contribution to the latter was distempering the cupboards, at which I was not very good. Ted remarked that I got more distemper on myself than on the walls.

The tough measures of 27 July had not satisfied the holders of sterling. In August there had been a further drain on our reserves of £24 million and with adverse trade balance still running at £48 million another crisis was never very far away. Henry Fowler of the US Treasury, anxious to avoid a British devaluation, had been touring Europe to rally support for sterling, but the price he exacted was a toughening of the voluntary prices and incomes policy which had not prevented a rise in earnings well above the hoped-for 'norm'. The new prices and incomes proposals, to which George Brown had reluctantly agreed and which were announced on 2 September, were a half-way house to a statutory policy. Under them the Prices and Incomes Board was to be made a statutory body with power to collect information and call witnesses. The Government was to take power to require advance notification of pay or price increases and to hold up their implementation until the Board had reported. The General Council of the TUC had grudgingly acquiesced and on 8 September Congress endorsed its report by 5,231,000 votes to 3,319,000. It also agreed to the proposal of the General Secretary, George Woodcock, that, pending the Government's legislation, the TUC should itself be empowered by Congress to vet pay claims by member unions. In this way it was hoped to show that the voluntary system could be made to work and that legislation was unnecessary. The Government proposals were published in November in a White Paper, 'Prices and Incomes: An "Early Warning System"' (Cmnd 2802).

On 10 November the Bank of England was to announce that support arrangements for sterling had been made with ten central banks and with the Bank for International Settlements.

Tuesday, 31 August. Back at work, after a hectic fortnight cleaning up Hell Corner Farm, with an OPD meeting on Singapore. We had before us an officials' paper on the effect of the break-up of the Malaysian Federation on our base. Their conclusion was that we should not rely on being able to stay much longer and should plan a phased withdrawal to Australia, trying to persuade our allies to share more of the cost on the way.

In the afternoon I got a message saying Jim Callaghan would like to talk to me at the Treasury. This is the third time he's asked me to come over for personal talks: he loves reassurance. He said he wanted to explain about the proposals on prices and incomes coming before Cabinet tomorrow. He wasn't going behind George's back as they were in agreement on this. He liked to talk to me because, although I was a strong left-winger, I was always prepared to listen reasonably to his difficulties. There had been a bad time with sterling during August. God knew how the psychology of these people worked. Now it was just a straight crisis of confidence. We had just got to face it that big business didn't like a Labour Government. The trouble was not, as we had always thought, with the bankers but with the big international companies who operated dispassionately in any country and had no national loyalties. It was almost impossible to curb their operations: if they were denied forward cover here, they merely instructed their agents in another country to get it for them. However, Western governments were now determined to save sterling. Devaluation, he insisted, would not help us (even Treasury officials were alarmed at the damage to Labour which would result from being automatically associated with devaluation: 'It would set democracy in this country back for years'). Certainly it would not help other governments. Fowler, US Secretary to the Treasury, was now going round Europe ostensibly to discuss monetary reform but also specifically to get European governments to agree that their banks should announce their willingness to take sterling into their reserves any time it looked under threat. This would be a big change in their current policy and the very announcement would be enough to end the threat to sterling once and for all. Prospects for success were bright. To clinch it, however, we needed to strengthen the incomes and prices policy. That was why they were proposing to introduce the 'early warning system' of statutory references to the Board. He believed that these two measures would mean an end to our sterling worries: the balance of payments was improving more than hoped and soon we should begin to be able to deliver our pledges.

I said that the sooner we disembarrassed ourselves of sterling's role as an international currency the better. The trouble was that on no front except my own ('And that's only because we have you as Minister,' he interjected) were we acting any differently from the Tories. We might even have another Leyton result at Erith.[1] On what could we fight the by-election: Vietnam? Immigration? Social service pause? Cost of living? He came back firmly: 'We fight it on the fact that we inherited a nation in debt. This year the trade deficit will have been cut to £300m. Next year it will have been abolished. I believe the nation will respond to that.' I pointed out that unfortunately we had not made this our priority in Opposition: rather we had pressed for expansion at all costs, including overseas borrowing if necessary. What was the consolation of solvency if unemployment was rising? He got very excited at this and sent for the figures to show that unemployment was actually lower than last year: 'I planned my Budget on the assumption of 360,000; in August, it was only 280,000. Can we really object if it *does* rise a little? How else can we make the economy work?' We both had to go and parted amicably.

A glowing reference to Harold during our talk interested me. 'You know, Barbara, he's tough: much tougher than you and I. You should see him handling the Governor of the Bank. The Governor comes in breathing fire and slaughter, Harold does all the talking and he goes out like a lamb.'

Wednesday, 1 September. A surprisingly easy passage for the prices and incomes proposals in Cabinet. Harold gave a pragmatic account of economic developments, utterly devoid of ideological analysis but remarkably optimistic. He didn't refer to Fowler's mission, but merely hinted at certain discussions for strengthening sterling which the proposals would help. Dick said we ought to discuss the general economic policy first instead of continuing to make important decisions *ad hoc*. The PM had said that 'with a fair wind' we ought to be able to consider controlled reflation after a few months. What were we going to do if there was not a fair wind? Were we going to be faced with more sudden panic measures? Prompted by me beforehand, Tony Greenwood asked when we were going to have the Chequers discussion we had been promised on economic strategy. Harold said this was important and ought to be held, but should be on general strategy of which economic policy was only a part.

[1] In fact Labour held Erith and Crayford comfortably at the by-election on 11 November 1965. The Conservative share of the vote was up by 4.9 per cent, but Labour's was up by 2.3 per cent while the Liberal share fell by 7.2 per cent. The by-election success brought the Government's majority back to two with a by-election at Hull pending.

Alternative measures such as import controls had been under very detailed study and there ought to be something to report soon. Crosland, while welcoming the proposals, pointed out that reflation, unless bolstered by new measures, could merely recreate the old problems, *cf.* the National Economic Review. Harold insisted that we had had to use financial measures last year because we had no others to hand, but this was the purpose of the National Economic Plan, to substitute positive steps.

Jim astonished everybody by asserting that he would not come to Cabinet again, whatever happened, asking for more deflationary measures. We had done as much as we ought to do in this direction. He also said he was launching an exercise to disengage sterling from its role as financier of international trade. 'The City is important, but not at the expense of industrial development.' (Can I have influenced him?) All this clearly helped to reassure Frank Cousins, who had merely said he sympathized with George's difficulties but thought the TUC would never buy a statement as vague as this one. Nor should we try to argue that such steps were automatically in the interests of trade unionists: they would never be accepted from a Tory Government. George said that he didn't want to discuss statutory powers of enforcement of any kind at this stage. When Jim (backed by Ray) rashly said that, if necessary, we ought to be prepared to take powers of enforcement, George exploded, 'I want to make it clear that I am only introducing these proposals on the strict understanding that this is *not* the first step to statutory wage control.' Harold backed him up, saying it would not work, hadn't even worked in wartime. Nor would price control on complicated commodities like textiles. George is to go to the TUC to sell the proposals to Congress first.

At the Labour Party conference, which was held at Blackpool from 27 September to 1 October, the Government survived two major attacks on its policy. A resolution moved by Clive Jenkins, General Secretary of the Association of Supervisory Staffs, Executives and Technicians [ASSET, later the Association of Scientific, Technical and Managerial Staffs, ASTMS], disapproving of the proposed new legislation on prices and incomes, was lost by 3,635,000 votes to 2,540,000 – too close for the Government's comfort because of the opposition to the policy by the powerful Transport and General Workers' Union. John Mendelson, MP for Penistone, also failed to carry a resolution calling on the Government to dissociate itself from 'American policies and military operations' in Vietnam, though here again the minority was substantial with 2,284,000 votes to 4,065,000. Harold Wilson, however, had received a standing ovation for a powerful speech.

In Cabinet our discussions were dominated by Rhodesia where the showdown with Ian Smith was coming to a head. The majority of the Cabinet was obsessed with the need to avoid UDI at all costs. Harold Wilson had gone to great lengths to try to reach agreement with the Smith Government and, following visits by various British Ministers to Salisbury, Smith himself came to London on 4 October for further talks, but with no result. It had always seemed clear to me that the differences of approach were insurmountable. Ian Smith wanted immediate independence on the racialist constitution of 1961 only modified in ways which did not undermine his determination not to see majority, i.e. *African, government within his life-time or, as he once put it, 'for a hundred years'. Harold Wilson had based his stand on five principles which he said must govern any independence constitution: 1) unimpeded progress to majority rule must be guaranteed; 2) there must be guarantees against retrospective amendment of the constitution; 3) immediate improve-*

ment in the political status of the African population; 4) progress towards ending racial discrimination; 5) the British Government would need to be satisfied that any basis proposed for independence was acceptable to the people of Rhodesia as a whole.

Faced with deadlock the Rhodesia Committee of Cabinet had drawn up a 'war book' of action it would take against the Rhodesian Government if independence were declared illegally, though Harold Wilson had already ruled out military intervention. But Smith was adept at laying false trails of possible compromise and some members of Cabinet were prepared to clutch at straws, believing that Smith could be detached from his hard-line colleagues in the Rhodesian Front like William Harper and Desmond Lardner-Burke. Matters were not helped by the jittery behaviour of the Governor, Sir Humphrey Gibbs, who clearly had no stomach for a heroic role. So the talks dragged on.

Monday, 8 November. The OPD [has] agreed on a further offer by Harold to meet Smith in Malta. The whole thing is becoming undignified. Tonight Smith has turned even this offer down. At a reception to Ministers at No. 10 at which Harold read the Queen's Speech,[1] I said to him that we had surely now reached our sticking point. He agreed.

The Queen's Speech was received with unreflecting murmurs from Ministers lubricated with gin and tonics. Harold was at his most unctuous. When this session's programme was through, he said, we should have completed 95 per cent of our programme. 'Except steel,' I whispered to Jennie Lee who was standing by me. 'I noticed that,' she replied. We both slipped away from the hot atmosphere as quickly as possible.

Tuesday, 9 November. State Opening. I arrived on the front bench at 11.20 to find it full, Frank Cousins being installed well up the line. I think, for all his grumbles, he likes all the ministerial paraphernalia more than he will admit.

At the Party meeting in the House that morning Mike Foot and John Mendelson launched a successful protest against the curtailment of an opportunity to discuss steel. Harold gave as the reason for steel's omission from the Queen's Speech the problem of priorities and challenged Members to say which of the measures they would omit in what may well be election year to make room for steel. No mention of Messrs Wyatt and Donnelly, but 'we know, tha knows'. Prompted by Harold, Mannie Shinwell staved off a revolt by agreeing to adjourn the meeting till tomorrow to enable discussion to continue. (What a change of treatment from the old Bevanite days!)

Thursday, 11 November. Woke to find Smith had made a last appeal to the Queen, saying that whatever happened they would never swerve in their loyalty. Her Majesty had sent a beautifully formal reply, saying she was confident that 'all her Rhodesian people will demonstrate their loyalty by continuing to act in a constitutional manner'. Harold has certainly got her superbly organized.

[1] The new legislative points in the Speech were on the extension of the manufacturing powers of the nationalized industries, the disclosure of political contributions by companies, the appointment of an Ombudsman and rating reform. But it reiterated that the Government 'will give priority to ensuring that balance in external payments is restored next year and that the strength of sterling is maintained' – and there was no mention of steel.

Ten o'clock Cabinet and I found that things had moved rapidly in the last twenty-four hours.

As we talked, at 11.20 am a message was brought in to the PM, who said, 'As of five minutes ago a UDI was declared.' A solemn moment. We then went into a discussion on tactics on the basis of the war book.

Friday, 19 November to Wednesday, 24 November. My first ever Food and Agriculture Organization [FAO] conference. Made a hit with two speeches calling for more action and less talk by FAO. Developing countries all over me.

Thursday, 25 November. Back home for Cabinet, worried about Rhodesia. Hinting darkly at imminent developments, Harold told us to stand by for an early Cabinet next week. Opposing Harold is like playing blind man's buff.

Next, the bread strike.[1] It appears the union has resisted all attempts at arbitration in any form, not only reference to the Prices and Incomes Board. George and Ray said the union was delighted with the success of this, its first strike for forty years, and had got the bit between its teeth. The strike was clearly seen as a recruitment drive. George added that it was also a rather sinister attempt by the master bakers' federation to use the union to break the Board's ruling on bread prices: the employers could have carried a refusal of price increase for bread out of fat profits elsewhere. Harold asked whether the union supported the Labour Party and realized what it was doing to a Labour Government. 'Oh, yes,' said George cheerfully, 'the union's been very good – supported the prices and incomes policy all along the line.' Grim laughter. Frank said he had warned us all of where we were heading: there ought to be some arbitration machinery side by side with the Board. Harold said impatiently that was a long-term question which wouldn't help us now since the union wouldn't go to arbitration anyway. We decided to sweat out the strike and approved George and Ray's decision to refer the claim to the Board over the union's head.

Next headache was on rate rebates.[2] Here again, Jim wanted a cut in the scheme, warning darkly that public expenditure was getting out of hand. We finally agreed on a compromise between him and Dick, but not before Houghton had said vigorously that all this came of trying to deal with the needs of the poorest piecemeal. To cap a long and hard morning, Tony Crosland introduced his memo on the public schools with the words, 'This is a strictly insoluble problem.'[3] More grimaces. We approved the proposed terms of reference for his Commission after I had wrung from him an assurance he wasn't trying to get a Fleming-type solution.

[1] Strikes had been taking place in certain bakeries in support of the Bakers' Union claim for shorter hours and a pay increase, including an immediate increase of £1 per week. On 25 November, Ray Gunter referred the claim to the PIB which produced an interim report in January 1966, recommending an immediate increase of 15*s* a week to be financed by a 1*d* increase on a standard loaf.

[2] Dick Crossman had been working on the long-term reform of the rating system which was proving very long-term indeed. As an interim measure he wanted to introduce rate rebates for the hardest-hit. His Rating Bill came before the House on 26 November. Describing it, he said, 'We are giving a short-term relief from this unpleasant tax while we make our plans to abolish it.'

[3] Tony Crosland had decided to set up a Public Schools Commission to advise on the integration of the public schools with the state system. Sir John Newsom agreed to serve as chairman.

Monday, 29 November. Unexpected summons to 10 am Cabinet. Harold reported that the group of Ministers dealing with Rhodesia had been meeting all weekend to consider an urgent request from Kaunda to send in planes to 'protect' him. If we didn't do it, wilder and sometimes more sinister elements from OAU [Organization for African Unity] would have to be called in and Kaunda didn't want that. They were therefore recommending that we send nine Javelins which could outclass Smith's Canberras and Hunters. He personally didn't think Smith was going to attack Zambia, but it was a good excuse for giving us squatters' rights and keeping other people out. With some grumbles from Houghton this was agreed. Harold has obviously been goaded by snide remarks all over the British press to the effect that Smith is winning.

Tuesday, 30 November. Another Cabinet: first item, Rhodesia. Harold reported a serious hitch in developments. Kaunda was not ready to agree to our conditions (*i.e.* that no other troops should be sent in without our permission) unless we sent not merely an RAF regiment, but also a battalion, and stationed it on the border. We were prepared to agree to the first, but wanted the troops at Ndola, 200 miles away. Kaunda was also insisting that, if power was cut off, we should occupy Kariba. Negotiations were still going on.

I left to prepare for PQs, which went well. For once I ate my supper in the Members' dining-room. As we talked, Harold walked up with a plate of veal and ham pie and chips saying he was due to dine at the Royal Society. He intended to arrive just in time to pay his tribute to Pat Blackett.[1] 'This way I avoid having to put on a black tie.' He was very pleasant and completely without self-importance. And he told us how 'one of the more irreverent members of the Cabinet' had said of me as I left the room, 'Look at her. She only has to waggle that bottom of hers and she gets all her own way.' He added, 'That is why we put her with her back to the wall.'

Wednesday, 1 December. At 3.30 pm, unable to contain himself any longer, Harold made his statement, though he could only report agreement to send Javelins. Kaunda is still standing out against troops, at any rate on our conditions. But Harold was very tough.

Thursday, 2 December to Saturday, 4 December. After Cabinet, down to Hell Corner Farm to start the removal agony. On Friday Ted and I worked till 9 pm scrubbing carpets and floor. On Saturday afternoon it, of course, poured. When the new housekeeper arrived at 5 pm chaos reigned and we were frantically trying to finish her room. She took it very well. Later, as we were consuming our first meal of the day, in the kitchen, the doorbell rang. Two Cabinet boxes! I got up at 6 am to cope with part of them. And then people ask why there are not more women in public life! I doubt the Chancellor has to do his own removing.

[1] Patrick Blackett, President of the Royal Society and Professor Emeritus at Imperial College since 1965, had become part-time scientific adviser to the Ministry of Technology in November 1964.

Sunday, 12 December. Intrigued by Alan Watkins's article in the *Spectator* on 'The Conservatism of Mr Wilson'. He brilliantly hits a number of nails on the head. It is quite true that Harold has not done much to undermine the power of the civil service (he was already placating them before the Election, modifying his threat to swamp them with outsiders) and clearly he is pretty matey with Burke Trend. When, for example, I was urging that we should try to bribe Rhodesian civil servants away from Smith, he was all in favour of our encouraging them to stay as he was sure they would be only too ready to swing over to us at the right moment and he couldn't imagine having anyone better than, say, a Burke Trend, in a key position there when Smith was overthrown. It is also true that he is 'highly reluctant to sack anybody' (*vide* Frank Soskice); that he is both kind-hearted and anxious to be liked. It is also true that he is no sweeping reformer, except in little things.

Monday, 6 December. First of my new weekly office meetings at the Ministry, designed to give me tighter control over the Department and to influence policy in advance instead of waiting for submissions to be put up to me at the last minute, or allowing officials to pre-empt the Ministry line at the multitudinous international gatherings which they attend. (The idea was Dudley Seers's.) The meeting was highly successful. I laid down the lines of work for the coming year. Now we shall plan our activities properly.

In the afternoon went with Oram[1] and my Under-Secretary, Ambler Thomas, to see Michael Stewart about our representation at UNESCO. For over a year the FO has been trying to get us to do more to counteract Russia's alleged manipulation of UNESCO for political purposes – of which my people can find no evidence. Thomas says this is a bee in the bonnet of Mr Greenhill, an Under-Secretary at FO, and Michael, of course, faithfully took his officials' line that we ought to have a permanent representative of higher grade and diplomatic experience in Paris. I managed to head him off it for six months.

Tuesday, 7 December. A long and onerous Cabinet.

We were going to slide over Rhodesia with barely a word as to how things stood when I said I wanted to ask some questions. First I wanted some more information about the Commonwealth peace force which Harold said they were trying to raise to guard 'both sides of the Kariba Dam'. The only reply I got was to argue how desirable it was to have such a force, but I was left as much in the dark as ever about how it could do its job. Secondly, I wanted to know more about the reported peace moves. Was it true that we were prepared to negotiate with Smith? And had not the time come for us to have a Cabinet discussion on our long-term constitutional objectives in Rhodesia? Harold said no one was negotiating with Smith. The ideas being discussed were that the Governor might get half a dozen people to join him in forming a Governor's council. It was obvious that there would have to be a period of direct rule, followed by a period of minority rule, but also there would have to be a period of majority rule before independence could be granted.

Then on to another headache: earnings related short-term benefits. Peggy's

[1] Albert Oram, Labour and Co-operative MP for East Ham South, was my Parliamentary Secretary.

scheme was voted down, though I backed her.[1] (Dick didn't because of the effect on public employees.) Peggy is becoming very bitter about the way her ideas are knocked about. She is particularly bitter about Dick who, we agreed at our end of the table, is obsessed with the claims of his own Department. So when he tried to get permission to build an extra 6,000 houses in 1966 at a cost of £19m on the grounds that the construction industry would not be fully employed, Peggy, Tony Crosland and I combined in opposing him, saying it was time that schools and hospitals had a turn. It was referred back eventually for further consideration.

Thursday, 9 December. Michael raised the question of our diplomatic representation at the Vatican and mouthed some phrases about this being the appropriate moment to raise it to ambassador status. I am glad to say he was well and truly trounced, Fred Peart and Tony Crosland whispering that the FO was full of Catholics. Only Longford made a few pathetic bleats in support. Harold was sympathetic. His motives stand out a mile. He has, in his own words, more Catholics in his constituency than any in the country. I was amused by the mixture of Harold's gamesmanship and Michael's subservience to his officials. But the rest of us had no doubt that the move would unnecessarily stir up a hornet's nest. The US has no representation at all! Harold tried to get through a suggestion that he should tell the Archbishop of Canterbury (who was opposed to the idea) that we would definitely do it later, but we headed him even off this and Michael meekly acquiesced. I am more than ever convinced that, if one shows some guts, the formidable FO is just a paper tiger.

Thursday, 16 December. George presided over Cabinet as Harold is in Washington. He certainly gets through business more quickly. Whether over a longer period the quality of our decisions would suffer is another question. The Americans [have] now agreed to a limited oil embargo, though not as much as we would have liked. George warned we might be faced with a cut off of oil to Zambia; also other retaliations before we were ready with a full airlift to Zambia. I protested that the Chancellor had made a statement about pensions to Rhodesians without Cabinet being consulted (even though Cabinet had met the same morning), and I was supported by both Frank Cousins and Douglas Houghton on this but George merely denied any knowledge of how it happened. When I asked whether this meant that the Rhodesian crisis had been taken out of the Cabinet's hands, he merely said, 'As the PM put it, we are at war.'

Tuesday, 21 December. Harold reported on his American visit to Cabinet. On Rhodesia he said there had been a 'complete turn-round in the American view' and they were now backing us enthusiastically on oil sanctions and were letting us have big planes for the airlift. When he arrived the Americans were still dithering, but 'once I met the President it went like a bomb'. Harold was full of beans about his trip: said the President was 'full of admiration' for the

[1] Miss Margaret Herbison, affectionately known as Peggy, MP for North Lanark and Minister of Pensions and National Insurance. She was widely esteemed for her conscientiousness and integrity.

behaviour of our Cabinet over the past year, had a lively sense of our parliamentary difficulties and thought our narrow escapes, majority-wise, were great fun. Obviously the two get on like a house on fire, and Harold couldn't resist adding that he had been asked to help illuminate the Christmas tree: 'the first time a PM has been asked to do this with the President since Churchill did it in 1943'. (This reference even crept into his speech in the House later.)

On Vietnam he had been impressed with the President's deep desire to get peace negotiations going and his anxiety that we should act as the peace-makers and take some new initiatives. It might be that we should have news of a new American initiative soon, but it was better he said no more about that at this stage. But the President had made it clear that he would warmly welcome any openings we could secure.

Later I talked to Harold on the front bench. He asked me when I was going away as he wanted to talk to me tomorrow. 'With our small majority I can't get rid of people at the moment and create more Reggie Pagets on the back benches, so I'm planning some sideways moves.[1] You have done a marvellous job in building up the new Ministry and I want to know whether you want to stay a bit longer or whether you feel frustrated because of the aid ceiling and would like to move.' He grinned at me affectionately and said, 'It would be an interesting job and you would have a good successor.' Intrigued, I asked him to tell me what he had in mind, but he said, 'Wait till tommorrow.' I wonder what he is plotting? He is always very warm towards me, his traditional greeting being, 'How's my little Barbara' or 'little Minister?' I have never seen him more relaxed than he was in his speech. Despite unusual fire from Heath, he still dominated.

At 8.45 pm phone call from Marcia. Could I come down and see the PM? Harold waved me into his room, boyish and slightly dishevelled. 'May I open my heart to you? You and I ought to talk more, only I'm so busy and you are, too. Have a whisky or brandy?' When I said I'd love a brandy, he said, 'It's the only thing that keeps me going. Fortunately I have a most intelligent doctor who prescribes it for me. It does something to my metabolism.'

He then said he had problems and I was the centre of them. 'Oh, I don't mean you cause them. But only your decision can help me out of the web. The others are against what I am going to suggest, which proves to me I am right. Bert Bowden and Ted Short are excellent bureaucrats, but they have no political nous at all. I ought to make a political shuffle and, if only our majority were even ten, blood would flow. If we win the election, it *will* flow. I have two incubi. Can you guess who they are?' I said, 'Tom [Fraser], of course.' He groaned and said, 'And how.' I said, 'You ask Ted about that. He is vice-chairman of the Traffic Commission of the GLC and they are going mad. So is Stephen Swingler.'[2] 'Don't I know,' he retorted. 'I often talk to Stephen. The

[1] Reginald Paget QC, Labour MP for Northampton since 1945, had been an Opposition spokesman from 1960 to 1964, but was not given a job in the Government. He held highly individualistic views and resigned the Labour Whip from December 1966 to June 1967 over the Government's Rhodesia policy. He was made a life peer in 1974.

[2] Stephen Swingler, left-wing Labour MP for Newcastle under Lyme, had already made a name for himself in the Commons as Parliamentary Secretary at the Ministry of Transport. He was a skilled parliamentary performer and a prodigious worker and was to prove an invaluable ally in my coming struggles in the Ministry. One of my first preoccupations was to get him his much-deserved promotion to Minister of State. He died tragically in 1969.

trouble is he is too loyal. Who is the other?' And I said Frank Soskice. 'Yes,' he replied, 'I always knew Tom was weak, but I was saddled with a shadow Cabinet, every one of whom expected a job.' He went on, 'I *must* have a Minister of Transport who can act. Tom has got a very strong Permanent Secretary whom Churchill got rid of in the Cabinet secretariat and brought in Burke Trend (though I'll get rid of Helsby before I'm through).[1] I am convinced he has killed integration. But we have *got* to have an integrated transport policy: I can't hold the Party otherwise. And the Party is the key to everything. Unless you accept my offer the reshuffle can't take place. I hope you will, but, Barbara, if you say no I shan't hold it against you. I know what you feel about Overseas Development, but I want you on the home side. I think you are the best person we have got. I want you to be Minister of Transport.'

I closed my eyes. Then I said, 'Who would go to ODM, because I really care about it?' He said, 'There are two possibilities and you shall choose. One is Tony Greenwood.' I said, 'But Tony is weak and you need a toughie on aid.' 'Tony', he said in tones of contempt, 'has no brains. I soon realized that all he is good at is public relations. But you've got a mind. The other', he added, 'is Fred Lee.' 'Oh, no,' I said. 'Tony wouldn't be too bad,' he replied. 'You've set the pattern for him to follow and he's got Dudley Seers.' 'And Andrew will keep him in line,' I conceded. 'What happens to the Colonial Office?' 'Merged with Commonwealth Relations. But, Barbara, I do hope you'll take it.'

I said, 'I'll have to have advisers and can I get rid of the Permanent Secretary?' He said, 'You can have anything you want.' 'I must think about it,' I said. 'Can I tell you tomorrow?' 'Yes,' he said. 'Ring me in the morning. And for God's sake say yes. I must have a tiger in my transport policy and you are the only tiger we've got.'

Wednesday, 22 December. After talking things over with Ted, his conclusion was: 'I don't see how you can refuse.' Already I had reluctantly faced that fact myself. Phoned Harold at 8.10 am to tell him I wanted to help if possible, but there were a few points I wanted to clear up with him. He asked me to come and see him before OPD. He was as pleased as punch at my acceptance. 'Tommy will help you. Your job is to produce the integrated transport policy we promised in our manifesto. I could work something out myself, given half an hour.' He hoped to make the announcement later in the day. I went away keeping it all bottled up inside me.

At 5 pm George Thom (my Private Secretary) told me shyly that the Private Office of MOT had been on the phone: when was I going to take over? So that cat was out of the bag! Apparently the announcement was to be made at 6 pm. I asked him to call the boys at ODM together in my room 'for a Christmas drink'. When they learned it was a farewell party, there was dismay. Andrew, who had heard from No. 10, came in shattered. 'I had fooled myself that there was no danger of your being moved.' I made a little speech and could hardly hold back the tears; failed totally when Andrew paid me the most moving tribute: 'We have learned to respect you. We had indeed become very fond of you.' The

[1] Sir Laurence Helsby, Joint Permanent Secretary to the Treasury and Head of the Home Civil Service. He was made a life peer on his retirement in 1968.

Economic Planning people were dismayed. Tears were pouring down Peter Ady's cheeks. We then had to let the press in and I was rushed off to TV where I could do little but stall. Homewards very, very sad, to Hell Corner Farm.[1]

Thursday, 23 December to Sunday, 26 December. Paper full of pictures of me. My appointment the sensation. The fact that I couldn't drive had almost, as Harold predicted when I tried to use this as an argument against appointing me, turned out to be an asset. Ted and I drove back to London so that I could kiss hands. Then into the Ministry with Tony to introduce him and say last farewells. I could hardly tear myself away from my beloved desk. (Andrew later sent me a letter I shall treasure all my life.)

So home at last to Christmas, punctured by various phone calls which I refused to take. Stephen Swingler nobly took over the ministerial comments on the road accident figures; also stood by for twenty-four hours for a meeting with George Brown about the railways' 'early warning' of their intended fares increase due to expire on 28 December. On Christmas Eve Stephen phoned to say all attempts to locate George had failed. He had been doing a tour of office parties and just wouldn't reply to messages. That morning he was still *hors de combat* and the meeting clearly could not be held. Apparently this sort of thing has happened before.

Wednesday, 29 December. Back to London to the press mobs waiting for me outside the Ministry of Transport. I had almost to fight my way through. The press poured after me upstairs and I had to let them photograph me in relays for an hour. But I refused to give interviews and, to placate the correspondents, had to promise a press conference next week. The place seemed intimidatingly masculine, the liftmen a bit gruff, and I noted that there was no welcoming Sir Thomas Padmore waiting at the door to greet me as Andrew had done when I first went to ODM.[2] But, undeterred, I smiled at everyone and was told afterwards that I was the first Minister of Transport ever to be seen smiling in the place.

After lunch held a meeting with as many of the top chaps as could be collected. By my usual technique of asking idiot-child questions I produced some interesting revelations. (I heard later from Stott[3] of GLC that some of his friends in the Ministry had told him, 'It was rather an unhappy meeting' – and gathered that this was to be taken as a compliment.)

I also discovered that they had one part-time economic adviser, Michael Beesly, in the whole Ministry. He worked under the 'co-ordination' Deputy

[1] In the reshuffle the most notable promotion was that of Roy Jenkins, Labour MP from 1948, first for Central Southwark and later for Stechford, Birmingham. He had made his name in the House as a formidable debater on the back benches and had been appointed Minister of Aviation outside the Cabinet in 1964. His performance had been impressive and he now came into the Cabinet as Home Secretary, a post which suited his reformist temperament. Frank Soskice became Lord Privy Seal, Tom Fraser was offered Aviation, but preferred to retire from the Government and Fred Mulley took his place.

[2] Sir Thomas Padmore was Permanent Secretary at the Ministry of Transport. He had once been tipped as going very high indeed in the civil service hierarchy but seemed to have lost interest and was blamed for letting the work of the Ministry drift under Tom Fraser.

[3] Director of Highways and Transportation at the GLC 1964–67, after which he became Traffic Commissioner and Director of Transportation.

Secretary, though the others had a right to use his advice. When I asked in what way they did this, the answer was that they would stop him in the corridor and ask for his views! This over, I took a large box of reading matter and went off to the country.

In the few days' break I took to sort out my ideas I practically had to build a transport policy from scratch. The Labour Party had always believed in an integrated transport system under public ownership and this had been the purpose of the Labour Government's 1947 Transport Act which set up a British Transport Commission [BTC] to integrate all forms of public inland transport (except air transport), to acquire the assets of the railway companies and the long-distance road haulage companies and to draw up area passenger transport schemes. The Act was fiercely attacked by the Opposition and the road haulage industry and when the Conservatives came to power in 1951 they lost no time in reversing it. The BTC was instructed to sell back its road haulage assets to private firms, competition was restored between road and rail and finally, in the Transport Act of 1962, the BTC was disbanded and its subordinate Executive transformed into four independent Boards for railways, London transport, docks and inland waterways.

But the Tories had not succeeded in denationalizing everything. The road haulage sales had hung fire. By 1956 less than 20,000 road haulage vehicles had been sold back out of 32,500 available for disposal and when the trunk services had been put up, only 528 out of 6,115 vehicles had been disposed of. The Government had bowed to the inevitable, recognized that the British Road Services [BRS] of the BTC were offering a co-ordinated network of trunk services which industry valued, decided to allow BRS to retain a substantial number of vehicles and merely reorganized it into five operating companies under the BTC, of which BRS Ltd dealt with general haulage. When the BTC disappeared in 1962 these assets were transferred to the Transport Holding Company [THC] together with the BTC's road passenger transport companies, shipping assets and travel agencies, with instructions that they were to be run on commercial lines. The THC had thrived and expanded and I had a formidable force to deal with in its managing director and later chairman, Sir Reginald Wilson.

Nor had the railways been denationalized, merely decentralized. The 1962 Act had wiped out some of British Rail's debt and then instructed it to pay its way. The Beeching Report, published in 1963, showed that this was to be done by drastic pruning of the network with over 2,000 stations and a third of the route mileage being eliminated. This had caused an outcry not only in the Labour Party, but among local communities.

Labour spokesmen had bitterly opposed the 1962 Act as leaving transport without any unifying authority of any kind and I therefore faced demands from the Party and the unions for the re-establishment of the BTC, for the re-nationalization of road haulage and for the reversal of the Beeching closure policy. While strongly believing in integration I felt we had to take account of transport developments since the 1947 Act. In the first place there was little evidence that the BTC umbrella structure had succeeded in integrating road and rail movements. Secondly the nationalization of road haulage had meant acquiring hundreds of small firms with inferior vehicles at excessive cost. It seemed better to encourage THC to continue its steady expansion of BRS by buying worthwhile firms and vehicles. Thirdly an explosion in the use of road transport – particularly the private car – had taken place. In 1947 there were only 3½ million vehicles on the road, including nearly 2 million private cars, so the railways played the predominant role in the transport of passengers and goods. By 1964 the number of road vehicles had risen to over 12½ million, including 8 million private cars, and the Road Research Laboratory was forecasting an increase to over 18 million cars by 1975. There had been a dramatic switch in transport of all kinds from rail to road, including a big expansion of C licences held by traders carrying their own goods. Recognizing that it was no use nationalizing road transport if own-account operators were to be left uncontrolled, the Labour Government in 1946 had at first announced that no C licence holder was to be allowed to operate beyond a radius of forty miles without special authority, but in the face of an outcry by industry it had lost its nerve and agreed to free own-account-operators from any restrictive licensing.

In such a situation it was no use trying to turn back the clock. I refused to be a King Canute, trying to force people onto railways which could not take them where they wanted to go. If the private car had brought the boon of mobility to millions of people, which it clearly had, then that boon should be available to everyone. We then must collectively face the consequences and deal with them through new arrangements which reflected the new facts.

In the first place we had to decide what size railway system we wanted in the new situation, how to subsidize it and how to get more traffic from road to rail. One obvious way was through the liner train concept which Dr Beeching had launched: the need to get away from small, slow waggon-load consignments of freight to a modern door-to-door through service by fast trains carrying containers, in which sundries traffic had been loaded at special depots for easy transfer from lorry to rail. But this hopeful development had been bedevilled by the question of 'open terminals'. The BRB *and the Government, anxious to get the highest return on their investment in the new container terminals, wanted them open to all-comers. The National Union of Railwaymen [*NUR*], fearful of redundancies for its members, wanted access limited to* BRS *and* BR *cartage vehicles. So the adoption of the new method had been stymied and this was one of the problems I had to solve.*

But it was the urban traffic problem which was the most serious. Movement in our towns and cities was seizing up. Public transport had been undermined by the flood of private cars and living conditions made miserable by heavy vehicles. How could we accommodate the new mobility without ruining the environment? One answer had been vividly expressed by Professor Colin Buchanan in his Report, 'Traffic in Towns', produced in 1963 when he was Urban Planning Adviser to the then Minister of Transport, Ernest Marples. The Report warned starkly that the number of road vehicles was likely to treble within the next twenty years and urged that 'unless steps are taken the motor vehicle will defeat its own utility and bring about a disastrous degradation in the surroundings for living'. His analysis was invaluable but his proposals for an elaborate and expensive restructuring of our cities to accommodate the car had been quietly buried by the Ministry. I was convinced we had to save the urban environment by an expansion of the road programme to syphon as much traffic as possible away from town centres, by the subsidization of public transport, by restrictions on the use of the private car in city centres and by the imaginative development of commuter rail services. Above all I believed it had to be done by the creation of new democratically accountable Passenger Transport Authorities with a remit to expand public transport and integrate road and rail services.

*I was particularly anxious to apply this concept in London where public transport was losing ground and where attempts to make the London Transport Board [*LTB*] pay its way had miserably failed. I already had sympathetic listeners in Maurice Holmes, chairman of the* LTB*, and in the Labour majority on the Greater London Council [*GLC*] under the chairmanship of Sir William (Bill) Fiske. The* GLC *also had a live-wire in P. F. Stott, its Director of Highways and Transportation. An added help was the fact that my husband was an alderman of the* GLC *and a member of its Transport Committee.*

One thing I had already decided and that was to bring more economists into the Ministry. Tommy Balogh had recommended Christopher Foster, a Fellow of Jesus

College, Oxford and an expert on transport, to head the team. I was determined to publish a White Paper outlining my policy proposals by the summer, so there was no time to lose. I also asked Chris Hall to join me again.

1966

Saturday, 1 January. A very pleasant dinner party with Christopher Foster and Stephen at Hell Corner Farm. The former had jumped at my invitation to come and talk. When I asked him if he would come to the Ministry he said yes eagerly, provided the status was right. Tommy had recommended him and I took to him, though I thought he was a bit young and brash. He will take a bit of breaking in. Spent the weekend reading and noting follow-up points and people to see.

Monday, 3 January. Into the office, seriously this time. Sir Thomas Padmore wanted to see me and I told him firmly that I wanted Foster to come into the Department and what for. He concurred eagerly and said he would go off and see Helsby. Embarrassingly he assured me of his complete loyalty. The more unctuous he became, the less I liked him.

At 4 pm off to No. 10 to see the PM as I had asked. 'Come in, little Barbara,' he greeted me affectionately. He was delighted with the publicity I had received and said, 'You see, I told you it would be an asset that you did not drive.' I told him bluntly I wanted to get rid of Sir Tom. I had my eye on Jones of Housing, who was a planner.[1] Harold thought it was a good idea, but didn't know what he would do with Sir Tom.

Tuesday, 4 January. Saw Stanley Raymond of BRB in afternoon informally and alone. (My Private Secretary, Bill Scott, has been insisting on sitting in at every confab, till I told him I would let him know when I wanted him. Stephen says it dates from the days when Marples used to run the Department from his own home and no one knew what was going on. Personally I think it is also a routine piece of PS spying in an intensified form.) Raymond was friendly and we got on well.

Wednesday, 5 January. Another private confab: this time with Maurice Holmes of the London Passenger Transport Board [LPTB]. After some polite skirmishing we got down to brass tacks when I invited him to let me have his ideas on London's role in a national transport plan. It then emerged he had done a paper for George Brown's Labour Party committee on transport and promised to let me have a copy. Cosy moment when Sir Tom said to me

[1] James D. Jones, the Deputy Secretary in charge of Planning at the Ministry of Housing and Local Government. He was a live-wire and I wanted to poach him from Dick Crossman to strengthen the planning side of my own Department.

casually, 'Bickerton tells me there are rumours that I am to go.'[1] I looked him straight in the eye and decided that some honesty was the best policy. I told him I had been under great pressure from my parliamentary colleagues to move him because he was held responsible for Tom Fraser's policy, or lack of policy. He spent half an hour trying to persuade me things would be very different now I had taken over.

Friday, 7 January. At 12.30 I dashed over to DEA to see George, whom I have been trying to contact all the week to clear my poaching of Foster. To my relief he was in his most ebullient mood, kissed me, said my line at Transport was what he had been begging them to take for ages and that he would help in any way he could. I could have Foster. But what I needed to do first and foremost was to get rid of Sir Tom. He was ready to offer me his key man, Douglas Allen, whom he had offered to Tom Fraser in an effort to save him: 'One of my oldest friends.' But the PM had not taken up the idea: 'Perhaps he had already made up his mind. He didn't consult me about the changes and I suppose he is within his rights in not doing so.' (Harold had told me George was furious about not being consulted.)

Monday, 10 January. Dined with Tommy Balogh who was full of the need for me to take Allen. I told Tommy that I needed a small political group on policy as well as the official administrative one, and we agreed to have the first meeting of it in his office on Friday: Stephen, John Morris[2] (who has arrived to take over from George Lindgren), me, Tommy, Christopher, Holmes and a few more.

Tuesday, 11 January. Visit from Helsby to discuss changes. He said it was difficult to find a niche for Sir Tom Padmore. If I still insisted, it would take a couple of months to make a transfer in an unspectacular way. 'It isn't usual to move a Permanent Secretary when the Minister changes. I don't say it can't be done, but it has never been done before.' He was friendly; I was regretful but firm. Lunched with Jock Campbell with whom I discussed construction costs.[3] He is desolate that I have left ODM.

Wednesday, 12 January. Lunch with Sid Greene, the NUR General Secretary, in a private room at the Great Northern Hotel – the red carpet out with a vengeance. He is a rather pathetic figure. I told him I would like one of his best men to come and help me plan an integrated transport system, putting the railways' angle. This obviously nonplussed him but he said he would think about it. We parted on most amiable terms.

[1] Frank Bickerton, Chief Information Officer at the Department.

[2] John Morris, MP for Aberavon and Parliamentary Secretary at the Ministry of Power, was my choice for the new Parliamentary Secretary at Transport which Harold had promised me.

[3] John (Jock) Middleton Campbell was that rarity – a Socialist businessman. He was chairman of Booker McConnell Ltd and of the Commonwealth Sugar Exporters' Association. He was chairman of the New Statesman Publishing Co. from 1964 to 1966 and became chairman of the Milton Keynes Development Corporation the following year, presiding over the new town's impressive development till his retirement in 1983.

Friday, 14 January. Meeting at Home Office on the Road Safety Bill.[1] Roy Jenkins called me in ahead of the others. I told [him] he was lucky his Permanent Secretary was retiring anyway.[2] He said that nonetheless he had had an emotionally exhausting time.

Back to the Ministry for a hurried briefing on Hull roads. Had asked James, Ministry of Housing planner, to come along to discuss a Humber Bridge.[3] He said this should follow agreement on a regional development plan for Humberside.

Then off to Cabinet offices for our private conspiracy meeting in Tommy's office. Had had a good deal of trouble with Scott about this.[4] Had merely told him I had a meeting, not with whom or what about. He was bursting with curiosity; muttered in my presence, 'I have no idea what the meeting is about.' When I ignored this he got even with me by suddenly informing me my meeting would have to be postponed as Sir Laurence Helsby wanted to see me and he had fixed 5 pm. I told him firmly my meeting could not be cancelled and I'd see Sir Laurence at 6 pm. He looked shocked at this and said, 'I'll say 5.30, Minister.' 'Say 5.45 and I'll arrive a quarter of an hour late', I retorted. At Tommy's we discussed our national transport plan. Over at 6 pm to Helsby to find, as I expected, that he was perfectly free at that time. Again he was very affable. The Permanent Secretary at Defence was leaving as soon as the defence review was finished – *i.e.* April – and Dunnett was going to Defence from Labour. There would be nothing out of the ordinary for Sir Tom then to go to Labour, but it would mean waiting three months. I said I didn't mind waiting two as long as it was all agreed.

Monday, 17 January. Off to Hull to speak in the by-election: photographers at station, standing room only at meetings. I told them categorically that, as soon as the development plan was decided for Humberside, they would have their bridge. Speeches went down well.

Tuesday, 18 January. Meeting with Maurice Holmes and Stanley Raymond over railway pensions. Raymond urged that he should be authorized to negotiate a wages grades pension scheme with the NUR so as to get Greene 'off the hook' over the PIB report.[5] I instructed my chaps to contact Treasury immediately over this. Later Raymond phoned to say the NUR had jumped the gun by calling a national strike for 14 February.

Later, while dining with Dick at the Garrick, I got a message to attend a

[1] My predecessor, Tom Fraser, had published a White Paper, 'Road Safety Legislation 1965–66' (Cmnd 2859), setting out proposals for dealing with drunken drivers and with faulty goods vehicles. It fell to me to carry the proposals into law. The provisions for breath-testing raised a storm of controversy.

[2] Sir Charles Cunningham had been Permanent Under-Secretary at the Home Office since 1954.

[3] John (Jimmie) Richings James was Chief Planner at the Ministry of Housing and Local Government.

[4] Bill Scott, the Private Secretary I inherited from Tom Fraser and who clearly resented my arrival, believed he had a right to keep an eye on all my activities and I was equally determined that he should not.

[5] In October George Brown had referred to the PIB a claim by the railway unions for a substantial improvement in pay and conditions which BRB was resisting. The report, just published, had angered the unions by recommending that the BRB offer of a 3½ per cent pay rise plus other improvements should not be exceeded except in the case of clerical workers who should get 5 per cent. The one bright note for the NUR was the report's statement that pension arrangements for the wages grades were inadequate and that joint discussions on a modern pensions scheme should proceed.

meeting at No. 10 on the strike at 9 pm. Found Harold and Ray Gunter there, but no George. Harold said significantly that we wouldn't wait for him as he believed he was 'not feeling too well'. At that moment George walked in, lolling his head aggressively, his speech thick and belligerent. When Ray suggested George and I should see the unions first, he squared up angrily, saying that Cabinet had agreed the day before to back the PIB collectively and that he wasn't going to have Ray waiting in the background to do his conciliation act: 'The nice cuddly Gunter coming in to save the day when the nasty Brown had turned them down.' Ray was all ready to pick a quarrel but Harold kept saying soothingly, 'Keep going, Ray, keep going.' They swopped some cynical calculations about the unlikelihood of the strike materializing and went on quarrelling about whether Ray should be present at the first talks or not. Harold's role was merely to try and jolly them along. He made no attempt to disguise his contempt for George's condition, accepting it as a cross he must bear and only once putting his head in his hands with sheer fatigue. It was an unedifying three-quarters of an hour, watched silently by Burke Trend and the two secretaries.

Wednesday, 19 January. Early phone call from George to say that as soon as he had left the meeting he realized he was wrong to have allowed himself to be jockeyed into seeing the unions without Ray Gunter and that he was going to insist on Ray being there. At Cabinet I asked him and Harold whether I should postpone my planned visit to Blackburn that afternoon. They both said they didn't know when the meeting would be held and that I could always come back for it. Off to Blackburn expecting to be recalled.

Thursday, 20 January. Phone call from Scott at 9 am to say a meeting was being held that morning: he had only been informed just before midnight, too late to get me back. I instructed him to enter a strong protest to George Brown and No. 10.

Friday, 28 January. George handled the meeting with the railway unions beautifully (despite the fact he had been up till 3 am celebrating the Hull result).[1] He told them we could not make offers under duress but if they would call off the strike and negotiate with Raymond, although he could make no promises, he would not ask them to do this if they were wasting their time. Had Harry Nicholas [of the TGWU] to lunch. He was very pleased I had asked him: said he had never received an invitation to talk to Tom Fraser at all until, just before Tom was sacked, Stephen Swingler brought them together. Even then Tom Fraser had nothing to say to him.

Monday, 31 January to Friday, 4 February. This might be described as 'living with George' week. It started with an early meeting on Monday with George, Jim Callaghan and Ray Gunter to discuss what we could offer to avert a railway strike. The attitude of the others was a perfunctory discussion of what the

[1] Kevin McNamara held the seat for Labour with a majority of 5,851 compared with the Labour majority of 1,181 in the General Election. The overall swing of 4.5 per cent to the Government was the largest at a by-election for more than ten years.

alternatives would cost; no examination of principle. I was authorized to tell Stanley Raymond he could offer two out of three fringe benefits: advancing the forty-hour week one month (£1m); an extra day's holiday, and a pensions scheme for wages grades (£4m). Only if desperate was he to offer a month's advance on pay (£1m). All this to be conditional on the strike being called off. When I reported to Raymond he said categorically that this would not do the trick as the men had been offered the pension anyway by agreement of MOT and Treasury. What the men wanted was cash. Checked up and found we had, in fact, authorized him to start negotiations on pensions. Was just minuting my colleagues to this effect when George phoned after lunch (a little thick in speech) to say he had very good reason to know that the men would settle on the fringe benefits alone. 'Sid Greene?' I asked, but he trumpeted, 'Don't press me, but I have it on good authority.' When I begged leave to differ he got truculent, bellowing down the phone, 'If you don't want to add your name to this, I'll add mine. But you go ahead with this and you'll get all the credit for ending the strike.' I told him it wasn't a question of who got the credit but of getting the results. As he continued his brow-beating (and one can't argue with George, only listen) I said I would try it, but we must clear it with our colleagues. He said, 'I'll do that. You just go ahead and get on to Raymond.' Raymond was appalled when I phoned him again, saying the NUR wouldn't look at it but he'd do his best.

At a policy meeting in the Ministry that afternoon I told officials we were getting nowhere fast with the transport plan and demanded detailed papers on a National Freight Authority [NFA].[1] They were alarmed when I said I wanted to integrate all freight. On Tuesday Raymond phoned to say the NUR had gone away to consider his offer but he thought the situation was hardening. On Wednesday we learned that the men had voted twenty to two not to lift the strike threat, though they were still willing to talk. Again Raymond assured me that the NUR Executive would have to get some indication he was willing to talk money. Tried to contact George for a meeting that evening but he dodged me as usual.

In the meantime I had very useful private talks with Raymond on railway policy. I told him I wanted to take the tin can of unavoidable deficit off the tail of public transport. To do this I wanted to put in consultants or a study group to identify the loss-makers so that we could give him a fair operational target. He was pleased with my approach and prepared to consider the study group, but argued effectively that 'identifying the loss-makers' had been Beeching's line

[1] The National Freight Authority was born of my growing certainty that the only effective way to integrate road and rail transport was through organizations responsible for managing both road and rail movements rather than by recreating a vast overlord authority like the BTC with separate road and rail executives under it. I wanted integration to be a reality on the ground rather than a theoretical concept at the top. This, I believed, involved different treatment for passenger and freight traffic. The integration of passenger transport should be the responsibility of regional or local authorities who alone could link town planning, road planning, traffic management and all forms of public transport in a coherent plan designed to strengthen and extend the role of public transport. Freight movements by road and rail, or canal, where appropriate, should be under a freight authority which, using up-to-date methods of freight handling including containers and liner trains, could offer an efficient through service. 'I am confident', I told the Party's local government conference, 'we can build up an expanding freight service under public ownership which can compete effectively with private haulage and help us make fuller use of our railway service.' Nonetheless my idea was strongly resisted in the Department while the railway unions resented the idea that liner trains should be taken away from BRB.

and that we must be more positive: 1) decide that the country wanted a rail system; 2) decide what kind and shape; and 3) decide how it should be paid for. Felt very cheered at progress.

Woke Thursday morning to hear that George had paid a surprise visit to the NUR to make a dramatic appeal to railwaymen to call off the strike. Had got an eleven–eleven vote on this. All this looked like near-triumph for George, but I suspected he had made things more difficult and was furious that he had done it without consulting either me or Raymond; both of us look and feel foolish. Raymond phoned me early to say as much and I told him I knew no more than he did. Raymond said, fairly enough, 'I must know how you want me to play it. I don't know how the First Secretary left it. Is it back in the Government's court? How much more than I offered did he hint at?' I promised to ring him after Cabinet.

At Cabinet Ray Gunter told me neither he nor the PM knew anything of George's intention and agreed he was impossible to work with. After a long Cabinet, in which we had the most spirited wrangle yet on Vietnam – Dick, Frank, Lee and me protesting at Stewart's statement of support for the renewal of American bombing,[1] even the Chief Whip being angry about it – the only reference to the strike was on the need to call the Ministerial Emergency Committee. Harold said the handling of the strike was in the hands of us four. Ray and I agreed we must find out what George had offered the previous night so that Stan Raymond could know how to proceed. Grudgingly George agreed to meet us at 6.30 pm at DEA. I raced over, cutting a meeting short, only to find George was not in his room and that his PS had been instructed to 'keep us happy' while he completed talks in another room. After ten minutes I went into the next room to find George drinking whisky with Terry Pitt of Transport House and already half seas over.[2] He thereupon came out to talk to us, thick of speech and at his most truculent. The only thing, he insisted, was to decide whether the eleven–eleven vote was good enough for us to proceed on the assumption that the strike threat was withdrawn. Ray Gunter, keeping his temper admirably under impossible provocation, wanted us to weigh things up much more carefully. George, claiming he ought to be congratulated on having done so well, finally admitted he had made 'one mistake': he had in the excitement of the argument let slip that there might be a fourth element in the offer – some more money. 'But dammit I was under great strain.' When Ray and I tried to point out that this slightly altered the situation, he got very abusive. (I wasn't surprised by his admission. George's way of taking the law into his own hands by his 'little mistakes' – *vide* Woodrow Wyatt and steel – are now becoming familiar. I felt like saying that Raymond could have achieved just as much if he had been allowed to offer money.) After a painful hour we drew up a statement for me to issue saying that in the light of the vote I had authorized Raymond to reopen talks. We also agreed that a month's advance in pay was openly on the list.

[1] President Johnson had ordered the resumption of the bombing of North Vietnam and the Foreign Office had issued a statement including the words 'Her Majesty's Government understand and support the decision of the US Government to resume the bombing which they had suspended.' This caused a major row in Cabinet and among our backbenchers.

[2] Terry Pitt was head of the Labour Party Research Department at Transport House, the Party's headquarters.

On Saturday morning Raymond phoned me to say that following protracted talks the NUR had passed a resolution saying the offer was unacceptable, but not mentioning a strike. It was agreed the position should be left to sweat over the weekend, though the meeting of Cabinet and NEC at Chequers on Sunday may give us a chance to discuss it.

Sunday, 6 February. Highlights of the Chequers meeting with the NEC were: 1) its unruffled harmony; 2) the intellectual superiority of Jack Jones [of the TGWU] over the rest of the trade union representatives; 3) total absence of references to public ownership in the policy document prepared for us. Tom Driberg raised the fact that there was no reference to foreign affairs either and was promised by Harold, at his most conciliatory, that another statement on that would be prepared.[1] The best discussion was on the general economic situation, in which Jack Jones and Mik starred.

Monday, 7 February. The start of one of the most exacting weeks of my life. Had Griffiths of ASLEF to lunch.[2] He told me he would be placed in a very awkward position if the Government conceded any more to the NUR over the strike. His members would want to know why he hadn't stood out. At 3 pm was called to PM's room for a meeting on the next steps to avert the strike. We left it that Ray, George and I should meet the NUR negotiating committee again to make a firm offer of the four points that had already been hinted at.

Thursday, 10 February. Set alarm for 2 am to finish speech [on the Road Safety Bill]: overslept and didn't wake till 4.45 am. Panic rush to get it finished before I had to leave for early meeting at DEA with George and Ray and the union negotiating committee. George put the four points firmly to them and we went round the same questions and arguments, Dan Kelly on the NUR side chipping in quietly and devastatingly whenever George looked like winning the day. The men then went off to consult their Executives.

While on the front bench, was summoned to see the PM. I urged him to make no more monetary concessions, though by this time we had heard that the NUR had turned down our morning offer by eighteen votes to five.

Harold said he might call a Ministers' meeting on the strike in the morning. Later I heard that George had called one for the morning at DEA with the whole NUR Executive. Bewildered, I sought out Ray Gunter, who was furious. He said this was George going off at half-cock again, acting without reference to anyone, least of all the PM. 'This is pure jealousy on George's part. He can't bear the thought of Harold ending the strike where he has failed.' He said he wasn't going to George's meeting and I said I wouldn't go either. At midnight got a call from the office to say the DEA meeting was on, Ray Gunter was going and I was asked to go.

[1] Tom Driberg, MP for Barking, and Ian Mikardo (Mik), MP for Poplar, were left-wing members of the constituency parties' section of the NEC. With Dick Crossman and myself they had been part of the Bevanite group which continued to have a strong hold on the local Party activists.

[2] Albert Griffiths was the General Secretary of the Amalgamated Society of Locomotive Engineers and Firemen [ASLEF] until his death in 1970, when he was succeeded by Ray Buckton.

Friday, 11 February. SHOWDOWN DAY! At 9.20 am walked into George's office at DEA to be greeted by a penitent and charming George. It was quite inexcusable of him not to have consulted us. His only exoneration lay in the fact that he had had an impossible day. After talking to Woodcock the idea had come to him quite late of having a last try to convince the whole NUR Executive. Into meeting at which NUR Executive – and no other union – was there in force. Carefully and courteously George did his best to convince them that the Government had gone as far as it could, though it had certainly not thrown over the Guillebaud concept of 'fair comparison'.[1] With the strike out of the way, we could discuss the other implications of the report with them.

We then retired to George's room, leaving the NUR to chew it over. For four hours the minutes ticked by while we waited. George and the rest started to drink, while I worked on some office papers. George's manner began to change rapidly: he got noisy and aggressive, abusing his officials in what he no doubt considered a jocular way and shouting at everyone. At 3 pm I said mildly I hoped I shouldn't be prevented from voting at 4 pm on the Second Reading of the Sexual Offences Bill.[2] This set George off on a remarkable diatribe against homosexuality. As an Anglo-Catholic and Socialist, he thought society ought to have higher standards. As Eric Roll[3] and officials argued with him good-naturedly, he got very passionate: 'This is how Rome came down. And I care deeply about it – in opposition to most of my Church. Don't think teenagers are able to evaluate your liberal ideas. You will have a totally disorganized, indecent and unpleasant society. You must have rules! We've gone too damned far on sex already. I don't regard any sex as pleasant. It's pretty undignified and I've always thought so.'

Just as we were feeling the long wait would never end, Sid Greene came in to say we had lost by twelve to eleven. George was deeply disappointed. I left him phoning Harold and went to vote. The Second Reading was carried by a comfortable majority of 179 to 99. I then heard Harold had cancelled his trip to Liverpool and we were to go to No. 10 to meet the NUR Executive at 6 pm.

Arrived to find a huge crowd of press and public outside. Harold, looking tired but excited, said to Ray and me that he assumed he had better play it very conciliatory at first. I agreed but urged that he must stand firm. He had whiskies waiting and, as the men trooped into the Cabinet room, he jumped up, dashed for the door and shook them all by the hand as they came in.

As the whiskies circulated, Harold took brandy and then started a very gentle, indeed rather hesitant, exposition of the political and economic difficulties involved and why we couldn't do more.

[1] In November 1958, the Conservative Government, faced with growing discontent on the railways, had set up a committee of enquiry under Mr C. W. Guillebaud, Reader in Economics at Cambridge, to study the relativity of railway pay to that of staff in other nationalized industries and in outside services and companies and to establish the degree of job comparability. In its report of March 1960, the committee found that railway pay had fallen substantially out of line and recommended adjustments. The Macmillan Government accepted the obligation to see that railway workers received 'fair and reasonable' wages but insisted that the railway system must be remodelled and management by the British Transport Commission decentralized. This was achieved in the Transport Act, 1962.

[2] A Private Member's Bill, introduced by Conservative MP Humphrey Berkeley, to implement the Wolfenden Committee's recommendations on homosexuality, notably to legalize homosexual acts between consenting adults in private.

[3] Sir Eric Roll, Permanent Under-Secretary at the DEA, 1964–66.

Harold then called on me, having already thrown me into the scales, as it were, telling them the reason he had appointed me was to get them the sort of transport changes for which they had been waiting. I spoke with the conviction I felt. Beeching, I began, had said he wanted to see them at the top of the wages league. (Nods.) But on what basis? On the basis of a skeleton railway service pared to the bone and operating on purely commercial principles. I didn't want a skeleton railway system. My researches already showed that we should never solve the transport problems of this country without a great expansion and improvement of public transport. (More nods.) But that must mean a new financial basis for the railways. Some dead wood would have to be cut out of the system, but it must clearly expand at other points, *e.g.* to deal with the commuter problem. You couldn't do this on the basis of 'paying its way'. We have got to identify the social cost element and provide for it in other ways than running up a general deficit. 'I'm not surprised the morale of railwaymen is low. I want to take the tin can off the tail of public ownership. I've told Raymond I'm coming to see him next week to work out the sort of railway structure this country needs and I'm determined to see that, before it is decided on, you shall be brought in on the ground floor. I'm working flat out on all this and I only wish I could have got further before this interim crisis broke on us.' I could see they were impressed, and Harold rubbed it all home by saying I was speaking for the whole Cabinet. He repeated his offer of a meeting on 11 March – though again stressing it wouldn't affect the money available for this round or for 1966.

We could feel the whole atmosphere changing. Some of them put questions to me, but when one of them tried to snarl at Raymond Sid slapped him down. Sensing the advantage, Harold suggested they might like to retire and talk it over. It was 10 pm and we reeled into Marcia's room while they trooped off to another one, Harold promising to send them sandwiches. Harold was delighted with my speech – 'What passion' – and almost optimistic. His son, Giles, joined us and we whiled away the hours chatting with George Wigg, Gerald Kaufman and Lloyd-Hughes.[1] Harold, with his high sense of drama, trooped us all upstairs to peep out at the crowds waiting in Downing Street. As time passed, Harold said, 'It looks hopeful. If we can't interrupt TV with a news flash soon, it would be better to go on all night.' At 11 pm Sid came out looking tired but distinctly perky for him. But all he would say, solemnly and officially, was that they wanted to ask some more questions.

By the time the men trooped in, bottles of beer, thick sandwiches, sausages and pies were circulating. Sid said the point that some of them wanted to know was, if the talks on 11 March revealed that the lower-paid workers ought to get more, could it be made retrospective? Harold decided the moment had come to get tough: he was sorry but there could be no more money this round. It seemed deadlock as the men trooped out again. I could only hope my instinct had been

[1] George Wigg, the Paymaster-General, was Harold Wilson's close personal adviser on matters generally but particularly security. Gerald Kaufman, officially the Labour Party's Parliamentary Press Officer, was unofficially a member of Harold Wilson's 'kitchen Cabinet'. He was elected Labour MP for Ardwick in 1970 and held junior posts in the 1974–79 Labour Government. Trevor Lloyd-Hughes was the PM's Press Secretary till 1969, then Chief Information Adviser to the Government. He was knighted in 1970.

right: that the chief thing we had to do was to convince them this really was the brink and that we were prepared to go over it.

Another painful wait, with Jim looking in from next door. Just as hope seemed dead, out came Sid. The strike was off by thirteen votes to ten! I hugged Harold and Ray. Peace with honour! I went home elated.

The results of Denis Healey's review of defence policy were published on 22 February. The White Papers (Cmnd 2901 and 2902) said the target was to reach a ceiling for defence expenditure of £2,000 million at 1964 prices by 1967–70, a cut of £400 million in our Conservative predecessors' estimate, from over 7 per cent of the GNP *to about 6 per cent. Our forces would be withdrawn from Aden when South Arabia achieved independence in 1968, but we would retain a wide range of commitments, including a military presence East of Suez. Economies would be achieved by abandoning a number of British aircraft projects in favour of the purchase of American F-111s, which would increasingly take over the strike-force role of the aircraft carriers in the 1970s. The plan for a new aircraft carrier was therefore dropped.*

On the publication of the White Papers Christopher Mayhew, MP *for Woolwich and Minister of Defence for the Navy, together with the first Sea Lord, resigned in protest, declaring that commitments should be cut rather than equipment. 'We cannot maintain a world role in the 1970s, including a presence East of Suez, on £2,000 million', he declared in his resignation statement.*

Monday, 14 February. Cabinet meeting on the Defence White Paper. The papers were already full of rumours that we were to drop the new aircraft carrier and that Mayhew might resign. Harold began by saying we would not be deterred by this from taking decisions on their merits. Nor would we postpone publication until after the Election as we mustn't look as though we were running away. Healey outlined his conclusions.

There was not a voice raised in support of the carrier. F-111 was a tougher proposition – the argument raged for over an hour. Dick and I pointed out that its sole use was for an East of Suez policy. The others appeared to give in, but, as I did not, Harold had a last crack at me. He was surprised to find I wanted a purely European policy. I retorted, 'Since you have maligned me, Prime Minister, by calling me a European' (laughs: through it all the atmosphere had remained remarkably genial) 'may I point out that I *do* want Britain to have a role East and South of Suez.' ('Good,' said Harold.) But, I added, I wanted it to be an economic rather than a military one. 'Don't let us forget that by adopting this policy we are deliberately sacrificing any increase in our overseas aid.' I was sorry to poach on Tony's preserve but he never puts up any fight for it. (Later he told me he thought my intervention had been 'irrelevant'.)

Wednesday, 16 February. Practically a whole day on railway policy. First, in the morning at Marylebone House, Raymond and other members of the Board demonstrated to John Morris and me the existing closure policy and how they thought it should be modified. Raymond had organized it very well. I was impressed and I think even my cynical officials were, too.

In the afternoon we met at the Department to discuss finance. I got Raymond to outline his ideas, then led him gently into accepting that we should have a joint study under a joint steering committee to identify the 'social cost' elements and give BR realistic financial targets.[1]

Friday, 25 February. With rumours of a General Election in the air, I decided I must make my speech to our local government conference at Birmingham a major speech on transport policy. I had already been asked by George Brown to submit my main transport proposals for the next five years and had included a new deal for the railways and the creation of a National Freight Authority. This, Dick told me, had been passed by the PM.

Caught my train just in time and was met at Birmingham by Joan Bourne, our Local Government Organizer, who said my Private Secretary wanted me to ring him urgently. When I did so, Bill Scott said that the Chancellor was very worried about my intention to mention a National Freight Authority and didn't want me to commit us to any public expenditure until I had consulted him first. I said that this would not mean any increased public expenditure, to which he replied, 'That isn't certain.' So I asked who had alerted the Chancellor anyway. To this he said frankly that 'certain people' in MOT had been alarmed by my mentioning this in my speech and had got on to the Treasury! Civil service intrigue can go no further. . . . I pointed out that the press release had already been made and there would be even more press comment if I left it out now than if I left it in. Scott had reluctantly to admit that might be so: it was purely a matter of 'political judgment'. So I went ahead and made my speech, which was well received.

Saturday, 26 February. Papers full of my speech. Glad I had the nerve to go ahead.

Monday, 28 February. Special Cabinet meeting at which Harold confirmed that the Election would be on 31 March and outlined reasons for it. He said he had already formed the view before Hull. On political grounds, this was a good moment according to the polls. But there were good national reasons, too. If we delayed till October we would face six months' electioneering which would be bad for sterling. Nor could we carry through much more legislation between now and October because of the Finance Bill. No one objected to the decision. Harold then said that, in order to meet the accusation that we were running away from the Budget, Jim intended to make a statement in the House assessing the economic situation, not offering any tax bribes, but saying he did not foresee the need for any 'serious' tax increases, announcing our mortgage proposals and also a betting tax to pay for them. We all agreed it was very ingenious, though we had doubts about the popularity of the tax statement.

Wednesday, 2 March. Meeting at DEA between George Brown, Ray, myself and three chaps from TGWU: Harry Nicholas, Alan Thompson[2] and Collier, to try to win their acquiescence in the reference of the bus pay claim to the Board. George handled it with the utmost tact and skill.

[1] The main aim of the joint review was to work out the cost to the BRB of the 'socially necessary' railway lines I wanted to subsidize, leaving the Board with a financial target it could hope to attain, but it also gave us the opportunity of probing the efficiency of BRB management which had been causing the Department increasing concern.

[2] Alan Thompson was National Secretary of the Passenger Services Group of the TGWU.

Thursday, 3 March. In the afternoon the EPC [Economic Policy Committee of Cabinet] passed my proposals for a new railway policy and National Freight Authority in broad outline. The anticipated attack from Jim never materialized (so much for the civil service's wrecking efforts!).

Tuesday, 8 March. Press demonstration of new Red Arrow single-manned buses with turnstile. Great press success. Having a woman Minister certainly does help publicity!

Wednesday, 9 March. Stephen and I were summoned to see Harold about concessionary fares on non-municipal buses.[1] This has arisen sharply in Harold's constituency. I pointed out that the Chancellor would want consulting about this as any increase in rates would attract rate support grant. But Harold doesn't like to leave any open sores unhealed. He therefore dictated a Minute promising a review. He asked me, 'Will you issue this or shall I?' As we left Stephen remarked, 'So that is how policy is made.'

The Election was a low-key affair, and on a relatively low poll (75.9 per cent) Labour was returned with an overall majority of 97, its share of the vote rising from 44.2 per cent in 1964 to 47.9 per cent. All the Ministers were returned, most with increased majorities, one of the few exceptions being George Brown, whose vote at Belper dropped from 6,312 to 4,274. This time Patrick Gordon Walker won Leyton with a substantial majority. For the Conservatives Edward Heath's majority was nearly halved and four former Ministers lost their seats, including Peter Thorneycroft and Christopher Soames. The Liberals' share of the vote fell from 11.1 per cent to 8.5 per cent. Only twenty-six women were elected, three fewer than in the previous Parliament.

There were few Cabinet changes following the Election, the most significant being the elevation of George Thomson who became Chancellor of the Duchy of Lancaster with specific responsibility for political relations with the European Community. At the same time George Brown was given oversight of our economic relations with the EEC. Jim Griffiths, veteran Secretary of State for Wales, left the Government, as did Frank Soskice and ten non-Cabinet Ministers. Jim Griffiths was succeeded at Wales by Cledwyn Hughes, while Lord Longford took over Frank Soskice's post as Lord Privy Seal. Dick Marsh was brought into the Cabinet as Minister of Power and Fred Lee moved to the Colonial Office. Douglas Houghton became Minister without Portfolio, but retained oversight of Social Service policy.

Monday, 4 April to Friday, 8 April. Back at work after one of the most boring Election campaigns I have ever experienced. It wasn't that the meetings were not well attended and, in Blackburn at any rate, I had more systematic heckling by a posse of Young Conservatives than ever before; but there was an air of unreality. I felt the campaign was merely an unavoidable hiatus in our work and I think this is what the country felt: they had made up their minds at the start and they remained unchanged.

[1] One of the Labour Government's first acts had been to restore to local authorities the freedom to arrange travel concessions on municipal buses for old age pensioners and others. This had been immensely popular but anomalies had arisen where municipal services giving concessions were operating side by side with non-municipal ones which did not and there had been a growing demand to enable local authorities to subsidize similar concessions on non-municipal buses. This was finally achieved in my 1968 Transport Act.

Had to go into the office on Monday for a meeting of Ministers presided over by the PM on the 70 mph speed limit.[1] Harold had refused to let me put out the compromise we had agreed (extension for two months) during the Election. Despite ferocious opposition from George Brown and Roy Jenkins, I got it reaffirmed. The reception was better than we dared to hope, thanks to my idea of coupling it with banning heavy lorries from the fast lane of motorways. (Approving leaders in *Guardian* and *Times*). Office meeting to discuss how to present the new railway policy in the interim period. Stephen had the bright idea that we should not announce the batch of railway closures and approvals (held up during the Election) till we were ready to announce the setting-up of the railway policy steering group and working-party of consultants. I sent for Raymond to explain this; also to tell him I wanted to improve workers' consultation in the railways and therefore to put a working railwayman on the steering group. Both he and Scott Malden[2] had fits about this, but eventually I got their agreement, provided the unions were given the responsibility of nominating someone, instead of my doing so as I had intended.

At Thursday's Cabinet we discussed the Queen's Speech. By this time Harold had issued his list of new appointments and reappointments. (Relieved I didn't have to go through the business of kissing hands again.) He had shown his usual skill in balancing Left and Right (David Ennals promoted as Army Under-Secretary at Defence, Fred Lee still in the Cabinet, though everyone relieved he has been moved from Power. I expect he will disappear completely when Colonies is merged with Commonwealth Office). He has kept up his modern touch by making Eirene White Minister of State at the Foreign Office: the first woman Minister at the FO, and it was an inspired move to put Judith Hart in charge of Rhodesia.[3] But the Right still holds most of the key posts. I would be more worried about making George Brown and G. Thomson responsible for the Common Market if Harold hadn't made a speech at the same time to the National Farmers' Union [NFU] saying we couldn't accept the European agricultural policy.

Long fight to decide what must be sacrificed in next year's legislation programme. Harold backed me up over the Road Safety Bill (which they had tried to exclude). Agreed that Consumer Protection should go to make room for it and Leasehold Reform; also the Ombudsman to be sacrificed if necessary, though Harold made mysterious references to fact that this might have to be retained if he was to make the civil service changes some of us were hoping for (glance at me). I must pursue this after the holiday: am determined not to let them renege on their promise to move Sir Tom. Off to HCF for week's break to do some reading.

[1] Tom Fraser had introduced an experimental 70 mph speed limit on roads which was due to expire on 13 April and I wanted to extend it for another eighteen months. Some of my Cabinet colleagues, notably Roy Jenkins, were restive about it but, despite opposition from my Conservative 'shadow', Peter Walker, I succeeded in getting the Order through the House. When the experiment ended in September 1967, I extended the limit on motorways indefinitely, while reviewing the limit on other roads. I had also earlier made permanent the trial ban I had introduced on the use of the fast lane of three-lane motorways by heavy vehicles.

[2] Peter Scott Malden, Under-Secretary at the Department, in charge of railways.

[3] Judith Hart, elected for North Lanark in 1959, had quickly become one of the left-wing group which supported Harold Wilson's candidature as Leader of the Party following Hugh Gaitskell's death in 1963. She had become Joint Parliamentary Under-Secretary of State for Scotland in 1964 and had now been promoted Minister of State at the Commonwealth Office, with particular responsibility for Rhodesia.

Friday, 8 April to Sunday, 17 April. Hard at work on National Freight Authority and White Paper policy. I've really got the boys thinking! It is amusing to see them trying to reverse the instinctive reactions which they imposed on Tom Fraser. What fascinates me about a Minister's job is the difficulty of knowing when to stand out against official advice. Some of it (*e.g.* on technical problems) is invaluable, and civil servants are also the reservoir of knowledge about past parliamentary battles, the reaction of interested organizations, etc. Yet there are limits to the purely technical, and even these types of judgment overflow into, or are influenced by, political and economic attitudes. When you are pushed for time (as you always are) it is hard to stand out against a strong submission. You wonder if you are being unwarrantably pig-headed – yet, if you fail to back your own judgment, you are often left defending something about which you aren't happy.

Tuesday, 19 April. Arrived at No. 10 early for meeting with PM. Harold greeted me affectionately, was very pleased with my publicity generally: 'It is going very well; I always thought you had a slight flair for public relations.' I then raised the question of Padmore, and he said the trouble was Ray Gunter wouldn't take him.

In the afternoon, a key meeting with the TUC General Council at which I outlined my policy. I said there was a great deal in their memorandum with which I agreed but I did not believe the way to get integration was to recreate the British Transport Commission. *I* was going to be the BTC. Integration would be achieved much more effectively on the freight side through the NFA and on the passenger side through regional transport authorities. They were clearly impressed and we had a most amicable discussion, Hayday in particular being very reasonable.[1] Ted learned from Geoffrey Goodman[2] afterwards that the unions felt they were really getting somewhere on transport at last.

Spent the afternoon on union meetings. First the NUR – a sad-eyed lot. My line went down well, though I said it was impossible to stop all closures and ended with an impassioned plea for open terminals for liner trains. 'If railwaymen won't use the railways, how the hell can we expect anyone else to? Other people may not have had the right to ask for this, but I have.' Stephen told me afterwards that even Frank Donlon, their President, who had been saying shortly before that he would never accept open terminals, was shaken. I offered to meet their executives and attend their union conferences.

The Queen's Speech reiterated the main planks of our policy: the setting up of a Land Commission to acquire land for the community; the promotion of comprehensive education; the introduction of rate rebates and a scheme to assist those of modest means with their mortgages; the control of private building. An Industrial Reorganization Corporation was to be created to stimulate the modernization of industry and the prices and incomes policy was to be reinforced. Steel was back in the legislative list. A Ministry of Social Security was to be set up to press ahead with the review of social security which was to lead to the new superannuation scheme. Most significant of all was Harold Wilson's achievement in getting into the Speech the first clear declaration that the Government

[1] Frederick Hayday of the General and Municipal Workers [GMW].
[2] Industrial correspondent of the *Daily Mirror* and a personal friend.

'would be ready to enter the European Economic Community provided essential British and Commonwealth interests were safeguarded'.

Thursday, 21 April. State Opening (televised), followed by a Parliamentary Party meeting on the Queen's Speech. From the truculent tone of some interventions on Vietnam, etc., it is clear the Party is in a different mood from the last Parliament.

Spent the rest of the day in a frantic game of cops and robbers over Padmore. Sent imperiously for Helsby and told him I must have [Douglas] Allen. Helsby tried to tell me it was too late because the First Secretary now had other plans for him (though it was George Brown who had advised me to see Helsby quickly). When I said I would see George, Helsby dropped all pretence at geniality and said he would advise the PM against moving Allen. Managed to corner George as he left the chamber: he denied Helsby's story and said irritably that he wanted to be left out of the whole business. 'I warned you this would happen. I've now got to look after my own interests. I warn you they won't do anything.' ('They' being apparently Helsby and the PM.) Nobbled Harold on the front bench. He was sulky from Tory attacks on him over Rhodesia and from our people's less than ecstatic reception of his speech. He said he had instructed Helsby not to see me until he (Harold) had talked to him – did Helsby just defy him? He also said that I was going to get Allen as Director-General, but I left for Chester worried and dissatisfied, instructing Tommy to fight my corner.

Monday, 25 April. Lunch with Dick, at my request, to discuss better co-ordination of the work of our two Departments. We agreed to meet officially soon to plan our role in the new Cabinet Committee on Environmental Planning and to co-ordinate our ideas on the regional organization of transport and planning. Dick asked me if MOT had been consulted on the siting of Chorley-Leyland New Town and I said I didn't know: we agreed it would be appalling if it hadn't. Chatting generally, Dick admitted, 'I'm not really a Cabinet Minister, any more than you are; I'm a Departmental one.' I pointed out that I frequently raised international points without much backing from anyone else, over overseas aid, for instance, and he apologized for not having backed me on this. But he agreed when I said, 'There isn't really a Cabinet, only a Cabinet clique of inner Ministers.' He told me he had sold the rights in two books for a large sum (£30,000), one on government and the other his autobiography, and advised me to do the same. He dictates his diary for two hours every Saturday and files the tapes, taking Cabinet Minutes home.

Thursday, 28 April. At lunch in the House, sat at same table as Neil Carmichael and Norman Buchan who were discussing the revolt of the 'new Left' against the 'old Left'.[1] They said the new MPs were bored with Zilly, Sydney Silverman and John Mendelson with their endless Early Day Motions which just debased the currency of protest. Something more constructive was needed. Besides,

[1] Neil Carmichael was Labour MP for Kelvingrove and Norman Buchan for West Renfrewshire. Both were of the moderate Left.

they made the mistake of not being sociable enough with the newcomers, some of whom even regarded Mike as pussy-footing. Later in the tea room I discussed same theme with Brian O'Malley[1] and Trevor Park, who said that Norman Buchan and Paul Rose[2] were the leaders of the new move. They believed the Left should specialize more and offer more informed criticism, but I reminded them that the function of the Left was to guard the conscience of the Party and insist that the Government, which was always in danger of being swamped by administrative compromises, did not lose sight of its principles.

After the 10 pm division, went to Jim's room at his request for a very hush-hush consultation on the Budget. He assured me that transport operators would be treated neutrally under Selective Employment Tax. I promptly asked him why: said I would be glad for A and B hauliers not to be given the tax back as I was seeking ways of getting bias unobtrusively into my transport policy in favour of rail. Couldn't he alter it? Reply: 'No, it's too late. The White Paper has gone to press.' In that case, I couldn't see the point of the consultation. Later I learned that three of my top officials had been consulted under oaths of secrecy and, when they asked whether they could discuss it with me, were told that the Chancellor would inform me when he thought it appropriate. I really do think the Budget procedure, which gives the Chancellor almost dictatorial power in matters greatly affecting other Departments, is inconsistent with effective planning and ought to be changed. I don't see why there could not be a general discussion in Cabinet of the various alternatives months ahead of the Budget, leaving it to the Chancellor to select at the last minute, but Otto Clarke[3] and Helsby, to whom I mentioned this, nearly fainted at the idea.

Monday, 2 May. There was a lot of uneasiness about the new tax but, with the enthusiastic support of Roy Jenkins and Tony Crosland, Jim got away with it. (Incidentally he had told me the idea was Nicky Kaldor's and Robert Neild's.[4] If it had only been the former's, I should have been a good deal more worried. He has a propensity for getting governments overthrown.)

Tuesday, 3 May. Lunch with Beeching in his very elegant, man-servanted house in Smith Square. (Nothing simple or suburban here.) An excellent lunch of scampi, lamb and strawberries accompanied by really superb wines. We talked transport policy all the time, Beeching laying down the law with an arrogance that comes, I suspect, from a clear mind that sees a logical answer to a situation and cannot tolerate any modification of it to meet human frailty. Though intellectually impressed by him, I am glad now we didn't put him in charge of drawing up an 'integrated' policy, as once mooted. It was typical of

[1] Labour MP for Rotherham since 1963, and a Government Whip. He became Deputy Chief Whip under John Silkin in 1967 and in 1969 became Parliamentary Secretary to Dick Crossman at the Department of Health and Social Security where he made a name for himself by his mastery of the complexities of the National Superannuation scheme. I found his political skill and acute mind invaluable when I became Secretary of State for the Social Services in 1974.

[2] Trevor Park, MP for Derbyshire South East, and Paul Rose, MP for the Blackley division of Manchester, were part of the new 1964 Labour intake. Paul Rose was my PPS from 1966 to 1968.

[3] Sir Richard Clarke, known as 'Otto', was Permanent Secretary at the Ministry of Aviation in 1966 and then at Technology from 1966 to 1970.

[4] Robert Neild, Cambridge economist, had been deputy director of the National Institute of Economic and Social Research before he was recruited by the Labour Government as Economic Adviser to the Treasury.

Beeching that, having contradicted everything I said during the meal, he then said abruptly, 'But don't think I am against everything you have done. I think you have done well to strengthen the economic side of the Ministry and are quite right to refuse to reconstitute the British Transport Commission,' and offered to help in any way he could as he showed me to the door.

At 4.45 went to see the PM in his room at the House at his request. One's overwhelming impression of him is always of informality to the point of rakishness. When Marcia puts her head round the door in the middle of a very private talk, he calls out cheerily, 'Come on in.' And he loves to pop out into his private Private Office, with Gerald Kaufman or Lloyd-Hughes hovering about in it under Marcia's dominance, to tell them about one of the latest outrages of the civil service machine. He seems to be running a private war with the civil service, despite the outward correctness of his relationship with it, and I feel he doesn't always come out on top and, when he does, it is merely as a result of his political astuteness. He wanted to talk to me about Sir Tom. He still hoped to get Allen for me but would have to clear it with George first: 'I told them not to fit you in until I'd seen George, who is coming at 5.30.' I could also have Jones as deputy. I grabbed his coat tails as he went bobbing about to tell him there was another matter I wanted to talk to him about. He is always so friendly and approachable it is difficult to be dramatic, even about Rhodesia. Finally, I got it out: 'Please don't be offended or think I don't trust you, but you know, don't you, it is something I should have to resign over, if it went the wrong way?' He flashed back, 'It is something I'd have to resign over – if it went wrong. But it won't. As a matter of fact, I don't believe the talks will get off the ground. The Rhodesian Front is being very vocal. I believe these boys would ditch Smith.' And on this note of his buoyancy, I left comforted.

Thursday, 5 May. A nightmarish day with more work to cram in than even a 24-hour day could accommodate. As I stood writing my speech for the Structural Engineers' dinner before Cabinet, Burke Trend came over and said, 'You're very busy, Minister.' I told him I had three things to do at once and just didn't know what the answer was. 'How many times have I heard Ministers say that,' he smiled. 'And it is getting worse. I think the trouble is that more and more things are being taken to the top – perhaps because Parliament is getting more vigilant about details.' He is always very nice to me, with something intelligent and sympathetic to say, and I can understand Harold liking him. Worked on my speech through a long Cabinet discussion on the Ministry of Social Security Bill.[1]

Tuesday, 10 May. Made history by going to a meeting of the NUR Executive – the first Minister of Transport ever to do so. At last I had got an invitation from Sid Greene – though he wanted it making clear that the initiative had come from me. I walked in relaxed and informal and spoke almost without notes and sitting down, only to find that they conduct their proceedings with great

[1] In order to get rid of the humiliating image attached to non-contributory benefits Peggy Herbison had been pressing for the merger of her Ministry with the National Assistance Board in a new Ministry of Social Security. When the Bill was enacted in August she became Minister of Social Security and the NAB was replaced by the Supplementary Benefits Commission.

formality and always stand up when they speak. I've noticed that the weaker men feel their position is, the more they insist on correctitude and protocol. I addressed them fluently, I believe effectively, and almost passionately. I have never believed in anything more sincerely than when I told them I was offering them probably the railways' last chance and urged them to concentrate on getting every available piece of traffic they could on to rail in order to justify my new network and the subsidy I was fighting for. The sat stolidly round the large table, though I could see some of them were impressed. I spoke for twenty minutes and answered questions for fifty. Some of the questions were pathetic, just as most of the members of that EC are, poor, rather distraught creatures, clinging to prejudice as a substitute for self-confidence. Afterwards Sid was bubbling with suppressed excitement and in that private room of his in the GNR Hotel really overflowed with *bonhomie* and exuberance, pressing drinks on us and hoping the food was to our liking, and getting as near as he dare to congratulating me on having so successfully put over the line he wants the NUR to adopt.

Met the NUR again at 4.30 pm at Ministry of Labour to discuss wages, conditions and negotiating machinery under Ray's chairmanship. We made a good, probing, non-committal start before I had to rush off to the annual dinner of the Federation of Civil Engineering Contractors. A major speech to make, with the banqueting room at the Dorchester crowded with members come to gawp at the woman Minister. Got home blind with fatigue. What a day!

Another black cloud was looming up in the threat of the first major strike by British seamen since the war. The National Union of Seamen [NUS] had legitimate grievances. In 1965 they had reached an agreement with the employers for a 25 per cent pay rise, part of which was to cover the inevitable overtime that has to be done at sea, and a number of ship's masters had been abusing this by putting the men on Saturday and Sunday work not normally done on those days. In protest the union was demanding the immediate introduction of a forty-hour week with Saturday and Sunday work paid as overtime. There was great sympathy with the conditions under which the men had to work, not least the antiquated provisions of the Merchant Shipping Act of 1894, but the claim was a clear breach of prices and incomes policy. Efforts to avert the strike by the offer of a court of inquiry into the seamen's grievances failed and the strike started on 16 May, the General Secretary of the union, William Hogarth, declaring that it would be a 'fight to the finish'.

Harold Wilson took the situation very seriously. It was, he said, 'a strike against the State – against the community', and on 23 May, when 527 ships had been immobilized, the Government proclaimed a State of Emergency. It also announced the setting up of a court of inquiry under Lord Pearson, a Lord Justice of Appeal, which produced an interim report on 8 June recommending the introduction of the forty-hour week over twelve months, instead of the two years the employers had been offering. The union, however, rejected this out of hand and further efforts at conciliation by the Prime Minister and the TUC, including the Government's announcement that it intended to set up a wide-ranging inquiry into the structure and organization of the shipping industry as soon as the Pearson Inquiry had finished its work, failed, Mr Hogarth declaring that the strike had become 'a fight with the Government and not just with the shipowners'.

A few days later an exasperated Harold Wilson astonished the House and the Cabinet with an attack on the NUS which, he said, was being influenced by outside pressure from a 'tightly knit group of politically motivated men'. Challenged to substantiate this claim he later listed eight Communists who, he declared, had been asserting pressure to prolong the strike, including Jack Dash, unofficial leader of the London dockers. In the meantime, thanks to the efforts of George Woodcock, the union and employers had been brought together again and, following an offer of more annual leave, the NUS called off the strike on 1 July, claiming a great victory.

Thursday, 12 May. Cabinet consisted of one item, the seamen's strike. The discussion wandered all over the place for an hour and then ended with the inevitable conclusion: we must stand firm.

Sunday, 15 May. Chris Foster phoned *re* Jones of Housing. I've lost my fight over Allen, George having decided to promote him in preparation for the departure of Eric Roll. Harold asked Dick if he would let Jones go and at first Dick bucked at the idea. But on Thursday he told me that he had decided it would be a good thing to have our Departments inter-linked in this way. He had therefore told Jones it was up to him.

Monday, 16 May. Won my battle to extend 70 mph experiment at HAC [Home Affairs Committee of Cabinet]. Delighted and astonished. The ease with which Roy capitulated indicates, I think, that public opinion is firming on this issue.

Tuesday, 17 May. Cleared my transport paper for EDC [Economic Development Committee of Cabinet] with George Brown. Though he had some reservations, he too said it was a pleasure to have a coherent transport policy produced at last. The PM having cleared our decision to continue the 70 mph speed limit till September 1967, it was decided I should take the Prayer against the limit in the House and make my announcement then. The extension was received remarkably calmly, reinforcing our view that the previous Tory outcry against it was largely electioneering. My first encounter with Peter Walker. It went well, partly because he was at the disadvantage of not having seen our press notice and the figures we had put in the Vote Office, his Whips' Office having failed to pass on the copies we had sent for him. So the Tories have their inefficiencies, too!

Thursday, 19 May. A day of bad news. First the office sent me a letter from the NUR giving the involved resolution they had passed on liner trains. Scott had jumped – almost gleefully – to the conclusion this was a flat rejection of open terminals. I decided it was folly to accept it as such and told John Morris to phone Sid Greene and ask him not to release the resolution till he had had my reply. Next blow: Dick is having second thoughts about Jones. Apparently his other planning officer, James, is going to UNO and Dick can't spare both. Into Cabinet determined to check up on what is happening in Rhodesia. Harold said that next week the fact-finding talks would move to Salisbury. I asked tartly, 'What facts are they trying to find?' Harold said equally tartly, 'Whether there is any basis for negotiations.' Harold is always so plausible it is difficult to fault him, but I am left with uneasy feeling that he is on a slippery slope and that it is he who will increasingly have to yield, not Smith.

An unhappy discussion about the seamen's strike. Ray said that seamen showed no signs of yielding and we were in for a long struggle which would certainly embroil the dockers: Jackie Dash just couldn't wait. We agreed to proclaim an emergency on Monday so that we could get powers to control prices, though I said there was no need yet to bring in the Navy to move ships.

At a meeting with Raymond on the NUR letter I told him the best way was to assume the letter did not mean rejection, as it certainly did not say so in terms. He should acquire as many cartage vehicles as he needed to dispense with hiring and then go ahead and open the terminals and risk a strike.

Later John Morris minuted me that he had spoken to Sid Greene, who said of course it didn't mean rejection: this was the most I could expect them to say in order to save face, and no, they didn't intend to publish it. So we may salvage something yet!

At dinner had an interesting chat with Dick and Mike Foot, Dick at his most outrageous and sweeping. He said he hated the whole system of Cabinet Government and didn't bother to play any part in it, outside his Department. He rebuked Mike for a 'reactionary' opposition to more back-bench committees, said he wanted them to help him against his own officials. I warned him that the fascination of administration was like a dangerous drug: one should not take too much of it. And I agreed with Mike that the main job of a back bencher was to keep banging away at principles on the floor of the House, not to indulge in administration by proxy. 'Of course we in Government have to translate principles into administrative detail, and make some compromises on the way, but the job of Parliament is to force us to change those details back into principles from time to time in order to see how far we've strayed.'

Friday, 20 May. What should have been a quiet day of catching up with detail turned into one of furore by the sudden release by NUR of their resolution. I was very angry with Sid Greene for not having warned me (he is either very weak or very devious) and with the BRB for telling the press that the resolution meant the NUR had turned open terminals down.

Monday, 23 May. Delighted to learn from the papers that Harold is sending Judith Hart to Zambia; at least, delighted that once again he is entrusting a woman with a responsible job, but anxious as to what her visit could mean. Then on to Buckingham Palace for a meeting of the Privy Council to clear the Proclamation of an Emergency over the seamen's strike. A marvellously equipped aide-de-camp met me at the door and accompanied me to the drawing-room with a great clicking of his spurs. Roy Jenkins arrived with thirty seconds to spare and urbanely explained he could afford to cut it fine because the Home Secretary was the only Minister allowed to travel in a police car. The Queen looked charming in light green silk and, as usual, tried to make informal conversation after the formal business was over. This time she was a little nervous about it, not sure what to say about the strike: 'I believe the berths won't fill up for quite a time.' It was all over in half an hour.

At night we faced a late sitting on the rest of the Transport Finances Bill.[1] The debate didn't amount to much, though the Tories filibustered till 1.30 am. As I sat yawning on the front bench, listening to attacks on me for not having produced my policy earlier, I realized what a drag our parliamentary procedure is on rapid progress of any kind.

Tuesday, 24 May. A vital day in the evolution of my policy. I met all three rail unions at BR's headquarters in order to let Raymond explain the proposed new rail network to them. My heart was in my mouth because I knew it meant the closure of 3,000 more miles of lines, although the outcome would be a network of 11,000 route miles instead of the 8,000 proposed in the second Beeching Report. I told Raymond to pile on the positive side of the policy and he excelled himself. I told them I had got my colleagues' agreement to the survey into railway finances and stressed this meant a subsidy – open and overt – to the railways, something we had refused to other nationalized industries like coal. I then asked for questions. There was a long silence while I waited, hardly daring to breathe. At last Sid said slowly, 'I am very pleased with what we have heard. Clearly there is going to be a very good future for the men who are left in the system. Our trouble is, as I expect you know, with the men who will not have a place in it. I know you think we are always moaning and are against change, but we have to deal with our members and we have to speak for those who are affected. I shall have to moan a lot more, but nonetheless I am pleased with what we have heard and not least for the fact that we have had it all explained to us so fully in this way, not like when the Beeching Report came out – that blue book – and the first we heard of it was when a copy was put into our hands two hours before publication.' The other union leaders echoed him in turn, ASLEF saying, almost pathetically, 'You must help us with our members.'

Tuesday, 31 May. Broke my Whit holiday at HCF to come to London for a meeting of the Emergency Committee on the seamen's strike. Judith Hart asked me to come and talk to her about Rhodesia. I was relieved to learn from her that my fears about her visit had been unfounded. She had been sent to try to persuade Zambia to make a complete trade break with Rhodesia, which they were now reluctant to do because they believed economic sanctions had failed and were bound to fail.

Thursday, 2 June. Up to London for another meeting of the seamen's strike Emergency Committee: the position is getting very threatening though we are taking every possible step not to be provocative. A meeting with officials on NFC.[2] Padmore and the rest are doing their best to get me to leave bulk freight (the biggest part of rail freight) under BR while Foster and Beesly are adamant that an NFC should control all freight. Behind all the official politeness there is obviously a war going on.

[1] The 1962 Transport Act had given the public transport bodies impossible financial targets and the revenue grants earmarked for British Railways for five years had run out ahead of time. I had to get them renewed pending the implementation of my new transport policy and to get similar help for London Transport and British Waterways.

[2] We were now talking about a National Freight Corporation which would be a free-standing corporation responsible direct to the Minister.

Bill Scott asked for a private word with me afterwards. He burst out into a torrent of explanation as to why the redraft of the White Paper was not ready as promised: in fact the Department hadn't got its heart in it and wasn't really trying because it was fed up with the recent promotions and transfers. (Jones is coming on Monday after all.) It wasn't only Jones's appointment. Feeling had been building up ever since 1959, since when a succession of people had been imported into MOT – including the Secretary – and nobody inside ever seemed to be promoted. Morale had never been so rock bottom. He apologized for his outburst – he was by now near to tears of rage – but I had told them all to speak out and he was doing so. The Association for the administrative grades was meeting that night and would probably demand a meeting with Helsby. I listened in silence and thanked him for telling me, but mentally I was commenting: 1) civil servants behave exactly like other trade unionists when their interests are threatened, even to the point of going slow; 2) that I could deal with morale *and* improve the staffing of the Department if only I had a free hand; that is, they obviously would not have given a damn if Padmore had gone provided they could have had some promotions up the line which is what I always planned; 3) our system is damnably unfair on a Minister who has to carry the can back for any failures of her Department yet is unable to make the staff dispositions which would enable her to deliver the goods. I become more and more convinced that our civil service system needs radical overhaul.

Monday, 13 June. Up early to see Jim Callaghan at No. 11 about my NFC paper. The Department had failed to make an appointment with him for me so I rang him early and he could barely refuse. I soon saw he was in a bloody-minded mood and I got nowhere. On our way to EDC I told him that Tony and I were discussing not running for the NEC.[1] He was taken aback and said instantly, 'I shall run.'

At EDC we spent most of our time on the Channel Tunnel. I'm all in favour of it because it could do more to put our railways on their feet than any other single step, provided we insist on through transit rights across France. Nor do I mind it being built by private capital provided it is operated by a public authority (as proposed) with profit sharing for Governments, some public equity and right of eventual acquisition by Governments. But Frank Cousins hit the roof about it: said he was in favour of the Tunnel but was not prepared to sacrifice his principles. When reminded that France was not prepared to raise public capital, so it was this or no Tunnel for years, he waved the argument aside rather than answering it. And as usual he got his facts wrong, claiming that the roads leading to the Channel would have to be privately financed as well. Willie Ross's main objection was that the Tunnel wasn't being built in Scotland and he remained unmoved by my pointing out that, linked to fast freightliners, the Tunnel could overcome many of the disadvantages of manufacturers sited a long way from Western Europe. The latter might even find it worthwhile to use our deep-sea ports like Liverpool instead of Rotterdam. George Brown ruled that the majority was in favour of going ahead but the matter would clearly have to be put to Cabinet in view of the objections.

[1] There had been grumbles on the Left of the Party that there were too many Ministers on the NEC and Tony Greenwood and I had been discussing whether we should run again.

With ten minutes left to go we turned to the NFC, and here I met the full blast of Douglas Houghton's malice and Frank's muddled militancy. Jim said categorically he wasn't prepared to agree my paper even with all my assurances that the transfer of assets, sharing of the deficit, etc., were for negotiation. When George postponed the discussion for another meeting I took Frank aside and tried to probe what his objections really were. It was impossible to get them clear.

Tuesday, 14 June. A bitter discussion on seamen's strike in Cabinet. The TUC has upset the applecart by suggesting a solution that would push the increase up from the proposed 5 per cent to 7¼ per cent and the owners wouldn't play. The general view was that we should stand firm. Frank, who sits in Cabinet tight-lipped and withdrawn these days, protested that we couldn't have an open breach with the TUC, to which Jim Callaghan retorted, 'The TUC isn't the Government: we are.' I said I thought we should put ourselves in the wrong if we were the ones who took up a rigid position now. But the others brushed that aside. Jim gave more dark warnings about what would have to be done if the P and I policy failed: 'I warn Cabinet someone will have to take drastic action – and quickly.' Harold said he would see the TUC and try to get them to recognize the impossibility of their suggestion, the crucial nature of the economic situation and the danger of unemployment if the policy failed. He was not taking a rigid position and would be ready to see the NUS and seek a point of compromise within the policy.

Over to No. 10 to see Harold with Tony Greenwood about our idea of not running for the NEC. Harold was as relaxed and friendly as ever, not seeing our proposal as a plot against him, but identifying himself with us as in the old days as Left-wingers: 'You are the people the rank and file want. They would much prefer you to the Norman Atkinsons.[1] Jim Callaghan is the one who might get beaten. He'd be wise not to stand. He barely managed to get on: I beat him first time.' We left it that we would think it over. I then had a private word with Harold urging him to make Stephen Swingler and John Morris Ministers of State: 'We're much more entitled to some than other Departments who are rolling in them.' 'I agree I made some mistakes. But it will take time to shed some of the existing ones. Leave it to me.' I told him about the trouble I was having with the White Paper. He said our chapter on the NFC was first-class. As for Jim, 'He's in a bad state. Getting too arrogant.' 'You ought to get rid of him.' He smiled a cunning smile: 'That thought had occurred to me. But not a word to anyone.'

Wednesday, 15 June. The famous Party meeting on East of Suez.[2] All Ministers

[1] Norman Atkinson, Labour MP for Tottenham, was an uncompromising left-winger. In 1976 the Left succeeded in getting him elected Treasurer of the Party, but he was defeated and replaced by Eric Varley in 1980.

[2] Hostility to the Government's East of Suez policy had been growing among Labour MPs of both Left and Right. They had joined hands to table a Motion for the Party meeting calling for a 'decisive reduction' in our military commitments East of Suez by 1969–70, including a withdrawal from Malaysia, Singapore and the Persian Gulf. The Motion was moved by two right-wingers, Christopher Mayhew and Joel Barnett, a pro-European, and strongly supported by the Left. Harold Wilson took no chances and to a packed meeting made a lengthy apologia for the policy which he issued to the press. The speech obviously influenced some of his critics to abstain and to his relief the Motion was overwhelmingly defeated by 225 votes to 54. The majority, however, was not a true indication of the unease in the Party.

had had a strong whip to attend. Harold read a carefully prepared speech and I watched Mike's face while he did so. Momentarily he was impressed, but then he sank into disbelief again. I can't say I found it very convincing myself.

Monday, 20 June. Harold's statement after Questions about Communist influence on the seamen's union took us all by surprise. I couldn't find anyone in the Cabinet who thought it very clever. Elwyn and Roy Jenkins both assured me they had not been consulted. Is it Ray or Wigg who is to blame or is it just Harold's idea? At EDC we returned to the NFC and I was again under pressure from Denis and Frank Cousins who attacked the whole idea root and branch, while others like Jay and Crosland said it would be better to postpone the White Paper until there had been more discussion. My only friends were George Brown and – this time – Jim (my officials having won over his officials since the last meeting). George manœuvred so brilliantly from the chair that the committee found itself agreeing to consider the rest of the WP later in the week on the understanding I would reconsider phrasing of NFC section on more non-committal lines. The result is that we shall get the WP after all, provided I can square people on the NFC. I thanked George afterwards and he said, 'They are bastards, aren't they?' At the Emergency Committee later we still found ourselves without any need to use emergency powers. As Denis Healey said, 'Much as we should like a problem to solve, we haven't got one.'

Tuesday, 21 June. To Cabinet for a long discussion on the seamen's strike. Harold explained that he and Ray felt that many members of the NUS Executive would have supported a return to work if it had not been for outside pressures which were also operating on the strike committees. That was why he had thought it necessary to make the statement he did. This was received in a pretty non-committal silence by all but Frank and me. I asked if we could be given more details of the conspiracy, to which Harold replied ponderously that there were some things that were better not revealed, even to the Cabinet. (Shades of Wigg!) Frank said tartly that he thought such a statement was hardly calculated to help end the strike. Harold took all this imperturbably (at any rate on the outside). We agreed that the provincial emergency committees should now be set up, even though there is no real need for them yet, in order to justify renewal of the Emergency Regulations. We also agreed in principle to proceed with the Channel Tunnel, Frank still protesting that, much as he was in favour of it, he would rather not have it than have it on the terms proposed.

It was 12.30 before we turned to the most important item of all: prices and incomes policy. George Brown had submitted a lot of papers examining the whole basis of the policy and outlining the amended Bill.[1] In a rather moving introductory speech he admitted there was a lot of scepticism about the policy, even, he suspected, among members of the Cabinet, and before he became any

[1] The Bill embodied the proposals of the previous year's White Paper. It established the PIB as a statutory body and provided for the compulsory notification of proposed price increases, dividend increases, wage claims and settlements. Failure to notify was punishable by fines. The Government had thirty days in which to decide whether to refer the increases to the Board and where it did so the increase could not be paid until the Board had reported or until three months after reference, whichever was the earlier. Non-observance of the temporary standstill, or pressure by a union on an employer to breach it, was punishable by fines.

more extended on it he wanted to be sure where Cabinet stood. 'Do we want to go ahead?'

Harold then announced that we would have a special Cabinet meeting soon to discuss productivity, on which he knew some members of Cabinet had ideas (a friendly gesture to Frank). I slipped out before the rather rambling discussion had finished.

Wednesday, 22 June. NEC meeting at which we were supposed to discuss the overhaul of organization Harold had talked about, but he didn't turn up. He had used this argument to persuade Tony and me (successfully) that there was no reason for us to decide not to run for the NEC again. He had told us he was going to propose the setting-up of a commission to look into the whole organization of Transport House and that he intended to devote more time to the NEC. He had even rung for Michael Halls [his Private Secretary] and instructed him to see that nothing interfered with his attendance at the next meeting. But in the event, no Harold!

Monday, 27 June. Got my new version of NFC through EDC. I don't like it, but it is the best I can get. A hair-raising report on Concorde: the costs are escalating madly; the commercial prospects are poor; the thing will run at a loss and there is doubt whether it will fly at all because no one knows whether the sonic bangs will make life intolerable. Yet, thanks to the crass inefficiency of the Tories who negotiated the agreement, we have no legal escape route. Since the Chancellor couldn't be there we agreed to refer the matter straight to Cabinet.

Tuesday, 28 June. At Cabinet Harold reported that the seamen seemed to be moving towards a settlement. The Executive had decided by thirty-one to eleven that the shipowners' new proposals provided a basis for negotiation. The additional nine days' leave would add 1.8 per cent to the cost, which would be exactly balanced by the savings from the productivity proposals. Frank said coldly, 'We are now moving towards a settlement we could have had a month ago, but the Cabinet was not willing to negotiate. The union has never been firm on the forty-hour week now or nothing.' He wanted to know what we would do if the employers offered more. Our industrial relations were bad: the Minister of Labour had lost his traditional role as conciliator and was now only an instrument of the incomes policy. Harold replied with elaborate politeness and restraint. It wasn't true the employers were longing to offer more; they had had to be pushed. Unappeased, Frank said icily, 'I thought I was the only one in Cabinet who wanted to negotiate on extra days.' Jim Callaghan got fed up: 'It is a little trying for the Cabinet to be continuously put in the wrong.' To which Frank retorted, 'You *are* in the wrong on this.' I whispered to Elwyn Jones [Attorney-General], 'Frank is systematically building up a case for resigning,' and he nodded.

We then turned to a joint paper by Gardiner and Longford on the reform of the Lords – excellent in tone about the need to reduce their powers, but also asking for a re-examination of their composition. There then followed a spirited discussion which quite put me in heart again. George, supported by Harold, Frank, Dick and me, was all for reducing powers but leaving composition alone. We carried the day. What surprised me was a speech by Roy saying the whole matter could wait: it wasn't a priority. I told him straight that the movement needed a pinch of radicalism occasionally to leaven our mass of pragmatism. (He told me afterwards that I had completely convinced him that he was wrong.)

Later Harold made his further statement to the House about the 'politically motivated men'. We all thought it was a bit thin.

Wednesday, 29 June. So America has bombed oil installations near Haiphong and Hanoi! What will Harold do now? None of us were consulted of course, but I was immensely relieved when he volunteered a statement to the House dissociating himself from it. It was a careful minimum of dissociation, however. I thought he was looking rather yellow. He is trading too heavily on his comparative youth and I believe his health will crack if he doesn't learn to husband it more. On the front bench he said to me triumphantly, 'So the strike is over. I know some of you didn't agree with my statement yesterday, but it did the trick.' We shall never be able to prove whether it did or didn't, but the effect on the Left will be enduring. In the evening I met the Transport group and outlined my transport policy. I was very encouraged by the welcome it got.

Thursday, 30 June. At Cabinet a long discussion on overseas affairs. I asked about press reports to the effect that we were hell bent on getting into the Common Market and it was now only a question of a few details. Harold said *The Times* report was wrong.

We turned to Concorde – a classic example of Tory incompetence. The cost of our share has risen to £250m. Nobody knew whether the sonic bang would affect sales; it might do so disastrously, whereas we were relying on selling 150 of the planes. The Attorney-General reported that we had no legal let-out; the treaty left us no loophole. So we might face compensation claims as expensive as staying in. There was general agreement that the economic case for withdrawing was stronger than ever. What the hell could we do? The only hope was that the French were as worried as we were about rising costs. It was agreed that the PM should sound them out during Pompidou's visit.[1]

On 3 July, the day before the publication of the Prices and Incomes Bill, Frank Cousins resigned from the Government, declaring in a long letter to the Prime Minister that the policy was 'fundamentally wrong in its conception and approach'. He was followed at Technology by Anthony Wedgwood Benn, who entered the Cabinet. Ted Short became Postmaster-General and John Silkin, left-wing MP for Deptford who had been made a Government Whip in 1964, then Deputy Chief Whip, was promoted Chief Whip in his place. Frank Cousins immediately resumed his duties as General Secretary of the TGWU and resigned his seat in the Commons in November 1966. In the resulting by-election the Government held the seat with a reduced majority.

In the meantime, despite an improvement in our balance of payments position, the run on sterling was continuing and we faced another crisis in defending it. On Tuesday, 12

[1] Georges Pompidou, Prime Minister of France, paid an official visit to the UK, attended by his Foreign Minister, Couve de Murville, from 6 to 8 July. The visit was part of Harold Wilson's continuing efforts to get Britain into the EEC.

July, Cabinet had been warned that the Chancellor would need cuts of at least £500 million, but a decision had been delayed owing to disagreement between Jim Callaghan and George Brown. On 14 July Harold Wilson was forced to make a holding statement in the House and bank rate was raised from 6 to 7 per cent.

Thursday, 14 July. A memorable day. When I arrived at Cabinet at 9.50 expecting a short meeting as we only had one item (Post Office reorganization)[1] to deal with, Tony Greenwood asked me what I thought of the proposal to lop £100m off overseas government expenditure. It was the first I had heard of it. Yet apparently this was to be a key meeting in beating a new crisis.

Overseas affairs were dealt with smartly and Harold settled down to unfold the main business. He said that the inner three – George, Jim and himself – had been holding urgent discussions. For a number of reasons, sterling had been under severe pressure. As a result the bank rate was being raised today and the special account provisions were being introduced, even though – as Jim would agree – the latter was really meaningless and was for presentation purposes. But these two steps would not be enough. They were all three agreed that it was no answer just to go on borrowing. We needed a fundamental appraisal of strategy. They therefore suggested that a statement should be made in the House today announcing that overseas government spending was to be cut by £100m. This would be in addition to the defence review cuts. Action was also necessary to deal with internal demand, but the ideas they had been discussing would take some working out and they were not ready to announce them.

Surprisingly, the National Opinion Poll showed us over 16 per cent ahead of the Tories, nearly three times what we had been at the General Election. He couldn't quite understand how or why! It appeared that the more unpopular the measures we took, the more popular we became. But now we must act regardless of popularity, or of the effect on Carmarthen.[2] The three felt that a further statement on the internal measures should be made as soon as he returned from America as it would be wise for him to warn the Americans of what we intended to do.

In the ensuing discussion Michael Stewart emerged in a more emphatic temper than I have ever seen him in Cabinet. He fought against the proposed cut in overseas expenditure ('mainly military') more vigorously than he ever did against the aid allocation under PESC. At one stage I thought he was going to threaten to resign! He said such a cut in our defence commitments would undermine our whole foreign relationships and ruin our influence. It would mean completely contracting out of our policy in certain areas. 'Yes,' said Harold unperturbed, '£50 million out of Germany and £50 million East of Suez.' I could hardly believe my ears! So even Harold now realizes we can't afford that role.

Gerald Gardiner asked mildly whether we really had to wait three weeks for the further announcement and I weighed in pleading that the new internal

[1] On 3 August Ted Short announced that the Post Office was to become a Corporation under a Board instead of a Department under a Minister. The aim was to prepare the way for the separation of telecommunications from the postal services.

[2] The effect was to prove disastrous. In a by-election caused by the death of Megan Lloyd George a Labour majority of 9,000 was converted into a 2,400 majority for the Welsh Nationalists.

strategy should be announced *before* Harold went to America. Otherwise it would look as if we had sought America's permission first. 'Let us tell the US: "It's our country; these are the remedies we propose and, if you don't like it, that's just too bad." That is the language our people are waiting to hear. It is the language that will sweeten any pill.' To my relief Harold was immediately swayed by this. Ministers were told that detailed discussions on items affecting their Departments would begin at once. Someone asked how we had got on with the French over Concorde and Harold said, 'There was no give at all by the French and it is clear that they will hold us to the full letter of the law.' So we can't shed prestige projects even if we want to.

It was finally left that Harold should make a general statement today with a fuller one to follow in about a fortnight. I was astonished at their willingness to accept even this much delay and wondered how they thought they could survive the inevitable run on sterling. I was, however, heartened by the belief that our stiff stand on Tuesday against sweeping cuts in government expenditure had had an effect.

Went on the front bench to hear the statement. It fell limply on an unimpressed audience.

In the tea-room ran into Harold on the prowl. He told me there was a great plot on by George and Jim to get rid of him. 'You know what the game is: devalue and get into Europe. We've got to scotch it.' He said Jim was in a bad state – seeing too much of Cecil King and always under the influence of the last person who had talked to him.[1] I said, 'You ought to get rid of him as Chancellor.' To which he replied, 'You know my views about that.' Into the House to hear Frank Cousins on the P and I Bill. He spoke with remarkable fluency and rather unattractive assurance – all his egoistic confidence restored. But the Left was ecstatic.

Harold Wilson's interim statement and the rise in bank rate had not stemmed the heavy sales of sterling. Faced with a dangerous run on our reserves Cabinet rushed through an emergency package which the Prime Minister announced to the House on 20 July. Explaining that the Government had been 'blown off course' by the seven-week seamen's strike which had checked the encouraging rise in exports, and by other factors, he claimed that action was needed to help the balance of payments, deal with the problem of internal demand and check inflation. The measures proposed included tighter hire purchase controls; a revival of Selwyn Lloyd's 10 per cent regulator; a 10 per cent surcharge on surtax; building controls; cuts in public investment, except for housing, schools, hospitals and advance factories; a tightening-up of foreign exchange controls. Most traumatic from the Labour Party's point of view was the six-month standstill on wages and prices increases, to be followed by six months of 'severe restraint', and the announcement that this was to be enforced by a new Part 4 to be added to the Prices and Incomes Bill.

Sunday, 17 July. Papers all full of sterling crisis, and news that Harold is curtailing his Moscow visit to make the promised statement on Wednesday of this week. So the dam is bursting, as I thought it would.

[1] Cecil Harmsworth King, chairman of *Daily Mirror* Newspapers and of the International Publishing Corporation [IPC], had turned sour on the Labour Government. Though the *Mirror* ostensibly supported it, he conducted anti-Wilson intrigues around his dining-table, finally declaring open war on him.

Monday, 18 July. 'Split in the Cabinet,' said the papers. There was no sign of it as we met the PESC Committee. Jim was at his most urbane and friendly in the chair. George sat beside him, apparently in agreement with all he said.

Travelled back to the House with Wedgie. We lunched so that we could discuss what was happening. He told me he was against a 1931 deflationary exercise. We should draw up the package needed to put the economy in order and then let the pound float. Otherwise we should deflate and still have to devalue later. I agreed with him and we worked out what the package should be. The office then rang to say that the Minister of Housing wanted to see me at 9 pm. Everything is now beginning to slip into place and I can see a major battle is on, highlighted by press reports from Moscow, where Harold is having a very unproductive time, that the PM is in a tough mood and intends to drive his policy through – those Ministers who don't like it must resign.

As 9 pm Dick arrived very much in the same mood as Wedgie. 'The first thing we must do tomorrow is to ask what the package is *for*.' We discussed what support we might get in Cabinet. Dick said he was going to talk to Crosland and Jay. I told him I was going to see George and he looked quizzical. 'You can say you have been talking to me.'

I found George brooding ominously in his vast room. He had drunk enough to be voluble, though not offensive. I told him I had been struck by what he had said that morning: that if certain measures were carried through, there would be no growth at all. At this he exploded: yes, that was true. And then he proceeded, almost in the same words as Dick, to say that he was going to have this out in Cabinet first and foremost: what was the package *for*, let us do what must be done, but for ourselves, not the bankers, etc. He knew he would lose, and then he would resign. I told him I thought he would win and he said, 'No, I can't win because a Cabinet can't sack the Prime Minister. You wouldn't have me for Leader, would you?' 'No,' emphatically. 'There you are then. Look, I'm not seeking allies. Let me make that clear. You asked to see me, not me you. But I'm not going to wear this. And you will side with him.' Just then Wedgie put his head round the door and George waved him in. 'We've got to break with America, devalue and go into Europe.' 'Devalue, if you like,' I said, 'but Europe, no. I'll fight you on that.' 'But I believe it passionately. We've got to go somewhere. We can't manage alone. That is what Pompidou said to us: "Devalue as we did and you're in." ' Wedgie and I tried to persuade him that, if he brought Europe into the argument, he'd lose the battle that really mattered. We could argue the Europe issue out later. He was very het up about it but we finally persuaded him. Wedgie: 'Are you doing this for Europe?' 'No, of course not. I'm doing it for Britain. Even if there was no Europe in it, I'd still do it.' 'Very well, then; that is what you should say tomorrow.'

We also tried to head him off the resignation talk. 'I've had an agonizing weekend thinking this out. Now the agony is over.' Me: 'Oh God, this fissiparous movement of ours.' He waved an arm, sitting on the table edge: 'Don't use your long words at me.' 'You'd destroy this Government.' 'Oh no, I shan't do that. I shall resign silently: no resignation speech. I'll just fade out of the picture.' We could neither of us see him doing that! Me: 'But there's no need to resign. We shall have thirteen votes in Cabinet.' 'But you can't sack the

PM.' 'No one's going to sack him. He'll have to accept the majority view. He always collects the voices.' Frantically George said, 'He can't do that. He won't do that. Look,' pulling telegrams out of his pocket, 'this is what I sent him yesterday and here is his reply. He won't budge. He can't budge.' 'Why?' 'Because he is too deeply committed to Johnson. God knows what he has said to him. Back in 1964 he stopped me going to Washington. He went himself. What did he pledge? I don't know: that we wouldn't devalue and full support in the Far East? But both those have got to go.'

Tuesday, 19 July. Went to bed at 3 am too tired to sleep. My first meeting was with the TGWU to discuss my proposals for an integrated passenger transport system. Jack Jones, who had asked for the meeting, couldn't come but Alan Thompson and his T&G colleague, to my surprise, welcomed my approach and left me a document recommending regional co-cordination of passenger transport services. A 5 pm dash to the crisis Cabinet. I had run into George at lunch. He told me he had talked to Harold, who had agreed to have the whole issue of devaluation out first before going on to details of the package. So we have won one point!

Harold started by saying that the run on sterling had developed unexpectedly in the last few weeks. It was hard to say why, but 'we are not dealing with rational people'. In addition to all the other factors he had mentioned before he added Vietnam: the gnomes feared the effects of the intensification of the war. Then the statement the French had made after Pompidou's visit, to the effect that we ought to devalue as they had done, hadn't helped – perhaps deliberately. Before we discussed the tough cuts we ought to consider the alternative. Would the cuts work? No one could say. Should we devalue? If so, a flat devaluation or a float? As he droned on no one would have guessed that a major political drama was being played out – one never does at Cabinet. I don't know whether it is a deliberate tactic on Harold's part or just that casual, low-key manner of his, but I always feel in Cabinet as if I were in a cocoon, cut off from the vulgar realities of political conflict.

Dick was the first to jump in with the case for devaluation. Roy Jenkins followed, quietly but convincingly. Douglas Jay would have none of it: there was nothing irretrievably wrong with the economy and devaluation had solved nothing in 1949. Crosland swung the argument back our way and it looked as though we were winning it. George weighed in with a passionate recapping of what he had said last night (minus Europe). But then one after another the 'do nothing yet' brigade mowed us down. I made an impassioned speech on political lines: 'Devaluation would be new because it would mark our freedom from monetary obligations to countries, *i.e.* the USA, who want political obligations in return' – obligations which prevented us from finding our new role in the world. When Gerald Gardiner came down against us, to say nothing of Tony Greenwood, while Cledwyn Hughes[1] called for really tough cuts to put the country on its feet, including cuts in the social services, I knew that we had lost. (Michael Stewart's and Healey's line was predictable.) The best speech

[1] Labour MP for Anglesey since 1951. He had been appointed Minister of State for Commonwealth Relations in 1964 and, following the Election in March 1966, had been promoted to the Cabinet as Secretary of State for Wales in succession to the Labour veteran, Jim Griffiths.

from our side came from Wedgie at the very end, but it was too late. Anyway, the others didn't want to know.

The opening discussion ended with a curious incident. When Harold summed up against us, George said cryptically that he would have to consider his position, though he wouldn't walk out ahead of us for fear of inviting comment from the press outside. Harold said calmly that these matters were not for discussion in Cabinet, but he hoped the First Secretary would do nothing without first talking to him. (George nodded.) And he added, 'If the decision had gone the other way, I should have had to consider my own position.'

Over a drink Harold said to me, 'You've been taken for a ride by the Europeans, who only want to devalue to get us in.' I said I was aware of their ploy and hadn't fallen for it – I was after something else. I suspect Harold will never really trust me again. Behind that blandness he never forgets.

Wednesday, 20 July. Back, bog-eyed, to Cabinet at 9 am where we proceeded to discuss the package, starting with a wages and prices freeze. The difficulties are formidable, not least in prices where statutory controls can always be evaded by changes in quality.

Harold's statement in the House went down quite well with our people, largely because of the Tories' attacks, which rallied our troops. But later in the afternoon the rumour began to spread that George was going to resign anyway. He had a long session with Harold at No. 10 and all sorts of people got in touch with him to persuade him not to. The story was that he objected to the deflationary cuts and their effect on growth and the rest of us were nearly bursting with frustration because we could not tell the real truth. It was not until late at night that George appeared on the steps of No. 10 flanked by the Chief Whip to announce that he was going to stay after all. So he has managed to get the best of both worlds and lessen the impact of the cuts on the gnomes.

Thursday, 21 July. Another Cabinet meeting. Dick and Douglas Houghton asked if we could have a report on 'last night's events' which had placed some of us in a very invidious position. Harold said calmly that he had had certain discussions with the First Secretary, who now accepted Cabinet decisions as much as the rest of us and would carry them out. George said sharply, 'What do you want to know? A letter of resignation was sent and not accepted. I finally withdrew it. That is all there is.' But we left him in no doubt we thought he had behaved pretty irresponsibly. Dick next pressed for the setting up of a ministerial committee, equivalent to OPD, which could keep in continuous control of economic strategy, so that we were not caught unprepared by one crisis after another: we ought to be studying now for instance the consequences of devaluation, if it should again become an issue. He had been asking for a long time for the holding of Cabinet strategy meetings, of the kind we had just been forced to have, as a normal thing. Harold said we would have Cabinet strategy meetings at regular intervals. The next would be in September and certain studies had already been set in hand for it, like a study of Britain as a world banker and whether we should get out of this role. He also said a ministerial economic strategy committee would be set up. So we progress!

We then turned to the gloomy picture of escalating costs on Concorde. Tony

Crosland protested that we were spending £250m on the plane with no hope of getting more than £100m back, and in addition it would need an operating subsidy. If we dropped the scheme, half our deflationary cuts would not be necessary. Harold said the French were determined to go ahead, but Dick insisted we should not agree to commit ourselves further until a full economic assessment had been made. Harold was in favour of the reappraisal and this was agreed.

Earlier Harold had reported on his visit to Moscow. Kosygin had talked privately to him in 'a quite fantastic way'.[1] No other Western leader had ever been given such an insight into Russian thinking. Kosygin had confided in him about all his problems. There was nothing he would like more, Harold was sure, than to reconvene the Geneva conference, but he couldn't. Very afraid of escalation and bitterly critical of the Americans. He believed Kosygin was anxious for him to carry a message back to Johnson. Kosygin had made it clear that he regarded Britain as a valuable go-between. 'If ever there were another Cuba situation, they would want our services.'

Friday, 22 July. An interesting day visiting progress with the Severn Bridge. All the workman I talked to said, 'We want more of these.' 'Humber next,' I replied. I agree with Wedgie that a country cannot live by economic return alone: we need vision and 'an act of faith' occasionally as well. I found the Almondsbury interchange almost as fascinating as the bridge. With its complex pattern of roads crossing each other at four levels and its carefully aligned, elegantly slim columns – reflecting new engineering techniques – it reminded me of the highest forms of architectural expression of the past. 'These are the cathedrals of the modern world,' I remarked. These windy bridges, however, play havoc with one's hair. While paying my sixth visit to the makeshift Ladies' to straighten up for the non-stop pressmen and TV cameras, I heard a voice through the partition (which I suspect was that of Kerensky, consultant for the Almondsbury interchange): 'Marples always used to sleep on these visits: this woman spends all her time in the lavatory.' When I ran into him after emerging, I saw a look of doubt and embarrassment in his face. Had I heard?

Monday, 25 July. Lunch at No. 10 with Pietro Nenni.[2] Harold came in with his now customary stance: a hunched Churchillian prowl accompanied by a brooding bulldog look. I had a quiet word with him about the weekend press. I told him I had been sickened by James Margach's[3] eulogy of George in his *Sunday Times* article 'When Labour's heart was touched'. He replied, 'I told you it is all a plan to get us into the Common Market. But the real threat is from Jim. Did you see Anthony Shrimsley's[4] article a few weeks ago in the *Sunday*

[1] On Khrushchev's resignation in October 1964 his dual post as First Secretary of the Soviet Communist Party and Chairman of the Council of Ministers was split between Alexei Kosygin, who became Chairman of the Council of Ministers, and Leonid Brezhnev, who became First Secretary of the Communist Party of the Soviet Union.

[2] Veteran left-wing Italian Socialist leader and Deputy Premier in the Centre-Left Moro Government. He entered Labour Party history in the 1948 Italian election campaign, which he was fighting in a popular front with the Communists, when thirty-eight Labour MPs sent him a telegram of good wishes and were disciplined by the then NEC.

[3] Political correspondent of the *Sunday Times*.

[4] Political correspondent of the *Sunday Mirror*, later Political Editor of the *Sun*.

Mirror?' 'But Jim isn't a common marketeer.' 'He is now: he has been got at; he has been seeing a lot of Cecil King.' I told him it was time we took steps to counter the plot. I intended to speak to some of my press friends. 'Only if you read something in the *New Statesman* this week, don't say you are going to set up a tribunal.' He grinned. Over the lunch table, bored with having to address Nenni through an interpreter, he continued his asides to me. He is obviously planning a reshuffle. I said, 'The most brilliantly daring move you could take would be to make me Foreign Secretary.' His eyebrows shot up: 'You would be better at doing a round of domestic ministries. Housing next. Dick doesn't seem to be able to get the houses built.' I suggested Crosland in Jim's place but he didn't like that at all. 'He's a European.' 'Not as dedicated as some.' 'I have my plans.' My guess is Gordon Walker for the FO on the continuing grounds that Harold is going to be his own Foreign Secretary.

Wednesday, 27 July. A day of fantastic strain. First to an NEC meeting, trying to draft on the way a speech for the press gallery lunch. At the NEC we decided to leave organization and discuss the crisis instead. I had to leave early to see journalists about my White Paper,[1] but I heard afterwards that Jack Jones made a bitter attack on the wages freeze and that Frank Chapple warned that, if one union broke line, it would be impossible for the rest to hold it. Saw a couple of journalists before lunch; got through my speech somehow with a splitting head, then returned to the office to face a massive press conference, TV and all. Not until I faced that sea of cynics did I realize what an ordeal a major press conference is. Then a mad round of recording and TV interviews, ending up at the BBC at 8 pm where I changed into full evening dress in ten minutes flat for the dinner to King Hussein of Jordan at Lancaster House, arriving with my face still plastered with TV make-up. A dash back to the House for a 10 pm vote on the Tory Motion of censure on our economic policy. Everyone was talking about the incredible, almost incoherent speech George had made.

Thursday, 28 July. A mixed press on my White Paper, the biggest disappointment being *The Times*, a welcome surprise being the *Mirror, Daily Mail* and *Sun*. I see now I made a mistake in not spelling out in the introduction that this

[1] In the White Paper, 'Transport Policy' (Cmnd 3057), I outlined the general direction of my policies: the need to come to terms with the motor car while not allowing it to ruin our environment. This, I argued, meant an expanded road programme to relieve the growing congestion; the preservation of an adequate rail network with subsidies for non-paying but socially necessary lines; the diversion of long-distance freight traffic from road to rail; and the encouragement of public transport, particularly in the urban areas. I announced the Government's intention to set up new comprehensive transport authorities in the conurbations and to provide financial help to make public transport more attractive by developing interchange facilities, new rail tracks, rapid transit facilities and so on. Major new facilities for London, such as extensions to the Underground, were also being planned. Outside the conurbation the Regional Economic Planning Councils were to be brought into the transport planning process through transport co-ordinating committees. Rural transport was to receive Government grants.

I also reported that details of the proposed new national freight organization were being worked out and that the Ministry was carrying out research into whether road hauliers were paying their true costs and what changes were needed in the licensing system. On ports the Government planned to give financial help towards a programme of modernization and development as an interim measure pending the re-organization of the ports under public ownership. I also indicated that the Government would finance a leisure network of canals for use by powered pleasure boats. Finally the White Paper described our new initiatives on road safety, including the cost/benefit analysis of various safety measures being made by my economists. It was published on 27 July.

was not the detailed transport plan, merely the basic policy decisions. However, my colleagues at Cabinet thought I had done very well.

Cabinet turned out to be another marathon as we argued the amendments needed to the Prices and Incomes Bill to enforce the standstill. We had before us the draft of the proposed new Part 4 of the Bill and, as the discussion proceeded on it, we gradually realized that we were proposing to take far-reaching new powers, *i.e.* to freeze prices on penalty of a fine up to £500; to compel an employer to refuse a pay increase on the same penalty; to apply Section 16 of the Bill (relating to employees) to these new provisions and to indemnify an employer for refusal to pay an increase provided by a contract. Dick was the first to exclaim that these powers went far beyond what might have been expected from the 'strengthening' of the Bill agreed in the previous Cabinet decision. They could mean that a trade unionist who brought pressure to bear on an employer to pay the increases he was forbidden to pay could render himself liable to a fine and, in default, to imprisonment. We had accepted these arrangements under Part 2 of the Bill in relation to the early warning, but it was quite a different thing to apply them to a standstill. Statutory fixing of wages had never been attempted, even in war, because everyone knew you could not send hundreds of trade unionists to gaol. Congress would throw the policy out; so would Party conference – and where would be the credibility of the Government then?

George, and others, argued that you could not have a situation in which an employer could be ruined by strike action as a result of being prevented by law from increasing wages while nothing was done to proceed against the strikers. I backed Dick strongly, but George was adamant. How else had Cabinet expected to enforce the standstill?

And so we went on, round and round for over two hours. At this point Harold had one of his bright tactical ideas. Wasn't the answer to make the Orders bringing these powers into operation subject to an affirmative resolution? In this way we could show that we were attempting to make the voluntary method work first – and we could hold that line until after Congress and conference. Then if we had to resort to compulsion later in the year we could justify this on grounds that we had tried the voluntary method and failed. Personally, I thought we were merely postponing trouble.

Sunday, 31 July. The Sundays are full of Harold's spectacular reception by Johnson in America. Henry Brandon in the *Sunday Times* was clearly intoxicated by the whole business, describing Harold's public performance as 'truly impressive'. Even its political correspondent James Margach, in an article on Harold's 'vulnerable position' at home, said: 'Nobody should under-rate his intellectual and moral courage' – a new note to be struck about him. But for the first time I am really afraid. It is clear from the Washington reports that Harold went there in an entirely different mood and for an entirely different purpose than he indicated to Cabinet in that long inquest on the crisis. Says Brandon, Johnson used the luncheon to 'bolster Wilson's credibility with the European central bankers'; Wilson 'to make it clear that he would not turn Britain into a little England or abandon Britain's world role'. So his assurances about being ready to devalue rather than deflate further were never genuine. As for his dissociation from the bombing of North Vietnam, Johnson now saw it 'in a different perspective and in a minor key'. No wonder the Left now hate Harold!

Tuesday, 2 August. At Cabinet Harold reported on his visit to Washington, from which it became clear that he had not really pressed at all the line he had promised us he would. In fact, when I asked him point blank whether he had discussed linking the pound and dollar and floating them both, he replied that he had not raised this as it wasn't an opportune occasion. Jim Callaghan supplemented by saying that 'the Americans have been of the very greatest assistance to us in every way.' When I asked in what forms, he became mysterious and said: 'The gold reserve figures will be out this afternoon; when I tell you they will merely have fallen by £25 million, you can guess what forms that assistance has taken.' So we are no nearer the independence he claimed deflationary measures would bring.

Lunch with Maurice Hackett, chairman of the South-East Regional Economic Planning Council. He told me how grateful the Planning Councils were to me for working with them so closely – the only Minister, apart from DEA, who did. Apparently they are worried about becoming merely pieces of window dressing. One of their greatest problems was lack of staff. I asked him to help me by pioneering conurbation transport authorities in his region. Discussing George, he said how difficult he was to work with. He couldn't understand his recent fiasco in the House because, in fact, he has been on the wagon for weeks.

Wednesday, 3 August. Made a point of being in the chamber to hear George's speech on a Tory Motion to recommit the P and I Bill to a committee of whole House. Everyone was agog to see whether he would flop again, his friends worried because he had insisted on staying up all night on the Standing Committee on the Bill. Heath's telling attack on our 'dictatorship' didn't help. But as soon as George got up I knew he was completely in command of himself and the situation. It was a great display of personal courage and an effective one. He made a better case for us than I would have believed possible. A significant passage in his speech was where he explained why we chose to add a new part to the Bill. We could, he said, have merely extended the scope of Part 2 but we decided that would be inappropriate because Part 2 was intended to be permanent, the standstill temporary. That was the first I had heard of our reasoning: the choice was never put to Cabinet.

Dinner with Dick in a corner of the Strangers' dining-room. We agreed that Harold probably would never trust either of us completely again. Harold obviously thought Dick was organizing a conspiracy. 'He said to me on Sunday: "No cabals, Dick." This is all due to Wiggery.' Dick said he thought Wigg had a disastrous influence on Harold, seeking intrigues everywhere and knowing everything that was going on. He had put Harold up to the Communist line over the seamen's strike. I said that, since there was a 'cabal' round Harold, we had better have one of our own. We would be suspected of one anyway. Two or three of us ought to meet more often. We discussed who and agreed on ourselves and Wedgie. Marsh was discontented about the inner group of three and how the rest of us were left in the dark, but it was difficult to know where he stood politically. Tony Greenwood was just a lightweight. I said, 'In the last few meetings you have been behaving like a Cabinet Minister again – and very effectively.' He chuckled: 'Yes, I have, haven't I? I made a note in my diary the other day: "I'm going to be a Cabinet Minister." ' Dick is a very influenceable person. He catches one's mood and gets carried away by it. For instance, he said he thought we ought to keep closer touch with the trade unions. I told him how I had made a big point of consulting them since I became Minister of Transport, and he suddenly said impulsively, 'You humiliate me. I am very ashamed because I've always said I am not interested in wages and all that sort of thing. I've never once seen NALGO. I shall put that right tomorrow.'

Monday, 8 August. Talked to Judith Hart about Rhodesia. She said it was all right: the proposals we were going to put at the resumed talks were quite unacceptable to Smith but would put him in the wrong. It was largely a presentational excerise, but there would be no sell-out.

Wednesday, 10 August. At an unexpected Cabinet meeting, Harold turned to the economic situation. The new ministerial committee on economic strategy would, he said, be meeting tomorrow to begin preparations for our September discussions. I interrupted to ask if we could know who were to be members of it. (I have been expecting the usual Cabinet note advising me of the membership for some time.) To our surprise Harold said tartly that it was not customary to discuss membership of Cabinet committees at Cabinet (the first I've heard of *that*) and that the usual notice would be circulated. I signalled to Wedgie was he a member and he shook his head.

Later I rang Dick and asked to see him, having learned, after great pressure on my office, the membership of the Economic Strategy Committee [SEP]. The list of Ministers was so appalling that I felt that the time for an open breach with Harold had come: the inner three (under Harold's chairmanship), plus the Foreign Secretary, Secretary of State for Defence, the Minister of Labour and the Lord President *i.e.* Michael Stewart, Healey, Ray Gunter and Bert Bowden. That meant that none of the devaluationists (apart from George) were on: not me or Dick or Wedgie or Roy or Tony Crosland. I fully felt Dick would have been on. When I asked to see him, he answered mysteriously that he could not see me till after 10 pm; we would meet then. I ran into Crosland in the corridor and told him how outrageous it was: we ought to go to Harold about it in a body. He agreed. I also discussed it with Roy Jenkins. He was in favour of our going to Harold separately. Then, as I walked through the division lobby at 10 pm, Crosland said, 'All our plans are now changed.' As I was trying to grasp what he meant, Harold came up grinning from ear to ear. Hadn't I seen the tape? Cabinet changes. I thought he was teasing as he often does, particularly when he went on to list them: a new First Secretary, Michael Stewart; George to the FO. Dick to be Lord President, Bowden to the CRO [Commonwealth Relations Office], Greenwood to Housing and Bottomley to ODM. I was stunned, but it appeared it was true. Wedgie and I took Dick aside. He wasn't too happy at leaving his beloved Department until we encouraged him about all he could do to modernize Parliament. He agreed this was the idea; that Harold had said to him, 'I have had a non-political Leader of the House for too long; now I want a political one.' He had also stressed that this gave Dick new power at Transport House. Wedgie remined him he would even be boss of broadcasting now. So he went away cheered.

All this explains the composition of the Economic Strategy Committee (on which Dick will now sit) and Harold's mysteriousness about it. He kept his secret well, that is what delighted him. He adores foxing the press. Making a hurried political assessment of the changes, I could see the theme behind them: getting rid of a hated Foreign Secretary; putting a steady chap, Michael, in charge of P and I policy; with George at the FO perhaps being ready to modify the East of Suez line? Judith will keep an eye on Bowden over Rhodesia (she assured me again this evening that Harold has been wonderful on this). They also mean housing is to be reduced in status: I know Harold's contempt for Tony's abilities. I know, too, he would not like to insult Dick by demoting his Department (even though Dick himself volunteered at Cabinet the other day that we had given housing too automatic a priority. He clearly believes 500,000 houses can't be built except at the expense of other urgent fields). Altogether it might be a great deal worse and the changes should improve the atmosphere in the Parliamentary Party. Dick told me they are only the beginning and that there are to be more changes in the autumn. I am ready to go away now for a badly needed holiday – surfeited with crises and excitements.

Thursday, 1 September. Had to interrupt my holiday for Cabinet, cursing under my breath. But I suppose it was unavoidable since Harold has to go to the TUC annual conference on Monday and the Commonwealth PMs meet next week. The items, therefore, were Rhodesia[1] and P and I policy. We had almost reached agreement with Zambia on the £7m aid offer in return for the cut-off of trade and the agreement had been on the point of signature when Kaunda called it off. He was stressing what was now known as NIBMR – no independence before majority rule.

Next a brief debate on P and I. From what Ray, Michael and Jim said, it is clear that they are only waiting for the TU Congress to be over to introduce Part 4. The voluntary system is working quite well, but Clive Jenkins's legal case is forcing our hands.[2] Even Dick did not cavil at the inference about Part 4, merely insisting that the Party meeting should be consulted first. Jim reported that 500 firms had not raised dividends; only thirty-six had. The Treasury was following up every one of them. So far it had only authorized three. It was going to be hard to hold prices as world interest rates were going up.

[1] Informal talks had been going on all the summer between officials of the British and Smith Governments, but without result. On 8 August Ian Smith had declared in Salisbury that it would be possible to keep Rhodesia 'in the hands of civilized people and not only for the foreseeable future'. Undeterred Harold Wilson launched the third round of abortive talks on 22–25 August. The day after they ended a Constitution Amendment Bill was introduced in the Rhodesia Parliament designed to give statutory backing to the powers of detention held under the emergency regulations, to reduce Africans' constitutional rights and to weaken the entrenched clauses of the constitution.

[2] Under Clive Jenkins' militant leadership as General Secretary the Association of Supervisory Staffs, Executives and Technicians [ASSET] had taken advantage of the fact that Part 4 of the Prices and Incomes Act, giving powers of enforcement of the policy, had not yet been activated. The Union had decided to take Thorn Electrical Industries Ltd to court for refusal to pay one of its members the increase due under an agreement negotiated on 12 July 1966. On 29 September the court found in its favour.

Tuesday, 6 September. Back to work meant lunch with Dick. He seemed like a stranded whale in the Privy Council office and said he hated being without a Department. He certainly seemed out of place in that rather formal splendour! We discussed the reasons why Harold had moved him. He is still dubious as to whether his new post will put him right on the inside, *e.g.* Bert Bowden (when Leader of the House) had never laid claim to membership of OPD. I told Dick he must push himself into everything. He had a tremendous opportunity if he would only take advantage of it: 'Now you can't help but be a Cabinet Minister; you're no longer a Departmental one!' He grinned and said he thought Harold's real purpose was to get back control over the PLP. He had systematically got rid first of Short and then of Bowden, who were messing things up. We plotted getting control of Transport House; Dick wants to chair the NEC Home Policy Committee and we agreed on Ian Mikardo as the chairman of the Organization Sub-Committee. He also confessed to me that his secretary, Jenny Hall, is typing the dictated instalments of his diary. How he reconciles that with the Official Secrets Act I'll never know. However, he can be the most indiscreet of men.

Good news on the liner train front: the TGWU have reached agreement with Reggie Wilson on 'guarantees' for the BRS men who use the terminals. So my efforts just before the holiday have succeeded in achieving a breakthrough. But, here again, the agreement only applies to an 'experimental' use of the London to Glasgow run. The trade unions really are the limit. They admit the guarantees are satisfactory, but they are still holding back from full participation by BRS, thus costing BR and the country something like a cool million in lost revenue. Then they preach about productivity and higher wages! What on earth right have they to waste money in this way as though we were all rolling in it?

Thursday, 8 September. Royal opening of the Severn Bridge. I risked wearing a daring new hat – very 'with it' – and I enjoyed doing so, even though Mother disapproved. Had a lively chat with Philip [Duke of Edinburgh] over lunch. He and I always argue like mad. I like his utter lack of stuffiness. The Queen, too, is much more relaxed and natural than her pictures show. I loved one moment at the Almondsbury interchange. Kerensky was explaining the model with great pride – 'The first of its kind in Europe' – and telling her all about the landscaping. 'There is a mental home just here and the road will be completely hidden from it.' The Queen turned to the Lord Lieutenant and chuckled: 'They'll need that mental home to accommodate the people who go mad trying to find their way through this.' Fortunately Kerensky didn't hear!

Back to a late reception at Lancaster House for the Commonwealth Prime Ministers' conference. George was rolling round distressingly sozzled: a dreadful beginning to his new job! He was very affectionate to me: 'The only Minister who really tried to make a go of my Regional Councils; they appreciated it very much.' I asked if he was pleased with his new job. 'I hate it. I didn't want it. It was an order: this or I go. He said he couldn't keep me at DEA after my little bit of business over resigning. Two years ago, when I wanted it, I couldn't have it. Now I don't want it I've no choice.' I tried to reassure him that he had got a very big opportunity and he said, 'You're very sweet,' and wandered noisily off.

My next encounter was with Dick, looking black with misery. He obviously isn't reconciled yet to the change. Really, I sometimes think Harold moves people round the chess board with complete frivolity. My mounting depression was capped by Harold himself into whom I ran just after midnight. He, too, looked as if he had quite a bit aboard. He was in one of his rather dishevelled, indiscreet states.

Friday, 9 September. Good press on the Severn Bridge – and my hat. It is almost incredible how much the spotlight is put on one's appearance by TV. Millions of people just talking about the HAT – and about the fact that I bowed instead of curtseying to the Queen. (To my surprise John London of the *Evening News* came out in my support.) The *Sun* had a nice photo of me facing the Queen but smiling past her. I was in fact smiling at one of Philip's cracks. When he saw my name as Minister of Transport on the commemorative plaque he said, 'That's pretty cool. It was practically finished before you came along.' 'Not a bit of it,' I replied. 'It is entirely due to me that it was finished five months ahead of schedule. Anyway I intend to be in on the act.'

Spent the morning with Edgar Pisani, my French counterpart, on Channel Tunnel. It was a quick-moving sophisticated affair. The French obviously came along thinking *we* were dragging our feet. But I went straight to the point and said we were ready to commit ourselves as a Government in principle that morning if they were. That took the wind out of Pisani's sails as he still has to get formal clearance. We agreed to meet in Paris on 28 October and I suggested we should say in the communiqué that it would be to 'finalize' the discussions. Pisani said as we broke up, 'Je suis ravi'. I find my open and direct method usually pays. At lunch we discussed Concorde. Pisani said that if he had known the cost beforehand and been Minister at the time he would not have been in favour of going ahead. He insisted that we must keep greater civil service control over the Tunnel and not let it get into the hands of the industrialists too much (welcome words!).

Tuesday, 13 September. Went to Zambia reception where Tom Mboya came over and we got into a deep discussion. As I listened, all Harold's clever tactics looked like a cheap and tawdry trick. I went away wondering whether I should still be a member of the Government in a few days' time, for I could never betray my belief in the rights of those Africans.

Earlier there has been a most distressing meeting of the NEC's International Sub-Committee. George was tight, amorous and truculent, full of bitterness about the FO. They were, he told me, 'a stinking lot. Up to now I've shown them my nice side but today I told them there is another side and if they force me to show it I will. I don't want rows but, if they insist, they shall have them. Today I went the rounds and you should have seen them: bored or downright rude.' In the discussions he warned that we must make up our minds about Europe one way or another soon. But he made two points of sense. He was, he said, trying to mend two sets of relations – with France and with Nasser, to whom he has sent a message.

Wednesday, 14 September. Phoned Dick in some distress. I reported what George had said about Europe and he was horrified. 'We've got a meeting on Friday on this with a paper on the economic consequences of going in. It would be madness to do so.'

Solly Zuckerman came to see me privately at Harold's request to say he wanted me to be a member of the new ministerial committee to decide the allocation of scientific and technological research.[1] We ought to distribute the £500m better – less on defence for one thing. We had an hour's interesting talk in which he told me he had been against the F-111, and still was. Harold had seemed against it at one stage but had been won over by the powerful defence chiefs' lobby. East of Suez would mean building up a whole powerful new apparatus of air power. He seemed to think Harold is swinging back again.

Monday, 19 September. The Rhodesia crisis is over – for the moment. Once again Harold has found a formula to satisfy the Commonwealth PMS.[2] Dick phoned to ask me to dine with him at the Garrick. It sounded urgent, but as we talked I was a bit nonplussed as to what it was all about. He said Harold had been very pleased with the way the weekend ministerial speeches had been synchronized and wanted Dick to do more 'orchestration'. Dick had replied that, if so, he must know what he was to orchestrate. Harold should consult one or two of us more. Harold had looked alarmed at this and said, 'So you want an inner Cabinet?' Dick and I agreed that there was one anyway and that we weren't in it. We puzzled yet again at the way Harold puts himself in the power of the Right wing: putting Stewart, for example, at DEA to follow George. I said that Harold would only pay attention to those of whom he was frightened and he was not frightened of us – he was too sure of us. If we wanted to be listened to we must frighten him – organize a group of our own quite openly. Dick agreed Harold made his own prisons and then complained he was a prisoner. He would tell Harold quite frankly that one or two of us were going to meet and discuss what we thought the Government's policies should be.

I asked Dick what had happened at the much-reported meeting of the new Economic Strategy Committee. Harold, he said, had had a shock when he was faced by a concerted effort by Stewart and Jim Callaghan to drop the idea of import controls. What the heck else did he expect from Stewart? 'By temperament he will be a complete Treasury man. I could have told him that.' However, George had been very good and the attack had been beaten off. I got Dick really sold on our reviving a sort of Keep Left[3] ministerial group, pointing out that he was the most vulnerable of us all now as he was thought to have more overall responsibility.

[1] Sir Solly Zuckerman, Chief Scientific Adviser to the Government.

[2] After a bitter dispute at the conference Harold Wilson succeeded in buying time for further talks with Smith on the understanding that, if he was not prepared to return quickly to legality, Britain would withdraw all its previous constitutional proposals and switch to NIBMR. It would also support mandatory sanctions in the UN. The conference had proved so traumatic it was not to be held again for two and a quarter years.

[3] In 1947 a number of Labour back benchers, including myself, founded an informal discussion group of critics of the Labour Government's economic and foreign policy. It got its name from a pamphlet, 'Keep Left', published in the same year among whose signatories were Dick Crossman, Michael Foot and Ian Mikardo. Its founder members were later to form the nucleus of the 'Bevanites'.

Thursday, 22 September. Dick has got his way: Cabinet agreed that he should conduct an inquiry into what improvements are needed in inter-departmental machinery in the field of home information services in order to secure better presentation of Government policies. George reported that there had been an overture from Gromyko to Dean Rusk for a meeting, apparently about Vietnam. It might amount to nothing and of course we could not openly interfere. On the other hand we should be rightly blamed by public opinion here if the hawks in the US scotched hopeful prospects without our having tried to use our influence. He would therefore be talking to Rusk about it when he went to New York. Europe apart, I think George will prove a good Foreign Secretary in the sense that he will have a mind of his own and not be ruled by the FO as Stewart was.

Thursday, 29 September. Off to Brighton for the Party conference.

Thursday, 29 September to Friday, 7 October. This was to be the conference at which the Party divided irreconcilably over prices and incomes, Vietnam and East of Suez. Yet it was remarkable for lack of bitterness. At NEC meetings on Friday and Sunday, Jack Jones argued tenaciously and with Mikardo and Driberg (sometimes backed by Willie Simpson) voted automatically against the Government on all issues, through prices and incomes and the economic statement generally to the statement on foreign affairs. But George Brown showed much greater flexibility than Michael Stewart ever did and this was later reflected in his speech with its new proposals on Vietnam.

I told Jack Jones I was going to move to reduce lorry drivers' statutory hours and he was very pleased with this. 'We will support you, though it won't be popular in all quarters!' Alex Kitson,[1] too, was highly delighted: 'This is what I have been asking for for thirty years.' Despite his fighting speech in the transport debate demanding renationalization of the road haulage industry, he was uninhibitedly friendly at the evening dance, expressing understanding of my difficulties and full confidence in what I am trying to do. Altogether I built some useful bridges with the trade unions: with Sid Weighell, assistant General Secretary of the NUR, who made a wonderful speech in the P and I debate in Sid Greene's absence; with the TSSA who were delighted that I dropped in at their cocktail party; and not least with the TGWU. One of their delegates, Pickering of the Northern Region, sent me a note asking for a few words with me about A licences and C licences, and the whole delegation was very gratified when I went and sat among them for a few minutes before carrying Pickering off for a cup of tea. He told me in his rough working-class way what Frank Cousins has told Chris Foster: that he doesn't believe we can enforce proper hours and conditions on private haulage without renationalization. Jack Jones and I parted on very friendly terms agreeing to meet for lunch for a private confab on my return from America.

Harold has had a mixture of hits and misses this week. But the interesting thing was his obsession with 'plots' against him. At the ITN cocktail party on the

[1] General Secretary of the Scottish Commercial Motormen's Union. When it merged with the Transport and General Workers' Union in 1971 he became an executive officer of the union and later Deputy General Secretary. He was elected to the NEC in 1968.

last night he dilated to me about Ministers who went a-whoring with society hostesses and was livid with Tommy Balogh for coming down specially to attend Pamela Berry's dinner (which Ted and I refused).[1] He even pursued Pam Berry out of the room to attack her for the biased reporting of the conference in the *Daily Telegraph*, which I thought a rather undignified occupation for a PM. 'Mrs Ian Fleming is another one,' he said darkly.[2] 'If any of you knew your job you would find out who attended that weekend meeting at her place last July when I was in Moscow. And if you were there, Barbara, I will accept your resignation now.' He said he knew what the ploy was – to make Jim Callaghan Prime Minister, Roy Jenkins Chancellor, and form a Coalition Government. Jim had lost his nerve during the crisis and badly wanted to change his job. 'But by making George Brown Foreign Secretary, I have cornered him. And George Brown was never the danger.'

On Wednesday we had an emergency Cabinet meeting at which we decided to implement Part 4 of the P and I Bill. I didn't oppose this.

Harold Wilson had agreed I could visit the United States to study new developments in passenger transport, freight handling techniques and highways policy. The visit lasted from 11 October to 21 October and included San Francisco, Sacramento, Los Angeles, Boston, New York and Washington. I was accompanied by my Chief Scientific Adviser, E. C. Williams, and my new Principal Private Secretary, Richard Bird.

Tuesday, 11 October. San Francisco is a disappointment. Partly because of the ever-threatening mist and fog, partly because of the parched brown of the surrounding hills (no rain from May to October), but chiefly because of the lack of care to preserve and highlight the city's best qualities. That elevated freeway across the water-front, for instance, cutting the view down Market Street to the Ferry Building Tower at the water's edge, is a civic crime. The outskirts of the city are one long sprawl of jam-packed hutches across which the freeways thunder. The signs on the freeways are bitty and inelegant. But the chaps at Sacramento were kind enough, and I found them impressive in their frankness and obvious efficiency.

Wednesday, 12 October. Fascinating day with the Southern Pacific Railway people and with Matson's, the pioneers of the container ship which has revolutionized their traffic to Hawaii. The railway people are only interested in freight and would like to shed their passengers altogether, but are bound hand and foot by controls. Here again the Americans were extraordinarily civil and generous with their time. Biaggiarù, the President of the Southern Pacific Railway, gave me an hour of his time and I was very impressed with the calibre of the younger executives. San Francisco was looking better in warm sun with clear skies. Its steep switchback hills with the old cable cars tugging up it give it a character all its own.

[1] Lady Pamela Berry, wife of Michael Berry, later Lord Hartwell, chairman and editor-in-chief of the *Daily Telegraph* and *Sunday Telegraph*. She gave lavish parties for prominent people, including Labour leaders.

[2] Ann Fleming, former wife of Viscount Rothermere and widow of Ian Fleming, author of the James Bond series of thrillers, who died in 1964.

Thursday, 13 October. Another fascinating day visiting the test track of the Bay Area Rapid Transit District [BART]. Here again I was impressed with the calibre of the chaps.

Sweet touch in San Francisco: they are starting a 'pedestrian precinct' in Market Street. Definition? Reducing the six lanes road to four in order to widen the sidewalk!

On to Los Angeles by plane where the City Governor had laid on a dinner party for us. I sat between Telford, the LA district chief highways engineer, and the Chancellor of the State Colleges of California (175,000 students of 'red brick' university status).

Friday, 14 October. A fantastic aerial tour by helicopter of big freeways with Telford. I enjoyed the lunging sensation; Richard Bird was nearly sick. They have over 500 miles of freeway already and are planning or constructing 1,000 more. Would that solve the traffic problem? 'No. We shall have to start building more when this programme is finished.' LA already sprawls about 75 miles north of the city centre, 75 miles south and 80 miles across. Apart from a few sky-scrapers in the city it is purely suburban sprawl.

Toured Sunset Boulevard with all its night-clubs and garish signs (the rich man's Blackpool-in-the-sun) before catching the midday plane to New York. We chuckled over the trimmings of the affluent society (first class); book matches printed in gold with our individual names, the Walt Disney film show and earphones for piped music all the time. But the meal, though lavish, was uninspiring. Williams got into conversation with Brigadier-General Carlton commanding the Fighter Wing in Vietnam. He called me over to meet him in the bar, where they had been knocking back endless drinks – the stewardesses turning a blind eye to the legal maximum of two. The General (well lit on a combination of brandy and benedictine) was beginning to talk wild: 'You got your job by your own efforts? I bet it had something to do with your undies.' Williams hastily headed him off the smut in which they had been indulging. I started to cross-examine him about Vietnam. 'Are you winning?' 'No. The politicians won't let us. I'm just a professional soldier. I just get wounded. I'm going to New York to collect the American Star and to testify to Congress. But the politicians won't listen to me.' Me: 'What do you think should be done?' 'We should take out China now.' 'Nuclear weapons?' 'That's not necessary. Just flatten all her ports and railroads.' 'And when you have "taken her out" what would you do with her?' But that was obviously beyond his political comprehension. He just sat there, a big, flat-faced man with extrovert eyes. He pulled out his daughter's photo to show us. Just before we landed he whipped out an eyebath and bathed his eyes. 'The cameras will be waiting,' he said bashfully.

Saturday, 15 October. In New York, lunched at Lord Caradon's. He is very distressed by George Brown's behaviour at the UN. His speeches have gone down well but he has been outrageously rude at social gatherings. So much so that the French and Nigerian delegates refused to meet him again. Hugh walked me back to the Drake Hotel to tell me he was appalled by the statement HMG had sent to Smith (in my absence) and said he couldn't possibly support it publicly. What would I advise him to do? I said he shouldn't take any unilateral action. If there was any resigning to do over Rhodesia a dozen of us should resign together. I asked him to let me have a copy of the statement.[1]

Monday, 17 October. Spent the morning with Commissioner Barnes, New York City Traffic Commissioner. The TV just 'happened' to be there, too. But I agreed with Barnes when he said he thought it was his duty to be accessible both to the public and the press. He agrees New York's transport problems can't be solved by traffic management and new highways alone. 'No thought has been given to mass transport on anything like the scale it has been given to traffic management.'

Friday, 21 October. A heavy day in Washington with Under-Secretary Boyd of the Department of Commerce – still in the running for the new post of Secretary for Transportation since Johnson has not yet confirmed the rumour it will be Califano instead. In typical fashion Boyd had laid on a succession of lectures and slide shows by his staff, covering every aspect of his departmental work. This took so long there was no time for the probing questions I really wanted. But I got one nugget out of the day which confirmed that Boyd will *not* be the new Secretary. Over the tea-break one of his staff said to me in front of him, 'We have all decided unanimously that you should be our new Secretary for Transportation.' Unperturbed, Boyd chipped in, 'That will be the first time any decision in this Department has been unanimous.

Saturday, 22 October. Arrived London 8 am (still only 3 pm New York time) to find a phalanx of pressmen and TV waiting. Bickerton and Chris [Hall] were there with a sheaf of press cuttings about my various statements in America. Even my most innocent remarks have hit the headlines. I teased them: 'You both look so worried, I know what you've been saying: "Look what she gets up to as soon as we let her out of our sight." '

After press conferences, etc., straight on to Chequers for the ministerial conference on Europe. I arrived late and so missed half of the morning conference at which the officials and economists had been giving their views on the consequences of our going into the Common Market. Everyone seemed to agree it would be disastrous to try and go in until we were strong, and there was far from certainty among the economists that even the long-term effects of entry would be beneficial to our economy. Tommy had put in a paper advocating an economic union with America instead (the 'Javits' solution).

After lunch officials withdrew except Burke Trend and we continued the discussion on Europe purely among Ministers. It was an excellent debate, aided by the fact that it was informal, everyone using Christian names, none of this 'The Minister of So-and-So' which makes Cabinet meetings so stiff and politically unreal. After the unenchanted attitude of the economists it seemed inevitable that we should dismiss any immediate commitment as economically dangerous, but the Europeanists fought back hard.

[1] Caradon had sent a telegram to George Brown to express his dismay at the size of the concessions made to Smith and his belief that they would arouse the 'strongest protest' in the UN and elsewhere. He concluded with the words: 'I have made it quite clear all along that I myself am opposed to granting independence to a minority Government in Rhodesia . . . I am not prepared to defend what is now proposed.'

I said that I had been interested to learn that morning the extent to which the economic options were open. The decision therefore was basically a political one. Politically we had cast ourselves for a separate role. Economically it wasn't proved that non-entry would be disastrous. So my alternative was to continue as we were, not finally shutting the door, but not trying to push it further open at this stage. Crosland had said, I went on, that, if nothing came out of this Chequers meeting, the effect on Europe would be very bad. But there had been no need for this meeting: it had been forced on us by the Foreign Secretary and I objected to being blackmailed now into the need for 'something to come out of it'. I agreed with Dick that our only available fall-back was to adopt a foreign policy appropriate to our economic strength.

Harold then 'summed up' on lines he had clearly already decided on, whatever the rest of us said. There was general agreement that there was no question of negotiating with the Six for some time, certainly not before the outcome of the Kennedy Round of trade negotiations in Gatt and negotiations in the IMF [International Monetary Fund] were known. Officials should in the meantime study our fall-back positions in depth – both Javits and 'going it alone'. But we couldn't just do nothing. We must keep the subject alive. As Harold insisted that no decisions would be taken that evening and that his suggestion would be put to Cabinet – and as I was by then blind with fatigue – I excused myself and left them arguing the minutiae.

Thursday, 27 October. A desperately hectic and exhausting day. I had stayed up till 6 am to finish a major speech for the Town and Country Planning Association conference – with a night trip to Paris to see Pisani ahead. Then, after one hour's sleep, on to Cabinet.

On to the TCPA, where I was too tired to eat much before going on to deliver my speech. I was even afraid I might not be able to read it! But my stamina came to my aid as usual and it went like a bomb. I *thought* it was good, though when one works through the night one gets too dazed to judge. But I never expected the rapturous reception it got. It is worth drawing on one's reserves for a special effort like this when it brings results. By the time it was over I was feeling positively lively again – ready for a rush visit to the Motor Show, a 'Motor Industry' cocktail party and speech, and a dash to the night ferry to Paris. We had a Departmental conference on the train over my brief on the Channel Tunnel before I got to bed at last and slept deeply for eight hours.

Friday, 28 October. Alighted into a cold Paris paralysed by a Metro strike. This meant I had no time at the Embassy for a bath before going to my talks with Pisani on the Channel Tunnel. They went well and soon we were holding our press conference. I like Pisani: he is dynamic and able and his staff obviously get on well with him. He told me he had been asked in his TV interview what it was like negotiating with a woman. He replied it was like playing tennis with a *gaucheur* – a left-handed person was used to playing with a right-handed one but the same thing didn't apply the other way round. Over lunch he told us a delightful story about how de Gaulle announced to his Council of Ministers the breakdown of the talks over Britain's entry into the Six in 1963. There was nothing on the agenda about the breakdown of talks. At the end, as de Gaulle rose, someone asked him what had happened. Pausing for a moment, de Gaulle said, '*Curieuse époque, Messieurs, où l'on ne peut pas dire, sans provoquer je ne sais quelles agitations, que l'Angleterre est une île et que l'Amérique n'est pas l'Europe. Je répète: curieuse époque.*' And he walked out of the room.

After lunch, to Fontainebleau to see a French method of loading accompanied cars quickly on to rail flats: a prototype of the shuttle service which will operate through the Tunnel. I told Scott Malden to get BR busy developing a British equivalent. These French will steal every march they can if one doesn't watch out!

Wednesday, 2 November. Dinner with Bill Fiske, Jane Phillips,[1] Ted [Castle] and some of their colleagues – and with Stephen – at the Festival Hall to discuss possibility of putting all London transport under the GLC in some way. They are very keen and I am interested.

Thursday, 3 November. At Cabinet George reported that he would be going to Germany. He had had a message from Gromyko about Vietnam which indicated it was worth his going to Moscow earlier than he had intended and he felt he must visit Germany first in case they thought he was entering some plot against them. Dick struggled his way through the item of parliamentary business, manful but inexpert. It is obvious he has a lot to learn about being Leader of the House. He certainly hasn't yet found the way of handling the Party meeting.

Then back to Europe again, of which I am getting heartily sick. Round and round we went again. Harold kept saying he would insist on conditions, so I challenged him: 'Do your conditions mean you want to amend the Treaty of Rome?' He replied that, if we could be satisfied on our two main points, the Treaty need not be a stumbling block. Finally he summed up that we needed to know more about the terms on which we could get in. He therefore proposed a series of steps: 1) a conference of EFTA PMS to be called in London for early December; 2) an announcement of our willingness to enter on appropriate terms and of the high-level visits at the same time; 3) a major speech by him to the January Consultative Assembly at Strasbourg; 4) high-level visits to take place early afterwards; 5) urgent study of the two fall-back positions to go on simultaneously; 6) consultations with the Commonwealth. A number of us said that our reaction to all this would depend on the terms of the statement that would have to be made when all this was announced, so it was agreed that George should prepare a draft for our next meeting. Harold is edging his way step by step towards his goal.

Saturday, 5 November. Off to Bradford University to receive my honorary doctorate of technology. Harold was in his element during his installation as Chancellor. In his purple velvet and gold-collared gown he looked, as one paper put it, like a medieval merchant prince. I gathered he had laid down strict instructions about the design of his mortar board. Trust him not to miss a trick! He had obviously been appalled at the sight of himself on TV in that floppy

[1] Chairman of the Highways and Traffic Committee of the GLC.

medieval cap he had worn at a previous academic occasion. But as always he disarmed by his total lack of side. When he had conferred my degree on me by a solemn handshake he almost winked and told me afterwards, 'I decided it wouldn't have done for me to tickle your palm.' He became the first ever D. Tech. in this country, so that makes me the third. He emphasized that my doctorate was at the University's suggestion.

Monday, 7 November. Second Reading of the Road Safety Bill. I took it very relaxed. Ran into Dick who told me he had just been at the RIBA [Royal Institute of British Architects], where they were raving over my speech to TCPA. 'At last we have a Minister of Transport who is thinking in planning terms.' He grinned: 'They told me your speech was much better than mine had been.' The Ministry of Housing, he said, had closed in on itself since he had left. How was Tony Greenwood doing? He pulled a face. 'They are saying that J. D. Jones got out just in time. *Your* Ministry will have to make the planning running now.' I said what a pity it was we were still not working together. 'Harold was a fool to move me,' he moaned. 'He couldn't see just what we could have done together. He just doesn't understand. All I am now is a fixer – and I was never interesting in fixing.'

Tuesday, 8 November. Ran into Judith who was pretty happy about the outcome of the morning's meeting of the 'Rhodesia X' Committee. (I learn it consists of Jim Callaghan, Gerald Gardiner, Douglas Houghton, George Brown, Michael Stewart, Dick Crossman and Judith herself, under the PM.) 'There will be no sell-out over Rhodesia. Everyone was unanimous that we cannot accept Smith's reply. It is only a question now of tactics presentationally.'

Wednesday, 9 November. At 9.30 am Cabinet to discuss Rhodesia and Europe. Smith's reply had not been circulated and we had only Bowden's oral report. The reply, he said, was 'clever but evasive' – and unacceptable.

Next: Europe again. We had before us George's draft of the procedure to be followed and of the sort of replies that should be given to questions on our attitude to the Treaty of Rome. We were all set for going over the old ground again when Dick burst in with a plea for decision. 'There is no alternative for this country to genuinely trying to get in.' He personally would not be sorry if the probes failed, but we must seriously try. Otherwise we would be ridiculed for our indecision. Jim Callaghan supported this and added that, if we were heading for an open break with Smith and all the economic strains of mandatory sanctions, it was imperative that we took some step to restore confidence; otherwise he wouldn't answer for the effect on the economy. An attempt to enter Europe, he was now convinced, would give a boost to economic morale. Harold agreed that Rhodesia and the probes were linked: the Governor of the Bank had told them that a move towards entry would strengthen sterling. And so it was agreed and Harold was told to lay before us a statement for the House the following day, to be followed by a big speech at the Guildhall. Dick said to me afterwards, 'Harold is so chronically indecisive.' Me: 'Indecisive or just clever at wangling his own way without an open split?'

Dick: 'Deeply indecisive. I know because I am now working closely with him.'

Official report on the UK economic situation at the end of October: 'The July measures have checked the expansion of the economy and brought a sharp and widespread rise in unemployment. The motor car and building industries have been the hardest hit. Perhaps the most significant development has been a change of mood in industry. Expectations are now gloomy and investment plans are now being revised downwards.

'Prices and wages have been far more stable in recent months, the gilt-edged market has risen and sterling has been faring better in the foreign exchange market. However, it is too soon to see significant results of the July measures in the balance of payments figures, which will probably show another large deficit for the third quarter.'

Classic picture of a good old Tory deflation!

Monday, 14 November. The Guildhall dinner. Harold had passed round the word that Ministers should only wear black tie – a gesture that the City didn't appreciate. Ted gathered that the reason was Dick had refused to go unless he could wear a black tie. Harold's speech was received with only perfunctory applause, despite his warm words about the Common Market. By the end of the meal I was nauseated by all the lavishness: gold microphones among the gold plate; Dr Ramsey, the Archbishop of Canterbury, proving himself a sycophantic servant of the Establishment in moving the toast to the late Lord Mayor. Gerald Gardiner wasn't much better: 'A lot of things need modernizing or improving in Britain today. The one institution which is quite incapable of improvement is the Lord Mayor's banquet.' I suddenly wondered what we were all doing there among our enemies.

Tuesday, 15 November. Cabinet again. Hours of it. We quickly disposed of the final draft of the WP [on prices and incomes policy]. It fixes a norm of nought. Powers under Part 4 of the Act can be used to deal with any settlement in 'clear breach' of the severe restraint criteria. Fiscal powers will be used to deal with 'any excessive growth in aggregate profits'.

[We then] turned to the agonizing reappraisal of public expenditure of which we had been forewarned by Jim in August. PESC had been sifting Departments' figures in a series of meetings and had submitted various proposals for cuts totalling (surprisingly enough) only a modest £277m. Nonetheless they were not pleasant to contemplate. Miserably, we went down the list. I have never known a more painful exercise. Keen as I am to protect my own programmes, I cannot ignore the effects of other cuts on our general policies.

First came defence. Here the reduction proposed was £50m and Jim congratulated Denis on being so co-operative. Roused by this, I asked whether this was additional to the £100m offered in the July cuts. Oh no, I was told. The latter was merely a cut in foreign expenditure and might even mean an increase in expenditure in pounds (*e.g.* the housing of the lads brought home). The £50m meant that our target of defence total in 1969–70 would be a real cut. I said tartly that this ought to be made clear to the Party – they thought they already had an £80m cut in hand. Michael accepted a reduction of £4.5m on overseas information, and this was agreed, but not before Dick had warned that this cut was really intolerable, particularly when we needed increased expenditure on information services to counter the effect on our influence of the proposed defence cuts. Next to roads. I breathed a sigh of relief when a cut of £6.2m on minor roads and car parks just scraped through, but they accepted this grudgingly, muttering that the roads programme was as inflexible as the defence one and that they would have to have a careful look at the long-term implications. (I see battles ahead.) On railways they asked for a cut of £5m in next year's deficit through an increase in fares and charges. I dare not resist this, though I warned it would have to be introduced in the period of 'severe restraint'. Small cuts in agricultural farm support, in ports and airports were seized on thankfully.

The biggest battle of the morning came on housing. The PESC proposal was for a cut of £15.9m in subsidies, including the postponement of the option mortgage scheme from October 1967 till April 1968. Tony fought hard against this – in vain, but he stood out desperately for 15,000 more approvals in public sector housing next year to offset the forecast slump in private building. Without this we should have no hope of reaching our target of 500,000 houses before the Election. Jim was all for re-examining that target and I felt (not for the first time) that we had been rash in committing ourselves to it. I objected to the tendency to label this as a 'Socialist' priority as though other programmes were not. What, apart from anything else, of the National Health Service? Jim agreed with me on this, saying that the Minister of Health had been the worst done by of any of us, but Harold urged that we should at least be able to say we had kept one pledge, and Tony, strongly backed by Dick, reminded us how solemn the pledge had been. Oh dear, I wish we had concentrated more at the outset in 1964 on the need to strengthen the economy before we attempted to do anything else. Why hadn't we set out a four-year plan, making it clear that it was dependent on economic recovery? After an exhausting discussion Harold got his way with the suggestion that a group of Ministers should go into the whole housing question, including long-term targets, on the understanding that, until they had done so, there should be no additional provision for public sector housing investment. We crept out of No. 10 at 1.15 pm feeling like wet rags, with only half the list gone through.

Thursday, 17 November. Cabinet again. On overseas affairs George reported his preparations for his visit to Moscow. Then back to PESC again. We continued our weary journey down the list of proposed cuts. Roy put up a fierce resistance to cuts of £3.5m in police services. 'The primary duty of a Government is law and order,' he said with savage intensity. Failure on this front could be fatal to a Government committed to radical penal reform. Harold was so visibly shaken that he proposed this should be put on one side till we had taken decisions on the remaining items.

We were all waiting for the major battle over family endowment. It was finally agreed that the cost of school meals and welfare milk could only be increased in September as part of a package deal, including an acceptable family endowment scheme, the details of which must be worked out urgently by the Chancellor of the Exchequer and the chairman of the Social Security Committee. So I relaxed, feeling a good deal happier.

Monday, 21 November. Sunday's papers are full of Roy Jenkins again. There is obviously a campaign on to run him as Harold's successor. Ted says it is all due to John Harris.[1] I was interested to read that Roy works at the Department only till 7.30 pm. My day's work is just beginning then. I think the explanation is that Roy carefully contracts out of anything ancillary, *e.g.* I never see him at Party meetings. Ambitious he may be, but he isn't going to sacrifice himself. Personally I believe he is temperamentally incapable of leading the Party. Despite all his care, his instinctive high-handedness will slip out – as when he and I were having a word the other day. Fred Blackburn[2] stopped to speak to me and Roy said impatiently, 'I've got to get away,' Fred walked away in a huff. When Roy and I had finished he turned on his charm smile and said, 'Now I suppose I had better go and placate Fred.'

Over to the Ministry of Housing for a confab with Tony Greenwood on integrating our activities. Richard Llewelyn-Davies[3] had told me at lunch that morale in the Ministry was low, largely due to the activities of the new Permanent Secretary, Stevenson, who is anti-planning. Tony was trying to put some heart back into his chief planner, James. When we met he proposed the setting up of a joint planning unit between our two Ministries, which I think is a good idea.

Tuesday, 22 November. As we waited to go into Cabinet I asked Dick if he was in hot water over his 'reflation' speech as the press implied.[4] He told me he had cleared the speech with the Treasury before delivering it! Typically, Jim was having cold tremors on seeing the big splash it got and the Treasury was washing its hands of all responsibility. 'Pretty mean treatment,' he said grimly. In Cabinet Michael reported that he was going to make a statement on his Prices and Incomes White Paper that day.

Next we rounded off the remnants of PESC. At the end Gerald Gardiner astonished us all by piping up with unaccustomed determination. He said it had been agreed we should go back to the defence item when we had seen what other cuts were involved. We were always told that defence expenditure could not be run down quickly because contracts had been placed. He gathered from the press we were about to place one for a sixth nuclear submarine. We were in time to cancel it. Why not do so? We were going ahead with a vast programme at a time when children in this country had not got enough to eat. The reaction was like a Bateman cartoon and I prayed fervently that Gerald hadn't been deterred from speaking up for ever more. Denis said coldly that he hadn't been given notice of this attack – and proceeded to demolish it. Harold smoothed everything down and said that this might be considered as part of the continuing review, but not in isolation. Jim paid another tribute to the way in which Denis was doing his best to run his own expenditure down. I asked for an assurance that the new submarine did not involve any departure from our

1 Former Research Officer and then Press Officer for the Labour Party, he had become Roy Jenkins's public relations officer.

2 Labour MP for Stalybridge and Hyde.

3 Professor of Architecture at University College, London, and later chairman of the Centre for Environmental Studies. He had been made a life peer in 1963.

4 Addressing a regional Party conference he had said the disappointing production figures were a warning that the July cuts might have gone too far.

decision not to order any more Polaris missiles after the order we inherited had been fulfilled – and got it. It was a hunter-killer, I was told scathingly.

Wednesday, 23 November. A lively hour with Transport PQs in which I had to hit back on freightliners. Then I heard with astonishment that Harold was going to make a statement on Rhodesia. I thought we were going to discuss this tomorrow at Cabinet. To my horror I heard him announce that Bert Bowden was going out to Rhodesia at the Governor's urgent request.

Thursday, 24 November. Before Cabinet I asked Gerald Gardiner urgently what lay behind Harold's announcement. He said that the Governor had been pressing hard for the Secretary of State to go out and there was a 'grave danger' of his resigning. Reporting to us, Harold covered the same ground and said that the House now realized a break was inevitable. Dick said complacently that the Tories were embarrassed by the visit. I could stand no more and begged that we should have no euphoria about the visit. The Secretary of State had been out in September and had come back convinced it was impossible to get anywhere with Smith. 'Sometime', I said passionately, 'we have got to turn and fight.' This shocked Harold. I was the only one to oppose the visit.

We then turned to the draft of the WP on the discussions with Smith to date, a factual record which I could not fault except for a grammatical error to which I drew attention. Said Harold: 'You'll make a good Leader of the Opposition yet.' I whispered to Wedgie: 'If I can't have any principles I do like a little punctuation.'

Tuesday, 29 November. Up early with so many things to do a man doesn't have to do (my dress to press, the housekeeper's journey home to organize, the dog to see to) before leaving for an appointment before Cabinet.

The first item was Rhodesia. Harold called on Bert to make a report. Smith had undoubtedly moved, though his phasing-in proposals would delay an African majority for one or two elections beyond the two or three Cabinet had been prepared to accept. I took the plunge. I said we should realize we were doing what we said we wouldn't do: negotiate with the illegal regime. If we could erode our position on that, where would the erosion stop?

Stung, Harold leapt in to reply. (I suspect he is deeply angry with me. If so, I don't care.) He said first that Smith's concessions showed how right it was for Bert to go; otherwise Smith would have come out with them afterwards, saying he was always ready to make these proposals if we would only have listened. I was right about one thing: there had been some erosion of our attitude on not negotiating before legality. But Rhodesia X was unanimous that we would be wrong not to explore any possibility of a real settlement.

At the House I just missed Harold's PQ on Rhodesia but ran into Judith. We had a quick confab behind the Speaker's chair, smiling sweetly at each other to fool the press gallery. I merely said, 'I have sent a warning shot across his bows.' She replied, 'I will do the same.' But as she said it I realized that neither of us would have any effect on him. In a curious way he is very tough and, fond of us both as he is, we would both be expendable. He is implacable when he has made up his mind to a compromise, though he spends a good deal of his natural adroitness trying to keep even those he has alienated as his friends. If only he would be as stubborn in *not* compromising! Ah, then we might have got somewhere as a Government. 'Resolute only to be irresolute' isn't quite fair. Perhaps the right phrase is 'resolute only to avoid a showdown'.

Thursday, 1 December. Flew to Paris for a meeting of the European Conference of Ministers of Transport. Scored a triumph by getting all the members to agree to ratify the European convention on drivers' hours. Even Germany, though temporarily without a Minister, agreed I had made an unanswerable case. Since Germany has been the main stumbling-block, the British delegation rejoiced mightily. On my arrival home I heard that the PM had flown to Gibraltar to meet Smith on a warship. Went into the House to hear the comments. Apparently Harold had been very impressive in the House announcing his trip. He had also reassured the Party meeting successfully. Everyone was suspending judgment – even Mike. What else can one do? Cabinet had endorsed the visit that morning while I was away.

On 2 December Harold Wilson, accompanied by Bert Bowden and Elwyn Jones, met Ian Smith, the Governor, the Chief Justice and two of Smith's colleagues on the British cruiser, the Tiger, *moored off Gibraltar. The aim was make a 'last' attempt to negotiate sufficient amendments to the 1961 constitution to enable Rhodesia's independence to be recognized and mandatory sanctions avoided. The constitutional details of the negotiations were so complex that Ian Smith had endless opportunities for creating confusion and delay. See Wilson,* The Labour Government.

Sunday, 4 December. A heavenly winter's day. I worked in bed from 7 am, waiting for the sun to melt the frost so I could finish planting my daffodils. Suddenly, a call from Richard Bird: a Cabinet meeting at 2.30 pm. I was trembling so much I could hardly eat my breakfast. I realize now why I have been so tense and irritable. Underneath I have been worrying myself sick. On the drive back to town I was so *distrait* I entirely forgot to eat my sandwiches. Arrived in good time to find a friendly crowd outside No. 10. Inside Elwyn was chatting about the trip. No, they hadn't been seasick. 'The Navy found us a soft spot in the Med – somewhere near Casablanca.' What did he think of the working document they had brought back? 'It's a package deal,' he shrugged. 'The best we could get under the circumstances.' Smith was not yet committed. Then I heard the familiar phrase: 'Will you come in, gentlemen, please.' Would it be for the last time?

Harold looked buoyant, despite the long hours of negotiation, preceded by talks with his own team till 3 am. He opened by introducing the document which had been signed by him and Smith, though at the end Smith had withdrawn his agreement to commend it to his Cabinet. It was therefore *ad referendum* to both Cabinets, though he and the Commonwealth Secretary *were* recommending it. It was clear they could reach agreement on the constitutional side. His breaking-points had been a return to legality and the broad-based interim Government. Smith wouldn't accept these without reference back to his Government.

In the end, despite the doubts and anxieties voiced by Michael and Fred and

Douglas and the two Tonys, I was the only one who opposed the deal. The rest heard me in silence and let the document through.

Out to the waiting crowds and the flash lights. I brooded all the way home miserably in the car. I do not believe we need have come to this impasse if there had been any real will for a 'kill' in the first place. The will has never really been there. And now we are in a situation where the only hope of getting away with our half-hearted measures lies in pretending our bluff is nothing of the sort. What a dilemma! I despise our timidities. Yet if I resign and expose them as such I shall give us the worst of all worlds. Not for the first time the agonies are intellectual rather than moral. What the hell is the *wise* thing to do? If others resign, I certainly shall. I mentally prepare for resignation all the way home. What a wrench to give up the architecting of my transport policy. Going back to the facile criticisms of the back bench will be so *dull*. But I shall not hesitate to do so if my natural allies in this battle feel we should take this course.

Monday, 5 December. We waited all day for Smith's reply. On the ticker-tape it said he had asked for an extension of time. None of us knew what was happening. Eventually came the 'No', accompanied by wild rumours that he had qualified it in various ways. Harold was due to make a statement at 7 pm and we were all there in force. There ensued a period of hilarity – the sort that always accompanies moments of high drama in the House. No Harold. The Opposition positively raced through a list of amendments to minor Bills, I suspect to embarrass us by leaving a hiatus before Harold was ready. Elwyn had to be fetched hurriedly for his item and arrived trying to read his brief as he ran. The House was in convulsions as he obviously searched for his place. It was the most bland piece of floundering I have seen for a long time.

Gradually the idea spread that Harold wouldn't be ready for some time and the House emptied. I went off for a drink with Dingle Foot, my tummy rumbling. I dare not take time off to eat. Back on the bench at 8.30 pm. The House had filled up again but still no Harold. Savagely I muttered to Dingle, 'He is cooking up a desperate last-minute wriggle out of it.' The House got restless and I said to Jim, 'Why hadn't Harold got a statement ready on the assumption Smith might reject? He is making us look indecisive again. It is no good acting like a Superman if you end by falling short.' Jim replied gravely, 'He *is* a Superman. I couldn't do what he has done.' In the end H. came dashing in, head down. To my utter relief there was no indication of running away in his statement. His control of the detail and the House was masterly. Jim's right: there is a touch of the Superman about him.

Thursday, 8 December. I missed Cabinet because I had to attend the Standing Committee on the Road Safety Bill, where I took a tough line over our proposal to make disqualification automatic for the new offence of drunken driving. Thanks to office meetings I also missed Harold's reportedly scintillating speech in the Rhodesia debate. Later I had a meal with Dick. We mused about Harold's character, Dick insisting that he lives very short-term. Said Dick, 'He hates working out the long-term implications as much as Nye did.' He had lived the negotiations on the *Tiger* with his whole being. Now he was living 100 per cent the other way. Dick didn't like his new moral attitudes. He is a tough cynic these days, is Dick. I asked him what had happened to the economic discussions in SEP [Economic Strategy Committee of Cabinet] and he replied that devaluation was being forced into the open again. Harold now realized that it was the only alternative to cumulative deflation. But the breach with Smith was likely to delay it. Harold had definitely intended to 'float from strength' next spring and without Rhodesia we could have done it. But the breach meant a setback.

Friday, 16 December. Visit to Manchester for my first discussion on setting up Conurbation Transport Authorities [CTAS]. Had a meeting last night on arrival with Alderman Alker, chairman of the passenger transport co-ordinating committee, and Alderman Blackwell of Manchester, together with Bennett, Manchester's transport manager, the town clerk and other officials. I was delighted by their unaminity on the need for these authorities and by their belief that the other municipalities only needed a push to come into line. At the transport offices this morning I was shown the progress with the rapid transit study which we are helping to finance (75 per cent) and was immensely impressed with the young project manager and also by the parallel studies between us, Manchester and BR on the integration of road/rail services. It will all obviously be much easier when we get a conurbation transport authority!

Tuesday, 20 December. A hectic day of pre-Christmas negotiations. First, Cabinet. I asked Dick how the Sexual Offences Bill had got through without a vote. He said that Dance, leader of the opposition to it, had been so sozzled he had failed to rise at the right moment![1] On overseas affairs George reported that Willie Brandt[2] had made a most impressive speech at the NATO meeting renouncing all nuclear weapons for Germany and struck a very different note from Schröder, the Minister of Defence. There is, he said, obviously going to be a divided Government there.

He gave a fascinating account of his meeting with de Gaulle, which had been arranged at Couve de Murville's suggestion.[3] At the end it was very difficult for him to make up his mind where de Gaulle stood. Was he keeping the door open? It was not agricultural policy which troubled him as much as the sterling area which, de Gaulle felt, gave us a privileged position. 'The other was the American thing – he made that very plain.' (Just what I said at Chequers!) De Gaulle had said France felt she might be 'annexed'. But he had great goodwill towards Harold personally, whom he obviously admired.

An exhausting meeting in the afternoon with Stan Raymond and Reggie Wilson over the NFC. Raymond tried to browbeat me when I told him I had decided to go for a free-standing NFC, but I stood out. After a stormy meeting of an hour and a half he threatened to bring the Railways Board to see me. I said OK. Then as we broke up he was all genial again. He will try anything on.

Wednesday, 21 December. Went to Transport House in the afternoon for the

[1] James Dance, Conservative MP for Bromsgrove.
[2] Chairman of the Social Democratic Party in the Federal Republic, Vice-Chancellor and Foreign Minister in the Federal Government. He became Chancellor in 1969 until 1974.
[3] French Minister of Foreign Affairs.

meeting with the National Committee of Lorry Drivers of the TGWU which I had suggested to Jack Jones at Brighton. Frank Cousins, Harry Nicholas and Jack met me on the steps and we posed smilingly for photographs. The lorrymen were sitting dourly round the boardroom table – one of the least oncoming lot I have met. But I forged ahead vigorously with a short introductory speech, dealing mainly with my proposal to reduce their hours. They welcomed this, if somewhat sceptically. One of them said, 'If you can give us the ten-hour day you'll do more than any Minister of Transport in history, but I doubt whether you'll be able to do it.' I replied that it all depended on enforcement, with which they agreed, though whether they'll accept the tachograph when the time comes I very much doubt myself. Then on to general questions and a rough hour and a half at which four of them in particular accused me of encouraging the railways to undercut their rates and ruin their industry. The same four demanded to know why I didn't renationalize road haulage and one of them was very rude. I hit back hard and gave as good as I got. Frank was magnificent, chipping in to tell off the most unreasonable of them and backing me up when I said that he knew, as an ex-Minister, that I couldn't overthrow the 1962 Act or deal with the Transport Holding Company till I had got parlimentary support for a new law. Frank said a few warm and friendly words at the beginning and the end, and this time they stood up as I left, giving me a good hand. Escorting me to my car, Frank said, 'The ones who didn't talk are the ones that matter and they were impressed. So were the others as a matter of fact.' He is a generous-minded chap.

Worked late at the Ministry clearing up papers while an office party raged in my room. I said flatly I wasn't taking any boxes home for Christmas.

Tuesday, 27 December. A heavenly Christmas, marred only by a grisly record of road deaths: fifty-six on the Friday alone. I chanced my arm on some very sweeping comments, and fortunately got away with it. I instructed Chris Hall to prepare a speech on road safety for my first lunch engagement after the holiday and then had to spend most of Sunday polishing it.

1967

Monday, 2 January. Back to work. George Brown has had a very bad press over his peace initiative on Vietnam. Serves him right. The suspicion is widespread that he only did it to stave off a demand by the Left that Harold should 'dissociate' himself from American bombing of Hanoi's surroundings with its civilian casualties as reported by Salisbury of the *New York Times*. Was Harold in the know, I wonder? Probably not. He would be too fly to fall for George's impulsive techniques. Nonetheless he has studiously avoided any further act of 'dissociation'.

Stanley Raymond is absolutely thrilled with his knighthood in the New Year's Honours List, for which I had pressed. I'm glad I succeeded in getting it for him.

Tuesday, 3 January and Wednesday, 4 January. A succession of exacting meetings at the Ministry on various aspects of policy. I told Sir Tom Padmore that I want a 'critical path' chart of our progress with the Transport Bill. He assured me he would be the progress chaser so I asked him to report to me every Monday morning with the aid of the chart. A pleasant lunch on Wednesday with Colin Boyne and colleagues of the *Architects' Journal*. They said the only trouble was they agreed with everything I was doing! Chris Hall's only caveat to that was that I am too pro-motorist!

Friday, 6 January. A busy day in Newcastle: Tyne Tunnel and all. Just as I was trying to rush into my press conference I got a message to ring No. 10. It was Harold, Cabinet reshuffling, to ask if he could have my PPS. Of course I said yes, but added, 'I thought it was one of my Parliamentary Secretaries you were after. Don't forget: I want you to make at least one of them a Minister of State.' 'I can't do that,' he moaned. 'I am having a terrible time already. You know me, I'm no butcher. I have had a horrible two days.' Sacking anyone is clearly misery for him.

Tuesday, 10 January. One of my biggest shocks over the Cabinet reshuffle has been taking Bottomley at ODM out of the Cabinet.[1] To call him 'of Cabinet rank' instead is a mere gesture, largely meaningless. Judith, too, though 'promoted', is moved from direct responsibility for Rhodesia. One by one

[1] The reshuffle was mainly among Ministers of State but Harold Wilson seized the opportunity of bringing Patrick Gordon Walker back into Cabinet, replacing Douglas Houghton as Minister without Portfolio in charge of the long-term review of social security policy. With the merger of the Commonwealth and Colonial Offices Fred Lee became Chancellor of the Duchy of Lancaster and was allocated to help Michael Stewart at DEA. The size of the Cabinet was reduced from twenty-three to twenty-one, with Arthur Bottomley keeping his job at ODM but outside the Cabinet.

Harold is abandoning his earlier idealisms. Were they only gimmicks?

Thursday, 12 January. The Cabinet, now slightly reduced in size so we have all more room to breathe, was opened by a homily from Harold. He wants more businesslike Cabinets (at last!) with less items brought to it and more solved in the Cabinet committees which he is going to reorganize. Three economic committees are to be merged in one. I certainly welcome all this. Patrick Gordon Walker was back in play, obviously at home. George Brown reported that press accounts of disturbances in China were almost certainly exaggerated. Mao and Lin Piao[1] were still in control of the situation. One outcome might be that China would be unable to prevent Russia from adopting a more positive attitude to Vietnam, which she obviously wanted to do. His own public overture was merely a cloak to more secret pressures he was exerting to bring the US and the Soviet Union together. Meanwhile, while we must continue to deplore the US bombing of North Vietnam, there was nothing to be gained by dissociating ourselves publicly. Johnson was resisting pressure from his hawks to escalate, and public dissociation would make it more difficult for him. Kosygin was clearly worried about escalation, too, and we attached great hopes to the outcome of his visit here. I said that, if our overtures failed and escalation took place, we should face a crisis over our own policy: a warning shot that some of us would not tolerate these 'secret pressures' indefinitely.

Monday, 16 January. Got my NFC paper through the new economic policy committee which will be known as EN. (Someone asked what the initials stand for and a wit replied, 'Economic Nonsense'.) We also had a paper in front of us asking for an increase in building licences for the private sector. Prentice[2] explained that there was surplus capacity in the building industry, owing to the cut-back in local authority activities, and he wanted to be allowed to authorize some building (like shops) which was classified as essential though less urgent. This was going through on the nod when I chipped in to remark sardonically that it was a strange outcome of our planning that we were holding back housing and things like swimming baths in order to build shops. This got quite a response, though Dick, for instance, said we had no choice till we could relax our restrictions on local authority expenditure. Wedgie passed me a note: 'We are knocking a hole in the economy and filling it with candyfloss!'

In the afternoon off to Germany to see the new social democratic Minister of Transport, Herr Leber; also pedestrian precincts in Cologne.

Wednesday, 18 January. In the afternoon I had my consultations with the three railway unions on the railway network map. I had approached it with some trepidation but it went far better than I had dared to hope. They were all clearly impressed with the tone of the foreword which I read out to them and also by the indication of the number of lines Raymond and I had reprieved compared

[1] Mao Tse-tung was chairman of the Central Committee of the Communist Party of China and Marshal Lin Piao was Defence Minister.

[2] Reg Prentice, Labour MP for East Ham North from 1957, had been appointed Minister of State at Education and Science in 1964 and Minister of Public Building and Works in 1966. In August 1967 he was to succeed Arthur Bottomley as Minister of Overseas Development, outside the Cabinet.

with what Beeching would have done. Of course they had to make some grumbling noises but that was inevitable. But suddenly Sid Greene went difficult. He insisted on saying that all grey lines were to be closed, despite my repeated explanation that they were merely to be investigated. Then he asked for a lot of information which we could not understand, and when I tried to spell it all out to him he said sulkily, 'I didn't hear. I wasn't listening.' I decided that the moment had come to lose my temper. 'This is a poor return for six months' hard work,' I said (and was horrified to find my lips trembling). Then I closed the meeting and swept out, leaving John Morris and Raymond to try and knock some sense into Sid. John told me afterwards my reaction had done good: the other trade unionists were embarrassed by Sid's behaviour. I replied that I wasn't going to lick anyone's boots.

Thursday, 19 January. A very brief Cabinet. Harold and George reported on their visit to Italy on their Common Market tour. George said the talks about our joining the EEC had gone as well as could be expected and indeed rather better. Arriving at the airport he had seen from the plane window what he could only assume was a demonstration on Vietnam. However, it turned out to be enthusiastic students waiting to greet our PM as 'the greatest federalist they had ever known'. Harold mildly corrected this and added generously that no one could have been tougher on agricultural policy than George. George in turn admitted that it would be unwise to rely on the Italians to stand up to de Gaulle on our behalf. I reported what I had been told in Germany by the head of the international section of the Ministry of Economic Affairs, namely that de Gaulle was determined not to have us in and that the Five would not be willing to risk disrupting the Market by defying him. In other words, we were wasting our time as long as de Gaulle was there. There was a moment's hostile silence, then Harold said, 'Well, Paris will show.'

Monday, 23 January. Met the TUC Nationalized Industries Committee on transport policy generally and the NFC in particular. The meeting went better than I had dared to hope, though what will happen with the individual unions is a different matter. Saw Dick in the evening. He wants to know what I can do in the transport field 'to help Bill Fiske'. I told him the GLC wants to take over London transport and he asked me to try and get something settled in time for me to announce it at a big London demonstration at the end of March. That suits me! As I have told my officials more than once, there is an electoral tide in the affairs of government which, taken at the flood, leads on to policy. Dick is very hurt by yesterday's article in the *Sunday Telegraph* about him as a Minister. He is hurt that his civil servants thought him a bully! Of course, he pretends not to be hurt at all. I took advantage of the talk to warn him about cuts in the roads programme. I said that, if the Government just tried to cut the programme, after he as Minister had agreed with the Cambridge planning conference that housing and roads must not get out of relationship, it would show itself to be illiterate. I said I was planning a balanced approach to transport, including improvement of public transport and highly unpopular measures like traffic restraint. I was even prepared to recommend increases in licence fees. But none of this would be tolerable without a big increase in the roads programme, and if I was forced to do the unpopular things without the latter I would resign. After a few highly illiterate remarks of his own, he showed signs of being impressed. He really has a terribly superficial approach to politics on occasions. But like all bullies (and he *is* a bully) he will cave in under pressure.

Wednesday, 25 January. In the evening I got a mysterious message from my office: 'The Prime Minister will be raising orally in Cabinet tomorrow the question of ministerial publications. This is not being notified to Cabinet Ministers generally.' I sought out Dick and we agreed that it was all due to last Sunday's story in the *Observer*.[1] Somebody has been blabbing again and my guess is that it is Dick himself. Later he too got a message and found the initiative has come from George Brown. Dick was in a very defiant mood and said if they wanted his resignation they could have it.

Thursday, 26 January. Opening Cabinet Harold said the Foreign Secretary wanted to raise a matter. George duly plunged into a fairly mild statement to the effect that he had been very disturbed by press reports that certain Ministers were signing contracts to write their life stories and were keeping diaries which might be used. This was bound to undermine confidence between colleagues and he thought it was undesirable. He personally had turned offers down. Harold was even milder, pointing out that it was no uncommon thing for people to keep diaries and to write memoirs. Non-members of the Cabinet could be just as bad as anyone else in embarrassing their colleagues by their writings after resignation – *vide* Mayhew after he resigned. Cousins, by contrast, had acted very honourably. There were certain rules which he had to interpret, but they could be evaded as Kilmuir[2] had shown. We must be sensible about all this but he thought it would be a good thing, not least to protect ourselves against some of the demands of the Opposition, if there were to be a fresh review of the existing conventions which could propose any changes, and he suggested that the Lord Chancellor might take charge of this. He didn't want to argue '*ad hominem* – or *ad feminem* for that matter' – but any private and personal recording of what went on in Cabinet was to be deprecated and contracts which might bring a Minister under any kind of improper pressure were obviously wrong.

One or two people then virtuously said they had brushed all approaches aside – Jim, for one – until Dick could bear it no longer and burst out with a speech of such disarming candour as to have us all rolling with laughter. Explaining that he had had his contract long before he became a Minister he said he had never attempted to hide it because it had been his lifelong intention to write a serious book on government. 'I was just about to write it when Gaitskell died and my political career began. Of course, it has been fascinating for me to see you all at work. I shall now be able to write from first-hand

[1] The Pendennis column reported that Dick Crossman was proposing to publish a book 'based on the diary he has kept for years'. It also reported that I was working on my memoirs.

[2] Lord Kilmuir, formerly David Maxwell-Fyfe, Conservative MP and Home Secretary, had been Lord Chancellor in Harold Macmillan's Government, but was axed with a number of his Cabinet colleagues in July 1962. In 1964 he had published his revealing political memoirs under the title *Political Adventure*.

experience. But', turning to Jim, 'it's Morrison I want to get at, not you. I want to debunk that odious book of his. And I've never hidden this. The one thing I am always accused of is candour.' He utterly charmed everyone. But, fighting back, Jim asked about his second proposed book: his memoirs. That really frightened him. With childlike charm Dick assured him he always kept his tapes under lock and key! And anyway what was written from a diary was likely to be far less coloured than those retrospective rationalizations in which memory played tricks, always to the benefit of the writer. Weakly Cabinet agreed to the inquiry almost in a mood of hilarity, though whether it develops more seriously remains to be seen. I have a contract with Weidenfeld[1] in my pocket which I haven't yet signed: a book of my memoirs. This is something I should never have thought of entering into if Dick hadn't urgently advised me to beat my colleagues to it! I shall have to consider whether to tell the inquiry about it or just let it drop.

Harold concluded this episode by suggesting that anyone who had anything which might be of interest to the inquiry might care to communicate with the Lord Chancellor. But I'm not going to stop keeping my diary – even if a word of it never sees the light of day in my life-time. I feel it is a duty I owe to history, however hard a chore.

Next we had a report on the Paris visit. George and Harold were clearly pleased with themselves. They said the talks with de Gaulle in the morning began rather frigidly. Harold had spent seventy-five minutes explaining that the sterling area wasn't a liability and that, thrown into EEC, it could actually prove a help. It was hard going till lunch when, as Harold and George talked one on each side of de Gaulle, the atmosphere suddenly changed. They were convinced they had made an impression on de Gaulle, who was particularly charming to George and made a positively fulsome after-lunch speech. During lunch he started meditating on the possibility of having some entirely new arrangement to accommodate Great Britain – a line which worried them a bit because they saw him using it as a get-out. They had no illusions that they had converted him. They thought the chief obstacle to our entry was that de Gaulle was frightened of disturbing the cosy little enclave of the Six. He knew that the Common Market would be transformed into something much wider if Great Britain came in. Nonetheless they both glowed with self-satisfaction.

Wednesday, 1 February. Met Bill Fiske, Jane Phillips and officers of the GLC to confront them with Maurice Holmes, who is asking for £7m a year of fare increases. I am going to ask my Cabinet colleagues for a bridging operation, not only because of the GLC election but also because we *must* break through the vicious spiral of rising fares, falling use of public transport, declining services, and so on. My aim was to make the GLC sit up and do something radical about parking. It isn't their fault that it has taken them two years to build up the necessary staff for effective traffic management. Nor is it their fault that they have to share their powers with the boroughs. The Tories, who are now hypocritically asking for a Traffic Commissioner for London, are responsible

[1] George Weidenfeld was chairman of the publishing house of Weidenfeld and Nicolson. He was knighted in 1969 and became a life peer in 1976.

for taking the powers away from the Ministry. But nonetheless it is time the GLC showed some fight. I left them absolutely scared by the thought of a massive fares increase and, I hope, ready to demand action.

Thursday, 2 February. Another Cabinet. Harold and George reported on their visit to Belgium which they obviously found rather depressing. George referred to these 'wearing' visits.

Then on to the Prices and Incomes policy. Eventually everyone agreed that Part 4 must go in July as promised and that Part 2 must be activated to take its place.

Friday, 3 February. Early Cabinet to discuss the Defence White Paper. I raised the East of Suez question. Both Denis and Harold had drawn our attention to the differences of wording on this in the WP compared to last year – showing clearly that Harold is cooling off on the 'world role' line. (This is just another confirmation of my view that he is now sold on going into Europe.) But I asked why there was no indication of the effect of this difference of emphasis on our procurement of aircraft, *i.e.* the F-111. Denis replied that the further review was of course taking into account what reductions in *numbers* would be required, but that personally he didn't think there would be any change in the *range* of aircraft needed. (Later I noted that this item was referred to in the Minutes as 'recorded separately'. I wonder whether it is in fact recorded anywhere – or just recorded and not circulated – and if the latter whether one has any right of access to the record? I daren't ask because of the hoo-ha over diaries.)

Monday, 6 February. Dinner at No. 10 in honour of Kosygin. Out of deference to our visitors dress was informal, but Mair Connor lent me her mink cape to tart up my short black dress.[1] It was a most variegated crowd of guests: Donald Stokes,[2] the actress Moira Shearer, politicians and – typical of Harold – Alf Ramsey, of football management fame, the real star. Donald Stokes made friendly noises saying he was delighted I was to visit Leylands soon and that I had really put buses on the map. Hugh Cudlipp[3] was there, bunched up and predatory in his smiling but unreal way. I always find conversation with him very difficult.

Then Kosygin arrived. He has a rough-hewn face, looks dour until you talk to him and then his face softens and warms. But I was only introduced briefly before Mary and Harold swept us all into dinner. How they managed to get so many into that fairly small dining-room is a mystery. Mary admitted that she had to send out for a horse-shoe table. I was between Rees-Mogg and a

[1] Wife of Bill Connor, who wrote a brilliant column in the *Daily Mirror* under the name of Cassandra for over thirty years until his death in 1967.

[2] One of the businessmen willing to work with the Labour Government. He had been made a member of the Industrial Reorganization Corporation the Government had set up in 1966 to help restructure and modernize industry and in 1968 became chairman of the British Leyland Motor Corporation Ltd. He was made a life peer in 1969.

[3] Former editor of the *Daily Mirror* and the *Sunday Pictorial* who had become deputy chairman of the International Publishing Corporation [IPC] and chairman of Daily Mirror Newspapers Ltd. In 1968 he succeeded Cecil King as chairman of IPC, serving until 1973. He was made a life peer in 1974.

member of the Russian entourage. I congratulated Rees-Mogg on his new job as editor of *The Times*. Opposite me was Tony Crosland, who confessed he has no time for the social round so he sends his wife Susan out to pick up any gossip for him. He obviously works very hard, contrary to the impression given by his rather dissipated appearance. But I was delighted to learn he needs – and tries to get – eight hours' sleep. We thereupon started a discussion as to how much sleep one needs. The Russian on my right said he gets three hours a night. Jim Callaghan said he gets six. I've been insisting on seven hours lately.

Then the speeches. Both Harold and Kosygin were mercifully short – friendly, but guarded. No loyal toasts on either side. And then we were streaming out. I found myself just behind Harold and Kosygin. Harold grabbed me and hissed, 'Don't let him go straight through and out. Keep him talking.' Obediently I swung round, confronted Kosygin and engaged him, somewhat desperately, in conversation. The interpreter obliged, poker-faced. 'It is about ten years since I was in Moscow. I suppose the traffic has increased enormously?' Yes, it had. 'What is the main aim of your transport policy in the Soviet Union?' 'To supply one car to every family'! 'Well, that is a good capitalist objective,' I replied. 'Here, I am appalled by the difficulties which will be created when we have reached that point. In this little crowded island. . . .' Kosygin broke into a charming smile, 'But you see we have plenty of Soviet space.' 'But what are you doing to encourage public transport? . . . That is my aim, as a Socialist. Are you extending that wonderful Moscow Underground?' Yes, they were extending it. But that was obviously, to Kosygin, a bit *vieux jeu*. We continued like this animatedly for what seemed like a quarter of an hour, while other people circled us at a respectful distance. Kosygin was warm, very natural and friendly. Then Harold, who had been foraging, surfaced with an odd-looking chap who had something to do with timber. Harold, who is in his unpretentious element on these occasions, started reminiscing about timber negotiations. And then suddenly Kosygin detached himself and I could go home.

Wednesday, 8 February. A day of non-stop consultations over the NFC. I had been mildly dreading it but in the event it all went too smoothly to be true. Then on to the Transport Users Joint Committee where I expected much more trouble since the CBI has been pontificating about the Government's first duty being to provide industry with the transport it preferred at the lowest cost. I said the Government's first duty was to produce a balanced transport plan which made the most effective use of our resources. That meant supporting a substantial railway network and then making the fullest economic use of it. But even here there was no real fight and they ended by agreeing we must use the railway system more, even suggesting the railways should cut rates to uneconomic levels to attract traffic! So, I thought to myself, the trouble will come from the unions. But somehow the joint team had put Jack Jones in the chair and he was at his constructive best. I threw them a number of points to brood on and make recommendations to me, including the form workers' participation should take. Jack seized on all this gladly and said they would let me have their views as soon as possible. He is undoubtedly, in my view, the most outstanding trade unionist of the day.

Thursday, 9 February. At Cabinet Harold reported on Kosygin's visit. There had been great cordiality and it had been clear that the Russians regarded us as the real mediators over Vietnam. Of course Kosygin had had to make tough speeches – he had to think of Moscow radio and his home audience. But he had been extraordinarily frank over China: what he thought of her went far further than any of us realized. Michael Stewart reported on his discussions with the TUC and CBI about P and I policy. Both of them wanted to return to a voluntary scheme. But he still stood by his view that we should reactivate Part 2 with additional powers.[1]

Friday, 10 February. Talks with Raymond and Reggie Wilson as to what we could do to force a decision on open terminals. Under pressure Reggie admitted that Chester of Tartan Arrow [TA][2] had put the cat among the pigeons by sending out a circular to its customers assuring them they were still a private concern and had not been nationalized! He also admitted that Tartan Arrow had taken some business away from the liner train by undercutting: he had put a stop to that. 'Can't you get 100 per cent ownership?' I asked in despair. No wonder the NUR were threatening to black the Tartan Arrow train! 'Only by spending £1¼m more than if we wait the two years,' he replied. In the meantime he would try and control Chester.

Monday, 13 February. Saw Moxley of the *Railway Review* over my reply to his article on open terminals. I really gave him the works! John Morris said afterwards that he had never seen anyone more completely routed. 'Let me say this: I wouldn't be married to you for any money but you will be Prime Minister one day, if your health holds out'!

At 5.45 pm got a message from the Department that Reggie has taken 100 per cent control of Tartan Arrow! I was flabbergasted. But I could see at once that this was going to be regarded as an act of appeasement by *me* since the railwaymen at York Way are blacking two Tartan Arrow containers which have arrived there by ordinary liner train pending the completion of TA's own terminals. Although this is an unofficial action which the NUR is trying to call off, the union executive still stands by its threat to black the special TA train when it is ready to operate. I got on the phone immediately to Reggie to tell him he must not announce the take-over at this stage – only to find he had issued a press statement on his own authority. I lambasted him for proceeding without consulting me. He said he thought I would be pleased, particularly as he had acquired control without the expenditure of any extra money. But he did agree (with tongue in cheek?) that he ought to have contacted me before releasing the announcement. I am now really in a mess! I shall be criticized for something

[1] Part 2 of the Act passed the previous August empowered the Government by Order to bring into operation for periods of twelve months at a time the power to demand the early warning of price, wage and dividend increases and to standstill them pending a report by the Board. The temporary draconian powers under Part 2 of the Act to enforce a wages and prices freeze followed by a period of severe restraint were due to lapse in August and a solemn undertaking had been given that they would not be renewed. The question was what would follow them. The Part 4 powers not only enabled the Government to halt increases, but to bring a wage or price down to the pre-freeze level.

[2] The Tartan Arrow road haulage company, launched by Mr Chester, was one of the firms in which the Transport Holding Company had bought a fifty–fifty share through a holding company. The THC had the right to buy out the firm after two years.

which I did not do but for which I shall have to take public responsibility: not the first time Ministers have found themselves in this situation.

Tuesday, 14 February. More to-ing and fro-ing at Cabinet about P and I policy. Michael reported that the TUC was still adamant that it would accept nothing more than a reactivation of Part 2 with some wider powers over prices, but not incomes. Faced with the argument that we should be back to stop–go, Woodcock says that would be better than abandoning free bargaining.

Went into the House for Harold's Questions. I knew he had one on open terminals and could guess that he would get a supplementary on Tartan Arrow. I tried to put him in the picture but he was supremely confident and barely listened. When I tried to sit next to him, George remained entrenched between us, waving me aside with, 'He'll manage better on his own.' So, for the first time in my experience at Question Time, Harold boobed. For the first time Heath asked a devastatingly simple supplementary which got his middle wicket: 'How many open terminals are in operation at the present time?' Without me to whisper to him, Harold floundered and said, 'I must ask the Right Honourable Gentleman to give me notice of that question.' Howls of derision. Harold came out growling about me and my open terminals.

Tuesday, 21 February. Spent most of the day struggling with my speech for tomorrow's Transport debate. There is little new to say at this stage. True, I have succeeded in getting the increase in London fares postponed; also I have got agreement in principle for a CTA for London. But the office stands over me waiting to snatch every page from me for clearance with all the departments and bodies concerned. Every word has to be weighed and qualified till the life has gone out of it. I don't get the feel of the occasion at all. Oh, for the carefree days when I made a speech on my own responsibility!

Wednesday, 22 February. One of the best NEC meetings I have ever known. Joe Gormley of the Miners had given notice that he wanted to raise P and I policy, and one after another the trade union members spoke from the heart: the rank and file were asking them why the Labour Government had gone anti-trade union. There was a growing move to contract out – even to disaffiliate. The traditional relationship between the two sides of the movement would crack if the Government persisted in its policy. I have never heard them speak better and Harold and Jim were clearly shaken. From their own point of view the unions are right. Yet I remain convinced that free collective bargaining (on the old model) and full employment are incompatible. What are the implications of all this? Possibly that an effective Labour movement will be driven to find another basis than the unions. And yet that would be a pity because one of Labour's jobs is to make the unions *political*. Left to fulfil a purely industrial function, they will become merely an arm of capitalism, as in America. I felt I was witnessing one of the great turning-points of history – all the more so because the union lads were too deadly serious to be captious or unreasonable. Where it will all lead is too early to say. I don't know whether we are just educating the unions or breaking with them. After this, a Party meeting on East of Suez and defence seemed small beer.

More frantic last-minute corrections to my speech as Minutes poured in from the office, and then into the Chamber, tense and exhausted. I didn't excel myself, and came out swearing that one day I would have the courage to resist all this office nursery-maiding, make an off-the-cuff speech and risk putting some cats among the pigeons. Stephen redeemed the day by a first-class winding-up speech.

Monday, 27 February. More union consultations over transport policy. Had a pretty smooth run with TGWU, GMWU and others over CTAS. Once again Jack Jones was in the chair, fair but firm.

The entire afternoon was spent with Stan Raymond briefing me on my meeting with the NUR Executive tomorrow on open terminals.

Tuesday, 28 February. Up early to prepare my speech for the NUR. At the office I told a disappointed Richard Bird and Scott Malden that I had decided to meet the EC accompanied only by John Morris as I intended to play a political opening line. (This was Ted's advice and I am sure he is right.) They bit back their disagreement but asked if they could come along and wait in another room on call, which I readily agreed. After a frantic last-minute collection of material for the speech we set off – a little late. Yes, there were the photographers. Sid Greene was waiting, smiling as usual, in his office. I told him I wanted a decision that day and was ready to go on all day and night if necessary. Still that non-committal smile from Sid. And so into the boardroom to face twenty-four hostile and suspicious men, sitting in a semi-circle round the big horseshoe table. [Frank] Lane [the President] in his vast mahogany presidential chair greeted me very civilly. Some of the members straggled to their feet; others remained stonily seated. Lane then made a perfect introductory speech from my point of view. I know he is as anxious for open terminals as I am (so is Sid) and, despite his rather dumb look and simple halting speech, he gave me just the lead-in I wanted: said I had indicated that there could be no more investment in freightliners unless the terminals were opened; that I had indicated I had in mind a package deal and that they would be interested to hear more details of it.

My speech lasted an hour and then the questions began. Before very long I was pretty near to despair. The questions were speeches as well and they showed an emotionalism – in some cases an irrationality – that boded ill for agreement.

At 3.30 pm Lane said he thought they had exausted all the points and they must release me. I thanked them for their courtesy in listening to me and stressed once again that I was on call all day. Then back to the office to work as best I could on other things while waiting for the result of this marathon. I was worried about the three-line whip on Defence, the Whips having made it clear that I could not be excused on any account. At 9 pm the call came: would I go back to Unity House? Off we ran, but it was only to tell me that the negotiating committee (to which the matter had been referred) was divided. I went in to the EC and made a brief, somewhat impassioned speech, begging them at least to keep the door open. And I left to vote, leaving the others behind.

In the House Healey was making a lamentable winding-up speech on defence. (Later we learned that there was the biggest ever mass of abstentions on our side: some said sixty-nine; our Whips said forty-five.) Back in Unity House I found the others sitting around in Sid's room, having a drink and waiting for the EC to make up its mind. At last down came Sid, the President and George Brassington [Greene's deputy]. Sid told me that the EC had adopted the [negotiating committee's] majority report [in favour of negotiations] by fourteen votes to ten. I jumped for joy. But, said Sid, it was too late to start negotiating that night. (He doesn't like late hours.) The negotiating committee was ready to come along to the Ministry the next day. We all went home jubilant.

Wednesday, 1 March. [When we resumed at the Ministry] Sid went straight into Tartan Arrow. They had been discussing their position. Some of them were for saying that there should be no Tartan Arrow trains at all. Others were prepared to accept that Tartan Arrow should continue on the basis that there would not be more than two trains a day. He couldn't say yet which view would win. Raymond launched into an eloquent exposition of the role of the private siding in railway business. It had always been its backbone. Tartan Arrow was an example of the modern private siding appropriate to the freightliner age. I asked Quick Smith, deputizing for Reggie Wilson who is on leave, if he could make an economic use of TA on the basis of only two trains a day, and he looked dubious.

Our side of the table betook ourselves to my room [at 1 pm]. We were all limp. Quick Smith went off to phone his office and came back to say he could probably agree to stick at four trains a day without too much difficulty. At 2.30 pm back we went; I was keeping an eye on the clock because I had to leave for the House at 3 pm. I then read out our terms and to our astonishment the balloon went up. Said Sid, 'I tell you now you haven't a cat in hell's chance of getting that through my members.' And Lane echoed mournfully, 'Not a chance.' We argued with them in vain: two trains were the limit. I expostulated that I could not justify this £750,000 of expenditure on TA terminals being kept underused: after all, it was in the public sector now. But no. They just sat grimly shaking their heads. As for our offer of job opportunities, Sid was contemptuous. If railwaymen went to work in TA terminals, wouldn't they become employees of TA and cease to be railwaymen? Silence on our part. We knew we were up against the nub of the problem: not just jobs, but jobs for members of the NUR.

It was by now 3 pm and my PNQ [Private Notice Question] gave us the chance to break off again. I dashed off to the House accompanied by John. When we got back Quick Smith had been doing some more telephoning. He admitted to me that in any case there was no chance of TA filling more than two trains, at least for the first year. This, then, was it. Over tea we rejigged our offer and back we went with it: two trains for TA, the whole position to be reviewed in due course in the light of the progress with freight integration. I was sure this formula would do the trick. So I announced our offer, confident of victory. Then we left them yet again to brood over it. We hadn't to wait very long before the call came that they were ready. We sat down cheerfully – only to be told that the committee had turned the offer down flat. 'I told you,' drawled Sid, 'that some of my members wanted open terminals and no TA at all. Well, that is now the decision of all of them.' At this I exploded. What on earth did they expect me to do with the TA facilities? They shuffled about, but said nothing. Sid shrugged. There it was: that was my problem. 'Do you really expect me', I cried, 'to go to the dispatch box at the House of Commons and tell them that I have sealed up £750,000 of the most modern freight-handling equipment in the country? This at a time when we desperately need more production in order to give a better standard of life to lower-paid workers, including your own? What sort of image do you imagine that would give to our railways? We'd all be a laughing stock!' Silence; more shrugs from Sid. 'Is that the view of all of you?' I demanded. 'Go on, speak up for yourselves. What do you expect me to do?' McFadden, who had been muttering to Danby, then blurted out unhappily, 'It's no good, Minister. We simply wouldn't get away with it to our members. They'd turn us down. Even if we accepted we just couldn't get it carried out.' I used all the eloquence of which I was capable: couldn't they dare to give their members a lead? The Government had to do that and risk unpopularity.

One by one they came alive. Lofkin, another nice chap, assured me with great sincerity that they *had* given a lead: they had accepted redundancies after redundancies. Now their members were fed up. When the railways got a new development at last, it was handed over to other people. To me their sincerity was patent. I began to feel that they were as desperate as I was: in fact, they said in effect that they wanted to accept open terminals but I had to help them out over TA. John Morris passed me a note: 'Is it quite impossible for BR to acquire TA?' But I had another idea. By now it was 8 pm and I could see I was too late for the concert I was supposed to be attending with the Queen, though Richard had sent for my evening clothes from the House. I told them we had better have another break while we all thought over what we had said.

By this time we were nearly hysterical. We were desperately hungry and I had nothing but another drink to offer them. One half of me wanted to tell the NUR to go and stuff it, but the other half of me *knew* that the negotiating committee were dead keen on getting agreement, if only we could help them out over TA. The thought of breaking now with open terminals so near was unbearable. We sat round the table in my room over our drinks, puzzling what to do. John repeated his plea that we should not rule out BR acquiring TA. I said that this was going too far, but what about BR acquiring 50 per cent ownership? I could feel in my bones that this solution was right because it would be a living instalment of integration – thoroughly justifiable. I expected a storm, but Quick Smith merely said rather mournfully that he couldn't take a step like that without his chairman's permission. All right, I said, let's get on to Reggie. 'But he's in Switzerland.' OK, get him on the phone. Swooning a little at this mad extravagance, Richard disappeared into the Private Office followed by Quick Smith.

In the hiatus we seemed to hang around endlessly, our tummies rumbling. We were still waiting at 9 pm. 'I'm afraid those chaps will just walk out on us,' said Richard. I could hardly blame them if they did. Quick Smith, it appeared, had been talking on the phone to Reggie for nearly a quarter of an hour. I swept into the Private Office. 'The chairman is OK,' said Quick Smith, and I took the phone from him. Reggie was perfectly serene. 'I am quite happy to do anything you think right.' He even thanked me for consulting him! 'Right,' I told them all, 'this is it. Let us get going.'

As we entered the conference room, the negotiating committee were sprawled round the table despondently, without even a glass in front of them. 'Good evening again, gentlemen,' I said briskly. 'Haven't you even had a drink?' Oh, yes: they had had that. 'I am sorry if you are hungry – so are we. I am sorry, too, that we have kept you waiting so long, but as I told you earlier I have no statutory power to play about with Tartan Arrow and I have had to consult those who have. Let me ask you first whether you have reconsidered your attitude?' No, they said. They couldn't do that. By this time they were looking really apprehensive. They could see an agreement slipping away. 'Right,' I said. 'I will come straight to the point. You want something simple you can take back to your members. I have obtained agreement from THC that BR shall acquire 50 per cent ownership of TA. That means that when your members get those equal job opportunities they will remain members of the NUR. That is really what you want, isn't it? It also means that BR will have 50 per cent membership of the Board and will be able to see there is no unfair competition. This is proof that integration is really on the way. This dramatic addition to the terms we have already offered you gives your members every assurance they can rightly ask.'

They sat up and brightened visibly and I sensed that the battle was over. Sid made a few noises. They would like an adjournment to consider what I had said. But we had not long to wait: within half an hour the message came that they were ready for us. They all looked different men as Sid told us they had agreed – he hinted unanimously – to recommend the package deal with its new element to their Executive. Winding up I said, 'Now go in to win. Please let me make one thing clear. If this is turned down, all bets are off. There will be no Stage 2, no increased investment in road vehicles, no road powers, no new plan for the workshops. It will be war.' They nodded.

I wished them goodnight and hurried off to the Queen Elizabeth Hall and – I hoped – food. As I swept out of the Ministry in my full regalia the press were waiting, but I left Bickerton to deal with them. At the Queen Elizabeth Hall the crowds were lined up waiting for the Queen to leave. Up the circular staircase I walked, past the curious eyes, to the foyer where I immediately approached the Queen to add my apologies to those Ted had given on my behalf. She said I must have had an exhausting time and, waving her hand towards a glass of champagne, said, 'You'd better have some of that.' But it was food I wanted. 'Where's the buffet?' I hissed to Ted – only to find it consisted of a few drying sandwiches! At that moment I felt my dress was a little loose and discovered to my horror that the long zip at the back of my dress had come undone. My little jacket would have disguised some of this fact. Nonetheless the curious crowd which watched my dignified entry up the staircase had probably been admiring the view of my pants. Tom Padmore was there, enjoying himself. 'Minister,' he said, 'my spies at the Ministry tell me that your conduct of these negotiations has been absolutely brilliant.' I couldn't help thinking, 'And where were you?' I know I could not have had such a crucial negotiation at ODM without Andrew

Cohen being at the heart of it. And so out to a very late meal at the Gay Hussar with Ted.[1] I was intoxicated with hope and the knowledge that I had done well.

Thursday, 2 March. A long day of waiting. At Cabinet Harold congratulated me on a 'memorable achievement'. I told him that I hadn't won yet, but no one would believe me. More congratulations at the House as I walked through the division lobby at 7 pm. At Cabinet we had had another of those tricky ideological conflicts to resolve. What salaries could Dick Marsh pay to members of the National Steel Corporation? If nationalization was to succeed he must get the best brains he could find. But nationalized steel would be in competition with 260 private firms and the salaries he originally proposed to suggest to us (with the Chancellor's agreement) would cut the top 150 people in the industry off from recruitment.

Melchett[2] himself would be prepared to act on a personal salary very much lower than this scale but he did not think he could get the right deputy-chairman for less than £20,000 to £24,000 and members for less than £15,000 to £19,000. How would this fit in with prices and incomes policy? First, the men serving would still be getting less than they were in their present jobs; secondly, they would be prepared to abate the substantive scales by 12½ per cent for a period of two years. Nonetheless we could all see where this was leading us: to a first-class row in the House which would make the row over judges' salaries seem like a storm in a teacup. I said that the Socialist policy here, as I saw it, was to give public ownership the status it deserved. If we could have a policy to bring down salaries in private industry to a fixed maximum, fine; but, pending that, publicly owned industries should be able to compete. And so it was decided, rather unhappily.

Our opening discussion had been on the state of the PLP [Parliamentary Labour Party] for which Cabinet officers were not present. Harold said we ought to discuss the recent abstentions on the Defence White Paper. Others might disagree with him, but he thought the time had come for him to address the PLP and tell them some of the facts of political life. He spoke mildly enough – indeed, I thought almost smugly. None of these dissidents would be in Parliament at all, he said, if it wasn't for him; they had queued up to have their photos taken with him for election purposes. It was time to pull them up sharp. Jim agreed with him. Dick and John Silkin put in a word for tolerance. 'I don't know any other way of keeping the Party together,' John said. George was pretty scathing about the Left: 'Are we all going to have three free consciences a year?' I urged that we should leave the loyalists to deal with the dissidents and not interpose any edict from above. But it was an unheated discussion from which no one would have guessed that a major storm was brewing.

With my mind still on the NUR I managed to hold two office discussions on other matters, sign letters and so on. By 8.30 Richard asked me whether he should ring up the NUR to see whether they were still in session: 'Do you

[1] Favourite Soho rendezvous of journalists, politicians, writers and other public personalities. Its attraction lay not only in the quality of its food, but the personality of its presiding genius, Victor, and in the Hungarian charm of its little private room upstairs where I, for one, organized many a conspiracy over a good meal.

[2] Julian, Lord Melchett, banker and agriculturalist, had been approached by Dick Marsh to be chairman of the nationalized steel industry. He was chairman of the British Steel Corporation from 1967 to 1973.

suppose they have just stood us up and gone home?' I said I didn't think so and then, suddenly, as I was working away at my desk, a phone call from Sid Greene. Terms accepted. 'I'm not supposed to tell you what the voting is on my Executive but in fact it was eighteen to six,' he said, barely able to keep the jubilation out of his voice. Now the dramatic moment had come, I could not believe it. 'Bring as many of 'em round as want to come,' I said. 'I could kiss you!' Sid said he'd be round as soon as possible.

Hasty calls to No. 10 and to Raymond and Quick Smith. Within fifteen minutes everyone arrived, just as a call came through from Harold warmly congratulating me and 'my team'. 'Tell Sid from me he's a great man.' By now the truth had really registered with me and I was jumping for joy. My officials were dazed: they had never lived through a drama like this before. 'Send out for some drinks,' I urged Richard as Sid and his merry men were shown into my room. 'I've brought ten of my Executive,' said Sid. As I shook hands with Lane, his honest face suffused with pleasure, I couldn't contain myself and gave him a big hug and a kiss, thanking him. The same for George Brassington. And for Sid, who blushed and said, 'Now, behave yourself.'

One by one the ten men filed in, all those fellows who had fought me so bitterly at the EC – even the Chinese Communist (who, Sid told me, had voted for me in the end). I beamed at them as I shook hands and they beamed back. You wouldn't have thought we had ever had any differences. The Chinese Communist merely said mournfully, 'You won't let us down, Barbara?' And so, at late long last, to bed.

Friday, 3 March. A deliriously happy – as well as interesting – day. I did my oft-postponed helicopter tour of Tilbury dock development. The Port of London Authority boys were delighted with my open terminals success, and George Perkins, the Director-General, told me the decision had come just in time. They could now go ahead with the freightliner terminal they are going to build inside the docks ready for the opening of the United States Line container dock next summer. At my press conference I was applauded. Said Richard, 'You can live on this for six months.'

But the day had been clouded by splash press reports of Harold's speech to the PLP meeting last night, which I missed.[1] It seemed entirely out of character, and the phrase about 'every dog is allowed one bite' was so crude it is difficult to understand how Harold could have so lost his touch. So this is what he was hinting at in Cabinet! We would never have guessed. The speech is reported very fully because Harold warned us he was going to release most of it. He was sick of 'slanted reports'. Really, he has less to complain of in that respect than most of us. But then, he is getting positively pathological about the press – and never misses an opportunity of complaining how anti-Government they are. Personally, I think they have been pretty generous to the Government.

Monday, 13 March. Office meetings on railway subsidies. The interim report of the railway survey recommends an elaborate procedure for assessing the loss

[1] Harold Wilson had delivered stern warnings to the Party meeting that the indiscipline must stop, including the often-to-be quoted phrase that 'every dog is allowed one bite', adding that if he makes a habit of it his owner may have doubts about renewing his licence.

on socially necessary black lines on the railway map, the grant to be paid for three years *in advance*. To my surprise I learned that the Treasury will raise no objection to this (one of the fruits of having put a Treasury man on the steering group). I was delighted with the report's emphasis on the possibility of cutting losses on a number of lines by operating economies such as singling the track.

Thursday, 16 March. Another Cabinet. Jim triumphantly reported that the deficit for 1966 was down to £189m and that as a result the bank rate was being reduced to 6 per cent. Nice to have something cheerful to deal with for a change!

Monday, 20 March. Went to the BRB for lunch. I had no idea what it was in aid of as it was merely a quiet Board lunch for John Morris and me, but then at the end Raymond presented me with a desk model of a freightliner and made a little speech thanking me for what I had done over open terminals. He is always very friendly to my face, whatever he may say to others, and I flatter myself he really likes me. At EN Committee I got my railway subsidies paper through without difficulty.

Tuesday, 21 March. The first of our Cabinet discussions on Europe. We had before us the report by Harold and George on their European tour, plus a full account of each individual meeting taken at the time. Harold stressed that this first meeting should not try and take any decisions: we must not rush this crucial matter. The first thing was to get the facts clear on the points of difficulty we saw about going in. The main ones were the Common Agricultural Policy [CAP], capital movements and the Commonwealth, particularly New Zealand, and the sugar agreement. Other difficulties had diminished as the tour proceeded, *e.g* regional policies presented no problem. We would be free to do as we pleased about Industrial Development Certificates [IDCs] etc., and any loss of European investment would, in his view, be offset by increased American investment here once the road to Europe was open. Even the sterling issue had been considerably clarified. Nor had de Gaulle raised the special relationship with America. The big problem was that France did not want to surrender her dominant position in the Community, and the Five would not in the last resort risk disrupting the Six in order to stand up to her.

And so, skilfully, he kept the temperature down and got us going through the details of the CAP. After two and a half hours it was decided we needed more papers for the next meeting: *i.e.* an assessment of the impact on essential British and Commonwealth interests of membership on different assumptions as to the conditions which might be expected to prevail over the next few years. Dick pressed for us to have the long-promised papers on the possible alternatives like the formation of a North Atlantic Free Trade Area or going it alone. Harold agreed that these must now be prepared. And so we parted amicably.

I thought Harold had manœuvred brilliantly. I remain convinced he is anxious to get in (we are obviously not going to have any draconian Socialist measures from this Cabinet) and he had succeeded in guiding us into a discussion of details which is more effective than anything else in making principles look less important. I got one good blow in, though, when I pointed out that the CAP would not only distort the pattern of our own agriculture, but also the world economy by its protectionism. The only way to defeat Harold's manœuvres is by coming back to these basic principles. Once again I have been meditating on the insidious pull of office. I believe Harold has got this Government off on the wrong foot by his desire to play a role on the world stage instead of concentrating all his skill and economic knowledge in making us economically strong. He has left too many of these issues to Jim, so the Treasury is as strong as ever and just as committed to orthodox policies and it is almost certainly too late now to change course. Yet the more disappointed I am over our policies in other fields, the more satisfaction I get from fighting for the right policies in my own. And the more painful becomes the thought of giving up my job to return to the sterilities of the back benches.

Wednesday, 22 March. Seat belt testing at the British Standards Laboratory premises at Hemel Hempstead. And another good spate of publicity. The joy of being a Minister is that one can *do* things.

Monday, 3 April. A meeting with the Home Secretary about our preparations for the Road Safety Bill. The East German breathalyser hasn't passed its tests, so we are dependent on the West German one. This means we can't get enough supplies to start before 1 October. This is the third meeting we have had on this: I am desperately anxious to implement Part 1 as soon as possible. I have now got Roy treating the matter urgently after a lackadaisical beginning by his officials. I made some more suggestions which he agreed to follow up.

Tuesday, 4 April. Prices and incomes came up again at Cabinet. Having announced the norm we now had to decide what powers we needed to supplement the TUC's voluntary scheme. I thought Michael Stewart's proposals were very mild: reactivation of Part 2 plus a bill to provide for six months' delay on reference to the Board instead of four as at present (and twelve as he had originally proposed) and to prevent retrospective payments of deferred wage increases and to enforce price reductions; all this only on a recommendation of the NBPI. I thought it would go through on the nod, but no. We were engaged in another passionate argument for over two hours.

We were drifting into a fine confusion when Jim suddenly clarified everything by coming out against any further powers at all, apart from reactivating Part 2. It was his reasons that did it. It was no longer necessary to take the powers because of the economic situation. The overseas position was not as important as it had been. And to cap the lot, 'An incomes policy in a free society won't work.' That brought us up sharply against the choice, and one after another we said that what we were deciding was whether to sacrifice growth. I urged that, if we faced political defeat either way, it was worse to be defeated for having failed to achieve growth, like any Tory Government, than for fighting for a new concept. Harold countered Jim's line by pointing out that 3 per cent growth next year would mean from £950m to £1,000m more national income. If the TUC's voluntary policy failed, wage increases could pre-empt £1,800m – at best £1,200m. This would mean higher taxation as well as severe cuts in public expenditure. The alignment was obviously finely balanced and in the end Harold summed up in favour of the package without the ban on retrospection, but with the threat of introducing it later if necessary.

On 11 April Jim Callaghan introduced a cautious but reasonably optimistic Budget, announcing that the balance of payments had improved as a result of the July measures and that he was repaying the £357 million loan from the IMF. He also anticipated a growth rate of 3 per cent. But he admitted that unemployment was too high in certain regions and that there had been a loss of output. 'Broadly speaking,' he told the House, 'the measures are doing what the Government expected of them, namely restoring our fortunes abroad while giving us an uncomfortable time at home.' He was not, therefore, prepared to make any major tax changes.

Monday, 10 April. Budget Cabinet. Just before I went in I was handed a heavily sealed envelope – a letter from Jim's Private Secretary to mine informing me that he was going to reduce hire purchase restrictions on motorcycles. Under the strict Budget secrecy arrangements Richard hadn't been able to send it on to me, even by dispatch rider. (It had arrived on Thursday afternoon after I had left for Blackburn.) So I had no chance to protest. I was furious. It really is ridiculous that the Chancellor should have this absolute power to interfere in the policies of other Ministers without consulting them. It is increasingly impossible to isolate taxation provisions from general policy and I made a mental note to press home Dick's point that there ought to be more Cabinet-wide general discussions on taxation policy. When Jim came to this point I interjected tartly, 'These are the most dangerous vehicles on the road. The result of this will be an increase in road casualties.' Jim merely waved this aside urbanely.

Tuesday, 11 April. Another Cabinet. We agreed Dick's recommendations that there should be ministerial appearances before the new Select Committees,[1] including the ones for nationalized industries, but not without a lot of grumbling from Jim, Michael and George, who thought it was a lot of nonsense and that we were being led into deep waters.

In to the Budget speech in the House. Jim's 'marathon' merely succeeded in boring the House and failed to get across the philosophy outlined in Cabinet. When he at last came to his mini-proposals, there was derisive laughter. In short, the whole exercise misfired, due I think to the ingrowing arrogance to which all Chancellors after a certain time are prone.

Wednesday, 12 April. The reception given to Jim's Budget speech has been disastrous. No one has a good word for him. After all the talk about him as the Crown Prince lately, the deflation of his ego must be terrifying.

Friday, 14 April. Woke to realize the GLC results would be out, so dressed to

[1] One of Dick Crossman's reforms as Leader of the House had been to obtain Cabinet's reluctant agreement to the extension of the Select Committee system by the setting-up of specialist committees of back benchers to monitor aspects of Departmental activities and to take initiatives in various general fields of policy such as agriculture. He had also persuaded his Cabinet colleagues to appear before the committees on request.

the news on the radio.[1] Catastrophic! Nothing less than a massacre. Yet I remained remarkably cheerful – I don't quite know why. Another challenge, I suppose. Richard, creeping in to collect me at 8.30 am, expected to find me in tears, I think. Instead I greeted him with, 'Well, we are in for an interesting time.' My officials didn't quite know how to handle the situation but I told them cheerfully that I had a simple philosophy of life: 'The best successes are always snatched from the jaws of disaster.' Richard looked relieved.

Tuesday, 18 April. At 5 pm I got the long-awaited appointment with Harold for which I had asked. As I waited outside his room at the House Marcia came by and I asked her how he was taking the election results. She said very well, though she looked depressed. (She is politically minded, as I am.) As always, Harold was utterly charming and disarming. But, pleasant as he is, Harold is difficult to talk to: you get half a sentence out and he interrupts and goes off at a tangent. Whether this is because he has a very quick mind and is way ahead of you, or whether it is because he hates to probe anything in depth, I'm never quite sure. But I am in the sort of relaxed relationship with him that enables me to chip in, tapping him on the knee firmly to stop him in mid course, and say doggedly, 'Harold, listen to me.' At which he grins and listens till he interrupts again. I think he knows I have considerable affection for him, even while I despair sometimes over his ideological limitations and am ready to resign, if necessary, if his tactical subtleties ever betray my beliefs. He knows, too, that I will always be honest with him – as I was on this occasion, telling him about the contract I have signed to write my life story. When he asked me if I had signed it after joining the Government, I said squarely yes. He took it very unperturbedly, saying that writing one's life was very different from a political book. Oh, Harold! But he took the precaution of saying I ought to let Gerald Gardiner know, because of his Committee, and that I would be bound by the rules. OK, if everyone is, so will I be.

Thursday, 20 April. Another Cabinet about Europe. We turned to two papers prepared by officials on the economic alternatives to going in (on which Dick had insisted): Go It Alone [GITA] and Atlantic Free Trade Area [AFTA] (the Javits plan). They were introduced by a covering paper by Burke Trend couched in language that made even the Europeans squirm (*e.g.* 'We feel that . . .' The Royal We?). Dick proceeded to slaughter this, and rightly, as 'tendentious', while Trend looked down non-committally at his blotting paper. As for GITA, this had reappeared as 'Abstention' which caused a lot of satirical comment. Even Roy supported me when I said that a less emotive word would be 'Non-membership'. The whole tenor of these official papers (on which Tommy had rushed agitated comments to Dick and me) was that it would be disastrous if we didn't get in, and Dick wasn't alone by any means in pointing out that this attitude could be more disastrous still because the third alternative, 'Exclusion', was very much on the cards.

[1] For the first time since 1934 the Conservatives had captured control of London, holding 82 seats to Labour's 18. This was of major importance for my transport plans for London since the new Leader of the Council, Desmond Plummer, was far less sympathetic to my ideas than the Labour GLC under Bill Fiske had been. In the rest of the country the county council elections were equally disastrous for the Government.

As always Harold trimmed brilliantly. On the one hand he insisted that 'AFTA *might* be on' if de Gaulle turned awkward and America got fed up with the EEC's attitude; on the other he once again tipped the balance in favour of going in: 'I believe the Russians want us in; they are afraid of a German revival and want us there to counteract it.' Then suddenly a storm flared up – from Healey's quarter of all places. Harold got over-confident. Denis was dilating on how dangerous it would be to 'play for a rebuff'. If we got it, morale in this country might slump, and he added, 'This emphasizes the importance of not coming up to the jump unless . . .' when Harold broke in, 'We *are* at the jump.' At this Denis exploded, 'Pardon me, Prime Minister, but some of us were always opposed to making these approaches at all and only agreed last year to what we thought was an unwise decision because we were assured that we would not be committed in any way. We simply cannot accept that we are compelled to make a decision now.' Harold hastily tried to retrieve his Freudian slip, but it looks as though Denis is going to be unexpectedly tough. Personally I think Harold and George have so cleverly set the scene that it will be impossible for Cabinet to come to any decision but to have a try. I think our best bet now is to get Cabinet committed to conditions that will ensure failure.

Tuesday, 25 April. Meeting with Stan Raymond on various matters. We have these regularly and he is so loquacious they can drag on for hours. I used to let him rattle on (the less sure he is of his ground, the more he pontificates) but now I've learned to pull him up politely but firmly. We had a long discussion on road licensing.[1] BRB want distance limits so as to tip the balance in favour of rail. The Department dismisses this with scorn, but Stephen is all for it and, the more I think about it, the more sure I am that quality licensing alone will not be enough. I promised to consider his ideas. Later Chris Foster told me he thought there was a good deal to be said in favour of a modified version of BRB's ideas, based on weight rather than distance. If we limited licensing to lorries of five tons and upwards we should eliminate the majority of vehicles, make enforcement possible (even with C licences in) and catch the bulk of the traffic in which rail is interested. If BRB didn't contest the licence, it would go ahead. If they did, they would have to show they could move the traffic equally expeditiously and economically. The three-to-five-ton lorries would be covered by our increases in excise licences. Stephen, John and I thought this was a very bright idea.

[1] Everyone agreed that the road licensing system must be overhauled, though there were deep differences in the Department about how it should be done. It was obvious that the Geddes Report recommending the abolition of all restrictions on carriers' licensing was incompatible with Labour's demand for an integrated transport policy, but equally the present over-regulatory system was unsatisfactory. I was considering two basic changes aimed at switching more traffic from road to rail. The first and most controversial was for 'quantity licensing', advocated in different forms by the TUC and BR, and designed to limit the number of private road haulage vehicles, including own-account vehicles with C licences, according to the need for them or to restrict the distance they could travel in cases where equally economical rail services were under-used. This was reinforced by a widespread belief that road hauliers were not paying their full 'track costs'. The second, 'quality licensing', was seized on thankfully by my more timid civil servants as less provocative though, as Chris Foster and his economists pointed out, it could be very effective in weeding out some of the large number of operators (over 84 per cent of the total) with five vehicles and less who, the unions maintained, were in many cases breaking the law over drivers' hours and other aspects of road safety. 'Quality licensing' meant enforcing much higher standards of

Thursday, 27 April. Great hoo-ha at Cabinet about Nutting's book on Suez.[1] Apparently he has dodged the rules by not seeking access to official documents. 'No doubt he kept a personal note,' said Harold grimly.

Then at last to the Common Market again. Harold spelt out the timetable: meetings all next weekend, including one at Chequers, two more Cabinets next week. He had no intention of rushing anyone. He also referred severely to a report that some 'anti' Ministers were meeting to concert their activities. That from him! I burst out at this that an atmosphere was being created publicly on the basis of certain assumptions. The press was full of stories that we were going to decide this weekend to apply. George had expressed a 'personal' view in favour of entry at the NEC meeting yesterday. Yet if those of us who opposed entry were to express 'personal' views against going in, we should be accused of not following Cabinet policy. Harold mildly rebuked George, who shrugged it off with a light-hearted semi-apology. They are very sure of themselves! So we wound our way again through the detailed documents. Harold once again facing the home truths only to say they were not insurmountable. The most important of all, on the balance of payments consequences, was left till Saturday. Harold assured me that he would not burke any issues in his speech to the Party meeting that evening. But, in the event, he made a rousing political call to go into Europe – and carefully released it to the press. After this we can only decide against entry by repudiating him. The whole long-drawn-out nonsense has been ruthlessly stage-managed, under cover of the soothing phrase: 'It is of course for Cabinet to decide.'

Saturday, 29 April. Up to London in a bad temper to another Common Market Cabinet at No. 10. The photographers were out in force for the 'historic' occasion. The walls of the Cabinet room were lined with officials, brought to answer our questions – unless their Ministers preferred to answer them themselves. As always when I am in a bad temper, I was at the top of my form, putting in some pointed ones. I extracted, for example, the admission that we would have to adopt the added value tax; that it would have to apply to all commodities including food, and that at the lowest it would add another 5 per cent to the cost of food. All this I dragged out of a brisk Nicky Kaldor and a reluctant Con O'Neill.[2]

Sunday, 30 April. Rose early [at HCF] to a wonderful morning of sunshine on the early blossom. The garden looked beautiful as I left reluctantly to pick up Dick for the Chequers meeting. When we arrived most people were already there drinking coffee in the cavernous great hall. Everyone was artificially gay.

Then up to the Cabinet room on the first floor. Eventually we reached the

vehicle maintenance, power/weight ratios and so on. This had a value from a purely economic point of view since my economists' study of track costs showed that a lot of congestion on the roads was caused by under-powered lorries, but it was also highly desirable from a road safety point of view.

[1] Anthony Nutting, who had been Minister of State at the Foreign Office at the time of the Anglo-French invasion of the Suez Canal zone in 1956 and had resigned in protest, had published inside revelations in *'No End of a Lesson': the Story of Suez* to show that the charge of collusion between Britain, France and Israel was justified.

[2] Deputy Under-Secretary of State at the Foreign and Commonwealth Office and an ardent advocate of Britain's entry into the EEC.

real debate. It took place on a paper by Harold and George listing the alternatives open to us and coming down flatly in favour of an application for entry right away. And so, after lunch (during which he had been particularly abstemious), George made the great opening speech for entry. The debate then ran pretty true to form – the big surprises being Dick Marsh's unqualified opposition and Wedgie's passionate speech in favour of a technologically united Europe. Cledwyn Hughes, who has been moaning to me privately about his fears for the development areas, toed the Wilson line predictably, while Willie Ross stood his ground grimly against. I felt more and more conscious that, however much we might protest, the issue was decided.

When my turn came I said that, like Marsh, I was interested to see how the argument had changed. Originally it had been: 'Can we afford to stay out?' Now it was that the economic case was unproven, but that the political case was overwhelming. Personally I thought it was an odd distinction: could the two cases be so separable? The big mistake we had made as a Government was that we had paid too little attention to economic policy and too much to playing a part on the foreign stage. Now we were paying the price. This move was necessitated by our failure to develop alternative economic policies to the Conservatives. It was a step which flowed logically from our decision to give priority to the defence of sterling; from our refusal to try and make a controlled economy work, based on import controls and on incomes equality as an essential part of an incomes policy. If we had devalued at the outset, as we should have to do on entry if crippling deflation was to be avoided, we should not be discussing our application today. And I warned that the latter was merely an intensification and extension of our present economic policy, which had hardly won us widespread popular support. It meant still more austerity because we would have to offset a bigger balance of payments burden to meet the effects of Common Market policy. So what were the political consequences? A threat to our political survival because we should not be able to hold out the hope of easier times after 1970; in short, pressure to reduce real wages to make us 'competitive' (*vide* the CBI's statement) plus the prospect of a continuing cut in consumption in the 1970s. And, worse still, the blurring of our political role through the adoption of a bi-partisan policy. We should not underestimate the effect of this on the morale of our own workers, who did not exactly rally to us when there was no discernible difference between the two parties. As for the foreign policy consequences, let us realize that we were deciding on the destruction of the Commonwealth: not only through the abandonment of preferences, but above all as a result of the immigration priority we should have to give to the Six. In exchange, we did not even offer our Party a new policy on Vietnam! We were being told it was impossible not to apply now that so many expectations had been raised. Yes, they had been – deliberately. The Prime Minister himself had made his views clearly known to the PLP and for us not to apply now would be a deliberate repudiation of him. I remained and had always been against entry but, like Bowden and others, I demanded the laying down of conditions as a minimum. At the very least this was an insurance against Heath's gibes if we failed. We must pin him down on the issue of safeguarding our essential interests and above all we must *not* give the impression of desperation – of having no alternative. To my surprise, Tony

Crosland, when his turn came to support entry, did so saying that he did not disagree with my analysis as much as I might suppose.

And so we worked our way through a day broken only by a modest lunch (Harold saying he didn't want us to go to sleep). We all felt nothing but thankfulness when Harold said about 7 pm that he did not intend to do a long summing-up. In any case there was no intention of recording a decision that day: that would be done, in keeping with tradition, only at No. 10 on Tuesday. But he did feel that he and George must prepare a draft of the statement to be made to Parliament for Cabinet to discuss at its next meeting.

Monday, 1 May. The office kept phoning to say they had not yet received the PM's draft of the Common Market statement. Would I get in early to read it before Cabinet?

Tuesday, 2 May. Arrived at the House at 9 am to be told that the statement would be circulated in Cabinet. We 'antis' feared the worst. As far as we could see only George and Dick had been consulted about the draft. But in the event we were agreeably surprised. Harold had done a brilliantly skilful job, managing to produce what he described as an 'unconditional application for negotiations about the conditions for entry'. Nonetheless we spent two hours amending it. What interested me was that we were led straight into the discussion of a statement implying an application for membership without any formal decision being taken at the outset. It was only at the end that Harold, having been extremely reasonable throughout, put almost as a formality the proposition that we apply. And only Dick Marsh and I dared to say no.

After Harold's statement to the House (which he handled well) I switched to tough party politics. At my suggestion I went to see Roy about the possible extension of traffic powers for the GLC. Since the Tory capture of the GLC, I have been considering my tactics carefully. As Ted suggests, I must keep the initiative on traffic management so I discussed with Roy whether we would be willing to transfer control of the traffic wardens to the GLC Traffic Commissioner, if asked. We agreed, after a most co-operative discussion, that, as we were going greatly to extend traffic wardens' powers, it would be difficult to separate their control from the police, to whom they would become full traffic auxiliaries.

Thursday, 4 May. At Cabinet Harold had the nerve to complain about the reports in the press about the attitude taken by individual Ministers on the Common Market. Once again we had to listen to his homily on the need for us all to fall in behind Cabinet decisions: as if we were the people who leaked! To brighten us up, Jim then reported that bank rate was being cut to 5½ per cent, though he could not promise it would last.

Monday, 8 May. Opening of the great parliamentary debate on the Common Market, followed later by Harold's appearance on *Panorama*. By all accounts it was a *tour de force*.

Discussion with Percy Clarke[1] about my party political broadcast on Wed-

[1] Director of Information of the Labour Party.

nesday. I complained that he hadn't given me much time, so he admitted that they had originally chosen Crosland to do it. Then a message had come from No. 10 that it had to be Barbara Castle. I told him I wanted to grasp all the nettles and to have three journalists grill me toughly about all the awkward issues.

Wednesday, 10 May. I quite enjoyed the filming of my party political. I had genned myself up well on my facts and, encouraged by Stanley Hyland[1] to 'be myself', I really let fly. The joke was that, having been warned by Hyland that a retake would be unwise (might lead to satirical Fleet Street comment) and that I'd better get it right first time, it was the journalists who made a mess of it and were pleading for a retake! I firmly said no and dashed off to office meetings on road haulage licensing. The office had very intelligently invited two of our traffic commissioners along to advise on the practical details. As a result of a first-class discussion, in which their contributions were very helpful, it became clear that the Foster plan for weight limits wouldn't work (the licensed vehicles would have to be limited to certain routes if they were not to compete with rail) and that we would have to adopt distance limits after all. The traffic commissioners seemed quite satisfied that this would work. Unfortunately I learned privately from Padmore that it looked as if we would have to drop our proposals for increasing the licence fee for heavy vehicles as our free and open discussions on this possibility had breached the very strict rules of Budget secrecy. Hauliers, scenting this development in the next Budget, would take out new annual licences the day before. This was an aspect that hadn't occurred to me and I think it is typically slack of Padmore not to have thought of it until too late. I cast round desperately for a way out and sent them off to explore the possibility of a completely separate additional licence.

The chips were down with some of our back benchers over the Common Market. When Harold Wilson had made his statement to the House on 2 May, Mannie Shinwell to loud cheers had promised him 'the most relentless and ruthless opposition', and the only left-winger to welcome Britain's application was Eric Heffer. When the debate opened a few days later thirty-seven Labour MPs, led by Mannie Shinwell and Michael Foot, had tabled an amendment refusing to support the White Paper, 'Membership of the European Communities' (Cmnd 3269), which included Harold Wilson's statement, because 'it fails to affirm in explicit terms Her Majesty's Government's adherence to the conditions laid down by the Labour Party'. An attempt at the Party meeting to get a free vote on the issue having failed, a three-line whip was imposed for the vote on 10 May, but this did not prevent thirty-four Labour Members from voting against the Government, while some fifty more abstained. Thanks to Conservative support, however, the Government Motion was carried by 488 votes to 62. Among the abstainers were seven PPSs including Laurie Pavitt, PPS to Michael Stewart, Alf Morris, PPS to Fred Peart, and Michael English, PPS to Douglas Jay. It was General de Gaulle who was to lower the temperature. At a press conference on 16 May he brushed Britain's application aside, implying that she was not yet fit to join without causing 'destructive upheavals'. His comments were described as a 'velvet veto'.

[1] Hyland, who was Deputy Head of Current Affairs for BBC Television, used to help the Labour Party with its party political broadcasts.

Thursday, 11 May. An astonishing outburst from Harold at Cabinet about the press. He was writhing with annoyance at *The Times* of that morning, which had splashed the large number of abstentions and votes against in last night's vote on the Common Market. 'To read it no one would ever guess we had a majority of nearly 500.' He muttered angrily that we ought to consider not giving facilities to the journalists of certain papers. 'We should refuse to talk to them: Ian Trethowan, for instance, is just a publicity man for Heath. If we kept them at arm's length, they'd come to their senses.' Frankly I was appalled. I think Harold is getting quite pathological about the press. The size of the opposition on the Market was legitimate news; the *Times* leader was fair enough. I think, too, that we get a pretty fair press as a Government – and pointed out how well the press had treated me departmentally. Other members of the Cabinet tried to persuade him that the line he proposed would be unwise, but he kept brooding over the fact that one commentator had called him a con man. Pressed for more details as to how he would operate his embargo, he switched to another tack and spat out that it was time some members of the Cabinet stopped talking to our enemies like Nora Beloff and feeding them with material designed to destroy him. I could stand it no longer and burst out, 'Prime Minister, you keep making this allegation. If it is true, ought you not to say openly who is doing this as otherwise some of us who feel ourselves to be totally innocent are left under a cloud.' To my surprise it was George who replied, 'The trouble is, Prime Minister, that if you did that the disclosure itself would find its way into the press.' Who on earth are they getting at? Having let off steam, Harold left the whole thing in the air.

Friday, 12 May. An interesting day touring the canals. Allen, General Manager of the British Waterways Authority [IWA], said I was the first Minister of Transport to do this for thirty years. I encouraged him to press ahead with the development of the amenity network.

Wednesday, 17 May. First an office meeting on British buses and a hard tussle with J. D. Jones, who is doing his best to head me off building the PTAS [Passenger Transport Authorities] on the basis of full public ownership. He wants them to enter into agency arrangements with the private bus companies. It was a wonderful example of how the civil service will pressurize a Minister to be apolitical. 'It is only, Minister, that I thought you handled the CTA discussions so well and managed to avoid alienating your opponents.' 'I've told you before, J.D., that one can spend so much time conciliating one's opponents that one ends by alienating one's supporters.' It was quite unpleasant for a time, with J.D. nearly losing his temper and making it clear how thoroughly he disapproved. 'Of course, Minister, it is your policy and we shall carry it out, but it is a different policy from that which you started with.' I told him it was nothing of the sort. At one point they were all against me, with only Stephen Swingler to back me, but I stuck to my guns.

Relations between Israel and her Arab neighbours had been worsening. On 14 May Mr Eshkol, the Prime Minister of Israel, had warned that a showdown with Syria would be inevitable if raids by Arab terrorists into Israel from that country continued. The crisis was brought to a head on 19 May when the UN Secretary-General, U Thant, bowed to pressure from President Nasser and withdrew the UN *Emergency Force which had been patrolling the Israel–Egyptian frontier in the Sinai and the Gaza Strip ever since the Suez crisis of 1956. Egyptian and Israeli reservists were immediately mobilized and pacific overtures by Israel turned down. On 23 May Nasser announced the closing of the Straits of Tiran, at the entrance to the Gulf of Aqaba, to Israeli shipping, thus blockading the Israeli port of Eilat at the head of the Gulf, Israel's outlet to the Red Sea. While Western governments hesitated about how to deal with illegal closure of what they asserted was an international waterway, Israel took the matter into her own hands and on 5 June fighting broke out between the two sides. In the Six-Day War which followed Israel routed the Egyptian and Jordanian forces and occupied large tracts of territory. Britain's declaration of neutrality during the war did not save her from an Arab oil embargo and from the economic consequences of the closing of the Suez Canal. Harold Wilson later claimed that the Middle East crisis of June 1967, was 'the biggest contributing factor to the devaluation which came five months later'. (Wilson,* The Labour Government, *p. 400.)*

Tuesday, 23 May. With a crisis looming in the Middle East I wasn't altogether surprised when an emergency Cabinet was called for 2.30 pm. But I was certainly surprised – as were the majority of us – at the proposition that was put before us. George began with a very clear and well-marshalled résumé of the events of the past few months. Israel could not afford to sit back quietly and allow her lifeline to Eilat to be cut. The only hope of restraining her was by an immediate and unequivocal statement by the maritime powers that they were determined to enforce the right of innocent passage through the Gulf. The Americans were determined to stand by Israel and we must join with them in making that statement tonight, hoping that other maritime powers would join with us. He was flying to Moscow that night and he needed Cabinet's authorization to make it clear before he went.

The reaction of most of us listening to him was one of utter dismay. I thought immediately, 'This is no better than 1956.' Apparently we weren't even going to wait for the Security Council to meet. George fought hard to the end: 'How can I bang the table in Moscow unless Cabinet gives me a clear remit before I go?' But that was the last thing Cabinet was in a mood to do, and eventually it was agreed that George Thomson should go to Washington to ascertain just what military dispositions the US intended to make; that he was not to commit us in the discussions which were to be *ad referendum* to Cabinet; that no statement was to be made till Cabinet had had his report; that under no circumstances were we to get tied up in an Anglo-American ploy – other maritime nations must be brought in – and that meanwhile Caradon was to continue his efforts to get the Security Council called and we were to make it clear that this was our first bet.

Tuesday, 30 May. Another long session of Cabinet on the Middle East. It became clearer every minute that [George] and Harold had dramatically shifted their position, and were now working for a compromise in which Israel would give up something, too. The reason for this *volte-face* soon became clear. The Americans had cooled down remarkably – Johnson had been having some trouble with Congress. The French, too, had been playing it cool. There was clearly no inclination by others to do anything at all. And there would be no commitments of any kind without further reference to Cabinet. And so we left it. I passed a note to Dick, back from a holiday in Cyprus: 'You have no idea what we saved you from last week.'

Wednesday, 31 May. Office meeting on road haulage licensing. I was enthralled by Heaton's brief. He reported that the officials' committee on transport had unanimously turned down my proposals for quantity licensing. It was far better for the railways to be made to try and attract traffic on to rail, rather than forcing firms to use rail where it was equally good, etc. . . . As for my intention to include C licences in the controls, the very idea turned them apoplectic. In a covering note Heaton had another desperate shot at getting me to change my mind. He wrote: 'I think she should be aware that a strong case can be mounted at least against the quantity licensing proposals on the grounds, *inter alia*, that they are of doubtful workability; at best the inquiries involved will be superficial and at worst they will involve an intolerable degree of interference with what is still in the main a free enterprise economy. . . . therefore, even though the Minister has decided otherwise, I do submit that it should be considered whether it would not be wiser to go simply for quality licensing and leave quantity licensing to be tackled at a later stage.' The tenacity of civil servants is astonishing. When one touches one of their sacred cows, they fight back like demons. When I met them round the table I said sweetly, 'I have read your Minute, Mr Heaton. I am going to fight on this. Would anyone like to lay odds that I will win?' Heaton, a shy man, blushed. I then spent an hour and a half with them amending their proposed document for Ministers.

Over a cup of tea in the House, I told Michael Stewart and Wedgie what was happening over road licensing. 'Every one of you is going to be briefed to turn me down. I have touched the sacred cow of C licensing.' They were fascinated, and Michael remarked that Alf Barnes, who was Minister of Transport at the time, had been got at by his civil servants in 1947 after we had all been mobilized to stump the country to defend the nationalization of C licences. I have hopes now that even Michael will back me up!

Thursday, 1 June. A massive agenda for Cabinet: eight items, which by our normal standards should have kept us there all day. In the event we were through by noon! We went through a succession of complicated business expeditiously and raised a little cheer when we finished it in two hours flat. 'Let's face it,' said Douglas to Wedgie and me, 'we had a better chairman.' Reason? Harold's gone to Washington and George was in the chair. We all agreed that Harold spins things out something terrible, interjecting a commentary of his own between every speech. 'Though to be fair,' said Douglas, 'he enjoys *listening*, too.' I said he conducted Cabinets like a don at an interesting tutorial.

A long, painful session with Stan Raymond over the mounting railway deficit. He came coldly into the room having been, according to reports, deeply 'wounded' by a tough letter I had sent him asking him some awkward questions about his long-term planning and financial control. However, I wasn't going to be deterred by a frozen smile and moved immediately into the attack. After an exhausting two hours I wore him down a bit.

Monday, 5 June. Took my road licensing proposals to EN. As I expected, I got a good deal of support for my quantity licensing proposals – including the C licences, though some of them were a little nervous about the economic effects. Only Douglas Jay faithfully trotted out every argument in his official brief and was promptly demolished by Harold Lever, who said he had never accepted that it was one of the fundamental human rights to have a C licence. (Douglas had actually described my proposals as 'a tremendous interference with the liberty of private industry'.) Ironically the biggest objection was to the financial provisions of the quality licence, which Locke[1] had pressed on me, backed by the rest of the Department, as ensuring that the small man would be eliminated and quantity licensing made unnecessary. We had a terrific discussion for over an hour, which then had to be postponed because Michael had another meeting, and I was told to elaborate certain points. I went away, not dissatisfied, to rub the Department's nose in it.

Tuesday, 6 June. At Cabinet Harold reported on his visits to America and Canada. He was full of the welcome he had had in the States: 'I have never before had the feeling that they needed us more than we needed them.' So we have got the best of both worlds – we have left the Americans grateful for not leaving them internationally isolated on the Middle East while not having to do anything ourselves, the Israelis having done it brilliantly for us.

On Vietnam Harold, emboldened by his reception, had apparently got away with some stern statements about escalation and insisted that we must hold ourselves free to take any initiatives for peace we felt necessary at any time. Johnson had taken all this very meekly: indeed there was a much less 'hawkish' atmosphere in Washington and they were obviously only too anxious for any moves for peace to be taken.

We then agreed to make provision for an interim increase in family allowances, Peggy complaining to me that Patrick Gordon Walker was utterly reactionary about all social security matters.

Wednesday, 7 June. Top for Questions. Despite some awkward ones, we wiped the floor with the Tories and I had the joy of announcing my proposed reductions in lorry drivers' hours. The Liberals were staggered when I said I intended to see them rigorously enforced and was going to make the installation of tachographs compulsory.

Dinner with Peter Shore,[2] Wedgie, Tommy, John Silkin and Dick. We all agreed we ought to meet regularly and keep in better ministerial touch. Wedgie was all for crystallizing our ideas into decisions, but Dick was as nervous as a

[1] John Locke, an Under-Secretary I had lured from the Cabinet Office, was one of Tommy Balogh's recommendations to me. He entered fully into the spirit of our transport policy and was working on the rationalization and expansion of passenger transport services under public ownership. I was so impressed with him that I persuaded him to come over to the Department of Employment and Productivity with me in 1968.

[2] Labour MP for Stepney from 1964. He had previously been Head of the Labour Party's Research Department and Harold Wilson had a high opinion of his abilities, making him his PPS from 1965 to 1966, when he became a junior Minister first at Technology and then at DEA. In August 1967, Harold Wilson brought him into the Cabinet as Secretary of State for Economic Affairs where he was responsible for prices and incomes policy. He was not considered a success at this and when DEA was wound up in 1969, he became Minister without Portfolio.

kitten at this. He had told Harold we were meeting and it was better to keep it all purely conversational. I suspect he has promised Harold we won't plot anything.

In our Election Manifesto we had committed ourselves to reorganize and modernize the ports through publicly owned Regional Port Authorities under a strong National Ports Authority [NPA], and I had reaffirmed this intention in my White Paper, 'Transport Policy'. The Party had set up a Port Transport Study Group under the chairmanship of Ian Mikardo which had produced in February 1966 a unanimous report on how the policy should be carried out. Sir Arthur Kirby, the dynamic chairman of the British Transport Docks Board, had given sympathetic evidence to the study group and I was proposing to set up a National Ports Organization [NPO] to prepare the way for the legislation. The negotiations had not been completed by the time my Transport Bill had to be produced, but on 29 January 1969, my successor at Transport, Dick Marsh, published a White Paper (Cmnd 3903) setting out the Government's plans and a Ports Bill, based on the White Paper, was introduced into the Commons on 26 November 1969. The Bill had passed all its stages in the Commons and was in the Lords when the dissolution of Parliament in June 1970 meant that the Bill lapsed and the policy was abandoned by the ensuing Conservative Government. In August 1966, however, we had enacted the Docks and Harbours Bill decasualizing dock labour on the lines of the Devlin Report.

With the period of severe restraint in prices and incomes coming to an end on 1 July 1967, the Government decided to activate Part 2 of the 1966 Act and to strengthen it by lengthening the period of standstill for a price or wage increase from three to six months. In the House Michael Stewart described the proposed new powers as 'strictly limited, of temporary duration and specifically designed to support and encourage the voluntary principle'. He argued that without them groups of workers in organizations not affiliated to the TUC would escape the discipline the TUC was exercising on its own members through the voluntary wage-vetting policy. Despite this some thirty Labour MPs abstained in the Second Reading vote on the Prices and Incomes (No. 2) Bill on 13 June. The Bill became law on 14 July.

Thursday, 8 June. At Cabinet George sketched in the details of Israel's tremendous triumph and said our main job now was to mend our relations with the Arab states. The Soviet Union was still maintaining a very moderate attitude diplomatically, in marked contrast with her propaganda statements.

Saw Jack Jones to ask him if he would take the vice-chairmanship of NPO. To my delight he agreed. Arthur Kirby put the idea in my head by suggesting Jack Cooper of the GMWU. I would have none of that and suggested Jack Jones instead. Arthur and the Department were a bit nervous about 'security': they obviously think he is a Communist. But we cleared all that; I got Ray to agree and spoke to Harold, who thought it was an excellent idea. The hope is beginning to form in my mind that I might persuade Jack to become chairman of the NPA in due course. The difficulty is that it would mean him giving up his trade union work.

Off to Glasgow, exhausted, on the night sleeper.

Friday, 9 June. A useful day in Glasgow seeing ports and freightliner terminals. The best bit was talking to Alex Kitson's Executive. Alex told me that what had finished Tom Fraser for him was the latter's refusal even to consider cutting lorry drivers' hours. He had given him the pure official reply. How my chaps must have sat up when I just told them I intended to do it!

Sunday, 11 June. A perfect summer's day – so, of course, I had to work! Spent the whole day at Chequers on a joint meeting with the NEC remarkable for its comparative harmony. True indeed that the steam has gone out of the prices and incomes controversy.

Wednesday, 14 June. A successful day at the conference. Herr Leber, the new Federal Minister of Transport, was an excellent chairman and is obviously a very different kettle of fish from his predecessor, Seebohm. As a social democrat and a trade unionist, he is very willing to back me up and I got my way in insisting we should go ahead with the ratification of the convention limiting drivers' hours while losing no time in preparing improvements to it.

Monday, 19 June. Saw Alex Kitson informally in my room in the House to tell him what I have in mind about road licensing. To my surprise he was completely receptive to the idea of getting as much traffic as is economically possible on to rail and was delighted that I intended to include C licences in my quantity control proposals. He said he was all against a blanket renationalization of road haulage which would mean our acquiring all sorts of dud lorries. He really is the most politically intelligent of all the trade union leaders with whom I have to deal. I am sure I shall have a much worse time with Frank Cousins.

Tuesday, 20 June. Another battle in the afternoon in EN on my road licensing policy. Dick, who had promised to come and back me up, slept through most of it! Harold Lever,[1] who had been tricked by his officials into signing a joint paper with Douglas Jay attacking me, did his best to retrieve himself. I had been astonished to see the document in view of the vigorous way in which Harold had dissociated himself from Douglas's 'nineteenth-century views', as he called them, on C licences. When I tackled him about this, Harold was his usual charming self – comically contrite and quite open about the fact that he had succumbed to officials' pressure against his own better judgment. I told him he really must learn to stand up to them: 'If you are ever going to make a good Minister, you must eat a civil servant before breakfast every day.' He said he agreed, but that, as he was having a struggle with the officials over something else, he had felt he must give way over this. In such ways are Government decisions taken! Eventually my paper was referred back for further consideration by officials, despite my insistence that officials were mulishly opposed on doctrinal grounds – not being Socialists – and that the delay would throw out the whole timetable on my Bill. I emerged weak with fury and frustration, but determined to fight to the bitter end.

On to Vincent Square for another 'keeping contact' dinner with Dick, John

[1] Harold Lever had been a Manchester MP since 1945 and had been appointed a Parliamentary Secretary at DEA in January 1967. In September 1967 he had been promoted Financial Secretary to the Treasury, and in October 1969 Harold Wilson brought him into the Cabinet as Paymaster-General, making him Tony Wedgwood Benn's principal deputy at Technology. Immensely likeable and highly intelligent, he was notable in the Party for his wit, wealth and generosity.

Silkin and Wedgie. Dick had told me in the morning that he proposed to invite Marcia. When I asked why on earth, he said it would make Harold happier – anyway, Marcia was as worried as we were about the way things were going. I told him emphatically that, if we could only meet with Harold's emissary keeping an eye on us, I wasn't going to come. And I added that it would be a darn good thing if Harold was afraid of what we were up to, then he might listen to us more; he only listened to people he feared. Dick rather agreed with this and said he wouldn't ask Marcia after all.

It was good to be in Vincent Square again in the sitting-room where we had had so many Bevanite lunches. The room is looking rather sad and neglected now because Anne spends most of her time in the country with the children. But she turned up this time to give us one of her excellent meals. John and Dick were in their now normal semi-hilarious states. I have never seen a pair who got on more happily together. They sail serenely through one party rebellion after another and hugely enjoy cheating the disciplinarians, among whom John counts Roy Jenkins. He says we'd have hell if ever Roy were PM. Of course we got talking about Harold again. I am quite open about my growing disappointment and distrust, but John insists that he still loves him, despite Harold's growls from time to time about the Left: 'Knock 'em off one by one.'

Thursday, 22 June. At Cabinet Harold reported on his visit to de Gaulle.[1] He said de Gaulle was 'terribly, terribly depressed and terribly, terribly friendly'. He had talked in an apocalyptic way about his belief that we were heading for a third world war: there was no possibility of a Middle East settlement without a Vietnam settlement. All in all de Gaulle had seemed more tired and bored than hostile, and Harold was now more optimistic about our chances of getting into the Six.

Denis sharply cut this euphoria down to size by saying there were no grounds for it at all and if we were not careful negotiations would drag on and on, sterilizing all alternative policies. Jim said that, in such a situation, it might be worth looking at some sort of association and Harold actually said he agreed – provided it took the form of a 'treaty of transition' with an assurance of full membership at the end. But it would be tactically fatal to show any interest in this at this stage. We should review the position in the autumn.

A pleasant meal in the evening at Admiralty House for Harry Lee Kuan Yew [the Singaporean Premier]. Denis was host and I was the only other Minister. Harry and his Defence Minister were in great good humour, cracking jokes that were more English than ours. They had spent the day arguing with Denis about our proposed withdrawal from Singapore, and they are obviously thinking of ways of at least keeping our officers there, while they provide the soldiery. The Defence Minister told me it would take him years to train officers of his own. No, our military presence wasn't colonialism. At least, Harry pleaded to me, don't announce far ahead that you are going: the result would be chaos.

[1] Indefatigable as ever in his pursuit of Britain's entry into the EEC Harold Wilson had suggested to de Gaulle that Harold should pay him a visit to discuss wider international issues, notably the Middle East. He flew to Paris on 18 June.

Tuesday, 27 June. First round of PESC discussions in Cabinet. I had been swotting up the details from six in the morning, but in the event all we had was a two-hour second reading, most of which was spent deciding whether we needed to cut as much as £500m at all. After Jim and Michael had pontificated about the general economic and financial situation, Tony Crosland weighed in with a magnificent speech, challenging the need for as big a cut and the assumption behind both Jim's and Michael's speeches that the consumer would no longer be prepared to be the 'residuary legatee' of other fields of expenditure. He claimed that personal consumption as a proportion of GNP was already higher in this country than in most industrially developed ones. We should reduce the proposed cuts and aim for an increase in personal consumption of no more than 2 per cent a year, which was the rate achieved in 1961–66, rather than the 2.2 per cent advocated. The alternative would be damaging inroads on our social policy. Most of the discussion ranged round this. Dick had phoned me in the morning to warn that this was our last chance to have a go on growth policies: in other words to advocate devaluation as an alternative, so I built my speech on this. Harold, however, was firmly behind the Chancellor. He believes we need a £500m cut to enable us to give a boost to personal consumption which he thinks is essential – the 'jingle in the pocket' theory. And so it was left, Harold promising that there would be at least two Cabinet meetings to discuss the details of cuts.

Wednesday, 28 June. In the evening Ted and I had decided on a little light relief by accepting George Weidenfeld's invitation to dinner to meet Senator Javits of New York. As usual I had to change into my 'long' in half an hour flat but, as I had just had my hair done, I felt more *soignée* than usual. Just as well: as we sailed into his sumptuous flat we found it full of wealthy women in beautiful chiffon drapes, ethereal and expensive. I don't often stray into this kind of society and when I do I always feel there is something deeply wrong with it. The women prattled in high, immune voices about their children, while George took me aside and said, 'You are looking marvellous. Here is the other book you ought to write: how you manage to look as you do with all you do.' At supper I sat between Javits and Lord Melchett – and the latter turned out to be the more interesting. Javits, for all his reputation as a man of progressive ideas, has that American veneer of bonhomie which always seems to indicate insincerity.

With Melchett, however, I had a long and fascinating conversation. He is young and very alive, and when I asked him why he had come into the public sector he said because it was so challenging. Life in the Bank was so secluded; it was fun to take on a real job. Of course he believed that nationalized industries should be given a remit and then left to get on with it. He was keen on his workers' participation experiment, too. Altogether it was what is called a 'brilliant gathering'. Not my crowd but I had fun, ending up with an argument with Peregrine Worsthorne who tried to make out that the Government's spirit was now broken. I would have none of it. He replied, 'Well, it obviously doesn't apply to you. Your morale is higher than that of any other Minister I meet.'

Tuesday, 4 July. Press conference on my Road Safety White Paper.[1] We were a bit nervous at the reception it would get with not enough sensational proposals to please the press. And the fact that I had had only two hours in bed didn't help. To make matters worse, I found there was a lot of TV, including *Twenty-Four Hours*. I was thankful to crawl to bed at 10 pm.

Wednesday, 5 July. Astonishing press on the WP! Never has a Government document had such praise. Everyone got the point – as we never thought they would – that there really is a 'fresh approach'. Ah well, that's politics. One can never tell. Thus heartened I went into my first battle with Plummer and co. on a PTA for London. Didn't get very far. Understandably they complained they hadn't time to think it out, but first reactions were definitely unfavourable. We agreed that officials should probe the details of my ideas and their alternative – which is to get all the power with no ultimate financial responsibility, something I told them wasn't on.

Thursday, 6 July. The key issue at Cabinet was the proposed WP on defence. Harold began by saying he had had a telegram from Johnson asking us to go slow on defence cuts East of Suez. This was the second time a foreign power had got to know Cabinet business. In these two cases, being the US, it wasn't serious. Nonetheless Cabinet business was secret and we should none of us chat about it at embassies, etc. Denis began by pointing out that the first £400m of cuts had been obtained by squeezing water out of the programme: the next £200m to £300m could only be got by a change in commitments. By 1970–71 defence as a proportion of GNP would have been cut to 5 per cent, while the rest of public expenditure would be up by 25 per cent. He offered a cut of £200m by 1970 and of £300m by 1975. So the WP, slightly modified, was approved.

A lighter note occurred at the beginning when Longford gave us his usual bleat about our giving time for the Abortion Bill.[2] I'm afraid he just sounds comical. But we did all agree that bills of this importance were really unsuitable for Private Members' time. Dick said there ought to be some 'pre-gestation procedure' and he was looking into it.

Monday, 10 July. Went to Bournemouth to open the new electrified service. Of course, there was a technical hitch! Worse still, we were half an hour late

[1] The main theme of the White Paper ('Road Safety – A Fresh Approach', Cmnd 3339) was that the present haphazard handling of this problem must give way to a scientific one. The growing toll on the roads could not be tolerated. If the accident trends continued, we could expect to see half a million casualties by 1970. But resources were limited. The Ministry therefore was applying cost-effectiveness analysis to help it choose the lines of action which would bring the best results for the money spent. But we also needed a better organization to see that the knowledge gained was applied systematically. A new Central Road Safety Unit was therefore being set up in the Ministry to disseminate the information gained by the analysis of accident reports. Five new Area Road Safety Units, which specialized in this work, were being set up and local authorities were being asked to appoint Road Safety Officers to apply the same techniques of accident analysis locally. Other action proposed included making the fitting of seat belts compulsory in some of the older cars; introducing a compulsory register of professional driving instructors; encouraging driver training for young people at school and raising the age limit for riders of two-wheeled vehicles from sixteen to seventeen years.

[2] The Medical Termination of Pregnancy Bill, known as the Abortion Bill, was a Private Member's Bill which had been piloted through the Lords by Lord Silkin and had now been introduced into the Commons by Liberal MP David Steel, who was to become Leader of the Liberal Party in 1976. The Government had decided to facilitate its discussion.

getting back and the press was waiting to ask whether I proposed to institute an inquiry. I brushed them off. I hurried back to the House to have urgent consultations, first with Wedgie and then the PM, about my carriers' licensing. Wedgie, while expressing sympathy with my aims, nonetheless took the technological line – transport was part of the whole production chain and manufacturers must be able to buy themselves into freedom of action if they wanted to, etc. We finally compromised on the point that I should be free to go to consultation on his suggestion as well as mine.

Then I dashed off to see Harold, five minutes late. He was in his outer office gossiping with Marcia, Brenda and Harold Davies. George put his head round the door, his face flushed, to wag his finger at me and say, 'Put a speed limit on other roads if you have to, but leave the motorways alone. I drove back at 100 miles an hour the other night – perfectly safe.' As usual Harold treated him genially, 'You'd better have your tape recorder, Barbara. Anyway the evidence is all on your side.' When we got into his room he added, 'Don't let them push you off the 70 mph.' 'If George goes driving at 100 mph in that condition, he won't last long,' I replied. 'One way or another, he won't,' said Harold. 'I was going to do a reshuffle a few weeks ago, but the time wasn't right – and it would have included you. Now I must wait and it isn't any use moving anyone until you have a place to move them to which has been cleared by a major vacancy.' 'That is as clear as the hieroglyphics on an Egyptian tomb,' I replied. 'It's meant to be hieroglyphics,' he retorted. 'I know who I want to move where, but until I can move someone somewhere else I can't have the place I want to put you.' 'Oh my God,' I moaned. 'What about transport?' You know CDS is active again?' said Harold darkly.[1] 'When I referred in Cabinet to a campaign against George, I knew that a conspiracy was afoot. The idea is to get Jim into the FO leaving the Chancellorship for Roy.' I said I would rather see Crosland as Chancellor than Roy. Harold said, 'Yes, he's different from Roy.' 'Roy will never lead this Party,' I declared. 'Well anyway, they have turned against Jim. Now I know what you want to see me about – PESC.' 'As a matter of fact, I don't – though I hope it is going to be all right.' 'It is about my carriers' licensing,' I said.

And then I told him about my long struggle. He poured me a drink and paced up and down, listening for once and asking questions. I told him I was playing a game of political chess – 'Like you.' Yet my politics was on a foundation of hard economic fact. There would be an unholy row with the RHA and the CBI but I believed it was time we had a row with the other side instead of our own people for a change. He heartily agreed with me that we shouldn't leave out C licences ('See my speech of 29 – or 30 – April 1963'). He told me I was doing a first-class job and said he could back me.

Thursday, 13 July. Into Cabinet for my great battle on carriers' licensing. Tommy had done his stuff briefing Dick and I knew I had Harold on my side.

[1] The Campaign for Democratic Socialism [CDS] had been formed by Hugh Gaitskell's supporters immediately after the 1960 Scarborough conference of the Labour Party in order to reverse the conference vote for unilateral nuclear disarmament. A prominent member was William Rodgers who some twenty years later was to defect to the SDP as one of the 'Gang of Four'.

But, even so, the outcome was anybody's guess. I finished my speech and then waited anxiously. Ray Gunter couldn't very well *not* support me, though he did so with a number of his usual pontifical warnings. Dick supported me 'on the margin and on political grounds'. But Jim was grudging. Of course he was in sympathy with my aims, etc., but the railways hadn't proved themselves. We should take my proposals in two stages: quality licensing now and quantity licensing in a later Bill if developments warranted it. Dick Marsh supported him and my heart began to sink. I appealed to Roy: 'Back me up.' And, purely on *quid pro quo* grounds for my support of the Sexual Offences Bill, he did! Then came two surprises. Michael Stewart said in his careful way, 'I agree after a great deal of thought and against a considerable weight of official opinion.' It was wrong to say that industrialists had a right to run their own transport in their own way. After all, they were using public roads, even if they were using their own vehicles. He believed the difficulties some had mentioned could be overcome, 'and that is the view of my Parliamentary Secretary'. Good for both of them! Then George, who I had thought would take the TGWU line, said no one had offered any real alternative ideas and, if we were trying to put stuff on rail at all, we couldn't leave out the C licences. Even Wedgie swallowed his doubts and supported me. This gave Harold his chance for his usual act of reconciliation. He understood the Chancellor's doubts. Couldn't we meet them by letting me go out to consultation on the basis that the appointed day for quantity licences would be fixed by Order under the Bill so that I was free to bring it in as soon as the railways were fit to take advantage of it? I jumped at this: actually I thought it was a good idea on merits and of course it saved the day.

Just as I thought life was easing a bit, I learned that the Tories are forcing a transport debate next Tuesday. I've told the Department I will prepare my own speech.

Friday, 14 July. Someone has sent an anonymous letter threatening my life and the police are insisting on giving me police protection. So Ted and I set off for HCF with Detective-Inspector Dobson in the car!

Tuesday, 18 July. Enjoyed myself in the transport debate and my speech delighted the troops. My 'shadow', Peter Walker, did me a good turn by presenting me as the nationalizing bogey. Slipped out during the debate to see Frank Cousins and Tonge, chairman of the port employers, about the problems of redundancy that face the industry as a result of containerization. They both want a national plan to deal with it, on the lines of the coal industry. I asked Tonge point-blank what he thought about nationalization of the docks. He hesitated, then said, 'God help me if this ever gets out, but I believe it is essential. Containerization will make the industry capital intensive instead of labour intensive and this calls for central decisions which only Government can take.' I wrote this down and handed it to Stephen for his winding-up speech (without, of course, quoting Tonge). As Stephen faithfully read out Tonge's exact words the Tories shouted, 'Rubbish!' What a pity we couldn't tell them where the remarks came from!

Wednesday, 19 July. An early call from Andrew Cohen thanking me for what I had already done to try and prevent the overseas aid programme from being cut to £205m and asking me to keep up the good work. Arthur Bottomley, bless him, had reported my support back to ODM who were delighted, knowing I am under pressure myself.

Thursday, 20 July. Zero hour for PESC. Since Tony Crosland's outburst at the weekend, it is pretty clear to me that he will get off very lightly.[1] I ought to do a bit more of that kind of thing myself! Jim began with one of his comprehensive surveys of the alternatives: in 1965 we had said we would limit the growth of public expenditure over the period up to 1970–71 to 4¼ per cent per annum. If the existing programmes were maintained the rate of increase would be 4.7 per cent (6½ per cent in 1968–69). From all this it looked as if we were in for a tough time. I was therefore relieved when he confirmed my small cuts plus charges. On housing we merely cut completions and the increased sale of houses by local authorities. On education Crosland argued successfully that he should be allowed some additional programmes as I had been. He got away with a reduction of merely £9m, plus a willingness to consider student loans instead of grants and the possible withdrawal of free milk from secondary schools. Kenneth Robinson got a cut of £10m but was allowed to offset against this the increased price of welfare milk. Harold launched a great spiel on how we could cut the drugs bill by being tough with the manufacturers. Kenneth held out no great hope of this, but nonetheless it was entered on the credit side as a potential saving of £10m. Peggy fought hard against her cut of £70m, arguing that it could only be achieved by a smaller increase in benefits at the next uprating (already postponed till 1969 at a saving of £124m) than was necessary to keep them in line with earnings. Harold, however, said that this reduction would allow account to be taken of half the earnings level.[2]

We then turned to overseas aid and wrung another £10m out of Jim. I couldn't understand what was happening. Since they had only got a notional £30m reduction in the railway deficit from me, plus £25m cut in my *additional* programme, I couldn't see how this gave us the £500m on which Harold had been insisting – or anything like it. Harold, however, totted it all up cheerfully to a rise of merely 4¼ per cent consistent with an increase in personal consumption of 2.1 per cent per year, even if some increase in taxation proved necessary. So the whole PESC agony of recent months had turned out to be largely a farce! Was it Crosland's piece of effrontery that did the trick? If so, I'm going to learn by it.

Yet, though relieved, I went away worried. We just are not solving the economic problem and our priority, in my view, should be more growth. I always said so, even before we came to power. The economic indicators are worse than they have ever been. Jim's orthodox policy just has not worked.

Saturday, 22 July. Sonya and Terry, who have been staying for the weekend,

[1] In a widely reported speech at Norwich he had made a vigorous defence of the social services.

[2] A few days later Peggy Herbison resigned from the Government giving the decision on family endowment as her reason. Judith Hart succeeded her as Minister of Social Security outside the Cabinet.

drove me over to Chequers – so as to have a look at it.[1] Harold, Dick, Silkin, Peter Shore, Wedgie, Tommy and Judith were already there in the small, smoke-filled study; Beattie Plummer[2] arrived with me: quite a gathering of the left-wing clan for the promised informal talk with Harold. To my relief Marcia, looking her usual well-groomed self, swept into the airless room, took a breath and snapped, 'The atmosphere here is disgusting. You'll asphyxiate them all.' Harold told her mildly that someone would have to fetch a key as the security men had locked all the windows. At last a waft of fresh air lightened the closeness and humidity.

To my delight I found Harold ready to plunge straight into a discussion of our economic difficulties. He said it was clear that Jim had got his estimating wrong and had over-deflated. He believed that production was on the rise again, but our short-term problem was to avoid a rise in unemployment this winter. That could be treated separately by a short-term injection of reflation. He therefore suggested we needed a programme of mini-works, whose criteria must be that they would at least stop unemployment rising, but must not carry over into the next financial year; the aim would be to save 100,000 jobs. For a start we should stop all further pit closures during this period: that would be worth 15,000 jobs. It was absurd to take steps which merely meant we had to spend £12 a week per man to put him on the register. Then again there must be mini-measures in the field of schools, hospitals, roads, environmental services which the local authorities would be glad to put in hand and he proposed to give them the all clear. He looked at me and said, 'I can see that Barbara is thinking of railway closures.' 'Even more of railway workshops,' I replied. 'I can put 500 men out of work at Inverurie tomorrow and ought to do so, if we are to bring down the deficit.' 'If you want to suggest a hold-up', he replied, 'and get in touch with the Chancellor, I think you'll find you are pushing at an open door.'

'On Monday,' he continued, 'the Chancellor will make a speech of impeccable virtue in the economic debate. Like the parson, he will preach on Sunday and start fornicating for the rest of the week. Economic righteousness on Monday next, and then the economic fornication will start.' But that would only be for the short term. For the medium term the problem was different: it was to solve our built-in weakness which arose from the fact that every time we reflated imports were sucked in. On the consumer goods side, he thought we should have a 'buy British' campaign. Why should all these Italian shoes be being sold in the shops? ('I could never buy British shoes,' moaned Marcia.)

We sat talking round his proposals which we found promising, adding notions of our own. It was Dick who said sternly, 'But do we really think, Harold, that this will be enough?' At this moment the girls entered for the orders for pre-dinner drinks. It was already ten to eight. We broke up into groups chatting. Said Dick to me, 'We must bring him back to this economic side after dinner. He will try to run away from it.'

Back upstairs we were all anxious to get back to the economic discussion. Harold kept slipping in and out, disappearing and reappearing like the

[1] My niece, Sonya Hinton and her husband, Terry. Over the years they acquired four children: Mark, Rachel, Paul and Laura.

[2] Beatrice Plummer, widow of Sir Leslie Plummer, Labour MP for Deptford from 1951 until his death in 1963, was one of Harold Wilson's few close friends. He made her a life peer in 1965. She died in 1972.

Cheshire cat. 'He's determined not to get back to it,' said Dick tightening his lips. It was getting late and I was finding it difficult to keep my eyes open in the close room. Outside a violent summer storm had broken out. Then suddenly, at 11.30 pm, Harold surprised us all by saying, 'And now I think we should talk about the subject we all know is there though we never talk about it: devaluation. I should like to hear all your views.' There was a stunned silence. Tentatively Tommy led off, saying it was no real solution by itself. Its purpose was to cut real wages and it would not succeed without the things we should have to do anyway: *e.g.* prices and incomes policy. We were sucking in imports because our costs were out of line. The danger was that, within a couple of years, we should be back in the same position again. The others appeared to be agreeing with him when I declared emphatically that I thought we should have devalued in 1964. We had cut real wages anyway and we hadn't had growth. Moreover I didn't believe that giving priority to defence of sterling was compatible with a prices and incomes policy. One was orthodox economics; the other political economics. It would have been better to identify the workers with the battle for their own standard of life instead of seeming to be fighting them. That was why I thought we should float and say to the workers: 'Now you're on your own. The defence of the value of your money can only be conducted on the factory floor.'

This stirred things up and the others began to chip in. Judith summed it up by saying, 'Harold, I don't mind cutting real wages if after a couple of years we've really got off the ground.' Harold said calmly, 'I don't rule out devaluation. This must be a political issue when it comes: we devalue to defend our independence.' And he added suddenly, 'God, why can't we have sane discussions about it like this in Cabinet? We couldn't, even if Cabinet were leak-proof, which it is not.'

And so, at half-past midnight, we broke up. I have never felt nearer to Harold or understood him better. He is *not* just a cynical schemer. He has his own clear views and principles; he is not afraid to defy orthodox opinions or the Establishment. At the same time he is very pragmatic, not stirred by great ideals. And he is terribly tempted to find ad-hoc solutions, at which he is very good. It is easy to complain that he hasn't found the right economic solutions. Few people, even on the Left, can agree what they are.

Tuesday, 25 July. In Cabinet Wedgie got agreement to the early publication of a WP on his Industrial Expansion Bill in order to dispel some of the misrepresentations about it,[1] and I got my Joint Steering Group on the railways report accepted without difficulty. My main anxiety now is about the NFC. The working-party consisting of BRB, THC, my people, the independents and Mr Burney, my financial adviser, had been chewing over the details for months. The timetable has slipped badly here and I have been too swamped in work to chase things up. Now they have presented a vast detailed report on how they think a free-standing NFC could be made to work and, frankly, the complexity

[1] The purpose of the Bill, described in its long title, was to put Government money into 'industrial projects calculated to improve efficiency, create, expand or sustain productive capacity or promote or support technological improvements'. To these ends it extended the powers of the National Research Development Corporation and the Industrial Reorganization Corporation.

of it appals me. Have I made a mistake here? If so, I would rather backtrack, at whatever cost in time or face, rather than push through something I am not happy about. I have called a full meeting on it for Friday and asked Jock Campbell and Tommy to come along.

Thursday, 27 July. I really am furious with my Private Office. Without consulting me they have cancelled my lunch with Dingle Foot on the grounds that I am too busy! I gave them a real raspberry. Private Office graciously fitted in ten minutes for him after the 10 pm vote on defence. He tells me that his 'little brother' has been told that we are selling another consignment of arms to South Africa and that he has to justify this at the UN. This he has refused to do and has rushed over here to see Harold, who has promised to inquire into the whole thing. It seems Harold doesn't know about it! I asked Dingle to keep me in touch, saying this could be a resigning matter. Dingle would certainly not be averse to this as he is expecting the push anyway. I should *hate* to resign, but if we really are sending more arms to South Africa I shouldn't hesitate.

A sizeable number of the Left abstained again on defence. They really are the limit. Can't they realize there has been a revolution in our defence policy and that East of Suez is dead? This is of epoch-making importance to Britain: something they would certainly not have got out of the Tories. It is a tragedy that they can never give this Government credit for anything.

Friday, 28 July. Another exhausting day. First our great meeting on the National Freight Corporation. Egged on by me, Jock Campbell spoke his mind. He didn't like the proposals in the working-party report; the whole set-up just didn't feel right. This encouraged some of the officials like Scott Malden, who have never liked NFC, to pipe up. I told everyone that they were free, if they wanted to, to go back to basic principles. Cuckney,[1] too, said he would have preferred a more gradualist approach, with the NFC more of a selling agency than an integrating one. Stephen wasn't there and John Morris, who had to leave for an adjournment debate in the House, left me a note saying he was worried. But Mills[2] and Foster fought back, backed most ably by Burney, who insisted in his clear and relaxed way that there was not all that difference between him and Jock. I finally said that we must meet again before reaching any decisions.

On to a hurried office lunch, consultations on carriers' licensing with the RHA (which again went remarkably peaceably), and finally to an exhausting meeting with Stan Raymond on the financial prospects of the railways (bad, of course). Scott Malden and Foster had put up a pretty cruel brief – their contempt for BRB is bottomless. I queried whether I ought to hand over to Raymond one of the briefs as suggested, but they insisted it was necessary. In the event it caused an explosion on Raymond's side and he went away furious. I wasn't happy about the whole thing.

[1] J. G. Cuckney, Managing Director of the Standard Industrial Group, was one of the independent members of the Joint Steering Group for our joint review with British Railways. The other two independent members were J. P. Berkin, formerly Managing Director of Shell Petroleum, and Professor A. J. Merrett, Professor of Applied Economics at Sheffield University.

[2] L. S. Mills was an Under-Secretary in my Department.

Down at last to HCF for a weekend with Phil, Colin and the babes:[1] not restful, but woman cannot live by administration alone.

Monday, 31 July. The House is up and I look forward to a slightly less tense week clearing up office issues before my holiday. A lot of consultations to fit in, and Herr Leber has just announced he would like to come over and see me. Since he is very interested in my ideas for carriers' licensing and other things – and since it would be useful to keep in step with another European country on the unorthodoxies of my policy – I am anxious for him to come.

Thursday, 3 August. A most fascinating discussion with Leber at which he revealed to us the outlines of the transport policy he is going to present to the Bundestag in September – very trusting of him, as it hasn't even been to his Cabinet. His policy is designed, as mine is, to put more traffic on to rail. One section of his proposals will help me particularly: the total ban he is putting on the movement of bulk materials by road over fifty miles. At my insistence we had laid on a big lunch at Lancaster House. I was glad to see Raymond back in his old friendly mood – after the stormy interview with him last Monday when he came to offer his resignation, saying that Friday's meeting had shown I had no confidence in the Board. Here again I had to tread warily as John Morris and the independents of the Joint Steering Group are pressing me to get rid of him. They believe there will be no improvement in BR management as long as he is chairman. But even they don't want me to sack him yet. We have still to discuss what to do.

Friday, 4 August. My last day before the holiday, and the worst of a terrible week. From 9 am onwards I rushed through a succession of office meetings. Everyone wants me to settle everything before I go away. The brief holiday is hardly worth the strain.

At last down to HCF for a few days clearing up. Then Ireland. I don't think I have ever been so exhausted in my whole life.

Friday, 11 August to Saturday, 26 August. A delightful fortnight in Ireland, despite the rain. And Ernie Evans of the Towers Hotel at Glenbeigh is a great find. He even got me pony-trekking in the mountains: the first time on a horse for twenty years! On the day before our return, Marje Proops[2] rang me to tell me I was 'Top of the Pops' in ministerial rating, according to a public opinion poll, and that she was going to do a piece about me in the *Mirror*. Could there be photos of me on holiday, please? So the photographer came pony-trekking, too. On Thursday evening I got a phone call from No. 10: where could the PM phone me on Monday at 10.30 am? I told them I would be back in London. Inevitably Ted and I started speculating. Did it mean I was in the reshuffle – maybe DEA? I had mixed feelings. I felt it would be disastrous for me to move from Transport at such a crucial stage. Yet DEA would bring me into the heart of economic planning – and I had plenty of ideas. All rather unsettling.

[1] My niece, Philippa Dobson, and her husband Colin. They had two children, Kathryn and Ben.

[2] Marjorie Proops, famous columnist of the *Daily Mirror*.

Monday, 28 August. The phone call, in fact, reached me at HCF where I was gardening in my sunsuit, wondering how long it would take me to change if it meant recall. But it was merely Harold telling me he was meeting my request to strengthen my Ministry by making Stephen Minister of State, while giving me Neil Carmichael as an additional Parliamentary Secretary. 'I think he is your kind of kidney.' For the rest, I would know tomorrow what he was up to. Of course, I was delighted about Stephen and Neil but had a curious sense of anti-climax about myself. Why had Harold changed his mind about moving me? Was it because I had been so outspoken at Chequers about devaluation and Rhodesia? Well, I ought to have learned by now that the expected never happens. I only hoped that the fact Harold hadn't sent me to DEA didn't mean that the old gang was to be at the centre of power.

Later that night the news broke. So *that's* why he hadn't moved me! He is going to do the job at DEA himself.[1] But that is meaningless unless he enforces a more coordinated policy. I am determined to force myself more into his inner counsels. His other lot haven't been so hot. And I've made up my mind to ask to see him – *soon*.

Thursday, 31 August. At last I got to see Harold. Tommy, looking browned and fit, came up to me as I was waiting outside the Cabinet room. He said he had been recalled from holiday for last weekend's confabulations. 'Do the changes mean a change of policy?' I asked. He shrugged. 'Devaluation, maybe?' He squirmed, 'Don't ask me, Barbie.' Then he added darkly, 'Jim stays.' Dick, he said, had been trying to get hold of me for us all to have dinner before the next meeting of SEP on Wednesday. 'One thing you must ask Harold is to put you on SEP. Let me know what happens.'

Then I was called in. Harold greeted me cheerfully. He had been taking a lot of exercise, thanks to his dog, Paddy, whom he obviously adores. 'And it is Paddy who is responsible for these Cabinet changes. There had I been brooding how I could get rid of Michael Stewart. This particular night Paddy started barking at 2 am. I went down to shut him up and couldn't get to sleep again. Then suddenly the idea came to me – why shouldn't I take over Michael's job myself? DEA will concentrate on economic planning, industrial policy in its widest sense, and regional development. But I shall now have direct access to industrialists and the trade unions instead of just having to give them formal luncheons from time to time. George Woodcock's gone away happier than he's been for years. And Tommy's ecstatic about it.' (That hadn't been my impression.)

As usual Harold wanted to talk rather than listen, but I battled to get a few words in. 'So there's going to be a change of policy?' 'Er . . . should we say, rather, that policies are going to be carried out more effectively.' I thrust in again, determined to have my say: 'But you'll need allies. Why don't you put

[1] In a mini Cabinet reshuffle Harold Wilson had announced that he was taking charge of DEA himself, replacing Michael Stewart who remained in the Cabinet as First Secretary with general charge of social policy. Harold was to be assisted by Peter Shore who jumped from Parliamentary Secretary at DEA to become Secretary of State for Economic Affairs with a seat in the Cabinet. Tony Crosland went to the Board of Trade and was replaced at Education by Patrick Gordon Walker, Douglas Jay leaving the Government. George Thomson was promoted to Cabinet rank, taking Bert Bowden's place at Commonwealth Relations. Arthur Bottomley was replaced at Overseas Development by Reg Prentice, still outside the Cabinet.

me on SEP?' 'I'll think about it,' fencing. 'There are certain people I want to keep off which I might not be able to do if you came on. But in any case SEP won't survive in its present form. What I want is to upgrade Industrial Policy, which Harold Lever has been chairing, into a full key Cabinet committee to deal with wide economic strategy.' 'Well, I should be on that – transport is vital to industry.' 'Oh, of course, you will be. I want to make more use of those Chequers discussions where we can thrash out ideas. And you had better come along to some of my informal Monday lunches – pretty simple ones, I might tell you. Every Monday I meet with my economic team and about every three weeks I have an outside Minister.' I tried again: 'Harold, some time ago you said you had thought of moving me.' 'Yes, to DEA, largely because of your success in dealing with the trade unions. And with your public impact. Michael had none. Nor is it ruled out for the future. I shan't be doing this forever.' He chuckled over my 'Top of the Pops' success. Me, doggedly: 'When you spoke about moving me I began to think what I'd do about prices and incomes policy. We've either got to wind it up or bring it back into a philosophic context.' He agreed.

He had enough spirit for his usual spate of cracks. He chuckled over his dog again: 'Gerald Kaufman says Caligula made his horse an Emperor. Paddy made the Emperor Minister for Economic Affairs.' And he was delighted with the picture of me in the *Mirror* riding on my Irish pony: 'The sexiest picture I've seen for a long time: I've stuck it over my shaving mirror.' So I left him – still wondering to myself whether he has got what it takes to pull it off. He has plenty of guts of a rather devious kind. And I'm very fond of him. He's flexible – and that's important. Cheeky – and that's good, too. But there is a lack of some element in his character I can't yet put my finger on. I wish him well.

Monday, 4 September. My last policy meeting on NFC. Having listened to, thought deeply about and probed all the conflicting points of view, from Jock Campbell to Jack Jones, I am convinced my original agreement to a free-standing NFC is right. And I now have a number of officials on my side. And Burney, who is very impressive, believes the proposals he has helped to draw up will work from a management point of view. Setting up a BTC would be easier for me, but it would mean in effect passing the buck. I want to make a real impact before I leave this job.

Wednesday, 6 September. I've another headache coming up. All my three independents on the Joint Steering Group, Berkin, Cuckney, and Merrett, together with Burney, came to see me to tell me they do not believe the proposals of the report will be implemented as long as Stan Raymond is chairman. Nor do they believe that I will be able to get anyone of stature to serve under him. After one and a half hours of their restrained and solemn unanimity I had to accept that I must force him to resign. The first step is to get him to agree to the publication of the Joint Steering Group report. Then, I suggested, we must draw the attention of eminent journalists to the fact that the report is a scathing indictment of BR management (not least of Beeching, they pointed out). I hope the comments in the press will bring a reaction from Raymond that will give me my chance. If not, I shall just have to have it out with him. What a prospect! For I like Raymond. But then I'm a Minister and he has to behave with me. With his staff, I am told, he is a bully and is incapable of delegation. But I hate the thought. Why do we all love being in government? It must be at least as much masochism as vanity.

Thursday, 7 September. Cabinet accepted a report of the Cabinet group which has been inquiring into the need to modify the powers of the House of Lords. It was unanimous in recommending that there could be no change in powers without a change in composition because we should only put up the backs of the existing interests and make relations with the Government worse, actually damaging the speed of Government business. We instructed the committee to report on composition as quickly as possible. In the light of their report we could decide whether to go ahead.

In the afternoon I had my press conference on the Inland Waterways WP;[1] reception quite good. But the surprise of the day was the success of my meeting with the canal 'enthusiasts'. It turned into a paean of praise for what we had done. Even their leader, Monk, produced verbal bouquets. And there was a real bouquet as well! When I returned to my room I found a huge bunch of beautiful roses waiting with a card from the IWA and the Pleasureboat Operators: 'Thank you for sharing our vision.' Well, well! It is nice to be loved now and then.

Friday, 8 September. Took a rare day off for Hugh's wedding.[2] I tried to keep out of the picture, knowing the interest of the press. But the *Sun* got a picture of me saying goodbye to the bride and groom in their car after the ceremony. Press caption: was I asking them why there were no seat belts?

Monday, 11 September to Saturday, 16 September. My official visit to Hungary. Actually there was little to see transport-wise and I only agreed to go because the FO were very keen. I am glad that they are trying to improve relations with Hungary, so I did my stuff valiantly but the formalities always get me down and the Hungarians were as formal as any I have visited.

Sunday, 17 September. Went over to Nettlebed to see Jock Campbell at his home. John Morris and Chris Foster were there. Apparently it was Chris's idea; he wanted us to discuss Peter Parker[3] and how to get rid of Raymond. Jock enthused about Parker and John seemed impressed with him. I couldn't make out whether or not Chris has doubts. The common consent seems to be that Parker has all the qualities of leadership for the job and is undoubtedly able, but there are doubts as to whether he will be tough enough. But in the meantime I have to get rid of Raymond. Oh hell!

[1] In 'British Waterways: Recreation and Amenity' (Cmnd 3401) I recorded a victory over the Treasury which had reluctantly agreed to keep open for pleasure cruising some 1,400 miles of non-commercial waterways which, without a subsidy, would have had to close. The White Paper also held out the hope of government help for schemes by voluntary bodies to restore disused canals.

[2] Hugh McIntosh, my nephew. My only sister, Marjorie McIntosh, had died in 1964 leaving three children, Sonya, Philippa and Hugh, to whom I had become 'proxy Mum'.

[3] A business colleague of Jock Campbell's at Booker, McConnell Ltd, of which he was a director, and like him a Socialist businessman. He had been a member of the British Steel Corporation since 1962 and had made a name for himself in the world of management as an up-and-coming young man of unconventional ideas.

Tuesday, 19 September. D-Day for the drink and driving campaign – or rather the drinking and *not* driving one.[1] Before my marathon of press conferences and TV performances I had a tense little office meeting about Operation Getting Rid of Raymond. Having thought a great deal about this, I have come to the conclusion it would be altogether too cruel – as well as too risky – just to sack him outright. In any case I have no power to do so: I would have to blackmail him into resigning. I think I could move him sideways into the chairmanship of the Freight Integration Council[1] without doing the latter too much damage. Inquiries into pension, compensation, etc., go on. The Chancellor has been squared.

Wednesday, 20 September. An exacting but triumphant day. In the afternoon I sailed into my conference room for a showdown with Plummer and his Tory cronies from the GLC about whether or not they are prepared to become responsible for London transport. Officials have been very despondent about the Tories' willingness to take this on. I had ready in draft a paper for HAC asking for authorization to impose a PTA on London if necessary. So when Plummer started by raising niggling queries about the questions officials had already discussed for weeks, I began to see red. I half bullied and half tempted, was half coldly angry and half utterly reasonable. Anyway, whatever the reason, they suddenly began to crack and say they thought we could reach agreement. I gave them till 6 October (my birthday) to set out in a letter their terms for a take-over, and we ended by joking together: 'Make it a good birthday present.' Coming out of the room, J. D. Jones said to me, 'I think we've won.'

Feeling pretty drained, I dashed to Liverpool Street to catch my train for the by-election eve of poll meeting at Cambridge.

Thursday, 21 September. I am sure one of the reasons why things are going wrong is that we spend so much time on trivialities in Cabinet. First we spent an hour on leakages. Gerald made a sensible report on the result of his inquiries, the main tenor of which was that the circulation of documents and disclosure of information should be on the wartime basis of 'need to know'. We agreed on some tightening up, but the real problem is that most men just can't keep their mouths shut. Cabinet Ministers blab. That is the long and short of it. I think it just gives them a sense of importance. Then we spent another hour discussing the report of the Committee on Ministerial Publications – an appalling document in my and Dick's view. Not only was there a lot of palaver about whether we could be stopped from keeping diaries or not, but there had been a suggestion that we should all sign an undertaking to submit all documents before publication to the Secretary of the Cabinet, not merely for security vetting (which is OK) but for his view as to whether we had violated the conventions of collective Cabinet responsibility – and be bound by his suggestions for deletion and amendment. We left it that [Harold] should prepare

[1] The breathalyser law was due to come into effect on 9 October and we were launching a publicity campaign to prepare motorists for it.

[2] I was proposing in my legislation to set up a Freight Integration Council [FIC] consisting of the chairman of the BRB and the NFC, two representatives of the unions representing rail and road workers and two independent members under an independent chairman to supervise the working of my proposals for freight integration and to propose any improvements if found necessary.

some recommendations to us in the light of the discussion. Dick and I will watch it – but I think we have won.

One bright spot: the unemployment figures are slightly down.[1] Harold made this announcement with considerable pride – obviously he believes the corner is being turned – that optimism again. It could be fatal. As he pointed out, it had been a gamble to fix two polling days on the day of the Ministry of Labour return, but the worst had not happened. I doubt whether it will help us much at Cambridge, however.

Friday, 22 September. Raymond obstinately refuses to give me an excuse for sacking him. He has even taken lying down my letter informing him that I have definitely decided on a separate NFC and has agreed to get into immediate working arrangement with Reggie Wilson (as the latter, a strong NFC supporter, had urged on me). But I am pressing ahead with selecting a successor. Had an hour with Peter Parker, certainly very attractive and intelligent. John Gunn was most impressed with him.[2] How can I know whether he is tough enough?

The Walthamstow result is appalling, Cambridge less so.[3] As predicted, it is obviously the working class who have defected. The only bright spot is that the Tory majorities are built on Labour abstentions, *not* on growing confidence in the Tories. If Harold has had a punch, Heath can't be feeling particularly happy.

Monday, 25 September. After a meeting of the IP [Industrial Policy Committee of Cabinet] of which, true to his word, Harold had made me a member, I had a word with Ray about the railway guards' go-slow.[4] Despite Len Neal's[5] efforts to stand firm, Ray has ordered an inquiry, even though the go-slow has not been called off first. I believe such capitulation will be disastrous and told him so. I said I believed that the NUR had a national strike in its system which would have to come out before they would face up to realities, and that it was better for us to have this out now instead of waiting for them to have us by the short hairs again on the eve of a general election. I *know* that if the guards get their bonus without having to give any increased productivity in return (and the vast majority of them are not doing second man duties anyway) we shall only have another claim from the drivers for an improvement in *their* differential. This isn't social justice, it is anarchy. Of course *Tribune* is backing the guards on the principle that true Socialism consists of supporting *any* industrial claim, regardless of its effects on other workers. But to me this is nonsense. The religion of Socialism is the language of priorities and that means daring to choose between one claim and the next, to work out proper relationships

[1] The register of wholly unemployed in Great Britain, excluding school leavers and seasonally adjusted, had fallen from 541,600 in August to 540,600 in September.

[2] John Gunn had become my Principal Private Secretary in succession to Richard Bird.

[3] At Walthamstow a Labour majority of 8,725 at the General Election was turned into a Conservative majority of 62. At Cambridge our majority had only been 991, but the Conservatives turned it into a majority for them of 5,978.

[4] It was a dispute about a productivity deal which BR complained the unions were not honouring.

[5] Leonard Neal, labour relations adviser to Esso Europe Inc., had been brought onto the British Railways Board to deal with the Labour relations side. He was knighted in 1974.

between the different members of society. Left-wingism that consists of burying one's head in the sands and avoiding all awkward choices just makes me sick.

Ray raised his eyebrows at me – so did Peter Shore a bit. I suspect Harold may have stepped in to stop a showdown. If so he is making another of his disastrous mistakes.

Tuesday, 26 September. *The Times* has a front-page story to the effect that my Cabinet colleagues were surprised at the tough line I had taken on the railway strike when it was discussed at a meeting of Ministers. I know where *that* comes from. Ray has been up to his malicious leaking again. Said Ted, 'Well, you know all the leaks come from him – everyone in Fleet Street knows.' Playing on the technical inaccuracy of the report, I got a denial put into the paper. As for Ray, I shall bide my time, but I'll destroy him yet. He is despicable and dangerous.

Thursday, 28 September. At Cabinet George gave a long account of his visit to the UN. He said he had come back very depressed about the prospects in Vietnam. The chances of a settlement now seemed very much more remote than in February and March – the Soviet Union just didn't want to talk about it, and when he had tried to discuss it with Gromyko the latter had politely said he didn't want to waste the Foreign Secretary's time. He had put it to Johnson in their personal talk that the bombing was now counter-productive from America's point of view. Johnson didn't agree with this, but maintained that there was no alternative in the light of American domestic policies. To my delight Dick hereupon launched into one of his rare and devastating attacks. The prospect George opened out to us was appalling – endless and increasingly destructive war. Hadn't the time come for us to review our policy? Public opinion in this country and in our Party was becoming increasingly bewildered. They just didn't know where we stood. Did we support the war or not? Of course we didn't approve the war, Harold snapped, but Dick pressed relentlessly on. Did we then approve of America's part in it? Some of us had remained silent as long as there seemed a chance of our acting effectively as intermediaries, but George had made it clear that was no longer the case. America just wouldn't listen to us – nor would Russia. So that at the very least we should make our position clear. But he couldn't for the life of him make out what our position was. Did we think America was fighting a just war or didn't we? Personally he didn't.

I backed him enthusiastically – so did Wedgie, and Harold got very cross. Our job as co-chairman of the Geneva Conference was to be neutral: we deplored the bombing as much as we deplored the infiltration from the North. Dick brushed this aside scathingly: that wouldn't wash any more. Harold kept asking, 'Just what would the Lord President have us do?' Dick faltered a bit here and said he merely wanted to get the position clear as a starting-point – now he knew the Foreign Secretary thought it was a just war. The rest of Cabinet listened almost in embarrassment. I passed a note to Peter Shore next to me: 'Speak up! Assert your rights as a *full* member of the Cabinet.' He scribbled back: 'Not yet.' That is the trouble with Cabinet meetings. There is something paralysingly anodyne about the atmosphere. It isn't 'done' to have any concerted move by like-minded men – unless, of course, Harold has organized it. Tony Greenwood sat in total silence and Peter was obviously inhibited by his own newness from speaking up. I know just what he is suffering from – a sense that he has been brought in for economic affairs and shouldn't intrude on some other Departmental preserve. This is the creeping disease of Cabinet government and Dick himself once suffered from it. There is only one cure for it (as long experience on the NEC taught me). You must just speak your mind and ignore the sneers.

After Dick had kept this up for a quarter of an hour, Crosland asked petulantly whether we couldn't have a properly arranged discussion some time, with a paper circulated, as some of them who hadn't spoken might have something to say. I supported this urgently and Harold said grudgingly, 'I don't see why not.' Peter whispered to me that he would speak up next time.

Off to Scarborough for what I am sure will be the most uncomfortable Party conference of all time. And who knows? I may be off the Executive. Dick's decision not to stand has concentrated the minds of the constituency parties on the belief that there are too many Ministers on the NEC. So there are, but my instinct is never to abdicate. If they want to get rid of me, let them work for it.

Sunday, 1 October. A lovely morning, but I had to work in bed till noon, preparing my speech. I have to reply to the Transport debate and it comes up on Monday afternoon, which means that I shall get it over soon, thank God. I don't know why, but I have never been happy speaking at conference – perhaps because I have been given so little chance to do so in the past. In any case, it is a very special kind of audience, something between the expertise of the House of Commons and the demagogy of a public meeting. At noon I wandered out into the sunshine with Ted, pursued by photographers till I shook them off by posing for a picture with a couple of donkeys on the beach.

Monday, 2 October. Another conference is launched! My best hat, the one I've had for two years, rose to the occasion triumphantly, and I was amused to read in the press that I had been out specially to buy it. It is fantastic how the yearly ritual is perpetuated. Conference routine, and the press comments, are as traditional as Hallowe'en or Christmas time. I got myself pretty keyed up about my transport speech during the morning, but when I got on to the platform in the afternoon I relaxed and made a better speech than I have ever done at conference before. As I sat down I thought it was just adequate and was surprised at the applause. My great breakthrough, conference-wise. Immensely relieved.

Our left-wing gang has revived another tradition, the great long collective table in the hotel dining-room at which we all sit – Wedgie, Mik, Tom Driberg, John Silkin, Tony Greenwood, and all the wives, and of course Ted and me. Over dinner I produced a good crack, 'Nye inspired a faith but could not build a church.' Wedgie says he is going to put it in his memoirs.

When Ted and I got back from the agents' dance, Tom Driberg was in the lobby of the Royal [Hotel] in a great state. Apparently George had come back from the dance in a fury and had had an unseemly brawl with the press, shouting at them about how he was being persecuted by photographers and saying, 'This is on the record.' His poor wife Sophie had stood on the stairs wringing her hands and saying over and over again, 'He *isn't* drunk.'

Tuesday, 3 October. Jim's great day. He was pretty nervous beforehand and almost pathetically grateful for the reference I had made to him in my speech, but in the event he had a triumph. It was no doubt partly due to him that the resolutions critical of the Government were mostly rejected, but I can't help feeling that conference *wants* to be reassured. It certainly doesn't want the old splits. There is no venom in this conference and the credit for this must go to Harold who has so assiduously kept the balance between Left and Right, both in appointments and in policies. Consensus has paid off here at any rate – though I don't think it is paying off in actual achievements. We are no nearer being able to reflate with safety than we ever were, as *The Times* has pointed out in a remarkable leading article.

The NEC election results reflect the general mood of the rank and file. Tom and Mik have jumped to the top of the list (despite the predictions of many journalists that I would walk away with it). But Tony Greenwood, Wedgie and I have held our seats, with me coming a comfortable third. Frank Allaun and Joan Lestor are on,[1] but perhaps only by grace of the voluntary withdrawal of Jim Callaghan, who has become Treasurer, and Dick. If Dick had fought it is an open question whether he would have knocked out Tony or Joan.

Wednesday, 4 October. Thank God, Harold has pulled it off, but in my view only just. Once again he has been saved by conference's longing to believe. But he did manage to convey real emotion in his piece about unemployment. It was a pity he couldn't stop at that point instead of bringing in every issue he thought Heath might make something of. As it was, I reached my emotional peak nearly a quarter of an hour before the end and sat irritated. But delegates clearly thought it was wonderful and the commentators called it a masterly piece of political management.

When it was all over I said to Harold, 'Now perhaps you will spare me that twenty minutes I have been asking for.' So at 4.45 pm I went into the sitting-room at his hotel where he was sitting with Gerald Kaufman and Mary Wilson. She was slumped in an armchair in her cardigan, refusing to be elated. I suspect she too is disenchanted about some of the policies. They both melted away and first I told Harold that I thought his speech was good, but too long, etc. I have always been on disrespectful terms with him. Then I told him that Ray was the source of many Cabinet leaks, quoting the bit about the railway strike. 'I know he leaks,' said Harold, 'but Roy leaks, too.' He really has Roy on the brain – I don't know why because Roy will never be Leader of as complex a Party as ours, torn between revolutionary principles and conservative instincts. Harold urged me to drop him a Minute about the railway strike incident so that he can set the leak procedure in motion, but I don't like the idea.

Finally I got on to the dreadful issue of Stan Raymond. When I told him that I had had a deputation from the independent members of the Joint Steering

[1] Labour MPs for Salford West and for Eton and Slough respectively. They were on the Left of the Party and had been elected for the constituency party section.

Group saying that Raymond must go, he thought that was conclusive. 'But I like Raymond,' I moaned, 'and this could ruin him.' 'You try reshuffling a Cabinet,' he said grimly. 'You'll learn to be tough.' I said I would like Harold to read the comments we had collected from various sources about Peter Parker and I would send them in his weekend box. As I left he said, 'If it will help, Raymond can have a peerage.'

Thursday, 5 October. George, unfortunately, had a walk-over on the Common Market. It helped him to live down his publicly paraded *Angst* about himself following his brush with the photographers. The 'Must George Go?' campaign has got lost in his breast-baring declaration: 'You must take me as I am.' I prefer the comment of Peter Shore's wife, who said quite seriously that he ought to have psychiatric treatment. Why should the rest of us – including the Transport House staff – suffer the exhaustions of George's maladjustments? But the most serious thing is that the anti-Common Market argument went by default. Frank Cousins did pretty well, but Alf Morris and Douglas Jay just did not ram home the implications of the document from the Commission. In effect, the Commission say that to get in we should have to devalue. I believe we shall have to devalue anyway. The real case against going in is that, if we do, we shall be hampered in being interventionist – and, if conference has voted for anything this year, it is for interventionism.

Friday, 6 October. My birthday, always spent pretty wretchedly at conference. This year it has been further darkened by an incipient feverish cold. At last we are on the train home. Conference has heartened me to take up the attack again on Vietnam in Cabinet. Dick and I were delighted that the platform was beaten on the Vietnam resolution as we agreed, if it *hadn't* been, we should have been left without a leg to stand on in our coming fight. Dick, egged on by me, is now afire on some of these larger issues.

Wednesday, 11 October. I find that I have forgotten to mention B for Breathalyser Day! This is an indication as to how coolly I have taken the introduction of the social revolution – the new drink and driving law – for which I am responsible. The fact is that, having gone into all the arguments myself very thoroughly, and all the medical evidence, I have just assumed that the new law was the most natural thing in the world. Yet, far from coming a cropper over it, I seem to be sailing through. Of course there have been another couple of threats on my life, but nobody takes those seriously. Apart from them, and from attacks in the expected quarters, the law has been astonishingly well received and the press and TV have done a magnificent job putting it across. I was astonished to find how interested the press were in my movements last Sunday, eve of B-Day. Tired after Scarborough and with a streaming cold, I had to fend off requests for photos. A sixth sense made me realize we should be followed to our local for our Sunday drink. I am certainly going to be shadowed from now on!

In the evening I made my first encounter with a tycoon. Ted and I dined *tête-à-tête* with Arnold Weinstock, Managing Director of GEC, and his wife in their flat at Grosvenor Square. I never got it clear quite how the invitation came – I suspect it was inspired by Chris Foster, who has been floating the idea of making Weinstock a part-time member of BRB in order to put the railway workshops on their feet. Chris maintains that, since Weinstock's forte is taking over and making a go of industries that aren't doing as well as they might, he could do the same for the workshops. The very idea horrifies Jock Campbell, whose type Weinstock very definitely is not, but I am prepared to consider any idea that may help us to make the railways thrive.

The manservant ushered us into a large, but not particularly lavishly furnished flat. Weinstock is a slim, darting, voluble, youngish man with glasses; his wife rather sweet and anxious to please and unpretentious. I wasted no time getting on to Weinstock's managerial philosophy. I gathered he admired me because I 'got things done'; that he is suspicious of management theories and has a simple formula: 'Give a man a job and tell him to get on with it and sack him if he fails.' Over the excellent meal, he talked and talked. He was one of the 1964 converts to voting Labour because he thought the Labour Government would get things done. Now he was disappointed, not that he thought the Conservatives would have done any better. It was all talk. Nor had he any time for the CBI and its Director-General, Stephen Brown. He represented no one. Everything was becoming too institutionalized and the Government was spending far too much time trying to square the CBI. It should do what it thought was right and damn the consequences. I drew him out a bit about nationalized industries. Here again he thought that earning a return on capital was the only effective measurement of efficiency, with which I agree. Hence my policy of separating out the social subsidy for the railways. Neither of us broached directly the question of his taking a job: I was trying all the time to calculate whether one dare let him loose on the workshops. His answer to my question, what would one do when faced with closing a workshop down in a development area, was 'more industrial training'. He couldn't understand why the Government hadn't done more of this. Moreover he believed one might reorganize the work so as to rejuvenate some of the ones that at present were not paying. He thought the workshops ought to be able to find a good role for themselves as subcontractors to outside industry. I am still attracted to the idea of using him – though one would run a terrifying risk. Altogether a mind-stretching evening, at the end of which we agreed that the key to good management was to find a genius and give him his head. Very simple really – if one can find the genius!

Thursday, 12 October. Dick came to see me yesterday to enlist my support for his proposals for reform of the House of Lords: George was being awkward and his fellow committee members were away and could not attend Cabinet. I agreed, provided he backed me over Vietnam. He grinned: 'Yes, I am a real Cabinet Minister now.' In the event the proposals went through Cabinet pretty smoothly. Personally I think they are pretty ingenious. No doubt the Left in the House will attack them, but I think the position of doing nothing and keeping the Lords impotent by keeping them ridiculous is no longer tenable. We should either abolish the place or reform it. And it is clear that the Liberals – and Tories too – will come out with proposals for reform even if we do not, and it would be unwise to let them get the initiative. Moreover, as Dick pointed out to me, he can't really reform Parliament without doing something about the Lords, and he added rather pathetically, 'I would like to get some real reform through before I leave this job' – his only consolation in this long, dreary year of non-departmental activity.

We even got the divorce law reform through, too, though Longford bleated as usual that if we gave a Private Member a Bill we would be violating our neutrality, while Ray added an unctuous disclaimer of the whole business.

A mad rush to catch my train to the North-West. James Drake, the new head of the Road Construction Unit [RCU], had come up to London in order to travel with me. He is a gloriously unpolished Northerner of blunt speech in a broad Lancashire accent, obsessed with roads and a real go-getter. Contrary to custom, I have prepared a long and careful statement on roads policy for my press conference and have inserted in it the need to give more emphasis in future to regional development.

Friday, 13 October. A most successful tour. It was a great moment to get out into the Pennines along the route of the M62 and to see, up in the hills, a Yorkshire RCU crane on the skyline – 'Colonel Lovell coming to meet us from the Yorkshire end.' This, the first east–west motorway, will revolutionize east–west links. I intend that there shall be more of these cross routes, instead of the endless radial routes into London. After a day talking to Drake, I can really begin to see how I can get better planning and priorities into the roads programme.

Scare about a bomb in my sleeper. The Preston CID were at the station to see me safely aboard. I slept well.

Monday, 16 October. Still on the search for the ideal chairman of BR, I saw Ronnie Edwards of the Electricity Council, strongly recommended to me by the office. He was very flattered and amiable but said he didn't think he was the man. Nor do I. I am more and more confirmed in my first hunch that Peter Parker is the only one who combines the ability needed with the 'charisma' we must have to put BR across. Just a tough businessman won't do.

Saw Harold to report progress on the [BR] chairmanship. I told him the office had produced a list of possible candidates with some astonishing names – everything from Jock Campbell to Keith Joseph![1] The list in my view reduces down to only two possibles, Duncan Dewdney, Managing-Director of Esso, and Peter Parker, on both of whom I had sent him particulars. Having seen Dewdney I didn't think he was on: a pleasant, competent chap, but no world beater. Harold wasn't too enthusiastic about either Dewdney or Parker (despite my plea for the latter) and produced some odd names of his own.

Friday, 20 October. The office is still very anti-Peter Parker, though I think Scott Malden is coming round. John Morris is very indecisive, but what influences me most is that Chris Foster is definitely against. Since he was in at

[1] Sir Keith Joseph, Conservative MP for Leeds North-East since 1956, had been Crossman's predecessor at the Ministry of Housing and Local Government from 1962 to 1964. He was also to succeed him as Secretary of State for the Social Services on the fall of the Labour Government in 1970 and was to dismantle Dick Crossman's national superannuation scheme in favour of an emasculated two-tier system.

the original meeting with Jock on this and, I thought, rather keen on the idea, I wonder if there is something about Peter Parker I don't know. Heaton, of course, wants Dewdney – very much his sort of man. They keep arguing to me that, if I go for Dewdney and he fails, he will be blamed, but that if I appoint Parker and he fails, all the blame will fall on me. Certainly it is one of the most important appointments I shall ever have to make. To turn everything upside down by sacking Raymond and then choose the wrong man . . .! My original instinct that Parker has exactly the right mix of qualities has been tempered by the doubt as to whether he is tough enough. His manner is almost too open and sincere to be true.

I must see Raymond next week. With the guards' dispute threatening a national railway strike, the moment hasn't been propitious up to now. We fixed on next Friday for the interview – which I dread. I've been sounding a lot of people (Dick Marsh, Greenwood and others) about a possible alternative job for him in their fields, without success. I hate the thought of a straight sacking: he doesn't deserve that from me.

Thursday, 26 October. In the afternoon I had a useful meeting at the office on road strategy. J. D. Jones has taken charge of this and we are setting up new machinery to co-ordinate highway planning with overall transport planning, something that had never been done before. J.D. is his usual enthusiastic self about this. The only thing that worries me is that we have got to put Neil Carmichael in charge of this and he is not yet fully up to the wiles of Highways division.

As we were discussing all this, I had an urgent plea to see Chris Hall and Bickerton privately. They came in to tell me that Chris had been lunching with Monty Meth of the *Mail*, who had told him that he was publishing the next day a firm story to the effect that Raymond was being sacked. And they also told me – under strict pledge of secrecy – something that they thought I ought to know. Monty had told Chris that he knew the story was correct because he had got it from Ray Gunter! Ray had taken him aside after a meeting with the railway unions and tipped him off. (Ted tells me this is a common practice of Ray's. Why does he do it? To get in well with the press.) But of course, they said, I must not disclose the source of their information or it would ruin the Ministry's relations with the *Mail*. A nice burden to place on me! The only way to deal with it, they urged, was for me to see Raymond at once. It was imperative he shouldn't first learn of his removal from a press story.

We had an urgent council of war and I said that, obviously, I must now offer him the chairmanship of the Freight Integration Council in order that we could present the story as one of transfer, and *not* sacking. I therefore got on to Harold for his permission, telling him of the threatened leak, while the office contacted Raymond to ask him to come and see me. Harold readily agreed, but we discovered to our horror that Raymond was attending an important meeting with the NUR to discuss the productivity deal. I told them to tell him to come as soon as he was free, but a few minutes later I had him on the phone. What was this all about? Was it important? Yes. Did I want him to come immediately? Well, before too long. (It was by now 6 pm and I was afraid of the *Mail* story going out in its first editions.) How long would his meeting last? 'Hours.'

I hesitated and then said that he had better come and see me at once and then go back. I didn't see what else I could do.

He arrived arrogant and irritable. Personally I believe he guessed what was in the wind because he has already had two meetings with Padmore skirting round the possibility of his removal. It was an unpleasant background against which to put him in the picture, which I did as gently as possible, offering him the new job. He went rigid with hostility: 'So you have brought me out of this important meeting with the unions to tell me I'm sacked?' I stressed once again that my hand had been forced and that I didn't want to present the story as a sacking but as a transfer. He talked about getting legal advice: as for the FIC, he couldn't possibly make up his mind off the cuff like this. After half an hour of this I told him to go away and think about it and we would meet the following day as originally arranged. He stalked out cold with anger to go back to his meeting. What an emotionally exhausting life I do lead!

Friday, 27 October. The press stories are just what I wanted: Raymond offered new job. But when I saw him again he wasn't in any more relaxed mood – and I can't blame him really. He was full of the fact that he wanted to know our terms, and have them considered by his legal advisers, before he would agree to anything. How furious he would be if he knew Reggie is to become chairman of the NFC! I had Alex Kitson to lunch to break the news about Reggie to him. He took it a bit hard at first because he dislikes and mistrusts Reggie. But I read him bits of Reggie's memo to me, outlining how he sees the NFC developing, and Alex was clearly impressed by it. 'He must have changed a lot,' he kept saying. He promised to take it away and study it. He was also tickled pink at my suggestion that he himself should become a part-time member of the NFC Board.

Monday, 30 October. Gave Frank Cousins lunch to break the news to him that I had decided to appoint Reggie Wilson as chairman of the NFC. I led into it gently by saying I understood he would consider a job in transport. The ideal job for him would be as chairman of NPA in about two years' time when he had retired. This obviously pleased him, though he said deprecatingly that in the normal way he wasn't in favour of filling these jobs with retired trade union officials, etc., etc. I gather he wouldn't mind giving up the TGWU a year earlier to take the job: 'Jack can carry on.' In the meantime, I went on, what about part-time membership of the Board of the NFC? I then hesitantly said I was thinking of Reggie as chairman, and to my surprise Frank said emphatically, 'You couldn't have a better man.' The Department is full of constitutional objections to my proposal to put practising trade union officials on boards, even as part-timers, but I shan't give up easily.

Harold has helped me by calling a Cabinet to clear my WP on Railway Policy. I explained that it was urgent to get this out quickly since my hand had been forced last week over Raymond's dismissal. Ray Gunter tried to make trouble over this. I know he hates me (Ted tells me he never disguises the fact when he's with journalists), but it was more than I could stand when he came out with a venomous attack on me for the way I had handled the dismissal – 'dragging the chairman of the Board out of an important union meeting to give him the sack'. Damn it, I should never have had to do it if Ray hadn't leaked to the *Mail*. So I snapped back that my hand had been forced by a leak which, according to the journalist, came from 'someone round this table'. The fat was in the fire at that! Must give names, etc., etc. Harold ordered another leak inquiry but nothing will come of it. I can't give my informants away.

Anyway, the White Paper went through and is to be published next Monday.

Monday, 6 November. Woke with a sick headache and a tummy as liquid as Niagara Falls. Wanting to heave is not a good state to be in at the dispatch box! I don't know whether it is something I have eaten or just the accumulated tension of the past few weeks. And things were not made any better by the fact that I had to see Stan Raymond again to agree what I should say about his position if it was raised – as it certainly would be – in today's debate. He came into my room icy cold and hostile, holding his hand out stiffly ahead of him for a reluctant handshake. When he saw John Gunn and Poland[1] with me, he said as insultingly as he could that he had his own legal adviser with him and that, if I were going to have advisers with me, he wanted his. So I sent them out of the room while I had a preliminary talk with him.

I began by saying how sorry I was that once again I had had to suggest he came to see me at a time of stress on the railways. But I had done it, as I had last time, in his interests as much as mine: it was a matter of concern to both of us that we should agree what I should say in the debate. He almost spat at me at this, asking me whether I was really saying that I had fetched him out of the NUR discussions to help *him*? I replied firmly that I had done just that, whereupon he hissed, 'I am preparing a dossier on all that and then people can judge for themselves.' 'What people?' I asked, going coldly grim myself. He shifted a bit at my change of tone and added lamely, 'You, for one.' 'I take it, then, that you will do nothing with that dossier until you have shown it to me. Otherwise, you know, I shall produce my own dossier.' He climbed down, saying yes. I then asked him if he had considered my offer of another job. He replied that he wasn't prepared to consider a hypothetical job for a body which hadn't even been created yet. Eventually we agreed a form of words. Altogether an unhappy interview.

And so into the debate, laced with Kaolin provided by the nurse at St Christopher House. My stomach wouldn't take more than a glass of milk. Peter Walker was at his most trivial. I rallied as vigorously as I could and people said afterwards that no one would have known there was anything wrong with me, but I knew I wasn't at my best.

Still feeling sick, I dragged myself into a meeting of the Overseas Sub-Committee of the NEC. One of the items was resolutions passed at Party conference, so this brings us right up against Vietnam. Personally I welcome it. The NEC has a duty to carry out conference decisions faithfully so we are heading for a crisis over the position of Ministers who are also members of the NEC. But the NEC could, if it asserts itself, influence the Government on this. I suggested that we ought to ask George Brown to discuss the whole matter with the NEC. Everyone thought this was a good idea.

[1] R. D. Poland, the Under-Secretary in charge of nationalized transport.

Wednesday, 8 November. Discussion in the office about next steps over the BR chairmanship. Heaton is for going ahead with Parker as quickly as possible. But they all think I should see Johnson first and explain the position to him. Scott Malden brought a report from Cuckney to the effect that Johnson may resign if I choose Parker. This made me see red and I told him firmly that I cannot give Johnson a power of veto in this way. I also told him that there seemed to be an absolute conspiracy in certain quarters to blacklist Parker and to encourage others to do so. I personally think that the independent members of the Joint Steering Group [JSG], having pressurized me into getting rid of Raymond, are now trying to dictate his successor and are turning a little nasty in the process. It really is absurd that, having rejected Parker as not having enough managerial experience, they should be so keen to put in Johnson who, they admit, is not over blessed with grey matter. What is behind their anti-Parker obsession? Jock Campbell says it is straight political: these people hate Socialist businessmen. He may be right. Certainly it smells and their attitude only toughens mine.

I arranged to see Johnson at 6 pm. He came in as full of old-world courtesy and respect as ever. I went through the agreed formula: I had considered him seriously for the chairmanship but, as he was sixty-one, his appointment could only be for a few years and another change so soon would be unsettling. I intended when the legislation had gone through to offer him the post of chief general manager and deputy chairman and consider him my anchor man in this situation, in which I knew that morale has been undermined by the JSG report and uncertainty. I had it in mind to appoint Peter Parker to the chairmanship. He had many qualifications, etc., and I knew that he would support him loyally, etc.

Then to my horror I realized that Johnson had been led – by whom? – to expect that he would get the chairmanship himself. Sitting grey-haired and correct in his chair, he asked if he could speak frankly. I said I wouldn't like him to do anything else. He then spoke bluntly for ten minutes about his disappointment. He had nursed a life-long ambition. 'What is that?' 'To be head of British Railways.' He must tell me that morale now was very low. They had had a succession of people from outside: Brian Robertson, Beeching, Raymond himself (when I expressed surprise at Raymond being called a man from outside, he said scathingly, 'Yes he came to us as assistant general manager'). He wasn't against people from outside. No doubt they did the railways good, but for the moment the railways needed a breathing space (I almost expected him to say, 'a healing period'). He must warn me that top railwaymen wouldn't take kindly to Parker's appointment. After all, he knew nothing about railways and had had no experience of running a big concern. In view of this he would like twenty-four hours to consider his own position.

By this time my estimate of Johnson had gone up 200 per cent. I had no idea he had so much guts – and certainly no idea that he was so keen on the job. Rallying from the shock, I told him I would be equally frank. How could I justify sacking a man of fifty-four in order to put in his vice-chairman of sixty-one?' 'ICI have just appointed a chairman of sixty-two,' he retorted. And so we went on. To lessen the tension I asked him if he had given thought, as I had asked him to do, to the railwaymen we might promote to the Board. Yes, he had, and brought out a list on which he talked very intelligently. He dilated about how we must seek out and bring on the young men and became less unhappy looking. Leaning forward, I said to him earnestly, 'Mr Johnson, are you prepared to be a member of this team?' He hesitated, then said, 'Ma'am, I would ask for a little time to think about it. If I give a decision I keep to it loyally so there is a lot involved for me.' Agreeing, I said, 'I can only say how much I hope the answer will be yes.'

When he had gone I sat there brooding, turning the pros and cons of Johnson *v.* Parker over and over in my mind. Then I said, 'John, open that cabinet. I'm going to have my first drink of the week. I need it. And ask Heaton to come in.' Over a whisky I discussed with him my impulse to send for Parker and tell him frankly of the new development. Perhaps he wouldn't want the job in these circumstances. But if I was going to switch to Johnson it must be *before* he gave me his answer. Otherwise he and I would know forever that he had got the job under blackmail. My reason must be, and be seen to be, that I had changed my mind because I had got a new insight into his qualities and ambitions. But Heaton counselled delay, repeating the injunction, 'Sleep on it.' My mind in a turmoil, I went home at 9 pm.

Thursday, 9 November. Apparently *The Times* is running a firm story about Peter Parker tomorrow – and a hostile one. I said [to John Gunn] I must see Johnson at 6 pm. He began by reiterating his own disappointment and the low state of BR morale. Though the fate of my policy hung in the balance, I felt curiously detached. I find this is a state that grows on me the more my troubles pile up. However, Johnson suddenly smiled and said, 'Of course, ma'am, I'll take the job you offer me – indeed, I'm honoured by it. And I shall do it loyally.' So he will, bless him. We parted on good terms.

Friday, 10 November. At 9 am Parker was smuggled into my room at the House. I told him that, after weeks of thought and interviewing people, I had decided to offer him the job – and I stressed that he was the only person to whom I had offered it. Then with brutal frankness I outlined the difficulties: he would have no deficit grant in five years' time; morale was low; there would have to be more redundancies. And in particular I told him all about Johnson. His reaction impressed me. He was honoured to be selected; he knew the choice would not be well received by the press – all the difficulties. These were manageable. But what would make his job impossible would be if he could not command the confidence of the Board and railwaymen generally. I asked him to talk to Johnson over the weekend, and would not let him give me an answer until he had done so. We both had a wry smile over a snide piece in *The Times.*

Monday, 13 November. I found to my surprise that I was lunching privately with the Home Secretary. When I asked my office what it was all about they said he had suggested this some time ago, but they had only just been able to arrange it. I met Roy at the Connaught Grill – excellent food, I remembered from the few occasions I have been taken to lunch there. Roy grinned as I arrived and repeated that he had suggested this some time ago – there was really nothing very significant about it; just the feeling we all ought to keep in touch more. I didn't dodge about, but asked straight out what he thought the Government ought to do about the mess we were in. He said that he thought devaluation was necessary and that, if we were offered another deflationary package, some of us ought to say, 'This is too much,' and be ready to go. But I left him in no doubt that I didn't think anyone could lead the Party but Harold. An affable and delicious lunch. Roy can be very charming when he likes.

At 6 pm Parker came to report on his talk with Johnson. Apparently it went very well and they have already established a rapport. Parker talked of him in glowing terms. His answer therefore was yes, he would take the job. I then broached the question of salary. We were reviewing salaries in all the nationalized industries but it would take a little time to complete. Would he start at Raymond's salary of £12,500? He looked at me squarely and said quietly and steadily, '*No*. That would be my first mistake as chairman.' It soon became clear to me that getting nationalized industries more in line with private industries was a key principle with him. 'Look,' he said unhappily, 'I want to help. But as a life-long Socialist I believe we simply can't make public ownership work by starving it of talent. A man like Johnson, for instance, as Chief Executive ought to get at least £15,000 and I won't take the job unless he does. I shall have failed unless in two years' time we have a first-class Railways Board. How on earth am I to recruit them under a ceiling of £12,500? I couldn't get a financial director under £18,000. I don't mind paying him more than I get myself, but we must begin an upward movement in salaries for all key staff and to do that I must have headroom. Why, they offered me £15,000 just for a board job in steel! The chairman of BRB ought not to get a penny less than £22,000. I am prepared to come for £17,500, provided Johnson gets £15,000 – and that's not the professional salary. But it is not the money I worry about for myself. After tax it will only make a few hundreds difference anyway. But I must have room to move up the men under me – it is the only way to get that upward boost in morale. I fought this battle on steel and my first job as chairman must be to fight it on railways.' I was very impressed by his manner and, as for the argument, I was already convinced, having backed Dick Marsh over the steel salaries. All I could do was to say that I would do my best – and tell Gunn I wanted to see the Chancellor and the PM right away.

Tuesday, 14 November. Arrived at No. 11 at 9.15 am. Jim was in a black mood and swept my argument aside brutally. 'Tell him he's got to start at Raymond's salary and then we'll see.' 'He won't.' 'Then we'll have to get someone else.' 'You won't get anyone else at that price – Dewdney would want £20,000.' 'Then bring back Raymond.' 'Really, Jim, don't be absurd. We'll just be without a chairman for weeks and morale will collapse. I can't get rid of the deficit for you unless you give me the tools.' The miserable interview ended abruptly as we went into Cabinet. I got my Freight WP through easily – but what use is that? Our carefully laid plans to launch it on Thursday, accompanied by announcements about Parker and Reggie Wilson, are now all awry. I asked leave to publish on Thursday, or later according to developments.

After Cabinet I had a hurried five minutes with Harold about Parker. He was receptive, as always, but merely said, 'You must talk to Jim.' 'I *have* done.' 'Then keep on talking. And the matter must come to Cabinet on Thursday.'

My spirits at zero, I went back to rally my forces, cancelling all my engagements in order to start the most intensive piece of lobbying I have ever done. I spent the rest of the day interviewing colleagues one after another and getting a surprising amount of support. Dick Crossman, Marsh, Gerald, Peart, Willie Ross, Cledwyn Hughes – even Michael Stewart – agreed that what Parker asked was reasonable. Only Roy asked for a *quid pro quo*. 'When we do come to discuss a package deal of cuts, don't press for cuts in Cabinet salaries,' he said grinning. 'Unlike most of my colleagues, I have four children and no private income.' I couldn't help wondering how he could afford that expensive lunch for me.

Wednesday, 15 November. More lobbying. To my delight Peter Shore has had no hesitation in saying he supports me. That leaves only Ray, Jim and, no doubt, George as implacable opponents. I've also cleared my paper for Cabinet.

Thursday, 16 November. Into Cabinet all keyed up for the battle over Parker. I had only managed to push this up to second item (after parliamentary business and overseas affairs) so I knew that it would be a close thing on timing, even if all went well. But as soon as we started Harold said, 'The Chancellor and I have an important statement to make. We must take it first and then deal with any other items for which there is time.' We all stiffened and Jim began heavily, 'I have decided that the pound must be devalued. If Cabinet agrees, the necessary machinery will be set in motion and devaluation will be announced on Saturday. This is the unhappiest day in my life.' We all sat very still.

He then elaborated on the recent run on the pound. We could arrange another massive loan, but the thought of going through the whole process again was sickening. He and the PM therefore recommended 14.3 per cent devaluation. This was the only alternative to further deflation, which would be intolerable. This figure, he had found, would be acceptable to other countries. Anything more would lead other countries to follow suit and then we should lose all the advantages. As it was, only a few, like New Zealand and Israel, would devalue along with us. But expansion was already going ahead rapidly – we should have 4 per cent growth by 1969 – and if we were to have an export-led boom we must take some of the steam out of the home economy. So bank rate was going up to 8 per cent and we would have to save £500m of domestic expenditure. There obviously hadn't been time to discuss the details of the package with individual Ministers, except the Minister of Defence who had found savings of £100m for 1968–69, a tremendous effort. In conclusion he said, 'This is the most agonizing reappraisal I have ever had to do and I will not pretend that it is anything but a failure of our policies.'

Harold elaborated on Jim's statement as he always does, stressing that, although the decision was a set-back, it would also be a relief to our people: 'They will feel that at last we have broken free.' The aim was not to create more unemployment, but to reduce it, and there would be still greater preferences for the regions. He also stressed that we must get our discussion through quickly. This was the most secret matter we had ever had before Cabinet and it was essential that Cabinet should not sit beyond its usual time. Comments, please. Some of us queried whether 14.3 per cent was enough and I urged that we should give earnest consideration to the possibility of floating. This was the only way to involve the man in the street in the defence of the pound, otherwise all the burden would be on the Government again. And otherwise, too, we should not be 'breaking free' at all, but merely committing ourselves all over again to the defence of sterling, though at a lower parity. In myself I felt great uneasiness at Harold's line: this modest devaluation just wasn't a break for freedom at all. I doubted whether it was anything like enough to cure our ills – Harold seemed altogether too complacent to me. But I couldn't get any support for floating, not even from Crosland or Roy, while Jim's main argument was that other countries wouldn't find it acceptable. Some thought 14 per cent might not be enough, but were persuaded by Jim that this was the only way to prevent other countries following suit. As for the proposed cuts, we were all asked to have a look at them. When Dick objected to our having once again to consider a hastily concocted package of cuts under duress, Harold told him tartly that he had taken the unusual step of consulting Cabinet three days in advance – they hadn't been consulted in 1949.

Harold then said that, as it was 1 pm and as it was imperative that no one should guess anything was untoward, Cabinet should dismiss, but that a few should stay behind to discuss an urgent item – mine! I was horrified. For one thing I lost a lot of my allies that way, and was left with Jim, Ray (an implacable enemy), Michael Stewart, Peter Shore, Dick Marsh and, of course, Harold. Moreover I knew that moment was utterly unpropitious. However, I made a passionate case in favour of meeting Peter Parker's terms. It was, of course, in vain. One by one my friends deserted me: Peter swung over completely, saying that devaluation altered everything, and Harold himself took the same line. He told me to see Peter Parker again and ask him to come at the tariff rate, though, of course, I couldn't tell him the new developments. What a task! And he added that, if necessary, I could bring Peter to see him that afternoon.

Back to the office to tell my troops the bad news about Peter Parker – and I couldn't even tell them why. It was hell! I sent for Parker and tried to persuade him, but he was regretfully adamant. So I asked him to come with me to see the PM. Harold had to be as vague as I had been, but promised him that before too long there would be a review of nationalized industries' salaries. Parker was as charming and as firm as ever. He was desperately sorry but he thought his proposals were the only possible terms for success. He would be misleading us if he said otherwise. As he left Harold said to me, 'He's impressive.' 'What do I do now?' I asked in despair. 'See him again on Monday. He'll change his mind when he hears the news.'

Friday, 17 November and Saturday, 18 November. Two wretched days sitting on my secret knowledge. I couldn't talk to anybody sensibly – least of all my journalist husband, Ted.[1]

9 pm Saturday: at last the news is out and I can relax and talk to Ted naturally again.

[1] My husband had had a long and distinguished career in journalism, including periods as News Editor of the *Daily Mirror* and Editor of *Picture Post*. He was currently between assignments on the *Daily Herald* and the *Sun* and was devoting most of his energies to local government.

Monday, 20 November. We missed Harold's broadcast to the nation last night. Apparently he took his 'breakthrough' line. I don't share his attitude. There seems to be a feeling abroad that he was too complacent by half.

I sent for Peter Parker again. 'Now you know why I couldn't win last Thursday.' What could he do to help now, I asked? He said he realized that devaluation made a difference and he thought the best way to meet it was for him to take a cut on his salary of 12½ per cent, which would leave him with no more than he was effectively getting at Booker's and only a little more than he had been offered for the steel board. This ought to help the Government out of its difficulty. But he couldn't surrender the principle, and above all he insisted on Johnson having his increase in recognition of the fact that he would be doing a new and much more responsible job. Harold has put the item down for Cabinet tomorrow so we have rushed through a paper strongly urging the new terms.

Tuesday, 21 November. An early Cabinet to discuss further the 'package' of economies which is to underpin devaluation. I was on tenterhooks because I knew the PM had an official engagement at 11 am. Then, to my horror, Jim did not turn up till 10 pm and the PM refused to take any of the economic items without him. Once again it was ten minutes before the end when my item was reached. Both the Chancellor and the PM said that an increase for the chairman of the BRB at this moment was out of the question, and one by one my allies deserted me again, Peter Shore being particularly vehement that this would be incompatible with the prices and incomes policy. Harold did make an attempt to get an increase for Johnson, but even this was swept aside. I left the room in utter despair. Harold called me back to say cheerfully that there were lots of people who would take the job at £12,500 and he had a particular name in mind. It was true he was at present having his salary made up by private industry but he was sure that that could continue in the new job. I was appalled at the suggestion that we should get private enterprise to subsidize our nationalized industry salaries, but Harold waved my objections aside: 'He is first class! You will like him. Ask Tommy about him.'

Wednesday, 22 November. I dodged the Party meeting on fuel policy to see Mr Wall, Harold's new name for the BRB chairmanship, but as soon as he walked into the room I was sure that he was not my man. I merely said to him that he was one of the names on my list and asked him to go away with my White Papers and think about it, which he agreed to do.

So the misery goes dragging on. It was a relief to get on to the front bench for the winding-up speech in the great economic debate. Harold's speech yesterday had been severely criticized in the press as too knock-about, just as his TV broadcast had been sized as too optimistic. The House was, of course, crowded and Anthony Barber[1] had made a similarly knock-about speech for the Tories amidst many interruptions from our side. It was therefore astonishing to see Jim completely command the House and get a quiet hearing. He spoke without flamboyancy, dealing meticulously with the different points that

[1] Conservative MP for Altrincham from 1965 until 1974, when he was given a life peerage. He was Chancellor of the Exchequer 1970–74.

had been raised, and then allowed himself a high moral tone peroration in which he frankly described devaluation as a defeat for the Government's policy. He clearly had the Tories almost eating out of his hand and our people gave him a great ovation too. But the more sophisticated of us could see his ploy standing out as obvious as the Albert Memorial. Tommy caught up with me after the Vote and hissed at me, 'Did you ever see the knife put more deliberately into a leader's back?' and he almost spat out the word 'Casca'. Jennie Lee said indignantly to me, 'That was a coalition speech.'

Thursday, 23 November. The press has not been slow to point at the contrast between Jim's speech and Harold's broadcast, and the rumours are already circulating about a take-over bid for Harold's job by Jim. This is given weight by an astonishing article in *The Times* business news by Peter Jay, its economic editor, the most distorted account of the past three years I have ever read. Its theme is that Harold was a great opponent of devaluation all along and even suppressed reports by his advisers in order to prevent the Cabinet discussing it. The implication is that poor innocent Jim was dragged along on the chariot wheels of an anti-devaluationist Prime Minister. Well, this does not agree with my memory of the facts. And, of course, Peter Jay is married to Jim's daughter. There is no doubt that Jim sees himself at the very least as the Crown Prince again.

At Cabinet, when we discussed the economic follow-up to devaluation again, Jim was curiously detached. I note that, in his references to the next Budget, he never once used the word 'I'. He obviously does not see himself as Chancellor by next March.

In the afternoon Wedgie and Wilfred Brown[1] called on me to urge co-operation, rather than competition, between the BR workshops and the railway equipment industry, which faces contraction. I told Wedgie we were wasting our time: until I had a chairman, none of this forward planning could be done. But I thanked him for backing me in Cabinet – the only one who did. He said he thought what I was asking for Peter Parker was right. Message from Wall: he doesn't think he is the right man for the job and isn't interested.

Harold has been on *This Week* falling over himself to correct the bad impression he made in the economic debate in the House. He said devaluation had been a 'defeat'. A pity he makes it so obvious that he is reacting to Jim.

Friday, 24 November. My last fling, before going off for the weekend, was to send a desperate Minute to Harold about the chairmanship of BRB. I'll have one last try to make Harold – and the Chancellor – see sense about those salaries.

Monday, 27 November. No reply yet from No. 10 to my Minute, nor from the Chancellor. I got John Gunn to put out feelers as to whether I could see the Chancellor. He reported that he thought something must be moving because the Treasury had headed him off, advising us to leave things alone for a bit as the Chancellor was seeing the PM the next day. It is hard to keep my patience when I know how desperate things are.

[1] Lord Brown, Minister of State at the Board of Trade.

Tuesday, 28 November. A good consultation in the afternoon with the unions on my final proposals on the PTAS, including the formation of the National Bus Company. Jock was there and we talked about the impasse over Peter Parker. The Treasury are still staving off our queries and my Department think this is a hopeful sign. I told Jock I had brought all this on myself by hesitating over Parker in the first place and not backing my hunch – 'The only time in my life I have ever been judicious: never again!' Jock was his usual charming self. It must have been difficult, he said, when even Chris Foster was advising me against. And then it emerged that Chris had twice tried to persuade Jock to recommend him for the chairmanship! If only I had known . . . the idea never entered my head that his advice was influenced in this way.

Wednesday, 29 November. Theoretically a day off, organized lovingly by John Gunn. In fact, of course, I catch up with jobs at the new flat in Islington, urgent Christmas shopping and arrears of work with Elaine, my constituency secretary. As I returned to the House in the afternoon I saw the posters: Jim's swop with Roy.[1] So *this* is why we haven't been able to get a reply from No. 10 and the Treasury to my Minute on Peter Parker. All our hopes that a constructive reconsideration was going on are dashed. Another urgent council of war on the telephone with the office, as a result of which it was agreed I shall hand Roy a personal letter at Cabinet tomorrow.

Thursday, 30 November. At Cabinet this morning Harold was looking very pleased with himself, chatting outside the Cabinet room beforehand with Roy and Jim as though they had all just had a birthday. His buoyancy and optimism are astonishing. I slipped Roy my letter of warm congratulations (genuine) followed by a plea for him to give my BRB problem 'highest priority'. He promised to get down to it as soon as possible, adding, 'What does Harold think of it?' I told him I was going to try and see Harold later that day.

A long discussion about what to do about the Common Market. For conflicting reasons we agreed to adopt George's proposed line: that we shouldn't treat de Gaulle and his rejection, announced two days ago, as though he were the Six by withdrawing our application, but let it go forward to the Council of Ministers meeting on 19 December and force a showdown.

My WP on public transport (grants and all) went through without a hitch, despite rumours that the Treasury were going to try and cut the grants.[2]

Back in the House I was determined to force a meeting with Harold. No. 10 was being difficult, and so I just marched down to his room. I realize I tend to be too tender with him and that he must be bullied into doing something – as Dick bullies him. It worked! Though he walked up and down wriggling out of my

[1] Roy Jenkins had become Chancellor of the Exchequer and Jim Callaghan had taken his place at the Home Office.

[2] The White Paper, 'Public Transport and Traffic' (Cmnd 3481), set out in detail the composition, functions and powers of the PTAS for conurbations outside London and announced a succession of grants to help public transport: not only capital grants for infrastructure, but also for the purchase of new buses, for the maintenance of rural bus services and towards the cost of subsidizing suburban railway lines which would become the financial responsibility of the PTAS. It also announced that the National Bus Company was to be set up to take over the bus interests of the THC.

arguments – 'Cabinet would never agree,' 'I think it is intolerable for Peter Parker to put you on this spot,' 'He's not the only one with principles,' etc. – I stood firm. In the end he said, 'If you can get Roy to agree, I'll back you in Cabinet. But it is asking a lot to expect him to reverse Jim's line in his first few days.' Maybe – but I'll try. I ask the office to fix up a meeting for me with Roy as soon as possible.

Monday, 4 December. At last I have got my meeting with the new Chancellor about Parker's salary. In his room at the Treasury Roy was already taking on a patina of Treasury toughness. He told me frankly that he didn't think he could go higher than £12,500, and said that anyway some people didn't think much of Peter Parker. I got angry at this. I knew the smears that were going round. One of them had been that Parker was 'available'. Well, he wasn't available on the wrong terms and I admired him for sticking to his principles. I didn't try any high-falutin' oratory, just told Roy I couldn't be held responsible for the tough remit Cabinet had given me to get rid of railway deficit financing if I wasn't given the tools to do the job. We argued for half an hour and then Roy asked me if I minded if he saw Peter Parker. I said I would welcome it – but would he please do it *soon*.

Tuesday, 5 December. White Paper day. I spent the morning interviewing key correspondents individually. Only Michael Bailey of *The Times* was sour. He agreed with a lot of what was in the paper, but that was what he had been asking for for some time, 'so I'm afraid we just take that for granted and concentrate on the criticisms.' I told him that that sort of attitude devitalized political life and sent him away feeling a bit ashamed. Anyway I've got my Transport Bill through the Legislation Committee of Cabinet this morning – all 169 clauses of it. It's the longest Bill since the war.

Thursday, 7 December. No Cabinet for a change. Ted and I lunched with Frank Giles of the *Sunday Times*, and Harold Evans, the editor, who are interested in publishing my memoirs. I referred them to my literary agent, Jean Leroy. Back to the House and found waiting for me the message from the Chancellor: 'He sees no reason to change his mind about Mr Parker's salary.' He is reported as not being impressed with Mr Parker. Right, I said to my chaps, no more delay: it's Johnson.

We sent for Johnson as quickly as possible and he arrived at 4.30 pm. I told him frankly that, as he knew, I would have preferred Peter Parker but that I had always had him in mind as a second choice and some people had always thought he ought to be my first choice. I had never offered the job to anyone else but Peter Parker and now I was offering it to him. He didn't beat about the bush, honest man that he is: said he would have worked loyally with Peter Parker, whom he liked very much, but was honoured to accept the job which he had always wanted. Then I phoned Parker. He was clearly shaken, but thanked me for what I had tried to do. He then gave congratulations and good wishes to Johnson on the phone.

So ends the famous Parker case. I will use him somewhere else if I get the chance, though I think BR was the ideal job for him. Oh, Barbara, you ought to be ashamed of yourself.

Sunday, 10 December. The papers are full of the story that the Government is about to change its policy on arms for South Africa. This obviously arises from George's replies to the AAM [Anti-Apartheid Movement] deputation last Thursday.

Tuesday, 12 December. A most disappointing day in Paris at the ECMT: no progress. I made a number of speeches, including two passionate ones on the need to ratify the European convention on drivers' hours immediately and the need to press ahead urgently with creating uniformity in our vehicle safety regulations. The effects were very discouraging.

On my return home I found the arms for South Africa issue had blown up to enormous heights. Apparently Jim dined at the House last night privately with the Under 40 group of Labour MPs and let his hair down about what he thought we needed to do to put the economy right. An interesting list: 1) drop the Industrial Expansion Bill (it is only a 'sop to the Left'); 2) freeze wages for eighteen months; and 3) reconsider our policy on arms for South Africa. All those present, whether from Left or Right, streamed out in consternation and went straight to see John Silkin to say they wanted to table a Motion. Since this merely endorsed the Government's present policy of an arms embargo, John gave it the OK. Seventy names were down in no time. We really *shall* have a row about this in Cabinet. If Harold has sold out on this, my resignation is only a matter of days.

Wednesday, 13 December. In the middle of the afternoon I received an urgent message to go and see the PM. Wondering whatever could be in the air, I arrived at his room at the House. 'Ah, little Barbara,' said Harold genially. When I walked into his room he was pacing about like an animal. 'What I want to talk to you about has nothing to do with official business. I know you never leak but perhaps you can be persuaded to in a good cause. Barbara, I'm in a real spot over South Africa. You know how I feel about this arms thing – and how I'm pledged up to the hilt. At OPD last Friday George and Denis fought for lifting the embargo and they got a hell of a lot of support. If I had put it to the vote I should have been defeated. So we agreed it should go to Cabinet, but not until a month's time. But the Party is in a terrific state and I intend to force a decision tomorrow. They are not going to trap me on this, which is what they are trying to do. George is in Brussels, but I've sent for him to come back. Let the Party be mobilized. And I wouldn't mind getting a letter from junior Ministers saying they won't stand for a change of policy. But remember, none of this must be traced back to me.'

I agreed to get Reg Freeson[1] to organize the letter. Also to get Michael Foot to try and table a PNQ.

[1] MP for Willesden East and PPS to Richard Marsh, Minister of Power.

Thursday, 14 December. Cabinet was postponed till 11 am so it was clear that George was trying to get back. But when we assembled Harold said with impeccable correctitude that of course we couldn't discuss South Africa in the absence of the Foreign Secretary, and unfortunately he was fog-bound in Brussels.

Friday, 15 December. George is back. As we streamed into the Cabinet room I heard him say to Denis Healey, 'It's getting worse and worse.' It was soon clear that he was determined to pick a fight. The knives were really out and the atmosphere was nastier than I have ever known in Cabinet. Undeterred for once, Harold weighed in equally grimly. He too had been suffering – and not just in the last few days but for weeks – from something that amounted nearly to character assassination. He wasn't going to take any more of it.

From our end of the table we threw in barb after barb, Wedgie saying icily that he had been acutely embarrassed at a meeting of the Science and Technology group, the day after Jim's remarks, by having quoted against him the fact that the Home Secretary thought the Industrial Expansion Bill was just a 'sop to the Left'. By this time Jim was abashed and George chipped in to point out that time was passing and could he move next business? We had beaten off the first attack and they were in disarray.

Harold summed up by first expressing his own point of view: he was against changing our policy. He then said he thought the feeling was eleven to seven against change, but George said tartly, 'Some of us can count and we don't make it out that way.' Suddenly Harold switched. The proposition that we should solve our problems by selling arms all over the world wasn't on. But we could say there was going to be a comprehensive economic statement in the New Year. In the meantime the policy remained unchanged. Our group was furious and went out utterly disconsolate. My only hope is that Harold intends to use the breathing space to do some more mobilizing. And it is true that there wasn't a majority in Cabinet for making no change.

Saturday, 16 December and Sunday, 17 December. Harold has circulated a Top Secret, heavily sealed document about the economic situation. Devaluation has failed to work and the situation is 'menacing'. Emergency measures will have to be taken immediately after the recess. Meanwhile he is just putting us in the picture. Certainly his optimistic talk of a 'breakthrough' has proved wrong. I wonder why exports are falling off so disappointingly? And our old friend, lack of 'confidence', is back again.

The weekend papers have been full of the most astonishing anti-Harold campaign I have ever read. And as the reports are almost identical it is obvious that they are based on an organized leak. Their tenor is that Harold, who was supposed to be as keen on selling arms to South Africa as anyone else, had seized the opportunity of the Party's outcry against it to stab George in the back and actually to get the Whips mobilizing support for Motions. On Saturday morning there was a call for me from Chequers. It was Harold, thoroughly chirpy. 'It is all going very well. This time George has over-reached himself. I am just ringing to say: no counter-briefing. George and his friends must have no alibi.'

Monday, 18 December. To my delight we were all suddenly summoned to an unexpected Cabinet meeting at 11 am – only item: arms for South Africa. So Harold is going to fight! As we waited outside the Cabinet room Gerald took the lead in saying to everyone that the scandalous stories in the press made it inevitable that we should reach a decision immediately. Otherwise Harold's position would be intolerable. At the meeting Harold lost no time in coming to the point – and I have never seen him so grim and white, whether from fear or deliberate anger it was difficult to tell. For twenty minutes he dilated on the press stories: their uniformity, their unscrupulous bias against himself. This was character assassination of the most overt kind designed to make his position in the House impossible and clearly coming from within Cabinet. But he must point out that it was not just his position that was at stake, but the position of the Government. He had a right to demand that Cabinet issue a statement repudiating the reports, if it agreed with him that they were grossly untrue. While George and Denis sat utterly silent, one person after another said that the only issue now was the position of the Prime Minister. The credibility of the Government depended on his credibility and Cabinet must be ready to restore it. And so it was agreed. The statement that afternoon should include a categoric decision: no arms for South Africa. So George has completely over-reached himself and has been defeated on every front. I suppose he must have been drunk when he did that systematic and grotesque briefing of the press.

Tuesday, 19 December. Press conference and TV on the road accident figures for October.[1] The figures are a triumph for the breathalyser.

Wednesday, 20 December. Over to the House with my speech on the Transport Bill still to read and shorten. It went quite well and it is clearer than ever that the Tories would have no real grounds on which to attack the Bill if it were not for the wear and tear tax which was forced on me in the last PESC exercise. Stephen Swingler did a first-class job winding-up – the best I have ever heard him.[2]

[1] Total road casualties in England and Wales in October 1967 were 12 per cent down on the figure for October 1966.

[2] The Bill embodied the new policies I had described in my White Papers and legislated for a revolutionary overhaul of carriers' licensing. First, it liberalized where control had become meaningless, freeing 900,000 vehicles under 30 cwt from licensing, their roadworthiness being enforced by other means. All other road haulage vehicles (about 600,000) had to have an operator's licence or 'quality' licence, which brought them under tough controls as to maintenance, drivers' permitted hours and other road safety measures, the aim being to stop operators scratching a living by buying a lorry or two without the resources to maintain them properly. And every firm had to have a transport manager responsible in law for the state of the firm's lorries, instead of the driver being left to take the rap if the vehicle was found unroadworthy. The second form of control proposed was

Sunday, 31 December. Christmas over. The party [at HCF] was a great success. Boxing night dinner over, I crawled to bed and barely lifted my head off the pillow for four days. The pain in my lower ribs when I coughed was agonizing. My doctor said she thought I might have fractured a rib coughing and that I ought to have it x-rayed.

During all this I kept getting requests to appear on TV about the marvellous reduction in the Christmas accident figures.[1] All I could do was to groan at the very idea and turn over in bed!

quantity licensing to apply to all vehicles of over 5 tons unladen weight (about 100,000), travelling over 100 miles or carrying certain bulk materials in order to ensure that where rail offered an equivalent service in terms of speed reliability and cost, the goods would go by rail. This, we estimated, would help British Railways to divert to them some 4,500 million ton-miles a year of road traffic in a few years' time, but as I did not intend to introduce this licensing until the freightliner service had developed more comprehensively, the Bill provided a separate appointed day for this group of clauses. In the event my successor, Dick Marsh, never brought them into operation because he did not approve of them, so the experiment in shifting goods from road to rail was never made.

The Bill also reduced the maximum length of the working day for drivers of buses, coaches and goods vehicles from fourteen hours to eleven hours, with exceptions up to a higher figure where specified rest periods were provided, and laid down that drivers might not spend more than ten hours at the wheel in any day instead of the eleven hours then obtaining. My plans for reorganizing London Transport and transferring responsibility for most of its services to the GLC were enacted in the later Transport (London) Bill, after I had left the Ministry, which received the royal assent on 25 July 1969.

[1] In the five-day Christmas holiday period road deaths were down from 158 in 1966 to 98, serious injuries from 1,507 to 1,013 and slight injuries from 4,285 to 2,918.

1968

Monday, 1 January. Crawled back to work feeling faint with the sharp pain in my chest and generally sorry for myself. The office had fixed up an appointment with the radiologist at Guy's.

Tuesday, 2 January. My GP, Dr Wigg, breezed in, having seen the x-rays to tell me I had had a pneumonia which hadn't completely dispersed yet. If I were anyone but myself he would have ordered another fortnight's rest but, knowing I wouldn't relax while Cabinet carved up my motorways, he would make a dispensation for that. But he wanted me to see the chest specialist at Guy's. In the meantime he got on to John Gunn and between them they cancelled all my appointments for the next ten days, except for Cabinets.

Wednesday, 3 January. Spent the day in bed and then went out – most reluctantly – into a raw night to dine at Dick's with Wedgie, Tommy Balogh and Peter Shore. But it was worth it. I wanted to know what the special group of Ministers, hand-picked by Harold to supervise this latest exercise in slashing, had been up to, and Dick said, 'Nothing. There are ten of us – far too many – and the result is that we take no decisions at all.'

We had been warned that nine papers were on their way to us for tomorrow's Cabinet, but none had arrived yet. 'You wouldn't have had any, if I hadn't insisted,' said Dick. 'They were going to circulate them tomorrow.' The Group of Ten Ministers were meeting in the morning to consider them before the afternoon Cabinet. The big thing, said Dick, was to insist on getting the defence cuts agreed before we would discuss any social cuts at all. 'Roy is counting on us to be tough on this.' 'And we must know what is to be done about taxation,' Tommy urged.

On details we had quite a ferocious argument. Dick was at his most truculent and offensive, but we hit back and had, by common agreement, one of the most successful discussion evenings we had ever had. It was 11.30 pm before I dragged myself home.

Thursday, 4 January. Spent the morning with the chest specialist at Guy's. He gave me a very thorough examination: result, no heart damage, no signs of lung cancer, a fractured rib – due to coughing – but, what worried them most, a shadow on the top right lung which must be cleared up before I went back to work. I'm to do nothing but Cabinets till Monday 15 January and then have another x-ray. Well, Cabinets look like taking a lot of time!

I raced through my nine Cabinet papers as best I could. The key one, of course, was Roy's summary of demands. It was prefaced by a Top Secret document explaining why we must reduce demand by £1,000m and how important it was to err on the side of toughness. In addition to the items in the package we must look further afield for other economies and be ready to re-examine any programme, *e.g.* Concorde. But it was followed by the toughest document on defence cuts I have read in the life of these two Governments of ours and, as I read it, I was ready to forgive anything. This boy means business on defence at last. He makes Jim's recurring bleats about the need to cut defence expenditure look utterly ineffectual. There it was all spelt out: paragraph 2: 'Our standing in the world depends on the soundness of our economy and not on a worldwide military presence. . . . I have therefore proposed . . . that drastic changes should be made in defence policy.'

When Cabinet at last met at 3 pm Roy was true to his own document. He began by pointing out that we had borrowed £2,000m over the last few years and that, if we were to have any status as a Government, we must begin to pay it back. In the current year we would run a deficit still of £300m which must be changed into a surplus of £500m in 1968–69. But we must also secure an increase in fixed investment of at least £200m. He couldn't put all this on taxation. He was therefore proposing as a minimum cuts in civil expenditure of £325m in 1968–69 (when defence cuts could not help) and £370m in 1969–70. But he made it absolutely clear that the fact that defence cuts had been made earlier did not mean that at this moment defence cuts should be somehow exempt – defence and civil cuts must be on a parity. The Foreign and Commonwealth Secretaries had put in a paper accepting reluctantly that some acceleration of withdrawal was necessary but insisting, with various dire warnings, that 'the earliest date for the completion of the rundown' in the Far East and the Persian Gulf 'would be 31 March 1972'. But Roy would have none of this. The decisive difference between 1970–71 and 1972, from a credibility point of view, was that the former was 'this side of the hill' in terms of the life-time of this Government.

And so the long rearguard action against the cuts began. It was a near thing. In fact I think we only carried the day with Harold's casting voice.

However, he was able to sum up without challenge that Cabinet was in favour of withdrawal from the Far East by March 1971, and that we should withdraw from the Persian Gulf at the same time.

And so to the F-111. Healey argued passionately that this was the last thing we should cancel if we paid due regard to defence needs. We had decided to keep this capability in the past, even after the decision to withdraw from the Far East. And the reason was that we needed it in the European theatre if we were not to have to rely on an instant nuclear response to attack.

For two hours the argument raged and Healey had some powerful allies. 'My God,' I thought, 'it is going to be close.' But Harold, who had backed Roy, summed up that by a majority – 'bigger than on the last issue' – Cabinet had agreed to cancel. Denis then desperately demanded the right to put before us alternative savings to secure the same result. Patient to the end, Harold agreed he could put in a paper outlining alternative economies. We dragged ourselves out at 7.30 pm: four and a half hours!

Friday, 5 January. The second round of our marathon started at 2 pm – the idea being that afternoon meetings give us more time to spread ourselves. I don't know what my doctors will say!

The first item was education, where Roy is demanding a three-year delay in raising the school leaving age. Longford hinted that he might have to 'consider his position' if this went through.[1] [But] it was carried by eleven voices to ten. We don't vote in Cabinet, of course, but Harold collects the voices carefully on issues that divide us as acutely as this.

And so to prescription charges. Peter jumped in with a compromise which, I suspect, he has cooked up with Harold. He accepted the point that those at work should pay for their medicine, but the chronic sick, expectant mothers, the retired and children should not. The loss of revenue on these far-reaching exemptions – which must go much further than the Tories' former ones – should be offset by a 6*d* increase in the National Insurance stamp. Eventually [Harold] summed up by saying that there should be a further study of the proposed compromise.

By this time it was the turn of roads and I was all keyed up to do battle when George, who had slipped out to attend an official function, returned very much the worse for wear. He said truculently that, as he wouldn't be with us next week, he would like Concorde to be discussed while he was here. So Concorde it was and George reported that the Ministers who had been discussing it were evenly divided. The Attorney-General had advised that there were no legal grounds for cancellation and that the £200m we should save if we did cancel would probably all be swallowed up by damages. So it was agreed that the best we could do was to try and prepare for the position where we could break, without damages, in 1969 by negotiating new conditions with the French – *i.e.* if by the summer of 1969 we had not got a minimum number of firm orders for the aircraft.

By now it was 7 pm and Harold suggested we should break up as good decisions were not made by tired Ministers. 'After the traumatic experience some Ministers have been through, they would have slaughtered you,' he reassured me afterwards. Maybe, but my whole instinct was to take roads then. Damn George and his temperament.

Tuesday, 9 January. When I walked into the Cabinet room I was dismayed to see Michael Stewart in the chair. Harold would be another three-quarters of an hour, he explained. I tried to get roads postponed, but in vain – and so I hadn't a chance. I made what some told me was a powerful case in favour of cutting back effectively. But no one would listen. Roy just said that my roads must make a contribution – £15m next year and £25m the year after. And everyone agreed. Without Harold there to make those mollifying modifications at which he excels I was led like a lamb to the slaughter. 'Right, I'll see that every one of these cuts falls on your development areas,' I hissed angrily at Peter Shore.

Thursday, 11 January. At last we caught up on some of our routine business in Cabinet. On the Race Relations Bill Roy once again won my respect. Without striking any philosophical attitudes, he is so much clearer-headed and naturally progressive – and more courageous – than Jim. Then back to the agony of the

[1] The raising of the school leaving age having been postponed, Lord Longford resigned and Eddie Shackleton became Lord Privy Seal and Leader of the Lords in his place.

PESC package. We really are devils for punishment! I thought to myself as we sat there hour after hour, exhaustively examining the implications of every cut, with a very high level of debate and conscientiousness, that we only really function as a Cabinet when we have failed and further retrenchment is necessary. If we only spent a quarter of this energy and time and cohesiveness in working out a strategy for success we should be in a very different position now. And, as Dick says, Harold must carry a lot of the responsibility for this.

A curious thing happened during Cabinet. Jim passed me the following note: 'Barbara – When you come back, would you like to have a general talk? I would – becos. I feel we have drifted further apart than usual. I have nothing to sell you – (or to buy!) – & I have more free time now than I ever had in the last 3 years! Come & see me in my splendiferous room in the Home Office!! Jim.' Then I happened to see on top of Peter's papers another note Jim had sent to him, all unctuous with praise of the line Peter had taken over prescription charges: 'Seldom have I heard an Economics Minister argue a social case more powerfully.' So poor old Jim is feeling insecure and is looking for friends. I told him I'd be glad to come and talk as soon as I was in full operation again.

Friday, 12 January. Into the fifth Cabinet meeting on the cuts at 11 am, and another to follow this afternoon! Although George is back, Harold said we would give him till the afternoon to recover from his flight, so we dealt with more details of the package till 12.15.

At 2.30 pm we resumed our meeting for the traumatic discussion on withdrawal from the Far East and Middle East. George wasn't there and Harold, punctilious and accommodating to a fault, said we must wait for him. He came in at 2.45 pm apologizing for keeping us. 'I made the mistake of trying to catch up on some sleep and colleagues will understand that I now feel much worse.' Nonetheless he proceeded vigorously, if rather thickly, to report on his talk with Dean Rusk. It was a masterly piece of dramatic rendering and we listened in silence as he thundered on for half an hour, merely raising an eyebrow at his more purple passages.

'I prefaced my telegram home', said George heavily, 'with some carefully picked words: "I had a bloody unpleasant meeting in Washington this morning with Rusk." No other words would describe the interview. And I must tell my colleagues that our relations with the US are now critical. Indeed, I would say this to the Chancellor: his proposals have probably already done so much harm that it is too late to retrieve it. Rusk is a soft-spoken man and was completely courteous but he told me not to measure his reaction by his decibels. He said in words that our decision meant that Britain was "opting out". It was the "end of an era". Rusk in particular complained of what he called "the acrid aroma of a *fait accompli*". I believe there is now a real danger of isolationism in the US with consequences which will be visited on our children and grandchildren. I can assure my colleagues that I put the case Cabinet told me to with all my force.' ('No one ever suggested the opposite,' soothed Harold.) 'But,' added George bitterly, 'I fought the wrong battle and I went back to our Embassy thoroughly sick with myself. There were two biting points with them,' he continued. 'The first was that they want to get some leeway on time; the second that they want us to keep the bird.' 'The what?' we chorused. 'The bird – the

F-111,' George banged back. 'And despite what I said earlier I am convinced that the only way we shall mitigate any of the consequences of our decision is to meet them on these two points. Their view was put to me most succinctly by Levy' (apparently a high official in the State Department) 'who said to me: "You're not going to be in the Far East. You're not going to be in the Middle East. You're not even going to be in Europe in strength. Where are you going to be?" There really isn't any answer to that. We've not gone pacifist: we've gone straight neutralist.'

After he had exhausted himself emotionally, he got down to more constructive details. The Americans, he said, attached more importance to our decision about the Middle East than the Far East. He thought they felt they could take care of the latter. 'They think they are on a winner in Vietnam and that the PM's visit to Moscow will bring them the outcome they are waiting for.' Harold raised a pleased eyebrow at this. I raised two. 'They really believe the Russians are waiting to move into the Middle East if we leave a vacuum and I would beg my colleagues to take this danger seriously. Above all they don't want us to announce the date of our withdrawal from the Gulf.' At last he had finished, and Jim jumped in to say that he had been very disturbed by what George had said. If it were true that the Americans were writing us off, he must warn the Chancellor of the financial and commercial consequences. America had been a very good friend of ours. If we lost her support and couldn't get into Europe, we should be without a friend in the world.

Heading off the claque, Harold promptly called on the Chancellor. Once again I had to admire Roy's courteous but steely inflexibility. Arguing quietly but firmly, he pitted intellectual reasoning against emotion. 'The Home Secretary and I have a fundamentally different approach. He wants us to continue as we have done for the past three years. I don't believe we can afford to do so.' The American reaction was predictable, but the hard truth was that the time had come for a fundamental reappraisal of our influence in the world. We could only regain it by regaining our economic strength. The important thing was to demonstrate that we had really changed course. Our determination to do so would be more likely to win back confidence – and the respect of America – than any 'muddled middle course'.

Harold then said it was time to turn to hardware, leaving the final decision on dates. But our misery was not over: we had to listen to a long, turgid presentation by Denis again of the reasons why we should not cancel F-111. After prolonged discussion, John Silkin passed me his tally of the voices: for the F-111, Healey, Brown, Stewart, Longford, Callaghan, Gunter, Marsh and Ross; against, Jenkins, Harold, Gardiner, Shore, Crossman, Crosland, Castle, Hughes, Greenwood, Benn, Peart and Gordon Walker. And so it proved to be. There was a dramatic silence at Harold's summing-up. Then Denis and George said heavily that they would have to consider their position, to which Harold replied cheerfully, in almost these words, 'That's all right. A number of Ministers feel they have to consider their position in the light of certain elements in the package. It is up to each individual Minister to decide.'

And so we trailed out, having made history. I can't believe it has happened – and I don't think either Denis or George will resign. And I think now we have got a package which will do a lot to hold the Party together.

Monday, 15 January. The last leg of our marathon. On the whole I feel much happier than I ever thought I would be. Roy has shown many of the right instincts and we are certainly a long way from the crude sell-out of 1931. The package is a sophisticated combination of principle and expediency and that is what politics is about.

In the lunch hour I fitted in a hurried visit to Guy's. My chest is clear but the specialist earnestly begged me to take a week's rest. And I must say I feel absolutely washed out. John Silkin, with his usual humanity, said to me, 'Your health comes first. Only you must put out an announcement tonight.' Actually he is not worried about Thursday's vote in the House on the package. 'I've spent £50 on lunches in the last few days and it's going to be all right.' He really is a wonderful chap. So I'm off to the country for a few days to get fighting fit. Actually, I don't mind missing the parliamentary debate. From Left to Right the reactions are predictable. Some people will go through the motions of outrage, but I don't believe this feeling will go deep. And I can watch it all on TV.

Tuesday, 16 January. As I thought, the reactions are pretty mild. No one can say we've sold out after those defence cuts.

Despite the Left's victories on defence and foreign policy reflected in the package there were growing signs of revolt on the social policy cuts, notably the reimposition of prescription charges, and on 16 January John Silkin as Chief Whip sent a letter to all Labour MPs informing them that the coming vote on the package would be a Vote of Confidence. This did not bring the critics to heel and in the vote on 18 January twenty-six Labour MPs, including Michael Foot, abstained on the Government Motion approving the package; among them also were two right-wing MPs who abstained in protest at what they considered was the lax discipline in the Party. The reaction of John Silkin took everyone by surprise. Without consulting anyone he sent a letter to all the abstainers informing them that they had 'endangered the existence' of the Government and that they would be suspended from all Party activities, including attendance at Party meetings. This unilateral and uncharacteristic action infuriated the Liaison Committee between back benchers and Government, particularly the chairman of the PLP, Douglas Houghton, and Harold Wilson hurried to mend the breach. He announced that he would address the party meeting on his return from Moscow and circulated a proposed Code of Conduct for it to discuss. In the event the meeting, held on 31 January, was something of an anti-climax. A Motion to suspend the MPs concerned was carried by 123 to 66, but the suspension only lasted until 28 February, when the Code of Conduct was agreed. This recognized Members' right to abstain on matters of 'deeply held personal conviction', but not on a Vote of Confidence in a Labour Government. If the Code was defied the Party meeting could be asked to suspend the Member or withdraw the Whip. The incident blew over, but the relations between John Silkin and his two main allies, the Prime Minister and the Leader of the House, had been seriously damaged.

On Vietnam Harold Wilson tried another of his initiatives. His visit to Moscow on 22 January was in pursuit of his self-appointed role as intermediary, but his long talks with Kosygin on Vietnam did not produce any positive results. He was also pressing ahead indefatigably with his attempt to get Britain into the European Community. At its December meeting the Council of Ministers had tamely accepted de Gaulle's veto, but various proposals had been put forward by the other member states for interim links between the Community and the four applicants: Britain, Ireland, Denmark and Norway.

One such set of proposals, made by the Benelux Foreign Ministers, was discussed in Brussels on 24 January and once again the five were sympathetic while André Bettencourt of France reserved his country's position. In the meantime my massive Transport Bill had gone into the committee. Peter Walker for the Opposition had declared all-out war on it and the committee stage was to drag on for months.

Friday, 19 January. Harold has had the most appalling press, both after his speech on Wednesday (described as 'lacklustre') and in the weeklies. It is now openly hinted that he may be on his way out – and not only because of Reggie Paget's demand that he should resign. What has brought this dramatic change in less than two years? Well, in the first place it is true that the conditions of the 1964–66 Parliament were ideally suited to Harold's temperament. They called for brilliant tactical skill, which Harold showed, and there was not enough margin of majority or time for a more profound strategy to evolve. After the 1966 Election different qualities were called for and Harold hasn't shown them yet. But he can't be saddled with all the blame. Jim threw himself with relish into his puritanical denunciations of running into debt. He adored pontificating about how we must 'pay our way'. And I used to wonder why we had changed our line so completely over the need for expansion first: hadn't we attacked the Tories for not taking a few risks to secure it? And we should have been willing to devalue from the start. I think Harold opposed it then because he was flattered by Johnson's exuberant welcome of a Labour Government. But he was more than underpinned by Jim – he was egged on. I won't stand by and see Harold alone penalized for it.

Wednesday, 24 January. John Silkin arrived at the NEC looking his usual cheerful self. But on the way out he admitted to me he had been having a hell of a time. 'Tell me the saga of The Letter,' I asked him. 'I thought it up over Christmas,' he told me. 'It was the only way to head off the demand for expulsions. And it succeeded. But the Liaison Committee was nasty – very nasty indeed. And not only Willie Hamilton.[1] Douglas Houghton is playing a double game. He is hand in glove with Jim to get rid of me.' 'What part did Harold play?' 'He was afraid that the plot to get me out would succeed.' 'It won't,' I assured him. 'I'll see to that.'

Thursday, 25 January. Stephen and I were due to see Dick and John Silkin in Dick's room at 7.30 pm to discuss tactics for the Transport Bill. No John. Message, he was so sorry he couldn't make it. And Dick was entertaining political columnists.

We talked for half an hour over large gins till I lost patience and told Dick irritably that I really had something important to talk to him about. As we walked along the corridor to the dining-room we ran into John matily strolling with Harold, with whom he had been dining. 'I'll join you for a drink,' he called. I felt nauseated. We spend three-quarters of our time in these personal pro and anti intrigues instead of getting down to real jobs. Dick was feeling grim, too. He told me neither he nor Harold knew that John was going to send the letter. You couldn't pin him down on anything. And you couldn't trust what he told you. So relations between Dick and John are clearly getting pretty

[1] Labour MP for West Fife since 1950 and a thorn in the flesh of all Governments.

strained. And I was immensely irritated about the impossibility of getting either of them to give serious attention to a routine bit of work like presenting the right public image over the handling of my Bill which is, after all, the major Bill of the session. And Dick may be brilliant but he is maddeningly erratic. After an exhausting hour we finally agreed that we should work for a guillotine on Monday week by having an all-nighter on Wednesday night to show how impossible life would be without one. This is something Stephen and I could have worked out perfectly well for ourselves.

Tuesday, 30 January. We continue to make astonishing progress in the Transport Bill Committee, all things considered. I cannot make out what Peter Walker's tactic is. We calculate that at this rate we shall be on schedule under the allocation I would have proposed if we had got a voluntary agreement. I can only play this by ear and I promised to tell Dick after the Wednesday evening session whether or not we need next week's guillotine.

In the afternoon I had my long-planned meeting with the railway unions on the Transport Bill. All that has come out of my original proposal to meet the representatives of the rank and file of the three unions – which would have meant something almost as big as a Central Hall meeting – is a meeting of the three union executives. When it came to it the union leaders objected to my appealing to the rank and file over their heads and said it was their job to pass the message down the line. The atmosphere was friendly but I thought it was ominous that the Communist hard core of the NUR Executive established itself on the back two rows and refused to come further forward.

Wednesday, 31 January. On target again on the Transport Bill Committee. I remain puzzled. Certainly the guillotine cannot be justified next week, but when I got on to Dick to tell him this I found that in his usual way he has taken the matter into his own hands and has put in some other business for next Monday anyhow. I do think he might at least have had the courtesy to consult me before he did it. But not our Dick. On the practical details of his work as Leader of the House he is pretty nearly a disaster. But of course he is saved time and again by the breadth of his ideas and by the rather blundering way he has pressed ahead with parliamentary reform. But I must say that it was more than I could stomach when he said that he and John Silkin had been discussing the Bill with the Tory Chief Whip, Willie Whitelaw, and that they were prepared to consider a voluntary agreement if I would drop part of the Bill. Dick passed this on to me as a serious suggestion and asked me to consider whether there was anything I could drop. I certainly have no intention of dropping anything.

Thursday, 1 February. George is still beavering away to get us into Europe and won't recognize any obstacles. He was full of the success of the Benelux meeting and assured me that the Commission was not hostile to the idea of this collaboration with members of the Six as I had suggested they would be. The French had not damned the idea but it is clear that the only co-operation likely to be achieved is in the technological field. And I repeated Wedgie's warning of last week that we don't want to go too far in this while getting nothing in return. George reported that the developments in Vietnam were much less encouraging. It was difficult to assess what the North Korean putsch meant – whether it was a serious military ploy or merely a softening-up as a prelude to negotiations. One of the real worries was what effect it might have on the American attitude to escalation and he didn't like the wording in a recent telegram to the effect that 'minds are being cleared in Washington' in preparation for the PM's visit. Well, of course, if there is escalation Harold will have to be true to his pledges or I shall walk out of the Government.

I had got up early to read up more carefully than usual the papers on Lords reform.[1] I am all the more suspicious about the proposals because Dick is now so sold on them. I know he has a fatal habit of getting carried away by short-term enthusiasms for a piece of work on which he is engaged and tends to lose sight of the rabbit. However, Gerald Gardiner urged the proposals on us very strongly, while Dick insisted that the negotiated scheme was actually a better one than we had originally proposed. Most of them were for going ahead, even Wedgie, who argued it was a gain on balance though not the end of the story. What we ought to do was to tackle the Honours system itself and to create Lords of Parliament who would be plain Mr and Mrs So-and-So. I cannot see Harold ever getting round to that!

Monday, 5 February. New developments about my wear and tear charges in the Transport Bill. It was always an administrative nonsense for me to create new machinery for levying these charges and anyway they were never part of my Transport policy, but I had to accept them in order to try and save my roads programme. And having done so I have incurred enormous odium with the road haulage industry (every time attacks are made on my 'monster bill' they always boil down to this one item), and at the same time I have had the cuts in the last economy round anyway. Such are the unfairnesses of politics. And now the Chancellor has got new ideas about the whole business. He wants to include the wear and tear charge in his Budget as part of a general increase in the vehicle licences. This development suits me all right except that it is closing the stable door when the horse has bolted and wreaked havoc everywhere. And of course I have got to keep completely mum about it and pretend this section will be in the Bill as planned. When eventually this charge comes out of the Bill we shall be able to romp home well within my proposed timetable and I can hardly wait to see Peter Walker's face!

Having been a bit worried by J. D. Jones's manner, which was a little *distrait* at our last meeting, I suddenly decided to have a private word with him. I have to keep reminding myself how important it is to civil servants, particularly when they are jostling their way to the very top, to feel they have personal access to the Minister. I tend to be so absorbed in my work that I don't think about these things, and if I do I consider them too trivial to bother about. But

[1] Since November 1967, a conference of representatives of the three main parties had been meeting to try to reach all-party agreement on a reduction in the delaying powers of the Lords in return for a reform of its composition and therefore an inevitable increase in its influence. The main proposal was for a two-tier House consisting of 'voting members' (*i.e.* life peers who were prepared to accept the responsibilities of regular attendance) and 'non-voting members' who could only take part in debates. Membership for the future would be by creation alone and a hereditary peerage would no longer carry the right to a seat in the House. The problem was how to give the Government of the day a working majority without undermining their Lordships' independence and it was proposed to do this by creating sufficient 'cross-bench' peers to hold a balance between the parties so that the Government had to win a majority among them to get its legislation through.

men are such touchy people and personalize things so much more than women do. This time I made a special effort to fit in ten minutes with J.D. privately and even then I had firmly to tell my Private Secretary I didn't need his presence nor that of anyone else. I told J.D. that I had been a little worried by his loss of his usual ebullience and wondered whether something had gone wrong with his wife, who has just been recovering from a serious operation. His face positively lit up with gratitude that I had bothered to inquire. He assured me nothing was wrong either with him or his wife or with relations inside the Department – a noble piece of self-restraint because I know Chris Foster nearly drives him up the wall. He in turn inquired anxiously about my health: said they had all been very worried about the way I had overworked before Christmas and added that there was one thing about me they all admired – I always kept my temper even when understandably on edge with overwork. 'And, he added, 'there are a lot of Ministers about whom one couldn't say that.' I think I will have this testimonial framed in letters of gold and hang it in Ted's room!

Tuesday, 6 February. At last I managed to get my resumed discussion with Peter Walker on a voluntary timetable. Things are really going swimmingly in Standing Committee and the much vaunted Tory uncompromising attack is turning out to be pretty hollow. True, they make malicious attacks wherever possible and endlessly keep repeating the prepared Tory scares about the Bill, regardless of the evidence one advances to explode them. But it is all pretty superficial and we are still well inside my own private timetable. However, I told Peter Walker that in the interests of the later stages of the Bill, on which I knew he would wish to make a very vigorous attack, we should conclude a voluntary agreement which would enable us to fix well ahead to our mutual convenience the time of the Wednesday sittings. He sat there nodding his head, perfectly amiable, and suddenly said he would let me have his proposed timetable and then we could see how far it approximated to mine. We all nearly fell off our chairs and afterwards my officials and I were trying to make up our minds what the Tory tactics could be. We may be walking into a hidden minefield but it certainly is not obvious yet.

Wednesday, 7 February. Went into the Party meeting to hear some of its second reading debate on the new Code of Conduct. I was just in time to hear a savagely sour speech by Charlie Mapp[1] who said that he objected to the degree of discretion given in the proposals to the Chief Whip. As the author of the liberal policy which had so obviously failed, the Chief Whip was the last person to administer the new one. The campaign to oust John Silkin steadily grows.

Ted, who had slipped in to listen to the proceedings of our Standing Committee, was full of a conversation he has had with Joe Haines of the *Sun* who lunched with Denis Healey yesterday. Joe told Ted he had been assured that at least a dozen members of the Cabinet were now convinced that Harold must go and were just waiting their opportunity. 'They have lost all faith in Harold and of course they are trying to argue that Harold had resisted devaluation single-handedly.' This canard is now being spread systematically in order to protect Jim and the right-wing junta. The dissidents, Joe said, have

[1] Labour MP for Oldham East.

not yet decided who the Leader should be, but apparently they are all agreed on the Deputy Leader. Me! Haines said that they believe that in any contest for the leadership in the PLP at this moment I would be runner-up; and they wanted me as Deputy Leader because I had always taken an independent line and was not just one of what they call 'Wilson's poodles'. Ted seems to think all this is very flattering, but I am not fooled. No doubt it would help a right-wing led Labour Government to have me as the captive from the Left.

Monday, 12 February. British Rail have concluded their long pay and productivity exercise with the unions and have produced a scheme which, though barely self-financing and therefore not really a productivity scheme at all, does mark a revolution in the wages structure of the railways and breaks away from the principle of comparability. Some grades will get as much as a 10 per cent increase; others nothing at all. The average will be 3½ per cent. The great gain is the increase in versatility. Chris Foster produced a gloomy report about its economic effects but politically I have no doubt we should go for it, even though it means £8m more on the deficit next year until the harvest of productivity gains is reached. Fortunately Ray Gunter and I were able to get it through Cabinet Committee. It only remains to be seen whether the unions will accept it. It gives them a much smaller minimum wage than they have been asking for. If they don't accept it, there is absolutely no hope of British Rail breaking even when it is on its own under the new financial regime next year.

The Transport Bill continues to absorb large chunks of my time. The Road Haulage Association and Aims of Industry are launching a massive campaign against the Bill on a scale not seen since they opposed the nationalization of road haulage in 1948 (financed by a levy of 4*s* on every vehicle). And Peter Walker has let it be known that he is paying £10,000 out of his own pocket to employ a research team to help him 'kill the Bill'. Belatedly I am trying to rally the meagre force of the Labour and trade union movement to counter this extensive campaign. I had Terry Pitt and Percy Clark over to the House to discuss the production of leaflets, information for MPs, etc. Then I went downstairs to rally my members on the Transport Bill Committee to do their stuff too. I got them to accept a self-denying ordinance about speaking in the committee.

Tuesday, 13 February. Peter Walker has produced a document alleging to set out the cost of the freight section of the Bill: £150m. Though supposed to be drawn up by professional experts, it is so wildly inaccurate that my officials are almost beside themselves. It continually fascinates me how civil servants, even when they have done their utmost to persuade one to accept a different policy, identify themselves with the success of the measure once it has been introduced. They are rushing to produce figures to show Peter Walker up and we had a council of war on how to counter the RHA campaign. They sat there solemnly advising me how far I can go constitutionally in using the Department to this end. Apparently I am not allowed to produce a popular version of the Bill while it is going through the House. Nor can I produce any ministerial pamphlets or leaflets counteracting it. But I can ask them to produce all the material on which Transport House do their stuff. And this they are now working on most enthusiastically.

They do all this although I continue to alarm them with the development of my policy – workers' participation, for instance. At a vast gathering of officials I told them the amendments I intended to produce in the Bill if I can. They warned me solemnly that I would have to 'go to colleagues' if I wanted to do anything as far-reaching as putting a practising union official on any of my boards, even part-time, or if I wanted to let unions elect their own workers' representatives. They also reminded me solemnly I might be up against the TUC. I have told them that as a first step I will circulate a document to all the transport unions, road and rail, and invite them to a discussion. To cover myself I will also invite a representative of the TUC. Then if I get agreement there, it will be difficult for Ray Gunter to stop me going ahead. Heaton, swallowing hard, murmured, 'Can we put up a paper to you first, Minister?' I said he could provided it included a draft letter to the unions.

Thursday, 15 February. We ended the Standing Committee on such a violent note last night that I felt I must go in today, even though it meant missing Cabinet. It was worth it for the blissful moment when I knocked Michael Heseltine off his balance.[1] He had been making great play with the special section which said Passenger Transport Executives would have the power to manufacture or produce 'anything' they required for their business. He had made enormous use of this last night saying it was the most monstrous clause which had ever appeared in any Bill. So I greatly enjoyed standing up and reading an identical clause word for word in the 1962 Tory Transport Act! Their discomfiture was delicious. My only regret was that I didn't think till afterwards to tell Peter Walker that he really wasn't getting very good value for his £10,000 if his 'experts' couldn't point that out to him.

I used the press conference to get over our answer to Peter Walker's phoney estimates. But I doubt whether a word of it will be used. In fact my sixth sense tells me we shall have a poor press on it tomorrow.

Off to Blackburn on the night sleeper, my first visit for two months because of my illness.

Harold has had a triumph in Washington. L.B.J. has made another 'I'm backing Britain' speech. Harold always said the storm over our withdrawal East of Suez would soon die down. And that daring speech of Harold's at the official dinner was, I am sure, no dash for freedom from the special relationship.[2] In fact, I suspect it was cleared beforehand with L.B.J.

Friday, 16 February. Off the night sleeper at Preston to my usual friendly welcome from the stationmaster. As we waited for him to come and escort me I chatted to the sleeper attendant about this and that. These attendants, too, are

[1] Michael Heseltine, Conservative MP for Tavistock, was one of the 1966 intake, but was already making a name for himself. He later succeeded Peter Walker as official Opposition spokesman on Transport.

[2] With the Tet offensive underway in Vietnam, President Johnson had told Wilson during their Washington talks that the ban on the bombing of the centre of Hanoi and Haiphong had been lifted. Wilson decided to turn his after-dinner speech at the White House banquet into an implied attack on the American 'hawks' over Vietnam by insisting that there could be no imposed military solution and urging the dangers of escalation. But it was tempered by a reiteration of his refusal to dissociate the British Government from America's actions or to call for an unconditional end to the bombing.

always charming and always have been, even before I became a Minister. This one said, 'You treat everyone alike. That is why you are so popular.' I have a natural inclination to do this, anyway – pomposity is, I think, my absolutely top pet hate – but also I make a conscious effort all the time to break through the cocoon of insulating material with which one is surrounded when one becomes a Minister. It is compounded of deference, obedience, comfort and convenience, much genuine will to serve and some downright hypocrisy and, if one is not careful, it cuts one off completely from ordinary people. It is designed to make one feel like God, and with a lot of Ministers it succeeds. I constantly remind myself that I am a very temporary God indeed and anyway only by leave of a lot of humble people to whom I try desperately to reach out from the inner recesses of the cocoon.

That is why I positively enjoy my visits to Blackburn, despite the physical strain. I come down to earth with such a healthy bump. Indeed, as I get out at Blackburn to walk across to the White Bull, I wonder what reception I will get from the ordinary man and woman who are not at this moment exactly enamoured of the Government. But within minutes I am being stopped by an elderly lady to bless me for all I am doing (the breathalyser?). In the shops the welcome is as friendly as ever. And I am soon in a lengthy discussion with a couple of workmen at the White Bull who seize the opportunity to air their own pet ideas. Interestingly, there are two topics which dominate all these conversations: my drink and driving Bill and 'colour'. Four times during the day people (most of them Labour) said to me, 'I've no colour prejudice myself but . . .'.

Monday, 19 February. I am feeling very pleased with myself because I have won a victory over the grants policy for the unremunerative railway services. Apparently the task of assessing the grants on these lines is going to be formidable. Some 300 lines or services will be involved and we ought to do a thorough cost-benefit analysis on each, as well as probing the possibility of economies. The Department tells me it simply will not be able to finish more than 100 of these studies by the time the new financial arrangements for the railways come into force in January 1969. So they have proposed a number of complex amendments to the Bill to enable transitional provisions to be made, the idea being that we should take another year over the business and then pay grants retrospectively on a complicated basis. I was appalled at the prospect and asked why we couldn't just fix a notional loss on each line based on BR's own assessment of what it was costing them to keep it open, limit the period of the grants on a phased basis and then phase in the new figure as the studies in depth were completed. To a man all ten of my officials present said it was impossible. I stuck to my guns for over an hour, though even John Morris was hesitant. Then they agreed to take my idea back to the Treasury and, lo and behold, they have now told me that 'the Treasury has agreed'. It just shows that it is worth backing one's judgment against the united horde.

At my weekly meeting with the troops on the Transport Bill I asked them if they were game for an all-night sitting this week so that we could really test whether the Tories were prepared to make progress on it. They were positively eager.

Tuesday, 20 February. Got through four clauses in committee this morning at a galloping pace. It just shows what progress can be made when both sides are in earnest about it. When at the end I announced that we would go on as long as necessary the following night, the Tories cheered loudly. I still can't make up my mind how they are trying to play it. Lunched with Alan Watkins of the *New Statesman* who said some very flattering things about my White Papers. He had read all four of them in the last few days and was astonished to find how good they were. I told him that of course they were as I had written most of them! The only thing we were at odds about was Peter Parker. Alan said he had met him in some dining club or other and thought he was too smooth by half. That is certainly the impression he gives and that is one of the reasons why I hestitated. But I am still convinced I was wrong to do so.

Wednesday, 21 February. The tempo of life is creeping up relentlessly to its pre-Christmas pace and my brief respite is rapidly coming to an end. The day started with an NEC meeting in which we had an illuminating discussion on the future of Mr Desmond Donnelly.[1] Nobody could hate him more than the left wing, but with an eye on their own fates Mikardo and others were all for letting his misdemeanours ride a bit. Joe Gormley and the right wing were thirsting for his immediate blood. Finally they were headed off by Alice Bacon's[2] suggestion that we ought to go through the usual routine of interviewing him first. The next argument was about who should interview him, and the general view was that it ought to be the Organization Sub-Committee. Said Joe Gormley with relish, 'With me on the Organization Sub-Committee he is halfway out already.' We all roared with laughter and Harold raised his eyebrows, murmuring under his breath, 'Another Jim Callaghan' – a wicked reference to the howler Jim has perpetrated in the House this week about the London murders.[3] In doing so I think Jim has given away his fundamental shallowness of mind. One can just see what had happened: the police had come and said to him triumphantly, 'We've caught him, sir,' and Jim instinctively aligned himself with the policeman's view. But what an incredible start as Home Secretary! He hadn't turned up to the NEC – I suspect because he has taken a bit of time off to lick his wounds.

I had to leave the NEC early, missing Frank Allaun's resolution on the economy cuts, in order to have an office meeting on Transport Bill amendments. We ploughed through the clauses up to Clause 23 in preparation for the coming all-nighter. And then I had hastily to read up my PQs as I was top for Questions today. Fortunately this ordeal has ceased to worry me and we sailed through Question Time with ease, considerably helped by the latest figures of the post-breathalyser accidents. The December figures are so dramatic that I

[1] Following the vote on the package Desmond Donnelly had resigned the Labour Whip and had been consistently attacking the Government.

[2] Alice Bacon, Labour MP for South-East Leeds, had been appointed Minister of State at the Home Office in 1964 and moved to Education in August 1967.

[3] Answering Questions in the House the previous day Jim Callaghan had been carried away into a testimony to the success of the police in these words: 'I am glad to say that less than three hours ago one of those responsible for the murder at Fulham was arrested in Bolton in Lancashire and that the man who committed the murder this morning in Acton has also been arrested.'

was rapidly raked in for two TV interviews.[1] Then back into the House for a few minutes in committee before going off to do another TV programme with the road hauliers of the South-West.

It was 10 pm before I got my hurried bite of bacon and egg and settled in for a long night's work. It was soon clear that the Tories were dragging it out, and at 6.30 am I called it a day (or night!) with a tart little speech clearly implying that there was no alternative but to guillotine. And so home at 7.15 am. I flopped on the bed next to Ted and murmured a plea for a cup of tea. While he got it I snatched three minutes' sleep before rising to bath and change and get a bite of breakfast before an early start.

I am delighted to find that I can still do a routine like that without difficulty. So I must have replenished my reserves successfully.

Thursday, 22 February. Got through a busy afternoon with only one snatch of sleep and even conducted a pretty intensive discussion with Robert Hickman about inland waterways over dinner. Penny Balogh had inveigled me into going and meeting him even though the Department had put up warning signals that he had been about the most vociferous of all the leaders of the volunteer enthusiasts. In fact, having founded the IWA [Inland Waterways Authority], he had then left it because he thought it was too moderate. He was a very difficult man to talk to, particularly when one was tired. But I struggled hard to keep my temper.

I get alarmed sometimes how easily as a Minister one gets impatient with the awkward customer enthusiast. If one is not careful one can become brutalized by office. Where does one draw the line between insensitivity and realism? It is all the harder to answer that because often when the Government is being at its most sensitive in its response to its own rank and file's warnings and demands (shown over the defence cuts) it discovers that it has merely created a new violent hostility elsewhere – say, among the defence workers who have been put out of work. I am meeting this same problem over the proposed reduction in drivers' hours. There are even members of the TGWU who are protesting at not being allowed to work themselves to death.

Friday, 23 February. Went along to the Privy Council office to have one of my regular quarrels with Dick about the legislative programme. As usual he is trying to push things out of the programme while I am determined to keep some things in. The battle over and settled by an honourable compromise, I stayed behind for a private talk. Dick is deeply anxious and unhappy about the way things are going. Harold barely troubles to consult him – he wasn't even brought into the discussions of the by-elections[2] and the public announcement was the first he knew of it. He says Harold is getting more and more suspicious and secretive. He had promised Dick when devaluation took place that this time he really would establish an inner working-group of Cabinet. But nothing

[1] And the improvement continued. In the first five months following the introduction of the breath test, road deaths fell by 799 or 22 per cent and serious injuries by 6,293 or 15 per cent.

[2] In three by-elections on 28 March there was a catastrophic swing against the Government. At Dudley, where a vacancy had been caused by George Wigg's elevation to the Lords, a Labour majority of 10,000 was turned into a Conservative majority of 11,000; at Meriden the Labour majority of 4,581 became a Conservative majority of 3,720 and at Acton our 4,941 became 15,263 for the Conservatives.

has come of it. Harold, Roy and everyone else are just running in parallel and Harold has completely lost control. When Dick tackles him about it he merely says to him, 'Do you really think there is anyone of them I can trust?' Once again we agreed that Harold has voluntarily made himself their prisoner. Indeed, Harold once said to Dick, 'Has anyone else ever brought so many of his enemies into a Cabinet?' I think Harold's trouble is that at bottom he just hasn't got faith in himself, despite all the air of bubbly india-rubber self-confidence.

Dick is clearly getting pretty desperate and relations between him and Harold are badly strained. Harold was furious with Dick for telling Margach quite openly that instead of a 'triumvirate' there was now a 'diarchy'. Of course Margach printed it, and when Dick cheerfully admitted that he had coined the phrase Harold was livid and told him that he was losing patience with him. To which Dick tartly replied, 'Well, I'm losing faith in you.' Dick clearly thinks we are moving relentlessly towards disaster and I see no reason to doubt that he is right. My only trouble is that I am so intellectually and emotionally absorbed with the evolution of my own Socialist policy in my own field that I haven't time to worry about my morale. Of course that is where Dick envies me. And he said so openly. He is wretched and idle and wishes he had a hundred times more work to do. 'Particularly', he added, 'as I have failed in the one thing I set out to do, to get an inner group going in Cabinet.'

At the door I couldn't resist putting to him again a question I had put to him a few weeks earlier. 'If Roy Jenkins became Prime Minister, would you serve under him?' He said no, he wouldn't. He was Wilson's man. He would just go away and write his book. But then he broke into one of those disarming grins of his. 'That's what I say now. But, you know, I can never be sure what I should say when the time comes.'

Monday, 26 February. The unhappiness of the Party increases day by day. Harold really has got his back to the wall and it is beginning to show. As I wandered past his room in the evening, he was standing talking to Tony Greenwood and held out an affectionate hand to me. 'I'm going to tell Mr Auberon Waugh that he has got his story in the *Spectator* all wrong. No one ever tried to stop your Transport Bill, did they, Barbara? I've told John Silkin we must send a denial.' I think he had been taking comfort in his brandy again and rattled on in a voice which could be heard by his retainers standing discreetly a few yards away: 'Roy's boys have had a busy weekend briefing the press. They are trying to give Roy all the credit for the prices and incomes policy when Peter Shore has done all the work on it.' The thought crossed my mind that it was rather an odd thing to be anxious to claim credit for. He said Jim Callaghan was furious at the pro-Roy briefing that was going on. 'Surely,' I said, 'after his clanger in the House about the murders he had finally ditched himself. He could never be Crown Prince again.' Retorted Harold, 'Don't use the word "never"' – Wilson's thirty-seventh law of politics is that political memories don't last longer than a week.' But he agreed that Jim had acted as Minister of Police, not Minister of Justice. Jim hadn't really wanted to go to the Home Office but Harold had insisted. 'Wilson's thirty-eighth law of politics is, if you must have a reshuffle, make it a bilateral one. If I had sent him to

Defence, as I first thought of doing, I would not have put Healey at the Home Office – or anywhere else, come to that.'

Wednesday, 28 February. I got in late to the Party meeting on the Code of Conduct, so I didn't hear John Silkin's explanation that he intends to move an amendment to it in due course. Apparently he has had a row with the Liaison Committee when he wanted, after consulting Harold, to extend the sentences on sixteen of those under suspension because of their action on Monday in voting against the increase in National Insurance contribution. There is a plot within a plot somewhere here that I can't quite understand. This is the first time that John Silkin has ever sought severer disciplinary powers. Perhaps it is merely that he and Harold have decided that the time has come to establish his authority. If so, he hasn't succeeded yet. If they are not careful they will get caught in the crossfire of the right-wingers who want to oust John Silkin as Chief Whip because he is too liberal and the left-wingers who don't want anybody to have any disciplinary powers at all. We got ourselves into another all-night sitting on the Transport Bill – by accident. Having received preposterous proposals from Peter Walker about the voluntary timetable, I now know it's only a matter of time before we have the guillotine so I don't intend to keep my people up all night uselessly. However, since the Commonwealth Immigration Bill[1] was going to have an all-night sitting in the committee stage, we decided we might as well stay all night in the Transport Bill upstairs, and we made some useful progress as a consequence. In fact at 5.30 in the morning I even had Peter Walker inquiring anxiously when I intended to call it a day. I am having to work out some very complicated tactics owing to the fact that only I know (and I can't even tell Stephen, let alone the Labour members of the committee) that the Bill will be radically altered as a result of the Budget speech. So of course this will affect the timetable. Keeping my chaps sweet without being able to put them in the picture is quite tricky.

With the existing powers on prices and incomes coming to an end in August 1968, Peter Shore and Roy Jenkins had been working out the next stage of the policy which was to be incorporated in the Chancellor's Budget strategy. Far from being able to say that the drug had cured the illness, they wanted to increase the dose. The proposed new powers lengthened the maximum delaying power on price and pay increases to twelve months where a reference was made to the PIB, *set a* $3\frac{1}{2}$ *per cent ceiling for wage and dividends increases; renewed the power to require statutory notification of pay and price increases and extended this to dividends and rents; took power to require price reductions, and to prevent excessive dividend distributions and to direct local authorities to moderate or phase rent increases. There had to be a twelve-month interval between settlements. One of the most controversial aspects was the statement that increases settled at national level must take account of increases at company and plant level and* vice versa.

[1] Under its own internal pressures the Kenya Government had announced its intention of expelling its large number of Kenya residents of Asian origin. When Kenya obtained its independence in 1963 many of them had opted to retain their British citizenship and had nowhere to go but Britain and in the three months ending January 1968, 7,000 had already arrived. With an unknown number still to come – potentially hundreds of thousands – the Government decided to legislate to control this influx by quotas. A special category of up to 1,500 vouchers a year was created for Kenya citizens, which allowing for dependants, meant some extra 7,000 immigrants.

Thursday, 29 February. Home at 8 am from my all-night sitting with not even a three-minute nap on the bed before going off to Cabinet. I was determined to keep awake for the key item – the future of prices and incomes policy. Reading the papers on it during the night, I had become increasingly uneasy. It seemed to me we were heading for an almost unilateral wage squeeze. And I just didn't think this was politically tenable except in the context of a wider Socialist incomes policy. So I was delighted when Dick drew me aside just before the meeting to ask me whether I had read the papers. 'Yes,' I said, 'and I don't intend to support the proposals, unless we get a Socialist Budget and that means at the very least a wealth tax.' Dick's face lit up and he said he had come to the identical view quite separately, and we agreed to back each other up.

Peter Shore introduced his P and I paper as toughly as ever Roy Jenkins could wish. I can't understand quite why he has become such an enthusiast for draconian measures and can only assume that Tommy Balogh has been getting at him. Peter argued that the increase in incomes per head for the year ended July 1968 seemed likely to amount to 6½ per cent at the rate we were going, and with devaluation pushing up prices it would be as much as 7, 8 or even 9 per cent over the coming year unless we did something drastic about it. The fact was that we could only afford an overall increase of 5 per cent, hence the need for further statutory powers. He recommended a ceiling of 3½ per cent with all increases up to this ceiling to be justified in terms of the present criteria.

I told them we had never known that type of P and I policy we were trying to pursue. There were two kinds open to us: the most overt type intended to secure a cut in real wages so as to make capitalism work; or the planned growth of wages as part of Socialist planning. I had always believed in P and I policy but only of the second kind. And I had always argued with my left-wing friends in favour of it. What we were talking about now wasn't a P and I policy at all because we were all saying we expected prices must go up. In fact the President of the Board of Trade in his heart of hearts actually wanted some price increases. Yet I had in my hand one of the latest PIB reports commissioned by us on retail margins which stated categorically that an increase in prices due to devaluation would actually bring uncovenanted bonuses to retailers if current retail margins were maintained. Weren't we prepared to take action on points like this? For me, therefore, the proposals were untenable except in the context of a rigorous restraint of incomes over the whole field. Dividends must be frozen too and the minimum provision for social equality in the Budget must be a wealth tax. I personally wasn't prepared to enforce the proposals unless I knew what was in the Budget. This must be a package for which we were collectively responsible. 'If this is another gambit to restore the confidence of capitalists we shall finally destroy the confidence of our own movement. This is our last chance and we are in mortal danger.'

Harold jumped in fussily at this point to say that it was quite impossible for the Cabinet to discuss the Budget proposals in advance. The Chancellor of the Exchequer was noting all we had said and we would have to leave it to the two of them to take our views into account. As time was running short he said the discussion would be continued next time. But before we moved on George

Brown said heavily that he was very concerned about the whole business and would want a chance to make his position clear.

Friday, 1 March. Interviewed Jessie Smith, a formidable and prominent Labour woman from Yorkshire, for a possible job on the British Rail Board. I am determined to put a woman on it because I believe that what the railways sadly lack is the practical touch. If I were chairman of BRB I would have an amenity officer whose job it would be to invite suggestions and complaints from the public and then see they were ruthlessly followed up. Perhaps my woman member could supervise this. Anyway, Jessie Smith is an imposing person in her own right and John Gunn was clearly impressed with her. The only trouble is her age. I am going to see Margaret Durridge at Jock Campbell's suggestion. She is on the Milton Keynes new town corporation with him and he says that though she is an Independent she is very go-ahead.[1]

Tuesday, 5 March. Another Cabinet meeting on P and I policy. George wasn't there. Peter reported [that] the CBI had reacted unfavourably to the idea of a ceiling: they wanted just criteria. It had been difficult to consult the TUC in advance of the Executives' meeting on 28 February. Woodcock, of course, was sticking to the voluntary policy. Cousins and Scanlon[2] just wouldn't take TUC vetting. He believed that the mood of the trade union group in the House about legislation was more understanding than it had been, but others were not so sure. Dick returned to the attack on the need for a package. He is weakening on the need for an egalitarian Budget (I think he has been convinced by Roy and Harold that it just isn't practical to get far-reaching tax changes in time) and is ready to take a milder P and I policy instead. I feel this gives us the worst of both worlds and I vigorously repeated my demands for a wealth tax.

Jim returned to his practical man line. We ought to accept that there would be a 5 per cent increase in incomes anyway whatever we did, so why stick to a ceiling of 3½ per cent? And how on earth could Peter Shore's system, with 200 civil servants trying to pick and choose between thousands of claims, be made to work? Crosland was inclined to back him, arguing that if we only got a 6½ per cent increase in wages this year we should congratulate ourselves. It would be manageable. Roy nearly burst a blood vessel at this. He said a system of free settlements now would mean an overall increase, not of 6½ per cent, but of 10 to 11 per cent. But everyone began to look more critically at the practicability of Peter's proposals. How many plant level wage claims were there? Thousands, said Ray vaguely and loftily. How many civil servants would be needed to deal with them? A few hundreds no doubt. Peter was sent back to look at all this again.

[1] In the event I was moved from Transport before I could make an appointment. My successor, Dick Marsh, was not interested in my idea.

[2] Hugh Scanlon had been elected President of the Amalgamated Engineering Union (AEU) on a left-wing ticket in 1967, beating the right-winger, John Boyd, by 68,022 votes to 62,008 on the second ballot. In 1968 the AEU amalgamated with the Foundry Workers to become the AEF, which in 1970 merged with the Construction Engineering Workers and the Draughtsmen to form the Amalgamated Union of Engineering Workers (AUEW).

Wednesday, 6 March. Had to attend NEDC where the CBI has demanded a paper from me estimating the cost of the proposals in the Transport Bill and the timing of their introduction.

After I had introduced my paper Stephen Brown [President] and John Davies [Director-General] of the CBI weighed in nastily. They are really getting uppish and hardly trouble to hide their hostility to the Government, even in such a collaborationist body as the NEDC. They said they were unconvinced by my figures, so I hit back tartly. The interesting thing about the subsequent discussion was the objectivity of everybody else. Sir Frank Kearton[1] even went so far as to say that 'by and large' my Bill was 'a move in the right direction'. He frankly welcomed the reduction in drivers' hours. So did Professor Robertson of Glasgow, who also admitted that the case for the abnormal loads charge was economically sound but pointed out it would create difficulties for development areas. Couldn't we have a charge tapering by mileage? By and large it all went very well and Peter was delighted at the way I stood up to the CBI.

In the Transport Bill Standing Committee, the Tories were obviously astonished that the guillotine has not been included in next week's business. I know that it is going to be and that Dick intends to announce a change in Thursday's business next Monday. In this way he has avoided giving the Tory Whips the tip-off today. (They always see next week's business confidentially on the Wednesday.) My own chaps are getting more and more restless as I cannot put them in the picture either. It is oppressive carrying all these secrets!

Thursday, 7 March. I was astonished to hear on the 8 am news a report to the effect that I had failed to persuade the Government to introduce the guillotine. Said the announcer: 'It is suggested that even some of Mrs Castle's colleagues have put to her the alternative of dropping certain parts of the Bill as Tory opponents have advocated.' So the Tory Whips have clearly gone straight to the press in breach of the strict confidentiality which attaches to their prior notice of next week's business.

When I got in to Cabinet, however, I heard Dick saying that he was going to announce next Thursday's guillotine that afternoon, after all. Apparently he and Harold couldn't bear to be accused of sabotaging my Bill. I expect the result of this will be another story in the press to the effect that I have had a violent row and managed to get my own way.

We turned again to P and I policy. Peter had circulated another paper, this time on the enforcement of the powers. He pointed out that there could be no hope of imposing any policy by statutory powers and sanctions if there wasn't a wide base of public support. But statutory powers would still be of great importance for dealing with the few groups who might try to get away with it. His conclusions were that prosecution would be difficult in any circumstances but that the Attorney-General thought it would be particularly difficult if powers were taken to prevent retrospection or if the Government were free to make orders without reference to the PIB, since the courts would be unlikely to be sympathetic in such cases. For the rest, enforcement had always been a difficult part of the policy. It sounded to me as though he was weakening and certainly a number of members of the Cabinet are.

[1] Chairman of Courtaulds and of the Industrial Reorganization Corporation.

Jim jumped in with a full-blooded attack on the whole concept of trying to control plant bargaining. How many of these bargains were struck each year? Thousands. How could inexpert clerical officers in the civil service judge between them? How many civil servants would you need to deal with them? George Brown backed him up, arguing that we couldn't be tougher on incomes than on prices, dividends, etc., but we didn't want to hold prices or dividends down. Dick Marsh categorically asserted that P and I policy would not work and we had better face up to it. Tony Greenwood supported Dick's and my demand for an ideological Budget.

The argument went round and round, but Jim kept coming back to the attack. He is obviously smarting all the time under the implication that he failed as Chancellor and is retrospectively justifying everything he did. 'What we do on this won't save the pound,' he snapped at Roy. 'I warn the Chancellor the dollar will fall sooner or later and the pound will be under pressure anyway. Strong measures of this kind may bring the opposite effect to what we require. let's forget the seamen's strike. We thought it bold and brave to stand out then, but it was catastrophic and led directly to the measures of July 1966.'

I could contain myself no longer. Jim's 'realism' is a little belated and comes at a moment when the only reality that matters is that if devaluation does come again we have really had it as a Government. Whatever mistakes we have made in the past, our first duty now is to survive. What we had to decide, I said, was what was economically necessary. We had never been frank with ourselves about this. We had talked about a P and I policy, when we hadn't meant that at all. Were we or were we not saying that real wages must actually be cut in order to make way for the increased investment in exports we require? If so, it was far better to say so openly. Only in that way had we the faintest chance of getting away with it, and of course we should not have even that chance unless we accompanied it by some redistribution of property. It was politically vital for sacrifices to be shared and that was the only context in which I, for one, was prepared to countenance an incomes and prices policy. This sharpened the whole discussion. Roy replied soberly. He said wage policy had been integral to our economic policy ever since 1964. Personally he had some scepticism about it in the long term, but immediately there was no alternative. He admitted at last that he was working for a slight fall in consumption and in real wages and finished tersely and emphatically with the words: 'If we are not seen to deal strongly with wages we can't avoid a second devaluation, world monetary confusion and the destruction of this Government.'

Despite this speech the majority of the Cabinet was still obviously disturbed, not so much by the size of the ceiling, as by the impracticability of Peter's and Ray's ideas. Peter just doesn't seem to have taken in the impossibility for the Government itself, through a mass of civil servants, to vet thousands of wage increases at the plant level and I am personally surprised that Ray has lent his name to this. Peter was sent away to chew the problem over and report again.

Uproar in the House when Dick announced the week's business including our guillotine. Heath leapt to the dispatch box with a spate of figures designed to prove that we had been making wonderful progress on the Bill and that the guillotine was quite unjustified. Dick handled it all with aplomb. But we are obviously in for a rowdy time and the fight is on.

Monday, 11 March. The *Daily Express* has an incredible feature article: 'Why Barbara is King of the Castle'. As I thought, the press is crediting me with having fought and won triumphantly a battle with my colleagues over the Transport Bill. Dick is a bit fed up about all this, having loyally supported me all the way through and not relishing his role as the ogre of the piece. Frank Allaun popped up to me in the dining room in the House to tell me that at more than one meeting recently – some with trade unionists and some with university people – my name has seriously been canvassed for PM. It is a flattering thought, but I don't take it seriously.

In the meantime I am mopping up a series of office meetings. One concerned Clause 45 of the Transport Bill in which we really are taking a fantastically wide extension of the manufacturing powers of nationalized industries.[1] Having won Cabinet approval for the general principle of extension in the Bill, I have sent my officials away to work on it and they have come back with the Bill drafted to give me practically limitless powers. It is amusing to hear them explaining solemnly that any attempt to define the powers in a Bill in order to limit them would merely lead to unwarrantable restrictions. Once again I marvel at the civil servants: these chaps really hate the whole idea of these manufacturing powers but, the policy having been adopted, they are taking the job of implementing it *au sérieux*. Hankey, Deputy Treasury Solicitor, assured me that the only way to control the use of the powers was by the provision officials had made for the Minister to approve all proposals for their use, to have the right to modify or withdraw proposals and the duty to publish them. The control in other words would be through the Minister. The CBI has been pressing for inclusion of a phrase to the effect that, in using the powers, nationalized industries must behave in all ways like 'a company engaged in private enterprise'. Hankey is against my accepting this on the grounds that it doesn't make any sense, but the others think it might have some advantages presentationally. The real safeguard is that I have got Bill Johnson to agree reluctantly to set up a separate subsidiary company to run the railway workshops. This of course would have to conform to the Companies Acts. But, having gone into all the pros and cons very carefully for an hour this morning, I have decided that an amendment to include the desired words would not do any harm and might do some good. I have asked them to consult the Scottish Office urgently and table a Government amendment.

Went along to Dick's room at 7.45 to discuss the Transport Bill guillotine to find no John Silkin there. Dick was in a sour and desperate mood. He had been dining with Aubrey Jones, who complained he had never been consulted on the new proposals for P and I policy. Dick wasn't too optimistic either about the Budget being radical. 'The trouble is,' he says, 'Harold and Roy will just think it is radical.' We sat there drinking and gossiping for nearly an hour waiting for John Silkin to turn up.

His failure to do so only heightened Dick's irritation. That was his trouble,

[1] The Clause (which became Section 48 in the Act) empowered the Boards and new authorities I was setting up to manufacture for sale to outside persons, or to repair for them, 'anything which the authority consider can advantageously be so manufactured, or . . . repaired by the authority by reason of the fact that the authority or a subsidiary of theirs have materials or facilities for, or skill [in that work]'. It was this Clause that enabled the railway workshops, for example, to manufacture for export or diversify their activities.

he said, he had to deal with a Chief Whip who was irresponsible. He himself was still seriously thinking of throwing in his hand: why didn't he just retire and write books and see more of his family? In these moods Dick is not a very reliable witness to anything.

Thursday, 14 March. Up early to get the day's speeches ready. As usual I haven't had time to prepare myself leisurely for the great debates that lie ahead, and before I could get down to my notes on the guillotine debate in the House this afternoon I had to work away on the big debate on Clause 45 in the Standing Committee.

We were late starting the [guillotine] debate because of a number of statements. Dick gabbled through his speech (he hates reading one), but his final touch of gamesmanship, in which he said he was awarding a skilful and hardworking Opposition with the accolade it deserved, a guillotine, nearly threw Peter Walker, who had to start his speech actually grinning instead of foaming at the mouth. And then we were away on a slanging match in the middle of which Mike Foot made one of the most scintillating debating speeches I had ever heard. It was 9 pm before I stood up, with the Tories interrupting me every other line. I think my speech was adequate; not one of my best performances, but it seemed to delight our own side.

I slipped out for a conference with my officials on the amendments to the guillotine Motion leaving Dick in charge, only to return to find the House in pandemonium.

With Eric Fletcher [deputizing for the Speaker] in the chair the Tories were allowed endless repetition and discussion on the merits of the Bill. Things weren't helped when the report of the South Kensington by-election came seeping into the Chamber.[1] When the Tories heard we had lost our deposit a great shout went up and Derek Walker Smith, who was on his feet, made the utmost of it. The Tory mood was getting really vicious and it was clear that they were going to fight it out.

Eventually we got the closure and, with the vote on the first amendment out of the way, Peter Walker moved that the House should adjourn. He began mildly enough. Then another rumour began to seep into the House: 'Friday has been declared a bank holiday.' At once the House became like a live thing, the Tories twisting and snarling and ready to spring at our throats. It was a real mood this time: the Tories thought they were really on to something. With the disastrous (for us) South Kensington result in their stomachs, and with the scent of a fiasco for sterling in their nostrils, they were definitely after blood. And on the face of it it looked as though we were trapped. Heath came to the dispatch box to demand to know what was happening and Dick had to promise that the Chancellor would make a statement at eleven o'clock tomorrow morning. This only added fuel to their arguments: with an important statement to take in the morning, what were we doing sitting up all night on a Motion to guillotine one of the most massive, 'expensive' and 'irrelevant' pieces of legislation of the whole Parliament? I was reminded irresistibly of the Profumo

[1] As anticipated, Sir Brandon Rhys Williams held this safe seat for the Conservatives, but the Labour candidate was knocked into third place and lost his deposit.

incident when the Opposition (though in a minority) suddenly feels at last that it is in control of the situation and has the Government in its power.

Eventually John Silkin jumped up and moved the closure, and as we wended our way through the lobby I wondered whether we should hold our own people sufficiently to win. John Morris and I looked at each other quizzically, agreeing that we really seemed to have an ill-fated star which linked my policies with a financial crisis at every turn. First I lost Peter Parker because devaluation was decided upon the very morning I went to Cabinet. Now we had a world financial crisis right in the middle of my guillotine debate. The result showed we had a reduced majority, but we got our closure and defeated the Adjournment Motion too. The Tories were in a violent mood when we got back to the chamber, clearly determined not to allow the debate to proceed when suddenly Dick rose to the dispatch box and announced that the Chancellor would after all make his statement immediately if he could be given an hour to prepare it. That would give us until 3 am and in the meantime we could make progress with the Motion. The temper of the House quietened immediately and Heath, despite some continued rumbles on his side, got up to welcome this decision, and so we settled down into humdrum repetition again.

I think Dick thought we should get the next amendment (on which after all we had made a major concession) by 3 am, but he reckoned without Michael Heseltine, who was obviously intent on spinning out his own speech until the Chancellor came. While he was pounding on, Wedgie Benn slipped on to the bench beside me and Dick and asked urgently if we could slip out to a meeting of Ministers. 'What on earth for?' snapped Dick, who really does get very testy these days. Wedgie whispered that there was some trouble about George and at this moment Harold needed 'some of his friends'. I was all for one of us going, but Dick would have none of it. 'It's your Bill and you want it. You have got to sit here and work for it'.

'What is the trouble with George?' I asked. Apparently he was in a furious mood and had been bellowing on the telephone to No. 10, insisting that Harold came over at once and pouring out insults to him on the phone. So Harold was calling a few of us together. I was very surprised at this because George had been floating in and out of our proceedings earlier in the evening in one of his pathetic but reasonably amiable moods. He had sat on the front bench beside me, talking rather loudly, it is true, and distracting me, but really being rather touching. He had seemed to me emotion-intoxicated rather than drunk. 'God, I'm tired,' he had said. And when I had commiserated with him about all the overseas journeys and other exhausting things he had to do he said it wasn't that. It was rather frustration. It was all right for me. Everything I did was under my own control, 'provided we are not too nasty to you.' It was my own guillotine Motion, but everything he did depended on a dozen other forces outside this country. What he could do depended on what happened elsewhere – 'and everywhere I look, I can tell you, my sweet, is pretty bloody terrifying.' I suspected he had been more upset than he would ever admit about the comments on his rejection of Con O'Neill and was emotionally compensating by finding alibis.[1] And then he went on to say that anyway, we had better face

[1] Sir Con O'Neill had hoped to become Ambassador in Bonn and when George Brown failed to appoint him he resigned from the Diplomatic Service.

it, we were getting old. He and I were getting pretty bloody well near to sixty, though it took some realizing. 'You don't look it and I don't feel it,' I replied soothingly and he agreed. He didn't feel nearly sixty at all, but then, he kept saying to Sophie, one day someone would find him out.

Altogether it had been pretty amiable stuff, even if delivered in his own unnaturally loud voice, and I hadn't been too worried either when he had skipped through the division lobby with me at ten o'clock, unbuttoning the back of my blouse. When I had chided him he had grinned like a schoolboy and would have given anyone who didn't know him an impression almost of euphoria.

So I was horrified at Wedgie's story and wondered what the hell had happened as I hadn't seen George again for some time. With Schoolmaster Dick, however, keeping a stern eye on me I had to sit where I was. Wedgie collected up Fred Peart, the only other Minister within sight, and slipped away.

As the clock crept towards 3 am the House began to fill, like a disturbed, paper-strewn beach with a spring tide coming in. Dick and I were in the strategic point behind the dispatch box when Harold appeared to a loud cheer followed by Roy Jenkins who squeezed in almost on my knees, very tense and gripping his papers tightly. You could feel anxiety on the benches behind us and a scarcely controlled exultation on the other side. This time you could sense them saying to themselves, 'It's a kill.' Then Dick rose to adjourn the debate temporarily (it having been agreed with Heath that we should be allowed to continue the guillotine debate afterwards). Heath, who, I think, is looking old and white-haired and rather strained these days, certainly has given way on point after point.

Roy rose and to our relief made it clear that the crisis which is closing the banks tomorrow is an American one and not ours.[1] The pressure and anxiety and anticipation slipped out of the chamber like air out of a balloon. When Heath tried to hint at effects for sterling, our side got its nerve back and was ready for him, patriotism on our side again. Roy handled every supplementary very skilfully, with Harold patting him on the back with an exuberance of bonhomie every time he sat down. I noticed for the first time that Roy has a funny little habit of fingering his buttock every time he stands up and I was relieved to know that I am not the only one who feels the strain on these kind of occasions. But he certainly came out on top. Once more we were a credible Government, and as the debate was resumed the Opposition became tedious again, but never terrifying.

Now, however, a new rumour began to circulate. 'You know George has resigned?' back benchers whispered to us. Frantically glued to my rack of

[1] During March there had been heavy sales of sterling associated with speculation about an increase in the price of gold. Attempts by central bankers meeting in Basle to reassure the panickers failed and speculation against the dollar reached fever pitch which affected us as Harold was determined to maintain our parity with the dollar. At 10.40 pm on Thursday, 14 March the Chancellor received a call from the US Secretary of State asking the Government to close the London gold pool pending the calling of a meeting of Central Bank and finance ministries' representatives in Washington the following weekend to discuss long-term solutions. This also meant closing the London Foreign Exchange and declaring a bank holiday and a meeting of the Privy Council had to be called after midnight to make the necessary Order in Council. Harold Wilson maintained he had earlier tried to find George Brown to put him in the picture, but for a long time he could not be traced. (See Wilson *The Labour Government*, pp. 506–12.)

having to listen to the incredibly boring futilities of the debate, I barely cared. But runners from our back benches kept bringing us reports of great scenes going on in the tea-room, where George was apparently holding court and announcing at the top of his voice that he had had enough of this 'bloody Government'. What on earth was the matter with him now? Apparently it had nothing to do with Roy's announcement of the closing of the gold market – he agreed with that – but the trouble was he hadn't been 'consulted'. Well, nor had I for that matter. Nor, as far as I could gather, had a large number of other Ministers. My only feeling was one of thankfulness that it wasn't worse. But not our George.

The next story was that he was out in the lobby telling the press that he was going to resign. The situation took on a note of farce as people came in to us saying, 'He's in,' then a few minutes later, 'No, he's out.' Then, half an hour after that, 'He's in again.' When at last we got our second division just after 4 am, he was in the lobby, still not drunk as far as I could make out, but saying to me and to everyone in turn, 'I'm voting for *your* Government.' I said to him quietly, 'Thank you for voting for my Transport Bill,' to which he replied, 'But you heard what I said? It's *your* Government I'm voting for.' I know he intended us to think he had resigned, but whether he had or not no one ever clearly established as the long night drew to its fantastic end.

Friday, 15 March. In bed at 6.30 am and up at 8.30 am. Just enough sleep to keep me awake for the special Cabinet meeting that had been called for 10 am.

Everybody was there but George. Harold said he 'might' be coming, but we would start without him. Roy then proceeded to explain the chronology of the night's financial events. He began by saying that, although this was primarily a dollar crisis, sterling was inevitably affected, too, because people who want to get into gold have to sell sterling to buy dollars to buy gold. So the pressure on sterling had been great for some time. He hadn't been able to say anything at Cabinet yesterday morning because at that time there was no sign that the crisis was about to break. After lunch he had learned that the US was going to take some emergency action. But he had no indication what. At 6 pm he and the PM had met and they had composed a letter to Johnson pointing out to him that, whereas we didn't want to do anything to make things more difficult for them, we had a right to ask that they should not do anything to make things more difficult for us. He had then sat at the end of the phone trying to contact Fowler in the States. It was 10.40 pm before he finally got Fowler on the phone, who then put to him a formal request on behalf of the US Government that we should suspend gold sales on the London market. It was a request we clearly couldn't refuse. Someone, he couldn't remember who, had then suggested that we ought to make Friday a bank holiday in order to stop dealings in the Foreign Exchange. The US request was in fact very fortunate from our point of view. It enabled us to comply quite correctly and to prevent what might have been a decisively disastrous day for sterling. The Palace had been informed that the Queen must stand by for a Privy Council, which was eventually held at 12.40 pm.

Harold supplemented this by explaining which Ministers he had contacted during the night and why. He had called the Cabinet meeting to put us in the picture and to decide the line our representatives (William Armstrong and Leslie O'Brien)[1] should take in Washington at the hurriedly summoned conference of gold pool banks this weekend.

At this stage Tony Crosland jumped in. He said he entirely agreed with the action that had been taken and recognized that the Prime Minister and the Chancellor had had no choice but to do what they had done. But he wanted to raise a wider point. During the three years he had been in the Cabinet we had never once discussed devaluation. It had been treated as an arcane subject which Ministers were never allowed to discuss collectively. So all the real economic discussions took place merely between the PM and the Chancellor. The rest of us were merely faced with the results when a crisis came and when the choice of action was inevitably limited. He now, he said formally and incisively, made a request to the Prime Minister that he should do what he ought to have done a long time ago: establish an inner group of Ministers which could keep in touch on all these vital matters. (I wondered for one wild moment whether he and Dick were in collusion!)

The complaint about our being left in the dark had its effect, as Roy then proceeded to take us utterly and completely into his confidence. He said he thought we were in the middle of an end to the sterling area.[2] This could be beneficial to us provided that it came about in the right way. If the sterling area collapsed we should be in an impossible mess. Four possible courses of action were now being considered by the US Government.

We then had a very esoteric discussion on which of the four courses we should try to stimulate. The discussion continued at a high level for a full hour. I sat absolutely fascinated, feeling I had been let into political adulthood for the first time. Why on earth Harold could not have had these frank and forthright discussions a long time ago, I couldn't think. Tired as I was, I struggled to keep my mind concentrated. Looking up I saw poor old Dick dead asleep. How I sympathized! He told me that he was too tired to sleep when we finished at 6 am this morning, so had merely walked home and had a hot bath. Even young Wedgie kept dozing off. If ever there was a justification for the guillotine it was this. The folly of trying to run a country by exhausting all your Ministers to death was highlighted. Politically speaking, as Denis Healey pointed out, the gold crisis may prove a boon to us, 'psychological windfall' as he called it. If the mighty dollar is trembling, who can be surprised if we have a weak pound? But I felt passionately that one of the mistakes of this Government is that it has never tried to educate at any rate the PLP rank and file in our economic analysis and philosophy. So I pleaded that we should take the Party into our confidence as we at last had been taken into the Chancellor's confidence in Cabinet. People at large were feeling bewildered because no one would give them an explanation. Shouldn't we start the great process of educating people in these mysteries? Most of Cabinet dismissed this as too ambitious.

I left Cabinet drained of energy and yet in a curious way elated. Have we at

[1] Sir William Armstrong was Joint Permanent Secretary at the Treasury and Sir Leslie O'Brien was Lord Cromer's successor as Governor of the Bank of England.

[2] A block of countries who, because of their close commercial and financial links with the UK, were accustomed to keep their reserves in sterling.

last achieved a breakthrough in the sense that we shall dare to discuss among ourselves the facts of life, such as the fact that the pound may be devalued in the next few days? Or have we at the very least at last persuaded Harold to install that inner group? I agree with Tony Crosland that I don't mind delegating these matters to a small group of Ministers provided that I feel someone is dealing with them in an organized and forward-planning way.

Back in the House people were still speculating about the fate of George. All I could tell them was that he hadn't yet woken up!

I struggled through a succession of afternoon meetings and sat under the hairdrier scribbling a 'light-hearted', off-the-cuff speech for the annual dinner of the Institute of Transport tonight. It would be tonight of all nights! However, I managed to struggle into evening dress and when it came to it I was really pretty scintillating. People came up to me in droves to tell me they didn't know how I managed it after all we had been through. Frankly I don't quite know myself.

Home at 12.30 and by this time it is I who am almost too tired to sleep.

Saturday, 16 March. Despite the fact that I woke at 7 am, I feel utterly exhilarated. Partly because I did well last night, but also because there is hope, hope, hope. Hope for the world if it learns a little financial sanity and hope for our philosophy if only we stop talking in Tory monetary terms and put it across. But whether there is hope for the Party under Harold even I am now beginning to doubt. George has gone.[1] What has Harold done? Put Michael Stewart in his place! Hasn't the man the slightest recognition of the fact that such an appointment will be like a red rag to a bull to our Party activists? And of course neither Dick nor I believe that Harold will really create that inner group. It is just contrary to his whole temperament.

Dick was on to me bright and early full of the whole thing. George's resignation didn't worry him a bit. It's such a patently meaningless suicide. He thinks the Stewart appointment is only short term. But I doubt it. Dick thinks that if Harold had had any guts he would have made him, Dick, Foreign Secretary. But Dick would also like Defence as an alternative. We agreed that Harold would not put either of us in a key post. We agreed, too, that George's phrase in the papers this morning – 'I don't like the way you run your Government' – was one of the most telling he could have produced because everybody knows it is near the bone. As my Ted said to me, it is a phrase that will go on re-echoing, and, as Dick says, this is the reason he himself would have given to Harold on any of the three recent occasions when he was on the point of resigning. However, Dick is to take over Michael Stewart's supervisory work – *e.g.* on Social Security – and that will make him happier because he will have more to do. Whether he will ever get Education, which he would love, remains to be seen.

My Ted tells me that he talked to Thomas Padmore last night about my future. Padmore said everyone in the Civil Service believed I would be moved because I am considered (not least by Burke Trend) to be a very successful

[1] The involved story of George Brown's resignation is told in Wilson, *The Labour Government*.

Minister. Padmore thought I should go to Education. Heaven preserve me from that! I leave that to Dick.[1]

John Morris phoned me this evening to say the *Evening Standard* is full of banner headlines: 'The struggle for power.' They say George Brown can't remain Deputy Leader in the new situation and that I will be one of the contenders, strongly backed by the Left. Frankly I think I haven't a chance except in a situation in which the right wing take over and want me there as a left-wing prisoner. Even the *Guardian* quotes me this morning as a possible bet. John said he would keep his ear to the ground and sound out some people about the possibilities. Well, I have no objection to that, but it is strange how uninterested I am in such intrigues. I have never tried to chat up Members in the tea-room. I could never go through the calculating climb to power that Harold did. Frankly I am not interested in that sort of activity. Usually I bury myself behind a newspaper trying to catch up with the day's overcrowded reading. In fact John Ellis[2] has ticked me off for not talking enough to the chaps; I enjoy many good working relationships with people – like with the members of my Transport Bill Standing Committee – but I am just too bored with it all to intrigue. I don't think personally I shall ever climb any higher because I only got where I am by a fluke. If Harold hadn't manœuvred his way to power I would probably be still on the back benches or a very minor Parliamentary Secretary in a right-wing Labour Government. I know how lucky I have been. If I were drafted I would take on any job, but I am not going to elbow, scratch or scramble.

On 19 March Roy Jenkins introduced his first Budget, a tough one designed to switch resources from home consumption to exports by taking another £766 million in taxation out of the economy in a full year. This was to be done mainly through indirect taxation: betting tax, gaming duties, petrol duty, taxes on wines, spirits (but not beer) and tobacco, SET and car licences were all increased. Purchase tax was increased selectively, going as high as 50 per cent on certain luxuries. There was no change in the standard rate of income tax, though there were some minor progressive changes, such as raising the age allowance for the elderly. Estate duty and tax avoidance measures were tightened up. Finally he proposed a once-for-all levy on private wealth through a special charge on unearned income which, at the top ranges, rose to pound for pound. This ensured the Budget an ecstatic welcome on the Labour benches.

Monday, 18 March. The great pre-Budget Cabinet meeting. Roy began by reporting on the Washington conference. We had got the $4 billion line of credit (of which only $1.2 billion was new money, though we could now use the $1.4 billion from the IMF more freely) and that was our main need.

Roy then turned to his Budget. I listened carefully. Yes, there was the expected emphasis on indirect instead of direct taxation. And, thank heavens, the fuel tax increase is to be rebated for buses again, leaving my fuel tax rebate untouched. (I doubt whether Jim would have done that.) Yes, dividend limitation – to be in the legislation outright. But I suspended judgment till he

[1] I did not succeed in getting Padmore transferred before I was moved from Transport.

[2] Labour MP for Bristol North-West (later for Brigg and Scunthorpe) sponsored by the TGWU. He was a lively left-winger and was Stephen Swingler's PPS from 1968 to 1970.

got to the special levy on unearned incomes. £100m! No punch pulling here. I felt a sneaking admiration – but was the first among his dazed audience to ask a question. Why had he gone for a temporary levy on unearned incomes instead of a permanent wealth tax? Sheer impossibility to get a wealth tax organized in time, he replied, but he hadn't closed his mind for the future – nor on estates duty reform. After that, I couldn't really withhold my support for the much watered-down prices and incomes policy. Most people were very complimentary to Roy. I must say he has a greater grasp of principle than Jim ever had.

And so to the formal agreement that we should go ahead with the P and I policy. Details still remain to be cleared up but the White Paper won't be finalized just yet.

Tuesday, 19 March. Budget day. Somehow I sat through my Standing Committee knowing what a bombshell was going to hit them in the afternoon about the wear and tear charge. At lunch Michael Stewart came over to me positively radiating gratification and whispered, 'The Budget we are going to hear this afternoon completely justifies the stand that some of us took.' He really has been an ally in Dick's and my battle for an 'ideological Budget'. Dick Marsh and Bob Mellish were holding forth in scathing terms about George Brown, telling the world that if George tried to claim he had resigned on policy grounds it would be the grossest distortion of the facts. I got on to the front bench early in order to be sure of a seat and watched the House fill up to an intensity of expectation greater than I have ever known on any previous Budget day.

Roy darted in in good time with a small, flat, battered red leather box and a large glass of water; no stage props of rum and milk for him. And another thing I could have blessed him for was that he eschewed all padding and pontification in his speech. Even so, the basic economic and monetary analysis, coupled with the tax proposals, took just over two hours. But he did not fall for the usual trick of trying to draw out the suspense. For once in a Budget speech there were only five minutes of it where I wanted to nod off. His unveiling of the proposals was absolutely masterly. He would give us a large gobbet of tax information followed by some minor technical reforms, building up slowly to the climax of his unearned income tax and the grand tax total of £900m. The sheer daring of it took everyone's breath away, won the reluctant admiration of the Tories opposite and brought our people to their feet waving order papers at the end. It certainly was an impressive performance, but more important still it depended for its effect entirely on its intellectual content and marshalling.

Its brilliance is proved by the fact that the most swingeing Budget in history left our people positively exultant. As soon as he had finished we at the Ministry rushed out our press statement claiming credit for the abolition of the abnormal loads tax. The Tories cheered jubilantly when Roy announced the wear and tear tax was being absorbed and pointed at me derisively, but I don't think they will be able to make much of it. Stephen and my Committee members were tickled to death at the news and the way I had kept it all dark. Having had a business sub-committee meeting yesterday to allocate the time on the Bill under the guillotine, we have now got to have another one to deal with the new situation.

Thursday, 21 March. We are to have a debate on Rhodesia at last. Harold promised me that we would make it clear that we were now backing comprehensive mandatory sanctions. Apparently we are going to abandon our efforts to get someone else to table the necessary motion at the UN. OPD has drawn up a draft resolution of our own which provides, in addition to comprehensive mandatory sanctions, for a number of measures I think ought to have been taken long ago, like a ban on the supply of radio and TV material and on travel by active supporters of the regime. Unfortunately it is too late in the day to try to 'outlaw Rhodesia from the civilized world'.

Off to Birmingham for a tour of the Midland motorway links.

Friday, 22 March. Birmingham. A brilliantly sunny morning. Chris Hall brought off a brilliant *coup* while I was touring the Midland links. At one viaduct which I was due to inspect a demonstration of road hauliers and drivers was waiting for me, banners aloft, with the slogan 'Hands off Road Transport'. I, of course, was whisked on to the road works by the officials accompanying me, but Chris and John Gunn got together, arranged for a site office to be made available for me and invited the demonstrators to depute ten men to talk to me. Then when I came down from the viaduct they sweetly asked me whether I would concur. Of course I did. Men, banners, photographers, reporters and I crowded into the small shed. One of the hauliers offered me a cigarette, another hoisted me on to the table where I sat showing my knees. They crowded eagerly round me to pose for a photograph, and with that instinct of mine I whisked one arm round the neck of the chief road haulier employer and the other round the neck of a lorry driver. The employer leaned his cheek against mine and cooed happily, 'My wife will divorce me when she sees this.' I then turned out the photographers, lit my cigarette and got down to talking with the men in the friendliest possible way, reporters listening, trying to alleviate their fears about the reduction in drivers' hours. If the press use all this, it really should be a scoop.

Saturday, 23 March. Woke early and wearily to catch train home. But my day was made by the *Birmingham Post*. There is that fabulous necking photograph headlined on the front page with the banner, 'Dears, don't get steamed up, says Mrs Castle'. Peter Walker hasn't got a cat in hell's chance against this!

Monday, 25 March. Peter Shore has had a shocking press for his performance in the House on the P and I policy last Thursday. Apparently he stumbled and mumbled and had our back benchers in a deep state of demoralization. No doubt Harold is in a similar state; after all, Peter is his personal import and many of us who like Peter wondered at the promotion. It is the old case of bringing in someone who is eminently an outsider (a back-room boy this time) and trying to make a politician of him in a vital post overnight. Moreover, he has a streak of arrogance which is deeply dangerous in politics. And I can't help feeling he is too much of a theoretician.

I had a successful meeting with the TUC Nationalized Industries Committee about workers' participation. Here again I want to forge ahead with meaningful experiments. It is not enough, in my view, to do what the Iron and Steel boys have done and put a rank-and-file worker from the industry on the Corporation (and on Group companies' boards) on the understanding that he then ceases to be a rank-and-file worker. I want him to go on my boards part-time while remaining a transport worker or union official. And I even had Hayday agreeing that it ought to be considered seriously: he almost outdid Frank Cousins. Sid Greene was all for the idea, too. They went away to consider it: most encouraging. With any luck, my Bill will have settled the issue before the NEC gets round to putting something concrete into the Party's document on Industrial Democracy. 'Intervention' means forcing the pace a bit, that's all.

As I sat on the front bench for the winding-up speeches in the Budget debate, Peter crept in and wriggled his way in next to me. The only word for his demeanour was 'cowed'. Poor devil! Politics is a merciless game and his morale wasn't improved by a further disparaging reference to him by Reggie Maudling, even though delivered in Reggie's gentle way. Fluent as he was, Maudling nonetheless failed to draw real blood – in my view because it was difficult for him to hide the fact that he would have done very much what we have. He knew perfectly well that the Tories' pre-Election bonanza in 1964 couldn't last and was preparing plans to 'float'. I suspect that Harold will have to move Peter from his present job somehow.

Tuesday, 26 March. While I was lunching in the House after Standing Committee, one of the Welsh MPs (I wish I were better at remembering names) came up to me to whisper that some of them wanted me as Deputy Leader of the Party. I tried to be friendly without seeming as though I was pushing my candidature. In any case, I don't think the left wing would go for me: Norman Atkinson told me in terms the other day the Party wouldn't wear a woman! But the issue doesn't arise, because George has decided to keep the job, though out of the Government. Ted thinks George will still emerge as the great leader of the unions against P and I policy. Personally I think he is too deeply discredited. And, as Michael Stewart keeps repeating, he was committed utterly to the policy.

Spent the afternoon at the Ministry on a TV colour recording for *Wheelbase*. This involved an unholy upheaval with my room turned into a TV studio, but it was worth it to counteract the appallingly one-sided view on my Transport Bill put over in the programme recently. Apparently the Commentator, Gordon Wilkins, has been hauled over the coals for it. He is no friend of ours and I enjoyed making rings round him. Personally I thought I did it rather well. The programme will be shown when we are at Windsor next week. I wonder if I can ask Her Majesty whether I can turn on the TV?

Wednesday, 27 March. A historic meeting of the NEC. The photographers were outside in force to snap George coming in to claim his place as Deputy Leader and the reporters were agog to know how he voted on Desmond Donnelly. George slipped into the room quietly and only spoke once when the Minutes of Home Policy Committee were before us. As anticipated, the Inquiry Committee which interviewed Donnelly (consisting of Joe Gormley,

Harry Nicholas and Frank Lane of the NUR) came out unanimously for expulsion. Mik argued persuasively that we should let the matter ride a bit. Only Frank Allaun and Tom Driberg (the latter rather hesitantly) supported Mik. Harold and George abstained.

Thursday, 28 March. Michael Stewart reported on the Falkland Islands in Cabinet. Apparently the aim of our talks with the Argentine Government has been to get the travel restrictions, which the latter had imposed, removed and to establish a more satisfactory long-term relationship between the islands and Argentina. He had skilfully found a formula to deal with the question of sovereignty, saying we were prepared to recognize Argentine sovereignty over the islands only if the islanders themselves considered it to be in their own interest. He was rather pleased with the way he had managed this so as to prevent talks being called off while firmly standing by the rights of the islanders. 'I thought', he says in his inimitable way, 'that I had better get firmly established on one stool.' 'Yes, we know,' Harold flashed back, 'you have raced ahead on your stool and have defused the situation.' It was the first time in a long time we had had a good laugh at Cabinet.

It was Jim Callaghan who asked solemnly whether the Falkland Islands were any use to us. Apparently none at all but there would be one of those absurd parliamentary rows if we were to try and disembarrass ourselves of them.

We were ending our meeting well ahead of time and quite happily when Harold of course had to return to his favourite theme of leaks. He said darkly that he has been collecting 'finger-prints'. He is livid about the stories that he is to wind up DEA and told us that he had instructed Gerald Kaufman to brief the press to the contrary. 'Your finger-prints were clearly there,' said Jim nastily and then proceeded to launch into one of the most unrestrained attacks I have ever heard from him. First he complained that Gerald Kaufman was supposed to serve the whole Cabinet and not merely the PM. Next he complained that some Ministers seemed to have political press officers to protect them – looking hard at Roy. It was all said as offensively as possible and Roy's face tightened with steely hate. 'If you are thinking of John Harris,' said Harold, 'he is a civil servant.' If so, said Jim, he wanted to know why Harris had been moved from his job at the Home Office without consulting Roy's successor and what was he doing now at the Treasury? 'It's none of your business, Home Secretary,' said Roy viciously. He and Jim outstared each other across the table. There is going to be no united front there to oust Harold. Jim is clearly getting quite neurotic over what he considers to be his grievances.

Friday, 29 March. A day of terrible mourning. The four by-election results cannot just be shrugged off.[1] The question is now raised insistently on every hand as to whether Harold can survive. Dick phoned me early to say he is just on his way to see Harold. What did I think he should say to him? A tall order! I

[1] The first shock was the Labour rout at Dudley which had been held by George Wigg for twenty-three years. The by-election, caused by his elevation to the peerage and to the chairmanship of the Horserace Levy Betting Board, turned his majority of 10,000 into a Conservative majority of 11,656. This was followed by Acton where a Labour majority of nearly 5,000 became a Conservative majority of 3,720 and another shock at Meriden with a Labour majority of 4,581 collapsing into a Conservative majority of over 15,000. At Warwick and Leamington the Conservative majority jumped from 8,697 to 21,922.

reply that there must be no collective panic. Maudling's statement on TV last night to the effect that there ought to be a General Election because a Government couldn't carry out the necessary tough measures unless it had the confidence of the country, begged all the questions. Any Government carrying out tough measures would have a violent swing against it. We must hang on at all costs in order to reap the fruits of those measures ourselves. Yes, said Dick, but there would have to be changes in the Government. If Harold didn't produce a different Government, the Party would insist that it was produced without him. The time had come for the Wilson Cabinet Mark 2. We agreed to lunch together.

George Thomas[1] came to see me first thing at the office: a private talk. Judith should have accompanied him, but had to go North. Their purpose was to beg me to shed some of my Departmental obsessions and mingle more with the boys in the tea-room to bolster up morale and to help fight off the attacks on Harold. I agreed that I don't do enough of this. One of the reasons is that I have felt as helpless as they do to influence events, even though I am in the Cabinet. So the bigger the mess the more I cling to the one positive factor in the situation, the importance of my own policies and above all the potential success of my Transport Bill. But I promised to force myself to give more time to the House and the back benchers in future. I reported part of the conversation to John Gunn, who at once took on board the importance of it and promised to do what he could to keep me more free. He really is a good lad, a civil servant at its best, highly intelligent and utterly loyal to the Minister without giving any indication of his personal views.

At lunch Dick plunged straight into the point. He had seen Harold. There is to be a fundamental Cabinet reconstruction soon and he had a message for me from Harold: 'You are to put the life into the Wilson Cabinet Mark 2. (Apparently Harold was delighted with Dick's phrase.) That was all Dick was supposed to tell me, but of course it all came tumbling out. Harold is to go for an inner Cabinet at last: six of us representing regrouped Departments: Dick, me, Roy, Michael, Harold and Fred Peart, who is to become Leader of the House. Dick is to be in charge of the Social Services as First Secretary. I am to be in charge of the Economy with Peter under me. (Who else, I wonder? Board of Trade and Labour as well?) My prime task is to win over the trade unions. The thought terrifies me. As I told Dick, it was simple at Transport because I inherited a policy vacuum. There had been nothing before me to queer the pitch. But to take over at this stage a mess of policies which other people had created would be a very different kettle of fish. Anyway, someone had got to do it so I might as well have a shot. Could we control Harold more in the future? 'If we go into this,' I said grimly, 'we'll have to meet socially and informally regularly as well as the weekly official meetings you say he plans. And the rest of us will just have to make Harold play it our way – or say we'll get out.' Dick doubts very much whether we can do anything with Harold, even under the new regime. He then swore me to secrecy about all this: I mustn't let Harold know he had leaked to me. All I could share with Ted was Harold's general message to me. Well, I shall keep my mouth shut – unlike Dick himself.

[1] Labour MP for Cardiff West and Minister of State at the Commonwealth Office. He became Secretary of State for Wales in 1968 and was elected Speaker of the House of Commons in 1976. Hebecame a life peer in 1983.

Monday, 1 April. The beginning of a fantastic week which has marked a major change in the direction of my career. My mind was on the coming Cabinet reshuffle. Thinking over my conversation with Dick on Friday, I had decided that for once I had to take an initiative *vis-à-vis* the PM. Up to now I have always stood back and waited for him to decide how he was going to dispose of me. This time I have decided to take a hand in shaping, not only my future, but the future structure of the Government. Dick thought this was a good idea so I rang up Harold bright and early at No. 10. I said I had received Dick's message and would like to talk to him. 'Did Dick tell you what I had in mind for you?' Faithful as always to my pledges of secrecy, I said Dick had given me only a generalized message. 'I have now got a different job in mind for you. By all means let's talk later on, but I am still sorting out my ideas,' he replied. 'That's the moment I want to talk to you,' I answered. He sounded a bit taken aback and then recovered and said, 'Certainly, come along.' And so I have asked his office for a time and this has been fixed for tomorrow.

Tuesday, 2 April. The message came from No. 10 that I was to stay behind after Cabinet in order to see the PM. Dick Marsh had one of his rare radical moments when he asked whether we couldn't reconsider our policy on Vietnam. Johnson's dramatic decision to withdraw from the presidential elections has really opened up the prospects of peace[1] and Marsh suggested we should use this to get ourselves off the hook of our Vietnam policy. Harold gave us his usual long exposition of how we had always been ready to act as mediators, adding that this was the last moment to change our role. I then had to go out of the Cabinet with the others, wait until they had left the building, and then creep back into the Cabinet room through the Secretaries' annexe.

'Well, what is it Barbara wants to say?' asked Harold, looking at me defensively. 'I want to tell you my ideas about what I think should be done,' I replied. 'Quite right, go ahead,' said Harold and then he paced up and down while I, for once, succeeded in making him listen. I told him that he knew more about the intrigues against him than I did, but I knew that unless he presented a different image of the Government the Party would demand a different Prime Minister. I was interested in reconstructing a Wilson Cabinet and thought that the reconstruction now ought to be fundamental and quick before the traumatic effect of the by-election results had worn off. So I thought he ought to create a small war Cabinet because we were politically in a wartime situation, facing defeat. It should consist of the PM, the Chancellor, the Foreign Secretary, the Minister of Defence, a Social Services overlord, an Economic Services overlord, the Leader of the House and also – for political reasons – Scotland and Wales. Such a small Cabinet would create such controversy that it would have to appear not merely as a Wilson circle, but intellectually credible, and therefore he couldn't exclude his able enemies like Healey. Harold couldn't contain himself any longer at this point. Still marching up and down he said, 'I am very excited by your suggestion. I think it has possibilities. I had

[1] In a broadcast the previous day President Johnson had announced a partial suspension of American bombing of North Vietnam and offered a total cessation of bombing if North Vietnam would respond. He then added that he would not run for another term as President.

been intending, in any case, to have an inner Cabinet.' I waved this aside. An inner committee of Cabinet just wouldn't do the trick. 'We have got to get away from those ghastly long Albert Hall-type meetings at which every member of the Cabinet speaks in turn and it takes three-quarters of an hour to get one item ventilated round the whole room.' Harold seemed impressed, and then went on to tell me what he had in mind for me: the first ever Lady President of the Council and Leader of the House, with time to spare from Departmental duties to concentrate more on the collective strategy of the Cabinet (of whose inner circle I would be a member) and above all to get down to the job of putting the Government's policy across publicly.

My heart and face dropped. I told him this just wasn't my cup of tea. I was a natural administrator and the thought of spending long tedious hours hanging about in Parliament as Dick has had to do filled me with dismay. He seemed very disappointed at my reaction, but I went on to argue that my real role was in the economic field. 'Why not give me DEA?' Harold said this had always been his idea, but now it was out because Roy wouldn't like it. The Treasury had a tough job to do; it must be allowed to do it. And he didn't want the Treasury upset. 'Have you talked to him?' I asked. He said no, but he was sure Roy wouldn't want a strong Minister at DEA. I fought back hard saying that my real talents lay in getting on with the trade unions and with the working-class rank and file. I wasn't particularly good at organizing publicity. I had only managed to project myself because I was *doing* things. This was the only way in which the Government's image could ever be put across. It must be seen to be caring for raising the standard of life of the people we represent and this didn't mean going back on the Budget strategy of the Chancellor. For instance, I said, jumping up myself and joining him in walking up and down, we had got ourselves into a disastrous negative stance over prices and incomes policy. What the Government ought to be doing was going out into industry and taking the initiative in asking industries what they could do to raise their own workers' wages by improving productivity. 'You know, Harold,' I said, 'I remember Nye once saying at a meeting of the NEC, "The trouble with these people is that they hate the working class." That's the image we have fixed on this Government. And our economic strategy will never succeed unless we get rid of it.'

By this time it was nearly 2 pm and neither of us had had any food. Harold was sipping brandy hard and the gin and tonic which I had taken on an empty stomach was beginning to make my head swim, and anyway I had an appointment at 2 pm. 'I'm excited by your ideas,' said Harold, 'but I want to see you as the first Lady President of the Council. Go away and think about it.'

The first thing I did when I got back to the House was to ring Dick and arrange to meet him urgently later on. I told him what Harold had offered me and he agreed with me that it was ludicrously inappropriate. I insisted that I ought to be sent, as Harold had suggested earlier, to DEA. Dick said he was dining with Roy that night and would put the point to him. He promised to ring me first thing tomorrow.

Exhausted and hungry, I collected Ted at 10 pm and headed for home. I had just slipped into a dressing-gown and poured myself a drink when the phone rang. It was John Gunn. The PM wanted to see me immediately. Noble Edward volunteered to run me down. Redressing hurriedly, we dashed down to the car, wiped the snow off the windscreen and headed for No. 10. Harold came along as urbanely relaxed as usual, greeted Ted affectionately and beckoned me into his room. There another shock awaited me. He had been deeply impressed by what I had said earlier about the need to take a positive initiative on productivity and to set the prices and incomes policy to a new tune. He would have loved to see me as the first Lady President of the Council, but it was true I got publicity for the Government by doing things. So his idea now was that I should be Minister of Labour.

My spirits thudded through my shoes again. 'Look here, Harold,' I said, 'I don't intend to be Maggie Bondfield Mark 2.'[1] 'Let's call in that whiskered fellow from outside,' said Harold and told Michael Halls to fetch Ted (to whom he had already sent out a drink). Ted came into the famous Cabinet room slightly dazed. He told Harold, as he had told me, that he thought the Lady President of the Council and Leader of the House was a wonderful job – but then he is romantic about the House of Commons in a way I am not. To me it is not so much the stage of history as a workshop. Harold outlined his new idea while I sat moaning with my head between my knees. I could see my whole hopes of at last getting into the inner Cabinet fading away simply because the Minister of Labour would not have rank high enough in the hierarchy (and anyway Ray Gunter's job plus prices and incomes, which Harold said would be transferred from DEA to me, didn't seem to add up to enough). 'We can call it something new,' said Harold. 'Ministry of Production?' 'No, that would overlap with DEA. The only possible name', I replied, 'would be Minister of Employment and Productivity.'

We sat there for over an hour while Harold paced round, sipping brandy and water as usual, and finally told me to go home and sleep on it. So we trailed back home, empty, hungry and, as far as I was concerned, heavy of heart. I had just got into bed, exhausted, when the phone rang. The Chancellor's Private Secretary: could I see him at 9.30 the next morning? Highly intrigued, I said yes.

Wednesday, 3 April. Roy greeted me cordially at No. 11. He wanted to see me, he said, before he left for Washington so that he could assure me that in resisting the idea of my going to DEA he had nothing against me personally. On the contrary, he thought I was one of the three outstanding Ministers in the Government and would be capable of doing any job in the Cabinet, 'including this one', but he wanted to avoid the Treasury being distracted by the recreation of the old battles which George and Jim had had, and if I were at DEA I would want to make it something positive. 'Relations between us would be bound to be strained and I should regret that.' I tried to assure him that I accepted the unavoidable need for his immediate strategy and would visualize my work at DEA as underpinning his, but he was clearly not convinced. He suggested that if Harold really had the courage to do so he ought to sack Jim from the Home Office and put me in his place, as I could couple the Home

[1] Margaret Bondfield was Minister of Labour in the 1929 Labour Government under Ramsay MacDonald, but lost her seat in the *débâcle* of the 1931 Election when the National Government was formed. She was the first woman Cabinet Minister in Britain's history.

Office with leadership of the House. We then had a rather hurried discussion about the need to reconstruct the Cabinet and he seemed quite impressed by my urging that only a smaller 'war' Cabinet would see us through. He wasn't keen on the idea of overlords and pointed out that even small wartime Cabinets had included some Departmental Ministers. I told Roy I thought Harold ought not to reach final decisions until he, Roy, had returned from Washington. We parted amicably.

I drifted into the Party meeting on Vietnam – poorly attended and lethargic – and called out Dick, to report developments. He said that we should insist on seeing Harold together: it really was absurd to carry on all these conversations bilaterally. He was hurrying off to a meeting himself but said he would phone the PM. Before I heard the outcome of this I got another urgent summons to No. 10. Harold was stumping round tight-lipped. 'I've just sent the Chancellor off with a flea in his ear. He has tried to tell me how to run my own Cabinet. I told him he had better remember who was Prime Minister.' I couldn't help grinning inwardly when I realized that Roy had taken me at my word and urged Harold not to settle matters until he had returned from Washington. In the event, my suggestion had greatly heightened Harold's determination to get the matter announced before the weekend. He asked me if I had thought over his Ministry of Labour suggestion which had increasingly grown on him. He could see me handling the industrial correspondents as well as the lobby, getting my picture in the papers and on TV and generally helping the Government's image. I sat there miserably saying I really wasn't going to be Maggie Bondfield Mark 2 and that I would rather stay at the Ministry of Transport. It was quite clear now that Harold had been frightened away from the idea of a smaller Cabinet. All he was talking of was an inner steering group. And we all know what that would amount to. He said Wedgie had been to see him with some ideas and clearly had not taken kindly to the notion that he might be excluded from the Cabinet. In fact, Harold hinted, he might resign. 'Why should I turn out my friends and make more enemies? The Wilson Mark 2 Cabinet will have a built-in majority. I am not going to be put again in the position I was in over arms for South Africa.'

I wanted to know who would follow me at Transport and when he said he might send Ray Gunter there I revolted outright. It really would have to be Stephen Swingler who succeeded me, with John Morris upgraded to help him. Only in that way could we get the Transport Bill through. The trouble here, Harold said, was security. Stephen had been doing some 'very stupid' things.

By this time I was due to leave for Windsor where Ted and I had been invited to dine and stay the night. When he heard I was going, Harold said I would have a pleasant time. 'But they unpack your bags for you there. Don't do what my sister did. When they opened her bag her corn plasters fell out.'

I left uncomforted. I certainly am not going to do a sidewards shift to Labour from my beloved Transport, even if Harold does rechristen my new job.

Windsor Castle is an incredible sight. Guards clank arms and a policeman salutes as one sweeps into a huge inner courtyard dominated by the old tower with its high grass bank covered with daffodils. Lord Plunkett and Miss Morrison were waiting to receive us on behalf of the Queen. A few steps took us into an attractive suite of rooms with the most fabulous view right down the park, the length of the broad walk to the copper statue. They told us it was known as the Minister's room, where they always put the Prime Minister. Soft-footed servants moved in silently and unpacked our bags, as Harold had said. We washed and went down a long, long corridor, flanked with Stubbs paintings and showcases full of marvellous porcelain, to the drawing room. It was a relief to find Arnold Goodman[1] there as well as the Italian Ambassador and the Canadian High Commissioner, and the Croslands joined us too. When the Queen arrived she went round seriously shaking hands and then stood talking to Princess Anne with an air of almost glum indifference. So I joined in one of my hearty conversations with Philip, who is always easy to talk to. Suddenly to my astonishment he remarked, 'I am very sorry Peter Parker never became chairman of the Railways Board. He worked with me, you know, on the Outward Bound thing and I thought he was absolutely first class.' I warmed to him at this and told him the whole drama of the devaluation *débâcle* and he was absolutely fascinated.

At this point the Queen came over and, as usual, as she talked her face relaxed into what can be her very charming smile. I can only conclude that she is either naturally shy or has inherited Queen Mary's glower without knowing it. She always gets animated when she talks about the children and one remark she made brought home to me vividly the basic horror of the royal life. Talking of Anne and Charles and how much they were enjoying school and University, she recalled that the first time she had ever joined in any collective activity was when she joined the ATS, during the war. 'One had no idea how one compared with other people,' she said simply. 'And of course there were a lot of mechanical things one had to master.' 'Did you enjoy it?' I asked. 'Oh yes, enormously.' And I really felt sorry for her when she went on to say she had received a large number of critical letters because of something I had said in Parliament about mothers not taking children on their knees in the front of cars. Apparently she had been in the estate car in Windsor Park with Andrew in the back and had taken Edward on her knee in the front seat. Some photographer had snapped her and she had been flooded with a hostile mail, saying Barbara Castle said she oughtn't to do that. Poor woman! I don't know which of us is more under the spotlight!

Thursday, 4 April. Rang Dick from Windsor to see how things stood. He had seen Harold after me and put to him an astonishing proposition. Why should not I become First Secretary as well as Minister of Employment and Productivity? Harold was taken aback with this piece of self-sacrifice, but Dick said it didn't matter to him at all. He would rather remain Lord President. He had got used to it and anyway he didn't want to give up his nice room. 'Would this make all the difference to Barbara?' Harold had asked. 'Yes, I think it would,' said Dick. 'Is she so status conscious, then?' 'No,' replied Dick, 'but she is power conscious and quite right.'

[1] Arnold Goodman, senior partner in Goodman, Derrick and Co., Solicitors, had been made a life peer in 1965 not only in recognition of the shrewd and generous legal advice he had given Labour politicians overthe years, but also of his remarkable capacity for insinuating himself into positions of influence – in the arts, the newspaper world and as an adviser generally. He was to play a big part in my later life when I was Secretary of State for the Social Services.

I felt an enormous sense of relief. To become First Secretary would certainly not be a sideways shift. The high status would transform the whole job, categorically ensure that I would be in the inner Cabinet and make the chance of succeeding in my tough assignment much, much greater.

I hurried back to London and into the Standing Committee of the Transport Bill. Messages kept coming in to the effect that I might have to go at any time to No. 10. I had to keep forcing my mind back to quantity licensing. The message came at last that I was to go and see the Lord President at 1 pm. Then on via his room to the Prime Minister.

Dick was holding his confab with his officials in preparation for his weekly lobby conference and was absolutely beaming at his own ingenuity. There was only a moment before I was summoned, but I told him we must see the PM together. And so we did – at long last. Why Harold puts these things off I will never know. Marcia came in, too, and we sat round talking brutally frankly about the power set-up in the Cabinet. I told Harold I would take the job on Dick's terms but begged him again to put Stephen in my place. Harold said he would check up on the record again and see how black it was but Stephen really had been dabbling in Eastern Europe too much. He couldn't risk giving Jim Callaghan (who had access to the security records) a weapon against him by bringing Stephen into the Cabinet if Stephen were in any way a security risk. Dick agreed with him on this.

I barely got back to my Ministry when I got another summons to see Harold. By this time all the messages were practically in code. I had to go to my room in the House and wait to be summoned from there. As I entered Harold's room his Private Secretary came up in great agitation and reported a telephone message from the Chancellor in Washington. 'Tell him I have nothing to say to him and I will let him know what happens when I am ready,' Harold snapped. So Roy is still clinging tenaciously. Harold confirmed that the job was now all sewn up and wanted to know who I would like to have as Parliamentary Secretary. He doesn't want me to keep Roy Hattersley who, he said, is a Jenkins man, but Dick said he is very competent and I could manage him. So I said could I please have Edmund Dell or, failing him, I would stick to Hattersley.[1] 'You are taking a big risk,' said Harold, shaking his head. 'Everything you say will be reported back to the Chancellor.' All I am anxious to do is to get a competent team.

Dinner with Jock Campbell and at last I got on to my night sleeper for Blackburn at 11.15 pm. I had just got into bed with my hot water bottle and warm milk when there was a tap at the door. The station-master held out a bit of paper. Would I please ring Whitehall 4433. I tucked my nightie into my knickers, pulled over a skirt and my coat and went out on the cold platform with bare legs. They opened the reservation office for me and got me No. 10. It was Harold just to tell me that he had decided after all that I should be Secretary of

[1] Roy Hattersley had been MP for Birmingham, Sparkbrook, since 1964 and Joint Parliamentary Secretary at the Ministry of Labour since 1967. He stayed with me at the Department of Employment and Productivity [DEP] until 1969 when he was promoted Minister of Defence for Administration. Edmund Dell, MP for Birkenhead, who had been Parliamentary Secretary at Technology and DEA and Minister of State at the Board of Trade, then joined me as Minister of State.

State for Employment and Productivity and not merely a Minister, even though this would mean a Transfer of Functions Order in the House. 'This will mean an early debate at which you can set out your new policy.' I must say life doesn't let up for a moment. At last to bed.

The reshuffle was a major one but only one person was dropped from the Government. This was Patrick Gordon Walker whose post at Education was taken over by Ted Short. For the rest it was a question of reshuffling the same pack. Dick Crossman was moved from his hated job as Leader of the House to take charge of a merger of the Ministries of Health and Social Security into a new Department of Health and Social Security of which he was to become the head, while remaining Lord President and therefore retaining his magnificent room. Fred Peart took his place as Leader of the House, where he was very popular, and Cledwyn Hughes moved to Agriculture. Ray Gunter became Minister of Power, replacing Dick Marsh who followed me at Transport. The merger of the Foreign and Commonwealth Offices into the FCO *was also going ahead.*

Friday, 5 April. Well, I am in the thick of it now, for better or for worse – probably worse. I am under no illusions that I may be committing political suicide. I have at last moved from the periphery of the whirlwind into its very heart. I hate the thought of leaving the Ministry of Transport. If I had stayed I think I could have made a really dramatic and mounting impact on road accidents, to say nothing of carrying through my transport plan. My fan mail has been growing, and I am about to change all that for the very focal point of unpopularity. And yet I know I couldn't do anything else. If I go down in disaster as well I may, at least I shall have been an adult before I die.

Saturday, 6 April. Got off my night sleeper at Euston at 7.30 am to find Douglas Smith, my new Private Secretary, and Charles Birdsall, my Chief Information Officer, waiting for me. Stephen Fay of the *Sunday Times* had even gatecrashed my sleeper last night and tried to get an exclusive interview, but I told him I was meeting the Sunday industrial correspondents later in the morning and refused to say anything before then. I took instantly to my two new chaps and swept them up in the car to John Spencer Square, talking over the weekend's plans. We invaded a startled Ted, who greeted us sitting up in bed. It is magnificent the way he takes all this in his stride.

Sunday, 7 April. Had Denis Barnes down to tea [at HCF]. Harold says he is the best Permanent Secretary in Whitehall. It is certainly going to be stimulating to work with him, but in this Ministry I shall be dealing with real professions, not the tatty set-up I found when I first went to the Ministry of Transport.

Monday, 8 April. Started my new life by a trip to Windsor to kiss hands. Mollie Wright, my delightful driver, picked me up at HCF and we bowled along happily, still well under 70 mph. Dick Marsh told me he started his new job as Minister of Transport by doing 90 mph on the M4. After we had all done our kneeling and kissing with expertise and aplomb by now, the Queen had her usual chat with us. As Secretary of State I have my own seal which they gave me to carry away in a locked leather box.

Into the new Ministry feeling as one always does in the first weeks of a new job, rather at sea. Harold has already laid on a meeting for us both with George Woodcock at No. 10 this afternoon.

I had a private lunch with some members of the lobby and sailed along to No. 10 feeling muzzier than ever. To my astonishment the usual little crowd of visitors in Downing Street cried out when I arrived, 'There's Barbara,' and gave me a cheer. No doubt the country already sees me as the sacrificial lamb!

George Woodcock's attitude to my appointment was surprisingly encouraging. I had expected him to be sceptical, not to say scathing, but instead he remarked that the merging of the execution of the P and I policy with what he called the 'theology' was a sensible development, of which he had felt the necessity for a long time. He warned me that I was in for a tough time. It was no good the Government expecting it could get everything it wanted. There would have to be a lot of 'dirty compromises' (a favourite phrase of his, apparently). He would help all he could, but I mustn't expect him to support me openly. If he did, he would only get into trouble with his own militants. 'I know,' I agreed cheerfully. 'I'm on my own.' 'Exactly,' he replied. But on the whole I thought it was a heartening start. George and I left No. 10 together and the press noted as a major news item that he was smiling at me. Apparently making George smile is quite something.

Then on to the Ministry of Transport for my hastily convened farewell party. I had planned to say all sorts of moving things about the way I felt on leaving the Ministry, but I was too drained to produce any of them. The nicest comment of all came – not for the first time – from Hankey who concluded with the most welcome compliment of all, 'What I shall always remember about you is your laugh.' I really felt desperately sorry at leaving them all.

Tuesday, 9 April. I got a bit of a shock when I walked into the Cabinet room to find that I had been allocated a new seat, as First Secretary, plumb opposite Harold. I looked nostalgically down to the bottom corner by the window between John Silkin and Peter Shore. No more friendly giggles now! I am flanked by Gerald Gardiner and Denis Healey who spends a lot of his time muttering under his breath and stabbing viciously at his blotter. I suspect his resentment against Harold is profound.

Harold began the meeting with one of those pieces of ingratiating conciliation which I find rather nauseating. He wanted to explain what the new 'Parliamentary Committee' of the Cabinet (as he called the inner Cabinet) was going to do: the descriptions in the press were nothing like what he had in mind. It was merely going to co-ordinate the political strategy of the Government with special emphasis on the presentation of policy.

Spent the evening on a succession of personal talks. First with Roy Hattersley. Tommy has assured me he is a snake and I must not trust him more than I can see him, but I intend to reach my own conclusions on this.

Later I talked to practically the whole of the Tribune group. They had sent a message to me yesterday asking to see me as soon as possible and I had clinched with it at once. We had a hard-hitting two hours over drinks, but there was no malice in it on either side. In turn Norman Atkinson, Stan Orme, Jack Mendelson, Russ Kerr, San Newens, Jim Dickens and Ian Mikardo urged the need to find some compromise.[1] (Mike Foot sent apologies that he couldn't come.) They said they could see me being politically ruined and they were desperately anxious that this shouldn't happen. Didn't I realize how practically impossible it was to police every productivity deal? The more they talked the more I realized that they lacked the desperate sense of economic urgency we had acquired in Cabinet, and when Mik said to me, 'Are you really going to put trade unionists in jail?' I flashed out, 'Yes, if I have to – and I will go with them, Mik.' I might too, if the gesture seemed appropriate. And I think they realized that, though they hate the policy, I was trying to lift it on to a different plane.

As we broke up Mik put his arm round me and said, 'You are a marvellous woman and we love you dearly, but even you can't make us think a cesspool smells like a rose.' I laughed ruefully and said we must talk again and often.

Wednesday, 10 April. At my suggestion Harold and I met Stephen Brown, President of the CBI. I can't have them saying my first act in my new office was to snub the CBI. Once again I thought Harold was unnecessarily unctuous. I think we are wrong to disguise the fact that we are on a different side of the fence from them on many issues. I always made this clear at MOT and I think they respected me for it. Anyway I didn't like the relish with which Stephen Brown, who is of course a leading light in the Engineering Employers' Federation, is shaping up for a showdown with the engineering unions. OK, maybe I have got to have a showdown with Hughie Scanlon, but that doesn't make me the employers' ally. Aubrey Jones floated in for a quick interview and I told him I would want all the help I could get in enforcing the prices side of the policy.

Two main industrial disputes were to occupy my time. The first was the municipal busmen's pay increase. Following sporadic industrial action by them in the previous year in support of the 'busmen's charter', the Employers' Federation had conceded a £1 per week increase in December 1967, which the Government had had to standstill and refer to the PIB. The Board's report, published in April 1968, endorsed the Government's view that the settlement was contrary to prices and incomes policy because it contained no productivity, but it also suggested that there was considerable scope for increased productivity in the industry and recommended that local productivity agreements should be negotiated. One possibility was that a two- or three-tier system of basic rates above the minimum should be introduced in the largest cities, varying with the 'effort and strain' involved in driving there. In a separate report the Board had already proposed the immediate payment of 10s a week bonus for busmen willing to move to one-man bus operation [OMO]. The TGWU, however, was demanding that the £1 agreement, backdated to December 1967, should be honoured unconditionally and that the 10s should be additional. When I took over my new job, I found that the standstill was due to lapse on 26 July and would have to be renewed unless agreement could be reached in line with policy. The negotiations which were to ensue were long and tortuous.

Discontent had also been simmering for months among the engineering unions. In

[1] Of that group of left-wing Labour MPs Stan Orme, AEU-sponsored MP for Salford West, was to accept office in the 1974–79 Labour Government, entering Jim Callaghan's Cabinet in 1977 as Minister for Social Security. Michael Foot, of course, was to become the mainstay of that Government.

October 1967 they had put in a claim through the Confederation of Engineering and Shipbuilding Unions for a new long-term agreement with the Employers' Federation. Its main demand was for a 'substantial wage increase for all adult workers in the industry'. It also called for improvements in fringe benefits and for the men's minimum rate to be applied to women (who at present came at the bottom of the hierarchy of rates – skilled, semi-skilled, labourers and women – in a special category of their own) and for women doing skilled work to be paid the skilled man's rate (though there weren't many of them). This was later watered down in the phrase 'steps should be taken towards the establishment of equal pay for women'.

In their reply in March 1968 the employers had flatly rejected a general all-round increase, improvements in fringe benefits or steps towards equal pay. All they would offer was an immediate increase in minimum earnings levels followed by four more increments at six-monthly intervals, graduated according to skills, the new levels to be consolidated into new minimum time rates in three years' time. The offer was conditional on concessions being made by the unions on productivity. The scene was set for a serious clash. The Confederation Executive insisted that nothing less would do than an all-round increase in wages, bringing the rate of pay of skilled men within the band of £15–£20 a week within the three years of the agreement, with proportionate increases for the semi-skilled and labourers; and on 1 May a specially convened conference of the Executives of the constituent unions passed a resolution calling for a one-day stoppage of work on 15 May, to be followed if necessary by an overtime ban and other sanctions. The resolution, however, concluded with the words 'The Executive Council expresses its willingness to meet the Engineering Employers' Federation at any time', thus leaving the door open.

Tuesday, 23 April. Harold called me to No. 10 to discuss a number of points. It became clear to me that the Parliamentary Committee is going to be very much less than an inner Cabinet. Its area of discussion is going to be circumscribed to the parliamentary and presentational aspects of policy. And it is going to report faithfully to full Cabinet. So all that remains of the Mark 2 Cabinet will be three key Cabinet Committees (SEP, OPD and the new Parliamentary Committee) and the fact that I shall be on all three of them. It is a pretty heavy responsibility to carry if my change of status is supposed to be the solution to all our cares!

Wednesday, 24 April. It was 6 pm before I could settle down to my crucial speech to the AEF National Committee [in Eastbourne]. At 8.30 I could see I was in for a late night so I told Douglas Smith I was going to Dick's for a quick meal, even though I had only got my opening paragraphs prepared.

To my surprise the conversation over dinner was very general and it wasn't until the coffee stage that we got on to what I suspect was the reason for the meal: a discussion of the work of the Parliamentary Committee. Neither Roy nor Dick thought the Committee could do much good. With my mind somewhat on other matters I hurried away, conscious once again of the curious coldness at the heart of Roy, despite all his obvious desire to please, and I think his genuine good will towards me. There is no natural warmth about him. Roy remains instinctively aloof even when he is being most sociable. I certainly don't think he could ever lead the Party successfully.

Thursday, 25 April. Three hours in bed, then off to the most crucial meeting of my new job. On the train I learned to my horror that they had asked me to answer questions and I hadn't had a moment to prepare my thoughts for this. It was like going into the lions' den without even an hour's training on the tamer's course. The delegates are the most hard-bitten lot in the trade union movement anyway. Secondly, there are only fifty-two of them on the National Committee, so it is hardly a mass audience. But thirdly, they were spread round vast tables filling the whole room. And fourthly, there was a battery of TV lights between me and them. And to cap it all, some twenty top-ranking industrial correspondents were scribbling away below me in force.

My speech went pretty well and, considering all the circumstances, I was quite proud of it. But the questions were an entirely different matter. I didn't really strike home until the last question, on workers' participation, when I really let myself go. To my surprise they rose to applaud me after that, even though the decibel rating wasn't as high as some I have received and even though twelve of them sat down ostentatiously. But I felt I had at any rate survived and not done any harm. And there might be some value in the national appeal I was making, as it were, over their heads. This was confirmed later by the effect my speech had on a lot of people on TV.

Friday, 26 April. Another crowded day and my USDAW speech yet to do.[1]

Sunday, 28 April. Off by helicopter to Margate [for the USDAW conference] and at last a bite of food (I don't seem to have had a normal lunch for weeks).

So into the conference hall where I found something like 2,000 people waiting for me. Immensely friendly with a bit of healthy barracking. I knew that somewhere out of my reserves I had got to draw a spontaneous response; to have started reading a speech in that atmosphere would have been fatal. I thought I did all right under the circumstances. Apparently I did better than that. Ernie Fernyhough said to me afterwards, 'Your predecessor here last year could never have done that.'[2] Apparently he was referring to Harold.

Monday, 29 April. Fabulously good press coverage for my USDAW speech. In the office had Harold Lever in to discuss the increase in mortgage rates.[3] Jarratt and I are trying to persuade the Treasury to allow us to refer them to the PIB.[4]

Tuesday, 30 April. In my absence in Eastbourne last Thursday the Parliamentary Committee decided to take the Transfer of Functions Order legitimizing my status on Thursday this week and to fit in an Opposition debate on rising prices the day before. This is totally disastrous. I have several key negotiations ahead of me this week. Scanlon, for example, has agreed that I shall meet the

[1] I had been invited to address the annual conference of the Union of Shop, Distributive and Allied Workers.

[2] Ernest Fernyhough had been a full-time official of USDAW before becoming Labour MP for Jarrow in 1947. He was Harold Wilson's PPS from 1964 to 1967 when he became Parliamentary Secretary at the Ministry of Labour. He remained with me at DEP until 1969.

[3] Despite the fact that bank rate had been cut to 7½ per cent on 21 March following the tough budget, the building societies had announced on 19 April that the mortgage rate was going up from 7⅛ to 7⅝ per cent.

[4] Alex Jarratt, who had been rising steadily up the civil service ladder, had been Secretary to the PIB since 1965. He became my Deputy Secretary at DEP in 1968 and in 1970 left the civil service to become Managing Director of IPC.

Confederation[1] on Wednesday morning; there is the municipal busmen issue to deal with too. It will take me all my time to prepare for Thursday's debate.

Wednesday, 1 May. One of the most nightmarish days in my whole history. It makes last week pale into insignificance. Of course I had done no work on my [prices] speech. At the office we spent a frantic one and a half hours collecting and checking a vast complexity of facts. Then into the Confederation meeting. I told them I was not negotiating, but merely seeking to identify what were the sore spots for them in the employers' proposals. Altogether I thought it was a useful meeting.

Back to my office to bolt a sandwich and make some kind of coherence out of my scattered notes. When Dick Marsh arrived at 2.30 for the busmen's meeting I was barely sane and didn't have time even to greet them all properly. I told Dick I could make only a few introductory remarks and then get off to the House. So I told the busmen we should have to operate another standstill, and then fled. In the car to the House I don't think I have ever been more petrified. This was my first speech in my new job there, and the spotlight would be on me mercilessly, and I have never in my whole life been worse prepared. In the event I survived – but only just. It had the makings of a good speech but I hadn't the time or the energy really to refine it and put it across.

And there was still a meeting with the engineering employers waiting for me. I thought their President [*i.e.* of the Engineering Employers' Federation], Jim Fielding, looked hard-faced. I drew them out on where they thought things stood on the engineering claim and I gathered they, too, are beginning to have second thoughts along a general increase line – a direction in which I encouraged them. As we sat together Charles brought me a copy of the resolution just passed by the Confederation Executive at its meeting this afternoon. They threaten industrial action, but what matters is the last sentence saying that they are ready to meet the employers again 'at any time'. I urged Fielding to make a quick and favourable response to this.

Thursday, 2 May. Got up early to work on my speech [in the 'transfer of functions' debate]. Over to the House for a quick coffee and biscuits. I laboured through my speech uneventfully – to be astonished later by the press coverage it got. Ironically the phrase which stirred up most excitement as being highly interventionist was one Denis Barnes had produced.

Then into a meeting of the P and I Committee where Hattersley and I battled hard to get the mortgage increase (which Treasury had approved without even informing me) referred to the PIB. Roy Jenkins was very apologetic about the non-consultation but stood out firmly against the reference, much to Hattersley's disgust. (I am constantly intrigued by Roy H.'s criticisms of Roy J. Is he genuine or just trying to draw me out?)

Monday, 6 May. One of my discoveries in my new job is that the Minister of Labour has always been furnished with security reports on the trade unions.

[1] The Confederation of Engineering and Shipbuilding Unions was the banding together for mutual support of some thirty unions large and small in the same field of activity. Its General Secretary was George Barratt and Hugh Scanlon was chairman of its Engineering Committee. It was colloquially known as the 'Confed'.

The first one on my desk was about the inner Communist clique in the engineering unions. Says Security, of the fifty-two members of the AEF National Committee, ten are Communist Party members and nine more are sympathizers. They have been holding secret meetings under the chairmanship of [Bert] Ramelson, the Communist Party's chief industrial organizer. All very James Bond but I gather that Denis Barnes doesn't take these Security boys very seriously.

Following a talk with Tommy on the phone last night, I have managed to see Harold at last. I reported to him some of my recent conversations with Roy Hattersley. Once again Roy H. has been expressing his anxiety to me that I am too much of a 'hawk' on P and I policy. Personally he hasn't a great deal of use for it and he thinks that we should categorically say that we will abandon it in eighteen months' time and not renew the Bill under Expiring Laws. How does all this fit in with the description I have had of him from both Harold and Tommy as Jenkins's running boy? Time and time again he has criticized Roy J. to me saying, for example, that he would not recognize a plant productivity bargain if he saw one and telling me I ought to be tougher with the Treasury. Harold was immensely intrigued about all this and suggested that I should ask to see Jenkins, taking Hattersley with me. I should then force Hattersley to spell out his views in front of Roy while I seemed to remain neutral. Nobody could then accuse me of having advocated a weakening of the policy.

Wednesday, 8 May. Late at night I got my meeting with the Chancellor with Roy Hattersley. All went according to plan. I made it clear that Hattersley was more of a dove than I was and drew him out. He spoke up unhesitatingly, so whatever his game is it is not just crude Jenkins sycophancy. Roy listened carefully and said that he personally doubted whether we could continue an incomes policy indefinitely. What was important to him was that we shouldn't weaken on it for the next vital eighteen months. If I would stand firm on that he wouldn't mind abandoning the automatic renewal powers. Well, well, it is all very curious.

Thursday, 9 May. I had my first informal meeting with the industrial correspondents at three o'clock. Ray Gunter played the industrials regularly and I want to keep the practice up. So, more genning up to do on all the things that might be raised. Then on to my first consultation with the CBI. The President, Stephen Brown, was a bit grim about the fact that I hadn't invited them before and he and John Davies muttered away with their doubts about my policy of intervention and on productivity. I never like being lectured by the CBI so I answered them back crisply, though courteously. At the end of an hour I had them agreeing with me almost dangerously. When they had gone, Fred Jones (who has come to me from DEA) said with a grin, 'Well, that went very well. Just as good as George Brown and a lot less noisy.'

Home at 10 pm. Ted will be up to the early hours waiting for the municipal election results but I am off to bed. I know that they will be pretty terrible anyhow.

Friday, 10th May. They *are* terrible![1] Indeed far worse than anyone contemplated. The whole country seems to have gone berserk and to cap it all Cecil King has dedicated his life and his newspapers to getting rid of Harold as well as wickedly hinting that we are on the edge of another financial crisis.

Sunday, 12 May. Tommy rang to ask if he could see me urgently at HCF on his way home from Oxford. He and I had a secret confab in which he hurriedly unveiled to me the points he had been urging on Harold as contingency planning in case another financial crisis should break and urged that I should insist on joining a small group of Economic Ministers where it is discussed. The group would not be likely to meet next week, but he wanted to put me in the picture in case it did. In fact, said Tommy, the basic economic position is not too worrying. Exports in April have held up pretty well, but the level of imports is frightening. It was criminal of Roy not to have slapped on hire-purchase controls and the regulator at the same time as the January cuts and the consumer boom had gone on alarmingly. On the financial side we face an appalling consequence of the loss of money due to the delay in announcing devaluation once the decision had been taken. Jim's carelessness, he hissed, 'had been crim-i-nal', bringing a loss across the exchanges of £100m. It was this that was now helping to cripple us.

Thursday, 16 May. I have been writing round urgently to all the appropriate Ministers seeking their agreement to more price references to the PIB and in fact getting an astonishing response, even from the Board of Trade. Already we have shifted MinTech on the price of Malory's hearing aids and they are now following up the PIB report. I have got the paint reference out of Crosland and look like getting household textiles, children's clothing and proprietary medicines in time for Tuesday's debate as well. I am stirring up the Ministry of Agriculture about the prices of tea and beer and have made an open appeal to Ray Gunter to get cracking on the surcharge on oil, which might bring petrol prices down. They are all falling into line beautifully though I am well aware of the rumbles among Treasury economists at my determination to make some impact in the prices field. Opponents of the Bill keep saying that I can't do anything about prices so I mean to show them that I can.

Aubrey Jones phoned me as he was leaving for America. He has seen Jim Mortimer who has agreed to join the PIB full-time.[2] Will I just 'mention' it to Woodcock, but on no account consult him in the sense of inviting him to put up other names. I am delighted with the idea of an Executive member of DATA on the Board; the Left really is going to start and sit up.

In the afternoon I have my first 'quadripartite' meeting. Apparently this informal gathering of George Woodcock, John Davies, Aubrey Jones and the Minister to discuss, without commitment and off the record, problems arising from P and I policy arose when George Brown tried to get these things

[1] Labour had lost 596 seats. The Conservatives had made a net gain of 535 seats and won 27 out of 32 London Boroughs.

[2] Jim Mortimer was a full-time national official of the left-wing Draughtsmen's and Allied Technicians' Association [DATA]. His agreement to serve on the PIB was all the more surprising because he had always opposed prices and incomes policy. He was to become General Secretary of the Labour Party in 1982.

discussed in NEDC and found that no one would talk openly. Although Aubrey couldn't be there I had a useful hour with Woodcock and Davies – all on first name terms and very relaxed. Once again Woodcock showed me considerable good will. When I told him afterwards about Jim Mortimer his bushy eyebrows shot up. 'Well, I am all in favour of experiments – very interesting. Of course he is a Communist.' We shook our heads at this. 'Well, he certainly was, and I think he still is. But I don't say he is any the worse for that. I am all in favour of experiments.' So that hurdle is over and the office cleared it too with the CBI. I now put the heat on to get it cleared with the PM and Security. I can't wait to see Stan Orme's face when this news of Mortimer's appointment comes through![1]

Saturday, 18 May. The tooth with which I have been trying to get to the dentist for about three weeks has flared up into an acute neuralgia. There is obviously an abscess on it. So it will have to come out – and it is a front too too. How am I either to stand this pain during next week's Second Reading debate of the P and I Bill or get the tooth out and a new one in in time for the debate? It *would* happen just now when I need to be on the top of my form. I tried to make progress with Bernard Ingham's[2] rough redraft of my speech with very little success. Bernard has tried to liven up the ghastly officialese of the Department but I wouldn't say I have got myself a Kennedy-type speech-writer yet. However, he is still very new, poor man.

Monday, 20 May. Off to the dentist at 4 pm where he had to give me gas and take the tooth out, popping another one in its place. Home early in not exactly the best condition for writing the most important speech of my life. I gave it up at 10 pm and went to bed.

Tuesday, 21 May. Up at six o'clock as things were really getting desperate now. Every line of the draft had to be rewritten. At 2 pm there was a last-minute meeting, including Tommy, to check up the final form. Still feeling groggy, I tossed down a brandy and hurried to the House. The chamber was crowded, with Harold, Roy, Dick and the whole phalanx on the front bench. Seldom has a Second Reading been such a major occasion, and of course I would be in a sorry condition when it came. Hardly able to talk with my new tooth in my mouth, let alone deliver a piece of oratory, my own voice seemed thin and unconvincing to me as I read my speech and it was clear I hadn't made any very great impact on the House. My only consolation was that Robert Carr, who came next, succeeded in boring the House almost unbelievably.[3] The brightest spot in the whole debate was George Brown's speech. He was back in his old scintillating form and, even more important, he was backing us on this policy. In fact I was astonished to hear him say that he was now a convert to the use of statutory powers and regretted that the Government was only taking them for

[1] Stan Orme was the left-wing AEU-sponsored MP for Salford West.

[2] When, to my great regret, Charles Birdsall retired, I brought Bernard Ingham over from the PIB, where he was Press and Public Relations Adviser, to be my Chief Information Officer.

[3] Robert Carr, Conservative MP for Mitcham, had been Parliamentary Secretary at the Ministry of Labour in the 1950s and Secretary for Technical Co-operation, 1963–64. He was my 'Shadow' in my new job and in 1970 became Secretary of State for Employment in the Heath Government. He was made a Life Peer in 1975.

eighteen months. When I thought how he had attacked the abandonment of a voluntary policy in Cabinet I could hardly believe my ears. He is a curious and rather tragic figure. I still think he has got one of the best brains and most robust characters in the whole leadership and yet he has thrown power away.

Wednesday, 22 May. Ended a busy day dining once again with the CBI, but this time on a small scale and very informally. I think it is the idea of Norman, the new President, and we ate in the private house used by De La Rue for their entertaining. On their side there were only John Davies, Douglas Taylor and Johnson, while I was accompanied by Hattersley, Jarratt and Barnes. It transpired that what they really wanted to talk about was the Donovan Report on the trade unions. Douglas Taylor, their hatchet man, is obviously worried that the Report, in his view, is going to be too soft. I think he would like legislation on the conventional Tory lines, but John Davies is a different kettle of fish. Speaking, as he said, purely for himself, he stressed that in his view the greatest need was to get a rationalization of the trade union movement. I said I agreed with this purpose but I thought the best chance of getting the climate in which progress on these lines would be possible was if we could have some new 'statement of intent', this time in the field of trade union policy, in which the CBI would commit itself to the view that strong trade unionism was in the national interest. Douglas Taylor nearly had a fit at this: he couldn't see the CBI accepting the need for the extension of trade unionism, among white collar workers, for instance. But John Davies's reaction was far less conventional. He by no means ruled it out of court.

Thursday, 23 May. In Parliamentary Committee we had a preliminary run-in on the Lord Chancellor's report on House of Lords reform. The ease with which they have got agreement in the talks with the Tories is to my mind highly suspicious and I told Harold I didn't like the whole thing.

Friday, 24 May. *The Economist* has a most peculiar article headed 'Barbara's dissonance'. The theme is that by the emphasis I am putting on the prices side of the P and I Bill I could precipitate another sterling crisis. Apparently I have now become 'the bogey-woman of foreign holders of sterling'. All the world was listening to my talk about prices and I had 'got to be stopped'.

All this, I suspect, is inspired by Treasury economists who, Harold has warned me, are after my blood. Well, I intend to have this whole thing out at Monday's SEP meeting. I have no intention of pushing through the Commons a Bill under which we deliberately strengthen our powers against prices if the Government as a whole doesn't believe in them. I have got to be left to play this my own way.

Monday, 27 May. First thing I did was to write an indignant note to Harold, saying my position was impossible if articles like the *Economist*'s were to go unrepudiated. I therefore asked for an early meeting between him, me and the Chancellor, to be followed by a confrontation between the economists of all the relevant Departments, so that we could agree what was the Government's economic strategy. When I handed it to him before the meeting of the SEP he looked up and said with a grin, 'If it's about what I think it is, I agree. Someone has been doing some deliberate briefing.' I didn't smile back, but replied grimly, 'I'm not going to put up with it.'

In the division lobby later Harold had a word with me about my note. 'There are two points here,' he said. 'First what our philosophy should be and secondly the briefing that is going on.' He then proceeded to explain his own view and I interrupted him rather rudely, 'I know your philosophy all right but what is the Chancellor's?' I repeated again with some irritation that the three of us must meet and thrash it out and Harold said he was in the process of drafting a Minute to the Chancellor. I am determined not to let him ride away from this.

Had a talk with Robert Carr about a possible timetable for the P and I Bill. He told me straight that he didn't think he could get his own members to agree to a terminal date. They were in a very belligerent mood and, whereas he personally thought the forty hours I offered him was perfectly reasonable, he would have to make a scene when I moved the Sittings Motion on the grounds that it was unreasonable to expect the committee to sit on Tuesdays, Wednesdays and Thursdays every week. Clearly he wants to be decent, but some of his own people want to put up a big show and of course we have got Mikardo and Ted Fletcher[1] to reckon with as well.

Tuesday, 28 May. After voting at 12.30 last night I had to work into the early hours rewriting most of my speech to the Industrial Society lunch today. To cap it all, the BBC and ITV were filming my speech – after three hours' sleep I know how I will come across! However, it all seemed to go pretty well. Cattell was in the chair.[2] He is as keen as mustard to become head of my Manpower and Productivity Division and I think we are going to be able to pull it off.

And so into the P and I battle. We got our Sittings Motion after about four hours. Mik is out to make the maximum trouble for me. The only consolation is that he is rousing the rest of my side against him very bitterly.

Industrial disputes came crowding in on me thick and fast. One of the most intractable was in the newly nationalized steel industry where the Clerical and Administrative Workers' Union [CAWU] and the Association of Scientific, Technical and Managerial Staffs [ASTMS] were threatening to bring their members out on strike against the British Steel Corporation's [BSC] decision to refuse them recognition and to give sole national negotiating rights to six big manual workers' unions. This was to prove the most difficult inter-union dispute with which I had to deal and helped to convince me of the need for the measures to deal with such disputes I later outlined in In Place of Strife. *In this case it was not a question of an employer refusing to recognize unions, but of a nationalized body having to choose between conflicting union claims. The Corporation believed that industrial relations would be improved if the number of unions with which it had to deal*

[1] Left-wing MP for Darlington and one of Ian Mikardo's cronies in the Tribune group. John Silkin had told me that the only way he could contain a left-wing revolt on the Prices and Incomes Bill was by putting two of their number on the Standing Committee, but that meant he had saddled me with two highly skilled filibusterers who caused me more harassment than the Opposition.

[2] George Cattell had been Personnel Director at Rootes before being sent to take charge of Rootes' Linwood factory.

was limited, but it had taken the precaution of consulting the TUC which had supported its selection of the six manual unions and group of unions of which the British Iron and Steel and Kindred Trades Association [BISAKTA] was the most important from the industry's point of view. For their part CAWU and ASTMS argued that the privately owned steel industry had always discouraged the organization of staff in unions and that they had pioneered in this field while the manual unions had not been interested. The big six resisted this claim indignantly. Ron Smith, BSC Managing Director for Personnel, had infuriated the two small unions by sending a circular to local managements telling them to encourage staff employees to join manual unions. In an Adjournment debate in the House Ted Fletcher for CAWU and Ian Mikardo for ASTMS denounced this as a breach of the Bridlington agreement – a formula worked out at the TUC's 1939 conference which prohibited poaching of one union's members by another and gave the TUC the power to arbitrate in membership disputes. The BSC's reaction was to pass the buck to me. With industrial action threatened whichever side it came down on, what was it to do? In the meantime Ian Mikardo and Russ Kerr, two ASTMS MPs, had asked to see me.

I was also in trouble with the engineering unions for having set up an inquiry to try to settle the dispute at the Rootes factory at Linwood, where the unions were demanding comparability with the Midlands car workers' rates.

Wednesday, 29 May. Met Ron Smith and Milne Watson, Deputy Chairman of BSC. Ron Smith began by saying doggedly that he would rather have a strike by ASTMS and CAWU than the major industrial row he would face from the Big Six if he were to recognize the former. I explained patiently that I didn't think this was the point. The trouble had been caused by the wording of his circular which seemed in definite breach of the Bridlington agreement, to say nothing of natural justice. Harold Walker,[1] I pointed out, had to take the Adjournment Motion on it that night. (I didn't want to get embroiled in this but Ray Gunter refuses to take the Adjournment and has told the House that the matter is my responsibility.)

After talking patiently and politely to them for some time, I got Ron Smith to agree that his wording had been unfortunate and that he would agree with us a form of words for Harold Walker to use in the debate, interpreting it more acceptably. Conrad Heron[2] believes the only way to solve this matter is for ASTMS and CAWU to have a strike and demonstrate just what is their strength among the supervisory and technical grades. The trouble with this cold-blooded realism is that, if a strike does break out and I have done nothing to stop it, I shall be blamed.

Harold has sent me a copy of his Minute to Roy about the *Economist*'s article. Whether I have goaded him into action or have been doing him an injustice all along I can't say. But it is an excellent Minute. In it, Harold spells out the economic reasoning on which he thinks we should agree. Roy stopped me in the division lobby to say he wanted to talk to me: could I lunch on Friday?

Into the P and I Committee with Mik being as awkward as he can again. Owing to an astonishing ruling by the Senior Clerk we found that we were in for nothing less than a Second Reading debate on the whole policy. We reconciled ourselves to an all-night sitting.

[1] MP for Doncaster and Joint Parliamentary Secretary at DEP.

[2] Deputy Secretary at the Department in charge of industrial relations. I came to respect his judgment enormously.

Thursday, 30 May. It was 8.30 in the morning before I agreed to adjourn the committee – and even then we had only got Clause 1. My mouth was acrid with tobacco smoke and I had put on seventeen layers of powder during the long night, but there wasn't even a minute to go home and bath and change as my first Cabinet committee was 9.15 am.

I just couldn't believe it when this evening jubilant Members (once again traipsing endlessly through the division lobby) told me that IPC had sacked Cecil King.[1] Absolutely incredible! But there can't be much consolation for Harold in it, for Hugh Cudlipp will now merely root for Roy Jenkins whereas Cecil King had no use for any of them.

I was settling in for another night's sitting when John Silkin sent for me. He and Willie Whitelaw had been patching up one of their secret deals. He has always said he could do a deal with the Tories over my P and I Bill and the fact is that, behind all the public fighting and trumpeting, these kind of arrangements are regularly made. If only the public knew how hollow so much of the Opposition anger is. What the Tories obviously want is to get home in good time for the Whit holiday. They finally agreed they would give me Clause 3 by 11.30 pm on the understanding that I would adjourn by then. If I did this they would have no complaint, however hard I drove them after Whit recess. As I was pretty exhausted myself, I agreed.

It all went perfectly to plan. So we got our Clause 3 and adjourned at 11.30 pm. I must say I could do with some sleep by now.

Friday, 31 May. An urgent message from Vic Feather asking if he could see me as soon as possible. I fitted him in for ten minutes before my lunch with Roy. He came to say he thought things were going badly on my front. The steel unions are apparently furious with me for seeing Mik and Russ, while Johnnie Boyd is apparently making trouble over the inquiry I have set up into the Rootes strike. I explained to Vic that I had done my utmost to see Boyd but that he wouldn't even reply to my urgent messages. Vic said that this was typical but that I would find the trade union world was like this. He was merely warning me in a friendly way because he wanted to help. Maybe he does, but even he with all his goodwill couldn't suggest any alternative. 'You have got the most difficult job in the Government, luv, far more difficult even than the Chancellor's,' were his last comforting words.

Roy was in a more relaxed and accessible mood than I have seen him in. He appeared genuinely friendly and anxious to work with me. We had a simple lunch together alone at No. 11 and agreed about a number of things. Roy assured me that he had told the *Economist* that he didn't agree with their article and he had no objection to the way I was playing the P and I issue. But he agreed we really ought to keep in regular touch.

Wednesday, 5 June. I saw the six manual unions about recognition in the steel industry. I used the fact that we were meeting at 1 pm to offer them drinks, which they found a pleasant surprise. In fact, it all went pretty smoothly. Dai

[1] Cecil King, who had been running an increasingly vicious campaign against Harold Wilson and the Labour Government, had recently called for a new Prime Minister, declaring 'enough is enough'. The board of IPC had decided the time had come to apply this phrase to him.

Davies[1] of BISAKTA was passionately eloquent, but not bitter, and even Danny McGarvey the Boilermakers' President was civil. They argued that ASTMS and CAWU never seriously started to recruit in the steel industry until nationalization came along and then horned in, offering militant opposition to the P and I policy. And Dai said flatly that his union would strike if these two unions got recognition – and sounded as though he meant it. The more I listened the more convinced I was that there ought to be independent machinery to settle recognition questions (as the Donovan Commission recommends). I told them I did not intend to set up an inquiry, but would watch the situation and intervene if necessary. But I shall have to handle this slowly and carefully, perhaps in the context of the Donovan Report when it is published on 13 June.

I've told Denis Barnes that we must release the Mortimer news tomorrow and that I have decided we ought to balance his appointment to the PIB with the part-time appointment of a union right-winger. He has come up with the name of Lewis Wright, which I think is a good idea since he is chairman of this year's TUC and also retires as the General Secretary of the Weavers in October.

Thursday, 6 June. Jack Jones came to see me at my request. Stephen tells me he has been lobbying MPs about the municipal bus situation and I have told my people we must try and get a settlement *before* 26 July. I don't want to use the powers in the Bill and only took them in order to put myself in a negotiating position. After discussions with Jarratt, Cox[2] and Barnes, we agreed that we might find a way of giving the municipal busmen their £1 by saying 10*s* was the OMO bonus and the other 10*s* in return for their being willing to negotiate a tiered system on the lines of the PIB report. I was to sound out Jack's ideas. Jack, however, was unforthcoming. Gravely serious, he said to me, 'If you use the new powers, Barbara, I want you to realize what it means. There will be no way of preventing my union from disaffiliating from the Labour Party.' All we should negotiate at national level was basic rates, leaving each employer to settle local productivity deals on top. The Government ought to get out of the picture and leave it to the unions to deal with the employers, 'who after all will have to obey your law'. We had to leave it like that, but I saw hope in that last remark. I think we should now try to persuade the employers to offer the £1 again on the basis of acceptance of OMO and of guidelines for local productivity bargaining, which latter Jack seemed ready to accept. I am determined, come what may, not to allow the inevitable leapfrogging which would follow the unconditional grant of the £1, but if we are going to have a major political showdown we must put ourselves in a strong moral position.

For once I enjoyed my fortnightly meeting with the Industrials. I got Charles first to hand out the notice about Frank's appointment as chairman of the Industrial Training Council. They remained noticeably unmoved as I reeled off a lot of statistics about our progress with training. I then said I had two appointments to announce to the PIB. Their faces were a study as they read the hand-out. Mortimer! 'Any questions?' I asked sweetly, hardly able to keep my face straight. Well, they said hesitatingly, isn't it an astounding appointment? I

[1] General Secretary of the Iron and Steel Trades Confederation.

[2] D. G. Cox was an Assistant Secretary in the Incomes Division of the Department.

then held forth about how it was Aubrey's idea and how I had satisfied myself that Jim would play the game over incomes policy even though he disagreed with statutory powers. After half an hour during which I rebuked them for any snide comments (*e.g.* about salary), they walked out still in a daze, John Grant of the *Daily Express* murmuring, 'Two notable scalps in one day.' After all, Lewis *is* chairman of the TUC.

They were still dazed – with admiration as well as surprise – when I received them at the reception we gave for the TUC later in the evening. The whole room was agog with the news about Mortimer. Mik at first said admiringly, 'Well, you've hooked a big fish.' Later he was shaking his head, telling me it was a stroke of genius but nonetheless unwise, because it would boomerang. 'You'll have the right wing against you now as well as us.' 'That is as it should be,' I replied, 'safety in comprehensiveness.'

Monday, 10 June. In the afternoon I had my first meeting of the new General Purposes Committee of my NJAC.[1] The purpose was to discuss my new Productivity and Manpower Division and I had the inspiration of introducing Cattell to them. The response particularly on the trade union side to my ideas was most encouraging. I got an insight into what the trade unions are up against from the reactions of Taylor of the CBI to the documents I had circulated. What shocked him was the statement that we intended to make our new Productivity services available to trade unions as well as to management. He was really taken aback when I said of course I would make the service available to shop stewards as well.

Worried by the effect on public opinion of the growing number of unofficial strikes, Harold Wilson and Ray Gunter had decided in 1965 to set up a Royal Commission under Lord Justice Donovan ostensibly to study 'Trade Union and Employers Associations', but in reality to counter Tory demands for far-reaching legal curbs on trade unions drawn up by Conservative lawyers and later set out in a pamphlet 'Fair Deal at Work' published in 1968. The TUC had been persuaded to collaborate with the Commission by the inclusion of George Woodcock in its membership, which also comprised industrialists like Sir George Pollock; a representative of the nationalized industries in Alf Robens, chairman of the National Coal Board; academics such as Hugh Clegg who had been a member of the PIB before becoming Professor of Industrial Relations at Warwick and Andrew Shonfield, Director of Studies at the Royal Institute of International Affairs. There was one woman, Miss (later Dame) Mary Green, headmistress of Kidbrooke School. The Commission reported in June 1969 (Cmnd 3623), and it fell to me to work out what should be the Government's response to it.

The Report's main finding was that the formal method of bargaining at national level had broken down because the real decisions were being made at company and plant level and that was where good procedure agreements were urgently needed if collective bargaining was to be orderly. This meant that companies should give far more attention to the industrial relations side of their business. It also required a strengthening, not a weakening, of trade unions. The majority of the Commission rejected the legal enforcement of agreements, not on principle, but because they believed it would be unworkable,

[1] The National Joint Advisory Council [NJAC] was a consultative body in the Department representing both sides of industry.

certainly until procedures had been reformed. They also argued that, if collective agreements were made legally enforceable, few such agreements would be made and the result would be more, not less, anarchy. A key proposal was that initially all large firms, and progressively the smaller ones, should be required by law to register their agreements with the DEP. *An Industrial Relations Commission should be set up consisting of representatives of both sides of industry to monitor procedure agreements and seek to improve them, though it would not deal with pay or conditions. One of its major tasks would be to arbitrate in disputes over trade union recognition and recommend which union or unions should be recognized. Here again the Commission did not rule out enforcement of its decisions in principle but decided, Andrew Shonfield dissenting, that initially acceptance of its findings should be voluntary and that the position should be reviewed in the light of experience.*

The Commission also rejected other Tory nostrums. It was against the prohibition of the closed shop and wanted the law on sympathetic strikes clarified in the unions' favour. It also wanted statutory protection against unfair dismissal and, contrary to the Tory view, it declared that unions should be self-regulating. However, it believed that the rules should be tightened up in certain respects and that in particular there should be a right of appeal to an independent review body by workers dissatisfied with the refusal of membership of a union or expulsion from it. The Commission's most controversial recommendation was that the historic protection of the right to strike given by Section 3 of the Trades Disputes Act of 1906 should not cover persons and combinations other than trade unions. This, by withdrawing immunity from leaders of unofficial strikes, would expose them to the risk of penalties. The minority, led by George Woodcock, strongly opposed this, but accepted that registration of unions should be compulsory and that unions which refused to register should incur financial penalties.

Tuesday, 11 June. An astonishingly good press on Cattell. I have obviously scored another bull's-eye with him following Jim Mortimer. At the Parliamentary Committee meeting of Cabinet I got clearance on the statement I am to make in the House on Thursday launching the Donovan Report.

At 4 pm we resumed the committee stage of the P and I Bill. As the long all-night session dragged on I spent most of my time outside the committee room, my head in my hands, trying to wade through several thousand words of documents for tomorrow morning's meeting of SEP. Really, it is grotesque how one is expected to master massive wodges of economic and financial analysis in one's odd moments and always at the last moment. And one is not at one's brightest at doing so at 3 am!

Wednesday, 12 June. After a night's bitter fighting I eventually tipped off the Tory Whip that I would adjourn as soon as possible if I could get Schedule 2 of the Bill. It worked like magic and we galloped through the last six amendments in about fifty minutes, having spent something like fourteen hours on the previous six. This time I had come armed with my toothbrush and a clean blouse. After a hot bath I got to SEP at No. 10 at 10 am. Here we were faced with a massive agenda and I had not even had half an hour's rest in bed.

The main items at SEP were first the monthly report on the economic situation. This shows that, as expected, the trend of imports for the first four months of this year had been considerably higher than forecast and there has been a renewed and exceptionally heavy outflow of capital. The balance of payments deficit for the first quarter is no less than £280m. Exports are in line with the forecast, but there is no strong upward trend yet. Once again both Roy Jenkins and Tony Crosland were extraordinarily complacent about these factors.

The second item was Peter Shore's paper produced by his Medium-Term Assessment Committee. Here again it was admitted that the financial statement underestimated the flow of imports. So the Treasury machinery is not as hot as all that! Roy insisted that this should be taken as a background for his paper on proposals for cutting back public expenditure within the limits for this year agreed in January. His main aim now is to reduce borrowing needs. I think we all recognized that we had got to keep public expenditure within the figure promised in January, otherwise the credibility of the Government would be completely undermined and there is no doubt that public expenditure is running at far too high a level in relation to our production. The result is that the Labour Government has had to levy a considerably higher level of taxation. As Roy put it, 'I think there can be no doubt that here lies the explanation of a lot of our unpopularity.' We agreed to allow him to draw up proposals on this basis and I staggered out of the meeting sleepily.

Thursday, 13 June. My first attendance at MISC 205, that mysterious inner circle on monetary policy. I found it consisted of the four I had agreed with Roy: himself, Crosland, Peter Shore and me, with, of course, Harold in the chair. I had got up early to read the papers about 'Brutus', the operation which will have to take place if we face another run on the pound and which even Tommy flinches from. Tommy had asked me to watch carefully what Roy said. He feared that it was 'just an empty exercise' because the Bank would never agree to Brutus. Tommy thinks we should carry it out even if the Bank doesn't agree, though he told me it would involve measures of 'terrible severity'.

Reading my papers, I realized how facile are some of the remedies which the Left peddles: as though interfering with a market economy, run by expert beneficiaries of the market economy, were as easy as voting a decision in Cabinet. The result of [Brutus] would be a big increase in unemployment and a spectacular rise in the cost of living. Worst of all, I simply couldn't see public opinion taking this from a Labour Government in its present state of unpopularity. The Tories would move in to the kill. What sickens me is Tribune's constant propaganda to the effect that every wage claim is sacrosanct and every industrial dispute noble. They are just not prepared to pay the price of economic independence.

Tuesday, 18 June. Had a word with Dick before SEP. He told me he was going to protest about the attempt to railroad us into decisions about public expenditure cuts for 1968–69 at such short notice. He had already seen Harold and Roy and got their agreement for a bit more time because he had flatly refused to rush through the social security part. He shook his head over Roy: 'The Balfour type: he has a terrible streak of lethargy. Look how wrong he was over consumer spending. The Treasury forecasts were all wrong. They made no contingency allowance in January for the rise in the cost of living or for new policies.' Then, again, Roy had got himself committed to an absurdly stringent borrowing requirement. Now we were all in a straitjacket. Dick thought we would need big policy changes to get big enough cuts – but when he suggested abandoning agricultural deficiency payments I hit the roof and he grinned. He told me relations between Harold and Roy were not good.

Things went in Cabinet as Dick predicted: we are to be given another week. But we started grimly down the list, of course everyone saying they couldn't give the Chancellor what he asked. Roy spelt out the targets. However, he didn't get away unscathed. There were some nasty remarks about the deficiencies of Treasury forecasting. We're not going to have it that everyone is out of line but our Roy. Dick insisted that it was no longer possible to trim without disastrous consequences and that we should go for big policy changes. Roy said these would not obviate the need for the present cuts, but agreed we might have to propose major changes next year. What on earth are he and Dick cooking up?

Lunched with Joan Lestor. She said, 'The rank and file have lost confidence in Harold. But who else is there? What about you?' I shied away from that one.

Thursday, 20 June. A pleasant private lunch at *The Times*. I talked to them frankly about Harold. It wasn't true that everything about him was calculated. On the contrary, he found it very difficult to dissimulate. If he didn't feel something – such as Honours, about which he had never been radical – you couldn't interest him. But he *had* cared genuinely about arms for South Africa. David Wood, the Political Editor, agreed.

A dispute had broken out at Ford's Dagenham over the job grading of sewing machinists under a job evaluation scheme negotiated by the unions with the management. The women had come out on strike claiming that they had been cheated in the assessment of the value of their jobs in relation to those of other workers, mainly men. There were, therefore, undertones of the equal pay issue in the dispute and though a claim for equal pay had not been put specifically by the unions when the agreement was negotiated, the AEF *now insisted on raising it. The Department had set up a Court of Inquiry under Sir Jack Scamp, chairman of the Motor Industry Joint Labour Council, who was widely used by the Department as a trouble-shooter. The women machinists, however, refused to co-operate with the inquiry or to call off their strike, which was causing increasing dislocation of production, and I had been pressed to intervene. One of the difficulties was that a number of unions was involved – the* AEF, TGWU, *Municipal Workers, and the National Union of Vehicle Builders [*NUVB*]. They negotiated with the firm through a National Joint Council [*NJC*], but there was considerable rivalry between them, which made a concerted policy difficult.*

Saturday, 22 June. Back by night sleeper from Blackburn, I went into the office for talks with the unions on the Ford dispute. Hughie Scanlon sent excuses and the only person we had from the Engineers was Reg Birch – God help us. Mark Young of the ETU [Electrical Trades Union] and Jim Conway of the AEF represented the National Joint Council of the unions at Ford's. I opened by emphasizing what wide terms of reference and powers the Court of Inquiry under Scamp will have, stressed the immense damage to our exports from the dispute, and asked them what they could do to help get the women back to work pending the inquiry's report. There then followed a most revealing show of inter-union manœuvring. From all this it emerged that Alf Roberts of the Vehicle Builders was annoyed that the equal pay issue had been raised at all. But it was clear that, now that it had been, he was not going to leave the field clear for the AEF. The weight of opinion was clearly behind me when I said that they couldn't just spatchcock the equal pay issue into an agreement that they had freely signed, and the young 'uns – Ken Baker of the General and Municipal Workers and Les Kealey of the TGWU – brought out the fact that the equal pay issue had not been seriously raised during the negotiations.

Unabashed, Reg Birch insisted that equal pay was the policy of his union. When Jack Cooper[1] intervened to ask whether his union was in favour of overthrowing a voluntary agreement Reg said dourly, 'Yes, if new issues have been thrown up since it was signed.' This, of course, is a recipe for anarchy, as the others well realized. When I asked that they should now urge the women to return to work, all Alf Roberts would say was that he would consult his Executive and probably couldn't do that till Tuesday. Swallowing my irritation, I once again stressed the useless damage to exports which is going on and managed to get him to agree to try and make it Monday afternoon. And that was where I had to leave it.

Afterwards, over a drink, they all told me privately that the trouble was that there were 'political' elements involved, meaning that the District Secretary of the Vehicle Builders and the shop stewards concerned are Communists, while of course Reg Birch will sabotage if he can. But they seem powerless to give any effective lead. The trouble is that the more they stand up to their militant rank and file, the more ground the Commies gain. As Conrad Heron put it to me, 'What a commentary on Donovan.' Certainly this particular case throws doubt on the efficacy of the Donovan remedies. Here was a new agreement negotiated on a company basis by a firm which is certainly taking a lot of interest in labour relations. The agreement was accompanied by a fully worked-out procedure agreement for dealing with grievances and disputes and for adjusting the details, if required. Yet the NUVB, more from muddle than malice, hadn't made use of it, though Les Kealey said angrily that, if the matter had been referred to the NJC Sub-Committee, it could have been settled without any strike taking place. What the hell does one do?

Monday, 24 June. Feeling tired and sick, I went through my regular quadripartite meeting with George Woodcock, John Davies and Aubrey Jones. In this informal setting they speak frankly and in remarkable harmony about things they will be quarrelling about publicly. George doesn't see the need for any long consultations about Donovan: in his view there is no need for the Government to legislate about the main proposal, the setting up of the Industrial Relations Commission. This could be done under royal charter. As for the Ford's dispute showing the weakness of the Report's recommendations, he won't have it. 'Of course you will have strikes under our proposals; there is no way of avoiding them.' All this may be earthy commonsense, but it is

[1] Lord (Jack) Cooper was General Secretary of the GMWU. He had been made a life peer in 1966.

not to my taste. If we are in business for anything, it is to change things and you only do that by trying. Even if you apparently fail, that is the only way to have any impact on events.

I was just heading for home to catch up with my reading for tomorrow when Douglas told me the PM wanted to see me. I found Harold upstairs at No. 10 in a new study, which he said he had taken over from the Church Commissioners! He was on the brandy – talkative and affectionate. He kept repeating how well I am doing, and was as usual obsessed with conspiracies. He told me he is going to raise leaks again at Cabinet tomorrow. My heart sank and I begged him not to waste any more time on then. Then I discovered to my horror that he was brooding on David Wood's article in today's *Times*.[1] 'I can't let a single remark drop in Cabinet without their using it against me.' The remark was in fact recounted by me at the private lunch I had at *The Times* last week. I passed it on in all innocence as part of a conversation which seemed very sympathetic to Harold, never imagining it would be used. And here is Harold brooding on it! Mind you, it is a lesson to me never to let down my defences with the press, particularly when they seem friendly. They are, after all, only professional scavengers. I begged Harold not to bother with these press comments – he could never prove anything anyway – but he kept repeating, 'I've got them this time.' I sometimes think he is going mildly off his rocker.

Tuesday, 25 June. At the meeting of MISC 205 we returned to the question of import controls. As Roy pointed out we need something ready for the danger period after 11 July if the June trade figures still show that imports are running too high. Roy's paper said the trouble about import quotas is that they are slow to introduce with the risk of forestalling before they can come into effect and they only affect the volume of imports gradually. The quickest and most effective method of imports control is by a surcharge (which is why we introduced it in October 1964 and got heartily blamed for it by left-wing critics who didn't seem to understand the technicalities). However, today the reimposition of a surcharge would be internationally intolerable. An import deposit scheme is quick to act and introduce and is less damaging to international confidence. The Treasury paper therefore came down in favour of this. After a short sharp discussion we agreed that planning on these lines should go ahead.

I asked how the Basle talks were going and Roy said not too bad but they would not be completed until early July.[2] Although they would not provide any more bridging money he agreed that they would be 'bridging' in confidence terms. We are therefore neck and neck in the race between the production of the June trade figures and the outcome of the Basle talks. If bad trade figures are published before the Basle talks are finalized, we may be in one super-insoluble and catastrophic mess. There we sat, the five of us – Harold, Roy, Tony, Peter and I – the only ones who really know what faces this Government.

[1] In his political column David Wood had referred to an exchange in Cabinet between Harold Wilson and a 'senior Minister' when, replying to the latter's plea that the Government must put something in the Queen's Speech that was electorally popular, the Prime Minister had replied almost despairingly, 'Is *anything* electorally popular?' In fact the article was not an unfriendly one.

[2] A meeting of the Bank for International Settlements was being held in Basle.

Considering the volcano we are sitting on we remain remarkably calm!

At the beginning of Cabinet, Harold said tensely and angrily that he had a serious statement to make. Once again he had to complain of leaks. Even a light remark he had made at the previous Cabinet meeting had been made the basis for a vicious article by David Wood. There just was no basis of trust between us any more. But the most serious leak had been of an item in relation to our discussion on the House of Lords. Not only had he been reported as wanting a short Bill to deal with powers, but six newspapers had carried an identical story of something he had said which was known and could only be known to two Ministers. This kind of thing could only be done in the deliberate pursuit of personal political ambition and he intended to have it out with the Ministers concerned.

As he spat all this out the rest of us sat horrified. He had never been so blunt and pointed in his accusations before. Heaven knows, we have all been bored to tears with his generalized complaints about leakages but this was something quite different. We passed on to the rest of the agenda in a kind of daze.

Wednesday, 26 June. Tommy Balogh threw a lunch party to precede his introduction in the House of Lords.[1] This was a historic moment I could not miss and I sat on the steps of the throne chuckling with delight as two of our Labour peers, Gavin Faringdon and Jock Campbell, lumbered up in their long robes with Tommy between them and then sat solemnly doffing their hats three times to the Lord Chancellor. I must say this is incredible mumbo jumbo for grown-up men to take part in but they really do enjoy dressing up even more than women and have an insatiable appetite for time-hallowed pantomime. Dick and I had a quick coffee in the smoking-room afterwards. He was full of Harold's outburst at Cabinet yesterday. Harold's attack, he said, was directed at Roy and him. Roy, said Dick, had been absolutely furious at Harold's attack. But Dick had gone off to Harold cheerfully to say that of course he had been responsible. We shook our heads together over Harold's neurosis and I secretly decided to go and tell Harold at the earliest possible opportunity that I was responsible for the leak to David Wood. This whole leak business would be like a bedroom farce if it weren't becoming a tragedy.

Then into the Commons to resume the exhausting marathon of the P and I Bill. My troubles were still not over. As soon as I got into the House the Whips warned me that the Government faced defeat again, this time on an amendment demanding equal pay. I sat next to Roy Jenkins on the front bench towards the end of Question Time and warned him we might be in a real mess. Would he permit me to use a carefully worded formula promising immediate discussions with the CBI and TUC on a timetable for phasing in equal pay? I scribbled down a form of words and after hesitating and swallowing hard he reluctantly agreed. In these ways is history made! I have thought ever since I came into this new job that the only way we can survive these tricky issues is to play them positively and play them long. When we reached Lena Jeger's amendment my announcement did the trick – but only just. It was 8 am before I could slip away to bed.

[1] Oxford had been pressing Tommy Balogh to return to regular teaching which conflicted with his almost full-time consultancy job at No. 10. Harold Wilson had decided the solution was to make him a life peer.

Thursday, 27 June. Into the office early to receive Prince Charles who is starting his royal training in earnest by a tour of Government Departments. Once again I am struck by what a charming, natural boy he is.

Then off to Cabinet where we started the long wrangle over trimming the 1968–69 public expenditure. We all of us get horribly bored with this kind of exercise.

I left them all arguing the details of who sacrificed what and slipped off for my urgent meeting with the National Joint Council for the municipal bus industry: the crucial confrontation between Alan Thompson, National Secretary of the Passenger Service Group of the TGWU, and the representatives of the municipal bus authorities. I had called it in an attempt to reach a settlement over the busmen's £1 claim before the current standstill lapses. My people had come up with proposals they had worked out with the union, that we should accept the payment of the £1 and a new 10*s* OMO bonus the NJC has just agreed on the understanding that there would be no backdating to last December. Not surprisingly Roy Jenkins is rather unhappy about this. We were willing to settle for the £1 if retrospection didn't take place but the 10*s* bonus on top of it was another thing. But to make matters worse my people advised me there seems little guarantee that retrospection will not take place in a number of instances anyway. Also we have now learned that the employers' side don't want to pay 30*s* at all. Eventually it became clear from Harris of Southend that the employers want to pay the £1 on 26 July and to include the 10*s* bonus as part of it and that they don't think they ought to go any further than that. Alan Thompson of course rejected this but even he could see how absurd it would be for the Government to be pressing the employers to pay more than they wanted to.

I ended up by suggesting that the 10*s* bonus should be paid as soon as they liked, and an additional 10*s* on the basic rate put in payment on 1 July without even waiting for the standstill to terminate. The Government would hope that authorities would not backdate it though they recognized retrospection could not be prohibited. Alan grumbled at this, said he doubted whether his delegate conference would accept it. However, he would go and discuss it with his Executive Council. Jarratt and I agreed that if we could get away with this we would be doing wonderfully, but I am far from hopeful, even though Alan Thompson squeezed Jarratt's hand as he left and said he would do his best. I decided to send him a letter setting it all out.

A remarkably good vote, all things considered, on the Third Reading of the P and I Bill. A majority of forty-four is really quite a triumph – we even had Mannie Shinwell getting up and making a speech congratulating me and explaining that he was going to toe the line. Harold called me into his room for a celebration drink with the Parliamentary Secretaries and the Whips. He was obviously feeling like someone from whom a cloud has been lifted. 'I have seen Roy and Dick and made my peace with them,' he whispered to me. But I believe that his incredible outburst in Cabinet will leave a scar.

I went back to my room in the House to clear some work with Douglas Smith. 'How is the Ford Court of Inquiry going?' I asked cheerfully, thinking that that little problem was settled for the time being. But not a bit of it. Douglas told me with a long face that several things had gone awry. First of all Jack Scamp had upset our plans by deciding that the court would meet in private and Douglas said the Dagenham women had been heard muttering as they left the court that if everything was done in secret they weren't going to go back to work. Secondly, Gallagher, Assistant General Secretary of NUVB, had decided he would have to consult his Executive before he could recommend a return to work.

I blew my top, saying emphatically, 'This is where I intervene.' Douglas began by looking dubious, but when he saw I had made up my mind he fell in with my plan, and anyway it was obvious that Charles Birdsall agreed with me, saying the press were getting impatient about the whole thing. First I told Douglas that Jack Scamp must be instructed to hold the meetings in public and he arranged for Denis Barnes to get cracking on this. Secondly I said I was going to see the women myself.

Friday, 28 June. I had to leave early to get to the Ministry. The Dagenham girls had already arrived and were waiting in an ante-room. Heron handed me a telegram which Ford's had sent last night to the Prime Minister pleading with the Government to intervene urgently. Of course the press think that I had called the meeting because of it, whereas I wasn't even aware of the telegram when I decided to act.

We spent the next half an hour doing some furniture moving – pushing back my big conference table and making an intimate circle of chairs. Charles said the press were besieging us outside and suggested I had a picture taken with the women before the talks began in case the talks went sour on us afterwards. When Gallagher duly arrived I saw him for a few minutes and got his agreement for me to meet the women first. In they trooped, looking rather suspicious. So I turned on every ounce of relaxing charm. I firmly ensconced myself on the sofa right in the middle of them and got them laughing and talking as the photographers trooped in. They were a nice set of women, obviously with a burning and genuine sense of outrage, and I could quickly see they weren't going to be budged easily. The press out of the way, we drew our chairs close together in a circle and got down to business.

After half an hour's patient questioning I elicited what was troubling them. Rose, the ring-leader, said categorically that they didn't trust the firm. They knew that their job evaluation profile had put them into Grade C of the job evaluation scheme, but the firm had suppressed it. When I told them that the Court of Inquiry would bring out all these facts, Rose said darkly, 'If the profile still exists.' Obviously she thinks the firm has quietly disposed of it. At this stage I sent for Gallagher, who came in accompanied by the NUVB District Officer, Blake, whom the Department believe is a Communist. I explained to Gallagher what I had in mind and he was perfectly happy. Blake tried to make difficulties saying we could never get the truth from the firm, but I smiled sweetly at the girls and said, 'Well, at least it is worth while having a try, isn't it?' They nodded their agreement and I suggested we broke up for lunch.

I cancelled a lunch with the Lord Chancellor and all my afternoon engagements and bolted a sandwich while we sent urgently for Blakenham and elicited from him what the real cause of the misunderstanding was. In the girls' case there had been two profiles. The first, which put them in Grade B, had been drawn up by Consultant's Assessors. When the girls protested this was too low it had then gone in accordance with the procedure agreement to the Divisional Review Committee on which sat three union representatives (including the Communist shop steward Friedman) and three representatives of management. At Friedman's insistence the profile had been considerably altered in the girls' favour. It had then gone up to the Central Review Committee for checking. The Central Committee at once saw that this case was what they called 'a flier', *i.e.* it was out of line with all the other grading assessments (now I know what Rose meant when she kept saying, 'They said we were a fly'). The Central Review Committee therefore rejected the amended profile in favour of the original one. Under the disputes procedure their ruling should have gone back to the Divisional Review Committee. But, as the case had come up late in the whole process, the Divisional Review Committee had been disbanded. The procedure agreement provided in these circumstances for a disputed case to go to the Consultant's Assessors for re-checking and finally to an independent adjudicator. It had been through this process and the adjudicator had found in favour of the original profile. But none of this detail seemed ever to have been explained to the girls – whether through deliberate mischief making by Friedman or Blake one could never establish, though I shouldn't be at all surprised.

Blakenham looked extremely worried. He said the one thing that mattered to the company was to preserve the present gradings intact. If the girls were upgraded nothing could prevent the thousands of men workers from demanding reconsideration of their gradings, too. Yet it was imperative to get work resumed before export orders were irreparably lost. He told me that in any case the firm had been reconsidering whether the 15 per cent differential between men's and women's rates wasn't too high. After all the women got 92 per cent of the men's rates at the company's other plant at Vauxhall, and he had indeed made tentative approaches to the union at the time of the negotiations to suggest that the differential might be narrowed, but the unions weren't interested. The firm would be willing to go up to 92 per cent as the very small price of peace. Conrad Heron told me he thought we could justify it on the grounds that the firm had reconsidered the economic advantages of women's work compared with men's. I called in the girls and asked Rose to tell Mr Blakenham equally frankly the suspicions of the form which she had voiced to me. She did so and Blakenham replied patiently and carefully. Gradually the girls began to grasp what had taken place despite Blake's efforts to confuse the picture by bringing in irrelevant points. I then told them that they could if they wished have the Divisional Review Committee reconstituted so as to examine their case again but they said they would prefer to go to the Court of Inquiry.

Somewhat mollified by the frank face-to-face talk with management, they then turned to their second point: 'We can't ask the girls to go back to work without having won something,' Rose insisted and the others echoed her words shaking their heads determinedly. Blakenham then spelled out to them the firm's willingness to look at the differential, and they began to prick up their ears. It would however, said Blakenham, have to be done through the proper negotiating procedure which meant the calling of the NJC. That couldn't be done at the earliest till Monday morning and the girls once again began to look dubious. Once again Blake tried to make trouble but Gallagher asked for an adjournment.

While they were out I sent the office chasing Mark Young, chairman of the employees' side of the NJC, and I also told them to make another effort to get hold of Reg Birch who had been lying low despite repeated messages from me to his office. Within half an hour the girls were back saying with relieved faces that they agreed. Mark and Reg were then brought in and to my astonishment they said they saw no difficulty about summoning an early meeting of the NJC. If the firm was ready to concede a narrower differential, they saw no objection. We then had a celebration drink together and the girls said nostalgically, 'We shall miss all this.' Everybody in the office was jubilant about the settlement. And so was Blakenham, who took me aside to thank me earnestly on behalf of the firm. But I was throwing no mental caps in the air. I could see the press sniffing round this settlement suspiciously. The best part of it from my point of view was the genuine rapport I had established with the women. I think I managed to make the Government look again as if it consisted of human beings and not just cold-blooded economists.

Sunday, 30 June. While I was trying to enjoy a little sunshine at HCF, Harold phoned me from Chequers to tell me Ray Gunter had resigned. He wanted to tip me off ahead of the official announcement because Ray might be dragging me into it. When Harold had talked to him he had been extremely bitter. His main attack was not on me but on Harold himself, complaining of 'lack of trust'. Said Harold, levelly, 'He thought I was getting at him in Cabinet last week.' (I thought that outburst would leave indelible scars.) But certainly one of the main reasons was that I had got his job. 'He thinks you are a bitch.' Harold suggested I might like to be ready with my counter-briefing of some industrial correspondents when the news came. Frankly, I am not very good at this kind of thing. However, Ted contacted two political correspondents, Ian Aitken of the *Guardian* and Harold Hutchinson of the *Sun*, for me. The latter was always one of Ray Gunter's closest friends. When I said mildly that I thought Ray just wasn't an administrator and that the Ministry of Power had probably proved beyond his abilities, Harold Hutchinson unhesitatingly agreed with me. In fact Ray had been talking along those lines, saying, 'I always go by instinct. Now I have to read all those papers.' I bet the press uses all this for another attack on Wilson. Yet he did have the courage to make the change at the Ministry of Labour, knowing that he was risking Ray's resignation at the time.

Tuesday, 2 July. The press, having had a field day on Gunter's resignation yesterday, is moving in for what it hopes is a kill. *The Times* has exceeded even its own malevolence towards Harold, but at the SEP meeting this morning Harold was extraordinarily calm. I have a hunch that he realizes where his own outburst last week has landed him and is now recognizing he must steady his own nerves and just keep quietly soldiering on.

I must say I didn't emerge with any great hopes for the future of the trade union movement from my first consultations with the TUC this afternoon on the Donovan Report. George Woodcock dominated the conversation, rattling on about his favourite theme so fully embodied in the Report. It was no good trying to have sanctions against unofficial strikes because they wouldn't work. Admittedly the voluntary policy wouldn't work either, but that was life! Vic Feather said nothing and when Bill Carron of the AEF[1] tried to hint that there might be a case for sanctions George slapped him down good and hard. I can't see any revolutionary changes being carried through unless the Government is prepared to impose them on an unwilling TUC. The ones I would go for would be compulsory amalgamations of trade unions, but we won't even get that.

Trouble was still rumbling on the railways. Wage increases offered by BRB in February had been turned down and the NUR had demanded a 9 per cent increase irrespective of any later productivity agreement. When this was rejected, and despite an improved offer made by BRB on 22 June, the NUR and ASLEF started a work to rule which caused considerable disruption. On 25 June Dick Marsh told the House of Commons that the Government would not intervene and pointed out that, following the introduction of subsidies for socially necessary lines, there was now no general deficit grant on which to draw. Any settlement, therefore, would have to be out of BRB's own resources. After further stalemate Len Neal went to the NUR's Annual Delegate Meeting at Penzance and on 5 July negotiated an agreement giving increases of between 3 per cent and 4½ per cent to be paid immediately but to be absorbed in the current pay and productivity talks. The agreement was vociferously attacked in the press as a sell-out, as my own settlement with the Ford women had been, but Neal's negotiating ability was triumphantly vindicated when the productivity talks were successfully concluded on 14 August in which twenty-three ways of increasing productivity were accepted by both NUR and ASLEF, fully offsetting the cost of the pay increases.

On 3 July I decided that the only way out of the impasse over union recognition in the steel industry was to set up a Court of Inquiry. Lord Pearson was its chairman and its terms of reference were 'to inquire into the causes, circumstances and effects' of the dispute over recognition.

At a meeting of the Bank for International Settlements in Basle agreement was reached whereby the BIS and the central banks would participate in a medium-term stand-by arrangement to offset fluctuations in the sterling balances of sterling area countries. Though not a loan, it helped to revive confidence in sterling.

Wednesday, 3 July. The NUR's delegate conference in Penzance has turned down the BRB's latest offer. So the Annual Delegate Meeting is not proving more moderate than the Executive Committee, as everyone had hoped. The eight o'clock news is full of the fact that the BRB is likely to suspend the guaranteed week. I decided it was time for us to jump in before any irrevocable step was taken. Dick Marsh therefore came over to the Department where we met Johnson and Neal. Both were in a pretty tough mood. Johnson believes that to suspend the guaranteed week is not only justified but there is an even chance that it will lead the dispute to collapse. On the other hand we can't rule out that it may precipitate a national strike. That being so, I said, we must be sure that we are all in a strong position presentationally. If a strike was inevitable, wasn't it better for the union to drift into it rather than for it to be precipitated by action by the BRB which the press would say had been

[1] Member of the Executive of the Confederation of Shipbuilding and Engineering Unions and of the General Council of the TUC.

provocative? After an hour's talk along these lines, in which Johnson and Dick Marsh seemed to be lusting for a showdown at the earliest possible moment, while Neal and I were more cautious, we agreed that the BRB should not take any action on the guaranteed week until Neal had at least expressed his willingness to meet the negotiating committee. He said he was willing to go down to Penzance. Eventually it was agreed that Neal should go, though Johnson didn't like the idea.

Dick Marsh and I were united on one thing, namely that we should leave the Board to fight this one out. For the rest I dislike that man increasingly, the more I see of him. As one of my conciliation people, Mr Marre, said to me mildly afterwards, 'The Minister of Transport *is* a hawk, isn't he?' There is something crude and cheap about him which I can judge for myself now I can see him against the background of my old job. None of us thought that anything would come of Neal's visit and if it doesn't, of course, we shall have to face up to a strike.

Thursday, 4 July. At Cabinet someone raised Gunter's personal attack on the PM.[1] Said Harold tartly, 'Give him a medal for saying it openly.' At one point he prefaced his remarks with, 'Knowing that anything I say will be reported outside . . .'. I do wish he wouldn't be so touchy.

Saturday, 6 July and Sunday, 7 July. An appalling press on the rail settlement. The Government is being blamed for a breach in the incomes policy and the BRB for going back on its tough line. Actually I think Len Neal was right to gamble on a more co-operative mood by the NUR. But in any case we weren't consulted. I quarrelled madly with Ted about the stupidity or downright malice of the press for not realizing that the key point was that the Government hadn't put up any more money and never intended to. He told me that once again the Government's PR has broken down. This is what comes of our being tough enough to tell the BRB they are on their own! As usual I rejected violently everything he said but mentally filed some of his points for future action.

Monday, 8 July. The bad press continues. I strode into the office and told Barnes and Charles that we've got to fight back. I asked Charles to arrange a succession of lunches with key industrial correspondents at which we can start disabusing them of some of the myths that have got around that prices and incomes policy has broken down – notably in the *Financial Times* leader today.[2]

The only ray of sunshine is that the Basle deal has been clinched. Naturally the pound has rallied at the reports. So presumably Brutus won't be necessary, after all. And anyway Crosland is launching into a series of public speeches attacking import controls.

Another desperate appeal from Jack Jones and Alan Thompson that I should see them about the municipal bus settlement. It was increasingly clear

[1] Following his resignation Ray Gunter had given press interviews and had made a series of appearances on TV bitterly attacking the Government in general and Harold Wilson's leadership in particular, being particularly savage about 'intellectuals'.

[2] In a front-page article the *Financial Times* had suggested that the Ford women's and railway settlements were a breach of incomes policy which would incite other workers to follow suit.

that the last thing they wanted was a showdown. Far from threatening industrial action if I extended the standstill they were obviously terrified at the very idea. 'Do you want to ruin the union?' pleaded Jack. 'The last strike cost us £2 million.' They maintained that the December settlement must be fulfilled: their rank and file would not stand for any less though they didn't mind what productivity strings I attached to it. When I asked whether they would insist on the £1 being retrospective, they argued that the date was part of the settlement. I told them that £1 paid retrospectively would equal an annual rate of 8 per cent increase and that it just wasn't on. Their men could get £1 immediately on the lines of the letter I had sent to Alan and that I was sure they could sell this to their members as opening the door to more money still from local productivity deals. This was the very furthest we could go. Jack then said urgently that he and Frank must see the Prime Minister. I think the union leaders are frantic to get out of the mess which they have got themselves in.

Tuesday, 9 July. At Cabinet I reported on the state of play of the bus settlement and warned them all of the fact that I had to give notice by Thursday of our intention to extend the standstill and what this meant. If the union organized official strikes against the employers, the Attorney-General might find himself forced to consider action under the Prices and Incomes Act. Nonetheless I recommended that we go ahead. But I asked that I should be allowed to announce our own offer at the same time. This led to quite a nasty little scene in which Roy asked tartly if I was trying to go back on what we had agreed; rightly or wrongly, everyone believed the incomes policy was crumbling. I snapped back that there was no crumbling on my part but I thought the only way we would get away with it among our own parliamentary colleagues was if we put forward a positive alternative. Crosland said we ought to have a discussion on the whole strategy I was pursuing as some of them couldn't understand some of the recent settlements, such as the 'total surrender' in the Ford's dispute. I could see what the influence behind all this was – the Treasury's assumption that I am soft on incomes policy. They really will never forgive me for the Ford's settlement. Eventually, however, it was agreed that I should go ahead.

Lunched with the *Financial Times*. John Elliott, their industrial correspondent, is a nice friendly chap, but the leader writer, Fisher, was one of the most unpleasant people I have met for a long time. He spoke in a slightly guttural way and I said to Charles Birdsall afterwards, 'They have got a bloody arid continental trying to run British politics.'

At five o'clock Dick Marsh and I duly dropped into Harold's room in the House for the promised meeting with Frank and Jack. Once again I was left with the impression that they were desperate men. Frank, of course, always gets apocalyptic on these occasions, but even he pleaded rather than threatened while Jack Jones kept bringing us quietly back to the possibilities of a compromise. At the end I was left in no doubt that if we would let the agreement on the £1 go through they would agree that it included 10*s* for the acceptance of OMO. When I asked about backdating they shied away nervously but here again I am sure that if we put on the heat they would abandon this too. I asked Jarratt to look into alternative possibilities, but he advised strongly that I should not be the one to press for them. The attacks on me from the Treasury are now quite overt. Roy has circulated a Minute which has infuriated my people, asking who was responsible for the fact that a railway settlement had not included what he had wanted to insist on as a minimum, namely that if pay and productivity talks were not concluded by 2 September we would back the Railways Board in withdrawing the increase. 'Obviously', he had written, 'we had lost control of the proceedings in Penzance.' Of course we had, but that was the price we paid for keeping out of it. He really can't have it both ways. Anyway in view of all this Jarratt advised me to take a hawkish line.

Wednesday, 10 July. In Parliamentary Committee I reported at Harold's request on the talk with Frank, and advised that we should stand firm on our own offer of a 10*s* OMO bonus and 10*s* on the basic, not granted retrospectively. Roy is now getting restive even about my package deal. But I told him tartly that I had made that offer with his full consent and the unions would undoubtedly release my letter to the press. It was far better for us to make a virtue of it.

Thursday, 11 July. Another dreary three hours at SEP on that wretched public expenditure exercise. Cutting out £300m is a miserable process. Wedgie, for instance, was nearly in tears at the suggestion that he should sacrifice £3m of his expenditure. His cut would mean slashing the work he was doing on computers, machine tools, micro-electronics, all of which were beginning to yield results. Healey has volunteered another £13m cut in defence so long as it is carried through with no publicity. He is always full of his own virtue in cutting the defence programme and said that, even after everybody's cuts, civil expenditure would be 0.7 per cent above the January target while defence spending would be 2.8 per cent below. But somehow I never trust his claims and have a sinking and perhaps unjustified feeling that a lot of his so-called cuts are totally unreal.

Roy is now out to cut Concorde, which would save £35m in 1969–70 and £53m in the following year. He wanted a firm decision minuted that we should abandon it. Wedgie said mildly that we had always been told by the Attorney-General we couldn't get out of it. In fact, he added, it was always intended to call the plane the 'Elwyn Jones' because he built it. However, we agreed we should have another look at the possibilities.

To cheer us up at the end Harold got Crosland to read us the trade figures for June. With exports up £9m and imports down £37m they are far better than any of us dared to hope, but those of us on the inside know it is far too early to get excited yet.

Monday, 15 July. As usual, my draft speech for the Donovan Report debate was no good. So we had a quick office meeting to try and decide how to present our non-existent line. Then on to another interminable meeting of SEP on public expenditure in 1969–70.

Later Jarratt came to me to tell me there had been an interesting development in the municipal busmen's dispute. Jack Jones had indicated to him that the TGWU would be prepared to accept a compromise involving the payment of a 10*s* basic increase retrospectively, but the other 10*s* in the form of the OMO bonus. I got quite excited at this and thought this was really a dramatic step forward. I therefore said Dick Marsh and I should ask to see the PM and the Chancellor urgently. We have got to make a quick decision before the NJIC meets tomorrow at 10 am. Harold readily agreed to see us and a meeting was fixed for after the ten o'clock vote. I went along to his room to find that the meeting was off. Apparently Roy had just refused to turn up although he had been in for the three-line whip and would have to be back again for another three-liner at 11.30. His only excuse was, Harold told me, that he 'had a social engagement'. The way that man refuses to sacrifice his social life to his political duties never fails to astonish Harold and me, but he obviously feels strong enough to get away with it.

Tuesday, 16 July. I was at No. 10 early for the delayed meeting with Harold, Dick Marsh and the Chancellor. Roy listened with his usual rather *distrait* air as I spelt out Jack Jones's latest offer. Doodling hard with his left hand, Roy said that he felt that we couldn't go as far as this without giving the appearance that the policy was 'crumbling'. Answering one of Harold's apparently relaxed, but really pointed, comments, Roy agreed that the alternative would probably cost us more – *i.e.* full retrospection at the end of the extended standstill on 26 December which would amount to an increase at an annual rate of 8.6 per cent. But he preferred that nonsense in December to a compromise now, for 'confidence' reasons. I went out of the Cabinet room to ring Douglas and tell him that Jack Jones's offer was turned down. Then back to the office to prepare my speech on Donovan.

It wasn't an easy speech to make for the simple reason that I have no policy to declare – and it is far from clear that all members of Cabinet want to climb on the Donovan bandwagon. Roy for one, I am sure, is anxious to give an appearance of toughness – again for confidence reasons. In the circumstances I think my speech was quite good and people like Russ Kerr told me so. I was just sitting on the front bench when I got a message that both sides of the National Joint Industrial Council [NJIC] wanted to see me urgently – could I manage 5.30? My heart leapt: it looked as though we might have won. None of my officials had a clue what the employers and unions had cooked up.

We all trooped into the large ministerial conference room where the full negotiating teams on each side were assembled. Frank was very jocular and I soon realized why. Harris, looking very solemn, announced that they had reached agreement unanimously to recommend a settlement to the Government. When we looked at its terms, our hearts sank. It was for the payment of 10*s* on the basic back to December with another 10*s* for OMO from 13 June on the basic. All this to be associated with readiness to meet under our Departmental chairmanship to discuss productivity guidelines for local deals, etc. Worse than the Jack Jones offer Roy had insisted we turned down! We sat dumbfounded wondering why the hell Harris had sold out. In reply to my point that this represented an increase of 5.5 per cent, Harris said miserably that they had argued all day and that they were convinced this was the very best deal they could get and that it would mean that OMO buses could start moving immediately. So Frank has successfully browbeaten them!

Urgent calls at No. 10 elicited that the PM would see us at 7.15 pm before his dinner for Kenneth Kaunda, and they had even managed to ferret out the Chancellor this time. I took Jarratt with us. Dick Marsh and I told what had happened and I said that we could certainly not accept the offer the NJIC had agreed. But we were in real trouble and our only hope was to try and swing Jack Jones's offer on to them instead. Finally Roy agreed that we should throw in Jack's offer, but not try 'too officiously' to keep it alive. What he would really prefer was that we should make the offer and be turned down.

Back in the House I found they were all ensconced with a drink. Frank was looking immensely pleased with himself and I am sure he was contemplating victory. When I said that the Government could not possibly accept their agreement, which meant an increase of 5.5 per cent at an annual rate, and that we would have to go ahead with the standstill unless they were prepared to talk on these two points, Frank effervesced, ending up ponderously with the demand 'on behalf of both sides' that they should see the PM. I told him that the PM was very tied up with an official engagement of Commonwealth and international importance and I thought it was unfair to ask him to interrupt it. Nonetheless they wanted to see the Prime Minister. I replied, 'Very well. I will ask our infinitely patient and courteous Prime Minister if he will see you, but it may not be possible till the early hours.'

We broke up with some cracks about finding fish and chips and I went into the dining-room to grab my first solid meal of the day. In the middle of it came a message: the PM would see me if I could go immediately. Abandoning my meal I dashed out into the rain where Douglas was waiting with a taxi. Harold and his guests were already at table and they had to fetch Harold out while I waited in the flower-filled drawing-room. I quickly recounted what had happened and said that Dick Marsh and I thought he must see them for presentational reasons, but I added a footnote of my own: 'You must NOT see him without the Chancellor.' When he returned to the dining-room, Michael Halls and Lloyd-Hughes came hurrying out. 'What is all this? We must not go through the old ritual of bringing the parties to No. 10 for a settlement. It is a trap.' I told them that I would not on any account ask Harold to see them without the Chancellor being present, and they went back somewhat relieved, leaving me with a higher estimate of their value to Harold than I had had before.

Back to the House in a chauffeur's mini and I went up to my room to wait for news from No. 10. Eventually the message came through that the Prime Minister didn't think he could see the parties at all as he wanted to get away from the idea that all unsuccessful negotiations ended with a ritual visit to No. 10. I at once saw the hand of Michael Halls in all this and realized that he was quite right. However, I had the unpleasant task of breaking the news to men who had been kept waiting around for three hours expecting their request to be met. I marched in for the most uncomfortable hour I have had for a long time. Frank hit the roof again, saying it was unprecedented for such a request to be turned down and they had all better go home. Harris miserably begged me to keep them talking. I knew that the time had now come to play my trump card positively so I told them that the Government had leant over backwards to reach a settlement; that we recognized the difficulties many of them had on the retrospection point and would be prepared to turn a blind eye to this if only the second 10*s* had been a bonus instead of on a basic rate. I couldn't have made it clearer and I saw Jack Jones whisper something to Frank who brushed him away brusquely, so I felt my main point had gone home. Frank, however, had the bit between his teeth. I took the chance to wind up the meeting and we said goodnight.

At 2 am a press conference, and finally to bed at 3 am. If only these people would leave me to play P and I policy as I know it must be played, I could have got a settlement. But I warned Dick Marsh as I warned Roy that the ships' tally clerks' interim settlement of something like 15 per cent will be coming along this week. I am willing to bet the Treasury will go soft here because the stoppage of the Port of London would have a disastrous effect on our exports. I am, however, not prepared to knock the busmen for six when they have already gone a long way to meet us only to sell out to the tally clerks because of their economic power.

Wednesday, 17 July. Frank Cousins is still playing it remarkably mild in the press, considering all his sound and fury last night. Nonetheless we all waited anxiously for the outcome of his special Delegate Meeting. The news when it came was pretty grim. Frank had of course defended the new settlement with the employers and attacked the Government hip and thigh. But he had advocated only local guerrilla action and had done his utmost to resist the call for a national strike, arguing that they would get their money in December anyway. Nonetheless the strike Motion was carried by 35 votes to 19, so the press are all full of the story that the Government and the union are set on a collision course for the first exercise of the penal powers. I am more than ever furious with Roy for not jumping at the Jack Jones compromise.

Thursday, 18 July. In the afternoon we had the tally clerks' issue before the P and I Committee. Although the employers and unions are only meeting today, I was determined that everybody shall be fully aware of it before we take any more decisions on the busmen's dispute. As I expected, both Roy Jenkins and Tony Crosland, who have been so critical about my being soft, said at once that we should not rule out the interim agreement automatically. 'Three months' trade figures would go for a burton if we had a Port of London strike,' said Crosland firmly. I told them equally firmly that I wasn't prepared to be soft on the tally clerks and tough on the busmen and we left the issue with that warning shot across each other's bows.

Saturday, 20 July. Dick [Marsh] tells me he has got rid of Tom Padmore a year ahead of time. He certainly goes up in my estimation! Perhaps I might have got further with my efforts if William Armstrong had been in charge instead of that awful creature Helsby.[1] Dick expected scenes with Padmore but instead the latter came along quite resigned to say to him that although he had been upset at first he now realized that it was the best thing that he should retire a year early in this way. He admitted that he had been thoroughly unhappy for the past three years because he hated the Department and was utterly bored with Transport.

[1] Sir William Armstrong had succeeded Sir Laurence Helsby as Head of the Home Civil Service.

Tuesday, 23 July. At 10 am Dick Marsh and I went along to see Harold and Roy about the busmen's situation. I reported that there had been no serious move from the trade union side and that it looked as though we should have to take the initiative. Jarratt had drawn up a list of possible alternative compromises, all based on the proposition that, though insisting that the second 10*s* must be in the form of a bonus for OMO, we could offer consolidation of the bonus into the basic rate under various conditions. These were listed in order of descending toughness. Roy actually had the cool nerve to say that he didn't think it was as essential as it had been to insist on a tough line because sterling was now a bit stronger! Eventually we agreed that Dick Marsh and I should see the union.

Wednesday, 24 July. The great day of the selection of the new Labour Party General Secretary,[1] and we were all there in strength. Jennie Lee began by reading a long report of the actions of the sub-committee instructed by the last NEC meeting to approach certain individuals. The sub-committee had decided unanimously (only George Brown being absent) that the first approach should be made to Alf Allen of USDAW.[2] It also unanimously agreed that, should Alf refuse, Tony Greenwood should be the choice. On this basis she and Sara Barker[3] had approached Alf Allen who, despite their repeated pressure on him, had finally turned it down. They had then in accordance with the agreement approached Tony Greenwood, saying it had been a unanimous decision to make him second choice. Tony had written agreeing that his name should be put forward and that he was ready to resign his seat if he were nominated and conference endorsed the NEC choice. This was then reported to the second meeting of the committee at which George was present this time (and drunk according to Harold's account to me). At this meeting George had suggested Harry Nicholas's name for the first time. Harry had clearly been as surprised as everyone and said he thought he was too old. But apparently this had been dismissed as irrelevant. However, bearing in mind their previous decision, the rest had decided to recommend Tony Greenwood to the NNC by four votes to two.

After a heavy silence in which everyone waited for everyone else, George Brown finally moved in saying ponderously that he wanted to move Harry Nicholas. After that it was just a question of watching the trade union votes fall into line. The members of the women's section of the NEC, dependent as they are on trade union votes, dared not demur, even if they had wanted to. Joe Gormley, who had been a member of the sub-committee, almost exploded at all this. He said he was frankly astonished at Harry Nicholas for allowing his name to go forward, he having quite early on been ruled out by age. Now, said Joe, he himself had been put in the position of appearing to recommend someone who wasn't a trade unionist and there couldn't be a greater crime than that. What right had the committee to switch its views in this way? Frank

[1] The General Secretary of the Labour Party, Len Williams, was about to become Governor-General of Mauritius and we had to appoint his successor.

[2] General Secretary of USDAW and a member of the General Council of the TUC.

[3] Former Women's Organizer of the Yorkshire Labour Party, Sara Barker had become National Agent in 1962. She retired in 1969 and died in 1973.

Chapple,[1] in his typically insulting way, said that the press had been carrying stories for weeks that Wilson was backing Greenwood and if we turned Greenwood down now it would inevitably be reported as a rebuff for Wilson. He personally wasn't a Wilson man by any means, but after all the man was Prime Minister so we couldn't have him insulted publicly. Peggy said promptly that we ought to pay no attention to the press. Jim Callaghan, of course, sat on the fence as usual while nonetheless insinuating he was going to vote for Harry Nicholas, while Harold made an elaborate explanation of how it was he who had originally proposed Alf Allen. Finally the horrible morning was capped by Eirene White's public switch. She said that some of them in the sub-committee had voted for Greenwood because they thought they were bound by their previous decision but if another name was now in the running they felt they were free to vote for him. It was clear that the day was lost – as indeed it was by twelve votes to fourteen.

I was furious, having already told the meeting that I thought it was intolerable for the sub-committee to invite a man unanimously to stick his neck out and allow his name to go forward only to rat on him. There was quite a scene at our end of the table when the result was announced, Ian Mikardo saying that it was the blackest day yet for the Labour movement, while even Arthur Skeffington shook his head over the lack of comradeship. My heart went out to poor Tony who, however, rose to the occasion magnificently. It must have been a terrible blow to him. Yet when they were called back into the room he said without a tremor in his voice that he congratulated Harry and wished him well, which brought a sympathetic round of applause from all those who had just done Tony dirt. I have seldom felt so nauseated by a meeting of the NEC and that is putting it very high indeed.

All day today we waited for news as the TGWU and employers met to discuss the ideas we had put forward. There was still no signal from them as I left for the dinner which Donovan was giving for his fellow Commissioners. We had just completed a very pleasant meal when I was called to the phone: could I leave immediately as the meeting had broken up and both sides wanted to see me and Dick Marsh 'to ask us a question'. They were tired and didn't want the meeting to be a minute later than 9 pm. I hurried back to the House to be joined by Dick Marsh in full evening dress. Nobody had any clue as to the outcome of the meeting, though I said grimly, 'Question, my foot. They want to up the ante.' We marched into the large ministerial conference room to find the two sides facing each other in full strength. Harris, speaking for both sides, said there was one point they wanted to put to us which he was sure would cause no difficulty. He then spelt out the exact lines of what we had agreed with Jack Jones and Alan Thompson the day before but with one vital addition: the 10*s* bonus for OMO was to be backdated to 14 December. I felt coldly furious. They must have known that to backdate a bonus which had not been fixed till 13 June would be to make nonsense of the whole thing. I turned to Frank and said coldly, 'Do you wish to add anything?' He shook his head. 'Very well, then we will have a short adjournment,' and I swept out of the room, followed by my troops. In Dick Marsh's room nearby it took us five minutes flat to decide that

[1] General Secretary of the Electrical, Electronic, Telecommunication and Plumbing Union [EETPU] and a member of the NEC of the Labour Party.

this proposal was impossible. Indeed John Locke said that both Alan Thompson and Harris had admitted openly, 'It won't take them five minutes to turn that down.'

We returned. I said that it was impossible for us to backdate a bonus for the acceptance of a principle to a date before the bonus had been agreed. The employers looked miserable but Frank truculently shrugged his shoulders. It was all over a few minutes afterwards.

Thursday, 25 July. I had to prepare an answer to my Private Notice Question on the [bus] dispute. The House took the news of the failure to agree much more calmly than I had dared to expect, though Eric Heffer exploded a bit. Then came the news: the TGWU Executive Council had authorized Frank to launch strike action on 13 August and they added a curious phrase to the effect that they would seek to achieve local agreements meanwhile.

Tuesday, 30 July. Up early to discuss workers' participation with Dick Marsh. He has scrapped all my ideas for putting Frank Cousins and the other Transport Workers' Union members on the Board of the NFC and wants to put on an official from the TUC instead while he sets up an independent inquiry into different forms of workers' participation. There really is an appalling slovenliness about that man's thinking which, put across brashly as he does, passes for smartness. He rattles out his objections to workers' participation in all its known forms without having any clear alternatives. He doesn't seem to have any feel for Socialist ideas at all, and he also has an appalling cynical defeatism which he parades as realism.

Thursday, 1 August. At the Parliamentary Committee of Cabinet I warned of the trouble we are heading for over the ships' clerks' preposterous interim claim. Roy and Tony said unequivocally that we could not afford a strike and if necessary we must climb down. I retorted that, if we did, P and I policy would collapse. I believe that the only way we can avoid this mess is, as I keep repeating, to 'play it positive'. I've therefore instructed my people to encourage the port employers to open talks with the dockers about Stage 2 of the Devlin decasualization scheme and try to get some real productivity. In this way we shall forestall the endless leapfrogging between the dockers and the ships' clerks. Apparently the London employers want to get cracking on this anyway.

Friday, 9 August. The national bus strike is off! Frank has told his chaps to go for local agreements along the lines he wants. Good luck to him. I'll go for some local agreements, too: my model ones. The important thing is that – miracle of miracles – I've now got the all clear to go on holiday!

Sunday, 11 August. Vico Equense, Italy. I can't believe we are really in the sun at last. Although the weather is misty for Italy, it is indescribably blissful compared with the wet misery we have endured in England during the last few weeks. The Savareses are as delightful as ever.[1] Fernando met us at the airport yesterday with the Public Schools Commission Report in his hand. As usual he is more up to date with what is happening in England than I am myself. Despite my warning to him that I wanted to keep off politics, I can see that we are going to spend endless hours chatting with him about just that.

As Ted and I were sunning ourselves on the beach, Charlie Forte, the restaurateur, arrived in a huge motorboat and anchored off our little beach. Fernando and Violetta went out to lunch with him on board and afterwards Fernando came to ask us if we would like a trip to Capri with them all. Of course we jumped at it. The Fortes turned out to be a large, delightful family and we got on excellently.

Wednesday, 28 August. Back to a full day's work at the office. I spent an hour discussing developments in the bus situation. Fifteen local authorities have reached local agreements with their union to accept the Castle package but at the NJIC meeting on Monday this week the TGWU had flatly refused to approve them and have proposed all sorts of modifications on the lines that Frank and Jack had indicated. Since then another agreement has been submitted to us by Blackburn which we shall be only too glad to approve, and I told officials to lay on a meeting in Blackburn for me tomorrow with my local TGWU to be followed by a press conference, the theme of which will be 'Who is interfering with free collective bargaining now?' I intend to rub it in to my local busmen that there is a £1 increase and £30 back pay waiting to be picked up at any moment in lieu of the December agreement as soon as their own union will approve it nationally.

Thursday, 29 August. It's worked! The Blackburn busmen have been eating out of my hand and I want to find a formula for bypassing the NJIC. I promised them we will let them know by next Wednesday whether their formula is on, so they reluctantly agreed to wait till then. They were delighted that my Department has responded so promptly and effectively with help on their local productivity deal. This is just the 'positive' image I want to give, and we parted affectionately. I take an impish delight in outwitting Frank – just as he has tried to outwit me.

The engineering pay negotiations had been stalemated all summer, with the employers insisting on a package which contained a number of tough productivity strings. The unions were getting restless and on 26 August the National Committee of the AEF had voted for a strike. It was clear that no one was eager for industrial action, but it was my job to ensure that the industry did not drift into it, or breach P and I policy.

Tuesday, 3 September. After the Bank Holiday weekend at HCF (wet, of course) I am off to the TU Congress meeting at Blackpool. The office was very dubious about my going without an invitation but I told them nobody could

[1] Fernando and Violetta Savarese, the proprietors of a charming little hotel at Vico Equense, were old friends. Violetta was the former ballet dancer Violetta Elvin, while Fernando was so interested in all things English that he was almost more English than she.

stop me turning up in the public gallery. They then tried to persuade me not to attend the P and I debate but I told them that was the only one I was interested in. I think it could do nothing but good for the papers to be full of pictures of me listening to a debate abusing my policy. The only snag is that, thanks to the SOGAT [Society of Graphical and Allied Trades] strike, there are no pictures! Anyway the Department has now entered into the spirit of the thing and have agreed I must attend the Fraternal Dinner, to which I received an invitation. The press, bored to tears with the dullness of the Congress proceedings, are building up a great story to the effect that I have come in order to negotiate with the engineering unions. Last Monday the AEF National Committee voted for a national strike, but only by thirty votes to thirty-one, and the irony of the situation is that it was Willie Simpson's lads, the Foundry Workers' section of the committee, normally classed as moderates, who carried the day by voting seven to two. Left to themselves, Hughie Scanlon's lot would have turned the strike down. I shall play down all this talk of intervention, and when I arrived at the Imperial Hotel I duly informed the press men who came crowding round that I had come 'to listen and to learn and not to comment'.

The Fraternal Dinner turned out to be just about the most boring event I have ever attended. But I mean to seize this opportunity to gen myself up on the details of the engineering pay negotiations. This pay claim is going to be a hell of a minefield to negotiate.

Wednesday, 4 September. I walked down to the conference hall in brilliant sunshine. (One of the press comments said later that I 'sailed along the promenade like Queen Elizabeth I surrounded by a bevy of young men'.) The papers are all full of my arrival and the press boys are watching my every move. Charles says they even have someone posted outside my bedroom door. They soon got their reward for their pains because I hadn't been in the Winter Gardens for two minutes when I ran into Johnnie Boyd who took me aside to give me a brief résumé of the engineering state of play. He reiterated Danny [McGarvey]'s assurance [to me last night] that there will be no strike. The ETU, GMWU, Vehicle Builders and Boilermakers are all going to insist on a ballot. This will mean a delay of about six weeks which will put Hughie Scanlon on the spot; he has been saying that there is no need for a ballot in the case of the AEF but the latter's rules only give the Executive power to act if there is no time for a ballot to take place. Moreover, the Confederation's rules provide for it. Hughie is already eating some of his words and one paper carries the story that there is going to be an approach to me to intervene in order to get him off the hook. I doubt that, but nonetheless Willie Simpson approached me to suggest I ought to talk to Hughie. (Here again the photographers had a feast day. It is perhaps as well that none of those photographs will appear!) Willie said it is a geographical accident that his foundry workers were represented by militants. Under his union's new rules the representation would be more moderate and the voting would be more like four to five against militancy when they come into operation next year. In the meantime he is clearly worried about developments. I sent a message to Hughie via Willie suggesting he come and see me in my hotel room that afternoon.

I then took my seat in the gallery at Congress amid the flashing of television bulbs to hear Sid Greene open the economic debate. He did so surprisingly well. But it was a terrible strain sitting there behind the TV cameras where I had a full view of the five monitors. Out of the corner of my eye I could see my own face appear from time to time on one of them. They had got me covered all right and I was afraid to yawn, sneeze or even smile. Such are the hazards of public life.

Hughie was very affable when he turned up in my room at the hotel. Douglas Smith, Charles Birdsall and John Fraser (my PPS)[1] had done a rapid transformation job. They had got one of the beds removed, had some easy chairs rushed in and a bar installed, so I was able to sit in the centre of my web unobserved. I drew Hughie out about what his minimum demands would be. He wouldn't tell me in terms, but it did emerge that the general increase is largely irrelevant. What really matters is the demand for the £15 minimum time rate rising to £20 at the end of three years. He argued that this would make little difference to the skilled man's actual earnings which are already over £20 a week, but once the new rates were consolidated they would become the basis for overtime pay and holidays. The real cost, however, comes when one is dealing with the unskilled workers and above all the women, whose earnings only run at 67 per cent and 56 per cent respectively of the skilled man's earnings because they cannot earn his premia. What amuses me is that, for all the AEF's talk about helping the lower paid and fighting for equal pay, they find their existence a bloody nuisance, and would be ready to settle for something which sold them out if politically they could get away with it.

We spent one and a half hours bottoming all this and I told Hughie I would get my people to cost the whole exercise much more accurately than obviously the employers have done or the unions are in a position to do. My aim is not to double-cross the unions but to work out constructively the best possible solution for them within the confines of P and I policy. I was relieved to find Hughie was not entirely negative about the productivity conditions which must accompany it.

When he had gone, Charles Birdsall dashed in to say that Hughie had told the press of his talk with me. He obviously finds it a help and not an embarrassment. We therefore decided that I must balance this with a similar talk with Johnnie Boyd. His approach is much less analytical. He thinks in terms of the employers improving their offer by a few bob under every heading and is confident that some 'give' on these lines would do the trick. Personally I doubt it and I am beginning to think there may be a constructive role for DEP to play in prompting the employers to make a dramatically better offer on the minimum time rates in exchange for the unions dropping the general increase claim completely. The first step is to get it all far more reliably costed than it has been so far.

Thursday, 5 September. We walked down early for the big debate in Congress on P and I policy. There I sat under the cameras' scrutiny while the debate wound its inevitable course. George Woodcock brilliantly lowered the temper as usual. Frank Cousins was even more confused and ineffectual than his norm,

[1] MP for Norwood, later Lambeth Norwood. With his shrewd mind and steady personality I found his help invaluable.

while Hughie Scanlon rattled off left-wing statistics like a machine-gun. Once again I was conscious of a curious lack of tension in the debate – I would call it a lack of reality. Certainly over my drinks in bars and at cocktail parties these last few hours I have met no personal bitterness from the trade unionists (except from Dai Davies who is breathing murder over me for having held the Pearson Inquiry on his BSC dispute). I personally was delighted that Jack Peel of the General and Municipal had insisted on pressing his motion of support for the TUC's voluntary policy.[1] In the event it just scraped through by 34,000 votes which was broadly what everyone had anticipated. As the result was announced the press men crept up on me in the gallery, sneaking into seats next to me and in front of me, waiting to pounce on me in the dark the moment I moved, to get my comments. We had a hurried confab and agreed that I should stick to my line that I was there merely to listen and learn and not to conduct a running commentary on the affairs of the TUC. But just as we were beginning to relax there came an urgent message from No. 10. Trevor Lloyd-Hughes said the PM was distressed to find I had refused to go on TV. It was imperative that I should state publicly and as tactfully as possible (for foreign consumption) that the Government intended to stand by its P and I policy. So we had to undo all Charles's work, summon a press conference and race over to the TV studios to do a recording for the news. Fortunately I made no slips and we got a message from No. 10 late at night that I had been 'word perfect'.

We hurried to our night sleeper train in the pouring rain, eating our belated sandwiches on the way and congratulating ourselves on two days' most useful work.

Friday, 6 September. Down to Dick's farm at Cropredy for our meeting on economic strategy. I picked up Tommy back from his holiday, rested and fit, and discussed the economic prospects with him all the way. Dick is all full of an official document produced at the Cabinet's request on the national minimum wage. In his usual way he has got carried away with it and has just dropped a terrible clanger by pretending it doesn't matter that some chaps can earn more on unemployment benefit than when they are at work. Dear Dick, he really is irresistible! Here he sits at Cropredy, revelling like Nye used to do in being a *kulak*. He insisted on taking me to see his new combine harvester and, with that disarming frankness of his, admitted that farmers buy a new machine every year, selling the old one second hand, because they get a 10 per cent allowance on it, and therefore make a profit. 'One of those little rackets in farming,' said Dick with relish. He is also revelling in his new heated swimming pool and we swam solemnly up and down for a good half an hour. What I love about Dick is the way he always enjoys everything that happens to or belongs to him. It shows a capacity for enjoying life which keeps him perilously and entertainingly human.

Despite all Jack Scamp's efforts at trouble-shooting, unofficial strikes in the motor industry were getting worse and both the Government and the employers were in despair.

[1] Jack Peel was General Secretary of the Dyers, Bleachers and Textile Workers, later part of the Transport and General Workers' Union. He was a member of the General Council of the TUC from 1966 to 1972.

Typical of the industrial anarchy we faced was the walk-out of twenty-two machine setters at the Girling Brakes works because, as members of the AEF, *they refused to accept the instructions of an* ASTMS *charge-hand. As they were key men producing a key component for the motor industry, their action led to 5,000 workers being laid off and to growing public hostility to the trade unions. It was this strike, in which a few men were able to do massive damage in a highly integrated industry, which led to the concept of the 'conciliation pause' I was later to embody in* In Place of Strife. *It also made me determined to revive the almost moribund Motor Industry Joint Council in order to compel the unions to face up to the chaotic situation which was doing so much damage to their own standing as well as to the economy.*

Meanwhile the inquiry into the inter-union dispute at the British Steel Corporation I had set up under Lord Pearson had reported in August (Cmnd 3754). It expressed its clear annoyance at the situation at BSC, *pointing out that 'the public reasonably regard with special disfavour strikes arising out of recognition disputes, or indeed any disputes between unions', and that was the reason why Donovan had proposed the setting-up of an Industrial Relations Commission to which they could be referred. In the meantime it condemned the arbitrary way in which* CAWU *and* ASTMS *had been excluded from national recognition by* BSC, *to which they had strong claims under any objective criteria, and came to the 'firm conclusion' that the decision was mistaken. Despite Dai Davies's threat to bring his steel union out on strike if* CAWU *and* ASTMS *were to be given negotiating rights, Pearson recommended that they should be recognized on condition that they entered into joint working arrangements with the other unions with regard to spheres of influence. The steel union,* ISTC, *was furious with this finding and with me for having set up the inquiry and it was clear that other unions as well resented any interference in their affairs, even by a fact-finding body.*

Monday, 9 September. Lunched with Donald Stokes and the top brass of British Leyland. He had sent a list of points he wanted to discuss with me that sounded like a high-handed catalogue of instructions to the Government, and Denis Barnes said he thought some of them were sheer cheek. But in conversation Donald was far more tentative and reasonable. Their main obsession – and who can blame them? – is the disastrous effect on them of the crop of unofficial strikes in the motorcar industry. This time the main threat to them is from the Girling Brakes strike. They agree the real answer is not to get over-dependent on one supplier and to build up more stocks, but point out this is about the most uneconomic way you can run a business. They are worried, too, about how to get the unions' collaboration in the essential rationalization they must carry through and I told them to 'do a Windsor'. In other words they should spend a weekend with union representatives explaining all the economic realities of their business to the unions and outlining their economic strategy. If it would help I would be delighted to come along. They thought there was something in this: as Donald put it, 'The unions still look on us as robber barons but there aren't any more robber barons. We are just management.' My aim is to get firms into the habit of collaborating with DEP on the forward manpower planning side.

At last some sun has come back to drenched England. The day has been so warm and balmy that I couldn't bear to go home without my usual constitutional round St James's Park. As I strolled across the grass a man's voice from beneath a tree said, 'Good evening.' I was just ready to walk on haughtily with my head in the air when he added earnestly, 'The best of luck to you.' I can't walk across the park these days without getting accosted but always, I am glad to say, politically.

Tuesday, 10 September. Rosie of Ford's sewing machinists is on the march again. She has written to me complaining that the ad-hoc committee set up following the court of inquiry had not given them a fair do.[1] For one thing the employers had insisted on putting forward the wrong profile, which didn't tally with Paragraph 114 of the Scamp Report. Checking up on this I found the paragraph referred to Friedman's profile which had never been accepted by the assessors. Unfortunately the company had not had the sense to challenge Friedman, so the Court of Inquiry had accepted his profile as being correct. So Rosie is pressing me to scrap the whole Report and set up a new inquiry. I am furious with the company for letting Friedman's profile go unchecked. Paragraph 114 will dog us for many months to come and I said we had got to find some way of getting it corrected. Really, these employers are intolerably lax. We go to all that trouble to end a strike which they said was costing them £30m worth of exports and they can't even manage to conduct their side of the inquiry properly.

Monday, 16 September. My battle of wits with Frank Cousins over the bus dispute continues merrily and I am amused to find how easy it is to get a settlement with local TGWU branches if only the national officers keep out of the way. Wigan, for instance, has come to a local settlement which we couldn't approve but have protested they don't want to defy the Government and have asked to see me. When they came I explained how anxious I was to help and how far I had gone in seeking a compromise. 'But the NIJC won't approve your agreement,' they pleaded, so we gently intimated that Burnley and other authorities had found a way round and they went off to explore the possibility of doing it themselves. At the end of the meeting to my surprise the TGWU representative came up to me murmuring, 'We will do our best to get your model agreement through.'

At lunch with Tommy and Derek Robinson I probed Derek's anxieties.[2] He said that he was finding it difficult to discover just what work the Department wanted him to do. On the future of P and I policy, for example, the Department had got to make up its mind on a series of options and then put them clearly to his Division so that it could work out the statistics on them. I said I would circulate a Minute to the effect that the Research Division must be represented on all my policy discussions and that no submissions should come to me without their comments on them.

[1] The court of inquiry under Sir Jack Scamp had reported in August (Cmnd 3749). It was satisfied that the machinists' present grading was not incompatible with the job evaluation results but, as the sewing machinists felt strongly that on five characteristics the markings on their job profile were too low, it recommended that an ad-hoc joint committee be set up to consider the machinists' profile. Unfortunately the Report had commented that 'in profiling the sewing machinists' job the assessors rated it higher than the benchmark on four characteristics and thus did not see the benchmark as a standard to be rigidly applied', and this had reopened the whole issue.

[2] I had appointed Derek Robinson, Senior Research Officer at the Oxford Institute of Economics and Statistics, as my Senior Economic Adviser. He had previously been Economic Adviser to the PIB.

Tuesday, 17 September. I called Heron and Marre in to tell them I thought we must do something about the catastrophic deterioration which is taking place in industrial relations in the motor industry. My attempt to call the Motor Industry Joint Council together to discuss Jack Scamp's third Report on the industry had come to nothing because of the indifference of both sides, and we would have to find some alternative. Heron nodded his head sadly in agreement and when I asked him what his solution was he laughed ruefully and said, 'I haven't one.' I said I thought the least we could do as a first step was for me to call both sides together under my chairmanship. They agreed this would be a good idea. As we talked a message came in from Donald Stokes on behalf of the Society of Motor Manufacturers and Traders [SMMT]. They were in conference in London and wanted to see me urgently. I told them I would see them the following day and asked the office to try and lay on a similar meeting with the Confed.

Wednesday, 18 September. The SMMT turned up in force for the meeting they had requested. They were clearly desperate men – saying that they had hardly had a strike-free day in the past few months, and the vast majority of them wildcat strikes. The unions, they said, had lost control completely over their shop stewards and their rank and file and they didn't think the situation could be improved until collective bargains were made legally enforceable. I then put my idea of a joint meeting to them. They were pretty sceptical but said that of course they would try anything.

Next was the turn of the unions. Despite my efforts to get Hugh Scanlon, George Barratt trailed in disconsolately accompanied only by a representative of the Confed and Les Kealey of the TGWU. They sat there helplessly while I spelled out my idea. Of course, George said he would play but Les Kealey told me frankly that the whole thing would be useless without the AEF. Eventually George said he would try and get the Motor Industry Committee of the Confed to come in force. They didn't like my having jumped the gun on them because they couldn't deny that the situation has become serious and it is clear they just don't believe they can do anything to influence it. But I shall go ahead nonetheless. I can see my only hope is to force the trade unions to face up to their responsibilities publicly.

Thursday, 19 September. Thank God the unemployment figures are slightly better.[1] Harold used this as an excuse at SEP to delay the discussions on the winter relief programme, though I warned them there was still no reason to doubt that unemployment would rise to 700,000 by next February. What he is up to Peter and I cannot make out, and we are determined to return to the attack on Monday next. We also had a gloomy document from Dick Marsh on London Transport fares. He says another £8m must be raised to make London Transport viable before it is handed over to the GLC and he just wants to give London Transport the go-ahead without any further reference to the PIB. I slapped him down hard on this whereupon he muttered that his whole policy would collapse. He really is appallingly negative. At every stage he throws in

[1] The register of wholly unemployed in Great Britain, excluding school leavers and seasonally adjusted, had fallen from 541,600 in August to 540,600 in September.

his hand on my Transport policy and I have to sit back and see it murdered before my own eyes. This is the sort of thing I can't forgive Harold.

Phone call from a dejected George Barratt. Scanlon is refusing to come to next week's meeting of the motor industry. Apparently he argues that it would be inconsistent of him to come and talk to the employers when they had not yet agreed to a pay settlement. Publicly he is going to argue that he has got a busy day anyway, dealing with twenty-seven outstanding references for York.[1] George wants to know whether in view of this I still want to go ahead. I say firmly yes. 'I intend to hold this meeting however many unions turn up, or even if none do.' George says if that is the line he will do his best. Afterwards I told Douglas Smith to get on to the employers and get them to postpone next Thursday's discussion of their outstanding references. I don't intend to let Hughie Scanlon off the hook.

Monday, 23 September. Still no meeting of MISC 205. But at SEP we had the Treasury's monthly economic report. The underlying trend in the economy shows, thank heavens, considerable improvement. Though imports were 'unexpectedly high' in August it is claimed that this was probably due to a big turn round in stock building in the second quarter, the biggest increase in volume in oil and semi-manufacturers. The unemployment trend is now downwards and industrial production is up 5 per cent on a year ago. True to Tommy's instructions, I asked if we could have a more detailed analysis of the import figures than this report gave and rather crossly Crosland said of course I could have it if I wanted it. I also pointed out that although retail prices had increased by just over 4 per cent since devaluation the rise in hourly wage rates had been somewhat smaller. And this spelled real problems for us in P and I policy. It was one thing to get a 1 per cent cut in consumption by increasing purchase tax on inessentials; it was another to hold wage increases below the normal cost of living. However, I am as aware as everyone else that there are some big wage demands in the pipeline, which may alter the picture.

We then turned to the report on possible measures to relieve winter unemployment. I stressed the fact that my Department still thinks unemployment will go over the 700,000 figure by next February and I strongly backed Peter Shore's demand for relief measures in those parts of the development areas where unemployment is likely to be particularly high. This would cost £21m and Roy said we just hadn't got enough allowance for it. He therefore insisted that the most he could approve was an expenditure of £10m in the Special Development Areas only, coupled with the expenditure of £1m at Barrow-in-Furness (which Wedgie has been pressing as the most effective way of reducing unemployment in shipbuilding).

Tuesday, 24 September. I was surprised to see in my Cabinet papers an item on P and I policy to be raised by me, so I phoned Harold early to ask him what line he wanted me to take. He explained that it was down in error and that he

[1] Joint discussion at York between the representatives of the AEF Executive and the Engineering Employers' Federation was the final stage provided for in the procedure agreement at national level. In 1968 the references averaged 28 per month. In a number of cases the claims or disputes were referred back to the firms concerned 'for final settlement domestically', or failure to agree was recorded.

intended to raise it himself because he wanted to tie Jim Callaghan down. Jim had been asking to see him for some days now but he had been staving him off until he could get a ruling in Cabinet. I told him about the proposed reference in my speech for conference to the consultations I wanted to launch with the trade unions on the next stages of P and I policy. I didn't intend to refer to it in Cabinet as I didn't want Jim leaking it and claiming credit for this overture.

In Cabinet the outcome of the P and I item was satisfactory. After I had reported on the engineering strike and got agreement that I should not intervene at this stage, Harold said smoothly that of course Ministers would be expected to stand by the P and I policy at conference. As we anticipated, Jim then chipped in to say he was glad the PM had raised this as he had been trying to see him about it for some time. He was afraid we were in for a resounding defeat on this issue: couldn't we at any rate hold out some hope that the policy would be reconsidered and studied before the end of 1969? Frank Cousins's vote might depend upon it. I said that I intended to indicate as much in my speech. Jim said he was very glad and Roy said he personally would have no objection. So that was that.

But the item on which we spent far the longest time was the Falkland Islands. It is typical of British policy that the fate of 2,500 people should occupy us for not less than one and a half hours. Michael Stewart has worked out the terms of a joint memo with the Argentine Government which recognizes our willingness to surrender sovereignty when we are satisfied that the interests of the Falklanders will be preserved. This, he said, was to be accompanied by a unilateral statement by us saying that we thought this meant we should only give up sovereignty when the Falklanders agreed we should. But it was only the memo which would be registered at the UN. Dick and Fred Peart promptly said there would be an absolute howl of anger in Parliament and everyone would say we had not only treated the Falkland Islands badly but paved the way for a betrayal in Gibraltar too. Yet, retorted Michael, we should certainly have a hostile reaction in the UN and there might even be armed clashes with the Argentines which – Denis Healey warned – we couldn't meet except by an enormous increase in expenditure. Really, the problem of winding up the last outposts of empire is almost ludicrously difficult. I thought to myself that this is a classic example of how on these so-called moral issues one can't win. Which should be our parliamentary priority? To defend to the last ditch the rights of a small group of people who want to remain Britishers? To do nothing which would increase defence expenditure? Or to observe UN resolutions? I tried to get the words 'views and' inserted before 'interests of the Falklanders' but Michael said this would be utterly unacceptable to the Argentine Government. In the end we sent him off to get an exchange of unilateral statements with the Argentine Government before we signed the memo so that we could see what there was in that and also to get their agreement that our unilateral statement should become a UN document too.

Wednesday, 25 September. Had a long meeting with Crosland and Cledwyn Hughes about P and I policy. I told them we had got to agree on a philosophy for my conference speech. Cornered, Crosland admitted that he thought prices would inevitably rise by 7 per cent. But then he thought wages would rise more than our assessment too. Personally he never thought that P and I policy could accomplish much. It is clear that he and Roy are getting ready to back out of it and certainly they would not dig in their heels to the tune of risking a major strike. This leaves me carrying an immense can. I have got to go on justifying a policy which three-quarters of the Cabinet no longer believe in, and pending its winding up I am being publicly bullied into enforcing it on the weaker brethren like the busmen and the railwaymen. My only consolation in all this is that we really are beginning to get people to talk and think about productivity.

Thursday, 26 September. My great meeting on the motor industry. I approached it with some trepidation, but Douglas Smith had arranged the chairs in a relaxed circle and in the event it turned out far better than I dared to hope. George Barratt began by explaining primly (and inaccurately) that, contrary to press reports, Mr Scanlon had hoped to be present, but that previous engagements had made it impossible. However, he hoped to be there at the next meeting. (I increasingly get the impression of how unsure of himself Scanlon is. He is always getting himself into difficulties by striking militant attitudes and then having to retreat from them.) The employers were articulate, lucid, firm but utterly reasonable in tone. Of course, they are obsessed by the need for legislation but they made out a sensible case for it and I was astonished to hear Les Cannon [of EETPU] say at one point that he personally would not be against it in certain circumstances. Drawing the unions out was much more difficult. They rambled on uneasily but they, too, had some telling points, not least the fact that, when they had taken a pay claim all the way through procedure only to be turned down after months of talk, the men had only to come out on strike for two or three days and the claim was conceded immediately. Gradually I drew them out on the procedure point on which Les Cannon and Les Kealey were particularly forthcoming.

After nearly two hours I pointed out that I must go and get my train to Blackpool for the Party conference and I suggested we met again as soon as possible. George Barratt got truculent at this and said he thought the unions and the employers ought to be left to get on with the talking on their own. But I brushed this firmly aside, saying that that might follow later on but that we had joint work to do together yet. The chap from Rootes said almost pleadingly that I had been 'like a breath of fresh air' and that he for one hoped I would continue to preside. And so it was agreed. We then spent a quarter of an hour wrangling about the date, the employers saying they were ready to drop everything to come any day I cared to name, the unions muttering that they had all got appointments they could not break. I finally got the unions to agree that we would meet on Monday or Tuesday after conference and I invited anyone from either side to put forward specific proposals as a starting-point. I went off to Blackpool feeling that we had done rather well since Conrad Heron keeps telling me that if I can get the unions to go on meeting under my chairmanship and to do anything radical about reforming the procedures, I shall have made a major breakthrough.

I then shut myself into my carriage to Blackpool to brood over two major speeches: the first on Sunday at the evening rally, and the second on Monday which Harold has succeeded in getting Conference Arrangements Committee to allocate to P and I policy. It is just my luck that, not having made a major speech or spoken at the rally at conference for years and years, I now have both to do on successive days.

Friday, 27 September. There is a lot of adverse comment about the discovery that Harold is not coming to attend the pre-conference NEC. I can guess what he is up to – he is determined not to be there when the row goes on as to whether Roy Jenkins and Michael Stewart should be allowed to speak at conference. I have some sympathy. I, too, can see the headline: 'Wilson rebuffed'. In the event we won on that point by fifteen votes to six, but only after Wedgie had moved an elaborate resolution establishing the principle that Ministers had no right to speak except as the invitees of the NEC. George Brown and Jim Callaghan put up a strong fight to keep Roy and Michael out, backed by Walter Padley, who is increasingly sour these days. Whether Jim and George are doing it just to spite Harold I will never know.

The mid-term Manifesto was before us in somewhat turgid form. George is now utterly reconciled to our presenting it because it gives him the occasion to make a great come-back speech. It has all appeared in this morning's papers anyway. The only lively moment on it was Jim's protest about the paragraph on devaluation about which he remains acutely sensitive. He wanted it reworded because he said it had not been proved that the currency was wrongly valued. Moreover, he added tartly, if we had devalued in 1964 as some people wanted to, we would never have got the trade unions and the country to accept the austerity measures and the tougher P and I policy we have had to adopt now – an ingenious line of *ex post facto* rationalization which, however, doesn't apply to devaluation in 1966 to which he was bitterly opposed.

After a brief excursion out into the rain I retired to my room to work on my speeches. Panic has now set in.

Saturday, 28 September. Just before I went off for a women's dinner, Terry Pitt came to bring me the composite resolutions. The key one is the short sharp demand by the TGWU and the Boilermakers for the repeal of the current Act and no more statutory restrictions on trade unionists. Terry says he thinks that Jim has actually been mobilizing support for this and I wouldn't be surprised. Terry urged me to hold out as much of an olive branch as possible.

Sunday, 29 September. This morning I still hadn't got a speech for tonight's rally, and what was more I had spent half the night on the loo. I don't know whether it was the café meal last night, or what.

And so into the fateful NEC meeting at which the P and I resolution came up first. A good job too because it brought into the open all the poison in the atmosphere. I had never realized that the opposition among the trade unions had been growing so bitter and so widespread. I began by saying I had hoped we might be able to ask conference to remit this resolution because of the gesture I proposed to make about the future of the policy. But one by one they swept this aside as totally inadequate.

As we took the vote on the TGWU resolution I was certain that we had been beaten and was astonished to hear Bert Sims say, 'It is twelve votes to twelve.'

Without a moment's hesitation, Jennie Lee in the chair gave her casting vote our way and there was an immediate feeling of almost tangible relief, not least, I suspect, among the trade unionists like Willie Simpson who had been forced to vote against their own convictions by their trade union Executives. Afterwards the supporters of the resolution were almost jubilant. I think they had got the best of both worlds: they had made a dramatic demonstration without winning and a number of them crowded round me afterwards saying, 'I wouldn't have your job tomorrow for anything. You will be whacked but, don't worry, you'll win the argument.'

And so to the rally, dosing myself heavily with chlorodyne and hoping I wouldn't have to make a hurried exit off the platform in the middle of my own speech! After the dramatic experience in the NEC it was a pleasant shock to find an enthusiastic audience who cheered Tage Erlander's account of the Swedish Social Democrat victory and greeted my own speech tumultuously.[1] They ended by shouting for Harold to give them a few words. This curious movement with its curious contradictions is all set for another unpredictable conference.

I was not so happy about my speech on P and I policy the next day. The TGWU Motion, moved by Frank Cousins, calling for an end to all incomes legislation, was carried by the astonishing majority of 5,098,000 to 1,124,000 and my speech answering the debate had clearly fallen flat. Hugh Scanlon had denounced the whole concept of the policy and threatened industrial action over the engineering claim. Harold Wilson, however, had a personal triumph with a speech in which even his snidest press critics admitted he had complete command of the conference; and I had the consolation of doing unexpectedly well in the elections for the NEC, moving to the top from third place in the constituency parties' section.

Sunday, 6 October. My birthday and a lovely autumn day. Mellow sun soon dispersed the mist and lit up the dahlias and chrysanthemums into vivid splashes of colour against the green of lawn and orchard and the bank of woods opposite. I dug hard in the garden, replenished by a good night's sleep and slowly the pain of my failure at conference began to fade and my fighting spirit to creep back. All right, so I mucked up my great speech (how clearly I can see now what I should have said!). OK, so I always muff my big opportunities. But these correctives to one's vanity are always good and I grimly determine to get down to the job of evolving a really Socialist and constructive policy for the future of trade unionism and of tackling unofficial strikes by revolutionary new procedures in the motor industry. As I've said before, doggedness is about my only virtue.

Monday, 7 October. Into the second meeting with the two sides of the motor industry. I was absolutely determined to move on to something constructive this time and we had prepared some proposals of our own. However, the employers had got together beforehand and Donald Stokes on their behalf put forward an unexpectedly far-reaching document. In it the employers, of course, reiterated their belief in the need for legal backing for collective agreements. But, this apart, the paper went a long way to meet the point of

[1] Tage Erlander was the Social Democratic Prime Minister of Sweden where his party had just won its first absolute majority since 1940 in the General Election held on 15 September.

view of the trade unions, offering to accept a closed shop and the system of 'check-off'[1] in their factories if in their turn the trade unions would guarantee to secure the honouring of agreements once they had been reached. To establish this new understanding in the industry they proposed the setting up of a new joint council for the motor industry consisting of the unions involved and the manufacturers both on the assembly and components sides.

The unions were clearly taken aback by all this. Les Cannon said rather feebly that he had half prepared a paper but that it wasn't finished yet. But the union reception was pretty good. George Barratt was dumbfounded while Hughie Scanlon, who had decided to turn up this time, was, all things considered, remarkably conciliatory. After a general discussion I urged the two sides to meet face to face next week to work out the details. Eventually we got the unions to agree to a press statement accepting the joint council in principle.

Tuesday, 8 October. The big item at Cabinet as far as I was concerned was Rhodesia. As Gerald [Gardiner] had warned me, Harold is now proposing to renew talks. He rattled on a bit about how worried he was about what would happen in Rhodesia unless there was a settlement. Of course everyone else agreed with him and Jim Callaghan even praised him for his courage in gambling his own reputation once again. I was the only emphatically dissentient voice.

Friday, 11 October. Faced with my determination to have new safety, health and welfare legislation in this Parliament, the office has come up with a new idea. Instead of struggling with a detailed Bill we should have a simple measure setting up a new independent authority which would co-ordinate the safety provisions in all fields. It obviously has great possibilities, though a few probing questions by me reveal that the difficulties have not yet been thought through. I told them to prepare a more detailed submission to me.

Monday, 14 October. This is the week we know we shall have to devote to the engineering dispute. In fact Douglas has depressed me by suggesting that nothing will be settled until the eleventh hour next Sunday night. I plunged into the day with a lively office meeting on the Donovan Report. Burgh has put in a basic paper which is nothing more than a catalogue of Donovan recommendations and our suggested reaction to them.[2] I held forth about the need for us to have our own discussions about whether we accept the Donovan analysis and above all our own philosophy of the role of the trade union movement in the present day. I insisted we must do a 'Windsor' weekend and fix 15 November on the spot. They went off reeling a little, but stimulated, I think, to produce various analytical papers on the lines I suggested.

I swept along the corridor to the library to start the engineering talks, braving a phalanx of TV cameras on the way. I was a bit nervous about how to tackle this, my first big conciliation assignment. Everyone is saying that if I settle this

[1] The unions had been urging that, to facilitate their work, employers should be willing to deduct members' trade union dues from their pay. It was one of the proposals for strengthening trade unionism I was to urge in my document on Donovan, *In Place of Strife*.

[2] John Burgh, Under-Secretary at DEP dealing with industrial relations.

one I am made for life; if I make a mess of it I will never live it down. Significantly as I entered the library everyone rose to their feet, even Scanlon, who carefully refrained from doing so when I last met the AEF Executive at the beginning of their negotiating marathon. I made a mental note that today he was in a very different mood. Perhaps he is mellowing a bit under his responsibilities.

I sat at the top table with the union phalanx on my right and the employers on my left and delivered a little homily about the importance of settling all this in the national interest. I then called on them to explain their difficulties. It was soon clear how thankful both sides were to be meeting across a table again. After two hours, when the discussion was getting ragged, I suggested they formed a joint working-party of nine a side to get down to details and adjourned the meeting so they could get on with it, saying that we would meet in plenary session at 10 am the next day.

When we left the office at 10 pm they were still at their working-party, the employers insisting that they were prepared to go on all night.

Tuesday, 15 October. In early to get a report from Conrad Heron. He said that they had broken up at midnight deadlocked on the issue of which came first, the hen or the egg, the offer of money or of productivity. The employers were adamant that they wouldn't put any more money down until they had got the conditions sewn up. They had also complained that Scanlon was in fact doing an Ian Smith: always ready to say what he disagreed with but never putting forward a possible alternative and they had challenged the unions to put their own ideas down on paper. I went into plenary session determined to back them up on this and find a way of swinging the unions round. However, to my astonishment I found it was unnecessary. Scanlon opened by saying that someone had to break the deadlock and that we were 'all indebted to Mr Boyd' who had got his secretary out of bed at six o'clock that morning to prepare two documents ('I didn't get her out of bed,' said Johnnie, 'her husband did' – and everybody had a good relaxed laugh). One was on productivity, said Scanlon, and the other on training. At this Fielding said the employers had been getting up early too and had produced another document to try and meet some of the unions' points. I suggested they go away together to try and match their documents up while I would stand by to call another plenary meeting if necessary. We must all give the negotiations complete priority, as I had done that morning by missing a Cabinet meeting. And so back to my office to start the endless hours of waiting.

I was all the sorrier to miss Cabinet because it received Harold's report on the *Fearless* trip.[1] Knowing that I was tied up with negotiations, Harold

[1] Indefatigably pursuing his attempt to reach agreement with Ian Smith Harold Wilson had flown to Gibraltar on 9 October for another *tête-à-tête* with Smith on a British warship, this time HMS *Fearless*. It was clear from the report of the talks that Harold was being drawn into more and more concessions to keep Smith interested. Ignoring a resolution just passed at Party conference demanding NIBMR, he had proposed that, once the new constitution had passed the test of acceptability, the control of its introduction, including the holding of elections, should come under a broadly based administration under Ian Smith, including some Africans. Smith had agreed to take the proposals back to his Government but once in Salisbury he started to back track on a number of points he had seemed to accept. Undeterred Harold Wilson sent George Thomson over to Rhodesia to continue the negotiations. Despite further modifications of the British proposals to meet Smith's objections. Thomson

typically sent me a reassuring message: 'Tell her we shall reach no decisions on Rhodesia.'

Later I sent for the Cabinet Minutes on this item, insisting that I must see them. Of course, the Cabinet had approved the statement handed to Smith and I doubt whether in my absence anybody raised a peep at it. I hope to God that Smith's rejection will put an end to this nonsense, but I am afraid he will merely try to go on nibbling away at our position. Cabinet agreed that no record of the *Fearless* talks should be published, which I regret.

I remained incarcerated in my room at the Department all day like the prisoner of Zenda, beleaguered by a horde of cameras and press outside. Eventually I decided to make a dash for freedom and food at 8 pm, joining Dick, Tommy and Peter for a little dinner party. Dick was full of his new job on which he launches in two days' time.[1] I found it all too easy to pump him (he, of course, swearing me to the secrecy he cannot maintain himself!) about the future of his subordinates. I discovered to my horror that he is going to take Stephen Swingler from Transport and I launched into a tirade at Harold's frivolity with his appointments. Of course Stephen deserves a move, but for us to spend seven months battling to get the Transport Bill through Parliament only to let it die administratively under Dick Marsh with none of its three originators left to carry it through is to me a total abdication of serious government,[2] and I told Dick I was going to see Harold and have a row.

Wednesday, 16 October. Into the office after OPD to do another stint of this wretched hanging about. At 3 pm I went over to the House to see Harold in his room. Of course I kept my word to Dick and didn't let on that I knew anything about Stephen. I merely told Harold that I wanted to talk to him about the appointments consequential on Dick's new job. Harold waved me aside saying none of these were being settled immediately. I then begged him to move Dick Marsh. He didn't believe in the Transport Bill; he was cynical, superficial and lazy. And, worst of all, the transport trade unions were up in arms about the whittling down of my policy. Harold pricked up his ears at this and, pacing up and down, asked where on earth I thought he could move Dick Marsh. I told him to give him the chairmanship of a nationalized board or anything. We had to break off so that Harold could go and tell the House about the Transfer of Functions Order he was tabling that day.[3]

Back at the office, one bright bit of news. The Blackburn bus undertaking has signed my model local agreement! I can just imagine Frank Cousins' fury. Most amusing of all, Alan Thompson had paid a rush visit up to Blackburn to try and stop the whole thing, only to be repudiated by the local secretary of the TGWU who insisted on signing the agreement in defiance of his own union. In fact he has told my local paper that the Blackburn branch has had no trouble with the management, only with the 'hierarchy' of the union. I now hope other

returned on 17 November reporting breakdown. Nonetheless he assured the House of Commons, 'We for our part are not slamming the door.'

[1] As Secretary of State for Social Services.

[2] John Morris had received well-deserved promotion in the April 1968 reshuffle, succeeding Roy Mason at Defence.

[3] The Order provided for the merger of the Foreign and Commonwealth Offices and also for the merger of Health and Social Security under Dick Crossman which became operative from 1 November.

Lancashire authorities will follow suit.

Thursday, 17 October. This time I simply had to attend Cabinet – particularly to give a report on the progress of the engineering talks. I told them the pace was slow but the temper low and that the employers were being pretty successfully hawkish. I pressed for and got the promise that the Foreign Secretary would make a statement on Vietnam next week so that we can discuss whether we should amend our policy. On Rhodesia, Harold said they had had no approach from Smith himself and that in the meantime he was paying no attention to what Smith said on the radio. I was glad to note that both Harold's and George's tone about Smith was now much more critical.

Another long wait in the office twiddling my thumbs and wondering what the hell Heron and the negotiators were up to. The whole attitude of the office in these conciliation cases is that I ought to keep out of it as much as possible and leave it to my official conciliators, and I am having to learn by experience how far I should follow their advice and when I should back my own judgment. Finally, when it was clear I would not be needed, I went off fairly late to bed.

Friday, 18 October. Still no news from the negotiators. Finally I lost patience at being kept in the dark and sent for Heron and Denis Barnes at 1 pm, demanding a full report. I wanted to be sure that the employers' offer on wages was within our overall percentage ceiling and I particularly asked what was being done about the principle of equal pay – a point I have been rubbing into Heron all along. I wasn't going to have them leaving *that* baby on the Government's lap. He was certainly watching the point about the ceiling, and on equal pay the unions had always understood that there would have to be some concessions by them on the women's differentials if they pushed up the skilled rate. They hadn't yet got down to this. He then dashed off to preside over the meeting which had just started again after lunch.

I was still brooding over my anxieties when Douglas came in to say that the unions had asked to see me about the question of equal pay. The employers had agreed to a £19 skilled rate for men in three years' time with £13 for the women. The unions had accepted the former and rejected the latter and were now asking to see me 'most unreasonably'. I absolutely exploded at this, telling Heron tartly that I had been warning everybody about this all along. So I was in a pretty savage mood when Hughie, Les Kealey and the others, including Marion Veitch, the only woman in their team, came in. Hughie told me unctuously that everything had been going perfectly well until the employers had come to the women's rate. The increase they offered here would actually widen the differential and was quite unacceptable. The unions wanted the women brought up to the labourers' rate (£15) in three years' time as a minimum. Otherwise they would break. I was furious with the employers for having allowed themselves to be manœuvred into this trap, particularly as I know that none of the unions really expected the women to get the labourers' rate. Indeed I had in my possession a note we had got privately from Les Kealey on what he thought would be a satisfactory basis for a settlement in which he included a figure of £13 16*s* 0*d* for women at the end of three years. Of course, it is part of our whole conciliation code in the Department that we never reveal these private comments that we elicit. But it didn't make my temper any better to know that he was now publicly going back on his own suggestion.

I therefore well and truly blew my top, telling them icily that I had been waiting for a long time to hear when they were going to start talking about the women and was shocked to find that they had left it to the very end. They knew that the employers had only a limited amount of money to offer and it wasn't my fault that the unions had pre-empted it all by pushing up the skilled rate. If they wanted to do something about the women, why hadn't they given up the general increase? Scanlon bridled angrily at this and said it was an impossible suggestion, but the effect of his militancy was somewhat undermined when Marion Veitch, who had been sitting silent during all the plenary meetings, suddenly burst out that she was glad to hear me talking in this way because she personally was ashamed of her male colleagues. So a ding-dong row ensued, Hughie trying to maintain that they would have broken anyhow if the employers had not offered more than £18 10*s* 0*d* and that it was the employers who were being mean. At this I said, 'Come off it, Hughie, you know that you have done very well – far better than you dared to hope at one stage.' He had the grace almost to grin at this but he was clearly nervous at the success of my attempt to turn the tables on him, and tried to maintain that the employers would never agree to rejig the package in favour of the women anyhow. I told him tartly that I was going to see the employers about this now.

I then called the two sides together and got them to spell out the deadlock. It was fascinating to hear Les Kealey actually accuse the employers: 'You shouldn't have offered the £19 if you weren't prepared to face up to the differentials. I told them that obviously the money had run out before they had thought of the women at all. But they could always alter the package if they wanted to. Hughie said passionately they weren't going to give up anything they had been offered and challenged Fielding to say whether the employers would be willing to rejig in favour of the women anyhow. Fielding dodged that one rather evasively but I told him that the employers should go away and think about it, and adjourned the meeting to enable them to do so. Afterwards I called in Fielding to see me separately. I told him he ought never to have agreed to go above £18 10*s* 0*d* until he had cleared up the differential issue first, and that he had now got to get us all out of the mess by agreeing to raise the women's figure if Scanlon's team would drop the general increase altogether. He wrung his hands at this and said he would never get the agreement of his principals, but I told him he was on a safe bet because the unions would just turn it down. I sent him off to do some telephoning around to get authority.

While I was having a drink and a sandwich with my officials (still reeling under the impact of my ferocity) Charles Birdsall dashed upstairs to say that Marion Veitch was holding forth to the journalists downstairs telling them of the little scene and, of course, getting all the credit for it. Charles was doing his usual magnificent stuff, seeing that the press got the picture right.

At eight o'clock, when the time limit I had given him had expired, Fielding came in looking limp. He was anxious to help, he said, but he couldn't get the firms he represented to let him do what I wanted. It was too dangerous. I harangued them for an hour without much effect till a message came from Scanlon that the union side were tired of waiting and that they were going to walk out, saying that the negotiations had been broken off. I therefore had to call a plenary meeting hurriedly.

I opened by saying that the employers had at my request been considering the *impasse* and that Mr Fielding had a statement to make. Fielding said rather limply that he had nothing to suggest and he was prepared to consider anything the unions had to propose. This, of course, brought all Hughie's scathing wit down on his head and there was an awkward hiatus. I had to jump in in order to rescue Fielding who, obviously grateful for the respite, got his second wind and went on to say far more than I dared to hope he would: namely that the employers were prepared to set up immediately a joint working-party on job evaluation for women as part of the settlement. Hughie, cheated of his manœuvre, was furious. The argument raged for a long time but Fielding, now thoroughly having got his nerve back, repeated that the employers had given the absolute maximum they could afford and that the unions had always known that they would have to make some concession on differentials if the employers went up to £19. Hughie, banging the table, said that they wouldn't give up the £19 nor the general increase. 'Very well,' I said sweetly, 'that's that.' We all know that tomorrow he has to face his AEU Executive. The question is whether he can get a motion for strike action on an offer by the employers which in some respects meets so much of the union's claim. We doubt very much whether he can and so our obvious tactic now is to sit tight.

I got back to HCF in the early hours ready to return at 7 pm tomorrow when we know the results of the National Committee meeting of the AEF.

Saturday, 19 October. As I drove up to the office in the evening I found an excited mass of pressmen and cameras. One journalist called to me through my car window that the strike was off, but by only two votes. When officials came in to report to me, however, it was clear that the position was not so definite. Scanlon had actually rung Heron to say with astonishing frankness, 'We have been defeated. We have postponed industrial action.' He said he wanted to report to the First Secretary but that would have to be after the Confed meeting, which was then taking place. He sounded very rattled. It was all very confusing. However, we were thankful for small mercies: strike action on Monday is now obviously off. Then Heron, who had been checking up on the progress of the Confed Executive meeting, came in to say that it was in total disarray. They had agreed that industrial action should be suspended but no date for its resumption had been fixed. There is to be a meeting of the combined Executive on Friday next. The employers were standing by on call in case there was any chance of reaching a settlement that night. What I had better do was to meet the Confed Executive, as they were requesting, and then ask for an immediate adjournment to consider what they had to say.

So we all trooped into the library where a very dejected body of men was waiting for us. Hughie was at his most subdued and most reasonable. He reported to me frankly that earlier in the day the AEF Executive Committee had unanimously recommended that the agreement so far negotiated, with the reservation of the women's wages, should be accepted, and that they should try to resolve the women's issue before Monday, otherwise strike. This had been rejected by the National Committee by two votes. This meant that the whole agreement was in the melting-pot. The Confed Executive had considered the position and decided on the lines Heron had already reported to me. I thanked him for his frank statement and said I wanted a moment to think about it.

Back upstairs we trooped to my office and I hastily agreed with my officials that we had obviously got to let the whole thing sweat. So down again we went to find the Confed Executive waiting meekly. I then delivered a few carefully prepared words. 'The situation,' I said, 'is obviously very complicated and cannot be resolved tonight. You have raised some very big issues that we shall all have to think about. We shall just have to leave it at that.' To my surprise they murmured their agreement. I thanked them all and was just rising to go when Reg Birch of all people said that they should all thank me for my efforts to get a settlement. There was a murmur of approval and I went the rounds shaking hands with everybody in the friendliest manner possible. Hughie and I parted as if we had been buddies for life.

But the night wasn't over yet. I still had to have my press conference. I told the press emphatically that there had never been a question of demanding equal pay in these negotiations. All that was at issue was an improvement of differentials in the women's favour, but personally I didn't believe equal pay was a question of narrowing differentials between the women's and labourers' rates. There oughtn't to be such a thing as women's rates at all; the answer lay in proper job evaluation for everyone, on which the employers had offered to set up a working-party as part of the settlement. And so home again to HCF in the early hours. Before I left Harold was on the phone from No. 10 congratulating me and my officials. He is always very good at that.

Monday, 21 October. Top for Questions, I had to make a statement on the engineering talks. At the office I met my negotiating team to discuss what I should say. Denis Barnes was as cool as ever and Heron as cheerful despite the past weeks of strain. My Questions went well and I had a sympathetic House.

Afterwards I went to see Harold again. I am furious that he fooled me about last week's announcement on the promotions and desperately anxious about the MOT now Stephen has gone.[1] Dick Marsh left to himself will let the whole policy disintegrate. So once again I begged Harold to move him and, if necessary, put George Thomson in his place. Harold said he was thinking about it. I also pressed him on Roy Hattersley's promotion, long overdue on grounds of common justice. If necessary I'd let him go elsewhere as Minister of State, though I'd much prefer to keep him. Roy H. has been bluntly frank with me about his desire for promotion and also flattering, saying he would much prefer to stay with me. 'The last six months have been my happiest in government. My relationship with you has been unrecognizably different from mine with Ray Gunter. You have always treated me as a Minister of State.' Harold was much more grudging about this. Anyway, he said, he hadn't got another Minister of State to dispose of at the moment.

[1] In a mini reshuffle Harold Wilson had announced two promotions to the Cabinet: Judith Hart, who became Paymaster-General, and Jack Diamond, Chief Secretary to the Treasury. When Dick Crossman took over his new Department of Health and Social Security on 1 November, Fred Peart succeeded him as Lord President of the Council. As I feared Stephen Swingler had been moved from Transport to become one of Crossman's two Ministers of State.

Lots of congratulations in the division lobby about the calling off of the strike, but Roy Jenkins and Tony Crosland passed me without a word. I can't decide whether they basically distrust me or whether they are just bad at PR.

Tuesday, 22 October. At SEP we had [a] paper on the Chancellor's proposed cuts for 1970–71. And here the protests and grumbles started all over again. I said it would be politically intolerable to raise (as the Treasury proposed) some £20m more in charges for school meals. Hadn't we put enough burdens on the lower paid? Crosland complained, and rightly, that we hadn't had enough time to study these complex papers: would the Chancellor please let us have a simpler one summarizing them? And were we certain the right political strategy was to put tax cuts before the maintenance of the social services? Grumbling that the decision could not be postponed beyond next Monday, the Chancellor agreed to give us a little more time.

At this point I got a message from the Department saying that the ships' clerks have unanimously voted to return to work. Harold, always anxious to get credit for me in Cabinet, asked me to read it out. Crosland whispered, 'Your second triumph in a week. You really did awfully well over the engineers.' He's a curious bird: says a lot of the right things, but never really fights. I notice he has an odd habit when sitting next to me of shaking his foot violently all the time. I thought I was tense but, by comparison with that, I am relaxed!

Thursday, 24 October. At Cabinet we had at last Smith's official comments on the *Fearless* talks. They were remarkably non-committal, in terms which made it impossible for Harold to refuse to send George Thomson out, merely saying the visit would 'assist the considerations of the Rhodesian Cabinet'.

The other big item at Cabinet was Michael Stewart's long-promised paper on the reconsideration of our policy on Vietnam. It doesn't really amount to much. He said America has already stopped bombing over a wide area and would stop completely in return for certain undertakings from North Vietnam. It would be fatal for us to make any overt statements now because we should be accused of trying to influence the American elections. The only thing we could do was to reconsider our position when there was a new American President. Denis Healey then surprised me by saying we ought to start disengaging ourselves from the need to make any comments on American policy. It was absurd that we should have gone rushing in to approve the resumption of American bombing when other of America's allies had got away perfectly happily with refraining from any comment at all. Our posture should be neither to defend America's position nor to criticize it. It was this old business of insisting on being the world's parson when we were ceasing to be the world's policeman. His outburst provoked a considerable response and Harold himself agreed that it should be possible to move towards this new posture with a new President. But he stressed and so did Denis – that this was very different from 'dissociating' ourselves from American policy and would not bring us any more thanks from the Left.

Monday, 28 October. At SEP we considered the Chancellor's paper on the level of domestic demand in 1970–71 and its implications for public expenditure, produced at the request of some of us that we should see the picture as a whole before going into detailed cuts. Eventually Harold summed up that we should settle the level of Rate Support grant[1] now and have a wider strategic discussion after the mid-term forecast was available.

Thursday, 31 October. Another glorious document has been circulated to me by our Security boys. This reports on the attitude of the Communist Party during the engineering negotiations. Scanlon, it says, did not seek the advice of the Party and had departed from that advice by agreeing to talk about productivity before pay. He had consolidated his position as President and had to some extent freed himself from Party direction. Interesting!

Prices and incomes problems continued to plague me. I had inherited an explosive situation in the building industry. In April 1967, the building workers had put in a claim for a new three-year pay agreement which my predecessor had brooded on so long that it had not been referred to the PIB *until May 1968. By that time negotiations for the new agreement were well advanced and when the* PIB *made it clear that it could not report before the old agreement had expired, unions and employers jumped the gun with an interim settlement providing for an increase in the standard rate of 3½*d *per hour for craftsmen and 3*d *for general workers, which was estimated to equal an increase of 3¾ per cent. The employers justified this on the grounds that important productivity concessions had been made by the unions, but the increase was above the ceiling, and in any case an additional 1*d *per hour had been paid in March as the final payment under the industry's cost-of-living scheme. This brought the overall increase for the year up to 4¾ per cent and the Government insisted that the cost-of-living 1*d *must be taken into account. This was rejected by a united front of employers and unions and on 4 November the Government decided to refer the interim settlement to the* PIB *and to issue a direction enforcing a standstill pending the Board's report. The 'builders' penny' was to become a political* cause célèbre.

Tuesday, 5 November. Address[ed] the trade union group [in the House]. I talked safely away about my desire to consult them on the future of P and I policy and on Donovan. Then I added what I thought were a few harmless remarks about my philosophy of the future of trade unionism: how it must be made strong enough to put its own house in order so as to fend off action from outside. The balloon went up! Stan Orme could not see anything but menace in the strengthening of the TUC, or of the national trade union leadership, or even of the disciplinary powers of shop stewards. Some of our left are just anarchists.

A document has been circulated giving the new membership of SEP. I gather that there are a lot of 'MISCS' of whose existence some of us don't even know! There is MISC 205, of course, which Dick hasn't cottoned on to yet; another MISC dealing with Rhodesia, of which I'm not a member (even the circulation of the Rhodesia telegrams is 'restricted' so that I can't get hold of them).[2] I've just discovered there is a nuclear MISC – heaven knows who's a member of it!

[1] The contribution which central government pays to local authorities.

[2] The Prime Minister's arrangements for dealing with Rhodesia were becoming more and more obscure and the formal committee on Rhodesia seemed to have given way to an informal grouping of Ministers sympathetic to Harold Wilson's views.

The documents belonging to any MISC are usually Top Secret. Fair enough. One simply can't have confidential discussions in a Cabinet of our size. So long as I am in the secret economic discussion I am content because, to do Harold justice, he always brings the conclusions of these inner discussions to Cabinet for final ratification. What it does mean, however, is that by the time things have gone as far as that it is very difficult for the rest of Cabinet to change them. All one can do is to decide whether the existence of the near *fait accompli* makes the continuation of one's membership of Cabinet impossible. And, in the event that it isn't, one can't be blamed for not having resigned earlier.

Wednesday, 6 November. My throat was so sore when I woke I decided to stay in bed. After all, I mustn't develop flu for our Guy Fawkes family gathering this weekend! As I lay limply there, dozing from time to time, a parliamentary storm was breaking, unbeknownst to me, over our decision to refer the building workers' settlement to the PIB. Harold Walker had to deputize for me in answering the PNQ. Well, it's just too bad.

Thursday, 7 November. The papers are full of the row over the building workers. Labour MPs of all points of view are rushing to put their names to a Motion on the Order Paper. The Department is as foxed as I am at why this particular reference should have caused such an outcry. As my sore throat is still acute I called in the doctor. Nothing serious but he wants me to stay in bed, which I do gratefully. Later I learned that Harold Walker had had a stormy time at the Party meeting but had handled it well. I really must go back to work tomorrow, and face the music.

Friday, 8 November. Phone call from the office to tell me on no account to come back to work. They wanted me to complete my cure over the weekend and, not least, wanted me to keep out of the way while Harold Walker saw the civil engineering side of the building workers this morning about the reference. I agreed reluctantly. The row seems to be concentrating on our inclusion of the 1 per cent cost of living bonus last March in the ceiling for this year and Alex Jarratt assured me that we had carefully checked precedents on this and cannot possibly rule otherwise. Anyway it would be good for Harold Walker to handle things on his own, which he seems to be doing very competently.

Mollie drove me down to HCF. It was a raw day and I felt almost as weak as if I was convalescing from a long illness. I arrived at HCF at lunchtime to find the central heating had failed and that [our cocker spaniel] Aldie had been pretty ill. He greeted me enthusiastically and then started sneezing great clots of blood all over the place. It was all so chaotic I barely had time to say hello to Phil, Ben and Kathryn. Eventually I took Aldie to the vet's by taxi, nursing his poor bloody nose on my lap while he clung to me all the way. Archard felt his nose tenderly and then told me he was worried by a small lump which had appeared there. It could be a tumour and if so it might be inoperable. I agreed that we will get him to the veterinary college at Cambridge on Monday somehow. What a homecoming!

When we came to bed Aldie never stirred from his chair. We went upstairs leaving all the doors open for him and knew how ill he was when he didn't attempt even to follow us upstairs. At last I fell into an exhausted sleep and woke early with a headache. When I slipped downstairs Aldie was lying at the foot of them, too exhausted to get up to us.

Monday, 11 November. Alistair and Ann[1] called for Aldie to take him to Cambridge before I left for work. He was clinging to us so closely that it seemed cruel to send him off again. My trouble in life is I get so attached to the familiar that I can hardly bear any changes in the family or in my environment. However, I threw into a bag an old evening dress for the Guildhall Banquet tonight. I only go to these functions to ensure that Ted has a good meal occasionally! Harold, of course, was speaking at the banquet and Ted chi-iked him about the fact that this time he was in white tie and tails. I remember how in 1964 he created a sensation by turning up in a black tie. Harold countered with the remark, 'When unemployment was rising I thought white tie was wrong. Now it is going down I haven't the same difficulty.' I told him I would have to slip away from Cabinet in the morning because I was due to see the building workers. He replied, looking mysterious, 'Cabinet doesn't matter. But there is a meeting on Wednesday morning you must not miss.' So MISC walks again.

Tuesday, 12 November. At Cabinet I reported on the building workers' row, pointing out that we were now moving into an acute phase of P and I policy. Up to now we had been dealing with relatively unimportant claims and had successfully managed to hold the line. In the next three months we would be dealing with some major settlements which could bring us into violent conflict, not so much with the trade union movement as with the PLP. Our only hope of getting through this phase was if we had ministerial unanimity on, and support for, the policy. Harold agreed we must all publicly support P and I policy and some – notably Fred Peart – complained I hadn't been backed up enough. It was also agreed that I must stand firm on the building workers' 1*d* and I then dashed off to see Aubrey Jones. I had to know what the Board's general reaction would be likely to be. We smuggled Aubrey into No. 8 by the back door.[2] He told me, in his usual rather languid way, that he had seen a rough draft of the report on the initial reference and it wouldn't help us at all in the short term. He couldn't see it justifying any interim increase at all! I told him categorically that there would have to be *some* increase and he agreed to try and get some short-term proposals worked out to justify it.

It was therefore with some anxiety that I went into the talks with the Building NJIC. The employers were pretty emphatic that they had been in the process of working out a good settlement when we made the reference. For the unions Harold Weaver, General Secretary of the National Federation of Building Trade Operatives, claimed that output had increased by 6 per cent this year and the unions had contributed to it by not insisting on restrictive practices. The inclusion of the 1*d* cost of living bonus in our calculations had been the 'bitterest blow of all' to them. I told them patiently that we had strictly applied the same rules to them as to everyone else: anyway, why not let the Board decide? In the meantime I was prepared to authorize 2½*d* per hour for

[1] Alistair McIntosh was the husband of my dead sister, Marjorie, and Ann was his second wife.
[2] No. 8 St. James's Square was the Department's HQ.

craftsmen, and 2*d* for labourers which might be uprated in the light of the Board's report, with my assurance that they wouldn't get less than this, whatever the Board said. Any uprating could be backdated to 4 November. What had they to lose? Though they hummed and hawed, I could see they were impressed and eventually they said they would have to report my proposal to the meeting of their Executives tomorrow morning.

Wednesday, 13 November. Got up at 6 am to read my papers for MISC 205. They consisted of a paper by Crosland pointing out that the October trade figures were disappointing and suggesting that we get all the material ready for the introduction of import quotas in December if the November figures show an equally adverse trend. Harold said we should merely consider mechanics at this stage and not have a substantive discussion on what we should do in ten days' time, but I said (having talked to Tommy) I thought there were two points to be made at once. The first was to consider introducing import deposits and quotas in parallel, not as alternatives. (Roy said he by no means ruled this out though he clearly hadn't considered it. Tommy may be right: Roy is getting *laissez-faire* advice; that is why he is 'soft' on prices and incomes policy which can only make sense on the basis of a much more interventionist strategy.) The second point was that we could not just control imports in isolation. It would be folly not to accompany it with the control of the outflow of capital to the sterling area. The realization of some of our overseas portfolio assets also seemed in order. Finally, as I couldn't be at OPD, I wanted to register my opposition to Denis Healey's request for an extra squadron of Harriers to reinforce our contribution to European defence. We hadn't withdrawn from East of Suez merely to expand our European burdens. (I detected a look of approval from Roy at this.) Peter backed me up strongly and so did Harold eventually, though he seemed remarkably relaxed in view of the adverse trade figures. It was agreed in the end that the Chancellor should put in a 'conjuncture' paper for our policy meeting in ten days' time.

All this time I had been choking back my tears about Aldie. Littlewort of the veterinary college had phoned me earlier in the morning from Cambridge and dashed all our hopes. Aldie, he said, had a tumour in his nose which had already eaten into the bone extensively. We had better face the need to put him away in a few weeks' time. It was a relief to get into the car and have a good weep with Mollie almost joining in. Then a hasty dab of powder on my nose and into battle again.

Message from No. 10. The PM wanted to see me. Would I go in through the Privy Council office so that the press wouldn't get the idea that I was bringing Harold in on the builders' row. Harold was sitting relaxed over a brandy in his upstairs study. As usual at that time of the day he was talkative. I put him in the picture on the building workers. The talk then drifted on to Rhodesia where Harold told me he didn't think a settlement was likely. I decided I owed it to him to make my position clear once again. 'You know, don't you,' I said, 'that I shall resign if a settlement is reached on *Fearless*.' Harold rolled his head in almost sleepy incredulity: 'You *can't* go.' He then tried to tell me that only Reg Prentice was likely to make trouble over *Fearless* and he was 'foolish'. His answer to Reg would be that if he really thought a point of principle was involved he shouldn't wait to see if there was a settlement or not; he should resign now. I said quietly, 'You're probably right, Harold. I ought to resign now.' 'No, no, no. You *can't* go,' Harold repeated, adding, 'Anyway there isn't going to be a settlement.' So we left it at that.

Thursday, 14 November. At the Department the building workers had asked to see me again. Despite the fact that their Executives have turned down my compromise, they clearly have no stomach for a fight. I had to listen patiently while they went over all the old ground again. Couldn't I just leave the 1*d* in payment on the understanding that it would be 'taken into account' when they came to apply the conclusions of the PIB report? After two hours of this I told them we would have an adjournment and I then said to my officials I thought we would have to bring the whole thing to a head, saying I would let the 3½*d* remain in payment on condition that they would agree to be bound by what the Board said about it and take off the cost of living 1*d* if the Board found against them. Jarratt and Heron said they saw no harm in this, though none of us thought the union would agree to such terms. I then called the chaps back and said we must come to finality. There were only two alternatives I could offer them: either the compromise already offered, or my agreement to leave the 1*d* in the payment on condition that, if the Board ruled that it should be counted towards the 3½ per cent ceiling (as I maintained it should), they would agree to accept the ruling 'for immediate application in the pay packet'. I told them categorically that I recommended them to accept the first. Then they asked for an adjournment and to the surprise of all of us came back and said they accepted the second. My heart sank! However, I said I must now put this to my colleagues and dashed off to the patiently waiting P and I committee. Another surprise: they all said that they thought I had done astonishingly well, provided it was quite clear that the 1*d* would come off at once if the Board reported against the union. So back to No. 8 and a most matey reunion with the chaps, who thanked me warmly for everything I had done! Rather dazed by now, I got Harold Weaver and Les Kemp of the TGWU to put their signatures to a press statement and insisted that they should flank me while I met the press. The press, too, were absolutely taken aback but Kemp and Weaver did their stuff, almost embracing me in front of the journalists. Altogether a good time was had by all. This industrial relations business grows more and more astonishing. No doubt there will be a row when the report comes out but that won't be my fault. I've done my best to advise them to take the 2½*d* and 2*d* before the Board reports on them.

Friday, 15 November. Harold phoned me early at the flat to congratulate me on the settlement. He added, 'I've got bad news for you. Smith has turned down *Fearless*. We are now in the position in which I wanted to be. We are clearly seen to have been reasonable while Smith has not. He will have no support from British public opinion now.' He then added jocularly, 'It is a good job for you and for me that your settlement was reached while mine broke down. Altogether a bad day for you.' I then had to hurry to the House to make a statement. The left wing were bewildered and appalled by the unions' decision to let the PIB arbitrate. They can see its role strengthening every day.

I had decided to hold a long discussion weekend to clear my ideas about the Donovan Report. In addition to myself, my two junior Ministers, John Fraser and a phalanx of officials, I had invited Peter Shore as Secretary of State for Economic Affairs, Campbell Adamsom (who was shortly to succeed John Davies as Director-General of the CBI*), Donald Stokes of Leylands, Jim Mortimer, Len Neal, Aubrey Jones, Professor Clegg of the Donovan Commission and Professor Robertson of Glasgow, another of the Department's trouble-shooters. After intensive discussion of a series of background papers a consensus emerged that we rejected the concept of 'collective* laissez-faire*' and were in favour of state intervention in industrial relations. The question was: intervention for what and by what means? It was wrong to assume that state intervention always meant using the law against the unions. Employers had greater responsibility for securing reform and state intervention could pressurize them, for example, to recognize and negotiate with unions or to accept workers' participation in management.*

Nor did state intervention necessarily mean sanctions. It should be positive rather than repressive. The most pressing need was to reform negotiating and disputes procedures, for until there were good procedures, workers could not be expected to observe agreements. That meant strengthening the trade unions. Here again the state should intervene to guarantee trade union rights and improve the machinery of collective bargaining, but it was also urgent to persuade unions and workers not to use their bargaining powers in ways which damaged the collective economic interest. If sanctions were to be used (and there were few cases where they would be desirable or effective), they should be specific and not general and should be administered by the Government.

In general we accepted the Donovan analysis, though we thought it had its weaknesses. Like Donovan we rejected the legal enforcement of collective agreements, the banning of sympathetic strikes or of the closed shop. But we were also deeply disturbed by the industrial anarchy which was doing so much harm to the economy and by the fact that so many strikes seemed to be directed more against the community than the employer. As Peter Shore put it, 'A dock strike is a blockade of the nation.' How could one bring more order into industrial relations without putting unacceptable curbs on what we called the 'primitive power' of workers to defend their own interests?

Gradually the idea began to emerge – stemming mainly from Peter Shore – that we could at least legitimately use the law to insist that, where workers downed tools in breach of procedure agreements which their unions had voluntarily negotiated, they should be made to accept a cooling-off period during which conciliation procedures could be given a chance to work. Such 'unconstitutional' strikes could be official or unofficial, but the principle was the same. But we agreed that in such a situation the employer should be compelled to revert to the status quo*. We also began to feel that where unofficial strikes seriously threatened the national interest, the Secretary of State should have the discretionary power to order a ballot. Finally we agreed it was absurd that disputes over union recognition should be allowed to create such havoc. We welcomed the Donovan proposal that an Industrial Relations Commission (which came to be known as the* CIR*), should arbitrate in such disputes, but, with the experience of the dispute in the* BSC *in mind, there was a general feeling that there must be some method of enforcing the findings. This primarily involved compulsion on the employer, but there would clearly have to be a means of dealing with attempts by unions to coerce an employer who was carrying out the* CIR*'s findings. Altogether there was a surprising amount of agreement between us, though some would have preferred to go further.*

Our 'Windsor' weekend on Donovan at the Civil Defence Staff College at Sunningdale has got off to a great start. After dinner we discussed the philosophy of industrial relations and decided to a man that we were interventionists (even George Turnbull, Deputy Managing Director of Leylands deputizing for Donald Stokes). The question was: intervention for what and how? John Fraser astonished everyone by a coherent and emphatic statement in favour of the enforcement of collective agreements against both management and trade unions and told me he thought the PLP would take it if certain pro-trade union measures were enforced, too. Jim Mortimer said we should intervene to protect the workers' interests and their right to bargain collectively, and also to ensure industrial expansion, on which their standard of living depends. He had gradually realized as an industrial negotiator that both unions and employers used false arguments in bargaining and in the event reached agreements at the expense of prices. 'The State ought to intervene to show you can get more if you produce more.' When I pointed out that this was an argument for P and I policy (and that personally I thought this was inseparable from Donovan) he didn't disagree.

Sunningdale is a government conference guest house run by Vice-Admiral Sir Nicholas Copeman. At dinner he told me a delightful story about two building workers who are laying a drain across the path to our sleeping quarters. This morning he told them they must finish it before I came otherwise I would freeze their pay increase or (even worse) he would lose his job. One of them looked at him meditatively and said, 'If she falls, the Government falls.' The path was finished in time.

Incidentally I learn that all Permanent Secretaries meet here for secret weekends from time to time. Neither junior civil servants nor Ministers ever learn what they discuss! The Whitehall network of top brass is powerful indeed.

Saturday, 16 November. Altogether a fabulously successful weekend. We can all see our way on Donovan quite clearly now. We agreed that we would never get anything positive out of the TUC and that the Government would have to risk giving a lead.

Monday, 18 November. Returned to the office, still a little tired after our intensive weekend, to find everyone full of it. Douglas told me that his phone had never stopped ringing: academics, trade unionists, etc., saying how useful it had been. Had a word with Heron and co. about the Girlings Brakes strike: a classic case of an inter-union dispute where AEF craftsmen refuse to work under an ASTMS foreman and where the men ought to be forced to go through a cooling-off period in order to enable procedure for conciliation to work. I am more than ever convinced that this is needed urgently.

By now I had received a message that there was to be an unexpected MISC meeting at 6 pm. My heart sank. At the meeting Roy and Harold were grave but calm. Roy apologized for only being able to give us a disjointed picture of what was happening. He had been sitting at the end of a phone, linking up with Paris, Bonn and Washington all day. France, it appeared, was resisting devaluation though the franc was on the floor and the pound with it. But no one believed it could be avoided and, if it came, it would probably be 15 per cent, which would compel us to follow suit. The only hope would be if Germany could be persuaded to revalue at least part way: that might just enable us to get through with further credit tightening at home. If the French devalued on their own, he believed our only course would be to 'float' plus 'tough measures'. The very fact that we had met must be kept deadly secret.

I said, as calmly and firmly as I could, that I believed a purely deflationary package, unaccompanied by any direct action on imports, would complete the erosion of our political base and that was just as important as any other factor of 'confidence'. Peter backed me up on this and Roy admitted that his advisers had considered whether the imports deposits scheme should be included in the package. They were divided on this, but had eventually decided this was not the moment to do it. He himself had not closed his mind and would be prepared to adopt such a scheme if next month's trade figures did not show an improvement.

Tuesday, 19 November. Another MISC meeting. Roy reported that the French and Germans seemed to be 'staring each other out'. The run on sterling continued serious: we had lost £28m already that morning. There was now some attempt to get the meeting of the Ten tomorrow. If so, he would propose to go himself with the Governor. On the package, he had been thinking over what had been said yesterday about the import deposits scheme. His advisers had been uncertain yesterday, but now they believed that, if we didn't do it, there would be such endless pressure wanting to know why we hadn't and urging us to do so that the position would remain dangerously unsettled. He therefore agreed that we should include it in the package. Immense relief!

Wednesday, 20 November. The news reveals that after midnight a decision was announced to hold the meeting of the Ten [Western Finance Ministers] tomorrow and that Roy was on his way to Bonn. It also reveals that all Couve has told the Assembly is that cuts in expenditure are going to be introduced in France. So the situation is still far from clear. One good thing is that all the foreign exchange markets are being closed, even, so it is said, New York.

Friday, 22 November. While I was working at the office, assuming I could dash for home soon, the message came that Roy was back, determined to make a statement. I hurried to the House, just in time. I thought he did very well, particularly for a man who had had very little sleep for several days. He certainly avoided the pitfalls Jim was afraid of and, on an impulse, I told him so because I believe in giving people encouragement when the truth warrants it. His face positively lit up and the warmth of his gratitude surprised me. I kept hearing repercussions of this for days afterwards. John Harris, for instance, told Roy Hattersley that the Chancellor had been deeply touched by my words.

At last Mollie and I got away to HCF. There was no Aldie lying in the hall. 'I'm afraid he is a very sick dog,' said Birdie.[1] There he was in his chair, inert, listless, his poor nose caked with blood and his eyes beginning to glaze. I dropped on my knees beside him, heartbroken. As I gently stroked his head, I knew I just wanted one thing: to get him out of his misery as soon as possible. When Mollie had gone, I rang the vet and, subject to Ted's agreement,

[1] My nickname for our housekeeper, Mrs Lilian Evans.

arranged everything for 9 am the next day. I do not remember ever having spent a more wretched evening. I tried to work and wept into my typewriter. Of course, it *would* be the night Ted was kept late at the office with the monetary crisis – as if I cared about that. When at last Ted came Aldie struggled out of his chair, wagged his tail feebly and followed us into the lounge where he flopped exhausted on to the rug. We left him there by the fire as we went to bed, loth to disturb him in the bit of comfort he had managed to find. But it meant that all the night I could hear his struggle to breathe beneath me. I lay awake sharing the last hours of his life with him and in doing so all the love and gratitude and memories of nine years welled up in me. It isn't only what he has been in himself but what he has shared with us. His beauty and his zest for life have been a gold thread running through our private joys and linking together all the things that matter to us in life. The loss of him stirred me to the roots of my being as I relived the poignancy of all the loves and losses I have ever known. Because he would never trot across the garden again, burrow into the soil beside us as we dug in the garden or jump on to my lap in the hammock on a sunny summer day, I felt as though all the simple, richly reassuring things of my life were at risk. He was our Lates and Penares, the symbol of our home, and he was about to be destroyed.

Saturday, 23 November. I got up early, exhausted with tears. Birdie was up, too, and we made some tea. Ted and I dressed wretchedly. Suddenly we heard a faint noise. Aldie was at the foot of our stairs, trying to drag himself up. I rushed to lift him but he growled, his body unrecognizably rigid with pain. I put him down and he hauled himself with a last great effort up the stairs and on to our bed. It was there that I said goodbye to him and Ted took him away.

Goodbye, our dear love.

Monday, 25 November. Woke exhausted. It is astonishing how the death of a dog can drain one. Even the good news from Douglas Smith that the AEF has accepted the engineering proposals failed to lighten my weekend. It was a relief to get back to work.

Harold decided after all to call a meeting of MISC 205. Roy reported that the pound had stood up well so far. France's decision not to devalue the franc has astonished everyone.

My Questions in the House went well and the Tory attempt to make play with the new measures fell flat. Then into the debate at which Heath over-reached himself and succeeded in uniting our side, while Roy did brilliantly. The Party meeting produced another surprise. Here again we had been expecting a stormy time whereas instead we had the most harmonious meeting I can remember for a very long time with everyone from Left and Right uniting to say that the crisis was not of our making and asking for greater pressure behind international monetary reform. At the end Harold and Roy were congratulating themselves on an easy passage at which I remarked gently, 'It wouldn't have been so easy if we hadn't introduced the imports deposit scheme.' They laughed and admitted it, Roy adding, 'I didn't take much persuading about it.' He is altogether friendly to me these days.

Message from Douglas Smith: the Engineering Confed Executives have decided to call off the strike action. They are seeking an urgent meeting with the employers to settle one or two technical points so that they can sign the agreement as soon as possible. Neither the productivity conditions nor the women's rates have been sticking points. So I DID succeed in avoiding an engineering strike and without selling out on P and I policy. But I don't suppose I shall get any public credit for it.

Tuesday, 26 November. Another early MISC. Roy reported that sterling is holding up well and is off the floor, though the outlook remains uncertain. We must be ready for any contingency. Brutus had been slightly modified but its introduction would be catastrophic. It would entail a severe reduction in our living standards and would severely disrupt world trade. An alternative, if we were faced with a run on our reserves that we could not meet, would be to float and the implications of this were being worked out. Finally there was the question of what, if anything, we should do about exchange controls in the sterling area to stop the outflow of capital, particularly to Australia. He would be only too glad to be able to save £100m capital outflow but we could not act on Australia alone and we had to consider the effect on the import of capital (which had increased recently) as well. Timing was all important and if we were in a position of strength at the time of the Budget we might be able to do something then.

I said I would like to know what we should take as the signal that the time had come to float. What were the indicators? And ought we not to meet regularly every week to study them, instead of meeting so spasmodically? We should also have a paper on exchange controls so that we could discuss the implications and timing. I personally considered that we should never be able to hold our own people's confidence if, at a time of rising unemployment, the drain of capital with its consequences for unemployment was allowed to continue. We shouldn't wait till we were in a 'position of strength' before we acted. Roy had begun to look irritable. He said he really couldn't have his busy officials taken off their current worries to produce papers, though he agreed the mid-November forecast should be revised. He couldn't exactly be accused, he said, of keeping his cards close to his chest: he had consulted far more than his predecessor had done. When we were moving into the devaluation crisis last November he, like the rest of us, had been kept in complete ignorance of what was happening. He really wasn't going to have all the alternatives discussed at this stage. Harold, however, as soothingly urbane as ever, suggested that realization of some portfolios might turn out to be a good alternative to restricting capital outflow. At the end of it all it was agreed we should have a discussion soon on a new forecast in the light of this week's happenings.

Wednesday, 27 November. The chief point at the NEC meeting was the new liaison committee between the NEC and the Government. Harold had nominated five Ministers to represent the Government, while from the NEC we had seven nominations in front of us, including two Ministers – Jim and Tony Greenwood. I supported the seven nominations and that was eventually carried (the Left voting against).

After various frantic decisions at the office (such as what to do about the above-ceiling settlement by Lucas's with their toolmakers), I got to the House to see Chris Foster. He came into my room for a drink as desperate as a man can be. He said morale at MOT had totally deteriorated since I left. Dick Marsh was not only lazy, but completely cynical. He had no ideas of his own on transport and spent his time saying how little he thought of mine. His only theme was efficiency, but he had no clear idea how to achieve it, so all that had happened was that they were landed with David Serpell as Permanent Secretary who has the reputation of being a bastard. I was sorry for Chris's wretchedness.

As I changed hurriedly for the diplomatic reception at Buckingham Palace, I wondered why on earth I let myself in for things like this. Having had a sandwich at lunch, I decided not to risk waiting for the buffet supper and have some food before I went. I'm glad I did. First we had to stand in line for nearly two hours while the royal party wended its slow way through our room. I am glad to report that the Queen's hair looked better than I have ever seen it. Margaret looked slightly *outrée* and Anne very promising. She was wearing a very slimming white gown and I noticed that her neck and back were quite beautiful. The Queen Mother, bless her, was as bouffant as usual, while the Duchess of Kent was the most enchanting of the lot. All this I could observe while they went down the diplomatic line opposite, we natives having rightly been waved to the other side as not counting. What I always marvel at – and muse about – in these contacts with the royal family is the utter naturalness of their entourage. The lords-in-waiting wander around in the most relaxed way, chatting everyone up. I couldn't remember the name of the older one who stood next to me, though I did recognize Plunkett who came up to him. 'You're in the doghouse,' said Plunkett to him, grinning. 'The Bruces were late. We had to start without them.' I gathered that my companion had had the American Ambassador and his wife to dinner before the reception. When I asked why they were late, he said affably, 'I suppose we gave them too much to drink.' Not for the first time I was able to see at first hand the secret of the British ruling class in action: they survive by just assimilating their enemies socially.

When the formal procession had passed we headed, thirsty, for the supper tables. All we had been offered so far was one glass of champagne (which I don't like and didn't drink). All my poor starving Ted got was one cocktail sausage on a stick. We escaped early and I heated him some soup when we got home.

The White Paper was based broadly on our Sunningdale discussion. Philosophically it rejected the idea that strikes were always to be deplored. 'There are necessarily conflicts of interest in industry', was its opening phrase. It stressed that 'the right to strike is one of the essential freedoms in a democracy and the existence of this right has undoubtedly contributed to industrial progress and the development of a more just society.' However, with the growing interdependence of modern industry the use of the strike weapon could have disproportionate effects on the rest of the community. The aim should be to direct the forces producing conflict to constructive ends. The need for state involvement to secure this objective was now recognized by both sides of industry.

The White Paper stressed the democratic role of collective bargaining. 'Collective bargaining', it said, 'is essentially a process by which employees take part in the decisions which affect their working lives ... it presents the best method so far devised of advancing industrial democracy.' But our present system had many defects, as outlined by Donovan. Many procedures were too slow and uncertain; the behaviour of management autocratic and arbitrary. The first step, therefore, should be to set up the CIR *suggested by Donovan to improve procedures on references by the Secretary of State. It would be set up initially as a Royal Commission and later made statutory. One of its key tasks would be to arbitrate in disputes about union recognition. It would have no juridical authority, except for obtaining information, nor would collective agreements be made legally enforceable. There would also be a register of collective agreements on Donovan lines. But if we were to improve bargaining structures we must first extend and strengthen trade unionism.*

The White Paper, therefore, was first and foremost a charter of trade union rights. Like Donovan it proposed to give workers the statutory right to belong to a trade union, statutory protection against unfair dismissal, clearer legal immunities for sympathetic strikes and safeguards for the closed shop, subject to the right to compensation from the employer for a worker dismissed for refusing to join a union on conscientious grounds. It went further than Donovan, giving unions a statutory right to certain information from employers and announced our intention to proceed towards worker participation in management. It also proposed a Trade Union Development Fund from which grants and loans could be made to unions through the CIR *to promote mergers, training and research.*

Like Donovan it proposed that unions should be obliged to register, though they should be free to frame their own rules, provided the coverage was adequate. The Commission had found no evidence of widespread abuse of union power, but, with the Government actively encouraging the spread of trade unionism, it was obviously just that a worker should have a right of appeal to an independent review body against refusal of membership of, or expulsion from, a union.

But there were four major ways in which the White Paper differed from Donovan.

1) It rejected the suggestion that, in order to reduce the number of unofficial strikes the protection of the right to strike given under Section 3 of the 1906 Act should be limited to registered trade unions and those acting on their behalf. Instead it advocated the Woodcock alternative of fining unions which refused to register.

2)It proposed to give the Secretary of State discretionary power to order a ballot where an official strike seriously threatened the national interest.

3) It maintained that the CIR*'s findings in recognition disputes should be enforceable by financial penalties against both the employer who refused to recognize and the union or unions who tried to coerce him not to carry out the findings.*

4) It proposed to deal with strikes in breach of procedure by giving the Secretary of State discretionary power to order a 'conciliation pause' of 28 days to enable negotiations to take place. During this period the employer would be ordered to revert to the status quo. *Enforcement would be through an Industrial Board, drawn from the employees' and employers' panels of the Industrial Court under an independent chairman. The Board would be able to impose fines on employer, union or individual striker as it found appropriate. The Board would also deal with the enforcement of strike ballot Orders or refusals to register. Fines would be recoverable through attachment of earnings and other civil remedies.*

It was this last proposal which caused a major outcry. The White Paper pointed out that 95 per cent of all strikes in Britain were unofficial and were responsible for three-quarters of working days lost through strikes. The vast majority of them were in breach of procedure and the number of these unconstitutional strikes was increasing in many industries. It also pointed out that the TUC *itself, in its document 'Action on Donovan', had recognized that the trade union movement had a responsibility to see that the strike weapon was not abused and that, where procedures were satisfactory, unions had an 'obligation to see that the procedure is adhered to'. It was hoped that the existence of the Secretary of State's reserve power would encourage unions to act themselves.*

Monday, 2 December. Spent nearly the whole day at office meetings discussing the first draft of my White Paper on the Donovan Report – three hours in the morning and two at night. Our document is really excellent for a first draft and all those concerned in the Department are getting quite excited about it. Ted Heath is trying to whip up the issue of legal sanctions following the Girling dispute and I am determined to advance the date of publication and also to do everything possible to prevent leaks in order to take everyone by surprise with our package. This means bypassing SEP on which there is more than one blatherer. So I asked the Department to arrange a meeting of the special ministerial committee on Donovan next week and to get on to No. 10 to see if Harold will agree that we should report direct to Cabinet. The message came back that the PM wants to talk to me urgently about this tomorrow.

Tuesday, 3 December. A meeting of MISC 205 to discuss the revised mid-November forecast in the light of the measures we have recently taken. Roy said our biggest danger was not from a low growth rate but from higher consumption and the disappearance of our balance of payments surplus. Controlling home demand was the core of the problem. Two hours having elapsed, we adjourned our discussion. Most of it is going to come up at SEP tomorrow anyway.

Wednesday, 4 December. Sure enough we went over a great deal of the same ground at SEP. Roy returned to his usual theme that the forecast showed we must curtail consumption. There then ensued a discussion in which various people tried to wriggle out of the implications for public expenditure of our present strategy without challenging it basically at all. Harold was in his most loquacious mood and the fact that the discussion went on for three hours was almost entirely due to his own insistence on commenting personally on every speech.

Finally, seeing that I was bursting with impatience, Harold called on me and I delivered my now routine speech on the need to change our strategy. I repeated what I had said at MISC: the need for stronger import controls and the check on capital outflow which, coupled with an imaginative Budget, would enable us to operate a tough incomes policy and continue to stimulate productivity. This would enable us to run a higher growth rate than we otherwise would. But first and foremost it would enable us to get a favourable swing in the balance of payments, which I agreed was an urgent priority. When we had achieved that (which could be early next year), we could then talk about rephasing our debts and realizing some of our overseas portfolio assets for debt repayment. I was certain what we needed was a short, sharp, tough pull. 'We cannot go on with an endless extended vista of hard slog.'

Roy came back immediately on this, saying quite courteously that he thought I had given a ruthless and penetrating analysis 'with much of which I would agree'. However, he thought that my alternatives were quite inadequate for the size of the problem we had to face, and he then proceeded skilfully to misrepresent what I had said. I could hear Jim Callaghan muttering through all this and whispering at one stage to Fred Mulley on my right, 'Do you think we can win the next Election?' Suddenly Jim burst out into a great theme, the practical details of which were less clear than his utterly defeatist psychology. He believed import controls and capital controls would only be marginal in their effects and that the position which faced us was pretty desperate. Of course the Chancellor was right to warn us he might have to take desperate action in 1970 and it wasn't his fault. On the other hand (mournfully) there would be urgent needs in industry that we couldn't meet without a high level of public expenditure. The whole problem was that we were in a vicious circle and that our problems were insoluble. He ended up by saying in his best dramatic dispatch box manner, 'I think we are heading for defeat at the next Election.'

After that helpful contribution, we were all relieved to find that our time had run out. It had already been agreed that we should continue the discussion next Monday and I, for one, escaped thankfully. I think Jim Callaghan is the most disloyal and damaging member of the whole Government.

I was late for my lunch with the Building Societies' Association. It was a small private affair: Mountbatten, Jim Peddie[1] and Frank Kearton were the other guests. Our poor hosts never got a chance to press their own problems because Mountbatten and I got into an argument. He greeted me by thanking me once again for giving attention, as Minister of Transport, to his Hampshire road. Then after lunch he launched an attack on the increase in public expenditure: Britain would never get back on her feet again till it was drastically cut down. I retorted that it was people like him who helped to push it up. What did he think it went on? Free trips to the Bahamas for Cabinet Ministers? It went on roads for one thing, and if he thought I was going to accept cuts in school meals or family allowances in order to enable people like him to get an inessential road to increase their own private convenience, he had better think again. He was rather taken aback at this and said what he had in mind was other sorts of cuts. Which ones? Well, cuts in the number of civil servants, for example. I was now in my stride – his aristocratic arrogance irritates me – and asked him who he thought were civil servants. Just pen pushers? They included people like driving examiners and I was proud to have increased the number of civil servants by 100 under this heading alone when I was Minister of Transport, thus cutting down the delays in passing driving tests. He retreated from the fray at this like one of his own disabled battleships.

Grotesque developments in the Girling Brakes dispute. As a result of my insistence the Court of Inquiry met again this morning to give the strikers a chance to give evidence, and this time four shop stewards turned up. But so, Douglas tells me, did a posse of women from the same factory who had come for the express purpose of protesting to the inquiry about the behaviour of the strikers and the AEF men at the factory generally. All this is absolute grist to Ted Heath's mill. My chaps had got hold of Scanlon and shut him up in a room

[1] Jim Peddie, a leader of the Co-operative movement, had been made a life peer in 1961. He was Deputy Chairman of the Prices and Incomes Board from 1968 to 1970.

with the four shop stewards at St James's Square where he argued with them for two hours, at last emerging exhausted having got their promise to recommend a return to work.

At 6.15 went in to see Harold. He had just read the first draft of our White Paper and was quite lyrical. He said we had obviously done a first-class job and a lot of hard work. 'As I said to Marcia, Barbara has not so much out-heathed Heath as outflanked him.' He is not only as keen as I am to get the report out quickly but he is even keener on stopping leaks. He is therefore scrapping the ministerial committee he set up and intends to call just three or four Ministers together as soon as possible under his chairmanship to discuss my White Paper. From there it will go straight to Cabinet. He is even prepared to call a special Cabinet meeting on 2 January if he can persuade Burke Trend to come back to work in time. Of course, I was pleased but a little nervous, too.

Thursday, 5 December. Glorious little incident on the Falkland Islands at Cabinet. As we had all foreseen, this has blown up into a great issue in Parliament. Fred Mulley said that Chalfont[1] had handled the matter out there very well considering we were in some difficulty as a result of our decision to agree to the transfer of sovereignty. Dick exploded at this and said it was a complete distortion of the Cabinet decision, so Harold sent for the Minutes. But Jim had come armed with them and read them out to prove that we had made it clear at the time there should be no transfer of sovereignty without the agreement of the Falklanders. This was why we had said we would not let the main memorandum be approved until we had Argentina's agreement to publish our unilateral document at the same time, giving it equal status. Dick said categorically we were committed by no previous decision and I pointed out that I had tried to get something about 'the wishes of the inhabitants' into the basic memorandum. Harold was equally firm and said our position was clearly open because all the discussions were *ad referendum* to Ministers. Anyway the Argentine Foreign Minister had been making it clear that he would not sign the memo if we insisted on publishing our unilateral document. 'Right,' we all said triumphantly. 'So the whole thing is off.' But why, Dick wanted to know, did we ever get started on this ridiculous thing at all when it was quite clear we couldn't reach agreement with the Argentine on conditions acceptable to ourselves? Once again the Foreign Office officials have been going beyond their remit. Harold informed us all this was part of the George Brown legacy. It was he who had started the overtures without even consulting the Prime Minister. We were all rather cross about the unnecessary storm having been raised and agreed with Harold when he said categorically we had got to avoid getting into these side rows during the next two years.

A lively discussion on Lords reform as well. Gerald has his Bill ready and wants to introduce it before Christmas. Jim came out with a typically defeatist speech. Why couldn't we drop the whole thing? 'I don't want to have to carry

[1] One of Harold Wilson's more eyebrow-raising appointments in 1964 was that of Alun Gwynne Jones, defence correspondent of *The Times*, as Minister of State at the Foreign Office with special responsibility for disarmament and with a seat in the Lords as Lord Chalfont. The appointment always seemed a dangerous gimmick and it backfired. Chalfont was never politically at home in a Labour Government and once out of office he came out in his true colours as a Conservative.

this Bill in the House.' Some of its propositions were only supportable on the grounds of party compromise and he would have to fight it line by line, clause by clause. The opportunities for mischief on both sides of the House were untold and the Chief Whip couldn't even agree to guarantee support. Now I happen not to like this Bill but, as Dick pointed out, Jim's *volte-face* was astonishing. He had been a member of the ministerial committee which had worked on it and had gone along with the general compromise. Dick believed that to abandon the Bill now would put us in an impossible position and he offered to share the parliamentary burden with the Home Secretary. This brought Jim climbing down somewhat shamefacedly and the vast majority agreed that it was too late now to abandon it. In fact I was the only one who thought we shouldn't go ahead with the Bill even after Christmas.

Saturday, 7 December. The papers are full of a grotesque run on sterling, engineered by a rumour that the PM is resigning and the Cabinet breaking up. Terry Lancaster rang me to say he was going to town on this in tomorrow's *People*. The rumour apparently came from a drunken broker at a luncheon party, making a feeble joke. These people, he was going to suggest, are not fit to be in charge of 'reserve currency'. But one cannot be surprised at these 'jokes' when the Lobby Editor of the *Financial Times* runs the story he does in today's paper, saying, 'It is reported that over the last fortnight several senior Ministers have been at loggerheads.' Roy and Harold are supposed to be at each other's throats while Roy and I are quarrelling too. Our relations are reported as being 'raw and bitter'. As Terry pointed out to me, the only person not quoted as quarrelling with somebody is Jim Callaghan, which seems to give a strong indication as to where the story comes from. Frankly I believe Jim Callaghan is capable of anything.

Wednesday, 11 December. The Cabinet meeting was supposed to be a short one to decide what Michael Stewart shall say about the Falkland Islands in the coming parliamentary debate. Michael started with a lengthy justification of the attempt to get negotiations on the Falkland Islands going at all. He insisted that it was important to try and reach an understanding with the Argentine, as we were in trouble with the Latin American states in the UN. He admitted that the possibility of a military raid by the Argentine on the Falkland Islands was not high, but thought it was essential to our interests to improve our relations with Latin America. One by one we all turned on him and he was soon assuring us defensively that he had left the Argentine Foreign Minister, Costa Mendes, in no doubt that we would not transfer the Falkland Islands without the agreement of the islanders. However, he believed he might get an understanding on the basis that we should sign the memo of understanding as it stood and he would then make a statement in the House of Commons setting out our interpretation of it. The memo and the statement would then be included in the same document and sent to the UN. The status of the memo would not be that of a registered treaty and we would not be legally bound by it. The rest of us would have none of this and most of them agreed with me that this way of doing things simply made us look devious.

Thursday, 12 December. At Parliamentary Committee I reported on the continuing row over union recognition by BSC and warned that Dai Davies's threat to bring the steel industry to a standstill might have to be taken seriously. Equally it was clear that if the two unions did not get the recognition the Pearson Inquiry said they ought to get they would once again provoke a serious disruption in the motor industry. At the moment I couldn't see any way out of the *impasse*, but it did illustrate the need for more effective powers to deal with situations like this than advocated in Donovan. Roy's only contribution was to tell me categorically that there must on no account be any strike in the steel industry as it would be economically disastrous. The one bright spot was the trade figures. These, thank God, are excellent and will make *The Times* look as foolish as it ought to do after all its hysterical nonsense about the need for a coalition Government.

The ships' clerks have at last accepted the port employers' interim offer, which is well above the ceiling but Roy won't allow me to standstill it because of the economic damage a dispute in the docks would cost. It really is impossible to continue the P and I policy if we are going to run away from the economic implications of standing up to the strong and always only clobber the weak.

As I expected, the PIB, in its report No. 92 published in November, had found that the building workers' interim settlement was incompatible with P and I policy since cost of living bonuses had to be taken fully into account in applying the $3\frac{1}{2}$ per cent ceiling. The unions were trying to wriggle out of their commitment to accept the Board's ruling and I was therefore forced to issue a Direction, operative from 20 December, standstilling the whole settlement pending a further reference to the Board.

Friday, 13 December. As the building workers are still dodging the honouring of their undertaking on the 1*d* I have had to publish my Direction in the *Gazette*.[1] The office advised that there was really no need to make a statement on this to the House as we didn't want to create a precedent for doing this every time a Direction was published. However, Douglas Smith rang to tell me that there had been a major row in the House at 11 am and Fred Peart had had to promise that I would make a statement that afternoon.

I easily beat off Tory attacks in the House during my statement. After all, as I pointed out, it was a simple question as to whether or not the unions should honour their undertaking and I could see Maudling was impressed. Eric Heffer, of course, threatened that my Direction would be fought by every parliamentary means and, as we know, there will almost certainly have to be a vote on it. It looks as though we are in for another rough parliamentary ride.

Sunday, 15 December. A most successful day at Chequers. Everyone agreed afterwards that it was the best meeting of Neddy that had ever been held. The CBI and most of the trade union chaps left before dinner, leaving only Frank Cousins, Jack Cooper, Alf Allen, Roy, Fred Lee and me behind. Harold had already plotted with me that we would have an informal chat with them after dinner about some of my proposals for action on Donovan. Once again the

[1] The *London Gazette* had been established in 1665 to enable 'Government departments and public authorities, lawyers and accountants to discharge their legal publishing obligations'.

Sundays are full of leaks about my proposals and Frank Cousins said to me pointedly over his gin and tonic, 'I hope there is no truth in those reports.' I countered by asking him how on earth he thought I could deal with the union problem in BSC. Could we really say in this day and age that two rival groups of unions should be left to fight out a recognition issue on the basis of seeing which of them could do most damage to the economy? He got truculently on the defensive at that and we were only saved by the dinner bell from a real up-and-downer.

However, over dinner everything went smoothly and it wasn't until we were sitting round the fire in the library that Harold broached my two main Donovan ideas: the discretionary peace pause in the case of unofficial strikes and my discretionary power to order a strike ballot in the case of official strikes. Frank of course bridled at the very suggestion, while Alf Allen said unhappily that trade unions just didn't like the idea of legislation at all, though he had to admit that there was some legislation (*e.g.* statutory minimum wage) which they were positively demanding. It was only Jack Cooper who said that a compulsory pause for conciliation might be acceptable provided that the right to strike was still there at the end of it.

At eleven o'clock I left them arguing about strike ballots and went to bed.

Tuesday, 17 December. I had been very distressed by the violent noises George Smith of the Building Workers is making about the builders' 1*d*. I had found him such a worthwhile chap I'm sure it isn't like him not to honour his word. So I sent for him for a private talk. He poured out his heart to me about a number of things and I pledged him my word that, as soon as we have got the 1*d* out of the way, I'll throw my weight behind the Phelps Brown recommendations and do my best to build up the unions.[1] I think he went away feeling mollified.

Thursday, 19 December. The whole of the morning was spent going through my Donovan proposals in MISC 230 created by Harold as a small, leak-proof group of the Ministers primarily interested: the law officers, the Chancellor, Fred Lee and Fred Peart. They all backed me unquestioningly, though Fred Lee has some queries about the conciliation pause. To my delight the law officers have thought out a form of sanctions which won't take strikers into the ordinary courts and which cannot possibly lead to imprisonment. We decided to work out further details of their proposed Industrial Board and Gerald told us that the Payne Committee Report[2] will be published soon providing for attachment of wages for the collection of all civil debts.

In the afternoon I saw George Woodcock. First Conrad and I raised with him the question of whether there was anything to be gained by asking the TUC to try and solve the steel recognition dispute. To my surprise he jumped at it

[1] In March 1967, my predecessor had set up a Committee of Inquiry under Professor E. H. Phelps Brown into the extent and effects of labour-only subcontracting in the building industry. The practice was being widely abused and was preventing the proper organization and training of labour in the industry. It was bitterly resented by the unions. The report (Cmnd 3714), which had been published in July, recommended ways of regulating it and of strengthening trade union organization.

[2] A Committee under Mr Justice Payne had been studying the problem of how to recover debts without sending debtors to prison. Its report in 1966 on the enforcement of Court Orders for payment of debts had advocated the deduction of the debt at source of income through the 'attachment' of wages.

eagerly. He told me he thought it was entirely right that the TUC should try to settle it and asked me to write referring it to them formally. I then saw him alone. On an impulse I have decided to take him completely into my confidence about what I am proposing over Donovan. He listened to my full résumé in silence and then, to my surprise, said that he didn't think there was anything there that need alarm the trade union movement. I could hardly believe my ears! But he urged me to take the TUC Finance and General Purposes Committee equally fully into my confidence and to see them separately at the next round of consultations (fixed for 30 December) instead of together with the CBI as planned. This shook me rather as I know that whatever I tell them will leak and I haven't yet been to Cabinet. That is why I had arranged to see the two sides together so that I could outline my proposals on an 'either–or' basis and let them argue with each other. But George assured me this might only stir things up. He knew I would be taking a risk in talking fully to the TUC before going to Cabinet, but he was sure it would reap dividends. The TUC would then never be able to say they had not been consulted fully before the Government had made up its mind. I agreed to think it over.

Just before he left I remarked casually that, after Christmas, I should want to talk to him about the chairmanship of the CIR. He tried to keep his face dead-pan at this but his eyelids flickered and I could almost feel his hopes rising.

A quick look-in at Harold's party for the lobby correspondents and then a dash for HCF. I've fifty people coming to the party on Saturday!

Monday, 30 December. Reluctantly back to work. Why does one always feel so muzzy after a holiday? I really didn't feel I had my wits about me enough to cope with my great consultation on Donovan with the TUC. After much thought I had decided to follow George Woodcock's advice and risk taking the Finance and General Purposes Committee fully into my confidence. So I began the meeting by solemnly telling them that I had originally intended to discuss with them merely a set of hypotheses but that eventually, recognizing the great importance of this issue to them as trade unionists, and being a great believer in consulting them at a formative stage, I had decided to be completely frank with them. But, as I had not yet put my ideas even to my Cabinet colleagues, I was taking a great risk and could only tell them what was in my mind on condition that no one in the room communicated what I had to say to any person or organization outside the room. If anyone there was not prepared to accept that condition, I would ask him to say so openly. Silence and portentous nods. Then George said they all accepted a pledge of confidentiality. So I went ahead – how effectively I can't say. I only know I felt lousy. I also followed George's advice by adding that I didn't expect comments at that stage, only questions, and would meet them later that week to hear their views. The atmosphere as I talked was quiet and serious. Even the questions were muted and there were certainly no attacks. At the end they agreed that they owed it to me to report their views to me quickly and even said they would come back on Thursday of the same week. Frank frowned a good deal but didn't say very much while George played it dead-pan. Nonetheless I was under no illusions as to what would happen when the press closed in on them.

Tuesday, 31 December. Of course the press is full of accounts of what took place yesterday. My main proposals have already leaked but the newspapers confirmed them and added some quotes from George and supposedly from other trade union leaders, allegedly made at the meeting, which I for one never heard. It is pretty clear that Frank at any rate has been talking to the press.

I had to repeat the same operation with the CBI. When they assembled I went through the same formula as I had done with the TUC. John Davies said, not unreasonably, that the CBI did not usually leak, but that accounts had appeared in the press on which their views had inevitably been sought. Of course they expected the same frankness from me as I had shown to the TUC, but he hoped they would not be prevented from commenting on what I was alleged to have said yesterday. I told him I thought his attitude was perfectly reasonable. Since the TUC had been reported as believing I had completely sold out to the employers' views, I could hardly restrain them from saying what they really felt. 'You can leave me to correct the impression,' said John with relish. And so, by heavens, he did.

Late that night Ted and I forged our way out to Mill Hill to attend Geoffrey Goodman's New Year's Eve party. I was anxious to go, partly because I like Geoffrey and partly because I hoped there would be some good left-wing contacts there. Sure enough the party, though select, was useful. Jack Jones was there and I was soon in a corner with him, busily discussing Donovan over a glass of wine. 'Why didn't you stick to Donovan?' he asked. 'Because I didn't agree with all his propositions,' I replied. 'Do you really want the protection of Section 3 of the 1906 Act withdrawing from unregistered trade unions?' Of course he didn't. OK. But if the rebel can amend the Bible, why can't the Government?

1969

Wednesday, 1 January. Dick has asked to see me. He was even willing to come to my Ministry so I knew it must be serious and about Donovan. I therefore asked John Burgh to join us. Dick was in one of his curious moods, unable to decide whether he wanted to be helpful or critical. He had already received my draft of the White Paper which, we had agreed in the office, must be sent out well ahead of Friday's meeting of the Cabinet, and was torn between a reluctant admiration of it and his pique at being excluded from the ministerial group which had okayed it. So he took refuge in the constitutional point: he wanted to warn me that other people not as understanding as he might make trouble about being faced with a *fait accompli*. They might argue that I had made a mockery of Cabinet. But his personal resentment kept creeping in: 'Why pay mc £9,000?' I retorted that he knew as well as I did that our oversized Cabinet could only work by delegating major decisions to sub-groups. He ended up by saying we must divide the job of fixing everyone else. Michael Stewart wouldn't be too pleased at being left out and Harold had better take the responsibility of squaring him. He himself was willing to fix Judith and Ted Short if I would speak to Tony Greenwood and Wedgie Benn. I said of course I would: I was sure they would understand. And so we parted.

Later I rang Wedgie about my proposals. He replied cheerfully, 'I'm your friend.'

Thursday, 2 January. Got up early to see Tony Greenwood. He was as unctuous as usual. He *had* been worried about my proposals but if I said the trade unions hadn't hit the roof that was a great relief. He is about as much use as a paper raft in an Atlantic storm.

In to another meeting of MISC 230 on Donovan. Taking my hint, Harold had brought Michael Stewart in, apologizing profusely for having left him out before – 'I believe you were abroad.' Michael supported my proposals completely and uncritically. Just as the meeting ended I got a message from Denis Barnes, who had been seeing Woodcock (at my request) to ask him when he thought I might talk to him about the chairmanship of the CIR without embarrassing him. (I didn't want to seem to be trying to bribe him to get the TUC to support my proposals.) Without hesitation George had said he would stay behind after my meeting with the TUC and added that he thought the WP was excellent and congratulated us on it. Wonders will never cease! But he went on to say that Frank Cousins was making trouble and wanted the TUC to throw out the whole document.

Saw the CBI briefly about my WP. 'We still think it is inadequate.' They wanted collective agreements made legally enforceable by the Government and they were very concerned about the provision for the *status quo*. Next I went on to the Finance and General Purposes of the TUC. All they could tell me was that they could not give me final comments because a special meeting had been called of the General Council for Tuesday next. However, they had welcomed a number of the provisions while entering caveats about the penal powers much as anticipated.

After the meeting my people smuggled George into my room and I formally offered him the chairmanship. Though he carefully controlled his reactions, I could see his eyes light up. He repeated that he thought the WP was excellent and he went on almost passionately to say that I had given the trade unions the opportunity he had always wanted them to be given and that our approach had been better than Donovan's. 'I wanted the Commission to be more forthcoming but I had to compromise.' He clearly inferred that my penal powers would act as an incentive to the unions to do the job themselves and for this reason he welcomed them and I hinted hard that he could save an unnecessary cleavage with the unions if he would only say as much. He obviously intends to help but no doubt he will do it in his own obscure way. He told me he would like to think over my offer overnight and would ring Denis Barnes the next day.

Friday, 3 January. The great Cabinet marathon. I spent some time introducing the WP because I wanted to spell out my analysis and philosophy. But the hounds were waiting to close in on me. No one criticized me for the way I had handled the consultations, indeed my critics went out of their way to explain (contrary to Dick's gloomy warnings) that they had no complaint on that score at all. But it was soon clear, too, that Dick's uncertain spurt of helpfulness had petered out and that he had completely swung over to a bloody-minded mood, egged on by Judith who was worried about the 'Left'. Jim opened the bowling by saying that the theme in the WP was all wrong. It did not deal in any substantial way with the basic theme of Donovan to the effect that penal measures were 'futile and harmful'. Crosland said he was uneasy about deciding this so hurriedly. He personally believed the rule of law should be extended to the trade unions but he wanted a series of papers spelling out why he had rejected the Shonfield arguments for giving legal powers to the CIR and the whole-hog line of the CBI.

After a general discussion all morning we got down to detailed proposals in the afternoon when, curiously, it appeared that the majority were prepared to support compulsory strike ballots (which I would happily withdraw) while digging their toes in on the conciliation pause. Dick came out against it openly, as did Judith, Roy Mason and Fred Lee. Unfortunately Peter (who was co-architect of it at Sunningdale) was away ill. But Denis Healey stuck by me staunchly: 'We are responsible for the nation.' 'Speaking for myself,' said Jim, 'I welcome 90 per cent of this White Paper' – but it was clear he would emasculate the rest. It was clear, too, that Cabinet did not intend to be done out of its right to argue and reargue the whole thing, and once again Harold climbed down hastily. He agreed with Dick that the difficult points ought to be referred to an Industrial Relations sub-committee and that I should prepare a set of papers showing how the conciliation pause would work, why I had rejected Shonfield and so on. We should get down to work urgently and report to Cabinet next Wednesday night.

Roy Jenkins stirred things up, too, by saying suddenly that, although he supported me, he only did so on the understanding that we should ACT on my proposals at once. He insisted that we should have a short interim Bill. Dick was all for this, too. I passionately resisted the idea: I for one am not prepared to put forward a shorter Bill in which all the emphasis will be on the penal bits. I could not imagine anything more detrimental to my whole philosophy. However, Harold said I should prepare a paper showing what a shorter Bill might contain.

Monday, 6 January. Ted and I had just turned off the light at midnight after a pleasant dinner with the Fortes when No. 10 phoned. It was Harold to warn me that Dick and Judith were being very difficult over the conciliation pause. Would I try and talk to them?

Tuesday, 7 January. The hard work I had put in on our Donovan papers paid dividends at the meeting of the Industrial Relations [IR] Committee. I had 100 per cent support from Fred Peart, Eddie Shackleton, A. J. Irvine,[1] Jack Diamond and Gerald Gardiner. The rest supported me on the conciliation pause but Judith and Fred [Lee] went on and on nattering about it so eventually I said crisply, 'Right. That means there are two of us in favour of Donovan minus.' That shook Judith and she went away looking worried. I was surprised that Dick wasn't there and disappointed, too – as I had assumed he was a member of the committee.

Douglas phoned with belated news about the meeting of the TUC General Council which had been taking place most of the day on my proposals. Vic Feather[2] had been in touch with Denis Barnes to tell him that he thought we should find the temperature pretty low at tomorrow's meeting with the TUC. Frank Cousins had come along breathing fire and slaughter and had tried to get a resolution through to throw my package out, backed by Danny McGarvey. George had had ready a statement prepared by the TUC office and eventually Frank had withdrawn his resolution in favour of it. Vic's advice was that I should just listen tomorrow and not argue and keep the temperature down. Vic said George delivered the General Council a little homily at the end of its discussion. He told them that they knew it would be very difficult to get any changes in industrial relations or in the trade unions themselves unless there were sanctions behind them: that there came a time in a society's development when action had to be taken to change things and that the Government had to pay attention to public opinion. All that is fine and dandy but I get a little tired of hearing trade union leaders talk sense in private while attacking us in public for doing the very things they know must be done.

Dashed home to change hurriedly for the Buckingham Palace reception for the Commonwealth Prime Ministers. It was an awful nuisance having to dress but the only way I could see of meeting my old friends during my frantic week.

[1] Sir Arthur (A.J.) Irvine had been Labour MP for Liverpool Edge Hill since 1947. He was Solicitor-General from 1967 to 1970.

[2] Deputy General Secretary of the TUC.

It was nice to see Indira Gandhi again:[1] I warm to her. She is a pleasant, rather shy and unassuming woman and we exchanged notes about the fun of being at the top in politics. When I asked her whether it was hell being Prime Minister she smiled and said, 'It is a challenge.' Oddly enough, I always feel protective towards her.

Every group I spoke to greeted me as the first woman Prime Minister to be. I hate this talk. First, I'm never going to be PM and, secondly, I don't think I'm clever enough. Only *I* know the depth of my limitations: it takes all I've got to survive my present job. Ted told me afterwards that Fred Peart was full of praise about the way I was handling Donovan, Cabinet and industrial relations: 'You know I could really serve under her, Ted.' Well, I'm grateful but I'm under no illusions that Donovan may be the political end of me with our own people. I'm taking a terrific gamble and there is absolutely no certainty that it will pay off. My only comfort is that I am proposing something I believe in. I see no objection in principle to asking the trade union movement to adapt itself to changing circumstances and my one aim is to strengthen it. One doesn't do that by clinging to things as they are.

Wednesday, 8 January. The meeting with the TUC went as Vic forecast. It was an almost absurdly constrained atmosphere. John Newton, General Secretary of the Tailor and Garment Workers, emphasized that it was a 'unanimous' document and said all they wanted to say. Frank sat with folded hands and his eyes on the ceiling, visibly restraining himself. Finally John Newton asked, 'What happens next?' I said, of course, that I would consider their document and report what they had said to my Cabinet colleagues.

Dashed over to Dick's office to discuss with him and Judith the modifications they proposed in the conciliation pause and tried to persuade them that (as my officials agree) their suggestions would be unworkable. Dick prowled around with all his signals still set at stormy while Fred Lee, whom they had invited, too, went over all the ground he had covered in the Industrial Relations Committee once again. At that moment the messenger came to say the PM wanted a word with me before Cabinet – which didn't improve their tempers. They think Harold and I are in cahoots behind their backs.

I reported Dick's mood to Harold, who was as surprised as I was to discover that Dick wasn't on the committee. Then hurriedly into Cabinet where I reported that IR was agreed on all the points except the conciliation pause and that, even on this, a large majority supported it. But if I thought the battle would therefore be brief I was soon disappointed. Dick was as intransigent as ever, even if illogical. Stung by my pointing out that the critics wanted Donovan plus on trade union rights but Donovan minus on their responsibilities, he said, 'We all agree we've got to do something about unofficial strikes.' He agreed, too, that he had no alternative proposals to make to mine, but that didn't stop him from opposing me. At the very least the WP should have 'green edges'.

[This] gave Harold his chance to say that, although there was clearly a majority of Cabinet in favour of the proposal, we couldn't settle the matter that

[1] I had had a long talk with her during my visit to India in January 1965. She was then Minister of Information, but she had become Prime Minister in the following year.

night but should resume discussion on this question of consultation the following day. He is clearly playing out a bit more line, confident that we should win in the end. Indeed he passed me a note saying: 'Including absentees, it is 16–7.' Tony Crosland, who wasn't there, had circulated a Minute saying he had been reassured by my comprehensive and 'excellent' papers. Nonetheless I am never as optimistic as Harold and wasn't going to count Crosland's vote until it was hatched.

Thursday, 9 January. Cabinet met at 9 am but still Harold didn't take the plunge. Dick still fought vociferously for his 'green edges' and time was short. Harold therefore summed up that the IR Committee should polish up the draft of the WP and further consider the points raised, adding ingenuously that of course the Secretary of State for Social Services should be a member of the Committee, indeed, it was all a mistake that he hadn't attended it before. 'I'm afraid I was forgetting that he is no longer Lord President.'

Friday, 10 January. All day in IR. At Judith's suggestion I took Denis Barnes and Frank Lawton, the Department's solicitor, along and they were absolutely astonished by Dick's bloody-mindedness and petty-mindedness. As we went through the draft he haggled over verbal point after verbal point until the rest were infuriated and even his allies were a bit ashamed. I really think Dick must be going through the change of life.

When it was all over bar the argument about the conciliation pause (which still remained unresolved) and the polishing, I dashed to the hospital to see Ted who is having a tumour (non-malignant, thank God) removed. Then back to the office for another late meeting with my chaps to tell them the points we had got to redraft and how. A lonely journey and a late one down to the farm.

Sunday, 12 January. A filthy wet day. It was wretched at HCF without Ted, though the news from the hospital is good. I hadn't even a dog to share my muddy walk with me. Worked hard on the redrafting of sensitive bits of my WP and then off to Chequers at 7 pm for one of the many dinners with Commonwealth Prime Ministers.

Monday, 13 January. After an early meeting in the office, wearily into yet another meeting of the IR Committee, armed with a series of redrafts of my own as well as the text which incorporates a lot of the points made at previous meetings. Dick was in more subdued mood. The office told me that I had been too patient with Dick and that I ought to get tough with him, but I know my Dick – he is quite prepared to exhaust everyone nervously and physically if he is in that sort of mood. However, when he tried to alter small words here and there, the rest got impatient with him. In the end it boiled down to one or two points where further redrafting would obviously be an improvement and one outstanding point of conflict: the last paragraph on the conciliation pause.

I had produced a draft which, while making it clear the Government stood by its own proposal, told the trade union movement in terms that it must show its own ability to get procedures observed if it rejected all other alternatives. Dick muttered that this sharpened the issue, rather than 'green-edging' it more. I said crisply that this was the difference between us and that I for one was not prepared to soften it any more.

At 6 pm George Woodcock came to see Denis [Barnes]. As he had left George had said, 'I genuinely believe Barbara has done a first-class job of work. The policy is excellent – very skilful.' It will be the day when he says that to the press.

Tuesday, 14 January. A meeting of P and I. [At] 6.20 pm [I felt] I had to have a few minutes to collect my wits before the vital Cabinet meeting at 6.30 pm which would decide the fate of my White Paper. I therefore said that Roy Hattersley would deal with the next item on OTOS [Overseas Telegraph Operators], on which, according to my brief, the case for standing out was watertight.[1] John Stonehouse protested that he hoped my exit didn't mean that there was nothing to negotiate. I said that Roy would always listen but that John would have to fetch tablets from Mount Sinai in order to refute the case that had been put to me, and swept out of the room. Even if I had stayed I wouldn't have altered my line.

Into the fateful Cabinet. We all agreed that the only outstanding difference left was on the conciliation pause, though I personally feel that the most dubious part of my package is the strike ballot. In Tory hands that really could be abused and, if only the TUC had done any real negotiating with me and urged that that should be dropped, I would have had a chance to persuade Harold to let me do so. However, it was soon clear that Dick and Judith were digging in on their alternative draft for the conciliation pause, designed to give this proposal edges as green as the Irish shamrock. I know that once we show hesitation about this we'll be forced off it without any TUC *quid pro quo* and the chance of the unions taking effective action themselves will disappear. I passed Harold a note: 'I hope to God this doesn't drag on. I have an important and long-standing dinner date.' He replied that his tactic was to let the opposition exhaust itself on this and then all would be plain sailing. My dinner must wait.

Exhaust themselves they did – and me. It was soon clear that Dick had more support than I hoped: Judith, Jim, Dick Marsh and Roy Mason, of course. But even Willie Ross had doubts about being too firm on it, while Peter, back from his illness looking fit, surprised Harold and me by some rather equivocal remarks, considering he was one of the authors of the idea at Sunningdale. However, I was backed strongly by Fred Peart, Gerald, Jack Diamond, Roy J., Wedgie, Michael, Ted Short and the two Georges, Thomas and Thomson, while Eddie Shackleton and A. J. Irvine said they had become enthusiastic as a result of the discussions in IR. Denis Healey and the two Tonys were absent but

[1] A dispute had broken out with the Post Office Workers' Union over a pay claim by overseas telegraph operators [OTOS]. The Government was offering 5 per cent backdated to July 1968, when other civil servants had had a similar increase, plus a further 2 per cent on condition that they accepted immediate changes in practice to increase productivity. The union wanted the 5 per cent without strings, deferring productivity discussions till July. The Government also wanted to reintroduce a semi-automated overseas tape unity relay [OTRU], which had been out of use for two years for technical reasons and the use of which it claimed had been 'bought' from the union when the machine was first introduced. The union contested this and demanded that an extra payment should be made for the re-activation of OTRU since it would mean the loss of 167 jobs and a reduction in overtime. On 20 January the union was to bring the overseas telegraphists out on strike and follow this with industrial action by all its members.

with Harold we were home and dry, Harold making it a clear majority. I told them, 'The old carthorse is stirring in its stable. If we show doubts it will turn over and go to sleep again,' and then wondered if I hadn't given a hostage to Jim Callaghan, who will no doubt repeat this to every influential trade unionist.

This issue settled, we did, as Harold suspected we would, race through the WP without difficulty.

Wednesday, 15 January. Into the office for final polishing. Ted rang me from hospital at 9 am to say he was coming out early and would like to join me for lunch. I told him that I was still without a title for my White Paper: would he do some hard thinking and ring me at my deadline of 10 am. He did so with a list of suggestions, among them 'In Place of Strife'. I knew at once it was a winner. Bless him, he really does have strokes of genius.

I knew I MUST have some rest before my press and TV ordeals. But first I called in George Woodcock to arrange about his announcement. I spilt a great yarn to him about how he could transform the whole atmosphere by what he said. 'You know, George, I really am not out to clobber the unions.' 'Of course you're not. No one could say that – or perhaps I should say they can't believe it even if they do.' He assured me he could deal with the press men perfectly well when they came to see him on Friday at Congress House. I hope so! I do want to make Dick and Judith eat dirt. Their assumption of superior concern for rank-and-file feeling has been almost more than I could bear. I have a hunch that I can carry people with me on this and I only hope that proves true. Of course, I am swept with doubt from time to time as to whether I have entirely misjudged reactions. If I have I shall have mortally damaged my political career. I am gambling a lot on this – but politically my conscience is clear.

It was a pleasant break to lunch with Ted, Julius Nyerere and Jamal (his excellent Finance Minister), and to renew old acquaintances.

Home early, where both Ted and I were glad to crawl to bed.

Thursday, 16 January. Woke refreshed and even had enough energy to argue about the Commonwealth conference at Cabinet.[1] Harold gave a general report saying everything had gone much better than predicted or than the press had implied. Harold assured me that we would not initiate any more talks with Smith.

Back to the office to prepare for the press conference on my White Paper: an intimidating experience because the lobby was there as well as the industrials and they were standing round the walls. I had refused to prepare a statement for hand-out, had rejected John Burgh's stiff form of words and ad-libbed on the record, stressing that this was a great advance for the trade unions. A lot of questions were designed to prove that trade unionists *could* go to prison and I told them off about that. After, Roy Hattersley congratulated me. 'Sometimes I think you do well, sometimes not so well. This time you did very well and I don't say so if I don't mean it.' He's a funny chap and I am never quite sure where I stand with him.

[1] The Commonwealth Prime Ministers' conference had at last been reconvened. On the Rhodesian issue the Government had been saved by Ian Smith's rejection of the *Fearless* proposals, so the atmosphere was more relaxed. The main bitterness was over our immigration policy.

Friday, 17 January. Back to another press conference, this time to announce George. Of course, it had leaked, so it wasn't news, but I elaborated it a bit. Then TV and more interviews with individuals. No time for any lunch at all.

Down to HCF heartened by two bits of news via Denis Barnes. First, Aubrey welcomes the setting up of the CIR and promises full co-operation with George Woodcock. Secondly, Jim Mortimer is ecstatic about the WP and says he is going to seek out people like Clive Jenkins and Mik to persuade them to support it. Whoopee!

Saturday, 18 January. Not a bad press, judging by the radio. Of course, George's attitude has not emerged as clearly as I hoped but I shall try to make the most of it when I meet the trade union group again on Monday. 'Miscellany' has one of its usual sour comments about the title of my WP, trying to make out it was one of Harold's tricky touches. If only the sourness of the press was ever balanced with real generosity. (Well, I can't complain about today's *Mirror*!) But I'm sure no one can take away the real impact of the title which says just what I wanted to get across: that I really am in line with Nye's philosophy. Always echoing in my mind are those words of his after our 1959 Election *débâcle*: 'The trade unionist votes at the polls against the consequences of his own anarchy.'

So successful had our Sunningdale weekend been on Donovan that I decided to hold a similar weekend discussion on the future of prices and incomes policy with a similar mix of representation from industry, unions, administrators and economists.

Tuesday, 21 January. Off to Sunningdale to discuss the future of P and I policy. Everyone invited had turned up, including Clive Jenkins who told me that the non-penal proposals in my WP gave the trade unions everything he and Jim Mortimer had been asking for in their recent book, of which he gave me a copy. Jim Mortimer went even further and said he thought the WP was 'marvellous'.

Wednesday, 22 January. The afternoon was spent seeing representatives of the weeklies. I don't suppose I have influenced a word they will write. Then a party for the chairmen of the PLP study groups with drinks in my room. We were joined by Vic Feather in the most euphoric state I have ever seen him in. I had told the office to fix a private evening for me with him. He accepted with alacrity. Clearly he is heady with [the prospect of] release from George's shadow over him. After a drink I took him off to dinner at a private room at Brown's Hotel where the euphoria continued with such intensity that I could hardly get a word in. Eventually I managed: 'Well, at any rate you can thank me for George's appointment.' 'Not only that, luv. Not only that.' He was full of reminiscences about Bradford and 'your Dad',[1] about which he had been talking to John Torode. I have never seen a man so frankly liberated. He spoke

[1] My father, Frank Betts, was a leading intellectual light among Bradford Socialists in the 1920s. As a senior civil servant in the Inland Revenue he had to keep his political activities under wraps, but it was widely known that he edited the ILP weekly, the *Bradford Pioneer*, and was producing plays for the ILP Arts Guild. He held discussion groups for young workers in our home and Vic Feather, then driving a milk van for the Co-op, was one of his discoveries, helping him to monitor the deeds and misdeeds of local Tory councillors for the *Pioneer*.

of Dad so vividly he reminded me of things and people I had forgotten long ago. His roots still hold him. I liked the way he didn't play mock austere: the way he asked for a particular cigar and accepted my offer to choose the wine without being pretentious in any way.

It was late before the conversation turned to shop and even then he wasn't going to be too serious. I touched on my WP. 'Why did you do it, luv?' But as I started to explain my aims for the trade union movement, he interrupted to say he would help in any way he could with trade union conferences. 'Let's keep contact like this.' I think he may turn out to be a very great General Secretary.

The dispute over union recognition at BSC had reached danger point. Although the TUC consultative steel committee had rejected the Pearson Report and refused joint meetings with CAWU and ASTMS, BSC had announced it was going to allow the two unions to recruit at all steel plants and to grant them local recognition once they had a 'substantial' membership. The 'big six' unions immediately threatened industrial action, but this was suspended on 23 January following my request to the TUC to intervene. On 7 February the General Council endorsed a document reaffirming that the two should have no rights beyond the limited local recognition they had had before nationalization. So the stalemate continued.

Attempts to solve the Girling dispute had also failed. Following talks by my Department with unions and management, the AEF Executive had urged the strikers to return to work, but with no effect, and on 20 November I had set up an inquiry under Professor Robertson.

Thursday, 23 January. In Cabinet I reported on the steel dispute. If the TUC failed I was standing by for urgent meetings with Dai on Saturday. [Then] I went off to catch my train to Blackburn.

Friday, 24 January. At the end of an exhausting day of interviews in Blackburn Douglas phoned. Dai has climbed down at last! Industrial action is now postponed indefinitely and the Finance and General Purposes Committee of the TUC is meeting on Monday to try and work out a compromise. This is an all-round triumph. There is no stoppage in steel yet Dai has succeeded in convincing everyone that my proposed reserve powers are necessary. Indeed, most people will think (as Douglas put it) that there wouldn't have been a climb-down but for the WP. Apparently Frank Cousins pressed as hard as anyone for a settlement though his union is one of the steel group.

I'm less happy about the PO dispute. Tom Jackson[1] has telegraphed me asking me to intervene but the office tell me there is a long-standing convention that one Government Department doesn't intervene between another and its employees. I feel there is something wrong here.

Saturday, 25 January. The weeklies are full of criticisms of the WP but the arguments are getting very confused and the whole attack is rather muted. I've foxed them all!

Friday, 31 January. 9.30 pm: Roy Hattersley has just phoned. The PO strike is over in circumstances which put a final peak of absurdity on the Stonehouse

[1] General Secretary of the Post Office Workers' Union.

saga. It was already clear last weekend that Stonehouse had been doing some extensive press briefing. The papers were full of stories to the effect that he had wanted to yield to the union's demands as reasonable but had been prevented from negotiating by the rigidity of the P and I policy and the obduracy of its custodians, Castle and Jenkins. Douglas phoned me early on Monday to say the matter was coming up at Parliamentary Committee that morning and that a new paper had been put in by the Paymaster-General. We were all astonished to discover that the *average* take-home pay of OTOs would actually be reduced as a result of the pay increases, net of the reduction of overtime, due to the reintroduction of OTRU. I said at once and they agreed that the Government could not possibly justify standing out on this basis. Apparently there was a P and I meeting last Thursday while I was in Blackburn at which no mention was made of the net reduction in take-home pay, so everyone agreed to stand firm.

Now Roy J. was absolutely fuming about the Stonehouse stories in the press [and] was not prepared to discuss Stonehouse's paper till this point had been cleared up. And so Parliamentary Committee started with a major row. After a long trouncing all round, John replied in his curiously flat and halting way, denying that he was responsible for the reports (though Ted tells me he has been approaching everyone in Fleet Street). Eventually Harold said that there could be no discussion about the merits of the dispute until John had publicly repudiated the press stories.

Tuesday's papers duly carried Stonehouse's assurances that he supported the Government line. When P and I met at 6.30 pm we were still hopeful of averting the strike and had told Jackson to stand by for a possible meeting that evening. However, Roy J. was as adamant as ever. He insisted that we could not negotiate a compromise now 'under threat of a strike'. John supported Roy saying we mustn't talk to the unions now and that anyway it was too late to stop the strike. (That I didn't believe.) So I was overridden and Roy ruled that it was hopeless to discuss a formula in that meeting.

Thursday's strike was unexpectedly well supported by the postmen, though patchy on the telephonists' side. At Cabinet John, sitting just behind me, launched into a long, painfully halting but determined counter-attack, finally ending by saying that he must be left to continue the negotiations as it would be an intolerable undermining of his authority for him to be taken off them now. Harold, tart as ever, asked John point-blank whether he had specifically raised the take-home pay issue at P and I and finally John admitted that he hadn't. But he got some sympathy from Ted Short and Tony Greenwood on the negotiating point and Harold summed up that he could remain in charge of negotiations subject to P and I's approval of a formula.

I had to be in the House that afternoon so was on the front bench when John answered his PNQ. To everyone's surprise he suddenly announced the suspension of the 4*d* post. As some of us agreed, the announcement seemed rather unnecessary and I couldn't avoid the suspicion that he was gratuitously stressing the effectiveness of the strike. Of course, the announcement provoked a great Tory storm and John capped everything by being vague about his constitutional powers. Later, having just arranged with Ted to go to our first movie for nine months, I learned that the Speaker had allowed a Standing

Order 9 (Emergency) debate on the constitutional issue and that there was a three-line whip. So there I was on the front bench again for the winding-up. I tried to put some fight into John but he wasn't going to play it that way. Instead we got treated to a great emotional piece about how he was the son of a PO worker and how deeply he regretted this 'unnecessary strike', which provoked a cry from our left wing: 'Blame Barbara.' So I wasn't feeling too pleased with him when he turned to me ingratiatingly as he sat down, 'I hope I didn't embarrass you.' To this I retorted, 'I am afraid you did.' My feelings weren't improved when I saw Tom Jackson grinning from his seat under the gallery.

The office sent me details of a new formula worked out by officials of the three Ministries in recognition of the union's fears that some of their people would be out of pocket – the best we could do. In return the union would advance the productivity deal from July to April. On Friday morning I went along early to P and I armed with this formula. Once again Roy was for letting it sweat a bit with the idea of 'perhaps' talking to the unions on Monday, but I did strongly support John on this. This got strong backing and Roy was overruled. John thereupon said he would be happy to invite DEP to send conciliators to advise him and to have Roy Hattersley take part in the negotiations.

At No. 8 Roy Hattersley and I talked to Denis Barnes and agreed that Conrad was our man. I had a word with them, stressing the importance of not agreeing to John's proposal to leave OTRU on one side. I also stressed that they must keep in touch with me and the Chancellor before any variants on our formula were agreed.

Ten minutes later Roy H. was back. The Paymaster-General had disappeared. Even his own office didn't know where he was. Eventually he was traced to the House of Commons from which he was reported as saying he wasn't visualizing a meeting with my people till 2.30 pm. We all looked grim at the news. It meant he must have contacted Tom Jackson privately about a meeting with the unions despite the delicacy of the situation and our desire to agree the exact terms of the overture with him. I told Roy to get down to the House at once and not let John out of his sight.

Roy H. rang me twice during the afternoon, the second time to say that he was convinced that a settlement was possible on our formula if they could go up to $1\frac{1}{2}$ per cent. Conrad agreed with him and the Chancellor was prepared to agree. So of course I said yes. I had just got down to HCF at 9.30 pm when Roy phoned me again. I have never heard him so outraged. Almost spitting out the words, he told me that the $1\frac{1}{2}$ per cent offer had been made; he and Conrad were convinced Jackson was about to agree to take it to his Executive when John chipped in without consulting anyone and said, 'I can see you aren't happy with this proposal. I have another suggestion to make.' He had then made the offer to withdraw consideration of OTRU at this stage (his proposal all along, on which he had been overruled by the rest of us). Jackson had jumped at it. The deal was clinched while Roy and Conrad sat speechless and helpless and the strike was off. 'So it's collusion,' I said grimly. 'Looks like it,' replied Roy equally grimly. I hurried into the lounge for the 10 pm News. There was Jackson beaming about his 'victory'. Next John, smooth and enigmatic as ever, saying there had been no breach of P and I policy. I dread what tomorrow's papers will bring.

Saturday, 1 February. Just as I thought, the *Sun* heralds John's 'personal triumph' – the implication being that success was inevitable once he was allowed to negotiate. I rang Harold at No. 10 and told him the story. He says he has already decided to hold a full inquiry into the whole business. Stonehouse has obviously been doing some ringing round.

Sunday, 2 February. The papers are just as we feared. Roy H. phoned to say he thought Stonehouse was going off his rocker. Whatever it is, I don't see how the Government can mend the position. Just as we were leaving for London, Roy J. phoned. In his usual languid way he said he thought we could never trust Stonehouse again. He personally was against an inquiry but he thought Harold, he, and I ought to discuss the matter as soon as possible. 'Stonehouse will have to go.'

Other highlights of the week included my dinner with Roy J. on Monday which took place in a private room at the Connaught Hotel – another demonstration of what he calls, with a smile, his 'expensive tastes'. It was fixed some time ago at his request and I was curious to know the reason for it. Roy certainly tries to keep in friendly touch with me. Once again he turned out to be far more relaxed than he sounds in letters and Minutes. The Department, for instance, were sure that he wanted to talk about the future of P and I policy with a view to persuading me to retain statutory powers at the end of this phase. In the event it was I who introduced it and Roy merely said he wanted to keep his options open, not because he anticipated disaster, but because one never knew. He admitted, with a smile, that I had always been a firmer believer in the policy than he was. Was he concerned with it, I asked, for presentational or economic reasons? 'A bit of both.' He took quite seriously my assertion that I didn't believe we could get a renewal of statutory powers through the House. On economic policy generally I repeated that I had always been in favour of floating. Here again he had no fixed objection. He just believed that the outcome would be so problematical that he didn't think we should float unless we were forced to.

At one stage he asked me what I thought of Tony Crosland. With my usual bluntness (which he encouraged) I said that his contributions were always intellectually brilliant but that they never seemed to lead to anything. He agreed at once. Tony, he said, was always against taking a decision until every intellectual avenue had been explored. He didn't seem to realize that there were certain situations in which one just had to act. Of course Tony had wanted to be Chancellor. Interestingly, Roy was very anxious that the rift between Dick and me should be healed. 'He has behaved badly,' I said grimly. 'He deserves to be sent to Coventry.' 'I know,' drawled Roy, 'but not for more than a couple of weeks.'

Tuesday, 4 February. We had been summoned to a meeting of MISC 205 so secret that no document has been circulated beforehand. We had to arrive early at No. 10 in order to read it. I discovered that Denis has now been added to the committee (another case of personal pique to which Harold has given in?). The paper was one from the Chancellor describing what we should have to do if we were compelled to 'float' – an exercise now named 'Hecuba'. A short inconclusive meeting which left me deeply disturbed.

Lunched with Alan Watkins. He has been running a series of attacks on me in the *New Statesman* and, as he has obviously been talking to Dick about Donovan, I thought it was time he talked to me. But it was a wretched meal. After pumping me as much as possible about the OTOs, he refused to concede that Harold had done anything but 'rush through' my WP. 'I think you are a dangerous woman. You are a button pusher like Kennedy and I don't like button pushers.' 'One can push a button to start Vietnamese peace talks as well as nuclear wars,' I pointed out. 'Doesn't matter. I am just against activists. I'm an old-fashioned Whig.' One interesting point emerged: Dick, he told me, is 'left out of things'. So that is what Dick is brooding over! And he held it as damning evidence against me that both Harold and Roy speak well of me. Harold praises me to the skies, so I must be supporting him (and Roy) in an inner triumvirate! I told him it was nonsense but he didn't want to know.

Wednesday, 5 February. The first meeting of the PLP on my WP. Of course, as usual, despite the great outcry against my policy, there were only about 100 people there. Surprisingly, the mood was far from bitter and there were a lot of compliments for my 'sincerity' – even 'Socialist' sincerity! – and for the great bulk of the WP. But there were almost non-stop objections to the three proposals they dislike most: the strike ballot, the conciliation pause and the attachment of wages, in that order, especially the latter. It is astonishing how much furore that has created!

Monday, 17 February. Another private chat with Vic Feather over a drink, this time at my request. He's been writing some pretty scathing things about the WP and I wanted to find out if he really is outraged about it and why. He seemed quite surprised that I should take his articles so seriously: after all, one was only for the Soviet paper *Trud* and the other for the *City*, which surely nobody read? I pointed out that they had been reported widely and were helping to create a real breach between the trade unions and the Labour Party. If the TUC felt so strongly about my proposals, why didn't they at any rate try to negotiate on them? Soothingly he assured me he would make a constructive speech on the WP at the Union Executives' meeting on 27 February, urging that they shouldn't get their criticisms out of proportion. 'It'll be all right, luv.'

Tuesday, 18 February. Meeting with building trades employers about the PIB reports and Phelps Brown. Mellish[1] and I tried to stir them up to a sense of urgency and I told them I would like there to be a meeting of both sides under my officials in about six weeks' time. I also inspired Bob to warn them that he was looking into the question of putting new conditions into Government contracts on the adoption of proper wages systems, conditions of work, etc. Egged on by me, he got quite enthusiastic about the idea. The employers also agreed to join our working-party on the reform of labour-only subcontracting and accepted that legislation would be necessary.

[1] Bob Mellish, Labour MP for Bermondsey, had been Dick Crossman's Joint Parliamentary Secretary at the Ministry of Housing and Local Government. In 1967 he became Minister of Public Building and Works. Later in 1969 he was to succeed John Silkin as Government Chief Whip.

Wednesday, 19 February. The afternoon was spent on the steel dispute. First Mikardo led a deputation of MPs (Russ Kerr, Denis Howell, Fred Mulley and himself) to put the point of view of the Two. Melchett, of course, has been running to the press spreading the idea that I am pressurizing him to adopt the TUC line, because he is anxious to find an alibi. I repeated to Mik exactly what I had said to the earlier deputation from the Two. He rubbed his hands at this and said he intended to point out to Melchett ('whom I like') that he had been misleading them. I retorted, 'It is not the first time, Mik, that people have tried to hide behind my skirts.' They all agreed that my attitude was perfectly correct and went away to plot trouble.

I then saw Melchett and Ron Smith again, feeling rather mad with them and determined not to give them an inch of advice which they could turn against me. However, it proved easy. They reported that their talk with George Woodcock had produced absolutely nothing. The Two were anxious to compromise but the Six were adamant. I told them we would stand by what they decided. They shook their heads sorrowfully and went away.

Thursday, 20 February. Dreadful news broken to me by Douglas. Stephen Swingler has died! The shock was all the greater because it looked as if he were round the corner from his pneumonia. He really was a triumphant administrative success as well as retaining his Socialist drive. A warning not to neglect bronchitis, particularly when one smokes too much.

Sunday, 23 February. Dick phoned me to say he has agreed with Harold to take Bea Serota[1] as his new Minister of State. Harold won't have Hattersley (whose claims I have been pressing) because he is said to have made three 'disloyal' remarks recently. Dick and I agree this is absurd because, although we don't think Hattersley is a particularly nice man, we know he will make disloyal remarks about anyone, including Roy Jenkins.

Tuesday, 25 February. President Nixon, who arrived yesterday on an official visit, made all the right noises at the airport. He even talked about the special relationship! Harold had some talks with him this morning, to which I was not invited. I don't know whether Jim was, after his angling last Thursday, but he certainly wasn't at the dinner at No. 10. When I arrived I found Michael and Denis there, Philip Kaiser,[2] Hemminger from Nixon's entourage, John Freeman,[3] Burke Trend and the head of our FO. Downing Street was a blaze of light and when I walked into the drawing-room I was dazzled by another flood of light behind which I could just make out a row of photographers and TV cameras.

[1] Beatrice Serota had had a distinguished career in London local government before she was made a life peer in 1967. In February 1969, following Stephen Swingler's death, she had become one of Dick Crossman's two Ministers of State.

[2] Minister at the American Embassy.

[3] John Freeman, former Labour MP for Watford, had disappointed his left-wing friends when, having distinguished himself in various junior ministerial posts in the Labour Governments of 1945 and 1950 and having resigned from the Government in 1951 with Aneurin Bevan over prescription charges, he gave up Parliament in 1955. Since then he had been editor of the *New Statesman* and British High Commissioner in India. He had been appointed British Ambassador in Washington in 1969.

As we waited I chattered mostly to Hemminger, whom I found intelligent and lively. We were all very poised and relaxed, like people who have arrived into the heart of the establishment. If we're honest, it is moments like this, when one is in the inner circle and conscious of not being awed by it, that are the consolation for all the work and strain. Then Harold whisked off downstairs to the front door, taking Michael with him, and was back with a very suntanned, eager-to-please Nixon, followed by David Bruce, the US Ambassador, Secretary of State Will Rogers, and Kissinger.[1] Nixon was geniality itself as he went the rounds being introduced. I found him surprisingly likeable. Harold was almost beside himself with exuberance. He held forth to Nixon at great length about me: what a success I had been at ODM, Transport and now at the toughest job in the Cabinet. 'She has to tell all the trade union leaders they can't have their wage increases and then she goes round kissing them – after she's won, I mean.' Nixon worked hard at trying to think of the right things to say: 'We'd better have her over in our country.'

At dinner I found myself between Will Rogers and Burke Trend, who, in this informal setting, seemed far more boyish and vulnerable than in his rather avuncular role in Cabinet. We had a natter about Cabinet affairs and then he said with impulsive jocularity, 'But it's all *great fun*, isn't it?' Dinner over, Harold rose to move the toasts and assured Nixon in a short speech that he wasn't going to make one. He welcomed him almost like an old friend already and Nixon replied in the same vein. Then Nixon disarmed everyone with an unexpected flash of wit about 'your new Ambassador to the United States'. He understood the Ambassador was supposed to have said some derogatory things about him in the past but, then, we all changed. Indeed their two roles had changed. 'He has become the new diplomat while I have become the new statesman.' Great applause.

There then took place a quick survey of the position in the Middle East. Just as we were warming up, Michael Halls slipped in to whisper something in Harold's ear. Harold interrupted to say that, if the President didn't mind, there were other Cabinet colleagues waiting outside who were anxious to meet him. No doubt they had sent in a signal of revolt because as we all trooped out to the drawing-room we found a sulky group. Dick and Tony Crosland muttered to me, 'We do object to being kept waiting.' So once again Harold had to cut the pleasantries short to suggest that we adjourned for a short talk in the Cabinet room. Indefatigably smiling, Nixon fell in with this again.

We all took up our usual places in the Cabinet room. There was a positively festive air about the whole proceedings with Harold making a few cracks before inviting Nixon to tell us what he would like us to talk about. Nixon rose valiantly to this unusual setting and atmosphere and responded by making some rather discursive remarks about general social problems, in particular the problem of youth and student revolt now manifesting itself everywhere, even Germany. What did we think it was all about? Harold made a few rather coarse jibes at Marcuse which irritated me, as his lapses into Philistinism always do, and I was delighted when Judith put him in his place, saying that as the mother of teenage sons she had decided she must make a study of Marcuse and that we

[1] Dr Henry Kissinger was Special Assistant for National Security Affairs to the President of the US from 1969 to 1975. He became Secretary of State from 1973 to 1977.

all ought to take him seriously because, as an apostle of violence, he was having a big effect on young people. Wedgie gave one of his scintillatingly pat little homilies on what technology was doing completely to internationalize the relationships of young people, to which Denis vigorously retorted, 'Rot.' Dick, soured again by having been left out of the dinner party, was twisting his lips at all this and I cried out to Harold, 'Let Dick say something: he knows more about Germany than any of us' – which Harold eventually did. Whereupon Dick delivered a brilliant cameo of a speech, culminating with the words, 'They are looking for a religion and we can't give it to them because it doesn't exist.' George Thomas nearly expired with indignation at this while Harold interjected primly, 'The Social Services Secretary, Mr President, is not speaking for the rest of us.' However, still no shocked reaction from the Americans. Nixon was beaming away while David Bruce looked positively inspired. In fact it all went like a bomb and, as Harold said afterwards, 'I don't suppose he'll get anything like that in Germany.'

Phone message to ring the office where poor Douglas is incarcerated for the night over the Ford's strike. He reported that the AEF has decided to make the strike official and that Heron would like to see me early tomorrow before my NEC meeting as things were looking black.

Fresh trouble had broken out at Ford's. Following negotiations with the union over their claim for a substantial pay increase, the company had offered a package consisting of an average pay increase of 8 per cent, with productivity strings, plus important improvements in fringe benefits: a £20 holiday bonus and a guaranteed lay-off payment for time lost owing to disputes outside the company. The fringe benefits were only to be payable on condition that the employee had not engaged during the previous six months in action in breach of procedure agreed by the National Joint Negotiating Committee [NJNC]. The company was also prepared to concede equal pay. The trade union representatives agreed unanimously to recommend the deal to the trade union side of the NJNC which adopted it by majority vote on 11 February. The AEF, however, had always opposed the penalty clauses and on 18 February its Executive rejected the deal as did the TGWU.

Unofficial action broke out at various Ford plants and on 25 February the AEF made the strikes official, followed closely by the TGWU, the Patternmakers and the Vehicle Builders. Despite this the trade union side of the NJNC reaffirmed its acceptance of the deal on 25 February by majority vote and asked the company to proceed to implement it on 1 March, as it proposed.

In December 1968 the Newspaper Publishers' Association had reached a settlement with the National Union of Journalists for a two-stage pay increase which seemed to us likely to have repercussive effects. In March 1969, I standstilled the agreement and referred it to the PIB.

Wednesday, 26 February. A 7 am phone call from the Whips. Could I get into the House by 8 am for a closure vote? Pandemonium. Got to the House to find they had been sitting all night but had made little progress because there were not enough of our chaps to get closures in the early hours. Heron came in to report on Ford's. At the NJNC meeting yesterday Ford's had suggested a ballot which had been turned down by the unions. Instead, they had announced the AEF decision to make the strike official. So it is total confusion. Jack Jones is going to try and get the backing of his Executive this afternoon to make their strike official, too, and there is talk of the whole matter being raised after the Croydon meeting of Executives tomorrow. Blakeman is almost at his wits' end what to do next.

Later I learned that the TGWU had turned Les Kealey off the Ford's negotiating committee and decided to make the strike of their members official. So it's a showdown! I had just got home after a session of the Parliament Bill when the indefatigable Douglas phoned. Ford's are applying to the High Court tomorrow for an injunction restraining the TGWU and the AEF from seeking to extend the strike! I was staggered: not least because we have argued in the WP that collective agreements in their present form are not legally enforceable.

Thursday, 27 February. At Cabinet I reported on the Ford's injunction, carefully making it clear (for Jim Callaghan's benefit) that I had had nothing to do with it. Gerald Gardiner was sure that the judge would not grant even an interim injunction on an *ex parte* application. Roy, doodling as usual, looked up and said with disarming candour that, although he had been responsible for our 'going soft' on these industrial issues in the past, this time he thought we must stand firm. Even Jim was put off his stroke by my blow-by-blow account of the disarray among the unions.

Roy Mason and I then rushed off to see Melchett and Ron Smith at their request. They reported to us their decision on trade union recognition in the steel industry which we duly said we would abide by.[1] My guess is that both sides will take it lying down, thus justifying Conrad's handling of the whole dispute.

Friday, 28 February. Worked all day on my speech for Monday's debate on my White Paper. Went home exhausted to HCF with the first (unsatisfactory) draft.

Sunday, 2 March. I was just preparing for the third go at my speech when Douglas rang. Gillan, head of Ford's Europe on the manufacturing side, had been on to Heron saying he would like to talk to me urgently. Could I manage it that evening? So we had to return home early to warm up the flat and prepare for our visitors. To everyone's surprise the judge gave Ford's an interim injunction on Thursday and this led to a hurried meeting of union leaders at Croydon at which Mark Young refused to take the chair. Blakeman and Gillan wanted to put us in the picture. When they arrived Blakeman looked a very unhappy man but not more anxious than Gillan, a dapper little man with a strong American accent who obviously feels out of his depth in the midst of British industrial anarchy. Blakeman reported that at Croydon Jack Cooper of GMW had taken the chair and had sent the following message to Ford's last Thursday: drop the writ, take out the penal clauses and negotiate. On Friday morning Blakeman had replied that the company would be more favourably

[1] BSC had decided to confirm national recognition of the Big Six, to continue local recognition of CAWU and ASTMS existing before Vesting Day and in addition to recognize them locally at those plants where, on 1 February 1969, they had in membership a majority of the grades concerned and where none of the Big Six was recognized locally for these grades.

disposed to withdraw the writ if the unions would order their people back to work. Ford's would then talk right away in the NJNC. Jack Cooper had replied that that was a very fair offer, but so far the company had had no response from him or the unions.

Gillan followed up Blakeman by mournfully shaking his head over the prospects for the company. Couldn't I at least persuade the unions to let enough workers into the plants to meet the export orders? The company held an IDC [Industrial Development Certificate] for a £20m extension at Dagenham but if they were faced with this kind of industrial trouble it was doubtful whether they would think it worth while building it. I told him the Government was as worried as they were about the development of what was clearly a political strike. The only way of coping with it was for the company to take their stand on their own commercial needs – not try and hide behind P and I policy.

At last I got rid of them at midnight and went bleary-eyed to bed. Not a good physical starting-point for tomorrow's debate.

Monday, 3 March. The great debate on the WP at last. I found it even more difficult than usual to condense my thoughts down to size and I was bombarded on all sides (Whips, PPSs, etc.) to throw out a lifeline to the doubters by stressing that consultations would continue on the controversial points. Altogether just about the most difficult speech of my life, but I survived: just. I was still scribbling the last sentences as I rushed down to the House by car. The votes against and the abstentions were more than we had anticipated, but then a lot of people took a holiday from responsibility in the happy knowledge that the Tories were going to abstain.[1] Passing the buck has now become an endemic disease in the PLP.

Tuesday, 4 March. To the Epicure to take Harry Nicholas out to lunch. After listening to his down-to-earth enthusiasm, I began to be glad that Tony Greenwood hadn't got the job after all. Tony wouldn't have been as practical and it isn't as though he had any great intellectual distinction to offer in its place. Harry volunteered that he should go and talk to Vic Feather to try and close the breach that I saw developing. We parted on genial terms.

Back to the office to see the Newspaper Proprietors' Association [NPA] and the National Union of Journalists [NUJ] about the journalists' pay claim. I had to explain why I couldn't accept the settlement without a reference. What interests me is that no newspaper has yet carried what I should have thought was a sitter of a story: 'Babs standstills Ted'. Could it be that this would show how impartial I am?

Suddenly I found myself with a free evening and phoned Ted to suggest we went to the theatre to see *The Ruling Class* by Peter Barnes. It was a joy to be entertained for a change – even if everybody did look at me in the bar.

Thursday, 6 March. The CBI has asked to see me again about the WP before going into consultation with officials over details of the Bill. Their attitude was an eye-opener. John Davies was in fighting mood and told me categorically

[1] The Ayes were 224 and the Noes 62, so there was obviously a large number of abstentions.

that, having read the WP, they were more alarmed about my proposals than ever. If I intended to ram trade unionism down the throats of managements who had built up perfectly good collective bargaining arrangements without it, I should have business up in arms against me.

The judge has refused to renew Ford's interim injunction! Worse still, he says they haven't got an agreement at all because the union Executives hadn't ratified it. Urgent plea from Gillan to go and see him, so we smuggled ourselves into the side door of Grosvenor House where Ford's have a company flat (so far we've managed to keep these meetings secret). Gillan was plunged in gloom. The company just couldn't afford their continuing losses. European subsidiaries were up in arms at the drying up of components from the British plants. He made it clear that, left to themselves, the company would have conceded a 10 per cent rise without strings: much cheaper than this struggle. But they recognized their responsibility to the P and I policy – 'which we support'. Nonetheless it was clear he was sagging under pressure from Detroit. Blakeman was much calmer and firmer. The judge's dictum on the agreement had made life very difficult for them. Never before had it been suggested that an agreement concluded in the NJNC had to be ratified by Executives before it became operative. When I quipped to him, 'This only goes to prove we should keep judges out of industrial relations,' he heartily agreed. The question they had to decide now, he said, was whether they should appeal. Backed by Conrad, I strongly advised against, but that didn't mean they should capitulate. They had a valid constitutional case, if not a legal one. I told him that the Cabinet was prepared to weather this particular storm; and on this note I left them.

Friday, 7 March. Ford's still haven't announced their decision not to appeal. Conrad tells me Blakeman has decided to keep this as a negotiating card. The AEF and TGWU are now trumpeting that they will not try to get their chaps back to work on anything less than a bigger increase without any strings at all. Conrad is going to move in with his usual conciliation roles.

Monday, 10 March. The Sundays were full of Mark Young's resignation from the chairmanship of Ford's NJNC. Jack Jones, who has been egging Hughie on, really does seem to have misjudged it this time. I had to make a statement in the House on the state of play and it went so smoothly we could hardly believe our ears. The Left were so subdued it was clear they were very uneasy about the whole business.

Tuesday, 11 March. The Ford talks are in a mess. To facilitate progress Blakeman has told the unions that the company will drop all legal action, but Reg Birch has had his way and the unions have put forward impossible demands. They want the March package in its entirety, minus the penal clauses and plus a larger wage increase. It is imperative that Ford's don't give way on this: if they do, we shall only have to standstill it whereas my strategy (as it was in the case of the engineering pay talks) is to keep the political element out of it and make this a straight fight with the employers.

Wednesday, 12 March. The Ford talks have finally broken down and I had to make another statement in the House. Leslie Blakeman has taken my advice and clearly offered the alternative of a return to work on the basis of the 1967 agreement with renegotiation from scratch. As a result the discussion in the House was a walk-over. In the tea-room afterwards several of our people came up to me appalled by the attitude of TGWU and the AEF. Roy Hattersley's comment was typical: 'One thing has been demonstrated in the House this afternoon and that is that we could get the penal clauses of the White Paper through at this moment.' I told him that the same idea had occurred to me and that I had already given instructions for an interim Bill to be prepared urgently.

Friday, 14 March. A successful afternoon with the Yorkshire Regional Advisory Council of the TUC (from which it was clear that they at any rate are not steamed up about the White Paper) and then back to the office, through the flashing of photographers' bulbs, to see Leslie Blakeman and [Bob] Ramsey. We went over the ground with Leslie over a drink and I asked him whether he had given any thought (as Conrad had suggested) to alternatives to the penal clauses. He said they had been working on a different form. The idea was that there should be two funds, one for lay-off benefit into which they would pay 4*s* per week per employee and the other for the holiday bonus into which they would pay 10*s* per week per employee. Both these payments would be suspended for all employees for any week in which there was unconstitutional action of any kind in the plant. Any surplus in the lay-off benefit fund would go into the holiday bonus fund, thus bringing the bonus above £25 (*i.e.* the additional £20 on top of the existing £5) if no unconstitutional action took place. His new plan sounded pretty ingenious and I went back to the empty flat quite encouraged.

Saturday, 15 March. Jack, Hughie and Les Cannon came in at 10 am. Hughie told me that the penal clauses presented the major obstacle; they wanted a 'total revaluation of the agreement' but recognized that this, together with the withdrawal of the penal clauses, must inevitably mean the suspension of some of the benefits – *i.e.* the £25 bonus and the guaranteed week. Discussions should take place with the company as soon as possible, either with me or without me. I assured them that Blakeman and Ramsey would be plenipotentiaries and that I would try to get them round.

After lunch Blakeman and Ramsey came in looking downcast at the reports of what had been said that morning. However, we sent them off to talk to the three while we settled down to wait. I was just giving up hope of getting down to HCF at all when they asked to see me. They had agreed a formula to be put to the trade union side of the NJNC the next day.

Sunday, 16 March. It was bliss to dig in the garden for a few hours. But at 2 pm Douglas was on to me. There had been a hitch in the NJNC talks. Could I come back to London and stand by? So I hastily swallowed my lunch and the noble Ted sacrificed his afternoon to drive me back. There then ensued another miserable period of waiting at the flat, uncertain even if I had time to eat, before the call came for me at 9 pm. Once again the phalanx of photographers was waiting outside No. 8. I wouldn't mind my job half so much if I didn't have to keep bothering whether I was groomed enough to face the cameras! Conrad Heron was grave. Jack and Hughie were now repudiating last night's agreement, whether as a result of outside pressures we didn't know. More hanging around and then eventually at 11 pm the two sides asked to see me to report an *impasse*.

Monday, 17 March. To the office to gen up on Ford's. Conrad told me that the two sides were deadlocked. I said impatiently that it was time we took charge. Conrad: 'They won't have us in.' Me: 'I can call them in separately.' Conrad was just agreeing with this when the message came that the joint meeting was breaking up. Right, I said, this is where I take over. I saw Blakeman and Ramsey first. The unions, they said, were resisting the idea of a collective penalty and insisting that only the guilty should forfeit their benefit. I soon realized that Hughie was in a genuine dilemma. He said, 'We accept some form of deterrent. What we objected to was that the deterrent should be on holiday pay.' Jack Jones added (much to my surprise) that they were prepared to look at some form of collective sanction in the case of the lay-off benefit fund, but not the holiday bonus. In other words they conceded both the principle of the deterrent and the principle of collective sanction. They looked desperate. Hughie confided in me that he was bound hand and foot by the instructions given to him by his Executive at York. What could he do?

When they left Conrad commented how anxious the unions clearly were not to break and I had a bright idea. Obviously the unions had to get some improvement of the holiday bonus over the existing £5 to satisfy their own people: why not split the difference and make the guaranteed bonus £15? If we stuck to the original idea of two separate funds, both of which could be at risk, we should still have a considerable deterrent as well as a great victory of principle. Blakeman was quite taken with my idea. He said that £15 would exactly fit in with some figures he had dug up which showed that a £15 holiday bonus guarantee would meet the situation exactly, leaving a pretty good incentive for good behaviour. So I dashed over to the House to see Harold and Roy who said I could go ahead. I even got a meal while Blakeman and the unions went into a huddle again.

Back in the office at 9 pm I learned from Conrad that Hughie was trying to push Blakeman up to £20 and I nearly hit the roof. However, apparently Blakeman was standing firm. Just as we were discussing the position Andy Kerr, our Chief Conciliation Officer, dashed in to say that the unions were on their way to meet the NJNC which had been standing by. Hughie had said to Blakeman that if he would make it £20 the unions would recommend acceptance; if not 'this is it', though even now he wasn't saying there was a formal breakdown. 'If you want to authorize £20, First Secretary, you must do it quick,' said Conrad. Hattersley was all for saying yes, while Douglas pointed out emphatically that the Chancellor and the PM had told me not to go above £15. In any case, I wasn't prepared to: it would have undermined all the credibility. So we had to stand by and wait anxiously, whiling away our time with coffee and chatter, hugely entertained by Roy Hattersley. At 12.30 am the three came in to see me to say the NJNC had adjourned till 2 pm. Hughie said he and Jack would have to hold delegate meetings and 'see what comes out of it'. And so to bed, not daring to count any chickens yet. Anything can go wrong in this game.

Tuesday, 18 March. Back at the office I found that the NJNC was still talking. At 4.30 pm both sides came to see me to tell me that the strike was off.

Thursday, 20 March. The main item at Cabinet was the PIB report on top salaries.[1] I got a surprising amount of support at Cabinet for my recommendation to accept the report. Some, like Fred Peart, were worried about the reaction of the PLP and I think Harold was, too, though he was impressed enough by my support to keep silent. I wanted to say that we would implement the first increase immediately (as it is within the policy anyway) but take our decision on the next two stages in the light of developments in the P and I policy. (As I expect we shall drop statutory powers this will enable me to put through the increases as planned.) But the majority, including Peter, had taken the bit between their teeth and insisted that I should go the whole hog and accept the whole report unconditionally. I protested strongly that this would make my position untenable under P and I policy, but I was overruled.

Saturday, 22 March. Another Security Service report on the Ford dispute. The more I read these reports the less confidence I have in our intelligence. The material is always mighty thin and most of it would be obvious anyway to an informed politician. I'm not surprised to read, for instance, that Scanlon was anxious for a prompt settlement – he had as good as told me that himself. Talking of Ford's, I got into the office on Wednesday to find waiting the most magnificent box of flowers I have ever seen with a card from Gillan: ' "Bloody" well done!' If that had leaked into the press I really would have been in trouble!

Monday, 24 March. Meeting with officials and Roy Hattersley on what we might put in an interim IR Bill. They told me in unison that their advice was not to try and do a package (which would just look like a gimmick anyway) but to go for a straight penal clauses Bill on the grounds that these were needed immediately. I shook my head and took them all on single-handed, telling them that I was not prepared to have my name on any purely penal Bill. One had to feel that a policy was right and that felt all wrong. Besides, the philosophy of it was wrong, too. My argument would be that three things were needed 'immediately': 1) the reform of disputes procedures, which we had set on foot by establishing the CIR; 2) change in the attitudes of management, which would flow from giving statutory rights to trade unionism; 3) a change in the attitudes of the trade unions. Faced with my flow of determination they all backed down.

I was invited to the meeting of the Cabinet–NEC co-ordinating committee in Judith's room. It was a pleasant and not unuseful occasion. But I don't think these meetings are going to heal the rift. But I had a word with Harry Nicholas about Joe Gormley's resolution on my White Paper at tomorrow's NEC. Harry

[1] This recommended that the salaries of Board chairmen in nationalized industries should be increased to £20,000 in three stages.

was very relaxed about it and said he thought Joe now regretted he had put it down. However, if it were pressed it was bound to be carried.

Wednesday, 26 March. At the NEC Joe's resolution was taken first. He said there was no need to reargue the merits of it. It was very reasonably worded and he couldn't see why I couldn't accept it. Other unionists argued the same way – even Andy Cunningham. I replied that that was clearly impossible. First, it said that the NEC couldn't support 'any legislation based on all the proposals in the WP' and it was obvious what the press would make of that. Jim jumped in to suggest in his smoothly plausible way that I had a point about the word 'any'. If that were dropped he saw no reason why I couldn't accept. Joe at once said he would accept that amendment and I could see Jim's trap closing. Tony G. passed me an amendment to delete this sentence and substitute, 'welcomes the Minister's assurance that she is continuing her consultations with the trade union movement' which I promptly moved. Then George Brown moved in, massively impressive, telling Jim bluntly that he must realize the Government could not be dictated to by the NEC on its legislation, so the passing of the resolution would be bound to create an open rift and would be so interpreted in the press. To this one trade unionist gave the usual bovine reply: 'We can't be dictated to by what the press may say.' They were obviously anxious to get it out of the way quickly as a matter of form, without rancour, and so we came to the vote. To my astonishment Jim ignored my pleas and voted against my amendment which was lost by fifteen to six: George Brown, Tony Greenwood, Wedgie and Arthur voting without hesitation with me, Jennie doing so with an overt protest, telling Mik, Tom Bradley, Frank Allaun and everyone within earshot, 'I'm a prisoner: that is what is wrong.' Alice must have abstained, as did Eirene White. The resolution was then carried by sixteen to five.

Just as I was eating a hurried dinner I was called to the phone to speak to No. 10 on what had happened that morning: Harold had had a full report (from Tony Greenwood, I gathered later, who was far more incensed about the whole business than I was) and was going to put it down as an item for Cabinet immediately on his return from Nigeria.[1] I told him what Wedgie had suggested to me on the train, that Harold should write at once to Jim: 'Dear Jim, As you are no longer prepared to defend Government policy in public, I assume you have resigned.' I could almost feel Harold recoil at this: 'I can't do that just as I am leaving the country for a week. But I intend to be very tough about it when I get back.' (I'll believe that when it happens.)

Thursday, 27 March. The papers are full of Jim's 'revolt' at the NEC yesterday. Well, they certainly didn't get it from me. I've merely registered another reason why I should despise him. He crept into the meeting on the future of P and I policy and slipped out early. Another press leak is Ronald Butt's article in *The Times* giving a detailed, factual account of the proceedings of the very committee we were attending! How the press get all this – whether from officials or Ministers – I suppose we will never know. At the meeting we were

[1] In May 1967 civil war had broken out in Nigeria following the Eastern Region's declaration of independence as the Republic of Biafra. Harold Wilson had decided to visit the Federal Government leader General Gowon to explore ways of ending the war.

all pretty well agreed that we must go for Part 2 powers only after the end of the year.[1]

But the highlight of the day was the PLP meeting at 5.30 pm. Stan Orme had warned me he was going to raise the PIB report on top salaries. The outcry was predictable. I had had no time to prepare a reply, but I took along the report of the Select Committee on Nationalized Industries and hurriedly ran through what it said about Board salaries. It was a gold mine. Then I looked at those who had signed it. A gift! John Horner, Trevor Park, Kelly, Russ Kerr and, of course, Mikardo as chairman. Mik wasn't there, but John Horner was and he played right into my hands. Nobody could have been more magnificently scornful than he was. Where was our sense of justice? Our sense of timing? 'The Government must consign this PIB report into the dustiest pigeonhole it can find.'

My reply was a walk-over: there was a real problem here from which they were running away. I quoted and quoted and quoted the Select Committee report.[2] 'Bad timing, John? You signed this and this and this in July 1968 – just as the latest P and I Bill was going through Parliament.' They all rolled in the aisles. John came up and said with a wry smile, 'That was a bull's-eye.'

Monday, 31 March. The papers are all full of Jim's 'defiance' and have whipped up a great furore about the 'showdown' Harold will have to have with Jim on his return and speculations as to whether Jim will be asked to resign.

Had a drink with Dick to suggest that he and the family might like to join Ted and me at Whitsun in touring the Italian coast in Charles Forte's boat.[3] He was delighted at the idea – and rather touched. I took the opportunity of sounding him out about an interim Bill, determined to make him feel this time he is on the inside. The only way to avoid trouble!

Tuesday, 1 April. When I was on the front bench, to my distaste Jim came and sat next to me. Of course the Tories opposite noticed us sitting in apparent harmony side by side and started pointing and calling attention to us, whereupon Jim put his arm round me. That will be in all the papers tomorrow! He really is a cool customer.

Wednesday, 2 April. Harold is due back tonight – and not a moment too soon. I have sent a message to No. 10 saying I want to see him and Roy Jenkins before tomorrow's Cabinet. The answer came back: 5.30 pm, in the House, where we are still making derisory progress on the Parliament Bill. Before that, however,

[1] The draconian powers of the 1968 Prices and Incomes Act to hold up wage and price increases for twelve months were due to lapse at the end of 1969 and we knew we could not get support for the renewal of this power over incomes. Roy Jenkins, however, wished to retain the powers under Part 2 of the 1966 Act to hold up increases for three months on reference to the Board. I was anxious for us to rely more on price controls than direct wage restraint to encourage employers to resist excessive increases and therefore wanted us to retain the 1968 powers over prices, but Roy Jenkins would have nothing to do with an 'asymmetrical policy'.

[2] The Report had said that the present rules about fixing salaries must be abandoned 'and a new start made towards fixing and paying a proper rate for the job'. Such a rate must be 'significantly higher than that which is now generally paid'. And it added, 'The State cannot afford to manage its public industries on the cheap. There is too much at stake.'

[3] Following some pleasant trips Ted and I had had on the Fortes' boat while holidaying at Vico Equense the previous summer, Charles Forte had offered us the use of it for a few days at Whitsuntide.

I had to see the TUC Finance and General Purposes Committee to discuss my proposed procedure for making references to the CIR. Here was one aspect of my policy with which the TUC agrees yet when I went into the room at Parliament Street, where they had been having a meeting first, they were waiting for me like a bunch of executioners. No one would believe that I have had something like a major row with John Davies because of my determination to let the CIR look at trade union recognition cases without being put into a straitjacket about 'criteria' and that I have been fighting their battles. Frank, as the most dominant personality, was once again in charge, bristling with suspicion and arrogance. John Newton suggested we should adjourn the meeting so that they could continue their discussion in the light of my clarification. As we left them to it my officials told me that Len Murray had come up to them to apologize for their behaviour. He at least realizes that the Government suffers a lot at the hands of the TUC.

Harold was strangely subdued when I joined him and Roy at 5.30 pm. He looked tired, though suntanned, and I urged that he should try and get some sleep. I told Harold why I had decided that an interim Bill was now both practicable and desirable but I was horrified when Roy went on to say that he wanted to announce it in his Budget speech. His argument was that he would have to say something about the future of P and I policy. If he were to pretend that we were not modifying it, and then a month or two later we were to modify it, it would look as though he had been forced off it. This would have the worst possible effect abroad. But he couldn't possibly announce any modification of the policy without at the same time announcing the decision to proceed with the interim Bill. His suggestion, therefore, was (and he was very firm about it) that he should make the two announcements briefly in his Budget speech and that I should elaborate on them the next day, making the major Government reply to Macleod.[1] Consternation! I asked for time to think about it. Could the Chancellor and I talk about it during the Easter recess? Roy, of course, agreed to this. I urged that we should bring Dick into the discussion of this strategy. Harold said Dick had asked to see him – along with me – that night and suggested that we should all meet at No. 10 after his dinner party.

Dick and I drove over to No. 10 together to find the presidential dinner party still in full swing. Roy joined us and eventually Harold came in in full evening dress followed by Michael Stewart. Harold isn't going to have any cabal without him. Harold must be desperately tired, having flown through the night, but brandy keeps him going. He had recovered his *élan* a little and paced the room pouring us drinks and telling us how firm he was going to be with Jim Callaghan the next day. The time had come to reassert control of the Party and the Chancellor's strategy would provide the foundation. Dick agreed that, given the dropping of the Parliament Bill and the announcement of November's uprating, the new package might do the trick, but he warned Harold that Jim might well resign. Was he prepared to face that, since a footloose Jim could enter into a most dangerous alliance with the machine at Transport House? Harold waved all this aside: the Party must realize that, unless they accepted

[1] Iain Macleod, Conservative MP for Enfield from 1950, a brilliant debater and tactician, who had held various posts in Conservative governments. His sudden death in July 1970, when he had been Chancellor of the Exchequer in the Heath Government for one month, was a great loss to the Conservative Party.

the package, they would be faced with an Election and a large number of them would lose their seats. It sounded a curious kind of threat to me. At about midnight I excused myself and slipped home exhausted and depressed.

Thursday, 3 April. There was an air of expectancy in the Cabinet as we assembled in Harold's room in the House. Harold had told us last night that officials were not going to be present while we discussed Jim's crime, but the drama was somewhat spoiled when we found Jim wasn't there. Was he just going to boycott the meeting? Did it mean he had already decided to resign? I was feeling desperate because at noon I had to make my statement in the House on top salaries and we still had to agree the line I should take. To my relief Harold was now obliged to take this first. My office had drawn up what I thought was a good statement. However, we had put back into it what I had always wanted to spell out, namely that we could only agree the first instalment at this stage; the rest would have to await the next development in incomes policy. After some discussion my line was agreed, though I could see that Harold was still hesitant.

In the meantime Jim had arrived – ten minutes late. He really is a cool one! Perhaps his coolness unnerved Harold. At any rate the thunderbolt never materialized and I heard myself listening to my astonishment to some very generalized and conciliatory noises indeed. It was Jim who pushed his own position firmly into the open by saying he had no reason to apologize for what he had done on the NEC. No decision to legislate on the WP had yet been taken by Cabinet and it had been agreed that the final form of the policy should only be decided after consultations with the TUC during which we were prepared to listen to their alternatives. Harold then said that he must now clearly reaffirm the Cabinet's decision to back the WP, which must be accepted as binding on them by every member of the Cabinet. Jim was just saying slowly something like, 'If that is how you are interpreting Cabinet policy, Prime Minister, some of us may have to consider our position,' when I got a call from the Whips to come on to the front bench immediately as one of our Questions was about to be reached. So I had to dash out not knowing whether I had been listening to a resignation speech. Later Dick and Roy both told me that Harold had beaten what looked ominously like a retreat and Cabinet had broken up in some confusion because Harold had to answer Questions, too. So much for the great showdown! Jim is clearly ready to play a tough game and this convinces me that an early showdown with him over my Bill is now inevitable. Otherwise Jim will *de facto* have become the Government.

My statement on top salaries went well. And so down to HCF for Easter. The beauty of the place always acts like a balm and I find it only too easy to throw off politics. When people tell me they don't know how I stand up to the strain (and sometimes ask me if I take drugs!) the answer is that I couldn't do it without my private moments in our retreat. Hell Corner Farm is the only drug I need!

Saturday, 5 April. The papers are full of the 'dressing down' Harold is supposed to have given Jim on Thursday. Harold has clearly compensated to the lobby for what he failed to do in Cabinet. The surprising thing is that the lobby has swallowed it so uncritically.

Easter Monday, 7 April. The weather has been beautiful over Easter, and with the house full with Sonya, Terry and their brood it was blissfully easy to forget politics. But I am not to have my promised week off after all. Roy J. phoned me yesterday. He chatted a bit first about the press reports on Friday of what was supposed to have happened at Thursday's Cabinet. 'I must say,' he drawled, 'Harold seems to have been a good deal firmer at his lobby conference than he was in Cabinet.' Next Roy invited me to come over to East Hendred for supper tomorrow, and said that he had invited Dick too. But he was very insistent that I should arrive three-quarters of an hour before Dick and told me Dick would not be staying to supper: he wanted to get back to Banbury. I didn't like this business of being manœuvred into a corner alone with Roy so I rang Dick to discuss tomorrow's meeting. He agreed with me that this was a crucial one and was surprised to hear that I was staying to supper. He had only opted out of supper because he didn't like to seem to be asking for hospitality. When he heard I was staying on we cooked up a ploy between us that he would breeze in and ask how late he was supposed to stay. I want Dick there not merely to keep him sweet by keeping him in the conspiracy, but also because I really will welcome his political judgment on the way Roy is proposing to handle the IR Bill. Incidentally we had a chuckle – rather a sour one – about the difference between Harold's behaviour at Cabinet last Thursday and the impression he manages to give through the press.

Tuesday, 8 April. I managed to get in a morning's spring cleaning before Mollie arrived to take me to East Hendred. I was most curious to get this new glimpse into Roy's environment. Their cottage is authentically old and beautiful with uneven floors, low doors and a number of rooms full of character. It is furnished with taste but by no means lavishly. With the good weather continuing, Roy took me out into the garden for our cup of tea, brought by a rather harassed-looking Jennifer in an old skirt and plimsolls. The contrast between Roy's poise and polish and her general air of rather untidy harassment is fascinating. The garden was rather neglected and Jennifer complained that she had to do all of it, whereupon Roy drawled that gardening really wasn't his strong point. 'It would be nice if you could do the lawns,' she pined plaintively.

Roy and I went over the old ground about his proposed tactics for combining the announcement of P and I policy and the interim IR Bill statement in his Budget speech. I told him that to rush out the two together would be to rob us of all the political advantages of modifying P and I policy. It would be fatal, too, if the PLP came to believe that my White Paper package was dictated by the need to pacify the IMF. Roy listened courteously, but obviously thought that his own anxieties had priority.

At this moment Dick burst in on us and went through a superb bit of play acting. 'What time do I ask my driver to come back?' he asked innocently. Roy got a bit flustered at this while I sat looking at my feet. When Roy, outmanœuvred, feebly asked Dick if he would stay to supper, Dick jumped at it. A harassed Jennifer went off to boil up a bit more rice and, as Roy went indoors to mix us dry martinis, Dick grinned at me. However, if Roy had only realized it, I was doing him a favour in bringing Dick in in this way. Within minutes Dick was agreeing with the whole of Roy's proposed strategy. I repeated all my anxieties, but Dick brushed them aside. I think his prime reason was that he is desperately looking for an excuse for dropping his Parliament Bill. The consideration which weighed most with me was that I thought Jim Callaghan has put us in an impossible position and forced us to make him declare his hand as soon as possible, which the early introduction of my 'penal' powers will do. Dick believes he may resign, not because he is a strong man but because he is weak and will find himself caught in his own trap. He may be right.

Warming to Dick's 'reasonableness', Roy was soon opening up everything to him, even giving him the full details of his Budget proposals as he had to me. I think such near-reckless frankness by a Chancellor must be almost unprecedented. We then worked out our tactical programme over the next few days and I was immensely amused to hear Dick plotting how we could keep other Ministers in the dark to the last possible moment. I remembered what happened to me over my White Paper when I did that to him! We agreed that we should jointly see Harold on Thursday afternoon, meeting privately ourselves an hour beforehand, at which we would finally decide whether to go ahead on the lines Roy proposed.

In a final private word after supper, Dick, Roy and I came down once again to the urgent need for setting up an inner Cabinet. Surely, we said, the crisis in the Party will force Harold to come round to this at last? Dick didn't query Roy's suggested membership of it: Harold, Michael Stewart, Denis, Fred Peart and the three of us. Roy insisted earnestly that Denis must be in but I noticed he didn't even mention Tony Crosland. As a *quid pro quo* for that I suppose we shall have to leave out Peter Shore. For myself I frankly didn't care who is in it so long as it is small and continuous.

Thursday, 10 April. I tore myself away from my spring cleaning to meet Dick and Roy at No. 11 as arranged. I have now resigned myself to accepting Roy's strategy and Dick is obviously quite enthusiastic about it. We were still arguing about this when we were told that Harold was back from the Scillies and wanting to see us.

Harold was quite firm that Roy must make the announcements on Tuesday and that I must follow with a major speech on Wednesday. If the TUC really had any alternatives to offer we could always keep our promise of continuing consultations by the device of having an 'appointed day' for legislation bringing in the penal powers. Vic Feather had asked to see him later that evening.

Friday, 11 April. I took Denis Barnes and Conrad Heron along with me to No. 10. Harold told us it was clear from his meeting with Vic that the TUC are not going to propose any definite alternative. Indeed, as soon as we got into the meeting with the Finance and General Purposes Committee it was obvious that they were barely going to mention their own document. They trooped into the Cabinet room, sorrowfully shaking hands with Harold as he stood by the door, but clearly in a subdued and somewhat defensive mood. Vic opened quite effectively on the TUC's behalf, touching upon the work they had been doing in holding TUC conferences and expressing rather a note of doubt about the effectiveness of the powers we proposed to take than any sense of outrage. He certainly didn't outline any concrete alternative. Harold Collinson of the Agricultural Workers was equally earnest and sorrowful. 'We don't come here as enemies.' Even Frank was visibly holding himself in. Oddly enough it was Sid Greene who was the most vituperative, saying that penal powers would never work. George Lowthian of the Building Trade Workers played right into my hands by stressing that the *status quo* would be invaluable and would do more in his view to avoid unofficial strikes than any proposition that had yet been made.

Summing up, Harold made it clear that the Government must be free to decide its legislative programme in its own time, and Vic said to him firmly, 'So we go away from here without any assurance either as to the content or to the timing of the legislation?'

Monday, 14 April. Budget Cabinet. The feeling on the whole was that Roy had been very ingenious, considering we were not offering anything very radical.[1] Then into our meeting of the IR Committee where everyone had been carefully genned up beforehand on the interim Bill proposal. So there was no real resistance to what I carefully described as the Chancellor's idea. However, to my intense relief, Crosland suggested that we should substitute the inter-union disputes procedure for the strike ballot in the short Bill as being more valid and more urgent. How I agree with him! I would have dropped the strike ballot months ago if Harold would have let me, but he clings to it – I suspect because it is a simple formula which has attracted a lot of public support. So I was able to report the IR recommendation to the afternoon Cabinet.

We had taken care not to circulate any papers beforehand, knowing our Jim, but he must have suspected what was in the wind because he took the announcement of the short Bill calmly enough. Indeed he was obviously looking for excuses not to make a resignation issue of it. The general line seemed to be that, if we were going to have the 'penal' clauses at all, it was better to get them out of the way as soon as possible.

A two-hour meeting of IR Committee to tie up the details; then over to No. 10. Harold had asked me to join him while he broke the news to Vic Feather.

Vic was as relaxed and friendly as ever. He didn't hit the roof when Harold told him the news – just sat there looking grave as he munched his sandwiches while I fell ravenously on mine. Once again I felt uneasy at Harold's cosy way of smoothing over all the issues, sitting there in that pretty green, white and pine study sipping brandy as though the mateyness would solve everything. However, Vic didn't bridle or declaim. He even entered into a discussion as to what kind of fund we might set up to absorb the penalties and promised to let us have his ideas. How far Vic is genuinely unalarmed at our proposals (he may

[1] The Budget took £340 million out of the economy in a full year by hefty increases in indirect taxation (3*d* a gallon on petrol, increased taxes on gaming and wine, an increase in SET and an extension of purchase tax to new items), but skilfully offset the political effect on our own people by increasing corporation tax, removing tax relief for interest on personal overdrafts and above all by raising income tax allowances so as to take 1 million of the lowest paid out of tax and to reduce tax for a further 600,000. There was also to be an autumn uprating of pensions and other benefits. The balanced package was completed by the Chancellor's announcement in his Budget speech that a) we were not going to renew the 1968 prices and incomes powers at the end of the year, but rely on Part 2 powers and b) we were to legislate immediately on 'some of the more important provisions' of my White Paper.

even welcome the new power they give to the TUC) I cannot tell. I only know that in public he will trounce them vigorously.

Tuesday, 15 April. Worked on my speech and then went into the House for Roy's Budget speech. To my astonishment Vic phoned to say that, as promised, he had been thinking over the idea of the fund and the only thing he could suggest was to devote it to industrial research. I asked him if it was worth trying it out in the speech and he said he saw no harm in it.

Wednesday, 16 April. A frantic rush again preparing my speech for the House at 3.30 pm: I had to rewrite every word of it. After a dicey start it went pretty well. At 5.30 pm Harold and I were receiving the TUC in the Cabinet room in the House, where they were clutching copies of my speech over which they had been brooding. They were grave rather than violent. Vic was quietly stern; he is developing quite an air of authority. What worried me most was the intransigence of people like Sid Greene and Sidney Robinson of the Boot and Shoe Operatives. (Frank wasn't there.) We went round and round the issue for an hour and a half and then they agreed to take the speech away and consider it properly.

Thursday, 17 April. The sun was shining brilliantly as I left Heathrow for Glasgow. The press interest in my visit to the Scottish TUC was phenomenal. Douglas warned me there were stories that chaps at the ferry to Rothesay were going to go on a lightning strike when I tried to board and I said OK, I'd face it out. Instead, smiles and waves everywhere with the crew posing for photos with me at the slightest opportunity. At Rothesay pier only two lonely demonstrators to whom I talked civilly and a crowd of women cheering madly. Officials of the Scottish TUC, led by the new President, Enoch Humphries, greeted me with every show of friendliness and I had quite a triumphal procession up to the hotel.

At the big dinner that evening there was a succession of short speeches which everyone kept light. John Matheson, chairman of the General Council, told me not to worry and to speak my mind tomorrow, while a number of chaps came up to me (GMW, I suspect) to tell me to stick to my guns. I began to have that Alice in Wonderland feeling again that I always get over this business of my Bill. Can it really be that I have outraged every trade union sentiment or are most of them going through an inevitable ritual dance of protest? Such friendliness to me as a person, yet such violently hostile resolutions.

Friday, 18 April. I went to bed relaxed, though I hadn't yet prepared a speech. Got up at 7 am to put a few headings together. I just can't bear those written speeches and hand-outs that put one's arguments in a set mould before one has even got the feel of one's audience. At last the great moment. Despite myself I was tense: the toughest audience in the trade union world, a vast battery of TV cameras and press. I didn't feel my usual resilience but apparently the speech impressed the press and most of the audience because of its content and above all because I went in fighting.

On by helicopter, in brilliant sunshine, to the Rootes factory at Linwood.

Here again, I learned later, the management had been fearful of a rough reception. But when the helicopter landed in its enclosed space I saw phalanxes of workers lining the wires. (It was their lunch break.) The managing director tried to wave me to a waiting car away from the wire, but I turned and walked towards the cheerful crowd – an old electoral instinct, I suppose. They waved and I waved back and one of the women called out, 'Come in at the workers' gate, Barbara', so I wheeled round, and so did the bosses, and we all walked through the workers' gate to a cheer. It was then that one of life's lucky flukes occurred. A young apprentice leaning over the wire called out to me, 'Give us a kiss, Barbara.' 'Of course,' I replied and held up my face. A great roar of delight went up and I prayed that the cameras had been around. They had! Only to my distress I found that, in reaching up, I had shown my petticoat under my red dress and then and there I swore I would find half an hour in my busy life to go to Marks and buy some new mini petticoats!

And so it went on all day: the women calling out, 'You do look nice', and some of the men booing mildly as I went through the 'militant' shops. (Apparently the Vehicle Builders are the militant boys here.) But no hostile demonstrations, only a young lad jumping down from the assembly line with 'Think again, Barbara' spelt out on his white jumper, clutching my hand earnestly while he said, 'Think again. We are your friends.' I held on to his hand asking *him* to think again because I was *his* friend, as my White Paper showed. And at the end of my tour I met, at my insistent request, some forty of the shop stewards over tea. Photographers tried to hang around but I said firmly, 'Press OUT,' and the men added, 'Management OUT,' so I repeated it. We had a good round-table conference for over an hour. These are my people in a way that the bosses never will be.

Saturday, 19 April. Another triumphal day, first with the Junior Chamber of Commerce at Edinburgh, then with a regional conference of the Scottish Labour Party. In both cases I spoke without notes – and effectively. So effectively to the latter that three-quarters of the audience rose spontaneously to its feet. The local Labour parties are obviously much more in tune with my White Paper than the trade union establishment is. But the most interesting moment came as I was waiting for my plane back from Edinburgh. An employee of the airport, dressed in some kind of airport boilersuit uniform, said to me, 'Did they give you a rough time at the Scottish TUC yesterday? No? I thought they would.' He turned out to be the TGWU convener, who went on, 'When I first read your White Paper my instinct was to throw it into the wastepaper basket. Then I read it again: three times in all. And I kept finding in it things I've been asking for in vain for years, even from a nationalized industry. More information; the check-off. As for strike ballots, I wouldn't dream of calling my lads out without taking a ballot first.' My Alice in Wonderland feeling deepens!

Wednesday, 23 April. After the P and I Committee meeting at noon Roy took me aside. He was desperately anxious that the effort to establish an inner Cabinet shouldn't fail. I told him that Dick and I were trying to see Harold, which was an obvious relief to him. He said he thought that it was far better that

Dick and I should press for this than for him to become embroiled; otherwise Harold would suspect an intrigue.

Thursday, 24 April. Had an early word with Dick. Harold is still dodging seeing us. Dick had suggested that we went out to Chequers about 6 pm on Sunday but Harold had made some excuse for saying no. Nor could he see us after Cabinet; we'd have to wait till after SEP next week.

Monday, 28 April. Off to Portsmouth for the annual conference of the Metal Mechanics. I was on form and, despite the fact that they have a number of resolutions down against my WP, I got a standing ovation. It won't alter the vote because they all are pre-mandated, but, I was assured, it would change attitudes.

Tuesday, 29 April. At last Harold has agreed to see us. He greeted us in his study and, almost before Dick could start on what we wanted to say, he chipped in to tell us he had some news that might make some of what we had to say unnecessary: he had decided to wind up the Parliamentary Committee and have an inner Cabinet instead, probably of seven people. We were taken aback. Never have the walls of Jericho fallen so easily! We explained why we wanted it: Dick said bilateral talks were not good enough, while I urged the need for a body that could give us both coherence and continuity of strategy, linking together all the key issues from Northern Ireland to the state of sterling. 'And if you are going to do that,' added Dick, 'you must clearly have in the inner group people you can trust and by definition that rules out Jim.' Harold nodded at that and then went on to say that the next thing he was going to do was to replace Silkin as Chief Whip. John was making an increasing number of mistakes (*e.g.* calling a vote of confidence on the Budget without consulting Harold) and the PLP was disintegrating. 'And he's lazy, too,' snorted Dick. I was appalled and told Harold bluntly that this Government was in no position to impose discipline because MPs no longer felt they had anything to lose. 'As long as they feel the Government has failed, they are in no mood to accept our authority and I can't blame them. The first priority is an inner strategy for success – then we can talk about loyalty.' I was brutally blunt and Harold took it extraordinarily meekly – as Dick and I said afterwards, he is in a completely new receptive mood. Dick wasn't as pro-Silkin as I was. He merely looked at his boots and then said gruffly, 'It all depends on who you are going to put in John's place.' Silence from Harold who tried to look vacant.

Our time being up, we all went downstairs and I went back to the office for a meeting on the drafting of the IR Bill. I am insisting on spelling out the *status quo* in the Bill.

I was working in my room in the House (three-line whip on the Post Office Bill) when Douglas phoned to tell me that Mr Silkin had gone to the Ministry of Works and that Mr Mellish had replaced him as Chief Whip. I thanked him, put down the phone and sat dazed. My first feeling was sadness. Only last night we had been plotting gaily how to get my Bill through and John had been saying how he would never desert Harold or the Left: 'They are my sort of people.' My next feeling was anger which rose in me slowly, coldly and massively. So *this* was what Harold had been hinting at this morning. He had known what announcement he was about to make and he hadn't even had the courtesy to tell us. Mellish! How the hell could I get my Bill through if the Healeyites had won their battle for a Chief Whip who would dragoon the Party and who would have no subtlety? I went in to Dick next door in explosive mood and suggested we eat together.

Over dinner I felt my anger rising coldly and uncontrollably. 'I'm through with Harold now,' I told him. 'Henceforth I dedicate myself to his destruction. I'm going to write him the sort of letter on which he ought to ask for my resignation.' He replied that he didn't blame me. Harold's behaviour had been inexcusable. 'Grotesque,' I spat out. 'Grotesque.' Apparently Harold had sent for Dick just before the announcement and had told him what he intended. Dick had warned him I would be very angry and that he couldn't blame me, at which Harold had looked very nervous. But who would I put in Harold's place? asked Dick. He added, 'It's only me or you.' I told Dick that I wouldn't shrink from leadership but that I had quite deliberately and consciously excluded myself from the running by my sponsorship of the Bill. ('I'm afraid that's true. If I thought you would take it I would back you.') I was, I said, ready to serve under Dick, but a) I didn't think he really wanted to take on such a burden ('That's right, too. I care about my family too much'), and b) there would be a number of issues on which I would fight him tooth and nail, like Rhodesia. 'What is left, then?' asked Dick. 'Just this,' I replied. 'I am now looking for an excuse to extricate myself.' 'So you've come round to my point of view. We must get ready for opposition – a Bevanite movement again.' 'No,' I told him emphatically. 'I'll never join the remnants of the Bevanites again. They are too negative. I've no use for political virgins.'

An unhappy meal, at which neither of us knew what must be the next step. I despise opposition for opposition's sake. I am convinced that my White Paper policy is the only way to give that injection of effectiveness into the trade union movement we used to talk about on the Left. I went off to write a more blistering letter to Harold than I would ever have believed possible, including the words: 'If the strategy is to railroad my Bill through Parliament by a Healey-type restrictive discipline of the Left, I will have no part of it.' At 11.30 pm I dropped it in at No. 10 on my way home.

Back at John Spencer Square I told Ted what I had done, adding, 'We had better take the receiver off the hook. I'm not going to talk to him tonight.' The words were barely out of my mouth when the phone rang. I hissed at Ted, 'Tell them I'm not at home and you don't know whether I am coming home at all.' As I said it I realized how near I had come to resignation. A Cabinet Minister must, by definition, always be get-at-able by the Prime Minister. Sure enough it was No. 10. Ted, wretchedly, tried to spell out my message and then we took the receiver off the hook. I went to bed and slept peacefully.

Wednesday, 30 April. I was just supping my morning tea when the phone rang. It was Douglas. He had been phoned early by No. 10. The PM wanted to see me. I informed him I would look in briefly at No. 10 at 9.30 am.

I walked into Harold's study unabashed, even though I was sure he would never forgive me. This time I don't care. I greeted him coldly. 'I thought we had better talk as soon as possible about your letter,' he said nervously. 'I tried to phone you last night but your phone was out of order.' 'Yes,' was all I said. He then went into an explanation as to why he hadn't told me about Mellish's appointment yesterday. 'I said I would come back to it later and then our time ran out.' That was a lie. Next he said he had hoped to talk to Dick and me last weekend at Chequers but that I hadn't been available. That, too, was a lie. I told him coldly that I thought we had now lost all chance of getting my Bill through. 'It isn't just your Bill,' he said gently. 'I am as committed to it as you are.' That, of course, is true. He assured me that the appointment of Mellish didn't mean that he was going to 'clobber the Left' but it was the middle-of-the-roaders who would give us our majority on the Bill – never the Left – and they had become disillusioned with Silkin. At this inconclusive point he had to go down to a meeting and I stalked out, having yielded nothing, went to Ginala and bought three new dresses to steady my morale. I am now really frightened at Harold's state.

I just got to the Party meeting on time. Almost every speech was against us. Harold, who slipped in and sat next to me, distracted me with his interjections. Then my turn came. I started rather hesitantly, but spoke from inner conviction and the crescendo rose out of my very vitals. I am always at my best when everything seems against me and at the end I got something very near an ovation. Afterwards people came streaming up to me to congratulate. 'Superb,' said Harold. 'Even better than your last one.' But I sense now that my triumphs demoralize him even further. And I have developed an odd capacity for making a lot of my failures (they seem natural) while I suspect the validity of my successes.

I was working at my room in the House when Dick suddenly dashed in to ask, 'How did it go?', sending Pat Edwards of my Private Office flying into the corridor in a flurry of civil service discretion. I told Dick briefly and he said Harold had rung him last night after receiving my letter. He was in a terrible state. 'I told him that he must see you and that his behaviour to you had been intolerable. He replied, "I shan't sleep tonight", and rang off.' Dick was sure I was right not to have melted. Anyway we are by no means sure yet of our inner Cabinet. I have told Ted that Jim is definitely out, but no announcement as to membership has been made. 'You watch,' said Dick contemptuously. 'Jim will be in.' We believe that Harold is going through one of his agonies of indecision. This time we mean to make him sweat it out.

Thursday, 1 May. Up early for OPD. The interesting thing is that Harold wasn't there. Michael reported that he had a 'tummy upset' but that he might manage to get to Cabinet.

However, when Cabinet met shortly afterwards, still no Harold. 'I've been upstairs to see him,' said Michael, 'and I was glad to find him surrounded by papers.' 'Sinister,' commented Denis audibly. Yes, it is in a way. It means, in my view, that Harold is dodging something. Is it that he is completely demoralized? It may be a psychosomatic illness to which I have contributed. Alternatively, of course, it may be that he is playing for time in which to settle the vexed question of the membership of the inner Cabinet, on which the rumours in the press now are that Jim is in. It is probably a mixture of the two.

Harold is terrified of leaving Jim out and terrified of telling Dick and me that he believes Jim must be in.

Sunday, 4 May. Harold has had a triumph at the Festival Hall. His capacity for comebacks is remarkable and I'm relieved. He really was becoming almost paralysed with indecision.

Monday, 5 May. At last the first meeting of the inner Cabinet! And, of course, Jim is in. We had a preliminary discussion as to how we should plan our work on what Harold said he was going to call the Management Committee. We agreed the meetings should be informal, frank and forward looking; that Burke should attend; there should be no Minutes but (as Dick wisely suggested) our decisions should be recorded. These would not be reported to Cabinet as they would be purely private ones, but we hoped that we would as far as possible agree on a united line on key issues. Harold said everyone should come 'without any external interest or *arrière pensée*' so that we could meet on a basis of trust – the nearest he got to a warning to Jim. [He] then astonished us by saying that each of us could appoint someone to act as our 'political cabinet': a politician, too, not a civil servant, if we wanted to. Altogether not a bad start.

Wednesday, 7 May. Arrived late for our second PLP meeting on the IR Bill, having had to attend that boring institution, NEDC. John Fraser intercepted me to say that in opening the meeting Houghton had dropped a bombshell, more or less saying that the Government would have to compromise over the Bill.[1] All speeches built on this (except Woodrow Wyatt's, which didn't help). The PLP clearly had the bit between its teeth. Everyone seized on Houghton's speech as though it was a lifeline. Fortunately this time it was agreed I shouldn't speak, but wind up at the end of the next meeting. But the mood of the meeting in its inchoate escapism only toughened my resolve. This Party must be pulled together somehow, but threats won't do it. Let's face it, our threats as a Government are no longer credible.

I rushed back to the office to be ready for the members of the PLP I had asked in for drinks at Joel Barnett's suggestion. They came pouring in, full of a speech which Jack Jones had made to the Economic group on my Bill. Naturally Eric Heffer was impressed, but when Joel started applauding, too, I began to get impatient. Eric spelt out Jack's ideas to me. They were facile and one-sided, but how does one explain this without seeming an utter reactionary? From the word go this was a meeting going to the heart of things. They were a disparate lot – Bob Sheldon, Jimmie Dickens, Mike, Jimmie Hamilton,[2] Joan Lestor, John Horner, Frank Judd[3] and, of course, John Fraser – but we were united in a desperate need to get down to fundamentals without personal recrimination. By the time they had all had a go at me about my Bill, from widely different points of view, I knew what was wrong with the Party. It is true, of course, as I

1 He was reported as warning the Government against believing that its determination to force things through the Party and the House of Commons was 'either necessary or desirable'. Nothing the Bill might do to improve industrial relations would 'redeem the harm we can do to our movement and to the nation by the disintegration or defeat of the Labour Party'.

2 Labour MP for Bothwell.

3 Labour MP for Portsmouth West since 1966.

said, with Jimmie Dickens nodding sagely, that the real trouble isn't my Bill at all: it is concern about the Government's whole economic strategy. The process of 'transference' is at work; Nye's remark after the 1959 Election came to my mind: 'People have rationalized their reasons for voting Conservative because they are ashamed of the real ones.' But it is equally true that we will not get out of our mess by disintegrating. That, too, was their fear – but they are making disintegration a reality.

Take Joel Barnett, for instance. Months ago, as I reminded him, he had told me that in my WP the Government had at last produced a policy which he could support wholeheartedly. Yet here he was panicking. I pointed out to them that there were as many views about my Bill in the room as there were people. If we were the Cabinet, we would be disagreeing passionately. Yet in the end we would have to cohere around *some* view, even if we all marginally disagreed with it. The trouble with the PLP, I told them, was that it would now only cohere *against* the Government. But the credibility of some of us was at stake. As Mendès-France had said, 'To govern is to choose.' Yet they were running away from choices. And I told Mike flatly that he had grown soft on a diet of soft options because he never had to choose. I told them, too, that I utterly rejected Bob Mellish's threat that, if they did not vote for the IR Bill, the alternative was a General Election. We had no right, I protested, to try and dragoon the PLP with the threat that otherwise we would destroy it. They had a perfect right to reject my Bill but, if they did so, they could not take away from me my right to destroy myself. 'You have a right to say you will not sustain the Government. OK, but then you must find yourself a new Government.' They were appalled at the idea. 'You mustn't go. You are too valuable. And, if you go, other people will have to go, too.' I told them that this was the inexorable logic of their attitude. I did not believe that there was a will in the PLP to sustain this Government in power. Joel was plunged into gloom: 'You've made me feel terrible again.' Of course I had. He had come in inflated with the euphoria of Houghton's phoney alternative. They couldn't even see that Jim and Houghton are playing in double harness, like a comic and his feed man.

In the end Mike pleaded with me desperately that at least we should postpone the introduction of my Bill until after the Special Congress of the TUC. I challenged him, 'And if the Congress comes up with nothing, will you back me then?' 'No,' he said honestly. 'There you are,' I replied, but the others rushed in to assure me that he didn't represent their view. And so we left it and parted, shaken deeply and near to tears. But I believe, now, we must postpone till after the TUC Special Congress on 5 June. That much at least they have a right to ask of us.

Thursday, 8 May. I was full of last night's meeting (and I'm encouraged by the fact that Ted sees Houghton's speech for the calculated political snare it is). I wanted to report it to Harold, Roy and Dick before we met in inner Cabinet with the snake, Callaghan, lurking in the grass. And so it was arranged. But first we had to go through Cabinet. Dick told me that Harold was determined to raise the constitutional issue of Houghton's speech. I thought this would be counter-productive, as all threats without action are. But nonetheless Harold went ahead and soon had Denis telling him it wasn't a constitutional issue at all.

It was a matter of 'political wisdom' and it was from that point of view that Houghton's speech should be condemned. Bob Mellish pleaded that there should be no dressing down: we must play for time, quietness and coolness.

Jim started to widen the issue on to the merits of the IR Bill, urging that at least we should not introduce the Bill until after the June congress. My heart sank: I can see Jim claiming the credit for this now, when we anounce that we will do it, and I wished Harold had never raised the Houghton matter at all. But suddenly Dick launched into a ferocious attack, obviously aimed at Jim. Some people, he said, believed they could get us off the hook by ditching Harold and finding another leader. That was obviously why Houghton had made the speech. Why else should he have done it in municipal election week? It wasn't a spontaneous speech, but deliberately calculated, written out and given to the press – and totally unnecessary in the middle of continuing discussions with the PLP. But the plotters had better realize that it wouldn't work: 'four of the inner heart of the Cabinet couldn't and wouldn't serve' under the supplanter. We would sink or swim together. 'Sink or sink,' interposed Jim. Dick rounded on him: how could he work with the rest of us when he believed the next Election was already lost? Defeatism that starts in the Cabinet spreads everywhere. 'If my colleagues want me to go, I will,' murmured Jim unctuously. Dick flashed back at him, 'Why don't you go? Get out!' We all sat electrified till Harold intervened soothingly, 'We don't want you to go. We think you should stay and be convinced.' Nonetheless I could see he was secretly delighted.

Roy, Dick and I sneaked into Harold's room after his Questions. We are now in the absurd position that, thanks to Jim, we have to have an inner 'inner Cabinet'. I told them what had happened last night and how sorry I was that the Houghton issue had been raised that morning as it had given Jim his chance to ask for the Bill to be postponed which I was going to press for anyway. But Roy and Harold were delighted with Dick for telling off Jim, and Harold assured me he would steer the discussion at inner Cabinet so as to indicate that he and I had already been discussing the possibility of postponing the Bill.

The inner Cabinet meeting half an hour later was a farce. Harold duly passed the ball to me to play about the postponement of the IR Bill. Jim welcomed this gravely, but we didn't get down to real strategy on the Bill with him there.

Friday, 9 May. Hell Corner was a glory of beech green and cherry blossom in the morning sunshine as I left early for No. 10. I felt utterly disinclined for a day-long tough confrontation with the NEC. Typically – for our movement – it turned out to be far more genial than tough. Joe Gormley, John Chalmers of the Boilermakers[1] and the rest made noises about the IR Bill, but didn't press them. Obviously, like the PLP, they are praying for some miracle from Monday's meeting with the TUC to save us all. Another utterly unscrupulous attempt by Jim to play to the trade union gallery over my Bill (we should stop describing the trade union movement as 'ante-diluvian' and 'the Government's job is to build up the popularity of the trade union movement') fell totally flat. Not a hint of a clap from anyone. When Eirene called on me to wind up, I moved in systematically for the kill.

[1] He had succeeded Danny McGarvey on the trade union section of the NEC in 1966.

I dealt with everyone in turn: Mik over P and I policy, the trade unions over their split personality ('We have just not worked out a philosophy of wages'), and finally Jim. I listed all the pro-trade union legislation we have already carried out and then turned to the NEC statement on Industrial Democracy. The document from Transport House said that the Government ought to have another sympathetic look at it. OK: so I had. And I found that every one of its proposals had already been implemented by the Government or were in my White Paper on Industrial Relations including the Trade Union Development Scheme. How I rubbed their noses in that! Here it was in the document drawn up largely under the inspiration of Jack Jones, Frank Cousins's lieutenant, yet all of them, including Frank, had poured scorn on it as a typical Government gimmick! And finally I rounded on Jim. With one of those premeditated bursts of anger which I occasionally organize, I told him he ought to be ashamed of himself for suggesting we had described the trade union movement as 'antediluvian'. On the contrary, we had deliberately and effectively built up trade union power and this was the aim of the WP. I wasn't going to enter into controversial details as we were in the middle of discussions with the TUC. No one would be more pleased than us if the trade union movement would do the job of reform itself. But it was no part of the Government's job to 'make the trade union movement popular'. Our job was to build up the strength, authority and status of the trade union movement so that it could make *itself* popular.

I was astonished at the warmth of the applause for my speech and by the plaudits I got afterwards. It is too good to be true! But what pleased me most was the reaction of people like Tom Bradley[1] and Joe Gormley, the repositories of the rights of the trade unions – and of Mik who, apart from saying that I was getting 'too tense', went out of his way to try to restore our old relationship. We ate our buffet lunch in the same corner together while he assured me that he had no doubts first about the value of most of my WP, and secondly about my sincerity. It was nice to be on the old warm terms with my old friends again.

Altogether a successful day with everyone united in trying to keep a Labour Government in power. But then I had to hang around till 8 pm for the private dinner with Harold and Vic. Eventually we had to smuggle Vic in through the back door of No. 10 because the press were still lingering outside. Over dinner Vic began by being truculent. He had sent Harold and me a copy of the TUC's document privately,[2] and when we began to criticize the part of it dealing with unconstitutional strikes as too vague he tried to get high-handed. I was rather snappy with him while Harold was at his most conspiratorial. Under pressure Vic admitted that the TUC document had 'soft edges', but maintained that if he had taken his proposals any further he wouldn't have got away with it. But he added, encouragingly, 'I don't mind how diamond-hard you go, so long as it comes from you.' And it is encouraging, too, that the whole General Council

[1] Labour MP for Leicester North-East and President of the TSSA. He had taken Ray Gunter's place on the trade union section of the NEC.

[2] The General Council were preparing a statement for Special Congress rejecting the penal clauses of the White Paper and setting out positive steps the TUC was ready to take to deal with the problem of strikes. Vic Feather's first draft was woolly on crucial points.

will be at Monday's meeting, which means that Hughie Scanlon and Jack Jones will be there. We agreed that this would be a 'crunch' meeting, but not a final one. I excused myself after dinner and left them conspiring over the brandy.

Monday, 12 May. Got up early to fly to Southport for the NUPE conference. These Government planes do cut down the travelling time fantastically: we really ought to have more of them for Ministers' regular use. At NUPE they gave me a genuine standing ovation, though I was by no means at my best. Back in London Conrad was waiting to brief me as we raced to the meeting with the TUC at No. 10 to discuss their document. Everyone was there and once again there was a pleasant surprise in the atmosphere. Even Frank contained himself, while Hughie seemed really anxious for an agreement. What a long way we have travelled from the first negative reactions by them all to the WP! After two and a half hours it was agreed that we should send the TUC our comments and questions for their next meeting on Thursday and then meet again next week.

Everyone is speculating as to whether Harold will or should now sack Jim. He certainly won't resign voluntarily and I am against making a martyr of him. When Harold called Roy, Dick and me together he started on his old tack of saying we should administer a collective rebuke, but Dick and Roy told him firmly that it was impossible for Jim to remain a member of the inner Cabinet. How could we discuss tactics or policy on the Bill with a spy in our midst? They insisted, too, that Harold should see Jim beforehand and tell him he was out of the inner Cabinet. Harold duly agreed and Dick was quite triumphant afterwards. I said I would believe it when it happened.

Tuesday, 13 May. An early P and I meeting ended abruptly and I found myself hanging around at No. 10, killing time for the 10.30 meeting of the Management Committee, when Jim arrived. An awkward moment, particularly as he came up to me at his most ingratiating to say, 'There was nothing personal about you in what I said on Friday.' I'm not good at pretending, so replied coldly that I wasn't concerned about my personal position: it was a matter of collective loyalty. Then he was called in to see Harold. So Harold was sticking by his decision after all! Yes, this had been the great moment, as we learned half an hour later. Harold informed us in Management Committee of what he had done and there was a long discussion as to what should be said publicly about it. I was alarmed when Harold began, 'By mutual agreement Jim is no longer a member of the Management Committee.' I really believe he was going to present it that way till we stopped him. As someone pointed out, it would look as though members of Cabinet could pick and choose their committees to save themselves embarrassment. Harold insisted that the main reason for sacking him was that he was working on the assumption that we were going to lose the next Election, but again we pointed out that we could hardly say that publicly. Nor was it possible to stress the disagreements over the IR Bill. Eventually we agreed that no reason should be given at all: let Jim do the briefing and put himself in the wrong. We then had a detailed discussion of the IR Bill. As Dick said afterwards, for the first time we really did get down to constructive team discussion, thanks to the absence of Jim.

On 19 May the General Council had finalized their statement for the Special Congress, headed 'Programme for Action'. Following our criticisms of their original draft they had firmed up their alternative proposals for dealing with the problems referred to in the interim Bill: inter-union disputes and constitutional strikes. The document pointed out that under the TUC*'s Rule 12 the General Council already had considerable power to deal with inter-union disputes. They could summon the contending parties to appear before their Disputes Committee and discipline a union which failed to accept its findings, either by reporting it to the next Annual Congress or by dealing with it under the disciplinary Rule 13,* i.e. *suspend it from membership. They were prepared to strengthen Rule 12 still further by laying down that no affiliated union should authorize a stoppage of work until the General Council had considered the dispute and that, where an unauthorized stoppage had taken place, the union concerned would be put under an obligation 'to take immediate and energetic steps to obtain a resumption of work'. This went a long way to meet the Government's demands, but the proposed action against unconstitutional strikes was still not firm enough.*

True, 'Programme for Action' defined and denounced unconstitutional strikes for the first time. It admitted that where discussions were going on under satisfactory agreed procedures and the status quo *was operating, there should be no stoppage of work and 'the workpeople are constitutionally in the wrong if they strike before procedure is exhausted'. If a stoppage did take place, 'the union should take action to ensure that the workpeople return to work while discussions take place'. What was at issue between us was how this was to be enforced. The General Council maintained that this could be done under a strengthened Rule 11 which already placed an obligation on affiliated organizations to keep the General Council informed about disputes and empowered them to intervene where the effect on other workers was likely to be serious. It also provided that, where an organization refused the 'advice and assistance' offered, it should be reported to Congress – a step which unions took seriously. The rule was primarily intended to deal with official disputes, but 'Programme for Action' now proposed to extend it specifically to cover 'unauthorized and unconstitutional stoppages' and to ensure that the disciplinary action of Rule 13 could be applied to recalcitrant unions.*

What the General Council had in mind was elaborated in Paragraph 42 of the document. The General Council, it said, would 'require unions to satisfy them that they had done all that they could reasonably be expected to do to secure compliance with a recommendation (or an award where this has been made), including taking action under their own rules where necessary.' They recognized that 'a few unions may need to review their own rules to ensure that they are in a position to comply with recommendations or awards by the TUC*.' Harold Wilson and I welcomed this proposed strengthening of the role of the* TUC *as an important step forward, but pointed out that it did not seem to be adequately reflected in the amendments to rules set out in the document. In particular the document did not spell out an obligation on unions to revise their rules where necessary and we pressed for the words 'may need to' (revise their own rules) to be changed to 'must'. Our demand for more amendments to Paragraph 42 and to Rule 11 was to take us nearly to breaking-point with the* TUC.

In the meantime continuing economic difficulties had forced Roy Jenkins to seek another line of credit from the IMF *in order to help him repay previous debts which were falling due. In order to raise the money he had to send a Letter of Intent to the* IMF *and its contents were highly disturbing to some of us. In it he committed himself to tough monetarist and fiscal policies designed to swing our balance of payments deficit into a surplus of £300 million, with obvious effects on unemployment, while committing himself to 'maintain the present degree of trade liberalization' and to abolish as soon as possible the restrictions on travel expenditure and the import deposit scheme, thus ruling out any alternative economic strategy. When the Letter was debated in the House on 25 June some forty Labour MPs tabled a motion demanding mobilization of overseas portfolio investment, further restrictions on capital outflow, the introduction of selective import controls and further cuts in defence, though most of them reluctantly toed the line in the vote.*

Tuesday, 20 May. At Management Committee I reported David Basnett's assurance to me last night that he thought the TUC would not proceed with its own proposals if we legislated for penal powers, even if they were suspended.[1] (The whole point of an inner Cabinet is that we should face facts frankly.) Harold said that there must be another meeting with the TUC after the Special Congress at Croydon and before the introduction of the Bill, even if that meant further delay, and that Dick and I with the Lord President and Chief Whip must work out alternative timetables. But there would also be strictly private discussions with a few key TUC people during the recess of which even the General Council wouldn't know. He was certain I must not interrupt my holiday as I should need all the rest I could get and was equally determined not to see anyone alone as he wasn't going to let them try and drive a wedge between him and me on the false assumption that he was a dove and I a hawk. Perhaps the way out would be for the Chancellor to be present as a hawkish watchdog in my place. I told Harold I would like to discuss the holiday arrangements with him so as to find a way out.

We then turned ourselves (except for Dick and plus Tony C.) into MISC 205 to consider the Letter of Intent of which the draft was handed round the table. Roy made it clear that we must have $500m as soon as possible because of the sums we had lost during the mark revaluation speculation. Whether he took the second $500m depended on whether we were prepared to go on carrying out the terms. I said I didn't mind our going for the money now provided it was understood we should have a full review of strategy immediately after the Whit recess. Roy accepted this, though it is clear that he has doubts about import quotas. All we have done is to postpone the real fight.

I was going through the lobby late at night when Stan Orme came up to me wild-eyed. 'What about your friend Johnnie Boyd now?' he almost raved. I was interested to see how appalled the Left are at the decision of the AEF Executive to turn down the TUC proposals: apparently this is due to an unexpected line-up of Reg Birch and Johnnie Boyd. Johnnie's vote swung it (Hughie abstaining as President) so the Left are furious with him. I can't help chuckling, though it is sinister, too.

Wednesday, 21 May. Got an urgent note from John Horner [Labour MP for Oldbury and Halesowen] urging that Harold and I should not make too much of the AEF vote as 'moves' were already underway. We had already decided not to refer to it at this morning's meeting with the TUC. The General Council were

[1] David Basnett was a member of the Executive of the General and Municipal Workers' Union and of the General Council of the TUC.

there in force again and Vic began, at Harold's request, by spelling out their answer to the points in our letter, particularly to our request that they should strengthen Paragraph 42. His speech didn't get us very far, because it was so complacent. First he warned us that a 'pre-requisite' of the TUC proposals was that there should be no penal clauses in our legislation, but I listened very carefully to his wording here and he did *not* issue an ultimatum in specific terms as Hughie and Jack had wanted him to. He assured us that there would be rapid intervention in disputes by trade union officers: 'that always happens anyway'(!) The TUC was *not* expecting the trade unions to write into their rules a specific reference to unconstitutional strikes as the existing rules were wide enough to cover this. As for enforcement, there had been 1,000 awards or recommendations by the TUC in the last thirty years and in only one case had the award been defied. Only two unions had left the TUC rather than accept an award in the last fifty years. As for the *status quo*, this should be written into procedure agreements which would be more effective than the conciliation pause which only provided for the *status quo after* a strike had occurred. They did not, he said, suggest a trade union veto on all managerial action.

We then went over the old ground, apart from the points that Jim Mortimer had put to me last night. I had asked him to come and see me privately and tell me what he thought of the TUC proposals. He said he thought they went a very long way but that there should be more guarantee of urgent and serious efforts to end unconstitutional strikes, because trade union officials were very busy men and simply could not take on fire-fighting work effectively. The Government should be prepared to give the TUC a chance to show if its proposals would work but only in exchange for a detailed and specific plan, including the recruitment of a large number of additional officials for the job. But when I put these points to the meeting, the trade union chaps shuffled impatiently and obviously thought I was being difficult. In turn they urged that they were doing as much as they could be expected to do. At noon, Fred Hayday and a couple more came up to Harold to make their excuses and slipped away, so we wound up the meeting shortly afterwards. I was outraged to see headlines in the evening papers later declaring that 'wild-cat' trade union leaders had walked out on us in disgust. Worse still, our people believed it and the tea-room was buzzing with alarm. I assured them that nothing of the kind had happened and that once again they had been fooled by an alarmist press. In fact the meeting broke up amicably after a good deal of banter by Harold in cricketing terms. What we needed was a wicketkeeper, he quipped. As Ronnie McIntosh [Deputy Secretary at the Cabinet Office] whispered to him, we needed a 'copper-bottomed wicketkeeper'.

Harold and I then talked privately. He astonished me by saying cheerfully that he didn't see how we could get a settlement with the TUC, but he and I were now too committed to back down. He therefore intended to make this an issue of confidence in *him* and, if we were defeated, he would stand down from the leadership. The Government would drag on for a time and he could use this issue devastatingly against Heath. He clearly visualized that it wouldn't be long before he staged a comeback. I was delighted that he was no longer talking about threatening to force a General Election. I'm sure, if a crisis *does* come, this is the only way to handle it. But he instructed me not to tell Dick 'at this stage'. I then said that I was willing to fly back from my holiday for the secret talks.

Elaborate arrangements had been worked out for keeping the Prime Minister in touch with me during my holiday on Charles Forte's boat. These included a timetable of the boat's movements day by day and instructions as to how to contact me through the ship's telephone service. Conversations with or messages to me were to be in a rough and ready code in which 'Eagle' meant the Prime Minister and 'Peacock' the First Secretary. Someone had obviously had great fun allocating the names, making Dick Crossman 'Owl', the Chancellor 'Starling', Vic Feather 'Rhino', Frank Cousins 'Bull', Hugh Scanlon 'Bear' and Jack Jones 'Horse', while the General Council of the TUC went under the unflattering pseudonym of 'The Zoo'. The message 'Auntie has mumps' meant that the Prime Minister wanted the boat to go to port.

Friday, 23 May. On board at last! *Maria Luigi II* is sheer luxury. As [Dick's] Anne put it, it really does make life easier to have four crew looking after six people! Charles has even sent us Gino from the Café Royal to wait on us, which he does day and night most deftly. I feel uneasy about the whole thing but no one else – not even Harold – sees any harm in it.

Sunday, 25 May. Off Ponza, which we find far more attractive than Ischia (and certainly than Capri) because it is less exploited. We swim from the ship three times a day even though the water is not yet warm. This holiday is proving an eye opener on Dick's character. He certainly wants his own way in everything and sulks childishly when he can't get it. And he bullies those two nice children of his like a Victorian father. He is revealed as deeply selfish. How many of his sweeping political denunciations are dictated by pique? When he is getting his own way, however, he is good company and Anne and the children are delightful.

Thursday, 29 May. Ischia. Dick, of course, was all for climbing Mount Epomeo. His physical energy is fantastic. Ted and I went with him, thinking to escape the sticky sirocco up there. We certainly succeeded: the '*multo vente*' blew the umbrellas out of their sockets at the little restaurant perched on its shelf of rock at the very top. Broom and pines and vines tumbled luxuriously down the precipitous slopes below us and we could see *Maria Luigi II* dancing on the water in San Montano bay 3,000 feet down. After our strenuous hour's pull up the mule track we were in expansive mood. The ham omelette, salami and tomato salad were excellent and we knocked back two bottles of local wine.

Inevitably, we became aggressive and Dick and I were soon in a violent political argument. He was in one of his most *Götterdämmerung* moods, foreseeing disaster facing the Party as a result of the IR Bill; the PLP in revolt and the Party smashed in the Election: another 1931 again. I told him the Party need not be split. My own credibility was at stake, but I could resign quietly, as could others like Roy who were equally committed. Perhaps even Harold (though I carefully did *not* mention my conversation with him). 'Then we really *are* in a 1931 situation,' said Dick dramatically. 'There will be two sets of candidates: one backed by the trade unions and Transport House and the other not. You and Harold have faced us with this situation. You can understand now why we were so angry when you did all this without consulting us.' (Only he doesn't speak coherently like this: it comes out in a rush and if he is challenged he interrupts after the first two or three words, then breaks off and charges off on an entirely different tack. For a so-called stimulator of argument, he is a great bludgeoner.) I retorted that Cabinet had been free to make up its own mind, and had done so: the only person who had been at risk was myself for they had been free to repudiate me. And I reminded him that it was *he* who was responsible for our facing a crisis at this particular moment. *I* had never been in favour of rushing an interim Bill. And I taunted him, 'Thank God I've kept a diary, Dick, so there will be someone to challenge the Crossman version of history. And, by heavens, I will!' We got quite violent for unless one stands up to Dick he steamrollers the truth, but if one refuses to be a doormat one has positively to shout him down. This particular row ended when the restaurant closed and we had to start the long, exhausting, tortuous drop to Fario. The storm over, Dick was – as usual – much more reasonable and spent the rest of the holiday telling everyone about how we climbed Mount Epomeo.

One interesting point emerged during a quiet moment of the row. Dick said he had never been part of the pre-war Left. The Spanish civil war just hadn't interested him: 'I was with Bevan and Dalton on that.' 'Just as you are not stirred by Rhodesia,' I added. 'Quite,' he said. And when we discussed how Cabinet might split on the IR Bill, with Jim, Dick Marsh, Crosland, Tony Greenwood and Judith leading the rout, he said reluctantly, 'I suppose I should go with Harold, you and Roy.'

Sunday, 1 June. We moored at Mergellina at 9.45 am to find the consul (commercial) waiting. Fortunately no press! It transpired that Douglas had tried to phone the ship to recall me to London and been told we weren't answering. After that he scattered cables all over the place which never reached us. At last we were airborne in an Andover Mark 1, a big, bumbling, military transport plane which had been rigged out to receive us.

Conrad said he and Denis Barnes had had a long private talk with Vic, who insisted that the TUC couldn't give us 'must' instead of 'may' in Paragraph 42 of the TUC document. Vic's own preference was for putting off the whole Bill till next session to give the TUC a chance to show what it could do. He expected the TGWU Executive at its meeting on Wednesday to back the TUC proposals with the proviso that they should be suspended if the Government went ahead. He also expected that the AEF National Committee would reverse its previous decision against them. But altogether he was in a pretty gloomy mood.

It was raining when we arrived in England but the great park at Chequers looked unbelievably beautiful in its fresh green. Harold called me into his room to talk while he changed his shirt after golf. He was in ebullient mood. He agreed with the line taken by Dick, Bob and me at our meeting last week that the guillotine motion should be made the issue of confidence. But the guillotine motion would be made an issue of confidence in *him* personally. If it went against him, the Party wouldn't split: those of us who resigned would do so quietly and the Government would merely gradually come to an end. I believe he is positively looking forward to being free to bid for the recapture of the leadership in Opposition. It is clear to me that, for all his rebukes to Jim, he is himself resigned to our election defeat and is preoccupied with how he can outmanœuvre Jim and thwart his ambitions.

He agreed with Conrad Heron's suggestion as to how we should play the talks, namely that he should begin by saying the Government's credibility depended on there being an interim Bill and challenging the rest to say what should be in it. In the event it all went very differently. The atmosphere was positively jovial from the start. You would never have guessed that Hughie had just come from a speech declaring all-out war on us. Harold is an excellent host on these occasions: relaxed, witty, informal, doing the honours with relish but without any kind of side. We all joked at Vic's assiduousness in fetching us all second drinks as we stood before dinner in the great hall. 'After all, he isn't elected yet,' quipped Jack. 'It'll be very different when he is.' But Jack agreed with me that Vic would make a good – possibly a great – General Secretary: 'The best we have had for many, many years.'

The roast duck having been dispatched (Harold was the only one who drank beer instead of the superb wine), Harold got down to business: 'How do you see things now, Vic?' We were launched on a vigorous but rather discursive argument and my heart sank. However, over brandy in the long gallery the issues began gradually to crystallize out. As the talk went on, the franker we all got, led by Hughie, who is a much more open character than Jack Jones is. 'Let us face the reality,' he said. 'The question isn't whether our scheme works or your scheme works. It is the fact that our people won't accept Government intervention.' He reminded us bluntly that he was personally in a very difficult position, having led his people in all-out opposition to the WP. Moreover, he faced an election in the union and he could be accused of a *volte-face*. But he was prepared to back the TUC proposals at whatever cost.

Harold replied equally bluntly. He was worried about two things. If there were no legislation the TUC would lose its nerve. With legislation the Government would find itself in certain strike situations with which it could not cope. 'In a sense we are both right and both wrong.' But the Government's credibility was indissolubly linked with legislation. We were prepared to give the TUC the first chance, and every chance, to show what it could do. But unless there were much clearer indications of what the TUC would do, we must have reserve powers. Would they make binding awards as in the case of inter-union disputes? Jack and Hughie tried to argue that the situations in unconstitutional strikes varied so much that there must be flexibility, but I brought them up sharply against the central point. Of course we had to analyse the different types of strikes. My Bill would distinguish, as their document did, between strikes caused by the action of management and the rest (hence the *status quo*). But in those cases where the TUC itself admitted that adequate procedure was available and the striker was constitutionally in the wrong, what were the TUC prepared to do to see that the unions got the men back to work? They dodged that by saying our proposals wouldn't be effective either. I told Hughie this was the crux: establishing the *will* of unions to deal with unconstitutional strikes, instead of hiding behind them as a means of extorting concessions on the cheap. And I challenged them, 'Is it penal powers you are against, or legislation?

Because the penal powers need never operate if the TUC delivers the goods.' They said firmly legislation, Hughie adding that his own people would never accept the principle of powers a Tory Government could use. 'They'll never use *my* powers,' I retorted. 'They wouldn't suit their book at all.' 'If you say that, Hughie,' said Harold very quietly, very conversationally, 'then you are claiming to be the Government. I will never consent to preside over a Government that is not allowed to govern. And let us get one thing clear: that means we can't have a Labour Government for I am the only person who can lead a Labour Government.' ('We accept that.' 'Agreed.' 'None of us has ever suggested anyone else,' they chorused.) 'Well,' continued Harold, 'there are two types of Prime Minister I have made up my mind I will never be: one is a Ramsay MacDonald and the second is a Dubcek. I'm not going to surrender to your tanks, Hughie.'

And so we went round in circles, Hughie and Jack remaining adamant – Hughie almost trying to instruct Vic that in his speech at Croydon he should commit the TUC publicly to abandoning its own proposals if the Government went ahead in any form. Vic sat sadly, saying almost nothing. Not, added Hughie, that the TUC would necessarily do nothing, particularly about inter-union disputes, but 'Programme for Action' would be torn up. It being now past midnight, I said, 'Since we are now in a crisis which is clearly irresolvable, may I go to bed?' Harold said there was still another meeting ahead of us: with the General Council on Monday, 9 June. 'Does this mean you will have an open mind, Harold?' asked Jack as they got out their diaries. 'As open as I think your minds are,' he replied. 'Fair enough.' 'What makes you think that is fair, Jack?' quipped Hughie. 'Come and see me before you leave in the morning,' said Harold as I slipped off to bed.

Monday, 2 June. Harold was eating breakfast in bed as I went in to see him at 8.15. 'It's about as black as it can be,' was his greeting. 'Those two only want the TUC proposals in order to avoid legislation, not because they believe in them.' I suggested the time had come for us to restore the initiative by sending [a] letter I had proposed, setting out our requirements for the amendment of Paragraph 42. If the Special Congress turned our letter down, they would be on the defensive when the crunch came.

I went downstairs to greet Conrad and Douglas and we strolled in the rose garden waiting for Harold to join us. It was a glorious June morning: cool breeze and a hot sun. When Harold came down I urged that Conrad Heron should prepare a detailed paper setting out the pros and cons for Sunday's Management Committee and it was agreed he should also fly out to Italy tomorrow to clear with me my letter for the TUC. Mr Ford, the consul (commercial), was waiting for me when I got back to Naples and we made complicated arrangements for joining up with Conrad at Herculaneum tomorrow.

Tuesday, 3 June. The weather had deteriorated disappointingly and we had to wait for the rain to stop before leaving for Herculaneum. After a hurried tour Ted and I had to leave for our rendezvous 'in the nearest café to the station' at 2.15. We were just traipsing despondently up Risena's main street when we were hailed by the consul's car. Out piled Conrad, Douglas and Mr Ford. Relief! We could now find somewhere tolerable to eat. So it was in a modest restaurant in Risena, over omelette and *vino bianco secco*, that what Ted called 'the Treaty of Herculaneum' was signed. Conrad's draft was just adequate, but needed pointing up at key points. Then they dashed off to catch a plane back to London, leaving us to splash our way back in the rain.

Rang Douglas at the office at 10 pm. The letter,[1] he said, had been dispatched to Vic who had hit the roof and was demanding to see Eagle. I might be wanted on the phone to discuss it with Eagle the next day.

Wednesday, 4 June. The weather continued poor. We made a choppy journey to Capri but I had to hang around on the boat while Ford rang London. Answer: no message from Eagle and it was not considered likely that I would be needed to speak to him that day. I wonder what he has decided to do?

*The Special Congress at Croydon on 5 June had endorsed the General Council's proposals by 7,908,000 votes to 846,000 – a majority of over seven million. Congress's 'unalterable opposition' to financial penalties had also been carried by 8,252,000 votes to 359,000. A third motion, welcoming certain proposals in the White Paper (*i.e. *the ones strengthening trade union rights), obtained a majority of nearly 8½ million. Although the General Council had rejected our pleas to strengthen Paragraph 42 and Rule 11, the size of the majorities for 'Programme for Action' and the tone of the debate had impressed the journalists present and the press reports had been very favourable to the TUC's initiative. This gave us an opportunity, if we had wanted it, to suspend the legislation in order to see what the TUC could do. I was therefore astonished to learn on my return from holiday that in my absence and without consulting me Harold Wilson had issued a statement over my name rejecting the proposals on unconstitutional strikes as inadequate. I found that he had, if anything, toughened his attitude and committed us still more deeply to the indispensability of the rule change.*

Friday, 6 June. Left Naples in the middle of one of the worst hailstorms I have ever seen! Douglas was waiting at Heathrow to explain why a statement on the Government's reaction to the Special Congress has been issued in my name without consulting me. The papers are full of it: the *Telegraph*, true to form, carrying the headline, 'Mrs Castle snubs unions'. I was furious. It has, in my view, reduced our room for manœuvre. Harold was very relaxed about it when I phoned him indignantly: said Vic had calmed down about our letter and that he was seeing him again that night. He felt it was necessary to do something to check the post-Croydon euphoria. All the papers, of course, are full of how far the unions have moved, so he said we had to toughen things up again. Harold certainly seems very firm.

[1] In it I repeated our view that 'Programme for Action' did not go far enough on unconstitutional strikes. 'The discussion of 21 May', I wrote, 'showed that the General Council do not regard Paragraph 42 as a commitment to ensure that where the TUC have recommended a return to work and persuasion by the union fails to secure this, the union will take action within its rules, including the exercise of disciplinary powers against members who remain on strike. Nor does the report provide that where a union fails to take such action, the General Council will instruct it to do so and, failing a satisfactory response, will take action against the union concerned under Congress Rule 13.'

Sunday, 8 June. It was hell tearing myself away from the garden at 4 pm to go to the office. As Ted said, 'On a day like this England is Arcady.' At the office all my officials were in shirt-sleeves.

Then into the Management Committee. Harold put them in the picture about the Chequers meeting while Dick sat doodling sourly. Harold warned that the TUC seemed serious about withdrawing its own proposals if we went ahead and circulated Conrad's paper. I was surprised at how depressed they all seemed. Denis, usually adamant, said Vic had manœuvred brilliantly. Roy was even worse. He said we were in a new situation. Public opinion had been favourably impressed by the TUC's efforts and that made our position more difficult. 'The PLP *has* lost its nerve,' chipped in Dick and then went on to warn Harold that, if he and I faced them with a showdown over this, Harold's position would be at risk and they would opt for a Government under Callaghan. This was received coldly by the rest of us. Michael Stewart passed me a note: 'It seems to me (if you will forgive the expression) that anyone who lets you down at this stage is a prize shit.'

Gradually Harold rallied them. Our line should be that we would give the TUC a try and take penal powers only on a suspended (and minimum period) appointed day. Vic had suggested to him that he should ask the TUC to set up a negotiating committee tomorrow for continuing talks. Roy looked pretty uneasy – 'shifty' was the word which came into my mind.

Monday, 9 June. In the event the meeting with the TUC was completely amicable. Vic reported on Croydon, saying that Special Congress had welcomed parts of the WP. On unconstitutional strikes the General Council had considered our letter but were reluctant to give commitments on things they couldn't do. Harold was as urbane and relaxed as usual. At Croydon, said Harold, the TUC had put its signature to the acceptance of binding awards in inter-union disputes. (Jack nodded at this.) But, continued Harold, on unconstitutional action you still use 'may' in Paragraph 42 instead of 'must'. It might be all a matter of drafting. The document could be strengthened. Vic replied rather wearily that he couldn't see what else they could do to strengthen Paragraph 42. 'When we say the unions "may" amend their rules, we are expecting action, not a permissive society.' Fred Hayday added earnestly, 'For the first time we have the weight of the TUC thrown behind the use of disciplinary action by the unions. Penal sanctions would make the situation worse. That is why we are against them.' Harold replied that we were not proposing the automatic use of sanctions, but it was all like a dialogue of the deaf until Briginshaw of SOGAT, who can hardly disguise his impatience with all these proceedings, suddenly erupted: 'We are not speaking the same language. We don't come here as penitents, but as co-operators. Some of us feel there is a tendency to string us along. If we strengthen Paragraph 42, will you definitely drop the penal clauses?' With barely a moment's hesitation, Harold answered, 'Yes.' There was a bit of a stir at this. Harold seized the opening to suggest a timetable: there should be another meeting on Wednesday evening; we should then report to Cabinet and meet the TUC again on Thursday evening or Friday morning.

And so to Management Committee. To my surprise the atmosphere was much steadier than on Sunday night and Bob (who had been left out on Sunday because his nerve couldn't be trusted) was one of the steadiest.

Cabinet was in much the same vein. After Harold had reported, Jim jumped in at his most ingratiating. The starting-point must be, he said, that whatever might be the disagreements about the tactics used, we would all agree that they had brought results. (I couldn't believe my ears!) Piling it on, he continued that this was a tribute to the determination of the First Secretary. On the whole a not unencouraging Cabinet.

Tuesday, 10 June. In early at No. 10 to see Harold. He is full of the reports in the *Guardian* and *Express* to the effect that Roy is weakening in his support of us on the Bill, and I reminded Harold how shifty Roy had seemed on Sunday night. We agreed the reports could gravely weaken our bargaining position.

Wednesday, 11 June. At the meeting with the full General Council we went over the old ground. Harold opened by saying there were a number of possibilities. Let us examine whether it was possible to strengthen their document. The effective part, we understood, was the change in Rules. Rule 12 had been fundamentally rewritten; Rule 11 only tinkered with. Could there be any improvements there? These details might best be considered in a smaller group which could report back to the General Council. Vic duly played up to this and we left them to appoint their group, my officials murmuring their admiration of Harold's handling of the talks as 'astute'. 'He's like an eel,' said Frank Lawton approvingly. 'He's handling Vic marvellously,' added Denis Barnes. While we waited for their reply I went into the drawing-room and wrote a draft of the amendments we needed to Rule 11.[1]

When we got into the negotiating committee we found that they, too, had been busy on an alternative draft: a few feeble words about disputes in general which they said they would circulate as an 'interpretative statement'. We swopped drafts and it was obvious they were appalled by mine – particularly because it spelt out the problem of unconstitutional strikes. After going fruitlessly over the old ground, Harold said we should go away and think over what everyone had said.

Thursday, 12 June. Management Committee was easy; everyone was so confident that, having promised to drop the penal clauses if we got a change of Rule 11, a settlement must be in sight. I told them that a rule change was the minimum for my credibility, particularly as the TUC words didn't even mention unconstitutional strikes. Cabinet was easy-going, too. Even Jim said that the

[1] I proposed the addition of the following new clauses to the rule:– 'd) Where a dispute has led to an unconstitutional stoppage of work which involves directly or indirectly large bodies of workers or which if protracted may have serious consequences, the General Council shall ascertain all the relevant facts and shall tender to the organization or organizations concerned their considered opinion and advice, which may take the form of an award or recommendation; in cases where, having regard to the principles set out in Paragraphs 20 to 27 of 'Programme for Action', they find that the workers are constitutionally in the wrong, they will place an obligation on the organization or organizations concerned to take immediate and energetic steps to obtain a resumption of work, so that negotiations can proceed.
e) Should the organization or organizations concerned refuse the assistance or advice of the Council under Clause (c) above, or not comply with an obligation under Clause (d), the General Council shall duly report to Congress or deal with the organization under Clauses (b), (c), (d) and (h) of Rule 13.'

offer we had made must be attractive to the TUC. If they were prepared to indicate that they were going to recommend our rule change to Congress, that ought to be enough for us to drop the interim Bill.

When Harold and I met before the resumed meeting with the General Council that evening, he was firm that only an amendment to rules would do. Meanwhile the General Council was meeting separately. It didn't take them long to tell us they were ready and our hopes that we might have split them by our offer were soon dashed. Fred Hayday was politely firm. There was no hope of proceeding on the basis of the alteration of rules as drafted. His colleagues thought a circular explaining how they would interpret Rule 11 would be as good, if not better. By this time we were all getting hungry and irritable so Harold proposed our usual break for beer and sandwiches.

As we trooped into the drawing-room for about the umpteenth time, Frank Lawton said to Denis Barnes, looking round at the magnificent floral arrangements, 'The trouble is that I'm getting used to this gracious living.' 'I'll never get used to these No. 10 sandwiches,' grumbled Denis as the usual doorslabs were wheeled in. 'Not even a plate or a paper serviette,' I moaned. Someone disappeared and came back with the nearest thing they could find, a coarse teatowel which I solemnly spread on my lap. At this point I was summoned to the study where Harold was imbibing his usual brandy and water. He was quite firm: 'This amendment to rule or we break.' The message came that the TUC was ready – and adamant. Harold therefore came straight to the point. We would report back to our colleagues and meet them again on Wednesday of next week. 'If your colleagues have second thoughts . . .' said Fred tentatively. 'For my part I am not prepared to recommend it to them,' was Harold's reply. And so we broke up. 'We've done very well tonight,' said Harold jubilantly. I myself believed that Cabinet and the PLP must be prepared to back us now that what everyone believed was a generous offer had been turned down.

Friday, 13 June. Met the CBI to put them in the picture. They were appalled that we should have offered to give up the legislation under any circumstances. I pointed out to them that failure to agree could lead to an increase in industrial strife instead of the opposite. But they are only interested in penal legislation at all costs. Down to HCF for a few hours' rest.

Tuesday, 17 June. The most traumatic day of my political life. Any hope that the TUC's intransigence would have hardened the attitude of the inner Cabinet soon disappeared and we had to go into Cabinet disunited and unprepared. Harold went over the old ground: we had offered to drop penal clauses in return for an amendment to rule and been turned down; we now had to consider alternatives for legislation. The First Secretary now had worked out a new version of the conciliation pause which he would ask me to explain to them. This I duly did. But the wreckers were not interested in the merits or demerits of my proposals. All they wanted was a settlement: peace at any price. Harold, however, was extraordinarily ebullient. Quite early on he passed me a note: 'Not to worry. Leave it to me.' So I sat silent while, one after another, the vultures moved in on us.

But it was Peter who shook everyone most. With an intensity of passion I have never seen from him before, he threw all his weight against us and for once he was impressive. What was I concerned with? Winning a victory over the TUC or reducing the number of damaging strikes? I was completely overlooking what we had succeeded in doing. Under Rule 11 we had now brought unconstitutional strikes under the ambit of the TUC. Secondly we have brought the whole of Rule 11 under Rule 13. The coverage of the TUC letter [or circular] was wider than that of our proposed amendment to rule: it covered official strikes as well as unconstitutional ones. The status of a rule was not important. There were approving noises to all this. (Dick said to me afterwards it was the only influential speech Peter has ever made in Cabinet.) But Harold and I knew how far it was from reality. Once again Harold interrupted grimly, 'I'm sorry; we've got nothing whatsoever on unconstitutional strikes. If the Cabinet has decided that we just capitulate, neither this nor any other Government can carry on.' By this time it was 12.30 pm and Harold had to leave. We agreed to resume the discussion on the IR Bill at 4.30 that afternoon.

At 4.30 pm Harold was still in as buoyant a mood as I have ever seen him. He is clearly determined to resign on this if necessary, but will go down fighting, probably believing that, if he fights, he will win. Personally I think he is right in this. In the resumed discussion some of the loyalists began to make themselves heard. Willie Ross, Cledwyn and George Thomas warned that Harold and I were being put in an impossible bargaining position. But the doubters were still on the attack. Ted Short's contribution was: 'We've got to take what we can get and make the best of it.' Roy Mason argued that the opinion polls were now swinging against too rigid a line by the Government. Judith made a muddled speech, something about going for a better formula than the TUC's vague one.

Roy sat silent through all this looking pretty worried. Before the resumed meeting he had sent a message asking me to come to his room at 4 pm. There he told me, with that evasive look he has been developing lately, that I would have gathered that he no longer thought that the fight was worth the cost. I replied that, yes, I had noticed it, but he would realize that Harold and I could not back down. If we could not get an acceptable compromise, we should both resign. He looked unhappier than ever, saying that this would have a very bad effect on the Party morale, 'More because of your resignation than Harold's, if I may say so.' He argued that the negotiations had now been strung out so long that a break had become unrealistic. I replied that it was impossible for Harold and me to capitulate. Unhappily, he said that they must go on trying to find some way of backing us up without leading to a crash. Exactly, I said. And, if we weren't backed up, there *would* be a crash. Now he was looking even more unhappy as a crash seemed inevitable.

Harold hit back more convincingly than I have ever seen him in Cabinet. He pointed out that it was now nearly 7 pm, at which hour he was supposed to be addressing the trade union group. What was he to say to them? If Cabinet wanted peace at any price, they had better find someone else to go and negotiate. He wasn't prepared to do so on those terms. This brought a rush of efforts to find a formula. Harold stood firm: he had better cancel the trade union group meeting and the meeting of the TUC tomorrow so that Cabinet could have more time to decide on the alternative policy if we were turned down by the TUC. Oh no, they moaned. Cancellation would set the press humming about a Cabinet split. Well, aren't we split? asked Harold. There was more agonizing. Jim made another speech about how he was prepared to work loyally for victory at the Election if only we could get this issue out of the way. (There's a commitment for you!) George Thomas grew more and more indignant about the way Harold and I were being treated, while even Roy was compelled to admit we were being placed in an impossible position.

Time moved relentlessly on. It was 7 pm. Harold sent a message to the trade union group that he would be a little late. Finally in our desperation a solution evolved that Harold and I should go to the TUC tomorrow with an entirely free hand to get the outcome we thought was right on the understanding that Cabinet would have a free hand, too, to endorse or reject our action when we reported back . . . I thought this was excellent – except, of course, that our enemies will brief the TUC. OK. If they harden them against us, we will break. As Harold and I dashed out to the trade union meeting, he said to me jubilantly, 'We've won.' In his hand he had a note from Gerald (who was on the woolsack) saying Harold would have his support in what he thought was right and that went for Eddie, too. That clinched it. I reckon that, if the showdown comes, we shall have a majority: Gerald, Eddie, the two Georges, Michael, Tony Greenwood, Willie, Cledwyn, Jack, Denis, Wedgie, Fred and me, with perhaps some people like Ted Short coming over to us when the chips are down.

The trade union group meeting didn't exactly restore my faith in human nature. Almost to a man (except for John Hynd [Labour MP for Sheffield]), the speakers were for prostrating themselves before the TUC. Harold, with nothing to say, said it too long-windedly. When we went over to No. 10 to meet Vic, Harold hadn't a card in his hand. But this didn't cramp his style. This time Vic had brought Harold a cigar and they were soon in their matey routine. 'I'll have nothing to say tomorrow, Vic,' Harold began. 'We've not yet worked out our alternative policy.' 'Pity,' said Vic. 'But can't we talk about your amendment to rule?' 'Is an amendment to rule ruled out on principle?' said Harold casually, lighting his cigar. 'No, I wouldn't say that,' said Vic slowly. 'But the trouble is that they think your wording rules out all freedom of action – leaves us no discretion.' 'Well, now,' said Harold, 'that's the last thing we mean. No doubt our wording is at fault – we tried to stick closely to your wording. I'm sure we could have another look at ours.' 'Do that,' said Vic. 'It would help.' I rang Douglas to tell him to get our chaps working on this point and to be at No. 10 early to discuss it before the meeting with the TUC, and went home in a kind of euphoria. Wouldn't it be heaven if we could get an amendment to rule after all?

Wednesday, 18 June. Up early to brood on the rewording of our amendment. I sketched out a form of words. It was a good job I did because Denis Barnes and Conrad Heron hadn't got anything ready when we met in Harold's study at 10 am. They all approved my redraft and Harold led us into the meeting with the TUC as cocky as usual. He began by saying that if last Thursday was their last word, the Government had to consider what form its legislation should take. We none of us wanted to have to go forward with legislation. But he did not believe a Labour Government could continue without either legislation or an effective alternative by them. An interpretative circular was not enough. 'That is still our position. If you rule out an amendment to Rule 11, I do not believe we can progress any further. If it is a matter of wording, we might move closer together.'

Vic had obviously done his stuff with John Newton as he had promised to do last night. Said John, 'We will consider any suggestions you put forward.' Harold said we were ready to circulate a draft (my draft) and to leave them to discuss it. And perhaps they would delegate responsibility to their negotiating committee to argue the detail with us. As we swept out of the room, Harold was firm that only an amendment to rule would do. When I asked nervously what we should do if they accepted our wording in some other form than an amendment to rule, he wouldn't entertain the idea.

The negotiating committee met us at 11.30 am. To our surprise they said the wording didn't present any difficulties. We could hardly believe our ears: a *volte-face*! But on the amendment to rule they were adamant. We went over the ground for nearly two hours. Sid Greene pointed out that they were afraid of creating a precedent: 'We wouldn't like to discuss amendments to rules with any other Government.' Jack Jones urged that we had made considerable progress. He insisted that it was possible for them to say that the agreement with us could only be changed in the same way as rules were changed – and pointed to the analogy of the Bridlington Declaration of 1939.[1] Harold was endlessly affable and endlessly firm. It was turned 1 pm and everyone was getting hungry and a bit irritable when Hughie leaned forward with one of those pieces of frankly taking us into his confidence which are rather touching, and I think impressive. The trouble in his union, he said, was that there were elements only too prone to say, 'A plague on both your houses – TUC and Government.' He had already had to recall his National Committee and, 'let's face it', he had only carried the day by a narrow margin. It only needed four votes to switch for the whole situation to be changed. 'If there is any suggestion that this is a gradual process of erosion, I can't guarantee what that vote will be.' But if we didn't insist on a change of rule and agreed to a binding undertaking in some other form, there would be no need for him to recall his National Committee. By this time I was urgently pressing Harold for an adjournment. 'Let us give them food and drink – no one to leave the building. We *must* settle something today.'

Over our doorslabs and beer, Conrad, Denis and I agreed that the last point made by Hughie had been a telling one. Could we not find something on the lines of the Bridlington formula? After all, said Conrad, that really had worked. Douglas was set busy turning up the details of Bridlington. I urged on Harold that, before we met the General Council again, we should find out from Vic whether they were willing to yield on the rule point. If not, *we* should go into the full Council and propose a 'binding undertaking', *provided that our words were approved*. After all, I had drafted them in the form of a rule so that they were as precise as we wanted them to be about unconstitutional strikes and, most importantly, included an amendment to Rule 13 to make the 'obligation' laid on unions (as against their acceptance of TUC 'advice')

[1] In 1939 the TUC had drawn up what were known as the 'Bridlington Regulations' governing inter-union relationships and prohibiting poaching between unions. Though not formally a rule of Congress, the Regulations had been strictly observed.

enforceable. Harold and I both agreed that to break now, when the TUC was accepting our wording and the concept of a binding undertaking, would put us in an impossible position with the PLP and even our own friends. And so it went. Vic and John Newton, summoned to the drawing-room, reported that the General Council had decided to 'stick' on the amendment to rule. Right, said Harold, and we swept into the full meeting. He told them we had been considering their arguments and were prepared to accept a binding undertaking equivalent to our proposed amendment with a covering letter which we had been drafting during the recess. Their relief was obvious; despite the leaks in today's press (particularly the accounts of the trade union group meeting) they had obviously been convinced of Harold's determination to break if necessary and they obviously didn't relish the thought of an open split in the Government with Harold's resignation. It had been a pure personal *tour de force* by him.

Once again we adjourned to leave them to finalize their approval of our words. As we waited restlessly we speculated as to which words they would challenge: almost certainly they would object to the reference to union rules and to the alteration invoking Rule 13. In Harold's study the press advisers had moved in, ready for the handling of a settlement. As the time dragged on, our hopes of agreement began to fade: we were certainly not going to accept any weakening of our draft. But suddenly they were ready, we joined the negotiating committee in the Cabinet room, and to our astonishment they had only two changes to request: first, the addition of the words 'if necessary' after the reference to union rules (no harm in that) and, secondly, the removal of the words 'having the same binding force as a rule of Congress'. Even on this they were convincing, Jack assuring us earnestly that there was no such thing as a rule of Congress. Harold said at once that we must adjourn so that we could consider their points. Once again we went through the Bridlington formula and I suggested we add a reference to the undertaking having the same binding force as the 'Bridlington principles *and regulations*'. To our surprise they made no demur and the deal was on.[1]

While they were reporting to the full General Council, Harold told Burke to summon Cabinet: 'And see that they are kept away from the TUC. I don't want them to know the news before we see them.' Adding grimly, 'I want to do some face washing first.' A depleted General Council told us that the deal had been confirmed 'unanimously'. The mood was one of relief rather than jubilation. Everyone agreed that no one should claim a victory.

Harold and I then raced down to Cabinet, which had been nervously twiddling its thumbs. Harold kept them in suspense as long as he could, saying that we had used our freedom of action to the full, but time was short and he couldn't spin it out as long as he would have liked to do. A ragged cheer went up as he announced the settlement. I insisted on putting in my spoke: 'Considering the background of press reports against which we had to negotiate, it is surprising that we achieved anything at all. In the end we have got complete acceptance of our formula and this is entirely due to the superb way in which the Prime Minister handled the talks.' Michael congratulated us warmly

[1] On 25 June the General Council issued a circular to all affiliated organizations setting out the agreement with the Government and announcing that the proposals endorsed by the Special Congress were being put into effect forthwith.

on behalf of all of them and Jim chipped in with a most odd form of words: 'I want to say that I will now dedicate myself to winning the Election,' or something like that. We hardly waited to listen to him and hurried out to the press conference, oozing contempt for the cowards from every pore.

The next climacteric was the PLP meeting. The room was packed and the cheer that went up was a self-conscious one – or was I being over-sensitive? Anyway I didn't wait for anything but Harold's announcement as he had landed me with appearances on TV. As we raced in the car to the BBC studios, I felt deflated to the point of tears. I told Douglas that we must have an office party tomorrow to 'celebrate' the fact that we should not be going through the agony of an interim Bill. 'If you can understand this, Douglas,' I said, 'I wish with one part of me that it was a farewell party tomorrow.' Yes, he understood, but he and Charles were almost as emotional as I was. 'Don't forget this, First Secretary,' he urged, 'you have achieved a great deal. The TUC will never be the same again: nor, might I add, will the Department. We have never had a Minister before like you.' It is these moments of sheer comradeship with a Minister which makes the civil service so remarkable. He and Charles could not have been more loyal or more comforting. But life is so irrational. Ted, who had been so depressed a few days ago at the thought of a breakdown, was now very subdued about the settlement. Of course, we know what the headlines will be: surrender. But government by headlines is the curse of British democracy.

One thing stays in my memory: Dick's moodiness as he sat next to me at the Party meeting. 'I hope that Harold will not be too hard on Peter,' was all he could say. He may have a bad conscience about his own part in this but he can't save Peter now.

Thursday, 19 June. A relaxed morning. Douglas suggested that I might at least retrieve some peace from the wreckage (though he didn't put it that way) so I went and had my hair done. Then into the office party where I thanked them all, high and low, for the work they had done, toasting them in champagne. 'I have spent the last few months delivering sermons up and down the country. You built the pulpit for me and it is not your fault that it has turned into a scaffold.' Yes, we have had an appalling press, but that was predictable. What angers me is that it is mostly turned against Harold personally instead of against a cowardly Cabinet, but that is just another example of an illiterate and prejudiced press. For myself, I don't care: a week is too short a time in politics to judge consequences.

Off to Eastbourne to the dinner party of the Socialist International. Thanks to the meeting Harold and I had to have with the CBI, I arrived late and hungry. Fortunately I was not too late for the excellent food. As I was still catching up with my eating, Eirene called on George Brown to move the toast to Albert McCartney, who retires from the secretaryship tomorrow. To my surprise George began by reaching out to me across the crowded room. 'I want to begin by saying a few words to Barbara. I know that the last few weeks must have been misery. But you have achieved a marvellous result. Barbara, you have been magnificent.' At that I nearly *did* break down. Afterwards Percy Clark of Transport House came up to me: 'You know that I think you were right.' Yes, a week is too short in politics to judge results.

Friday, 20 June. Down to HCF to bury myself in the garden and recuperate. After all, there are more important things than political set-backs – like getting the garden ready for our silver wedding party.

Monday, 23 June. A dash to Scarborough to attend the annual banquet of the Confederation of Engineering Unions. They were all waiting for me in friendly formation and I met with nothing but kindliness as I went round having drinks. We had just sat down to dinner when Reg Birch came up behind my chair. 'I've only just seen that you are here. How are you?' 'Fine, thank you.' 'So you ought to be. Of course you've won. You know you've won.' I've never met a more amusing combination of old-world charm and tough Communism.

Tuesday, 24 June. Harold called me into the Cabinet room ahead of the others. 'You and I must keep together. I am the only friend you have and you are the only friend I have. I'm like the elephant: I may appear to forget but I never do.'

Wednesday, 25 June. Tommy has sent me a paper on economic strategy. He says Peter's paper on the trend of imports shows, rightly, that direct action to check our propensity to import is urgently necessary. These obvious conclusions from the paper hadn't been included because the Treasury had insisted they were left out. Despite Roy's astonishingly euphoric speech today in the House on the Letter of Intent, Tommy is full of gloom about our prospects. And Roy's optimism is all the more inexplicable because of two papers that have been circulated to us: one from the official committee on PESC and one from the Medium-Term Assessment Committee. Both find that we can't sustain the 3 per cent growth in public expenditure we planned last autumn for 1970–71 and Roy wants cuts of £400m.

Monday, 30 June. A meeting of the Management Committee to soften us up on the new PESC exercise. For once I had had time to read my documents and I was determined to go in fighting. Roy was as smoothly plausible as always. As anticipated, he said we needed a £400m cut in public expenditure. I came in heavily at this point, quoting the two reports to show what, under our present strategy, the political scenario would be as we came up to the Election: growth down, unemployment up, investment down, imports above target, £400m cuts in public expenditure PLUS automatic increases in taxation due to the natural effects of inflation. How could we hope to win on this basis? I was as ready as the next to face tough policies but not in support of a self-defeating strategy. I believed we were on a 'rake's progress in reverse'. It was one thing to keep in line with PESC; quite another to cut back on our own planning made as recently as February just as we were getting inflation under control – particularly following the most optimistic speech I had ever heard the Chancellor make in the House. Our only hope was to alter our whole strategy, go for direct control of imports and capital exports plus a renewed drive to revive support for a prices and incomes policy.

I grabbed Dick afterwards to say that he, Peter, Tommy and I must meet urgently. This was a vital turning-point in the history of the Labour Government. Did he realize that, if we threw the Election away, the Tories would come in just in time to reap the benefits of the vast assets of his earnings-related pension scheme, while we would have incurred the odium of putting the contributions up? Yes, he said, he did realize it and said he would arrange the meeting I suggested tomorrow. He and I should then ask to see Harold and stiffen him against Roy's orthodoxy.

Tuesday, 1 July. Dick and Peter duly came along to my room for a drink. (Tommy couldn't be there.) We put Peter in the picture and I lectured him on the need for him to take a positive stand for once on economic strategy; Dick added that he had made a tremendously effective speech in Cabinet against me on the IR thing ('Of course she's forgiven you') and he should be equally effective on this. Peter confirmed that his misgivings about the trend of imports were very real and that he thought we ought to have a new strategy. Dick told me that he had arranged for him and me to see Harold tomorrow and that we must try and win him over to our side before Cabinet.

Wednesday, 2 July. We resumed our discussion in Management Committee on Roy's strategy. Roy plunged right in, saying that he wanted to answer fully the points I had made. 'I don't begin to think,' he said, 'that this is the right moment to change our basic strategy.' Things on the whole had gone better since the Budget than he anticipated. 'I think our strategy looks *more* like working than I thought ten weeks ago.' At the end of a long discussion Dick said that he thought Roy had had the best of the argument with Barbara on the possibility of getting off the tramline. So once again Dick's great revolt collapsed and I was isolated, though unconvinced. Harold assured me cheerfully that I could raise it all again in Cabinet.

After the meeting Harold called Dick and me over to say that, as he had to dash off, our talk would have to be postponed. I no longer saw any point in it anyway as I am clearly not going to get any support. But Harold did close the door and talk to us very intimately, very privately for two minutes about his plans for reconstructing the Cabinet. We couldn't go on with a Cabinet in which we were afraid to discuss anything of importance like basic economic strategy because of disloyal leaks. He knew who was responsible because their 'fingerprints' were on the stories. Tony Crosland's for instance; he was giving Peter Jenkins all his stories. We must restore the Cabinet's cohesion and unity; he was planning a major reconstruction and some of our friends would have to accept demotion 'or else they know what they can do'. Dick Marsh was another disloyal lightweight. As for Peter and Judith, they were a great disappointment. Peter was the complete bureaucrat while Judith did nothing but talk vague nonsense like 'participation'. He hoped we agreed with all this. Dick nodded encouragement (so much for his transient defence of Peter).

Thursday, 3 July. Over the old ground of PESC at Cabinet. Roy had obviously been thinking hard over my criticisms and weighed in with a rather different emphasis. He said that there was no question of a public expenditure crisis and that he wasn't proposing any cuts for the current year. He was not taking a pessimistic view of the balance of payments outlook. We should probably be in current account balance for the first six months of this year and the indications were that we were moving into a period of export growth. We should probably achieve 3 per cent growth this year, but there was always the paradox that, to the extent that one succeeded in switching resources to the balance of payments, one created greater pressure on resources. The budgetary prospect for next year, therefore, was a daunting one. Hence his proposals to cut public expenditure. And so it was agreed that Roy should go ahead and seek his £400m cuts. He is to have bilateral talks with Ministers. But in forcing him to discuss strategy like this I have made him give immense hostages to fortune in these detailed forecasts.

I can't make up my mind whether my winding-up speech in the debate on our settlement with the TUC was a triumph or a disaster. I suspect I shall get a bad press though Harold assured me it was the best speech I had ever made in the House. Roy Hattersley, too, was surprisingly (and I think genuinely) congratulatory. Certainly it was the roughest ride anyone could have. It was Harold who got me off to a noisy start by whispering that the Tories had fought the Leicester by-election[1] *against* the breathalyser. He also nearly drove me mad by chattering to me all through Heath's speech and, when I finally protested, he said it wasn't worth listening to, anyway, which was patently wrong because it was one of the best speeches Heath has made.

Tuesday, 8 July. A lively evening at Pam Berry's to meet Kay Graham of the *Washington Post*. Of course, Roy was there – he can always find time for a social occasion. When we dashed back to vote I slipped in to see Harold about Aubrey. Aubrey had been to see me earlier in the day to show me a copy of a letter he has sent to Harold explaining that he has accepted an offer to become a director of IPC. It won't operate till next March and I urged that it should be kept dark till then. He was perfectly happy about this if Harold could arrange it with Hugh Cudlipp. Harold agreed to have a try.

Monday, 14 July. Aubrey asked to see me again to say that Hugh Cudlipp was coming to see Harold at 7 pm to tell him the announcement about Aubrey's appointment must be made immediately. He told me he would be only too glad to keep his new job dark, if Cudlipp could be persuaded to agree, adding that he wouldn't take the IPC job, even at this stage, if Harold would offer him something else – 'Make me a sort of Averell Harriman dealing with our entry to the Common Market.' I managed to see Harold for a few minutes to tell him all this. He said he had nothing to offer Aubrey: 'Chalfont is in charge of the Common Market negotiations and he's very good.' Anyway, 'I am less of a devotee of Aubrey's than you or Tommy.' I told him I knew all Aubrey's faults, but nonetheless thought he had put the PIB on the map as no one else could have done. The announcement of his departure would finally undermine its standing. Harold agreed to try and get Cudlipp to delay the announcement and suggested that Aubrey might in any case carry on part-time after March. He then asked me whether I minded losing Hattersley to take Gerry

[1] In November 1967 there had been a by-election in Leicester South-West following Herbert Bowden's elevation to the Lords. The Conservatives won the seat from Labour.

Reynolds's place at the Ministry of Defence.[1] I said that on the contrary justice to Hattersley was long overdue and that he would be ideal for Gerry's job. I urged him to see Hattersley as soon as possible.

It was a late night in the House on the Finance Bill and I was working in my room at 2 am when Harold suddenly phoned. Could I go down and see him? He was sitting in his room surrounded by boxes, looking very boyishly dishevelled and positively frivolous. It is curious how relaxed he becomes the worse the problems that press in on him. He greeted me affectionately. His main purpose was to tell me that he had had no luck with Hugh Cudlipp, who had been very uncooperative about Aubrey. He then dilated about his ideas for Cabinet changes. He was going to do something root and branch – connected with the overhaul of the machinery of government. As for Crosland, he was one of the main sources of the leaks. Did I know that, at the time he and I were having our showdown over the IR Bill, Callaghan had promised Crosland the job of Chancellor in his Government? There was a secret pact between them based on their joint disloyalty. I said I was all in favour of a smaller Cabinet.

Friday, 18 July. Polly Devlin of *Vogue* to interview me. While we talked David Bailey wandered nonchalantly round taking photographs. He is a very self-possessed young man. 'Fine,' he kept saying through his chewing gum as he pushed the camera up to my face. 'Absolutely fine.' 'What's that gauze for?' I asked. 'To make the picture softer.' 'Thank God,' I replied, thinking of the lines. 'I'm always kind to women,' he said, tousling Polly's hair. 'Ta ta, Barbara, thanks a lot.'

With the penal clauses out of the way I was anxious to get ahead with putting the rest of In Place of Strife *on the statute book, but I ran into snags. I found that the* TUC *was less enthusiastic about Donovan than it had made out to be. Though it had acquiesced somewhat half-heartedly in the setting up of the* CIR, *it remained deeply suspicious of any interference in the running of union affairs or any hint of sanctions against unions. I was soon in difficulties, therefore, over the Donovan proposals that unions should be compelled to register and that union members should have the right of appeal to an independent review body against expulsion from a union or refusal of membership in it.*

Meanwhile Vic Feather had been throwing himself loyally into the task of carrying out the 'solemn and binding undertaking' the TUC *had given the Government, jocularly known as 'Solomon Binding', and had turned himself into a one-man fire-fighter.*

Monday, 21 July. Lunched at Lloyd's: the first woman to do so, they told me proudly, apart from royalty. It was fun. The evening was taken up with my private meeting with Vic, John Newton and their officials about next session's IR Bill. They were obviously touched by my desire to discuss the difficulties with them frankly and responded in kind. We did some useful work on details before coming to the explosive issue of the compulsory registration of unions with its financial penalty. Vic said the TUC wouldn't like it and, after all, why was it necessary? There was a financial penalty already in that only unions which registered got tax relief as friendly societies and that could mean a lot to

[1] Roy Hattersley replaced Gerry Reynolds as Minister of Defence (Administration) on 15 July and Edmund Dell, MP for Birkenhead, came over to my Department from the Board of Trade as Minister of State.

some of them. But he was surprisingly mild about it and I began to wonder if my fears were exaggerated.

Tuesday, 22nd July. By arrangement with Harold at Management Committee, I proceeded to tie Cabinet down on the commitment we had made in April to reactivate Part 2 of the P and I policy when the present legislation expires. Cabinet had agreed that the Chancellor should announce this policy in his Budget speech and I had elaborated it in the same debate but, I added drily, 'Other things he also said with Cabinet agreement at that time were later repudiated by Cabinet.' So we ought to get the policy specifically confirmed before I went any further with my consultations.

In the afternoon Harold sent for me. He paced up and down his study saying that he knew I had made it clear that I didn't want to move from DEP, and he respected my reasons, but the reconstruction on which he was working was bound up with fundamental changes in the machinery of government and he wanted to put a proposition to me. He wanted to merge more departments and get a smaller Cabinet. He'd thought over Mikardo's idea of a Ministry of Nationalized Industries but it meant splitting functional Ministries, like Transport, which had a large private sector as well. So you ended with more splitting, not less. (On this I heartily agree with him.) So he was on another tack: merging Transport with Housing and Planning. (Again I agree, though I suspect he is, as always, thinking largely *ad hominem* – how to downgrade the individual Ministers he doesn't like.) Then there was DEA. It must go. Peter was only a bureaucrat. MinTech, where Wedgie had done well, could absorb some of its functions and some from the Board of Trade to become a Ministry for Industry (thus, I noted approvingly, downgrading the Board of Trade). But its regional planning responsibilities should go to Housing which would then expand into a new regional planning ministry, absorbing housing and transport. The trouble with these mergers was that he had so few giants capable of coping with them: in effect only Denis and me. And I would be far better than Denis. 'And you'll be responsible for your old love, Transport, again,' he said enticingly. I was divided in my reaction: hating the thought of going from exciting trade unions to dull local authorities, but attracted, as always, by the challenge of a new and bigger job. But my dominant nagging thought was that I must avoid the danger of becoming Harold's gimmick-maker. Unless I stayed at one job long enough to carry a policy right through, I should cease to be regarded as an efficient trouble-shooter and be seen as a bit of a show-off. So I asked if I could talk it over with Ted and he said of course. Ted shared my divisions and my doubts and eventually, after a long talk in bed, we agreed I should say no.

Wednesday, 23 July. At the NEC we agreed to set up a Campaign Committee but, as usual, after a long discussion, we filled it with the old dead-beats again. The only good point is that Harold is to add three nominees and I'm delighted to learn from him that he intends to include Wedgie. Later I asked to see Harold to tell him my reactions to his reconstruction idea. I said I thought it was excellent, but for Denis, not me, as it would really be disastrous for Harold and for me if there was any suggestion at all that I was running away from DEP. I always find it hard to resist Harold when he gets an idea into his head but he wasn't in a pressing mood because he has decided after all not to announce his reconstruction till after we return. Incidentally, he laughed at the press reports that he intends to make Jim Leader of the House: 'Can you see me putting him in a job where he could spend *all* his time intriguing in the tea-room?' I expect his ideas will go through a lot more changes before he comes to a decision and I'm yet to be convinced that he will downgrade Tony Crosland.

Thursday, 24 July. In between Cabinets I had my meeting with the TUC on the future of P and I policy. As anticipated, they had come to argue against the reactivation of Part 2 powers and I didn't think there was much steam in it. But a warning shot came from Hugh Scanlon, who suddenly said to me at the end of the meeting, 'How would you feel if it was said that this was a breach of the Government's agreement with the TUC?' I looked at him and said, 'I would feel total incredulity.' The other TUC boys looked uneasy and I don't think they thought much of Hughie's intervention.

Friday, 25 July. Home to prepare for the silver wedding party tomorrow. It is a gloriously relaxed feeling to know that a caterer will be moving in at 8 am to do the work, and I strolled around having my photo taken with Ted for the *Sunday Times*. The garden looks glorious, the good weather still holds. We filled the bath with champagne bottles and Ted ferried ice from High Wycombe in a plastic dustbin, while I filled the house with flowers. It *could* be our most memorable party ever.

Saturday, 26 July. Woke early to a glorious morning. The caterer and her minions were soon setting the bar up on a corner of the lawn, putting the little round tables and gilt chairs under the trees, and decorating the lunch table under the awning even better than I could have done it myself. And although the sun clouded over, it remained beautifully dry and warm so that people lolled on the grass just as we had dreamed. Harold joined in the fun in a relaxed way, making suitable cracks as he planted the commemoration tree, while our Tory friends were enchanted with Mary Wilson. An idyllic party in which I was actually able to join because I wasn't in the kitchen rustling up food. At 6 pm, as the last guests were saying they ought to go, the first raindrops fell. God's watch must have been slow!

Monday, 28 July. The House is up but we face a frantic week of Cabinet business before any of us can go on holiday. First, Management Committee: a meeting for which I had asked so that I can get clearance to go ahead with preparing an equal pay Bill. Roy was not unsympathetic to my paper, indeed he said he had no objection to equal pay in principle: 'I think it is both inevitable and right.' He wouldn't, however, accept that it necessarily corrected inequalities and would like a survey made of its social effects. Dick backed me manfully, saying that the largest area of deprivation was the fatherless family. Equal pay was very important because he was greatly concerned at the increasing disincentive of social security payments. Another important poverty group was the spinsters. Roy replied that the economic effects would be bound to be adverse, at which I pointed out that the formula I was proposing would add only about 5 per cent to the wages bill spread over five years. What worried them was my desire to get it cleared at Thursday's Cabinet. Harold said I must wait till 4 September, doing the survey in the meantime. He would then say in his speech to Congress that I was about to enter into consultations and I could cap it with a speech at the Labour Party conference. I am tickled at the way he manages to look after both of us these days.

Tuesday, 29 July. The crunch Cabinet on PESC. The battle went on so long that we all had to cancel afternoon engagements and meet again at 3.30 pm. Roy began by saying he was now prepared to settle for £300m as the 'absolute floor'. He must warn us, however, that as a result the Budget prospect was a 'daunting one': increased taxes of some £280m in Election year. While we were all trying to think up painless taxes and congratulating ourselves on his malleability (one might almost say softness from the point of view of his own policy), it soon became clear that the battle was not over.

At the end of exhausting hours we reviewed where we stood. If Roy was to reach his 'absolute floor' of £300m we had to find £8m more from the 'sensitive areas'. One by one the very people who refuse to fight for a change of strategy turned on the Chancellor. Dick, of course, wouldn't accept that the exact cuts asked for are necessary. Tony Crosland said in his breezy way that the Chancellor had done 'jolly well': he should settle for £292m. I sat silent because *I* believe we are not doing enough if we are going to support – as Dick and Tony Crosland do – the orthodox strategy. Cornered, Roy finally said (with even slim Jim advising him to take £292m) that he would do so on the understanding that any bonuses that might come, say from an airport tax, would accrue to him. And so another PESC agony was over with Cabinet having squeezed a bit more water out but having once again dodged the basic choice between orthodoxy and an alternative strategy. Roy's last gloomy word was that he couldn't guarantee we wouldn't face a difficult situation in January. Personally I think he should have stood firm on his own beliefs.

Wednesday, 30 July. Day-long Cabinet to clear up a back-log. Another long evening with Vic and his friends. Our talk before supper went happily enough. I led Vic back gently and unobviously to my IR Bill and the crucial point of financial sanctions for the non-registration of unions, but he merely shrugged. On the independent review body he hinted that the TUC might even be ready to appoint its own Ombudsman. Over supper he was at his gayest and most entertaining: I think my officials delight in his broad Yorkshire humour. And then Len Murray and his aide, Ken Graham, came clean with us: if we went ahead with any financial sanction there would be an unholy row, however illogically. They agreed that the registration point had never been covered in Harold's and my talks with the TUC; nonetheless a financial sanction here would be considered a breach of faith and arouse real anger. If no compulsory registration meant no Bill, the TUC would choose that, they said, though they would consider this, too, as a breach of faith.

Thursday, 31 July. Into Management Committee where I reported on the problem which faces us on next session's IR Bill in the light of the TUC's reaction on registration. I pointed out that, without even this in the Bill, it would be difficult to justify all the strengthening of union bargaining power. The alternative seemed either to postpone the Bill on the basis that we were waiting to see how the TUC kept its undertaking (a course I opposed) or to go for a more limited Bill dealing with appeal against unfair dismissal and one or two other items of individual rights, including the statutory right to belong to a trade union. The general view seemed to be that we couldn't risk another major row with the TUC and that a selective Bill might be the only answer. Harold said that he and I should be given latitude to negotiate the best arrangements we could with the TUC.

Monday, 1 September. I travelled down to Portsmouth for the Trades Union Congress in the same train as Harold because I wanted to hear his speech to the TUC. He insisted on my reading it on the way down and I thought it read a bit flat – not a flicker of humour or warmth anywhere, nothing but solid fact and stern warnings. In particular I pointed out that, by linking equal pay to 'restraint' in incomes, he was asking for trouble. (We in DEP don't think you can include moves towards equal pay within the norm.) But he refused to take this out and said something about Roy being worried about this part of his speech because he would be 'pre-empting' what Roy wanted to say himself to the Labour Party conference. I wondered what was going on. Something to do with the IMF?

As I feared, Harold's speech fell flat. Apart from everything else, he delivered it in such an offhand monotone that it nearly sent everyone, including me, to sleep. I just couldn't understand his manner in view of his ebullience on the train. In the evening I did the rounds of four cocktail parties and two annual dinners. Vic was doing an even madder round than I was. After a few choice words to the General and Municipal Workers' dinner crowd – in which I said that I was that despised of the trade unions, a politician, which meant that I had to legislate where they failed to negotiate (applause) – Vic, Eirene and I swept on to the AEF dinner. Hughie greeted us warmly, and before I knew where I was he and I were doing a duet at the microphone. It was he who suggested the song 'Are you lonesome tonight, do you miss me tonight?' In memory, he said, of the long hours we had spent together at No. 8 St James's Square and at No. 10. He's a curious fellow. He may make tough speeches but he's never become sour as Frank has. Nor do I think he is as calculating a revolutionary as Jack Jones.

Tuesday, 2 September. The press are full of the cool reception of Harold's speech and John Torode of the *Guardian* has the theory that Harold was deliberately talking to the country through the TUC. In order to talk tough without getting a hostile reaction from his audience he had to talk flat. Torode may be right and Harold may be a far more sophisticated politician than I am or than I give him credit for. But that unfortunate use of the word 'restraint' brought the reaction on the equal pay issue that I anticipated: no thank you to the Government for deciding to make progress, just attacks from Frank Cousins and others for linking equal pay with P and I policy. It is so absurd because we know we shall have to make advance to equal pay an exception to the norm.

Wednesday, 3 September. The day of Vic's first major speech as General Secretary. He introduced the debate on industrial relations in a speech far more competent, confident and even sophisticated than any I have yet heard him make. Indeed as a performance it was better than Harold's. But it was also far less tough on what the trade union movement must do to keep its pledge on strikes. I said to George Woodcock, sitting next to me in the public gallery, 'A good speech.' 'A good speech for Congress,' he replied, 'but I would have hammered home the implications of the agreement as the Prime Minister did.' Jack Jones instead rubbed in the warnings: 'The Croydon declaration did not promise to do the dirty work of the Government.' And he waxed eloquent on his favourite theme of democracy: 'The corridors of power are not in Congress House or even in Whitehall but in the streets where our people live.' Exactly. But, as I pointed out to industrial correspondents afterwards, those streets are not his constituency: they are the Government's. And a Labour Government can't get elected on 11 per cent of the votes as Hughie Scanlon did to the presidency of his union. Altogether not a heartening week politically.

At the TUC annual dinner I ended the evening singing at the microphone again. This time it was Les Cannon's idea and he brought a willing Hughie in as well. I suggested the only song whose words I could remember – 'We will overcome' – and we had a riotous time improvising on it. Les made up a verse, 'She will give us Part 2', ending, 'She will overcome.' Not to be outdone, I seized the mike and sang solo, 'We will build a new Bill.' The audience – and Hughie – took it enthusiastically. Only Frank, who had refused to join in the singing, turned sourly away.

In trying to make my Bill as water-tight as possible, I was faced with two definitions of equal pay. The first was the ILO definition: 'equal pay for work of equal value' and the second the EEC formula of 'equal pay for the same work'. The former struck me as too vague and the latter too restrictive. The ILO definition did not indicate how 'value' should be measured or enforced while the EEC phrase, 'the same work', was clearly inadequate. John Locke, who did an excellent job on the Bill, suggested that 'equal value' should be linked to job evaluation schemes and firms' pay structures and drew up provisions which would outlaw any discrimination in them on grounds of sex. We also widened the phrase 'same work' to make it 'like work' defined as 'of the same or broadly similar nature' as men's and we laid down that comparisons could be made with the work of any man in any of the same firm's plants, wherever situated. Equal treatment must also cover terms and conditions of employment as well as pay; except for pensions which were being dealt with in separate legislation. One of the points on which I insisted was that the law should be easily enforceable by the women themselves. The Bill therefore gave them right of access either individually or through their union to local industrial tribunals on which trade unions had equal representation with employers. Equal pay was to be phased in over five years.

Thursday, 4 September. It was a haggard Departmental team that I took back to London at 8.24 am. Most of them had been up drinking and talking till the early hours. I spent the morning on an office briefing meeting for the equal pay discussion due in Cabinet this afternoon. I queried John Locke's definition of 'equal pay for the same work' and got him to agree that it must involve equal basic rates in any job evaluation scheme.

The discussion on equal pay went much better than I had dared to hope. Opening it, I stressed that we had run out of delaying excuses. The position now was that there would be a move to equal pay anyhow and it was far better that we should control it and get credit for it. A five-year phasing in was the maximum we could get away with. Eventually Harold summed up that there was overwhelming support for me in principle though the date of any announcement must be agreed with the Chancellor.

Friday, 5 September. The all-day session of the Management Committee at Chequers went extremely well. Harold opened by saying we should concentrate first on the strategy for winning the Election, though he hadn't decided yet when the Election should be. Bob jumped in to say that the key issues in the Election would be the cost of living, unemployment and the high cost of mortgages. With the National Institute [NIESR] having produced a very gloomy forecast that morning, what could the Chancellor tell us about the economic prospects? Roy replied that the Treasury was by no means as gloomy as the National Institute was. The balance of payments results for the second quarter were very good, though there was a 'weak and worrying' sterling position due to French devaluation and the July trade figures. The National Institute was too pessimistic on the unemployment figures for the beginning of next year: 'I'm not pessimistic.'

After lunch we got down to some concrete issues, notably the future of P and I policy. I agreed with Roy that we couldn't run away from implementing Part 2 powers but I believed that the only way of avoiding a sterile confrontation for little economic advantage – 'the bloodshed of a political Passchendaele to gain a yard of economic ground' – was a war of movement to catch the TUC off balance by going for the merger of PIB and the Monopolies Commission into a new body. The asymmetrical prices policy which Roy feared would then come in an entirely different context. All Departments agreed on the merger except the Board of Trade. Roy didn't blench at this – I think his loyalty to Crosland is subordinate to his loyalty to me – and said it should certainly be considered, though he couldn't obviously commit himself at this stage. Harold told us that in any case he was working on a major Cabinet reshuffle designed to achieve a smaller Cabinet linked to the reform of the machinery of government. He still intended, however, to put mergers and consultancy services under me. Harold went on to say, to our surprise, that he thought the time had come to bring Jim back into the inner Cabinet: 'I think he is behaving now.' He also told us that George Brown was very anxious to come back into the Government and had had two long talks with him. The only snag was that he would only come back as Deputy PM (and presumably at the FO) and that wasn't on. (Harold won't sacrifice Michael now.) So George had said he would soldier on on the back benches until, perhaps, the eve of the Election.

An amusing moment when we were discussing relations between the Government and the NEC. Harold said he thought Tony Greenwood was at risk in this year's elections at which I said I thought I would be off the NEC myself this year. A chorus of dissent and Dick bet me £5 at 5 to 1 that I would be on. Others said, 'Top of the poll.' Eventually I took bets of £1 evens that I would NOT be top of the poll and had six half-crown bets at 5 to 1 on my retaining my membership. I wrote it all down and we gave it to Burke to keep for us. I don't suppose he's ever done a job like that before!

Wednesday, 10 September. Farewell party at the office for Charles Birdsall who is retiring, whom I shall miss terribly, then off to Blackburn, this time followed by the *Observer* photographer. No one can complain that I haven't put Blackburn on the map! But I get terribly sick of this endless 'projection' of me. Kenneth Harris may not believe it, but I am really a very reserved person and I squirm inside when I am asked to talk about myself or put myself on show. Of course I like being reported so long as it is about what I *do*, rather than introspective.

Wednesday, 17 September. Meeting with CBI on equal pay. They came breathing fire and slaughter but I suspect that most of them were more convinced than they were prepared to admit when I said that they would face an irresistible pressure for it anyhow. But the highlight of the day was another private evening meeting with Vic and his chaps. Everything went smoothly before supper when we discussed innocuous things like what they really had in mind for the period for the phasing in of equal pay. (Three years, said Vic.) Vic had brought boxes of chocolates all round for me and the lassies who prepare our supper. 'Terry's Golden Feather', he pointed out proudly and we teased him about the fact that they were soft centres.

But the balloon went up when I got on to the IR Bill. Registration? Leave it as it is now, said Vic. Those that don't register don't get tax exemption. But as usual he hadn't thought it through and was appalled when he realized that, under Donovan and us, registration would depend on unions having better rules than they have now. He was hostile, too, about individual members of unions having the right of appeal to an independent outside body though he was responsive when I suggested we could withdraw this from the Bill if the TUC appointed its own Ombudsman. (Len Murray, however, was shaking his head. After all, Jack and Hughie have already turned down the idea of any appeal to the TUC.) Vic was even touchy about references to the CIR and he absolutely hit the roof when I got on to the clerical workers' dispute with BSC asking if he was going to intervene. 'I'll intervene when anyone is laid off because of it and not before. But no one is laid off. The management are liars.' Finally Vic went touchily away, leaving a sour atmosphere. His own officials looked embarrassed and unhappy. Vic is obviously an exhausted, over-stretched man not very far from collapse in my view. He hasn't had a holiday for years and he is really sensitive about Solomon Binding.

Friday, 26 September. Off the night sleeper from Blackburn to catch an early train to Brighton for the Party conference.

Saturday, 27 September. As Ted arrived and we went into the bar for a drink I was anxious to know whether the opponents of P and I had managed to include anything about it in the composite on industrial relations. Mik, whom we had joined, said no, but he and Clive Jenkins insisted that the wording in the composite about 'basic trade union rights' covered it and that conference would be very annoyed if I didn't reply to the points on Part 2 powers that would inevitably be raised in the debate.[1]

Sunday, 28 September. Harold turned up specially for the NEC because last night I had warned him that P and I policy might come up on the composite on industrial relations. What am I to do? I had asked him. I can't renege on the Government's policy, even if I wanted to. Yet, when the crucial moment came, Harold was out of the room. (Whether by design or accident I shall never know.) Fortunately Mik didn't raise P and I policy, as I had thought he might do. So it just went through: accept.

Monday, 29 September. Conference opened as flatly as the rally had finished last night and I spent the morning putting the careful finishes to my notes. As I rose to speak confidence came flooding in and I know that I did well, despite the fact that Jack Jones was gesticulating to Hughie across the gangway at some of my remarks, notably my references to the CIR. His grumbles erupted into an audible outcry as I came to my bit about Part 2 powers. But I swept on regardless to the climax of my announcement about equal pay, which brought me the nearest thing to an ovation this conference has yet seen. Afterwards I went into a conference with the industrial correspondents about the details of our plan for equal pay (we really have got an excellent formula).

But already the air was full of the 'revolt' by Jack Jones, meekly followed by Hughie, on what I had said about Part 2 powers. As the night went on it became totally clear to me that Jack is furious at my announcement about equal pay which robs him not only of a grievance against the Government, but of some of the leadership on industrial issues which, I am now convinced, he wants exclusively concentrated in the hands of the unions.

Tuesday, 30 September. To my relief I am top of the poll again for the constituency section of the NEC. In the normal way I wouldn't have cared, but Jack's attack on me made it important this time. The equal pay story has been swamped in the press by the 'row' story.

At the civic reception Alex Kitson seized me. The AEF delegation, he told me nearly in tears, had decided to vote against the 'Agenda for a Generation' despite the statement. It wasn't really Hughie's fault: he had been overridden. Why did I have to say what I did about Part 2 powers? Alex moaned. I told him how Mik and Clive had insisted that I must deal with P and I policy and, that being so, I couldn't let the Government down at a moment when the Chancellor had backed me on equal pay. He wrung his hands.

Wednesday, 1 October. It is clear that Jack and the AEF have not been pacified and are going to vote against 'Agenda' unless George Brown says the right

[1] The composite resolution, moved by Harry Urwin of the Transport and General Workers Union, congratulated the Government and the TUC on having reached agreement on industrial relations and added: 'Conference declares its unalterable opposition to any legislation which would curtail basic trade union rights, including penal sanctions on workpeople or on trade unions in connection with industrial disputes.' It was carried *nem. con.*

things in the economic policy debate. But that meant crawling, which George refused to do.

Friday, 3 October. Yes, Jack and Hughie voted against the document. Up to the very last they tried to find a way out, Jack going to the rostrum asking whether the NEC would amend the document before publication to take account of conference's views. But Eirene refused to budge beyond her rather guarded commitment. At the vote there was some confusion as Jack and Hughie consulted each other across the gangway but by now their protest has been defused. One thing I noticed: they both stood for the ovation to Harold last Tuesday. Not that I am deceived.

It had long been clear that a statutory prices and incomes policy could not work in the face of mounting hostility from the trade unions, but the problem was how to avoid a rush back to an inflationary free-for-all. The answer lay, in my view, in retaining the educational role of the PIB *but set in the wider context of the need to promote industrial efficiency, productivity and accountability and to curb the power of dominant firms – not least their power to strike monopolistic bargains with their unions in the knowledge that they could pass on the cost of inflationary settlements through higher prices. In other words I wanted to switch the emphasis from control over incomes to control over prices. I therefore wanted to merge the work of the* PIB *and the Monopolies Commission in a new body, the Commission for Industry and Manpower [*CIM*], to which the Government could refer for examination purposes prices and dividend increases and pay settlements, the use made of a dominant position in an industry, specific practices which distorted competition and proposed mergers. The Government's power of reference should not be limited to the 'technical monopolies', but apply to all major firms,* i.e. *some four hundred major industrial firms and financial institutions. Tony Crosland was strongly resisting the merger, but Roy Jenkins was also opposing the 'asymmetrical' powers I was proposing to give the Commission to regulate prices, but not wage settlements.*

Roy Jenkins was also insisting that, when the tough powers of deferment given by the 1968 Prices and Incomes Act lapsed at the end of the year, the Government must retain the power under Part 2 of the 1966 Act to refer pay settlements to the PIB *and to defer their introduction for three months pending the* PIB*'s report. He argued that he needed this for 'confidence' purposes, but I saw it as a bridging operation pending the setting up of the new body and the introduction of the new long-term policy.*

In the meantime on 5 October Harold Wilson had announced his Cabinet reshuffle linked to a reorganization of the machinery of government. There was some doubt as to whether the reorganization had dictated the reshuffle or whether the Prime Minister's political preoccupations had governed the shape of the new machinery. DEA *was wound up, and two new super Departments were created: a Ministry of Technology to subsume the Ministry of Power and the industrial responsibilities of the Board of Trade, to which he promoted Tony Benn; and an environment empire of Local Government and Regional Planning of which Tony Crosland became overlord, assisted by Tony Greenwood as Minister of Housing. In this way he was able to move Crosland from the Board of Trade where he was impeding my plans, to remove Tony Greenwood from the Cabinet and to downgrade Peter Shore to Minister without Portfolio, though still in the Cabinet. He also seized the opportunity to get rid of Dick Marsh, whose place at Transport was taken by Fred Mulley, and to retire Fred Lee from the Duchy of Lancaster to make room in the Cabinet for George Thomson who was again put in charge of* EEC *negotiations. Judith*

Hart also left the Cabinet to become Minister of Overseas Development in Reg Prentice's place and Harold Lever was promoted to the Cabinet in her former post of Paymaster-General with responsibilities at MinTech. Kenneth Robinson also left the Government. The net effect was to reduce the size of Cabinet from twenty-three to twenty-one. In the reshuffle of junior Ministers, Edmund Dell became my Minister of State and Dick Taverne Financial Secretary to the Treasury. Reg Prentice was offered the post of Minister of State at MinTech, but resigned after a couple of days.

Wednesday, 8 October. Management Committee to consider prices and incomes policy and the merger. Once again we all agreed that Part 2 must be reactivated.

We then turned to my new proposal for a comprehensive IR Bill minus penal powers. Harold is obviously worried about this. He can see us pushing through a charter for the trade unions next summer in the middle of the worst outbreak of strikes since we came to power. His solution is for me to prepare a comprehensive Bill while having tougher powers (*e.g.* on compulsory registration) ready in reserve. Roy's hatred of the unions came bursting out. When I said I would have to go into consultations officially with the TUC, he said tartly that I should avoid this as far as possible. 'The more impotent one is, the more important it is not to get into a close embrace that will reveal one's impotence.'

Thursday, 9 October. A tough Cabinet. We should never have got the merger through if Harold had not dedicated himself to it from beginning to end. Undeterred by the big guns brought against us, he summed up that we were agreed there should be a reference to the merger in the Queen's Speech in 'rather general' terms which Fred, Roy Jenkins and I should agree. When Crosland chipped in to say that surely the President of the Board of Trade should be consulted about the wording, too, Harold said blandly, 'Of course.' On this rather confused note we ended, but we've gained our main point.

Another victory gained was over the supply of Wasp helicopters to South Africa. On balance OPD had been in favour, led by Tony Crosland and Roy, with Harold apparently concurring on the grounds that these were replacements and that it was a pure accident that these helicopters had been included in the shopping list we had turned down in 1967. They could only at great expense be adapted to riot control. But a number of us hit back and we won, Michael Stewart helping a lot by saying what trouble it would cause in the UN. I am convinced that the cynicism of a number of our colleagues is one of the main reasons for the demoralization of our rank and file.

Wednesday, 15 October. Tommy was full of gloom about Harold's reorganization of the machinery of government: says the Treasury has been 'terrifyingly strengthened'. Tommy agreed that we couldn't change the economic policy this side of the Election, but what were we trying to win the Election for? The Treasury was swinging to the Right and Roy was no one's friend but his own. I pointed out that Harold now backed Roy in everything and we agreed this was alarming. I said we must resume our regular private meetings as a group and Tommy cheered up at this.

What interests me most about Harold's reorganization is the way no one believes it will shift the balance of power in the Cabinet. Certainly Harold has skilfully removed Crosland from the Board of Trade, where he was getting in my hair, to a job which will keep him very busy dealing with local government machinery. As Harold put it to me with relish, 'It will stop him meddling so much in economics.' I am more than ever convinced I was right to refuse his job.

Thursday, 16 October. Back to public expenditure at Cabinet. Roy presented the proposals of officials for cutting expenditure in 1971–72 by £355m. Most people accepted their cuts, Denis grudgingly agreeing to push his defence figure up to £60m. But the real debate raged over overseas aid, on which Judith had been hinting darkly beforehand that she might resign. On the main principle there was near unanimity: that we had got to announce our intention to move towards 1 per cent and give better proof of it in the figures for 1971–72. Harold appalled me by suddenly saying cynically that, as we only got credit for the quantity of our aid and not its quality (*e.g.* interest-free loans) we should increase the quantity and reduce the quality. It is this Philistine streak in him which reduces me to despair and arouses the distrust of so many people. I weighed in vigorously. So Harold was isolated ignominiously.

Monday, 20 October. Sudden meeting of MISC 205. I guessed that it was about import deposits and I was right. Roy said that a decision had to be announced the next day. He had discussed the matter with the Americans and the IMF when he was in the States, and they obviously thought it was reasonable that we should keep the scheme on and their attitude would have a big influence with GATT [General Agreement on Tariffs and Trade]. He therefore believed that we should go to 40 per cent instead of 50 per cent at the end of the year. His aim would be to phase the scheme out gradually with a view to eliminating it completely by December 1970. I was the only one to raise a critical voice. I was appalled that we should reduce the cash deposits to 40 per cent of the value of the imports instead of 50 per cent by the end of the year. Harold said Cabinet must be consulted and he asked Burke to call a Cabinet for 9.30 am tomorrow.

Tuesday, 21 October. At Cabinet I was astonished at Roy's behaviour. Obviously nettled at the effectiveness of my attack on him yesterday, he made a very different explanation of what he intended to do on import deposits. I could hardly believe my ears as he said that the effect of the relaxation on imports would be so marginal as to be negligible. He also assured Dick that he had no intention of relaxing further by any given date. He played on the awful trouble we would have with EFTA (which he had hardly mentioned yesterday) and didn't mention the attitude of the Americans and the IMF. I made my great spiel again but his evasions had countered most of my points. Only Wedgie and Fred backed me, Wedgie making a far better case against any relaxation at all than I had been able to do.

Into Management Committee. Crosland and Wedgie have joined us and Jim is back, determined to show that he hasn't been intimidated by the PM's displeasure.

Wednesday, 22 October. In the evening Ted and I went to a reception at the American Embassy. I felt that I owed it to the poor, harassed ambassador, Annenberg. In the event I enjoyed it enormously, which seldom happens to me at cocktail parties. But there were a lot of trade unionists there and I found myself in a corner with Fred Hayday in expansive mood after a few drinks. He told me that he knew we were going through a difficult time over strikes but that I should play it quietly. 'If the strikes go on, you will find the General Council split and things will be possible which were impossible last summer.' Vic was there and friendliness itself. He came over to me to say, 'You look tired: take care of yourself.' I retorted that he had better take care of himself, too. 'I've just been paying you another public tribute,' I told him. 'Thank God someone is, luv.' 'It must be hell.' 'It is killing, luv.'

Thursday, 23 October. I reported all this to Cabinet and we had a long discussion about the industrial situation. Militancy seems to have grown up spontaneously from the shop floor. Personally I think the explanation is very simple: Roy Jenkins's austerity has applied only to one section of society. Moreover, he has been the first to climb down whenever strike action threatened our economic recovery.

Tuesday, 28 October. The Queen's Speech went down well.[1] It was gratifying to stand at the bar of the Lords and hear the Queen read out the historic decision on equal pay. Harold's speech in the afternoon didn't go down so well. There are times when he seems positively determined to bore the pants off everyone. I was surprised when he started to dilate on strikes, stressing that other countries were in the same boat as we were over the rash of unofficial strikes. He was so obviously exposing himself to the taunt that he was doing a *volte-face*, as the titters from our own back benches showed.

Wednesday, 29 October. I was going to cut the PLP meeting when a message came from No. 10 that the PM wanted me to be there to answer any points on P and I policy. The meeting was sparsely attended and the atmosphere flat and I couldn't help remarking that the PLP really only comes alive when it has something to attack. Then suddenly Charlie Pannell, of all people, said that he hoped the Government wasn't going to create an unnecessary row by insisting on pressing ahead with the Part 2 Order. As I expected the argument has now switched to the line that as the powers are so mild it isn't worth the row! Norman Atkinson followed with a thoughtful philosophic speech. I answered Norman in kind philosophically. I pointed out that the lack of philosophic argument in the Party wasn't entirely the fault of the Government. Look at the attendance that morning: the PLP was just not interested in discussing anything constructively. And I stressed the importance of keeping up the *educational* momentum of P and I policy. Later I was staggered to read great stories in the press that I had 'harangued' the meeting and stuck my neck out again in

[1] Despite the imminence of a General Election, it was full of meat. It announced that we were going to legislate on equal pay, the setting up of CIM, my new Industrial Relations Bill, labour-only sub-contracting, amendments to the Merchant Shipping Act, civil aviation and the reorganization of the ports on the basis of public ownership.

support of a detested P and I policy. Really! The trouble is that we are all now at the mercy of Houghton's reporting to the press.

Wednesday, 5 November. To lunch with the Chancellor. Roy was as friendly as usual – positively jocular. In these relaxed moments I quite warm to him, though my instinctive reticences, born of the Bevan *v.* Gaitskell days, would always prevent my making a friend of him. One exchange, I thought, was very revealing. Roy was saying that I really ought to have a 'grace and favour' residence as he has at No. 11. There was George Brown's flat still empty – I really ought to have it. The idea doesn't attract me. I prefer the more modest comforts of our own flat. So, apparently, do Roy's children who, he said wryly, have insisted on moving out of No. 11 so that poor Jennifer has to commute between two homes. 'Not that I will be here myself very long,' he added. The reason, apparently, is that he thinks no one ought to be Chancellor for more than three years. So, even if we win the next Election, he doesn't want to stay in this particular job. But if we win the next Election under Harold, Roy will clearly have little chance of becoming PM. I thought this remark showed that, in the conflict between the ambitious politician and the lover of the good life, for Roy the good life would always have a head start.

The other major point in our discussion was P and I policy. I told Roy that I thought a 3½ per cent norm was no longer conceivable. The only hope of the policy was that it should keep in touch with reality. That was why I wanted to produce an 'unconventional and imaginative White Paper', giving something like 10 per cent increases for the lower paid with the rest being asked to accept 6 per cent increases. 'If I got a 6 per cent increase in incomes overall I should be perfectly satisfied,' said Roy ruefully. He promised not to close his mind to my ideas and to put one of his less conventional chaps on to the job of arguing it out with my people. As he showed me downstairs we ran into Jennifer. She was full of alarm that I should ever consider taking a Government residence. 'The Ministry of Works' responsibility stops here,' she exclaimed, sweeping a gesture to the top of the stairs from the official entrance. 'Above here there are eleven rooms, every one of them full of dust, and I am supposed to deal with them. It is enough to make me a feminist.'

Thursday, 6 November. I missed Cabinet as I was delivering my speech to the Institute of Directors at the Albert Hall. It went down very well. I had worked hard on Bernard Ingham's basic draft, and only left in one of his many references to the way power had passed to the shop floor (which I had developed rather carefully in my speech to the Industrial Society the other day). Later I was astonished to see this headlined in a number of newspapers, including *The Times*. Yet my speech to the Industrial Society had barely been reported! It is a revelation of the way the press can create a totally misleading atmosphere by lifting one paragraph out of a balanced speech.

Monday, 10 November. Saw the CBI on the IR Bill, purely at this stage to indicate its scope. I played it rather cleverly, not giving them any details and asking them to reserve judgment until the consultations on the exact contents began. I was getting away with this nicely when Douglas Taylor asked if, on trade union recognition, we were still going to have penalties on employers though we had dropped them against unions, and I said yes. Campbell Adamson[1] drew himself up at this and thundered that, if that were so, they couldn't exactly refrain from comment, even at this stage. I shrugged at this (some CBI thundering will help me with the TUC).

Tuesday, 11 November. At Management Committee we spent a lot of time on what Harold should say in the House about the Civil List.[2] Edinburgh has put his foot in it again and we agreed that the question of what to pay the Royal Family was something we didn't want stirring up this side of the Election. But Dick said angrily that he thought Philip's speech was a constitutional breach, while I urged that Harold shouldn't say anything that would prevent us widening the argument after the Election. Why, after all, should the Civil List be increased to enable Philip to play polo, when his wife was one of the richest women in the world, and who enjoyed tax concessions that other people were denied? The rest were rather in sympathy with all this and I think we may have influenced some of Harold's answers to supplementaries. Eddie passed me a note suggesting jocularly we might refer the 'Royals' to the PIB. I had already been thinking about this quite seriously, but when I proposed it it was laughed out of court.

Wednesday, 12 November. At OPD we discussed the Duncan Report.[3] Even Michael said he didn't like the over-blunt division into 'areas of concentration' and the 'outer areas', but it was clearly the way it was stated rather than the idea which he objected to. I urged that we should not accept Duncan's geographical division either but wait till we had finished our survey post by post. Harold, too, deplored Duncan's division of the world 'literally into black and white'. But my best bit of work was on Duncan's reference to the need for an urgent start with a new HQ for the FO. What, I asked, was this Whitehall Development Plan Committee, to which the officials' covering note referred? Just where did we stand on the plan for rebuilding Whitehall which seemed to be rolling onwards like a juggernaut without any of us having discussed it properly? It's all right, Harold said, we agreed that it couldn't be carried out for the time being on economy grounds. Blow that, I exploded. Why pull the FO building down at all? Give them a new one on the South Bank. From St James's

[1] W.O. Campbell Adamson had been seconded to DEA as an industrial adviser in 1967 where he had served as Deputy Under-Secretary of State and Coordinator of Industrial Advisers until 1969 when he became Director-General of the CBI.

[2] In an interview on American television on 9 November Prince Philip had said that the royal finances would 'go into the red next year' because payments to the royal family under the Civil List had not kept pace with inflation. This caused an uproar at home and on 12 November Harold Wilson had to make a statement to the House. He made a skilful apologia for Prince Philip's remarks by pointing out that the Civil List would move into deficit by the end of 1970 while pointing out that a number of the royal expenses had been transferred to Departmental Votes, and by announcing that he had agreed with Her Majesty's advisers that a new Select Committee to examine the Civil List would be appointed at the beginning of next Parliament. In the meantime any deficit would be covered 'from funds available to Her Majesty from sources other than public funds'.

[3] In August 1968, the Government had set up a Committee under Sir Val Duncan 'to review urgently the functions and scale of British representational effort overseas' in the light of Britain's changing international role. One of the main conclusions of its Report (Cmnd 4107) was that from the point of view of diplomatic representation overseas countries could be divided into two broad categories: 'advanced industrial countries' with which we were likely to become increasingly involved, and the rest of the world, or 'outer area'.

Park bridge there was one of the loveliest vistas in any capital city in the world. Millions of people enjoyed it every day, including me. It entranced me every time I walked to the office from the House. Were we really going to be guilty of monstrous vandalism by putting modern buildings in Whitehall instead? To my delight Roy backed me enthusiastically and Harold agreed we should have a paper on the whole thing. Nothing I have achieved in Cabinet has elated me so much for a long time.

Monday, 17 November. Highlight of the day was my PIF [Prices and Incomes] Committee on the White Paper. All we should do at this stage, I said, was to discuss the quantitative guidelines. I dismissed a norm of 3½ per cent as utterly unrealistic; no norm at all as a complete abandonment of the policy. And urged the only alternative: a realistic range of 2½–5 per cent. Roy said he would prefer 3½ per cent, no norm and a range in that order, but stuck out firmly against anything higher than 2½–4½ per cent. To my surprise Dick as well as Peter backed me warmly. So did many others. At the end Roy, stretching it a bit, summed up that he thought the Committee favoured either a norm of 4 per cent or a range of 3–4½ per cent.

Tuesday, 18 November. The office rang to say that the Chancellor was putting in a terrible report of PIF to Cabinet. Could I go over and see him and try to keep the 5 per cent issue open? So I dashed over to No. 11 where Roy and I had a friendly argument. He stuck out quite toughly at first and then, as he often does these days, he suddenly melted and said that, although he was willing to do a private deal with me then and there on a 2½–4½ per cent range, he would have no objection to my reopening the 5 per cent: 'though', with a grin, 'if you go and make one of your great speeches and sweep Cabinet off its feet, I shall have to come in hard for no range at all.' And so we left it amicably.

Wednesday, 19 November. Dinner with CIR, this time with me as host. The main idea was to discuss the next references but the main interest of the evening lay in a very frank discussion about the trade unions. Alf Allen and Will Paynter[1] objected to my saying in my Institute of Directors speech that power has passed to the shop floor. They don't welcome this development a bit. I replied, George Woodcock backing me, that I wasn't recommending this as much as pointing it out as a fact and was saying that, since the unions wouldn't do anything to contain this development, management would have to do so 'and follow power down the line where it has gone'. It is clear that Alf and Will are bitterly anti-Jack Jones and think he is destroying traditional trade unionism. I said I would believe they were serious about it when one of them – any of them – spoke out openly about the dangers. George was with me all the way, not least on P and I policy. 'I've always been in favour of this though I've stressed that we can't get it quickly.' George is in great form these days.

Thursday, 20 November. By insisting on rejecting Roy's offer of a deal and fighting for 5 per cent I nearly lost the whole day at Cabinet! Once again we

[1] William Paynter, former Secretary of the NUM, was a Communist with a record of service in the International Brigade and on the hunger marches of the 1930s.

weren't discussing the wording of the WP though I had circulated my powerful redraft on the low paid to show how it would fit in with the concept of the range. A number of them took fright, led by, of all people, Jim Callaghan! The best hope in my view was a range of 2½–5 per cent as we might then just hold some settlements at 5 per cent, particularly in the public sector. If Harold had summed up arithmetically I should have been lost. Instead he took the 'sense' of the meeting as being in favour of striking a compromise between the Chancellor's anxieties and the view of the responsible Minister, 'who really has had great successes in operating the policy'. (Murmurs of Hear, Hear.)

Monday, 24 November. Early SEP meeting to discuss the WP on public expenditure over the next five years. This piece of forward looking is causing us a lot of trouble. The hottest argument raged over overseas aid. Judith had put in an excellent paper. Roy retorted that a commitment to raise official aid to 0.7 per cent by 1975 would mean raising it to £500m in that year, something we couldn't risk with our balance of payments so precarious. All he was prepared to do was to add £20m in 1972–73 and another £20m in 1973–74, reckoned in real not cash terms. Dick, never an overseas aid enthusiast, grumbled about this: 'I realize the skill of this lobby.' Others maintained that our record compared favourably with that of stronger countries than we were.

It is at moments like these that I despair of this Government, and I crashed in: look at the figures in Judith's paper. They showed that our aid as a percentage of GNP had actually gone down compared with the Tories! What on earth had we bothered to set up a special Ministry for? This wasn't a sentimental lobby: it was an economically realistic one. In fact, it was still true that the aid programmes helped the developed countries as much as, if not more than, the developing ones. Where would international trade be without them? So Harold had to agree to refer the whole issue to Cabinet.

Tuesday, 25 November. When the PESC discussions were resumed in Cabinet Roy began by announcing that he was prepared to increase his offer to £25m and £35m [on overseas aid] over the two years in question in view of yesterday's discussion.

Wednesday, 26 November. A meeting of PIF to discuss my revised draft of the P and I White Paper on which I have spent long hours. I am very pleased with my rewrite of the section on the low paid which even Jarratt and Locke haven't been able to fault seriously. Roy was my biggest difficulty here, saying that if I went on like this I would produce the most inflationary WP ever. He wanted a paragraph inserted to the effect that the low paid would only be entitled to pay above the normal range where this was necessary to give them 'reasonable' standards. I had to agree to look at this, though John Locke and I are determined not to include anything so nonsensical.

Thursday, 27 November. Got my draft WP through Cabinet without too much difficulty. Harold, I am sure, is wise to insist on Cabinet approval before the draft is circulated to the TUC and CBI for consultation: he is determined not to have me isolated and betrayed this time. He pointed out that this was only a basis for consultation; that PIF would have to discuss a final draft next week for Cabinet to clear on Monday 8 December, ready for publication on the 10th or 11th. So we only made a few amendments. For the rest of the document was accepted to a man, Jim merely saying he was glad the WP was flexible about the police.

The WP on public expenditure went through smoothly, too.

Tuesday, 2 December. A victory for the girls at OPD! Michael had put in an innocent-seeming paper saying that he was about to convey to the South African Government Cabinet's decision taken in October not to supply them with Wasp helicopters. It would be helpful if he could tell them at the same time that we would be prepared to replace two Buccaneers they had lost in accidents in accordance with the policy we had agreed in 1965. He was backed warmly by Denis and Roy Mason and it was literally going through on the nod when I asked quietly what this policy decision in 1965 was and how did it compare with what we had said when we came in in 1964? I thought we had only agreed then to fulfil the Buccaneer order on the grounds that we couldn't cancel existing contracts. The supply of two new Buccaneers was a very different kettle of fish. Great flurry as Harold sent for the relevant statements. He then read out what he had said in the House on 24 November 1964: no mention at all of replacements, only of the supply of spares. To do him justice, he positively chuckled at the discovery. It then transpired that the statement of 31 May 1965 was a purely private one to the South African Government, in which we had said that we would be willing to replace items lost through accidents, though not through normal wear and tear. (I suspect this private message was never even agreed in Cabinet.) Anyway I was on an easy wicket in pointing out that the supply of two Buccaneers now, following our line in 1964 and 1967, would come as something of a shock to the PLP. Hesitation all round. Judith then followed up by asking equally sweetly whether the South African Government had requested the supply of these planes? Michael had to admit they hadn't. So our victory was complete. Harold summed up perfectly happily that our Chargé d'Affaires was not to raise the matter with the South African Government.

I was also encouraged later in the day when I saw the TUC on my draft WP on prices and incomes. As usual the Department was all for my playing it quietly, but I've got a bit tired of this advice. Of course, we knew they had to make noises about Part 2, though we were convinced that the row would be largely a ritual one, but I was determined to get them discussing the merits of the policy of the WP apart from the powers. I therefore opened rather unusually by giving them a summary of the philosophy and main points of the WP. They were a curious group: the Economic Committee led by Tom O'Brien of the Cine Technicians' Union with the two power houses, Jack and Hughie, sitting back modestly while he made all the running. They knew he would have to toe the Congress line, which he did rather unconvincingly. The General Council, he told me, still stood for the 'complete repeal of the P and I Act'. I would not, therefore, expect them to engage 'at this stage' in any discussion.

The Government, I replied earnestly, wanted to enter into a constructive dialogue with the trade union movement. 'How would YOU', I challenged them, 'deal with the problem of the low paid? How would YOU suggest a Government should control demand if the money paid out in incomes exceeds what is produced? These are economic problems that face any type of society.' Hughie, essential innocent that he is, was goaded by all this into coming out of his corner. If I wanted a philosophical discussion, he said, no one would welcome it more than he at the appropriate time. For the moment all he would say was that he did not accept that a P and I policy could redistribute wealth or help the lower paid. Nor could he accept that wage claims could ever be inflationary. They were obviously relieved when I said that there wouldn't be time for any further consultations before the WP was published.

Wednesday, 3 December. Main business at Management Committee was to plan the parliamentary timetable over my WP and Part 2. I'm going to have a horrible time of it! On to Industrial Policy Committee where Jack Diamond (who never agreed with the merger anyway) and Harold Lever (reflecting MinTech's determination not to have anyone interfere with 'its' industries) fought me every inch of the way on the powers and scope of the new body. We got agreement to include the 400 large firms, but had a wrangle over what constituted the 'public interest'. I suppose I am lucky to get as much as I have, with no powers over incomes and theoretically far-reaching powers over prices, particularly with Crosland waiting in the wings to make a row in Cabinet.

The Parliamentary Labour Party was becoming increasingly restless over the Vietnam war. Feeling had been brought to a head by allegations released by three American soldiers on 18 November that in March 1968 they had witnessed 'point blank murders' by American soldiers of Vietnamese women and children in the My Lai village in the 'Pinkville' (the American code-name) area of Vietnam. Over thirty Labour MPs tabled a Motion calling on the Government to express its 'deep concern' and there were immediate demands for a debate before Harold Wilson went to Washington. On 24 November the US Army ordered a court-martial of First Lieutenant William Calley for his responsibility as platoon commander for the 'premeditated murder' of 109 villagers at My Lai, and the Government was forced to concede a two-day foreign affairs debate of which the first day was primarily devoted to Vietnam.

Thursday, 4 December. One of the main items at Cabinet was the coming two-day debate in the House on foreign affairs. Harold said that he had decided to open on the second day in order to be able to answer Heath's speech on the first, but I begged him to reconsider this. He ought to set the whole tone of the debate by a statesmanlike wide-ranging speech, not merely react to Heath's debating points. Above all we must recognize that our usual line on Vietnam just would not do any more. This was a war the Americans could not win and most Americans knew it. Wedgie backed me up strongly. Harold was clearly shaken. He agreed at once that he would open, assuring us that he would make a philosophical speech stressing the moral dilemma that faced all of us. He also promised we should have a full discussion on Vietnam during the recess, which is more to the point.

At PIF we finally approved my draft WP, with the exception of my new prices chapter. I've stayed up late two nights rewriting this and have now got it much more on the lines that Tommy and Aubrey want. In fact, I'm very pleased with it. But of course the rest (particularly Roy and Harold Lever) nearly hit the roof. After a fierce argument it was agreed that their officials and mine should meet to agree the draft. I told John Locke to get cracking at once and not to yield anything of substance. As time is now so short he would have to travel to Bristol with me for my party engagements tomorrow to go through what was agreed. Roy tried to get me to put his 'reasonable standards' phrase in the low paid chapter but I successfully out-argued him.

Monday, 8 December. My P and I WP sailed through Cabinet.[1] Our biggest argument was about the section on public service salaries. I agree that it would be intolerable to operate a P and I policy which merely penalized the public sector – that is the Tory policy, not mine. So I didn't mind some loopholes. Harold then summed up that the WP should be published on the 11th and that the Part 2 Order should be laid before the House late that day – which was accepted without a murmur by anyone.

Wednesday, 10 December. Long discussion at SEP on the future of Concorde. Everyone, including Wedgie, now agrees that for the first time we have a choice as to whether we continue the project or not, because the costs are escalating beyond all reason and give us a good case legally. Everyone is convinced that Concorde will be an economic flop. Roy Mason was emphatic about the folly of the whole project. [He] was all for having a confrontation with the French on the facts before June. Wedgie, chastened as he was and admitting the scheme ought never to have been started, couldn't agree to this. Eventually we agreed that we should review the project in June.

Thursday, 11 December. My great – or terrible? – day for the publication of the Prices and Incomes WP. Press and TV were waiting to fall on me but I had to go through the agony of part of Cabinet first in order to get approval for my consultative document on CIM. At last I escaped.

A formidable phalanx of the lobby and the industrials was waiting for me over at the House. Introducing the WP I made a strong case on the danger of a

[1] The White Paper, 'Productivity, Prices and Incomes Policy after 1969' (Cmnd 4237) confirmed that the more stringent controls over prices and incomes would be allowed to lapse at the end of the year, but that the milder early warning and delaying powers of Part 2 of the 1966 Act would be renewed pending the setting-up of the new Commission for Industry and Manpower to discharge the educational role of the long-term policy. Its function would be to examine specific pay and price increases in the context of wider questions about the operation of a firm or industry: 'how, for instance, it is tackling the problem of labour costs, whether it is making full use of capital equipment, whether it is investing adequately and whether its pricing policies generally are in the public interest.' In the meantime the White Paper laid down guidelines for the coming phase of the policy. Pay settlements should fall within a range of $2\frac{1}{2}$–$4\frac{1}{2}$ per cent a year, the higher range being intended to help the low paid and facilitate the move towards equal pay. It went even further and admitted that in certain cases the introduction of equal pay, or fair treatment for the low-paid groups, would only be possible 'through pay settlements which on average work out above the normal range'. It also set out the conditions for price increases and price reductions, but since I was still arguing with Treasury about the powers CIM should have, I could not be specific about my intention to give it strong powers over prices and none over pay settlements. All I was allowed to say about the latter was that 'the Government hopes it will not be necessary to perpetuate these delaying powers in the legislation to set up CIM'. This equivocal statement led the TUC promptly to reject the White Paper and gave me great trouble in the House.

prices and wages explosion if Part 2 powers were not reactivated – too rapid de-escalation of the present powers could be psychologically dangerous. I think this is totally convincing but I got a foretaste of the arguments I am to meet when John Torode said smoothly that I had made a powerful case, but what would be changed when the new body came into existence? How could I justify abandoning all powers then? I have no answer to this as long as I cannot say that effective powers over prices (and therefore indirectly over incomes) will be retained in the new legislation – and as long as I know that I will have to fight a pusillanimous Cabinet to create an effective role for the new body. However, I don't think I came out of press or TV interviews too badly.

At 5.30 pm into a crowded PLP meeting to outline the contents of the WP. I didn't make my most effective speech though as usual I rallied under hostile questioning. It obviously isn't going to be easy to get the Part 2 Order through. The discussion was postponed till next week.

Sunday, 14 December. Spent the weekend preparing for a ghastly week ahead, including a meeting of the NEC, for which Joe Gormley has tabled a resolution condemning the Government for reactivating Part 2. To cap the lot the press has been full of stories to the effect that I have railroaded my colleagues into hanging on to the remnants of a P and I policy which they are anxious to ditch, so the Party is being brought to the edge of a crisis again purely to save my face. Harold is far more angry about these stories than I am – I'm just resigned to the fact that I am going through a bad patch press-wise and there is nothing I can do about it.

Tuesday, 16 December. At the PLP meeting on the Prices and Incomes WP Houghton opened the proceedings with a remarkable statement saying that there were some very different issues facing us this time compared with the summer. The first was the economic one. Were we going to pre-empt the Chancellor's freedom of action in the Budget? The second was the issue of confidence: whether the Government made it a vote of confidence or not, in fact the Party and the Government would be in total disarray if we were defeated on Wednesday. Then Roy turned up and made a vigorous and effective intervention claiming the importance of the policy. But I was horrified at the irresponsibility of so many who spoke, notably Brian Walden who seemed to think he was on a winner when he claimed that he just couldn't understand why, if it was so important to have powers over prices now and to prevent a wages explosion (which he thought were powerful arguments), it wouldn't be equally important to have those powers in a few months' time. Even if he were right – and I think the answer that we must de-escalate in a controlled way is a good one – couldn't he with so much at stake take us on trust enough to wait and see what the powers of the new body will be? After all, he is not opposed to a P and I policy. The political irresponsibility of the PLP frightens me. The opposition to us was so contradictory it was just a rabble.

Scribbled the first parts of my speech for Wednesday's debate between office parties. What a business!

Wednesday, 17 December. Got up early to continue my jottings for the speech, then had to dash to the NEC where, to my intense relief, Joe Gormley announced that he was going to withdraw his motion. Later, on the front bench, I turned to Jim sweetly and said, 'How did you get Joe to do it, Jim?' He smiled a rather secretive smile and then his self-satisfaction overcame him: 'Well, I just told him that I wouldn't be able to support him this time.' What a Freudian slip! – a clear confession that he had told Joe he *would* support him over my industrial relations proposals last summer.

Thanks to his respite, I even got a peroration to my speech sketched out, and I thought it went down quite well. By this time I was too exhausted to care anyhow. Roy's winding up was masterly. The most nauseating part of the debate was Brian Walden's speech – brilliantly destructive, the most able bit of rhetoric I've heard for a long time but saturated with political vanity. How can any serious politician risk bringing down his Government on a debating point, however cleverly expressed? I just couldn't do it. We won easily by twenty-eight votes.

Thursday, 18 December. More P and I problems in the afternoon. The gas workers are on the march for an increase of 18 per cent and of course Harold Lever wants to capitulate. He argues we shall face strikes if at any rate we don't allow the Gas Council to offer 14 per cent. But, if we do, how can we prevent the unofficial strikes now threatening in the electricity supply industry over their unions' settlement of 10 per cent? So we said: 10 per cent for the gas workers and no more. Then the building workers are on the rampage, having reached a settlement for an annual increase of 10 per cent, or $8\frac{1}{2}$ per cent on earnings. Jarratt is all in favour of our being tough but I am very reluctant to seem to keep picking on the building workers. I therefore suggested that I should see both sides and try, under threat of a standstill, to try and get them to strengthen the productivity side of the deal by accepting a firm commitment to the introduction of job evaluation. This was agreed.

Christmas parties have started. [At] No. 10, where Harold was entertaining the lobby, I'm afraid I had a tiff with Ian Aitken over his stories about Cabinet hostility to my P and I policy. He said it was the duty of the press to be irresponsible. Very well, I said, then you must accept that the press is irrelevant. 'If I were to ring you and check up on the story I was proposing to write, would you tell me whether I was right or not?' asked Ian. No, I said flatly, I wouldn't. There you are, then, he retorted. It got quite heated. I'm sure I would get a much better press if I were to leak, but I simply can't do it. I have an irremovable blockage about that sort of thing.

Tuesday, 23 December. At last we are on our way. With fourteen adults and six children to cater for over Christmas there is a hectic time ahead and I have a bilious reaction from the strain of the past weeks. But I have a hunch that this is going to be a great Christmas.

Wednesday, 24 December to Sunday, 28 December. And so it has proved to be. None of us has had flu. And the children are in the seventh heaven. Sonya's American friends who have come to stay say they too have never had a

Christmas like it. Even the clearing up was fun. I dread to think that anything might happen to Ted. How could I ever face life if I lived a solitary, self-contained widow's life? Politics is only tolerable if one has human interludes like this.

1970

Monday, 5 January. Back to the office with my usual sense of guilt at having had a few days off and full of ideas for catching up. I immediately set in train my plan to have a weekly 'Sits and Snags' meeting to progress our work. Of course the problem is to find a regular time when we can all meet: I have Cabinet committee meetings every morning, even including Mondays if I'm not lucky. Eventually I gave up in despair and asked Douglas to lay one on for tomorrow for a start. Spent two hours catching up with constituency letters.

Wednesday, 7 January. Meeting with Harold Lever on the gas claim. His Department is all for allowing the Gas Council to go for 14 per cent. We pointed out that, if we went above 10 per cent, we should alienate Les Cannon of the Electricians' Union who really did a job getting the electricity supply boys to accept that figure. After careful consideration I decided we should stick to 10 per cent and risk strike action.

Tuesday, 13 January. We were astounded to read in the papers that the Gas Council had settled with the union on a 14 per cent increase. Yet Edmund Dell was due to attend SEP yesterday in my place to insist that we didn't allow the Gas Council to go above 10 per cent. Had SEP lost its nerve or had Henry Jones defied us?[1] The latter, it transpired, from the note Polly from Private Office was waiting to give me. I was furious. I am sure we shouldn't have had a strike if the Gas Council had stood firm, but now we might well have one if we were to standstill the settlement. The office recommends standstilling, but Douglas agreed with me that it was now impossible.

Harold Lever, reporting to Cabinet, said Henry Jones had written to him saying the wage deal would mean that £15m extra costs would have to be passed on in higher prices and they were proposing a $4\frac{1}{2}$ per cent increase in the bill of domestic consumers. Everyone in Cabinet was angry. They all felt the Gas Council had behaved intolerably. The line we should now take generally was that there would be no price increases if employers gave unjustified wage increases – as Frank Cousins had argued in Cabinet years ago. We shouldn't standstill the wage increase but make a reference to the PIB to find ways to compel the Gas Council to absorb the extra cost. I'm delighted at this change of line because it greatly strengthens the case for 'asymmetrical' powers for CIM.

Naturally enough, the gas settlement has made Ted Short's position far more difficult with the teachers. Privately Alex Jarratt thinks we shall now have to make some further concession to them, possibly through a short-term

[1] Sir Henry Jones, chairman of the Gas Council.

reference to the PIB on their interim claim. However, Ted is taking things pretty calmly at the moment and only asking that we should try and persuade the teachers to accept arbitration, and so it was agreed.

My main meeting in the afternoon was with the builders.[1] I told my Department firmly that, if we weren't going to standstill gas, I certainly wasn't going to standstill building. Why pick on them twice, particularly as they have clearly made an effort to carry out the recommendations of the PIB? The meeting went marvellously. I told them that the last thing I wanted to do was to weaken the NJC machinery. When I had cut off the penny I had asked them to go away and see how they could make progress under the PIB report while at the same time promising that the Government would act on the Phelps Brown Report. Both of us had kept our promises but their agreement was too vague in two vital respects and now I wanted them to help me to help them. They nearly fell over themselves in their eagerness to accept my request that they should send me a letter elaborating their assurances on job evaluation and work study. Even George Smith and Les Kemp, who like to make ferocious noises, were disarmed. My officials were agreeably surprised by the outcome.

Spent the rest of the day with Harold Lever and Jack Diamond settling the terms of reference to the PIB on gas, seeing Henry Jones and drawing up a very tricky press statement. Sir Henry was terribly nervous when he came in, taken aback by the reference, and then spent a lot of time assuring us that he hadn't contemplated early price increases: anyway not before the summer. There wouldn't be price increases even then, I told him firmly. Jack Diamond has played along marvellously, saying he was prepared to commit the Treasury on this occasion not to press for price increases. The Gas Council must just get down its costs. If only the Treasury will co-operate by being more flexible in future, I think we may be able to get somewhere.

One interesting footnote: as he left Sir Henry thanked me for not standstilling them, adding, 'though I don't think there would have been a strike if you had'(!). So once again we had been misled by sponsoring Departments – just as we were over the water undertakings.

Wednesday, 14 January. Long discussion in Management Committee on our political strategy for the next months. Harold said that we should take an autumn Election as our assumption, though there was always the possibility of seeing a favourable opportunity earlier. Roy outlined his view of our economic strategy. In 1970, he said, we should be able to hold – and ought to hold – to a balance of payments surplus of £450–£500m. It was important to keep to this target as he wanted to announce a debt clean-up at the time of the Budget. Our investment position had improved quite a lot, though it was not very high compared with other countries. Growth at 2 per cent had been disappointing in 1969 but was likely to be 3 per cent this year or a little more. Earnings were likely to add strongly to consumer demand and there would be no great room for manœuvre in the Budget. We shouldn't build up too great expectations about it but stick to the psychology of gradualism. On unemployment the picture was confused: probably there had been no real change for the past two

[1] The building unions had accepted an offer by the employers of a three-stage pay improvement which was in breach of our policy and were resisting the productivity strings the employers wanted to attach.

years. He was not sure there was anything we could or should do about this as labour demand was high, except for certain limited areas. I asked immediately what he was going to do about the import deposits scheme. If growth rose this year more than last, the imports figure was bound to be affected and I personally had been sorry we withdrew the travel restrictions so soon. It didn't help me to hold the wages front when the papers were full of how some people could now have a winter sports holiday. I hoped we weren't going to do any further relaxations of the import deposits scheme. But I had everyone against me.

We all agreed that a Maudling-type give-away Budget would be disastrous, though I said it was essential we exempted more people from income tax. I wanted to put before Cabinet a paper suggesting a group of strategic price references (Jarratt's idea). Roy said he was not against three or four key price references though he would be strongly against deliberately unbalancing the economy. It was agreed I should put the paper to Management Committee first.

Fred Mulley came to see me to say he wanted to make Peter Parker chairman of the new Ports authority and that Peter was very keen, though he thought he had a prior obligation to me. I was delighted [and] promised every support.

Thursday, 15 January. An agonizing struggle over CIM in Cabinet. I had to report on the result of the discussion with the CBI. They have, I gather, been bitter: Edmund tells me he has never seen them in more hostile mood. Campbell Adamson is saying that our proposals will damage our relations with industry irretrievably. We discount this (though we expect a terrible fight in the House) but, of course, this gave Tony Crosland his chance to try and reopen the whole policy. He proposed amendments which sounded plausible but which, I pointed out desperately, were designed to reverse the whole intention to cover large firms. After an hour of acrimonious wrangling, during which most people were out of their depth, it was left that I should have another attempt at redefining the 'triggers' for references though Harold confirmed that the decision on the four hundred firms couldn't be reversed.

Sunday, 18 January. Call from Derek Andrews[1] at No. 10. Harold had been trying to get hold of me before he leaves for America in a few days' time. 'I think the PM rather favours the IPC Reed merger and wouldn't like any decision to the contrary to be taken before he gets back.'[2] So Hugh Cudlipp has won him round!

Monday, 19 January. One of the most ideologically revealing meetings of SEP we have ever had. First Dick made a bid to be allowed to amend his Pensions Bill in committee to permit the National Superannuation Fund to invest in

[1] D. H. Andrews was one of the Prime Minister's Private Secretaries and was responsible for home affairs.

[2] Following the dramatic sacking of Cecil King from the chairmanship of IPC, Hugh Cudlipp, the journalistic genius of the *Mirror* newspapers, who succeeded him, felt the need for some reinforcement on the management side. He had therefore accepted a proposal by Don Ryder, chairman and chief executive of Reed International, for a merger of the two companies. Though this should clearly have been referred to the Monopolies Commission, Harold Wilson was anxious not to do anything to alienate the *Mirror* newspapers who were the only ones supporting the Government.

equities, as had been visualized in the Labour Party's 1957 document, 'National Superannuation'. Having carefully read my papers beforehand, I couldn't get as excited about it as Dick proceeded to do because, of course, as he admitted, this would really make very little difference: at most £100m of equity investment might be involved in the first few years.

The next item confirmed me even more deeply in my gloom. Roy had circulated a memo for submission to Neddy as our revised assessment of the medium-term economic prospects in the light of the recent talks with industry. It was an appalling document. The switch of resources into the balance of payments, it said, had now largely been achieved and it should be possible to combine an average annual rate of growth of just under 3 per cent over the period to 1972 with a continuing surplus. Wedgie followed with a MinTech paper: what he called 'the first report of my Department as a central Department'. In it he urged that there should be no major change in the industrial or fiscal framework for some time so as to give greater confidence to industry. When we could relax, the priorities should be the easing of the down payment of hire purchase. We must find more sophisticated methods of demand management than 'just bashing the mass production industries'. In taxes we should lighten the burden on highly qualified men and mineral development. The best way forward was through creative dialogues with the large firms, which he was undertaking, rather than by harrying them through bodies like CIM.

Peter jumped in and saved the day. He really is justifying his position in Cabinet by reading all the papers and thinking things through. He pounced on Roy's paper as disastrous. Were we really going to say we could only hope for a growth rate of 2.9 per cent compared with the 'wedge' of 3 to 4 per cent given in 'The Task Ahead'?[1] This was the lowest projection ever published, and compared with rates of 4 per cent and more in other European countries. It implied no reduction in unemployment, though the present level in certain regions was unacceptable. He believed there were real possibilities of faster growth. I backed him up strongly saying that this projection would be explosive and incite the unions to press even bigger wage demands as the only means open to them of getting reflation. As for Wedgie's paper, a dialogue with industry by a sponsoring Minister could not be the sole instrument of Government policy. Tony Crosland endorsed everything I said.

Roy hastened to conciliate us all. Of course he would alter the paper in the light of our remarks. As for unemployment there was still a high level of vacancies over two-thirds of the country. He would strengthen the regional side of the paper and consider putting in a 'wedge'. And so, with Harold endorsing the call for a more cheerful picture, it was left. I wish I had a macro-economist to help me draw up a counter-Treasury policy! I have never seen the SEP in such united revolt. I believe we are now running the country below its productive potential but the problem is always to mount a sufficiently concerted and authoritative attack by the rest of us to have some practical impact on Treasury policy.

[1] On 26 February 1969, Peter Shore, then Secretary of State for Economic Affairs, had presented the Government's Economic Assessment to 1972 to the House. It was published as a Green Paper called 'The Task Ahead'.

Thursday, 22 January. I spent most of Cabinet scribbling notes for my press conference this afternoon on the launching of the CIM consultative document.[1] Bernard Ingham is terrified lest we shan't be able to convince the press that our Department is competent to deal with monopoly policy. Oh yeah? If I can't make more use of the new body than the Board of Trade has of the Monopolies Commission, I'm not the girl I think I am.

I avoided any major disasters at my press conference, though obviously most of them were out of their depth.

Monday, 26 January. Another good Sits and Snags meeting at which I instructed Ken Barnes to let me have a draft outline of what he would like to be in our WP on the employment services, without waiting to clear policy at official level. I am determined to make our new manpower services plan one of the key points of my activities this year and get it adopted before the summer ends. It may well prove to be my most important monument in this job. I am reinforced in this determination by the report I have got from our Research and Planning Division on their examination of industrial training. This confirms the suspicion I have had for a long time that our industrial training leaves a lot to be desired. But I am even more reinforced by an outstanding note on our employment services I have received from Robert Keith, our Director of Establishment. And it was a pure accident that I have had it at all! It was only because I was introduced to him at Bernard Ingham's Christmas party, learned he was full of ideas on the employment services and asked him to send me a document that I have got it.

His paper is most exciting, not only for his comments, but because it sets out a piece of history, showing how officials in the Department spontaneously generated a review of the employment services as far back as 1963. The result was a report of a working-party (purely official), chaired by James Dunnett, then Permanent Secretary, which outlined the need for reform. What fascinates me about all this is the light it throws on the way government works in this country. Here was a group of officials who, independent of ministerial initiatives, initiated studies of their own Department's inefficiencies and made suggestions, waiting for a Minister to pick them up. Keith's paper points out that the employment services 'because of staff retrenchments' languished in the 1950s (Ian Macleod?) until two favourable influences began to be felt in 1963 – first, 'the managerial impulse of Sir J. Dunnett' and, secondly, the Swedish 'active manpower policy'. The return of a Labour Government obviously made an immediate difference. As Keith's paper puts it, 'in the changed circumstances of 1964 onwards we built up the total staff engaged on employment service work from 7,000 in 1963 to 9,200 in 1969.' But, as it also points out, progress was limited because the employment services never

[1] Announcing the merger between the PIB and the Monopolies Commission the document proposed to extend the Government's powers under the Monopolies Acts so as to enable the new body to carry out efficiency audits of all major firms where competition was not effective enough to protect the public interest. References to CIM could be triggered off by price increases or price levels or pay settlements or other situations which indicated that there was an abuse of market power. The Government would have a reserve power to require the notification of price increases, pay settlements or increased dividend declarations before they were implemented but would not have power to hold them up pending an investigation by CIM. It would, however, be able to freeze prices or call for their reduction on a recommendation by CIM. The new body would also rule on proposed mergers.

attracted 'a worthwhile lobby in Whitehall, Westminster or the media . . . Lack of reaction from the TUC in particular has been a loss.' But I think the trouble lay in the fact that the old Ministry of Labour was regarded, not least by Ray Gunter, as mainly a conciliation service. Certainly he was never interested in anything but the 'smoke-filled rooms' side of it.

The real chance came when we changed the Ministry of Labour into the Department of Employment, stressing the positive side of its responsibilities. Now I have more time I am pushing them for all I am worth and working overtime to deal with them myself.

Having read Keith's document I realize, for instance, that Denis Barnes should never have advised me to accept even our modest cuts in public expenditure and in the expansion of our manpower. This way we'll never replace those badly sited, ugly pre-Keynes Ministry of Labour offices or be able to raise the standard of our services. One of the things I have always deplored has been this Government's surrender to Tory agitation about 'bloated bureaucracy'. Unless we fight on this one we have one hand tied behind our backs in carrying out our plans.

Trouble was looming up again at Ford's. In the pay negotiations in the National Joint Negotiating Committee the unions were demanding parity with Midlands rates at all plants. Rejecting this the company offered at the meeting of 27 January an increase of 2s *per hour, worth from £4 to around £5 15*s *0*d *per week, together with the introduction of equal pay in two stages to be completed by March 1972, the whole agreement to be effective for twelve months. The offer was to prove acceptable to the majority of the workforce except at Swansea where an unofficial strike broke out, supported at Halewood and involving in all some 4,000 employees. The action threatened to disrupt production at other plants.*

Wednesday, 28 January. The press conference went very well. John Locke has produced an excellent background document and the correspondents couldn't find a chink in our armour. He really is bright, that boy!

Back to that familiar seventh-storey room at Grosvenor House where Gillan and Bob Ramsey were waiting for us. Bob assured me quietly that the £4 offer was their final one, even if it meant a strike. Gillan concurred sombrely. But Ramsey was not totally without hope. There were signs that some of the plants wanted to accept the offer, notably Langleys. Why not resurrect the idea of a ballot? I asked. We talked about this for some time and agreed that, if unofficial action started on Monday, I might see Jack and Hughie privately and suggest to them that a ballot might get them off the hook and be entirely consistent with their 'shop floor democracy' line.

Monday, 2 February. A long meeting of Management Committee to discuss political strategy. Harold, while pretending that Selsdon Park[1] had played right

[1] At a Conservative policy-making conference at Selsdon Park Edward Heath had set the note for the coming Election campaign by breaking with the middle-of-the-road tradition Harold Macmillan had created. As Margaret Thatcher was to do nine years later he called for a radical new medicine for Britain's ills: more incentives, lower taxes, cuts in public expenditure, tougher competition, no subsidies. People – and industries – were to be forced to stand on their own feet; all this was to be stimulated by membership of the European Community.

into our hands, was all for vigorous counter-attack based on rousing people's fears about Tory policy. I cut through the chatter impatiently. I said that we couldn't really plan our counter-attack until we had worked out our own themes for the Election and that meant knowing what would be in the Election Manifesto. It was imperative that we worked out its main lines soon and it ought to be drafted by *us* in Management Committee before the NEC got their hands on it. I suggested that we all ought to put in papers for systematic discussion over the next few weeks, meeting twice a week if necessary. This was on the whole well received, though Roy said languidly that he hoped we wouldn't do anything so exacting as meeting twice a week – an all-day conference at Chequers would be better.

I thought one of the shrewdest remarks was made by Wedgie when he said there was a danger of the Tories looking as though they were dealing with the next five years while we were only dealing with the next few months. He strongly supported my demand for an analysis.

Tuesday, 3 February. The main discussion in Cabinet was the Europe WP.[1] Despite the modifications that have been made in the document, the cost of entry stands out in all its stark unpleasantness. And what interested me were the shocked reactions of some of the most devoted adherents of going in. Harold added that there were no policy decisions in the document at all, no arguments for or against joining. Jim surprised me rather by complaining that one of the concluding paragraphs did not quite keep Harold's remit because it concluded that the political considerations would still outweigh the economic ones. We agreed that that should be toned down. Denis Healey stressed that the argument of growth was the key to the question, yet Table 14 showed that membership was not necessarily synonymous with growth: some EFTA countries had done better outside the Market than those inside. And he urged that we shouldn't exaggerate the political benefits. But the biggest surprise was Roy Mason. I am a pro-European, he said in effect, yet this document would cause me to pause. Harold maintained that all these points were a matter for the debate. 'Nothing here changes the grounds on which we decided to go in.'

Thursday, 5 February. The amended WP on Europe went through without much trouble. Harold reported on his visit to Washington and clearly is pretty pleased with Nixon. He described it as 'by far the best visit I have had to the US' – not least because he was at last going from a position of economic strength. He was very encouraged by Nixon's line on Vietnam. He was sure he was committed to early withdrawal (something which John Freeman has confirmed in his annual review).

[1] The White Paper, 'Britain and the European Communities: An Economic Assessment' (Cmnd 4289), was a brutally frank analysis of the economic consequences for Britain of Community membership. Its conclusion was that the maximum overall balance of payments cost of entry arising from the agricultural policy, our financial contribution, trade and capital movements and so on, would lie within a range of £100 million to £1,100 million, a high figure for the time, with additional effects on the cost of living due to a rise in retail food prices of between 18 per cent and 26 per cent. It did not deny that the 'impact' costs of entry would be considerable, but relied on the 'dynamic' effects on growth to enable us to bear the cost.

Lunch with John Davies, Ted and the Netherthorpes.[1] It was merely a personal friendly overture on John's part following his retirement from the director-generalship of the CBI, and confirmed a suspicion I have always had that, despite our official 'rows' and confrontations after which he has gone out to the press and denounced me, he really rather likes me. I have certainly always liked him. He still nurses ambitions of getting into the House and I don't think he will be just a conventional Tory if he succeeds. One thing he said which particularly pleased me: 'When we used to come to meetings under your chairmanship, we were merely conscious that we had a chairman – not that she was a woman.'

Friday, 6 February. Great battle with Denis Healey in P and I on Armed Forces' pay. We all agree the PIB has done a first-class job in its report, but I can't agree that we should give those chaps 25 per cent all at one go. There would be no hope of holding any other wage increases! Under pressure Denis has agreed to staging, giving 20 per cent in the first year, but we in DEP say this is still far too much and that 16 per cent is our maximum. Denis fought with his usual long-winded tenacity and that mixture of Yorkshire bull terrier and Irish twister that is so typical of him. Finally Roy summed up that officials from all the Departments concerned should meet and work out the implications of a 16 per cent staging. I went back to the office and warned John Woolfe to fight hard.[2] We know that Denis will produce figures showing the maximum anomalies unless we are a match for him.

Tuesday, 10 February. At SEP I introduced the report of the mergers panel, recommending that the Reed/IPC merger be referred to the Monopolies Commission. MinTech officials agreed and only the Board of Trade had reservations on the grounds that delay would cause uncertainty. But I was totally isolated. Harold jumped in to say that he hoped we would look at this thing politically. He knew of various highly politically motivated plans to take over IPC. If that happened we should be left without a single friendly newspaper. Roy said he entirely agreed. The case for reference was marginal and it was therefore overwhelmingly desirable to save the *Mirror* and keep it under its present direction. He was supported vehemently by Denis Healey, Michael, Peter, Wedgie and Roy Mason. So that was that.

Thursday, 12 February. Spent two hours of Cabinet discussing a whole spate of public sector pay claims. Denis, having failed to move us in P and I, had put in his paper on the Armed Forces, Dick one on the nurses, Ted on the teachers and Stonehouse on the Post Office. It certainly was a grimly inflationary retinue and Roy opened with a typical Chancellor's sermon. The consequences of such high claims on our competitiveness and on prices could be very serious. We were heading for a runaway consumption boom in the summer and more July 1966 measures. Was that what we wanted? 'This is the last moment we have a chance to stop the avalanche and do something about it.' We should stand by

[1] Lord Netherthorpe had been President of the National Farmers' Union from 1945 to 1969.
[2] Assistant Under-Secretary in the Incomes Division of my Department.

the offers we had already made and say that this was the most we could afford.

Harold then went round the table calling on the Ministers concerned to deal with their papers [and] then called on me. Brutally frank as always, I said that I appreciated the Chancellor's anxieties, but the fact was that Cabinet had as a deliberate act of policy decided to dismantle our prices and incomes powers. Moreover, even when we possessed them, we had undermined our policy by refusing to act – on economic grounds – against the strong. Nothing would be more intolerable than to try to resurrect the policy against those who were not in the position to wreak so much economic damage. Were we prepared to standstill some of the private settlements – the Ford's £4, for instance? Or the 20 per cent we expected would have to be given to the seamen? Or the docks? If so, I would be perfectly ready to do some standstilling. But, if not, I would resist any attempt to stop the 'avalanche' by having a blanket policy towards the public sector claims: we should consider each one on its merits, as we did the private ones. I then went down the list. On the Armed Forces I was totally unconvinced that the staging I suggested (16 per cent and 9 per cent) was disastrous or unfair. As for the nurses, I still believed we could and should treat them as *sui generis*. The best thing was to go for a one-year settlement of 20 per cent. As for the teachers, Ted had borne an unjust burden very stoically. We should offer £100 interim and announce that we were referring restructuring immediately to the PIB. On the PO we should make the sort of calculations we did in the private sector and decide that it wasn't worth standing out against 1.7 per cent more at the cost of a national postal strike.

There was widespread support for my general approach. Only George Thomson wholeheartedly supported the Chancellor. Harold then came in with his favourite theme: we must look at it politically. Timing was the essence of our problem, particularly as events had now made a spring Election impossible. We should aim to postpone the results of some of these claims as far as we could: he would rather win the Election and have a November Budget than have July measures and lose the Election. We ought therefore to see how far we could phase some of the increases, postponing the second stage till January. It was all pretty crude and Roy reacted loftily: 'I would rather lose the Election than jeopardize our economic success.' *That* didn't sound sense either. I am convinced there is a way between Harold's gimmicks and Roy's self-interest and it consists of getting the right balance in one's policy and then sticking to it. Anyway, none of us thought Harold's approach was practical.

Eventually we agreed to go for a one-year settlement for the nurses at 20 per cent; add 1.7 per cent to the postal offer as our final breaking-point; and to accept Ted Short's alternative to my proposal – *i.e.* to move from an interim offer to a restructuring dated from October (which I don't think the teachers will accept). On the Armed Forces I would have won if Harold hadn't intervened to suggest a three-stage phasing: 16 per cent now, 4 per cent later this year and the balance next. The Chiefs of Staff had clearly influenced him. I was sure it was a nonsense but some of them fell for it.

Later that day a phone call from Denis. Could he come and see me urgently? He knew it was a nonsense, too, and came to suggest that he would settle for $18\frac{1}{2}$ per cent this year, the balance next. That suited us better at DEP because we certainly don't want the idea to get abroad that people can have increases every six months, but I beat him down to 18 per cent plus the withdrawal of the Northern Ireland special allowance from all those who would get their full increase this year. When it was all settled he could hardly conceal his satisfaction at having got away with so much. He knew as well as anyone that I ought to have defeated him in Cabinet.

Monday, 16 February. The Ford situation is developing into a farce from the unions' point of view. After decisive votes at Dagenham and Halewood last night to accept the offer, Swansea is still on strike and Jack and Hughie are clearly on the spot. Having nailed their colours to the 'parity' mast, they are now hoist with a democratic vote that repudiates it. We are intrigued to know what they will do.

Went home after a late vote determined to nurse a streaming cold in bed for a day. I am tired of my own over-conscientiousness. They can manage without me for twenty-four hours!

Tuesday, 17 February. Conrad phoned with the latest Ford developments. Farce is becoming tragedy: Jack has decided to make the Swansea strike official. At the AEF Executive this afternoon Reg Birch's attempt to reject the offer and call a strike was only defeated by Hughie's casting vote – against Birch and two anti-Scanlon moderates. (Internal union politics again.) The issue goes to a delegate conference on Friday. If the Swansea strike goes on much longer there will have to be massive lay-offs as the plant makes axles for the whole company. Conrad agreed with me that I will almost certainly have a PNQ tomorrow. I set about trying to draft a form of words. I can't even have twenty-four hours' peace.

Wednesday, 18 February. Back in the office I learned that Jack hasn't made Swansea official but has sent a message of support pending assurances from Ford's that they are ready to discuss parity. More face-saving, but I must say he cuts a poor figure and my opinion of him as a trade union leader has gone down. His one idea of militancy is 'give 'em the money, Barney', totally devoid of any political strategy, unless his aim really is anarchy. Just as I was leaving for lunch, Conrad came in with the latest news: Moss Evans[1] had now indicated that the union was in favour of accepting the offer and had recommended Swansea to return to work immediately. It justified this on the grounds that the company had agreed to discuss parity, but in fact all that Bob Ramsey had said was that the company was always ready to discuss any issues the union cared to raise and privately he has told Moss Evans he won't agree to any joint working-party on parity.

Monday, 23 February. At Management Committee we discussed my paper on the strategy we should follow over P and I policy in the coming months. I was determined to do two things: 1) rub in the fact that the 'wages explosion' was not so much a reaction against P and I policy as against the Chancellor's; and 2)

[1] National Secretary for the automotive sector of the Transport and General Workers' Union. He became National Organizer of the union in 1973 and General Secretary in 1978.

compel them to tell me not to make standstills. I don't intend to be blamed for wrecking Roy's strategy by going soft.

The upshot was that Harold said we were agreed there should be *no* references of key wage increases, but we should continue to stiffen employers' resistance to excessive demands by emphasizing the inescapable link between wage and price increases and by making selective price references, not necessarily excluding nationalized industries. 'We must roll with the punch on wages but we can't do it with prices too.'

Tuesday, 24 February. Off to Oxford, to St Hugh's for a dinner they had belatedly decided to hold for their Honorary Fellows, of which they had made me one. It was a peculiar sensation walking into the place as the guest of honour. The principal went out of her way to be charming to me and showed me the building extensions with great pride. The first thing we ran into as we walked into the main building from the garden was an undergraduate conversing in a quiet corner with her young man. *A deux* and at 7.30 pm, too! The principal explained that the young men could stay around, unchaperoned, till 11 pm. Student revolts? Yes, they had been threatened with one only this week. The young men had been planning a 'sleep-in' as part of an attempt to get the hours extended till Midnight! However, the powers that be got to hear of it in time and it had been scotched. The Senior Common Room was crowded with old, new and Honorary Fellows, all in their best long gowns. Plenty of drinks (and not just sherry!). There was the Gwyer,[1] a frail, gentle figure in a wheelchair – aeons away from the ogre I had known when she was principal. I liked some of the young Fellows enormously. Oxford must be a very worthwhile place these days.

Shock No. 3 came when we sat down to food on High. It was absolutely superb! (What the undergraduates were eating I don't know.) Certainly the SCR has got itself a first-class chef. And an excellent cellar, too. I congratulated the current bursar on her purchasing. The students looked very young and girlish and not a bit impressed by us. Back in the SCR for more drinks. There was a bit of a flurry because some Oxford students had invaded the Clarendon only that night in an effort to examine student files. I couldn't get excited about an issue like this. At 10 pm Mollie called for me and I tore myself away. Really a traumatic experience. I felt like a former Japanese prisoner-of-war who had returned to find the old place had been turned into a well-run night club.

Friday, 27 February. Dick phoned to ask if we could postpone the SEP meeting on my plan for reforming the employment services so that he and I and our Permanent Secretaries could meet first and discuss it.[2] 'Your officials have outmanœuvred mine. My Permanent Secretary has only just put me in the picture. If I am to take over the cash payments I might want to hive off all my

[1] Miss Gwyer had been Principal of St Hugh's College, Oxford, when I was an undergraduate there from 1929 to 1932.

[2] As part of the manpower service I wanted my Department to provide I was hoping gradually to transform the employment exchanges into modern, attractive job centres which would out-rival the private agencies. An essential part of the plan was to transfer responsibility for dole payments to Dick Crossman's Department which was already responsible for the other social security benefits.

cash payments into a separate Board.' But he was very relaxed about it and I readily agreed.

Monday, 2 March. Second Reading of the Safety and Health (Employed Persons) Bill. Went quite well. I slipped off the front bench for my confrontation with Dick over passing responsibility for dole-paying to DHSS. William Armstrong was there at Harold's suggestion, as well as our two Permanent Secretaries, and a good job, too, for, having listened to Dick's diatribes in his quiet, pallid way, Armstrong suddenly swung in on our side, reminding Dick that DEP had been doing this job patiently as his agents for years and implying that it was he who ought to be grateful to us. Dick was at his most outrageous, twisting bad-temperedly from one argument to another and finally ending up by hissing at the wretched Clifford, 'I know my officials have entered into a conspiracy with DEP over this behind my back and I resent it. I shan't forget it.' The civil servants merely lifted their eyebrows at each other. I suggested that William should try and think out a way to help us all over the interim period, and so we broke up, Denis Barnes remarking good-naturedly to me after Dick left, 'He really is impossible, isn't he. He changes his ground so much.' Dick's temper really has deteriorated in recent years.

Wednesday, 4 March. At Management Committee I reported on our progress – or lack of it – with the IR Bill. John Burgh is worried because the timetable for consultations is slipping. We are now faced with the fact that we may fail to introduce the Bill before Easter as arranged. My rather confused thinking has slipped into a clear pattern. I'm now sure we must go ahead with a genuine attempt to get the Bill through – strikes or no strikes – partly for the sake of our own people, but to a very great extent on merits. This is our positive answer to the problem of strikes. I think the whole argument about the penal clauses has precipitated much more constructive action by the unions themselves: oh yes, tentative at this stage but nonetheless real. Oddly enough, too, the fact that the Tories are making such an issue of it, putting such emphasis on making agreements legally binding, has given some employers furiously to think. They are beginning to realize (with my help) that this isn't the simple panacea they once believed, so they are beginning to brush up their ideas about the responsibility of management. I'm now therefore all in favour of getting the Bill on to the floor of the House as soon as possible so that I can spell out the constructive approach and force the Tories to reveal their true policy. I don't give a damn whether this produces some embarrassments for me: after all, this is the way things go in life – seldom in a straight line. One often produces one's best results obliquely, as the fall-out, for instance, from apparent defeat on a major issue. 'Treat those two impostors just the same' is still my favourite philosophy.[1] Anyway Management Committee responded clearly, cleanly and on the whole well. They want a Bill, but a good Bill, and are prepared to sacrifice some time to get it.

[1] From Rudyard Kipling's *If*:

If you can meet with Triumph and Disaster
And treat those two impostors just the same . . .
Yours is the Earth and everything that's in it
And – which is more – you'll be a Man, my son!

Thursday, 5 March. Final check-up in Cabinet on the outstanding issues of my CIM Bill. Life has been so impossibly hectic that I haven't even been able to read through the latest text. So it was a shock when Elwyn suddenly pointed out that, under Schedule 1, financial penalties could be levied on trade unionists for refusing to attend or give information to the Commission's inquiries. Did this mean that, hypothetically, Clive Jenkins could go to gaol a) for refusing first to attend an examination of a pay increase, and b) for refusing to pay his fine for non-attendance? Answer, yes. Panic all round, with Bob Mellish giving us his usual doom-laden warnings. However, as I pointed out tartly, 'There is a limit to scuttle.' You can't set up a statutory body and then refuse it the normal powers to do its work. So it was agreed that this bit should stand – trade unions *should* be covered – but that we should look at the wording of the next sub-sections carefully from a presentational point of view.

One piece of comfort by Roy: bank rate is down to 7½ per cent.

Sunday, 8 March. Got up early for our all-day meeting of the Management Committee at Chequers. I read the file of papers for the meeting on the way there in the car. Chequers's park was brilliant in the sunshine and snow – I'm getting almost fond of the place! Jimmy Margach has a curiously confusing story in the *Sunday Times* about our 'secrecy' over the meeting. The explanation, Harold told us as we gathered in the library, was that Dick had absentmindedly got his instructions wrong. When Margach approached him with a scoop about the meeting, Dick had forgotten that the press were going to be informed in the usual way and had gone all mysterious! Dear Dick, our compulsive communicator, knows no happy medium between telling all and telling the wrong things. In the morning we had a normal Management Committee meeting. Very useful, as we had time to deal in depth with such issues as the Tories' law and order campaign. Jim is in his element here: he has an instinctive feel for the pragmatic reactions of the ordinary man. Also, temperamentally, he is in tune with the median common denominator.

After lunch I curled up on my favourite seat in the corner of the sofa by the fire in the library. Jim next to me, almost nodding off. Harold began by going round asking us all when we thought the Election should be. Denis: 'First half of June if possible; failing that, end September or early October.' Fred: 'We've never had a June Election in our history.' Wedgie: 'Have our battle plan for June; delay if necessary.' Dick: 'I can't see a Budget good enough to go in June. October, unless in June the prospects look marvellous. Be ready to carry on till March if necessary.' Peter: 'At earliest possible moment: late May. Catch the other side napping.' Roy said he wanted to pass at that stage. Jim: 'As soon as we think we can win. Do our organizational planning for June, our policy planning for October.' Me: 'Of course we all want to go when we think we can win. The real question is: when will people feel best? I suggest that is likely to be after a holiday, when the higher supplementary benefits are in payment and equal pay is on the statute book.' Harold: 'I'm afraid of delay. I remember how the City has invoked a run on sterling before and it could do it again.'

Harold then asked us on what issues we thought we should fight and this time started with me. My heart sank because I thought that at his pace we would never get on to the Budget. However, I said that we had got to fight on the type of society in which we believed, and stop making the balance of payments the be-all and end-all. Of course, we should claim credit for the surplus but say, as I had been doing in South Wales, that this wasn't an end in itself. It was a chore we had had to do, but it was merely a base for something else. Our over-riding priority, therefore, should be a massive increase in supplementary benefit, coupled with tax reliefs at the lower end of the scale which would help many on basic pension as well. The rest were shocked at my cavalier treatment of the balance of payments. Jim said it was essential to give it priority. Bob declared it 'the one winning bull point'. Peter, too, was in favour of stressing our balance of payments achievement as the only basis for safeguarding employment. Roy passed again, saying he would prefer to speak at the end. So Tony Crosland took the bit between his teeth. Yes, we should fight on our achievements. For the future: 'A continuation of existing policies, improved as much as we could afford.' But the key question really was what we *could* afford and he didn't think he could avoid discussing the Budget.

The rest of us seized on this opening to give Roy the benefit of our Budget views. Dick plunged in. To win, we must regain our working-class vote and the Budget must do it at one jump by helping 75 per cent of those below the average wage through minimum earnings relief. We should fight on a 'class redistributive Budget' plus fear of the Tories on issues like trade union reform. Wedgie: 'Yes, fear of the Tories is our best hope. Our theme must be that we trust people. The responsible society. Reflate selectively and by stealth.' Michael: 'Do something to help people who are just in the income tax range. If necessary pay the price of increasing SET.' Bob: 'Don't do a Stafford Cripps on us, Roy.' 'I read it all in the papers this morning, Bob,' snapped Roy. (He obviously blames Bob for all the stories that he is being pressurized to reflate through the Budget.) Peter: 'It is essential that we get the elixir of expansion into the economy. Go for 4 per cent growth.'

At last Roy spoke and it was soon clear he is not contemplating anything like Dick's 'class redistributive Budget'. He insisted that we had invested so much political capital in solving the balance of payments that confidence in the Government depended on our maintaining a good surplus. The very worst political prospect for us would be if, through an over-generous Budget, he had to use the regulator in the autumn. And he told Dick there was one fatal flaw in Nicky Kaldor's minimum earnings relief scheme: it sharply raised the marginal rate of tax just at the point where chaps began to earn overtime. It was far better not to do too much in the Budget and reflate selectively in the summer by other means if the outlook was propitious. Harold said he thought we had pressed the Chancellor enough, and as it was now nearly 6 pm we began to break up, with me complaining plaintively that we hadn't even begun to discuss future policies.

Monday, 9 March. Began the week by jumping feet first into a violent argument with Dick in SEP over my new policy for the employment services. He was at his most outrageous: distorting it for his own ends in order to defeat me over the transfer to him of the cash payments. He made great demagogic play with his claim that it wouldn't be to the benefit of the unemployed. All I wanted was to set up posh new offices to deal with the easy cases. He was unctuous about the 'socially disadvantaged' who, he tried to make out, would be tucked away somewhere out of sight under my policy. Weak with rage, I nonetheless hit back vigorously, pointing out that my policy was going to enable me to do something for the difficult cases for the first time – *and* in the posh new offices. 'The Social Services Secretary tries to make out that he is the most socially disadvantaged member of the Cabinet but in fact he always manages to get the plums for his own services while I have been doing his job of paying cash benefits for years in detriment to my own.' (Burke Trend grinned into his notes.) Unfortunately Harold had to leave early and unfortunately, too, William Armstrong, who is on my side, has done a Minute in which he has put all the emphasis on a compromise scheme that lets Dick off the hook. Harold actually thought he was helping me by saying that we must do what Sir William suggested.

Tuesday, 10 March. Got my CIM Bill safely through Legislation Committee except for the point about penalties. I myself believe we can word the Schedule far less provocatively.

With Easter looming up Heathrow was threatened with serious disruption by two disputes. The first concerned a pay claim pressed by the TGWU on behalf of firemen. The men had imposed restrictions on working which had led to their suspension by the British Airports Authority [BAA] on 13 March. The second arose from an agreement concluded in September 1969 by BAA with a Canadian and American firm, General Aviation Services Ltd [GAS], to provide handling services to airlines using Heathrow airport. Despite the conclusion of an agreement between GAS and the TGWU initiated by John Cousins, the TGWU organizer at Heathrow, shop stewards had refused to endorse it and airport employees had been blacking GAS services. On 11 February a meeting chaired by a shop steward, Ian Stuart, decided to extend the blacking and this had led Peter Masefield, chairman of BAA, to seek an injunction in the courts against Mr Stuart to stop him 'procuring' workers for the action. The political atmosphere was heightened by the fact that the Government had approved in principle the proposal of the British Overseas Airways Corporations [BOAC] to take over British United Airways [BUA], a decision which was bitterly attacked by the Opposition as curbing the scope for independent airlines. On 17 May I announced that I was setting up an inquiry.

Sunday, 15 March. Clive Jenkins has played right into the Tories' hands by threatening a strike if independent airlines try to wreck the BOAC bid for BUA. The air is thick with Tory demands for legislation to control the 'arrogance' of the trade unions and Ray Gunter has joined in, denouncing this assumption of extra-parliamentary power. Even John Cousins has attacked Clive and this is the clue to what really is at stake – not a revolutionary bid but an inter-union row. That is why Clive is linking his attack on the independent airlines with an attack on BAA's decision to give a sub-contract to General Aviation Services. Conrad tells me that Clive and co. were reconciled to the contract when, after discussion with GAS, they were satisfied that it would observe good terms and conditions. Then John Cousins double-crossed them by negotiating a closed shop for the TGWU with GAS! So, robbed of his union's right, Clive is making a great ideological issue of it – and throwing in a threat to the independent airlines for good measure. Where all this will lead in political terms, God only knows. Clive has certainly done enormous damage to the Labour Government. I believe now that the Tories will win the next Election, thanks to our 'friends'. But I also believe that the result of their doing so will be to strengthen the move towards a modern version of syndicalism.

Tuesday, 17 March. Conrad came over with Douglas to the Equal Pay Bill Committee to discuss Heathrow. The mass meeting, called by an anonymous group of shop stewards at Gatwick yesterday, had called for an inquiry into GAS. It was clear that Jack Jones wanted to get off the hook of the firemen's strike on which John Cousins has impaled him. So it looked as though the way were clear for us to go ahead. But the National Joint Council for Civil Air Transport (which deals with the Air Corporations' staff and is led by Mark Young and Clive) wasn't meeting till tomorrow afternoon. So he suggested that I should make a statement of my intention to set up an inquiry in the House just before tomorrow's debate on civil transport (at which the Tories have put a censure motion down on the BUA take-over). I said at once that this would look far too much like reacting to the Tories' censure. Why not announce it straight away? Douglas agreed with me and Conrad said he was prepared to be persuaded that we were right.

Wednesday, 18 March. I was just in the middle of SEP when I got an urgent call to ring Douglas. He told me that we had run into snags over the inquiry. Clive and Mark Young were declaring that they would not co-operate unless BAA withdrew the legal action pending against the chief shop steward, Stuart, which is due to be heard on Friday. BAA was adamant that, although it was ready to suspend the action, it wouldn't withdraw it entirely. Vic had asked to see me urgently. So had Jack Jones. He assumed it was on this point. Was it possible for me to get back to the office?

I found Conrad and Andy Kerr[1] very disturbed: they could see real trouble ahead. But when Vic arrived he couldn't have been more relaxed. He had come ahead of Jack, he told us, to let us know that Jack wanted wider terms of reference so as to enable the whole labour relations at the airport to be reviewed. No mention of the action! And Vic chatted on happily about the mess John Cousins had made of things. He was a neurotic, and Jack would be only too glad to be rid of him, but it couldn't be rushed. When Jack arrived, he was at his most friendly, too. Yes, he wanted a wider inquiry as the only basis on which he could get the chaps to go back. All was sweetness and light. So they went away, waving happy ta-tas to us, leaving us bewildered but relieved.

At 5 pm Conrad called me out of an office meeting to report on the reactions of the NJC. The workers' side had unanimously agreed that they would not co-operate in the inquiry unless two conditions were met: 1) the existing legal action was 'abandoned' and 2) the inquiry only covered industrial relations within BAA and *not* the NJC. The reason for the latter, said Conrad, was that they were determined to keep Jack Jones off their territory. Apparently his

[1] Andrew Kerr was a brilliant negotiator in industrial disputes. He had become the Department's Chief Conciliation Officer in 1968.

predatory ambitions are fiercely resented by other unions. Here was a pretty mess! Clive and Mark were on their way to the office, hotfoot from Gatwick, and Conrad suggested that our only hope of breaking the deadlock was to try and get everyone to agree to have an inquiry limited to the firemen in the first place on the understanding that talks would continue on the terms for widening the inquiry later on. I said try by all means and went back to my meeting where we were discussing, appropriately, the problem of how to deal with secondary boycotts. The trouble is that the number of actions by employers under this heading has been increasing in the last few months and it is no longer true to say that they only cover recognition disputes.

The meeting over, back came Conrad and Andy with long faces accompanied by Frank Lawton and Jim Barnes of the Board of Trade. They had phoned Vic, who agreed our line: limit the inquiry to the firemen at this stage. But Jack, apprised of the stand which Clive and Mark were taking on the legal action, had clearly decided he couldn't afford to be less anti-penal clauses than they. His attitude now was that the 'abandonment' of the legal action was the first problem that had to be solved and that there could be no inquiry covering the firemen only. BAA must drop the present action. After an inquiry it would be free to bring a new case but only on actions by the shop stewards taken *after* the inquiry. Frank explained the innerness of all this: BAA apparently have accumulated a lot of evidence against Mr Stuart which they have been compiling since last September, including affidavits of his attempts to induce breach of commercial contract. If they withdrew, rather than suspending, the action, they would lose the right to use this evidence for all time.

We talked round the problem for a long time. We suspect Masefield of having other motives than industrial ones. In fact Jim Barnes said in terms that Masefield was anxious to prove to the Tories that he was a strong manager who could stand up to the unions. After all, his contract ended this May. He might well be preparing the ground for a return to private industry. (I have seldom heard a civil servant more outspoken.) All this echoed what Vic had said to me this afternoon when he phoned to tell me, rather mysteriously, something he thought I ought to know: that Masefield had lunched with Ernest Marples yesterday. Eventually we agreed that I should go out to my dinner with Geoffrey Goodman and Monty Meth while Conrad continued his efforts to bridge the gap between the two sides, and I would be recalled if things went wrong.

I was just relaxing happily in Victor's cosy little private room at the top of the Gay Hussar when the call came. It was Douglas to say that the talks had foundered and they needed my help. Could I be back at 9.30 pm when the Attorney-General would join us? Elwyn listened gravely to all we had to say and then commented that it would be very serious for the Government to be seen interfering with a case in the courts. I insisted that my next step must be to see Masefield, though I promised I would merely probe and not say anything that could be considered pressurizing. Where was Masefield? Gone home to Reigate, leaving George Hole and Ewart with full powers to speak on his behalf. I said grimly that I wasn't talking to any of Masefield's merry men without him there and risk being accused afterwards of saying and doing things

I hadn't done. So Douglas phoned to fetch him back and I went to the House for the 11.30 pm vote, seizing the opportunity to put Roy Mason in the picture. He was only too thankful to leave everything in my hands.

At 11.45 pm Masefield and his chaps trooped into my room. Whatever he felt, Masefield was polite enough, though hardly cordial. I felt he regarded this meeting as a bit of tiresome ritual which courtesy demanded he should go through. I pointed out that we had reached complete deadlock. How did Masefield see things developing? He said that he thought there were three points on which we could make progress: BAA were willing to hold up any extension of GAS services while the inquiry was held and to give an undertaking that the legal action would be completely stood over and that they would not in any case seek any damages. Conrad went patiently over the difficulties about the legal action: the unions were adamant that 'standing over' was not enough. Masefield insisted that he couldn't be expected to withdraw the action without an equivalent *quid pro quo* from the unions. I asked him what he saw as the final outcome if agreement was not reached over the terms. 'Impose an inquiry with Government backing,' he replied. He was sure that, if the Government set up an inquiry on the terms he suggested, the unions would co-operate. 'And if the gamble fails?' 'Close the airport.' I pointed out that, if that happened, the Government would take the blame. We needn't imagine that either BAA or the Government would be applauded for standing firm. The press would be indignant about the sufferings of the travelling public at Easter time. Everyone would say it was absurd to close the airport over such apparently small differences. However, I was careful to add, we would continue to do our best to persuade the unions to accept BAA's terms. It was 2 am before Masefield and his troop retired thankfully.

'Let's have a drink,' I said to my chaps as we sank exhausted into our chairs. At times like this we are just one anxious united team. And, anxious as we are, we always manage to have some fun. Jim Barnes continued to mutter about Masefield's machinations while Conrad, Andy Kerr and Frank Lawton weighed up the negotiating possibilities. 'Never mind about your negotiations,' I interrupted them, 'and give a thought to my political problem instead. It seems to me that there are only two courses open to me, and there is not much time. Either I can impose an inquiry, and in doing so endorse Masefield and his line, or I can refuse an inquiry and endorse Clive. I find both equally unattractive.' Suddenly something clicked in my mind and I said I believed my only course was to say publicly that I thought Masefield should have met the unions over this small difference on the understanding that BAA would be free to bring in a new action if the findings of the inquiry were defied. They agreed unanimously. And so to bed.

Thursday, 19 March. I was under the drier at Xavier's, getting my hair done for the weekend, when Douglas phoned. Conrad and Frank Lawton had an urgent point to put to me and would travel with me in the car to Cabinet. Frank then told me that he had learned that morning that Peter Pain[1] had advised BAA and GAS that any pressure on them by the unions (or the Government!) to abandon

[1] Highly respected lawyer who had become a QC in 1965. He later became a judge of the High Court.

their legal action would constitute 'a clear contempt of court'. I said we ought to tell Vic about this contempt of court point. In any case I was sure I ought not to spell all this out in Cabinet. Instead I would try and get a meeting with the PM and Attorney-General immediately afterwards.

It was 1.15 pm before Elwyn, Arthur Irvine (the Solicitor-General) and I joined Harold in his study. As soon as I outlined the situation, he realized its seriousness. 'One thing we must avoid,' he said, 'and that is a rebuke by the court to the Government.' On the other hand, he could see the political danger to us if BAA went ahead with its case: BAA *v.* Stuart could become as emotive to the trade unions as Rookes *v.* Barnard[1] and become the focal point of pressure on us to legalize inducement to breach of commercial contract in the IR Bill. On the whole Harold was inclined to endorse my line: it all depended on the wording of the statement on which I must keep in closest touch with the Attorney-General.

I was over at the House having a belated lunch in the cafeteria when Douglas phoned. Total deadlock had been reached at the morning's meetings. Could the Attorney-General and I come along at 3 pm? It was a gloomy group which assembled in my room and we talked round the problem for nearly two hours, getting nowhere. Elwyn was as urbane as usual although, poor chap, he had other problems on his mind. He certainly attached considerable weight to Peter Pain's warning and didn't like the rough draft of my statement which the office had prepared. I didn't like it either. This view was fortified when Andy brought the news that Masefield had decided to issue a press statement that night. We couldn't find out its exact terms. As for the action, BAA would decide whether to ask for an adjournment or not at 10.29 tomorrow morning. Where was Masefield? Gone home to Reigate to change for a 'do' at the Hilton at which he was going to talk about the Jumbo Jet Age. The possibilities of *that* for mischief-making were obvious! I decided I must see Vic and Jack immediately – the only thing I could think of to help me to decide what to do. I said I would appeal to them on the political net: surely they would realize the danger for them was as great as for the Government? Then I would see Masefield. Douglas hurried to the phone and said Vic and Jack would be with me at 6 pm. Masefield had been more difficult. He had just got home, was changing for his speech and didn't at all fancy being called in by me. He tried to suggest he should come and see me after his 'do' but Douglas had told him that wasn't on. So he had reluctantly agreed to come at 6.30 pm.

As I waited, I jotted down some notes. I just didn't know what to expect. But when Vic and Jack walked affably into the room I felt a sureness of touch come back to me again. I saw them without officials. As I poured them a drink I said to them, 'I wanted to talk to you privately about a danger that faces all of us. Everything I say is strictly between us until we decide what to do publicly.' They agreed. I then said we had all three of us hoped we might have got an agreement on the lines we discussed yesterday. They nodded. But, I went on, difficulties had arisen over the legal action. Vic had been right to warn me that

[1] A classic case in trade union history. In 1963 the House of Lords had ruled that Mr Rookes, a non-unionist who had been sacked because the unions at his place of work had threatened to strike in support of the closed shop, should be compensated by the union. This revealed a gap in the Trades Disputes Act of 1906 which Harold Wilson promised to close. This he did in the Trades Disputes Act 1965.

Masefield was under Tory influence. It was not only impossible to budge him over the action; his counsel had warned us that any pressure brought on him, either by the unions or the Government, to withdraw the action would be a contempt of court. Vic looked grave. This meant that, whatever I thought of Masefield's actions, I could not publicly deplore his stand. Yet Clive and Mark were equally adamant. Masefield was threatening to make a press statement that night. I would be cross-examined by the press and I would certainly have a PNQ in the House tomorrow. Yet what was I to say? Jack looked up at once and said, 'You could say you were going to set up an inquiry anyway.' I could hardly believe my ears! But what was the use of that if the unions refused to co-operate? Jack and Vic replied almost in unison, 'We would do our best to see that they did co-operate.' I felt a great hope swelling up in me.

We talked for some time about how to handle the situation. We were like friendly conspirators deciding how to defeat a common enemy. 'I wanted you to know that I wasn't behind BAA's determination not to withdraw the action,' I explained, and they said, 'Of course.' How could we deal with Mark and Clive? Leave them to us, they said: 'You and your friend Clive,' said Vic mockingly. 'I told you what he was like.' I pressed my bell. Conrad, Andy, Frank and Douglas nearly fell through the door behind which they had been waiting. I said I now wished to dictate a Minute of my meeting with Mr Feather and Mr Jones. I then spelt out what we had agreed. I could see that Conrad was incredulous and slightly alarmed. What would the NJC say? 'Leave them to us,' said Vic. 'We'll be available.' And, leaving details of their movements, they left the room.

I was euphoric, damn all Conrad's doubts. How now to handle the BAA? It was a slightly lofty Masefield who walked into the room in evening dress followed by his team, barely trying to hide his irritation at having to go through what he obviously considered a charade, anxious to get to his dinner and his press statement. We talked round the position a bit and then I took pity on him. I had, I told him, decided that I was going to announce that night that I was setting up the inquiry – on the following conditions: 1) that the BAA had assured me it was prepared to accept the outcome of the inquiry; 2) that tomorrow morning they would ask the court to adjourn the case for three months; 3) that he himself would issue no press statement, though of course he would be free to comment on and amplify my announcement; 4) that I would ask the inquiry to comment urgently on the firemen's dispute. He rallied quickly and said at once that he would accept all my conditions. As I let him go, wishing him well with his speech, he took me aside to thank me for my help with every appearance of sincerity. I think that, whatever he might have been planning in the way of a showdown, he was genuinely relieved. And to a certain extent, of course, events had proved that he was right to stand firm.

Conrad then rushed off to summon Mark and Clive and, at my suggestion, to get Jack and Vic back into the building to help us deal with any storms. I was about to settle down to some work over a curling sandwich when Douglas said, 'First Secretary, why don't you let Frank take you to his club for a good meal?' I rose to the idea but then we discovered that, as Frank's club was the Athenaeum, its kitchen had more or less closed for the night! Eventually Frank, Douglas and I slipped out of the back door for a quiet meal in the Italian restaurant opposite, during which we had a delightfully relaxed talk about the family and other influences in our lives.

When we returned at 10 pm Conrad reported that the usual French farce situation was operating: everyone concerned (except Masefield) was in the building, accommodated in separate rooms between which Conrad and Andy were moving with bits of paper and lots of soothing advice. (I really do love Conrad on these occasions: he is unrivalled for his patience, charm and clarity.) A remarkable thing, we discovered, had happened. Mark Young and Tudor Thomas (chairman and secretary respectively of the union side of the NJC) were insisting on going through the terms of reference line by line and word by word. Of course, they hadn't committed themselves to co-operate with the inquiry but, if they intended to condemn it outright, why bother with the terms of reference? I settled down to a few hours' wait, wading through some work to the accompaniment of muffled laughter from my private office. (Mercifully we had found Clive was in Scotland: perhaps he was as thankful for this divine accident as anyone else.) At intervals Conrad came in to report. Mark and Tudor were insisting that there should be no mention of the negotiating machinery in the terms of reference. All right, I said, see Jack and if necessary bring in Vic, who was also waiting in a separate room. The minutes dragged on and eventually Conrad came in triumphantly: Jack had agreed to modify the terms. (So he HAD kept his promise!)

It was by now nearly 1.30 am and the press, said Bernard, were getting frantic because he hadn't been able to tell them anything. 'Bring them in,' I said. Some of the trade union chaps were already drifting away. 'I'll play it as quietly as I can,' Tudor Thomas had promised Conrad. I went along the corridor for a wash and saw another figure walking wearily towards me. It was Vic. 'Where's the gentlemen's, luv? God, luv, I'm tired.' I thanked him for what he had done (and later learned that he said all the right things to the press downstairs. He, too, had kept his promise).

Eventually, at 2 am, the press came tumbling, tired and irritable, into my room. I commiserated with them and we handed round a press statement. The first question was what had happened to the legal action. My patience snapped. 'Look,' I told them, 'if you want to wreck hope, you can and there is nothing I can do to stop you. But the important thing to emphasize in all this is that BAA has bound itself to me to abide by the findings of the inquiry. If you could find it in your journalistic hearts to headline *that*, the airport could be open at Easter instead of closed.' They took it very well.

Everyone gone, I tried to pick up the remnants of my weekend arrangements. I was too tired even to want a drink. Douglas and I smiled at each other. 'You know, First Secretary,' he said, 'we ought to design a special tie or have campaign medals struck to mark these occasions.' We played with the idea: one medal for Ford's strike 1968, another for Ford's 1969. 'Of course,' he said, 'there's the Ford's women, too. Perhaps we ought to have a military cross with bar.' I left him to his couch at the Ministry while I went home to creep into bed beside a sleepy but still sympathetic Ted. He *is* a dear.

Friday, 20 March. Extraordinarily euphoric still at 8 am. And ready for an exacting day. I suppose there is nothing so stimulating as an action which one feels instinctively one has survived. I think we shall survive this and that the unions *will* co-operate.

Monday, 23 March. Not a muff from Clive or Mark over the weekend! We kept our fingers crossed. But it was a near thing: even the firemen, with John Cousins and Jack urging them to return to work, have only agreed to do so by one vote. So George Hole's smug claim that the firemen were longing to go back to work and would do so at one word from Jack has been disproved. Anyone who tries to be facile about industrial relations soon comes a cropper.

The Ayr by-election result has cheered everyone up, but at Management Committee I was glad to see that Harold was anxious not to appear euphoric about it publicly.[1] I suggested we ought not to be euphoric about it privately either: my feeling is that we still have a very hard row to hoe with public opinion. (Anyway I am anxious to persuade Roy that everything depends on his not giving us a 'neutral' Budget.) I asked acidly if we were going to discuss the unemployment figures: the headlines about the worst March figures since 1963 weren't exactly our best lead into an Election period.[2] Harold said we had discussed the economic situation at Chequers and shouldn't go over that ground again. Roy added that he thought the trend was now slightly upwards. Trying to talk reflation, even in Management Committee, is like banging one's head against a wall of cottonwool.

Wednesday, 25 March. Over to No. 11 for a drink with Roy. As I suspected, he wanted to talk to me about the Budget, though he stressed that I shouldn't let any of our colleagues know he had taken me into his confidence. He thought it was quite wrong that the first any Cabinet Minister knew about the Budget was the day before and that until then the Chancellor should keep his secrets locked up in his breast. But this didn't mean he should consult everyone: there were some of our colleagues in whom he wouldn't dream of confiding.

He then spelt out fully what he proposed. 'I suspect I am not going as far as you would wish.' He intends to give away about £229m and to take back nothing in exchange. He thought it was psychologically vital that he should have a Budget which didn't have a single increase in tax, and on that I agreed with him. The vast majority of his tax reliefs would be income tax – £170m, the reductions very much orientated on the lower end of the scale through the personal allowances. To be able to afford the cost he would have to curtail the reduced tax band, but no one would be worse off and those on the lowest incomes very much better off. Roy said the rest of the money would go on a number of modest measures, such as to reducing surtax on unearned income marginally (which will help a number of better-paid workers). On the whole, given Roy's strategy, I don't think it is a bad Budget.

Friday, 10 April. The opening of the new government training centre at Durham went like a dream. Some trouble with unofficial strikers waiting to boo

[1] In the South Ayrshire by-election caused by the death of Emrys Hughes, Jim Sillars held the seat for Labour with a swing of only 2.5 per cent to the Tories.

[2] The number of wholly unemployed in Great Britain, excluding school leavers, had been rising gradually from 2.2 per cent in May 1969. In March 1970 it reached 2.5 per cent.

me at the gate. The car swept by but when I got out I turned back and walked to the gate to talk to them. Result: a friendly little cheer when I left. As I told Douglas, in politics accessibility is all.

Saturday, 11 April. The first real spring day, though everything is still terribly backward. No daffodils out yet. I worked in the garden [at HCF] till I ached. Memory of the day: little Ben (not three yet) and Printer[1] playing with a large ball. Ben's conversation with Printer really ought to be tape-recorded. Those two creatures understand each other. Printer is a Ben dog as you might say. There is a glorious, self-sufficient, take-life's-knocks-on-the-chin-and-smile charm about both of them which is irresistible.

Tuesday, 14 April. Budget day. Roy had complete mastery over the House as he spelt out our economic success, but lost some of it when the Tories realized that his tax concessions were so limited. I still think that psychologically he is striking the right note of sustained growth, much as I would have liked him to do more. We have now invested so much political capital in his strategy we had better stick with it. I was surprised how depressed my Ted was with the Budget: he thought there wasn't a vote in it. Well, we shall see tomorrow how well it has gone down.

Wednesday, 15 April. Vic's friendly reaction to the Budget has set everyone speculating whether he is ready to co-operate with a voluntary P and I policy. I certainly don't intend to rush in with any public statement because I know how delicate this flower would be. I would rather probe the possibilities privately.

Friday, 17 April. A good day at Wakefield, opening a new government training centre. I love these sallies into the field. But I returned home to disaster. Ted had just learned from one of his sponsors that he had not been rechosen as an alderman of the GLC. I have never seen him in a more desperate state. He was knocking back whiskies when I arrived and almost shouting aloud with the pain of his humiliation. 'Everywhere and by everybody I am rejected. Why? I am arrogant enough to believe that I am as good as, or better than, the dozens of people I have helped, yet no one – absolutely no one – helps me. At every stage of my life I have failed. Why? I ask myself. Why? Why?' There were tears of sheer despair in his eyes. 'You can't possibly understand. How could you? You have gone on from success to success. I have gone from rejection to rejection. What am I to do with myself? I go back to London with you. How am I to fill my time? You've no time to spare for me: how could you have? How could Reg Goodwin ask me to put my name forward and then leave me to be humiliated in this way? I could have been deputy leader of the group: I've been asked to run as leader before now. I could have led the attack on Tory policy. I know I am one of the most effective people they have got.' (He is, too.) 'And now this.' He moaned with pain. My heart ached for him until I thought it would break. Yet there was nothing I could say, nothing I could do: only listen exhausted for two hours with my head between my hands and then at last get him to bed and

[1] The young black and white cocker spaniel we had acquired following Aldie's death.

cradle him in my arms. I lay in the dark, the tears running down my cheeks. Everything turns to ashes when he is hurt in this dreadful way: Hell Corner, my job – everything. 'April 17th,' he had said. 'Make a note of it. This day I died: here inside me.' Shouting: 'I am dead, do you hear? Dead inside. And I hope tomorrow I don't wake up.' When at last he slept I dedicated myself to getting him the recognition he deserves. I'll see Harold, Reg Goodwin – anyone. I will not have Ted destroyed in this way.

Saturday, 18 April. Ted in control of himself again. As we went out to work in the garden in glorious April sunshine no one who didn't know him well would know that anything was wrong with him. But I know the inner wound is far too deep to heal quickly. It will probably never heal at all unless I do something. My resolve to confront Harold is as strong as ever and I have arranged to see him at 10.15 on Monday morning. If necessary I would have gone out to Chequers to beard him there.

Monday, 20 April. When I went into his study to see Harold he was full of his speech for the Scottish TUC – one which he told me was causing him more trouble than any he had yet made. But then he switched abruptly: 'This isn't what you came to see me about; it's Ted, I presume.' So Ted's interview in the *Times* diary had had its effect! I had cringed when I read it and wished Ted hadn't poured out his heart on the phone to the *Times* chap so freely. But apparently Ted's instinct to communicate is sounder than my instinctive reticence.

I found myself fighting back the tears: 'Harold, I've never asked you for anything for myself and I never will . . .' He interrupted to say of course we must do something for Ted. He was anxious to strengthen our debating strength in the Lords: would Ted be interested? I knew he would, but my heart sank. I didn't have to be a Lady myself, did I? I asked. I couldn't bear that. 'Only on Palace occasions,' replied Harold urbanely. 'You'll always be Barbara Castle in your constituency.' I told him I was sure Ted would be superb in the Lords and Harold rattled on, thinking aloud. He'd like to find a Government job for Ted. It would take a bit of time to sort things out but meantime I could tell Ted something would be coming his way.

As he hurried into Management Committee I rushed to the phone to ask Ted to come to the office as quickly as possible. I couldn't wait to put him out of his misery. He was like a man transformed. I hate the thought of being associated with the Lords even in this indirect way, but I would risk anything – even losing my seat – to give Ted a break at last. God knows, it is his turn. Later he phoned me from the country, still in a euphoric dream: 'And on the third day they rolled away the stone . . .' he crooned. Oh God, Harold, don't let me down now. It would break my heart.

Thursday, 23 April. Final stages of the Equal Pay Bill. It was an empty House and then suddenly, as we got to the third reading, it came alive as one speaker after another warmly congratulated me on a 'historic moment'.

Tuesday, 28 April. Into the Standing Committee on the CIM Bill, both morning and afternoon. The Tories are trying to make heavy weather about our taking in the large firms, but Edmund demolished them in a long, impressively argued speech. In the evening had Douglas Houghton in my room for a drink to plan how we should handle the IR Bill in the PLP. I explained to him what was in it – and not in it. He didn't foresee any difficulty.

Wednesday, 29 April. At Management Committee Harold said he wanted to talk about the Election date. He then deployed all the arguments for and against a June Election, which had now become at least a possibility. He was immensely amused at the press speculation which has arisen from the announcement by Harry Nicholas that we are all to meet at Chequers on 17 May. Apparently the request for this meeting came from Harry (and 17 May was the only date Harold had free) but Harold is enjoying the panic this has caused in Tory quarters. Heath, he said, had become almost a maniac. He had heard that Heath was going round talking of the Labour Government as 'this riff raff' and generally showing signs of nervousness. But the fact was that we faced a difficult choise about the Election date and he would welcome our interim views, though there was no question of making a final decision at this stage. The responsibility for fixing the date clearly weighed heavily upon him.

Jim, suddenly all sunny about our prospects, said he thought we would win whichever date we chose. On the whole he would go for June. Wedgie said he was worried about possible developments in the US. He had found great anxiety there during his visit: the economic situation was apparently much worse than it appeared. Roy commented that he would like more time to think out the economic implications of the two dates, having just returned from his holiday. Bob said the PLP was evenly divided into three groups, members who weren't running again preferring 1971! I said that there were certain risks in an October date but certain *facts* against June, like the importance of people having their summer holidays under their belts, supplementary benefits actually in payment, time to do something about unemployment in certain regions, and the fact that, although the spirit of our activists was reviving, we hadn't had time to rebuild the war organizations on which everything depended. There were some nods at all this. And so we left it for the time being, but it is clear that some of them are now afraid of leaving things till October and are ready to risk June, a view with which I do not agree.

At last I was able to turn to my IR papers and swot up the details for tomorrow's press conference.

The Industrial Relations Bill was published on 30 April and included all the promised extensions of trade union rights – statutory right to belong to a union, the right to have CIR rulings on union recognition enforced against an employer, right of appeal against unfair dismissal – except the specific legalisation of inducement to breach of commercial contract. The Bill also improved the provision periods of notice under contracts of employment, amended the Wages Councils Act to strengthen voluntary collective bargaining and made it clear that collective agreements should be conclusively presumed not to be intended to be legally binding unless the intention was stated in writing. It also put £3 million at the disposal of the CIR for a Trade Union Development Scheme under which grants or loans could be made to promote amalgamations, finance training schemes and help unions provide better facilities and services.

Monday, 4 May. [At Management Committee] we turned to discuss the timing of my IR Bill. I've been pressing for the Second Reading before Whit in order to kill the gossip to the effect that the Government isn't really serious in trying to get the Bill on the statute book. Now Bob and Fred are raising difficulties and I've minuted Harold about the dangers of changing our line now. Harold was sympathetic, but Tony and Denis began to sneer. When I said that I thought we could turn the Bill to our electoral advantage and that our boys were rearing to go, Roy chipped in with a superior smile to say that he really didn't think anyone would lose any sleep if the Bill weren't introduced. I saw red at this. Harold said promptly that it was time other Cabinet Ministers made some speeches about the Bill which the whole Cabinet had agreed must be introduced. On timing he said we should wait and see the feeling at the PLP meeting this week and decide at Cabinet.

During the proceedings I passed Harold a note: 'It is Ted's birthday tomorrow. Any chance of your being able to give him some hope for the future?' Harold replied, 'My hope of last Wednesday collapsed – but I have two others including a new one I started this morning.'[1]

Monday, 11 May. Managed to get Robert Carr to agree a voluntary timetable for the rest of the CIM Bill. So a guillotine won't be necessary and we shall be able to get the IR Bill into committee on 16 June. I'm sorry it couldn't be earlier but that should still give us some time for fun in committee before the summer recess.

Tuesday, 12 May. Off to Hastings early for the Labour women's conference. The debate on equal pay was pretty flat – another example of how our movement is so schooled in protest that it doesn't know how to celebrate victory. Everyone is agog with the 7 per cent lead for Labour in the Gallup poll. This, coupled with the excellent local results at the weekend, has started the bandwagon really rolling for a June Election. There are still some doubters including me. What we have to do now is to wait for the NOP poll on Wednesday next. But a tide of emotion is rising which is very unsettling. Somehow I got down to the afternoon session on the CIM Bill. Everyone has been caught napping by the unprecedented switch of support to us.

Wednesday, 13 May. [At SEP] I returned to the attack on my plan for reforming the employment services. Dick has had time to reflect on this and become a little ashamed of himself, so it was agreed without difficulty that I should be allowed to proceed with the separation of the employment and benefit services *within* DEP. But Dick still stuck out that I should play it down in the wording of the consultative document as otherwise it would become obvious that one day benefit paying would pass to DHSS. I am determined to play it *up*. That is the whole idea. Harold said we must agree the drafting between us, so I still see a

[1] In fact the General Election intervened before Harold Wilson could keep his promise, but he never forgot it and when he became Prime Minister again in March 1974 he lost no time in reopening the matter with me. Ted became a life peer, as Baron Castle of Islington, on 26 June 1974.

struggle ahead. However, I won a notable victory at Social Services Committee. It was agreed I could announce *now* that we will legislate before 1975 for equal treatment for women in employers' pensions schemes.

Wild rumours are circulating about the NOP poll. Bob assured me it would show a lead for us of 5.6 per cent. In the event it has turned out to be 3.2 per cent: enough to keep up the Election fever. A packed PLP meeting saw a presentation of the thinking behind 'Yesterday's Men', which most people think clever and legitimate, but wrongly timed for a June Election.[1] The truth is that we've all been caught on the hop by the sudden swing of opinion our way.

Thursday, 14 May. At Management Committee (no officials present) Harold came straight to the point: the Election date. He said he had always been in favour of a summer Election if he saw the way clear. Now all five polls put Labour in the lead: averaging a 3 per cent lead between them. The borough election results were far better than he had dared to hope and if we went to the country now we ought to get a majority of over twenty.[2] If we waited we should have to endure a £2m advertising drive by the Tories throughout the summer which could have an effect. Moreover, the register would be less stale. 'Thanks to the Chancellor's foresight over the travel allowance,' he added, quipping all the way through, 'many Tories will be on holiday in June.' On the other hand, we should get it over before the wakes weeks. All in all, therefore, he thought we should go nap on 18 June. What were our views?

Agreeing, Dick said the important thing about the NOP poll was that it showed 65 per cent now expected us to win, a most important psychological factor. Tony Crosland, typically, put it, 'Obviously you have made up your mind and of course we will all back you loyally.' Jim was more direct: 'I think June is right.' No one demurred. In fact we began planning as if it were all settled, but Harold wasn't going to let us dodge sharing responsibility. 'Everyone agreed? Right: then no one will be able to claim the virtue of hindsight.' After some deliberation we decided he shouldn't make the announcement before Monday: let the Tory demoralization continue over the weekend. Harold is now carrying 'inner Cabinet' government so far that he said our committee should continue to meet throughout the campaign.

Then into Cabinet to which Harold didn't disclose the date. Dick and Roy then announced their new compact to increase the supplementary benefits by 8*s* instead of 7*s*. In return Roy has insisted the increase shan't be introduced till November instead of October – the same date as last year. What matters from an Election point of view now is that the Order will have been obtained before we rise. We agreed, too, that Dick's new pension scheme can't possibly be introduced for administrative reasons before April 1973, though here again there is to be 'consultation' about the timing.

[1] Theme of a £60,000 publicity campaign, worked out by Labour Party supporters in the public relations world through the Party's Voluntary Publicity Group, which was planned to continue through the summer in preparation for an October Election. The first stage attacking Tory leaders was to have been followed by a second one on 'Labour's Winning Team', but this was overtaken by the June Election.

[2] In England and Wales Labour had made a net gain of 443 seats, mainly at the expense of the Conservatives, and in Scotland had gained 57 seats with the Scottish Nationalists losing 27.

On Monday, 18 May, the Prime Minister announced from No. 10 that Parliament would be dissolved on 29 May and a General Election held on 18 June.

Monday, 18 May. Crisis over the Heathrow dispute which could cost us the Election. The report of Robertson's committee of inquiry is in our hands and shows a unanimous view a) that the firemen ought not to get more than BAA's offer of 12*s* 6*d*, and b) that there is no reason why the GAS contract should not go forward. I had a word with Harold about it yesterday. He suggested that I try and get publication delayed by persuading Jack to say his union had changed its mind and wanted to give evidence after all. Ingenious! And it worked! The response of Jack and Vic when I called them in was instantaneous. Jack, they worked out, would make an official approach to Vic asking him to call the unions together. I then called my officials in to say these gentlemen had a request to make to me. Jack solemnly explained that 'last Friday' he had sounded Vic out about the possibility of their giving evidence even at this late hour. He did it superbly and Denis Barnes and the rest of us could hardly keep our faces straight. Denis said he thought the committee would find it difficult to turn down a request of this kind (all of us carefully refraining from mentioning that the report was already in my hands). Vic then went off to draft a letter to me hurriedly. I must say this for Jack's reaction: it wasn't that of an enemy of a Labour Government. He wants us to win, even at some cost to his own union position. I think my civil servants were surprised at how readily he co-operated.

Wednesday, 20 May. A quiet NEC: we don't discuss the Election Manifesto till next week. Off early to HCF for, I hoped, a few days away from it all. But it was not to be. I'd hardly arrived when Harold was on the phone. What was I doing about the retail price index figure out tomorrow? Some industrial correspondent had tipped off the Tories that it was up two points and Heath was issuing a statement at midnight. I said I hadn't even seen the figure and he nearly hit the roof. 'Doesn't anyone know there is a war on? You'd better blow your officials out of the water.' He said he would have to draw up a statement for me to issue in my name and very cross he was about it. I contacted Douglas and told him he must keep me in touch with all news: if there were bad news, all the more reason to alert me. He said he would send down regular boxes. Bang goes my peace! Lucky Dick, away in Malta.

Saturday, 23 May. Went out to buy some plants and on my return found that No. 10 had been ringing me frantically. Harold was furious again: what was this about holding up the reference of motor repairing to the PIB? If P and I on Tuesday didn't clear it, he would announce it himself on his own initiative the following day. Some Ministers were just not behaving as if there were an Election on and were leaving it all to him. 'Well, Harold,' I replied sweetly, 'it is a presidential campaign.' 'Yes it is,' he retorted – perfectly seriously. Then Douglas rang to say he had drawn up terms of reference: if I agreed them we would clear them with MinTech and issue the announcement ourselves on Wednesday: the only instance in my memory when Harold as PM has violated Cabinet procedure and imposed his will. (All our Departmental briefs were against the reference.)

Another snag: this time about the retail price index.[1] The June figure may be announced on polling day! Apparently the figure is automatically published as soon as it is ready and the statisticians tell us it could be ready any time between 17 June and 23 June. They would get nasty at any suggestion it should be held up. We agreed to discuss this on Tuesday. By this time my lunch was cold and Ted in a bad temper. Some holiday! And an Election special to write yet.

Tuesday, 26 May. Back to work. Reactions at P and I Committee to the capital sharing paper were not unsympathetic but the general view, with which I could not really disagree, was that we hadn't done anywhere enough study of the details to be able to make even the most general reference to it in the Manifesto. I would be bound to be asked questions about it I couldn't answer. But everyone wanted a full interdepartmental study launched.

Wednesday, 27 May. Arrived at the NEC with a sheaf of drafts to go in their third rewrite of the Manifesto which is still innocent of any mention of the key issues of the campaign. All Harry Nicholas did was to look irritated when I produced my pieces but Harold insisted that they be circulated. We then settled down to rush the whole thing through for our press conference that afternoon. Fortunately my pieces were accepted almost without amendment. Having done my whack, I left at 1.45 pm as I had to make a statement in the House on equal pay and pensions. I left the rest soldiering on wearily. (Not a bit surprised later to learn that the press conference was nearly a shambles. Certainly Harold was less than his usual relaxed self in presenting the Manifesto on TV.) My statement went like a bomb. Great rush of work with Janet, then over to the office to the little party I gave to celebrate the completion of the Equal Pay Bill.

Thursday, 28 May. Brief Cabinet. On the Election Harold said he thought there was too much complacency about and that we should none of us take anything for granted. I pleaded that we should all of us think of ways in which we could make our departmental policies more concrete for electioneering purposes – *e.g.*, I had got my Department to do me a detailed paper on how the Tory industrial relations policy would have affected the Pilkington strike. Their finding: it would not have stopped the strike and might well have made matters worse. Could we have from Treasury some concrete examples of the effects of the Tory tax proposals compared with our measures in the Budget? 'We can get all this through Transport House,' said Crosland irritably. But I am appalled at our lack of good material with 'bite' as we go into the campaign. I've never felt less well equipped for an Election but the others (Harold apart) seem so lackadaisical. Off to Blackburn to start my campaign.

[1] In fact the figure, which was published on 18 June, showed an increase of only 0.4 points in May over the previous month compared with an increase of 2.1 points between March and April, so it would have helped us if it had been published earlier. Nonetheless, Ted Heath was making great play with the rise in the cost of living, the retail price index having risen by 6 per cent since May 1969.

The Heath Years 1970–74

The atmosphere of the Election campaign was puzzling. On the one hand Ted Heath, stiff and uncharismatic, had had an unsympathetic press while Harold Wilson was sailing through the campaign radiating presidential bonhomie backed by favourable polls. On the other hand I sensed an undercurrent of detachment among our own activists and Party audiences. As early as 13 June I was writing in my diary: 'I wish there weren't another five days before the Election! I don't believe those poll figures and although Heath is making such a pathetic showing personally and is getting such a bad press, I have a haunting feeling there is a silent majority sitting behind its lace curtains, waiting to come out and vote Tory.'

The turning point came on 15 June when freak trade figures pushed us into the red to the tune of £31 million, thus enabling Heath to throw doubt on the genuineness of our balance of payments surplus to which Roy Jenkins had sacrificed so much. On Election day my fears were justified when, on a low poll, Labour's vote dropped by 5 per cent while the Tory vote rose by 4.5 per cent, giving Heath 330 seats to Labour's 287. The Liberals lost seven of their thirteen seats. An interesting commentary on the Election appeared in the *Guardian* a few days later in an article headed 'How Roy Muffed It' by Peter Jenkins, normally a Roy Jenkins fan. In it he argued that the expenditure figures just published by the Central Statistical Office showed that production and consumption were both stagnant on polling day, so that Roy could have budgeted more generously for growth – and for the Election.

But it was too late. Installed at No. 10 Heath lost no time in putting into operation the tough new strategy he had worked out in opposition at a private gathering of Tory leaders at Selsden Park. All Labour's policies were to be reversed. There would be no government intervention in industry and no subsidies. Firms must be made to stand on their own feet, helped by higher profits and lower taxes, financed by dramatic cuts in public expenditure: all the apparatus of the 'incentive society'. Union power must be curbed and Britain toned up by the rough winds of competition which would blow from the European community, of which Heath was determined to make Britain a member at whatever cost.

In his first budget the Chancellor of the Exchequer, Anthony Barber, fleshed out the new strategy which he described as 'a fundamental reform of the role of government'. Labour's modest interventionist machinery was swept away. Financial support for industry was cut, as were the capital programmes of nationalized industries and public expenditure. Charges were introduced or increased over a range of public services: prescriptions, school meals, museums. Grants for public transport were cut back. Local authorities were to be compelled by law to raise council house rents and reduce housing subsidies. Even food did not escape when the Government decided to make the consumer rather than the taxpayer support agriculture by switching from deficiency payments to the EEC system of taxes on imported food, even though Britain was not yet a member of the Community. The savings thus achieved enabled Barber to cut the standard rate of income tax by 6*d* (2½ new pence).

This was hardly the 'One Nation' formula of moderate Tories and the result was inevitable. As working people studied the effects of the package they realized they had lost out. Prices had been deliberately pushed up, though Heath had fought the Election on a promise to bring them down. They set out to recoup their losses and the inflationary upsurge began.

There then ensued a remarkable series of U-turns by Heath. He is a humane man and he twisted and turned as he faced the consequences of the tough new Selsden Park strategy. His first reaction to rising inflation was to restrict growth, the classic answer. Despite the record balance of payments surplus he had inherited, he refused to expand the economy. Output stagnated and unemployment had risen by over 40 per cent by the end of 1971. Alarm bells began to ring in industry.

Heath dramatically reversed his priorities. There must be help for the lame ducks of industry, whom he had previously announced would be left to sink or swim. When the prestigious Rolls-Royce company faced collapse, he astonished his supporters in the House of Commons by nationalizing it through the unprecedented device of a one-clause Bill. But there was more to come. A few months later, to the sardonic delight of Labour MPs, his Minister of Industry, John Davies, former Director-General of the CBI, introduced an Industry Bill giving the Government power to help firms in difficulties, including the right to acquire shares in such firms in return for financial help.

These measures were accompanied by a dizzy reversal of economic policy. Tackling unemployment became the new priority. In a Maudling-type dash for growth Heath floated the pound, cut taxes yet again and increased public spending. But the dash did not last long. Inflation rose and when the balance of payments surplus he had inherited turned into a record deficit, Heath panicked again. By December 1973 credit had been restricted, interest rates raised and spending plans cut back sharply.

Through all these changes of policy the Government never lost sight of one of its primary aims: to curb the 'monopoly power' of the unions. For some time Conservative lawyers had been working out plans to put the unions in a legal straitjacket. Their ideas were embodied in an Industrial Relations Bill, which brought the law into industrial relations to an extent unprecedented in our history. Under it, every legal device was adopted to weaken the unions. Workers were given a statutory right *not* to belong to a union, the closed shop was effectively outlawed, as were sympathetic strikes. A list of unfair industrial practices was drawn up and unions which indulged in them could be brought by their employers – or by individuals – before a new National Industrial Relations Court (NIRC) under a High Court judge, Sir John Donaldson. Unions defying its rulings could be fined for contempt of court.

Most serious of all was the Government's resurrection of the 'doctrine of agency', first propounded in the Taff Vale judgment of 1901. In this the House of Lords had shocked the unions and surprised the House of Commons by ruling that railwaymen on strike at Taff Vale were acting as agents of their union, which must be held responsible for their actions, and it mulcted the Amalgamated Society of Railway Servants for heavy costs and damages. The judgment roused the whole trade union world and was reversed in the Trade Disputes Act of 1906 which restored the protection unions had enjoyed. Now the Heath Government was putting back the clock. Unions, it argued, must be held financially responsible for their members' actions, which meant that a union's funds would be at risk from any action by its members. To enforce this a new system of registration was proposed. Unions could only register if they drew up an approved set of rules policed by a new Registrar. The rules must lay down clearly who in the union had the right to call a strike – and in what circumstances. The Bill then limited the right to strike to registered unions and their members and officials 'acting within the scope of their authority' – a far cry from anything proposed in Donovan or my own *In Place of Strife*.

The Bill was bitterly, though vainly, fought by Labour MPs and the TUC. When it became law the unions set out with calculated non-cooperation to make it unworkable. Some unions like the TGWU refused to register, thus losing their legal rights. They also refused to recognize the court. The situation quickly moved from tragedy into farce. The TGWU was the first to be caught in the legal net. Dockers up and down the country were blacking lorries carrying goods to container depots outside the docks because they could see their own jobs vanishing. It was a problem which could only be solved by carefully worked out compromise, but conciliation had given way to legal machinery and the employers took the union to the NIRC. The court ordered that the blacking be stopped and, when the dockers persisted in it, fined the union for contempt.

But the blacking continued and so did the applications to the court. This time the TGWU decided to fight and the case went up the legal hierarchy. To the Government's embarrassment the Court of Appeal under Lord Denning ruled that the shop stewards involved were not agents and revoked the fine. Undeterred, Sir John Donaldson and the court decided to proceed against individual dockers – the very opposite of what the Government had intended – and issued orders for the arrest of three London shop stewards defiantly picketing the new container depot at Chobham Farm and eager for martyrdom. Disaster – and a nationwide walk-out at the docks – was only averted by the mysterious intervention of the Official Solicitor, a legal official of whom few people had heard until he was wheeled out to save the day. On his representations the Court of Appeal hurriedly set the arrests aside – a rescue operation which one of the disappointed shop stewards bitterly denounced as a 'bloody liberty'.

But the farce rolled on. Sir John Donaldson had the bit between his teeth and when the picketing of the depots continued, the court committed five London dockers to Pentonville. This brought 85,000 dockers out on strike. There was uproar in the Commons and the House of Lords reversed the Court of Appeal's ruling at record speed, making the union once again liable. The unrepentant dockers were released and carried shoulder high by an enthusiastic crowd outside Pentonville.

The farce did more than anything else to discredit the new Act and serious newspapers began to question it. But the legal juggernaut rolled on. When the Amalgamated Union of Engineering Workers refused to call off a strike to secure recognition at Con Mech (Engineering) Ltd the court sequestered £100,000 of the union's assets. The Government had earlier added the richest touch of comedy: faced with a threatened railway dispute over pay, it applied to the court under the provisions of the Act for a compulsory ballot and cooling-off period on the argument that there was serious doubt whether the union's members supported the dispute. This theory was quickly exploded. In the ballot the railwaymen voted six to one to escalate the dispute into a national strike. Two months later the Government was forced to compromise. The railwaymen got another £2 million. Lord Devlin, a High Court judge, complained that the courts were being brought in to make judgments on matters that were totally political. 'The prestige of the judiciary . . .' he wrote, 'is not at the disposal of any government.' Even Sir John Donaldson admitted that parts of the Act had been 'thoroughly misconceived'. The assumptions behind the Act had been proved wildly wrong and the Government began to hint that amendments might be necessary.

With his legal curbs on unions in disarray, Heath turned to other ways of limiting their bargaining power. His first step on taking office had been to wind up Labour's Prices and Incomes Board as another example of government interference in industry, which he so despised, but with inflation galloping ahead and industry pleading for action he was forced to change his tune and was driven stage by stage to a full prices and incomes policy. His first step was to clamp down on wage settlements in the public sector, which led to a series of bitter disputes as one by one the dustmen, power workers, postal workers, miners and railwaymen came out on strike. From all these encounters, except with the postal workers, the Government came out bruised. In February 1972, after a seven-week strike and a Declaration of Emergency, the miners won a spectacular increase of 25 per cent. By that time wage settlements were running at twice what they were at the end of the previous Wilson Government and more working days were being lost through strikes than at any time since the general strike of 1926.

In desperation Heath tried conciliation. In a series of tripartite talks with the TUC and the CBI he tried to persuade the unions to accept voluntary wage restraint, offering a range of inducements, including a Christmas bonus for pensioners and special treatment for the low paid. He even agreed to insulate workers from price rises through 'threshold agreements' under which every 1 per cent rise in the cost of living above the threshold of 6 per cent would lead automatically to an increase in wages. But it was too late. Heath had driven the unions back into the arms of the Labour Party. At the beginning of the year a Liaison Committee of representatives of the TUC, the Labour Party's National Executive and Labour MPs had been set up to work out agreed economic and social policies. The unions would accept nothing less from Heath. They demanded partnership in the running of the economy and the withdrawal of his hated measures such as the Industrial Relations Act, taxes on imported food and statutory increases in council rents. Even a chastened Heath could not stomach that. These, he said, were matters for the Government.

In November 1972 the TUC broke off the talks and the same afternoon Heath announced a freeze on wages, prices and dividends. The man who had said in the Election, 'We utterly reject the philosophy of compulsory wage control' had embarked on a fully fledged statutory policy, reconstituting a Price Commission and Pay Board to enforce a new Pay and Price Code. By October 1973 he was feeling his way towards refinements of what he clearly saw as a permanent policy, proposing a 'flexibility margin' of 1 per cent to deal with special cases. He instructed the Pay Board to produce a report on pay anomalies and a further report by the end of the year on pay relativities between different groups of workers to see which workers were falling out of line.

The scene was now set for another battle with the miners. In July the NUM conference had rejected the Government's pay policy and set out to recover the ground its members had lost since the settlement of 1972. The miners were in a powerful position, owing to the Middle East crisis and the huge increase in the price of oil, which had put a premium on coal. In September 1973, they introduced an overtime ban, which was already having an effect by January 1974. But there was worse to come. On 1 February the NUM balloted its members on a national strike. On a high poll 81 per cent voted for a strike. This time Heath decided to turn and fight. An Election on 'Who Governs Britain?' seemed his only hope.

Meanwhile, the Labour Party had been studying Heath's failures and its own previous defeat. The first lesson seemed obvious: no government – and certainly not a Labour one – could operate a successful industrial relations policy, or wage restraint, without at least the acquiescence of organized workers. This was all the more true in a period in which left-wing union leaders like Jack Jones had been encouraging local union democracy by building up the role of shop stewards on the factory floor. In the Liaison Committee old wounds were healed as the participants worked out a new 'social contract' between a Labour government and the unions. Under it, Labour leaders pledged to repeal the Industrial Relations Act and never again to introduce a statutory incomes policy. It was to be government by consent or not at all. In return the unions pledged to co-operate with a Labour government in solving its economic problems, including inflation – though it shied away nervously from any suggestion that this included an incomes policy. If, they argued, the Government were to build up the standard of life of working people through such measures as a child endowment scheme to help mothers (later to be known as child benefit), an end to queue-jumping in the NHS by phasing out pay beds, the strengthening of the social services, a radical new deal to help pensioners and the disabled, and a fairer tax system, it would find the unions would respond responsibly and sympathetically. It was Jack Jones, steadily emerging as the most dedicated supporter of co-operation with a Labour government, who proposed the setting up of a new Advisory Conciliation and Arbitration Service (ACAS) to settle disputes on a voluntary basis. The CBI welcomed the idea and ACAS later played an important role under successive governments.

But, the unions insisted, industry must also co-operate with the Government in increasing production and reviving manufacturing strength. This theme was taken up by the Labour Party NEC, which in 1973 produced a new industrial strategy based on greater worker participation in industry, enthusiastically endorsed by Party Conference. It rejected old-style public ownership as inadequate since it tended to saddle the taxpayer with declining industries, and called for the setting up of a National Enterprise Board with government funds, to invest in profitable companies in return for a controlling equity interest. National economic planning must be underpinned by a new system of 'planning agreements' at company level to be concluded by the Government with all major firms as a condition of receiving government aid. The agreements would give government, and workers through their trade unions, a say in deciding the planning objectives of the firm – its export, pricing and investment policies.

But Conference's apparent unity behind the new strategy hid dangerous rifts. Harold Wilson supported it enthusiastically but the Party's 'moderates' had been secretly mobilizing against what they considered dangerous left-wing tendencies inspired by Tony Benn. Their ideological leader was Roy Jenkins, who aroused the same devotion among his followers as Hugh Gaitskell once had. But, unlike Gaitskell, the 'moderates' had become fanatical pro-marketeers, believing, like Heath, that Britain's problems would never be solved without the shock stimulant that membership of the EEC would bring. They despised the anti-marketeers as 'little Englanders'. The Left in turn accused them of playing coalition politics.

Harold Wilson had personally become a convert to Britain's membership of the Community and had only been saved from a show-down in his last government by President de Gaulle's veto of his application before negotiations could begin. De Gaulle's resignation in 1969 had given Heath his chance. On taking office he had lost no time in opening negotiations, reaching agreement on the terms of our entry a year later. The Labour Party immediately split. The anti-marketeers denounced the terms as a sell-out, winning the support of the Party Conference, a majority of Labour MPs and most of the unions. The pro-marketeers fought back, making it clear that they would put Europe first. In a speech widely interpreted by the press as an attack on Harold Wilson, Roy Jenkins called for 'honesty and consistency' in the Party's policy. George Thomson, former Minister for Europe under Wilson, wrecked the Party's official line by claiming that Heath's terms were as good as any the Labour Government could have achieved.

Wilson was in an agonizing dilemma. He had always seen it as his prime function to weld the Party together after the damaging splits of the Bevanite years, sacrificing many of his own political preferences to this guiding principle. Now party unity was under threat again – and so was his own leadership. Jim Callaghan had come out against the terms and Wilson told some of us privately that he, too, was going to reject them, even though he knew it would destroy his credibility. This he did at a special Party Conference in July 1971 in such a low-key speech that both pros and antis complained of his lack of leadership. Later, he endorsed Tony Benn's device of a referendum on Britain's membership as the best way to defuse the situation. This later became Party policy. Bitterness came to a head when, in October 1971, sixty-nine Labour MPs led by Roy Jenkins defied the Party Whip and voted for Heath's motion, approving entry on his terms and giving him a majority of 112. On Europe the political coalition had become a reality.

As he had anticipated, Wilson was mercilessly pilloried in the pro-market press. His old ally, the *Daily Mirror*, came out against him, deriding him as a 'tethered sacrificial goat' to Party unity. Newspaper after newspaper harped on his 'loss of authority'. On 20 October 1971, *The Times* swelled the chorus by declaring that he must never again be Prime Minister. By contrast Roy Jenkins was glorified as a 'man of principle'. The more fanatical pro-marketeers began to campaign for a change in leadership. There was increasing talk of the need for a new centre party and in 1972 Dick Taverne, Labour MP for Lincoln, whose local Party had passed a vote of no confidence in him because of his vote to support Heath's terms, resigned the Labour Whip to fight as an independent Democratic Labour candidate. He held the seat in a by-election though he lost it at the General Election of October 1974.

The strain on Wilson began to tell. He became dispirited and more than once hinted at resignation. But Roy Jenkins had no stomach for political in-fighting: after a series of major political speeches, which the press applauded as an attack on the Left, he resigned the deputy leadership, leaving his supporters dismayed. Denis Healey gladly stepped into his shoes as Shadow Chancellor while Michael Foot, who had run Jenkins close in the elections for deputy, increasingly emerged as a conciliator.

It was therefore a bruised and shaken Harold Wilson who prepared for a general election in January 1974. Ted Heath had created a crisis atmosphere by declaring a State of Emergency (his third in three and a half years). Dramatic precautions had been taken against the consequences of the miners' dispute. Restrictions had been placed on the use of electricity and shopkeepers were selling their goods by candlelight. Industry had been put on a three-day working week and the country had been made to feel it was at war. No one could be sure how voters would react and whether Heath's political gamble would pay off.

1974

Tuesday, 1 January. Another wonderful Christmas over. Ted festooned Hell Corner Farm again with ivy and old man's beard; my food was a success and I even managed to squeeze in the children's play on Christmas Eve.

On Sunday, the family gone, we gave our adult party. Everyone said it was our best yet. There is no doubt that Ted and I are very good at giving parties. Ted, of course, is the supreme giver of himself and I am happy to dash around feeding everyone. HCF looks so lovely on these occasions with the log fire greeting everyone as they walk into the dining room, the flames flickering across the polished tiles. I remember John Freeman saying to me years ago how he envied us – particularly Ted – for our capacity as hosts. Some people, he said rather wistfully, would like to be able to give out as we do, but they just can't.

Yesterday we set off for Southampton to spend the New Year with Phil and Colin and are just recovering from their New Year's Eve party.

Thursday, 3 January. Terry Pitt has become a menace. With three weeks to do his redraft of the campaign document he has left it to the last minute as usual and has called a meeting of the redrafting committee, of which I have been made a member, today. I am not going to curtail my bit of holiday still further to be there. Terry had to rush his 'redraft' down to Southampton by train yesterday and it turned out to be almost the same wording which we criticized so strongly at the December joint meeting with the Parliamentary Committee.

Friday, 4 January. My hopes of a week's rest after Christmas have been dashed as the Liaison Committee with the TUC has been called unexpectedly for this morning. It is all part of the emergency atmosphere. I make my way to London by train without too much difficulty, though the trains are running spasmodically. The meeting was at Congress House, so Sid Greene was in the chair. The parliamentary side was strongly represented – Harold, Denis, Jim, Wedgie, Reg Prentice, Mik, Bob Mellish, Douglas Houghton, Ron Hayward [General Secretary of the Labour Party] and me – but the trade unions were terribly thin on the ground: only George Smith [General Secretary of the construction workers' union, UCATT] in addition to Sid and of course Len Murray[1] and his officials. When I arrived Wedgie was reporting on the campaign document as it had emerged from yesterday's redrafting committee, which our visit to Southampton had forced me to miss. He was rubbing in how closely it conformed to the joint statement agreed with the TUC.[2] (One piece of good

[1] Len Murray had taken over the general secretaryship of the TUC from Vic Feather in October 1973.

[2] 'Economic Policy and Cost of Living'.

news: Mike [Foot] has apparently completely rewritten Terry Pitt's mediocre draft.) Jim, who had also arrived late, then chipped in, pointing out that, although the campaign document was now pretty good, it had one serious weakness – its own lack of reference to incomes. Without this our posture at the Election would not be credible. Could the TUC help us on this? He thought something like the reference in the TUC *Economic Review* for 1972, setting out the terms for voluntary incomes policy, would be a great help.

Harold's turn next. It was true, he said, that this point could be thrown at us during the Election; it had already been thrown at him by Robin Day and others on TV yesterday. Denis then came in, putting it in the sensible way he always does on these occasions. What was lacking, he said, was a statement of *intention* by the TUC – 'something going beyond what you *think* might happen'. Of course it had to be a realistic statement. We were not asking for any reference to 'norms' or rigid commitment to an incomes policy. But what we needed was an indication that, if the Labour Government fulfilled its side of the compact, the TUC for its part would try to make the economic policy work. Our side kept up the barrage while the trade union boys sat silent: after all, we outnumbered them by eight to two. It was as though safety in numbers had given MPs the courage to reveal their secret thoughts.

Sid then called on Len Murray, who was at his most impressive. He began fluently: 'I must say after listening to this discussion that if you are relying on some commitment by the TUC to some kind of incomes policy you have got to think again. There ain't going to by any statement like that.' Some of the statements round the table had seemed a bit Bourbon to him – as though some people had learned nothing and forgotten nothing. He then gave us a lecture on the pitfalls of incomes policy. This did not mean that the TUC did not recognize the problem or refuse to try to help solve it. 'We have said to this Government time and again that if it would do so and so, the TUC would respond. God help us, we cannot go beyond that.' The greatest disservice the TUC could do a Labour Government was to pretend it could do more than it could: the disillusion from that would be far more damaging than the refusal to make impossible promises in the first place.

His speech relaxed the tension. It was as though, not for the first time, each side had listened to the other's problem and had realized it was well-nigh insoluble. So somehow we had got to get through by the solvent of mutual sympathy. Harold took up the challenge: we must study the words in the TUC 1972 *Economic Review*. And Len nodded vigorously when Harold added, 'What we need is more the creation of a mood than a compact.' The give and take grew every minute. Sid summed it up by saying, 'We want to be able to say when we see the document that we are in agreement with the policy and will do our best to help implement it.' He added, 'This has been a very valuable discussion.'

We then turned to the current economic situation. Harold treated us to a long résumé of his statement of yesterday on the miners' claim and his TV interviews, which we had already read or seen. Only one new point. Harold does not think Heath wants an Election, 'though his Pearl Harbor boys do'. The trouble was that Heath had a very low flash-point: if he lost his temper he might go for one.

I made my way to Marylebone pretty satisfied with the morning's work, except that all our constructive decisions have been taken in the absence of the representatives of the two most powerful unions in the country.[1] Nonetheless, I think Len knew he was speaking for them. Perhaps he can deliver the goods. At the station, when my train eventually crawled in, the ticket inspector (who of course recognized me) was very bitter about ASLEF.[2] I can't blame him: he is losing, he told me, £40 a month. But the most significant fact I discovered was that his take-home *basic* pay is £25 a week. Rates like that, in a still affluent society like ours, are the breeding ground for militancy.

Wednesday, 9 January. Heath has conceded a recall of Parliament to discuss the emergency, so there is talk of a General Election on the 'Who Governs Britain?' issue. I have established a 'hot line' to the constituency on the effects of the three-day week and have been tied to my desk for two days, taking the calls. Wedgie's elaborate plans for monitoring the effects of the fuel crisis don't seem to have cut much ice in the constituencies. My 'hot line' idea has had much more effect – he does love to overorganize things. He has made a great splash with his figures on coal stocks to prove the three-day week is not necessary, but the *Sunday Times* has repudiated them. At Information Committee [of the National Executive Committee] yesterday I urged him to get off this tack now and concentrate on possible solutions to the miners' dispute: for example, the coming Relativities Report of the Pay Board on which I have been having secret confabulations with Derek Robinson.[3] But Wedgie would have none of it.

Thursday, 10 January. The Speaker called me early – immediately after Enoch Powell – so I threw away my notes and debated ad lib, only returning to my notes to read from the Pay Board's terms of reference to prove that the special increases likely to be proposed under the Relativities Report were intended to be part of Stage Three. In the corridor I ran into Dick [Crossman], breathless with walking up the entrance stairs. He sank down beside me while I tried to interest him in the Relativities Report. He looked ill; said his tummy was in a bad way. 'They tell me there is nothing they can do: they give me three months or three years.' My poor, darling Dick. I chatted to him as normally as I could, going out of my way to praise his last column in *The Times*, at which he brightened up.

Friday, 11 January. The joint meeting of the National Executive Committee and Parliamentary Committee to finalize the campaign document was again

[1] Jack Jones and Hugh Scanlon.

[2] For several weeks the Amalgamated Society of Locomotive Engineers and Firemen had been operating a ban on Sunday overtime and rest-day working in order to secure better terms for its members under a pay package offered by British Rail and broadly accepted by the other rail unions.

[3] In 1973 Mr Heath decided to make his statutory pay policy more flexible. In the White Paper on the second stage of the policy (Cmnd 5205) he announced that the Pay Board would be asked to report on anomalies that had arisen during the first stage and also to look at the problem of pay relativities and of groups who felt they deserved special treatment in order to improve their relative position in the community. The Anomalies Report was published in September 1973. The Relativities Report, due at the end of the year, had not yet appeared. Derek Robinson, now a deputy chairman of the Pay Board, had chaired the inquiry into pay relativities.

held in the Churchill Hotel, where apparently we have an ally in the manager, who does us well. Michael Hatfield in *The Times* is this morning trying to stir up trouble with a story about how the valiant moderates are going to have a showdown about the need for us to commit ourselves to an incomes policy. It really is pathetic how *The Times* has to invent its heroes and villains. In the event Mike's redraft (which in itself was sensible and constructive) went through practically unchallenged. Frank Allaun was waiting to pounce on the reference to arms reduction and nuclear policy. We had a straight vote on whether we should include the specific figure of a £1,000 million reduction target – and those of us who supported Frank won, to Jim's amiable grumbling. For the rest, we again solved our problem by reverting to former compromise texts as though they were Holy Writ. The longest argument was over the references to public ownership, on which I had scribbled a substantial redraft in order to spell out the reasons why we are going to acquire sections of profitable industries. Mik welcomed my redraft at once, but Frank, backed by Joan Maynard[1] and John Forrester,[2] suspected that I was providing loopholes for *not* taking over profitable industries. After some patient explaining and the incorporation of some words by Mik, with Harold backing me vigorously and saying that we must not go back on the commitments of his conference speech, we reached agreement. Reg Prentice protested that he thought the nationalization list was too long, and Roy Jenkins clearly had some anxieties, but none of the Right put up much of a fight.

Some of our time was spent dealing with Denis's dire warnings about the economic holocaust we should inherit when we took over and how we could incorporate some reference to this in the document. But we *did* agree that the pensions and food subsidies commitments should stand, come what might. I am beginning to suspect that Denis will be an even more stubborn deflationist than Jim. He has, unfortunately, more backbone. He doesn't give up easily.

Monday, 14 January. Back to work because the recess has been shortened. I still think that Heath may announce an Election on 7 February on the 'Who Governs Britain?' issue and I am trying to get my Blackburn boys to get going on the postal votes.

Monday, 21 January. Meeting of the Social Policy Committee of the National Executive Committee at which we made progress with our disablement policy. Dick phoned to ask if I was free to have dinner with him in the Members' dining room. Though inconvenient I said yes at once. He looked haggard and weak. When I said that I was going to buy him some wine he said, 'Not much for me; I'm not allowed alcohol with my tummy.' But then he rallied enough to encourage me to buy an excellent half bottle of dry white wine, of which he drank a glass. He began by ordering some food, but only ate a mouthful. My heart ached for him. We talked relativities, in which I have at last persuaded him to take some interest. He guessed that the source of my information was Derek Robinson, with whom I talk regularly on the phone. Derek is very keen

[1] Miss Joan Maynard, Labour MP for Sheffield, Brightside. Member of the NEC since 1970.

[2] Deputy General Secretary of the Amalgamated Union of Engineering Workers – Technical and Supervisory Section – and a member of the NEC since 1972. He died in 1978.

for his report to be used in the miners' dispute and is keeping me genned up about when it will appear. But Dick was *distrait* and seemed to find it too much to concentrate even on light political gossip. 'My tummy is playing me up; no, I've no pain, thank God, but endless discomfort. And then I get so tired. I spend most of the week down in the country. Anne likes that.' I got him talking about his new TV series to try and cheer him up, but, frankly, I don't think he will live to do it. My poor, poor Anne! Their friends feel so helpless.

Wednesday, 23 January. I stood up about twenty times trying to get in on Heath's questions so as to deal with the Relativities Report, but Selwyn [Lloyd, the Speaker] didn't call me. Ran into Willie Whitelaw behind the Speaker's chair and he was fuming about the fact that I hadn't been called. 'Former Employment Secretary and a Privy Councillor and not called! I think it is intolerable.' He even tried to rope in the Tory Chief Whip who was passing by and I had to say mildly that really Selwyn was usually very kind to me. I am puzzled by Willie's friendliness. Is he still grateful to me for bailing him out over my recent intervention[1] or does he need my questions for some ploy of his in the Cabinet?

Thursday, 24 January. Another determined attempt to get called on the PM's questions in the House. To my astonishment, no luck. Even surrounding back benchers protested to me about it. So after questions I went to Selwyn and asked him mildly if he could not see me where I sat. 'It looks as if I can't,' said Selwyn, puzzled. So he hadn't noticed me! His failure to call me was also off-putting for BBC 2, which had booked me to record a piece for this Sunday's *Westminster*. However, the recording went ahead and I was able to rub in my points about the Relativities Report.

Tuesday, 29 January. Derek Robinson has changed the whole climate over the Relativities Report[2] by saying over the weekend that it *could* be used quickly to deal with the miners' dispute. And Derek Ezra [chairman of the National Coal Board] is reported in the *Guardian* as having asked the Government to use it. I have spoken to Len Murray as to what would be the TUC attitude to my pressing the Government on this. He said that it would be perfectly okay for me to trail my coat, though the TUC had not discussed the Relativities Report yet and would be chary of getting themselves involved in the proposed machinery. He could not see the TUC being willing to sit down with the CBI: they had had no confidence in them recently. He was obviously very pleased that I had consulted him and thought that this was the way things should be done.

Armed by this talk I went into the chamber determined to get in on the PM's supplementaries this time. As advised by Selwyn, I had a word with the Speaker's secretary – only to discover to my horror that it wasn't Selwyn in his

[1] During his speech in the debate on the three-day week on 10 January, Mr Whitelaw, Secretary of State for Employment, refused several times to give way to Labour MP George Cunningham, and then gave way to me. When Mr Cunningham protested, I defended Mr Whitelaw by pointing out that I was 'one of his predecessors who had to handle prices and incomes policy'. It was clear to me at the time that Mr Whitelaw wanted to give me the chance to press my point about the Relativities Report, which I duly did.

[2] The report (Cmnd 5535) had been published on 19 January. It recommended a procedure for considering claims for special treatment under pay policy.

chair but his deputy. Although I stood up time after time it looked as if I was going to be unlucky and Willie started gesticulating at me frantically. That man's desire for me to get in on relativities can only mean that I am helping him to play some game in Cabinet. He obviously wants desperately to settle with the miners. At last, after some signals of my own to the Speaker's secretary, I was called and made my point[1] to some 'Hear, Hears' from our own side. Afterwards David Ginsburg [Labour MP for Dewsbury] came into my room to tell me that not only had I put a first-class question, but that Willie had told him how pleased he was with it. Well, well!

I was leaving the House later with John Silkin to have dinner with Reggie Paget (who apparently loves cooking for people) when I got an urgent message to go and have a word with Harold. Harold, brandy in hand, was dictating a letter to Heath following up my point and wanted my advice on it. I warned him that we must not commit the TUC on machinery though I was sure we could make capital out of the 'exceptional' cases principle. I left him dictating to Doreen.

Wednesday, 30 January. Harold's letter to Heath has got great prominence, but I am alarmed at the unguarded way he has gone overboard for the whole report, with none of the reservations I had urged on him. He really is the most reckless tactician, always getting himself into corners. As I suspected Heath has seized back the initiative, saying he will apply the report to the miners if the TUC will say openly that they accept both the principles and the machinery: just the trap the TUC wanted to avoid! I went on *Nationwide* to discuss the issue and did rather well, arguing that Heath should go ahead and apply the report himself.

Thursday, 7 February. Get into the House early to prepare my notes [for the economic debate]. In comes Roy Mason. 'There will be no debate today, love. Parliament is to be dissolved tomorrow.' I feel cheated. Everyone in serious huddles. Some Tories are obviously distressed. 'No one wants this Election,' one of them told me.

Saturday, 9 February. Heath announces he has sent the miners' dispute to the Pay Board himself. Just what I advocated! If Harold had only listened to me he could have had the credit for the idea. But Heath's move has taken a lot of the wind out of his own sails.

Sunday, 10 February. Drive to Blackburn with Ted and Alison[2] to start the campaign.

[1] I reminded Mr Heath that both Derek Robinson and Sir Derek Ezra were pressing for the report to be used as a basis for a settlement with the miners and I demanded: 'Will the Government face up to their responsibilities, take the initiative and take the necessary steps to secure a settlement on the report – or is the nation to be sacrificed to the Prime Minister's blind bigotry?'

[2] Mrs Alison Morris, then my constituency secretary.

The Election campaign was launched in an atmosphere of bitterness when the miners, despite the pleas of their President, Joe Gormley, refused to suspend their national strike. At midnight on 9 February every pit closed down. Labour, first off the mark with its Manifesto based on its campaign document, fought the Election on the understanding it had reached with the unions. Mr Heath fought it on the need for 'strong government'. When Mr Wilson referred to the existence of a 'Social Contract' with the unions, Mr Heath poured scorn on it and demanded to see the piece of paper on which it was written. Mr Wilson replied that he was referring to the joint statement with the TUC *of February 1973: 'Economic Policy and the Cost of Living'.*

Mr Heath's riposte was to try to turn the Election into a 'vote against disruption'. While promising amendments to the Industrial Relations Act, he insisted that its essential structure must be maintained. In the Conservative Manifesto, he declared war on 'a small number of militants' who 'manipulate and abuse the monopoly power of their unions' and hinted that social security would no longer be paid to strikers' families. Inflation was the main enemy. He would press ahead with pay and prices policy, 'if necessary stiffening it'. The time had come, he said, to tell the extremists: 'We've had enough.'

Harold Wilson's determination to widen the issues was helped by the official announcement in mid-campaign that the index of retail food prices had risen by 20 per cent in the previous year: the fastest rise at any time since 1947. It was also helped dramatically when Mr Enoch Powell announced that he would not seek re-election as Conservative MP *for Wolverhampton because he would not be party to an 'essentially fraudulent Election', adding later that he had cast his postal vote for Labour because it was the only party offering the people the chance to vote in a referendum on whether they wished to remain in the Common Market. Another blow came three days before the poll with the publication of the trade figures showing a £383 million deficit.* The Times *described this as 'the largest monthly trade deficit that Britain has known'. The following day the final indignity was heaped on Mr Heath when Mr Campbell Adamson, Director-General of the Confederation of British Industry, called for the repeal of the Industrial Relations Act because it was 'surrounded by hatred'.*

Mr Heath's growing difficulties were increased by his own belated decision to refer the miners' claim to the Pay Board in its new guise as a 'Relativities Board'. The miners' union took full advantage of this to press publicly their arguments to be treated as a special case. Public opinion was already swinging to their side when, towards the end of the campaign, the Pay Board discovered that the Coal Board's figures had consistently overstated the miners' earnings. This made the disparity between miners' pay and average manufacturing earnings £3 a week greater than had been supposed. The following day a further discrepancy in the Coal Board's figures was discovered which widened the gap by another £2 a week. Harold Wilson maintained this had turned the Election into an unnecessary farce.

Nonetheless throughout the campaign the polls consistently gave Mr Heath the lead, though the lead varied from 1.5 per cent to 6 per cent according to the particular poll. A feature of the Election was the resurgence of the Liberals. At one point Mr Jeremy Thorpe, their leader, talked of a 'landslide' – even the possibility of a Liberal Government. On polling day morning (28 February) the Harris and National Opinion Polls were still giving Mr Heath a decisive victory. But as the results began to come in that night the picture changed. With a swing to Labour in the North and Midlands and a big upsurge in the Liberal vote to 19.2 per cent, it was soon clear that Mr Heath's gamble had failed. He had exchanged a working majority of fifteen for stalemate. By Saturday morning, 2 March, Labour had emerged as the largest party with a majority of four over the Conservatives (301 seats to 297), but thirty-four short of an overall majority. Ranged against it were fourteen Liberals and twenty-three 'others', including seven Scottish Nationalists, two Plaid Cymru and twelve Ulster Unionists.

At first a stunned Mr Heath refused to relinquish power. With 38.2 per cent of the voters behind him to Labour's 37.2 per cent, he turned to the Liberals, offering them a coalition with a seat in the Cabinet. Liberal MPs decisively rejected his overtures. At last on 4 March Mr Heath admitted defeat and Harold Wilson was called on to form a government.

The biggest surprise in the new Cabinet was the inclusion of Michael Foot. His appointment as Secretary of State for Employment was seen as a brilliant move. With Tony Benn at Industry, Peter Shore at Trade and myself at Social Services, the Left was given its usual niche in a Wilson Cabinet, but once again it was denied the key posts of Treasury, which went to Denis Healey, and Foreign Office, which went to Jim Callaghan. Roy Jenkins was partially back in favour as Home Secretary and Reg Prentice was steered from his shadow post at Employment, where he riled the trade unions, to Education. Newcomers to the Cabinet included Merlyn Rees at the Northern Ireland Office, John Morris as Secretary of State for Wales, Eric Varley at Energy and Shirley Williams in a new department as Secretary of State for Prices and Consumer Protection. Tony Crosland, who had always hankered after the Treasury, became overlord of the new super-department of the Environment which Ted Heath had created. Fred Peart went to Agriculture and Roy Mason to Defence. Willie Ross remained at the Scottish Office and Ted Short became Lord President of the Council and Leader of the House of Commons. New to the Cabinet were also the former Labour Attorney-General, Sir Elwyn Jones, who moved to the Lords as Lord Chancellor, and Lord Shepherd, who became Lord Privy Seal and Leader of the Lords. David Wood of The Times *commented that the Cabinet reflected Harold Wilson's 'loyalty to old colleagues'.*

Sunday, 3 March. Looking back over this curious Election I realize what an ambivalent state of mind I have been in. I never expected us to win, but equally I did not think that Heath would get away with his contrived scenario. Quite early on I told Ted that I thought it might be another 1964 – certainly no landslide for the Tories. Even when the polls were consistently against us – and a *Liberal* landslide seemed to be building up – this contrasted with the reception I was getting in my own constituency. Never in all my nine Elections can I remember such warmth of personal greeting as I got as I went around Blackburn.

Of course there were moments of anxiety. I was worried when the Liberals decided to put up against me, as otherwise I knew most Liberals would have voted for me. Fortunately their candidate, Frank Beetham, turned out not to be very popular, even with his own party. Then there was the National Party, which had polled 4,000 in the municipal elections. With a majority of only 2,800 I hadn't enough margin to cope with that! Kingsley Read, the National Party candidate, had been very skilful in rousing support on local issues like redevelopment, which some of our lads on the council had messed up. But somehow, despite it all, I was quietly confident, not least because of all the intensive work I had done in the constituency in the past two months when I was warning Tom Taylor and Jim Mason[1] that an Election was very probable. So I spent over half my time out of the constituency – in the South-West,

[1] Treasurer and Chairman respectively of the Blackburn Trades Council and Labour Party.

Yorkshire and all over Lancashire. It was a risk I felt I could afford to take, even if it reduced my majority.

The turning points of the Election were the announcement of last month's price rises; the appalling trade figures; the discovery that the miners had actually been claiming too little; Campbell Adamson's gaffe over the Industrial Relations Act and Enoch Powell's statement that he was voting Labour. Even in 1970 *we* never had such a series of catastrophes. But the weather was nearly a disaster for us when, at 6 pm on polling day, a bitter wind turned into the worst snow-storm I can remember at any election. Even with cars to take people to the poll it wasn't fit to ask a dog to turn out in. Yet my valiant knockers-up ploughed on. At 8 pm I told Ted firmly that I was abandoning the futile exercise of trying to get people out by loudspeaker and I too joined in the knocking up. We all got soaked. The irony of this Election is that the three-day week, Ted Heath's gimmick, saved us from potential disaster as, with so many people not at work, we had had a record early poll. In some stations the poll was already 60 per cent by 6 pm. And the immigrants, bless them, whom we had organized brilliantly, turned up trumps. The existence of a National Party candidate actually helped us. There was a roar of applause at the count when we found Read had lost his deposit.

The result, therefore, is better than any of us had dared to hope, though stalemate means there is bound to be another Election soon. I told Tom and Jim as we chewed over the events on Friday morning that I had intended this to be my last Election, but Jim said that, with another Election coming before long, they just would not release me. So here we go for a bumpy ride. Everyone was astonished when Heath did not resign immediately: he has got a bad press over it. But when I rang Harold this morning he agreed with me that he will be forming an administration before many days have passed. He was chuckling over the situation: some of his old spirit seems to have come back. He is already planning his amendments to the Queen's Speech if Heath manages to cook up a deal with the Liberals. 'Footwork is my strong point,' he murmured modestly. 'That's just what Peter Jenkins wrote yesterday,' I replied. 'We shall go ahead with our full Manifesto,' he continued, 'and dare the Liberals to defeat us. I shall work much more as a committee, keeping myself freer than I did before. And no more lobby briefings: just the *Mirror*, the *Sunday Mirror* and the *People* will have access to me.' 'Oh, Harold,' I murmured, my heart sinking. 'No,' he said firmly. 'There will be no more of those off-the-record discussions of what the Government is going to do. Instead, Government decisions will be all on the record – preferably announced in the evening in time for the 9 pm news.' 'That sounds okay,' I replied, relieved. So long as he doesn't renew that vendetta with the press! Certainly Harold is the only man for this tricky hour. It could be that he has really learned the lessons of last time. As he put it to me: 'After all, we are all experienced Ministers this time,' adding, 'Don't go too far away during the next few days.'

Monday, 4 March. My last day of freedom before I return to the treadmill. I spent it writing letters and walking the dogs in the snow. Tommy [Balogh] phoned to ask me to join Mike and Peter [Shore] for dinner at his house tomorrow. Brian [O'Malley][1] phoned to arrange lunch. Mik phoned to say some of the bods were meeting in his office tomorrow afternoon prior to the NEC meeting on Wednesday morning. At 6 pm Radio Blackburn phoned: it looks as if Heath is going to resign. So Harold will be summoned to the Palace at any moment. I wondered how I would get up to town if I were summoned to No. 10 as Ted has already departed for council[2] work in London. Decided to ring Harold. Got him at the House. He said crisply, 'It looks as though this is it. No, don't come up to town. I am not having anyone come up; I shall just make my announcements later. You'll be Secretary of State and I assume you will want Brian and the rest of John Silkin's team.[3] Yes, Social Services.' 'Brian, yes please. But he must be a full Minister.' 'I'll be announcing the junior appointments later,' was all Harold said. 'Just report to your office in the morning.' And he added with a chuckle, 'You'll be at the Elephant and Castle.' 'God,' I groaned. He was crisp and confident and didn't sound as though he were ready to negotiate anything with anyone. But I shall fight hard to keep my promise to Brian; he is worth ten of the other juniors. It is amusing how one can talk about terms before the event and when it comes to it everything melts away in the excitement and urgency of the moment. But if Harold is more self-assured this time, so am I. A year or two at Social Services and then it will be retirement – or a bigger bid. I am already scratching my head as to whom I can appoint my political 'cabinet'.

Tuesday, 5 March. Still no announcement, so Ted and I drove up to London leisurely. On our way Ted and I kept stopping to listen to the news on our portable radio. At noon there it was: Mrs Castle, Secretary of State for the Social Services. I hardly felt my pulse quicken. How very different from last time! I can't quite analyse my mood. I feel supremely confident that I can do this job and I should have hated to be left out. But there is no stardust left. There is even regret that my private pleasures are to be sacrificed again. Perhaps I shall adjust, but at the moment there is a kind of dread at the resumption of a feverish round of meetings and paperwork. I decide to keep my dental appointment and Ted and I continue to discuss whom I shall have as my political adviser. He comes up with an excellent idea: Jack Straw.[4] I ask him to arrange a meeting.

[1] Brian Kevin O'Malley had been Labour MP for Rotherham since 1963. He had been Deputy Chief Government Whip from 1967 to 1969 when he became Parliamentary Secretary to Dick Crossman at the Department of Health and Social Security. He had already made a name for himself in the House of Commons for his political flair, his debating skill and his mastery of the complexities of Dick's National Superannuation Scheme. While the Labour Party was in Opposition, he and I had worked closely together in the sub-committee of the NEC which was producing an amended Crossman plan. As a result of our ministerial partnership, my respect for him was to deepen into warm friendship.

[2] Ted was an Alderman of Islington Council.

[3] Following my defeat in the elections for the Shadow Cabinet for the second time in 1972, and my decision to retire to the back benches, despite Harold Wilson's willingness to keep me on the front bench, John Silkin, MP for Deptford, had become shadow spokesman for the Social Services in my place.

[4] Jack Straw had hit the headlines in 1969 when he became the first left-wing President of the National Union of Students for fifteen years, defeating a lethargic leadership which had reduced the NUS to little more than a travel agency. Jack set out to turn the NUS into a proper union for students, campaigning on the aim to make the NUS 'respected but not respectable'. But it was as a young councillor in Islington that he had met my husband and

Back at the House I find Alison in chassis, wondering what is going to happen to her. Sir Philip Rogers, my Permanent Secretary, has been on the phone. I ring and tell him I am going to keep a lunch date (with Brian O'Malley). Arrange for him to bring some people of the Department over to the House at 3 pm for a short chat before I have to go to the Palace to kiss hands. Then I take Ted and Brian over to St Stephen's for lunch. Brian tells me he is not too keen on coming with me just as Minister of State. That would mean he was no further on than he was three-and-a-half years ago when Harold had already promised that rank to him. It transpired he wanted to be a full Minister of Pensions and I promised I would try to get it for him. He certainly deserves it. He is the only man who can help me to get a national superannuation scheme painlessly.

Sir Philip (whom I now recall from his Cabinet Office days) could not have been more gentle and accommodating. I think I shall get on with him. Brian tells me that Lance Errington, the second Permanent Secretary whom Philip Rogers brought with him, is very good. It was amusing to see how patently anxious they were not to appear to be swamping me with that 'companionable embrace'![1] A few hurried words with them about urgent matters and then off to the Palace to kiss hands – a very muted affair this time: no tea and cucumber sandwiches (and I was dying for a cup). Obviously the Palace is economizing too! I was in the old coat in which I had been campaigning for three weeks; Wedgie and Mike looked as though they had been camping. Sir Martin [Charteris, the Queen's Private Secretary] and the rest were as friendly as ever and we stood in groups chatting for an unconscionable time. At last Harold arrived. Still we waited. I was anxious to get down to work but seized the opportunity to have a word with Harold about Brian's desire to become a full Minister of Pensions. Harold said he saw no objection to that. The Privy Council itself seemed a long and boring affair, though the Queen played her part as pleasantly as she always does. It was comical to see Mike balancing on one knee. Most people walked back normally to their places instead of feeling their way backwards as one is supposed to do. Only Wedgie, Mike, Fred Peart and I affirmed, Roy [Jenkins] clutching his Bible rather self-consciously. There was a moment's fun with the Queen's chaps when they asked those with a Bible if they would mind returning it this time if they had already had one. (More economy!) My chief delight was to see Harold Lever[2] there, leaning heavily on his stick, and I gave him a big hug. He said that he and Diane had been thrilled and relieved to find I was back in the Cabinet – so obviously some people had had doubts.

Our first Cabinet at 5 pm. The first shock was the sight of the inside of No. 10.

impressed him with his grasp of an argument and his enjoyment of a debate. Ted also liked him very much as a person – as I was to do. Jack had qualified as a barrister, but his thoughts were on politics. When I retired from Parliament in 1979, he was to follow me as Labour MP for Blackburn.

[1] While in Opposition I had been asked to address a seminar of senior civil servants at the administrative college, Sunningdale, on the relationship between Ministers and civil servants. I did so with some enthusiasm, telling them that the civil service had become a state within a state and stressing the need to strengthen the political power of the Minister against the administrators' 'companionable embrace'. On 10 June 1973, the *Sunday Times* published the speech under the title 'Mandarin Power'.

[2] Harold Lever, who had earlier suffered a slight stroke, had been brought into the Cabinet as Chancellor of the Duchy of Lancaster in the special role of economic and financial adviser to the Prime Minister. As his appointment brought the number of Cabinet Ministers above the number entitled by law to receive a salary, he was unpaid.

Heath must have spent a bomb on having it done up. Gone was the familiar, functional shabbiness. Instead someone with appalling taste had had it tarted up. New old gold carpeting everywhere; white and silver patterned wallpaper; gold moiré curtains of distressing vulgarity; 'nice' sideboards with bowls of flowers on top. It looked like a boudoir. An attendant came up to me to say solemnly that, if I didn't like the new chairs in the Cabinet room, they had kept my leg covers from the old chair and could bring them back![1] No need: the old brass-studded chairs have given way to expensive new leather-covered ones. An interesting insight into Ted Heath's personality.

The next shock was to have Harold say as we assembled round the Cabinet table that he thought we might adopt the custom of calling each other by our first names, adding with a smile to Wedgie, 'So you get your point at last.' How some of us urged this greater informality last time! There was a cheer, only Tony Crosland drawling languidly, 'At least let us call each other by our *sur*names.' No one took any notice of him and Harold was soon calling on 'Michael' to give us his report on the mining dispute. The whole atmosphere seemed transformed by that simple gesture at which the new Secretary of the Cabinet, John Hunt, sat smiling discreetly. He is a far less obtrusive character than his predecessor, Burke Trend – less charisma and therefore I think he will fit better into the new mood. He had already reminded me of the work he did for me on my Railway Steering Group when I was Minister of Transport. Very good work, too. I hope it is not vanity to assume that a lot of this change is due to my 'Mandarin Power' article. (In fact later in the day, when I met some more of my senior officials at the Department one of them said to me shyly: 'I was at that famous talk of yours at Sunningdale, so I really got the message.')

Harold's next remark was: 'I should make it clear that it is not compulsory to smoke in Cabinet', puffing clouds into the air from his pipe. More laughter. I notice there is a curious little box in the corner above the picture rail. Perhaps it is an air conditioner. If so, I shall really thank Ted Heath for that.

Mike gave us a rather sombre report on the miners. He said that he thought that what we should do was to authorize the National Coal Board to negotiate. Should we give them any indication of our limit? The Pay Board report[2] wasn't helpful because it proposed to give the faceworkers *more* than the NUM had asked and the surface workers (except for the ex-faceworkers) less. He didn't think the NUM would stand for that: the militants on the Executive Committee mostly represented the surface workers. The miners' full claim, including fringe benefits, was £138 million compared with £113 million for basic increases alone, while the Relativities Report went up to £98 million. He would try to settle at £113 million but might be forced further up. We agreed that the NCB

[1] In the 1964–70 Labour Government I had repeatedly complained to Harold Wilson that I had laddered my tights on the rough legs of the Cabinet chair I occupied. On one occasion when yet another pair had been spoiled I tossed him a jocular note: 'I shall sue you!' When I arrived at our next Cabinet meeting I found he had had the legs of my chair specially swathed in cretonne.

[2] The Pay Board report, 'The Relative Pay of Miners' (Cmnd 5567), had appeared on 1 March. It recommended exceptional increases for mineworkers consisting of a new allowance for every shift worked underground and a smaller personal allowance for surface workers who had previously served a qualifying period underground.

should be told to go ahead and to give Mike and Harold *carte blanche* to settle. I urged that we should make it clear we were rejecting the Pay Board report because I understood (I have had this from Derek) that a large number of unions, far from boycotting the Pay Board, were hoping to get in on the relativities act. There were nods at this, particularly from Denis, who nonetheless maintained that it was essential for us to settle with the miners in the next twenty-four hours. So there was complete harmony in our first Cabinet. We were urged to get on with our bids for the Queen's Speech.

It was a pleasant relaxation to go out to Hampstead to dinner with Tommy at Old Bank House; a lovely place, so he can't be as hard up as he likes to make out. Mike was there, modest and diffident, Liz Shore, Peter's wife, went down on her knees and salaamed when she saw me, murmuring: 'My boss, my boss.' I hadn't realized that, as Dr Shore, she is one of my employees! Tommy, said Catherine, had been called to No. 10, and when he came in beaming we realized why: he is to be Minister of State at the Department of Energy in charge of North Sea oil! Harold really does seem to mean business this time. Dick and Anne joined us after dinner. He looks so ill; my heart aches, but one dare not even murmur a word of comfort to Anne, she is so apparently unruffled and bright. Perhaps that is the only way she can keep going and keep Dick going. He is still doing his TV programmes, although he is so weak that the effort is obvious. I told Dick and Liz I didn't want Shirley Summerskill in my team: she just didn't carry enough weight. Who could I have on the health side? David Ennals, they said, so I went and phoned Harold, who told me David was already earmarked. Back I went and we mused again. 'What about David Owen?' said Liz. Back I went to the phone. 'I like that idea,' said Harold approvingly. 'Let me think about it.'

Wednesday, 6 March. Up early to a 9.30 am meeting of the NEC, called specially so that we in the Government can reassure them that this time we really mean to keep in touch. Jim, bright and relaxed in the chair,[1] had worked out some ideas for doing this. Harold made a little speech assuring the NEC that 'this time I am going to run this Government very differently'. In the Cabinet he now had 'the most experienced team in living memory', and he added with relish, 'They are going to do the bloody work while I have an easy time.' His job was to be the 'deep-lying centre half, not scoring all the goals'. We were going to act as a team. 'My job is to be the custodian of the Manifesto. I have already recruited a political team at No. 10 which will have access to all the documents. I am asking all my colleagues to appoint political advisers to their private office.' Wonders will never cease! I don't think it is euphoria (in fact I feel flat and positively reluctant about my own return to office) but I have a hunch things are going to be very different this time. We *could* turn out to be the most successful Labour Government in history. It is a good move that Harold has not put Roy [Jenkins] back at the Treasury and an inspired move to put Mike at Employment. Harold concluded by saying, 'Our relations with the press will be proper, formal, correct and on the record,' and then went on to spell out how he intended to keep any planned leaks for *Labour Weekly* and to build it up. The keeper of the

[1] Jim Callaghan was chairman of the Labour Party for the year 1973–74 and therefore presided over the NEC.

Manifesto! So at last he is blossoming out in the consciousness that his long ordeal in keeping the Party together is being vindicated.

Over to the House for a Party meeting. The thing that astonished me was the extent and the warmth of the congratulations I received. As our people streamed out of the meeting they queued up to grasp my hand and to tell me how delighted they were I was back in the Cabinet. It was as though they wanted to make good for all the humiliations I had suffered in being thrown off the Shadow Cabinet. Perhaps, like Harold, I shall be vindicated too. Though I do believe that our new concordat with the trade unions is far more hopeful than the arm's-length relationship we had last time. Thanks to the shock they have had under Heath they may at last prove that *In Place of Strife* was wrong.

Back at the office a hectic round of meetings to clear the Queen's Speech. We had a two-hour mass meeting with officials to discuss the uprating [of pensions and other benefits].[1] The brief officials had given me said that, with an effort, they could get the increase into payment by 1 September. Brian and I told them that this was politically unacceptable. After a lot of arm-twisting they agreed they might advance the date to 22 July, though they told us there was a lot of discontent among the staff about the pressure of work. They warned that, with such a date, a number of pensioners might get their increases in arrears. *Tant pis*, was all we said, and they went away a bit dazed. All I have to do now is to get it through Cabinet. I already know the Chancellor is talking about an autumn uprating and Jim has said that that is all we promised at the Election.

I am losing no time in appointing staff. I rang up Brian Abel-Smith[2] this morning and said simply, 'Will you come to me?' to which he replied equally simply, 'Of course.' What a relief! He is unmatchable. I also saw Jack Straw in the flat: he is Ted's brilliant idea for my political adviser. He was clearly keen to come, though asked for time to talk to the chap he is in chambers with. (I have mentioned him to Harold; no problem there.) But things were very dicey about David Owen. I rang him to ask him if he would come on the health side and he asked if he could come and see me. When he did, he did a Brian O'Malley on me: said that he quite enjoyed being on the back benches; had a lot of things he wanted to do; really didn't think it was worth his while to come merely as a Parliamentary Secretary, which would mean no advance for him on last time. But he added, 'It isn't that I don't want to work with you. In fact I should enjoy that.' I listened patiently, merely saying that I really did need someone with his knowledge and ability on the health side. I told him the line I thought we ought

[1] In its Election Manifesto the Labour Party had committed itself to bring 'immediate help' to pensioners, widows, the sick and unemployed by increasing pensions and other benefits from £7.75 to £10 a week for the single person and from £13.50 to £16 a week for the married couple: the largest increase (28 per cent) since national insurance was introduced. It had also committed itself to increase ('uprate') pensions and benefits annually in proportion to increases in prices or in average national earnings, whichever was the more favourable to the pensioner. These pledges were the outcome of a sustained campaign on behalf of the pensioners by Jack Jones, and formed part of the Social Contract entered into by the Labour Party with the trade unions.

[2] Professor Brian Abel-Smith was and is Professor of Social Administration at the London School of Economics. He had been senior adviser to Dick Crossman as Secretary of State for Social Services from 1968–70. From the academic and administrative posts he had held and the research work he had done, he had incomparable knowledge and experience over the whole field of health and social security.

to take on health issues and he agreed one hundred per cent. He was obviously wavering and then asked for time to think. He would ring me later that night. When he did it was to say that the last thing he wanted to do was to embarrass me. So he would come. But would I do what I could to see that he really got the next vacancy as Minister of State? I said that of course I would: repeated that Harold had assured me the only reason he couldn't make David a Minister of State now was that he was already over the statutory number and couldn't risk legislation to increase it. (In fact I have had a tough time with Harold, who has sent me a message: 'Tell the Secretary of State to stop badgering me over O'Malley.' But he really is in a difficulty over Ministers of State.) To my immense relief David said that on that basis he would come. So that is one hurdle passed.

Thursday, 7 March. Our first real Cabinet. I notice ironically that I have been moved down to the end of the table: no longer the central position I had as First Secretary. Not to worry: I'll be back. I'm no has-been, though I am surprised at my own detached mood. I work as hard as ever but wonder all the time whether the game is worth that mass of paper work. I keep saying to Ted, 'Do you know, I'm *bored*!' What on earth has come over me? I'm ten years older, of course, but my energy is as great as ever: my intellectual grasp seems stronger and I feel completely on top of the job. But I shrink from the idea of meeting the press; have no inclination to try and sparkle; just want to slog on doing a good job. And I deeply resent the work that comes between me and the garden – and the dogs.

After Cabinet I had a word with Harold about Brian O'Malley. He told me categorically that he couldn't – or rather wouldn't – make him a full Minister. Too many other people who also wanted to be full Ministers would be offended if he did. I couldn't move him. I went away weary and depressed to tell Brian the news, wrapping it up as effectively as I could. 'Then he's gone back on his word,' said Brian tartly. 'I don't think I like people who go back on their word.' I begged him to think it over and he said he would like the night to think it over.

Friday, 8 March. Brian phoned early, as promised. Reluctantly he agreed. I am delighted. He is very able. So now I have a really effective team. Harold is to make Alf Morris a Parliamentary Secretary for Disablement[1] and has offered me another Parliamentary Secretary to console me for the other rebuffs. So, from his list, I have chosen Bob Brown. But having seen this morning's further list of appointments I am terrified lest David Owen retracts. It really is absurd how many newcomers Harold has made Ministers of State. No wonder he has run out of his number! I am sure Eric Heffer, for one, would have been glad to start as Parliamentary Secretary, though I am very pleased he is in the Government.

Off to Blackburn to fulfil my promise to come back as quickly as possible.

[1] Alf Morris, Labour MP for Wythenshawe, had won a national reputation by his work for the disabled and in particular by his success in putting the Chronically Sick and Disabled Persons Act on the statute book as a back bencher in 1970.

Monday, 11 March. An early visit from William Armstrong,[1] charm itself. He raised no objections at all to my recruiting Jack Straw – even talking in terms of £8,000 a year. And of course I could have Brain Abel-Smith. I said to him that the whole mood seemed to have changed in the civil service: could 'Mandarin Power' have had anything to do with it? 'That and other things,' he replied. He had really come to tell me that Philip Rogers is due to retire this summer but could be persuaded to stay on if I wanted him to. I asked for time to think it over: 'Though I get on well with him. I am not out to do a Tommy Padmore.' It was all most amicable. William is – and always has been – almost too accommodating to be true.

At the eve-of-the-Queen's-Speech reception at No. 10 there was the usual euphoria for the first Queen's Speech of a new Government, though I still found the tarted-up rooms an irritant. It was good to see Michael Meacher [MP for Oldham West] there, as modest as ever and a little overwhelmed at being Parliamentary Secretary at the Department of Industry. I told him I would have liked him to come to me but Harold had said he was booked. I am not sure Industry is the right assignment for him, but no doubt it will do him good. Ran into Denis, who was very truculent about my proposed July date for the uprating. 'I shall fight you on this.' 'Cabinet will decide,' I said hotly and went away determined to win.

Thursday, 14 March. Some fun at Cabinet over Harold Lever, whom Harold called 'the Duke'. What else do you call the incumbent of the Duchy of Lancaster?

This is only our third Cabinet, but public expenditure is already rearing its ugly head. Denis had put in a memo saying that the economic situation the country faced was possibly the worst we had ever faced in peacetime. Unless something was done inflation this year would be over 15 per cent and the balance of payments deficit would jump to £400 million. There was no scope for increases in living standards this year: the threshold agreement would probably be reached by April, with the agreements being triggered nine times during the year. In order to clear the way for his Budget decisions it would be necessary to decide the total level of public expenditure by the end of the week. There would have to be increases in the prices of nationalized industries; defence should be cut by £250 million and prestige projects reviewed; in his view Concorde should be cancelled. In the meantime, he asked Cabinet to accept that for 1974–75 there should be no increases in public expenditure apart from subsidies – and of course the pensions uprating. Wedgie came in first about his beloved Concorde. He could not have been more disingenuous. All he asked was that we should cash in on the previous Government's refusal to disclose the facts and that he should be allowed to make an early statement revealing those

[1] On 10 April 1974, it was announced from No. 10 that Sir William would be leaving the public service in July to join the Midland Bank with a view to succeeding to the chairmanship the following year. Not only did Harold Wilson confirm the previous Prime Minister's consent to these arrangements under the two-year rule which prevented senior civil servants from taking without permission certain sensitive outside appointments immediately after leaving the Service, but he allotted Sir William a life peerage in his New Year's Honours list of 1975. Thus rewarded Lord Armstrong quickly used his freedom to campaign against the Labour Party's proposals to nationalize the banks. In 1978 he was to become prime mover in setting up a committee of top industrialists to mobilize public opinion against further nationalization generally.

facts. No one could – or did – object to that, though Denis did say wistfully that he would have liked to be able to announce cancellation in his Budget. Wedgie has lived to fight another day.

Reg Prentice was very reluctant to accept the December cuts,[1] even for this year, as their effects were proving even worse than had been visualized. Denis hastened to assure him that, if he had an autumn Budget, he would look at this again. I entered a firm caveat about the proposed increase in electricity prices[2] which Eric, like other Ministers of Power before him, was positively anxious to encourage. If there were a 25 per cent increase as suggested, I said, the position of pensioners would be intolerable and I would want to press for a big increase in supplementary benefit heating additions.

On defence (how history reverses the roles!) Denis was all for our completing the immediate withdrawal from East of Suez, while Roy Mason was full of the difficulties.

It was eventually accepted that there was no escape from Denis's formula for public expenditure in 1974–75, and that we would look at his proposals for later years when his further memo was circulated.

Next into my battle over the date of uprating. I felt on the top of my form. Mike was very helpful, saying he was briefed by his Department to support me. Peter Shore backed me too. Typically, Shirley, Reg Prentice and Jim suggested that we might go for 1 September as an intermediate date for the uprating, but Harold clearly was on my side. He suggested that the needs of demand management might change: we might even be faced with an increase in unemployment before too long. There were three decisive factors: first, the effect on the TUC and the need to win support for the Social Contract; secondly, the possibility of an early Election; thirdly, the fact that we might need an autumn Budget to expand demand. At this Roy came in to say that, as a former Chancellor, he believed he should support the Chancellor, but he wanted to ask him whether he really stood firm on this. Here Fred [Peart] passed me a note: 'Stand firm, you will win.' And sure enough, to my astonishment, Denis's opposition collapsed. He was prepared to 'concede', adding that he rejected 1 September as a 'soggy compromise'. I could have hugged him! I went away to receive the bewildered congratulations of the Department, Brian O'Malley whistling his astonishment at my victory.

Monday, 18 March. One of my inspirations – to appoint Jack Ashley as my Parliamentary Private Secretary [PPS][3] – has gone down very well. When I put

[1] On 17 December 1973, the Conservative Chancellor of the Exchequer, Mr Anthony Barber, announced some £1,200 million of cuts in public expenditure for the year 1974–75. Among the major items were cuts of £182 million in education and £111 million in health and social services.

[2] Under Mr Heath's prices and incomes policy the prices of nationalized industries' products had been held down and the industries had run up huge deficits, which had begun to alarm the Conservative Government. In order to correct this, Denis Healey proposed stiff increases in a wide range of their prices. In his Budget statement of 26 March he announced an increase in electricity prices of 30 per cent. One argument was that this was essential to secure fuel economies.

[3] Jack Ashley, Labour MP for Stoke on Trent, South, had gone totally deaf following an operation in December 1967. The courage with which he had carried on his parliamentary work, particularly for the disabled, had won widespread admiration. His affliction had brought home to me how seriously the needs of the deaf had been neglected and I determined to do something about it. Though he was centre-right in many of his political views, we were to work together harmoniously and creatively.

the idea to Ted he dismissed it as 'sentimental', but my instinct told me he was wrong. If I am to be head of a 'caring' Ministry, I had better start by showing I care myself. And I have taken the precaution of consulting Philip Rogers and Graham first, explaining that the appointment of a totally deaf man would add to our difficulties. Were they prepared to take on the extra burden involved in communicating with him and including him? Of course, they could not say no. And Jack is thrilled. Harold, too, instinctively warmed to the idea. It is the sort of gesture that appeals to him.

At last I have had to submit to the ordeal by photographer. The press have been clamouring for the 'at work at her desk' sort of picture but I have not been in the mood for it. Having been unable to stall it off any longer, I had my hair done first. But my irritation with all this side persists. Later I got into trouble with the office over my long-delayed first press conference when I discovered it clashed with Mike's speech in the House on the Tory motion on prices and incomes policy. I threw the only tantrum I have done in over six years of government, telling Graham[1] and Peter Brown[2] that their job was to save me from my own stupidities, like forgetting there was a historic parliamentary occasion on this day. I was tired of missing every dramatic moment in the House and they must just take into account that, if such an occasion arose, I was in future going to put the House first. Peter was very patient but very serious and I eventually struck a bargain with him: he would delay the conference for three-quarters of an hour if I would undertake to leave the House not one moment later that 4.55 pm. So I sat through Mike's speech, feeling like a truant but enjoying every minute of it. It was a *tour de force* and he made Carr look like Johnnie Boyd in an off moment. When I crept out to Admiralty House the press was waiting *en masse*, well lubricated by Peter in the meantime. Late as it was, Peter insisted on taking me aside to impress on me: 'I want some of the old Castle charisma this afternoon. Don't forget this is the largest uprating in the history of national insurance. Give it to them.' He was like a film director with a star who needed encouragement. I wonder what dear Dick would make of that? Thus encouraged, I went in with all sails flying.

Tuesday, 19 March. The main business at Cabinet was Mike's memo on his discussions with the TUC. In fact it soon became obvious that there was no need for a Cabinet at all, particularly as the Tory great attack had collapsed yesterday. (I suspect that Harold had only fixed our meeting as a cover for an emergency discussion if the Tories had defeated us. Their reluctance to do so takes some getting used to.) Mike's memo makes clear that the TUC is very willing to play along with the continuance of incomes control until a voluntary policy can be worked out. Len, at any rate, is clearly determined to make the Social Contract work.

Did a whirlwind tour of receptions in order to get the measure of international feeling about the renegotiating of the EEC terms and found the

[1] Graham Hart, my Private Secretary.

[2] Director of Information in the Department. He had been Chief Information Officer at the Ministry of Housing and Local Government when Dick Crossman was Minister and Dick was so delighted with him that, when in 1968 he became Secretary of State for Social Services, he insisted on Peter Brown being transferred to him. Subsequently Peter Brown served under Dick's successor, Sir Keith Joseph, and I had inherited him.

Germans apprehensive and the New Zealanders quietly satisfied with our line. At last on to the 'Husbands and Wives' dinner,[1] where Mike, to my sympathy and satisfaction, fell asleep. It is comforting to know that others feel the strain as much as I do.

Wednesday, 20 March. More office meetings, including a rather forced initial meeting with Lewin and Stevenson of the BMA. I was at my most charming because, as David Owen says, we shall have to have some showdowns with these lads soon.[2]

Thursday, 21 March. As I thought, Wedgie's retreat on Concorde was only to fight another day. He told Cabinet: 'I am not asking for any decision today.' (He knows he would have lost if he had.) The figures were still not agreed, he said, particularly of the social costs of cancellation. Moreover it would be intolerable to announce it without wide consultation with the unions first. All that Denis could salvage was permission to say in his Budget speech that we would stop production at sixteen planes and that there would be no further development or production.

On industrial relations Mike ran into trouble over his proposed transitional arrangements[3] and particularly over picketing, on which even Jack Straw has briefed me to persuade him to drop them. There was no time to discuss them thoroughly, so Harold proposed that a group of senior Ministers should look into them later that day before getting the proposals urgently to the TUC.

Incidentally, my family planning proposals went through without demur, not even Bob raising a murmur about my wish not to impose prescription charges.[4]

One of the issues which was to take up a great deal of my and Alf Morris's time was mobility for the disabled. Knowing as we did that money was limited, it was to test all our ingenuity. The invalid tricycle, which had been issued to some 21,500 disabled drivers, had been a boon, but it had two major defects: it could only help those fit to drive and the disabled driver could not carry a passenger. So he or she travelled alone. The Disabled

[1] The left-wing members of the Cabinet – Michael Foot, Wedgwood Benn, Peter Shore and myself – had decided to try to meet weekly over informal dinner in order to keep in touch. To allay Harold's suspicions of a 'cabal', wives (or husbands) were invited as well. The only non-Cabinet Ministers were Mrs Judith Hart, Minister of Overseas Development, John Silkin, Minister of Planning and Local Government (John Silkin entered the Cabinet in October 1974) and Lord Balogh. The description 'Husbands and Wives' dinner enabled us to book these meetings openly through our Private Offices without alerting the civil service network to the fact that regular political discussions were taking place.

[2] As soon as I took office Dr Walpole Lewin, chairman of the Council of the BMA, and Dr Derek Stevenson, secretary of the BMA, asked to see me to demand a review of the consultants' contract with the NHS. Officials told me that the BMA had been pressing this for some time and that feeling was running high. I therefore agreed to set up a Joint Working Party under Dr Owen's chairmanship to examine the possibility of a new contract, on the understanding that the working-party should also deal with the Government's commitment to phase private beds out of NHS hospitals.

[3] In keeping with the Government's Election pledge to repeal the Conservatives' Industrial Relations Act 'as a matter of extreme urgency', Michael Foot had been having discussions with the TUC on the scope of the alternative Bill and on whether it should extend trade union rights on such matters as picketing. His Trade Union and Labour Relations Bill, repealing the Tory Act, was presented on 30 April.

[4] Under the Conservative Government Sir Keith Joseph had announced his intention to introduce, from 1 April 1974, a comprehensive family planning service under the NHS, but he intended to impose a prescription charge on the family planning supplies dispensed. In the Budget debate on 28 March I announced that family planning supplies would be free. I also announced that prescription charges generally would be abolished for children up to sixteen years of age and for women from the age of sixty.

Drivers' Association had launched a campaign to get the tricycle replaced by a specially adapted car, for which war pensioners and a few others were already eligible. The case was a strong one: a four-wheeled vehicle was obviously safer than a three-wheeled one, it overcame the problem of loneliness and – most compelling – a mass-production small car cost no more, and increasingly less, to produce than a specialized tricycle. The Association had backed its campaign with alarming assertions that the tricycle was unsafe.

It was these arguments that had led Alf Morris to endorse the disabled drivers' campaign. Just before the Election Harold Wilson had thrown in his support. So, although there had been no Manifesto commitment, the Government was committed morally. Yet the problem, as often happened, was not as simple as it seemed. The invalid tricycle was originally visualized as a substitute for the walking capacity an individual had lost: an extension, in effect, of the artificial limb. But a car was a development of the quality of life of which a large number of other people dreamed. Above all, it was obvious that once the Government provided a car which could take a passenger, it could not logically refuse that vehicle to the most seriously disabled of all – those unfit to drive. As there were thousands of these 'disabled passengers', who at present received no help with their mobility, the additional cost would be considerable.

My predecessor, Sir Keith Joseph, had bought time by referring the whole issue to Lady Sharp who, as Dame Evelyn, had been Permanent Secretary at the Ministry of Housing when Dick Crossman was Minister, with instructions to take account of 'available resources'. Her report, 'Mobility of Physically Disabled People', had landed on Sir Keith's desk in August 1973. He had not published it. My first aim was to get Cabinet consent to my publishing the report, which I did on 25 March. I also published at the same time the reports of tests on the tricycle which had been carried out at the Department's request by the Motor Industry Research Association [MIRA]. These showed that, although some design modifications were needed, there were no reasons on grounds of safety alone why the tricycle should be withdrawn.

Lady Sharp found that the case for replacing three-wheeled vehicles by four-wheeled ones was unanswerable. But in order to keep down the cost she proposed that eligibility for a car should be limited to those disabled people, whether drivers or not, who in effect needed a vehicle to support themselves or their families. In this way the additional cost would have been kept down to £3 million over and above the £10 million already being spent on the vehicle service, including the private car allowance. Existing holders of a tricycle, who did not qualify for a car under the new criteria, would be able to keep them as long as stocks lasted but no new tricycles would be produced.

Neither Alf Morris nor I found this acceptable. We disliked the proposed needs test and we knew that, despite the campaign against the tricycle, those who possessed one valued it. Our civil servants and special advisers were unanimously opposed to the Government providing cars, not only because of the cost, but because a large administrative machine would be needed to buy and service them. They wanted us to 'get out of cars and into cash' through a mobility allowance available to drivers and non-drivers alike, which beneficiaries could then use in the way that suited them best: for taxis; as payment to a neighbour for the use of his car; to help buy a car themselves. The trouble, as Alf Morris and I well knew, was that we would be unlikely to get a high enough mobility allowance out of the Treasury to enable disabled people to buy a car, yet those who demanded cars expected the Government to provide either the capital or the vehicle. We had to find an answer to all these points.

Sunday, 24 March. Phoned Harold from Hell Corner Farm to see if he was willing for me to make the statement on the Sharp Report tomorrow. No problem there, though he says he wants an early meeting with me and Alf to discuss an idea he has for giving the disabled their cars at half the estimated cost. He is clearly determined, if he can, to fulfil the promise he made to the disabled drivers when in Opposition. He said he intended to get Harold Lever working on his idea: some pact he thinks he can enter into with Morris Motors. 'As you know, I don't intend to have a DEA; Harold is better than any DEA,' he told me. I said it had occurred to me we could link the provision of cars for the disabled with the cancellation of Concorde. Why not open a government factory – or get Morris Motors to open one – in Bristol to absorb the redundant men? In this way we could finance the cars out of the social costs of cancellation. He liked the idea. I next asked him if he would arrange for Cabinet Ministers to meet his 'think tank' so that we could know what it was up to, and he said that arrangements for such a meeting, with graphs, etc., were already in hand. Finally I asked him if it would be all right if I were to invite Bernard Donoghue's team[1] over to drinks to meet my political adviser and Ministers, and he said, sure, though Bernard hardly had a team as yet.

Over to our neighbours, the Pawsons, for drinks at lunchtime. Tony Keable-Elliott[2] seized on me and we annoyed everyone by talking interesting shop for ages instead of engaging in small talk like the rest. Tony gave me a lot of ideas I shall follow up and promised he would come and give evidence to our working-party on the consultants, 'though I shall get into terrible trouble'.

Monday, 25 March. Budget Cabinet was a very comradely affair.[3] Denis had an engaging frankness which disarmed any criticism. He began by saying that this

[1] In addition to the 'think tank' which Mr Heath had set up in Cabinet Office in 1970 under Lord Rothschild, Harold Wilson had decided to establish his own personal group of political advisers under Dr Bernard Donoghue. The need for such a policy unit servicing the Prime Minister had been urged by Mrs Marcia Williams, Harold Wilson's political secretary, in the light of her experience of the Labour Governments 1964–70, described in her book *Inside No. 10*. While Mr Heath visualized his Central Policy Review Staff [CPRS] as helping the Government as a whole with iron detachment to improve its collective decisions, she wanted to arm a Labour Prime Minister against the civil service by giving him a 'small core of highly qualified, highly expert individuals' to help him initiate policy instead of having it imposed on him by the machine. Dr Donoghue had previously been senior research officer in PEP (Political and Economic Planning) and a lecturer at the London School of Economics. During the two stormy years in which I held office during 1974–76 I never found that either the CPRS or Dr Donoghue's unit had any noticeable effect on the decisions we took. These depended far more on the political muscle and (expertly reinforced) political will of individual Ministers.

[2] Dr Robert Anthony Keable-Elliott FRCGP, Member of the Council of the BMA and chairman of its General Medical Services Committee. One of the ironies of my long struggle with the medical profession was that Tony Keable-Elliott was our neighbour in our remote country retreat. As we both did a lot of gardening we would often discuss our departmental disputes informally over the garden hedge, to the alarm of my civil servants.

[3] The Budget reversed nearly all the Heath Government policies. One of his main aims, Denis Healey told the Commons, was to recreate the 'sense of social unity'. His Budget raised the threshold for payment of tax, introduced a new higher rate of tax at a lower starting point and raised the highest rate of all from 75 per cent to 83 per cent. Corporation tax was increased and tax relief withdrawn from mortgages of over £25,000 a year or for second homes. More redistributive measures were promised for the future: a gifts tax in the next Budget and a wealth tax as soon as the administrative details had been worked out, with a Green Paper on this in the summer. But in its effect on demand the Budget was neutral – even slightly deflationary. Though unemployment was running at the seasonally adjusted figure of nearly 575,000 or 2.7 per cent, excluding school leavers – an alarmingly high figure by the standards of 1974 – the Chancellor said it was too early to talk of expansion. In February the trade deficit had reached its highest recorded figure, giving a total deficit of £800 million for the first two months. Inflation was rising and the first aim, he argued, must be to reduce the Government's borrowing requirement, which had mounted to over £4,000 million in the previous year. So there could be no hope of immediately restoring the Conservative Government's cuts in public expenditure of December 1973. Indeed, defence spending was to be cut by a further £50 million. The increased spending on pensions – with £200 million

was an interim Budget in the sense that it was impossible to gauge how things would develop over the next few months, and it had also been impossible to work out complicated administrative changes, like a wealth tax, in two weeks. An autumn Budget would therefore be inevitable.

Tuesday, 26 March. I am still trying to get a meeting of my political team every Monday morning at 11.30 am (Brian O'Malley takes life comfortably and does not get back from Rotherham till then), but so far something has always happened to prevent it. I thought it was symbolic of the new co-operative attitude of civil servants that, without consulting me, Graham had called the meeting for noon today instead. (Only this morning I ran into Fred Peart and his Private Secretary, who said, on being introduced: 'We are all frightened of you.') It was a useful meeting.[1]

I was afraid I wouldn't be able to keep awake through the Budget speech and at one point I did almost doze off. But then it was so packed with meat I perked up. I thought Denis did very well and the Tories sat silent, clearly not certain whether it was a case for jubilation by them or not. Slipped out towards the end to do urgent constituency letters and get ready for a protracted official meeting which had been called, first to prepare for my uprating statement tomorrow and secondly to deal with a complicated submission on the interim pension arrangements we should introduce next April.[2]

more for the house building programme and £500 million for food subsidies – must, he said, be covered by increased tax. So he increased the standard rate of income tax by 3 pence, raised national insurance contributions from 5 per cent to 5½ per cent and put up the duties on drink and tobacco. Nationalized industries, which had been forced to run up massive deficits under the Heath policy, would, he announced, be authorized to increase their prices. The net effect was designed to reduce demand by some £200 million by the end of the year and to cut the Government's borrowing requirement by £700 million. But a substantial deficit remained both on trade and internal borrowing. To finance this the Chancellor announced that the Bank of England through the clearing banks had negotiated a massive ten-year loan of $2½ billion from foreign banks and had arranged an increase in short-term financial help under the 'swap arrangements' with other central banks. 'Borrowing is more sensible in economic terms than trying to cut imports by massive deflation,' Denis Healey told the Commons. 'But no one should imagine it is a soft option.'

[1] The meetings became a regular weekly fixture at which we discussed policy with no officials present. In addition to Ministers, those attending included the Parliamentary Private Secretaries, my political adviser and the special advisers. Later I also invited two research assistants at Transport House, who were dealing with social policy and who found it invaluable to be kept in touch with the Government's ideas and problems.

[2] For some years all parties had been agreed that the Beveridge scheme of national insurance, with its provision for flat-rate pensions in return for flat-rate contributions, was out of date as the level of contribution needed to finance a decent pension put too great a burden on the low paid. In 1969 Dick Crossman, as Secretary of State for the Social Services, had produced an earnings-related scheme of national superannuation, but this had not become law when the Conservatives were returned to power in 1970. Sir Keith Joseph, Crossman's successor, abandoned the scheme in favour of a two-tier system consisting of the flat-rate state pension plus an earnings-related pension on top, both to be financed by earnings-related contributions. This became law in 1973. Under it, every employee had to qualify for the second pension, either by belonging to an approved private pension scheme, or by becoming a member of the inferior 'State Reserve Scheme'. In Opposition the Labour Party had bitterly attacked Sir Keith's proposals as a sop to the insurance industry by setting the standards of approved private schemes too low and making the Reserve Scheme less attractive still. Sir Keith had himself described it as being 'of modest dimensions'. One of the most obnoxious features of the Reserve Scheme was that it was to be 'funded', *i.e.* contributions were to be invested and the level of the reserve pension determined by the yield of those investments, instead of current pensions being financed out of current contributions, plus an Exchequer contribution, as in the basic state scheme ('pay as you go').

In our Manifesto we had pledged ourselves to replace the Conservatives' 'inadequate and unjust' long-term pensions scheme with a comprehensive one of our own and this was to be one of my major tasks. My first

Wednesday, 27 March. [An] early meeting of Legislation Committee [on my Uprating Bill]. I had to point out that one vital clause was still being negotiated with Treasury. This is the clause that fixes the date of the next uprating after this. If we are to fulfil our Manifesto promise of annual reviews the date included must not be later than 22 July. The Treasury has suddenly insisted that this limits the Chancellor's power of manœuvre and that Sir K.'s present wording of 'not later than 30 Nov.'[1] must stand. This would throw doubt on the whole validity of our uprating and I am determined to fight this to the death. John Gilbert[2] had to reserve the Chancellor's position. So when I got to NEC at 10.15 I soon got a message saying that arrangements had been made for me to discuss the matter with the Chief Secretary [Joel Barnett].

The meeting with Joel was exhausting. For over an hour he argued with a blind Treasury insistence that the Chancellor must be free to have a later Budget next year. This did not mean, we were assured, that the Treasury wanted to go back on our policy of annual reviews, merely that the Chancellor must 'keep his options open'. His options to do what, I asked. To move to a sixteen-month review next year? Not at all, said Joel. First patiently, then passionately, I pointed out that that was just what his suggestion of inserting the November date in the Bill would mean. The Treasury official who was sitting next to Joel interposed that my arguments were 'impressive', but Joel didn't give way. Finally, we broke it off, Joel shaking his head and saying, 'You are a terrible woman.'

I got to the Cabinet office late for Harold's meeting with the TUC. The TUC's main preoccupation was about the repeal of the Industrial Relations Act. Sid had said there was 'some anxiety', but Mike explained that he was pressing ahead with this with the utmost urgency. He clearly charms them with his friendly sincerity and Jack Jones nodded approvingly at everything he said. But Hughie returned to this, not unnaturally in view of the fine he faces over Con Mech.[3] Mike, trying to control his irritation at their failure to realize that he was as frustrated as they were by the procedural difficulties (how I sympathize!), repeated that he was rushing the legislation through as quickly as possible and hoped to introduce the repeal Bill by 1 May.

problem, however, was that Sir Keith's Reserve Pension Scheme was due to come into operation on 6 April 1975, and I had to decide what to do about the Reserve Pension Board, which had already been set up, and whether to allow the Reserve Scheme to start as planned until we could work out, and introduce, our own 'pay as you go' scheme.

[1] In his Social Security Act of 1973 Sir Keith Joseph had provided for an annual review of pensions and other benefits in order to keep them in line with price increases over the previous twelve months. Pensions were to be adjusted 'not later that 30th November each year'. Since we had advanced the date of our uprating to 22 July, our next increase would have to be in July 1975, if our own promise of twelve-monthly reviews was to be kept.

[2] Dr John Gilbert, Labour MP for Dudley East, was Financial Secretary to the Treasury.

[3] From September 1973, the Amalgamated Union of Engineering Workers had been in dispute with Con Mech (Engineering) Ltd over union recognition. In October 1973, under the Industrial Relations Act provisions, the union had been fined £75,000 for contempt of court for refusing to call off the strike. Despite the fine the strike had continued until the beginning of March and the firm applied to the NIRC for compensation. Although the Labour Government had announced its intention to repeal the Act, the court on 28 March made an award of £47,000 against the union. With the union refusing to obey the court, Scanlon knew its assets were at continuing risk until the Act was repealed. And so it proved. When the money was not paid, the court sequestered the AUEW's assets. The result was the calling of a national engineering strike. This case – as so many others under the Act – ended on a note of farce when on 8 May the court accepted £65,000 from an anonymous donor to discharge the union's debt. One theory was that a group of employers had put up the money. The Act was eventually repealed in July and the NIRC disappeared.

Back in the House I tried to contact Mike or Wedgie but couldn't reach either. Then I thought of Bob Mellish and eventually tracked him down in the Strangers' bar. I took him into a corner, bought him a drink and told him the whole tale. His response was instantaneous and complete.

Thursday, 28 March. Put on my best dress for the Cabinet official photo and hoped the tiredness wouldn't show too much. As it was cold the chairs had been set out in the upstairs reception room at No. 10, instead of outside. We had all been given a set place and Shirley and I found ourselves on the two outside seats of the semi-circle. 'You wait till the women of the movement learn about this,' Shirley called out to Harold. 'Not to worry, Shirley,' I called back. 'We can do a pincer movement on him. His days are doomed.' Harold just grinned, but I hope he was a bit embarrassed.

[In Cabinet,] turned to my item, Ted Short introducing it under Parliamentary affairs. Bob interrupted him to say we were faced with a new tactical situation in the House. The Tory Shadow Cabinet had had a reappraisal of its tactics and was clearly not going to try and defeat us at this time, but to give us enough time to get into difficulties. We must go to the country as early as possible. That meant we must always have immediate political points in mind. Harold followed him to say he agreed with the Chief Whip. I was all set for a protracted debate when Denis astonished everyone by saying sweetly, 'I have decided not to press the point for the reasons given by the Chief Whip.' Relief!

Went into the Chamber with a pile of scribbled notes and found I wasn't nervous at all. I really believe that, before I am through this stint, I shall be speaking in the House with ease and even eloquence.[1] The only bit that dragged was the long piece on family planning on which the Treasury had had to clear every word. I can't wait to hear Mike handle a speech in which expenditure implications are involved!

Friday, 29 March. If I survive, I think I am really going to find my feet in this job. But it is a big 'if', with the papers full of my family planning announcement, gleefully seized on by the *Mirror* as Barbara's 'free love'. My friend, Tom Wood, who took me back to Blackburn, told me the Catholic Bishop of Salford is already on my tail. But I never had a moment's hesitation that the family planning service must be free.

Monday, 1 April. A very useful meeting with my Departmental Ministers: at last I have got this [weekly meeting without officials] on to a Monday morning basis and Private Office is fully reconciled to it. They have also laid on drinks for Bernard Donoghue and his team this evening, as I asked. Donoghue turns out to be a pleasant – almost ingratiating – chap, but I wonder how much authority he will wield with the PM.

[1] Referring to the record increase in pensions and benefits, I told the House: 'I refuse to underestimate the size of our achievement in our first three weeks – a shift of £1,250 million of resources to the underprivileged at a stroke.'

Tuesday, 2 April. Up early to go to No. 10 for a meeting with the PM on the Sharp Report. In addition to Alf Morris I took Brian A-S. along so that he could develop his thesis about the need to move to cash allowances. Harold asked me to open and I did so by pointing out the financial difficulties of moving from invalid tricycles to cars. Brian had estimated that up to 500,000 people might qualify for cars if we included, as I feel we must include, disabled passengers. On the other hand I said that I did not feel we could move to cash allowances, which would merely favour the middle class. No ordinary poor disabled person would ever be able to afford the capital outlay on a car at any level of cash mobility allowance we could afford. There really must be state intervention to ensure that cars were produced for these people cheaply and in bulk. 'We cannot leave the disabled at the mercy of the car market.' Harold and Alf entirely agreed with this, while Brian sat mum. I suppose that advisers feel themselves to be such non-elected animals that they dare not throw their weight about. Harold had brought in Bernard Donoghue, but he sat mum too. 'You know I made a speech on this,' said Harold and turned to an official to say: 'Ask Albert Murray[1] if he can turn up my speech.' 'I have it here, Prime Minister. We study your lightest word,' I replied sweetly. Harold almost blushed.

After a discussion we agreed that my Department should do a crash job on seeing the motor manufacturers and working out what it would cost to supply a car which they would be willing to take back second-hand at a good offset. This is a favourite idea of Harold's of which I don't see the point myself. But Harold also liked my idea of arranging to manufacture these cars at Bristol and elsewhere as part of the 'social costs' of cancelling Concorde. Harold also insisted that we should start by merely providing cars for the present categories: disabled passengers to come later. But much as I sympathized with Harold's desire to provide cars rather than cash allowances (which obviously pleased Alf), I was wary of a euphoria which could overlook the enormous long-term cost. I am not going to have such a large slice of my budget pre-empted in this way. So I put in a caveat to the effect that some of the 'social costs' money of Concorde would have to come my way to help finance this (to help finance Harold out of his political difficulty, I might have added). Not unnaturally Joel exploded at this and said he wasn't going to have the Concorde savings spent before they had even been incurred. 'I am merely reserving my position,' I replied. Fortunately Joel and I are very fond of each other, following our long battle together in the Select Committee of 1972–73 against the Tory tax credits scheme.

Lunched with Peter Jenkins (of the *Guardian*) at the Ritz (a greatly overrated eating place in my view) and told him why I felt so much happier in this Government. I spelt out how much Harold had changed: as the 'custodian of the Manifesto' he just couldn't twist and turn any more. Peter and I mourned Dick, still clinging tenuously to life after his collapse last Thursday. I said impishly that after all I should have the laugh of him, for I would be writing the second diary: the diary of the third Labour Government which would make the

[1] Albert Murray, former Labour MP for Gravesend, had been brought by Harold Wilson into his personal office to help with constituency and party political correspondence.

fears and frustrations *his* diary would reveal seem old-fashioned.

Almost unnoticed by busy non-Treasury Ministers a deep world recession was developing. The massive increase in the price of oil had not only given inflation a boost everywhere, but had thrown world trade out of gear. In 1974 the oil-producing countries were sucking in extra money from the rest of the world to the tune of $60 billion which their economies were unable to absorb. As their surpluses accumulated unspent, world demand was reduced.

The oil price increase dealt a body blow to Britain's already ailing economy, adding nearly £2,500 million to her oil import bill in 1974. Although in his Budget Denis Healey had rejected 'massive deflation' and rightly chose to finance Britain's deficit by borrowing, there was no organized international attempt to recycle these surpluses and Britain remained highly vulnerable. The Social Contract was the Government's main hope in trying to get inflation down and maintain our competitiveness. In its few weeks of office the Government had taken a number of steps to fulfil its side of the bargain with the trade unions. The TUC was anxious to respond to this new 'climate', but the pent-up resentment against Mr Heath's statutory incomes policy was proving irresistible. One group of workers after another put in for 'catching-up' wage increases, led by the nurses, who were demanding a fundamental review of their salaries. Other NHS workers were following suit. The doctors were restive. Michael Foot struggled at the Department of Employment to hold back the tide.

Since an Election clearly could not be long delayed, Harold Wilson was preoccupied with issues which could affect the Government's popularity. One issue on which he had set his mind was devolution. He was firmly convinced that a radical devolution of power to Scotland, and to a lesser degree to Wales, was the only way to head off the Nationalists, who were threatening the Labour Party's survival in some of its traditional Scottish strongholds, and to defuse their growing clamour for separatism. To prepare for this he had to set up a Royal Commission on the Constitution in 1969, first under Lord Crowther and later under Lord Kilbrandon, to examine the possibilities. The Kilbrandon Report was published in October 1973, setting out seven alternatives. One of Harold's closest advisers on devolution was Lord Crowther-Hunt (formerly Dr Norman Hunt), a member of the Kilbrandon Commission and a keen devolutionist. In October 1974, Harold Wilson was to bring him into the Government as Minister of State at the Department of Education and he was to help Ted Short guide the Cabinet through the constitutional intricacies.

Relations between the Government and the National Executive remained sensitive. Trouble was liable to flare up at any time. It did so over the question of Chile where, in September 1973, the Socialist President, Señor Allende, had been murdered and his Government overthrown by a military junta. To the Labour Party this was the Spanish Civil War of the 1930s all over again. Party conference promptly passed a resolution demanding that the British Government should withdraw our ambassador from Chile, give all possible assistance to refugees from that country and withhold 'all aid, loans and credit from the military régime'. The Labour Government had gone a long way to meet these demands. It had embargoed all future arms sales to Chile, ended aid and adopted a sympathetic attitude to the refugees, but it had to decide what to do about naval contracts entered into by previous Governments and whether to allow the vessels being built or refitted in British yards to be delivered to the Chilean Government. In this it was embarrassed by the stand it had taken in Opposition. In a debate on 23 November 1973, it had called on the Conservative Government to 'prevent any sale of arms to the junta . . . and to withhold future aid and credits from the present Chilean régime'. Mrs Judith Hart had declared from the Opposition front bench: 'We do not believe any of the ships being built should go there, although my understanding is that the trade union movement is taking effective steps here.' In fact, Cabinet was told, there had been little or no trade union action against naval contracts, but only against four Rolls-Royce engines belonging to Hawker Hunter jet fighters of the Chilean air force which were under repair at East Kilbride, where AUEW *workers were refusing to handle them. Despite Mrs Hart's speech, Cabinet decided the practical difficulties of cancellation were too great. On 10 April Jim Callaghan told the House the contracts would be fulfilled. The* NEC *remained unconvinced. At its May meeting, with resolutions of protest pouring in from local parties, it called on the Government to reconsider its decision 'even at this late hour'.*

Departmentally one of my main headaches was what to do about Sir Keith Joseph's earnings-related second 'reserve pension' scheme. Should I bring it into operation the following year, or abandon it? Abandonment would mean at least two years' delay before people could start to earn their extra pension and that seemed politically dangerous. Yet the scheme had serious disadvantages. In the first place contributions would be high. Employees would pay 5.25 per cent on their earnings up to a ceiling for the flat-rate pension and 1.5 per cent on top for members of the state reserve scheme. In return they would get a meagre second pension which would take forty years to mature; women would get smaller pensions than men and widows only 50 per cent of their husband's entitlement. Most serious of all, since the scheme would be funded and the yield from investments uncertain, there would be no guarantee that the second pension would keep in line with prices as the basic pension did.

Thursday, 4 April. I went along with Brian to see Edmund Dell in his role of Paymaster-General [to discuss what we should do about Keith Joseph's pension scheme]. We met at the Treasury, where Edmund was flanked by Joel and the officials with whom we had had our earlier argument about the uprating date. They obviously now treat me with a healthy respect. For our part we were extremely wary, knowing the Treasury. Edmund started by saying, 'I take it we are all agreed that another half per cent on the contributions would be enough to pay for the new and higher basic state pension.' We thought it was a trap, but after half an hour of argument if became clear that Edmund was genuinely concerned that we should have an interim scheme that was politically tolerable. He didn't think we should throw away the chance of getting higher contributions for the new and higher basic pension, but equally didn't think we could justify appropriating the Reserve Scheme fund unless we offered improved Reserve Scheme benefits. 'I am speaking purely for myself – and I don't think officials are agreed on this – but I would have thought we must and could do something to shorten the maturity period out of the extra money we would get from putting contributions up,' he told us. This was an unexpected development which I said we must consider – and anyway I had to go to Cabinet. So we broke up, agreeing to meet again at 8.30 pm. I took Brian, who was muttering, 'I don't like it', into the waiting room with my officials, Alec Atkinson and Douglas Overend. 'How much would a half per cent on the contributions raise?' I asked. £630 million; and with the Reserve fund as well the National Insurance fund would have an enormous surplus,' they replied. 'Exactly,' I retorted triumphantly. 'It is just the old Treasury ploy to make the national insurance scheme carry the burden of demand management.' I sent them off to work out the figures to illustrate this.

When I arrived at Cabinet I found that we were all to parade ourselves in the garden for the benefit of TV. 'The idea is to show that we are a team,' said Harold to me. No one had told me and I hadn't even put my full make-up on! I told Shirley how much I liked her new hair style. 'I had to do something,' she replied. 'I got so many letters telling me how terrible my hair looked. I was letting the Party down, they said.' We strolled around in the garden casually forming and reforming groups, the cameramen trying hard to get me and Shirley together with Harold. 'We're not posing,' he snapped.

On Parliamentary business Bob reported that the Opposition are to put down an amendment to my Uprating Bill calling for pensions to be reviewed every six months. Bob was all for throwing in the sponge; we would be sure to be defeated on it and he couldn't even be sure of whipping our boys into the lobby against it. I was much more cautious, saying I had so many other things I needed to do in my field which would cost money that it would be better to turn and fight. If defeated I could always use this as an alibi when they pressed me to do more for the disabled, etc. Jim said it wasn't even clear that six-monthly reviews would be administratively practicable. It was agreed that I should put in a paper after consultation with the Chancellor and the Chief Whip.

Jim reported on how his statement on the EEC renegotiations had gone at the Council of Ministers.[1] In view of the thunderings in the press about the 'rudeness' of his speech and its disastrous effects, he sounded positively cheerful. He said the public reactions had been 'very strong', the private ones 'much more balanced'. The one point on which they would all part company with us was on the renegotiation of the Treaty of Rome. 'I think our approach is right – to see how far we can get, by changing the policies of the Community, to meet our Manifesto commitment – and I will of course report back to Cabinet.' Jim's statement was received without a murmur from anyone, especially when Harold said Cabinet ought to meet for a whole day in the Easter recess to discuss our proposals so as to be ready for the next negotiating round.

Finally we had a very interesting revelation of Roy Jenkins's mind. He brought up the question of the Speaker's Conference.[2] This, he said, had had unfinished business left over from the last Parliament and he was thinking of reconstituting it. But before he did he wanted to discuss how we should handle the matter of the single transferable vote. If we did not include it in the terms of

[1] In its Election Manifesto the Government was committed to try to secure 'major changes' in the Common Agricultural Policy [CAP], new and fairer methods of financing the Community budget, acceptance of our opposition to Economic and Monetary Union, the retention by Parliament 'of those powers over the British economy needed to pursue effective regional, industrial and fiscal policies', safeguards for the interests of the Commonwealth and developing countries; no harmonization of VAT which would require Britain to tax necessities. At the Council of Ministers meeting on 1 April, Jim Callaghan set out these terms in a tough speech which brought a particularly hostile reaction from the French Foreign Minister, who said that any terms involving a renegotiation of the Treaty of Rome would be unacceptable.

[2] Since 1916 all-party conferences of MPs under the chairmanship of Mr Speaker had been held periodically to consider questions of electoral reform. Speaker Lloyd's Conference, set up in 1972 to consider various aspects of electoral law, had come to an abrupt end with the dissolution of Parliament in February 1974, and had not finished its work. It was not to resume it and the Speaker's Conference was not brought into play again till July 1977, when Jim Callaghan as Prime Minister was anxious to win the support of the Ulster Unionists by increasing the number of Northern Ireland constituencies. Speaker Thomas's Conference then duly recommended by a large majority that the twelve Northern Ireland seats should be increased to a minimum of sixteen and a maximum of eighteen.

reference we should look as though we were the only party not interested in electoral reform. As the Liberals were very likely to propose its examination, it would be better for us to take the initiative. He suggested therefore that we should get the Speaker's Conference to examine it in a 'low-pressure way'. Bob Mellish looked alarmed at this, while Mike came in emphatically: 'Once we get into this it will grow and grow and grow. Why hasten the conference at all?' Nodding approval, Bob added that he was darn sure the Speaker was in no hurry to have [it] reconstituted. Willie Ross, in his lugubrious way, pointed out that all this was linked with the Kilbrandon Report, which had itself recommended a form of proportional representation as the only way of eliminating the perpetual Labour majorities in Scotland and Wales which devolution would produce. If we were not careful we could see the end of any possibility of a Labour Government. Harold [agreed we should] let this sleeping dog lie as long as possible. So we sent Roy away with a flea in his coalition ear.

One of my first acts had been to invite the staff side of the Departmental Whitley Council to my office for informal drinks. But I soon found that they wanted much more than that: Philip Rogers had not exaggerated when he warned me they were seething with discontent (a) about Heath's pay freeze and (b) about the way the Tories had cut down staff. Result: they had taken industrial action – unprecedented in the civil service – a couple of years ago. Now they are just not prepared to take my rush uprating on board without some 'tangible' gesture on my part, *i.e.* a bonus. My Department have been warning me off this, but I told them we must wait and see what the mood was. So when I saw the staff side this afternoon I told them I wanted to meet them informally, but I realized there were a number of things they were bursting to raise with me urgently and I certainly wasn't trying to fob them off with a drink. Naylor,[1] the chairman, and the other full-time officials responded very pleasantly and were particularly pleased when I said I intended to send Bob Brown on a tour of the local offices and that I hoped they would invite him to meet their Executives. But they weren't to be headed off their bonus and it was soon clear that the elected members were in a nasty mood. And, of course, being good negotiators, they quoted against me the tribute I had paid to our staff in the House with the words: 'On an uprating the Government gets the glory but they get the work.' I talked with them for an hour, giving nothing away on the bonus and chi-iking them on the obvious fact that they couldn't agree among themselves who should get it anyway. 'If you were able to give me good precedents, I'd jump at it,' I told them, 'but I can't be the one to create the precedent.' I left them to Bob Brown, promising to meet them again very soon.

At 8.30 pm, at the end of an exacting day, we had to go into another long conference with Edmund Dell. Well briefed with figures by my chaps, I soon punctured Edmund's previous 'offer' to improve Reserve Scheme benefits in exchange for pinching the Reserve Scheme funds *and* putting the basic contributions up. 'How much would your improvements cost?' I asked

[1] Mr B. H. J. Naylor of the Society of Civil Servants [SCS] was chairman of the staff side which included representatives of the SCS representing the executive grades and of the Civil and Public Services Association [CPSA] representing clerical workers. The SCS later became the Society of Civil and Public Services.

sweetly. 'I haven't really costed them,' he replied. '£5 million?' Edmund looked uneasily at his official, who replied equally uneasily, 'I doubt whether it would be as much as that.' '£2 million?' 'That would be nearer it, Secretary of State.' 'So,' I said, rounding on Edmund, 'you want to make us raise another £600 million and give us £2 million back. And you call *that* making the move politically more acceptable!' Edmund had the grace to grin. He really is too honest for the Treasury. The truth was, he confessed, that he didn't think Option B was politically acceptable anyway and would much prefer us just to postpone the whole Reserve Scheme. So the chorus in favour of this grows all the time. I look at Brian; he nods, and within minutes we had agreed that this was what we would do.

But then a thought struck me and I marched after Edmund into his room next door, followed by Brian and a trail of officials. 'But if we do postpone the Reserve Scheme,' I asked, 'what level of contribution would you visualize for the state pension?' '5.85 per cent,' he replied. I exploded. 'But don't you see that would be the worst of all worlds? It is certainly not on politically to put the Reserve Scheme into cold storage, deprive people of two or three years of earnings-related benefits and then put up their contribution rate for the state pension to a higher rate than it would have been under Keith Joseph.' To his eternal credit Edmund not only saw the point immediately, but took it seriously. He started poring over our tables of figures with his officials, and I left him at it, stressing the urgency of the need for me to make an announcement in next week's debate.

Friday, 5 April. Down, thankfully, to Hell Corner Farm, where I am determined, despite the red boxes, to do some gardening.

Dick has died and a great abrasive, tonic force has gone out of my political life. I shall miss him terribly.

Monday, 8 April. A very useful meeting of my Ministers which I have now turned into a working lunch. I told them, *à propos* of a list of appointments to the Central Health Services Council which David Owen has worked out for me, that what he had done was to reduce the number of women by one. 'I do not intend that, when I leave this job, it shall be found that the number of women in public posts is actually less than when I came into it,' I told him. Humbled, David said he'd have another look at it.

Tuesday, 9 April. Up early for meeting with Edmund Dell. We went along prepared for a protracted struggle to get Treasury to accept a contribution rate for the basic scheme of $5\frac{1}{2}$ per cent instead of the 5.85 per cent on which they had originally been insisting. To our surprise, after a token resistance, Edmund capitulated. I nearly hugged him afterwards, saying what a joy it was to have at the Treasury a Minister who looked at things politically and who knew and cared about social insurance schemes. He beamed happily and I felt a warmth towards him I have never felt before.

Then into Cabinet. On foreign affairs Harold reported on his visit to France for what he called a 'working funeral'.[1] It was noticeable how he curbed his

[1] The funeral of President Pompidou.

once familiar desire to chat, merely contenting himself with saying he had had an hour with Nixon, who had spoken 'very frankly'. Then to Wednesday's debate on the National Insurance Bill embodying the pensions increases. Ted Short reported that there seemed no way of preventing an amendment calling for six-monthly upratings being in order under the Money Resolution.[1] We would have to amend it first, which would clearly be impossible. I reported that there were no administrative difficulties in the way of six-monthly upratings either, though the additional cost would be £250 million a year, which I would clearly prefer to spend on something else. Other people (and I can't blame them) were anxious about more money being spent on the OAPs. Personally I agree they have had their share on this round. Denis's attempt to get us to say that, if six-monthly upratings were forced on us in the House, we should announce that we would reverse them after the next Election, was repulsed as the piece of Treasury nonsense it was. Finally it was left that, if we were defeated on this, we must accept it without commitment either way as to its continuance. I was left with the unhappy job of working out with the Chief Whip how we should handle the mechanics of a defeat.

Finally on to Chile. Jim's report on his discussions with the Party groups was ambivalent, despite his care to appear objective. We were left with no clear indication of the Party mood. He admitted that over one hundred Labour MPs had signed the Motion on the Order Paper against the delivery of the vessels, but added that there were only twenty-seven at the meeting, of whom five had spoken out against his proposal for going ahead with current contracts and two had spoken for. He described it as a 'fifty–fifty mood', adding that he had been surprised to discover the extent to which we were embroiled in the sale of arms generally. 'Fifty per cent of the capacity of our naval dockyards is for foreign ships,' he pointed out. (A shrewd diversionary note, this.) Flatly he continued that Chile might cut off our supply of copper if the contracts were broken. This formed 20 per cent of our supply. The ships concerned were not part of a government-to-government contract: they had been ordered direct from the shipbuilders. It might need legislation in the House to cancel delivery. We might have to impound the ships – an action which had never been taken before. It wasn't a question of cancelling export licences, as none were required. For the future, arms licences had been stopped. Taking all this into account, his 'strong recommendation' to Cabinet was that the warships should be allowed to go to Chile.

Listening, I thought it was a masterly demonstration of Jim's technique. Clearly it impressed his listeners. Roy Mason hastened to add that the meeting with the Party groups had been 'low-key'. I thought that no one could stand out against this weight of argument and was all the more impressed when Mike spoke up with a kind of defiant desperation. 'Some of us', he said, 'still hold the view we expressed last year.' The awkward fact was that the ships were going to continue to go to Chile through a long period. Even more important than our

[1] Any Bill involving public expenditure must be headed by a Money Resolution outlining the purposes for which the expenditure may be made and the committee stage of the Bill cannot be taken until the Money Resolution has been agreed to. Proposals for expenditure can only be initiated by the Government, but careless drafting can enable the Opposition to move amendments widening the area of expenditure, as in this case. Governments soon learn to draft Money Resolutions very tightly.

sales to Latin America (which Mason had said would be at risk) was to stick to the view we took in Opposition. Otherwise we lost credibility. Only Wedgie backed him up. Even Peter sat silent. I myself wondered whether to suggest that we try to draw a distinction between the ships that were merely being refitted and were already at sea and those that would take some years to complete.

But while I hesitated Harold ruled that the overwhelming view of Cabinet was that the contracts should be fulfilled. I was sorry afterwards that I had not pursued my idea. I have no doubt that we should not take great economic risks over fulfilling the ships contracts unless the feeling in the Party is very strong. Maybe Jim has misled us over this; time will show.

Cabinet ended early to enable those of us who wanted to to go to the service of dedication Harold has arranged in the crypt. The whole idea makes me cringe. Is he really a believer or is he doing a Mary Whitehouse? But when I raised the matter at my ministerial meeting last week Brian O'M. (who is a Roman Catholic) had smiled at me rather shyly and said that he thought no harm could come of it and it might do me good. So I went along with Brian and sang the hymns right lustily as I always do. Actually the sermon, by some bishop I didn't recognize, was a masterpiece and I quite enjoyed myself. It interested me how few people were there.

As I was coming out Harold W. asked me if I could spare a moment as he wanted a word with me. We went to his room in the House in great comradeship. He poured me a drink. It was quite like old times. As I sat in that familiar room, with Harold pacing up and down, drink in hand, five years just melted away and we slipped back as naturally as breathing into our old affectionate and slightly conspiratorial relationship. Only this time we were both tougher and more relaxed – subtly more sure of ourselves. Harold no longer glanced at his reflection in the windows as he walked up and down. When Harold told me he was going to the Scillies for ten days at Easter I retorted, 'Thank God you are at last learning some sense. Do take plenty of exercise while you're there and get really fit.' 'I've lost a lot of weight,' he replied, proudly patting his tummy. 'So you have,' I replied and added cunningly to encourage him, 'Ted Heath is getting terribly fat.' 'Isn't he?' said Harold, pleased.

Then he sprang his surprise on me: 'You know how short I am of debating talent in the Lords, and you remember how I always intended to put Ted there, though you had objections to being Lady Castle. Well, you could always insist that you wanted to be known as Barbara Castle, and I hope you wouldn't let that stand in the way because I intend to make some elevations soon and I want to include Ted in them. If Heath can have some resignation creations I can have some non-resignation ones.' I said without a moment's hesitation that I was thrilled for Ted and whatever it cost me I wouldn't stand in the way because it was his turn now. God knows he had sacrificed enough for me. But, jumping up and joining Harold in his perambulation, I grabbed him by the arm and said why didn't he seize this opportunity to strike a blow for women's lib. that would win the hearts of every woman in the land? Why didn't he announce that I would *not* share Ted's title but would be 'gazetted' as Mrs Barbara Castle, or whatever the word was? If necessary, I said, I could go and talk to the Queen and I was sure that I could win her over to my side. 'I don't think it is a question of the Queen,' replied Harold. 'I think that legislation would be necessary and I couldn't get that now. But if we are returned with a proper majority I intend to legislate on Honours anyhow – I want their Lordships to be called Life Peers or something.' 'Yes, Harold,' I cried excitedly, 'what we need is for everyone in the Lords to be Mr or Mrs So-and-so, LP instead of MP.' 'We could do it that way and give those who wanted to the right to retain their title instead,' he agreed.

I felt something remarkably like hope and happiness rising in me. Are we really at last going to do something bold? I asked him if I could speak to Ted? Of course, said Harold, adding: 'but don't you go and persuade him out of it.' Could I ask Jack Straw to make very hush-hush inquiries as to how I could remain Mrs Castle? Of course. We then chatted matily about how well the Government was doing. I enthused about the quality of Brian O'M. and David Owen, adding that it really was a scandal that David should only be a Parliamentary Secretary while Eric Heffer was brought straight from the back benches as Minister of State. 'I know,' agreed Harold, 'but you realize the reason was political.' I said I had an excellent team; we planned to do so much, if only we got the chance. 'There's life in the old girl yet,' I quipped as I almost skipped from the room. 'There's life in the young girl yet,' Harold called after me.

Saw Jack Straw at the office. He was as pleased for Ted as I was and thought the Islington Party would be glad, too. 'Ted has been a very conscientious Alderman.' He hurried straight off to check about legislation. It's very useful having a barrister!

Officials came in excitedly to say that the Opposition's first amendment on six-monthly uprating of pensions had been ruled out of order, but that they had put down another one merely providing for 'consideration' of the need for legislation and that was going to be called. Brian and I agreed that this put a different complexion on things. As someone very recently a back bencher it fascinates me how much consternation an Opposition can cause in a Department by its activities.

'Husbands and Wives' dinner in the private room at St Stephen's was rather drab. Only seven of us turned up. No explanation of Tommy's whereabouts. I wonder how he is getting on? I myself felt muzzy with all the complicated insurance formulae I have been studying. Ted is working very late at Islington Council's Planning Committee tonight, so I shall have to wait till morning to tell him the news I am bursting to share with him.

Wednesday, 10 April. Ted was pretty whacked when I took him his morning tea, which may explain the subdued way he took the news. 'It is ten years too late. I don't know whether I could do it now.' I told him firmly that he had got to snap out of his deeply ingrained instinct for running himself down: he could out-debate those deadbeats in 'another place' any time he tried. But, though he is pleased ('I was only thinking the other day that my real problem is loneliness'), neither he nor I are going really euphoric till it actually happens. It has been snatched away from us so often before.

At Cabinet a long discussion on Mike's Bill to repeal the Industrial Relations

Act.[1] Mike reported that, although he was personally in favour of including his picketing proposals in the Bill, he recognized that this might not be possible in the present parliamentary situation. Much the biggest difficulty arose over the safeguards for individuals affected by union action. The TUC strongly objected to a generalized provision, which they found insulting and unnecessary; they wanted it restricted to the closed shop situation by a formula dealing with the position 'where a union had behaved unreasonably in refusing or expelling a member and he had as a consequence of the action been dismissed'. Elwyn saw no objection to this. But it was interesting how meekly Mike in his paper had accepted the law officers' dictum that there could be no retrospective quashing of actions which had already started in the National Industrial Relations Court by the time the Second Reading came. Even to take that date had seemed to them to be straining things a bit. It was Bob who started an agitated protest on this. Did this mean that the fines levied on unions in the Con Mech and GAS cases must stand?[1] 'Incomprehensible!' Wedgie backed him. The only hope was an amnesty. 'The constitutional difficulty', said Harold, 'is that we can't get it through Parliament.' The more we studied it, the more intolerable the situation seemed, particularly when Sam Silkin pointed out that NIRC had announced that the whole of the property of the Amalgamated Engineering Union [AEU] would be sequestered if the union hadn't paid its fine by the end of this month. Mike seized the opportunity to ask if he could not have continued conversations with the lawyers about the possibility of limiting the dangers of the damages, even if the court cases went on. This was agreed.

Next, Cabinet promptly endorsed my line [on the amendment to the National Insurance Bill]. When I said we could not refuse even to 'consider' six-monthly upratings, Denis said, 'Of course. Accept.' But I got into trouble when I proposed my interim solution on the Reserve Pension Scheme, even though Edmund Dell supported me. Crosland complained that he had only had my paper the day before. Ted Short, who wasn't there, has circulated a letter fussing about the political effects. Harold said I could easily get away

[1] The problem of picketing was to bedevil the Government throughout its period of office. The unions were anxious to adapt the right to picket to the needs of the motorized age by enabling pickets to stop vehicles for the purpose of peacefully persuading the drivers to back their strike and Labour's Manifesto had promised this. On 22 March Michael Foot had told the Commons that a provision to this effect would be included in the Bill to repeal the Industrial Relations Act, but he had reckoned without the police and the Home Secretary, both of whom vigorously resisted any interference with the discretion of the police to prevent obstruction of the highway. Long wrangles took place in Cabinet and the only reference to picketing in Michael's amending Bill, the Trade Union and Labour Relations Bill, was a reaffirmation of the legal right in furtherance of a trade dispute peacefully to picket another person at his place of work 'or any other place where another person happens to be, not being a place where he resides'. The TUC was unhappy at the failure to authorize the stopping of vehicles and kept up the pressure on the Government.

[2] For Con Mech, see footnote to page 439. In its last throes the NIRC had also been pursuing the Transport and General Workers' Union, whose members had been 'blacking' General Aviation Services [GAS], a Canadian owned company brought in to provide ground handling services at Heathrow. After a prolonged industrial dispute the British Airports Authority had withdrawn GAS's concession and the firm claimed compensation against the union of nearly £2 million. The NIRC had found the TGWU liable and the union had appealed. Before the appeal could be heard, Sir John Donaldson announced that a full hearing of the compensation case would be held in his court on 15 July and refused the union's request for an adjournment. However, on 11 July the union took its request for an adjournment to the Court of Appeal and won. Twenty days later the NIRC was abolished and outstanding cases passed to the High Court. On 1 May 1975, having heard the union's appeal against liability to pay compensation, the Court of Appeal found in favour of the TGWU with costs.

with another two or three weeks' delay. 'If Geoffrey Howe[1] gets difficult Barbara can deal with him in that charming way of hers and with that throbbing voice we all admire so much.' So that was that! All those late sessions gone for nothing.

[In] my Second Reading speech, I got away without making my announcement on the interim pensions scheme perfectly easily. Indeed, the House seemed quite impressed when I promised it 'early after Easter'. So much for the anticipatory fears a Government has! But it was at the committee stage that I really began to feel a mastery of the House. I managed to accept the six-monthly review amendment while reducing its significance. I then had the satisfaction, when the vote came, of seeing the Tories defeated by thirty votes. (David Owen whispered to me, 'I'm afraid we've won. It really is time we had some defeats in the House so that we can argue that it is impossible to carry on. We must have an Election soon.')

Sunday, 14 April. One of the loveliest Easter Sundays I can remember. The sun shone. Everything went perfectly. The garden [at HCF] was not only a picture, with its great splashes of daffodils, the cherry blossom unfolding and the flowers on the magnolia tree shining like white lights; it was also a children's paradise. And soon it was full of children, laughing, shrieking, sliding down the slopes, playing hide-and-seek among the trees, searching for the little eggs the Easter bunnies had 'laid'. Ted went to fetch Great Gran, whom we ensconced on the terrace wrapped in a rug, holding her latest great-grandchild in her arms. Of course there had to be a run down 'rabbit hill' to collect primroses; another run through the woods where the rapturous children rolled me in the leaves. The lunch which Eileen[2] and I cooked for sixteen of us was a great success. And Great Uncle Ted presided over it all with his usual benignity. I feel so rich on these occasions, my heart stretching to embrace this large, diverse, loving and ever-growing family. This is what I promised you, Marjorie, and this is what I have performed. And I pray that we shall always be able to keep HCF just for this: a place of wonder and delight and peace, not just for the family, but for others who need a refuge and an escape.

Monday, 22 April. Up to London early for a meeting of the Liaison Committee with the TUC. The two sides faced each other across that rather bleak boardroom at Transport House which makes it so difficult to engender enthusiastic intimacy. The TUC anyway are hardly noted for forthcoming enthusiasm at the best of times, and this time their ranks were rather depleted: no Hughie, George Smith or Sid Greene. Jim, in the chair, exuded his usual urbanity. The purpose was, he said, to decide what the work of the Liaison Committee should be: what should be the discussions here and what was better dealt with by direct contact with Ministers. Personally he thought we should concentrate on the longer-term issues. But it soon became clear that the TUC was anxious for the Liaison Committee to keep overall control of the processing of current policy. Wedgie jumped at this. He was already, in his Depart-

[1] Opposition spokesman for the social services.

[2] Mrs Eileen Wells, our housekeeper, loyal guardian of our cottage and of our two cocker spaniels; famed in the family circle for her superb crême caramel and her home-made bread.

ment, working on such things as the new Industry Bill, he said, and he would welcome the opportunity of making a progress report to the Liaison Committee. Jack nodded approvingly, but Ron, always election-conscious, said that he hoped we wouldn't get bogged down with too much research, as in June we might be fighting for our political survival.

Jim kept harking back to the longer-term issues: the priorities for a five-year government. 'We must be free to have wide-ranging political discussions, too.' (I suspect he realizes that the TUC have not yet faced the really tough issues that lie ahead.) Alf Allen was as helpful as usual. 'There won't be a long term,' he pointed out, 'unless we are able to sell what the Government has achieved and what *we* have achieved in the Social Compact.'[1] Jack pointed out that there was a lot still to be done on the things we are already committed to do. The TUC side would like to be aware of what was being produced in the fields of social insurance, prices, etc. Jack went on: 'As far as the Social Compact is concerned, one of the most important things from the trade-union point of view is the establishment of the Arbitration Conciliation and Advisory Service [ACAS]. If we are going to avoid an extension of conflict when Stage Three ends it is essential that ACAS should be in being.'

Harold said it was important that Ministers should rush out White Papers on those issues on which we should not be able to legislate if an early Election came. I whispered to Bob, sitting next to me, 'Do you favour June or October?' 'June,' he replied, 'because things will be much worse in October. These folks won't be able to hold their bloody shower.' 'Then there won't be time for White Papers,' I retorted, [and] suggested that the way out was for the Ministers with vital matters under preparation to prepare brief paragraphs covering these points which could be brought before the next meeting of the Liaison Committee so that we could reach agreement on them before the Manifesto was prepared. 'We must have a paragraph on dealing with inflation, too,' said Jim, ever hopeful. 'Inflation will be dealt with direct with the Government,' replied Harold firmly.

At my ministerial working lunch I reported on what had happened and asked them all to get busy preparing paragraphs in their respective fields, particularly Brian on our long-term pension proposals. The passage in the last Manifesto had been too vague. If we played our cards properly we could get the Party committed next time to the sort of scheme we wanted.

Amusing meeting with Campbell Adamson and two of his buddies from the CBI. C.A. said they wanted to discuss what was going to happen about the Keith Joseph pension scheme. It was amusing because, in contrast with his two companions, C.A. was at his most truculent. It is clear why, of course: even my officials said that his visit might be to collect my thanks for his having won the Election for us! Despite C.A.'s truculence the discussion was mild enough, his companions protesting that they recognized there had to be improvements in Sir K.'s terms for recognizing occupational pension schemes. They clearly hope that, apart from these tougher conditions, I am going to keep Sir K.'s scheme.

[1] At this time there was still some confusion as to whether it was a Social Compact or Social Contract. The latter finally won.

Tuesday 23 April. Visit to South Ockendon, where things have clearly greatly improved following the Robert Robertson scandal way back in 1969.[1] Although Dick refused an inquiry then (Brian A-S. tells me Dick felt it would be too disastrous for morale, coming on top of Ely), he carried through a lot of improvements which have changed conditions there. The Inskip Report is horrifying and fully justifies my pressure in the House about R.R.'s death – a pressure for which all the credit must go to Barbara Robb and Brian A-S. As David Owen has urged on me, we shall obviously have to give mental health much greater priority – even at the expense of other, far more popular, developments.

The evening papers are full of Mike's speech to the AUEW conference. He got a standing ovation before and after it. This is a personal triumph, helped not a little by the announcement that the Government is to cancel the £10 million tax debt incurred by unions which lost the tax relief on their provident funds by not registering [under the Tory Industrial Relations Act]. The decision came as a surprise, since it had not been before Cabinet, as some of us were quick to tease him with when he joined us for the 'Husbands and Wives' dinner at Lockets. 'Give me £10 million and I could have the nurses eating out of our hands,' I said mockingly. Nonetheless I think it is a brilliant move.

But the evening soon degenerated into acrimony. Mike and Judith were insisting that we must reopen Chile at the NEC tomorrow, for which Alex Kitson[2] had sent in a resolution. Mike was saying we must send a deputation to Jim about it from the NEC. Ted and I retorted that that was a recipe for undermining the Government and bringing us into public ridicule as a divided movement just as we were shaping up for the Election. I insisted the Hawker Hunter issue was an entirely different one: 'We shall win in Cabinet on that.' What was more, we deserved to win because the workers involved were ready to risk their jobs. 'I'm not going to be a party to imposing unemployment on workers who have not asked for it, just in order to satisfy our middle-class consciences,' I added tetchily. But though we quarrelled, it didn't go deep.

Wednesday, 24 April. I think Ted and I must have had some effect on Mike, because in the event he was very mild over Chile at the NEC. Jim asked permission to leave the chair so that he could speak to it and made a long speech which clearly impressed his trade-union audience. I suspect it impressed the Left, too, because when he had finished there was quite a silence before anyone intervened. [At the end of a long discussion] I passed Mike a note: 'Is there

[1] In March 1972, Miss Barbara Robb, chairman of AEGIS [Aid for the Elderly in Government Institutions], launched a campaign for a statutory inquiry into the death three years earlier of Robert Robertson, a patient at South Ockendon Mental Hospital, which police enquiries had failed to explain satisfactorily. She was also disturbed by more recent incidents. In this she was strongly supported by Professor Abel-Smith and I took the matter up in the House of Commons. Sir Keith Joseph later agreed to set up a committee of inquiry under Mr J. Hampden Inskip, QC, which reported to Sir Keith in March 1973, and stressed the unsatisfactory conditions under which the staff had been working at the hospital. On taking office I immediately decided to publish the report as Dick Crossman had published in 1969 an equally disturbing report on the ill-treatment of patients at Ely psychiatric hospital (Cmnd 3975). In the meantime improvements had been made at mental hospitals as a result of the work of the Hospital Advisory Service which Dick Crossman had set up. I published the Inskip Report on 14 May (H. C. 124).

[2] Alex Kitson was now Executive Officer of the TGWU and a member of the trade union section of the NEC.

going to be a vote, because I am already desperately late for a Departmental meeting?' 'Of course not,' he replied. So I slipped away well satisfied. I am confident we shall now win on the Hawker Hunter issue, as I said last night. When I saw my office I told them they must *not* arrange Departmental meetings on the mornings of the NEC.

Earlier the NEC had agreed Harold's suggestions for greater liaison with the Government, arrangements which, he pointed out, went much further than any we had had in the last Government.

At Social Services Committee of Cabinet Ted Short agreed my proposals for the interim pension provision without argument: another unnecessary delay! I had then to rush into the Pay Committee of Cabinet, over which Mike presided as though he had been running an incomes policy all his life. The first issue was whether he should use his consent powers[1] in favour of three groups which would have certainly had special treatment by the Relativities Board: teachers, nurses and postmen. Officials had been looking into ways in which some relaxation might be given to them on a selective scale, and the suggestions for the nurses suited me admirably because they fitted in well with the proposals in the Briggs Report.[2] But officials had recommended that the relaxations should not be made because they would do more harm than good. Bob Sheldon, for CSD,[3] was against them, too, and Michael was obviously far from keen, but I weighed in strongly behing all three of them and carried the day, despite some sardonic remarks by Mike about my total disinterestedness. He is taking his role as guardian of the Pay Code so seriously that he is becoming more rigid than Jim Callaghan was in his Chancellor days.

[But] I met a stone wall [over] my plea to be allowed to give my staff a small leave bonus as compensation for the rushed uprating. I warned Mike that an overtime ban had already begun and that we risked having the uprating delayed by several weeks. I might have been talking to myself for all he cared and he outdid Bob Sheldon in warning about the 'repercussions'. Only Gerald Kaufman[4] spoke up on my behalf and he did so passionately. It would be 'insane' to risk our greatest achievement yet – the uprating – by a piece of nonsensical cheese-paring, he urged. But it was all in vain. In his best headmaster tones Mike told me to go away and try to persuade the staff side that their grievances were met by the proposed improvements in overtime (which haven't even been finalized yet). If that didn't work I could come back to the committee. 'It will be too late,' I said despairingly.

At Robin and Brian Thompson's[5] annual cocktail party I ran into Jack Jones

[1] Under Mr Heath's Counter-Inflation Act 1973, the Secretary of State was empowered to give a 'consent' overriding the restrictions of pay policy 'in exceptional circumstances'.

[2] A committee on the structure of nursing education had been set up by Richard Crossman in 1970 under Professor Asa Briggs. Sir Keith Joseph had sat on the report. On 6 May I announced that the Government had accepted the main recommendations. The £18 million Michael Foot was persuaded to allocate to the nurses under his consent powers enabled us to expand the number of nurse tutors and clinical teachers and to strengthen the career structure on the lines Briggs had proposed.

[3] Robert Sheldon, Labour MP for Ashton-under-Lyne, had been appointed Minister of State, Civil Service Department, in March 1974. In October 1974 he became Minister of State at the Treasury.

[4] Gerald Kaufman was now MP for Manchester, Ardwick and Under-Secretary of State at the Department of the Environment.

[5] The Thompsons are solicitors who do a great deal of work for various trade unions. Their party is one of the highlights of the political year.

and told him about the serious danger to the pension increases from the overtime ban. 'Tell them it's outrageous,' he said, clearly furious that his pet uprating was in jeopardy. 'They must call it off.' (No sympathy here for trade union militancy! I was too fair and honest to tell [him] that I could probably have got the ban called off if only Mike had yielded one tiny bit.)

Thursday, 25 April. I arrived late [at Cabinet], having had an early and unhappy meeting with the staff side, trying to persuade them that what I had to offer them in terms of career structure and improved overtime rates warranted them calling off their ban, even though I couldn't give them the cash bonus they had asked for. One of the trade union team admitted grudgingly that I had put a good case, but the unions have got themselves hooked on this cash bonus and it was clear they would lose face if they just succumbed meekly. Officials handed me a situation report showing that the ban has spread like wildfire through the regions and that in some areas the staff are refusing to work with casual labour or to handle the uprating at all, even in normal hours. The result could be disastrous.

Just as Cabinet was breaking up I intervened with my unhappy news. I poured it out in one minute flat, saying that I believed a small concession must be made if we were to have any hope of saving the [uprating]. To his credit Denis nodded understandingly at this. I went on to plead that Michael, Bob Sheldon and I should be instructed to look into it urgently. Harold agreed, but added that I must report back to the next Cabinet. It will be *far* too late by then. It is only at moments like these that I resent Michael's role as the favoured son of Cabinet.

Friday, 26 April. Up early to read my papers for my first Sunningdale.[1] My original idea was that I wanted time with my staff to consider some of the policy issues for the Health Service. It was Brian A-S. who suggested we should use the opportunity to examine the effects on our policy generally of Denis's proposed restraints on public expenditure. At first I thought that the whole enterprise was going to be a gigantic flop. There was a general and rather discursive discussion during the afternoon. But after dinner (thanks partly to the wine) the whole thing came alight and we found ourselves as Ministers engaged in a liberated argument about social security priorities. It wasn't until later that I realized what an effect this had had on my civil servants. Lawrence Brandes, one of my Under-Secretaries who had been with me at the Department of Employment, said to me in the bar at 11.30 pm as we had a belated nightcap, 'It was totally fascinating. We are all saying it is the best show in town.'

Morning came somewhat harshly. Having begged for an early morning cup of tea, I found it cooling on my doorstep when I had given up all hope of it and had emerged to venture into the spartan bathroom for my morning bath. But

[1] I was resuming my Departmental weekend conferences at the Civil Service College, Sunningdale, to discuss policy in greater depth than is possible during the working week. Sometimes I invited outsiders to join in the discussions. On this occasion the conference was to be an internal one to enable Ministers and officials to consider what our priorities should be in the field of health and personal social services in the light of the money we were likely to be allocated in 1975–76. The only 'outsider' invited was Mr Laurie Pavitt, MP, chairman of the Health Group of the Parliamentary Labour Party.

the discussion begun over dinner continued in a lively way over breakfast and we had a stimulating morning discussing Health Service priorities. One of the highlights came when David Owen, who began by saying with that disarming smile of his that he knew the Department disagreed with him, said that he thought the restraints of public expenditure meant that we should just have to be more interventionist. Consultants, doctors and the rest would have to realize that, when they were prescribing drugs or demanding hospital beds for their patients, they were making economic decisions. Dr [Henry] Yellowlees, my Chief Medical Officer, followed on immediately to say, 'It may surprise Parliamentary Secretary when I say that I entirely agree with him.' He was sure this was a time when 'my profession and his' would respond to this kind of argument if only they were brought into the consideration of it. 'Give them the data: put an edited version of our papers to them.'

One of the things that has come out of this weekend is that I have commissioned a new social survey, based on the papers before us, which will spell out with brutal clarity the size of the need in the field of health and social services and the agony of choices. And I think I succeeded in making the whole thing *fun* in obedience to my basic belief that the cardinal sin among politicians is pomposity.

Monday, 29 April. It was odd to go back to St James's Square, where our meeting with Mike and Bob Sheldon over the leave bonus for my staff was to be held. The liftman looked at me closely and said, 'It is Mrs Castle, isn't it? You look ten years younger!' Odder still to be in that ministerial room, scene of so many traumatic moments. I told Mike how grateful he ought to be to me for having left him such an aesthetically decorated room. But his mind wasn't on aesthetics and we spent a tense hour hotly arguing about the bonus. Mike still stands out against the thought of giving a consent, saying at one point that I didn't realize how difficult these issues were for him. At this I retorted, 'You are only just starting. This hasn't got anything on the builders' penny!' His people came up with the idea that we should approach the national staff side to see if they would be prepared to use part of their flexibility bonus under Stage Three to cover this. 'What?' I scoffed, 'Do you really expect a national body to use its money on behalf of a sectional one?' 'But we've got to *try* it, Barbara,' said Mike desperately. The Civil Service Department man quietly pointed out that once we had offered a bonus in this way we should not be able to withdraw it if the national side disagreed. So it was decided that private approaches should be made by CSD to the secretary of the national side. As we left the liftman still eyed me curiously. 'I can't get over it: you *do* look ten years younger.' 'It is not being here,' I quipped. 'Poor Mr Foot looks ten years older.' At the exit I ran into Frank Lawton, the Department's solicitor. The years rolled back as we greeted each other with great affection.

Tuesday, 30 April. I won Jack Ashley's praise again by the firm way I told an office meeting we must do something positive about battered wives. One by one I am trying to take his pet projects on board. But the highlight of the day was the deputation I received from the staff side of the Nurses and Midwives Whitley Council over nurses' salaries. Outside the building a thousand nurses demonstrated, whipped up by the Confederation of Health Service Employees [COHSE] and the National and Local Government Officers' Association [NALGO], and I was told that they had almost stormed the gates. I am glad to read that Mike is reporting to Cabinet in favour of selective increases for the nurses at least. But Griffiths, chairman of the staff side, soon made it clear that Briggs is not the priority. What they are bitter about is that there is now no Relativities Board for them to go to for a fundamental revaluation of their salaries. What they want is the assurance of an independent review. I replied as sympathetically as I could without promising anything. Afterwards David Owen said to me, grinning, 'You really are an old poker-face. You never even gave them a hint that something might be on the way.' 'When you have been through the fire as I have,' I replied, 'you will learn not to count on anything until it has been confirmed by Cabinet.'

Wednesday, 1 May. At the restive Parliamentary Party meeting on Chile I asked Harold if he had had my note about how I could arrange to remain Mrs Barbara Castle when Ted goes to 'another place'. He said yes and obviously is not going to raise any objections to what I propose, so I shall get my letter off to Godfrey Agnew[1] right away. But he said the announcement cannot be this week, so our plans for a double celebration on Ted's birthday this weekend have come to naught. I *long* for the uncertainty to come to an end so that I can allow myself to dare to revel in Ted's happiness.

Thursday, 2 May. When Cabinet met – minus officials – Harold said he thought we ought to have a discussion about our Election options. No decision would be made – and indeed he himself hadn't made up his mind. But reading between the lines, I sensed that he was seeking support for his own strong inclination to go for June. I was surprised how many there were (Shirley arrived late) who were all for a June Election – and strongly too: Eric Varley, Willie Ross, Reg Prentice, Tony Crosland, Roy Mason, as well as Mike and Peter – so the polarization was not on ideological lines. Mike admitted that he would be unhappy not to have got the repeal of the Industrial Relations Act through the House. Nonetheless he believed we could and should take the TUC into our confidence about the difficulties which would increasingly face us if we were to struggle on as a minority government.

Harold then chipped in to say that the TUC would understand if they could see how all the other aspects of our policy that were so important to them depended on our getting a real majority. Ministers should pour out White Papers in the next few weeks. We might even force the Tories to vote on some basic issues of principle, such as North Sea oil and gas (Eric nodded) or land. 'Or', he continued, 'we might bring matters to a head by just putting down a Motion of support for a referendum on the Common Market.' Roy snapped in at this point: 'I hope you would not try to make this the pretext, Prime Minister. I must tell you you might not find this the clear basis for unity you seem to think.' Harold hastened to reassure him that he certainly would not wish to embarrass anyone.

At this point I could no longer contain myself. 'The more I have listened to

[1] Sir Godfrey Agnew, Clerk of the Privy Council.

you, the more you have confirmed me in favour of September rather than June. What we shall be doing is to deny ourselves the parliamentary platform which will be essential if we are to demonstrate the basic difference between them and us.' Jim came in emphatically: 'I am horrified at the suggestion that this Party should be plunged into another Election in a matter of weeks.' The organization and money were just not there. And what if the result was a repetition of the stalemate we had now?

After an hour of this Harold summed up. The Cabinet was divided, but there was just a slight balance of view in favour of September. There was, however, one point none of us had mentioned and that was if the Tories thought they were safe from an early Election, they would be tempted to bring the knives out for Heath, just as they had done for Alec Douglas-Home when he, Harold, had said there would not be an Election in 1965. What he had to decide was whether that would be to our advantage or not. I still think Harold has made his mind up for June, though he repeated no decision had yet been made.

At last officials were called back in. I got my way on the consent for nurses' pay: one breakthrough for my long-term policy! I also backed the consents for teachers and postmen.[1] But, by the time we got to the leave bonus for DHSS staff, Harold and Ted had had to go to the Party meeting. Bob wasn't there. So it was a tired, tetchy and truncated Cabinet which had to deal with the overtime ban which now disastrously threatens my uprating. Mike is still holding out desperately against having to give a public consent on this. The TUC, he says, is more rigid than the Pay Board in wanting no exceptions at all to the Stage Three policy. The unions are obviously afraid they could not hold their own people if a gesture was made to any one of them. But Mike's Department have been trying to think of a way out and have come up with the idea that we should approach the national staff side again, the first soundings having proved disastrous, to see if they would agree for the leave bonus to be met out of the 1 per cent flexibility allowance, only this time against Mike's promise that they would be compensated later when the statutory pay policy no longer operated. Well, that's as good a device as any and I felt I had better accept it as Jim and Denis were making noises of opposition to any leave bonus at all.

Friday, 3 May. In to the office early to talk about the next steps over the leave bonus. Then into an office meeting on Sharp. Dear Alf may be very impressive in his obvious sincerity but when I had waded through his agonizing for fifteen minutes I had to take charge of the policy myself, finally sending Brian A-S., who is superb, away to produce a comprehensive submission along the guidelines I had laid down. These were based on the following principles: (1) all those in the existing categories must retain their right to a vehicle: either car or (if they preferred) tricycle; (2) new categories should be entitled to a mobility allowance, which we should introduce as the first phase in our long-term disability income policy – *i.e.* as part of the payment for the extra expenses of disablement; (3) we should further explore Brian's idea for a rent-a-car scheme. I think the office were relieved to have some clear guidance at last.

[1] On 6 May Michael Foot told the Commons that he proposed to authorize additional payments above the Stage Three limits to nurses and teachers, but not postmen.

Slipped away from the office after lunch to buy Ted's birthday presents. Those two darling dogs were awaiting me longingly at Hell Corner Farm, and as soon as I had swallowed my cup of tea I changed into my old things and braved the north-east wind to take them for a walk. Despite the cold wind everything is unimaginably beautiful. The bluebells are out; the beech is at its most tender green. I picked cowslips and crab apple blossom and filled the house with flowers. My love affair with the countryside will not end until I die.

Sunday, 5 May. A quiet birthday party for Ted: just Eileen and me and a meal at home. We have decided to reserve his celebrations till the great announcement is made. Neither of us will have any peace of mind until it is. Jack Straw has done his stuff with the Privy Council and it looks as though I shall be able to do a Beatrice Webb,[1] thank God.

Tuesday, 7 May. At last I am able to announce our interim pensions proposals and what we are going to do about the Tory Pensions Act.[2] My Parliamentary Questions and statement in the House caused me no difficulty, despite our apprehensions that there would be an uproar over the postponement of the Reserve Pension Scheme. Suddenly I am at ease in Parliament. I don't know why. Perhaps because I am aware that I am on my last lap politically, so I don't worry any more. But Mike's speech on the Second Reading of his Trade Union Bill was a disappointment. Even the parliamentary giant can't score every time.

Wednesday, 8 May. Tough time with BMA deputation over their superannuation scheme. Keable-Elliott was the most impressive of them and I had some sympathy with their case: told Brian to see what he could do about it. It will help us to be tough over pay if we can do something here. In the evening was positively fêted at a reception of the General Nursing Council. *They* at any rate are thrilled over Briggs.

Monday, 13 May. Office meeting on Brian A-S.'s examination of the possibilities of negative income tax.[3] He had to admit defeat, though is still hoping to work out a limited scheme for pensioners. But the main event of the day was my

[1] In 1929 when Sidney Webb was created a peer by the Labour Government and became Lord Passfield, Beatrice Webb refused to use her title.

[2] On 7 May I told the Commons that the Government had decided to scrap Sir Keith Joseph's Reserve Pension Scheme, due to come into operation the following April. Instead the Government would introduce its own, much more generous, earnings-related pensions scheme as soon as possible. Sir Geoffrey Howe denounced my decision as 'flat-footed and doctrinaire'. The pensions industry was dismayed. But Labour MPs welcomed the prospect of a better scheme and were particularly delighted by my statement that employees' insurance contributions would not go up again next April, as Sir Keith had planned, but would stay at the 5.5 per cent which had been fixed to cover the July uprating – a point on which I had won my battle with the Treasury.

[3] Negative income tax was a more radical form of the Tory tax credit scheme. Although its basic mechanism was broadly the same – the replacement of personal tax allowances by tax-free weekly cash credits – its purpose, unlike the Tory scheme, was to redistribute income in favour of the poor. Despite its attractions, particularly in reducing means testing which was one of the goals of our social policy, we finally decided to apply this approach only to children through our child benefit scheme, plus a premium for single-parent families. For other groups we decided to adopt the more flexible approach of progressively extending cash benefits as of right to neglected groups such as the disabled and of steadily lifting pensioners out of dependence on supplementary benefit through our new pensions scheme.

mass meeting at the office with the Royal College of Nursing. They mounted a massive array of speakers and arguments in support of their impressive report on the state of nursing. In effect, through Mrs Newstead's speech at the end, they gave me an ultimatum: announce the setting up of an independent inquiry or they would have to tell their members to withdraw their labour and be re-engaged as 'temporaries'. And she added they thought it was only fair to give me three weeks to meet their demand. I replied as best I could, having enormous sympathy with their case, and promised to meet them again in three weeks' time. I then told officials we must get the decision cleared quickly so that I could make an announcement *before* the three weeks were up.

Wednesday, 15 May. Dick's memorial meeting. I was in a panic. I have never found these personal tribute meetings easy and kept remembering how I had boobed at Kingsley's memorial. Harold was in the chair and read a pleasant speech – too long, of course. Brian A-S. read a polished and very charming one. Then it was my turn. I ad libbed rather desperately from headings, but gained in assurance as I went on. Tony Howard followed with a competent speech without much heart in it. Poor Mike, who was due to wind up, wasn't called till it was already 1 pm. He cut his losses and merely said a few words. Afterwards everyone said I was the only one who had conveyed the essence of Dick. I was glad because I loved the old boy and was relieved when Anne wrote and said she was sure Dick would have done the same for me.

Monday, 20 May. Up early to get to the Liaison Committee with the TUC. Mike gave a warning that we might have a number of defeats in committee on the Bill [the Trade Union and Labour Relations Bill] on the pre-entry closed shop, disclosure of information and independent review machinery. 'In my opinion,' he said, 'we should press on with the Bill, even with these amendments, making it clear we will raise these matters at Report stage or when we have a majority. It is essential that we should get the main purpose of the Bill.' Harold agreed.

We then turned to Wedgie's report on the work of his Department, which painted his reforming efforts in glowing terms.[1] Wedgie told us he hoped to publish details about the public monies received by the first twenty companies in two weeks' time. Only Alf Allen came in from the trade union side: 'The intentions are very welcome, though there is some anxiety about the reper-

[1] In his paper Tony Benn had seized the opportunity to jump the gun on industrial policy. Although three weeks earlier he had circulated a Minute to the Prime Minister promising a Green Paper in the summer after consultation with colleagues 'through the normal machinery in the usual way', his paper set out his own proposals in considerable detail. These were much more specific than the Manifesto, which had itself gone much further than any previous one in its attitude to public ownership and intervention in industry. Not only, the Manifesto said, would the Government take over mineral rights and the aircraft and shipbuilding industries, but it would acquire profitable sectors and individual firms in those industries where a public holding was essential to enable the Government to pursue its economic aims. Included in the list were sections of pharmaceuticals, road haulage, construction and machine tools. The Government would create a powerful National Enterprise Board [NEB] 'with the structure and functions set out in Labour's Programme, 1973'. There would be a new Industry Act and a system of planning agreements 'which will allow the Government to plan with industry more effectively'. What Tony Benn's paper did was to put his interpretation on this policy before Cabinet had considered it. The firms to be included in the planning agreements' system, it said, 'will initially number about one hundred, controlling about half of manufacturing output'. Government aid would be increasingly channelled through these agreements. The NEB would be initially formed out of existing government holdings in industry 'and will then

cussions on employment.' I often wonder what the unions really feel about Tony; I suspect their real hero is Mike.

Harold passed me a note about Ted: '*Operation Ted*: Announcement likely Thurs or Friday this week.' Cheers!

In the afternoon I helped Harold receive a deputation from the nurses, which covered the same ground as they had done with me. I welcome anything which will persuade Cabinet to give me that independent review of their salaries!

Tuesday, 21 May. The Confederation of Health Service Employees [COHSE] and the National Union of Public Employees [NUPE] are a bit offended at my seeing the Royal College [of Nursing], which they feel has stolen the initiative, so I have to agree to see them too – individually. Albert Spanswick [General Secretary of COHSE] warned me that the nurses would insist on an interim payment: something that had *not* been raised with me originally by the staff side. This inter-union rivalry is a curse. I listened courteously. Alan Fisher [General Secretary of NUPE] was his usual reasonable self and I could understand that he had to make his mark. But I really do seem to have walked into a pack of trouble. Unions always seem to let their pent-up frustrations explode as soon as there is a Labour Government. Later I received a deputation from Blackburn nurses. There are deputations everywhere, even though I have already promised to consider their case urgently. After all I have now been in office for the grand total of eight weeks!

Wednesday, 22 May. Another deputation from nurses, this time led by Bob Mellish. Two nurses from COHSE were so rude he apologized for them – then they went out and leaked an attack on me to the press. I shall need the patience of a saint to go through these provocations. In the evening snatched a few moments to go to the Africa Day reception at the Commonwealth Institute, where I was almost mobbed by African women fans. Teelock, the Mauritian High Commissioner, asked me when Ted and I were coming to Mauritius: they had been trying to get us there for so long. 'We could come in August,' I said on an impulse. 'Good,' he replied. 'I will tell my Prime Minister.'

Thursday, 23 May. It is now clear there will be no June Election. I passed Harold a note [in Cabinet] pointing out that Blackburn has its September holiday in the week starting 16 September: I didn't want him calling an Election for 26 September! He tossed me a note back saying, 'I killed one PPS by not knowing about Leek.[1] I should not like to kill a former PPS. I have retained

move to purchase key sector leaders in manufacturing industry'. In addition to the nationalization of the aircraft and shipbuilding industries, which would require specific legislative authority, the Industry Act would empower the Government to extend public ownership by the acquisition of individual companies 'through a full parliamentary process'. All this would be underpinned by a new system of consultation with the trade unions and a bold extension of open government. One example of book-opening he had in mind was to publish details of the 'massive programme of public subsidies' – some £3,000 million over the previous four years – showing the amounts received by leading companies.

[1] Harold Davies, Labour MP for Leek, had been Harold Wilson's Parliamentary Private Secretary in the previous Labour Government. In calling the Election in June 1970, Harold Wilson had uncharacteristically overlooked the fact that the date clashed with the wakes week in Leek when some 15,000 miners, potters and textile workers took their annual holiday. Harold Davies's vote fell by nearly 9,000 and he lost his seat.

your note for my file though I expect my already very exhaustive list will include it.' To my relief Cabinet then endorsed the decision of Social Services Committee to give the nurses their independent review. I have already sounded out Lord Halsbury,[1] who is tickled pink to do it and told me it ought not to take too long; he could probably let me have the report by the end of July. He has gone away to start work on it. I also won another victory with the Cabinet's agreement to back-date the nurses' increases in due course to this very day. The way is now clear for me to ditch my 'shadow', Geoffrey Howe, in this afternoon's debate.

But our biggest discussion was on Concorde, on which Elwyn reported the findings of his Committee of Ministers. On balance the committee would prefer the project to be cancelled, provided the agreement of the French Government could be obtained. Failing that, we should go ahead with the completion of sixteen aircraft at a cost of £360–£400 million. (The cost of cancellation was estimated at £120 million.) Wedgie's speech was moving and eloquent. We all agreed, he said, Concorde should never have been started, but to go for cancellation now, after having spent £545 million, would mean we should have nothing to show for an expenditure of £800 million. The TUC and the Confederation of Shipbuilding and Engineering Unions [CSEU] were strongly against cancelling. 'For us to go for rupture would be wrong.' Denis put up a brave fight against impossible odds: 'Public participation must not be made to seem a device for spending money on white elephants.' There are bound to be public expenditure restraints. We should take the decision that we shall seek cancellation. Wedgie's most enthusiastic supporters turned out to be Peter and Mike. So although Roy Jenkins supported the Chancellor ('Giscard was never in favour of these planes'), we proceeded to endorse Elwyn's recommendations. I had my deep doubts but I sat mum.

When I returned to the office with the good news about the inquiry into nurses' salaries, we hurriedly called the staff side together so that I could inform them before this evening's debate. I unfolded my answer: yes, there would be an inquiry, Halsbury had agreed to chair it and – bull point – the increases would be back-dated to the moment I was speaking to them. They were clearly thrilled. Even Spanswick was impressed and said he would consult his Executive Committee immediately. I then went with relish into the Chamber to listen to Howe's dirge on the state of the NHS. In my reply I played with him, developing an effective attack on the mess the Tories had got the NHS into and leaving my announcement about the inquiry to the very end. There were cheers from our side and a Tory back bencher shouted, 'Why couldn't you say so earlier?', obviously furious that I had shot their fox. It was one of the more enjoyable episodes in my difficult life. And, to cap it all, tomorrow is the Whitsun recess!

Monday, 3 June. Back to work refreshed, but to bad news. Despite the speed and completeness with which I have met all that they asked, COHSE are

[1] John Anthony Hardinge Giffard, third Earl of Halsbury, industrialist, scientist and Fellow of the Royal Society, had been chairman of the Review Body on Doctors' and Dentists' Pay since 1971. We hoped that the appointment of such a prestigious figure to chair the independent review of nurses' pay would convince the nurses that the Government was taking their grievances seriously.

demanding an interim payment and are bringing their members out on strike. And this a union that has never gone on strike before, the union that was expelled from the TUC for registering under the Industrial Relations Act! It makes me sick and I am determined not to give way. The nurses have already had their increases under Stage Three and are getting threshold agreements, which they just ignore. To talk about 'starvation' among their members in view of all this is tommy rot. I am determined that Halsbury's report shall make a big impact and don't intend the effects of it to be frittered away by payments on account.

Sunday, 9 June. Got up early to do an hour's weeding and take the dogs for a walk before catching my train to Swansea for the Labour women's conference. I hated leaving HCF, with its garden looking so inviting in the June sunshine, but I got through a lot of work in the train. At the Dragon Hotel I joined Harold and his retinue for a meal in Harold's suite. The PM (late, of course) was in his most relaxed mood – though cross about the Common Market article in the *Sunday Times*.[1] (I wonder who briefed them for it?) I think Harold loves power as much as anything because it enables him to play Father Christmas. He nodded approvingly in the direction of John Morris, saying to me, 'You were the making of that man and he's doing very well.' He then chuckled over the news he had just had that Joan Lestor had run into Frank Judd at Lusaka airport, where they were both on their respective official business: Joan for the Foreign Office and Frank for the Ministry of Overseas Development! Neither are the conventional PM's idea of a junior Minister, but I think it is the joker in Harold which makes him delight in promoting unexpected people – and, as in these cases, he is so often proved right. He was tickled pink when I told him I thought I had solved the dispute over the uprating by telling the unions I was going to go to the House and say I accepted that I had asked too much of my staff and that the uprating date must be delayed. It was the kind of ploy he instantly appreciated and he went into a long companionable reminiscence about how he and I had solved the railway dispute in the last Labour Government. At one point he twinkled at me: 'Don't breathe a word but by next Thursday we shall have completed our first hundred days!' The only sour note was provided by Mary, who slipped sullenly into the room without greeting anyone. She sat silent through our rushed meal, her nose in her plate. I had a sympathetic word with her in their bedroom afterwards. 'Of course I hate it,' she told me. 'But then I always have. But I do my job.' Then she added, almost as an afterthought, 'But I'm glad for Harold. He needed this. He went through such a rotten time.' Nonetheless I feel Harold has an incipient revolt on his hands in that quarter.

Monday, 10 June. Woke at 6 am, still ebullient. What has come over me? A kind of liberation. John Morris had greeted me affectionately last night, saying

[1] A perceptive 'Insight' article in the *Sunday Times* had reported on Harold Wilson's 'calculated, consistent – and so seemingly successful strategy . . . to keep Britain in Europe, though on cheaper terms'. It detailed how the Prime Minister had composed the European Strategy Committee of Cabinet so as to leave the final word with him and Jim Callaghan and described how some 250 civil servants working on the renegotiations were producing a

in astonishment, 'You look younger than ever.' 'The vitamin of power,' I replied.

Back at the House I got the good news: CPSA has called off the overtime ban. So my ploy has worked.

Tuesday, 11 June. My statement in the House on the ending of the dispute was a walk-over. Osmond[1] didn't like my insistence on including a reference to the fact that relationships with the staff had been worsened by Tory policy over the past three years. Geoffrey Howe didn't like it either. But, as I said rather wildly, 'History is history and facts are facts.' I don't like Harold's dull reiteration of the virtues of this Government, as though there were no difficulties. But equally I am not going to let this Tory lot get away with the fact that their policy *did* make matters worse. I woke at 6 am this morning with a sharp pain in my chest. 'This is it,' I thought and I felt pretty groggy. But I suspect that it is merely that I have had a punishing weekend. As John Ellis once put it, I am as tough as an old boot. And anyway I would prefer to go out like a light.

At Lockets the 'Husbands and Wives' dinner was more thoughtful than usual. First Peter reported on Jim's speech in the House on Europe[2] and admitted regretfully that Jim had been extremely skilful, so that it was difficult to fault him. Nonetheless the scenario is being built up, with Harold's help, to enable us to stay in. We agreed to have a row in Cabinet about Jim's lack of consultation. I then had a bit of a row with Wedgie, whom I love but whose unctuousness about 'open government' irritates me, perhaps because I sense the ambition that motivates it. Wedgie had acted smartly in the Home Policy Committee of the NEC yesterday to get approval for the public release by Transport House of his report to the Liaison Committee with the TUC on the work of his Department. He must have gone out immediately and released it to the press, because this morning the papers were full of it and this afternoon Heath had been chasing Harold about it at PM's Question time. Harold had fielded it loyally but I bet he is mad.[3] Wedgie told us loftily that he believed in taking the people into our confidence, etc., adding that he wasn't trying to get anyone's share of the money that was going because he wasn't allowed to do

flow of papers to prove that one of the anti-marketeers' key demands – the need to amend the Treaty of Rome – was unnecessary.

[1] Mr M. W. M. Osmond, my Department's solicitor.

[2] In the House that afternoon Jim Callaghan had reported on his second meeting with the Council of Ministers in Luxembourg on 4 June and had implied a considerable softening of his own attitude towards the renegotiations. In particular he stated: 'We do not propose to renegotiate the Treaties. . . . When I started out on this road I thought that it would be necessary to propose some amendments. . . . But why should we go out of our way to make trouble if our objective can be secured without it?' Speaking for the Opposition front bench Mr Geoffrey Rippon welcomed this as 'a considerable advance' (Hansard 11.6.74).

[3] Tony Benn's decision to go public with his plans before he had fought them through Cabinet was to backfire on him. It created a storm in Parliament, industry and the press which his enemies in the Cabinet were to use to clip his wings. Mr Heath had been very effective in the House that day, demanding to know the constitutional position of Benn's document. 'Have the Government now handed over complete control of their policy to Transport House?' Harold Wilson's reaction was to let it be known that he would take charge of the discussions on industrial policy himself and he took over from Ted Short the chairmanship of the Cabinet Committee on Industrial Development, claiming later that he had decided to do this several weeks earlier. But neither industry nor the Tories were appeased. The questions in the House continued and Mr Ralph Bateman, new President of the CBI, announced that industry would campaign relentlessly against any further nationalization or intervention.

anything anyway. And tomorrow at the PLP meeting he intended to distribute copies of his industrial policy blueprint to the MPs there. I told him that he might not be trying to pinch my share of the money but he *was* trying to pinch my share of the glory. I, too, could make a great speech at PLP tomorrow about my plans, but I could only do so by embarrassing my colleagues who knew the money was not available for the expansion in public expenditure they would need. And I went into a great passionate diatribe on my old theme: my belief in the doctrine of collective responsibility. I could, for instance, have avoided all my trouble with the nurses if Mike had been able earlier to give me my independent review of nurses' pay. But I recognized that Mike had immense difficulties in moving in orderly fashion from a statutory to a voluntary incomes policy. The socialist virtue lay in knowing when one had to keep one's mouth shut.

Wedgie disarmed me when he suddenly said, completely naturally, 'But you are able to *do* things, Barbara. I am in a Department where, at present at any rate, I can do nothing but talk.' I clutched his hand sympathetically. When he is honest like this I will back him to the hilt. And I heartily endorsed his suggestion that we ought to have a special Labour Party Conference on the Market terms before putting them to a referendum.

Wednesday, 12 June. The sharp pains have subsided, leaving me with a general tenderness around the chest and a horrible sense of nausea. Graham and Jack have become quite concerned about me and want me to take a day or two off, but there is too much on in which I am interested. If I could survive the TV programme on political advisers yesterday I could survive ordinary meetings. Graham and Jack have struck up a great friendship. Yesterday, as I got ready for the TV interview, Graham said to me, 'I must admit, Secretary of State, I was against the idea of a political adviser when you mooted it, but now I think it has worked very well.' I don't know whether to be flattered or worried by the fact that No. 10 positively insisted on the programme being done, provided it was done by *my* advisers! Jack and Brian Abel-Smith have a sensible moderation about them that would reassure any viewer. Nonetheless I find the strengthening of my political team – and our weekly lunches – invaluable. I even risked letting the BBC record our lunch discussion yesterday, on the understanding that Jack and Brian would vet the result and report to me. Jack says our discussion on butter tokens[1] has come over very well and the BBC are chuffed to have got what they consider to be a scoop. There was one delicious moment yesterday when, anxious to bring everyone in, I turned to Bob Brown and said, 'What do you think, Bob?' The wretched chap had just taken a mouthful of sandwich and went red in the face trying to swallow it quickly, while the cameras trained themselves on him. I couldn't keep my face straight: in fact, with the cameras behind my back, I laughed outright. Jack tells me the BBC has tactfully edited this bit out.

[1] Butter tokens enabled one pound of butter per month to be bought at 9 pence per pound (later 12 pence per pound) less than the normal price. The scheme had been introduced by the European Commission in 1973 as an attempt to deal with the 'butter mountain' created by the high prices under the Common Agricultural Policy. Eligibility was restricted to those receiving means-tested benefits such as supplementary benefit and family

At PLP meeting this morning Wedgie insisted on doing his bit first and I was glad to let him because I wanted to see what he laid on. As promised (or threatened) last night, he had lots of copies of his statement of Departmental work ready for distribution and he spoke just as he had done at the Liaison Committee with the TUC. He had an approving audience – then dashed off to look into the explosion that had just taken place at Bristol. My account of what we were working on went well. The only trouble was that there were only about thirty people there out of some three hundred Labour MPs. As Bob [Mellish] said savagely and audibly, 'This shower only turns up for a row.' Well, according to this morning's papers there will be a Tory row over Wedgie. They obviously see in the publication of his document the electoral opportunity they have been waiting for. This is the point at which we should close ranks against the crude Tory blackmail we shall be subjected to. But I wonder how Harold will react? I am under no illusions that the right wing of the Party is bitterly against the Wedgies of this world – and indeed against large parts of the Manifesto.

Meeting with the staff side of the Whitley Council section which deals with the Professions Supplementary to Medicine [PSMS][1] to discuss their request that they, too, should have an independent review instead of merely being tagged on to the nurses' increase. Mike, bless him, has turned up trumps and agreed that they can, provided it is done by Halsbury instead of Mike having to announce a succession of special reviews. I got the delegation to agree that the nurses' announcement should be made first. It was a pleasure to deal with such a gentlemanly lot. The NUPE chap told me with relish that the staff side of the Nurses and Midwives Whitley Council had yesterday rejected the demand for an interim increase for nurses. That won't restrain COHSE, which is crudely on the make for increased membership. I am astonished to find that Cronin[2] is one of the parliamentary representatives of COHSE, so he is not coming out against their militancy in the way he would come out against other militancy.

Thursday, 13 June. Heath has really got his teeth into Wedgie, and there are great stories in the press that Harold has decided to take over the chairmanship of the Cabinet committee dealing with economic policy. Only a few of them have the grace to mention that he decided to do this as long ago as last April. Ralph Bateman, new President of the CBI, has seized on the issue to make his mark as a truculent defender of private industry. When we got to Cabinet I wondered what on earth was happening. There was a *distrait* air about the Cabinet room. Harold stood chatting to one or two people; there were no officials to be seen. Finally Harold said he had been waiting for everyone to arrive (Roy Mason and Wedgie were missing and Denis had been replaced by

income supplement, so many pensioners were excluded. Brian O'Malley and I strongly opposed this 'tokenization' of poverty as humiliating and niggardly. Moreover the administrative cost was out of all proportion to the benefits. We persuaded the Government to withdraw the scheme in December 1974.

[1] The seven professions supplementary to medicine comprise chiropody, dietetics, occupational therapy, orthoptics, physiotherapy, radiography and remedial gymnastics. Speech therapists and helpers are also covered by the NHS Professional and Technical Whitley Council 'A' and they were included in the pay review.

[2] John Cronin, Labour MP for Loughborough and a successful consultant surgeon, was not usually classed as left-wing.

Joel), as he wanted us to have a discussion without officials present, but he suggested we got on to our ordinary business until the others turned up. Officials were called back in and we went through parliamentary business for next week.

At last, at 12.15 pm, we got to our private session. Harold walked circumspectly all round his theme, which seemed to be that we were doing very well as a government, that we were not 'co-ordinating' our information about our achievements sufficiently and that it might be a good idea if we had an early meeting between the Cabinet and the NEC to co-ordinate policy. I have no doubt that all this is *à propos* of Wedgie, who wasn't there. I remember now that Wedgie told the PLP meeting yesterday he was going to Blackpool today for the Post Office Engineering Union conference. Surely Harold not only knew, but had agreed his absence from Cabinet? But whatever the purpose, it all turned out differently from what no doubt Harold had intended. Crosland complained that no one except Harold could get any press coverage anyway, however many handouts one put out. He grumbled that he had made a detailed speech on the rating problem at the NALGO conference and not a word had been used, even in *The Times*. (How I sympathize!) Then Mike took most of the remaining time with a long speech on our strategy on the EEC and Jim took the rest of it in a tetchy reply, saying (he does go feminine at times) that he refused to be hamstrung over the negotiations and that if he was going to be criticized in this way he would chuck in his hand and someone else would have a go. With a number of us trying to speak, Harold closed the meeting in some disorder, saying we should have to have a full-day meeting of Cabinet before we met the NEC. Everyone said 'Hear, hear' to that. As we were all leaving the room Jim said again to Tony Crosland, 'I shall chuck in my hand.' I turned and said mildly, 'Don't talk like that, Jim,' to which he replied, 'I mean it; I won't have this interference.' I lost my temper. 'We have a right to know.' 'Then you must find someone else,' he snapped. 'Okay,' I retorted. 'I'm ready, for one.' And I swept out.

Jim's petulance is all the more childish when one realizes what a gargantuan effort Len Murray, Jack Jones and others are making to create a reality of the Social Contract. The Economic Committee of the TUC has turned up trumps with a document[1] which, as the NALGO conference makes clear, they will have some difficulty in getting through Congress. They make Jim's tribulations look like small beer. But the real question mark is what everyone – including Mike – will do about Mick McGahey's latest demand on behalf of the miners:[2] pure market economy blackmail. Will Mike find an excuse to resign, or will his honesty and charm succeed in drawing the destructive poison out of the miners'

[1] In its document, called 'Collective Bargaining and the Social Contract', the TUC paid tribute to the achievements of the Labour Government and called for an orderly return to voluntary collective bargaining when statutory controls were abolished. In particular it stressed that the twelve-month interval between major settlements should continue to apply. 'Over the coming year,' it added, 'negotiators generally should recognize that the scope for real increases in consumption are limited and a central negotiating objective in this period will be to ensure that real incomes are maintained.'

[2] The Scottish miners, under the militant leadership of their President, Mick McGahey, were supporting the equally militant Yorkshire miners in demanding £20-a-week pay increases. At the NUM conference in July the £20-a-week demand was narrowly defeated, but a Scottish resolution opposing all forms of incomes policy, voluntary or statutory, was carried.

claim? If he solves *this* one, I will acknowledge his superiority for ever.

The political row over Tony Benn's ideas continued unabated during the summer months. Tory spokesmen saw it as their major weapon in the coming election, which they feared they were going to lose. No opportunity was lost of building up Benn as a bogeyman and, for his part, he continued to make challenging speeches about his policies. On 7 June he told a Nottinghamshire miners' gala that his officials were investigating the books of the twenty biggest companies and their 4,000 subsidiaries as part of his determination to reveal the extent of public subsidies to private industry. His Tory 'shadows' took up the trail, flushed out the names of the firms concerned and started a scare that Benn was proposing to bring them all into public ownership. 'Benn Widens his Grab Net', screamed the Daily Express *headline on 26 June. 'Ready to pounce on 4,000 little firms.' The* Financial Times, *while reporting Benn's claim that the investigation did not mean that the firms were listed for takeover, added that the Opposition saw the list as 'further evidence that Mr Benn is pushing ahead ominously fast with his interventionist plans'. Tony's announcement in July that his Department was going to put money into workers' co-operatives seeking to launch a daily newspaper in Glasgow and to reopen production at the former Triumph motorcycle factory at Meriden were greeted in the press as further dangerous pieces of 'Bennery'.*

Denis Healey and Harold Wilson, worried about the effects of all this on industrial confidence, rivalled each other in trying to restore the image of the Labour Party's belief in a mixed economy. In May the Chancellor assured the annual dinner of the CBI *that the Government had no intention of destroying the private sector or encouraging its decay. At the end of June Harold Wilson told the Socialist International conference at Chequers that 'private industry must have the necessary confidence to maintain and increase investment'. But with labour costs rising, share prices falling and industry complaining that its cash flow had been hit by the Budget and price controls, the* CBI *reported that business pessimism was growing. On 22 July Denis Healey announced an interim package of measures to check the inflationary tide and the rise in unemployment. The rate of inflation, he said, had risen to 16.5 per cent, but this was not due to excessive wage increases. The* TUC *guidelines had stressed that wage increases should merely keep pace with price increases. This meant that the Government must do everything in its power to keep prices down, particularly as Mr Heath's threshold arrangement meant that every rise in retail prices above the threshold brought an automatic wage increase. The threshold had already been 'triggered' six times. The rise in nationalized industry prices following the Budget had added 1.5 per cent to the Retail Price Index and he now proposed to wipe out that increase in other ways. He therefore cut* VAT *from 10 per cent to 8 per cent, released £50 million for food subsidies and introduced £150 million of domestic rate relief. He also increased the needs allowance used for calculating rent and rate rebates and rent allowances. To help company funds he doubled the Regional Employment Premium and raised the ceiling under the price code for annual increases in dividend distribution from Mr Heath's 5 per cent to 12.5 per cent. The effect of this, he said, would be to put back into the economy the £200 million of demand he had taken out in March. But he was still not prepared to risk reflation on any dramatic scale. In fact, he claimed, money supply was now under the strictest control it had known for many years. (A month later economist Peter Jay was to complain in* The Times *[23 August] that the Bank of England was superimposing a financial crisis on the economic one by contracting the money supply too quickly and too drastically.)*

In my own field the solution of one problem merely gave way to another one. The settlement of the dispute with my staff over the uprating, by the offer of extra leave rather than a cash bonus and the promise of longer-term improvements in their pay structures and conditions for which the staff had been agitating, meant that the vast majority of pensioners and others got their increases on time. The Halsbury inquiry into nurses' pay, set up on 7 June, had lost no time in starting work. Later it agreed to undertake a similar inquiry into the pay of radiographers and other groups 'supplementary to medicine'. It promised that the report on them would follow as quickly as possible after the nurses' one and here again the Treasury had agreed to back-date the increases to 23 May. But this did not satisfy some of the unions – notably COHSE *and* ASTMS. *They launched a widespread campaign, backed by industrial action in a number of hospitals, to force the Government to pay an interim increase. I was entirely at one with Lord Halsbury in resisting this, agreeing with him that the first ever thorough evaluation of nurses' pay must not be jeopardized. But with protest action spreading and Lord Halsbury's committee refusing to be hustled, the situation became increasingly dangerous.*

Disruption in the Health Service was spreading to other fronts. Every section of the service was joining the clamour for higher pay. On 11 June consultants and other hospital doctors in the BMA, *meeting in national conference, called for mass resignations from the* NHS *unless their Review Body came up with a big pay increase and unless the Owen working party, which I had set up, reached speedy agreement on a new contract for senior staff. Urged on by the chairman of their negotiating committee, Mr Anthony Grabham, they called on the* BMA *to set up its own employment agency to hire their services back to the hospitals if mass resignations became necessary. Meanwhile the undercurrent of discontent among the Health Service unions over the issue of pay beds erupted at Charing Cross Hospital. This time it was* NUPE *that took the lead. The new £16 million teaching hospital, completed in 1972, included a private wing on the fifteenth floor – the penthouse suite. Feeling against the privileged services provided in the private wing – built by* NHS *funds – had been running high among the non-medical staff, from nurses to porters, fed by the discontent over pay, particularly among low-paid workers like kitchen staff and hospital orderlies. The local* NUPE *branch at the hospital, representing this group and 1,000 strong, was led by Mrs Esther Brookstone, a medical secretary, soon known to the press as the 'battling grannie' for her fight to close the private wing. At the beginning of July the union worked out a compromise with the Area Health Authority [*AHA*] under which for the time being the private patients would be transferred to general ward beds, releasing private wing beds for* NHS *patients, with only emergency private cases being admitted from then on. Some consultants objected and the* BMA *stepped in. Mrs Brookstone gave the* AHA *till 4 July to carry out the compromise. Otherwise all domestic, laundry, portering and engineering services would be withdrawn from the private wing. The media protrayed her in fighting mood: 'Give in . . . or we will starve patients out', the* Daily Mail *reported her as saying on 2 July. The* BMA *threatened retailiation. There were questions in the House. The* AHA *panicked and the problem landed in my lap. Meanwhile sporadic action against pay beds was being taken in other hospitals.*

The Charing Cross dispute turned the pay beds issue into one of urgency. With the Government admonishing the unions to leave the phasing out of pay beds to Parliament, it was clear that the necessary legislation ought to be in the next Queen's Speech. Discussions in the Department, therefore, were intensified.

Tuesday, 18 June. 'Husbands and Wives' dinner at Lockets was a restricted affair: no Wedgie. I am afraid we dealt with him rather critically in his absence; Mike in particular is furious with him for pushing his plan for a special conference of the Party on the EEC terms. Mike is obsessed with the need to win the next Election and is bitterly opposed to anything that might disrupt the

Party before then – and is therefore bitter about Wedgie. What interests me is how imperious Mike becomes in these discussions, getting positively irritable. But I don't object: I welcome the fact that Mike has developed such authoritativeness.

Wednesday, 19 June. Snatched an hour off in the evening to go to the wedding of the Teelocks' daughter: a Hindu ceremony at the Commonwealth Institute. Very colourful and posh. The Mauritians were full of our suggested visit there in August, so it looks as though it is on. Got back to the House in time for Denis's winding up on the £10 million clause of the Finance Bill, on which the Tories, goaded by our jeers on their phoney war, have threatened to beat us at last. Denis made one of his most effective knockabout speeches and we were all in a high state of excitement when the vote came. When the tellers announced our defeat there was a roar of delight from our benches. I sat on the front bench clapping my hands exuberantly and crying, 'Election, Election!' The Tories looked more frightened at their own recklessness than elated by their success and Carr's tepid intervention brought more jeers from our side. There was no doubt who *felt* they were the top dogs.[1]

Friday, 21 June. Off for an official visit to Kettering hospital. It was a hot and exacting tour but I sailed through it, taking all the lobbying by the different groups of staff in my stride. On my arrival, closely trailed by press and TV, I saw a small, rather pathetic little group at the door, standing silently carrying a banner: 'They won't show you the laundry.' I promptly broke ranks and went over to have a little chat with them, saying of course I would call in at the laundry. (Later I did so and found that it was old and inadequate. The chap who had been leading the lobby linked arms with me affectionately.) During my tour a group of nurses were waiting to hand me a letter. It merely said the patients wanted them to get more pay. I held a little meeting, gathering them round me. 'Do you realize that you have already got an increase?' I asked them. They shook their heads, bewildered. 'Well,' I said, 'you have. The Government has already agreed to accept the report of the independent review body and to back-date your increase to 23 May. So you are entitled to it *now*. We are only waiting for Lord Halsbury to put a figure on it.' They dispersed, astonished.

Monday, 24 June. Couldn't be in the House to hear Harold make his statement about that nuclear warhead test.[2] Jim this morning denies any knowledge of it. 'It is the PM's sphere and he plays these matters close to his chest.' It is a relief to know that the test is in the past, but appalling that these things can be done without the knowledge of Cabinet. Despite Harold's low-key explanation there will be a row in Cabinet on Thursday.

[1] The clause was successfully reinserted in the Finance Act 1975.

[2] Harold Wilson told an astonished Commons that a nuclear test had taken place a few weeks earlier. This, he said, had been arranged by the previous Government and was necessary to maintain the effectiveness of Britain's nuclear deterrent. But, he assured the House, it had been conducted fully within the provisions of both the partial test ban and the non-proliferation treaties.

Wednesday, 26 June. Teddy's day. I had told the office weeks ago that they must keep this afternoon as free as possible so that I could do full honours for him at his induction into the Lords. In the event there was an NEC this morning. I got up early to have my hair done and arrived late. Bob and others said approvingly, 'You've been to the hairdressers.' To which I replied, 'This is Ted's day and I shan't be able to stay for all these Motions that have been pouring in.' Ted was terribly nervous when I left home and I secretly prayed for him. Ideologically I hate the House of Lords but, as a wife, I know what this means for Ted and I don't intend to let anything spoil it. It is his great chance to take part in Parliament and it is a poor socialism that leaves no room for the illogicalities of love.

Thursday, 27 June. At Cabinet Harold warned us that we were in for a period of intensive work: Cabinets twice a week, as there were a lot of policy decisions to be taken before the summer recess. We all know what that means: White Papers must be got out before the Election. I have been struck how effectively Harold has been delegating work in this Government. It has been a joy to have brief and comparatively infrequent Cabinets which have largely endorsed what has been thrashed out in committees or by letter, with Harold foregoing his passion for making running chat on every subject.

Mike raised the question of nuclear tests, saying he had written to Harold asking for a paper on how, when and why the decision to hold a test had been reached without the knowledge of Cabinet. He wanted a proper discussion of the whole question. 'It has always been the convention of Cabinet that certain things are not discussed in Cabinet: for example, the 1967 nuclear tests. No policy decision has been taken on these tests. That decision has got to be taken by Cabinet when we get the Defence Review, which will be a very fundamental reappraisal. If we had refused to do this test we would have been closing an option. I could not consult Cabinet because a leak of any kind would have very serious effects for reasons I can't give now.' It was the old argument and it didn't convince Mike. He continued to press the matter. 'Many of us have been put in a terrible position of defending a policy decision in which we had no part.' Bob came to Mike's support. Even Reg Prentice expressed concern, while I pointed out that the French didn't seem to need all this secrecy: they just calmly announced their tests were taking place. To my surprise Jim then backed us. Quite a victory!

We turned to Concorde. Wedgie never gives up and Elwyn reported that Wedgie was now trying to by-pass Cabinet's previous decision, maintaining that a number of events had occurred which put cancellation out of the question. Wedgie wanted permission, if the French showed any sign of resisting cancellation, to go ahead with the sixteen without any further reference to Cabinet. Harold backed Wedgie by saying that he had talked to Chirac [the French Prime Minister] in Brussels yesterday (who incidentally wants to defer progress on the Channel Tunnel). He had taken the opportunity to ask Chirac non-committally what the French reaction would be to cancellation of Concorde and Chirac had replied tersely, 'Négatif'. It was clear he would resist strongly. Harold therefore suggested that the Ministers concerned should now prepare the brief for his meeting with Giscard on the basis that we were *not* going forward with cancellation, the brief to come back to Cabinet before his meeting with the President. Jim agreed. Denis grumbled. 'We must seek to limit our financial commitment to the utmost possible.' (Chirac has been talking of building two hundred planes!) Roy [Jenkins] thought the decision was 'absolutely disastrous' and I was amused when he added, 'The French get their way to an alarming extent.' Denis chipped in sourly: 'What if the French say "négatif" on [reform of] the CAP?' Wedgie wasn't to be deterred: we should be guided by 'simple common sense', he said, *i.e.* his constituency considerations, I suppose! Harold said it was sensible to bring all these issues together at the same time and so it was left.

Tuesday, 2 July. At Cabinet I was interested when Jim said, 'I haven't read any of my Cabinet papers.' So I'm not the only one who sometimes slips up! We moved to our long-promised discussion on the progress of Jim's negotiations with the EEC. Jim made a long defensive statement which Mike countered with a critical one. I thought Peter was most impressive when he pointed out we couldn't continue to drift over participation in Community policies pending renegotiation, as on 1 January we were supposed to introduce tariff changes which would concede some of our basic principles. In 1975, too, the whole basis of the budgetary contribution would be changed. He maintained we must make it known now that we would not move along these lines until a satisfactory basis of renegotiation had been agreed. Jim got tetchy about this, and a lot of us were bursting to speak. As it was 1.15 pm Harold said we must resume the discussion next time.

The 'Husbands and Wives' dinner at Charing Cross Hotel was a tetchy affair, too – Mike almost snarling at Wedgie from time to time. When Wedgie started saying darkly that Jim and others were heading for a coalition, Mike told him not to be 'hysterical'. The most important thing was the Election. 'We must win it with the people we disagree with.' When John Silkin said gloomily, 'By the time the next Election comes the whole of the atmosphere is going to be in favour of a coalition,' adding that Jim was in favour of one, Mike snapped, 'You have been wrong every time. The idea of Jim going into a coalition is a washout.' To change the subject Peter asked Thomas [Balogh] if he thought we were going to be in an economic crisis before long. Thomas replied, 'No one can answer that. Arab money is accumulating in London at £300 million annually. The situation is now almost inconceivably dangerous. The only person who has been acting in a constructive way is Harold Lever. You will all be terribly lucky if your spending programmes are not cut.' When I chipped in sadly with 'I *am* cut – in the NHS,' it was my turn to get the rough side of Mike's tongue. 'Don't listen to her,' he almost shouted. 'Quash her.' I am fascinated by Mike's current mood. He is so passionately dedicated to the success of the Government that it is as if his nerves are on edge about it. (Mind you, he has bullied me affectionately all the time I have known him.)

Wednesday, 3 July. The papers are full of Ma Brookstone's activities against private patients at Charing Cross Hospital. The Department is all for keeping out of it and leaving it to the Area Health Authority, but my bet is that Geoffrey Howe will try to make capital out of it through a Private Notice

Question. So I set off for an official visit to Leybourne Grange Mental Hospital, expecting to be called back – and so it proves. I have to cut the tour short and leave behind a tempting buffet lunch, making do with a few sandwiches in the car. A quick confab in the office over the draft officials have prepared, which David [Owen] and I find far too moralistic and admonitory. We tone it down and make it clear that we sympathize with the aims of the agitators, though not their methods. Despite this my reply goes smoothly and I get a cheer from our side as I say emphatically that it is our policy to phase private practice out of NHS hospitals. It is astonishing how a simple statement of principle heartens our own lads, who get disheartened by the cautious conditionals in so many ministerial statements.

Hurriedly I dress in my décolleté for Jim Callaghan's annual diplomatic banquet at the Royal Naval College, Greenwich. I haven't normally much time or inclination for these dress-up do's, but I have always wanted to see the painted ceiling there. I am not disappointed. I like the long low-ceilinged entrance corridor, all white, and the banqueting chamber itself is magnificent. Jim makes a brief, relaxed and highly competent after-dinner speech to that glittering audience. His poise in these matters is remarkable. (Harold would have written every word of it.) Our programmes warn us that after the meal there will be the Beating of the Retreat, but does *not* warn us that it will be out of doors on a bitterly cold July evening. Judith and I, both bare-shouldered, huddle under my flimsy stole in the evening air, with Ted's arm round us, as the Royal Marines wheel and weave and drum backwards and forwards across the grass between the two wings of that elegant building against a darkly clouded sky. We have probably caught pneumonia but it is worth it. Ted and I are suckers for history. The Navy insist on pouring strong drinks down us afterwards.

Thursday, 4 July. Of course the BMA are after me because I refuse to condemn the NUPE lads and lasses at Charing Cross in the unequivocal terms they demand. And the press join in. That I can take, but there are signs of panic from the AHA. First I have to accommodate Cabinet.

We then returned to our great debate on the EEC. (I was interested to see from Cabinet Minutes later that this was considered so sensitive as to be 'recorded separately' and so not circulated.) Denis opened with an attack on Wedgie. 'What is the purpose of this discussion? Here we have Tony Benn last night ostentatiously abstaining on his own front bench against a "take note" vote on the EEC regulations.'[1] Harold added severely, 'For a Cabinet Minister to abstain on a PM's Motion is quite intolerable.' But Wedgie wasn't going to

[1] Pending renegotiations there was an uneasy situation about how to deal with the flood of regulations, directives and other documents coming from the European Commission. The House of Commons had set up an all-party Scrutiny Committee to decide which of them were important enough to merit parliamentary debate and on 3 July two debates had taken place under this procedure on a 'take note' Motion by the Government. Tony Benn was on the front bench waiting to deal with the second debate on regional policy when anti-Market back benchers staged a revolt on the first Motion to take note of the guidelines on economic policy which the Commission was proposing, demanding their rejection. When they forced a division, Tony Benn openly abstained in sympathy. Bob Mellish, as Chief Whip, was so incensed that he sent back benchers home, leaving Tony to talk out the debate on regional policy.

take this lying down. 'Every single member round this table abstained last night,' he snapped, 'because none of them appeared.' But Bob snapped back at him, 'Everyone knew it was a one-line whip. But in the event there was a vote. You were there and you are a Cabinet Minister.'

It was interesting that Wedgie got no support from anyone on his behaviour last night. Mike obviously thinks he is obsessed with ambition. The rest of us, who are on his side on policy, are getting a bit sick of his clear determination to strike attitudes publicly whenever he can, regardless of our old friend collective responsibility. Wedgie therefore went on to widen the argument. He claimed that he fully supported what the Manifesto said about renegotiation but he didn't believe that renegotiation would achieve the Manifesto's aims. 'Membership is deeply damaging to Britain's interests. Control of the steel industry has passed from this country: on prices, for example. Shipbuilding capacity and investment could not be engaged in without the consent of the Community. The responsibility of Parliament is undermined.' Harold intervened coldly. 'You reject the Manifesto.' So the discussion ended inconclusively, with Jim resentful again about the suggestion that he wasn't toeing the party line. But it at least put some warning shots across his and Harold's bows.

Back to the office to film the programme on special advisers. In the middle of all the fuss Peter and Jack came in to say the press were still chasing the *Private Eye* canards about my having recently been in a private wing in University College Hospital [UCH] under an assumed name. (Rumour has it that the operation was gynaecological!) Peter said he wanted to scotch it once and for all. 'But I have never been in UCH,' I said, bewildered. 'Can I say then,' asked Peter, 'that you have never been a patient in UCH either publicly or privately?' 'Yes,' I replied. 'Ted was in there some time ago for a hernia operation, but he was in a public ward. And of course I visited Beattie Plummer [our friend] in the private wing.' 'That must be the source of it,' said Peter and went off triumphantly.

But in the middle of all the pressures the words 'UCH' rankled in my mind. I have already told Jack in confidence of the time I had sinus trouble as a result of a visit abroad as Minister of Overseas Development. I had gone to have it treated through the NHS, but the office had insisted I had a private room so that I could read Cabinet papers and hold office meetings. I thought it was in the London Clinic. When I got home I told Ted what had happened and he suddenly said, 'Of course your operation in 1965 was in UCH.' The full horror of my position then swept over me: I had lied in all innocence. I could see what the press would make of this. No one would believe that I had not gone into a private room through choice, but through necessity. I went to bed submerged in wretchedness and doubting whether I would sleep.

Friday, 5 July. Woke with a start at 5 am. All my miseries came flooding in and I knew further sleep would be impossible. Got up, made some tea and forced myself to work my way grimly through one of my boxes. When the newspapers arrived I found that the UCH story was on the front pages, together with an interview with the sinus consultant, Kingdom, who had now gone to the reckless length of allowing his name to be used about his treatment of me. Left home at 9 am, feeling physically and nervously exhausted before I started. Ted hugged me consolingly as I said, 'This is going to be one of the worst days of my life.' At the office there was an embarrassed reticence about the atmosphere. 'Where's Graham?' I asked. 'Checking about the Private Notice Questions,' replied the girls. Oh, God, I thought, spare me that! I couldn't even begin to turn my mind to the details of today's negotiations before I cleared up my own affair. At last I got Graham, Peter Brown, Jack and Philip Rogers assembled in my room. 'Peter,' I said firmly, 'I owe you an apology.' He looked surprised. 'Last night I unintentionally lied to you and I do not lie to my press officers. I tried to phone you to tell you not to put out my denial but I could not get hold of you.' Peter almost laughed at my agony. 'There's nothing to apologize to me about, Secretary of State. We didn't put out anything that was inaccurate. All the queries were about recent operations. The stories *were* all wrong anyway. Don't think another thing about it. I believe the story is dead anyway. But I want to get a statement out from you today to finish it.'

We then discussed how I could check up on the details of what actually happened. Philip said he would get on to the Ministry of Overseas Development and Jack was dispatched to turn up what he could from the cuttings. Graham then came in with the first good news of the day. 'The PNQ is refused,' he said in his genially laconic way. My spirits began, if not to rise, at least to calm and they steadied still more as a result of Peter's unruffled loyalty. 'I do not share your views about private beds, Mrs Castle. But this Department is not going to have you hounded. You have done no wrong.' And he made me laugh when he told me that he had to get Dick out of a similar mess when Dick had discovered that Anne [Crossman], unbeknown to him, was a member of BUPA! I began to feel ashamed that I hadn't taken Peter into my confidence. He was obviously in his favourite Svengali element and he kept saying to me, 'You are about to enter into crucial negotiations and you are going to win. We'll settle this other nonsense and I want you to put it out of your mind and do what only you can do.' They were all so charming, gathering round to defend me, that I wondered once again at the unique quality of the British civil service: the capacity of its top people to develop a genuine loyalty to a Minister who wasn't here yesterday and will be gone tomorrow.

But the physical damage was done. At an office meeting to discuss our strategy over Charing Cross I had such a headache I could barely concentrate. And this on a day when I needed all my wits about me! The message was that the AHA chairman and Mrs Brookstone's merry men had asked to see me, but that the consultants at Charing Cross were standing aloof. There was also an insulting ultimatum from the BMA in the post threatening industrial action on Monday if I did not intevene. I said I should reply to the AHA that I would be glad to see them, but only if the consultants came along too. I should then set up immediate, but separate, meetings with the BMA and the national leaders of the unions and should ask Len Murray to come along with Alan Fisher and Albert Spanswick.

Various people dashed off to make phone calls. At intervals Jack and Peter came in with drafts of my statement on my treatment at UCH. They said they had tracked down my Private Secretary of the time, John Rednall, who couldn't remember the details of Departmental advice to me at the time, 'And, unfortunately, Secretary of State,' said Philip Rogers, 'your then Permanent

Secretary, who would have given the advice, is dead.' But they had established that the Department had *not* paid for the private room. Peter and Jack asked me whether I could be sure that I had not received private treatment on any other occasion, as it would be fatal to have other incidents unearthed by the press bit by bit. 'It isn't the press,' I replied grimly. 'The Tories undoubtedly would employ private detectives to do us dirt.' I couldn't remember any, but then my memory could be deceiving me. Jack went off to contact Colin-Russ, who, even though he had only been our doctor for a few years, would have all my files.

Then back to an office meeting to discuss the state of play on the other negotiations. The report was that the Charing Cross consultants had agreed to come along with the rest. The BMA had also agreed to come. Would I phone Len Murray myself, please? Which I did, only to learn from him that it was impossible for him to get out of engagements that afternoon. 'In any case, Barbara, I doubt if I could be helpful. After all, Congress is in favour of getting rid of private practice.' I explained to him that that was not the point. I was in favour of getting rid of private practice too, but the right way was to negotiate a new contract with the consultants that would recompense them for loss of pay. Surely that was a good trade union principle? Len saw the point at once and said he would talk to Alan Fisher: the best he could do. Graham then gently reminded me that John Donne (chairman of SE Thames Regional Health Authority) was coming to see me over a snack lunch.

Jack came in with the report from Colin-Russ, who, it appears, has been immensely co-operative. There was, said Jack, another occasion on which I had had treatment: from a Mr Scott of Guy's who had written about me to Colin-Russ from an address in Guy's, Keats House, which would seem to imply that the treatment had been private. Did I remember it? No, I replied desperately. Jack went off to find out more. Until this was cleared up, my statement had to be held up. Somehow I got through my lunch with John Donne and his administrator, who had come to tell me of the desperate difficulties of their Regional Health Authority. As I ate a couple of sandwiches I thought, 'Thank God for the obstetricians' banquet tonight. I shall be starving by then.' Little did I know what lay ahead of me!

Before I knew where I was it was 1.30 pm and all the Charing Cross contingent had arrived. I tried to rally my thoughts. Jordan-Moss[1] had had the good idea that I should start by asking them whether it was true that they had nearly reached a compromise earlier and if so what was it? (We knew that they had almost agreed to move some of the private wing patients into other parts of the hospital, but then the consultants had gone to the BMA for advice and had been sternly told to sit tight and concede nothing.) As the chairman of the AHA, Mr Meyer, walked in, followed by his troupe, I thought how much nicer they all looked than they had appeared on TV or in the press. (Probably they were thinking the same of me!) Granny Brookstone turned out to be a pleasantly unaggressive person who was clearly bewildered by all the publicity she had attracted and very aggrieved by the nature of some of it. She was accompanied by a thin little girl in a white overall, who turned out to be a medico-physics

[1] Nick Jordan-Moss was Deputy Secretary at the Department.

technician, and a subdued little chap with fuzzy hair: the porters' supervisor. Meyer was deprecatingly grateful for my intervention; his administrator was a friendly, competent chap. Even the two consultants were mild and unassuming: obviously not cut out by nature to conduct a confrontation war.

I began by telling them that, as I had already said in the House, their local dispute was for them to settle. All I could do was to try to clarify the issues. Was it true that they had at one point almost agreed on a compromise? Meyer said, 'Yes,' outlined it and explained that since then the consultants had turned it down. I then pitched rather sternly into the two men about why they had turned it down. Were they refusing to move patients because their treatment might suffer? No. (Here Granny B. intervened to say almost pleadingly that she had never asked, and never would ask, that the interests of any patient should suffer.) There stand was upon the law and order principle, they said. The law allowed private practice and until it was changed it should be enforced. (All good BMA stuff.) When it *was* changed they would abide by it, even if they didn't agree with it. Did they realize that the NHS Act did not *require* me to allow private beds? [I asked.] It merely empowered me to authorize them when – and to the extent that – I as Secretary of State thought it reasonable. That shook them a bit. So, I said, I could have withdrawn authorizations immediately on taking office. If I had done so, would they have accepted it? No, they said, rather cornered now, because they thought private practice within the NHS benefited their private patients. So, I pressed them, 'Your objection is not on law and order grounds at all? You are merely fighting the Government's policy?'

While they digested this I turned to Granny B. Didn't she know that the Government was committed to phasing out private beds? What right had she therefore to disrupt the whole hospital? Disarmingly, and almost apologetically, she replied that she was no politician, but the fact was that her members didn't trust any of us. They were fed up with staff shortages and the fact that people like them had to wait months for beds, while people 'like this pop star', she added contemptuously, throwing a copy of the *Daily Mirror* across the table, could waft themselves up to the private floor, putting demands on the kitchen staff with their extra menus, simply by paying for it. She wanted a full inquiry, not just into pay, but into the whole situation in the NHS. Her silent companions nodded grimly. All they asked was that the privileges of the fifteenth (private) floor should be shared by NHS patients so as to shorten the waiting lists. They had *not* asked for the floor to be closed: merely for some of the beds to be made available to NHS patients.

I turned again to the consultants: 'What is your reply?' They shrugged. They didn't have to reply, they said. '*We* are not making any demands. We are merely standing on the *status quo*. Why should we compromise?' 'Even if it means closing the hospital?' I asked. They shrugged again. Again I could see the hand of the BMA. I told them I was now due to see the national leaders of both sides. Would they wait? As they left, David said to me, 'Those consultants are bastards.' Typically Philip interjected, 'I though they were all bastards.'

I saw Alan Fisher, Albert Spanswick and his President with only David and Philip present. They were in immensely emollient mood, obviously wishing to be rid of this incubus. Finally Alan, backed by the others, said that there might be a way out if the report of the Owen working party on private practice could be speeded up. I said I would see what I could do about this.

But the BMA, who came next, were a very different kettle of fish. They had rung up to say they were bringing the hospital consultants' breakaway union[1] with them: unity forged in the face of the enemy! In they trooped, about one dozen strong. Lewin was as tight-faced as ever, Stevenson as touchy and truculent. They were flanked by the authoritative – and authoritarian – top brass of the profession, and it was soon clear where the rigidity of the Charing Cross consultants came from. Lewin began by reading me a lecture. They had been shocked by my failure to denounce NUPE's action in unequivocal terms. I reminded them of their ultimatum to me: their threat to take industrial action – 'Everyone from top to bottom of the profession is apparently prepared to damage the Health Service to secure his ends: there is no difference between you.' I reminded them that we did not live in a dictatorship: I had no power to compel anyone to provide services. The idea obviously appalled them; I could feel the 'Gad, sir, these upstart trade unionists must be whipped' atmosphere.

They tried to be lofty about the 'law and order' principle, and once again I had to tell them that the law had given me complete discretion. I could have ruled out private beds from the word go, but I hadn't. This led to some nasty exchanges about the role of the working party (David Owen had said to me earlier that they might be coming to announce that they were walking out of it – the last thing I want). One of their chaps, who is a member of it, tried to make out that the outcome had been prejudged. When David and I reminded him that there had never been any secret about the Government's policy, he pretended that the BMA were going into it with an open mind while we were not. Anything further from an open mind than these chaps showed would be impossible! I then told them that the Charing Cross situation ought to have been dealt with locally: after all, my responsibility as Secretary of State was to *all* the patients in the hospital, not merely to the private ones. They nodded at this (they had to). But, I said, it had become clear that the Charing Cross consultants were acting under the orders of the BMA. The issue had to be settled nationally and my position was clear: I believed that it was wrong for any changes in the NHS to be made without proper negotiations with the appropriate union. They didn't exactly like the application of this word to them. Lewin put it pompously in a different way: 'We don't think our people at Charing Cross should have the burden placed on them of defending what is a matter of principle.' Mr Astley (the sort of man to be conscious that he held your life in his hands) kept looking up to say, 'I will never agree to any compromise.'

Finally, having established that there was no point of clinical freedom involved at Charing Cross, and having reiterated that I had no power to shoot recalcitrant trade unionists on sight, I told them what Alan Fisher and the others had said about speeding up the working-party report. Lewin pricked up his ears at this. Two hours having now elapsed I suggested a break while they considered this. 'And someone must find you a drink,' I said genially. 'You deserve it.'

While I gulped a cup of tea in their absence Peter Brown and Jack came in

[1] A number of consultants had broken away from the BMA and formed the Hospital Consultants and Specialists Association. It claimed to represent 7,000 consultants out of the 11,000 working in the NHS.

again to talk about my private treatment. Apparently they had unearthed that Mr Scott was the chap at Guy's to whom I had gone in 1968 about some trouble with my chest. 'God, I remember,' I groaned. 'I got 'flu very badly while down at HCF that January and the local doctors said I must have an x-ray. So the office sent me round to Guy's for one. For God's sake, it was the out-patients' department. I remember going there one afternoon. And they found a shadow on my lung. And the specialist told me to go back for a check-up.' 'But on the second time did you go round to his private room?' they asked. 'I can't remember,' I replied, 'but if I did, he probably asked me to and didn't charge me for it.' After a further rather wild discussion Peter said firmly, 'We must put this statement of yours out now or not at all.' We decided to stick to the wording we had worked out: that I 'normally' had treatment through the NHS. 'I seem to have spent my life queueing in out-patients' departments,' I said desperately.

There then ensued a lengthy lull during which someone, blessedly, produced some sandwiches. It by now being 7 pm, I said to Henry Yellowlees, 'We're not going to get to that banquet, Henry.' 'No, Secretary of State,' he replied sadly, 'and it would have been good food.' We chewed our way through some dry bits while the BMA, godlike, took their time. 'I wouldn't blame Granny if she walked out,' I remarked. But it was all so unreal I didn't care.

It was 10 pm before the BMA came back. ('Has anyone taken them drinks?' I hissed to Graham. 'Yes,' he replied, 'but we are running out of it.' 'There's some in my room,' hissed back Philip. 'Help yourself when you can get at it.') Lewin was obviously very pleased with himself and lost no time in saying triumphantly that the BMA was only too ready to help speed up the findings of the working-party. Provided that I agreed to state more categorically than I had yet done that I deplored the action of the union (with which by now I was feeling increasing sympathy), and that I committed myself to *no* reduction in private beds meanwhile, they were prepared to agree that the working-party should report by 31 August. I seized on the first point in white cold temper by now. 'You had better spell out first, Mr Lewin, exactly what you want me to say that I haven't said. What am I – St Joan faced by her Inquisitors? What exactly is it you want me to recant?' They looked nonplussed. But David seized on the last point, appalled. How on earth could his working party produce a report by August? The BMA themselves had originally said the discussions would take eighteen months. August, they surely knew, was impossible. And as he talked it became clear that the BMA's ploy was to kill the work-load studies which we had intended to be an integral part of the discussion on their contract and which Halsbury, as chairman of their review body which would have to price the contract, had welcomed. We would be faced with straight financial blackmail. Gradually David got them to agree to a November date as more reasonable. ('And that will still cost us a lot,' he whispered to me.)

I then turned to their second point, seeing a way of turning the tables on them. I couldn't possibly commit myself not to reduce the number of private beds, I told them, except in the context of a Charing Cross settlement. Remember I might be under pressure from the House next week to do something like ordering the withdrawal of half the private beds. Wasn't it possible for there to be a little give on both sides there to make a settlement possible? At this Lewin and his friends looked crestfallen. Eventually we made another break so that we could both try to work out a form of words that might do the trick.

When at last the BMA came back again with their proposed amendments to our draft statement, I was ready for them. Yes, I would reiterate my condemnation of the industrial action; yes, I would be prepared to promise not to introduce any arbitrary reduction in the number of pay beds while awaiting the working-party report. But I could only do that in the context of a Charing Cross settlement. And then I played my trump card: Alan Fisher [and Albert Spanswick had told me they were] willing to call off the action nationally that night if only we could settle Charing Cross. They were clearly shaken. Wasn't any give in their attitude possible? I asked, pressing my advantage. David followed it up. Did we need to talk about reducing the number of private beds there? Couldn't they be merely redistributed? Some of the BMA boys were for going to the stake for no compromise, but again it was the hospital consultants who were nodding at what we said. Finally the BMA agreed to go and talk to the Charing Cross consultants and we settled down for another wait.

Back at last came the BMA, again looking like cats that had got at the cream. They had worked out a formula that did just what David had suggested: did not reduce the number of private beds but *did* redistribute them through the hospital.[1] We said we would try it on the Charing Cross team, though I personally doubted whether Ma Brookstone, who had by now been cooped up for seven hours while we worked out her fate with the BMA, would find it tolerable. We then agreed the final wording of the statement with the BMA, and Lewin, looking mighty satisfied, got up to go. As he started shaking hands all round we said to him, 'Hey, Mrs Brookstone hasn't agreed this yet. There may be a hitch on which we shall need to consult you.' He seemed outraged at the very idea that Ma B. could upset anything *they* had decided, but agreed to stay.

'You are very near agreement now, Mrs Castle,' said Peter as we waited. 'In my experience,' I replied, 'the biggest snag comes just before the dawn.' It was by now past midnight and Peter was getting edgy lest I miss the press. 'The TV boys have already gone,' he told me, 'but the press are hanging on. As soon as this thing is settled I want you straight down there to see them. Those BMA fellows will be talking their heads off to the press and it is essential you put the key points of the agreement across.' I told him we hadn't got an agreement yet, and, sure enough, when Ma B. and her two companions came in we soon ran into difficulties. I explained what had been agreed, laying enormous stress on the fact that by her efforts she had got the date of the report advanced by several months. (Lewin himself had suggested to me that I might use this argument with her – the BMA wouldn't mind.) And I made as much as I could of

[1] The formula they proposed was: 'With regard to the distribution of private beds at Charing Cross Hospital, when private patients are treated for clinical purposes in special units elsewhere in the hospital, the equivalent number of beds in the private floor will be occupied by NHS patients, thus releasing acute beds elsewhere in the hospital.' In the statement we eventually agreed, I also reiterated my call to all concerned to leave the phasing out of beds to the Government, accepted the speeding up of the work of the Owen working-party with a view to trying to reach agreement by November and undertook not to make any 'arbitrary reduction' in the number of pay beds meanwhile. In return for this the BMA and HCSA agreed to call off their threatened work to rule on the understanding that the other parties would also call off their action against private patients in any NHS hospital involved.

the fact that the private floor would become a mixed ward. But she was no fool and soon realized that they hadn't got the magic formula on which they had pinned their hopes: the release of twenty private beds for the NHS. 'All we have got is one for one,' she complained. 'Yes, Brooky,' explained one of the consultants – now free from the shadow of the BMA to renew his normal friendly relations with Ma B. and her staff – 'but you know that the private floor is always under-occupied. In future these beds will not be kept empty. When we move a private patient to a specialized unit, as we do frequently, we will move an NHS patient immediately into the empty bed.' Could they guarantee a minimum number of NHS patients there? No, they must trust him to play fair. How quickly could they move in NHS patients? Tomorrow, starting with four. Could they make it six? Yes, they could, said the administrative officer.

Eventually, whether she was just tired and fed up with the whole business or naturally moderate, Ma B. said she was inclined to accept if her companions would. They were far more unhappy about it all. Timorously but tenaciously they maintained that in reality they had got nothing and when they reported back the settlement would be rejected. 'You have got the advancement of the date,' I said gently. 'And you have now got a mixed floor instead of a private one.' I could see that this was the bull point with them, so I clinched the business by suggesting we write the words into the statement: 'thus ensuring it becomes a mixed floor'. It did the trick. We started shaking hands all round. Ma B. thanked me profusely, saying she had said some hard things about me and that my statement in the House condemning them had made her very angry. But now she had met me she had formed a very different impression of me. The tense little girl was bitter about her pay and I assured her the medico-physics technicians *were* going to get their increase.

Peter kept tugging at me saying, 'I want you down there with the press before it is too late.' David reminded me that the BMA were still waiting in another room. I told him to go and report to them that the agreement had been clinched. There was no need for me to consult them again as we had not deviated in any detail from what they had agreed. Peter [was] almost beside himself with impatience. At last he was able to grab me and rush me downstairs, where a handful of reporters were watching the clock desperately. A hurried interview and three short radio recordings during which I fended off provocative questions and played it absolutely straight with the BMA. Then upstairs again where I hoped to relax over a celebratory drink, only to find David waiting with a face of doom. 'You ought not to have gone down without seeing the BMA,' he told me. 'You are in deep trouble there.' 'For God's sake, why?' I asked, bewildered. Apparently they had been expecting me to go into them, like a subject to a reigning monarch, to get their final blessing on what had been concluded and were blazing mad to learn I had gone to talk to the press without doing so. David said he had just about quietened them down by a grovelling apology and officials had been 'magnificent'. Apparently Philip Rogers had ticked them off in his mild way while Henry Yellowlees had lost his temper and torn a strip off them. It was now clear that officials were as contemptuous of the BMA's whole behaviour as ever we could be.

In an effort to retrieve the situation I, too, went into them with profuse apologies. Lewis was bridling like a petulant child, Stevenson was spluttering and the rest of the consultants stood around brooding like Henry Moore monoliths. I finally pacified them by sending Stevenson off to talk to the Press Association, who were still standing around, and sent Peter Brown chasing to see if there were any radio people left. And off at last went Ted and I to drive to HCF. Having been on the go by now for nearly twenty-two hours I was terrified that I might doze off and so encourage Ted to fall asleep at the wheel, so I forced myself to keep awake by screeching tuneless songs at him until at last we turned into the blessed home lane. The delight of the waiting dogs was, as always, an antidote to the unrealities of the day. To bed at 4 am.

Saturday, 6 July. Woke, still exhausted, at 9 am. I had barely rallied my senses before a spluttering Stevenson was on the phone. Had I seen the papers? The worst had happened, as he knew it would. The papers had got the BMA attitude all wrong. His telephone had never stopped ringing. He was in terrible trouble with his members and must therefore send me a letter to put it right. He then read out a letter beginning with a vicious attack on me for having kept them 'imprisoned' in a room while I scooped the press. I listened patiently, then, with infinite gentleness, gradually soothed him down. I told him that I would gladly send him a letter in reply confirming his interpretation of the agreement, but would it really have the effect he wanted if it appeared as just part of a row? That floored him and he sobered down. He said he would try his hand at a redraft and phone again – which he did, right in the middle of my breakfast. The redraft was fine – except for a still slightly petulant introduction. 'Why don't you just say that you had hoped to have a better opportunity to talk to the press than was possible owing to the lateness of the hour?' I said soothingly. 'If you will do that I will be glad to send you a reply by hand on Monday confirming your understanding of the agreement unreservedly.' He capitulated, took down my form of words and agreed to do as I said. I returned to my congealing bacon and eggs and breathed again.

Monday, 8 July. The *Daily Telegraph* carries the story that the breakaway consultants, who are meeting in London today, are complaining they have been 'outfoxed' by Mrs Castle. That won't help me over my statement in the House today, for, of course, Geoffrey Howe has put down a Private Notice Question. I insist on including in my reply to the PNQ that I am circulating copies of the correspondence [with the BMA] in the Official Report [Hansard]. This manœuvre succeeds in foxing Howe who, of course, does not know what the correspondence contains. His supplementaries were, therefore, muted and cautious and the whole exercise went swimmingly. Bob Mellish had approached me anxiously beforehand. 'Is it going to be all right, you darling?' He was immensely relieved and congratulatory when I got through so easily.

Tuesday, 9 July. In the afternoon Brian and I trooped over to the Treasury with our officials to discuss, at Denis's request, the family endowment scheme on which I have been working so hard. Denis, after some of his rather mawkish jocularity, which always irritates me, then suddenly proceeded to lecture me. It was all right my coming forward with all these plans, he said, but there was no money for any of them. Gradually I felt cold fury mounting in me. I told him at last that I resented being brought over for a lecture: 'Here's Barbara again with her begging bowl.' I told him that the commitment to a child endowment scheme was in the Manifesto, which *he* had helped draw up.[1] If he now wanted to repudiate the commitment he had better tell Cabinet. He climbed down somewhat at that; said it was all very difficult and Cabinet would have to decide its priorities in the light of the public expenditure exercise. We left it that officials should continue their discussions on the plan without commitment to timing, etc.

Wednesday, 10 July. Spent the morning chairing my first meeting of the Women's National Commission.[2] Apparently I delighted them all by my robust determination to build up the Commission and to get the Women's European Committee wound up. Dr Thornton, the Commission's secretary, had such a bad cold she had almost lost her voice. I have never known me catch a cold from someone so quickly that it develops in a few hours, but that is what happened – by the evening I had such a sore throat that I too could hardly speak. Perhaps my fatigue had made me vulnerable. I was in a wretched state when, at 6.15 pm, I met Alf Morris, Jack Ashley, Jack Straw and a phalanx of officials in the House to try to settle our policy over the Sharp Report. Alf has been getting nowhere over this and Brian Abel-Smith has taken charge. Brian is pressing us to go for cash payments instead of cars and I can see the sense of it. But the trouble is that, finance being so stringently short, this means that we could not afford to extend to disabled people who can't drive the big cash allowance (£300 million a year) that it would be necessary to give the existing disabled drivers instead of cars. And Alf and I are haunted by the knowledge that very few disabled people would be able to buy their own car on £300 a year anyway. Elizabeth Johnson [of my Private Office] has been urgently reminding me that we must get a decision soon if we are to clear the policy with Cabinet before the recess, so I said to everyone as we assembled, 'This is jury service. No one leaves this room, eats, drinks or sleeps until we have settled our policy.'

Two-and-a-half hours later I was regretting this. I felt ghastly; my mind was going round and round as dizzily as the argument. Alf had produced a complicated scheme for enabling existing users of invalid tricycles to commute their allowance into a large enough sum in the first year to enable them to buy a car and suggested that this provision be extended to disabled non-drivers who needed a car to get to work or education (Lady Sharp's idea). I don't like these

[1] In the Manifesto we had said we would 'help the low paid by introducing a new system of child cash allowances for every child, including the first, payable to the mother'. I was working on this 'child endowment' scheme, which was designed to combine child tax reliefs and family allowances in a new cash payment to the mother and which was later to become known as the child benefit scheme. In the meantime I was pressing the Chancellor to agree to a substantial increase in the family allowance, which had not been increased since 1968 and which stood at £1 for the second and subsequent children in a family.

[2] In 1969 Harold Wilson, always anxious to promote the status of women, had responded to United Nations pressure and created a Women's National Commission representing all the leading women's organizations in the country. This replaced the Women's Consultative Council, originally set up by Mr Heath in 1962 to disseminate information about the European Community as part of his drive to get Britain into the EEC. The terms of reference of the Commission were 'to ensure by all possible means that the informed opinion of women is given its due weight in the deliberations of Government on both national and international affairs' and the Government

arbitrary categories. But my idea of extending a mobility allowance to every disabled person as the first instalment of our disablement income scheme was slapped down by officials on the grounds of cost. They clung doggedly to their determination to get the Department out of the responsibility of providing cars. Finally, almost in despair and my head swimming, I said we would go for Alf's idea. '*Without* offering cars in lieu?' queried Philip. 'Yes,' I replied firmly. Brian O'Malley took me off to eat and bought me a superb bottle of wine, which cheered me up but didn't do anything to get my boxes cleared. When I went up to my room to start on them Jack Ashley came in to tell me both he and Alf felt it was politically impossible for us not to offer cars to existing users of tricycles. Would I allow Alf to reopen the point? I groaned and said 'Yes.' What with votes on the Trade Union Bill and my boxes, it was 2 am before I got to bed.

Earlier I had had to give an hour to the RHA [Regional Health Authority] chairmen, hearing their views on our proposals for the democratization of the NHS.[1] They are all against our making any changes at all until the new bodies have settled down. So even this modest instalment of reform is running into difficulties! The only bright note in the day was that Dick Bourton [Deputy Secretary at the DHSS] had managed to get Treasury to cough up £47 million to offset price rises in the NHS and thus avoid the threatened reduction of services. And Treasury have promised to let us have another supplementary estimate later if this sum does not prove enough to do the trick.[2] This meets one of the major worries expressed to me by John Donne last Friday and the RHA chairmen were duly grateful. Dick Bourton used the opportunity to get a dig in at David Owen, whom officials find irritating. Could I please tell Parliamentary Secretary, Bourton asked, to leave these things to him as Parliamentary Secretary had nearly upset the apple-cart by going direct to the Chief Secretary? These things were far better left to officials, as it had been necessary to twist the rules. I listened soothingly. I like David and am glad of his endless policy initiatives, even if some of them are only half thought through and, having started them, he drops them suddenly. I would far rather have someone who thinks for himself and stirs things up, for out of this good always comes.

Thursday, 11 July. The BMA doctors, meeting in Hull, have excelled themselves. The *Daily Telegraph* and others carry the headline: 'Doctors jeer at

had appointed one of the co-chairmen since its inception. On our return to office Harold had asked me to take this on.

[1] The Labour Party had bitterly opposed Sir Keith Joseph's reorganization of the NHS as administratively top-heavy and managerial. Party conference had called for its administration to be democratized and in our Manifesto we had said we would 'transform the Area Health Authorities into democratic bodies'. My difficulty was that the new structure was due to come into operation one month after we took office. Most of the new officials and authority members had already been appointed. It was too late to unscramble Sir Keith's eggs and another immediate reorganization would have been disastrous for morale. David Owen and I had therefore worked out interim proposals to make the new structure more democratic by increasing the number of local authority representatives on the Health Authorities to one-third and by including on them, for the first time in the NHS's history, two elected representatives of the rest of the staff in addition to the doctors and nurses who were already represented. We also proposed to strengthen the role of the Community Health Councils. Even these modest modifications had caused alarm among the existing membership of the Authorities.

[2] In the event the supplementary estimates for the NHS during the year amounted to over £642 million in England alone.

Castle's cash transfusion.' As Wedgie said to me, 'Could there really be any other group in the country that would jeer at £47 million?'[1] How I am going to cope with that bunch of mavericks, without even any margin of money to jolly things along, I don't know. And David has worried me by suggesting that he is working on the idea of allowing consultants to continue to work full-time in the NHS and do private work *outside* the NHS hospitals. I will never put up with that: it would be a direct incentive to build up a private service outside the NHS. It is clearly essential that I should keep in closer touch with David's negotiations, though he resents any feeling that he hasn't got a completely free hand. It is going to be a tricky situation to handle, particularly as I have to spend so much of my time on these blasted strikes.

This afternoon was an example. First I saw Clive Jenkins, at his request, about the medico-physics technicians, who are threatening to stop the kidney machines by coming out on strike. I have got colleagues to allow their pay revaluation discussions, held up by Ted Heath's pay policy, to be resumed, but the negotiations have got bogged down in the Whitley Council machinery. Clive told me the offer in Whitley had been derisory. He was worried about what might happen. Could I speed things up? I said I'd try and then seized the opportunity to tell him off about the radiographers. He's bringing them out on strike, too, for an interim payment and I told him he knew that that was impossible. He huffed and puffed a bit and then said he would see what he could do, but didn't I realize how high feelings were running? I said I thought it was because the rank and file had not been encouraged to appreciate just what was being offered them.

Next I had to see Miss Maddocks, staff side secretary with the Whitley Council that deals with the Professions Supplementary to Medicine [PSMs]. She wriggled in her chair uncomfortably as I told her we had to do something about the nonsense of the radiographers' threatened strike. Her union, NALGO, is not involved in this action for a change and she said that one of the troubles was inter-union rivalry: Society of Radiographers versus ASTMS. Perhaps I could see the staff side? I said (on official advice) that I thought it would raise expectations if I invited them to see me. Could she arrange for them to invite me? She said she'd try and was clearly unhappy about the whole thing, as the press is full of horror stories about the danger to patients.

Friday, 12 July. Up early to go to Blackburn, though I wasn't really fit. But with an Election in the offing I dare not fall behind with my interviews. Somehow I got through the day and on to the night sleeper where I dosed myself with pills and linctus and slept heavily. But I found the strength to give a press interview condemning the doctors for 'playing politics'.

Monday, 15 July. The BMA have reacted rather interestingly to my Blackburn

[1] On 3 July a meeting of doctors, dentists, nurses and midwives had urged the Prime Minister to set up an independent inquiry into the NHS, claiming that an injection of £500 million was needed to save it from disaster. At the meeting Dr Stevenson maintained that '£40 million is neither here nor there'. Mr Walpole Lewin told the meeting that the BMA had drawn up plans for sanctions in the event of any of the three crises facing the NHS not being solved. These were: the under-financing of the NHS, the future of the private practice and new contracts for consultants.

hand-out about the doctors playing politics (which I gather from Jack Straw alarmed Rogers and Yellowlees!). Lewin and Stevenson are very upset (I would say worried) by my accusation and have asked to see me. Just the reaction I anticipated – and wanted!

We are still agonizing over the Sharp Report. The office is fighting tooth and nail and I must say that I am rather overwhelmed at the prospect of our having to provide something like 11,000 cars a year – and to service them. This is what would be involved in making cars available for all the existing categories – to say nothing of extending them. B. A-S. takes the line that the provision of a car goes far beyond the 'prosthesis' of substituting an invalid tricycle for a leg and enters the wider realm of social dreams. I entirely agree with him that *all* the disabled should have help with mobility: the chance, for instance, to hire a taxi to get to some social event. The trouble is that, once you get away from the idea of a vehicle, you get away from the qualification of ability to drive – and provision for non-drivers becomes alarmingly expensive. I don't think we can get out of this difficulty without spending some money and I say we must send an SOS Minute to Harold urging him to allow us to provide cars for existing categories, *plus* the beginning of a mobility allowance for other groups as the first instalment of a mobility allowance that would eventually enable us to move completely to cash: cost £25 million. I hope that his recognition of what he himself said to the Disabled Drivers Group before the Election will swing him to our side. I think it is time the disabled had a look in.

Tuesday, 16 July. Up early to have my hair done; then into Cabinet. (We never seem to meet before 11 am these days.) The main item was Concorde again, and Elwyn introduced the brief for the PM's meeting with Giscard which, he said, had been unanimously agreed by the Ministerial Committee. I had read it with mounting irritation. Conscious as I was of the public expenditure pressures, I was furious at the way we were drifting into a more and more expensive commitment to Wedgie's toy and my fury exploded as I heard Elwyn obviously trimming our resolution not to proceed beyond sixteen planes. He wanted the phrase to run: 'But any agreement to authorize further production or development must clearly define the commitment of the parties.' When he added, 'It will be a real battle to hold them down to sixteen,' I thought the time had come to do something. I could see we were drifting inexorably into an open-ended commitment that would knock all our public expenditure plans for six. 'When some of you round this table see what the public expenditure cuts are going to do to the NHS and other social services, you will weep,' I declared passionately. I knew I had impressed Cabinet and Harold said that all these points must be borne in mind. We were definitely limited in our commitment to sixteen aircraft. I felt I had achieved something.

Wednesday, 17 July. Another COHSE deputation on the nurses' campaign for an interim pay increase. These industrial disputes are exhausting all my time. I listened patiently, explained endlessly – and kept thinking to myself how remarkable it is that these 'militant' unions always seem to come out on strike when there's a Labour Government.

Thursday, 18 July. [At Cabinet] we turned to a discussion of the proposed increases in Members' allowances. I supported them as a step towards the proper treatment of MPs' secretaries, whose conditions and pay, I pointed out, continue to be scandalous. But when we turned to the suggestion that Peers' allowances should be increased too, I interposed: 'I want to declare an interest; I oppose.' Wedgie, whose wit is a relief from his tendency to excessive seriousness, said he wanted to declare a *non*-interest.[1] He too opposed. We were overruled on the basis of sob stories about some of our Labour stalwarts in the Lords, who came from the North and were out of pocket from the cost of staying in London. I replied that the real answer was to review the whole system so as to introduce a differential rate between Peers living in London and those in the provinces. Harold said we would ask the Top Salaries Review Board to do just that – for the next round.

Monday, 22 July. Into confabs over the works engineers and radiographers who are threatening to close the NHS down. At the Ministers' lunch the MPs had united against me to say that I must concede an interim rise for nurses and radiographers. I told them stubbornly that the situation was not as simple as that. I agreed with them that it was important to have these disputes settled before the Election (and to have a payment in hand for the nurses), but I did not believe that a panic concession on interim payments would necessarily settle the disputes and that our only hope was to get Halsbury to report on the nurses earlier. He has promised to give me a firm date for the nurses' report next week, but I said I would see him before then to discuss the whole problem with him. This we proceeded to arrange.

Tuesday, 23 July. To the disapproval of the Department I insisted on taking an hour off on my way to the office to try to buy a swimsuit for my holiday. All the ones I have got are ten years old! Of course I have left it too late and there wasn't a swimsuit of my size to be had. When Pearl picked me up she said would I please hurry to the office as they had laid on a meeting with Halsbury. I found him waiting for me and I settled down for a long persuasive talk with him. Having outlined my problem I asked him how he could help: perhaps by producing an *interim* report on the nurses earlier? But he wouldn't budge: an interim report would take as long as a final one. Finally he said reluctantly that he would discuss the position with his committee. On an impulse I asked whether it would help if I were to come and address the committee myself? To my surprise he said it would. So I shall have the fight of my life there!

Wednesday, 24 July. The discussion [on devolution] at MISC showed how deep are the waters into which we have got. Officials clearly don't like the idea of devolution at all and have come out for legislative devolution as being, though

[1] In the early 1960s Anthony Wedgwood Benn had conducted a long campaign to renounce the peerage he had inherited from his father, the first Viscount Stansgate, which had robbed him of his membership of the House of Commons as MP for Bristol South-East. As a result of his brilliant tactics a Joint Parliamentary Commission was set up to consider Lords reform. This led to the passing of the Peerages Act 1973, which authorized the disclaimer for life of certain hereditary peerages. Within minutes of its becoming law, Benn had surrendered his. Some time later he announced that he was dropping the 'Wedgwood' from his name. Unrepentant I continued to call him 'Wedgie' and Dick Crossman once told me: 'You are the only one who is allowed to call him that.'

dangerous, less so than the sweeping ideas on executive devolution that Norman Hunt had pressed. Willie was as gloomy as usual: we ought not to have gone as far, he said, but, having started the whole inquiry, we had roused expectations we could not resist. 'It will now be impossible to avoid Scheme A [legislative devolution].' But he hinted darkly it might lead to the break-up of the UK. John Morris was far more enthusiastic. Expectations had been built up and we could be in grave difficulties in a few years' time if we did not meet them. A directly elected assembly was essential and had in any case long been part of the Welsh Labour Party policy. It was the haves who were for the *status quo* and the have nots who wanted a greater say. Roy Jenkins clearly disapproved of the whole business: 'I am horrifed at the idea of rushing into a decision in the last fevered weeks of July which could affect the shape of Great Britain for a hundred years.' He didn't like the effect of all this on law and order and in any case doubted whether it would influence many votes. Eric and Edmund supported him, but Ted Short said testily that he had spent months on this and time and again had pledged a White Paper before the Election. It was impossible for us not to make a statement soon. Eventually Harold ruled that Norman Hunt should submit a modified form of Scheme A for consideration next week. I raised the dangers of introducing a single transferable vote and was assured we would not be recommending this.

The papers are full of Marcia's installation in the Lords yesterday,[1] which I did not get time to go and see. Ted tells me she did it impeccably and with dignity. Whatever else one thinks of her she certainly is a remarkable personality. Personally I always got on well with her, but it is astonishing how many people are outraged at Harold's gesture – including Mik. It is typical of Harold that he should have gone to watch his own handiwork. The cheeky chappie is also a stubborn one. But Ted says their Lordships are disgusted at *The Times* for its profile on Marcia today, revealing that she has two children by Walter Terry. So dog has at last eaten dog! But the hack journalists of the right-wing press must be desperate in their determination to discredit Harold if possible.

Thursday, 25 July. Our joint meeting between Cabinet and NEC on the draft Manifesto took place in the large dining room at No. 10. Looking round the oil paintings on the walls Joan Maynard asked me, 'Is this where you have your Cabinet meetings?' 'God, no!' I replied. 'The Cabinet room is much more austere.' The atmosphere of the meeting seemed relaxed and genial enough.

The real trouble broke out when we came to the Common Market bit. Once again I realized what Harold is up against and what trouble he will be in if he tries to shift the delicate balance in the party in any way. Fred Mully, in the chair, reported that Jim had sent a message to the effect that he was in favour of a commitment to a timetable for the referendum, but it ought to be a general one of twelve months. Harold seized the opportunity to say we ought to add something to the effect 'and in any case not later than four months after the completion of the negotiations'. This roused Roy J. 'I wish to place on record my deep-seated and continuing objection to a referendum and therefore my

1 On 24 May Harold Wilson had announced fifteen new life peerages. Marcia Williams took the title of Lady Falkender and made it clear she would continue to work as his political secretary.

preference for keeping the options open.' Shirley supported him. Reg P. said he spoke as 'an agnostic about the Market', adding, 'I have supported the referendum but think now I was wrong to do so. I do not see how, given the sovereignty of Parliament, the referendum can be binding.' Denis suggested we should fix a time limit (*i.e.* by the end of 1975) and leave the Government free to have an Election or not. Harold climbed down: 'I would prefer to wait till the chairman of the Party is here. We are taking no decision today.' And so it was left: the grumbling appendix which, to everyone's relief, has not yet become acute.

Friday, 26 July. The first round of the battle over next year's public expenditure White Paper. Denis introduced his paper to Cabinet in less provocative terms than Jim used to do in the same role. He reassured us by saying there would be no settlement of individual programmes before the recess and that we could not do everything at once by trying to close the *whole* of the balance of payments deficit by 1978–79. Nonetheless we must begin to progress towards it and it was necessary to fix a public expenditure increase limit of $2\frac{3}{4}$ per cent in demand terms. I insisted that it was impossible to agree the figure of $2\frac{3}{4}$ per cent until we had seen the effects of this on the individual services. Harold then summed up in phrases that gave us all something for which we had asked: we must take the $2\frac{3}{4}$ per cent as a 'guiding principle', but we were only committed to a procedure of examination by officials, not to its detailed outcome.

Monday, 29 July. Bob held a noon drinks party to celebrate his promotion,[1] inviting the lobby and Ministers. Everyone was talking about Roy Jenkins's disastrous speech on Friday.[2] When Ted and I saw him on TV I said, 'That has cost us the Election.' Eric Heffer, Mik, Syd Bidwell *et* Tribune *al.* haven't made things any better by rushing into public attacks on Roy. One of the pressmen asked me if I was going to join in the fray. I replied no: I thought we should none of us make speeches on anything but our Departmental work between now and the Election. Ian Aitken of the *Guardian* tried to incite me into an indiscretion, but I merely replied that I liked Roy and thought he was badly advised.

I was *distrait* during our Ministers' lunch, being conscious that I had a major job on my hands that afternoon trying to persuade the nurses and radiographers to accept Halsbury's date.[3] First the nurses. The staff side listened

[1] On 26 July it had been announced that Bob Mellish, as Government Chief Whip, was to become a member of the Cabinet instead of merely attending by invitation. The appointment was to be personal to him. David Owen was made Minister of State at DHSS on the same date.

[2] In a speech at Haverfordwest, Roy Jenkins, while rejecting the 'febrile coalition talk', urged that the Labour Party must win over the 'great body of moderate, rather uncommitted opinion' in Britain and implied that this was being alienated by the left-wing views in the Party. For some time a group of middle-of-the-road and right-wing Labour MPs had been meeting to discuss how to counter the growing influence of the left-wing Tribune group of MPs and this move was formalized on 17 December 1974 by the establishment of the 'Manifesto Group' of Labour back benchers under the chairmanship of a prominent pro-marketeer, Dr Dickson Mabon.

[3] Owing to the growing threat to the Health Service from industrial action by nurses and radiographers, I had been to see the Halsbury Committee a few days earlier to plead with them to give me an early date for the publication of their report on nurses' pay. I also suggested that the committee might, on the basis of that report, be able to make proposals for interim payments for radiographers and the rest at the same time. The committee

attentively, but only made a non-committal comment. The PSMS were more forthcoming. After considering what I had said they called me back while Miss Maddocks read a statement warmly welcoming the date *by a majority*. The sting was in the tail. The three unions that really matter (the Society of Radiographers, ASTMS and COHSE) had reserved their position. I have told my chaps I must now mount the biggest exercise in individual contact with the unions, leaders and executives that I have ever done.

We started tonight with a series of meetings with the key chaps in my room at the House. Clive [Jenkins] first. 'Will you help me?' I asked, at which he spat out 'No'. He then proceeded to be as insulting as he knew how and told me his union would enter into widespread and destructive industrial action immediately. I was furious enough inside, but my show of temper was deliberate. 'All right then, go ahead,' I told him. 'I can't stop you destroying me and the Government. If that is what you want, it is war.' We screamed at each other like fishwives and officials sat cowed at the most unholy row they had ever heard. I thought Clive would walk out, but he lingered on. As I had guessed, this was the only way to treat him and he was clearly shaken by my determination not to budge. 'I've asked you to meet my members,' he said, 'but you haven't even had the courtesy to reply. You have behaved abominably.' I told him that was a lie and that I was willing to meet his members now – tomorrow if he liked. We finally agreed on Friday. He still hung around muttering and I almost had to throw him out, knowing that his enemy, the Society of Radiographers, were waiting in the wings. In came the Society's Secretary, Denley, and the President. They were polite, but tough. No, they didn't think they could persuade their members to accept Halsbury's date for their interim. Over drinks they softened a bit and said they would see what they could do, but would like me to meet their national council. Finally Albert Spanswick and his President. Albert was positively mellow and I think they will accept the nurses' date. All this took over three hours and I was limp at the end of it. And it was going on all week!

Tuesday, 30 July. Up at 6 am to struggle through my massive brief on the National Superannuation White Paper which we are bringing before Cabinet today. I had to be in the office early for the first of my round of talks with individual union executives: today with COHSE. Once again I spelt out the case for awaiting the Halsbury report on 16 September. They were immensely friendly and one of them said he was impressed by my obvious sincerity. They grumbled about the Whitley machinery and I promised to consider any proposals for change once the nurses' problem was out of the way. Later I learned that they had agreed to my compromise positively enthusiastically – one success I badly need to brighten a troubled week! But at Cabinet I had another success too. National superannuation went through with only a few manœuvres, pretty half-hearted ones, by Denis to whittle it down and to my joy he agreed that the White Paper ought to be published before the TUC Congress.

promised to consider my difficulties sympathetically and later agreed that I could announce that they would produce their report on nurses in the week beginning 16 September, on the understanding that there would be no interim increase before then and would produce an interim report on PSMS at the same time.

One thing that interested me was the total lack of interest in Cabinet in discussing my scheme. Remembering from Dick's days how complex these matters can seem to outsiders – and how long Dick took to expound his own scheme – I had gone to a lot of trouble to sketch out a summary, but before I had finished delivering it Harold interrupted to say that I really shouldn't assume that my colleagues hadn't read their documents. All I can say is that that is exactly my experience! But Cabinet – and particularly Harold – is in the mood these days to settle everything in committee, so Cabinets get shorter and shorter and the discussions on major policy items more perfunctory. The others were teasing me afterwards about my long oration. Said Bob, 'I said to Tony if she goes on any longer we'll all be old age pensioners.' But I didn't care: I've won and we've got a first-class scheme through with few compromises, despite PESC.

Lunch with Conrad[1] was a matey affair. He called me 'Barbara', sympathized with me in all my difficulties and eventually promised to do what he could to help. His trouble was, he said, that the staff at the Department of Employment was very thin on the ground because of the hiving off. He could ill spare Douglas Smith, for whom I pleaded. I told Conrad that the job I offered could lead quickly to a larger remit: to help sort out the whole Whitley machinery and to evolve a pay policy for the public sector in the light of the new pay policy. He could see the importance of that, particularly as he has no doubt that the voluntary pay policy will break down and that we shall be back to a statutory one before long – under any government. 'Isn't the civil service a remarkable thing?' he mused. 'Here am I, well known for my views on the need for a statutory incomes policy – and yet in this job. And Robert Armstrong [the Prime Minister's Principal Private Secretary]: he enjoyed working with the previous PM and had built up quite a loyalty to him, yet Harold keeps him on.' I replied that I had always said that I didn't mind what a civil servant's political views were provided he was open about them. It was nonsense to expect any intelligent man to be apolitical. What I liked was to surround myself with civil servants of differing political views and then get them arguing about policy. In that way I was really able to work out the pros and cons.

I asked Conrad how he got on with Michael Foot. 'Oh, what a charming man,' he exclaimed, but I detected something less than idolatry. 'How does he get on with the administrative side?' I asked. 'Ah, well, his only policy is to find out what the unions want,' he replied. One thing nearly drove them to distraction. When Michael had a major speech to make, they put up briefs which they doubted whether he even read. 'We ask: is there anything else you want to discuss with us? He won't put up even an outline of his speech, but will suddenly say he is going out for a walk. He will be gone for about an hour and a half and when he comes back he has obviously worked it all out.' I said I thought that that was the best way to prepare speeches, but Conrad shook his

[1] Conrad Heron had become Second Permanent Secretary at the DEP (renamed the Department of Employment) and now worked with Michael Foot. My aim in taking him out to lunch was to persuade him to persuade Michael to release one of his top conciliators – preferably my former very able Private Secretary, Douglas Smith – to help us at DHSS with the spate of industrial disputes we were experiencing. The difficulty I met was that, since my day there, most of the original functions of the old Ministry of Labour had been hived off to independent bodies. The conciliation work had gone to the new ACAS [Advisory Conciliation and Arbitration Service]; training to a new Training Services Agency and health and safety to the Health and Safety Executive.

head and said it led to all sorts of slips, 'like his remark about Donaldson,[1] for example'. I insisted that that was a small price to pay. Even the most cautious of us were liable to indiscretions which then dogged us for the rest of our lives. I said that what had astonished me was the way Michael had sturdily shouldered his share of unpopular decisions. 'Ah,' replied Conrad, 'but do you think he will really stay put when the going gets tough?' I said I did. Clearly here is a civil servant who thinks that Armageddon is not far away, yearns for a coalition and thinks the only answer is to contain the unions in a framework of legal restrictions.

After various office meetings, including a discussion with Dick Bourton about how we could get more money under PESC for the NHS, Norman Warner (who has now taken over as my Private Secretary) phoned to say that the Home Secretary was in his room if I would like to see him now. On an impulse I had decided to talk to Roy, whose speech and its repercussions are still headline news. Roy greeted me as warmly as he is capable of and I went straight to the point. 'Roy, I wanted to have a word with you in the greatest friendliness because I am fond of you. I think that once again you have listened to very bad advice. I have been struck by how harmonious we have been in this Cabinet. You know my views on Europe: I've always been against entry and hope the negotiations will at least get us out of the grandiose implications of the Treaty of Rome. But if the people voted to stay in, I shouldn't leave the Government. I'd stay in and try to make the best of it. Of course the press is waiting to egg you on: you are their mouthpiece for Europe and they are using you. But your friends ought to know better. They are driving you into a course that can only ruin your political career. . . .' At this point, red in the face with sudden emotion, Roy said violently, 'What makes you think I care about my political career? All that matters to me is what is happening in the world, which I think is heading for disaster. I can't stand by and see us pretend everything is all right when I know we are heading for catastrophe.' More calmly he added, 'It isn't only Europe. It is a question of whether this country is going to cut itself off from the Western Alliance and go isolationist.' I was frankly puzzled. 'I simply don't see where you get that fear from. Are you suggesting we are going Communist?' No, it wasn't as crude as that. At this moment the division bell interrupted us. As we made our way downstairs I persisted: 'But what exactly do you want the Government to do that it isn't doing? What is *your* remedy for our troubles? Personally I think the basic dilemma today is to get people to share responsibility instead of confusing short-term militancy with the need for fundamental change. But that problem remains whether we are inside Europe or outside it.' He had no answer. Awkwardly he said, 'Let us have a talk some time', and disappeared thankfully.

No. 10 Committee Room was crowded for Harold's end-of-term speech to the PLP. He read every carefully prepared word of it and I found it pedestrian. But Ted [Castle] said the people sitting round him praised it as extremely skilful. I was sitting on the platform next to Tony C. As Harold went through a long catalogue of our achievements in government it began to be obvious that

[1] In a Commons debate on 7 May, Michael Foot had said that part of the Conservative approach to industrial relations was to rely upon '. . . some trigger-happy judicial finger'. Asked if he was referring to Sir John, he said, 'Of course I am referring to Sir John Donaldson.' The Opposition attacked the phrase as 'unparliamentary'.

he was singling out Shirley for special and repeated praise. The rest of us got barely a mention (except Jim) and some Ministers none at all. Tony C. began muttering, 'Shirley 3, Jim 2, Barbara 1, poor Tony nought.' We soon got the giggles over Harold's patent manœuvres. I whispered to Tony, 'He's making a bid for the pro-marketeers and of course he isn't going to mention Roy.' Tony started to keep a list of mentions, and as we passed housing and land without a single reference to him he scribbled at the bottom of it, 'Unfair to To-to!' I consoled him, 'You are now classed with Michael and Wedgie,' who hadn't been mentioned either, despite the big point Harold made of the repeal of the Industrial Relations Act. Afterwards Ted said to me that from Harold's speech it was clear that our Election slogan was going to be 'Shirley for Queen'.

Our last 'Husbands and Wives' dinner before the recess was a bit thin on the ground, as Mike was having a celebratory party for the repeal of [Ted Heath's] Industrial Relations Act.[1] We were on a three-line whip and as John Silkin and I dashed for his car at one division bell (that is the beauty of Lockets: it is on the bell) we were followed out of the restaurant by Roy Jenkins and Reg Prentice, who stood on the steps looking helplessly around them. 'Quick,' we said, 'jump in.' Still they stood bewildered, and we almost had to drag them in. 'I didn't realize you were dining there,' said Roy vaguely. Neither of them had the grace to thank us; perhaps they were embarrassed at being caught in a conspiracy. They had clearly no idea that *our* conspiracy was going on in a private room! As we dashed through the division lobby John said to me, 'That is why I can't bear these right-wingers. They are arrogant, selfish and . . .' 'Insensitive,' I added. I am personally convinced that Roy hasn't got it in him to lead the Party – only to do a Gaitskell and divide it. And once again I realized that these right-wing and left-wing allegiancies are due as much to the chemical reaction between people as to ideology. To get back into that cosy room at Lockets, with Tommy, Katherine, Wedgie, Caroline, Judith, her Tony [Hart], Rosamund [Silkin] and Ted [Castle] was like getting back into a different world from Roy's.

Wednesday, 31 July. First a long, wearying meeting of the Ministerial Committee on Industrial Development to finalize the White Paper on industrial policy.[2] I had presumably been invited because of the pharmaceutical industry, which David has persuaded me ought to be left out of the list of acquisitions by the

[1] The Trade Union and Labour Relations Act became law on 31 July.

[2] The White Paper which was eventually published, 'The Regeneration of British Industry' (Cmnd 5710, August 1974), was very different both in tone and content from the Green Paper Tony Benn had proposed three months earlier. Its emphasis was all on the need for government 'partnership' with industry. There would be no statutory requirement on a company to enter a planning agreement. Financial assistance for these agreements would be additional, not conditional. The full range of help under the Industry Act 1972 would 'of course' continue to be available for companies not covered by them. There was no mention of extending planning agreements to one hundred companies: the Government would be 'selective' in its initial approach. The role of the trade unions was played down: the agreements would be bipartite, not tripartite. They would be concluded between the Government and the company, with the unions being brought into close consultation. The extent of public ownership was carefully circumscribed. The Government's proposals for public ownership, said the White Paper, were those listed in the Manifesto. In addition, the NEB would be used to extend public ownership into profitable manufacturing industry, but only by agreement. If in any case it proved necessary to acquire a company compulsorily – for instance, where an important company was in danger of collapse or of passing into unacceptable foreign control – this would normally require a specific Act of Parliament. These proposals represented 'the whole of the Government's policy for public ownership for the next Parliament'. The NEB's

NEB, as the acquisition of a single British firm would do nothing to secure the across-the-board control of the drugs industry that we need if we are to get the drugs bill down. There [was] a lot of esoteric talk about planning agreements, during which Wedgie said that he had never visualized them being statutory but that he needed some leverage to make the big companies play along with him. He therefore believed that all regional aids should eventually be channelled through them, except the Regional Employment Premium. Otherwise we should find that we could only get firms in by offering expensive additional inducements. I could hardly hear what was going on, but Harold summed up that, although the whole system of regional aid required review, the present system should remain in being for a further year. To my surprise Wedgie did not mention the pharmaceutical industry. In fact there seemed to me to have been merely minor disagreements.

There was barely time to have a quick briefing meeting in Harold's study for our great confrontation with the BMA and the Royal Colleges over the state of the NHS. I advised him to be sympathetic but to ask them to break down the figure of £500 million they had asked to be pumped into the NHS. If he did so he would find they had just not worked it out. The deputation streamed in, about twenty strong. Harold replied rather sketchily, leaning heavily on his brief to explain why we didn't think a full-scale inquiry into the NHS was necessary.

He then asked me if I would like to add anything, and I plunged in. I said they had made an impressive case, but as I listened I couldn't help wondering – and I didn't mean any offence – why the dog had suddenly started barking in the night. (Some of them had the grace to smile at this.) I then read out the comment that Stevenson had made at the time of the Tory December cuts in public expenditure and added, 'If those were the headlines we were getting now we should feel there wasn't any problem.'[1] I thought the reason for the sudden crisis mood had arisen from four things: (1) the chaos caused by the NHS reorganization, to which one of them had referred; (2) the trouble caused by the industrial action stemming from the last three years' pay policy; (3) inflation; (4) the December 1973 cuts. The first three were being remedied, and the important thing was that the Government had guaranteed to inflation-proof the NHS and also would meet any extra expenditure arising from straight pay increases. It was also considering the whole question of public expenditure. I believed therefore that the crisis could, and would, be largely defused. An inquiry wasn't necessary, but I would be glad, as soon as we knew the final figures of public expenditure, to hold conferences with the profession and the health authorities to work out with them how the money available could be put to the best use. Lewin and Stevenson seized on my speech and said it was 'most

main job would be to discharge the functions of the old Industrial Reorganization Corporation in promoting industrial efficiency and profitability. Power to establish these new instruments would be taken in a new Industry Bill. This would widen and make permanent the power in the existing Tory Act to acquire share capital in a company in return for financial assistance, but, as in the Tory Act, it would have to be by agreement and subject to the same parliamentary control. 'We need', declared the document, 'both efficient publicly owned industries and a vigorous, alert, responsible and profitable private sector.'

[1] In his crisis public expenditure cuts of 17 December 1973, the Conservative Chancellor, Mr Anthony Barber, had announced that expenditure on the Health Service in 1974–75, instead of increasing as planned, would fall by £111 million, of which £69 million would be in capital spending. Dr Stevenson's public comment had been: 'The Government's need to cut capital expenditure is understood, but the effect on the Health Service will be particularly felt because of the need for more hospitals.'

important'. If what I had said could be spelled out in an agreed communiqué they thought it would go a long way to meet anxieties. Harold handed me over to them and thankfully disappeared.

By now it was 7 pm and I could see my pleasant and relaxed dinner with Reggie Paget disappearing down a long corridor of tedious statement-drafting. And so it proved. As Henry Yellowlees, Jack Straw and Peter Brown kept coming in to me with reports of Stevenson's impossible niggling I was near to explosion. At one point Henry came in muttering, 'I'll kill that man Stevenson one day – I swear I will.' Finally I *did* explode and threatened to leave. Peter was assigned to the job of calming me down while Norman also kept an eye on me anxiously.

At last the agreed statement emerged and I swept into the impatient and disgruntled press conference flanked by Lewin and Stevenson. They played it absolutely fairly and down the line and I think the press were astonished – and disappointed – to find us so harmonious.

Thursday, 1 August. The press is full of Wedgie's announcement about the nationalization of the shipbuilding industry. He can't complain that he has had none of his own way! But we have also got a good press for our meeting yesterday. Arrived at No. 10 at 9.15 am for the meeting with Clive about the radiographers.[1] He was chatting with Harold in his study, which depresses me these days since Heath reclothed it in its expensive trappings. Harold went straight to the point and Clive was in an emollient mood. He explained how ASTMS had always opposed the radiographers' case going to the Halsbury inquiry and wanted a chance to negotiate their pay. If ASTMS and the Society of Radiographers both came to us and asked for the radiographers' reference to be withdrawn from Halsbury, would we agree? Thinking rapidly, I said of course (though I thought my Department would have kittens). I had no objection to scrapping Halsbury, Whitley or any other machinery, I said, once it was clear that the unions as a whole wanted something else. Clive said he would have a word this morning with the Society about this. But clearly knowing they wouldn't agree, he kept murmuring about an earlier interim payment anyway. I told him it was impossible. Clive was still murmuring 'interim' when Harold showed us out.

Once again I bolted a sandwich in my room in the House before departing for Camden Town and my meeting with ASTMS on the radiographers. It had been Clive's idea that I went to his office for the meeting and I had readily agreed, telling my Department I would go anywhere to get a settlement. Surprise, surprise: the TV and press had been informed of the meeting (which Clive had originally told me would be kept secret) and were waiting at the door! So was Clive, who greeted me with the utmost friendliness. Over drinks, Clive told me that the Society were not keen on his idea of withdrawing the reference. It was now up to me, he said, to convince his members, who were waiting for me, to await their interim payment. I would see how young they were and in what a militant mood.

[1] On 30 July I had persuaded COHSE to await Halsbury's report on 16 September and not to renew the nurses' industrial action, but ASTMS had rejected this and was threatening to step up the radiographers' action, causing severe disruption in hospitals.

He was right. There were about thirty of them and there was no reverence about them. Some of them stood up as I came in, others ostentatiously kept their seats. I was surprised how many young women there were among them and it was they who openly sneered as I spoke. It was quite an ordeal. I spoke off the cuff and without histrionics, starting with: 'Mr Chairman and fellow trade unionists'. (Sneers at that.) As I expounded my case, I had to struggle against more sneers, head-shakings and audible jeers from several of them. On my feet, I suddenly thought up a new idea. Talking about the Government's pledge to get the results of the inquiry into payment as quickly as possible, I said I would undertake to call the Health Authority Treasurers together well before 16 September to satisfy myself that everything possible had been done to speed up the payment machinery. Clive played it completely fair and did not try to influence them.

When I had finished the bitterness broke out as they had their turn and as I listened to their tirade I resigned myself to total failure. But I wasn't going to take it lying down and lashed out when some of them distorted what I had said. I think my passion surprised them. Just as I was despairing a young man stood up and congratulated me rather patronizingly on my 'eloquence'. But how, he said, did I expect them to persuade their members to wait for six weeks for an interim payment of which they did not even know the amount! They had been 'had' before. This struck me as a ray of hope: they would accept the delay if they had some indication of the sum. Clive followed this up (seeing it also as a ray of hope, I think) and asked me whether I could ask Halsbury to say what percentage increase they would get as an interim. I said of course, but I couldn't give any guarantee and warned them that Halsbury was getting fed up at being pushed around. At this point I had to leave and left Jack and Gillis behind to draw up an agreed statement. Clive accompanied me to the door and once again we were photographed shaking hands. I was limp with the effort and dubious of the outcome. In the car Philip [Rogers] was shaking his head about the 'vicious' young women, who clearly frightened him.

The meeting with the Society of Radiographers was in their office and here, too, the TV cameras were waiting outside. This was no modern, with-it Camden Town office but a traditional building in the heart of Harley Street land. The National Council was older, too, and much more polite. No sneering as I spoke and I knew I was on safer ground because the Society had turned down Clive's attempt to withdraw the reference. So I was able to play on this, saying they had got to make up their minds: they couldn't have their Halsbury cake and eat their Castle interim. (They smiled at that.) But when discussion came they, too, spoke of a sense of frustration among their members which they doubted whether they could contain and they, too, stressed how much it would help if Halsbury could indicate the size of the interim. I told Harold what had happened and asked him to invite Halsbury to see him.

I still wasn't through: there was the BMA to see again. Henry Yellowlees has begged me to fit them in before my holiday to discuss their pay. With statutory control of incomes dead from midnight on 25 July[1] they are on the warpath for an immediate re-reference of their pay to their Review Body to get another

[1] Section 6 of the Prices Act 1974 gave the Government power to abolish the machinery of a statutory incomes policy. The Order abolishing the Pay Board came into effect on 26 July.

instalment of pay to top them up. Henry assured me they had agreed to a short meeting, really only to be able to tell their members that they had made their mark with me as soon as possible after the end of the statutory policy. But once again he had underestimated them. They [came] streaming through the door, a dozen strong. No sign of yesterday's bonhomie: they were grim and politely threatening. Tony Keable-Elliott the most reasonable. But there was no doubting Grabham's mood of barely restrained viciousness. They had noted, he said, that militancy paid on every hand and warned me that they, too, had learned the lesson and, unless they got satisfaction soon, they would act on it. There was a lovelessness about that bunch that made me sick. Just as they arrived Norman brought me a piece of good news: the Society of Radiographers had agreed to call off its industrial action and wait for Halsbury! As I shook hands with Lewin and Stevenson I said, 'You will be glad to know the Society has called off its action.' 'At what price?' sneered Derek Stevenson. 'No price,' I replied sweetly. 'Just my eloquence.' Not a word of congratulation from either of them.

After nearly an hour of their interrogation I reminded Lewin politely that I had other things to do. Even so he clung on. Eventually it was agreed I should send them a letter setting out the new position under a voluntary policy, though I warned them the Government would want to stick to the twelve-month rule.

Friday, 2 August. More work over the now routine sandwich under the hair-dryer; a quick shop for a swimsuit [for my holiday] and then back to No. 10 for Harold's meeting with Halsbury, whom we smuggled in through the back door. I warned Harold that Halsbury was touchy, but in the event he could not have been more anxious to please, saying how disturbed he had been over press reports that he had threatened to resign. 'I told the press that my relations with the Secretary of State could not be more cordial,' he assured us. He had been trying to work out a formula to help and thought he might say that the radiographers' interim would be a 'substantial proportion of the nurses' settlement'. I seized on this and then, with typical caution, he backed away from it. I pressed him time and again, pointing out that it had been a triumph to get ASTMS to suspend their action even for a week to see what he produced and I was sure that, if he could say what he had originally suggested, it would do the trick. We left it that he would go back to his office to work something out and I phoned Philip to keep in touch with him and get him to stick to the words he had suggested if at all possible. In the car to HCF at last! Only one box between me and freedom and rest for a whole two weeks. On the way I noted with irony that Terry Lancaster had a piece in the *Mirror* building up Shirley as Harold's darling, the centrepiece of the next Election and potentially the next PM. What on earth is Harold up to? I haven't had a word of recognition from him about my efforts in the last three weeks. Yet I have done as much as anyone to save the Government from catastrophe. Philip phoned to say Halsbury refused to stick to his original words.[1] Hell!

[1] Lord Halsbury was only prepared to hint that his report on nurses' pay would be linked with a parallel but interim recommendation for other Health Service workers, including radiographers. This was not enough to prevent industrial action by the radiographers but, while I was away, David Owen had talks with their union, ASTMS. He assured them that high-speed arrangements were being made by the Department to ensure that the

Saturday, 3 August. The papers are full of Wedgie's supposed defeat in Cabinet over industrial policy. I wonder what happened after I left – or is it just another press ploy? Jimmie Margach phoned and congratulated me over the way I had 'cooled things' in the past few weeks, which must have been gruelling. When I told him that all I had had for my pains was a great spiel by Tim Raison on the eight o'clock news attacking me as the most disastrous Minister of Health in history, who had gone around 'lighting fires' through the whole Health Service, he was indignant. Ted [Castle] should get on to Bill Hardcastle, he said, and demand I be given the right of reply on *World at One* tomorrow. Ted did this, only to be told by Bill, regretfully, that he has got Harold on *World at One* tomorrow and simply couldn't fit in both of us. Harold ought to deal with it himself. I rang Harold this evening and he said 'That's odd, saying they couldn't have you as well as me: they have been trying to get Bob Mellish tonight to go on the programme.' Another example of the media's prejudice against me? Anyway Harold agreed to deal with it.

The happiest moment of the day was this morning when Henry Yellowlees came on the phone to speak to me, swearing to Ted that it was nothing to do with work. 'Forgive me for troubling you,' he said. 'I had written a note to you for the box only to find you weren't having any more and I can't blame you. I didn't want you to go away until I had told you how much I admire how you have behaved in the past few weeks and what you have achieved. The whole Department agrees with me. I have never known a Minister maintain themself as you have done in this difficult time. Have a good holiday.' I was so touched by his warmth I thought I was going to cry.

Off to Mauritius tomorrow! We are staying first with the Governor-General, then with the Prime Minister, and the fleet is in. We shall either be submerged in a boring social round or have the time of our lives.[1] The big thing is that I shall be right away from all this.

Friday, 23 August. Back from Mauritius I find that while I have been away things have gone amiss on a whole list of policy matters which it is essential to get right before the Election. The Chancellor has closed the door on my making any announcement about existing pensioners[2] when the White Paper on our new pensions scheme appears, despite the fact that we are still discussing this with the Treasury. Another miserable meeting about Sharp. The Treasury has had kittens about Alf's commutation idea,[3] not so much on the grounds of cost as of its implication that we are still committed to providing cars or their equivalent. Alf is away in Italy, so, if we are to get anything out before the Election, I must act. Says Elizabeth primly, 'He knew it was coming up, Secretary of State, so he shouldn't have gone away.' (It is a deep-rooted feeling

radiographers received their interim pay increase recommended by Halsbury, back-dated to 23 May, in their September pay packets. As a result the radiographers called off their industrial action on 17 August.

[1] We had the time of our lives.

[2] Brian O'Malley and I believed that existing pensioners would be resentful if they drew no benefit from the new scheme. We had therefore been working out proposals to give them notional credits under the scheme as though they had been contributing to it over a previous period of, say, ten years, but the Treasury refused to commit any more money.

[3] Alf Morris was working on an idea whereby the disabled could 'commute' their mobility allowance into a lump sum to enable them to buy a car.

among civil servants that they have done their duty if they have dumped the problems in Ministers' laps before going away themselves.) I say desperately that I am perfectly prepared to get the Government out of the car-providing business, despite the political difficulties, *provided* I have the political *quid pro quo* of a mobility allowance for all disabled persons with the same medical entitlement. This would scotch the Tories, who wouldn't dare to attack our failure to give cars to disabled drivers knowing that we had extended the mobility allowance to disabled people who can't drive. The cost of giving *them* cars as well would be prohibitive. Even Dick Bourton admitted there would be something very valuable in it for the Treasury. Though the cost would be over £20 million, we should be out of the car business for ever and the long-term implications would be clear and containable. I adjourned the meeting while I myself dictated a letter to the Chancellor.

Next to PESC. Bourton said he thought he might get another £100 million for the NHS, though he had conceded that the Sharp proposals should be taken out of it. I sat up indignantly at that and he looked crestfallen. Just before I went away he had asked me what were my priorities in my PESC list, and I had said, 'The NHS,' adding mischievously that my Cabinet colleagues had a vested electoral interest in the other items, like disablement policy and child endowment. But I can see that officials' hearts are not in my battle to get more money. I suspect that they thoroughly sympathize with the Treasury's traditional retrenchment attitude to public expenditure.

Monday, 26 August. Spent Bank Holiday Monday ploughing through my boxes at HCF. The lassies in the Private Office (in charge while Norman Warner is away) have almost begged me to work down here this week as the Department generally is so thinly manned. But I find from papers in my box that the private practice question has reached crisis point. I have been worrying for some time what David was up to on this issue and how the talks in the Joint Working Party were going on – all the more so since we have got ourselves committed to producing its report by November. The papers consist of a long, desperate Minute by Philip Rogers saying he knows officials ought to have let me have their views on pay beds earlier, but they have all been so busy. Now they feel they would be failing in their duty if they did not let me know how opposed they all were to the phasing of private practice out of NHS hospitals. His Minute was accompanied by a succession of submissions about the legal, constitutional and practical objections to phasing out. There was also a copy of a letter to Philip from Sir Douglas Logan [Principal of the University of London] saying that the disappearance of part-time consultants from NHS hospitals would seriously damage medical education. So the forces are mobilizing against us as they did against Nye – only this time the party would not tolerate the sort of concessions that Nye made.[1] Our job is going to be even harder than his.

[1] Aneurin Bevan, as Minister of Health in the 1945 Labour Government, had a long and bitter struggle with the medical profession over the introduction of the National Health Service in 1948. He was helped by the remarkable alliance he struck up with Lord Moran, President of the Royal College of Physicians, who was anxious to help him to attract top specialists into the new and untried service, which the profession was threatening to boycott. It was as a result of Lord Moran's advice that Nye agreed to allow NHS doctors to earn fees from private patients and NHS specialists to have the use of some private beds in NHS hospitals at the discretion of the Minister. Contrary to what the BMA was to assert in its later battle with me over the phasing out of these

Along with all this came a Minute from David saying rather sourly that he supposed officials had a right to put forward their views, but he was annoyed because this meant that they had not produced the document on the policy of separation of private practice from the NHS for which he had asked. He had himself, however, produced two papers – one of them for the Joint Working Party meeting on 4 September – which he was intending to discuss at an office meeting on Wednesday. Could I let him have my views before then? I read all this very carefully and, although I admired David's initiative of ideas, I grew alarmed as I read some of his proposals.[1] I wrote a long Minute in reply, saying I wanted an office meeting myself on all this next week. I can see that the time has now come for me to get fully involved in David's work on this, though he much prefers to be in full and independent charge. I shall have to handle him tactfully.

Monday, 2 September. Back full-time at the office. Spend most of my time preparing for my crucial meeting with the Chancellor tomorrow about my bids for PESC. Dick Bourton is gloomy about the prospects – even suggests that Denis will insist on my postponing the pension plan, due for publication next week. I gird myself with grimness for the fight.

Tuesday, 3 September. In the event the two hours with Denis were a pleasant surprise: no pawky humour from him; no irritating digs. We just sat down, Denis flanked by Joel Barnett and his key officials, Baldwin and Widdup. I was flanked by Brian [O'Malley] and Alf, Errington and the rest. Denis began by saying that my bids took up the whole of the contingency fund for 1975–76 and then drew up an agenda of items for us to deal with. I interrupted to say, 'You have left out the housewives' disablement benefit.' 'Oh, no, that's agreed,' replied Denis, brushing it airily aside. I looked at my officials, who have been bringing me messages, ostensibly from the Chancellor, to the effect that he couldn't accept any commitment to a disabled housewives' benefit and, if I didn't fall immediately into line, he would take the whole thing into Cabinet (where I know only too well I shall have few allies in my efforts to pre-empt some of the PESC discussions). 'But I thought you had reservations, Chancellor,' I said sweetly. (In fact I have been compelled by these peremptory messages from Treasury to write them into my document for the Social Services Committee.) Denis looked puzzled. Joel shrugged: 'We reached agreement.' Widdup then protruded his head reluctantly to admit that he had been the author of the diktats. 'You haven't seen this yet, Chancellor,' he said. I felt like

private beds, this concession was not a 'condition' on which the profession agreed to participate in the NHS. On the contrary its violent opposition to Bevan's proposals continued and was only broken down at the eleventh hour by Nye's clear determination to go ahead and by his offer – again on Lord Moran's advice – to embody in amending legislation his frequently repeated pledge that he did not intend to introduce a whole-time salaried service by regulation. The story is told in detail in Michael Foot's biography of Bevan.

[1] In my Minute I told David that two aspects of the paper he had prepared for the Joint Working Party caused me particular anxiety. The first was his proposition that we would allow up to three years for phasing out pay beds in order to provide time for alternative private accommodation outside the service to be built up. Our aim, I said, should be to discourage the building up of the private sector, not encourage it. The second was that we would consider, as one version of the new contract, allowing consultants to opt for a full-time contract, plus the right to practise privately outside the NHS. This was in direct conflict with my policy of encouraging consultants to devote their whole time to the NHS.

exploding at this impudence of Treasury officials, but restrained myself. 'Well, yes,' drawled Denis. 'I'll have a look at this, but I don't see any difficulty.'

Discussions went well for a time: no suggestion of postponing the pensions scheme (we are no nearer solving how to latch in existing pensioners); agreement between Denis and me to sacrifice the Christmas bonus in favour of two pension increases next year, starting in March; a warm welcome by Denis for my new line on invalid vehicles ('I like your new approach'), if only we could find some way of reducing the initial cost. But the real crunch came over family allowances and the child endowment scheme. Denis is trying to get the family allowance increase down to derisory levels and to get me to postpone the introduction of child endowment for a year. I told him that both propositions were totally unacceptable and we agreed to leave these issues for the fight in Cabinet. I also warned Denis that I would not be content with the present allocation for the NHS. (I am determined not to let him do a 'divide and cut' exercise between the social security and health sides of the Department.) He just noted that. Altogether I went away not too dissatisfied.

Tuesday, 10 September. Up early for a hair-do, ready for my terrifyingly imminent exposure to press and TV [on the launching of the Pensions White Paper]. I begin to get a bit trembly: how will our pensions policy be received? The more I reread it, the better it strikes me, but one never knows what reaction one will get. This is the great moment for which Brian and I have been working for months – a make-or-break moment – and I almost panic at the thought of the technical minutiae on which I could be tripped up. Then into Cabinet for the deferred discussion on EEC regional policy.

I slipped away hurriedly to join Ted at St Bride's for John Graham's memorial service.[1] The singing was so beautiful I don't know how Sandy didn't break down and howl. Then a whole bunch of us, led by Bob Edwards [editor of the *Sunday Mirror*] and Sidney Jacobson [editorial director of the *Mirror* newspapers], proceeded to the Press Club for drinks and lunch, which I had to abandon half-way through in order to get back to the lobby conference on the pensions scheme at 3 pm. By that time I was feeling pretty tense, but I survived, while Brian was waiting to jump in brilliantly to supplement, with complete mastery, what I said. I had stressed that he had done all the detailed work and I am so grateful that he doesn't in any way resent the fact that it is inevitably called the 'Castle' scheme. Who said that men will never work under women?

Back to the office for a series of meetings with individual leader-writers. Peter has organized these three days like a martinet. 'I arranged for Mr Crossman to do this for his scheme, Mrs Castle, and I want you to agree to do the same.' Of course I acquiesced meekly. And all the time other Departmental problems came crowding in on me, notably a continuing argument with Treasury over the wording of our press statement on Sharp, due out on Friday. I had carefully written the statement within the terms of the agreement I had made with Denis, even accepting that the total sum for the mobility allowance could only be £15 million. Every over-expansionary phrase had been toned down, but that did not stop the miserable Widdup from sending ultimata about

[1] John Graham, political correspondent of the *Sunday Mirror* and a long-standing Fleet Street friend of my husband, Ted, had died suddenly of a heart attack. He left a young wife, Sandy, and a small baby.

other passages, because they made me sound like a human being. Even Norman began to be outraged. In the end, by making a few minor concessions, I got most of what I wanted left in, but it was infuriating and wearisome.

At last I managed to get away, very late, to Russell Harty's party. He was terribly anxious to help me in the Election and very willing to speak at my main meeting. A lot of the acting world was there. Frankie Howerd was all over me; Jill Bennett intrigued. 'We thought Russell was making it up when he said Barbara Castle was coming,' said one of them. I explained that every minute of my day was earmarked by my officials, adding laughingly, 'They have to know where I am wherever I go so that they can get in touch with me. I could never have an affair.' Later Jill came up to me and said dreamily, 'I have been thinking over your problem. I've solved it. You *could* have an affair. You should say that you have regularly to attend a hypnotist and the whole essence of your treatment is that no one should know.' I told her that, if she thought that would hold off a Private Secretary, she didn't know the nature of the breed! I shouldn't be surprised if someone on TV doesn't now make a play out of it.

Wednesday, 11 September. More individual interviews on pensions. The *Financial Times* seemed friendly; Malcom Dean of the *Guardian* said openly, 'We like this scheme.' Then into a drinks session with City editors which Peter had specially laid on. To my horror he insisted on my making a little speech, but I needn't have worried. They were exuding friendliness. It was quite clear that most of the journalists there were very impressed and the crowning moment came when the CBI chap came up to me and frankly said that they warmly welcomed our whole approach! Brian and I began to have our tails up. 'I think it is going to be a wow,' I whispered to him. The vast press conference in the afternoon was an ordeal, but there was one thing Brian and I congratulated ourselves on: we took them all completely by surprise. No leaks, despite the continual earlier probing by John Cunningham of the *Guardian*. Then TV. The ITN chap was relaxed and helpful, but Hardiman Scott would not give me an inch to say anything about the merits of the scheme. He kept pushing me into a corner with snide questions like, 'Isn't this all just an electoral bribe?' I am beginning to share Harold's suspicions of the BBC.

A switch now to Halsbury and how to get the [interim] lump sums [we have worked out with Halsbury] into payment by the end of this month. The Treasurers say they cannot do it unless they get the figures at once. I say that if necessary I will have to see Halsbury again.

Thursday, 12 September. An excellent press for the pensions scheme, actually helped by the few sour comments of people like Geoffrey Howe. Even the Life Assurance have welcomed it! And Len Murray has said the right things. That is the great bond between Brian and me: we like to be politically clever as well as competent. Harold was delighted; greeted me at Cabinet with the words: 'Wonderful publicity. I am going to send you a note of congratulations, including Brian, of course.' We were almost back on the 'little Minister' terms. Perhaps I am beginning to come out of my eclipse.

At the office I rewrote the press statement on our disablement proposals.[1] I had intended to get Alf to deal with mobility at tomorrow's press conference, but he is committed to be in Liverpool, so he will hold a separate press conference there. With disablement out of the way, the only issue remaining before I can relax is Halsbury.

Friday, 13 September. The press conference on the disablement proposals went well. When I asked if there were any questions there was silence. Then one journalist said, 'We are stunned.' So it has worked! I should have thought this issue would have been of wide human interest, calling for TV, but once again the BBC didn't want to know. I think they are getting terrified of the effectiveness of our succession of announcements and are clearly determined to play them down. By contrast ITN agreed to put me on their midday programme live if I could get to the studio on time. With a rush I did, only to hear the interviewer say as he introduced me, 'We have already heard similar proposals by the Conservatives from Sir Geoffery Howe.' I was staggered: the Tory Manifesto is carefully non-committal on its disablement policy. Yet apparently Sir G. has rushed in to announce an identical disablement benefit, saying unctuously that he is glad the two parties agree on this at last. In the car I muse to Peter: 'Someone must have leaked.' But later, in the train to Lancaster, the penny dropped. We must have sent the usual advance copy out of courtesy to Sir G. yesterday! I could have kicked myself.

A succession of hurried office meetings. First with Halsbury himself, who told me with pride that I should receive the nurses' report on Monday after all. I thanked him profusely and got the office drafting a letter to the PM asking for urgent consideration of the report as soon as it was received, so that, hopefully, I could announce the Government's acceptance on the nod.[1]

[1] In 1973 there had been a revolt in the House of Commons against Sir Keith Joseph's failure to improve the social security provision for the chronically sick and disabled. He had been compelled to accept a new clause in his pensions legislation instructing him to review their needs and to report to Parliament by October 1974. This had given Alf Morris and me the chance to press for major reforms and on 13 September, after a long struggle with the Treasury, we were able to announce three important new benefits. (House of Commons paper No. 276.) These comprised a non-contributory invalidity pension to be introduced the following year for people of working age who had never been fit to work, including a 'pocket money' pension for the in-patients of mental hospitals; an invalid care allowance for those forced to stay at home to look after a severely disabled relative, to be introduced in 1976–77; and an invalidity pension for disabled housewives, which it was planned to introduce as soon as the problem of assessing incapacity in these cases had been overcome. We had already announced that invalidity pensioners would be able to qualify for additional earnings-related benefit in our new pensions scheme.

We were able to report at the same time the outcome of the protracted discussions over the mobility allowance. Treasury had at last agreed to pay a mobility allowance of £4 a week covering all the qualifying disabled, whether they could drive or not, to be phased in over three years for some 100,000 disabled, including children, at an initial additional cost of £15 million. In return we had given up the idea that the Government itself might commute the weekly payments into a lump sum, where the disabled desired it, which could be exchanged for a Government-provided car. Instead we undertook to continue to produce the invalid vehicle for those who wanted it, to improve it and to consider what advice and other help we could give to those who preferred to save their allowance to buy a car. The disabled people's organizations warmly welcomed the mobility allowance and said that they would be getting in touch with the motor manufacturers to try to work out a hire purchase scheme.

On 5 September I had also announced that we were going to set up an Institute of Hearing Research to give the problem of deafness the greater study and prominence it needed.

[1] The report recommended an average pay increase for nurses of 30 per cent, backdated to 23 May, together with improvements in overtime and holidays. This was in addition to the threshold payments they had received. As I had requested, Halsbury had worked out the lump-sum payments nurses should receive on account and recommended an interim award for the professions supplementary to medicine. The Government accepted the

Monday, 16 September. Had to get up at 6.30 am to get to No. 10 for the joint meeting between Cabinet and NEC on the Manifesto.

When we came to my section I was ready with an extensive rewrite. Even Denis nodded approvingly, for, of course, I stuck to what had been cleared with him. There was some teasing as I read on and on, but Bryan Stanley[1] whispered to me, 'Your redrafts are a great improvement. Stick to your guns.' Later, over the lavish buffet lunch Harold provided for us, Bob kept up the teasing: 'You should have heard us at our end of the table,' he cheeked. 'She'll never stop, we said.' Ted Short said quietly, 'She is one of the few Ministers who do their homework.' No one could say that of Fred Peart, who had failed to produce any section on agriculture at all and was sent away to draft something; or of Tony Crosland, whose section on housing was so inadequate that he spent his time profusely thanking Frank Allaun, Joan Maynard and me, consecutively, for the additions we suggested.

At lunch I had a hurried word with Harold about Halsbury. With the report due later today, I want agreement to announce that it will be published tomorrow and also a rapid indication of the line the Government will take on it. Harold washed his hands of the whole business and said that if Mike and Denis would agree a line, so would he. So Mike, Denis and I took our salmon and excellent wine to a little table in the drawing-room to talk it over. Mike was emphatic that we must publish and announce our acceptance of the report as soon as possible. Denis, entirely naturally, said that at least his people must be allowed a look at it, though he didn't see any difficulty. As we grew mellow over stilton and burgundy Denis said, 'You must admit I am the most political Chancellor you have ever had.' 'I do,' I replied, 'and I appreciate it.'

Back at the office I called an urgent meeting over Halsbury. Crises abound, of course. Peter said he didn't want to call a press conference tomorrow. It was too risky before everything was cleared with Treasury. I told him the report *must* be published tomorrow or there would be distorted leaks. So we must just go ahead and gamble. Raymond Gedling reported the PSMs had gone away satisfied with their proposed lump sum interim payments (£80 and £60), but there was a terrible snag with the nurses. Thanks to Halsbury's restructuring, which cuts out the juvenile training rates, a few student nurses would only be entitled to a lump sum of £20 if there was not to be a claw-back of overpayment when the increases came into the regular pay packets. The only way out of this would be to make the sums for the nurses £80 and £20. Inconceivable! I put my head in my hands and groaned. These student nurses, of course, are the COHSE lot. Peter insisted that the very mention of £20 would wreck the reception of the whole report.

We went round and round the problem. How many were affected? We didn't exactly know. Perhaps ten thousand. Perhaps less. But there would be a sprinkling in every hospital. News came in that the staff side had asked that some formula should be found for lifting this group, too, to £60. Another of my

report, which was published on 17 September, and agreed to make extra money available to cover the £170 million cost. The nurses were delighted and Albert Spanswick of COHSE commented: 'We never expected to get increases of this rate.'

[1] General Secretary of the Post Office Engineering Union and a member of the trade-union section of the NEC.

chaps said the Treasury would never stand for it – to say nothing of the Public Accounts Committee. I said the only way out was to take the payments for this group out of the computer and pay them manually. Could this be done? It was possible, but difficult, and anyway the pay clerks are now threatening to go on strike unless they get a cash bonus for doing the work. Of course this is ridiculous, but their union, NALGO, is sore because ASTMS made such a good running over the radiographers. In the normal way I would sweat this out, but, with the Tories waiting to ridicule the Social Contract in an imminent Election, I have not much room for manœuvre. I send Norman away to try to contact Len Murray to help us over the pay clerks and Gedling away to try to persuade the staff side to agree to leave this small group out of the computer and to meet me to fix their lump sum after we have all had a chance of studying the report.

I then sit down to wait. Message: there have been hitches over duplicating the report and its delivery is delayed. Message: Len Murray doesn't want to see me till he has talked to Audrey Prime.[1] Message: the staff side are bogged down over the problem of student nurses and want to see me personally. I agree to see them, and at 8 pm the staff side troop in, pretty jaded by three-and-a-half hours' non-stop belly-aching. I order Norman to open my drinks cabinet and they perk up noticeably. They are not aggressive: in fact, pleased with what they have heard of the report. But they are desperately anxious how to deal with this small group. So am I. But I explain to them it is going to be difficult enough to get Treasury acceptance of the report without their paying over the odds on it as well. I could not possibly commit the Government to this myself. They see the point of this. Would they like me to delay the payment to everyone, I ask. Vigorous head-shakings at this. Then, I say, the only hope is for them to agree to take this group out of the computer and to meet me on Thursday to discuss, in the light of the report, what extra we might do for them. Reluctantly they agree and go away. The report still not having materialized I go home. It arrives at 10.30 pm. Being pretty washed out by this time I say to hell with it and go to bed.

Tuesday, 17 September. Good news begins to roll in: Mike has accepted the report enthusiastically, the Treasury with resignation; the PSMs have accepted the £40 [interim payment] for helpers. We go ahead and draft a press statement.

So at 4 pm I sail into my press conference, still reading the report frantically on the way, and have an easy ride. When I ask for questions after my announcement of the Government's acceptance of the report there is a silence. 'We are stunned,' says one journalist at last. That phrase again! Then into TV after a make-up girl has tried to patch up my haggard face. As I am about to face the cameras Peter comes and whispers to me, 'Remember, no smiling. You are still too coy. Norman [Warner] tells me his children mimic you when you smile.' So I speak sternly to the interviewer. When I get home Ted says to me, 'Very good interview, but I wish you had smiled more. After all, it was good news!' Who'd be a politician? Well, I would, for one.

Wednesday, 18 September. Sudden call at short notice to a Cabinet meeting.

[1] Miss Audrey Prime of NALGO was the secretary of the staff side of the General Council of the National Whitley Councils for the Health Services.

When I arrived, a little late, Harold was announcing the date of the Election: 10 October. Officials had been turned out of the room and we had a discursive chat. Harold said Parliament would be recalled on 22 October; the State Opening would be on 29 October. 'I don't want any of you sitting next to a telephone after the poll. If we win I would not expect to make many changes in a winning team. Just catch up with your sleep after the poll and be at your office desk on the Monday morning. If it is stalemate I shall call a Cabinet at 2.30 pm on the Friday afternoon.' He told us he would be making the announcement that afternoon, so that he could make his broadcast tonight. That would mean Heath would get his right of reply tomorrow. 'I wasn't going to have him broadcasting at peak viewing time on Friday night.' In the rather rambling political discussion which followed everyone was calm. I don't think anyone was certain we would win, but no one seemed to doubt we were right to go to the country – or that, in choosing the date, Harold had taken every conceivable consideration into account.

Sunday, 22 September. Catch a train to Blackburn, leaving Ted to bring up Janet[1] and packing cases by car. I read up my background briefing on the way and do two meetings on my arrival. Am on top of my form. This pleases me immensely, because I am determined to make this my last Election if the results will let me – I want to go out on the peak, not in the trough, of my ability. I hate people who hang on, keeping the young ones out.

A chastened Mr Heath fought the Election in conciliatory vein. Gone was the confrontation of February. Nervous Conservatives and Liberals, worried by Labour's lead in the polls, had been toying with the idea of a Government of National Unity. The Conservative Manifesto echoed the theme of 'putting Britain first'. A Conservative Government, it said, would not reintroduce the Industrial Relations Act 'in the interest of national unity'. Other policies would be toned down. A prices and incomes policy was essential, but should if possible be voluntary. Even food subsidies would be retained for the time being. Pensions would be increased at six-monthly intervals. For the rest, public expenditure and money supply would be rigorously controlled. There would be no 'narrow partisan spirit'. After the Election a Conservative Government would consult other party leaders about policy and invite people from outside the Party's ranks to join in overcoming Britain's difficulties. 'The nation's crisis should transcend party differences.' Mr Heath's new tone disturbed some of his own activists and muted his attack.

The Liberals also took up the theme of national unity. In June the Liberal leader, Mr Thorpe, and his Chief Whip, Mr David Steel, had rashly offered to go into a coalition if no party won a clear majority. This aroused the fury of the rank and file and had to be toned down. Nonetheless Thorpe continued to insist that all parties must try to come together on an agreed policy. He talked confidently of lifting the Liberal vote from the six million of February to eight or ten million.

For its part the Labour Party flatly rejected all coalition talk. The Government continued boldly to elaborate its own policies. The Social Contract remained the cornerstone of Labour policy. Michael Foot issued a consultative document on his proposed Employment Protection Bill which met many of the unions' long-standing demands for an extension of workers' rights. The Labour Manifesto was in the main a

[1] Janet Anderson, my new constituency secretary.

recapitulation of the proposals of February with three additional promises: to create elected assemblies for Scotland and Wales, to set up a Co-operative Development Agency and to ensure open government by replacing the Official Secrets Act with a measure to put on public authorities the responsibility for justifying why information should be withheld. In my own field the Manifesto renewed the commitment to a new system of child allowances, or child benefit, a new pensions scheme and the phasing of private beds out of NHS hospitals.

The Conservatives were embarrassed by internal disputes. On 5 September Keith Joseph attacked incomes policy in a speech which reflected the growing support for monetarism among Tory back benchers. Worried by the opinion polls, the Conservatives put up Margaret Thatcher to promise to peg mortgage rates at 9.5 per cent. (They were then 11 per cent.) The Labour Party, too, had its embarrassments. The Common Market issue was still festering. The pro-marketeers in the Cabinet had reluctantly concurred in the pledge to hold a referendum or election within twelve months on the outcome of the renegotiations. Then, early in the campaign, Shirley Williams startled her colleagues by announcing that, if Labour took Britain out of the EEC, she would not be able to stay in the Cabinet or active politics. The following day Roy Jenkins echoed her.

In the campaign Labour's leaders denounced 'gloom and panic' talk. Britain, said Mr Wilson, faced crisis but not catastrophe. Denis Healey claimed that the balance of payments deficit, apart from oil, had been halved. So had the rate of growth of money supply. Sterling was strong and funds were flowing in. The worrying facts for the Government were growth, which had not fully made up the fall during the three-day week, and unemployment, which in September had risen to the seasonally adjusted figure, excluding school leavers, of nearly 612,000 or 2.7 per cent. Industry remained jittery, complaining of cash shortage. Some big firms, like Ferranti, ran into trouble and had to be helped by the Government. Nonetheless, as the country went to vote, the opinion polls were still giving Labour a comfortable lead. This was confirmed as the earlier results came in, showing Labour gains. They also showed the Liberals slipping everywhere, with their vote dropping to below six million. But when the counting was over Labour's absolute majority was down to three. Its lead of forty-two seats over the Conservatives had been eaten away by the 'third force' parties, the Scottish Nationalists polling particularly heavily and gaining four seats. The 'others', therefore, held the balance: Liberals (13 seats), Scottish Nationalists (11), Welsh Nationalists (3), Northern Ireland MPs (12). I myself was back with the highest majority I had ever had: 7,652.

Thus precariously reinforced the new Government faced up to its problems. Problem No. 1 was the renegotiations with the EEC. Expert Wilson watchers had already detected that he was determined to keep Britain in the European Community if at all possible. And although the Labour Party conference continued to be tough over the terms, there were signs of weakening among Labour MPs. In the new session they proceeded to elect an avowed pro-marketeer, Cledwyn Hughes, as chairman of the Parliamentary Labour Party and four pro-marketeers topped the poll in the election for the back benchers' Liaison Committee with the Government. Harold Wilson's most serious threat came from the dedicated anti-marketeers in the Cabinet, of which I was one.

Meanwhile my own showdown with the medical profession was coming to a head. With statutory incomes controls abolished, both consultants and GPs were getting restive about their pay. Like the nurses before them, they were pressing for an interim pay increase, for fear that a pay freeze might be slapped on before their annual review of pay could take place in April 1975. They were at the end of the queue for the catching-up pay increases that were taking place and I was determined that they should not lose out as a result of their having to wait twelve months for their turn.

But the situation was complicated by the consultants' demand for a new type of contract currently being processed in the Joint Working Party under David Owen. Since we had promised the report by November, there was no time to lose. Of the 11,500 or so consultants in the NHS, *some 5,000 had full-time contracts which forbade them to do private practice. Of the rest, the majority had opted for 'maximum part-time' contracts under which they were allowed to do private practice but were expected to devote 'substantially' the whole of their time to the* NHS. *Though they contracted to do the same eleven sessions a week as the whole-timers did, they received only 9/11ths of the salary, recognition of the fact that the demands of their private patients would be bound to affect their availability for* NHS *work. This differential in pay for equivalent sessions had rankled for a long time and the* BMA *was determined to get rid of it. It was therefore demanding a 'closed' contract of ten sessions a week for maximum part-timers and whole-timers alike, with extra work attracting extra pay, the whole-timers allowed to do private practice and an end to the differential. David Owen and I could see merit in a more 'work-load sensitive' contract which would enable us to reward the whole-timers more adequately. Many of them worked long hours of unpaid overtime manning up unattractive areas and unpopular specialities like geriatrics, which offered no rich pickings to part-timers seeking private fees. But there were dangers too. The* BMA*'s aim was to encourage the spread of private practice and to discourage whole-time work. To combat this aim it was essential to maintain the differential and reform the system of merit awards under which some £10 million a year was secretly allocated by a professional panel in additional payments to the medically distinguished. Under it a top consultant with a large private practice could get as much as an additional £8,000 a year. The whole-timers received only a minor share. We wanted to use the money on a new system of 'career supplements' which would recognize, not merely medical eminence, but dedicated service generally to the* NHS. *The breakaway consultants of the* HCSA *wanted to go even further than the* BMA, *demanding that payment should be by fees for 'items of service'. It was clear that storms lay ahead.*

The junior hospital doctors were restive, too – and with stronger cause. The men and women in these training grades had for years been expected to work excessive hours, filling in among other things for the part-time consultants' absence on private work. Their career structure was too narrow at the top. A 'junior' often had to wait till he or she was thirty-six to get a consultant post. Yet the consultant in situ *was not anxious to see the consultant grade expanded too much as this increased the competition for private work. There was a great deal of sympathy in the Labour movement for the juniors' grievances. In July the Government had recognized this by agreeing that the extra duty allowances to which they were entitled after 102 hours at work or on call should be paid after eighty hours. But the juniors, too, were set on a new type of contract which would define their working hours more closely and prevent health authorities from exploiting them. They had launched a campaign for a basic working week of forty hours, with all hours above that being counted as overtime. In September the Trades Union Congress had passed a resolution supporting them. Yet, unless carefully handled, their demand could create difficulties for pay policy. The Department's officials had been negotiating uneasily and the juniors' discontent had reached boiling point. In the new session the problem was to land on my desk.*

Tuesday, 15 October. Into our first Cabinet. No agenda. No officials taking notes, only John Hunt. Harold was very chirpy: said he thought we would like a general chat on the position following the Election. Personally he thought the tiny majority was manageable – after all, we had beaten the Tories by forty-two seats. His view was that we should act as though we were facing a full-length Parliament. He wasn't going to make any big changes in his 'winning team'; we should tell junior Ministers to stay at their posts and get on with it. As far as the Queen's Speech was concerned we should 'go absolutely straight ahead with our Manifesto'. He then tried a bit of whip-cracking. Ministers had been free during the Election – and indeed for some weeks before – to write articles and generally to trail their own coats. We must now have 'a more cohesive Cabinet, following all the rules'. He didn't even look at Wedgie!

Back at the office I called a meeting to discuss the social security headaches that lie ahead: the timing and size of the family allowance increase and, not least, what is going to happen to the child endowment scheme. All these have got to be settled urgently – ahead of PESC – so I have to go to see the Chancellor. Officials were very gloomy, saying that inflation had already boosted the bill for our policies and that the Chancellor was likely to be tough. We discussed what, if anything, I should yield on if I am in a corner. I am not likely to get any mercy from Tony C. or Reg if I appeal over the Chancellor's head to Cabinet – certainly not before the whole PESC is discussed.

Whatever our worries they are nothing to the Tories': they are in real travail over the leadership. Edward du Cann has been trying to jump the gun through the 1922 Committee,[1] but I have bet Ted that Heath will still be leader when the next Election comes. He's incredulous and has bet me two to one, but my hunch is strong.

Wednesday, 16 October. Into another tense office meeting, this time over our policy for phasing out pay beds. We are in for a major row here, and the officials have already passed me, with gusto, a letter from the Royal Colleges and the BMA which is practically an ultimatum to us not to touch private practice – or even pay beds. 'This is a declaration of war,' I said sternly, looking round the table. 'No Government could accept instructions to ignore its own Manifesto.' Things haven't been made easier by Halsbury's antics. In an interview in the magazine *Pulse*, he has blabbed in confidence to a journalist (Stevenson, who also writes for the *Mail*) about the doctors' interim pay claim,[2] saying he couldn't see how he could possibly defy the Government's policy on the twelve-month rule. The journalist has leaked! Naturally the doctors are furious, arguing that their case has been prejudged.

Monday, 21 October. Douglas Allen pays me a courtesy call as he has now taken over as head of the civil service. We have quite a useful chat. He asks first whether I still want Philip Rogers to go in February and I say I think we should get a new chap to take over at the beginning of a new administration.

[1] Edward du Cann, MP for Taunton and chairman of the 1922 Committee comprising all back-bench Conservative MPs, seemed to be trying to force Mr Heath into an early statement of his intentions on the leadership. Du Cann called a full 1922 Committee meeting for 22 October while there was still a strong anti-Heath mood following the second Election defeat. This tactical manœuvre leaked extensively to the press, but was defeated when the 1922 Committee's executive decided to hold the full meeting on 31 October, two days after the Queen's Speech. The full meeting set up an inquiry into procedures for electing a leader and invited Mr Heath to address them on 14 November. Although du Cann was criticized by some MPs for his conspicuous plotting, he was re-elected unopposed as 1922 Committee chairman.

[2] As chairman of the Doctors' and Dentists' Review Body, Lord Halsbury was considering an interim pay claim by doctors in breach of the twelve-month rule of pay policy.

Tuesday, 22 October. [A] long meeting with the Chancellor [which] was more productive than I had dared to hope. He agreed without demur that there must be another uprating of pensions and benefits in April next year and in return I agreed to accept the basis of 'historic' calculation of the relationship to average national earnings, instead of the 'forecasting' method we had sought.[1] The main thing is to have got the timing agreed, particularly in view of Denis's introductory homily to the effect that he now faced bids for public expenditure of up to £1,000 million *more* than the $2\frac{3}{4}$ per cent increase he was planning would justify.

My real battle came over child allowances [later child benefit]. First he delighted me by saying he was prepared to drop his figure of 25–35p increase in family allowances next year and go for my figure of 50–60p instead, but only, he added menacingly, if I were prepared to postpone the introduction of child allowances till 1977 and accept his proposal for a lower figure of £1.86p for the first child when the scheme did come in. My jaw dropped. I knew that my priority must be an adequate increase in family allowances next year; also that the Department do not think it is physically possible to achieve child allowances in 1976, but to have a lower allowance for the first child as well was intolerable. I told him as much, adding I had expected him to ask *either* for postponement of the scheme *or* for a lower allowance for the first child, but not both. 'Which would you choose if I gave you a choice?' he cracked back. After a moment's hesitation (and to my officials' relief) I replied, 'Postponement.' 'Only because you know you can't bring it in on time anyway,' he twinkled. There then ensued a complicated discussion about when we would have to decide the actual rates of child allowance anyway and we eventually agreed that we would tell Cabinet that we had decided to fix those later. I felt a great sense of relief.

To our surprise Denis then turned to my health budget, a subject which I had been told wouldn't be raised. He said sternly that we couldn't have a penny more for the NHS, at which I said, outraged, that if he intended to leave me out of the construction industry rescue operation I would take it to Cabinet. Philip came in gravely with a warning about the consequences of freezing the health capital programme and Denis suddenly said, 'But you haven't put in a paper saying what you need.' We denied this vigorously and he repented, smiling: 'Put one in now and we'll have a look at it.' We went out congratulating ourselves on what we had achieved.

Thursday, 24 October. The meat of the morning [in Cabinet] was the row between Mason and Jim over last night's stories that the Foreign Office had told off the Ministry of Defence about the naval visit to South Africa. Jim apologized to Roy about the reports and assured him they had not been inspired by him. Nonetheless, he said, the publicity given to the visit – and the

[1] In our uprating legislation, the National Insurance Act 1974, we had bound ourselves by law to increase pensions and other long-term benefits at least yearly in line with the movement of average earnings or prices, whichever was the more favourable to the pensioner. But there were two ways of calculating this movement. Under the 'historic' method, the increase was based on the movement of earnings and prices over an appropriate past period and was a process of catching up. The 'forecasting' method involved estimating the future movement of prices and earnings up to the date the next increase became payable. At a time of rising prices the forecasting method was obviously more favourable, but with the Chancellor promising another uprating in nine months' time instead of twelve, the time lag was not so serious.

propaganda use which the South African Government had made of it – had been very embarrassing to him diplomatically. We had agreed last March, as part of our arm's-length attitude to South Africa, that we would oppose sporting and cultural exchanges and not allow goodwill visits by the Navy. Operational requirement visits should only be made sparsely and on a very muted basis. That was obviously not what had happened this time. Personally he doubted whether the Simonstown agreement[1] was worth militarily the trouble it was to us diplomatically: we ought to review the need for it as part of the Defence Review. If the security interest was marginal, we should scrap it. He wanted however to warn us that he intended to veto the Motion coming before the UN to expel South Africa. He thought it essential to preserve the principle of universality in the UN; otherwise there might be moves to expel all sorts of people, including Israel. He thought it was essential to make our attitude to South Africa clear, and he hoped Cabinet would agree he should do so along the lines he had indicated when he made a speech in his constituency the following day. In the discussion no one opposed Jim's intention to veto expulsion; everyone agreed we should review Simonstown urgently and that Jim should make his speech.

I tried to get into my section of the Queen's Speech dealing with the NHS a reference to phasing out pay beds, because I want Cabinet committed to that so that I can get extra funds for the new whole-time consultants' contract when the time comes, but Harold said this wasn't appropriate for the Queen's Speech. 'Mention it in the debate,' he said.

Monday, 28 October. Raymond Gedling [Deputy Secretary, DHSS] and Philip asked to see me, full of grim foreboding about Halsbury. Raymond reported that Halsbury had told him in confidence that he wasn't going to be browbeaten into resignation by the threats of the BMA. Instead, to show his independence of mind, he was going to recommend that the twelve-month rule should be breached in their case – and then resign! We couldn't imagine anything more embarrassing for the Government. I said that I thought the PM ought to be brought in.

An awkward session with Dick Bourton, who had come to report what he thought were his great achievements over PESC. He told me proudly that he had got another £30 million for the NHS next year, but it was to be non-recurring. The Treasury refused to allow us any more for subsequent years. Nonetheless this, together with a few other things, meant that, together with my £25 million from the reflationary package, I had in fact got the additional £100 million for which I was pressing. And he sat back well satisfied with himself, awaiting my applause. Part of the deal was, of course, to be that I accepted the offer and would not argue the matter any more in Cabinet. I gulped; then said tactfully that I thought he had done very well, etc. Nonetheless I could not give up my right to demand that Cabinet look at the PESC

[1] The Simonstown Agreement was signed with South Africa in 1955 when the Royal Navy ceased to be the owner and occupier of the Simonstown naval base near Cape Town. Under the agreement the Royal Navy retained the right to use the facilities of the base in peacetime and Britain's allies were given the right to use it in war. In return Britain agreed to conduct joint planning and naval exercises with the South African Navy. Following the Cabinet discussion Jim Callaghan announced in Cardiff that the agreement 'should be brought to an end or allowed to wither on the vine'.

programmes *as a whole* before reaching a decision. All along I had resisted the attempt to set one side of my Department against another, or me against Education, in a series of bilateral deals. How could I accept this offer when I had still no idea what was going to happen to defence, roads or any other programme? (And although Dick Bourton's figuring *sounded* impressive, I was far from clear from his rush report what I had actually gained.) So I still wanted to go ahead and put to Cabinet the paper on social priorities.

Bourton bridled angrily. He was obviously deeply affronted. His reputation as the great fixer on behalf of the Department's interests had never been challenged before. (Philip keeps coming to me and saying how marvellous Dick is at getting more than our share out of the Treasury and how wise it is to leave him alone to get on with it, etc.) Dick then warned me darkly that, if I were to question the offer in any way, it would be withdrawn. Maybe, I said, but that was a risk I was prepared to take. I had no idea, for instance, how much Education was going to get. 'A mere £15 million next year and a *cut* of £160 million by 1978–79,' said Dick triumphantly. Maybe, I repeated, desperate by now but still placatory, but I really couldn't commit myself in the short time I had had to study this. And I hurried off to No. 10 for Harold's eve-of-Queen's-Speech reception, leaving him in high dudgeon.

Tuesday, 29 October. At PLP meeting on the Queen's Speech there were no great complaints from the rank and file. I whispered to Harold that I was in trouble over Halsbury and that we were faced with the possibility that he might come out against the twelve-month rule. I then went off to have a hilarious State Opening lunch with Ted and Joan Woodman[1] in the Lords, where we fought for food at the most lordly buffet it has ever been my hard work to queue for. I got back to my room to find an urgent message waiting for me: the PM had taken my remarks about Halsbury so seriously that he had called an urgent meeting at No. 10 to discuss the matter that afternoon. Michael, Malcolm Shepherd and Edmund Dell were waiting in Harold's study. I explained our problem and urged Harold to see Halsbury, who thought a lot of him. Everyone agreed with our analysis that Halsbury must be got to resign, but Harold insisted that I should see him first and that *he* should only be brought in as a last resort. So another dirty job lands on my plate.

Wednesday, 30 October. I went into the NEC not expecting any great drama. We discussed how to re-establish liaison between Party and Government, and decided to reconstitute the top-level Liaison Committee while keeping the Campaign Committee as well. I was getting restive as I had an official visit to pay at 2 pm and could see myself missing lunch again, but I felt I must stay for Mik's Motion on South Africa. This was couched in such offensive terms that I did not see how any Minister could vote for it, but I reckoned without the completely slap-happy, let's-have-the-best-of-both-worlds attitude of some of my colleagues. Mik then proceeded to move the resolution: 'That the National Executive Committee deplores the Government's action in holding the recent combined naval exercise with South Africa, which is directly contrary both to Party policy and to clear assurances given by the Government itself; and calls

[1] A family friend.

upon the Government to ensure that the Ministers concerned do not repeat this gross error.' There was a chorus of approval by Lena and co. I said that, as Jim couldn't be there that day, we should postpone the matter so that he could be asked for an explanation, at which Lena snapped, 'Why should we? He knew this item was coming up and it was up to him to be here.' I protested that Jim had already made a statement making it clear we were reviewing Simonstown in line with Party policy, whereupon Joan Lestor moved, and Judith seconded, that we should insert at the beginning that we welcomed this statement, before going on to the rest of the Motion. Even this geture of solidarity with the Government was too much for Lena: it would only weaken the resolution, she said. So the addition was put to the vote and only scraped through by eleven votes to ten, the Ministers voting for it, Mik against. (Mike, alas, wasn't there.) It was clear to me that most of them were hell-bent on having a row with the Government and nothing would stop them.

I plodded on, pointing out that we could have a Motion which reiterated Party policy without attacking the Government and so making it impossible for some of us to vote for it. Could we not delete the words 'the Government's action in holding', which would then leave us free to have time to sort out who was to blame? (I knew, for instance, that Harold and Jim had both been unaware that the visit was to take place, as the Cabinet as a whole had certainly been unaware.) This suggestion was rejected overwhelmingly (though, to do him justice, Wedgie voted for it), and Ron did not help by saying that he was sure the whole international as well as national Labour movement was waiting for us to denounce the visit in no uncertain terms. When the Motion was put to the vote I – and I believe Shirley – abstained, but the rest of the Ministers – Wedgie, Joan and Judith – voted for. As I got up to go I said angrily and audibly, 'I don't like this attempt to get the best of both worlds.' Walter and Wedgie joined me in the lift. Wedgie was seeking to justify himself as ingratiatingly as always. 'What we ought to do', he said to me pleasantly, 'is to distinguish between past actions of the Government for which we all share responsibility and *future* actions which we must retain the right to try and influence.' 'Exactly,' I replied, 'but that is just what the Motion did not do. I do not believe you had any choice but to abstain, as I did.' 'Well, duckie . . .' he shrugged. Walter, of course, was full of socialist righteousness.

Thursday, 31 October. Went into Cabinet without having seen my *Times*, so was surprised when Harold beckoned me upstairs to his study before the others came. He was blazing mad at the *Times* front-page story, with its usual line about how he had been 'snubbed' and 'defied' at the NEC yesterday. The story also reported my conciliatory role, so I was Harold's blue-eyed girl that morning. Harold said he wasn't going to tolerate this kind of behaviour; his authority would be completely undermined. I tried to head him off a show-down, but he wouldn't listen and marched into Cabinet room, turning officials out while he let fly at full blast. He was not going to accept such open defiance of collective responsibility, he declared. Some Ministers had better realize that they would have to choose between freedom on the NEC and responsibility to Cabinet. They couldn't have both. He would be in touch with those concerned.

Wedgie sat silent; so did I. Mike tried his usual emollient line. He was in favour of collective responsibility, he said, and agreed it was necessary to sustain it. This had always been Nye's view. But there were problems about the relationship between Cabinet and NEC which couldn't be dealt with properly in the way Harold suggested. His way 'could lead to a furious row'. He hadn't 'any simple solutions to offer' but thought we should have a meeting to discuss it. Harold replied that it was really a matter for the Liaison Committee with the NEC, while Jim gave us a gloomy bit of philosophizing about whether or not Ministers should be members of the NEC. He personally doubted whether it was possible to reconcile the two roles and was ready to come off the NEC himself. He hoped other Ministers would too. There were murmurs of disapproval at this from Mike and Wedgie; and so it was left, uneasily.

It was so late by the time we got on to the Defence Review that the meeting spilled over into the afternoon. But we did reach a decision on Simonstown. Roy [Mason] had put up a spirited defence of the agreement, but Harold and Jim were having none of it. The only problem was the legal one: there was no provision in the agreement for unilateral abrogation, so if we went ahead without discussing it first with South Africa we could be in breach of international law. We also wanted if possible to avoid retaliation from South Africa. So it was agreed that we should announce that we were entering into consultations with South Africa 'with a view to terminating the agreement'. Harold was determined to show the NEC that their great attack on the Government was unjustified.

One nasty little moment at the beginning of the afternoon meeting: Mike held up the *Evening Standard*, with headlines about how Harold had ticked off the recalcitrant Ministers that morning. He asked furiously who was responsible for this atrocious leak. Harold replied smoothly that it hadn't come from No. 10. Joe Haines, on his instructions, had merely told the lobby – who were clearly going to follow up the *Times* story – that the matter had been discussed at Cabinet, but nothing else. A likely story. I know my Harold and I bet he was determined to do a tit for tat. It is hard to blame him, though whether he is wise is another matter.

Friday, 1 November. Up early to try to knock out some headings for my contribution to the Queen's Speech debate. Jack Straw and Brian A-S. had put up long drafts for me, but I can't use other people's words, so I just took the essence out of them. It went swimmingly. I touched briefly on the NHS and our commitment to phase private beds out of NHS hospitals, adding, 'We shall act on that this session.' The House was empty, of course, and I went down to HCF thinking to myself that the debate wouldn't rate a line in tomorrow's press. To my astonishment my announcement was retailed on the news as a great new event and was accompanied by violent reactions from the BMA and the HCSA. David was interviewed about it on TV and did very well. I went contentedly to bed.

Saturday, 2 November. The papers are still echoing with my 'announcement'. Life really is very odd. I should have thought all I had done was to repeat the obvious.

Monday, 4 November. On the eight o'clock news I learned that consultants in the North-East have started to work to rule and were breathing fire and slaughter about me. Ted was obviously worried but I felt strangely relaxed, not to say euphoric: probably something to do with all the heavy gardening I had done. Digging always tones me up and sends me back feeling ready for anything. I told Ted things were turning out just as I wanted. First, a fight on this issue would put me back right where I wanted to be in the NEC stakes. Secondly, whatever the militant unions did now on the pay bed issue it would be the consultants who had started the industrial action. Ted seemed relieved at my cheeriness.

My mood held when I arrived at the office to find an atmosphere charged with menace. Henry Yellowlees wanted to see me urgently, so I said David must be there too. I have never seen Henry so white with anger. He is a very nice chap and not given to doing battle with me, but this time he was really steamed up. He said grimly that he agreed with some of what I was trying to do and had tried to help me to the best of his ability, but by my speech on Friday I had wrecked his credibility with the doctors and he thought he ought to have been consulted. Even David looked shaken. I said to Henry as gently as I could, though firmly, that I was extremely sorry if he had not known what I was going to say, but the fact was that we had all discussed at some length the sentence we should try to get into the Queen's Speech on this. The PM had ruled that the Queen's Speech was not the right place for it but had added that I should deal with it in the debate instead. This I had done, on the basis of a draft speech put up to me which I had assumed had been circulated to all concerned, including him. If it had not been, I apologized, but it was routine for this to be done and I just had not time myself to chase up Private Office. 'Do you realize I only got down to this speech at 5 am on Friday morning?' But I would instruct Norman to see that Henry was shown everything I proposed to say on the NHS in future.

Henry calmed down at once and the colour came back into his cheeks. Then Philip came in, even more beside himself than Henry had been. 'I must tell you, Secretary of State, that I believe the Health Service is in more danger than I have ever known.' I spoke soothingly to him too, but I made it clear by my manner that I was not alarmed. It is so obvious how against this change they all are and I can guess what councils of war they have been holding behind my back. David cheered up and said it was all his fault: he ought to have kept Henry in the picture. I congratulated David on the magnificent performance he had given on TV on Friday night.

We then went into a meeting about the next steps. I told them cheerfully that one could never make any real change in society without a row, but we must look at the things in our favour, as well as the dangers. One of the advantages for us was that it was only when there was a row that the public started to listen and I thought there would be a mass of feeling in the country on our side. The doctors had put themselves in the wrong by their hysterical reaction and even Philip seemed inclined to agree with this. David said dramatically that I had got to make up my mind on the crucial issue: how much time I was prepared to allow for the phasing out. We had fortunately circulated to the BMA his paper on the new forms of contract on Friday, before the storm broke. We spent a good deal of time discussing his second paper on the timing of phasing out. He wants us to allow at least two years, but has also worked out an ingenious plan for moving to 'consolidated' waiting lists by January, under which private patients would have to wait their turn with NHS patients in the medical priority queue. After some chat, with a circle of frightened officials around me, I said we would have to discuss this further at the ministerial lunch. In the meantime press office reported that the BBC were after me both for the nine o'clock news and *Nationwide*, on which they had arranged to interview some of the rebellious consultants. Peter Brown was all for my going on; Philip, typically, for my lying low. The more we discussed it the more convinced I became that I could not let our case go by default. And so it was arranged.

We spent the whole of our ministerial lunch on David's paper. Finally, after a protracted argument, we agreed we should not commit ourselves to a precise period of time in the document – 'Never give hostages to fortune,' I said – [and] decided to insert words like 'over a reasonable period, taking account of all the local circumstances'.

By the time I was on my way to Lime Grove my light-heartedness had come back. I felt almost frivolous. Who are these people to dictate that nothing shall be changed, even by a duly elected Government? To hell with them! I felt on top of the whole situation – and it showed. I knew I had never done a better performance and all the comments I got in the House afterwards confirmed it. I was helped by the fact that the interviewer was tough, knew his stuff and gave the two consultants from the North-East a gruelling time. Seeing these rather tatty creatures twisting and turning and changing their ground reinforced the sense of certainty I had had all day. I may fall flat on my face, but it is better to go down fighting than meekly submit to that autocratic lot.

Tuesday, 5 November. Among all this I had to brief myself for the great PESC discussion in Cabinet. Brian A-S. had drawn up an excellent paper for me to submit on the need to review our priorities in expenditure, which, with a little pepping-up by me, read very well. Denis, in opening the Cabinet discussion, made great play with the fact that the policies he had agreed would mean an increase in public expenditure of £3,000 million over the figure for 1975–76 which the Tories had published last December. He emphasized how much he was doing for me in the social security field and said he would need 'larger and faster cuts in defence' if he was to cover everything. On that basis he asked for general acceptance of the outcome of his bilateral deals with different Ministers. Harold called me next and I had not only to move my paper on priorities, but also, on the Chancellor's insistence, to present the paper embodying what he and I had agreed in the social security field. So naturally that made me look as if I had been very well treated (which was no doubt what he intended). Nonetheless I made an impassioned speech about how we had failed to rejig the Tory priorities (*e.g* law and order and roads), while our expenditure on the NHS was going to fall disastrously from 4.2 per cent growth annually under the Tories to 2.8 per cent under us. (I thought this must surely bring Mike up in arms on my behalf.)

Next came Judith, asking for an increase in overseas aid to a figure next year of £30 million. She needn't have worried: every speaker who followed her, Reg

P., Shirley, Roy Jenkins *et al.*, insisted that, whatever else suffered, overseas aid must go up to avoid world catastrophe. (What a difference from the miserable battles I had with Dick Crossman, Frank Cousins and the rest of them when I was at the Ministry of Overseas Development!) But I got no similar sympathy. Harold in summing up said that there was general support for the Chancellor, but Denis should now consider the detailed points and meet the Ministers concerned to see how far he could accommodate them. He should then bring back any unresolved points to Cabinet. I clutched at this life-line and bore it back to the office, where I instructed officials that I was not going to throw in the sponge. I told them to draft a very short list of the items that we should concentrate on trying to get.

In the afternoon I had to face Halsbury. I was dreading it, but it went like a dream. I think in fact he welcomed the whole business coming out into the open and warmed up gratefully when I told him I brought a message of 'affectionate sympathy' from the PM, who wanted him to know he still had confidence in him. Nevertheless, 'I made a mistake and I have got to pay the price,' chipped in Halsbury cheerfully. 'Of course I can see I ought to resign.' 'We *all* drop clangers,' I murmured, 'but . . .' Of course, he saw the point. So we parted, both feeling relieved.

At the 'H and W' dinner at Vitello's I insisted on talking about '*l'affaire* Simonstown', which has now become a *cause célèbre* in the movement. And of course Wedgie is the hero again. Harold has told me smugly that he has received letters from all three Ministers, which are 'entirely satisfactory', adding that Michael [Foot] had been 'most helpful'. But apparently Harold had had to send Joan's back for redrafting before he could accept it. I expect I have once again done myself damage with the Left by my attitude, but I can't help it. I really do find it intolerable for us to be heading down the road of splits again when they are so unnecessary.

Thursday, 7 November. In the afternoon I had to receive a deputation from the BMA, led by Dr Astley, steaming with fury at my House of Commons speech. To strengthen their attack they had even brought Dr Brian Lewis, Chairman of the militant HCSA, and his colleagues with them, dropping their traditional rivalry. I was my usual patient, reasonable self. I stuck by my right to phase out pay beds, but said I was certainly not going to rush into it without consultation, if only they were ready to discuss it. They kept bringing in their demand for a new contract as a test of whether the Government was prepared to safeguard their 'freedom and independence'. I kept telling them that the right place to discuss that was in the Owen working-party, where they could discuss private practice too. Would they get back into the working-party and try to speed things up? Eventually they simmered down. At the end of all this both Henry and Philip seemed to recover their nerve a bit.

Monday, 11 November. Budget Cabinet.[1] Denis gave a long, slow exposition in

[1] The main aim of Healey's autumn Budget was to improve the increasingly desperate financial position of companies. This he did by relaxing the Price Code and deferring corporation tax on profits arising from the abnormal stock appreciation which inflation had caused. For the rest he painted a daunting picture. Oil prices had now increased fivefold in just over a year. The $60 billion surplus in the hands of the oil-producing countries was

his best Ministry of Defence style. There was a shocked silence at first – whistles through the teeth when Denis said the borrowing requirement would have to be doubled, Peter in particular expressing dismay. Shirley and others commented that the Budget would be less severe than people were expecting, Jim describing it as 'agreeable'. Not when people realized how much prices would go up next year, retorted Denis. It struck me that the Treasury are back on their old track of trying to solve inflation by putting prices up. It has never worked and I think the result this time will be disastrous. Mike liked Denis's vigorous refusal to precipitate a world depression by being too deflationary. Mike meekly let pass Denis's claim that unemployment should be kept 'under a million'.

I launched into a great speech about how unwise it would be to assume that 'realistic fuel pricing' would solve our expenditure difficulties, as it would be essential to accompany this with rises in the incomes of the hardest hit. I reminded them that Denis had *not* managed to protect *all* families: we were doing nothing for the three million with one child. I wasn't just trying to grab more than my share, I said, because, if I had been consulted on tax changes, I might well have urged him not to give his £280 million higher tax allowances to pensioners who work; there were only 220,000 of them and the money could have gone to meet the cost of doing something for the first child. All this reinforced the case for the Anti-Poverty Strategy Committee which I had urged the PM to set up. (He refused to do so last summer.) We really must have the chance to influence tax policy at the formative stage, I continued. And what about the disabled with invalid vehicles, who were going to be faced with petrol at 75p per gallon? We must discuss all this at Chequers. There were murmurs of agreement. (When I got back to the office I discovered that No. 10 had phoned to ask us to work out something on petrol for the disabled. So I had really shaken them!)[1]

Halsbury has sent Harold his letter of resignation – exactly on the lines I

still depressing world trade. Unemployment and inflation were rising everywhere. With our trade deficit on current account running at about £4,000 million, he had begun to draw on the $2½ billion loan. Resources must be switched into investment and exports. The public sector borrowing requirement, estimated in the spring as amounting to £2,733 million for 1974–75, had doubled as a result of his July measures, wage increases and other cost increases. His proposed reliefs would push it up to the 'disturbingly large' figure of £6,300 million. To attempt to close it in the abnormal world circumstances would mean a fall in output and a massive increase in unemployment. Nonetheless it must not get out of hand. The increase in public expenditure must be held down to an annual average 2¾ per cent over the next four years in demand terms. Wage increases must be confined to what was needed to cover the cost of living, as urged by the TUC. Otherwise the Government would have to take other steps to curtail demand. Energy conservation was vital. To this end fuel prices must continue to go up to their economic level by eliminating subsidies to nationalized industries. He also proposed to increase VAT on petrol from 8 per cent to 25 per cent. The elderly, those on low incomes and families would be cushioned by another increase in pensions and benefits in April and an increase in family allowance. There would also be higher tax allowances for the elderly at a cost of £280 million in addition to another Christmas bonus. Meanwhile the Government was pressing ahead with a capital transfer tax to replace estate duty and with a new tax on the development value of land. The administrative problems of a wealth tax, outlined in the Green Paper, were being referred to a Select Committee. The proposal to lower the starting point for the investment income surcharge from £2,000 to £1,000, which the Commons had rejected in the summer, would be reintroduced, as would the retrospective tax relief on trade union provident funds. As a result of these measures he estimated that retail prices would rise by about 1½ per cent and output grow by 2 per cent a year. This would mean a 'modest' rise in unemployment, though the level would remain well below one million.

[1] We later decided to pay a £10 a year tax-free petrol allowance to all disabled drivers of invalid tricycles and Ministry-supplied cars.

urged on him. But No. 10 have agreed not to announce it until Halsbury has had a chance to tell his committee tomorrow. He has agreed to urge them to stay on, but Raymond Gedling (who is in close touch) thinks the committee has decided to breach the twelve-month rule anyway. They also have the right to go ahead and publish their report without a chairman (or so Gedling says), so our ploy to play for time by getting the new chairman to reopen the whole thing may not work. The BMA has now called outright for Halsbury's resignation (so he would have had to go anyway), but the HCSA is demanding the abolition of the whole review body. Personally I believe that might be a good thing: we will have to argue cash over the new contract if we are to have any chance of getting it accepted. But the Department is in a panic over the whole idea. Our troubles in this field are not over!

Tuesday, 12 November. First I was top order for Questions and they went swimmingly. They have no terrors for me any more. Then the Budget. At my office meeting we cleared my letter to the Chancellor: my dogged attempt to get something more for the Health Service out of the PESC round. I told officials it was outrageous that the Chancellor should be able unilaterally to give £280 million away in tax reliefs to the elderly, without even a word to me about the social priorities – and even Dick Bourton agreed.

Wednesday, 13 November. My main job today was my massive uprating statement in the House,[1] followed by a press conference. I prepared meticulously all morning in the office, as I always do on these occasions, pepping up Peter's press statement, checking on this fact and that, thinking up new pitfalls. To my relief there was to be no TV, so I could concentrate on the substance without worrying whether my hair was okay and went into the House feeling relaxed. Our side roared its approval of my statement and I had the refreshing experience of hearing Frank [Allaun] pay a glowing public tribute to me. I got over tricky points like the non-announcement of the child allowance scheme without disaster.

Thursday, 14 November. I was just leaving for Cabinet when Pam rang from the office. Someone had phoned from the Katherine Knapp home to say Mother had been taken ill; would I phone them. It was the nice deputy matron who answered. Mother had had difficulty with her breathing and they had sent for the doctor. She had given her a pill and she seemed better, but I ought to know. Arranging for a message to be got to me as soon as the doctor had been, I went into Cabinet feeling *distrait* and telling the office to cancel my afternoon engagements anyway, so I could go down.

Cabinet over, I hurried to the German Embassy for a private lunch with the Ambassador: the usual preparatory lunch for an official visit to the country

[1] I spelt out in detail the Chancellor's announcement that long-term pensions and benefits would be increased by about 15½ per cent the following April – eight and a half months after the last increase – and that there would be a further increase in December 1975. Short-term benefits would be increased by about 14 per cent. Family allowance would go up by 50 pence at the same time and would be extended to the first child under our new scheme 'in due course'.

concerned.[1] The Ambassador was accompanied merely by his labour attaché (who has worked hard for the reciprocal agreement I shall be going to sign). I was flanked by Norman and by my official who had negotiated the deal. The conversation at lunch ranged over wider fields. I seized the opportunity to warn the Ambassador about the mood of the NEC about the impending speech of his Chancellor to our Party conference.[2] I had that morning heard on the radio the report of comments [Helmut] Schmidt had made about what he was going to say to conference: how he was going to warn Britain that we would be cutting our own throats if we decided to leave the EEC. The Ambassador's excellent wine made me fluent, and I told him earnestly that his Chancellor faced a walk-out – or at best a slow handclap – if he tried in any way to lecture us about Britain's attitude to EEC. He had been invited as a *fraternal* delegate, not as a head of government. The best thing he could do from the point of view of his own objective of keeping us in the Market was to talk to us as a socialist to fellow-socialists. I waxed quite eloquent, adding, 'Why should I, as an anti-marketeer, give you such excellent pro-Market advice?' We all laughed, but the Ambassador was clearly impressed and told me that everything I had said would be conveyed to Schmidt.

After lunch I headed for Penn, picking up my brother Jimmie on the way. At the home, as we walked towards Mother's room, we heard singing. She was sitting bolt upright in bed, her cheeks pink, looking about sixty years old instead of ninety-one. 'It's my Barbara,' she said as I went in and instantly demanded to know when she was coming home. She didn't want to be in bed; there was nothing wrong with her. Edna [my driver] was enchanted with her – as they clearly all were. But when I phoned the doctor he said she had had a pulmonary embolism; it might recur at any time and one day it would be too much for her. Little Mother! Reconciled as I am to her approaching death, the sharp prospect of it brings my childhood right back into my consciousness and with it my sense of her as a mother: endearing, much loved and totally exasperating. Time is the oddest thing. There have been many moments in the last few years when it hasn't seemed to exist as a barrier of distance and when the past has been as vivid as the present. Perhaps I too am approaching the threshold. Into nothingness? No, back in a circle to where I began.

Sunday, 17 November. Chequers park looked beautifully peaceful as we arrived for the all-day strategy meeting, but the network of policemen showed that security was there in full force. As we came in by the side gate several policemen came out of the lodge to ask our names and search the boot. Inside the house it was clear that Heath's favourite internal decorator had been at work again (he must have spent a mint of money), but this time she had made an improvement by stripping the dark oak panelling (which I had always found

[1] I had arranged to visit my opposite number in the Federal Republic, Herr Arendt, Minister of Labour and Social Welfare, in order to sign a reciprocal agreement which would give all UK visitors to West Germany free urgent medical treatment under the German sickness scheme. This was necessary because the German scheme, unlike the NHS, did not cover the self-employed.

[2] The NEC had decided to invite Helmut Schmidt, leader of the German Social Democratic Party and Chancellor of the Federal Republic, to deliver fraternal greetings on behalf of all international delegates to our Party conference. Owing to the General Election our conference had been postponed from October to November.

oppressive) in the great hall. I liked the light wood, the careful display of china treasures and the urns of flowers in every corner of hall and landings, but it made everything look so much more *feminine* – another clue to Heath's character? Every room I went into seemed to have been lavishly repapered; *we* would never have dreamed of such extravagance. I was shown into the little bedroom I had stayed in that time in 1969 when Harold had brought me back secretly from Italy and memories came flooding back about that traumatic confrontation with Jack, Hughie and Vic. So near and yet so far – near in time, only five years ago, yet a century away in knowledge and experience gained in the meantime. The Cabinet was very largely the same then as it is now, yet we could not have been more different in approach.

This mood continued as we met in the library. I was proud of the success of my suggestion that we should all put in papers ranging over the whole field of strategy. Most Ministers had done so. They were succinct, concrete, very revealing and undoubtedly helped to concentrate our minds. As the discussion unfolded, revealing problems of almost insurmountable gloom, I had the quiet feeling that so much expertise, sense and conviction of purpose *must* enable us somehow to win through.

During the lunch interval Harold seized the opportunity to talk to me about Jack Ashley. He was tickled pink with his own cunning, taking me aside to say that he had to appoint a Privy Councillor and, having promoted Brian O'Malley to PC as the senior Minister of State, he was left with only Roy Hattersley or Bill Rodgers,[1] and he wasn't going to elevate either of *them*. So he had had a brilliant idea: guess who? As I puzzled he said triumphantly, 'Jack Ashley.' I was dumbfounded with admiration and told him how delighted I was. Denis also took the chance to tell me, in the light of my references to the need for an anti-poverty strategy, 'I was wrong about my tax concession to the elderly in the Budget. I'll admit it to you but I won't do so publicly.' This is what I like about Denis – his sudden bits of fairness and frankness.

Monday, 18 November. At Bonn officialdom was there in force to greet us. Nicholas Henderson, our Ambassador, rode in the car with me to the house of Mr Hibbert, Minister at the Embassy, where I was to stay, and I spent the journey reiterating my story about how disastrous it would be if Helmut Schmidt were to make a propaganda speech about the Common Market when he addressed the Labour Party Conference next week. Henderson listened attentively, but these diplomats are clearly out of touch with Party feeling on this issue: they just can't see what anyone should worry about if the German Chancellor makes a pro-Market speech to us. Henderson apologized profusely about the fact that he could not put me up himself as he was deeply committed to other engagements outside Bonn during my stay. That did not worry me at all – protocol is an obsession of small minds. And the Minister's house turned out to be lavish enough in all conscience, with a luxurious bedroom for me

[1] Roy Hattersley was then Minister of State at the Foreign and Commonwealth Office. W. T. (Bill) Rodgers, MP for Teesside, Stockton, was Minister of State for Defence. Both men were prominent members of the Gaitskellite wing of the Party and Bill Rodgers, in particular, had been an effective organizer on behalf of Hugh Gaitskell and later Roy Jenkins and consistently hostile to Harold. Both were appointed to the Cabinet in September 1976 in Jim Callaghan's first major reshuffle.

overlooking the woods to the Rhine and the Peterberg. They told me ten times that that was where Chamberlain had talked to Hitler.

Up early for the signing ceremony with Herr Arendt. Arendt was waiting for me in his office with all the charm I had been told I could expect from him: 'the most popular member of the Government'. He is a rather impishly avuncular figure, an ex-miner with no heavy pretensions to administrative genius, but he has, I suspect, made a number of breakthroughs in his field of labour and social welfare.

The signing was quite a moving affair. I have never signed an international agreement before – with the TV cameras flashing, the carefully prepared duplicated document, the flanking signatures by ambassadors, the solemn exchange of signed volumes. 'This will go into the treaty archives of the Foreign Office,' said Henderson picking up our copy. Then Arendt and I shook hands for the photographers and someone brought champagne – at 9.30 am!

Wednesday, 20 November. Cabinet this morning was for the purpose of allowing us a more relaxed discussion of the Defence Review, in keeping with Harold's promise not to rush us over some of the difficult issues. The main rub came over nuclear policy, on which Harold was clearly expecting trouble. He needn't have worried: Mike's comments were so muted as to be almost token. Harold prepared the way carefully by saying that, though we would keep Polaris and carry out certain improvements at a cost of £24 million, there would be no 'Poseidonization and no MIRV'.[1] The nuclear element represented less than 2 per cent of the defence budget but it gave us a 'unique entrée to US thinking' and it was important for our diplomatic influence for us to remain a nuclear power. Germany, for instance, would not like it if France were the only nuclear power in Europe. And he stressed that the policy was in line with the Manifesto and that the decision on it in Defence and Overseas Policy Committee of the Cabinet had been 'unanimous'. Other people took the same line, Jim echoing the importance of a nuclear capability for our world influence ('In other words, we must not go naked into the conference chamber,'[2] Eric whispered impishly to me). Mike came in almost hesitantly. He admitted Harold was trying to keep within the compromise of the Manifesto on this, though we were committed to get rid of the nuclear bases. 'We shall proceed to negotiate this within the overall disarmament talks,' Harold countered promptly. Mike then said that he remained of the view that we should rid ourselves of nuclear weapons, but recognized that he was in a minority and so would not press the matter. Peter and Wedgie said nothing.

I was more emphatic than Mike. It was not only that I was a nuclear disarmer, I said, but I thought the decision was self-contradictory within the context of our own defence strategy. What we were saying was that we needed nuclear weapons in order to exercise influence, yet intended to let them

[1] 'Poseidonization' meant the costly conversion of existing Polaris submarines to carry the Poseidon missile developed by the United States. Poseidon carries ten to fourteen MIRV [multiple independently-targeted re-entry vehicles] warheads each of 50 kilotons.

[2] A reference to one of the most famous sentences in Labour Party history, uttered by Aneurin Bevan, supporter of the Campaign for Nuclear Disarmament, when at the Labour Party Conference in 1957 he opposed a resolution calling on the British Government to ban the bomb. The gripping story of how Bevan shattered his left-wing friends is told by Michael Foot in his biography.

diminish in credibility by refusing to keep them up to date. This exercise in defence futility was not cheap: £24 million a year over ten years meant £240 million, 'and I could use that myself'. ('So could I,' parried Tony C. as usual.) The debate then died away. Harold summed up cheerfully, saying that Cabinet, with a few of us expressing dissent, had endorsed the policy and he added unctuously that he was extremely grateful for the constructive spirit in which those who disagreed with the policy had put their views. He then took himself off, looking pleased with himself, as well he might. The fact is that the spirit of the Campaign for Nuclear Disarmament no longer walks the land.

Denis has turned down my last desperate effort to get another £16 million for the NHS, which is needed to restore the Tory cuts last December. He has also rejected my plea for £1 million more for community homes and £7.8 million more for a limited scheme we have worked out to give family allowance to first children in one-parent families at least. His letter was positively nasty in tone and at the meeting of officials which I had hastily called Dick Bourton sat smugly with an 'I told you so' look on his face. 'I am afraid your letter has made things more difficult, Secretary of State,' he said. 'Treasury officials have noticeably hardened their attitude to us.' I ignored this and said that our only hope now was to concentrate on getting a scratch scheme of family allowance for first children, without which I thought we would be in deep political trouble. David agreed sadly that we must accept Denis's ruling on the NHS (after all, he has given us £35 million) and I asked Brian A-S. and the rest to draft a last-effort paper for PESC Cabinet next week, concentrating purely on our special family allowance scheme.

A quick visit to the Disablement Income Group sherry party, where to my surprise and delight Mary Greaves [a former Honorary President of DIG] thanked me for all we were doing for the disabled. 'Such a breakthrough.' I hurried back to the House. In the division lobby Joel came up to greet me affectionately. 'You've just sent me a horrid reply,' I pouted, tweaking his ear. 'You should never have sent your letter,' he replied with a poor show of severity. 'All I want is £7.8 million to save this Government from catastrophe,' I pleaded, nestling up to him. 'Just £7.8 million.' 'Just £7.8 million,' he echoed, appealing to those who were around. 'She's a terrible woman. We give her everything. I can promise nothing. I'll see, I'll see.'

Thursday, 21 November. Second Reading of our Uprating Bill[1] today and I haven't even started to prepare my speech. Officials have produced their usual well-meaning and factually thorough draft, but it isn't in language I could use. But first I have to get through Cabinet. Fred has come back from Brussels, flushed with what he considers a satisfactory deal over beef and sugar, but which some of us can see as the thin edge of the wedge of capitulation over one of our major negotiating objectives: the transformation of the CAP. The discussion confirmed my worst fears.

My Second Reading speech went without a hitch. I felt relaxed and I think I sounded it. It was a bore having to rush and change for the Lancaster House

[1] The Social Security Benefits Bill embodied the increase in pensions and benefits we had announced. It also provided for two new types of disablement benefit: the non-contributory invalidity pension and the invalid care allowance.

dinner for the Standing Committee of doctors of the EEC, but I was hostess. At first, with the debate on our Bill still going on, I was tempted to ask David Owen to deputize for me. Then I thought this was the worst moment to appear to give a slight – however unintentionally – to the BMA. Besides I am uneasy about what David is up to over the consultants' new contract. I think he has some exceptionally good and radical ideas, but he chops and changes them too easily. I certainly intend to keep an eye on things. So I ironed my gold dress in the Lady Members' room and climbed into it hurriedly.

In the event I was extremely glad I had made the effort. Walpole Lewin, this year's President of the Standing Committee, was delighted I had gone and even Derek Stevenson was affable. Henry Yellowlees just said, with those speaking eyes of his, 'Thank you, Secretary of State.' Chatting to Lewin over dinner, I found him much more compatible than I had ever done before. At one point he said to me with conspiratorial mateyness, 'I think we are going to solve our little problem, Secretary of State; we *must* do, because otherwise the consequences for the NHS could be disastrous.' I wondered what David had been up to: near agreement, indeed! After the guests had left, with profuse handshaking, David and his wife, Ted and I stood chatting for a few moments. I always get on well with David; he has a disarming way of suddenly grinning at himself. Jack says David treats him well too, but not the people lower down the line. But once home my suspicions flared up again. Waiting in my box was a long paper on the consultants' contract with a note from Norman: could I please clear it that night, as it had to be circulated at once in the weekend boxes so that it could be dealt with by the Economic Policy Committee of the Cabinet on Monday. The consultants had threatened that, if they did not get a firm offer next Wednesday, they would take industrial action. I glanced at it hurriedly and saw that it seemed to be weakening considerably the additional inducements we wanted to offer the whole-time consultants in the NHS. I threw it in my box. 'Clear it tonight? Not on your life!' I, too, intend to have it in my 'weekend box' – that euphemism for ten or twelve hours' work. If civil servants can get enough knotty problems into the 'weekend box' they feel they have done their job and can go home with a clear conscience for two days' rest.

Friday, 22 November. To my train to Doncaster for Brian O'Malley's annual dinner at Rotherham. It is hard to have to go these long distances after a heavy week, but I felt I owed it to him and I am very fond of him. In the event I enjoyed myself thoroughly. From the word go I felt among friends. The dinner was excellent, the attendance a record. Brian saw I had plenty of excellent wine and my tiredness seemed to vanish. I hadn't prepared a word of my speech, but when I got to my feet I felt on top of my form. I played with them, made them laugh and made them cheer. Then instead of going round solemnly shaking hands with everyone, I swept Brian on to the dance floor and jived round the room joining every group of dancers in turn. I insisted on going into the kitchen and shaking hands with the girls there, wanting to buy them a drink, which the Mayor then insisted on buying them instead. (Anyway, they got it.) Back in the Mayor's parlour the local Party chairman said to me, 'You know, if you hadn't been a politician you would have made a great actress.' That is what Peter Brown always says to me. I know what they mean. It isn't that I play a part; it is just that every now and then everything clicks into place and I identify myself emotionally with my audience. I love them, want to hug them, teach them, inspire them and carry them with me along the road of euphoric faith which, after all these years, I still tread.

Monday, 25 November. Had to get up to town early for a Cabinet – yet another, but the only one this week because of Party conference. When we turned to PESC Denis said he had concluded his bilateral talks with individual Ministers satisfactorily and the strategy was now sewn up, including the cutting of nationalized industry subsidies. Only two issues remained outstanding: defence and my paper.[1] Barbara had come forward with a new proposition at the last minute and, although the amount asked for in 1976–77 was small, he had accepted that the proposal might – 'I only say might' – push up the following year's figure by £100 million. ('No!' I called out.) This could only be met by calling on the contingency reserve and he thought it would be better to wait until next year before deciding anything as we would then know better whether we could accommodate it. ('That will be too late administratively,' I called out again.) Denis ploughed on with some details of the bilateral talks, stressing that Cabinet must face the facts not only that nationalized industry prices would go up, but that his proposals involved an increase of school meal charges of 3 pence each year from April 1975. Reg nodded approvingly at that. All this played into my hands.

Harold then called on me to introduce my paper, 'as briefly as possible, please'. I refused to be flustered and made a telling speech, quoting how our expenditure on family support in real terms was planned to *decrease* steadily up to 1978–79. I said that the matter could not wait, as I was under pressure in the House . . . At this point Tony C. interjected sneeringly, 'We are all under pressure in the House.' I saw cold red and retorted quietly, 'I should be glad, Tony, if you would contain your hostility till the end of my speech for a change.' Everyone laughed. I then repeated, 'I am under pressure in the House to announce our proposals for the introduction of the child allowances scheme and I must do so soon.' I pointed out that the decision to raise prices deliberately *before* we had extended family allowances to the first child meant that we were absorbing all the family allowance increase almost as soon as it was granted and making the one-child family catastrophically poorer. I recognized the expenditure restraints: that was why I had been casting round desperately for a way in which we could at modest cost hold our political front and salve our consciences. Harold then went round the table and every Minister in turn explained what sacrifices he had made. (Judith wasn't there because she had won her battle on overseas aid and I am glad.) Tony C. continued his elegant spite. Barbara had talked about pressures in the House, he said, but the greatest pressure was on housing. Anyway he was against having any more ad-hoc measures to relieve poverty until we had a proper system of social monitoring. Shirley's promised great battle on my behalf dissolved into a few wet words. She was worried about the withdrawal of subsidies until we had made some better provision for the children of poor families, but if it couldn't

[1] I had put a paper to Cabinet appealing against Denis's refusal to let me introduce a family allowance for the first child in one-parent families, known in the department as 'Special FAM'.

be done in my way it should be done by taxation (*e.g.* by treating maintenance allowances as earned rather than unearned income). Perhaps Denis could look at this in his next Budget. Mike tried valiantly to support me but was obviously ignorant of the minutiae. Peter and Wedgie were silent.

Denis then came back with a promise that he would see what he could do in his next Budget. I could not contain myself at this, so Harold called me in again. I said, passionately this time, that our whole social policy was based on the fact that relief through the tax system did not reach the poorest who most needed help. I did not object to social monitoring; indeed, I had asked months ago for the setting up of an Anti-Poverty Strategy Committee of Ministers. It had been refused. Everyone knew that tax reliefs were a loss of revenue that meant a loss of money for public expenditure. Reg had drawn up his programme on purely educational grounds, as he was entitled to do, but he had agreed to help pay for it by putting up the price of school meals. The odium of this did not fall on him: it all landed on my plate to try and meet the social consequences. I think this drew blood, for Denis came in again. He welcomed the idea of setting up an Anti-Poverty Strategy Committee [and] he assured me that when he referred to being willing to consider dealing with this in his next Budget he meant that he would consider introducing my idea then. 'It takes over a year to prepare these things,' I moaned. It was Harold who came to my rescue. If he had really 'summed up' he would have ruled that Cabinet thought a decision should be delayed. Not a bit of it. He said the view of Cabinet was that we should consider anti-poverty measures as a whole. He would set up the proposed committee immediately. My proposal should be the first item referred to it and the committee should report on it before Christmas. Denis and Joel got very restive at this. Surely Cabinet had agreed they should go ahead with the Public Expenditure report on the agreed lines? 'But you won't publish before Christmas,' said Harold cheerfully. They hummed and hawed a bit and then Denis agreed that, if this item were to be added, they could 'fudge' the White Paper sufficiently. And so I had won, to Tony C.'s obvious chagrin. I went back to the office to gloat over Dick Bourton.

We also had another office meeting on the consultants' contract, this time about our paper for EC(P) [Economic Policy Committee of Cabinet]. David was once again nibbling at the possibility of our surrendering the whole-timers' differential. He said that without a concession on this the talks would break down: he is obviously feeling browbeaten by some of the militants. I said, 'So be it', and reminded him yet again, 'I, too, have my breaking-point.' David vacillates a great deal, sometimes pressing the consultants' case for them and talking gloomily about terrible 'disruption' in the NHS unless we give way, then, later, suddenly and inexplicably perking up and saying he thinks a break is inevitable anyway. The profession have sanctions in the blood and must get them out of their system. I warned him that we were going to have great difficulty with colleagues over the new contract he was so cheerfully advocating and that our only hope of getting it accepted was if it was clearly seen to achieve our social ends and not merely as a straight pay increase. Jack Straw and Peter Brown, who seem to be in ideological cahoots these days, sat nodding at me approvingly from the end of the table. I sent David and the boys away to put a new draft paper up to me.

Tuesday, 26 November. The week's work is disrupted by the delayed Party conference. Brief it may be going to be, but it is playing havoc with my Departmental work.

Wednesday, 27 November. Up at dawn to have my hair dressed before going to Central Hall [where the conference was held]. Result: a charming photo of Harold and me on the platform. Edna, my wonderful friendly driver, told me that Pat [John Silkin's driver and her flat-mate] had said Harold and I were obviously playing footsy under the table. It was to be my brightest moment of the conference. I had to sit on the platform wading my way through a succession of boxes sent by a devoted office. Either Wedgie has less work than I have or he has different priorities. As I arrived for every session at the platform entrance, struggling upstairs with two or three of those ton-weights of work, he was out in front, mingling with delegates as they arrived, slapping them on the back, speaking at every fringe meeting there was. His ambition grows by the hour. I believe it is so dominating that it could be his undoing.

Thursday, 28 November. I was a bit nervous about the NEC election results, though I thought I must surely survive after my record at DHSS. I did, albeit without distinction – slipping a place and coming behind Mik. The old Tribune pull – and indifference to me – is still clearly working. But the big surprise to some (not to me) was that Wedgie went to the top, pushing Mike to second place. As the cheers greeted this, Harold turned and drawled at me, 'He is becoming quite a young hero, and I think it is a pity.' His ambition was in both our minds. Shirley has plummeted from top to bottom of the women's section: the price she is paying for that declaration about the Common Market she made during the Election. Okay, so why shouldn't she pay the price of her honest beliefs too?

'*L'affaire* Simonstown' came up in the afternoon. The great campaign to defend the three defiant Ministers was a bit of a damp squib, largely because Harold had had the genius to propose that one of them, Joan Lestor, should answer the debate.[1] She was pretty nervous about it, being a conscientious lass and not prepared to exploit the opportunity for her personal self-promotion. When she was muttering to me what a difficult speech it was going to be to make, I suggested she tell conference that there could hardly be any serious split between Government and NEC because it was Harold himself who had suggested that she should reply. This she did. She did pretty well, her manner as always being excellent.

Saturday, 30 November. Helmut Schmidt's day. When he arrived on the platform to sit next to Harold, I thought how handsome and relaxed he looked. His speech was masterly: it was a joy to hear how skilfully he dodged all the pitfalls and how cleverly he played on those emotions in his audience which

[1] An emergency resolution was moved by the Liverpool Toxteth Constituency Labour Party 'supporting those NEC members who censured the Government over the South Africa manœuvres' and calling for the Party's policy on South Africa to be implemented in full. Joan Lestor accepted it with reservations on behalf of the NEC, welcoming Jim Callaghan's statement on the need to end the Simonstown agreement. The resolution was carried without dissent.

were most likely to be favourable to him. He followed the blueprint I had given him via the Ambassador, line by line and embellished it brilliantly, even managing to incorporate the socialist appeal to 'solidarity' into his throw-away sentence about our membership of the Common Market. Above all he had them rolling in the aisles and once again I was surprised to realize what a good sense of humour Germans have. As I listened I felt almost guilty. If I had not sent all those warnings he might have boobed. Instead, I had helped him to strike one of the most effective blows yet for our membership.

My own speech on Friday morning was received politely but tepidly. I am nonplussed by my continuing failure to get over in conference. I had never felt more relaxed and the content was good, even if predictable. Ted said my voice sounded thin – not an accusation that is usually made. Perhaps it is that those blasted fixed mikes are too high for me. Whatever the reason, I left conference feeling depressed. Wedgie, of course, got an ovation for a rousing speech. It is no good my being rousing about anti-poverty strategy when I know what a struggle I have to get every penny out of Cabinet. And I could not be demagogic about pay beds, with the negotiations with the consultants in such a delicate state. On the contrary, I chose my words with great care: I was not going to have Henry Yellowlees complaining that I had rocked the boat. I suppose that in the end I am, and always shall be, more interested in results than in striking popular attitudes.

Monday, 2 December. Up early so that I could visit Mother in hospital on my way to the office. She has had to have a clot in her leg removed. She lay crooning in her bed and greeted me. 'It's my Barbara.' Then she sang to me in a high voice all the songs she said Dad had sung to her. When I whispered to her, embarrassed, 'You will wake everyone up,' she retorted, 'They are not asleep and they *like* my singing.' When I went out of her cubicle to talk to the other patients in the ward they assured me it was so. 'Sometimes we join in. She's marvellous.' Sister and nurse were very touched when I repeated what Mother had said to me: 'They are all so kind to me – just like the sister I never had.' I hope and pray she will die with dignity and not be reduced by a stroke into a vegetable.

At the office I went into a succession of meetings on subjects which had been piling up while I was at conference. First on the democratization of the NHS, on which David has been conducting a running war with officials. Philip, of course, is pretending that there is no difference of approach except on timing, but it was soon clear that he doesn't want any changes at all. I supported David in his view that we must build up the operational strength and independence of the Area Health Authorities and progressively reduce the RHAs to a strategic planning role in which they will become little more than the regional arm of the DHSS. I agreed with him too that we must get away from the present position in which the money which is available for the NHS is distributed automatically among the regions on the basis of a weighting formula which takes little account of our national redistributive priorities. I liked his idea that we should go for workers' participation on AHAs in a big way, in order to reassure the doctors that they were not merely being placed under local authorities. David is a curious mixture. He has excellent ideas but less good follow-through.

Next into another of our mass meetings with officials to discuss the latest state of play over the consultants' contract. About twenty officials troop in on these occasions and sit round like vultures, waiting to gobble every word. Why they all have to turn up I'll never know, for they seldom contribute anything. We went in detail through the paper I am putting to EC(P)[1] tomorrow and once again I had to spell out what I thought we had conceded to the consultants and made it clear to David what were *my* breaking-points: *e.g.* the need to maintain the differential for the whole-timers and to redistribute the old distinction awards on a basis that would reward service to the NHS. David went through his usual gloomy gamut about how the consultants would break tomorrow, etc. I told him I had always thought they would break, that we would have to carry the argument into the field of public debate and that I thought this would be no bad thing. Peter [Brown] and Jack Straw sat at the end of the table nodding their approval vigorously.

It was afternoon before we got down to the discussion of my speech for this evening's half-day debate on the NHS initiated by the Tories. It went smoothly until we got to the point where I was supposed to admit frankly that we faced a *reduction* in capital expenditure on the NHS in later years. I protested about being pitchforked into such a traumatic announcement ahead of a general orchestration of announcements by other Ministers and again Peter and Jack were on my side. But the alternative of making a cataclysmic statement to the House one afternoon soon was equally unpalatable. We went round and round the problem for two hours. Finally I suggested an alternative form of wording and told them, 'Geoffrey Howe won't be expecting this and, as I shall be following him, he won't have a chance to comment effectively. Yet we shall have cleared the way for discussion with the health authorities.' And so we

[1] David Owen and I had come to the conclusion that it would benefit the NHS, as well as being fairer to consultants, to accept the idea of a 'closed' contract. We proposed that this should consist of a basic ten sessions (half days) per week with additional payments for regular extra sessions, for emergency work, for domiciliary and exceptional consultations and for administrative and educational duties outside the normal working hours. Whole-timers, who would still be barred from private practice, would all have a basic ten session commitment plus the right to extra payments if they worked excessive hours, as many of them did. In addition they would be paid a 'complete commitment' allowance, equivalent to the existing 2/11ths differential. Consultants still wishing to practise privately could either retain their existing contracts or move to a new contract consisting of the same ten sessions at the same rate of pay as the whole-timers less the differential, but expressed as '8 plus 2' so that a consultant whose private practice workload was in danger of prejudicing his NHS work could be asked by the health authority to drop one or two sessions with a corresponding reduction in pay. If he did, he would not be eligible for our proposed new system of career supplements to replace the secret 'merit award' system as these awards ran out. These supplements would be of two types: a service supplement administered by the health authorities to reward exceptionally responsible and dedicated service to the NHS and a medical progress supplement awarded on professional advice to those making a major medical contribution to the NHS, including research and teaching. In our paper to EC(P) we justified this restructuring of salaries as a strengthening of the NHS as it would encourage the whole-timers we needed to man up the unpopular specialities and neglected areas. At the same time it would enable us to define more closely the part-timers' contractual obligation to the NHS. Under the present arrangements they had been free to fit in their private work at times that suited their private patients rather than the NHS. Though many of them worked devotedly for their NHS patients, in practice the health authorities had no control over this. But it would clearly be wrong to introduce extra payments for extra work if the basic commitment had not been clearly spelt out. As we put it in our document, the new standard contract of ten basic sessions would normally constitute a 'five-day Monday to Friday working week, from 9 am to 5 pm, including meal times'. It was this that particularly enraged the consultants' negotiators, who wanted to move away from an open-ended, professional-type contract without accepting the disciplines of an industrial-type closed one.

broke up. I did some frantic last-minute writing, snatching the last pages from the typists just before reaching the House at 7 pm.[1]

In the event, my speech went swimmingly. It made Howe's hotch-potch of unrelated comments look cheap. As I said scornfully, Howe had been 'long on gloom and short on remedies'. But of course the House was nearly empty and I had paid a big price in nervous energy. The evening crowned by a pleasant meal with Brian O'Malley. He insisted on buying me a Christmas dinner and a nice bottle of wine and talked with an affection that has been even more deepened by my visit to Rotherham. This stimulating intercourse of minds, warmed by our deep friendship, is the great consolation for all the stresses, strains and incredible rush of work we go through.

Tuesday, 3 December. Woke after a heavy sleep, still exhausted, to face my meeting of EC(P) on the consultants' contract. David swears that if we don't get clearance for our offer this morning he faces a walk-out of the Joint Working Party this afternoon. Officials had briefed us that we were not going to face serious opposition from my colleagues, but they had clearly not done their job properly because the reality turned out to be very different. Mike was in the chair as the custodian of pay policy and, as one colleague after another denounced the proposals as a violent breach of the Social Contract, he refused to come to my help. Albert Booth, speaking for Mike's Department, was the most devastating critic of all. To hear him denounce the continuation of a differential in favour of a whole-timer would have made Nye Bevan turn in his grave. I pointed out he was arguing on the same lines as the most militant consultants were and that I had been fighting for the retention of the differential as vital to our whole policy. All Mike could do was to pronounce gravely that my far-reaching proposals must go to Cabinet.

David was plunged in gloom as Edmund Dell tore us to shreds on behalf of the Treasury. To pay the consultants overtime would lead both to massive pay increases and to repercussions everywhere, he declared. Mike was obviously biased against me and as I pleaded in vain that the new contract would enormously strengthen the NHS (1) by enabling the health authorities to ensure that consultants really did work the hours they were committed to, (2) by meeting genuine grievances of the consultants and (3) by giving long-overdue incentives to the men who worked in under-staffed hospitals and less popular specialities, I thought ironically that Nye never met the obstruction from the Attlee Cabinet that I was meeting from the Department of Employment under Mike. I wonder if Mike one day will write the story of Barbara's battle to bring Nye's reforms up to date with as much approval as he wrote about Nye's compromises!

Back at the office we had a council of war. I refused to be gloomy, pointing out that one seldom got away with a major new idea on the first round. We could yet win in Cabinet. Our trouble was that we were under such pressure

[1] I pointed out that some £450 million additional money had already been made available to the NHS in the current year to cover rising costs, including pay increases for nurses and others, and I announced that next year the Government had decided to restore some of the December cuts of the previous Government. (£19 million on capital and £10 million on revenue.) But I added: 'I must warn the House that the outlook for the next few years is not encouraging. As things now stand it will not be possible to maintain this increase in expenditure in real terms over the next few years.' (Hansard 2.12.74, col. 1214).

from the consultants time-wise that we had not had enough elbow room to win colleagues round gradually. David went into his meeting of the Joint Working Party expecting to be torn apart for not having produced a firm offer, but came out positively cheerful. The negotiators had apparently accepted his explanation that the Government had not yet had enough time to consider their ideas and had agreed to postpone industrial action, though they wanted a decision on 12 December – or else.

Wednesday, 11 December. Another meeting with the office on the consultants' contract. We discussed what we should do if Cabinet decided tomorrow on a cut-off of all salary increases at £10,000 a year. They thought even the consultants could be got to wear it, provided it applied to absolutely everyone. This is, of course, my line. I have said all along, and still believe, that it is Toryism, not socialism, to hold public sector salaries down while doing nothing at all about the much vaster incomes in private industry. David has sent holding replies to the Joint Working Party negotiators, telling them the Government needed more time to consider the new demands they are now making, but they have made it clear they will expect an answer tomorrow. If I can't get a decision from Cabinet by the time he meets them, then heaven knows what they will do. David reported that they were now asking for extra payment for merely being 'on call', while some of them, like Lewis, were insisting that there should be a joint study of a complete 'items of service' contract and he had promised this. I told him that I should have enough difficulty getting through Cabinet what we had already agreed; to add anything else would just wreck all our hopes. As for a piece-work type contract, the idea was inconceivable and we should do nothing to encourage it. He is, in fact, reconciled to there being a break, whatever we do – and he almost welcomes it. It is clear that nothing less than complete capitulation by the Government on all their points will do the trick.

At my request Jack Straw has been working out a 'maximum incomes' policy and has been in touch with Derek Robinson and others. He is entirely with me on this and has beavered away, coming out in the end in favour of 100 per cent tax on increases above a certain level of income. He really is an invaluable help to me.

Thursday, 12 December. This is the day on which I have to do battle over top salaries. This was supposed to be today's priority in Cabinet, but as usual Harold allowed it to be pushed to bottom place while other matters were argued interminably, among them Harold's report on his EEC summit,[1] for which Mike was waiting avidly, clutching a copy of the communiqué in his

[1] On 9 and 10 December a meeting of heads of government of the nine members of the Community and their Foreign Ministers had been held in Paris on the initiative of the French President, Giscard d'Estaing. The communiqué which had been published (Cmnd 5830) was impregnated with determination to move to greater European unity. On economic and monetary union the Heads of Government affirmed 'that in this field their will has not weakened and their objective has not changed'. Mr Tindemans, Prime Minister of Belgium, was invited to submit an urgent report on European union. They called for the renunciation of the veto in the Council of Ministers, for direct elections to the European Assembly as soon as possible and for an extension of the Assembly's 'competence'. They decided to activate the European Regional Development Fund from January 1975, allocating Italy and Britain the largest shares, and held out the prospect of adjustments in Britain's contribution to the Community Budget – one of our renegotiation points. Harold Wilson had signed the communiqué, inserting merely token references to the fact that renegotiations were still going on.

hand. It went on for nearly an hour and a half and Harold was at his worst – wordy, defensive and repetitive. On inflation, Schmidt had stressed that unemployment was the worst danger. He was planning massive reflation. Harold also gave us a sketch of himself embattled against Giscard, who had organized the whole thing so abominably that we couldn't even get texts translated properly. At last Harold got to the Common Market renegotiations and I had to strain to catch his rambling résumés. It is a familiar technique: when Harold reduces everything to a boring, and almost bored, low key, I reach for my critical faculties. He had, he said, quoted the Manifesto extensively. There had been proposals on what to do about the Community's institutions, but he had 'washed his hands' of them, because until we decided whether to stay in, we were not involved. In any case, they were 'on ice for twelve months'. On the budget it had been 'very tough indeed'. We faced French intransigence.

Finally, a formula had been agreed about a 'corrective mechanism' for our contribution to the budget based on our line about making it a percentage of GNP. Even Schmidt had been difficult here. The discussion on the Regional Fund had been a 'squalid wrangle'. Eventually they had worked out a three-year temporary plan which gave us 28 per cent in return for a 15 per cent contribution, but he had remained detached about all this because, until we decided to go in, it didn't affect us. 'I was more concerned to get freedom to use our own national aids.' This was one of the aspects of the problem of sovereignty. The second was fiscal policy. The move to greater surrender of sovereignty was much less than he had feared. There was, for example, to be no harmonization of VAT. On industrial matters, he had reminded them sharply that there could be no interference with public ownership. But the fact was that economic and monetary union was 'as dead as mutton'. True, they had insisted on putting some words in the communiqué which retained it as their 'ultimate goal', but 'I made it clear it was a goal we do not share'. He had let it go because it was like the form of words always included in disarmament agreements – about complete disarmament being the ultimate goal. But it did not mean any more than that.

But Mike was not to be put off so easily. 'I am', he said gravely, 'deeply disturbed about some aspects of the communiqué.' There had been serious concessions on the issue of parliamentary sovereignty. None of this had ever been discussed in Cabinet. It was no use Harold saying that [economic and monetary union] wasn't *our goal*: 'the communiqué says the exact opposite'. Some of us had sent Harold a memo saying that Cabinet must face up to these issues. Before anyone else could speak Harold jumped in again with another long justification of what he had done. He repeated, *ad nauseam*, that he had not swerved one inch from agreed policy; on every issue Cabinet's position was 'totally reserved'. At this I said quietly, 'If we reserved our position on all these points, ought not the communiqué to have said so?' Even Eric murmured agreement on this. Harold floundered, saying there was a passage indicating that he had made our position clear in the discussions. He searched through the communiqué and at last produced a few wet words which obviously did not meet my point. Wedgie then came in equally simply: 'Is the communiqué the policy of HMG, so that we are all bound by it?' Harold snapped back, 'We have accepted the communiqué and reserved our position.'

Peter was much more dramatic. Having read the communiqué, he said, 'I can only register my own feelings of absolute shock. Our credibility in the country has been greatly undermined. The relaxation of the veto strikes at the heart of parliamentary sovereignty.' Harold got really tetchy at this. 'I resent the suggestions that Jim and I are little innocents abroad. What I did was explicitly in terms of the Manifesto.' It was clearly time for some of the pro-Europeans to come to his defence and they duly did. First Harold Lever and then Shirley said they thought he had done very well and hastened to assure the anti-marketeers that there was a lot in what Harold had told us that they regretted, but they had to accept the compromise position of Cabinet, etc. Harold came in yet again; he talks us down by sheer repetition and it works. By this time it was turned noon and the two crucial items on the agenda had not been touched. I was furious; it looks as though Harold is reverting to his old garrulity: a sure sign he knows he is on a collision course with some of us. (We used to get the same thing over his talks with Ian Smith.) Mike said stubbornly that it was a pity we hadn't had this discussion before the summit talks. An urgent discussion about how we should handle the referendum issue was necessary. Roy tried to demur at this but Harold overruled him. There *were* some aspects of the referendum we should discuss and he would arrange this early in the New Year.

At last we turned to top salaries. Mike has put in a paper saying that the proposed increases (particularly for chairmen of nationalized industries) would wreck the Social Contract and demanding a cut-off for increases at income levels of £10,000 a year. He has also ferociously attacked my proposals for the consultants' contract. Gradually, a consensus emerged in favour of a 'severe staging' for top-salary people, plus an announcement that we were freezing our own salaries for twelve months and some action in private industry. Harold then produced a draft staging document he had hurriedly prepared.

By this time it was 1.30 pm. Harold turned to my item on the consultants' contract: could it be postponed yet again? In despair – because I certainly didn't want the new contract discussed in that atmosphere – I said I would try to hold the lions at bay for another week, though please could I be top item, really top item, next time? Everyone laughed, Harold said yes, and we broke up.

At a hurriedly convened meeting later that afternoon, I told David Owen and officials just what had happened and said we must put a supplementary paper on the new contract to Cabinet. After all, we don't mind so much having consultants' increases staged if everyone else is being staged. The essential point is to establish the principle of the new contract. But once again I had to warn David that we could make no more concessions to the consultants – some of whom will not be satisfied until they have got complete payment by items of service established, with every difference between the whole-timer and the private practitioner ironed out. David seems to be edging inch by inch towards acceptance of the latter, but I would rather resign than accept it.

Monday, 16 December. Harold has circulated his draft of the statement on top salaries. Said David when he saw it, 'This is the end of the Social Contract.' I was furious at its tone and contents. It certainly was much more muted than

I thought Cabinet had intended and it totally failed to reflect our determination to produce a policy for curbing increases in the private sector, pending the production of the Royal Commission report on the *level* of top salaries. It was mercifully accompanied by a memo from Mike, saying that he was disturbed by the decision to go ahead with the announcement of our policy on top salaries before consulting the TUC and urging that this should be reconsidered.

Tuesday, 17 December. Mike on the phone, full of anger about top salaries. Harold had replied to his Minute by saying it was too late to postpone a decision as he was seeing the national staff side that afternoon. So Mike had hurried over to see him and had got a promise that the matter could be reopened at Thursday's Cabinet and that no announcement would be made meanwhile. Would I back him up with another Minute? I said of course.

Wednesday, 18 December. At the NEC Mike passed me a rough scribble of a letter to Harold which, he hissed, he hadn't sent yet. It expressed his deep concern that it transpired that Harold was not, after all, willing to reopen the top salaries issue completely on Thursday – just some consideration of the amount of the staging. In the letter Mike said that, if the announcement went ahead, the Social Contract would be in ruins and he would have no alternative but to resign. My eyebrows shot up and he looked unhappy and hesitant: obviously he is deeply uncertain about what to do. I scribbled an alternative sentence for him, 'If this goes ahead I believe it will make my job impossible', which, I pointed out, would hold a threat without committing him. He wavered and put the sheet away, so whether he sent it or not I do not know.

Thursday, 19 December. Harold called Cabinet for the unusually early hour of 9.30 am and, true to his promise, had put my consultants' new contract item at the head of the agenda. Much good did it do me! In fact, once again, it was only reached well after noon because the first two and a half hours were spent on top salaries. Whether Mike sent that resignation threat or not I do not know, but his pressures (and mine) had had an effect, because Harold began by saying that Mike had made such a strong case for reopening the matter that he, Harold, was going to break all the rules and allow it. Unfortunately for Mike, though, he was really too late. Harold had seen the [national] staff side, given them the broad outline of the proposed staging and so was in an impregnable position to fend off any great change. But he suggested we should vary our decision as follows: on nationalized industry salaries we should say that we were going to await the Diamond Report[1] before considering their increases; on the civil service we should 'honour our agreement' about comparability.

[1] One of the ideas to come out of the discussions in the Liaison Committee with the TUC before the February Election was the setting up of a Royal Commission on the distribution of income and wealth. The unions wanted to spotlight the unequal distribution of wealth in Britain and the way in which top incomes managed to avoid the restraints of incomes policy through such means as expense accounts, income from investments, capital gains and top-hat pensions schemes. The Royal Commission had been duly set up in August 1974 under the chairmanship of Lord Diamond, former Labour MP for Gloucester and Chief Secretary to the Treasury under Harold Wilson from 1964 to 1970. He had been made a peer in 1970. The Commission's terms of reference were to inquire into 'such matters concerning the distribution of personal incomes, both earned and unearned, and wealth, as may be referred to it by the Government'.

When at last we turned to my item the atmosphere could not have been worse for me. Cabinet was irritable and listened impatiently. But I ploughed on, telling them that unless we reached a decision that morning, I would face a walk-out of consultants the following day. And I spelt out the advantages of the new contract to the NHS as well as to some very hard-worked and underpaid men. Edmund Dell once again attacked my proposals viciously, unfairly and unscrupulously. I was, he said, wanting to pay consultants for work that had been unpaid before. The rest of them looked as though they neither understood nor cared. Then Mike came in. There were great dangers in the new contract, he said. It was hardly the right time to introduce an expensive new pay structure for a highly paid group. My heart sank. I thought I was finished. Then he said reluctantly (obviously ignoring his Departmental brief) that if, however, Barbara felt this was the only way she could deal with the difficult situation she faced, perhaps they ought to allow me to go ahead on the understanding that Cabinet was not bound by the findings of the Review Body on the cost and reserved the right to modify them in line with any other decisions we were taking over salaries.

Harold seized on this lead. Cabinet, he thought, was willing to agree with this, but I must clear with colleagues my Department's evidence to the Review Body on the new contract and Cabinet would wish to examine this critically. The outcome would depend on the decisions we took on higher salaries generally. Tony C. then said nastily that there had been no provision made in PESC for the cost of phasing out pay beds (with which Edmund had made great play) and he hoped that no steps would be taken in this direction until the point had been cleared up as to how it was to be paid for. Harold ruled that there should be no progress on this until Cabinet had discussed the timing in the light of developments on the new contract. So my hands are tied on every point! But I was relieved to get anything at all.

Back at the office I reported the position to another of those mass meetings of officials. David said he did not think it would have been possible to reach agreement in the Joint Working Party anyway. He thought the negotiators would reject the contract, so we should be ready to issue it after the meeting I am to have with them tomorrow and should make arrangements to see that every one of the 11,000 consultants got a copy. There would be disruption for some weeks, but he really didn't think our offer was too bad and he was not too pessimistic about the ultimate outcome. I sent them away to draft the necessary documents.

Friday, 20 December. Just before my meeting with the Joint Working Party [JWP] was due to start, Henry suggested it would be a good idea for me to see the independent members of the working-party, who, in general, supported me. In came three of them: Hunter, McColl and Dr Revans.[1] They told me they thought it was a good contract. The chances of the profession as a whole accepting it were 60–40; in the case of the negotiating committee it would be the

[1] Dr Robert Hunter (later Lord Hunter), Vice-Chancellor of Birmingham University; Professor Ian McColl, Consultant Surgeon to Guy's Hospital; Dr John Revans (later Sir John), then Regional Medical Officer, Wessex Regional Health Authority.

other way round. As academics, they particularly welcomed my clear rejection of the principle of a 'fee for item of service' contract, which they said would ruin the NHS. David smiled at me and said generously, 'You see, you were right.'

There were some fifty people round the table in the big meeting room [for my meeting with the JWP]. Already, before they knew I was coming to the meeting, they had informed the Department that the Joint Working Party was bringing with it Lewin and Stevenson of the BMA (not members of the JWP), the leader of the HCSA and the Secretary of the British Dental Association [BDA]. So clearly they were not visualizing an ordinary negotiating meeting of the JWP. In fact it was clear they had come prepared for a showdown. They had already threatened to take industrial action unless the Government announced a 'full statement of its position' on 20 December and they had come along prepared to walk out. We had made a copy of the contract proposals available to them half an hour before the meeting was due to start. I walked in, expecting to be able to explain the proposals quietly to them. Instead I found them lined up for war.

I asked them to take [the proposals] away and study them, discuss them with their members and then come back and talk them over with me after Christmas. In the meantime obviously I must release the proposals to the press. It would be fatal if they were to be leaked in garbled form. But I wasn't asking for their answer then. We had, I ploughed on, made arrangements for copies of the contract to be sent to all consultants, so that they could have an informed discussion with them. There was a fussy explosion from Derek Stevenson: really, was I proposing to appeal to their members over their heads? Outrageous! I said I thought they would have welcomed their members getting the facts on which to base a judgment. However, I did not wish to undermine their authority in any way. I was therefore prepared to arrange for them to send the copies out under the BMA's name at government expense.

I pleaded with them: 'Look at how far we have moved from what you originally feared. There was talk at first that I was going to abolish private practice and impose a whole-time service. The contract shows how different is the reality.' 'Yes,' said Lewis viciously. 'What Mrs Castle is saying now is very different from what she was saying earlier: it is much worse.' Something snapped in me and I said coldly, 'If that is to be your attitude there is nothing for us to do but to submit this matter to public debate.' And so we broke up and I went off to see the press, ending up in the ITN studio at 10 pm.

It was past 11 pm when Edna and I got down to HCF. At least the consultants are not due to strike till 2 January! I am determined to put the family Christmas first meanwhile.

Friday, 27 December. Despite its inauspicious beginning this has been one of the happiest Christmases we have ever had.

1975

Thursday, 2 January. My hopes of two days' rest have been shattered. Last night the *Today* programme was on to me for a recording for this morning – the consultants' D-day [on sanctions] – and Ian Gillis has told me I shall be in great demand all day by the media. So I get up early and hurry to London for a succession of appearances, starting with the *Jimmy Young Show* and ending with Llew Gardner late at night.

The Llew Gardner show was quite arduous: it went on for an hour and I felt I was beginning to flag at the end of that busy day. But the sweet make-up girl had done her usual brilliant job on me so all was well. At the end of the recording Llew said to me wryly, 'Game, set and match to Blackburn: three goals to nil.' When I got home I found Ted glued to the set, following every word avidly. He was thrilled with it.

Monday, 6 January. Back to a crowded day of work at the office. David is very proud of the job he has done with the press over the consultants' contract – and rightly. Certainly, it has produced a most helpful leader in the *Observer* – of all places. 'I headed off Nora Beloff anyway,' he chuckled. My long talk on the phone with John Fryer of the *Sunday Times* has also brought results – but not in their editorial comment, which is particularly snide about me. I believe I am in for a sustained 'it is time Barbara retired' campaign in the press. It is not that I am noticeably older than Jim Callaghan or Mike Foot: merely that I am a woman and so more vulnerable to the 'surely she's getting old?' kind of talk.

I arrived at Home Policy Committee of the NEC without anticipating anything significant: I had even forgotten we had to elect a new chairman. I had assumed that Jim would continue in the job, but he wasn't there, being on his tour of Africa. The meeting was sparsely attended and when Ron asked for nominations for chairman Frank Allaun promptly nominated Wedgie. John Chalmers seconded. Denis Healey equally promptly said he thought a Minister ought not to be in the chair and he was backed by Shirley. Denis then proposed a succession of people, who refused. And so, by default, Wedgie went unopposed into the chair. I think Frank Allaun would have got the job if he had played his cards less precipitately.

Tuesday, 7 January. Got to the International Committee in good time to make sure Mik got the chairmanship. I need not have worried: he was not opposed. I am amused to read the great press headlines about Wedgie's election yesterday: the *Mail* excelled itself with 'Benn's New Power Grab', while the *Mirror* talked of his 'triumph'. In fact, if the press were a little more literate, and not given to what Nye called 'the politics of demonology', they would realize that there is growing up in the NEC a new coalition between Right and Left behind the doctrine that Ministers should take a back place on the NEC. I think we have managed to defuse the Government–NEC confrontation because Harold is managing to keep a close liaison with the trade unions.

I hurried from Transport House to St James's Square for a meeting with Mike to discuss what I could say to the GPs when they come to see me tomorrow. There is no doubt we shall be faced with sanctions unless we can satisfy them that, their interim pay claim having been kiboshed by their Review Body, they will be sure to get their full award in April.[1] Of course, Mike hummed and hawed about how we could not give any group of workers an 'absolute guarantee', but he was obviously sympathetic and to my relief volunteered a form of words to the effect that we would not treat them any worse than we had treated the civil servants under the Top Salaries Report. This means that no doctor will have his increase staged, as those on salaries above £13,000 will, because he doesn't get that kind of money. I had myself told Gedling we should press for that formula. [Mike's] most reassuring words were that he had no doubt that the doctors would have to get their money in April. I as good as intimated to him that I would resign if the doctors were picked on for a unilateral application of an unspoken incomes policy.

Back at the office we spent several hours preparing for the other showdown we face tomorrow: the unexpected ultimatum from the junior hospital doctors.[2] David was very good as we worked out our line. But he and I both became tense as we turned to the consultants' contract. It is clear that David is edging me remorselessly towards a concession on career supplements; he even wanted me to volunteer it. This I refused to do. Eventually we agreed that we would in due course [accept] the Royal Colleges ['offer to use them] as our mediators.

Wednesday, 8 January. A most successful day. First the junior hospital doctors turned out to be nice, young, reasonable chaps, though one of them was obviously learning to be tough. They were primarily concerned with the fact that officials had fobbed them off on an exact date for their new contract. They melted when I said there had been a genuine misunderstanding – that I was *not* trying to stall on the date and that we should proceed to discuss the most feasible administrative timetable for introducing it. Nonetheless, it became clear as we proceeded that the crucial point was not so much the date as the fact that they wanted to produce a definition of the new contract that would enable them to go to the Review Body for some kind of payment for the hours they work between forty and eighty, instead of giving the second set of forty hours free as they do now. David had wisely warned me beforehand that I could not afford to be put in the position of appearing to argue that they must work eighty hours for their basic pay, for both David and I (and the TUC) think that their

[1] Despite Lord Halsbury's resignation as chairman, the DDRB had pressed ahead with its examination of the doctors' and dentists' demand for an 18 per cent interim pay increase. It found (Cmnd 5849) that the case for special treatment in breach of the twelve-month rule had not been made out, but gave warning of its 'firm intention' to recommend substantial catching-up increases at the annual review in April.

[2] They had told the press that, unless I gave them a written assurance that they could have a forty-hour week from July 1975, they would start an immediate work-to-rule.

present hours are outrageous. But all we conceded was that we knew they would go to the Review Body arguing for a hefty overtime rate, while we would go and argue for a modest one. They merely grinned at this and cheerfully agreed to insert a paragraph into our joint communiqué saying that each side would make its separate approach. But, as always, it took ages to agree on the communiqué.[1]

All this meant I was late for the GPS, who eventually came trooping in, looking very serious. Tony Keable-Elliott was their sole spokesman and he made out an impressive, reasonable but firm case. In reply I spelt out, slowly and carefully, the problem that no government could ever give them 'cast-iron guarantees' about accepting the report of their Review Body. But I went on to detail the assurances we had worked out with Mike, reading the words he had agreed. They were obviously impressed. They asked to retire, but Henry was sure we had done the trick. And so it proved, though Tony warned me sternly that he could not guarantee what his chaps would do when he reported back tomorrow.

At 10 pm I collected four weary members of my staff into my car, which meant I had to sit on Jack's knee. In this undignified posture we toured London, dropping them off at Victoria and King's Cross and finally arriving at home. I took Jack and Edna upstairs to have a celebratory drink with Ted. I love these dear people, and, despite my tiredness, an unaccustomed euphoria came welling up in me.

Thursday, 9 January. At Cabinet everyone greeted me warmly: 'You are having a dreadful time.' Harold congratulated me on yesterday's victories. 'I said when I read them that you were pursuing Marlborough's strategy.' (I haven't had time to read up my Marlborough.) He congratulated me in Cabinet too. Wedgie, as always, was warmly adulatory. I am sorry if I think it is a bit calculated, but he certainly does it very well, making one feel successful and wanted just when one needs it most. Perhaps there is a human justification for the formula. I really ought to try it more.

On the way to St Christopher's Hospice[2] for a long-promised ministerial visit, Henry travelled with me in the car and reported mysterious cloak-and-dagger overtures from Astley and Stevenson of the BMA. They wanted to see him – very hush-hush. Was it all right for him to go? I said, of course. My settlements with the juniors and the GPS have obviously had an effect. The *Evening News* also carried a story that David Owen is to see the BMA secretly with new proposals, and Henry explained elaborately that Astley had been trying to speak to David on the phone. I think David rather fancies the idea, but I have told him sharply that there must be no private enterprise. All *démarches*

[1] We announced that from July 1975 each junior doctor would be issued with a personal contract stating explicitly the 'units of medical time' for which he had contracted to be on duty. The contract, effective from October, would be based on a standard working week of forty hours with a further commitment to meet the needs of the Health Service at the discretion of the employing authority. The implications for the juniors' pay would be dealt with by the Review Body in April, with each side giving separate evidence as to what the implications should be.

[2] An independent hospital specializing in terminal care. Beds were available for NHS patients through contractual arrangements with the regional authority.

vis-à-vis the consultants must be discussed and agreed collectively, otherwise we shall find ourselves in a mess.

The people at St Christopher's were overwhelmed that I had come despite all the pressures on me. I told them – and meant it – that it was a refreshment to get out into the field and see them at work. They are the most marvellous bunch of people I have ever met. Dr Saunders particularly impressed me. As I toured the wards I could see for myself what their extraordinarily sensitive approach to terminal illness means to the patients. This is medicine as it ought to be – patient care at its most loving and comprehensive. It took some of the nasty taste of the dispute out of my mouth. It was late when I got on my night sleeper to Blackburn.

Friday, 10 January. Norman phoned to report the outcome of Henry's talk with Astley. Apparently they want to know whether I will agree to modify the existing contract instead of proceeding with the new one and have set out four additions they want to make to it, including payment for extra sessions. Henry, it appears, is inclined to nibble at this, but Philip has said emphatically that he doesn't see how I could possibly accept. I agree with him. I can see us being inched into a trap, ending up with getting the worst of both worlds. Of course it would suit the consultants to stick to their 'open-ended' contract, with the lack of supervision it entails, if they can get overtime on top of it.

Saturday, 11 January. I am quite enjoying the Party's annual local government conference at Manchester. My group's discussion this afternoon on the NHS and the reorganization of local government went very well, though I was irritated to find the press, radio and cameras hanging on my every word. No doubt they are hoping I shall let drop some indiscretion about the dispute with the consultants. But I kept mum. David brought with him the draft of Monday's statement on the dispute which I have volunteered to make to the House in order to forestall Geoffrey Howe (who has written me yet another letter and who is obviously trying to set himself up as a go-between). I tell David I will take the statement to bed with me and we agree to meet at 9.15 in the morning to finalize it.

Sunday, 12 January. David Owen and I met early, a little bleary-eyed after a late night of social activities. I had rewritten a large part of the statement and we agreed the final points. In a Minute to me outlining Astley's proposals for amending the existing contract,[1] David had commented that this was a very dangerous development, but, typically, this morning he seemed to be wavering. 'I think you will have to concede extra sessions,' he said at one point. I headed him off this sternly by quoting his own Minute at him. It was his turn to take one group session of the conference and he spoke extremely well. He is an able lad with a lot of good radical instincts, but he needs stiffening.

Monday, 13 January. It was a mad rush to get to the House in time for the

[1] Dr Astley wanted extra payments for family planning sessions, for sickness and exceptional leave, for 'out of hours' work and for being on call to be included in the existing contract without any of the reforms we wanted to see.

statement and I was a bit breathless, but it was a walk-over.[1] Geoffrey Howe made a mess of things, and, while choosing my words carefully so as not to exacerbate the situation, I didn't give an inch. Ted, in the gallery as usual, was delighted. He said my case sounded so reasonable. But there is no doubt that opinion among the consultants is hardening. They are voting against the contract overwhelmingly, even though many of them are drawing the line at sanctions. We had another office discussion as to what Henry might say to Astley and Stevenson. I told him to send them a copy of my statement and to tell them I would be glad to meet them again to deal with any points in it they wanted clarified. We also discussed how we could clear up the widespread misunderstandings that have arisen and decided that the first thing was to see the three presidents of the Royal Colleges tomorrow and see how they could help. We are anxious now to try and save the new contract, because otherwise we could be manœuvred into concessions on the existing one that would leave us with all the disadvantages and none of the advantages.

Tuesday, 14 January. Ted Short presided over Legislation Committee like a headmaster, giving everyone a bad report because they had not got their legislation ready on time. When it came to me I said innocently that our two Bills (the new Pensions Scheme and Child Benefits) were ready, or almost so. Ted, who had been getting ready to tell me I couldn't have the Child Benefits Bill this session, said primly, 'Barbara has got us over a barrel again.' I protested that I couldn't help it if I was a good girl and had done my homework, at which everyone laughed and Bob Mellish said, 'There is only one answer to Barbara: why don't we give her her own parliament?' Ted said we would have to get the approval of Cabinet, but I bet I win.

The meeting with the presidents of the three Royal Colleges on the consultants' dispute was a poor do: they were so terrified of being accused by the BMA of selling out the profession, as it was alleged they had done to Nye in 1948. All they did was to say I must emphasize my willingness to negotiate. My statement yesterday had been helpful, but they feared it would not be enough to get the sanctions called off at the CCHMS meeting on Thursday.[2] They would not, however, agree to our issuing a joint statement after the meeting, as a vehicle enabling me to repeat my willingness to talk. Afterwards Norman said to me how shocked he had been at their feebleness; here they were, the leaders of the profession, frightened even to say 'Boo' to the BMA goose. But Henry has had his further meeting with Stevenson and his deputy, Gullick. They were, he said, impressed by my statement yesterday, but wanted a number of points 'clarified'. We decided that I should send a written reply which they can use at their meeting on Thursday.

I was flagging by now, after a fortnight's non-stop pressure, so I went home to bacon and egg and an early bed.

[1] I was able to report my settlements with the GPs and the junior doctors. On the consultants' dispute I reiterated that the Government had no wish to impose a new contract on them and was willing to ask the Review Body to cost the new contract before the consultants committed themselves to it.

[2] The Central Committee for Hospital Medical Services is a committee of the BMA which looks after the interests of senior medical hospital staff. It consists of eighty-five members elected by all consultants in the NHS on a regional basis and its main job is to determine policy. Proposals discussed in the Joint Negotiating Committee are usually referred to it for approval.

Wednesday, 15 January. A hurried hair-do and into the car, finishing dressing as I went along to Lancaster House for the inaugural reception of International Women's Year. Rather to my surprise it went like a bomb; Princess Alexandra was utterly charming, with a softness and naturalness her mother never had. She worked very hard at questioning and talking to everybody. Harold came along with Mary [Wilson] and Marcia [Lady Falkender] in tow and stayed to the very end, obviously enjoying himself. Jim was there, and I was particularly touched that Len Murray should accompany Marie Patterson and Ethel Chipchase.[1] The press interest was greater than I'd expected and I did endless radio interviews. By the time it was all over I had no time for lunch. I swallowed three of Edna's digestive biscuits before hurrying to the department for six TV interviews for foreign parts. I could have done without this Women's Year lark at this particular time. The irony of it is that I have always found these women's issues a bore, but, having taken on this job as co-chairman of the Women's National Commission at Harold's request, I intend to make a go of it. Mary Wilson said to me, as we escorted her and Harold from the reception, that she was always telling Harold's office they ought to make more use of her. 'With the Leader of the Opposition a bachelor we have an advantage we ought to exploit, but they won't listen to me.'

David and Henry came over with the draft of their letter to Stevenson. I thought it was very good but changed the emphasis here and there, making it warmer in tone and eliminating anything that sounded a bit truculent.[2] Afterwards, David told me Henry had been tickled pink by my attitude and now had his tail up, having been very depressed yesterday. 'The trouble is', said David, grinning in his handsome, boyish way, 'that the office don't understand our rows. They don't realize that we can argue like that but that basically we agree.' I replied that if we had had someone like George Godber,[3] who would have argued ferociously with us, we should not have had to conduct so much of the argument between ourselves. He took the point: 'Yes, I shouldn't then have felt I had to put so much of the medical point of view.' He chuckled and said, 'I've been talking to John Morris and we both of us agree that you . . .' He let the sentence trail off, as he often does. 'But a year-and-a-half of you is about as much . . .' He grinned affectionately. In the division lobby I tackled John Morris: 'So you and David have been swopping notes about how terrible it is to work for me,' I teased. 'Not a bit of it,' he laughed. 'It was marvellous. You taught me everything. One-and-a-half-years? I managed two-and-a-half, but I was nearly dead at the end of it. I have never worked so hard in all my life.'

[1] Respectively Chairman and President of the TUC and Secretary of the Women's Advisory Committee of the TUC.

[2] I stressed yet again that I was anxious not to hold up the consultants' pay review due in April on the basis of their existing contract. If, however, we could agree the general outlines of the new contract over the following few weeks, I would ask the Review Body to put some financial figures on it at the same time so that the consultants could decide whether they wanted to go ahead with it. But I insisted that the differential was not negotiable. I said I could not enter into detailed negotiations while sanctions were continuing, but was willing for there to be an 'initial clarification meeting' within the Joint Negotiating Committee. Stevenson replied at once accepting the offer.

[3] Sir George Godber, a formidable personality, had been Chief Medical Officer at the Department from 1960 until he retired in 1973.

Thursday, 16 January. A short night's sleep and then into Cabinet. We have had a good press for our women's reception yesterday and now Italian TV want a picture of my Ted washing up! They say it will encourage Italian women to strike a blow for equality. The *Evening Standard* said that yesterday I looked as though I had just come from Elizabeth Arden's hands. If only they knew! I haven't had time to sew on a button, or get enough sleep, let alone have a face massage. The gossip writer said, 'How does she keep so young?' Answer: because I am fully extended, intellectually and emotionally, all the time; yet, when I get down to HCF to the dogs, the garden, the woods and my home, I can revert to nature in five minutes flat. I love my dual personality life and both sides are equally important to me.

Before Cabinet Bob said to me, 'Ask Ted Short to read out the letter he has had from John Stonehouse; it is a scream.' But in the event Ted was abrupt about the message he had received and said he was not at liberty to disclose it. The British Consul-General was chasing Stonehouse and his lawyer round Australia, but it seemed inevitable that a Select Committee would have to be appointed to get him expelled from Parliament.[1] Wedgie went up in my estimation when he said he hoped we would proceed cautiously. He himself was one of the few people who had been expelled from the House of Commons and he knew how complicated the matter could be. On what grounds were we doing it? Not because of any crime Stonehouse had committed: that had not been proved. His long absence? Other MPs had absented themselves for longer periods (Harold Lever ducked self-consciously at that one!). He thought we should show some compassion for a sick man and that someone should go out to Australia to try to talk to him. When Harold argued that we could get Stonehouse for contempt of the House in passing himself off as dead, Elwyn nervously counselled caution. But Harold insisted that a Select Committee could take into account all Wedgie's points. 'Then we must be careful not to appoint a hanging jury,' I said and Roy backed me on this. Harold summed up that Ted should talk to the Speaker and to the Opposition and keep us in touch as to how we should proceed.

Finally to the Channel Tunnel. Personally I am relieved that Tony Crosland has decided we can't go ahead. This is not only anti-Common Market prejudice. It is a kind of earthy feeling that an island is an island and should not be violated. Certainly I am convinced that the building of a tunnel would do something profound to the national attitude – and not certainly for the better. There is too much facile access being built into the modern world. Something should remain difficult to achieve. Typically, Tony would have preferred to have kept the scheme ticking over without commitment, but the reaction of the companies has made that impossible. So the crunch has come. Jim's was the only discordant voice. We were, he said, putting ourselves in a very difficult position with the French: 'They will use this kind of thing to damage us.' He

[1] Some two months earlier John Stonehouse had disappeared, faking his drowning on Miami beach. He was eventually discovered in Australia, which he had entered on a false passport. He claimed that he was being blackmailed and had suffered a 'brainstorm', but later it emerged that he was in financial difficulties. Pressures had been put on him to resign his seat and in his letter to Ted Short he had agreed to do so. Later he changed his mind and the problem of what to do about the absent MP was to plague the Commons for months. It was finally settled in August 1976, by his trial and imprisonment on eighteen charges involving theft and false pretences. He then resigned his seat and Privy Councillorship.

was worried about Tony's proposal to handle it 'in this brusque way'. From his diplomatic experience he warned us that we should always 'as far as possible avoid getting into the position of being the *demandeur* with the French: they will screw you to the limit.' I thought this was a very revealing comment from someone who is now working hard to get us into Europe. It was Tony who pointed out that the French had far more to gain from the project than we had: they did not face the need for a highly expensive rail link. Fate had made us the *demandeurs* once again and Cabinet agreed we must be ready to face paying the price of blame. The theory is that the project can be reopened in five to ten years' time, but I don't think Tony is fooled by this.

Friday, 17 January. An all-day meeting at Chequers of the Ministerial Steering Committee on Devolution. The implementation of the White Paper has raised so many difficulties that Harold has widely decided we should all get away and concentrate our minds on solving them. The papers we had to read were a foot deep. First we had a Second Reading debate over the whole field which, despite the fact that Harold said we were all now bound by the White Paper, enabled the doubters over the whole business (Roy J., Reg and Elwyn) to air their views again. The debate crystallized round the question of timing. They none of them liked Ted Short's haste. Tony C. was all for procrastinating: other options ought to be considered.

Wedgie gave us another of his apocalyptic summaries: the drive for devolution, he said, was 'part of the collapse of confidence of the English Establishment'. The trade unions knew where the reality lay: they didn't want devolution to destroy a centralized trade union movement. 'Industrial democracy brings power far nearer to where people are than any talking shop in Edinburgh for the SNP.' He also warned that we could take no decision on these matters until the central issue of whether we went into Europe had been decided. 'If we are in the Common Market it means the break-up of the UK; if we are not, we can retain centralized government.' I had sympathy with him when he ticked off Roy J. for one of his more pontifical speeches about sovereignty. Roy had been saying that sovereignty came from the sovereign, from whom it had passed to the sovereign's Ministers. Wedgie described this contemptuously as a 'feudal fiction', adding, 'We didn't get our authority as Ministers by kissing hands but by winning votes.' What interested me most in the whole discussion, though, was the extent to which Willie is now committed to making devolution work, on the sensible principle that, having been overruled in the first place, he wasn't going to get left out on a limb by the doubters now.

Monday, 20 January. I had not expected any great public interest in our resumed meetings of the Liaison Committee with the TUC, so when I arrived at Congress House at 10.30 am straight from HCF and struggled out of the car in mac and boots, with hair dishevelled by the pouring rain, I was dismayed to be snapped by a battery of waiting cameras. Jack Jones followed me into the building and when I moaned that the cameras had caught me with my tight tweed skirt pulled up over my knees he said almost humanly, 'That should make for good publicity.' I realized after a moment's thought that the news hounds were there expecting a major row – the only reason they ever turn up in strength. Denis's recent speech about the need to tighten the pay guidelines of the Social Contract must have made them lick their chops with expectancy. But the media will never understand this baffling movement of ours and they certainly do not understand the deep-rooted new concordat between the Government and the trade unions. They may envy it, and that is perhaps why they watch hungrily for it to disintegrate.

But when I looked round that panelled room where we meet, in such unrelieved acres of lavish woodwork, and saw Harold chatting to Jack, Denis to Len, and Hughie creeping in almost deprecatingly, I knew there wasn't going to be any row. Only Wedgie and George Smith were missing. Sid Greene was late, so Jack was voted into the chair while the rest of us quipped, 'That'll muzzle you.' Bob Mellish said to me wonderingly, 'Do you realize we haven't met since July? That shows you how time flies.' And as soon as Jack took the chair I realized how important it was for us to meet. Here is the Government, beset by so many economic difficulties it would have sunk us in 1964–70. Here was the trade union movement which had contributed so much to our 1970 defeat. And here was Jack Jones in the chair, who had always been considered by my officials, when I was at Employment and Productivity, as the archetypal trade union villain and who had in fact been arid and negative then. But today Jack sat in the chair as an almost gentle and certainly benign influence. I believe he is the greatest voice in the trade union movement today in favour of what I have always wanted to see: the trade union movement being made socialist. And what is more, he is someone who realizes that politicians have to operate in the real world as much as trade unionists do: in the world of the possible. I wonder if Ted Heath understands how much he has done by his crude clumsiness to create this miracle? I suspect the Tory Party is beginning to realize it.

Len Murray opened by introducing the TUC document outlining what would be the TUC *Economic Review*, 1975. His tone was conciliatory. On the international situation the TUC was 'greatly appreciative' of what the Government had achieved. Domestically the overriding priority was to maintain employment. As far as the Social Contract was concerned, defence of living standards remained 'the root of the guidelines'. As for the Budget, their minds were open. It was all very low-key. Denis immediately asked if he could come in and then proceeded to give us a twenty-minute speech of political shrewdness plus economic gravity. It was a difficult job, in the face of the suspicions he had aroused among the unions.

He began by saying that this meeting was 'very well timed'. The Government was facing some very difficult problems. But he repeated with impressive emphasis his belief in the Social Contract and when he said it was 'the reason for our success so far' it carried conviction. After all, it was a Chancellor speaking – and no Chancellor in Britain had ever said it before. Then he grew grimmer. The world was now in recession. Employment was the main consideration. There was no chance of pulling out of the recession this year. The threat to jobs came from outside Britain: we had got to get a bigger share of world trade. In March 1974 our trade deficit had amounted to 4 per cent of our GDP. The oil deficit had added another 4 per cent. We had cut the trade deficit by 2 per cent, but this still meant that a 6 per cent deficit had to be covered by borrowing. 'We are spending 6 per cent more than we are earning.' (Echoes of Jim's arguments to Cabinet in 1966! But Denis was arguing in an entirely different political context and speaking a different language: the sort of political language the unions were prepared to listen to.) The borrowing we had made was entirely on commercial terms, Denis maintained, but that meant that inflation could jeopardize it. In the three months to August 1974 inflation had been running at 8 per cent. In the three months from September it had jumped to 19½ per cent. In the same period earnings had risen 28½ per cent. The oil producers were simply not prepared to put their money into a country where its value could be undermined.

If inflation undermined commercial borrowing, Denis continued, one of two things would happen: either we should have to reduce the standing of living by 6 per cent, or we should have to start borrowing from institutions which would impose terms, like a statutory incomes policy, which a Labour Government would find unacceptable. Jack had said in a recent speech that unions could bankrupt firms by excessive wage demands. 'You can also bankrupt a nation by excessive wage demands.' The union leaders watched him transfixed as he spoke, Len Murray in particular being barely able to refrain from nodding at this point. 'That is why', Denis continued bravely, we simply had to get wage settlements down. He concluded on a note of appeal. He was not, he repeated, making recommendations, merely asking them to see his problem, though he would understand it if they said he did not understand theirs. Above all, he concluded, 'we must maintain our unity'. (Vigorous nods from Jack in the chair.)

There was a long silence when he had finished. It was Shirley who broke it first, adding some agonizing details of the rate of inflation to underline what Denis had said. Another silence; then Hughie came in, almost writhing in his seat as he tried to combine honesty with moderation and to curb his usual confident truculence. He welcomed Denis's frankness, he said, 'but it does not soften the blow'. Emboldened, he continued: 'I fundamentally disagree with you.' The disagreement, it transpired, was not with Denis's outline of the difficulties: rather with his proposed cure. 'Slumps are caused by the inability of workers to buy back what they produce.' Hughie groped desperately. 'Somehow we have got to bridge the difference between us.' And then came the crux: 'We are prepared to uphold the Social Contract' (a great breakthrough, that, for Hughie!) 'as we agreed it.'

Harold then assured us that the Government was not seeking to change the guidelines and I came in with a brief speech to remind them that the Social Contract was concerned with maintaining living standards – not merely for wage-earners, but for all those whom we were in politics to protect. 'We could have a situation in which we had maintained the living standards of wage-earners and yet had breached the Social Contract because we had reduced the standards of the weakest in our community.' Jack was almost at bursting-point, nodding his agreement vigorously. But by now it had turned 12.30 pm, so he had to sum up with great self-restraint. The discussion, he said, had been very valuable and we must continue it. 'We must disabuse the people of the idea that the Government is trying to force the unions to go further. We must implement the guidelines and above all we must go forward together in understanding and unity.' When we had all said Amen to that we broke up. Cynics might say we had achieved nothing by the morning's talk, but those of us who, like me, have lived through the traumas of the past few years, know differently. Winning consent is a slow process, but I myself am convinced it is the only way. And anyone who heard Hughie this morning would know that we progress. We left Congress House fortified in the belief that, if there is an answer to this country's problems, it lies in this inchoate union between our Government and the unions.

At our ministerial lunch we had a long discussion on pay beds. David is all in favour of a two-to-three-year phasing-out period, with us legislating next session. I believe we cannot hold the unions as long as that, though my trouble is that I have got no allocation in my PESC programme for the cost of phasing out and I simply cannot find the money from the inadequate amount I have been allowed for the NHS. I suggested that I should hold the fort by announcing a short Bill this session to take the necessary powers, to be followed next session by a more complicated Bill to enable me to regulate the private sector of medicine. Brian A-S. attaches a lot of importance to that – and so does David in theory, though, when cornered, he is liable to say suddenly that regulation will prove extremely difficult. The rest of them were all in favour of my not attempting legislation this session and I accepted their judgement – only to be faced shortly afterwards by a note from Jack to the effect that Bernard Dix of NUPE had been on the phone to him warning that their branches were getting restive, not least as a result of the consultants' action, and were threatening direct moves to force phasing out. The suggestion from Dix was that I ought to see Alan Fisher urgently. 'Of course you will have to see him,' said Philip anxiously.

A long official meeting then ensued on what Henry should say to the consultants at the 'initial exploratory meeting' he is to have with them on Thursday in the Joint Negotiating Committee. He began with a show of life, saying he wanted Ministers to decide if they were really going to entrust this job to him rather than take it on themselves, because if they wanted him to do it they really must allow him to play it his own way, 'though of course within your strictly defined parameters'. Otherwise, he added, he might find that he had let us down. (What he really means, I suspect, is that he fears we might repudiate him.) Of course David and I said we didn't want to go into ministerial discussion but to keep the talks within the more hopeful context of the JNC. But it is clearly going to be a tricky operation, because Henry does not intend to take detailed orders.

Tuesday, 21 January. As someone said afterwards, an historic Cabinet! In it the Labour Government slid easily into a solution of the difficulties which threatened to split it only two or three years ago, while Harold announced a fundamental change in our constitutional convention as casually as if he had been offering us a cup of tea. The occasion was a morning-long discussion on how we should handle a referendum on the EEC. Ted Short had circulated a stack of papers and official reports on the logistic questions which we should have to decide, but we barely referred to them. Instead we spent over two hours on the central political point: how we could deal with the imminent split in the Cabinet – already looming as a result of Peter Shore's latest speech, following Tony Benn's Bristol letter and Roy Hattersley's riposte.[1] Ted began by saying that we ought to aim at a referendum in June, otherwise we should be pushed very near our deadline of October. He hoped the Referendum Bill could be approved by 25 March. Then Harold came in quietly: 'As soon as we have made our decision on the terms I am going to recommend that the minority should be free to campaign in the country on their own point of view.' And he added, 'This is unprecedented.' But in his long-winded way he proceeded to justify it, qualifying his proposal with the implied rebuke: 'But this must apply only after the campaign starts.' And he thought we should issue some guidelines to prevent the argument from becoming unruly and personalized. There was a long silence when he asked for comments. I think the reason was that people like Mike, Wedgie and me were secretly jubilant, while the pro-marketeers were reluctant to accept openly the course of action they knew was inevitable. Gradually acceptance spread through Cabinet. Roy Mason uttered gloomy warnings: 'The media will personalize our differences, even if we do not.' But when Harold asked him rather sharply what he would propose, he admitted he could not see any other way. Tony C. said grudgingly that the PM's proposal was 'more attractive than either of the alternatives'. Mike thought the proposal was right.

I struck the first note of positive enthusiasm. I was glad, I said, that Harold had come to this conclusion. It was endemic in the decision to have a referendum. The alternative of a General Election was never open to us – not merely on the grounds of timing, but because people did not divide on this issue on party lines. And I was not gloomy about the consequences. Tomorrow, I said, the NEC was discussing the same issue and Ron Hayward was suggesting that, even after a special conference on the renegotiated terms had made its views known, every member of the Party should be free to campaign on his or her individual views. Our tolerance as a Cabinet would encourage the whole Party to be tolerant. The proposal was all the more necessary because I did not believe that either of the extremes Harold had visualized would happen: either that the terms would be so marvellous that we should all agree to accept or so terrible that rejection would be unanimous. I believed that the outcome of the negotiations would be 'a messy muddle in the middle'. They laughed at this and there was more laughter – relaxed, not bitter – as I went on to say that we would all then use the outcome to justify the line we had always taken anyway. 'So all Jim's hard work is irrelevant.' We wouldn't, for example, get the EEC to abandon the CAP. What we would be offered would be a bit of freedom to add a few national aids on top. So we would be back where we started years ago. But there was no reason why we should treat the situation tragically. I was prepared

[1] The battle of words between Ministers over renegotiations had already broken out. In December Tony Benn had published an open letter to his Bristol constituents declaring that 'Britain's continuing membership of the Community would mean the end of Britain as a completely self-governing nation and the end of our democratically elected Parliament as the supreme law-making body in the United Kingdom'. Roy Hattersley had followed with the counter-claim that the loss of sovereignty was minimal and was outweighed by the benefits of membership. Peter Shore, in turn, had produced a detailed analysis of the economic disbenefits Britain had already experienced.

to accept the nation's verdict, whichever way it went. I certainly wasn't going to let such an unimportant thing as the Common Market wreck my political work or my Party's socialist unity. (Shirley gave me a wry little smile at that.)

Fred, of course, took up my reference to the CAP with heavy indignation. I had never realized that all he had been doing was to negotiate as he was bound to do. 'I have not changed my basic position.' (Does that mean he is going to vote *against*, after all?) Peter's contribution was as astringent as usual. Harold's proposition, he said, was a generous one: '*very* generous, because the negotiations are not going to succeed. I do not expect to be in the minority.' But the healing thing was that we were all committed to accept the verdict. If, for instance, it went against his own views, he did not know whether or not Harold would still wish him to serve him ('Perhaps it would involve moving you to another post,' chipped in Harold genially): whatever it was, he, Peter, would accept the outcome and do whatever was required of him. Denis was pretty relaxed about the whole idea. The Party, too, must be ready to show tolerance and those of us on the NEC must use our influence tomorrow to get the same freedom for individual members of the Party. There shouldn't, for example, be a block vote at the special conference. He didn't think it should be held at all. Mike demurred at this. With the Government expressing a view, Parliament expressing a view, and every organization in the country doing the same, it was only right that the Party should express a view as well – but that did not mean the imposition of Party discipline. Wedgie was even more euphoric than I had been. 'The knowledge that we are free to express our views makes us much more relaxed towards the whole renegotiation.'

Roy J. was deeply dubious: 'The idea Harold puts forward is a very difficult one.' Some of them would be in a very uncomfortable position, just as he had been as deputy leader when he had felt he must resign. But even Roy didn't oppose the solution outright. Jim was characteristically Cassandra-like. The referendum would not necessarily be a healing exercise. 'I suspect that brotherly love will wear a little thin.' What he did urge was that the campaigning should not begin until the terms were known. His position, he said, was made impossible when members of the Government started publicly opposing membership in principle and thus breaching the compromise we had reached in the Manifesto. 'The negotiations are being made more difficult because the EEC believe whatever they do to meet us will not make any difference.' That is why he was taking over more of the negotiations himself. 'At least they believe it is not impossible to convince me at the end of the day.' (Some of us winked at that.)

As Harold started to sum up, Ted Short pointed out: 'This means that we are formally committing ourselves to a referendum, not a General Election.' Roy J. muttered some subdued token reservations at that, but the rest of us just took it as obvious. Harold then said he would submit a draft of his statement to Thursday's Cabinet. He would say that we would publicize the views taken by the different sides in Cabinet but make it clear we would all abide by the referendum result. Here again there was no reserving of positions by the Europeanists and I suspect that Shirley is now sorry she nailed her colours of resignation to the mast so precipitately during the election. Once again I was struck by our astonishing harmony. It really does look as though Harold's long period of humiliation has not been in vain and that the Party's unity is emerging as an exercise in genuine party democracy. There was, for instance, the quite moving moment when Wedgie, in the middle of his speech, turned to Shirley and said, 'When she said what she did during the Election I was very angry, but I don't think now that it did the Party any harm.' My morning was also made by a friendly note John Silkin tossed to me:

To Barbara in admiration *21-1-75*

In EEC matters the rôle of B.C.
Is to show that, in Cabinet, there is a key
To the problems, the troubles – above all the riddle
Of Pro and of Anti – and those in the middle.
For Barbara's answer to those who are tense
Or up-tight, is just simply to use commonsense.
Love,
John

Wednesday, 22 January. Denis arrived late at the NEC meeting and left early, having obviously timed his brief attendance to be present during the discussion of Ron's memo on the referendum and to beat off what he obviously thought was going to be the imposition of Party discipline. He need not have worried: harmony seems to have broken out in the NEC as well as Cabinet, just as I predicted yesterday. So another crisis in the Party has been passed peacefully. I suspect the will to unity in the Party, which strengthens every day, is being fed by the growing confusion in the Tory ranks over the leadership.[1] Despite the fact that Margaret Thatcher is now giving Heath a hard run for his money, mine is still on Heath's victory. You can't find two Tories to agree on an alternative to him.

Another meeting with the presidents of the Royal Colleges on the consultants' dispute. This time they had brought their whole conference body, but nothing new emerged and we went over the same old ground, with them emphasizing that I must treat these sensitive individualists, the consultants, gently and me replying that I was only too willing to negotiate. After various other office meetings Henry came to see me in my room in the House (where we are incarcerated by a running whip on the Finance Bill) to rehearse once again what he should say to the BMA negotiators at the 'initial exploratory meeting' tomorrow. He has obviously got himself quite keyed up over this and

[1] The revolt against Mr Heath's leadership had been growing among Conservative back benchers. As early as 13 October *The Times* had given it impetus by declaring that 'it is not possible for Mr Heath to remain as leader of the Conservative Party'. After manœuvres in the back bench 1922 Committee elaborate new election procedures had been devised by a group headed by Lord Home and the demand that Mr Heath should submit himself to them became irresistible. To win on the first ballot a candidate needed to get the votes of at least half the Conservative MPs and have a lead of forty-two votes over the nearest rival. Heath loyalists like William Whitelaw refused to run against him and Heath opponents prevailed on Margaret Thatcher, the rising star, to stand. At the first ballot she and the maverick right-wing Scots MP, Hugh Fraser, were the only challengers, and on 4 February Margaret astonished everyone by polling 130 votes to Heath's 119, with Fraser a bad also-ran with eleven votes. The result was enough to kill Heath's hopes, but not enough for an outright win by Margaret. Under the rules new candidates could join in for the second round and an unseemly scramble was to ensue, with 'Stop Thatcher' candidates putting forward their names.

his personality seems to have toughened up quite considerably, though he still lapses into self-deprecatory diffidence from time to time.

Thursday, 23 January. [At Cabinet] we went through Harold's draft statement on the Common Market referendum word by word and line by line. Then there was a great argument as to whether the Government should provide background information on the issues when the time came. Peter insisted that it was impossible to provide information that accurately summed up the cases of the two sides, but I did not agree with him. 'The major source of information must be under our control,' I said. After much to-ing and fro-ing Harold said a group of Ministers must look into the whole thing and report to Cabinet.

Finally we cleared the White Paper on Public Expenditure. Denis has toughened up the words about the grim options that lie ahead of us, but no one could object to that. Perhaps it will help to show the unions that if they go on pressing unreasonable wage demands they will only suffer a cut in the social wage. But I was dismayed to discover that Denis has dropped the idea of a popular version which he seemed to have agreed to when I raised it at Chequers. Once again all the talk of the need for education and persuasion seems to have come to nothing. Late as it was, with everyone edgy to get away, I insisted on raising it. Denis raised all sorts of difficulties, but to my relief Harold ruled that the Presentation of Government Policies Committee under Bill Price[1] should have another look at it. Harold at any rate can appreciate the importance of what I am talking about.

While Henry was incarcerated with the JNC we had an office meeting on pay beds. Philip, Henry and Brian A-S. have produced a long detailed paper about the measures we might take to control the private health sector and prevent it expanding excessively when the phasing-out takes place. To my surprise David exploded violently. Some of the propositions in it he found quite intolerable, he said. Quantity control, for example, was just not on. Having first welcomed the idea of controls he now seems to have swung to the other extreme. It was ironic to hear Philip explaining to him that we really must regulate standards in private nursing homes, while Raymond Gedling said that when the department started to license nursing homes for abortions we rejected some as unfit, though gastrectomies had been performed there for years! So David quietened down. I said gently that I thought the paper was right to put all the possibilities before us so that we could examine them, even if only to reject some of them. But I thought we ought to have a Sunningdale to do it and invite sympathizers from outside, like Laurie Pavitt and John Dunwoody, and perhaps some discreet people from the unions. This idea alarmed Philip, lest the BMA should hear of it, but I said that we could have parallel discussions with the BMA as soon as I had announced our intention to legislate. We all agreed that we should not broach the pay beds question publicly until the consultants' dispute is out of the way, but that we ought to waste no time in getting a paper to Cabinet, particularly as I persuaded them that we must get a quick one-clause Bill through this session, followed by a control Bill later. I convinced them that this was the only way to prevent the eruption of serious trouble with the unions.

[1] William Price was Labour MP for Rugby and Parliamentary Secretary, Privy Council Office.

The announcement of our intention to legislate, plus some immediate reductions in under-used pay beds and discussions on a common waiting list, would lower the temperature. Philip said he liked the sound of this package and they went away to redraft their paper to Cabinet.

At 5.30 pm Henry came out of the JNC looking limp and harassed. 'How is it going?' I asked. 'Terrible,' said Henry, mopping his face. He then settled down to spell out in detail the consultants' 'shopping list' and the objections to the new contract he had wrung out of them. Philip and Raymond shook their heads derisively as Henry ploughed on: the consultants wanted the lot.[1] What is more, they were waiting for my reply. Henry said he assumed I would just say 'nothing doing', but David, just before he had to dash off to the House to take a debate, took a different line. He said I should seize the opportunity to get on record the fact that they accepted, however reluctantly, that my two cardinal principles (retention of the whole-timers' differential and rejection of items of service contract) were non-negotiable. Apparently Henry, in opening the meeting, had started toughly by asking them if they did accept this: otherwise there was no point in going any further. (He's developing quite a backbone, that man!) Then, said David, we should go on to say in general terms that, although I could make no detailed comments at this stage, I saw nothing in their proposals to prevent fruitful negotiations from taking place. I liked this approach: it would put paid to the myth of my 'take it or leave it' attitude. But I said we must also reiterate the common objective between them and us of getting a more defined contract, otherwise I could see us being manœuvred into accepting their new aim, which was to keep the present open-ended, undefined and unpoliceable contract and just add extra payments onto it. After David had gone we sweated for an hour over the wording of my reply. We are now so terrified of putting their hackles up with the wrong phrase. At last we were ready to send Henry back into the lion's den, while I went home to pack for the night sleeper to Blackburn.

Monday, 27 January. Another office meeting on those dratted consultants. Henry reported that, when he went back to them on Thursday evening, they had mulled over my message, were clearly disappointed with it and had almost pleaded with him to get me to elaborate on it, saying they appreciated I hadn't really had enough time to think over their points. Conciliatory as always, I agreed to elaborate on it and we talked endlessly round the problem before Henry and co. went away to have a shot at another draft.

Tuesday, 28 January. At last we have resumed our weekly dinners. I must say it was pleasant to walk into that private room at Lockets again, even though there weren't many of us who could manage to turn up: just Mike and Jill Foot, Tommy and Katherine Balogh, the Silkins and me. We had a good discussion

[1] The consultants had switched their efforts to improving their existing contract. In this they went well beyond Dr Astley's four points, demanding in addition an emergency recall fee, new capital allowances for cars and phones, amendments to their incremental scale and superannuation improvements. They also wanted the maximum part-timers' commitment to the NHS 'clarified' to mean an obligation to attend for nine sessions of three-and-a-half hours each, including travel time, rather than whole time, *i.e.* eleven sessions. Above all they insisted that an 'absolutely fundamental' precondition for the lifting of sanctions was the Department's willingness to support a substantial pay increase for consultants in their current pay review.

on the economic situation, which we all recognize is deeply serious. What delighted me was to see no sign that Mike is going to throw in the sponge on what has become an increasingly difficult task for him, thus falsifying Conrad Heron's prognostication that he would quit when the going got tough. Instead Mike told us of a policy he has been working out in his Department for dealing with inflation by (a) massively increasing subsidies to hold the cost of living down and (b) a big increase in taxation. I found this an odd doctrine, but Mike says Denis, of whom he thinks quite a lot, had not turned it down out of hand.

I was late getting to the dinner because Henry had asked to see me urgently. The BMA has been in touch with him about my clarification letter, which they want further 'clarified'. After some discussion we decided Henry could give them assurances verbally on certain points but that I should not send them another letter. These clarifications of clarifications are becoming slightly ridiculous! The key question they asked is, as we anticipated, whether sanctions would have to be lifted before negotiations could begin. David suggested a useful formula: namely, that I had gone as far as I could reasonably be expected to go and that it was now for the BMA to take a public attitude. Henry went away well satisfied. His tail is slightly up again because my letter had clearly had an effect on some, at any rate, of the negotiators.

Friday, 31 January. Another meeting in the office about the consultants. Henry reported that there had been no further noises from their representatives. Both David and I are getting restive at the delay and David made menacing noises about how we must really explode the notion that the consultants were 'working to contract'. They were doing nothing of the kind: they were breaching it, since even the maximum part-timers were contracted to work 'substantially whole-time' for the NHS. I cheered Henry up again by saying I would not do anything precipitate to wreck his talks.

Monday, 3 February. Stevenson's deputy, Gullick, has written to Henry to thank me for my long letter of 28 January.[1] Having considered it carefully they asked whether a second clarification meeting would be possible as the first one had 'run out of time'. Henry has also minuted me saying that he now suspects that the negotiators have been so impressed by the reasonableness of my letter that they are trying to avoid publication of it at all – under plea that it is part of the clarification proceedings which we have agreed shall be confidential. The profession is clearly divided down the middle and my letter would split them further. I said at once that I didn't think I could refuse them a second clarification meeting, though Henry should fire a warning shot to the effect that a document of some kind must be published in due course.

Tuesday, 4 February. That the meeting of the Legislation Committee of Cabinet was up to something special was clear from the crowded room. Even

[1] In it I welcomed the professions' acceptance of the fact that I was not prepared to budge on the whole-timers' differential and that a system of payment by fees for items of service was ruled out. I also reminded them of my anxiety to reform the system of merit awards. On pay I gave them the same assurance as I had done to GPs, agreed that their incremental scale ought to be improved and said I was ready to consider changes in their

Ted Short had arrived by the time I got there. Conference Room A – scene of so many of my traumatic ministerial experiences – is a lofty, beautifully proportioned room overlooking Horse Guards Parade; it is the old Treasury boardroom. The ceiling is attractively moulded, and the whole setting is more appropriate to some leisurely eighteenth-century discussion than to the miserably involved technical details of domestic problems that we conduct there. Behind the chairman's seat is a red velvet throne topped with gilded moulding, last occupied when George III presided over one of the board meetings. It is now roped off to prevent the representatives of the people from sitting on it. It was in this room that I had my struggles with Dick Crossman and Judith Hart over *In Place of Strife*. It was here we used to wrangle over the horrible petty details of prices and incomes policy in 1968 and 1969. If X group of workers got 2*d* on their hourly rate, wouldn't Y group immediately demand the same, etc., etc.? Yet what strikes me now is how much less traumatic our policy problems seem. There is no reason why they should, because, God knows, they are as difficult as ever. Perhaps it is just that I am older and more relaxed. Probably, though, it is due to the fact that when we fell in 1970 the Tories made an even greater mess of things than we did, so we don't feel as desperately on trial as we did in 1964–70.

'All the first eleven are here this morning,' remarked Ted from the chair as Jim Callaghan, Shirley, Peter, Mike, Wedgie, the Lord Chancellor *et al.* squeezed themselves into the chairs round the big baize-covered table. Everyone grinned, for the subject that had brought us there was not the approval of a motley group of Bills but the crucial issue of the sovereignty of Parliament in the context of the EEC. Ted, in opening the discussion, reminded us in that staccato way of his that Legislation Committee last July had asked for some further study to be done on the problem of how 'Community secondary legislation' could be made subject to some formal parliamentary scrutiny. Hence his paper, which confronted us with two choices: either to try to get the amendment of Article 189 of the Treaty of Rome (so as to subject decisions of the Council of Ministers to the subsequent approval of the British Parliament), or to strengthen the procedure for discussing matters before they went to the Council. Ted solemnly read out the extract from the Manifesto dealing with the issue of sovereignty. One of the aims of renegotiation, it said, was 'the retention by Parliament of those powers over the British economy needed to pursue effective regional, industrial and fiscal policies'. The committee must decide just exactly what that entailed.

Ted then called on Jim, who, a bit taken aback, said he had really just come to listen; but Jim was soon warming up to his typical pro-Market theme. There was 'no chance whatever', he said, of getting the Community to agree to amend Article 189. The concept of directly applicable Community law was central to the Community system. 'If we intended to challenge Article 189 we shouldn't have made our application in the first place.' But, he insisted, 'it would be regarded as an act of bad faith to raise this now'. Mike, sitting next to me, was writhing in his seat. He spoke with his usual mixture of gentleness and firmness. It wasn't fair of Jim to suggest that some of us were only raising this at the last

superannuation scheme. I hinted that a payment for being 'on call' might be possible, but only within the context of a 'closed' contract.

minute, he said. As Ted had pointed out, we had raised it as long ago as last July. It would be intolerable to argue that it was now too late. The right of Parliament to retain control had been at the heart of the Party's fight against Heath's European Communities Bill which took us into the Market and everyone round the table had voted for the amendments we had put forward in Opposition to assert that right. But this was really a matter for Cabinet. Bob returned to the nitty gritty of the problem of even trying to retain the remnants of parliamentary sovereignty. How was he to keep Ministers in the House late night after night voting on these wretched directives? Ted Short, summing up, said that we had decided no decision should be reached.

Late that afternoon in the House someone said to me, 'Have you heard the news? Margaret Thatcher has swept to the top in the leadership poll [on the first ballot].' I fear that I felt a sneaking feminist pleasure. Damn it, that lass *deserves* to win. Her cool and competent handling of the cheaper mortgages issue in the last election campaign gave us our only moment of acute anxiety. All right, it was a dishonest nonsense as a policy, but she dealt with it like a professional.

Wednesday, 5 February. The papers are full of Margaret Thatcher. She has lent herself with grace and charm to every piece of photographer's gimmickry, but don't we all when the prize is big enough? What interests me now is how blooming she looks – she has never been prettier. I am interested because I understand this phenomenon. She may have been up late on the Finance Bill Committee; she is beset by enemies and has to watch every gesture and word. But she sails through it all looking her best. I understand why. She is in love: in love with power, success – and with herself. She looks as I looked when Harold made me Minister of Transport. If we have to have Tories, good luck to her!

A delegation from the TUC about pay beds. Their representations were very low-key, though Alan Fisher warned me we must announce our policy before their union conference in May. I suspect they were not more ferocious because we are busy fixing up a secret dinner with them to discuss how we can best implement our policy. This gives me a great peace of mind, because I am not willing to go along with David's ideas about a protracted phasing out until I have sounded out the unions, whose members are getting restive about our failure to announce progress.

Another insight into Roy Jenkins's character. I had asked him to see me about an immigration case in my constituency. He kept me waiting (which I didn't mind, because I knew he had been at a Cabinet Committee), but when I was summoned into his vast and rather gloomy room at the Home Office he didn't trouble to apologize. In fact, he was obviously angry that I should have dared to bother him and told me immediately that he wasn't going to argue over the evidence: he supported the immigration officer without question. But, in view of the fact that Roy Martin[1] had written in his letter to me that he was prepared to 'stake his life' on the reliability of the chap concerned, he was prepared to give him a chance to prove himself right. 'But tell him from me that, not his life, but his reputation, is at stake and if I am let down he must never put a case to me again.' It was all done like a judge lecturing a prisoner

[1] Roy Martin had been my political agent in Blackburn from 1960–68. He had then become an officer of the Race Relations Board in the North-West and later of the Commission for Racial Equality.

put on probation, and I was out of the room in five minutes. I found the whole process illuminating. Not for Roy any tortured doubts about the reliability of the immigration officer. And he had begun by telling me severely that none of the rest of his Cabinet colleagues ever troubled him on matters like this. 'I only have to see you because of your pertinacity on behalf of your constituents.' I have no doubt that this quality of mine does not make for my being loved, but I should have no peace with myself if I did not fight for those I believe to be in the right.

The newspapers are all full of the Tory leadership farce. So many brave warriors have now crept out of hiding to rush to climb on the second ballot bandwagon! Margaret looks the epitome of cool courage compared with them. In the House I ran into Stephen McAdden [Conservative MP for Southend East] and whispered to him, 'How did you vote?' 'For Margaret, of course,' he replied loudly. 'I think she might win,' I said. 'I am sure she will,' he replied.

Thursday, 6 February. At Cabinet Harold reported on his visit to the US. Despite his new-found caution he could not resist a little touch of the old self-satisfaction at the way he had been received by President Ford. Relations with the US, he said, were 'as good as they have ever been', adding typically, 'The ceremonies of welcome went far beyond anything I have had before.' We then went into a long discussion on how we should conduct the count in the EEC referendum. Ted was recommending a central count, despite the cost and the difficulties. This was the only way to show that it was a national issue. The views of Cabinet divided predictably: the pro-marketeers went for centralism (the two Roys, Shirley, Harold Lever, Roy Hattersley and Reg Prentice, backed by Denis, Fred, Elwyn and, surprisingly, John Morris, who said the Welsh group had been unanimous that this was the only way to prevent separatism); the rest of us supported Mike in wanting a count by counties. Only Wedgie was for a constituency count. But the voices were close: ten to eight.

At the office I ran into Henry, who was looking jaded. He had been awake since 5 am, he confessed, brooding over the consultants' problem. I began to feel quite worried about his health. At another of our now almost daily meetings on the consultants he put forward the idea that, instead of my amending my letter of 28 January, it might be possible for me to reach agreement with the negotiators on a joint statement. This would obviously have much more weight in getting the profession to call off sanctions. Peter looked very disapproving at this. He didn't trust the consultants' representatives further than he could throw them. But Henry insisted that my reasonableness had made a great impression on them and that they were in an entirely different mood. It would be difficult to agree a statement but it would be a 'great prize'. I said I was prepared to have a shot at it, but I repeated I was getting uneasy about the delay. We must aim to get a document to Gullick next Monday with a view to a statement in the House on Wednesday – the only day of the week that is not likely to be swamped by Tory leadership ballot news. Henry looked worred but said he would try.

Friday, 7 February. While I was in the House attending the Abortion Bill debate, Norman phoned to say Henry was having anxieties again about our proposed timetable. Could I possibly fit in another meeting that afternoon? Henry was as apologetic as usual: he knew he was being a great nusiance to me, etc., but he was worried that I was trying to rush things too much. He then went on to explain that the draft joint statement would be in my weekend box. No doubt I would want to discuss it on Monday. Then he had to get it to the consultants' leaders, who might want to suggest some further changes. At that I exploded: 'Oh no, we can't go on allowing them to erode my position bit by bit like this.' It really was all getting a bit undignified. The process would never end. I had a feeling that the issue might erupt publicly at any time. I really wanted to bring matters to the crunch now. David was as impatient as I was, but finally I said that the decision should be postponed till Monday, when I would have had a chance to see how near we were to agreement on a joint document.

In the corridor outside my room I found Peter Brown and Ian Gillis lying in wait. Peter asked me if he might phone me this weekend after I had had a chance to study the document. I said of course, though naturally I was puzzled. There certainly are wheels within wheels in this Department!

Sunday, 9 February. True to his promise, Peter phoned. He told me, crisply and firmly, that he thought that to issue a joint statement would in itself be catastrophic. He could just imagine how Stevenson would handle it. The BMA had had the impertinence in their part of the document to reopen the whole question of what they claimed had been agreed in the Owen working party, even though I had made my own position clear. My letter to them on 28 January had been a first-class document. That was why they were so afraid of having it published, as it would show how reasonable I had been. He still thought the right way was for me to send my own letter unilaterally and then publish it. Peter then maintained that there were a number of my officials who were against the whole idea of a joint statement, but might not have the courage to say so round my discussion table. I thanked Peter for his comments, which I found very useful. As I went back to my work I began to appreciate why Dick thought so much of Peter Brown. He is not only politically shrewd, but, if he identifies himself with a Minister, he throws himself wholeheartedly into the job of serving him (or her).

I duly phoned David to get his reactions to the document Henry had sent us. His first comment was that it was 'not too bad', though we should need to toughen up our part of it. The trouble about trying any redrafting was that, according to a Minute from his private secretary, it was 'agreed Gullick–Yellowlees, subject to ministerial approval'. I hit the roof at this. I seized the opportunity (without mentioning my talk with Peter) to say that, if this was so, it made it impossible to issue a joint statement at all, because any amendments by me would now take on a dangerous significance. David rather agreed and said he had never been keen on the idea anyway. We agreed sadly that it was going to be tricky handling the next steps. David believes there will be no withdrawal of sanctions until the consultants have seen the colour of our money in April. He has also changed his tune about the phasing out of pay beds, having been talking to NUPE leaders on a recent visit to the North. 'I am now convinced that three years is too long,' he told me; 'two years is the maximum, if we can get that. But I think this whole thing is blowing up.' I'm glad to hear him face this fact.

Monday, 10 February. Another long office meeting on the consultants' contract. I began by asking Henry what was the exact authorship of his document. Had it been jointly drafted by him and Gullick? He said firmly, 'Not in the sense you warned me about. So no one can say, if you reject this document, that there is any kind of a split between you and me.' I then asked whose idea it had been to have a joint statement and he said emphatically, 'Theirs. It was entirely their idea.' Peter's eyebrows shot up so far at this that I thought they would fly off his face. I plodded on patiently. I said I was concerned at the fact that the format of an agreed statement meant that the BMA set up the scenario and I was put in the position of merely reacting to it. Peter nodded vigorously at this; Philip gave a half-nod, while Raymond tried to hide his agreement by stabbing, head down, at his blotting paper. Henry was not upset. He had, he said, been in two minds whether to recommend this course of action to me at all. I said I felt in my bones we should miss the boat if we didn't get our own statement out quickly. We must act now. David supported me on this and so did Philip, so I sent Henry away to report on these lines to the negotiators and tell them I wanted to make a statement on Wednesday. Henry himself volunteered to tell them he had felt unable to advise me to accept their idea.

Some hours later Henry asked to see me, looking grim. He said Gullick's reaction had been pretty violent. He had threatened to reveal publicly that I had been asked to do this and refused. I snapped back that this revealed the negotiators in their true colours. They were not trying to reach a settlement but to score points. Henry should tell them that I would regard their revelation of the advice my own CMO had given to me as a serious breach of our agreed confidentiality and would openly describe it as an act of bad faith. Philip nodded approvingly at this and even Henry seemed impressed.

Tuesday, 11 February. With an urgent decision to be taken on my letter to the BMA, I had to cut the meeting of the International Committee of the NEC once again. Trying to fit in Party appointments, to say nothing of making occasional appearances in the House, becomes increasingly impossible. Departments remain firmly convinced that they have the first – and almost exclusive – call on their Minister's time and with so many crises popping up it is hard to blame them. Henry reported that Grabham had asked to see me urgently that evening with a last plea that I should delay my statement to the House. I replied that of course I shouldn't refuse. I wasn't going to have them say I had been high-handed. I believed I might even convince him that the course of action I proposed was wise. We then discussed my proposed letter; I had practically rewritten the whole draft. As usual, we spent ages on it, with one person after another wanting to query this word and that. Finally we got it done and agreed we should let Grabham have a copy confidentially.

A Tuesday Cabinet, because Harold is off to Moscow on Thursday. Another long discussion on the EEC referendum. There was a circular argument about what we should do about providing the information which will be necessary for people to reach a decision. Harold summed up that there had been no time to reach conclusions and that Ted should put alternative paragraphs in the draft White Paper he will be circulating.

I had my meeting with Grabham and Gullick in the House. The manner of both was extremely conciliatory. In return I spelt out in the most friendly way why I had not been able to accept a joint statement and why I felt it was urgent to make a statement in the House as quickly as possible, in the interests of consultants themselves. (This obviously impressed Grabham, who all along has stressed the importance of getting an early increase in pay from the Review Body.) I laid this down the line: how I was fearful we should miss the boat on this round of pay increases; how I was willing to meet their point on an incremental scale; how I was anxious to submit joint evidence with them on other things. I also said I did not wish to jump the gun on them. I was ready to postpone my statement for a day or two to enable them to draw up their comments in reply and would be glad to place their statement along with mine at the same time in the Commons library. They were clearly considerably shaken. Grabham said I had been 'most persuasive', though of course they could not commit their fellow negotiators. They went away clutching my letter and very glad I had agreed not to make a statement tomorrow.

Elizabeth said to me, 'Have you heard the news? Mrs Thatcher has walked it.'[1] I have had a growing conviction that this would happen: she is so clearly the best man among them and she will, in my view, have an enormous advantage in being a woman too. I can't help feeling a thrill, even though I believe her election will make things much more difficult for us. I have been saying for a long time that this country is ready – even more than ready – for a woman Prime Minister. The 'it's time for a change from the male sex' version of the old election slogan. After all, men have been running the show as long as anyone can remember and they don't seem to have made much of a job of it. The excitement of switching to a woman might stir a lot of people out of their lethargy. I think it will be a good thing for the Labour Party too. There's a male-dominated party for you – not least because the trade unions are male-dominated, even the ones that cater for women. I remember just before the February election last year pleading on the NEC for us not to have a completely producer-oriented policy, because women lose out in the producer-run society. The battle for cash wage increases is a masculine obsession. Women are not sold on it, particularly when it leads to strikes, because the men often don't pass their cash increases on to their wives. What matters to the women is the social wage. Of course, no one listened to me: even to suggest that the battle for cash wage increases might be a mirage is to show disloyalty to trade unionism! I believe Margaret Thatcher's election will force our party to think again: and a jolly good thing too. To me, socialism isn't just militant trade unionism. It is the gentle society, in which every producer remembers he is a consumer too.

The first fall-out from the Thatcher news came quickly: it clearly put Harold on his mettle. At a dinner for the New Zealand PM at New Zealand House Harold not only made an amusing speech. He was more relaxed than I have

[1] To win on the second ballot for the Conservative leadership a candidate only required an overall majority (139 votes). The result announced on 11 February was: Thatcher 146, Whitelaw 79, Howe 19, Prior 19, Peyton 11.

seen him for a long time, making impromptu jokes, wandering around talking to everybody and conducting the Maori choir in the singing with the relish of a schoolboy on holiday. Nothing like a bit of sex challenge for bringing the best out in a man. Ted and I then went on to Buckingham Palace for a late reception. I couldn't quite make out what it was in aid of but when I saw that all the literati had been invited from the theatre and the media, from Alec Guinness to Robin Day, I suspected it might not be unconnected with the threatened row over the Civil List.[1] (Incidentally, this matter has never been to Cabinet.) What more apposite than a bit of royal softening up – particularly as the refreshments were modest in the extreme, demonstrating that the royal economy drive is really on: nothing but whisky and some almost undrinkable white wine. Not even a canapé in sight. The Royal Family were waiting in line in force. Prince Charles was as forthcoming as ever, and we joked about how he had lectured me when I was Minister of Transport for introducing the seventy-mile-an-hour speed limit. When with routine courtesy I asked him how he was, he said he was very well, adding for no apparent reason, 'I enjoy my job very much.' Altogether a great night of royal salesmanship. But it was good fun.

Wednesday, 12 February. The papers are full of Margaret Thatcher, who is looking as radiant as a bride. Who wouldn't after such a successful courtship? But the only effect on Harold is to make him scintillate too. I slipped into the House to hear him make his announcement on the Civil List. As he passed Jim and me where we sat on the front bench he whispered chirpily, 'I am in for a rollicking.' 'Did you know about this business?' I asked Jim. 'Not a word of it,' he replied. 'Who *does* decide about the Civil List?' I asked, but he only shrugged. But Harold was on the top of his form, congratulating Margaret impishly and obviously ready to take on all comers from either side. No sign of his being constrained, as some feared, by a woman Leader of the Opposition. Margaret, naturally rather tense, made a not very notable intervention, but one which augurs that she will fight every issue with a populist political slant. When I left, Harold was going great guns. Sex moves in a mysterious way its wonders to perform!

Thursday, 13 February. Harold has had his best press for years. So the first fall-out from Margaret is pure gain to us. Nonetheless I remain convinced she will prove formidable and will have us fighting for our political lives. Right: that will be good for us.

Saturday, 15 February. When at last I got down to HCF I found the BMA statement in reply to mine in my box. Norman's comment on it was that it was 'rather disappointing'. I think it is shamefully irresponsible. It is not only that the statement says it thinks it is 'unlikely' that sanctions will be lifted because I haven't gone far enough; its whole tone is calculated to make the retention of

[1] On 12 February the Prime Minister announced an increase of £420,000 in the Civil List payment to the Royal Family, £150,000 of which the Queen had offered to pay. He defended it by saying that about three-quarters of it was to meet wage and salary increases, mainly for manual and clerical staff. The most serious threat of back-bench revolt came not from the left-wing Tribune group but from the centre-right Manifesto group, who put down an Early Day Motion that '. . . Parliament should have full information concerning the effects of the Sovereign's immunity from taxation which she enjoys not only on the Civil List, but on her private wealth'.

sanctions inevitable. Every conciliatory gesture I have made has been played down. When I phoned David about it he retorted, 'They are impossible. They are weak men and frightened of the HCSA.' He was convinced we had got to forget the new contract and concentrate on getting a good pay increase for the consultants on the present one. One thing he told me was new to me: that last year it was the BMA who had refused to press the Review Body for a change in the incremental scale. Now they are making it a test of my good faith! The trouble is that they don't give a damn for the younger consultant and are more concerned with getting a higher ceiling at the top, while we are more concerned with giving a boost to the chap at the bottom: another reason why they are so mad with me! I spent a good deal of time rewriting the draft statement for me to make on Monday.

Mike has made a speech justifying the miners' increase.[1] All I can say is that it has made it even more inescapable that we should do something generous for the consultants. Personally, my sympathy for the miners has completely run out. I can't help remembering the very moving interview which Sid Weighell of the NUR had on *Midweek* on Thursday night. 'What *am* I to say to my railwaymen who move the coal the surfacemen have loaded? Is their job really worth so much less?' One thing is certain: the miners' settlement has given inflation another dangerous upward twist and brought nearer the demand some members of Cabinet will make for restraints on pay increases. All I know is that I am not going to have wage restraint introduced *now* at the expense of my GPs and consultants, who are at the end of the line. Wouldn't it be ironic if I had to resign because Cabinet refused to give them a proper increase?

Monday, 17 February. Henry and Philip liked my redraft very much. David had some different drafting of his own out of which I incorporated some points. Henry didn't agree with me that the BMA statement was as bloody minded as I thought it was. He said that the negotiators had obviously been very divided over it. When he phoned Gullick about it on Friday Gullick had replied that it was 'now being retyped for the umpteenth time'. He thought the fact that there had been no leaks of my letter over the weekend (which David had gloomily forecast) was a sign that they were trying not to close the door. It was just that they were incapable of giving leadership. In the House my statement went extremely well.[2] Even Geoffrey Howe, with Margaret sitting watching him, didn't try to make any serious political mileage out of it, while our people backed me enthusiastically. I then managed to stay on for a snatched quarter of an hour to listen to Wedgie move the second reading of his Industry Bill. The Tories were giving him a sustained barracking, but he ploughed on, declaring his faith like a young martyr at the stake. (He always gives one the impression of being youthful, despite his grey hairs.) But I do wish he could manage to

[1] A settlement had just been reached which raised the basic rates of 246,000 miners by up to 35 per cent, with bonuses in addition for increased output. Michael Foot had defended it as being necessary to carry through 'a much needed . . . reform of the pay structure', which did not conflict with the Social Contract.

[2] I reported some of the discussions which had been taking place in the 'clarification' meetings on the new contract and repeated that certain principles, like the whole-timers' differential, were not negotiable. I added that we did not wish these discussions to hold up the consultants' pay increase due in April and announced that I was giving evidence to the Review Body in support of that increase and of important improvements in their incremental scale.

sound less like a lay preacher helping everyone else to find the right road to God.

Tuesday, 18 February. Eric Heffer had a rough ride winding up on the Industry Bill debate. He didn't make a great speech, but he did have the vital political stamina to plough on regardless to the end. Our majority, in the event, was quite comfortable, some of the Welsh Nationalists having switched. As it has happened, we have coasted through most divisions so far with an easy margin, but all that may change as Maggie leads her troops into a real fight. Life should be fun with an embittered Ted Heath on the back benches, together with the other ex-frontbenchers Maggie sends to join him. Her progress continues to be a triumphal one.

Wednesday, 19 February. Spent the whole morning at the Women's National Commission. I must be getting feminist in my old age! Then into an office meeting on pay beds. We all agree that I must get a paper to Cabinet quickly, so that we are ready with an announcement, either if we can get into talks with the BMA again, or if the unions break out of the restraints their leaders are desperately trying to keep on them. David is now convinced that we cannot hold the position for three years, but he gets quite tetchy at the idea of our trying to control the *quantity* of beds in the private hospitals that will undoubtedly spring up everywhere. He is far more reactionary about this than my officials are! I say firmly that I see no reason why I should not announce that I intend to keep the number of private beds to the level of the pay beds currently allowed in the NHS. I am convinced that we have to got to fight like hell to prevent the building up of a vast empire of private medicine. And with not enough money to keep the NHS expanding and improving as it ought, our whole policy is in danger.

Thursday, 20 February. Harold is back from Moscow, immensely proud of his achievements and of the communiqué.[1] And of course he is full of the welcome they received from the Russians. 'They laid themselves out in an unparalleled way by all the standard tests' (*e.g.* column inches in *Pravda*). On parliamentary business Harold surprised us by saying suddenly that he wanted to explain what would be his parliamentary strategy in view of the election of a new Tory leader. As far as Thatcher was concerned: 'I shall answer every question in the spirit in which it is put. If it is a genuine request for information I shall be informative. I want to concentrate on policy. I don't want to get into the situation I was in with Heath: confrontation.' So obviously he has been giving some anxious thought to it!

As I worked late at the office, news came through that the CCHMS had refused to withdraw sanctions; but they haven't extended them and they have asked to see the PM. I can't help feeling this is not a bad sign and Henry tells me Grabham tried hard to get them to negotiate with me. So my talk with him seems to have worked. I had to rush into TV interviews and a press conference.

[1] The long communiqué set out an agreed programme of Anglo-Soviet co-operation, particularly in the economic and scientific fields. Both sides agreed 'to aim at achieving a substantial increase in the level of trade'. Britain announced the provision of just under £1,000 million of credits for trade over a five-year period.

We shall have to give careful thought to where we go from here.

Friday, 21 February. To Sunningdale, where we are to have the first of our consultation meetings on the new strategy we need to cope with the financial straits that now face the NHS. This one was with the regional chairmen as a whole. With one or two exceptions I didn't find them a particularly impressive lot. I get the feeling that these appointed bodies are like a fifth wheel on the coach. They neither speak as elected representatives nor do they have the expertise of their own officials. And their attitude to the Secretary of State and the Department is necessarily pretty subservient – they want to keep their jobs! Nonetheless I found the two-day talks valuable, not least because they enabled me to set some time aside to study the details of the grim options that are now open to us. Anyway, the chairmen told me afterwards they had enjoyed themselves enormously.

During the weekend David, Philip, Henry, Norman and I discussed the answer the PM should send to the BMA. Philip and Henry said they thought he must turn down the request for a meeting, but David and I agreed we must take a more positive posture and constantly keep putting the ball back in the consultants' court. I liked Norman's idea that the PM might say he would see them if they would withdraw sanctions and I went back to Hell Corner Farm to draft what I think is a rather clever version of it.

One amusing moment came when David said to me, 'These people still think they can divide Harold from you, but I keep telling them yours is the strongest political alliance in the whole Government. You stood by Harold when no one else did. You really have a special relationship.' I hope he is right!

With the TUC guidelines being breached on every side, inflation had begun to run away. Over the twelve months to December average earnings had increased by 29.1 per cent and by January retail prices had risen by nearly 20 per cent over the previous year, with more increases in the pipeline. Output was falling and by 10 February unemployment had reached 734,000 or 3.1 per cent, with nearly another quarter of a million people on short time. Though the trade deficit was improving there were signs that this was due not so much to an improvement in Britain's industrial performance as to a big jump in our export prices which would eventually make us uncompetitive. World trade remained depressed, aggravated by competitive deflation among major industrial countries determined to keep out of deficit at all costs. West Germany insisted on remaining in surplus over the whole period. Sterling was under intense pressure and our reserves were shrinking, necessitating further borrowing. The press began to talk of national bankruptcy.

There was growing agreement in the Labour movement that something must be done. The argument was about what was necessary. With the CBI's latest survey reporting a slump in business confidence Harold Wilson had hastened to assure firms that Tony Benn would not be allowed a free hand to intervene in industry. Denis Healey was planning new stimuli for private industry. For its part the TUC was divided on the need to strengthen the guidelines and was calling for some reflation to save jobs. A new school of British economists, the Cambridge Economic Policy Group, led by Mr Wynne Godley, Director of the University of Cambridge Department of Applied Economics, had produced a challenging new analysis of the conditions for economic recovery, in which import controls played a crucial part. This was to dominate the political argument.

On the NEC apprehension about the crisis was growing. At the March meeting of the

Home Policy Committee Geoff Bish, the Party's Research Secretary, produced, 'with the agreement of the chairman' (Tony Benn), the first of what were to become four-monthly Economic Reviews, setting out 'some of the possible options available to the Government'. The most notable thing about this first Review was the priority it gave to tackling inflation and its bald statement: 'The reality of Britain's position today is that there is very little room for any improvement at all in personal living standards over the next four years.' It also rejected the idea that the Government could simply reflate its way out of unemployment. But it also rejected conventional deflationary policies or the belief that private industry could be bribed to invest in British industry to the extent needed. The answer, it argued, lay in more government intervention in industry through planning agreements, which must be enforced, if necessary, and through the NEB, *which should be given greater powers. In the short term, to stop the rot in manufacturing industry, import controls might be inevitable. He was already planning a severe budget and another £1 billion of cuts in public expenditure in 1976–77.*

Meanwhile the renegotiations of Britain's terms for membership of the EEC *were being hurried on in preparation for a decision at the Dublin summit on 10 March. The anti-Market members of Cabinet found the terms that were emerging totally unacceptable and started to prepare their counter-attack in the referendum campaign which was to infuriate Harold Wilson. In my own Department the negotiations with the consultants for ending their 'sanctions' dragged on endlessly. It was clear that the dispute would only be settled by the Government's willingness to implement in full their Review Body's pay award on their existing contract, due in April: the first review since statutory pay controls had been abolished. Although believing that voluntary restraint on pay increases was essential if the 'social wage' was to be safeguarded, I was determined that consultants, junior doctors and* GPs *should not be penalized by being the last in the queue in the free-for-all pay round.*

Saturday, 1 March. Looking back, I think this has been quite one of the most impossible weeks I have ever had. More than once in the past I have said to myself, 'The pressures this week are intolerable; next week *must* be easier', only to find that the following week has been worse. But this time I really do think I have had to crowd more into seven days (in the form of major policy statements, key speeches and policy crises) than I can ever remember and I have been top for Questions as well. There have been moments when I have felt my head would burst – and moments when my temper definitely has burst. It hasn't so much been the lack of sleep (I can manage pretty easily on five hours a night these days) as the relentless pressure of rushing from one piece of major exposure to the next, without even five minutes to relax and take a breath. It has been the endless worry as to whether I would even have a whole garment and an unladdered pair of tights to wear. Poor old Ted pointed out to me at mid-week that his jacket was torn and that he had a missing button which he couldn't get sewn on. My riposte was to pull out my winter coat, whose lining is falling apart for want of a stitch, and tell him how embarrassed I was when people at functions insisted on helping me into it. Any woman in public life really needs a seamstress and hairdresser to travel with her everywhere if she is to have her mind free for higher things. The Queen does, and, for all her public protestations, I suspect Margaret Thatcher has something much nearer to that than I have.

Monday started early, as I had to be at the Liaison Committee with the TUC at the House of Commons. I arrived a little late to find Wedgie in the chair and a full complement of the trade unions – even Hughie. The subject was ostensibly to discuss the draft of the TUC's *Economic Review*, but we all knew we were bursting to talk about inflation and what on earth the trade unions were going to do to help us about it. Jack Jones spoke with an almost pleading anxiety: 'The fact that we are trying has had an effect. Even the miners' settlement could be much worse. All we can do is to use what influence we can and I hope we shall not fall out on the basis that the unions are backsliding.'

Then came the surprise of the morning as Hughie stirred into speech, writhing in his chair as he always does when he feels strongly about something. 'What we should do is some straight talking within the TUC itself,' he said. 'The position has already been breached. If there is a free-for-all my union wants to be part of the all – and I am talking about the trade union movement.' We all knew, he went on, that his union had abstained on the Social Contract vote at Congress because it wanted to see what the Government would do, but at the meeting of his policy committee last November they had taken a line 'that can only be interpreted as concurrence'. But the guidelines meant 'only one increase a year and that within the cost of living, and if we mean that why don't we say so?' Wonders will never cease! The rest of us could hardly believe our ears, while Alf Allen murmured, 'I concur with that.' (Later someone pointed out to me that Hughie must be sensing the right-wing winds beginning to blow through his union.) Harold said the Tories were moving into a monetarist policy which would highlight the warning of what was the alternative awaiting us.

And so we broke up, still friends, the unions still pleading with us that they were doing their best, and with every one of us aware of the unions' difficulties. Perhaps Hughie's *volte-face* may signal a tougher line by the TUC in support of the guidelines before too long. But I still think Michael's public reaction to the miners' settlement was too soft and tolerant. I still do not see any alternative to a voluntary policy, but I despair at the Government's failure to orchestrate a firm exposition of what is necessary for the Social Contract to succeed and what steps we will have to take if it doesn't. I am more convinced than ever of the importance of my pamphlet on the social wage.[1]

I slipped off before the end in order to fit in an office meeting on the reply Harold should send to the consultants. It was cleared by No. 10 with barely a change. We next had a long ministerial lunch, with, as usual, so many items of interest that we ran over time. We had to discuss the social wage document, of which Brian A–S. had done another redraft along the lines we suggested. We agreed it is shaping up nicely now and that we should put it in the hands of a popular journalist to decide how to present it. I am desperately anxious to get it out quickly before Denis's axe falls.

It was late when I got home that night with only half my box work done. Submissions on this and that go on showering onto me and I just cannot get the necessary time to do any work in depth. For instance, I have to make a major

[1] Denis Healey having failed to produce a popular version of the Public Expenditure White Paper, I had decided to do one myself. I believed we were failing to get across to working people the cash value to them of the social services and how wrong it was for them to think of the taxes they paid as a pure loss. Brian Abel-Smith had worked out a series of useful illustrations. For example, when a woman had a baby she was entitled to free maternity services worth £300. We estimated that this 'second wage' was worth about £20 a week for every member of the working population.

statement on mental handicap policy tomorrow at a conference called by the National Society for Mentally Handicapped Children. I then tried to master a detailed background brief for the questions it has been agreed I should take at the conference. Really! A detailed Finer statement to produce on Friday;[1] a detailed mental handicap statement to make on Wednesday; a massive detailed brief to master on the Pensions Bill which we were to launch for press conferences on Thursday; a major speech on the social wage to make on Saturday (and a day centre to open on Friday!). No human being could be expected to do all this *in addition* to PQs and all the urgent routine office work. If I survive I deserve to be hailed as a genius.

I was a bit late for the private discussion dinner [on Wednesday] arranged for us by the NHS unions. Everyone I had suggested was there: Terry Parry (in the chair), Alan Fisher, Audrey Prime, Geoffrey Drain, Clive Jenkins, Peter Jacques, Renee Short,[2] Laurie Pavitt and my lot. Terry had insisted that on the union side only members of the General Council of the TUC should be there. It was a cosy, amiable meal in Victor's top room at the Gay Hussar, though we had to rush things a bit as we had to get back to vote on the Civil List. But we managed to cover all the ground, in addition to eating a good meal. The whole idea of the operation from my point of view was the education of David Owen, with whom I have been having such difficulty over the pay beds policy. In the event it was intriguing to see how completely he swung behind the unions' view. When I, leaning over backwards to present every side of the case (including his previous view), said that the profession would be expecting at least three years for phasing out, he promptly agreed with the unions that eighteen months would be the absolute maximum. So when we came to the issue of controls over the private sector of medicine I wasn't going to be caught again and said firmly that I thought I would be entirely justified in saying that I intended to limit the increase in the number of private beds outside the NHS to the figure at present obtaining inside the NHS – *i.e.* four thousand. Clive said he thought that would be acceptable to them, whereupon David said at once that this was undoubtedly the right course! Well, I'm delighted to have him committed. As I told him the other day, he is rather like Dick Crossman in that he likes to put up a line of argument purely for argument's sake, only to abandon it later – and he agreed cheerfully.

Sunday, 2 March. We broke our weekend's peace to go up to town for dinner with Mike. Since we can no longer afford our weekly Lockets dinner this is the only way our little group can keep in touch. As usual, Jill served up a superb meal and the red wine flowed. To our surprise, when Ted and I arrived (first as usual) Mike was solacing himself with classical music on the hi-fi. I hadn't realized he had that side to him. But the arrival of the Shores, Baloghs and Benns soon put a stop to that. Peter, who is off to foreign parts again in the morning, wanted above all to talk about the Dublin summit and the EEC. He

[1] The Finer Committee on One-Parent Families, which had reported in July 1974 (Cmnd 5629), had highlighted the financial difficulties of one-parent families and recommended a new cash benefit for them, plus generous child allowances.

[2] Terry Parry, General Secretary of the Fire Brigades Union; Audrey Prime, NALGO; Geoffrey Drain, General Secretary, NALGO; Peter Jacques, TUC; Renee Short, Labour MP for Wolverhampton North East.

was all for postponing a decision at Dublin if possible. But after I had listened to the discussion for a couple of hours a clear picture of what we ought to do crystallized in my mind.

I said I disagreed with Peter that we must play for time. The first question we had to answer was, under what auspices should we conduct our anti-Market campaign when the time came? I – like the rest of them, no doubt – was being approached by various anti-Market bodies to speak for them. Were we all going to fragment ourselves by appearing on non-party platforms, while the Government conducted a concerted official pro-Market campaign? If, I continued, Mike said we should wait for the terms and then swing the official Party machine onto our side, so that we all spoke at meetings arranged by Ron Hayward, he was overlooking two things: (a) Ron would never put Harold willingly at risk, so he was likely to drag his feet, and (b) Jim had manœuvred Ron into agreeing to call the special conference as late as 17 May and Ron would be unlikely to organize anything until after that date. That would leave us approximately three weeks in which to do our stuff. The moral of this was that, first, we needed a decision on the terms as quickly as possible, so as to leave us time to counter-organize, and, secondly, that we should create our own auspices. These should take the form of a Cabinet-level brains trust of all those members of Cabinet who came out against entry. 'This is the only way to counteract the authority of a Cabinet decision to stay in,' I maintained. We should form a committee as soon as the result of renegotiation was known and offer ourselves as a brains trust to anyone who would like to organize a large meeting for us. If necessary, my secretary would help with the organizing. Peter agreed I might be right, Mike demurrred, but Wedgie got quite excited and backed me in his enthusiastic way.

Monday, 3 March. Back to work, positively refreshed by last night's dinner. We had another crowded agenda for the ministerial lunch. The troops were delighted when I said I intended to have a blitz on NHS spectacles[1] and suggested I should see Marcus Sieff[2] to ask his advice on how I could get a top designer to design new frames which we would then have mass-produced. David said rather wryly that (a) it would cost more money (which I deny) and (b) that top officials were already so overworked that he hesitated to ask them to take on any more. In any case the Department was very weak on this side and we really ought to get someone in from outside as a procurement adviser. I thought this an excellent idea and Alf pointed out that he and Jack Ashley had had the same trouble with the Department in trying to get a more 'cosmetic' hearing aid under the NHS. The Department's instinctive reaction was that private industry should make the beautiful things and the NHS the ugly ones. I said I was determined to change all that. David promised to let me have a paper in three weeks' time. He also had the excellent idea that I should ask Hugh Cudlipp to suggest someone to write up our social wage paper, on which I am

[1] I was horrified at the extent to which even working-class families spent large sums on private spectacle frames because the range of NHS spectacle frames, particularly for women, was so limited and unattractive. I believed that attractive mass-produced frames need not be more expensive than unattractive ones and that in any case costs could be reduced by promoting the new frames for export.

[2] Sir Marcus Sieff was chairman of Marks and Spencer. He was made a life peer in 1980.

keener than ever, following the reception of my speech at Scarborough. At the Sextet meeting which followed I told Philip what I intended to do about the journalist and the procurement adviser. He just swallowed and said nothing.

The consultants have written back to Harold asking him to reconsider his refusal to see them. We decided to postpone consideration of our next step until we have had a chance to study the reply. About eighty Tories have signed an Early Day Motion calling for the appointment of an independent adjudicator to handle my dispute with the consultants. I said I would have no objection at all to the dispute going to ACAS, particularly as this would compel the consultants to spell out just what they thought it was about. This tickled Henry enormously, but Philip was worried at the idea of ACAS handling a dispute in which a Minister was involved and wanted to think about it.

David came to see me about the paper on the 1975 pay recommendations for the non-industrial civil service, which was due to come before the Cabinet working group this afternoon.[1] He was deeply anxious about the way the economy is developing: 'I don't think the Government's economic strategy will hold.' The problem of this 26 per cent pay increase was appallingly difficult. He had no doubt we would get industrial action if we tried to tinker with the findings of the Pay Research Unit, yet equally there was no doubt about the damage this increase would do.

Certainly, at the top of the scale the increases recommended are absurd: Assistant Secretaries go up from £8,850 to £11,000, while even Principals go up to £7,550, more than many a consultant gets! When Philip came to discuss the matter with me last Thursday I told him then, 'I expect my salary will fall behind everyone else's for years ahead, but that doesn't bother me: I have a comfortable living and a fascinating job. I don't give a damn about status and differentials.' 'That is a sentiment I honour,' replied Philip. 'But I have to tell you that if the Government does not accept this award it will, I am afraid, just not be able to get its business done.' I shrugged and replied, 'Then let people chase mirages. One day the stick will come down to earth with a thud.'

I went along to the working group meeting on the pay recommendations, quite clear what I must do. Malcolm spelt out the predictable civil service view; then Mike came in emphatically. At last Tuesday's MES, he said, the members had agreed to adopt a stronger attitude to pay increases. This was the first test. The increases were not by any stretch of imagination within the TUC guidelines: 'comparability does not figure in those'. Indeed, we were about to try to convince the railwaymen that comparability with the miners was not on. He therefore suggested we should try to get the increases reduced by 5 per cent. He wouldn't propose to overturn the Pay Research Unit, but would approach the TUC and ask for their support with the staff side. Denis said at once that he supported Mike. The MES paper, he said, showed that private sector settle-

[1] The determination of non-industrial civil servants' pay up to the top grades was based on agreement reached following the report of the Priestly Royal Commission on the Civil Service (Cmnd 9613, 1955). This recommended that pay for this group should reflect 'fair comparison with the current remuneration of outside staffs employed on broadly comparable work, taking account of differences in other conditions of service'. The Pay Research Unit [PRU] was set up to undertake fact-finding on job comparisons and on pay and conditions of service. On 14 April it had recommended an increase of about 30 per cent since the last award in January 1974: an annual increase of about 26 per cent. This applied to roughly 500,000 white-collar and non-industrial civil servants ranging from clerks and cleaners up to the Assistant Secretary grade.

ments were tending to fall off, due no doubt in part to the rise in unemployment. It was the public sector settlements which were now the problem, because the public sector was insulated against unemployment. It was here we must stand firm. On this award we should if necessary go to arbitration and have the full increase forced upon us. That would be better than conceding it.

I came in here – quietly for me – saying what David and I had agreed earlier and pointing out that I would consider the attempt to introduce a unilateral form of incomes policy at the end of a pay increase spree and at the expense of the public sector as 'contemptible'. Moreover I warned them that if I were to be forced now – because the Government was panicking – to go back on a pledge to the doctors which I had made with Mike's full connivance, I should be forced to resign. I repeated that we had one of two choices: either to back-track on our decision on top salaries, which was the cause of all our troubles, or to sweat it out till the end of the first free year's round of increases and then work out a much tougher set of criteria. But what we couldn't do – suddenly, arbitrarily and one-sidedly – was to ditch the machinery we had set up to deal with these cases. Tony [Crosland] urged again that 'we can't decide in forty-five minutes that fair comparison should go'. Mike, replying to me, claimed that 'the fact that we made a mess over top salaries doesn't mean we should repeat it now', to which I retorted, 'Of course, it does mean just that.' I was interested in Mike's plea: 'This is a decision about the whole pay policy of the Government – if it has a pay policy.' Finally we agreed that the matter should go to EC(P) [Committee on Economic Policy] for consideration in the wider context of what other demands are coming forward and our likely response to them. I certainly intend to be there and to force Michael to take a more comprehensive and more logically philosophical view. But I continue to admire him for the stamina he is showing in his fight to preserve the Social Contract, with all the unpopular decisions that involves.

When I reported to David he looked gloomy. He was particularly amused at my description of Crosland's line. 'That's the trouble with him,' said David. 'I think he has the best mind in the Government, but he just can't come to decisions. That is why he has never got to the very top.' I suggested to David we should put up a paper to EC(P) and he agreed to go away and have a shot at it.

Treated Ted and Brian O'Malley to a steak in the House. Brian and I talked companionable shop while Ted no doubt puzzled over the deep sense of political mateyness there is between us. We *enjoy* our politics. Afterwards I said to Brian, 'I have an idea. Later this year, when we have got pensions out of the way and I have done as much as I can for the NHS, I've told Harold I wouldn't mind becoming Leader of the House. What about being my Chief Whip?' He was tickled pink at the idea, but thought the Party would fall to pieces before then because Bob had shot his bolt and there was no real leadership from the Whips' Office. I think he and I could do a terrific job together dealing with the Party in Parliament in what is bound to be a period of increasing strain.

Tuesday, 4 March. David tells me he is mounting quite an exercise to get the paper on pay policy for which I have asked produced for EC(P). I enjoy working with him, too. He is very different from Brian and me, but he does bubble up with ideas and I find we interact very productively. I am supremely lucky in my team – but then I told Harold the people I wanted. David has sent a Minute challenging (quite rightly) Dick Bourton's conventional Treasury-type reaction to a paper Denis Healey has circulated about the next round of the perennial public expenditure review. Denis just wants to take this year's distribution of the spoils between Departments and whittle it down a bit. Dick Bourton obviously believes this is right, but David insists that this is the moment to demand a fundamental re-examination of the Tory priorities we inherited. He and I agreed that the top brass in our Department have a sneaking sympathy with the restrictions the Treasury are trying to put on us (and on public expenditure generally), but I told David to go off and draft a reply to Denis saying we wanted a basic reassessment of priorities. David certainly does work prodigiously. Not all his ideas are sound by any means, but he stirs things up in an entirely healthy way.

At last I have got Private Office to earmark time for me to go in and hear PM's Questions. I want to keep in some kind of touch with the developing drama on the Tory benches. Margaret's election has stirred up her own side wonderfully: all her back benchers perform like knights jousting at a tourney for a lady's favours, showing off their paces by making an unholy row at every opportunity over everything the Government does. Today they were baiting Harold. Everybody kept glancing at Margaret to see when she would take him on. She sat with bowed head and detached primness while the row went on: hair immaculately groomed, smart dress crowned by a string of pearls. At last she rose to enormous cheers from her own side to deliver an adequate but hardly memorable intervention with studied charm. Roy J., sitting next to me, groaned and I said, 'She's not quite real, is she?' As he agreed, I added, 'If she would only occasionally come in with a smut on her nose, her hair dishevelled, looking as if she had been wrestling with her soul as I do.' He gave me his slow smile. 'I wouldn't say that your hair is ever dishevelled. If that is to be the criterion, then Shirley would win every time.' 'That's why everyone likes her,' I retorted. 'Men never feel at ease with a woman politician who looks as if her hair has just been permed.'

Settled as we are in the House for four nights on a three-liner on the Finance Bill, I have seized the opportunity to ask Hugh Cudlipp over for a drink, to try and enlist his help in getting a popular-impact version of all the work we have been doing on the social wage document. He began by saying that he had guessed why I had asked him over: it was to do, as Dick Crossman had asked him to do all those years ago, a popular version of the 'Better Pensions' plan. When I told him it was something much more difficult that that, and handed him Brian A–S.'s basic social wage document on the social wage, his eyes glazed over and he said he would have to take it away. He left with an elaborate round of hand-kissing, making a particular fuss of Brian.

Wednesday, 5 March. I was immensely touched when I got to my room in the House this morning to find a bunch of freesias and tulips on my desk. Who on earth? A card explained the plot. It was Private Office's recognition that today was exactly one year's anniversary of my entry into the job. Ten of them in Private Office and the Letters Section had signed it: 'To the Secretary of State on your first anniversary with us – we've enjoyed the first year enormously and look forward to more. Best wishes from your *very* obedient servants[!]' I sent Janet out to find me an equally impish reply card and she came back with a very suitable one – something to the effect that it wasn't that I had forgotten the anniversary: I was merely in good time for next year! I scribbled on it my thanks for their flowers, card and 'belated obedience', adding 'three surprises at one go'. I get very fond of my civil servants (or at any rate some of them). The outside world has no idea how human they are.

Lunch with the medical correspondents. Though I had had little time to prepare, I rather enjoyed myself, teasing John Stevenson of the *Mail*, who was sitting opposite (and who is my most persistent persecutor at press conferences). The chairman told me that it was a record attendance, to which I replied sweetly, 'Barbara-baiting is a national sport.' Norman (whom I took for a quick, vigorous walk round St James's Park afterwards) told me that the speech came over well. We ought to use it again, because obviously even these expert correspondents hadn't yet grasped the simple facts I gave them about the financing of the NHS. We were both intrigued by the way Stevenson pursued me through and after the lunch – all the way down the stairs – pleading with me to take some new initiative to resolve the consultants' dispute. We both got the impression that the BMA is getting worried and is desperately anxious to get off the hook.

Further evidence of this lies in the reply the BMA have sent to the PM. Far from spitting in his face, they have urged him to reconsider his refusal to see them until sanctions have been lifted and have now dredged up a rather injudicious answer to a Parliamentary Question Dick Crossman gave some years ago.[1] At a meeting with officials we discussed a draft reply for the PM to send yet again. Henry is nervously feeling the way to a further 'give' on our side, though his initiatives collapse as soon as he sees they aren't popular with the rest of us (including Ian Gillis, who was holding a watching brief for Peter. Where *does* that man get to?). David was all in favour of our sweating it out. Henry looked like a grateful basset hound when I said that in any case the tone (if not the content) of the PM's reply should be conciliatory.

Norman tells me Cudlipp has sent a message: (a) he does think our material can be made into a popular pamphlet and (b) he is finding someone to do it for us. I have laid my plans for Hugh to do the popular version of 'Better Pensions' for us. Life is rather fun. And oddly enough I don't worry about my burdens half as much as I used to do.

In the division lobby late at night Wedgie said to me, 'I have done nothing but think about what you said about the referendum last Sunday. You are absolutely right: we must set up an anti-Common Market mini-Cabinet as soon as the terms are known. At the very least we could then issue an authoritative statement. It is essential that our impact should be co-ordinated. But the first question is, who would be the members of it?' We agreed to continue the discussion at the meal we are all to have at Peter Shore's on Sunday night.

[1] The consultants were still trying to get the maximum part-timer's commitment to the NHS defined as being limited to nine half days a week and had quoted a written reply which Dick Crossman had given to a Parliamentary Question in 1969. Officials assured me that the reply had been misinterpreted.

Thursday, 6 March. Home at 1 am again. Four nights on the Finance Bill this week! The proceedings have been punctuated by a series of Parliamentary storms as Margaret's back benchers have been demonstrating their new-found political virility. But the papers are full of the row she has created by sacking the Director-General of the Conservative political machine, Michael Woolf, while our people tell me that Margaret's party political broadcast last night was such a sweetly calculated bit of femininity that it was nauseating. Well, it is too soon to say how she will make out.

Friday, 7 March. Great panic because I just have nothing to wear for today's opening of the new Queen Mary's hospital at Sidcup. At the last minute I was frantically stitching the bow on my old black dress and decided I should just have to carry off my shabbiness with aplomb. Despite the consultants' threatened boycott of the opening it went off well. I just didn't notice whether the consultants were there or not and addressed myself to the nurses in the audience instead. More work at the office and then off to speak to Woolwich Labour Party. The funny thing is that, despite the short nights and endless strain, people are always telling me how well I look. The secret, as I've said before, lies in the fact that the older I grow the more philosophical I become – the more at ease in speaking to and meeting people All right, I sometimes get so strained that I blow my top, but once the pressure is relaxed I bounce back again.

Saturday, 8 March. Once again we broke our weekend to come up to London for a Sunday night dinner of our group, this time at Peter's. This is becoming quite a habit, but it wasn't such a wrench to leave HCF in the March sleet. With the EEC issue coming to the crunch, we have at least been driven to recognize the need for something more organized than the dilettantish discussions we have had up to now. The Foots and Harts were there, but no Silkin, no Baloghs, and – at the last minute – a message from Wedgie. He was sorry, but he felt so exhausted he thought he had better go to bed. So even his ever-youthful energy is feeling the strain!

Bereft of my ally, Wedgie, I tried to get Mike and Peter interested again in my proposals for organizing our opposition to the Common Market. Fortunately Judith was enthusiastic and said she thought a lot of non-Cabinet Ministers would like to sign a common statement, while Jill Foot got quite excited about the idea. They agreed with me that we must issue the statement promptly and that, between us, we could organize the brains trusts I proposed. Mike and Peter sat shaking their heads, but Judith and I are determined to pursue this at Lockets on Tuesday. These meandering men!

Tuesday, 11 March. In the evening we revived our Lockets dinner, at which Judith and I pressed the points I had been making on Sunday night about the need for us to organize a 'Cabinet [Ministers] Against the Market' group and be ready to present it at a press conference as an authoritative alternative to the inevitable pro-Market line of Cabinet as soon as the decision was known. Once again Peter and Mike seemed a bit diffident, but Judith backed me nobly and we worked out a plan of action to the last detail. Wedgie was given the job of drafting a statement for us to issue and John undertook to check the list of anti-Market junior Ministers and MPS which Jack Straw had hurriedly drawn up for me. We also agreed to meet at our flat for dinner next Sunday and that Jack Jones, Clive and Mik should be invited, so that the whole exercise between Cabinet Ministers, junior Ministers, MPS and unions could be co-ordinated. I went home feeling that something concrete had been decided at last.

During the debate on the Referendum White Paper in the House I thought Margaret made an effective speech. One of our Whips, sitting next to me, muttered, 'She's just a clever little lawyer.' Well, that is more than you can say about a lot of our Ministers – or the Tory ones.

Wednesday, 12 March. More office meetings on the consultants. Henry has fallen for the idea some of the profession have put forward that an independent 'fact-finder' should be asked to adjudicate on just what the facts are in the dispute. Of course, I would have nothing to do with it, but didn't object to Henry probing as to what Grabham and co. thought the terms of reference should be. That would at least pin them down as to what they thought the dispute was all about.

Took the night train to Blackpool to open the new maternity unit at the Victoria Hospital.

Friday, 14 March. A most successful day at the Victoria Hospital. I followed my usual practice of stopping to talk freely and friendlily – for instance, to a waiting deputation of anxious mothers, wanting to lobby me about the proposed closure of their hospital. I had some nice photos taken of me talking to them, banners and all. They were overwhelmed that I should stop and listen to them. I also insisted on seeing a couple of junior doctors who had been breathing fire and slaughter about me and demanding to talk to me. I gave them a drink, chatted for half an hour and sent them away in an entirely different mood, with the result that they told the press I was quite different from what they had expected. Finally I held a reception with representatives of every level of staff at the hospital. Norman has at last managed to persuade health authorities that this is what I want and although I gather there were some mutterings on the health authority about it, it went famously. Porters, laundry-men, kitchen staff, nurses, radiographers were all given drinks and chatted to me delightedly as I circulated among them. And as the official ceremony went well, with both Sidney Hamburger, the regional chairman, and me making informal and jolly speeches, I went home feeling very satisfied with everything.

Sunday, 16 March. Everybody seemed to decide to turn up at the referendum conspiracy meal at our flat. In the event it meant catering for over twenty people and I had to come up early from HCF to get the food ready. Despite all the preparation I did beforehand, I was inevitably on the go looking after everyone and missed some of the discussion that was going on. Jack Jones was a bit apprehensive of the taramosalata, though he had two helpings of goulash, but his wife, Evelyn, tucked enthusiastically into everything and appeared in a more human light than I have ever seen her. Clive Jenkins arrived with a couple of bottles of champagne, which was a welcome reinforcement. When I finally joined them after the meal, Mik was in charge and was holding forth about the blitz we must make on the NEC next Wednesday. They were all trying to draft a Motion for the NEC (of which we should have to give a week's notice) and getting nowhere fast. I piped up and said my usual piece: how our most effective counterblast to the Establishment was to come out as *Ministers* and to organize our group under the heading 'Cabinet Against the Market'. Clive was most enthusiastic about this. Wedgie produced the draft statement for the Cabinet Ministers' press conference. Mik said at once that this ought to be the basis of an immediate Early Day Motion[1] and of the Motion for the NEC. And so it was agreed. Jack Jones pledged that the unions would swing into line with us, but he was very anxious for us not to undermine the all-party basis of the anti-Market campaign, as he thought we should need every vote we could get. We broke up late with everything organized. I felt I had done a good evening's work and I knew the concept of 'Cabinet Against the Market' was a winner.

Monday, 17 March. When we assembled at No. 10 for the start of our Common Market marathon I passed Eric Varley a note: 'I'm bored before we start.' We had a pile of papers from Jim in front of us, explaining under the seven headings of the Manifesto targets what he claimed we had achieved in the renegotiations. I groaned at the thought of the tedious charade that lay ahead. We all knew that everybody had made up their minds and that nothing anyone said would change anything. And so it proved with the pros (including Harold and Jim) putting the best gloss on everything and being challenged line by line by us. On economic and monetary union, for instance, Harold insisted that it was dead, while Mike pointed out that the Paris communiqué had said the exact opposite. It all took a long time and when we adjourned at 1.30 pm we still hadn't reached the issue of sovereignty. Harold, stressing that this was merely an exploratory stage and that no firm decisions were being reached till tomorrow, said we must meet in the morning at 9.30. Groans went up from every side and voices were heard asking whether our misery could not at least be alleviated by coffee. Harold said he would see what could be done.

Later it was the turn of the PLP to be consulted. But first I got the horrible news that the Second Reading of our Pensions Bill has been switched to tomorrow and I have nothing prepared! No time to do anything about it before the PLP meeting, which I felt that, for decency's sake, I must attend. But that, too, turned out to be a ritual. Harold made a low-key introductory speech, running through the Manifesto shopping list like a bored housewife at the grocer's. I suspect that that is his way of playing fair. I had to leave before the end, but I gather Jim had no such scruples and made his own views plain.

Tuesday, 18 March. Up at 6 am to sketch out my Second Reading speech on the Pensions Bill. As always, the office is pleading for a text so that they can clear it with Treasury. I send them a few pages and tell them I will have to finish the rest somehow in Cabinet. I arrived a little late at Cabinet to hear Ted Short droning his way through the sovereignty issue. Peter was soon dressing him down,

[1] Back-bench MPs can table a Motion on the Commons' Order Paper on almost any subject they choose. They then collect as many signatures as possible in the hope of forcing the Government to allow an early debate on it. Since this does not often happen, the main value is propagandist.

complaining that the treatment of this had been 'the most regrettable feature of the whole negotiations'.

At last Harold said the time had come for him to go round the table and get our views, adding – to general approval – that he thought he ought to make his statement to the House the same day. This gave me the opportunity to work away at my pensions speech, as I knew pretty predictably what people would say. I merely kept half an ear open to see how the doubtful ones would vote: Willie Ross, for instance, who was okay anti in his usual lugubrious way; Merlyn, who (as Eric Varley had predicted) came down on Big Jim's side; and Eric himself, who hadn't opened his mouth during the two long discussions. He merely said tersely that he remained opposed to membership, largely on energy grounds (which he didn't specify). When my turn came I said no one would be surprised to know my view was against. As soon as the result was known I passed Eric a note: 'Some of us are having a press conference this afternoon. Would you like to come along?' He muttered something about considering it. As we broke up I said to him again outside the Cabinet room, 'We're meeting at 5.30 pm. Let Peter Shore know if you are interested.' I saw Robert Armstrong [the Prime Minister's Principal Private Secretary] hanging around, but didn't care. We have nothing to hide. Anyway, history has been made this morning. We actually had a break at 11 am for coffee to be served!

Spent the rest of the lunch hour finishing my speech for Second Reading over a sandwich. Considering all the difficulties, I was rather proud of it. But in any case, with Harold making his statement today, I knew no one would be interested. Just my luck to have one of the most important items of our social policy taken in the House on trauma day! Just before I went to the House Norman came in looking sheepish. He had had a message from No. 10: would he please tell me that the PM did not wish me to attend the press conference that afternoon. My eyebrows shot up, but 'Thank you' was all I said. Had Eric gone running to teacher? Or was Robert Armstrong eavesdropping? Either way, it was pretty contemptible and I intended to take no notice of the message.

In the House my heart went out to Harold as he ploughed his way through one of the longest and dullest statements he has ever made. Tory sneers and jeers greeted every line. We anti-marketeers on the front bench tried to hide our feelings as the pro-marketeers cheered. As I anticipated, the House emptied rapidly when the long questioning was over. When I stood up to move the Second Reading of my Bill there was not a single Labour MP on the benches behind me! I got through the speech easily, then slipped upstairs to join the others at the 'Cabinet Against the Market' lobby conference, which Peter conducted with relaxed bonhomie. Then down to the Grand Committee Room to a meeting of anti-Market Labour MPs called by Douglas Jay. There were about eighty of them there and volunteers were quickly at work collecting signatures for the declaration[1] we had tabled as an Early Day Motion. So our plan had slipped smoothly into action, and there were over a hundred signatures on the Order Paper before we went home.

[1] The declaration welcomed the referendum. It stated that 'it is the true interest of the British people to regain the essential rights which permanent membership of the Common Market would deny them, namely the right of democratic self-government through their own elected Parliament, the right to determine for themselves how they impose taxes and fix food prices, the right to pursue policies designed to ensure full employment and the

But the work of the Department has to go on. The BMA is now pleading for a meeting with me and is clearly distressed by the increased militancy being shown by the HCSA. The BMA now argue that they want to clarify 'misunderstandings' they say exist about the consultants' commitment under the existing contract and of course I said at once that I must see them. This is something very different from negotiations and, if they are getting worried about the way they are losing public support, it is my duty to try and get them off the hook. We had to have an office discussion about all this. David is against my trying to get sanctions lifted before the Review Body reports: he is sure the Government will have to clamp down on the Review Body award and thinks that sanctions will give me the excuse I shall need for not implementing it. Backed by Philip and Henry, I disagreed. I said I would meet the BMA the following day and have an adjourned meeting on Thursday if necessary.

But my stresses and strains are still not over. Tomorrow I am due to address a *Financial Times* high-level conference on pensions policy and I haven't prepared a word yet. Elizabeth suggested I ask Brian O'Malley to take my place, but I wasn't having any. I am already acutely aware of the conspiracy by the Tory front bench to keep me out of the pensions picture. They have been blackmailing Bob to try and get me not to go on the Standing Committee, claiming that the proceedings will be more protracted if I go on. I know Brian would love to handle the whole thing himself, but, as I told my officials, I am always sent in to do the dirty work and intend to get a few of the sweets of policy as well. Of course, I know what the Tories are up to: they want to maintain the 'ogre' image of me which my pensions policy and my conciliatory Second Reading speech today disprove. In his winding-up speech Kenneth Clarke [from their front bench] even went to the lengths of talking about the 'O'Malley Bill'. That decided me: I'll do the FT conference tomorrow if it kills me and I'll sweat out the committee stage, whatever the cost. I just gave in to my tiredness and went to bed.

Wednesday, 19 March. My speech to the *Financial Times* went like a bomb, despite the fact that I had had to get up at 5 am. I even survived some pretty tricky questions and afterwards Alec Atkinson, the Deputy Secretary, said I had covered myself with credit. Frank Byers, who took the chair for me, told me that Geoffrey Howe was 'a hundred per cent' behind our pensions policy and he obviously hadn't much time for Norman Fowler's[1] equivocal line.

But I still had to go through the misery of resumed talks with the BMA. They came in, noticeably subdued: Astley, Grabham, Lewin, Stevenson and Gullick. We went through the first stages of explaining what I thought was the consultants' commitment under their current contract with elaborate patience and mutual courtesies. I couldn't help feeling that if they had only shown half this civility on 20 December we would never have had this dispute. But as soon as we thought we had got one point cleared up and agreed, they were at their old game of changing tack. They nodded approvingly when, for instance, I said that I was not in any way seeking to change the existing agreement – and then

right to seek co-operation and trade with other nations in a world-wide framework'. It urged MPs to campaign for the withdrawal of the United Kingdom from the Common Market.

[1] Conservative MP for Sutton Coldfield and one of the shadow team on the social services.

tried to manoeuvre me into accepting that the existing agreement meant that a consultant's contractual programme was only for nine sessions a week instead of eleven: something which would, of course, immediately destroy the whole-timer's differential. After over an hour of this I suggested we should adjourn, that I should try to put their contractual commitment into words and that we should meet again the following day. Although they had previously welcomed the idea of an adjourned meeting, Stevenson sat up at this and started protesting with all his old petulant arrogance. Really! Mr Grabham had flown back from Majorca specially for this meeting. Anyway, added Lewin, they had only just started. They wanted to discuss with me the additions to the existing contract I would have to give them if sanctions were to be called off. I groaned and sat back while they reeled off the old shopping list, which I had already told them we could discuss when negotiations were resumed.

After another hour of this (while officials for my next meeting stood waiting outside in the corridor) I told them quite sharply that I had another important engagement. Why didn't we meet again when we had all had time to consider how far we had got and what I might be able to do to meet their points? Still they spluttered and finally I asked Henry to take them down to the waiting room to try and get some sense out of them. He kept coming back, head in hands, saying they were 'impossible'. They were now apparently quarrelling among themselves as to exactly when they wanted to meet me again and what they wanted me to do. Finally they were appeased. I was to send them an interim reply to their letter and offer to meet them for exploratory talks. But they had now changed their minds and didn't want this meeting to take place till after Easter.

In the meantime I had had another urgent meeting on pay beds, officials telling me that I am compelled by law to increase the charges for them on 1 April. The formula to which I am tied works out at an increase of 60 per cent.[1] I can just imagine how this will be interpreted. Mrs Castle out to kill private practice again! After a long discussion I told them to find a device for reducing the increase to 50 per cent, but nonetheless this will mean trouble.

By now my early start and lack of sleep were beginning to tell. Blissfully I managed to pair at 9 pm and had just got home, cooked myself some food and was watching the 10 pm news when the phone rang. It was Harold, angrier than I have ever heard him in my whole life. He was almost beside himself. The venom poured out of him. He had generously allowed us to disagree publicly on the Common Market and what had we done? 'Made a fool of me,' he declared. When he had talked about freedom to dissent he hadn't meant that we should rush out and hold a press conference and organize an anti-Government campaign. No one had done more than he had to keep the Party together and he had been pilloried and he had had enough of it. I tried to interrupt the spate but he swept on, finally spitting out the words, 'So this is all the loyalty I get. No one would have brought you back into Government but me.' At that something snapped in me and I retorted, 'I have never been so

[1] Under the Health Services and Public Health Act, 1968, the Secretary of State for Wales and I were compelled to fix pay bed charges every year to reflect the average cost of in-patient services at hospitals. We had to take into account rising costs, improvements in the services and a contribution to capital expenditure.

insulted in my life. I thought you had chosen me on merit. I am the best Minister you've got and you can have my resignation in ten minutes flat.'

He began to climb down. 'You can have mine. Of course I chose you on merit. But this campaign you are organizing is intolerable. Some of us are having a meeting in my room in the House. You can come if you like.' I groaned. Was I never going to get any let-up? Besides, I felt so angry I didn't care what he did or said. 'Harold,' I moaned, 'it is pouring with rain and here I am, marooned in Islington, without a car.' 'You should be in the House,' he snapped. 'Come if you like; it's up to you.' And he slapped down the phone. 'I'm damned if I'm going,' I thought, but then I knew he had knocked all sleep out of my mind anyway. I didn't give a damn whether he sacked me or not and I was utterly uncontrite about what we had done, but I realized that he was, after all, Prime Minister and I owed him some courtesy. So when Ted came home I got him to run me down to the House.

A gloomy scene met me as I entered Harold's room. Harold was sitting in his chair, obviously in a shattered state. Mike sat at one end of the table opposite him; Jim at the other, head in hands. 'Have a drink,' said Harold morosely and as I helped myself he added, 'I was very insulting to Barbara just now and I apologize. I withdraw what I said.' I went over and kissed him affectionately on the forehead. 'And I'm sorry if I have upset you, but I am afraid I can't withdraw,' I replied. 'Don't I get a kiss?' said Jim gloomily. 'God knows I need it.' So I kissed him too and sat down next to him. 'I can't understand why Barbara is so chirpy,' he almost groaned. 'Because I don't think the situation is tragic,' I replied. 'Harold, you must wear with pride this freedom you have given us.' Harold had obviously calmed down a bit, but he was still in a pretty neurotic state. So for over an hour we had to listen to him. He wasn't going to accept Barbara's resignation or anybody else's, because he did not intend to preside over a rump Government. He must represent the whole movement or nothing at all. But his position was intolerable. Here we had approached Eric Varley within minutes of Cabinet's decision having been taken, inviting him to join a press conference that had been clearly prearranged (who the hell did tell tales, I wonder?). The thing which obviously hit Harold was the fact that we had got it all worked out beforehand. If he knew I was responsible for the whole plan, I really would be finished! For the fact is that the speed and cohesion with which we have acted has had a big effect on the press.

As he went bitterly on I gathered that another piece of our plan of action has fallen into place: Mik has sent the Motion for next Wednesday's NEC with all our names on it and has released it to the press.[1] It is this Motion, calling for the Party to campaign actively against staying in the Market, that has made Harold declare that, unless it is withdrawn, he will resign. How could he carry on? he demanded of us. What would be his position at the special conference? If the NEC recommended that the Party should back withdrawal, would he even be allowed to speak? It was intolerable and if this was the position in which we wanted to put him, he would resign. 'I'll resign with you,' said Jim lugubriously. At this moment Ron Hayward – for whom Harold had also sent – drifted in and proceeded to make delphic, and hardly deferential, utterances. If

[1] It rejected the terms as falling 'very far short' of the Party's objectives and its final paragraph recommended to the special conference that the party should campaign for Britain's withdrawal from the Common Market.

the NEC instructed him to launch a campaign, campaign he would. 'Out of our deficit?' said Jim. From Ron's manner – at moments almost impertinent – I couldn't make out whose side he was on. I made soothing noises from time to time, but I couldn't help thinking that Harold ought to have foreseen all this. How could the right to dissent have any meaning, I asked him, unless it also included the right to make dissent effective? Weren't the pro-marketeers going to organize? At this Harold said he was as angry at their – particularly Roy's – organizing efforts and said he was going to try to stop them too, which is absurd. Why shouldn't they organize? But Harold went on with his dark hints as to what would happen to the Party, and not least to the Left, if he resigned. 'Some people would go straight into a coalition,' he spat out, adding, 'Roy would, like a shot.' I felt pretty unrepentant, but to my surprise Mike suddenly said, 'Of course, we shall have to take account of what you say, Harold. I don't think things are as tragic as you make out, but clearly we must consider what you have said. We cannot go any further tonight.' 'I shall make this the main business at Cabinet tomorrow,' declared Harold, at which I groaned. 'Oh no, Harold. Don't you know we ought to be talking about economic strategy? Don't you realize the Chancellor is demanding savage cuts in public expenditure which could split this party far more than the Common Market could? We are in a 1966 situation again.' 'If we are in a 1966 situation,' said Jim gloomily, 'this party is finished.' And so at 1 am we broke up. My patient – and fascinated – Ted was waiting outside Harold's room. Mike grinned and shrugged, saying to him, 'Harold is in a bad way.' Mike, too, had apparently been summoned as I had been, but no one else.

Thursday, 20 March. True to his word, Harold swept all the other items off the Cabinet agenda. As we opened he sent officials out of the room. He was calmer and clearer-eyed, but nonetheless still obsessed with his grievances. He had shifted his line from last night, drawing a distinction between the Motion on the Order Paper and the NEC resolution – though he had a side dig at the fact that 'someone' had approached Eric about the press conference, describing the whole pre-preparation of the anti-Market campaign as 'sly'. But then he went on to attack a 'leading pro-marketeer' (unnamed) who was also to be involved in a campaign. (We all knew he meant Roy.) Some people were preparing a 'pro-Market coalition with the Tories'. (Again we knew he meant Roy.) And then he changed tack, saying dissenting Ministers were perfectly entitled to make their position clear: the statement we had issued was okay. The real trouble was that the Ministers were trying to 'pitch the Party line against the majority view of the Cabinet'. This was so different from what Harold had been saying last night that I had to modify what I had planned to say, particularly as Jim had the nerve to say that no one had ever objected to our campaigning. But Mike came in next in his most moderate vein. The NEC, he admitted, did present 'special problems'. We should have to see how they could be overcome. 'If you say to me, Harold, that you feel very strongly about it, of course I take that into account and concede that I may have been wrong about it.' I was positively taken aback by this concession, having been much more unrepentant about things myself last night and being still unrepentant this morning. But as I listen to Mike these days the more conscious I am that, as they grow older, these Foot brothers all merge into one collective Foot type: rational, radical and eminently reasonable. They even speak in the same voice and the same terms; they are natural Liberals. No wonder Paul Foot has rebelled against his elders!

The rest of Cabinet clearly wanted to gag the NEC, Denis suggesting that Ministers who were members of the NEC should steer it away from a collective position and should try to steer the special Party conference away from taking a view either. Jim even went so far as to say that Ministers ought not to vote on the NEC resolution. This was too much for me. I pointed out that it was impossible for Cabinet to try to silence the NEC, which considered itself as co-custodian of the Manifesto. After all, the NEC had drawn it up jointly with us and spelt out the conditions we would demand for continuing membership of the EEC. How could we stop it from ruling whether in its view the conditions had been fulfilled? If we even attempted to, we should destroy the unity of the Party. And surely it was equally absurd to give Ministers freedom of action and then say they couldn't exercise that freedom on the NEC? There was a Motion down anyway. Were we going to be told we must vote against it when we agreed with it? Even the guidelines Harold had drawn up recognized that dissenting Ministers would be free to campaign because they talked about 'campaigning Ministers'. And for good measure I asked whether, if Cabinet had decided no, anyone believed Roy Jenkins would have meekly stayed silent? Hadn't the European Movement already organized four hundred meetings?

I think my speech had some effect and they started to cool down. Jim suggested that the moral was we ought to shorten the referendum campaign. Once again Mike played an emollient role. We should not try to take any decision here and now, he urged. 'The problem is not insoluble.' It was clear, he continued, that Ron Hayward had some idea as to how things might go at the special Party conference. We must have a resolution before that conference and a recommendation from the NEC; nothing could stop that. But that did not preclude speeches from both sides. The Prime Minister and Foreign Secretary could, he was sure, be allowed to state their case. If Cabinet would leave this matter for the moment there could be talks over the next few days over a possible statement by Ron which could supersede the resolution before the NEC. It might be we could all back this, but no decision either way should be taken at the present time. And so it was left and Cabinet adjourned at 1 pm, not having dealt with a single item of Government business. During the morning I was dispensing Polo mints on either side of me. Harold Lever, who sits opposite, tossed me a note: 'While we are still speaking – have you a sweetie?' I tossed him one back with a grin.

It was a very disgruntled Mikardo who joined us as the Dissenting Ministers gathered in my room at the House at 7 pm. After all, all he had done was what we had all agreed and here he was, being typecast as the Machiavelli again. And what he had done was based on the Dissenting Ministers' own statement, which happened to include a call to the Party to campaign for a 'no' vote. So he began by demanding truculently that he be told 'what has happened since last we met'. Mike replied gently and diffidently. There had, he said, been a 'commotion in Cabinet'. And he spelt out Harold's anxieties, ending with the plea: 'What we could do is to have a statement by Ron *re* procedure, etc., which at the same time would establish the NEC's rights.' Mik remained grumpy. He had been one of the originators of the proposal of the 'right to differ' in the Party, he maintained. It wasn't the Left who had tried to split the Party. What was wrong with the Motion? It only 'called on' the Party to campaign, it didn't 'instruct'. Peter tried to soothe him down: 'If the Party machine is brought into action a situation would be created from which we could not recover.' There would be a great current of feeling and he feared for the Party itself. Wedgie was conciliatory too. 'What really happened was that Cabinet misjudged the feeling in the movement. Having said that, the agreement to differ applies here too. We must have NEC guidelines and at conference facilities must be given to Harold and Jim.' Mik looked grim and unconvinced. Mike ploughed on: 'Of course the NEC must not be silent. All I suggest, because I want a solution that does not bring the collapse of the Government, is that you should take the resolution we have signed and lop off what we said about a campaign. All these organizational matters should be dealt with in Ron's statement. If that statement is taken first the resolution can be fought over afterwards.' He ended pleadingly: 'If we knock Harold through the ropes, we also knock the referendum and the Labour Government.' 'Are you saying he will go for a national government?' asked Dick Clements,[1] exchanging some eyebrow-raising with Wedgie, who then muttered, 'There are two ways of destroying the Party.' Mik remained stubborn. 'Let's move the resolution first and then have a document from Ron.' No, Mike insisted. We should have Ron's statement first. 'Let's try and get them to the bloody conference, Mik.' 'Let's get our victory before we are generous,' retorted Wedgie. And so it was left, rather uneasily. Mik, still grumpy, gave us details of the five working parties he was setting up among the MPs: one for the preparation of material; one on the House of Commons side of our activity; a public relations committee; a working party on the running of meetings and a fifth on contacts with Transport House. We agreed to meet regularly in my room at the House during the campaign. 'Let's call ourselves the DMS,' grinned Judith. 'My office thinks it is a Cabinet committee.'

Monday, 24 March. Our monthly meeting of the TUC Liaison Committee. The only item on the agenda was a discussion on the EEC, which turned out predictably routine. Harold didn't even bother to turn up. At the end of this inconclusive discussion we issued a neutral – not to say neutered – statement to the press.

At the office we returned to the tortuous question of our discussions with the BMA. We went through the officials' draft of our interpretation of the Option Agreement,[2] and I ruled out the possibility of a joint statement. It would take a

[1] Editor of *Tribune*, which was to be the voice of the anti-marketeers in the campaign.

[2] An agreement reached between the Ministry of Health and the Joint Consultants Committee in 1955 and reaffirmed in 1961. Its purpose was to reassure consultants who wanted to retain the right to do private practice that this would not bar them from whole-time posts in the NHS provided they were willing to give 'substantially the whole of their time' to their NHS work and to give it priority on all occasions. Hospital boards were therefore instructed, when making whole-time consultant appointments, to offer applicants the option of taking a maximum part-time contract instead of a whole-time one, if they so wished. Moreover the applicant need not declare his choice until after the appointment had been made and could move from one type of contract to another, unless there were compelling reasons why the hospital had to have a whole-timer. I was prepared to

month of day and night talks to agree that! Instead we decided to put our view in the form of a letter to the BMA. I ruled that we shouldn't offer any answer to the BMA 'shopping list' of demands at this stage. My heart sinks at the thought of the long, arid arguments that lie ahead.

Tuesday, 25 March. Harold has gone off to the States, so Ted Short presided over Cabinet, which thereupon proceeded at a cracking pace. Nonetheless, there was such an accumulation of items, thanks to Harold's obsessional monopoly of the last Cabinet, that we had to have a spill-over meeting in the afternoon. In the morning we started with civil service pay, on which we came to the reluctant conclusion that there was nothing to do but stand by the principle of comparability, despite Mike's mournful warnings. We next turned to the draft White Paper on the EEC negotiations, which Peter described as 'riddled with value judgments which make it almost impossible to take it seriously'. So we anti-marketeers let it go through with a shrug of indifference. We then had a long discussion on the draft guidelines which Harold had drawn up for Ministers' conduct during the referendum campaign and, if he had been there, he would have been a bit taken aback at the unity with which we dispatched some of them, agreeing they were far too restrictive and inflexible.[1] Roy, in particular, said he would be bound to appear with members of opposite parties and it was absurd to say we couldn't even appear with Tory back bench MPs. We all backed him up and Ted Short said he was sure the PM 'wouldn't take umbrage' if we altered this. As for the handling of ongoing Community business during the campaign, we again united in rejecting the idea that dissenting Ministers couldn't answer Questions or attend Brussels meetings. 'How are departments to be run?' asked Wedgie, quipping that Harold's proposals would establish 'no go areas' and take dissenting Ministers into 'protective custody'. It was much better, we agreed, to rely on Ministers' good sense.

In the afternoon we at last turned to Denis's public expenditure proposals. His determination to cut £1 billion off the programmes for 1976–77 has come as a traumatic blow so soon after the January White Paper and I am furious at the lack of planning and proper forecasting it reveals. The discussion took its predictable course: most of Cabinet resigned to the inevitable and all of us conscious that *something* had to be done to stop the inflationary drift. Denis gave his usual wordy piece of self-justification at the end. 'The things we counted on haven't happened: the Social Contract and reflation by other countries.' Of course, he got his way and those wretched bilateral talks with the Treasury are to begin.

reaffirm this agreement, but the consultants were pressing me to interpret the commitment to give 'substantially the whole of his time' as meaning nine half-day sessions a week, instead of the whole-timers' eleven sessions, with the obvious inference that any time worked over nine sessions ought to attract extra pay. This I was not prepared to do as it would have destroyed the existing pay differential in favour of the whole-timer.

[1] Harold's document stressed that Ministers should avoid personalizing the argument. There should be no direct confrontation on a platform or programme. No Minister should appear with an MP of a different political party 'or with the representative of any organization he would not in other circumstances be seen dead with'. Ministers, including non-Cabinet Ministers, should not be free to speak against the Government's recommendation in parliamentary debates and dissenting Ministers should not handle ongoing Community business during the referendum campaign either in Brussels or Parliament. It was Eric Heffer's insistence on speaking in the European debate on 9 April which led to his sacking from the Government.

After all this my chance of getting Cabinet to agree to advance the pension uprating date from November was minimal. I did my best, stressing that by October we would be spending £500 million less on benefits at an annual rate than what was necessary to restore purchasing power. Some of our lads backed me, but the rest put up no resistance to the Chancellor. It was hopeless. Altogether a dreary afternoon. Why, oh why, won't Harold get off his backside and really go for a public presentation of our problems, appealing publicly to the rank and file of the trade unions? We are drifting to disaster.

Wednesday, 26 March. Of course, the photographers were there in strength when I arrived at Transport House for the NEC. I was a little late and the TV cameras were just leaving. They swivelled round and said: 'Here she is.' 'Surely you didn't think I wouldn't turn up?' I replied sweetly. The press were there in force, hoping for a great row over the EEC. One chap even asked me for my comments on it before we started! But once again their hopes were falsified. Yesterday Mike told me he had been in touch with Ron and agreed a statement with him which he had then cleared with Mik. Mike's hard back-room work paid dividends. We found Ron's statement[1] waiting for us on the table, and Ron proceeded to speak to it quite eloquently. His advice was 'the sooner we have the special conference the better', and we were most of us glad that he had managed to get a hall in London for 26 April. Ron's second point was that he thought we ought to put to conference an NEC statement rather than a resolution (*i.e.* implicitly, that it would be better to have his statement – very conciliatory in tone – rather than Mik's resolution). Thirdly, he set out his proposal for giving Harold the opening speech at conference, followed by an anti-Market NEC spokesman, another pro-Market speaker and an anti-marketeer to wind up. As for the use of the Party machine, he suggested that any campaign would have to be organized by local parties, though there should be no disciplining of dissidents.

Harold had turned up in a much more temperate mood and was choosing his words carefully. 'The speaking arrangements seem okay to me,' he said, 'though I reserve my position at this stage.' I could see us drifting into a situation of total harmony behind Ron's line (with the media claiming a walkover for Harold and capitulation by us), when Wedgie dared to raise his voice. (It was like swearing in church.) He didn't object to Ron's statement but he thought we ought to clarify Ron's references to the Party machine. 'Of course, we shouldn't bully minorities or prevent the Party's press department from putting out speeches from either side. What we are discussing is whether the majority of the Party should have the right to produce its own literature in its own cause.' To this Ron retorted, 'The Government has decided to give money to both sides. I also know that the Party is in the red. If you want us to produce literature – which we know that only the antis will order anyway – you will put us even deeper in debt.' Then Mik moved in to stop the rot. First, he

[1] Ron Hayward had produced a draft statement which he suggested the NEC should put to the special conference in place of Mikardo's Motion. The statement paid tribute to Ministers' efforts in the renegotiations. Though it rejected the new terms and opposed Britain's continuing membership of the EEC, it dropped all reference to a Party campaign against membership and called for tolerance of differing views in the 'great debate'.

protested that the Motion which had been tabled was not *his* Motion: 'I didn't even draft it, I was just the postman.' (I could almost feel Harold pricking up his ears at this: so the dissident Ministers were behind this one too?) What we ought to do, said Mik, was to put the Motion to the NEC and then decide whether to put it or Ron's statement to conference. As for the last paragraph of the resolution about campaigning, which had caused such offence, it had been widely misinterpreted – he believed deliberately. He had personally always supported the freedom to dissent and had never intended the paragraph to mean that we should beat local parties over the head. So he welcomed Ron's paper as spelling out the libertarian attitude and supported it 'one hundred per cent'. The reference to 'freedom to campaign' would be in the context of Ron's paper. This clearly foxed the pro-marketeers. Shirley hedged and Harold trimmed. 'I have never', he said, 'argued at any time that the NEC should not make a recommendation to conference.' ('That's not true,' I hissed to Mike.) 'My desire,' Harold continued, 'was always that we should have a free debate and a comradely debate. I am deeply concerned about putting the reserves of the Party behind a campaign. I am also concerned about the wording, though I certainly believe the NEC has the right to say that certain objectives (for example, on the CAP) have not been met.' Finally, despite his obvious efforts not to relapse into his previous hysteria, it burst out of him: 'I am concerned that certain Ministers on the NEC should put their names to a resolution committing the reserves of the Party to fighting the Government line.'

Wedgie then suggested, with every appearance of trying to be helpful, that we should add bits of Ron's statement to the resolution for conference purposes and he was backed by Bryan Stanley, who is clearly going to remain toughly anti. At this point it was clear that the dissidents were making all the running. We had succeeded in getting the whole discussion concentrated, not on whether the NEC was pro or anti the terms, but on what form our opposition should take. Jim could obviously see the trap into which Harold had walked. 'I think I have been treated less than fairly,' he complained. 'I thought when I came here that the first thing that would happen is that I should be asked to give a report on the negotiations.' The resolution was tendentious in parts, he maintained, and, he added viciously, 'It is in the same language as the Motion on the House of Commons Order Paper – a remarkable coincidence.' But even he was forced to claim that he had never doubted the NEC must express a view. It was the reference to campaigning he complained about.

At this Mik made a brilliant move. He suggested that we should begin by adopting Ron's paper on procedure which accompanied the draft statement. No one could object to that as it ensured that Harold would speak at conference and adopt it we did – unanimously. After that it was only a matter of time before we won. Shirley in desperation moved the deletion of the last paragraph of our Motion about campaigning. Mik was relaxed: 'I would like it as an addendum but it is not madly necessary.' This time it was Wedgie who stepped in to stop us giving away too much. He said he didn't want to jeopardize our unity, but must support the inclusion of this paragraph. All it meant was that literature must be available from Transport House for local parties to use. Sid Weighell came in snappily. 'My union is split down the middle on this issue. We're going to ask both Tony Benn and Shirley Williams to address us. You know this paragraph is dangerous, Mik, and that is why you won't take it out.' 'I take that as a personal attack,' said Mik coldly. I then suggested we should leave in the paragraph but insert after 'campaign' the words 'on the lines of the General Secretary's statement'. Harold rather liked this and so it was agreed.

But another tussle lay ahead. Harold urged that we should not vote on Mik's Motion. It should merely be accepted as the majority view. (Once again this showed how successful our tactic in tabling the Motion with eighteen signatures had been. It conditioned the pros to surrendering the issue without a fight, as Jim kept tetchily observing.) We antis then in turn expressed our sympathy with Harold's aim. Nonetheless, we could see the danger of not having a clear record of the NEC view minuted. I therefore suggested that we should record that 'the following resolution was passed by a majority'. The Motion, I said, must have the same authority as the Cabinet decision. Harold didn't quite like that, but, after a lot of humming and hawing, my suggestion was approved.

Thursday, 27 March. No Cabinet. Cabinet government barely exists any more and is certainly going to be broadly in abeyance until the referendum is over. We antis noted that the popular version of the Government White Paper is being cooked up somewhere behind the scenes. There is no pretence about getting it approved by Cabinet.

Tuesday, 1 April, to Wednesday, 9 April. Trip to USA.

Having been invited to lecture to the Harvard Medical School on the British Health Service, I had decided to make a quick visit to the United States. I particularly wanted to study their 'certification of need' system of controlling hospital developments, as I thought this might encourage the fainter hearts in Cabinet who were worried about my own proposals for licensing.

On my return I found that Denis Healey's retrenchment plans were well advanced. On 15 April he introduced a Budget to cut back private consumption and to reduce public expenditure in 1976–77 by £900 million. Wage increases, he argued, had outstripped price increases and inflation threatened to undermine our national credibility. The balance of payments gap must be closed: in 1974 the rise in oil prices had helped to push it up to £3,800 million. Government borrowing must be reduced. If nothing was done the Public Sector Borrowing Requirement [PSBR] would rise to over £10 billion in the coming year. Resources must be switched to exports and investment. His Budget package, therefore, was double-edged. On the one hand, he announced a number of measures to increase the funds of private industry and to promote the training services provided by government. These would cost money. On the other, he introduced swingeing increases in taxation to reduce demand. Here indirect taxes took the lead, with the top rate of VAT going up to 25 per cent on less essential items, beer taking another 2 pence per pint while the tax on spirits went up by a record 64 pence per standard bottle. Income tax went up, too, by 2 per cent on the standard and higher rates of tax bringing the standard rate up to 35 per cent, only partially offset by a modest increase in personal allowances. These changes, he claimed, would reduce the borrowing requirement by £1,200 million. They would also push up the index of retail prices by $2\frac{3}{4}$ per cent. Most chilling of all was his admission that unemployment could reach one million by the end of the year. The only consolation for me was his commitment to introduce child benefit by April 1977 and his undertaking to extend the family allowance to the first child in one-parent families one year earlier.

On the referendum front my relations with Harold Wilson had become very strained. He would clearly not easily forgive the Dissenting Ministers for having organized their opposition to his renegotiated terms so promptly and effectively. His anger was deepened by the fact that, not only had he been outnumbered on the NEC, *but he clearly faced defeat at the special Party conference which had been called for 26 April. But before then he was to suffer further chagrin in the House when on 9 April, in the vote on the terms, he was only to get his massive majority of 226 with the help of Tory votes. Of the 315 available Labour* MPs, *only 137 supported him and 170 voted against. But the campaign of the 'antis' was hampered by the fact that they had to operate through the National Referendum Campaign, an all-party umbrella organization through which the Government channelled the public funds which the Referendum Act, which became law on 8 May, was to make available to each side in the campaign. Moreover the funds – £125,000 each – were derisory when compared with the money raised privately by the pro-Market umbrella organization, 'Britain in Europe' (see page 608).*

Thursday, 10 April. Another of those wretched PESC Cabinets. They are getting so drearily familiar! Denis reported he had reached agreement with Ministers on some £870 million towards the saving of the £1,000 million he was demanding, but the bilateral talks had still left him short of what he needed. Tony C. was edged into accepting a bit more of his share. I made a vigorous speech about the consequences to the NHS of the cuts the Chancellor was insisting on from me, but I got no support – not even from Mike, the custodian of Nye's memory. I told them flat that I couldn't take the additional £16 million for dental and ophthalmic fees, but Harold merely said we would discuss increases in charges when the time came. My trouble is that everyone remembers how successfully I fought for the roads programme when I was Minister of Transport and I get teased mercilessly. Bob has a favourite crack: 'What we ought to do is make Barbara Chancellor and then no one would get a penny.' Eventually we managed to get the total cuts up to £900 million and Denis weakly said he would be content – reluctantly – with that.

Friday, 11 April. I was astonished at the size of the anti-Market rally in Manchester. They came pouring into the Free Trade Hall, nearly two thousand strong. Everyone spoke well except me. I felt curiously listless. Perhaps it was jet lag, but I think it was also that I cannot get attuned to the over-simplified extremism of the anti-Market case. Peter was impressive and well received, but Wedgie, with a more fluent flow of rhetoric than I have ever heard from him, was the hero of the hour. There was a more revivalist atmosphere than the movement has known for years.

Monday, 14 April. Up at 6.30 am to get to London for pre-Budget Cabinet. It went predictably. Denis spelt out his economic analysis and measures competently, if a trifle wearily. Everyone shook their heads, but no one protested seriously. We all know that we have little alternative.

But it was all preceded by a very early meeting of EC(P) to discuss my paper on the Doctors' and Dentists' Review Body's report on doctors' and dentists' pay.[1] To my surprise, even the Treasury made no objection to accepting my

[1] The report, produced under the new chairmanship of Sir Ernest Woodroofe, had been in our hands since 1 April and was later published as Cmnd 5010 on 18 April 1975. As anticipated, it found that the pay of the

paper. Once again we were in a 'no alternative' situation. My decision to offer the staging of salaries above £13,000 (contrary to David's and the Department's first advice) defused any opposition Mike might have been contemplating. I even got him to agree to recommend to Harold that, since the recommendation was unanimous, it need not go to Cabinet and that I should be left free to play this Government acceptance of the report at any point in my negotiations with the consultants that I felt was right.

Tuesday, 15 April. I have insisted on keeping this morning free to attend the Standing Committee on the Pensions Bill. I was on my feet – frequently interrupted, but received with excitement by our own side – for nearly an hour. After the committee Brian, Alec, Alf and I went to celebrate over lunch.

I dreaded the Budget speech in the House because (like many others on the front bench) I always find the compulsion to doze irresistible. Denis seemed a bit tired by the time he limped home. But Margaret Thatcher's riposte was pretty shallow, though I continue to admire her impeccable grooming, even under strain. Query: is such polished coolness an enduring asset or will it be her downfall one day?

Back into consultations over my meeting with the BMA negotiators tomorrow. Henry ventured the suggestion that the BMA was now pretty anxious for a settlement before the Review Body report is published. Apparently they don't want to be in the position of still operating sanctions when the Government has to make up its mind whether to authorize their increase of 30 per cent. They neither want a Government refusal of the money, nor an ultimatum to give up sanctions as a condition of obtaining it.

Wednesday, 16 April. I dared to hope that the talks with the BMA would not take too long. But my hopes were shattered. We started our talk at 4 pm at the Department. The BMA's 'clarification' group had swollen this time to seven people and it was significant that they started by asking whether a wider group of representatives, which was standing by, could come to the office and wait in another room so that they could consult them if necessary. So they obviously meant business! Though Grabham and Astley were flanked by Lewis, Lewin and Stevenson, mercifully none of these three contributed a word the whole night. It was amusing to sit opposite Brian Lewis, who only a short while ago was castigating me on every TV programme he could reach, and find him transformed. Indeed, they were all transformed. Elaborate courtesy was the order of the day – a painstaking patience and determination to reach agreement if at all possible. If only they had been like this on 20 December! But the trauma was not over yet. Anxious they may have been for an agreement – and time and again Astley and the others were clearly ready to say yes – but with Grabham they had a fanatic in charge, he was determined to try to exact his pound of flesh.

professions had fallen 'so substantially behind those of comparable professional men and women, both in the public services and in the private sector, that a measure of structural adjustment is now essential'. It therefore recommended 'catching up' increases averaging 30 per cent, including threshold payments. My paper to EC(P) recommended that the Government should accept the report, subject to the staging over two years of the increases on salary levels above £13,000, as had been done in the case of top salaries. This was agreed and the date of the announcement was left to me.

And so began another of those wearying marathons. They said our draft on the Option wouldn't do and put forward some amendments. I said their amendments wouldn't do and we started suggesting modifications. They asked if they could discuss it among themselves and at 5 pm we retired, leaving it to them. Tim Nodder came up to say that he had overhead Grabham saying, 'If we reach this about midnight—' and we all groaned. Their old arrogance, their belief that they can command the attendance of the Secretary of State for as long as it suits *them*, may be more muted, but it is still there. Norman started to lay in food. It was soon clear what Grabham was up to: he was once again trying to insinuate into the draft a form of words which would imply that the maximum part-timers' commitment is only for nine sessions a week: the perfect jumping-off point for getting rid of the whole-timers' differential through the side door. Neither David nor I would have any truck with it. They twisted and turned endlessly. Finally we sent down a form of words which we insisted was our last concession; and they accepted it.[1] Relief all round. We even started drafting our press notices.

Philip and Henry, who had been beginning to clutch their heads with despair, perked up. We might get to bed at a reasonable hour! But we still had to agree the letter on future modifications of the contract – and that was to go on for another seven hours. We chewed the chicken legs Norman had rustled up for us, while Philip and Henry shook their heads over the incredible behaviour going on below. Every line of our draft was queried; endless petty little redrafts kept coming up to us. By 4 am David was beginning to lose his temper, but I told him we would see it through to the bitter end – even though Norman announced tragically that we'd run out of tea. Jack Straw was superb; Norman imperturbable. We then came to the crunch: the passage dealing with the payment for extra sessions. Once again it was clear what Grabham was up to: to get a passage which would link the new extra payments, not to a more precisely defined commitment, but to the existing contract as defined in the Option letter. I exploded. That, David and I agreed, *would* be our breaking-point.[2]

Philip and Henry suggested at this point that perhaps they had better join in the discussions and try to convince the negotiators that it just wasn't on. So down they went. When they came back it was with a form of words which they in their innocence obviously thought was not too bad, but David and I rejected it instantaneously. Whatever the plausible arguments with which Grabham tried to wrap it up, it would have committed us to basing the entitlement to extra sessions on the present 'flexible' one, not the new closed contract. 'This is

[1] The letter I agreed to send to Dr Stevenson repeated my acceptance of the Option Agreement but rejected Mr Grabham's interpretation of it (see footnote, page 583). Instead it said: 'The maximum part-time contract has been interpreted in a variety of ways and not always in terms of notional half-days. Where it has been so agreed it has normally been nine, but occasionally ten or eleven. The process of assessment should be conducted flexibly so as to provide both that the consultant will give substantially the same service and time overall as he would have done had he opted for a whole-time appointment, and also to allow him to accommodate his other work.' For full text see *British Medical Journal* 26 April 1975.

[2] In a second letter, which I agreed to send to Dr Astley, I reiterated the improvements in the existing contract I had already told the House of Commons I was willing to make and said I would be ready to discuss other improvements as soon as sanctions were lifted. Their request for payment for extra sessions, however, could only be discussed against a clear definition of the consultants' contractual obligations and an agreed programme of duties. For their part the consultants agreed to discuss the reforms in the merit award system for which we had been pressing. See *British Medical Journal* as above.

the crunch,' snapped David. 'We had better break. No bad thing if we do.' Philip and Henry looked anxious at this. I stood up. 'I had better go down and tell them this myself,' I said.

It was 5.30 am. The BMA contingent looked surprised as I walked into the room. I spoke as calmly as I could. We had made a lot of drafting compromises during the night, I pointed out. (Nods.) But we were still no nearer a solution, I added. It was getting on for 6 am. They would be aware that shortly I would be due at a very important Cabinet. (More nods, apprehensive this time. They obviously thought their Review Body report was coming up.) I really could not be expected to devote any more of my time to this. (Nods again.) We had better break. Even Grabham looked alarmed. (He had obviously made all the running.) He attempted another round of plausible argument. I told him that what they were clearly trying to do in rejecting our last form of words was to say that a modified contract should mean the same flexible commitment as the existing one but with payment for extra sessions. That just wasn't on. I had gone as far as my colleagues would allow me to go. I must tell Cabinet that agreement could not be reached. Panic. They asked for time to talk among themselves again. Back upstairs we went. Within half an hour it was all over. They had capitulated. Lewin asked me anxiously what form of words I needed to help me in Cabinet. I told him they must say categorically that they would recommend withdrawal of sanctions at the meeting of their Central Committee on Friday – and added as an afterthought, 'unanimously'. They fell over themselves to agree. We shook hands all round. I went upstairs chuckling. Little do they know that the DDRB report is not coming up at Cabinet and that Harold has given me full freedom to play the acceptance of the report when and how I think fit. 'She's got more stamina than the five of us put together,' said David affectionately.

Jack Straw drove me home, slapping his face from time to time to keep awake. It was 7.30 am when I got to bed. Mercifully Cabinet wasn't till 11 am, so I set my alarm for 9 am.

Thursday, 17 April. I awoke feeling remarkably fresh after one-and-a-half hours' sleep. We had to have an office meeting to plan our course of action following the meeting of the consultants' Central Committee tomorrow. Peter reported that we had had good press reactions to our agreement. After going round the problem for some time we decided we couldn't really decide till first thing tomorrow, which means an early meeting, despite the fact I have only had one-and-a-half hours' sleep in the past two days.

Friday, 18 April. Climax day. Will, or will not, the consultants' committee endorse the lifting of sanctions? At our early office meeting we had to try to decide how things would go and when we should release the Review Body report. David and I were in favour of publishing it today on two alternative formulae: if the decision of the Central Committee wasn't known by 3 pm (the latest time for answering the written PQ we had inspired), we could say the Government had accepted the report 'in view of the unanimous recommendation to lift sanctions.' If we *were* known and favourable, we could say 'In view of the decision to remove sanctions—' Once again we went through elaborate discussion of the possible combinations of events and contingencies. There was a mood of hilarity in the air. We know we have got a trump card in our hands in the Government's acceptance of the report. Once again I was struck by the remarkable sense of solidarity one's civil servants get with one in a crisis. Certainly, they are all very warm towards me. Anyway, it was a great cops and robbers day of an 'if they go here, we go there' kind. We decided to make all the contingency planning we could and decided to meet again at 1.30 pm. I was just leaving the office for the House when Henry rushed down to catch me in the car. He had spoken to Derek Stevenson, who had expressed surprise that we should have any fear of the outcome of the morning's meeting. Hadn't we heard that a thousand consultants in the south-east had already called off sanctions? Didn't we realize that this particular group contained some of the most active militants who had started it all? Right, I told Henry, get on to Derek again and tell him it is vital that I have the result by 2.45 pm. And tell him I mean 2.45 pm – 3 pm would be too late. He rushed off eagerly. 'This is a happy day, Secretary of State,' he said to me. 'Never say that,' I warned. 'That is always the moment when things go wrong.'

When we reassembled back in my room we heard that the consultants had decided to reach a decision before they adjourned for lunch, but were still arguing. Once again we had to adjust our contingency plans. But it seemed clear that a decision was in the bag. At 2.15 pm the message came: decision in favour of lifting sanctions carried by thirty votes to two, with six abstentions. A walkover! 'Press conference and TV at 4 pm,' said Peter. 'Then make-up girl at 3.15 pm,' I replied. We scattered to our jobs: getting the answer to the PQ over to the House, redrafting the press statement, getting ready for all the tricky questions at the press conference. At 3.30 pm still no make-up girl. 3.45 pm before she arrived. And so, at the end of several weeks now of intense strain – and of this week of forfeited sleep – I ended up as I know all these 'triumphs' end up: in rush, disorder and anti-climax. The girl tried to slap something on my face and bring some order into my disordered hair in fifteen minutes flat, with agitated emissaries knocking at my door: 'the press have been waiting for twenty minutes' and 'the BBC have missed their early editions'. Something in me snapped and I went into the conference churned up, tense and strained. Of course, I got through it all, as old pros do, but what should have been my relaxed moment of achievement was ruined.

My dear Private Office gathered round me like clucking hens over a chick. 'What a sad end to a good week,' said Norman, sad himself. Evelyn asked me anxiously if I felt all right. 'I just want to get down to the country,' was all I could say. Back in my room I felt utterly drained. I put my head in my hands and said to Norman, hovering protectively over me, 'Go away.' He slipped gently out. Then I howled my heart out – the first time I have cried for years and years. After ten minutes I felt better and wiped my eyes and started to sign the pile of letters waiting for me. One by one they drifted back into my room tentatively. The best thing of all in this incredibly demanding week has been the genuine affection I feel for them and which I think they feel for me.

Looking back over the consultants' dispute, I ask myself what are the lessons? First, I believe, as David said, that they had a dispute in them and that I couldn't have avoided it anyway. Secondly, that if one has a conviction that a certain course is right, the only thing to do is to stick to it, whatever the risks. All through this dispute I have stood firmly by the determination not to give way on the differential for the whole-timers. I think that without me David would have been edged off it. Certainly Henry would – and there is still a tough battle ahead. Grabham won't give up any more easily than I will. Philip and the rest never shared my sense of the importance of this principle: I doubt whether they ever understood why I attached so much to it. But once Philip and co. took on board that this was my sticking-point, they made it their own. Thirdly, the fascination of this whole game lies in recognizing when one is in a weak position and when one is in a winning one. Sometimes I got it wrong. For instance, at the end we were in a much stronger position than any of us realized. I could – I now believe, looking back – have got away with much tougher wording in those final letters than I did, even though we did not give anything fundamental away. Fourthly, these medical specialists are a breed all their own: they really do believe, as one of the presidents of the Royal Colleges put it to me, that they are in a position of 'special authority'. (I would put it that they think they are God.) Finally, that there is never a conclusion to anything. One just gets through one situation in a winning or a defeated position then picks oneself up and gets ready for the next fight that will surely come. I pick myself up now in a situation in which I have broadly won the first round. But I am under no illusions about the way in which Grabham is coming out of his corner to try to defeat me in the next round. As David and I have agreed, this is the moment to go into the attack on pay beds.

Saturday, 19 April. After a good night's sleep I feel fighting fit again. Anyway, HCF always cures any neurosis or strain. And this morning one of the most comical incidents I have ever experienced left me laughing for hours. At 8.30 am I went downstairs from our bedroom to the loo, opened the door and saw two bright eyes staring at me from the lavatory pan. It was a sweet little baby rabbit sitting at the bottom of the pan, with its nose and ears just above the water line. I was shaken to the core! I shut the door and went back upstairs to Ted, asking him seriously, 'Do you think I could possibly have DTs? There is a rabbit in the lavatory pan.' He was so scared at the very idea that he had to drink his tea before he went to have a look at it, saying, 'We'll set Printer on it', while I moaned, 'Oh, we couldn't do that. It wouldn't be fair after all it has gone through.' 'We're infested with the things,' said Ted angrily. When he peered into the loo he called out, 'It's drowned anyway'. I peered over his shoulder nervously. Its eyes were shut, its ears were flattened against its head, and it had gone limp. 'Well, it was alive when I looked at it,' I replied. 'If you want to kill it, why don't you get some more water and make sure it really is drowned?' But Ted would hear nothing of it: he *knew* it was dead. So he went and got his gardening gloves and a bucket and scooped out the limp rabbit, walking firmly down our long garden to throw the corpse over the hedge into the field. I was in the study working when I heard a roar of laughter from Eileen, watching through the kitchen window. At the hedge, calling on Printer to stand by, Ted tipped over the bucket. Out scuttled the rabbit, shook itself and was through the hedge before either Ted or Printer realized what was happening. 'It's pure *Watership Down*,' I chuckled. 'Once again, cunning rabbit outwits stupid man and dog.' It made our day. That rabbit *deserved* to escape, for Ted remembered that yesterday Printer had chased a baby rabbit through the garden and they thought it had escaped on to the road. Instead, it must have swerved into the house, through the dining room and into the downstairs loo. It must have been hiding in the corner all the time we were going to the loo last night and then somehow got into the pan. I shall never go to the lavatory again without remembering it sitting there. The dramas of the countryside are endless.

Sunday, 20 April. It was a terrible wrench to leave HCF on the first day of warm spring sunshine we have had this year. The garden had never looked lovelier, with its spread of daffodils and narcissi. All I wanted to do in the world was to get down to some real hard gardening. Things weren't made any better by the stuffiness of St Ermin's Hotel where we were holding our Dissenting Ministers' press conference, but the conference seemed to go quite well. As always, I marvelled at Wedgie's fluency and I got in a few digs myself. Later we all assembled for food at the Benns'. Their home in Holland Park Avenue is just what one would expect: roomy, comfortable, shabby and littered with political mementoes and some pleasant cultural bric-à-brac. Caroline is clearly no *cordon bleu* and seemed worried lest her cooking was not up to the standard of the rest of us. I suspect she and Wedgie normally get by on mugs of tea and bread and cheese. But it was great fun and they were lavish in everything.

After dinner we discussed (of course!) the strategy of our campaign. Having watched the report of our press conference on TV I said that we were in danger of being given 'equality of trivialities'. We ought to insist on some serious, in-depth programmes on TV. Peter said that all that was being organized by the National Referendum Campaign and that we ought to get ourselves represented on it. I was worried about the superficiality of our campaign so far, but when I said I thought we were going to lose the vote Wedgie, Peter and Michael turned on me. They clearly genuinely believed I was wrong; so I offered to lay some money on it. I also said that I thought Peter Jenkins was right when he wrote in the *Guardian* on Saturday that the referendum would decide the whole political direction of the Labour Party and that Harold, if the Europeanists won, would become the prisoner of the Right. Once again they all turned on me. They just wouldn't have it that Harold would move us all out of positions of influence: Mike insisted that Harold ('though I agree he is naturally to the Right politically') would stick by his regular tactic of conciliating his critics. I don't think I am naturally defeatist or gloomy by nature, but I often marvel at the complacency of my left-wing colleagues. Wedgie was at his most brilliantly ingenious again, telling us how he is intending to answer Questions tomorrow by challenging Margaret Thatcher to say whether the Tories accept the referendum. I almost began to believe in his capacity for party leadership.

Monday, 21 April. I am always taken by surprise at the way the press manage to work themselves into a lather about quite insignificant political occasions. I was therefore astonished to find, when I arrived at Congress House for our routine monthly meeting of the Liaison Committee with the TUC, that the cameras were there in force. They really had persuaded themselves that something portentous was about to happen – all in keeping with today's headlines to the effect that the TUC were going to tell the Government off about the Budget or vice versa. I could have told them better: the TUC are not looking for a showdown with us. They know only too well the alternatives they face. Instead, when they have awkward decisions to take, they prefer to run for cover, and today was no exception. The Government, NEC and the PLP were there in force for this much heralded 'historic' meeting on the Social Contract, but there were, apart from Len Murray and his officials, only *two* members of the General Council of the TUC: Jack Jones (who had to take the chair) and David Basnett. So we were, as it were, talking to the converted for nearly two hours. But the proof that we've done nothing to get at the root of the problem came later in the day, when the papers reported Hughie Scanlon's speech at his union's annual conference, denouncing the Budget as a breach of the Social Contract and warning that his members would insist on catching up with the price increases.

Later in the day I called in at the meeting of the National Referendum Campaign in the House. Neil Marten [Conservative MP for Banbury] was in the chair. He's a pleasant chap, but I can't see us ever getting much drive behind our plans under his leadership.

Tuesday, 22 April. A good morning's work getting my Child Benefits Bill through Legislation Committee, and enthusiastic endorsement by Social Services Committee of Cabinet for my paper on pay beds.[1] I can now go ahead making my statement to Parliament whenever I like.

Wednesday, 23 April. The papers have been full of the row over Geoff Bish's document on the EEC.[2] Jim Callaghan has been reported as threatening to move a hundred amendments to it at this morning's NEC, while the International Committee has reversed the decision of the Home Policy Committee that a copy of the Government White Paper should be distributed to every delegate to the special Party conference as well as Geoff Bish's document. So the cameras were out in force when I arrived. And sure enough, we spent the best part of the morning on it. Ron began by warning us that it would cost over £1,000 to distribute copies of the Bish document. Another £600 to distribute the White Paper as well. That morning he had received a hundred amendments from Jim Callaghan. Would the NEC please tell him how they wanted to deal with them? Mik moved that we should distribute Geoff's document and I supported him, pointing out that it would be one-sided if conference was not even allowed to know that the anti-marketeers were able to argue a detailed case. Mik's amendment was carried by fourteen votes to ten. Shirley then moved that we also distribute the White Paper. Again we all argued immensely

[1] David Owen and I had agreed that a statement of our intentions to legislate on pay beds was needed urgently to end uncertainty and I had to obtain Cabinet agreement. I made the statement in the House on 5 May. See footnote, p. 599.

[2] Geoff Bish had prepared a document for the Home Policy Commitee, 'The Renegotiations: An Appraisal of the Terms', which was hardly flattering in its analysis. The committee had recommended that the document should be distributed to the special conference, along with the Government White Paper.

courteously. Was it really necessary, I asked, to spend £600 on the White Paper when the Government's case was going to be distributed through every door? Wedgie had an idea. Why not ask the Government if they would give us copies to distribute free? Ted Short said he would have to look into this. Mike appealed to Jim to recognize the right of majority in the NEC, just as we had recognized the right of majority in Cabinet. For the first time Jim hit back viciously. No, he would not, he said, because the NEC had not handled this matter properly. A document ought to have been drawn up by the appropriate committee, where it could be examined and argued; this one was riddled with major inaccuracies. Once again it was Wedgie who was the conciliator. He was genuinely moved, he said, by the desire not to put Jim into the position of having to criticize a document issued by the NEC. We should therefore issue the document as an information paper and make it clear that it had not been endorsed by the NEC. That struck most people as eminently reasonable, but, with Jim still muttering protest and demanding that we go through it and amend it even if it took all day, Wedgie's proposal was only carried by thirteen to seven. Harold, incidentally, had carefully absented himself.

A late night on the Referendum Bill. At least we got one consolation: the House voted down a national count by a hundred majority. Peter, Wedgie and I were whipped reluctantly into the lobby to vote against additional money being given to both sides in the campaign and helped to defeat a proposition which would have given us a bit more of a chance to hold our own. What is £125,000 against the millions the European Movement can whip up?

Thursday, 24 April. Harold has effectively de-natured Cabinet. Whether he is just trying to clear the decks for the referendum, or whether it is a deliberate ploy to take any kind of control out of the hands of the anti-marketeers, I don't know. All I know is that Cabinet agendas have never been thinner and this morning's was a record: not a single item of business, apart from next week's parliamentary business and foreign affairs. So we met at 11 am and were out before noon.

At 7 pm we had our weekly meeting of Dissenting Ministers in my room at the House. Wedgie once again was bubbling with ideas for press conferences, questions we should put publicly to the Commission, etc. I groaned at the thought of another ruined Sunday and we agreed to make final decisions about our next press conference at the end of Saturday's special Party conference. I said that I thought we should go for more *visual* impact and outlined my idea for taking Joan Lestor, Jo Richardson [Labour MP for Barking] and myself to Brussels on a much publicized shopping spree that would get the prices issue bang on to TV. Tony Banks and Frances got ecstatic about this and Frances had the bright idea of taking some children along. But Wedgie was more obsessed with political in-fighting and suggested that as soon as it was clear that the special conference was going to say no we should requisition a special meeting of the NEC to plan a Party campaign against the Market.

Friday, 25 April. In the evening I went to speak at the Tribune meeting on the Common Market: the first time I have ever been asked to speak at a Tribune meeting at Party conference. It was nice to have the breach healed on an issue which I can endorse wholeheartedly. No one knows how painful it had been to be treated as a political pariah (not of Mike's choosing, I hasten to say). Much of what I did in 1964–70 is now being echoed by Mike, than whom there is no one more scrupulously operating an incomes policy (and incidentally no one currently more acquiescent about the high unemployment figures). Wedgie spoke first, getting a massive reception for a typically brilliant speech which contained a number of what I can only call distortions about the Community. I was, as usual, inhibited by my agonizing inability to say anything if I am not a hundred per cent sure that it is fair. I got a warm enough reception but slipped away early, doubting myself as usual. It was a balmy night and it was a curiously pleasant experience to be on my own, without the constrictions or comforts of an official car. So I strolled up Whitehall and Shaftesbury Avenue, enjoying the sense of normality as I caught a No. 19 bus.

Saturday, 26 April. The special Party conference on the Market went just as I thought it would. It was better attended than the press had made out it would be. The debate lacked thrills because everyone knew the result was a foregone conclusion, but the vote for the NEC recommendation was only two to one (actually 3,724,000 to 1,986,000).[1] Of course the press had been preparing for this by predicting a sweeping victory for the antis beforehand so that they could report a less than sweeping victory afterwards. Nonetheless, I think the pros have made some headway in the constituencies and of course they have captured (or always had) the GMWU, the UPW and the NUR.

My seniority on the NEC placed me between Harold and Mik on the front row of the platform. Harold was very tetchy before his opening speech: whether it was nerves or his resentment against me I couldn't say. At one point he reached out his glass for water and said nastily, 'And leave the jug here.' I poured him a glass of water and waited till he was on his feet before moving the jug away. (I'm not going to have a large glass edifice between me and the cameras. Two of us can play at that game.) Harold made a down-beat speech, contrary to the exhortations of the pro-Market press. He was obviously unhappy before he began and even more unhappy at the lukewarm reception he received at the end. My heart went out to him because I am very fond of him. Perhaps that is my trouble: I am not ruthless enough. His own speech over, Harold relaxed and more than once voluntarily placed himself in a heads-together-for-the-cameras situation with me. (Of course, the papers won't use such photos *now*. It would spoil their prepared scenario.) At one point I said to Harold, impulsively, but genuinely, 'The antis are saying that your speech was very skilful.' He jerked into a gesture of disbelief. 'And so it was,' I continued on my healing mission. 'You lowered the temperature. They are saying Roy made a great mistake in raising it.' Harold came to life. 'I intend to play it low-key throughout. The decision is purely a marginal one. I have always said so. I have

[1] The major unions voting in favour of Britain's membership of the EEC were the General and Municipal [GMWU], the railwaymen [NUR], shop and distributive workers, and post office workers [UPW]. Against were the Transport and General, engineers, miners, public employees and firemen. ASTMS representing white-collar workers voted against, but APEX [Association of Professional, Executive, Clerical and Computer Staff], also white-collar, voted for.

never been a fanatic for Europe. I believe the judgment is a finely balanced one.'

During the conference David chatted to me about office work as though the EEC bored him. He was tickled pink about the ending of the consultants' dispute. 'It is the first time the BMA has ever been defeated by a government.'

Monday, 28 April. The press conference on the Child Benefit Bill[1] went off remarkably smoothly. Peter almost grumbled: 'They let you off far too lightly.' But I am having trouble with David over pay beds. At the office meeting to discuss Lawrence Brandes's general registration plan for the private sector David, who told the trade unions at our private discussion dinner with them that he was in favour of quantity controls, has switched his ground again and insisted that he was against the whole idea. I suppressed my irritation and listened patiently. Out it all came gradually. He didn't think the private sector would prove a menace. The one thing to do was to leave the private promoters to burn their fingers, separate them 100 per cent from the facilities of the NHS and let the pressure of high costs do the rest. I told him I thought it was an arguable case, but politically untenable. Henry, of course, backed David, but, to my surprise, Philip said almost reluctantly that he thought I was right and David wrong. David shrugged that he didn't attach much importance to it either way and we then went on to discuss details in preparation for the statement on our pay beds policy which, we all agree, I ought to make as soon as possible, preferably next Monday, to stop the speculative stories that have started to run.

Sunday, 4 May. Ted's birthday party! Mercifully the sun shone. The garden looked enchanting. The food, on which Eileen and I had slaved all yesterday, was a triumphant success. Teddy was very happy and everyone enjoyed themselves, most of all Tony Keable-Elliott, who stayed a long time and seemed to revel in the relaxed atmosphere, as he always does with us. I *love*

[1] The Bill provided for a new cash benefit, payable to the mother for every child in the family, to be introduced from April 1977, when family allowance would disappear. The benefit would also progressively replace child tax allowances, thus transferring their benefit from the husband's pay packet to the mother's purse. The great advantage, I pointed out, was that some seven million first or only children would be covered for the first time, that the mother would get an income of her own to feed and clothe the family, and that families too poor to pay tax would receive the benefit of child tax reliefs. But there was no rate of child benefit included in the Bill as I had not yet agreed this with the Chancellor. All the Treasury would allow me to say was that if, as a starting point, we replaced the child tax allowances for children under eleven (then running at £240 a year per child), the rate of child benefit which would involve no extra cost to the Exchequer would be about £1.94 per week and that every 1 pence above that would cost about £6½ million per year. We should therefore, when the time came, have to decide the rate 'in the light of the economic prospect at the time'. The Bill also abolished the wage-stop and provided for the interim payment from April 1976 of family allowance for the first child in one-parent families: what I had been fighting for as 'Special FAM'.

Although the Bill was widely welcomed, there were two time-bombs ticking away under it. The first was the ruling Treasury convention that cash payments like child benefit counted as public expenditure while the loss of revenue from child tax allowances did not. This meant that some of the public expenditure 'cost' of the scheme, which was to come from the contingency reserve, represented the conversion of tax reliefs into child benefit, so it seemed greater than it was. The second was that the switch of child tax reliefs from the pay packet to the mother's purse meant a reduction in take-home pay for the wage-earner, thus rousing the deepest instincts of male chauvinism. Jim Callaghan's Government was to use these two factors in April 1976, after my removal from the Government, to justify an attempt to postpone the introduction of child benefit indefinitely.

giving parties, even though Eileen and I staggered to bed so tired we could hardly walk.

Monday, 5 May. Still a bit flaked out, but utterly relaxed. I have got the great pay beds debate in the House today. We worked away clearing the statement of policy[1] with every Department that tried to put a finger in it – including the PM, who had cabled some amendments from Jamaica. 'He can't have enough to do at that Commonwealth Conference,' grumbled Norman. It was irritating to have to read large chunks of my speech because every word of the text had had to be agreed, but the content was sufficiently meaty for me to get away with it. Obviously the Tories were furious, but the TUC health group whom I met beforehand were delighted and even the BMA was mild in its reaction, thanking me for the courtesy of informing them beforehand and for my promise that the details would be negotiated. David made a first-class winding-up speech in seventeen minutes flat and I thumped him on the back enthusiastically. I continue to believe we are a good corrective for each other. Then I had to turn my attention to occupational pensions, on which I have to make a major speech in Standing Committee tomorrow.

Tuesday, 6 May. Up early to finish wrestling with the technical details of my Standing Committee speech. By now I was pretty drained, but it all went well. I still managed to inject a little teasing into the technicalities.

Standing Committee over, I had to turn my mind to another group of technicalities – this time research into hearing problems for a TV programme with Jack Ashley on the deaf. The pressure continues relentlessly, but it is really my own fault. I will insist on starting new policy initiatives, on checking and challenging every detail of policy action that is put up to me, and on taking on an ever heavier load of speaking engagements of every kind. I am even planning a series of overseas visits to promote our exports in OPEC countries! What interests me is that I feel more than ever the urge to work flat out, even though I have definitely made up my mind to retire at the next Election and am reconciled to the fact that, when the referendum is over, Harold may well ditch me. I have a yen to go out at my peak and get a deep joy every time I chalk up another achievement – as on pay beds – before I go.

Wednesday, 7 May. For the second week running there is to be no Cabinet – and no Cabinet committees. Okay, so Harold and Jim are away in Jamaica, but Ted Short is here in full charge and the ordinary business of government ought to be going on. We Cabinet Ministers do not even know the business for next week until we hear it at the PLP meeting and there is no discussion of who should speak on what. It is all very eerie and it is anybody's guess what Harold is up to. The press is full of rumours about the reshuffle he is contemplating when the referendum is over. Brian O'Malley, with whom I had a meal, is

[1] I announced that we intended to legislate to phase out pay beds as soon as possible. I would therefore be consulting the medical profession about the detailed provisions for phasing out and on the extension of my licensing powers over the private sector. In the meantime I was proposing to reduce the number of authorized pay beds, then 4,500, by about 500 where these were under-used and I urged consultants to introduce common

worried. The press stories are that Wedgie is to be moved to my job and that he, Brian, is to be moved to Education. We agreed that the press is usually wildly wrong in its sensationalist speculations, but the fact remains that Harold, in this pre-referendum period, is effectively governing without a Cabinet, if governing is the right word.

All this speculation is part of the almost hysterical anti-Wedgie campaign that is building up. Tonight in the Lords Watkinson[1] has made a swingeing attack on him, more or less threatening a strike of the whole of British industry unless Harold gets rid of him, while Keith Joseph has called him a 'dracula'. But Ted tells me that by far the most telling speech in the Lords debate was one by Robbins, who made Ted's blood run cold with his gloom about the economy. On every hand there is the feeling among our own people that the economy is out of control: a mood which is fed by Harold's absence, making irrelevant speeches about commodity agreements (which are contrary to everything we have done in the EEC), at the Commonwealth Conference. Joel Barnett is in a near-neurotic state, making no attempt to disguise his belief that we are on the edge of disaster. Brian [O'Malley] tells me Joel has been to see Harold, begging to be released from the Treasury. He wants out before the crash comes. The outlook for public expenditure programmes is bleak indeed. I spent the morning soldiering on to complete our draft of the social wage document, but I have a feeling it will never see the light of day. Things have gone too far for that.

Yet the unions go cheerfully on with their demands, as though none of this had anything to do with them. Brian O'M. told me he had just had a meeting with the TUC social insurance committee which had left him in despair. They had unfolded a list of social policy items on which they wanted immediate action, such as increases in unemployment benefit, which would cost millions. I said to him, 'We have heaped goodies on them, but they have delivered absolutely nothing in return.'

The one bright spot in the day was the meeting I had called at the office on export promotion. We know that the OPEC countries have more money than they know what to do with and are itching to spend a lot of it on health care. But they want to buy complete health packages: whole hospitals and equipment plus a training programme for the necessary staff. Were we really taking advantage of this, I asked? David tells me that Sam Davies of our Export and Industries Branch of Supply Division is struggling to cope with inadequate staff and against the deep-rooted conventionality of the Department. I said that David and I ought to go on a series of overseas missions to sell our whole health image. Davies jumped at this and signed me up at once for a visit to Nigeria, which, he says, has the largest social expenditure budget of them all. I told Norman to lay this on for September. I am determined to keep this field under my control, despite David's obvious irritation at my intrusion.

Wednesday, 14 May. I continue to wrestle, through all my Departmental preoccupations, with the minutiae of the anti-Market argument, on which I am

waiting lists for their NHS and private patients. The Government had agreed to make extra money available to compensate health authorities for any loss of revenue from private beds.

[1] Viscount Watkinson, former chairman of Cadbury Schweppes Ltd, became President of the CBI, 1975–76.

struggling to brief myself. The inadequacy of the anti-Market machine, and of the money that has been made available to us, continues to manifest itself. For the pro-marketeers the highly professional and well-endowed European Movement has swung into action. Janet tells me that Roy Hattersley's secretary has told her that Roy has received a vast tome of speaker's notes from them and detailed briefing on every conceivable aspect. I have to do my own reading as best I can, referring points to Jack for checking from time to time.

Thursday, 15 May. Cabinet again at last. Harold was in extraordinarily benign mood, saying he thought the referendum campaign was going as he had hoped it would. Everyone was behaving themselves and had eschewed personalities. But some members of Cabinet had complained to him that the guidelines were inhibiting them from taking part in important meetings and TV programmes, because of the no-confrontation principle, and were asking that in the last week the guidelines might be let up a bit. He thought that was reasonable: 'It will all be forgotten as soon as it is over.' Roy [Jenkins] was the one who pressed this particularly hard.

Wednesday, 21 May. Off to Southampton for a TV programme on the Common Market: me, Clive Jenkins and Richard Body [Conservative MP for Holland with Boston] against Willie Whitelaw, David Steel and Roy Grantham.[1] It got a bit rowdy but I thought we antis won hands down. It occurred to me as I listened that the antis – so clearly outnumbered in the country and with all the Establishment against them – have managed to corner fifty per cent of TV time, as though we were level-pegging: very different from the showing we are given in the press. Which is another reason why I always thank the Lord for TV. And we have managed to put the Establishment on the defensive. No mean achievement.

Thursday, 22 May. Harold has reluctantly agreed that I may make my statement on the November increase in pensions today, but has vetted every line of it and of my press statement to render them as low-key as possible.[2] Nonetheless, it was well received and I have got away with murder, knowing as I do what Denis is preparing in the way of public expenditure cuts. The documents which have been circulated for Cabinet visualize a cut of 'at least £2 billion' for 1978–79, compared with the PESC White Paper last year. My Department has been studying the implications for our budget, which, if there is to be any expenditure on the NHS at all, will this time have to include cuts in social

[1] General Secretary of APEX, member of the TUC General Council and the Executive of the pro-Market Labour Committee for Europe.

[2] I announced that the next uprating would be in November, instead of December as originally planned, but that there would be no Christmas bonus. In keeping with the Government's promise, pensions and other long-term benefits would be increased in line with earnings. Using the 'historical' method of calculation (i.e. the movement of earnings over the preceding eight months up to March 1975), this would give an increase of 15 per cent. Short-term benefits such as sickness and unemployment, which were linked to prices, would go up by 13 per cent. Supplementary benefit would be increased in line with insurance benefits. I was also able to confirm the concessions I had wrung out of the Chancellor: heating additions would be increased and the amount of earnings disregarded in calculating the right to supplementary benefit would be doubled, to the special advantage of the single parent. The new non-contributory invalidity pension would come into operation at the same time. The cost of the total package would be over £1,000 million.

security plans. Philip Rogers and co., of course, see no alternative to cuts. Errington even hinted hesitantly at our office discussion that we should have to amend the legislation which compels us to increase pensions, etc., in line with average national earnings if that is more favourable to the pensioner than prices. So I went to Cabinet prepared to fight with everything I have got. 'I shall resign first,' I told Errington. My officials watch developments nervously, not knowing how much longer I shall be their boss. But Cabinet began surprisingly harmoniously. Harold was at his most affable, in marked contrast to last night, when he had been almost viciously curt with me. Seeing him stroll through the lobby, I had gone up to him. 'Hugh Cudlipp really has done a first-class job on the social wage document,' I said diplomatically, knowing his affection and respect for Hugh. 'Then it mustn't be all Barbara Castle,' he had snapped back. 'The Departments of Education and Housing contribute something to the social wage too.' 'We can include chapters from them,' I replied. 'Then it will have to be shortened,' he almost spat out, pushing past me. 'Harold really has the knives out for me,' I told my Ted afterwards. 'It may have been the brandy talking,' he replied. And Ted may have been right, because this morning Harold could not have been more genial.

The first item was Harold's own paper on the future procedures for dealing with public expenditure. Here it was, all we had been asking for: a timetable for dealing with public expenditure in the wider context of economic and political strategy, with the whole process starting at an early stage in the annual round. In introducing it he particularly referred to the criticisms Tony C. and I had made in the past and called on us to comment on the way he had tried to meet them. We both of us welcomed his proposals wholeheartedly. I merely asked (a) that the preliminary discussions should include tax policy and (b) that in future procedures the forty-eight-hour rule for the distribution of the discussion papers to Cabinet should be replaced by a one-week rule. 'We have today,' I said, 'two major public expenditure papers in front of us dated 19 May. Today is the 22nd. In practice, I got my papers in my box last night, because I had to await the office briefing on them.' Denis fell over himself to accept my first point; Harold agreed that my second one was legitimate. (In fact I discovered later both points were officially recorded in the Minutes.) But Harold was clearly very touched by the enthusiasm with which we had received his paper.

But it was in a different mood that we turned to Denis's paper on the survey of public expenditure after 1976–77. The picture he painted for us could not have been grimmer. It was backed by long official papers setting out the economic assessment for the next few years. What we ought to plan for, said Denis, was the implication for individual programmes of a £3 billion cut in public expenditure by 1978–79 and then study the consequences of our overall political policy. (My officials have welcomed this approach as the only way of getting the right assessment of priorities.) In fact, said Denis, he hoped that only a £2 billion cut would be necessary, but, if we didn't like the effect on certain programmes of such a cut, then we had to have in front of us an indication of what would be the effect of cutting other programmes even more drastically. The assumption of the illustrative figures was that inflation would be as bad in 1978–79 as now. 'If we are able to get the inflation rate down, the prospects for public expenditure will be better, but we have no policy for this at present.' I began to wonder what was the point of the whole exercise.

Harold summed up a sombre morning by saying we would resume the broad economic discussion after the recess. He insisted that we had taken *no* decision on future guidelines, but the general view seemed to be that officials should start their exploratory work. We could then have a whole day at Chequers in July to examine it. And he accepted my plea that, when we did meet, we should have various costed and worked-out options before us. So far so good. But I still feel we are drifting to catastrophe. I can't feel anyone has got a sufficient sense of urgency. Why, for instance, wait till July before the PM calls the sort of conferences with union representatives for which I have been pleading (and with other sections of society)? 'We ought to have held this morning's discussion in public,' I said to Shirley afterwards.

After all this, the weekly meeting of Dissenting Ministers in my room seemed almost euphoric, despite the usual hectic confusion. John Allen,[1] who has taken to materializing at these meetings (apparently NRC have appointed him their press officer), mooned about ineffectually. Bob Harrison[2] told me he had cleared my Brussels trip to examine the cost of living there provided I was prepared to make it all-party by going with Mrs Neil Marten. I agreed and got Janet to phone Sonya to see if we could borrow her little Rachel to go with us – Frances's idea. She is most enthusiastic about my trip.

Wednesday, 28 May. Great comings and goings over the Brussels trip. Sonya has done her stuff over Rachel's clothes, dressing her in Marks and Spencer's clothes so that we can compare their prices in Brussels, Jack Straw has got out a food shopping list from the *Daily Mirror* Shopping Clock. But at the last minute John Allen has tried to mess everything up by getting Enoch Powell to come along to the same press conference at which we are to report our findings. Jack Straw, Bob Harrison and I agree it would be ridiculous for Enoch and me to cancel each other out, but for some unknown reason John Allen refuses to budge and Neil Marten will not assert his authority. So I tell Jack I am going to phone Enoch, who is always very civil with me. He agrees at once that it would be absurd for us to upstage each other. He is free to go to the press conference on the previous day instead and thinks it is much better for him to double with Jack Jones on that day. 'Tell them we both agree that that is best.' I get Jack to convey this message to Allen and go to bed.

Thursday, 29 May. Up at 6.30 am to catch the plan to Brussels. Rachel is thrilled to bursting-point and behaves beautifully. Joan Marten turns out to be a very pleasant person. We work hard at our shopping and do everything as scrupulously fairly as we intended to do. Jack met us at the airport back with the news that Enoch was going to appear with me the next day after all – John Allen had flatly refused to alter anything. 'What the hell does that man think he is up to?' Jack asked. We were both furious – and not a little mystified. Whose side does he think he is on? 'Someone recommended him to us,' says Neil

[1] Son of former Labour MP for Crewe, Scholefield Allen, he had until recently been a research assistant at Transport House. He had also helped Harold Wilson unofficially.

[2] Of the TGWU, seconded by Jack Jones to the National Referendum Campaign.

weakly. We get back to the flat where Sonya cooks Jack a meal while he does some converting of our prices and weights into British terms and I wade through a big box. A happy but tired little Rachel goes to bed.

Friday, 30 May. A mad rush to get ready for the press conference. We all meet at the Waldorf, where once again Jack and Neil's two experts do all the work. One of them comes in with the news that the opposition have obviously got wind of our shopping trip and have trumped our ace by sending a housewife to Oslo so as to claim that prices are even higher there, though Norway is not in the Community. Then we get the message: Enoch has cancelled, refusing to wreck my show. At the last minute John Allen puts in an appearance – what to do I'm damned if I know. 'So all you have succeeded in doing is to lose Enoch,' I remark to him coldly. He just shrugs indifferently. The conference goes well: Rachel does her stuff as to the manner born. I beat back a hostile barrage from the journalists. Afterwards I say to Jack, 'We have a traitor in our midst and we both know who it is.' 'Of course,' he agrees. Once again I feel frustrated in having to work through an umbrella organization over which we have no real control.

True to form, the press have built up the Oslo lass and sneered at us. They have totally ignored the counter-statement Jack rushed out for me last night saying, 'What have Oslo prices to do with it? No one is asking us to join Norway.' The press have also ignored Neil Marten's report of a poll which NRC commissioned in New Zealand, which shows that 52 per cent of those polled think New Zealand would be better off if we came out. With such a conspiracy of the press against us, how can we win? But I have a feeling we have shaken public confidence in the Establishment case so much that we shall drive large numbers of yesses to abstain. I dash up to town to do a *Nationwide* phone-in at Lime Grove. Hopefully, in the end, it will be TV that counts.

Saturday, 31 May. Jack [Straw] phones to say he has just seen in the *Guardian*'s referendum diary of yesterday a tendentious and malicious piece purporting to explain why Enoch did not turn up at the press conference.[1] It could only have come from one person and confirms all our suspicions. I tell Jack to tell Bob that the person must not be present at any of our future discussions. I am not going to reveal my plans in front of a spy.

One nice note among the sour. In my box I have been reading the diplomatic report from Ghana by the High Commissioner, Stanley, on Joan Lestor's official visit there. It positively radiates excitement about her 'outstanding success', talking of the great effect she had on the Ghanaians with her 'enthusiasm, interest and easy informality'. I have seldom read in any diplomatic report such praise of any Minister. Yet I've no doubt some of the Jenkinsites sneered when Harold appointed Joan. 'Easy informality' is not their line.

[1] The report said that John Allen, 'the long-suffering anti-EEC official', had tried to arrange a compromise whereby Enoch appeared at the morning press conference and Rachel and I at a special one in the afternoon, but I would not have it. So Enoch refused to turn up. 'Barbara and her niece steal the show (and disgust the assembled international press) with the Brussels shopping basket and infant underwear.'

Sunday, 1 June to Friday, 6 June. The climax of one of the oddest fortnights of my life. It must be unprecedented for a government to extend the Whit recess in order to allow all comers, including Dissenting Ministers, to campaign against its policy. I flatly refused to do any anti-Market meetings during the Whit weekend. My sense of values held firm. But after that I was in the campaign up to my eyebrows.

The biggest occasion of all was the Oxford Union debate. The President had written to me weeks ago to ask me if I would participate with Peter Shore, ranged against Heath and Thorpe, on the subject, 'This House says Yes to Europe'. He had added that TV had shown great interest. Of course, I jumped at it. The Union has never been my favourite audience and, as the day drew nearer, all my old phobias about Oxford came flooding back. I was hampered too by my inhibitions about the crudities of our anti-Market case. (And I am *not* referring to Enoch, who, throughout everything, remains intellectually sophisticated.) I happen to believe deeply that membership of the EEC will fatally dilute some of the main motive power of British social democracy and give a great fillip to consensus politics. But my spirit cringes at some of the statistical distortions which bring such tumultuous applause from Labour audiences. Life is more complex than that and there is no doubt that the terms Jim and Harold have got effectively blunt the edge of a simplistic attack. Even my Ted said to me the other day that he couldn't get particularly steamed up about the issue! So I was like a fortress divided against itself and as the day of the debate grew nearer something like panic began to rise in me. I set all Tuesday aside to sketch out my speech (which I was determined not to read) and was still in a state of mental confusion by the time I had to rush to catch the train. Peter Shore was at the station, relaxed and casual, remarking: 'I really ought to jot down a few ideas.' I have never envied him more – never been more conscious of the fatal flaw in my make-up which has always prevented me from realizing my full potential. Give me a soap box at a street corner, or a hostile crowd of cocky inebriates at an annual dinner, and I can be masterly. But give me time to worry about the intellectual niceties of my case and I can become paralysed. As the train steamed into Oxford station I felt paralysed.

Dinner-jacketed undergraduates met us at the station: all politeness and importance. At the Randolph Hotel the BBC were waiting: would I mind being made-up now, before dinner, as there was so much making-up to do? I had decided to wear the sixty-year-old Edwardian blouse I had discovered among Mother's things – all mutton-chop sleeves and meticulous beading. 'My suffragette blouse,' I explained defiantly. (If only someone were threatening to forcibly feed me for my views, I should have no fear!) I arrived at the Union just in time for the elaborately organized photograph. It was a sunny evening and the queues for the debate were already long as I arrived on the lawn, head held as high as Anne Boleyn's on her way to the scaffold. (My terror had been made worse when Tony Keable-Elliott had informed me at HCF last week that his son was intending to queue 'for hours' in order not to miss the debate.) Then out of the President's room walked Jeremy, to tumultuous cheers from the queueing undergraduates. He gave them an American footballer's hand-held-high clinch. But the most revealing moment of all came when Heath walked on to the lawn. The catcalls of delight were uncontainable. It was a near pandemonium of enthusiasm and I suddenly realized what we were up against. Heath was the hero of the hour, as he had never been as PM.

At dinner I sat opposite Jeremy, facing the window. The queuers for the debate gawped in at us as they filed past, scanning the long table which was crowded with celebrities. I felt like a Christian being looked over by the Romans on their way to the arena. Jeremy was obviously in his element, cracking jokes and telling historical anecdotes. At one point we got on to Margaret Thatcher. Jeremy leaned forward and said to me with great deliberation, 'The lady *will not do*.' It certainly seemed to be Heath's night! And so it proved, when at last the protracted meal was over and the BBC had completed its last frantic whirl of making-up. A deadly calm of despair came over me as we filed into the debating chamber. The Union was packed to the ceiling; even the standing room had run out. Peter and I were greeted with catcalls and boos; there was warm applause for Jeremy and a crescendo of adulation for Heath, who took it with a new dignity.

The opening undergraduate speeches were fair enough. Then Peter opened for us. He said nothing particularly new and rather rambled on, completely unworried. I didn't think he did particularly well, but later Ted told me it came over very well on TV. Next Jeremy – and I suddenly realized he was out for a purely debating kill, and he did it brilliantly. His merciless cracks against us had them rolling in the aisles. At one point he turned and tore into us. If we thought membership was so disastrous, what would we do if the vote went against us? Resign – or hang on to office to operate a policy in which we did not believe? Enormous cheers from the audience. 'What answer should I give to that?' I asked Peter nervously. 'Ignore it,' he replied blandly. Then it was my turn. As I got to my feet every word I had prepared seemed irrelevant. I forgot all about TV, concentrating all my efforts on that overwhelmingly hostile audience, wishing with all my heart that this numbing paralysis would leave me so that my natural debating powers could assert themselves. All I could do, I said to myself, was to get through it somehow and not *look* afraid. So I hit out. I had decided to concentrate on the issue of internationalism: the biggest appeal for the young in the EEC idea. The very title of the debate. 'This House says Yes to Europe,' was typical of the sloppy thinking which dominated the pro-Market case, I said. It was necessary to define our terms more closely than that: 'Joad, thou shouldst be living at this hour.' For what did we mean by 'yes'? Yes on any terms? 'Yes,' called out Jeremy, so I turned on him. Exactly. His Party had been in favour of entry even on the reactionary inward-looking terms negotiated by Heath. So it ill became him to quote the Lomé convention in aid of the 'internationalism' of the Community. He had voted for entry without *that*! Lomé had only been produced by the people who had rejected the Heath terms. By common consent it had been a triumph for Judith Hart and she remained implacably opposed to our entry. Why? Because even Lomé was not real internationalism: it was neo-colonial paternalism.

But as I began to get into my stride Jeremy was biding his time and he leapt up to interrupt. 'Since the Right Honourable Lady thinks the Community is such a deplorable institution, if the country votes to stay in will she resign from the Government?' There it was: there was no escaping it. The audience went wild with delight. Hoots and catcalls drowned any attempt at reply. I turned and faced them, waiting for the row to die down and then said emphatically and slowly, 'If Britain votes to stay in the Common Market, my country will need me more than ever.' I was rather proud of it – and I meant it anyway. But the audience shrieked with derision, while Jeremy did a little jig in his place, turning his eyes heavenwards and drawing a mock halo round his head. By now my time was nearly up, and I had hardly got through half my material. I galloped to a close and sat down to the thinnest applause of the evening. Peter's congratulations were perfunctory. I knew I had been a flop, but my only feeling was one of relief that I had survived at all.

But the most remarkable phenomenon of the evening was Heath. The audience was all his, and he responded to it with a genuineness which was the most impressive thing I have ever seen from him. He stood there, speaking simply, strongly and without a note. They gave him a standing ovation at the end, and he deserved it for the best example I have ever seen of The Man Who Came Back. Then, mercifully, we were able to escape to the President's room for drinks and the slow stain of the misery of failure began to come through into my soul. Everyone was congratulating Heath and I did too. Then, about midnight, we heard the result: they had wiped the floor with us. Peter and I drove back to London and I just wanted to die. I don't mind being beaten – except by myself.

Wednesday, 4 June. Last night's debate is the talk of the town. Ted tells me it was superb TV, Heath coming over particularly well. A lot of papers have quoted my reply to Jeremy, which Ted says was 'splendid'. But what *didn't* come over on telly was the attitude of the audience, so no one would have guessed what we were up against.

Friday, 6 June. I didn't bother to go to Blackburn for referendum polling day, though Ted put in some work at Islington. Janet said to me, 'There are lots of letters about the TV debate.' 'Hostile,' I said, resigned. 'No,' she said. 'Only one against. The rest are very congratulatory.' And so, to my utter astonishment they were – even from people who said they didn't agree with me. Apparently that reply of mine seems to have been a sensation. What interests me is the contempt they express for Jeremy. His Union debating style proved counter-productive with a non-Union audience.

Sunday, 8 June. Congratulatory letters still pouring in: balm to my bruised soul.

On 5 June the referendum campaign had reached its predictable result. For some time it had been clear that the verdict would be Yes, helped by the professionalism of the well-heeled 'Britain in Europe' campaign, dire warnings by British firms about the danger to jobs of a No vote, the prediction by the polls of a Yes victory, but above all by the confusion of Labour supporters when they saw their trusted Prime Minister, Harold Wilson, in conflict with their romantic hero, Tony Benn. The confusion was compounded by the cross-party alignments on the two rival platforms. If it was off-putting to see Roy Jenkins in public pro-Market harmony with Edward Heath and Jeremy Thorpe, it was equally bewildering to see Michael Foot consorting with Enoch Powell and right-wing

Tory MPs *like Ronald Bell at anti-Market press conferences. The strength of Harold Wilson's appeal was that he kept out of sight, relying on the published popular version of the case for staying in Europe to pull in the loyal Labour vote.*

In this unheroic stance Harold Wilson was aided and abetted by the very press which was fond of castigating him for his lack of 'principle'. On the eve of the poll they came out in strength to praise the Government's line. The Daily Mirror *produced one of its famous four-page spreads to whip up pro-Market feeling and reproduced a* VE *Day cartoon by Philip Zec showing a wounded soldier pleading with the politicians not to throw away the 'peace in Europe' he had helped to win. Commentators everywhere hinted to the fearful that a vote against the Market was a vote for Tony Benn's domestic policies. When the result – a two to one Yes vote on a poll of about 65 per cent – was announced, the* Guardian *reported that the result had been received with satisfaction in financial circles. 'The first beneficiary was the Government,' it commented on 7 June, 'which took the opportunity to announce the issue of a further £1,100 million of short-dated government stock to help finance its massive borrowing requirement.'*

The count was held on a county basis, Ted Short having failed to convince the Commons of the virtues of a central count. In the event this strengthened the pro-marketeers' claims because it showed that the vote in all areas approximated very closely to the national result of a 68.3 per cent Yes vote against a 32.8 per cent No. Even Scotland produced a Yes majority, though a 10 per cent smaller one. There were some slight variations on party lines, strong Conservative counties recording a higher than average Yes vote and turnout and strong Labour ones a lower than average, but the differences were so minimal as not to counteract the local effect of a national result. Only in London, where the turnout fell as low as 49 per cent in the five most Labour boroughs, was there any hint of the massive indifference to Europe which was to manifest itself four years later in the direct elections to the European Assembly.

The pro-Market press was naturally jubilant. Peter Jenkins in the Guardian *on 7 June described it as a 'Euroslide victory', adding that 'The case is now closed.' The* Daily Telegraph *congratulated Harold Wilson on his successful gamble, while the* Daily Mail *declared that 'the effect of this thunderous Yes will echo down the years'. For the most part the anti-marketeers accepted their defeat gracefully, Tony Benn declaring: 'I have just been in receipt of a very big message from the British people. I read it loud and clear. . . . By an overwhelming majority the British people have voted to stay in and I am sure that everyone would want to accept that.' Only Enoch Powell struck a defiant note, declaring that the result was 'provisional' and reminding the country of the words in the Government's own pamphlet: 'Our continued membership will depend on the continuing assent of Parliament.'*

It was not until October 1975 that the accounts of the campaigning organizations were available, whose publication the Government had provided for in the Referendum Act, hopefully as a protection against excessive spending by either side. The White Paper giving the accounts (Cmnd 6251) showed that this disincentive had not prevented 'Britain in Europe' from spending nearly £1.5 million on the campaign, compared with just over £133,000 by the NRC*, including the £125,000 from the Government. The list of contributions to 'Britain in Europe' funds, notably from industry and the stock exchange, filled eight columns of the White Paper, while the* NRC *could only muster seven private contributions, mainly from individuals, the largest sum being £1,377 from the Transport and General Workers' Union.*

Press predictions that Harold Wilson would lose no time after the referendum in reshuffling his Cabinet were quickly vindicated. On Monday 9 June he switched Tony Benn from Industry to Energy, replacing him with Eric Varley. He demoted Reg Prentice from Education to Overseas Development, though forced to keep him in the Cabinet, and replaced him at Education with a right-wing pro-marketeer, Fred Mulley. Judith Hart, losing Overseas Development, decided to leave the Government. Meanwhile the economic storm clouds grew ever more menacing. Inflation had reached 25 per cent and Denis Healey was desperately negotiating with the TUC *over a tough voluntary incomes policy and was pressing ahead in Cabinet with his plans for further public expenditure cuts in the longer term. Jack Jones was using all his influence to help the Government.*

Monday, 9 June. Harold had called a Cabinet for this, the first working day after the referendum result. No agenda. No background papers. The sun was still shining brilliantly when I left HCF and yet I was glad to get back to reality. I remain astonished at the new sense of work vitality which possesses me. I am lured into taking on more and more burdens and instead of wanting to wind myself down from the limelight of responsibility, I am attracted to it like a moth to a flame. Perhaps it is like the drowning man who sees all his life's history concentrated before his eyes. I know I have not much longer to operate in the febrile, exacting and fulfilling world of power and some instinct makes me want to make the most of it.

To our surprise Fred was there, dark blotches under his eyes from the shock of the rail crash in which he was involved. We all commiserated with him. Harold swerved past me without a greeting into the Cabinet room and, when he had called us to order, it was in his best 'I'm going to get tough now', prime ministerial mood. I felt it didn't bode good to any of us Dissenting Ministers, though I doubt whether he will do a clean sweep immediately. That wouldn't be his style: he prefers picking people off one by one. As we waited outside the room I had asked Wedgie, 'Have you heard anything?' He had shrugged in his boyishly disarming way, 'Not a word.' The pro-marketeers as a whole, though not wholly avoiding looking like the cats that had got at the cream, were patently trying to restrain their jubilation. No gloating.

A brief discussion of the Stonehouse debate due on Thursday. Ted Short was on the whole in favour of going ahead with it but I protested that, since Stonehouse had tried to return to this country, however speciously, the public would condemn us for trying him *in absentia*. Shirley and others agreed with me though Eric Varley, who is clearly a secret pragmatist – not to say opportunist – whispered to me, 'If we postpone the by-election, we are less likely to win it.' Bob said robustly that we had been guided by the Select Committee all along and ought to be also on this point and so it was agreed.

I have been interested to read in my box a letter from Wedgie to Harold setting out the steps he is proposing to take to establish warm and intimate relations with the Industrial Commissioner of the EEC. He has lost no time in sending Spinelli a personal telegram and even phoning him 'to express my good wishes'. That lad really is brilliant at taking avoiding action! Here am I, ready to accept that I must co-operate now with the Council of Ministers, but still nursing reticences and unhappiness about the Market, while Wedgie has been able to do a complete about-turn emotionally without any sense of inconsistency. I was just brooding on this in my room at the House when Judith came in, somewhat distraught, to borrow a cigarette. She was to be moved, she told me, from Overseas Development. I was taken aback, having been lulled this morning into a false sense of security by Harold's failure to announce any changes in the Government. Judith said Harold had offered her Transport, but she wouldn't take it. Where was everybody, I asked. In Tony's room, she replied. I went along.

Tony Benn was sitting at his desk, a figure of tragedy, surrounded by a cortège of political advisers: Michael Meacher, Joe Ashton [Labour MP for Bassetlaw and Tony Benn's PPS] and other figures I could barely make out, because the curtains were drawn against the brilliant sun. The heat was stifling. 'Have you heard anything?' I asked. 'Yes,' he replied, 'I am to be moved to Energy.' I was staggered, my first feeling being that it was the cleverest move Harold could make. Wedgie said he had talked to Eric [Varley], who had been offered Industry. Eric had written to Harold saying he would not take the job if Wedgie were to resign, as he seemed to be contemplating. It must be a straight swap or nothing. Wedgie was clearly hesitant. Harold had demanded an instant reply and Wedgie had been 'very rude' to him. He thought he was at least entitled to twenty-four hours to think it over. We all supported him on this. Apparently Michael [Foot] has been in and was ready to act as go-between.

As we sat mulling things over Judith was sent for by Harold again and came back saying she was back at Overseas Development after all. Great rejoicing all round. Had I heard anything? they asked. No, I said. 'Then you are all right. It is clear that you, Peter and Mike are not to be moved.' I consoled Wedgie: 'At least Harold has moved you to another power point in the Manifesto.' 'Yes,' he replied gloomily, 'but I shall have no part in the negotiations with the oil companies. Harold has made it clear that that will remain with Harold Lever's committee.' 'But as Secretary of State they can't keep you out of the picture,' I replied. 'And if things are going the wrong way, you can bring it to Cabinet. It gives you a better resigning position.' I think he had already made up his mind to accept, however reluctantly. After an hour of this I could not stand any more of the airless, sweaty heat, so Ted and I went off to eat with Judith and Tony Hart. We speculated as to why Harold had changed his mind over her job and decided he must have offered it to Reg Prentice as demotion and had been faced by a row. Judith said the rumour was that Roy Jenkins had threatened to resign if Reg Prentice was moved out of the Cabinet. Whatever the reason we rejoiced that she was back at ODM. 'Though Transport would have been a challenge,' said Tony Hart almost wistfully.

Tuesday, 10 June. The newspapers are full of Wedgie's 'triumph' at Questions yesterday, the first time the proceedings of the House have been broadcast live. Some of the most ecstatic comments were from enemy papers. 'Big Benn is the star of the air!' said the *Sun*. 'Commons radio starts with sparkling Benn cut and thrust,' said the *Financial Times*. 'Benn a hit in radio Commons,' said the *Daily Telegraph*, while even Andrew Alexander talked about his 'dignity and skill'. Which confirms my view that (a) the press are doing more than anyone else to build up Wedgie and (b) that you have got to have certain attributes to be a successful rebel: you must shine on the platform and in the House. Wedgie does both, which is why he can get away with murder.

Alex Kitson came to see me about a health matter and spent the first quarter of an hour talking politics. He was very disturbed about the rumours that

Wedgie was to be moved, and about the result of the referendum, but said that Harold could always rely on Jack Jones's 'blind loyalty'. (It fascinates me how completely Jack has forgiven Harold for his part in the *In Place of Strife* saga. The breach between Jack and me has been partially healed during the anti-Market campaign, but I don't think he will ever completely trust me again. Alex remains my devoted slave, hugging me when he arrived. How much loyalties in politics depend on stray incidents! The only thing Alex stubbornly remembers about me is that I was the Minister of Transport who *volunteered* the reduction in lorry drivers' statutory hours.) Alex said that Jack got into trouble with the T and G Executive for his loyalty to Harold. He had had a rough time with them. 'He's the boss,' said Alex, 'so we are loyal to him. "Blind loyalty" if you like.'

Having been up till 1 am this morning at the House, I paired so as to be reasonably fresh for the Report stage of our Pensions Bill tomorrow. I got to the flat at 8 pm. I had just got out of my clothes into something cool and was planning to eat my bacon and egg while I watched *Edward VII* on TV when the phone rang. No. 10. The PM would like to see me at 9 pm. 'We will send a car.' This is it, I thought. We were all being premature when we thought Wedgie was going to be the only one to be dealt with. I dressed again, as relaxed as I always am when disaster strikes. My head went up as I worked out how I would act when Harold told me he wanted me out. He had the right to do it, just as he had a right to move Wedgie. After all, Harold was the referendum victor and there had been little doubt that he would exploit his victory. Not excessively, that is not his way, but to the maximum extent compatible with what the Party would tolerate. And as Ted has pointed out to me several times in the last few weeks, Harold has an excuse in my case on the grounds of age. So when the car came I walked down to it with all the poise I could muster, feeling like Anne Boleyn walking to the scaffold in the TV series on Henry VIII: my Dorothy Tutin to Harold's Keith Michell? 'Henry feasted while Anne died,' I thought to myself. In the car I chatted nonchalantly to the driver. My thoughts were racing. I have got to go soon. What better way than when my political allies can argue that I have been victimized? But do one's political friends care when it comes to the crunch? I felt very lonely. I doubted they did.

The meeting was to be at the House, though if Harold thought that would disguise the comings and goings he was being very naïve. The private secretary greeted me apologetically: did I suspect sympathy? As I waited in the anteroom I felt – or imagined – that Ken Marks [Labour MP for Gorton and Harold's PPS] and Doreen, one of the secretaries, were embarrassed in their elaborate friendliness. 'Come in, please, Secretary of State,' the message came at last. It was 9.20 pm. Harold was pacing up and down in his shirt-sleeves, enjoying himself. 'Sit here,' he said, indicating the chair next to his. He played out the drama, knowing full well what I was thinking. 'Barbara, as I am always loyal and never more loyal to anyone than to you, I wanted to see you to say that I want to take your junior Minister.' I was puzzled while he grinned. 'Alec Jones,' he explained. 'I want him for the Welsh Office.' 'But he's very good,' I protested mildly, 'and we have the Report stage of the Pension Bill tomorrow.' 'But I'm going to give you the one you asked for in the first place: Michael Meacher.' The significance of that remark did not dawn on me then for I was very pleased. 'Oh, he'd be first-class.' 'Right, then,' he said. He was too busy to offer me a drink.

'These reshuffles are hell,' he said, resuming his pacing. 'None of you know what ulcers they give me. All this multilateral moving about. But it's going very well. When it is all over you will say that the old boy has not lost his touch. It is pure poetry.' Then he added defensively, 'What I have done about Wedgie – he's accepted by the way – has nothing to do with the referendum. I planned it as long ago as Easter. And I've dealt with Reg Prentice. I have offered him the one job he cannot refuse: the one he resigned from because he said he believed in it so much.' So Reg has got ODM after all! In the Cabinet I suspect. Otherwise Harold would have faced Roy Jenkins's revolt. I tried to recapture some of our old relationship. 'I must say your move for Wedgie was brilliantly cunning,' I told him. 'I said to myself: "The old basket has outmanœuvred us again." You have moved him to another power point in the Manifesto.' 'I've moved him to a job where he will be commanding millions of pounds' worth of oil as it comes flowing in,' replied Harold. 'I told Wedgie he ought to accept,' I continued. 'You are a good girl,' he replied. 'I could never get you to be a bad girl even in the days when you and I were younger.' (I am always amused by this myth he perpetuates between us. As I remember those days, he never even tried to make a pass at me.) 'But', I persisted, 'there is one sour note in what you have done: you must not move Judith from ODM. Apart from anything else, she did marvellously. Do you realize how much what she achieved at Lomé helped you in the referendum campaign? If she hadn't, you would have been extremely vulnerable.' He got restive, looking at the clock and moving to the door. 'I have got an announcement to make at 10 pm.' I could see the point of that and left, shooting out to the waiting car, thankful to be free at last to cook my bacon and egg, for I was starving.

Back at the flat I had just shed my hot clothes again (we are never equipped for a heat wave in this country) and had started to cook my long-delayed bacon and egg (too late now for *Edward VII* but just time for the 10 pm news) when the phone rang again. I cursed. It was Wedgie. 'Barbara, Harold has moved Judith from ODM after all. He has offered her Transport and she has refused. We are all here in my room, except Peter, and we are going to see Harold to tell him we won't take it. Will you come?' 'Oh, God,' I groaned, 'I haven't got a car. And I'm starving. Look, I've just come back from Harold and he is making the announcement at 10 pm.' 'Never mind then, duckie. We'll go without you.' 'No,' I shouted, 'but the news is just starting. We must listen to that first. I'll ring you back.' Clutching a charred bit of bacon I hurried to listen to the news. Yes, there it was: Reg P. for ODM. No mention of Judith. I grabbed the phone, only to be told by the House of Commons switchboard that Wedgie had put his absent button on. 'We have been inundated with calls from the press trying to reach him' (for, of course, his new job was announced at the same time).

I was distraught. I must get down to the House to support Judith, but taxis are almost unobtainable in Islington. In despair I phoned Ted at the town hall. 'I have to get down to the House. Can you leave your committee and take me?' 'Of course,' said Ted, identifying himself as always with the dramas in which I am involved. I hurriedly re-dressed, gulping the rest of my charred bacon.

Twenty minutes later Ted arrived, announcing, 'I can't take you in my car as I'm out of petrol.' I groaned. Never had a wife a husband who managed to combine complete loyalty with patches of practical unreliability more exasperatingly. The times I have found in a crisis that he had a flat battery, was out of petrol or had forgotten to blow up his tyre . . . 'I'll get a cab,' he shouted, hurrying downstairs, obviously dreading the worst for me. When I followed him I found him standing in the middle of the road, trying to flag down the most unlikely vehicles. 'It's too late, too late,' I shouted, in despair at the feeling that I had let Judith down. Wasn't she feeling as I had been feeling just an hour or so ago? Then, as always, Ted's luck – the luck of the happy-go-lucky – held. A taxi drew up. On the way down I told Ted the whole story. He was immensely relieved for me. We raced up to Wedgie's room to find the usual crowd of mourners sitting behind drawn curtains in that steamy heat. Judith was holding court. 'Am I too late?' I panted. No, they said. 'Mike and Wedgie are seeing Harold now.' I raced downstairs to Harold's room, sweeping the private secretary aside. 'I'm going in to see the PM,' I announced and walked in. Harold was sitting in his chair, glass in hand, looking tired. Ken Marks was watching, fascinated. 'You were here only a short while ago,' said Harold amiably.

The atmosphere was relaxed as Mike and Wedgie greeted me with pleasure. But it was soon clear that, in his inimitably gentle way, Mike was laying it down the line. 'We're not trying to blackmail or threaten you, Harold. You have the right to make what appointments you choose. But then other people have the right to decide their position in the light of those appointments.' Harold gave us the old routine about the agony of these reshuffles. 'None of you know the job it is: the multilateral dispositions that have to be made. None of you know what this does to me.' We said we did. 'But', said Wedgie, 'you must realize that during these past few weeks the seven of us have worked as a team. We are not going to leave anyone on the battlefield.' Harold tried to make out that the Ministry of Transport was a worthwhile job. 'Look what Barbara made of it.' 'Not outside the Cabinet,' said Mike firmly. Harold was keeping his temper very well. 'I've never discussed Cabinet changes with anyone before,' he said mildly. 'Has no one else threatened to go on strike?' I murmured impishly. He had to admit they had: we knew Roy had laid it down the line on Reg Prentice's behalf. It helped to make our intervention less of an impertinence. 'But I'm already over the number of Cabinet posts,' Harold complained. 'I'd have to legislate.' 'You can do it if you want to,' said Mike tenaciously. 'Unless', said Harold slyly, looking at me, 'I were to give Judith Social Services, which she has had before.' 'You can have my job for Judith,' I replied promptly. 'That's no answer,' retorted Wedgie. 'We're not leaving Barbara on the battlefield either.'

The circular argument went on, Mike leaving Harold in no doubt that, if Judith were demoted, we would all resign, 'and Peter is with us on this, too'. I spoke eloquently, though I can't for the life of me remember what I said. Wedgie gave one of his amusing little homilies. 'I'm really quite a simple guy, Harold, and I'm certainly not after your job. You once called me an Old Testament prophet and that is just what I am. There are just certain ideas that I think ought to be spelt out and I spell them out.' After nearly an hour of this I suddenly took pity on Harold, having to show infinite patience after a long and exacting day. 'We shan't solve this argument by trying to beat this man into the ground physically,' I told the other two. 'I think we ought to have some mercy on Harold and leave him alone to think over what we have said.' 'There *are* two boxes to do,' said Harold, still mildly. As we got up to leave Mike repeated without menaces that we were not prepared to see one of our team sacrificed. We would like to see Harold again tomorrow if necessary. At the door I said to Harold warmly, 'Thank you for your courtesy,' and I meant it. Outside Wedgie and Mike hugged me enthusiastically: 'You were magnificent.' 'Barbara was magnificent,' they told the crowd waiting upstairs. God knows why. 'Not more than these two,' I replied. Judith thanked us effusively. 'We've told him we shall return to the attack tomorrow,' said Mike. 'I think we are going to win,' I assured Judith. And so to bed at 1 am. 'My early night,' I groaned. But my conscience was at rest.

Wednesday, 11 June. At the office I warned Norman, in strictest privacy, what might happen. 'You may find yourself not only without a Parliamentary Secretary for the Report stage of the Pensions Bill this afternoon, but without a Secretary of State.' 'That would be a great pity,' he replied. But I went ahead, briefing myself on some of the complex amendments I had to move, just in case Harold did give in. Then suddenly Norman came into my room to say that Mrs Judith Hart was making 'a personal statement on Rhodesia' that afternoon. I was flabbergasted. At the House I put my head into Mike's room and asked him if he knew what was happening. He was as bewildered as I was. 'I've been in touch with Harold again and said we would want to see him today to settle this matter,' he replied. 'But I now hear that Judith has been making statements all over the place.' 'She is making one in the House now,' I replied. We hurried down. Judith came into the Chamber rather coyly, notes in hand, and slipped deprecatingly into a seat on the front bench below the gangway. Anyway, one mystery was soon solved. She was making her personal statement *after* Jim's statement on Rhodesia, not on it. As she spoke, announcing her resignation from the Government rather emotionally, I couldn't help wondering what it was all supposed to be in aid of. What was she trying to prove? That she personally has been victimized[1] or that there was a great political point in the return of the Ministry of Overseas Development to Foreign Office tutelage? I certainly deplore that and I am nauseated by the cynical way in which Harold plays ducks and drakes with this whole question of overseas aid. He made a great political point in 1964 about his intention to create a separate Ministry of Overseas Development 'with a seat in the Cabinet'. And he gave me the job. As soon as he had moved me from ODM to Transport he demoted my old Ministry to outside the Cabinet (though it was still a separate Ministry). When we came back to office in 1974 he made ODM a separate Ministry again, giving Judith Cabinet status and charge of her own department. Now, to fit into his reshuffle jigsaw puzzle, he has put Reg P. *in* the Cabinet but as Minister of Overseas Development *under* the FO. It is this kind of behaviour that makes one despair of him. He subordinates all considerations, not only of principle

[1] In her statement she said: 'Frankly, I can see no reason for the Prime Minister to sack me from my Ministry.' (Hansard 11.6.75, col. 419)

but of administrative effectiveness, to his balance of power manœuvrings. If Judith had stuck to this point, I would have applauded her. As it was I felt slightly embarrassed.

Afterwards I learned that it was her political adviser, Tony Banks, who had told her she must make a statement. Mike was furious. 'It's bloody nonsense,' he said to me in the division lobby. 'Here we are, bringing pressure on Harold to put her in the Cabinet at Transport, and we would have won.'

The penny has now dropped about Michael Meacher. Glad as I am to have him at DHSS, his transfer is just part of Harold's determination to denude the Department of Industry of all its former devotees. And one of the things that shocks me most is the removal of Joan Lester from the Foreign Office. She was obviously a breath of fresh air in that airless institution and I gather that her move was due to personal representations by Jim to Harold. He had found her behaviour 'embarrassing' to him. I shan't forgive Jim for that. She is to go to Education: again, a move no one can really complain about unless they are in the know. But Joan working to Fred Mulley . . .!

Thursday, 12 June. Wore my new striped kaftan dress to Cabinet and the enthusiasm with which it was greeted cheered my morale. In a private word beforehand Peter told me: 'Of course I would have been with you over Judith. What a mess she has made of things!' Cabinet agenda was so light we did not meet till 11.30 am, and even then Harold was late. Jim and Harold launched on a long dissertation on the Middle East, which was as usual mumbled and difficult to follow. The minutes ticked by and then suddenly, when Harold turned to Denis for comments, Denis burst out with all his suppressed anxieties about the state of sterling. 'This morning we have had the most severe attack on sterling we have ever had. It has cost us 500 million dollars to hold the rate even here. *We have got to stop the slide.* I have been talking to the central bankers in Paris and the real reason for this run is the widespread feeling that we lack the will to deal with inflation. If the railways strike materializes – or, worse still, if we give in to the NUR – the position would be untenable. I am beginning to think that I cannot wait till July.' We just sat silent and worried.

I have decided to outdo Wedgie on the EEC. The Council of Ministers will be discussing social matters next week and so will be attended by social service Ministers. There is nothing of any great importance coming up, so the office had assumed we would be sending the Parliamentary Secretary. Alec Jones's transfer to the Welsh Office gives me an excuse to announce that I shall go myself. I'm sure Hindmarsh [Under-Secretary in the DHSS International Relations Division] will be furious at my intervention, which adds to the zest.

Friday, 13 June. NALGO has come out flatly against private medical practice at its annual conference and has called on local branches to oppose all planning applications for private hospitals. If I hadn't made my statement on pay beds last month, we should be in grave trouble now with the unions.

Monday, 16 June. Before I could go to Luxembourg I had to attend another all-day meeting at Chequers, this time of the devolution committee on which Ted Short is trying desperately to force the pace. Harold has got very fond of these

Chequers meetings, and it is certainly a pleasanter place to meet than No. 10. The significant thing about this meeting was the attempt of Denis, Roy J. *et al.* to back-track on the whole devolution idea, on the grounds that the Common Market referendum result in Scotland showed that the Scots Nats were a busted flush. Ted was furious because there have been extensive leaks in the Scottish press to the effect that the Government was retreating from its original plans.

I had to leave early to catch a Defence plane to Luxembourg. On the way John Fraser [who is now Under-Secretary of State at the Department of Employment] and I swopped notes on the line we should take tomorrow on the directive on Equality of Rights for Women in Employment – one of those pretentious pieces of EEC 'legislation' which can be as grandiose as you like because everyone ignores them when it suits them. The bit that concerned me was the reference to complete equality of treatment in pension rights, which was a nonsense as it stood and would have cut right across our new Pensions Bill. We arrived at Luxembourg in time for the President's dinner. This year the Irish are heading the Council of Ministers and President Ritchie Ryan has been working desperately hard to make an impact with everyone. Luxembourg was as pretty as a picture and looked prosperous. I put on my favourite Mauritian dress and swept into the club where the dinner was to be held, feeling full of mischief. Of course, there was considerable interest in the appearance of this British anti-marketeer and over dinner I got into a lively discussion with the French Minister of Finance, trying to explain to him in my erratic French how counter-productive I thought these ill-thought-out directives were. 'A law is a law and should be drafted with the intention that it shall be enforced,' I said. He was greatly amused. All I know is that I have no time for the shambling discussions and hypocritical attitudinizing of which I have had so much at these international conferences. If Britain is in the Common Market, for better or for worse, I want to see that the EEC institutions develop some of the intellectual discipline we have to have in our own Government.

Tuesday, 17 June. True to my intentions, I took the day's discussions *au sérieux*. In fact I made quite a powerful speech, pointing out the implications of the proposed wording about pensions equality. They were clearly staggered when I told them that to equalize the retirement age of men and women at sixty in Britain would cost £1,400 million, 'which my country just has not got at the present time'. But what shook them even more was my revelation that, as the words stood, it would not be possible for any of us to go on insisting that the family allowance must be paid to the mother and not the father. They just hadn't thought the thing out at all. My old friend, Walter Leber, chuckled at my energetic denunciations and backed my amendments. The Commissioner hastened to say he would consider them. The young Irish chairman of the Council egged me on. So, after a wordy debate it was agreed the Commission should take this bit back. I then excused myself gracefully and returned early to London, leaving John Fraser to wrangle for hours over the other points about employment. I was told afterwards that, at a late hour, when the discussion had been going in fruitless circles, the chairman had rapped the table and said reproachfully, 'Gentlemen, what would Barbara Castle say if she were here?'

Worked late on my papers for Friday's crucial Cabinet meeting at Chequers on economic strategy which some of us have been pressing for. The implications for public expenditure are quite terrifying.

Wednesday, 18 June. Quite a show in the press about my EEC debut! And of course my pro-Market ministerial colleagues are teasing me mercilessly. At Legislation Committee (where I had to fight to prevent Ted Short from knocking my Pay Beds Bill out of next year's programme) I whispered to Mike, 'Have *you* got an economic strategy for dealing with the crisis?' 'Some of us ought to meet tonight,' he replied. 'I am trying to fix a dinner somewhere. Can you come?' Of course, I said I could and would, even though it meant missing the Report stage of the Sex Discrimination Bill and getting David to move an amendment in which we were interested. But with the pound still weakening, and with the AUEW, despite some rather feeble efforts by Hughie to prevent it, voting at its conference to reject the Social Contract, I had no doubt that economic strategy had overwhelming priority. Before we met at the Gay Hussar I had time to read the document on strengthening the voluntary pay policy which Mike has circulated for Friday's meeting. I also read the TUC's draft statement for Congress on 'The Development of the Social Contract', which has already been through the Economic Committee and is going to the General Council on 25 June.[1] The TUC has certainly gone further than it ever has in spelling out the minutiae of a voluntary incomes policy and has even put its toes in the waters of 'norms', flat-rate increases and the Heathian formula of a combination of flat rate and percentage increases. But, as Peter Shore said tonight, can it deliver?

Friday, 20 June. Woke at 5.30 am in one of the depressed moods I get rather frequently these days. With Ted away at Bristol I could make myself a cup of tea and brood. I am now almost pathologically anxious to finish my job. With the press seeking to edge me out – and with some right-wing back benchers obviously speculating on when I shall go – the last thing I want to do is to hang on. What pains me is the way the press pick me out for sacrifice while ignoring the longevity of the others in my age group. Why do the press hate me so? I know I do not find fraternizing particularly easy, but then, equally, I am always civil and co-operative. My only problem is to find the right time and reason for going. I do not deserve to be humiliated. And there are one or two initiatives I want to get launched in the Department before I go so that my successor can pick them up (if he or she is the right sort of person). I want, for instance, to force the Department to reform those wretched NHS spectacle frames and I want to get a great export initiative going in the health field. *Nothing* will be done unless I am there to drive it through. Look at Tony Crosland for instance, still waffling about without a housing policy after fifteen months!

As Edna raced me to Chequers for our all-day meeting on economic strategy I was amused to read in my *Guardian* that 'at this time most of the Cabinet

[1] The first draft of the document embodied six main aims: the need to fix a target for inflation to be achieved by mid-1976; a figure for pay increases, related to this target, in the form of a flat-rate money increase; a cut-off point for pay increases in the case of very high incomes; radical action to limit price increases through the Price Code and subsidies; a major reduction in the level of unemployment in 1976; and the maintenance and development of the Social Contract. At its meeting on 25 June the General Council agreed that these points should be defined more specifically.

probably favours a statutory policy', the only real exceptions, it said, being the PM and Mike! (I suspected Harold would be furious at this right-wing build-up and sure enough he was.) There was a mass of documents before us: from Mike, spelling out various ways of toughening the guidelines; from Denis, giving figures of the effect on take-home pay and unemployment of the various alternative policies; from Shirley, suggesting a 'phased norm' for pay increases and demanding that breaches of the norm in the public sector should not be met from increased expenditure. (In the NHS that would mean no inflation-proofing of pay rises beyond the norm and in transport it would mean passing on the excess in fare increases.) There was also a massive document by officials spelling out the advantages and disadvantages of the different courses, *including a statutory policy*. Reg, Roy and others have been demanding that this course of action shall no longer be ruled out of order and I for one welcomed bringing this out into the open, so that they are forced to show their hand. But what interests me is how a norm of some kind is now widely accepted, even by the TUC.

It was a beautiful day and it seemed criminal to proceed to incarcerate ourselves in the long room, with its dark panelled walls and sombre oil paintings. As I looked out on the park with its lush grass, and watched the cows graze under the big bosomy trees, I wondered why it is that crises always occur in that incomparable weather in which the English countryside seems to exude a placid security. Harold called on Mike first to introduce his paper, which he did quietly and without histrionics, but with obvious total commitment to the need to face what had to be done. He began by dismissing a statutory policy, which, he said, 'is only possible with a consent that does not exist'. What we had to do was to get TUC support for a 'fixed target figure' for pay settlements and he hoped the CBI would be able to give it clearer support. He accepted that a norm of 10 per cent would be better than 15 per cent, but he warned us that it would be difficult enough to get 15 per cent and he didn't think that 10 per cent could be made acceptable.

Denis came next, more sombre than I have seen him for a long time, but still sticking firmly to a voluntary policy. The problem, he said, was more urgent than any of us realized. There was not a minute to waste. 'We must have a credible policy by the end of July.' And if we were to get inflation down to single figures, we couldn't go beyond 10 per cent for wages or £5 per week. The problem was how to get compliance. The Government would have to play a central role and prevent public service employees breaching the norm. It also meant the end of review bodies, and we should have to find some way of ensuring that the private sector followed suit.

When Harold threw the discussion open to general debate Tony C. made one of his drawling contributions in which he always manages to make everyone else sound a fool. Harold Lever spoke vigorously. Workers' net take-home pay had stagnated since 1972, he argued. 'We are suffering from a wage paper-chase that has got to stop.' There had to be a government pledge that 'one way or another we are going to enforce it'. 'What do you mean by that?' cried Mike. 'What I say.' 'But what do you *mean* by enforcement? How are you going to do it?' Harold from the chair tried to silence Mike, but Lever insisted that Mike's question was perfectly fair and he wanted to answer it. 'We could do it if necessary by a sanction against the employers, making it illegal to pay. There need be no reciprocal penalty against the unions.' 'If Harold really doesn't mind interruptions,' I intervened, 'can I say to him, as someone who has had to operate a statutory policy, that I was always told it was impossible to put a penalty on the employer unless one also put a penalty on the union which tried by striking to force him to break the law.' There were murmurs of agreement at this, but Lever said he was unconvinced.

My turn next. I thought I spoke rather lamely but I ploughed on. I welcomed the fact, I said, that some members of Cabinet had forced the issue of a statutory policy into the open, because this forced us to study it on its merits. And when we did so, as in the official paper, we found that it had as many disadvantages as any of the alternatives. What emerged was that the only solution to our problems was to win consent. In fact we were already beginning to succeed. The TUC document was an astonishing step forward in its acceptance of our analysis. Now we all knew the problem was to secure compliance, right down the line. It would be wrong for us to leave this to the TUC. 'It is for the Government to win support for the choice the TUC has made: we need an orchestrated Government effort to get this across.' This was the only way to set the crisis in the wider context of our social and socialist economic policies, and so break away from the exclusive concentration on the role of wages to which Wedgie had referred. For months I had been pleading that we should bring home to people the importance of the social wage and how the exclusive concentration on the cash wage was putting it in jeopardy. But we had never begun to get down to this seriously. I stressed the need for a Public Relations Unit to be set up, manned mainly by outside experts in communication. It should be given the job of organizing conferences to be addressed by the PM and other Ministers; preparing graphic material for newspapers to drive home the alternative scenarios that faced us; getting out the social wage document; drafting our White Paper. My speech was received in silence and I thought, 'Well, at least I've tried.'

A few more speeches followed mine. The climax came with Elwyn's. He made the most powerful case against a statutory policy I have ever heard him make. It was a remarkable change from his attitude in 1968 when I was put in charge of the statutory incomes policy Peter Shore had drawn up. I don't remember hearing Elwyn warn Cabinet then of the dangers of legal pay curbs on unions. I thought he would express agreement with what I had said to Lever about the impossibility of having a unilateral legal sanction against employers (it was he who always used to stress this). Certainly he did spell this out and then suddenly, to my astonishment, he turned it into an attack on me: 'I am interested to hear that Barbara is now converted to this view.' I was furious. 'I was too bloody loyal, that was my trouble,' I flashed out. 'Never again!' There was a roar of laughter. 'We all have skeletons in our cupboards,' said Elwyn patronizingly. 'I inherited Peter's policy,' I cried, 'and I had to get it through Standing Committee with half our own side against me.' Peter, to his eternal credit, nodded.

'We'll break for lunch now,' came in Harold. 'Back here at 2.15 pm prompt.' I crept out of the room feeling heartbroken. I would never, I felt, live down the myth that I had been the originator of all evil in the 1966–70 Labour

Government. The unfairness of it almost crushed me. I went downstairs into the great hall, where they were gathering for drinks, still seething. But the first thing that happened was that Harold came up to me, drink in hand, to say how much he liked my idea of the Public Relations Unit. He was all over me. As for Elwyn's intervention: 'We know who was disloyal, don't we? Remember how Jenkins ratted?'

People drifted into the buffet lunch. As I veered into a corner, Mike greeted me with great affection. 'Very good speech,' he said, 'Well done.' He nodded conspiratorially. 'The best speech on the Left,' drawled Tony C. I was staggered. So my rather muted vein had been more effective than a flow of oratory! Jim came up to me. 'I have been thinking about what you said about the problem of the NHS ancillary workers. I think we will just have to get some separate way of dealing with the low-paid through something like the wage councils. I'm afraid I've lost faith in collective bargaining, and, as you know, that is a strange confession to come from me.' Harold Lever came up to congratulate me on my contribution and I hissed at him, 'I'll never forgive Elwyn for that unwarranted attack.' 'Don't worry,' soothed Lever, 'you know we all know you carried the can for the lot.' As we sat perched on our chairs eating our cold collation off our laps Eric came and sat next to me. He seems to seek me out and poured out his heart defensively to me about Wedgie.

Back in the long room the discussion came quickly to a close. Finally Harold summed up. This was not a normal Cabinet, he said, and no decisions would be recorded, but the general view seemed to be that we should aim at a wages norm of 10 per cent. And time was running out. There had been an overwhelming rejection of a statutory policy, but the Government would have to be tough with the public sector. There would be no more money for the nationalized industries if they broke the norm. We might consider giving these industries a total wages bill and then letting them get the advantages of any increased productivity they could produce. He also, despite Mike's disagreement, came down in favour of some form of monitoring body. And with that we sent Mike, Denis and Shirley off to negotiate with the TUC. I was thankful that I myself was free to head for home.

As we broke up Malcolm [Shepherd] said to me, 'How is Ted's health?' 'Marvellous,' I replied. 'Good,' he said, 'because we are thinking of him as one of the peers' representatives at Strasbourg.' I was thrilled and assured Malcolm with everything I had got that Ted had never been fitter. I went back to HCF, hugging to myself an excited hope that Malcolm had asked me not to divulge at this stage.

Great excitement at HCF. Swallows have started to build in our front porch. I almost began to feel that they must be a sign of good luck! It was fascinating to watch the pair of them come and go, bringing bits of mud and straw to weave their home. At night they perch one on each side of their little edifice to sleep. We peer round the curtain to look at them, afraid to turn on the light.

Monday, 23 June. Yet another chewing over of the TUC document on the development of the Social Contract at the Liaison Committee at Transport House. The cameras and reporters were waiting as I arrived. One journalist asked me the usual idiot questions about what I thought was going to happen, ending with, 'Will the meeting be friendly?' To which I replied, 'Of course.' And friendly it was, but miserably ineffective too. The only trade unionists there, apart from junior officials, were Jack Jones and Len Murray. Hughie, we were told, was at his union conference; David Basnett abroad. No explanation from Alf Allen, Sid Greene or anyone else. And no explanation, either, why Denis did not bother to turn up. Harold arrived late to hear Len introducing the TUC document. Len hovered uneasily between endorsing it and putting up a show of belligerency. Jack Jones – lone, valiant and almost tragic symbol of the defenders of the Social Contract – came in next. 'We are anxious to help you,' he said. But then he too went into the counterattack. 'Some speeches coming from members of the Government are not helping us to get acceptance of it. It is quite wrong to lay all the blame on wages, as if the unions were the only criminals in the community.' I left Transport House wondering whether our meeting, with its sparse attendance, had not done more harm than good. This impression was confirmed when Roger Carroll of the *Sun* phoned me to ask whether the virtual trade union boycott of the meeting meant that the Liaison Committee had served its purpose and was about to wind up. I said of course it was not.

In the course of the morning, encouraged by what Jack Jones had said, I tossed Harold a note: 'Could you give a personal push to the social wage document? It has been bogged down with Treasury officials for over a month.' He nodded and pocketed it.

Wednesday, 25 June. Slipped away to have a couple of hours at Wimbledon: the first time I have played hookey for months. After all, it may be the last time I can watch it in style in the royal box at the Centre Court: with strawberries and cream to follow! The sun shone and it was all perfect Wimbledon, but it was rather exasperating to have to watch Rosewall and Feaver when roars of excitement were coming from Court No. 1 where the unseeded Stewart was beating Nastase. But it was all very brief, as I had to get back to office meetings, followed by an eve-of-poll meeting in the by-election at Woolwich West.

The whole day was made particularly happy by the fact that Ted tells me he has been selected for the European Parliament. I am *thrilled* for him. For the past five years I have been putting up a little prayer: 'Lord, I have had a good run for my money. It is Teddy's turn. Please let something go spectacularly right for him.' It looks as though my prayers are being answered. It reminds me of the skipping song we used to sing as children! 'As I go out, you come in.' I wonder what on earth I shall do with myself when I'm retired and Teddy isn't! I wonder if the adjustment will be as easy as I found it when we went into opposition last time?

Throughout June fears about inflation had been causing the pound to slide. On 30 June it took the biggest nosedive yet to a 28.9 per cent depreciation rate since it was floated in 1972. The press highlighted rumours that the Middle East oil interests were about to join the rush to sell sterling. Curiously, it was reported that the Bank of England was 'inactive' in supporting the pound. Wrote John Palmer, then Business Editor of the Guardian*: 'Most foreign exchange dealers are startled by the government's willingness to let the pound fall so low.'*

Whatever the reason for the run on the pound, it helped Denis Healey clinch a historic deal with the TUC *for a voluntary incomes policy. In this he had an unflinching ally in Jack Jones, who secured overwhelming endorsement of the policy from his own union conference. But there were arguments in Cabinet and with the* TUC *as to what form the new pay limit should take, Denis Healey talking of a 10 per cent increase and Jack Jones urging a flat-rate egalitarian one. There were also fierce arguments as to what powers were needed to enforce the policy. Some powers – such as the use of the Price Code – were uncontentious, but Denis Healey hankered after statutory powers to make it illegal for employers to breach the policy. This was resisted by some of us in Cabinet and by the* TUC *as the thin end of the wedge of a full statutory incomes policy. At a crisis Cabinet on 1 July Denis Healey insisted that he must make an immediate interim statement to stop the rot in confidence. In it he announced a 10 per cent limit in increases in pay and dividends in order to bring inflation down to 10 per cent over the coming year. On powers all we would allow him to say was that if no agreement was reached in carrying out the policy, the Government would legislate to compel employers to toe the line.*

Two days later the General Council of the TUC *endorsed a pay limit of £6 per week, but only by a majority of nineteen votes to thirteen and in the absence of powerful opponents like Hughie Scanlon. Thus armed Denis Healey returned to the attack, urging that, in order to give credibility to the agreement with the* TUC*, the promised White Paper on the policy must announce that the Government would legislate at once to secure these reserve powers. But he met with tough resistance, led by Michael Foot, and the White Paper, 'The Attack on Inflation' (Cmnd 6151), published on 11 July, contained a compromise. Legislation, it said, had been prepared and, if the pay limit was endangered, Parliament would be asked to approve it immediately.*

But the battles were not over. Denis Healey struggled to strengthen his package, this time by seeking to announce his proposed cuts of £2 billion in public expenditure in the debate on the White Paper on 22 July. Following strong resistance by some of us he was overruled, though he insisted on warning the House that the existing public expenditure programmes for 1977–78 and 1978–79 were 'quite unrealistic' and would have to be reviewed to make way for the expansion of exports and investments he anticipated.

Despite the TUC*'s acceptance of the policy, the Tribune group of Labour* MPs *was restive and in the debate of 22 July some thirty-six Labour left-wingers defied the Whips to vote against the White Paper. The Opposition officially abstained, complaining that the Government had failed to cut public expenditure. Challenged during the debate as to what he would do if the Government produced its threatened Bill containing statutory powers against employers, Michael Foot, who was winding up for the Government, admitted frankly: 'If such a Bill were to be introduced, I would hardly be the proper person to do it.'*

Thursday, 26 June. A most peculiar Cabinet: no item at all on the agenda apart from parliamentary business and foreign affairs. There was a short discussion on the appointment of our representatives to the European Parliament. It now looks as though the Social Democrats will be the largest party there, but Peter is furious because the parliamentary party has decided that the British Labour Party shall apply for membership of their group. The trouble is, he says, that the other European socialist parties are federalist. This is certainly a problem we shall face very shortly: whether to go for direct elections and all that means. I personally am torn. Does accepting the result of the referendum mean that we merely go through the motions of membership and in fact continue to stymie the development of democratic control of the Community? It is a horrible dilemma, not least because some of the younger anti MPs now see no alternative for us but to go in and run the whole European show ourselves. And there is an equally important tactical point for us to bear in mind: how to help Harold in his now patent desire to break out of the clutches of the pro-marketeers, now the referendum campaign is over, and to resume a central position in the Party again. As I put it to him during one of our now frequent conspiratorial chats, 'That is why I went to Luxembourg. I don't think we should let the pro-marketeers corner Europe, because in doing so they corner you.'

I was back at the House, waiting to vote my way through the evening, when Norman rang in some agitation. No. 10 had just come dramatically alive over my social wage document. Harold now wanted it finished by Monday and published in time for a press conference he is giving on social policy on 12 July. Panic stations! Treasury have sent back a turgid redraft and we are all furious – just another example of the way Treasury officials assume they can do every Minister's job better than he can himself. I sat reading through the redraft almost in despair; then I minuted Norman not to wait for any more clearance by Treasury, but to get on to David Tattersall [a journalist on the *Daily Mirror*] tomorrow, give him both documents, ask him merely to incorporate any new bits by Treasury and get the whole document into a uniform style. All this meant I was late to bed.

Friday, 27 June. Up early to face a gruelling day at Weston-super-Mare, every minute of which had been packed with official visits and talks. I was surprised how perky I felt. My spirits have risen: I must say it is rather nice to be in favour with the PM again! Even the news that we had lost Woolwich West didn't dampen me; I had expected it. By-election losses and runs on the pound no longer frighten us as they used to in 1966, I think because everyone knows the Tory Party isn't beginning to be a runner as an alternative government.

Saturday, 28 June. Jack Jones has rounded on the 'Left' – obviously a reaction to the Arthur Scargills of this world, who are up to no good at all. It is remarkable how Jack Jones has thrown his hat over the windmill in an overt and unequivocal determination to save the Labour Government. This makes me all the more furious at the botch-up over my social wage document.

I am desolate because the swallow in our HCF porch has deserted her eggs. On Friday night, when I arrived home, I found her sitting snugly in her nest, unperturbed by the dogs' high decibels. Yesterday she was nowhere to be seen and had not returned even at night. No sign of her today. I wonder all day what can have happened to her. Our porch is suddenly emptied of life.

Monday, 30 June. Rushed up to the office to deal with the social wage document, only to be told by Norman that David Tattersall is walking the Pennines and won't be back till Wednesday. So that is why I could not get hold of him yesterday! I go through the Treasury draft myself, marking the bits I think we should include with ours, and then hand the whole thing over to Brian Abel-Smith to knock into the sort of shape David Tattersall can deal with on his return. No. 10's timetable now is that we have till Wednesday to clear our draft.

In the evening I run into Mike at the House. 'How are things?' I ask conventionally. 'Terrible, terrible,' he mutters to my surprise. Drawing me aside he tells me that the pound is 'crumbling', that there is to be a Cabinet early tomorrow, that Denis is talking of statutory controls on employers – though not workers – and that he is just off to see Len Murray with Denis and Shirley, Jack Jones being away at his union conference. So the crunch has come earlier than we thought. 'You'll just have to give us a lead tomorrow in the light of your talks,' was all I could say.

Tuesday, 1 July. Cabinet assembled at 9.30 am. To my surprise, there were no cameras waiting outside No. 10. So the press has been taken by surprise as much as we have, despite the fact that the papers are full of the worst-ever run on the pound. It was an apprehensive lot who gathered outside the Cabinet room and John Silkin whispered to me as we went in, 'I have never attended a Cabinet more reluctantly.' I thought to myself, 'Crisis always strikes in the sunshine,' and, according to Denis, crisis it certainly was. The pound, he told us, had fallen 1 per cent yesterday and this morning it had reached its lowest devaluation ever: 29.2 per cent. The worst thing was that it was now going down versus the dollar, and we could face a disastrous withdrawal of funds at any time – just what he had kept warning us of. We simply had to stop inflation in its tracks. We had made enormous progress in our discussions with the TUC: they were now ready to link wage increases to a *forward* target of inflation of 10 per cent by September 1976. This meant there must be a limit on wage increases of 10 per cent or £6 per week, over the coming year. The TUC had not yet agreed that sum and Jack was still talking of £8. The question was: how could we create confidence in compliance with this policy by the unions? Yet unless he, Denis, was able to make a statement that afternoon which carried conviction, the run on the pound would continue and the withdrawal of funds would start. This is why he had been discussing with the PM, Shirley and Mike the need to impose a legal sanction on employers. They were a law-abiding lot and he was sure they would comply with the law. Nothing less would restore confidence.

[After a long discussion] Harold summed up that the general view was that we must make a statement today, but it should be in such a form that it would help us to keep the TUC in play. Denis insisted that we must spell out the wages target of 10 per cent 'which we have not done before'. If confidence was to be restored we must make it clear that we were determined to secure compliance and must spell out all the sanctions we had in mind. Harold ruled that a small number should draft the statement on behalf of Cabinet: Denis, Shirley, Mike and Peter. And so it was agreed.

I made the office rearrange my engagements so that I could be in the House to hear Denis's statement. I thought it was a pretty ineffectual one, but the Tories roared their ironic delight as the possibility of sanctions against employers was read out. Denis fielded the supplementaries superbly and the protests on our side were fairly muted. But I am not fooled. This is how it all started over *In Place of Strife*. I remember how Charlie Pannell congratulated me after I had explained it to the trade union group, but that didn't mean that he or anyone else stood up in my support once the fury started slowly, but surely, to escalate. Meanwhile I am still doing battle with Ted Short about the inclusion of my Pay Beds Bill in next session's programme. Doesn't the Government realize that this is an essential political sweetener for the unions?

Wednesday, 2 July. To the House for my long-overdue appearance before the Select Committee on Violence in Marriage.[1] Back in my room, with half an hour to change for an official dinner, I found Norman, Brian A-S. and a couple of our Departmental chaps waiting for me with the latest draft of the social wage document. Apparently David Tattersall had come back from his holiday only too keen to help. He had measured every word and line of the text in order to fit into a popular pamphlet and the result had to be approved by me before I dressed for Jim Callaghan's annual jamboree to celebrate the Queen's birthday. This is the great diplomatic event of the year, at which Cabinet Ministers are expected to help Jim out as co-hosts, and we had all been allowed to pair by the Whips, even though we were in the middle of a three-line whip on the Industry Bill. I flicked through the document, making a number of suggestions and then had less than five minutes to change. But I wanted to go because the dinner was at Hampton Court Palace, which I haven't seen since I was a child and even then I never penetrated inside. Ted – already dressed up in his glory – was marvellously patient as I changed. At last we were on our way, with me busily trying to catch up on the work in my two boxes on the way.

It was a gloriously sunny evening and, despite the absurdly intense pressures, I managed to enjoy myself. Hampton Court was everything I had hoped; the meal was good, and I enjoyed quarrelling with my Luxembourg neighbour about the European Community as I looked up at the high ceiling in the dining hall. 'I do hope they play the Post Gallop,' he said as the band rattled on in the Minstrels' Gallery. 'I have never heard anything like it.' And so they did. We then all trooped through the Tudor courtyard to the garden, with its long avenues and beautifully kempt lawns, to hear the marines play The Retreat as they marched and wheeled in perfect formation on a perfect summer evening. I was interested to watch the diverse diplomats – the one in front of me looked like Haile Selassie – studying the whole performance with rapt attention, while Ted and I tapped our feet approvingly to the tunes, unashamedly patriotic. 'This is one of the reasons why I am anti-Market,' I whispered naughtily to my neighbour, as he applauded the Englishness of it all. I love my home and country with a fierce protectiveness. It was nearly 1 am before we got back to our flat and as we drove up a young figure emerged from the shadows. It was Paul Chapman [one of the team of special advisers] with yet another urgent document from the devoted Brian Abel-Smith. I thanked him, yawned and went to bed, setting my alarm for 6.30 am.

Monday, 7 July. There really couldn't be a crisis, I thought, as I got up early on a perfect summer morning to finish spraying the roses before I left for town. The caress of the sunshine, the gentle greenness of orchard and woods, belied all the tensions that lay ahead. Somehow I tore myself away from it and hurried

[1] As a result of my pressure a Select Committee had been set up in February 1975 to consider 'the extent, nature and causes of the problems of families where there is violence between the partners or where children suffer non-accidental injury'.

to my hot room in the House to await Peter, Mike and Wedgie to discuss what we should do if we were faced with a Chancellor and Cabinet determined to impose statutory controls. To my surprise and delight Eric Varley was there too. Someone must have told him we had arranged to meet and I wondered why he had come to a meeting with us on this issue when he had so carefully detached himself from our group over the referendum campaign. There is something ineffably nice about that lad, even though he is far from being 'Left' in the traditional sense of the word.

Mike began by reporting on the progress of discussions with the TUC. The Economic Committee, he told us, was meeting that morning to discuss the final draft of the TUC document, which was 'a good document'.[1] I said that the threat of statutory powers had obviously concentrated the unions' minds wonderfully. What we needed was enough threat to make the voluntary policy work. If it looked as if Cabinet was going to beat us on the issue of including statutory powers in the package, we might propose as a compromise that we insert a paragraph in the White Paper to the effect that we would review the working of the policy with the TUC after, say, a three-month period and decide what further strengthening of the powers was necessary. Peter supported me strongly on this, but Mike looked doubtful. Wedgie and Eric said little. We left it that we would keep in touch and co-ordinate our line. We don't want any unilateral gestures. As Eric had whispered to me at the last Cabinet, 'If Mike can accept it, so can I.'

After a busy day we started the Report stage of the Child Benefit Bill at 10 pm – such is the pressure of parliamentary business up to the recess. It soon became clear that the Tories were determined to keep us late, dividing on all sorts of amendments, even though they were only keeping fifteen of their own people there. It also soon became clear that the Tory party is speaking with two voices. While Margaret is trying to get kudos by demanding tough controls of public expenditure, her lesser cohorts are busy attacking the Government for meanness on a number of specific issues. Kenneth Clarke on the Tory front bench indulged in more political hypocrisy than I have heard for a long time. We eventually got the Bill at 3.30 am. Dawn was breaking when I finally got to bed at nearly 5 am.

Wednesday, 9 July. After nine hours' sleep I am a different woman, ready for the day of tough policy meetings at the Department that lies ahead. The first meeting was on how to control private practice once we have phased pay beds out of the NHS. I have told the Department that our only hope of getting the legislation into the next Queen's speech is for us to get the policy cleared up before the recess and a consultative document issued so that Instructions can go to counsel. The Department has obviously been having agonies of indecision over the private practice policy, not least because officials are divided, Lawrence Brandes wanting to be tough, Gedling dithering and Philip uncertain about everything except the need for some sort of control. So the submission they have made to me consists merely of a list of problems matched by tentative suggestions or just plain question marks.

[1] The document, called 'The Development of the Social Contract', accepted a flat-rate pay increase limit of £6 a week and declared: 'The TUC will oppose any settlement in excess of this figure.'

I opened the meeting by saying firmly (and optimistically) that we would not conclude it until we had reached a decision on every one of the points. It didn't matter whether the decision was perfect. We were merely drawing up a consultative document. And so we went through the key points, every one of them bristling with difficulties. To my relief, David no longer spent his time declaring that in his view the policy of control would never work. Instead he put forward a lot of constructive and useful points. When in this mood he is invaluable. He is undoubtedly extremely able. It is his erratic changes of line that disturb everyone and make my job difficult. I have always believed in giving my Ministers of State their head, merely drawing the reins to myself again when vital policy decisions are at stake. And they appreciate it. David said to me with his charming smile the other day, after Harold's mini reshuffle, 'You nearly lost me to the Treasury. Denis wanted me to take the job of Financial Secretary. Don't worry, I refused. I told Denis that a Financial Secretary had no authority. I'd rather stay where I am, where I can get something done.' 'I would have told Harold to ban the move,' I quipped back. It is David's occasional arrogance of manner that gets him in bad with officials. It is a fault he shares with Roy Jenkins. I think Brian and I humanize him.

For nearly two hours we went down the list of queries. As I looked round that table, flanked by anxious and – in some cases – hostile officials, I thought once again how desperately a Minister needs allies if any real policy changes are to be made. The policy we thrashed out began to take workable shape and, as we proceeded, we began to plan fundamental and long overdue reforms in the *quality* controls of private nursing homes and hospitals, as well as quantitative ones. At 12.45 I had to admit that we could not meet my deadline before lunch. Rejecting my usual tray of cheese and lettuce, I disappeared to the House, where I joined Eric Heffer and Caerwyn Roderick for steak and kidney pie in the Members' dining room.

Back at the office we had another long lession on private practice, finally concluding the major points for the consultative document. It was David who pointed out that we might have to postpone the final phasing-out date from November 1976 as originally agreed, because otherwise we would be cutting off earnings from pay beds during the very year when we were limiting consultants' earnings under the pay policy. So we might be laying ourselves open to claims for compensation. The path to reform is immensely complicated! Home to read my papers for tomorrow's crucial Cabinet.

Thursday, 10 July. In my box was a note from Norman: would I arrive at Cabinet early, as there would be a redraft of the White Paper on pay policy waiting for us at No. 10 which we were expected to read before Cabinet. So I arrived at 9.45 am and was ushered upstairs to the large reception room, where coffee was waiting for us. The second draft was much superior to the first, and, of course, in both drafts there were alternative passages in brackets on reserve powers. But I was still shocked by the total lack of any indication of a socialist strategy. The sections on unemployment and public expenditure were pure Treasury orthodoxy – not even a mention of the NEB.

In Cabinet Harold was at his most businesslike. We had got to get the White Paper agreed that morning; we would go through it paragraph by paragraph.

But Wedgie intervened to say that some of us had not been in the intensive discussions with the TUC and CBI this week. Could we be told what had happened? Denis, looking rather irritated, skimmed through the events rapidly: there had been agreement with the TUC on the £6; the 'only issue left' was whether the cut-off for increases should be at £10,000 or £7,000. When some of us raised our eyebrows at this he added hastily that the TUC were at first not prepared to discuss any legislation at all, but had later agreed to penal sanctions through the Price Code, legislation to relieve employers of their contractual obligations and the selective application of the rate support grant. The CBI had finally agreed to the use of the Price Code, but were urging that we should have reserve powers against the employer. They didn't like the £6 and preferred a percentage figure. 'We must get on,' intervened Harold.

We went through the other paragraphs, making relatively minor changes, until we came to paragraph 38 on 'action on employment', where I was poised to make a row. But Wedgie got in first. 'I move we delete paragraphs 38 to 45,' he said sternly. 'The strategy in these paragraphs is entirely pre-Keynesian.' No one supported deletion, not because I (and I've no doubt Mike) didn't agree with him, but because we thought the right way was to amend the paragraphs radically. Even Harold Lever was disturbed by them. There must, he said, be a clear commitment that, if workers would co-operate in the pay policy, 'the Government will get these horrific levels of unemployment down'. Harold Wilson and Denis were soon agreeing to redraft, incorporating references to the NEB. Next we turned to the section on public expenditure. I pounced angrily. The paragraphs, I said, contradicted themselves. First we argued that a pay policy was an alternative to cutting the social wage; next that we had to review public expenditure anyway. I moved the deletion of the sentence which referred to that. Harold said that we should be discussing this question on Monday at a special Cabinet on the medium-term economic assessment, so the sentence was merely a statement of fact. It did not commit Cabinet to any specific decision. I persisted. Wedgie backed me. 'Is this policy an alternative to public expenditure cuts, or is it, as I believe, the first step?' he demanded. 'We've got to do both,' retorted Roy J., giving the game away. Harold insisted the sentence must stay in, but said there could be some redrafting here as well. I nagged on. What target date had Denis in mind when the paragraph talked about the need to 'eliminate' the balance of payments deficit? He hadn't got any specific date in mind, he replied irritably. And so I was overruled, but my suspicions were unallayed.

By this time it was 12.30 and we broke for coffee, refreshing ourselves for the tussle over reserve powers still to come. I went up to Mike and Peter and said, 'We ought to meet immediately after Cabinet to discuss our line. I'll get my secretary to lay on some sandwiches.' They agreed, but Mike said diffidently, 'I should tell you that I cannot say I will necessarily resign. Jack Jones has been pleading with me to remain in the Government whatever happens.' 'That's why we must talk,' I replied. The tussle began at 12.45 and did not end till 3 pm. Denis opened, fighting hard for his reserve powers. The TUC had gone a long way but it was 'absolutely essential that the White Paper carries conviction with our creditors'. Last year the Trades Union Congress had carried the Social Contract policy by an overwhelming majority, yet it hadn't been observed.

What could we expect to happen now, when the General Council yesterday had only carried the policy by nineteen votes to thirteen? We needed reserve powers on employers in the legislation to make the policy work and to give it credibility.

Harold supported him. If the White Paper was not credible we could be bringing Parliament back in August to deal with another run on the pound. He was totally opposed to criminal sanctions against workers, but sanctions against employers were not the same thing. Elwyn then asked what sanctions there would be on employers? Harold replied, 'Presumably a limited fine and no limit on indictment.' Mike said the TUC thought that they had gone very far. If we were to upset what had been agreed with them, the whole atmosphere might change. If we took reserve powers there would be an angry debate in the trade union movement and almost certain defeat in Congress. What would that do to sterling? 'We can't run an incomes policy without the support of the trade union movement.'

My line was to cast doubt on the 'credibility' argument. If it was compliance we were worried about, who was likely to rat on the policy? If it was the employers, why would they be doing it? Employers in this straitened economic situation were hardly likely to be rushing around pressing wage increases on their workpeople. If they ratted it would be because they were under pressure from a strike or threat of a strike. So what would be the scenario in which we would be going to Parliament for authority to activate these reserve powers? A situation in which the policy was being violated as a result of strike action. Was it really credible to try and get Parliament to invoke powers against an employer because he was under a threat? Peter spoke in very similar vein. Roy Jenkins backed Denis except that – typically – he would have preferred a 10 per cent figure rather than the flat rate. Wedgie read a piece from the Manifesto which he was carrying as he arrived – duly getting himself photographed.

As the contributions rolled on Eric and I began to keep a tally; for reserve powers: Ted Short, Denis, Shirley, Crosland, Prentice, of course (he said he would have been willing to go the whole hog), Roy J., Malcolm Shepherd and Fred Peart. Against them Mike, me, Bob, Eric, Peter, Wedgie, John Silkin. Eric was resigned to our defeat, and then some surprising things started to happen. First, Fred Mulley said he was very unhappy about throwing away our agreement with the TUC. Could we not merely say that we had a Bill ready which we would introduce if the policy looked like breaking down? This would mean that we would not be legislating right away, but would be giving the TUC the chance to deliver the goods. Soon Merlyn was coming down in favour of the same idea, followed by John Morris and finally – biggest surprise of all – by Harold Lever, the author of the whole idea of powers against employers. More surprises. Roy Mason came out vigorously against reserve powers. So did Elwyn and Willie Ross. Eric and I became jubilant. It was clear we had won hands down. But Harold who, I suspect, had all along been plotting for a compromise, summed up with his usual cunning when he is determined to get his own way. Apart, he said, from the four who wanted a compromise, Cabinet was evenly divided for and against. (The truth was that, leaving out the four, we had won by ten to nine.) He would like to know what the Chancellor felt. Denis promptly squeezed the maximum advantage out of his defeat. Of course, he said, he would have preferred to legislate for reserve powers now. 'Cabinet's attitude imposes a major problem for me personally.' But he would accept Cabinet's decision, provided that we announced that a Bill was already prepared and would be introduced immediately there was a breach of the policy. And if that happened it wouldn't be a question of legislating *reserve* powers; the powers would operate immediately. And, of course, if the package failed to restore confidence in sterling, we would have to use the powers right away. 'We are meeting on Monday,' soothed Harold, 'and can consider the position then in the light of reaction abroad.' For good measure Denis gave us a parting shot with a glare at me. 'Cabinet will appreciate that as the package is weaker than I would like, that will make it all the more necessary for us to be tough over public expenditure.' I was about to protest when Harold hastily wound things up. 'We shall be discussing that too on Monday.'

We broke up, longing for food. 'Can we still have those sandwiches of yours?' asked Eric and I said, 'Of course,' telling Mike, Peter and Wedgie to come along to my room immediately. Over sandwiches we agreed that we had been manœuvred into a trap. We couldn't even be sure that Denis would not welcome a run on the pound as a justification for slapping on the reserve powers right away. I asked Mike how he thought the TUC would take the compromise. 'They'll be very relieved,' he replied, grinning with relief himself. He would have been in an impossible position if we had lost.

[Back at the office] Jack and Brian A-S. came dashing back into my room. Could they have an urgent word with me about Monday's Cabinet? They had been studying the Chancellor's paper and the accompanying Treasury paper on the MTA [medium-term assessment] which had arrived while I had been in Cabinet. Did I realize that the Chancellor was going to demand an immediate decision on the £2 billion cuts from 1978–79? He wanted to announce it in the anti-inflation debate next week. I thumped the table furiously. 'So he lied to me this morning. He tried to fool us that no decision was imminent.' I could now see the whole ploy. Denis had kept this back until he had got the White Paper, trying to wangle reserve powers out of us as an *alternative* to public expenditure cuts, knowing all the while that on Monday he was going to demand his full public expenditure cuts as well. At this moment Norman came in to tell me Cabinet had been recalled for 6.30 pm. 'What on earth? – perhaps it is only so that we can approve the redrafts,' I said. 'Give me the papers. I will raise this in Cabinet.' As I read the MTA I made another discovery. The proposed economic strategy is based on our eliminating the balance of payments deficit by 1978. So Denis had lied to me about that too. We had been conned and I was determined to let Denis – and Cabinet – know I knew we had been.

When I arrived at No. 10 the cameras were still hovering. Harold, having got his way, was at his most affable. He and Denis, he said, had seen the TUC and the CBI and given them an indication of the decision of Cabinet. They had both accepted it. Denis then went into a rather emotional spiel about how essential it was to handle the decision properly. It was imperative, therefore, that there should be no talk of 'victory' by anyone over anyone else – no gloating that the Chancellor had been defeated. We nodded solemnly, shocked at the very idea of such caddishness. I began to wonder how I could raise my point about public expenditure. In this atmosphere any criticism of Denis would seem an indecency. But at last I got my point in by asking how we had redrafted the section referring to the policy as being an alternative to public expenditure cuts. 'When I got back to my office this afternoon,' I ploughed on, 'I saw the Chancellor's paper and the one on the MTA. In it Denis is asking us to decide on Monday to accept the £2 billion cuts *as a minimum* so that he can announce it during *next week*'s debate. So it would clearly make us look ridiculous if tomorrow we were to publish a White Paper holding out the hope that this pay policy is an alternative.' 'That bit has been rewritten,' replied Denis triumphantly.

Nonetheless, a sense of hopelessness engulfs me. The only strategy that will be before us on Monday will be one which commits us to unemployment levels continuing at 3 per cent right up to 1978–79, after which, say the Treasury, things should improve economically. But they certainly won't improve politically for us. This is a scenario for another Tory victory just in time for them to reap the harvest of our bitter self-sacrifice. And the price will be the destruction of all our social policies, so that a Labour Government will preside over the biggest cuts in public services since 1931. There *must* be a better way of running a Labour Government. I still back a voluntary wages policy, plus more daring and adventurous appeals to social conscience than we are ever likely to get out of this carefully 'balanced' (*i.e.* highly conventional) Government. And we are under this difficulty: that none of us are equipped with the sort of economic advice that enables us to stand up to the dubious expertise of the Treasury.

Friday, 11 July. I rearranged my day so that I could be present in the House for Harold's statement on the White Paper.[1] I squeezed in between Harold Lever and Jim Callaghan. Lever kept up a running commentary in my ear and I reciprocated, saying to him at one point, 'Do you know what target date Denis has set himself for eliminating the balance of payments deficit?' Lever didn't, so I told him, '1978.' 'But that's ridiculous,' he replied, adding, 'Let's have lunch together next week. Let me talk to you.' I told him I would welcome it. On one thing we agreed: that Thatcher with her prim and carefully modulated diction flopped. I was reminded of Jeremy Thorpe's words to me at the Oxford Union: 'The lady will not do.' Jeremy didn't 'do' today either. Too fluently slick by half. Incidentally, I noticed how cleverly Harold exploited Cabinet's agreement that we should help Denis as much as possible. He kept referring to 'reserve powers' as though we had already taken them. But the Left remained strangely muted. After all, Harold holds the trump card of an agreement with the TUC.

It was lovely to get home to HCF and find Ted waiting for me, full of interest in his great adventure. He is so sold on parliaments he is obviously ready to be sold on this European one. He told me that by far the most impressive British figure at Strasbourg was Peter Kirk. It is total joy for me to see Ted so fulfilled,

[1] In introducing the White Paper Harold Wilson described the TUC's agreement to the pay policy as 'unexampled in peace or war by the free democratic trade union movement in this country'. He listed the 'battery of weapons' that would be provided by the legislation to enforce the policy, such as the use of price controls and the rate support grant as sanctions against recalcitrant firms and authorities, and reiterated that legislation had also been prepared, 'for introduction if need be', to make it illegal for the employer to exceed the pay limit. On the prices side the Government was extending strict price controls and intended to ensure that price increases for a range of essential goods did not exceed the 10 per cent. It had also decided to delay the phasing out of food subsidies announced in the Budget and to limit rent increases.

even if he is now in favour of directly elected European Parliaments, providing the timing is right. I am ironically amused by all this. These are the political nuances beneath the monolithic surface of party loyalties.

Saturday, 12 July. The press on Harold's statement isn't too bad, though the 'foreign reaction' isn't as clear-cut as I would like it to be. We could yet be faced with a crisis on Monday – and who can say who will have engineered it? I'm amused to see, incidentally, that Harold has launched the Public Relations Unit I suggested to him. Of course I shan't get any credit for it.

Sunday, 13 July. After a happy day of gardening, work and lunch with our friend, John Fane, at Wormsley House – during which we read the scaffold speech of his regicide forebear Colonel Scroop and admired Cromwell's boots, I suddenly found that my Ted had been hit again by the press. This time it was the *Observer*, which, in a leader, picked him out for attack, saying he ought not to have been chosen for the European Parliament. Ted pretended not to care, but I know that it has taken the gilt off his bit of long-overdue gingerbread. I was so angry I could have killed the leader-writer. Because, of course, under the guise of dispassionate comment on matters of public interest, whoever it was was merely earning his bread and butter by promoting his newspaper's party line – *i.e.* to boost the Liberals. To pick Ted out for a sneer, saying he ought to give way to 'more vigorous and better informed Labour men', when what the *Observer* really wanted was that old European hack, Lord Gladwyn, is an old party trick: attack a policy you don't like under the guise of a dispassionate comment on an individual Minister's or representative's ability. I've suffered from it myself.

All this is made worse by the excitement with which Ted has come back from Strasbourg. He is thrilled to have been put on the political committee, is ready to devote himself flat out to the new work and is even planning to take a fortnight's refresher course in French! I suppose the *Observer* would prefer anyone whose name isn't Castle.

Monday, 14 July. Peter [Shore] phoned me yesterday to see if I could come to lunch. He had a few people coming in to discuss what we should do about the MTA [medium-term assessment] and public expenditure. I just couldn't face ruining another Sunday at HCF, even for that, so I arrived at Cabinet at 10 am, not having had a chance to co-ordinate strategy with anyone. Another grim morning milling round our economic miseries lay ahead. In my brief Jack and Brian pleaded with me to try and get any announcement of the £2 billion figure of cuts delayed until Cabinet had had a chance to study the detailed consequences. Officials, on the other hand, advised me to accept the Chancellor's recommendations, as they believed there was no alternative. This is exactly why political advisers are so necessary. I have no doubt that most top officials are conventional and conscientious Tories, so *they* are never going to encourage me to challenge the Treasury's fiat.

Harold opened by congratulating himself on this new approach to the public expenditure: 'it has never been done before'. Here were ordinary Cabinet mortals being let into the secret statistics of the MTA before we had to decide such mundane things as cuts. That would come later; we were merely deciding the 'global amount' today. We would have an all-day meeting at Chequers on 25 July to work out the details of the cuts. Then in the autumn we would put the finishing touches to the PESC exercise. Denis then covered familiar ground. There was 'severe imbalance' in the economy, he said. We have got to close the balance of payments gap by 1978 – not very clear why. And he once again returned to the innuendo that public expenditure had got out of hand, not just relatively, but absolutely. It had grown from 42 per cent of GDP to 58 per cent over the last twenty years, he maintained, and in the last five years particularly had galloped ahead. We couldn't go on diverting manpower from productive industry at this rate. We couldn't go at the balance of payments more slowly because that would mean increasing borrowing. So, of the prospective yield of growth over the next few years we should have £600 million left to share between private and public spending. And we couldn't take it all in public expenditure.

Criticisms then came in quick succession. I launched into a speech which had them grinning at its impudence. The sentence that had most struck me in the whole MTA paper, I said, was to the effect that: 'by 1978, following the elimination of the balance of payments deficit, the strain on resources will be very severe. By 1980 the situation should have eased.' That, I told them, was the scenario with which I had become so familiar during my years of service in Labour Governments: a Labour Government coming into power, accepting all the adjurations to put the country's house in order, reaching a climax of sacrifice in election year which ensured our defeat and then watching the Tories inherit the harvest we had sown and proceed to squander it in a burst of public popularity. The Treasury, I continued to appreciative laughter, found Labour Governments perfect material on which to impose their rigidly orthodox patterns, which they never managed to impose on any other Governments. The reason was that we were instinctive Puritans. We came in, lavished a bit of money on the poor and then had an immediate guilt complex because we were naturally masochistic moralists who didn't really believe life should be fun. So we were receptive of the argument that our only duty was to be tough. Tory Governments never made this mistake. They knew that government was the art of the possible – which was why they kept us out of power so successfully. We had only scraped back in February 1974 because, fortunately for us, the Tories were led by another moralist who wrecked his party with his fanaticism. (The knowing grins round the table showed that the shafts had gone home.)

What we ought to be doing, I continued, was to start the other way round, by asking the question, 'What will improve the standard of life?' Nothing the Treasury proposed ever in any circumstances improved the standard of life. As Denis shook his head vigorously I asked him: What course of action in the MTA document will improve the standard of life? A successful pay policy won't: we are now told it makes public expenditure cuts even more necessary. Eliminating the balance of payments deficit won't. That too, Denis has just told us, will make it even more essential for us to dig a "hole" in the economy to make way for the additional exports. No wonder people get cynical and uninterested. Whatever they do, the Treasury says more deflation is necessary. We all know that the only things that will raise the standard of life are increased investment and increased productivity. So why don't we enter into open discussions with the TUC and CBI about the choices we have to make if we are to reach these goals – just as we did over pay policy?' I agreed with Tony C. It was wrong to assume that people would automatically prefer cuts in public expenditure to higher taxes. It depended on which cuts and which taxes. We needed urgently to work out a comprehensive plan with the TUC and CBI.

So far we on the Left had made most of the running in the discussion, but the Chancellor's allies soon hit back. Denis replied at length, obviously torn between a determination to be tough and a lack of confidence in his own remedy. Why had there been such a big change in the outlook since last December? 'We did not expect so deep a recession.' The Germans and Japanese hadn't done nearly enough reflating, but he still thought the world upturn should start next year. As to unemployment, he admitted it would be 'above' 3 per cent till late 1977. He agreed we must move in the direction of a national plan, but the CBI was pressing for cuts in public expenditure. He then went off into a little tirade which was very revealing. A lot of people, he said, believed that too much of the resources of the nation were going on the public services. 'Barbara's social wage document will be very double-edged for us, though I'm in favour of publishing it.' People would be shocked, not pleased, when they saw how much we were spending on the social services. 'Which ones?' I demanded. 'Name them.' 'Oh yes,' he replied. 'Schools for one, and other forms of education.' Suddenly as I listened to him I lost heart totally. Harold Lever tossed me a note adjuring me not to look so miserable. I tossed him one back: 'I see no reason for the existence of a Labour Government. We have adopted the Tory *mores*. The only difference is that we carry out Tory policies more efficiently than they do.' He shook his head, but I felt I had lost all stomach for the fight. As I had said earlier, when Ted Short was moaning that he was worried about our abandoning the Manifesto, it isn't a question of not implementing it; we are committing ourselves to putting it into reverse.

Finally Harold said that the list of priorities would be discussed at Chequers. In the meantime, he continued, the views in Cabinet as to whether Denis should mention a sum in his speech next week were neck and neck. The balance seemed to be held by those who would be influenced by the way the statement was worded. It was 'absolutely necessary' that something should be said in the debate, but two or three Ministers should have a look at the wording and report to Cabinet later in the week.

Tuesday, 15 July. We had Cabinet today because Jim and Harold are due in Brussels on Thursday for a great Council of Ministers' post-referendum recap. We are in a mess because at the press conference introducing the Anti-Inflation White Paper Harold said that the Reserve Powers Bill would be published before the Commons debate, even though it was not intended to introduce it unless the voluntary system failed. Mike is furious: Cabinet has never agreed this. He has written to Harold demanding that publication should be deferred at least until after the Trades Union Congress: otherwise Len Murray's position will be impossible. Harold trimmed on this this morning, saying that the Bill should not be published during the debate next week, though Ministers should proceed to agree its text on a contingent basis and 'without prejudice'. He knows he has boobed.

Wednesday, 16 July. I am very glad that Douglas Allen has proposed Pat Nairne to me as Philip's successor. David Owen first mentioned him to me, having formed a very high opinion of him when Nairne was Denis's Private Secretary at Defence. Denis too raves about him. When I met him I took an instant liking to him and am sure we shall get on. I think too he will be far less the conventional civil servant than Philip, loyal as the latter has been.

Having paired all day I was able to go with Ted to George Weidenfeld's late-night party for Françoise Giroud.[1] I had had my hair done, put on my kaftan dress and felt ready to enjoy myself. I always find George's sophisticated little parties fun. Everybody who is anybody is there, his elegant Chelsea flat is an aesthetic delight, the drinks are good and the conversation spicy. I felt – and looked – young and gay. It did me good.

Thursday, 17 July. Went to the royal garden party with Ted – much against my inclination as I have a lot of work to do, but he took the line that it might be the last time we should take tea in the royal tent. It was a pleasant sunny afternoon and we enjoyed strolling round the garden till the time came for tea. The royal tent was packed with High Commissioners and their magnificently garbed wives of various hues. The general crowd were roped off some distance from the tent like animals in a compound and, the Queen having walked through the people and done her stuff for over an hour, they stood gawping at us favoured few as we drank our tea and iced coffee and ate the Queen's delicious raspberries and cream. I am glad to say that Ted and I share all the interests of normal people. No intellectual snobbery about *us*. Ted in particular adores ceremonial and will never willingly turn down a festivity.

Mike has reported victory over Denis's statement on the economy. Denis has climbed down and the fatal figure of £2 billion cuts does not appear.

Monday, 21 July. The press has an odd sense of values. There were no cameras or reporters waiting outside Congress House when I arrived for the Liaison Committee meeting, and yet this was one of the most revealing meetings we have ever had. The press could have learned a lot if they had only probed. They could have learned, for instance, that this time the trade unionists were there in force, even Hughie, whose mute presence was an eloquent testimony to the almost total collaboration we are now getting from the TUC with the pay policy. The agenda of the meeting was to discuss the TUC's document, 'The Development of the Social Contract', and the White Paper on pay policy due to be debated in the House in the afternoon. Jack Jones presided over the meeting like a lynx-eyed guardian of the policy. So we had the ironic situation of people like Mik being in the role of chaps who were defying the trade union movement and getting rebuked by Jack. (My mind went back to the Party conference of 1970 when, to Alex Kitson's distress, Jack dismissed me contemptuously in a talk with him with the words, 'She's lost all political credibility.' Alex begged

[1] Secretary of State for Women's Affairs in the French Government. Weidenfeld and Nicolson had just published her book *I Give You My Word*.

then that I should be forgiven for *In Place of Strife*. Now Jack is denouncing Mik for opposing wage restraint! Such are the strange twists of politics.)

At the office I had to curtail the ministerial lunch so that I could meet the BMA before the opening of the Commons debate on the Anti-Inflation White Paper. They came in all their solemn majesty, with Lewin flanked by Tony Keable-Elliott and a representative of the junior hospital doctors, to tell me how much they disapproved of the flat-rate formula and, above all, the cut-off at £10,000, and to ask me a series of detailed questions as to what we intended to do about increments, pension rights, merit awards, etc., under the pay policy. It was a familiar atmosphere: the incredibly complicated fall-out there always is even from an apparently simple pay policy formula. I staved them off, saying all these things were still being examined, but I would convey their views.

Instead of listening to the debate I sloped off to the flat to cook patés, etc., for Sunday's pensions party,[1] which is now the talk of the Department. I adore entertaining, but fitting it in to the pressures of ministerial life does create difficulties. Norman has entered into the spirit of the thing, 'I'll have to produce a fictitious list of engagements for you, Secretary of State.'

Tuesday, 22 July. My back aches and I feel bilious. It must be end-of-term strain. If my great, rich endowment of health and strength ever melts away I shall be in the soup.

Lunch with Harold Lever at Eaton Square. We ate in elegant isolation amid the colour and grandeur of the formal dining room. The pictures, porcelain and silver must be priceless. Even Harold's exquisite ties must cost a bomb. I have never indulged in the politics of envy and there is such a disarming honesty about Harold I always warm to him. We discussed Reg Prentice's troubles at Newham[2] and I told him I thought he, the PM and others who had written in support of him had been wrong to interfere. He agreed in principle, but added, 'If we hadn't, he would have been out; it's as simple as that.' On the contrary, I said, I was sure that the intervention would be counter-productive. Harold then destroyed his own case in support of Reg by telling a jocular story about himself: how he had disagreed with his own local Labour Party about the Common Market and had said he could not conform to their views on this, but had told them they had a perfect right to get another MP if they found his views intolerable. Result: there had never been a move to unseat him. 'Exactly,' I said, 'and that is what you should have said in Reg Prentice's case.'

But when we came to discuss economic strategy I found Harold had lost his old cheeky independence of attitude. He just couldn't keep still, jumping up

[1] Brian O'Malley and I had promised the Department staff who had worked on our new pensions scheme a party to celebrate the passing of the legislation. The Social Security Pensions Act 1975, embodying the scheme, received the Royal Assent on 7 August.

[2] For some time the Newham North East constituency Labour Party had been restive about the political attitude and statements of Reg Prentice as its MP and had called a special meeting for 23 July to discuss a Motion calling on him to retire at the next General Election. A letter of support for him had been sent to the constituency Party signed by twelve Cabinet Ministers and 160 Labour MPs. The previous day Harold Wilson had thrown his weight into the fray. In a letter to Labour MP Neville Sandelson, a Prentice supporter, he had declared that if the Motion was passed he would feel it his duty as leader and a member of the NEC 'to raise the question of action by small and certainly not necessarily representative groups who have secured a degree of power within a constituency'.

from the table time and again during the meal to hobble up and down as if to relieve an intolerable tension. He was also firmly committed to the new right-wing line that the level of public expenditure had become excessive and that it should be curbed as a desirable end in itself. I'm afraid I shan't find him much of an ally in Cabinet, but our talk did inspire some ideas in me of how to fight the new line. When I got back to the office I scribbled Brian A-S. a Minute asking him to get me a breakdown of the rise in public expenditure in recent years between transfer payments, acquisition of assets and goods and services. I bet I shall find that the increase has gone mainly on transfer payments, which are merely a way of redistributing private income to pensioners and others. I also asked for an analysis of the increase in manpower in the public services.

I got back to the House in time to hear the opening of the second day's anti-inflation debate. Geoffrey Howe was in quite good form, but Denis and Harold behaved like a couple of schoolchildren on the front bench, chattering, shouting comments and generally conducting themselves with levity. Mike, next to me, was writhing with disapproving embarrassment. Margaret sat with her air of knowing primness, immaculately groomed as usual, in a new dress. The general view was that she flopped yesterday. But I had to miss Harold's speech and most of the debate. Later the House was buzzing with excitement about Ted Heath's speech – by common agreement the best he has ever made. Apparently it made Margaret look like a tinny amateur and speculation began to circulate as to whether she could survive. When I went in to hear the winding up, there she was in another new dress. Two in one afternoon was a bit much! But I had to suffer the agony of watching Mike flop – and I knew why. I too have suffered from having to address two entirely different audiences at once, the enemy in front and the ex-friends behind. The Tories, of course, were waiting to pounce and jeer and Mike battled on against their derision and the unbelieving silence behind him, getting wordier and wordier. A flash of the old Mike came when he suddenly admitted that of course sanctions against an employer constituted a statutory policy to which he had always been opposed. And he dealt with dignity with his own position, saying simply that of course he was not the person to deal with a Reserve Powers Bill if it ever had to be introduced. As he finished to pandemonium I congratulated him genuinely on the way he had battled through, but he pushed past me, head down, muttering 'a terrible speech'. One of my front-bench colleagues reported almost with relish that Dennis Skinner had been heard remarking that that was the end of Michael Foot. I only know that he has matured before my eyes during these past months and to me he is worth half a dozen of the negative Left.

Wednesday, 23 July. I had to leave the NEC meeting early to attend a meeting of MISC 91, the ad-hoc group of Ministers who are dealing with pay policy. At the committee we went through some of the detailed points that Mike will have to deal with this afternoon at the Second Reading of the Remuneration, Charges and Grants Bill. (What a name! Some bright spark must have been determined to get as unidentifiable a title as possible for the new incomes policy.) I wasn't able to hear Mike's speech in the House as I had committed myself to a rather absurd dinner John Langford-Holt had organized. It was a private gathering of the 'Class of 1945': the MPs of all parties who had been elected in 1945 and who had survived. It seemed mean to refuse to join in, but I was sure it would be a bore and I was feeling rather annoyed with myself as I changed hurriedly. In the event, it was one of the most hilarious gatherings I have ever attended in the House. Everybody but Burnaby Drayson [Conservative MP for Skipton] turned up out of the twenty-two survivors, including Harold [Wilson], Jim [Callaghan], Fred Peart and the Speaker, Selwyn Lloyd. As soon as I arrived we were rushed up to Selwyn's rooms for a photograph and we were all in festive mood. As the only woman there I was fêted, petted and teased. I was sandwiched at dinner between Hugh Fraser and Derek Walker-Smith. Wine flowed and we were all mateyness itself. No one listened to the brief speech Selwyn made and when they forced me to my feet to say a few words I could hardly make myself heard for the ribald din. As we streamed through the division lobby at 10 pm, the libels started to circulate. People wanted to know what we had all been up to. 'You should have seen Barbara flirting,' said Fred wickedly, while Harold himself, I was told, had assured everyone that Hugh Fraser had put me over his knee and spanked me. Certainly everyone was high, but not as high as that! I can see I shall never hear the end of that dinner.

Thursday, 24 July. I had a bit of a struggle to get my consultative document on pay beds through Social Services Committee of Cabinet, but I think I've managed it. Most of the points raised were pretty trivial. (Treasury, for instance, which has been very good at making extra money available for my budget to meet the cost of phasing out pay beds, wanted to be sure that the licensing system would be self-financing.) Ted summed up that the committee endorsed the 'main aims' of my document, so that gives me everything I want: total separation of pay beds from the NHS by a date to be included in the legislation; the withdrawal of private out-patient facilities from NHS hospitals; and a licensing system which will ensure that the total of private beds outside the NHS after separation will not exceed the total number of private beds inside and outside the NHS in March 1974. The only retreat I have made is on the final date for separation, largely because David has made some valid points about the difficulties involved in going for November 1976 as I had originally visualized. I agree with him we must have greater flexibility than that in order to meet the problem of consultants who would face a sudden and considerable drop in their income if pay beds disappeared almost overnight, so I am happy to leave the date for further negotiation. I do believe that I am on my way at last!

Sunday, 27 July. The great Pensions Bill party. When Brian and I volunteered this months ago we had no idea how many were involved in the production of the Pensions Bill. Private Office, given the job of preparing the list of invitees, came up with a hundred! So I had given the office the job of dividing the invitees into two groups: one for HCF, the rest for London. (They said there was great rivalry to come to HCF, except among the lawyers, who plumped for London. There must be a moral in this somewhere.) Brian and Kate [O'Malley] arrived last night. Mercifully, this fabulous weather held and this morning we were all busy, putting a bar out in the garden, freezing the drinks as much as possible, while I put the last mad touches to an ambitious cold buffet. Prompt at noon the guests started arriving: I suspect they must have been counting the minutes while they dallied in the lane. It went like a bomb, even the prim Errington waxing poetic about the garden (which Ted had brought to a peak of perfection, despite the drought) and about our kindness in inviting them all. 'What we will never understand, Secretary of State,' said Tom [Crawley of my Private Office], 'is how you can bear to tear yourself away from all this to come to the office.' 'Don't you realize, Tom,' I replied, 'that the whole point of this party is to make Private Office more sympathetic to my needs?' Brian and Kate slaved away carving ham, beef and chicken, while I mobilized Eileen and whomsoever else I could to make salads. They all wandered round the garden, drank a lot of wine, ate a lot of food and thoroughly enjoyed themselves. I told them they were none of them allowed to leave until they had dossed down on rugs on the lawn, slept off the alcohol and had a cup of tea. It was about 6 pm when they started to leave. I loved it – and I think they did too.

Monday, 28 July. Letters have come pouring in from Errington and others about Sunday's party. There is no doubt that they are all very touched by the trouble we took. Jack told me that he had heard one civil servant at the party remark to another, 'Have you ever been invited to a party like this by a Minister before?' To which the reply had been, 'Never. I once had to call at a Minister's house and was given a glass of sherry, but that was all.' What apparently pleased them most was that we included everybody: from the Deputy Secretary to the humblest clerical officer. And, of course, my beloved driver, Edna, was there with her pal, Pat.

Thursday, 31 July. Brian is still hankering after a 1977 starting date for the pensions scheme. The trouble about this is that an early date might well jeopardize its success, and, moreover, it would mean a frontal battle with Treasury, who would use this as an example of Barbara trying to get more than her fair share of resources again and would insist on taking the whole question of whether we should even have a 1978 date to PESC. As I talked over the problem with Norman I suddenly saw what I must do: write to Joel [Barnett], saying that he knew we wanted a 1977 date, but, in view of the expenditure restraints, I was ready to drop this – provided he would let me announce a firm 1978 date at my press conference next week to introduce our popular booklet on the scheme. Norman chuckled at this and readily went away to draft it.

A miserable meeting with officials to brief me for the wretched Chequers meeting on Monday about public expenditure.

Saturday, 2 August. The heat wave continues. Why on earth are we going to Corfu for our holiday? The dogs were so limp with it I persuaded Ted to take us to the river so that they and I could swim. Printer, who normally takes to the water like a duck, took fright at something and we had a job to get him in. I think it is his sight which distorts simple things like stalks of grass and floating thistle seeds into terrifying objects. I am now convinced he is going blind and my heart aches for him. But when we threw an enormous bough into the water he suddenly overcame his fears and went in after it time and again, dragging it with enormous effort up the bank. He is a fine, lithe little retriever and I love him dearly.

Sunday, 3 August. Another brilliantly sunny day. What is all that nonsense some scientists are talking about an incipient ice age? I cannot remember more consistently hot weather in all my life.

Monday, 4 August. It was still stinking hot as we drove to Chequers. With Eileen away, I had a rush getting breakfast, clearing away, locking everything up and packing the dogs' things. So I felt limp before we started the day and ill-prepared for the discussion. The staff at Chequers oohed and aahed over Printer and Brandy as we drove up to the door. I took them in to see Harold and they sniffed their way cheerily round the furniture in the great hall. It was Harold who, as he fondled Brandy, reminded me we had had both the dogs at the time he came to our silver wedding party at HCF six years ago. I had forgotten that! He never forgets a dog. As we assembled in the library everyone was in shirt-sleeves, but even with every window open we could not keep cool.

Harold opened by telling us he wanted us to work through to a late lunch. The aim of the morning's work was to get 'as near a consensus as possible on priorities': first, our priorities for reductions in expenditure; second, those items we would put first when reflation became possible. Denis then gave us one of his long economic *tours d'horizon*, all about how this year 35.7 per cent of GDP was going on public expenditure in resource items: 58 per cent if we included transfer payments. Before throwing open the discussion, Harold issued a warning. We must all limit our speeches to ten minutes and would we please note we were *not* to reopen the general discussion on MTA: merely to indicate what were our priorities for cuts. I was furious at this, since my brief from Brian A-S. challenged the need for £2 billion cuts and called for a mix of increased taxation. I realized that once again we were being manoeuvred into accepting Denis's whole premise, which we were supposed to be there to examine thoroughly.

At last, as it turned 2 pm, Harold summed up: (1) There should be a meeting on unemployment in September. (2) A committee would be set up to consider areas of reflation. (3) Estimates should be produced of the increased unemployment resulting from any cut. ('You can't do that,' jumped in Denis, horrified. 'We can and we shall,' retorted Harold.) (4) There should be a review of staff levels in the Civil Service and of ways of controlling them. The priorities emerging for safeguarding were housing (but not housing subsidies), industrial retraining, and inner cities. The lowest priorities were transport and higher education. There was also a view that there should be more selectivity in social security payments, and JASP[1] should look at this. (I didn't protest. Let them look by all means: they will find the results politically suicidal.) And so we broke up. 'Lunch,' said Harold. 'A drink, I hope,' gasped Denis. We poured downstairs in the greatest amiability. Joel thanked me for what I had said on defence. 'To imagine we can go to the Party with these cuts and not include defence is ridiculous,' he told me. He knew ways in which we could save £400 million on it. 'Give me the details and I'll blast away at them,' I said, but he replied that he was intending to use them himself. (I'll believe that when I see

[1] Joint Approach to Social Policy [JASP] stemmed from a report produced by CPRS, 'A Joint Framework for Social Policy', which had been published by HMSO in June 1975. The report advocated regular meetings of Ministers concerned with social policy to co-ordinate their approach.

it!) I seized the opportunity to tell him of the letter that was on the way to him about the pensions scheme starting date. He was taken aback at my offer to give up the 1977 starting date in favour of a firm commitment to April 1978. 'Your number two won't like that,' he said. 'I know,' I replied. 'He'll be furious with me, but I think the most important thing is for me to announce a firm date on Thursday and I know you won't give me 1977 ahead of PESC.' Joel seemed impressed and said he would consider it. Later, in the House, I told Brian of my ploy and he was tickled pink, entering into the conspiracy with relish.

At the buffet lunch I sat in the same corner as Mike. Denis and Joel joined us and we chi-iked each other over a glass of wine. 'At any rate, you've got to admit I'm the only political Chancellor you've ever had,' said Denis again. 'Oh yes,' I cheeked back, 'but it all depends *what* politics.' My trouser suit – the only garment fit to wear I could find at HCF – caused a lot of favourable comment. One of the civil servants whispered, 'Every time you come to Chequers, Secretary of State, you wear an even more distracting ensemble. It isn't fair to the secretaries.' Bob said, 'Very sexy.' Fred: 'I always went for her.' Denis said, 'She is just the size of my first girlfriend. I can tuck her under my armpit' – and proceeded to do so. Life is certainly full of surprises! There was I, hair dishevelled, freckled face steaming in the heat, in a cheap mail-order suit, with bare feet and sandals – and in my sixties too! I wouldn't have thought I had a scrap of sex attraction left.

Harold Lever has sent me a Minute (copied to the PM) saying he is 'greatly troubled' by my proposal to take licensing powers over the private sector of medicine. I have sent him a firm answer back and am praying the PM will ignore him.

Tuesday, 5 August. At Social Services Committee we made further progress with David Owen's pet campaign against smoking. He is very touched that, smoker though I am, I should humour him on this. We agreed he should make his statement this week. I'm certainly leaving it to him, as I am hardly an example of desirable behaviour in this field! Later this evening the *Sun* was on the phone to the flat asking whether it was true I was going to ban sponsorship of sport by cigarette manufacturers. How these things leak! I always tend to blame officials – leaking happens so regularly – but I suppose it could be an interested Minister in each case, doing some log-rolling. Today we were top for Questions and we sailed through. It really is extraordinarily easy to fend off an effective probe by back benchers when the attacks are disseminated over such a wide range of diverse and detailed subjects. It is when a co-ordinated campaign on one specific and clear-cut issue gets going that Parliament can be effective.

Our Questions over, I sat next to Harold for his. This gave me a full view of Margaret, who slipped into her place as demurely tight-lipped as ever and glossy with her best suburban grooming: fresh flowered summer frock and every wave of her hair in place. How *does* she keep her hair so unchangeably immaculate? It all adds to the feeling of unreality about her political leadership. Somehow that also is too bandbox. She never risks anything: just sits there listening to Harold with a carefully modulated look of disapproval on her face, then produces one regulation intervention per Question time. When she is ready for this great act she starts to lean forward slightly and an atmosphere of 'wait for it' builds up behind her. When finally she rises our chaps cheer ironically. She ignores them and fires her shaft. It never completely misses but is never (or very, very rarely) deadly. The lads behind her cheer lustily. Once again their tame bird has laid her egg.

My main Departmental business of the day was the traumatic one: would I or would I not agree to raise dental and ophthalmic charges? The Dental Rates Board has now let us have the details of the new dental fees and David has been bombarding me with the need for me to make up my mind before the recess, so that, if charges are to be increased, the necessary regulations can be laid in time. I have been waiting for him to produce a sweetener on the ophthalmic side in response to my demand that we should produce a more attractive range of NHS specs. Now the submissions are before me, comprising a move from cost-related charges to (increased) flat-rate ones, with some concessions to children on specs (which will be very popular). But the submissions assert that to try and improve the range of spectacle frames would lead to increased costs, which we couldn't afford, and get us into difficulties with the manufacturers. I astonished them all by saying briskly that (1) it was clear that we would have to raise charges, because I wouldn't get any extra money out of the Treasury; (2) all Ministers would be expected to sacrifice at least one sacred cow anyhow (it was always part of the public expenditure cuts ritual), and this would be mine; but (3) the Government would never get away with a succession of dreary negative policies. Our policy must have some charisma. 'It is when you are hard up that you most need that bottle of champagne,' I said. A new breakthrough on spec frames would be our touch of charisma.

Dick Bourton looked shocked at this last point. He had put an offensive Minute on the file to the effect that the public would consider any titivating of frames as 'frivolous' at this time, but David suddenly changed tack and supported me. So we agreed that we should keep this in the statement and I instructed Norman to fix a dinner with Derek Rayner[1] after the holiday at which David and I could seek his advice on how to organize the production of more fashionable frames. Brian A-S. tells me Rayner is brilliant and loves advising government Departments on these things. (We also want to use him on the general medical procurement side.) Finally we decided that it would be politically advisable to make the statement before the House rose, otherwise we should be faced with it as first business after the recess. 'Treasury won't like this reference to NHS spectacles in the statement,' warned Dick Bourton, but I sent them off to polish up the statement and to draft a letter to Joel, in which we put the political choice squarely to him (copies to other members of the Cabinet) and made it clear what a sacrifice I was making. No hiding of my light under a PESC bushel for me!

Wednesday, 6 August. The *Daily Express* has got me on the front page as the villain of the anti-smoking campaign. How the press does miscast one! I worked at home all morning waiting for Norman to phone me with Joel's reply to my letter on the pensions starting date. Finally he rings at 12.30 pm. The

[1] Sir Derek Rayner, joint managing director of Marks and Spencer and a member of the Ministry of Defence procurement management executive board.

reply from Joel has arrived. It is as cunning as I might have guessed. I can announce 1978 as the firm date *provided* I postpone for one year the very three items Brian O'Malley had been willing to offer in order to get a 1977 date, thus giving a saving of £26 million in that year. I explode. 'So he is trying to pre-empt savings from me before Cabinet decides the cuts!' My naturally militant instinct is to tell them to stuff it and then have the battle out in Cabinet. But a hunch tells me I must control my belligerence and talk it over with Brian.

I race down to the House to have lunch with him. *His* instinct is to go for a firm date at any cost, and as we talk I can see the wisdom of it. We are both anxious about the lack of support we have had from the TUC over the pensions side of the pay policy and we suspect the hand of Jack Jones, who has never, as a ruthless egalitarian, seemed to have much sympathy with occupational pension schemes. Indeed, we recall, it was Harry Urwin, his second-in-command, who, when we were working out our pensions policy in opposition, joined other trade unionists on the NEC in supporting a flat-rate pension. So we dare not rely on TUC backing if I take this to Cabinet: the TUC might prefer to give priority to the big increase in unemployment benefit they are beginning to demand. We asked ourselves how the Treasury had hit on the three concessions we were prepared to make. 'Our officials must have told them,' I said indignantly. 'It's not disloyalty,' said Brian. 'It is just how the whole civil service works.' Finally Brian suggested a compromise. We would accept postponement of the invalid care allowance and of the abolition of the half test, but not of the improvement in short-term benefits for married women, which, we agreed, was much more sensitive.[1] We summoned officials to my room in the House and I phoned Joel, away home in Surrey. After a bit of our usual sparring I put the proposition to him, developing a ploy that had just occurred to me – namely, that we might even find ourselves before the Equal Opportunities Board if we were to continue to give women unequal benefits for the same contributions when the scheme came in. Finally he said, 'I'll think about it and ring you back in five minutes.'

Five minutes! We sat for two hours in that baking room, twiddling our thumbs, getting negative reports from Norman from time to time, and increasingly resenting the Treasury autocracy. Finally we discovered that the necessary Treasury officials had been in the House of Lords all the time and had only just assembled under the chairmanship of the Permanent Secretary to consider our proposal! I decided the moment had come to do a piece of my deliberate temper losing. I phoned up Joel's Private Secretary and tore a strip off him. He cringed. I told him I wanted an answer in ten minutes flat. A quarter of an hour later, when our hopes were at zero, Norman phoned. 'You've won.' We just grinned and I said, 'The press conference is on.' That means another day off my holiday, but it's worth it.

Back in my room I continued wading through the last minute pre-holiday boxes that keep pouring in: six already today. They included some very

[1] The 'half test' was part of the unequal treatment of women under the existing pension arrangements. Under it a woman who had been contributing for a pension while at work could not receive a pension in her own right, unless, after marriage, she had paid contributions or been given credits in half the weeks between marriage and her pension age. This was particularly hard on women who had married, or re-married, late in life. Even more iniquitous was the provision whereby a married woman at work, even if she opted to pay the full national insurance contribution as the men did, only received a reduced rate of benefit if she was sick or unemployed.

important submissions on the major issues David and I have been raising in the last few weeks. Norman has been doing his stuff remarkably, peppering me with comments and suggestions helping me to see through some of the difficulties. He advised me to accept a Minute from Philip about the export drive, which suggested we put Sam Davies as Under-Secretary in charge of a new export division under [James] Collier, while setting up a working group on procurement under David to try and get the regional health authorities buying their requirements centrally. This would give a stronger industrial base to our export drive in such things as medical equipment. I accepted Norman's advice on these things, though insisting that Derek Rayner should be asked to advise David's group. I am continuously impressed by Norman's radical instincts and good judgment.

Thursday, 7 August. Woke at 5.30 am again. I can't sleep in this heat. Had my hair done, did some hurried holiday shopping and then swept into the press conference on our pensions booklet. It was crowded and to my relief was in the Fish Room at the Admiralty, where these occasions always seem much more relaxed. 'Please go to town when you speak,' pleaded Peter. 'You've achieved something to be proud of. It *is* a good scheme.' So I held forth euphorically and all went swimmingly. Brian had drafted the press notice so cunningly that the postponement of the two items Joel had forced on us seemed the most natural thing in the world, and no one questioned it. They seemed quite impressed that the increase in the women's short-term benefits is to come into effect immediately. So our great anxieties about the postponements were groundless. And we have got the Government committed to start the pensions scheme in this Parliament, instead of postponing it. Altogether a good session's work, as Peter emphasized to me. As he saw me to the car and wished me a good holiday I said with a wicked grin, 'Poor old Dick Crossman will be turning in his grave with envy.' 'He'll be pleased,' said Peter gravely. 'Don't you believe it,' I retorted. 'That chap had no chivalry.'

Norman clambered desperately into the car with me to clear one last point. The PM had read my statement on charges and wanted it postponed till we came back. We grinned. 'So you've won again,' said Norman. 'I wouldn't be too sure,' I cautioned. 'It may be that he is merely backing the Treasury.' Anyway, I have made my noble gesture and Cabinet will not now be able to blame me for the consequences of the delay.

HCF at last, with only a few hours to go before the holiday. But as Ted and I listened to the news there came the reports of a new disastrous run on sterling. 'I don't believe in this holiday,' I told him. 'You watch: there'll be a crisis Cabinet yet.'

Saturday, 9 August to Saturday, 23 August. A perfect fortnight in Corfu. I slept about nine hours every night and had an afternoon snooze on the beach as well! The consultative document on pay beds was published on 11 August.[1] I preferred to have it come out in my absence than to hold things up.

[1] The document, 'The Separation of Private Practice from NHS Hospitals', elaborated the statement I had made in the House on 5 May. I repeated our commitment to legislate to withdraw pay beds and the private use of

Wednesday, 27 August. Settling down at HCF – if settling down is the word, for the hot summer days continue distractingly. A box was awaiting my return on Saturday night – even before my fortnight was up! I catch up in a leisurely way with arrears of departmental work or laze in the hammock. It is too hot for gardening. The dogs don't want to stir for a walk until the cool of the evening. I cannot remember a summer like it. On Tuesday we have Mother over for lunch to celebrate her ninety-second birthday. Members of the family make special trips over to see her and she gives us her familiar confused but endearing repertoire: singing 'Old Soldiers Never Die' and reciting the love poem Dad wrote to her seventy-odd years ago. It always moves me very much. On Sunday, as Ted, Eileen and I were dozing in the garden, Sonya and Terry *mit* brood suddenly materialized, asking if they could camp overnight at the bottom of the garden on their way home from their holiday. Altogether a week of rich enjoyment of HCF.

It was good to be home and back at my boxes. Holidays always bore me after a couple of weeks. Among my papers I find a letter from Malcolm Shepherd finally endorsing the appointment of a Chief Social Work Officer of Deputy Secretary rank in succession to Joan Cooper. Victory! It has taken me about six months, but I've won, overcoming all the resistance from the department. Malcolm has been very good, telling me he was totally convinced by my argument that we had to strike a better balance between the medical and the social work side of the department. So the long, slow process of loosening the grip of the medical professionals on the department has begun – just as I managed at Transport to reduce the dominance of the highway engineers.

The social wage document is still hanging fire. All attention has been concentrated on the production of Geoffrey Goodman's 'popular' version of the anti-inflation White Paper: not the same thing at all.

Wednesday, 3 September. The £6 pay policy has been 'overwhelmingly' endorsed by Trades Union Congress. Quite a landmark! Jack Jones has delivered magnificently. The Government must now deliver too. And that should mean no slashing public expenditure cuts.

Wednesday, 10 September. Another long day's meeting at Chequers: this time on devolution again. There was a mound of bumph to read on which functions should be devolved and which not. As Shirley said to me as we arrived, 'And so boring too.' There was also a paper by CPRS, gloomily questioning whether the whole devolution package was viable. There is no doubt that officials as a whole

out-patient facilities from NHS hospitals. The date for the completion of this process would be set out in the legislation, 'bearing in mind that the Government first announced their intention in March 1974'. I was willing to consider making certain highly specialized procedures, such as radiotherapy, available to the private sector on a contract basis at full economic cost, provided no fees were paid for such services to individual members of NHS staff. But the main part of the document dealt with licensing. First, I intended to strengthen the Government's powers to regulate the quality of nursing homes and other provision for patients in the private sector. Second, I intended to see that private developments did not jeopardize the needs of NHS patients, by, for example, absorbing 'any undue proportion of scarce skills'. To this end I proposed to set up a licensing system to ensure that, after pay beds had been phased out, the volume of private provision for short-stay patients (*i.e.* [acute] medical, surgical and maternity cases) would not substantially exceed the number of NHS pay beds and beds in private nursing homes and hospitals at March 1974.

are deeply alarmed at the whole exercise. Philip Rogers asked to see me last night to urge that we shouldn't rush to publish a Devolution Bill, but allow plenty of time for consultation on the further White Paper we are to produce. He said that officials in the devolution committee doubted very much whether we would be able to get away with devolving a lot of social policy powers and hardly any economic ones. And there is no doubt, either, that the anti-devolution minority in Cabinet is stubbornly determined to fight against it to the end.

By 4 pm we had gone through the long, dreary details. 'Aren't we going to discuss the CPRS paper?' asked Denis innocently. Ted nearly exploded. It was asking us to go back on everything we had agreed. Harold backed him up: 'We can't discuss the reversal of the White Paper.' Jim drawled, 'I am beginning to be converted to the least possible devolution.' Denis battled on stubbornly. We should at least have in front of us in October an 'alternative model' produced by CPRS. Ted would have none of this: we had considered all the possible alternative models before picking on this one, he maintained. But with Fred Peart, Roy, Malcolm, Fred Mulley and others making approving noises of support for Denis, Harold was forced to go through the list of items on which CPRS suggested we should ask officials to do further work. We agreed one or two of them. I said that what we needed in October was a document drawing together what we had so far agreed, so that we could see the whole picture. The decision would then be a political one. 'Thank you for your help,' Ted said to me afterwards. He really is deeply committed on this. Philip Rogers admitted to me wickedly that officials talk about him 'Short-circuiting' the timetable.

I think the implications of devolution *are* worrying, but (a) we have no alternative in view of the feeling in Scotland and (b) it is a bit much for Roy Jenkins and co. to express their alarm at the break-up of the unity of the UK when they have done so much to destroy its sense of sovereignty by impaling us on the horns of the EEC. For instance, when we were discussing the devolution of responsibility for the Health Service, someone pointed out that this meant the Scots could wind up the NHS if they wanted to, go over to private insurance and lure our doctors away. Was I prepared to accept that? 'Of course, I hate it,' I replied. 'But if you decide to make a constitutional change like devolution you must accept the implications, just as we decided to make a constitutional change by joining the EEC. I can assure you the BMA is licking its chops at the prospect this offers of lucrative pickings from private medicine in the Community.' That silenced them.

Saturday, 13 September. The papers are full of the rowdyism at Reg Prentice's meeting last night. The antics of the Trots play right into his hands.

Sunday, 14 September to Wednesday, 17 September. Off to France for an official visit to my French counterpart, Mme Simone Veil – hopefully to help promote the export of medical equipment to France. Norman isn't coming with me because he is still on leave. I never felt less like a foreign trip as we drove to the airport through driving wind and rain. And I only had summer clothes with me too! In the event it turned out to be one of the most satisfying adventures of my life. Reason: I found all my latent love of speaking French, however ungrammatically, surge up in me. Indeed, I just couldn't talk English even when other people were speaking it to me! So it was fun. I felt young and I looked young. I had no nerves, no shyness, no agonized sense of reserve as I so often do. I went right out to meet everybody in my most relaxed mood and they responded warmly.

It is always a joy to stay at the British Embassy in Paris. The Faubourg St Honoré is in any case my favourite street in Paris and to step into the courtyards of the Embassy is to step out of all the modern noise into the eighteenth-century elegance of de Charost. Napoleon's sister lived here and she filled it with its elaborate furniture. I must say I like splendour – so, incidentally, do Communist governments, who usually preserve theirs carefully for the greater glorification of the people's take-over. My relations with the Tomkinses [the Ambassador and his wife] were soon humanized by the fact that they have two blue roan spaniels. With this common bond – and with the help of their attractive teenage daughter – we spent a relaxed family evening talking dogs and Dutch elm disease. Wedgie, we were told, was due the next day, and I was amused by the flutter of mixed apprehension and curiosity this evoked.

Up early the next day. I was rushed to the big new hospital at Clamart, where Mme Veil was waiting. She turned out to be an elegant, rather shy woman in her late forties. I thought the words 'cold charm', which *The Times* has used to describe her, were about right. She is *très sérieuse* and used the occasion of my visit to see some of the hospitals, like Clamart, that she hadn't seen. The Antoine Beclerk was a well-designed modern hospital belonging to the vast 'Assistance Publique' group for the Paris area and seemed well equipped. But it struck me that in France they are still putting nearly all the emphasis on hospitalization. There is no family doctor list system like ours; there are vast out-patients departments and no health centres. I can't imagine how the link with the community services is made, though Mme Veil has responsibility for social welfare as well. Another thing that struck me as we marched miles round the hospital corridors was how clinical and austere it seemed: no colour anywhere, no warmth of atmosphere. The few patients we met in the out-patients seemed sunk in self-obsessed gloom. They don't have the system of wards: two beds to a room at the most.

In between visits I had some long chats with Mme Veil in her car. I congratulated her warmly on her courage over her abortion law reform and she seemed pleased. She is extremely popular with the public, even those who disagree with her, because they feel she is completely honest and straightforward in what she says and does. She is a Jewess and her horrifying experiences in German concentration camps are no doubt responsible for her air of reserve: besides, she is a jurist and therefore no demagogue. But as the day went by she began to melt, and when we concluded the long day with a sumptuous dinner in the private room of a restaurant, she really unbent. She made a friendly little speech of welcome after the meal and I decided to risk all and reply in French. She positively beamed her delight and we parted on terms of mutual warmth.

When I got back to the Embassy Wedgie had arrived and came into my room for a little chat. He seemed untypically subdued, as though he suddenly realized he had been shunted onto a track where he couldn't play the demagogic politics he loves so much. Why was he there? Well, he thought it was time he met his European counterparts, so he was doing a tour of Energy Ministers. I get the impression Wedgie doesn't like administration very much, which means he won't be a very good administrator, but at least he won't get swamped in administration as so many of us do.

Monday, 22 September. Woke at 5 am with agonizing tummy pains, which necessitated several trips up and down the stairs and across the cold tiles to the loo. So I left HCF in no state to face my meeting with Minister Petrovsky of the Soviet Union to launch our joint committee under the Health Co-operation Agreement. Of course, I got through it somehow, helped by the fact that he is an extraordinarily agreeable, fatherly and uninhibited old boy. He is a surgeon, which perhaps explains why he does not seem constrained by the political aloofness of most Soviet visitors. Our Dr Reid told me that, on the trip to Oxford yesterday, he had on an impulse invited Petrovsky to his own home, where they had a most matey and relaxed time.

Cabinet was on unemployment, as promised at the last Chequers meeting. My main aim was to see that DHSS got its fair share of any increased expenditure that was going, whether on work creation or the package to stimulate the construction industry. Tony Crosland overreached himself in his efforts to hog all the money for housing. He had put in a paper attacking the work creation scheme and saying the money ought to be put to housing improvements instead. But his sarcastic ribaldry in introducing it was so selective that it enabled me to shoot him down. What was wrong, I said, in spending £30 million on painting old people's own homes, helping them with their gardens, manning day centres or providing transport for the disabled? In any case it was the most effective way of getting young school-leavers off the dole. That was why, contrary to its normal approach on this sort of thing, the TUC were strongly backing the work creation scheme. But I supported Mike in saying that we had to go further and draw up a package to help the construction industry. But it must be the industry as a whole, not just housing. We had, for instance, in DHSS a backlog of maintenance work in the NHS amounting to £100 million, to say nothing of the long-overdue fire precautions we could not afford to introduce. So Denis gave way and agreed to consider a construction package to follow soon.

In the evening, still weak from my tummy, I had to go through an official dinner for Minister Petrovsky at Lancaster House. He admired the room's ornate beauty. 'This once was the home of a royal personage,' I said mischievously, 'but now it belongs to the people.' 'That is familiar with us,' he replied.

Wednesday, 24 September. Woke in the early hours with my tummy in a dreadful state. I knew I would have to give in and call our doctor; otherwise I should not be on my feet for Party conference. He diagnosed an infection of the bowel and put me on antibiotics. This meant a great flurry of cancelling all my engagements. Worked in bed, feeling very ill.

Thursday, 25 September. I insisted on getting up, for there were a number of things I could not afford to miss. First, Cabinet, at which the main business was my own paper on putting up dental and optical charges. I had a tightrope to walk here. If I insisted they must *not* go up, Denis would pounce and say the money must come out of my PESC allocation, and I just cannot spare that £16 million. We shall build no health centres at all if I lose any more money! On the other hand, David and I have carefully constructed a package of charges designed to make some important concessions (and thus reduce the saving). I had to defend it against a threatened Treasury demand that the savings were not big enough and that I must give up more. So I delivered my proposals in a flat, quiet tone, helped by my state of physical weakness. Then, to my astonishment, the storm broke. Denis welcomed my proposals as 'courageous', but our lads at last came out of their corner fighting to defend the NHS. Mike said he thought that to increase charges would be disastrous. (Of course! I suddenly realized the old bogey of 'teeth and spectacles' had rung a bell!) Wedgie said that, listening to me introducing my paper, he had realized what was meant by the phrase: 'Working without enthusiasm.' Were we really going to tear the movement apart for £16 million? Even Peter said gravely that he thought it would be a 'real mistake', because of the movement's emotive association with the NHS.

Others followed. Only Reg Prentice could not get the cuts in public expenditure increased quickly enough. Then Malcolm Shepherd, to my surprise, said he didn't like the increases either. Could he not come along to my Department and look at ways in which we could make administrative economies instead? He was sure he could find ways of saving the necessary £16 million. Unfortunately Harold had had to leave. (I am sure he would have grasped the political sensitivity of this and found a saving formula.) I insisted that any administrative economies possible had already been identified and earmarked to offset the £16½ million cut already made in the health budget. Tony C. objected to the reopening of the PESC decisions in this way. Other people had to deal with sensitive issues, he muttered: none more sensitive than rents, etc. But Mike snapped at him, 'Some of us have to deal with the effects of these decisions on the pay policy. We've helped you over rents.' Harold Lever told me that I could find the money by postponing the phasing out of pay beds – he would! Fortunately Denis nodded when I said that if we did not act, pay beds would be phased out by the unions anyway, but in a disorderly way. Finally Ted ruled that the decisions should be postponed till the Cabinet on 14 October, to enable Malcolm to see what he could do.

Somehow I got through the farewell lunch to Petrovsky and the press conference. Then a rush to the Treasury to discuss the 1977–78 and 1978–79 PESC with Joel Barnett. We went through the 'options' for cuts on the social security side which officials had prepared: Joel wants £500 million from this side alone. I told him I would offer £100 million by reversing the decision to phase out the earnings rule (which has never been my priority), but nothing more. Nonetheless, we went down the list (*e.g.* abolition of maternity grant, ditto death grant). I just gave Joel a withering look. 'Ah well, I didn't think you'd accept that,' grinned Joel. 'I'm glad she gave *you* that look and not me,' whispered one of his officials. Postponement of the introduction of the child benefit scheme? I countered that by referring to a table in our briefs which showed that our family support provision, despite child benefit, will actually be going down. The suggestion that we should save by postponement was therefore a Treasury fiction. Joel said hastily that he would look into this. His main aim was to get me to agree to switch from the historical method of calculating the pension increases (which, with the fall off in inflation, would now begin to benefit the pensioners) to the forecasting one, which would save the Treasury some £500 million. Brian and I had agreed we would resist this ferociously. Of course, Joel said, 'Then we'll have to get more savings from the health side.' Suddenly I had a good idea. We were talking about the 1976 uprating, yet the proposed public expenditure cuts were related purely to 1977–79. Was there to be a mini-PESC for 1976–77 for Barbara only? I would consider moving to the forecasting method once the 1976 uprating was over and we had given pensioners a fair turn of the wheel in their favour on one round. Peter Baldwin [Deputy Secretary, Treasury] and Joel looked at each other, saying that wouldn't be enough, but we agreed that we should all go away and look at it.

Friday, 26 September. Everyone has been predicting terrible rows at this conference. Certainly there have been floods of resolutions denouncing the Government's economic policy and expenditure cuts and demanding massive increases in expenditure on this and that. But there were few signs of dissension at the NEC meeting this morning. On the Finance Committee report, we were faced by a resolution of Shirley's saying that, in view of the Party's acute financial difficulties, Ministers should 'consider' meeting the whole of their expenses at conference this year and the trade union boys should ask their unions to meet their expenses. This led to an involved argument, from which it emerged that some union rules would make this difficult. Eventually it was left that Cabinet Ministers only should 'consider' this. I think it is right that those of us who are comfortably off should fork out generously at this time, but I felt aggrieved by two things. (1) Why keep picking on Cabinet Ministers, as though we were Croesuses? It should be done on ability to pay and I bet Mik's income is bigger than mine. (2) I wish it hadn't been sprung on us at the last minute. If I'd known I would have to find £110 or so for conference, I would have told Ted we couldn't afford Corfu as well.

But the main item was to discuss the proposed statement on jobs and prices – and, indeed, whether we should have a statement at all. Mike took the lead on this. He knew, he said, that there were many passages in Geoff Bish's draft which would offend both sides. It committed the Party, for instance, to support of the £6 policy, with which it was clear that Mik at any rate would disagree, but equally it embarrassed the Government by stating that 'the most urgent need is for the Government to introduce temporary restrictions on imports'. So why present a statement at all? Mike asked. He didn't think Harold was right in suggesting the Liaison Committee with the TUC had asked for it. 'We could have amendments moved from both sides that could get us into a great tangle.' Harold said he thought a statement was essential, but wanted the drafting done by a small committee. That didn't find any support at all. Wedgie said he favoured the statement being made unchanged and in its entirety. When Mike said he did not believe that import controls were 'anything like a full answer to the problem of unemployment' Wedgie said smoothly, 'The statement does reflect the views we have discussed with the TUC.' Joan Maynard supported the statement: 'The real cause of inflation is not wages but lack of investment.' (No mention of not eating the seed corn!) Frank Allaun echoed her dutifully. Mik, surprisingly, backed Mike. But the general view was that the NEC must not be the only people not to have a view on this issue; so that meant going through the document line by line in the afternoon. At the lunch break Mike seized on me almost desperately. 'Come and lunch.' 'Dodging the press?' I asked. 'Not only them,' he replied. I was grateful for his company as we both awaited the arrival of our spouses. 'They're fools to insist on having a statement,' he grumbled over lunch as he ate restlessly. 'We offered them a way out.' He is a very unquiet person these days, but I sense in him an absolute determination to see his job through: an approach I respect and share. His desire to lunch alone with me was significant. This is no situation in which the traditional camaraderie of the large companionable table of the Left could survive.

As we went through the document line by line in the NEC I was surprised by two things: (1) that Mik should let the passage on the £6 limit go through, merely repeating his sour comment that he wasn't going to waste time arguing it; (2) how much Denis was prepared to give to get agreement. He did get some important changes on such things as import controls, entering a caveat, on which the NEC supported him, because he warned of the danger of 'anticipation'. He and I both successfully resisted a snide attempt of Mik's to insert the words, 'and urge the Government not to introduce any further measures increasing the level of unemployment'. Denis protested at the word 'further'. I made quite a little speech, saying that if I thought the aim of this Government was deliberately to increase unemployment I would have resigned from it long ago. But on other points Denis gave away much more than I expected him to, and he was rewarded for his pains by getting the same line-up against him on the final vote as he would have got anyway, Mik, Frank Allaun, Joan Maynard, John Forrester and Nick Bradley (the Young Socialist delegate who sits next to Joan and does everything she tells him to do) voting against the final text as 'inadequate'. In the hotel lobby afterwards I was intrigued to hear Geoff Bish pitching into Denis in passionate complaint that he had given away too much. So much for the politics of demonology that the press is so prone to! If I had been Denis I would have crawled up to my room wanting to die and moaning to Ted, 'I'm a failure.' I suspect Denis has no such self-doubts, which is why he deserves to survive more than I do.

Went to bed still nursing my tum.

Sunday, 28 September. More work [on my boxes] in bed in the morning, followed by a stroll in the sun on Blackpool's magnificent sands. I must be getting set in my ways, because I can almost see some virtue in the place. Then into the usual long, gruelling afternoon session of the NEC to discuss the composite resolutions. The resolutions are all demanding massive expenditure increases, and Geoff Bish remarked to me that we really would have to adopt his idea of having a kind of large-scale tote erected at the back of the platform at conference. Every time one of these resolutions was passed we should ring up the cost on the tote, so delegates could see what the total was amounting to. 'And we should also ring up what this expenditure would mean in terms of increased taxes and insurance contributions,' I agreed. Really, the irresponsibility of delegates infuriates me. I agree with Bish: how can they call on the Government to obey conference decisions when they refuse themselves to do any realistic arithmetic? They must learn to choose: either they can continue to pass these resolutions as a relief for their own souls, knowing full well the Government cannot meet them all, or they must impose some revolutionary self-discipline on themselves.

In the evening we had our 'Any Questions' eve-of-conference meeting, designed to give delegates the chance of quizzing four Ministers: Mike, Joan, Eric Varley and me. Despite the fact that I had been living for days on antibiotics, the water wagon and boiled fish (or perhaps because of it), I positively scintillated. Nice to end my conference career on a high note – for I have decided not to run again next year for the National Executive.[1]

Monday, 29 September. Highlight of the day was Mike's speech answering the unemployment debate. Since the unions had been streaming to the rostrum to express alarm, he had a horrible job and triumphed by taking the challenge full on, giving all the emotional voltage he had got. Conference rose to him with a standing ovation, only Mik and co. remaining on their posteriors. Afterwards some people sneered: 'A virtuoso performance, but it had no content.' But I myself, sitting next to him, had been almost reduced to tears by his utter dedication and sincerity. Conference over, I had to go and address one of the many fringe meetings: this one by the Labour Campaign for Mental Health. It seemed so off the main political stream that I cursed myself, not expecting anyone to be there. In the event, about a hundred people turned up and, despite the antibiotics, I found myself on form, laying about myself as once again they asked for the 'massive injection of resources' into their own pet interest. I have been impressed to find – as on Sunday night – how many of our people are involved in constructive do-goodery. Yet these same people will vote to a man for some of the larger lunacies that will be peddled in some of the resolutions this week. This is what political commentators fail to understand: that conference is an essential piece of catharsis for our activists frustrated by the limitations on our actions imposed by reality.

Tuesday, 30 September. I went down to conference quite serenely to hear the NEC election results. Ted has been worrying that I shall be thrown off. Well, it may be so, but I should find it very odd at a time when the papers are full of my row over phasing out private beds. Ted's argument is that the sustained press sneers about my age have reappeared again and will have some effect. Also I am clearly not on Tribune's slate. Ted tells me that at the Tribune brains trust on Sunday morning Judith said she didn't think Ministers should be on the NEC anyway (having ceased to be a Minister herself), while Stan Orme argued that it

[1] In the event I was persuaded by Ian Mikardo, among others, to stand again. I remained on the NEC until October 1979, when, having left the House of Commons and been elected to the European Parliament, I decided not to run. As a result of a proposal by Tony Benn I became an ex-officio member of the Executive as leader of the British Labour group in the European Parliament.

all depended on the Ministers and then gave a list of the Ministers who *should* be on and omitted me. The only book Mik has been running this year is for bottom place. I put 50 pence on Denis surviving, finding it difficult to believe that the party would be irresponsible enough to inflict this public humiliation on their Chancellor. Ted put 50 pence on my being bottom – for which I was comforted to find the odds were sixteen to one against. But Ted proved to be right. Though my vote went up by 20,000, Wedgie and Mike sailed to the top with over 500,000 each. Mik dropped a few, but still got 6,000 more than I did, while Joan Lestor and Frank picked up thousands more. Even Eric Heffer, coming on to the Executive for the first time, beat me by 5,000 votes, while poor old Denis was nowhere, being only second runner-up even though he got 1,000 more than last time. The big increase in voting all round was symptomatic, I suppose, of the Party's mood of protest, though with typical illogic local Parties put Jack Ashley, a well known right-winger, in first place as runner-up, giving him 28,000 more votes than Denis! Such are the quirks of democracy.

It was against this erratic background that Harold launched into his major speech. He was obviously proud of it, having shown me some of his best cracks yesterday. But I thought it was one of the worst he has ever made: flat, uninspiring, unfunny, unphilosophical. It only came to life when he ended up with a long and rather obscure diatribe against the machinations of both Left and Right and the odd thing was that conference rose to it, cheering him constantly, the two wings in turn. This movement of ours really is unpredictable. Then on to the debate on economic policy, which gave Denis the chance to make the speech of his life. I couldn't help thinking that there is nothing like defeat for bringing the best out in one. He got a standing ovation and deserved it.

Wednesday, 1 October. Wedgie's turn. The debate was on industrial policy. Judith opened with what I considered a pretty banal speech. Wedgie had decided to play it *sotto voce*. I got the feeling he is trying to shape up more seriously for the leadership. It was, as usual, an impressively fluent speech and brought conference to its feet, only Ted grumbling that he didn't think much of it. In the afternoon it was my turn. As usual I tensed up in quite an absurd way: not so much nervous as unrelaxed. Jack and Ted urged me to make a scintillating speech, but I was conscious of walking a tightrope between the mood of conference, which is calling for the total abolition of private practice, which I opposed, and of the wider audience, including the BMA, which would be waiting to pounce on anything I said about pay beds. In the event, my speech went quite well. I got a lot of applause and it was a pleasant change to have the unions queueing up to congratulate me on what I was doing. But I could still have kicked myself for not being able to make an off-the-cuff speech with the sort of panache I had displayed on Sunday night. No one will ever believe that all my life I have been cursed by this lack of self-confidence, which only disappears in certain circumstances and before certain audiences. Once again, I contrasted myself unfavourably with Shirley, who followed on pensions, making an effortlessly fluent speech on the basis of a few scribbled notes and who was warmly congratulated by Harold.

During the afternoon the rumour ran around that Mik, who was speaking at the Tribune meeting that night, had issued a hand-out savagely attacking Jack Jones and the TUC and claiming that the poor had got poorer under this Government: straight Child Poverty Action Group propaganda of the kind Denis has repudiated. In any case I had decided to go to the Tribune meeting, Mik having told me there was to be a debate between him and Mike. But first to the *Mirror* party, where I congratulated Jack Jones on his speech on pensions. He exuded friendliness. 'What do you think of Mik's attack on you?' I asked. He bridled suspiciously: 'What attack?' 'He's accusing the trade union movement of selling out,' I replied. He shrugged angrily. But I suspect that by alerting him I was responsible for what happened afterwards. Ted and I got to the Spanish Hall at the Winter Gardens at 9 pm, in time to hear Neil Kinnock make the funniest collection speech I have ever heard. He's a find, that boy. The hall was packed, the TV lights picking out the baroque moulding at the back of the platform, which gave the whole scene an air of dramatic intensity. The plaster Spanish villages towering on the walls above the speakers' heads added a final touch of incongruity. Mik proceeded to read the speech he had handed out, piling selective statistic on selective statistic to give a hostile distortion of the work of the Government. Suddenly out of the crowded aisle where he had been standing leapt Jack Jones, up onto the platform, jabbing an accusing finger at Mik like an Old Testament prophet pronouncing his doom. As Mik had the microphone and Jack had not, all we could hear were a few snatches of what Jack said. 'I detest these attacks on the trade union movement' was all I caught. But he stood there for a full minute, jab following jab with inarticulate shout after inarticulate shout. It was electrifying. The audience split into pro- and anti-Mik arguments and there was pandemonium, which Dick Clements in the chair eventually managed to quell, appealing to Jack as an 'old friend' and saying that Michael would be answering Mik. Jack sat down heavily on the end seat on the platform to which Dick Clements invited him and didn't utter a word after that. Mik finished rather lamely to tumultuous aplause from parts of the audience. A few people tried to give him a standing ovation.

I wondered how Mike could possibly turn the emotional anti-authority tide. But once again, he dredged up immense energy from somewhere. It must be from his spirit, because it can't be from that emaciated frame of his. He even managed to make the pay policy sound like a socialist crusade, Jack nodding his approval frequently. The audience rose to him. He exuded clearness of conscience – just as I did in the speeches I made to the PLP on *In Place of Strife*. Only a few people remembered, as I did, the contrast between Mike's speech that night and the speeches he had made at Tribune meetings before he became a member of the Government. One of them was a woman sitting in front of me, who hissed, 'He's sold out,' and gave the communist salute. To everyone's surprise Dick Clements did not call on Jack to speak. The meeting broke up to the 'Red Flag'. That dramatic incident was the talk of the hotel when we got back.

Thursday, 2 October. At the Granada buffet lunch I got into one of my familiar arguments with Joel, asking him if it was true that the Treasury was now asking for expenditure cuts of £5 billion. 'If so, I know one person who will walk out of the Government,' I said. 'Of course,' he replied, 'it would kill the Government.' He tried to pooh-pooh it on the grounds that all the Treasury had done was to point out that, by omitting to mention interest on the national debt in its PESC documents, its proposals would not reduce the borrowing requirement to the extent anticipated. But I know what that means. Denis will come to Cabinet and say that, in view of this, a saving of £3 billion will be the minimum. I simply am not prepared to accept the sort of cuts they are planning for me and feel deeply apprehensive of what faces us when we return. 'I would accept pretty drastic economies,' I told Joel, 'if it was in support of a positive industrial policy. The Government must choose what it is going for: either the soft welfare line or the tough line of industrial reconstruction. What our people won't accept – and I won't accept – is a policy of messing about with everything: a little inadequate bit of investment plus slashing welfare cuts.' He's a nice chap but I don't think he grasps the political realities.

Friday, 3 October. At conference Mik made a bitter little speech on defence, deliberately down-beat. I find it hard to decide what makes him tick these days. Then 'Auld Lang Syne' and home – to enjoy my birthday in private peace. I thanked the Lord it didn't occur in conference this year and so robbed the commentators of their annual jibe at the 'ageing Mrs Castle'. Why did I ever put my birth date in *Who's Who* in a rash moment all those years ago?

Tuesday, 7 October. Highlight of the day was the dinner I gave to Derek Rayner of Marks and Spencer. With memories of Aubrey Jones in my mind, I had suggested a private room at the Stafford Hotel for the rendezvous. Present were David and I, James Collier, Brian A-S. and Norman, who was there to record the words of wisdom we hoped to get from Derek on centralizing procurement policy for the NHS as the basis for a great export drive. Rayner stressed that we must take the medical profession along with us in any changes in procurement of equipment, etc., we might want to make. At one stage I summed up his advice: 'Fix your target and then make the consultants think they had suggested it.' 'Exactly,' he chuckled. I had a bright idea. Since the French do a lot of 'cultural' self-promotion, sending their top specialists round the world to talk on this and that, why didn't we do the same? Why didn't we suggest to our top consultants that they should make trips to various key countries overseas to talk about their specialities and we would pay for it? It would not only help exports, but help to defuse the tension in the NHS which the BMA, aided and abetted by Tory spokesmen, are once again working flat out to build up. There is, for instance, a great campaign being launched in the press to suggest that half the top people in the NHS are emigrating. The others thought my idea was good and I told Norman to work on it.

With world recovery still fragile and patchy, the economic outlook remained deeply worrying. At home the £6 pay limit was holding remarkably well with the promise of nearly halving the rate of increase in earnings over the coming year and a big reduction in the rate of inflation, even if not quite to the Chancellor's target of 10 per cent. But with world trade flat and workers' living standards being cut, deflation was deepening. Output had fallen and unemployment continued its relentless upward trend. In October the seasonally adjusted figure had risen to over one million or 4.6 per cent and even the CBI *was forecasting that it would reach 1.25–1.5 million by the end of 1976.*

In this situation the NEC *remained restive about the Government's economic and industrial strategy. With other countries balancing their trade by deflating and with the export surplus of* OPEC *countries still running at between $40 billion and $50 billion, it was clear that the world crisis would only be solved by far more imaginative lending and recycling policies than the international institutions showed any sign of developing. This intensified the problems of the weaker economies like Britain and made it extremely unlikely that we could rely on the revival of world demand to stimulate industrial production. In any case our industrial problems were so deep-seated that some fundamental restructuring was necessary.*

The NEC, *therefore, continued to press its alternative strategy on the Chancellor. This laid increasing emphasis on the need for selective import controls to give industry a breathing space to rebuild itself. In October the* NEC*'s statement on industrial strategy, 'Labour and Industry', had been put to the Party conference. Geoff Bish's first draft had been softened in tone, but the statement nonetheless declared that the Industry Bill then going through Parliament fell 'very considerably short' of the Party's original proposals and called for further legislation to provide powers to ensure that companies entered into planning agreements. It also stated that the* NEC *was considering a number of ways in which the banks, pension funds and insurance companies could make a greater contribution to industrial investment. The statement was carried overwhelmingly by conference, not a voice being raised against it. Indeed, it was the moderate trade union leader, David Basnett [now General Secretary of the* GMWU*], who moved a parallel composite resolution calling among other things for the planning agreement system to be supported by 'indirect sanctions' of the kind the* NEC *had been calling for. And it was he, too, who in a forceful speech a few weeks later declared that workers and trade unions ought to have a say in the management of pension funds in order to ensure that they were used more effectively to promote social and industrial needs.*

Undeterred Denis Healey pressed ahead with his more orthodox policies. The battle over public expenditure cuts continued in Cabinet in preparation for the Public Expenditure White Paper of February 1976. On industrial policy the Government hurried to bury the last remnants of Bennery. With conference over, it held a tripartite meeting at Chequers of government, unions and CBI *to work out a consensus industrial policy. The result was a new White Paper, 'An Approach to Industrial Strategy' (Cmnd 6315), of which the keynote was collaboration with industry. Though making a token obeisance to the new instruments – the* NEB *and planning agreements – to which the Party conference had attached so much importance, it laid its main emphasis on a sector analysis. Within this framework, ran the argument, both government and industry would adapt their policies to ensure success. It found a willing collaborator in the* TUC. *Despite the bold words of the* TUC*'s* Economic Reviews, *most union leaders were not prepared to enter into an alliance with the Left against the Government, alienated by the Left's hectoring tone.*

Meanwhile the latent discontent in the Health Service had erupted into open war. This was fed from three sources: the consultants' anger over my consultative document on pay beds; the juniors' discontent over pay; and the general low morale, due partly to worry about lack of funds, but above all to frustration at the top-heavy administrative structure Sir Keith Joseph had introduced. The press wove all three issues together to build up a picture of the imminent 'collapse' of the NHS. *When on 7 October the breakaway consultants in the* HCSA *published figures claiming that 300 consultants were preparing to leave the* NHS *for jobs abroad, the press took up the emigration scare with enthusiasm.*

'Patients Put in Peril as Doctors Emigrate,' declared the Daily Mail. *'Scandal of the Sick Health Service,' echoed the* Sun. *Even* The Times *expressed concern. In vain I pointed out that most years some 500 doctors emigrated from Britain and 200 returned and that the figures had been at their worst in 1965. There was some increase in intentions to emigrate, but no one could say whether they would materialize – there had been some falling off since the April pay award. Nonetheless the medical profession seized the opportunity to press its grievances. The BMA renewed its demand for an inquiry into the state of the NHS. Sir Rodney Smith[, President of the Royal College of Surgeons,] declared that the Service was at the 'point of no return'. Opposition spokesmen blamed it all on me, Norman Fowler, a junior 'shadow', denouncing me as 'the midwife of chaos' to a delighted Tory conference.*

At the same time trouble had broken out again among the juniors. As we had agreed, the new contract I had negotiated with them in January had been priced by their own Review Body. But, as I had also warned them, that did not mean that there would necessarily be any extra money available to finance the 'closed contract' for which they had asked. And so it proved. Though the Review Body reluctantly accepted that supplementary payments should start after forty-four hours of work, to replace the extra duty allowances payable after eighty hours, the introduction of pay policy meant that the same amount of money had to be spread over a wider span. As the juniors had had a 30 per cent increase in April, all the Review Body could do was to redistribute the money already available for 'overtime'. They had done so to the best of their ability but, although most juniors were better off as a result, about a third of them suffered the fatal word 'detriment'. In other words, they were actually worse off. Although their own negotiators had grudgingly accepted the report, it was a recipe for conflict. And within days of the report being known, unofficial action on an 'emergencies only' basis had broken out in a number of areas. The BMA hurried in to blame the Government.

Meanwhile the pay beds issue was rumbling on. I believed it was essential to legislate quickly to clear the air and persuaded my colleagues to include the following paragraph in the Queen's Speech of 19 November: 'Legislation will be introduced in the course of the session to phase out private practice from National Health Service hospitals. Consultations will continue on My Government's proposals to strengthen and extend existing powers to regulate nursing homes and hospitals outside the National Health Service.'

The BMA's response was to call on all senior hospital doctors, from consultants downwards, to ban all NHS work except emergencies. Similar action by the juniors was made official at the same time. Some people in the Cabinet began to get cold feet. Harold Wilson schemed with his old friend, Arnold Goodman, to force a compromise.

Wednesday, 8 October. Woke to a major blast of hostile publicity on the NHS. On the eight o'clock news the BBC built up a small unofficial strike by some junior hospital doctors into a vaguely generalized indictment of the state of the NHS (the inference being that I was responsible). The *Daily Telegraph* and other newspapers splashed stories about massive emigration of consultants and warnings of the 'collapse' of the NHS. I soon had the *Evening Standard* and *World at One* on the phone: would I give interviews, etc.? I rang Norman and told him to call an office meeting at 10 am when we would decide our whole strategy. Peter was there, firm in the view that a blitz was being deliberately organized by the profession to coincide with the health debate on Thursday at the Tory conference. He agreed absolutely that I ought to have a press conference that day. David demurred a bit at this, but said it was 'a matter for your political judgment'. My political judgment backed Peter's, and so it was agreed. A mad rush to check up on a whole catalogue of detail and to get my reply off to the BMA to their memo on my consultative document. I suggested that the ostensible purpose of the press conference should be to announce my reply to the BMA memo.

In the event, the conference went well, helped by the fact that I had suddenly realized we ought to have a press statement. Most of the press get things woefully wrong unless they have something written down on which they can draw heavily. This meant I had to spend my lunch hour scribbling out the statement myself, choosing my words carefully about my willingness to discuss the consultative document with the BMA and my invitation to them for talks. 'It's no good telling the BMA that we have already erected the gallows and that all they can do is to discuss the thickness of the rope,' I quipped. So the drafting was tricky: how to suggest they could discuss anything, while not suggesting I was running away on pay beds? Anyway, it seemed to do the trick, foxing the hostile press. Then into a succession of radio and TV interviews – quite like old times.

Thursday, 9 October. Very good press coverage, which has successfully defused Rodney Smith's sour press conference yesterday. It is now clear that I was right and David wrong and that we have drawn the poison out of the situation before Norman Fowler can get to his feet at the Tory conference. At Cabinet Bob Mellish was ecstatic about my handling of the attacks. 'That "keep cool" line of yours is first-class.' He has the political nous to realize that all this outcry has been organized, but whether Harold will is another matter. He has asked for a full report. Of course, the right-wing press is using the occasion to call for me to be sacked and I know this campaign will be redoubled as the days go by. The *Mirror*, bless 'em, have got a first-class leader in my support. So I must just fight back with everything I've got.

Saturday, 11 October. The papers are full of Margaret Thatcher's triumph at the Tory conference yesterday. I was struck by how blooming she looked after what must have been a week of intense strain: the vitamin of power again. Success in politics does as much for a woman's looks as falling in love. It *is* falling in love – with success and power.

Monday, 13 October. The *Observer* had an interview with Margaret Thatcher yesterday in which she suggested that she managed to cope with all domestic chores herself, as well as do her political work. 'At weekends I cook and do some housework because there is no one else to do it,' she told Kenneth Harris. Sorry, but I don't believe it. Okay, she's not a Minister now, but she *is* Leader of the Opposition, and the amount of reading she must have to do is enormous. Or doesn't she? Because I find that I just can't fit in regular domestic work. Cooking is a special-occasion luxury that I do about six times a year. For the rest, it is done by Eileen, and very well, too. As for housework, it's fun. Nothing more satisfying than a good spring-clean. I'm positively longing to resign so that I can turn out Mother's storage shed. But when I have work to do at the level I have – and presumably Margaret has – it is quite impossible to do one's own chores. Shopping becomes one of the great unattainables.

First office meeting this morning was on the junior doctors. The *Daily Telegraph* has been excelling itself again, talking about my 'crude blackmail'. Since I have merely been carrying out the Government's pay policy, which Michael has refused to modify to give the juniors a bit more money, I find this a bit much. Unless I can budge Michael I think we face a long spate of official industrial action, which will, of course, be blamed on me and my 'tactless' way of handling things. I have had about enough and am determined to fight for my own hand. When David suggested that we draft a letter to Mike, setting out the situation objectively and suggesting that as I was carrying out Government policy the Chancellor and Mike ought to make this clear, I said this was not good enough. I said firmly that I would write to Mike, asking that we accept a 'no detriment' clause. 'Then,' I said acidly, 'if he refuses we can leak that Barbara was overruled by Cabinet.' David looked shocked at this, but I know that both Jack and Norman think that the dead-set which the press is now making at me must be taken seriously.

In fact, it is interesting to note that even David now realizes there is a press conspiracy against me which is getting out of hand. I have spent some time this weekend reading the long 'consultative document' on future health and personal social services planning, on which David has spent a lot of time. David has been all for our taking a tough, realistic line about the 'restraints' on expenditure that lie ahead, arguing that people will only respect us if we tell them the truth. The succession of distorted and viciously hostile stories with which the *Daily Telegraph* has been leading all the past week has shaken this simple faith. He even volunteered this morning that he thought our letter to RHAS on the capital allocations for hospital-building in the next few years (drawn up inevitably on the most pessimistic assumptions) ought not to go out in the present hysterical atmosphere. So I chalk up victory number one. David even said to me this morning that he thought we ought to hold up his precious consultative document. I was grateful for David's sudden access of political realism. 'What do you think the Tory press would make of some of your phrases?' I asked him. 'Like "medical benefits might fall"?' He agreed gloomily.

David has obviously been particularly shaken by the *Daily Mail* and *Daily Express* splashes today: 'Axe to fall on hospitals' and 'Hospitals Face Cash Swop Crisis'. Someone has obviously leaked the, as yet unpublished, report of the working party he set up to discuss the reallocation of resources to the needier areas.[1] But, once again, it has been turned into a personal attack on me. 'Social Services Secretary Barbara Castle is about to deal another hammer blow to morale in the NHS,' said the *Express*. I think David suddenly felt, as I did, that the British press would again kill the hope of intelligent decisions in our democracy. He insisted we must rush out a press reply at once and only

[1] This was one of David's most important contributions to the work of the Department. The Resources Allocation Working Party [RAWP], manned by civil servants, NHS administrators and medical academics, was set up in May 1975 to secure a fairer distribution of NHS capital and revenue resources among RHAS, AHAS and districts. David had long argued that the NHS had failed to iron out the wide discrepancies in health care between different parts of the country and was determined to get a new system of allocation related to need. RAWP's first interim report, published in August 1975, became the basis of the new policy and caused an outcry from the richer areas.

smiled ruefully when I said, 'Henceforth I am going to deal with our NHS problems politically. No more nobility for me. This open government lark is a catastrophe.' Norman nodded approvingly.

We spent most of the ministerial lunch discussing how we could hit back. Jack reported that Ian Wrigglesworth, Roy Jenkins's PPS, is anxious to table an Early Day Motion supporting me. Would we draft one for him? We drafted it and sent Jack Ashley off to collect the maximum number of signatures. In the lobby a lot of our people made friendly noises to me.

Our last office meeting of the day was on (three guesses!) PESC: this time the discovery by Treasury that they will need cuts of £5 billion, not £2 billion or £3 billion, to get any reduction of the borrowing requirement. Philip, Dick Bourton, Errington, Nick Jordan-Moss, David, Brian O'Malley, Michael Meacher and I met in my room as at a wake. The reason for the change in the calculation is that Treasury has overlooked the increase in the interest on the national debt, which arises (1) from the increase in the borrowing requirement and (2) from the fact that our very success in counter-inflation policy puts up the *rate* of interest in real terms. Can you beat it? As I put it, 'Our success in defeating inflation creates the need for more deflation.' Officials just smiled nervously. I held forth passionately. This had been my experience throughout the ages of my ministerial responsibility. Whatever one proposed – or did – was inflationary and had to be curbed. I saw Nick Jordan-Moss almost grinning his agreement. (As a former Treasury man he ought to know.) 'The only thing to do', I concluded, 'is to fly by the seat of one's political pants. Send for my abacus.' Brian said that if anyone tried to change the pension calculations from the historical method to the forecasting one, they could count without him. David merely looked gloomy.

I challenged Philip and Dick Bourton to produce the document now being circulated by Treasury outlining their proposals for £1,000 million more cuts. First they maintained they hadn't seen it, second that it wouldn't affect us anyway. 'We understand that nothing more is being asked from this Department.' 'Then where is it coming from?' I asked. 'Housing,' they began, but got such a groan from Brian that they stopped short. 'We really don't know, Secretary of State,' they said lamely. I replied that all this was no consolation for me. If nearly £500 million was to be asked from the health and personal social services under the across-the-board 'formula' procedure to help reach £3 billion cuts, I would be told I was damn lucky to get away with this when the total target went up to £5 billion. 'And I just won't accept the formula cuts,' I said firmly.[1] Philip and Dick wriggled and then Philip added, 'I sympathize, of course, Secretary of State, and of course we must defend our Departmental interest. But I must say to you that I have come to the conclusion that we shall have to accept the formula cuts.' So the whole exercise of trying to get real priorities in spending cuts will, if officials have their way, become a pantomine. I have never had any doubts that three-quarters of my officials have been half-

[1] The Chancellor's proposal, first outlined to Cabinet in May, was that savings of £3 billion should be identified for 1978–79, out of which a selection should be made to achieve a saving of £2 billion. Cuts would also have to be made in 1977–78. As a starting point he proposed a formula for across-the-board cuts of 5 per cent and 10 per cent in revenue and 15 per cent and 20 per cent in capital for 1977–78 and 1978–79 respectively. These would apply to goods and services but not to social security. As this would not give him the total he required, further savings of £1½ billion would have to be negotiated with Ministers on a more selective basis.

hearted in their defence of our services against cuts. But they had the grace to look ashamed when I said, 'How could the Treasury lose £3 billion? And how can anyone have any faith in their accountancy after this?'

As we broke up I told Philip that I wanted to see a copy of the new secret Treasury document right away. He pretended to agree but added, 'If we can get hold of it. There is really nothing to get hold of till the Chancellor has formed a view on it.' As we went through the division lobby that evening David said to me, 'I'm afraid that public expenditure has got completely out of control.' I don't agree with him. I think that it is the *reductions* in public expenditure that have got completely out of political control. The whole stage is being set for the most massive deflation in our history. Later, when Norman arrived with a couple of boxes, he confirmed my view. Barely maintaining the pretence of Civil Service objectivity, he told me, 'I must say the behaviour of some top civil servants over this is incredible.' I am convinced that Dick Bourton had a copy of the new Treasury document on his lap all the time he was talking to me. Officials have made up their minds about the cuts and are trying to get Ministers to carry the can. When I said I must see the document Norman replied, 'I am doing a note of this meeting which will say you demanded this forthwith.' Later over food Brian and I agreed we would resign together over this if necessary. 'In the end things become very simple,' said Brian. 'It is merely a question of whether we want to do a Philip Snowden.'

Tuesday, 14 October. The most important part of the day was the private dinner at the Gay Hussar with the health unions to discuss our progress on pay beds and other things. Victor had done his stuff in that charming upstairs room of his, all draped with Hungarian embroidery – as cosy as a peasant sitting room. Alan Fisher, Geoffrey Drain and Peter Jacques were there. Audrey Prime should have come, but it turned out that she had been laid out with flu. So Jack, Brian O'Malley, David and I outnumbered them. With the latest IRA outrages filling the press, I said cheerfully at one point, 'This place should be the next target for a bomb.' The Community Land Bill was going through the House, so we had been lucky to be allowed to pair at all, and at one point yesterday Norman had said to me, 'If your Whip won't pair you we will have to switch it to Lockets.' And lo and behold, Lockets was the target for an IRA bomb last night! Such is the precariousness of London life these days. This time it was the TUC's turn to stand the treat and they had ordered an excellent meal.

It was one of those discursive discussions out of which certain hard points of importance suddenly crystallize. And so we found ourselves getting down first to the nitty gritty of the 'participative management' exercise in the NHS which excites me so much. I was delighted to find that Alan and Geoffrey, far from entering stiff union caveats on this experiment, shared my excitement over its potentialities. They were all for my setting up the press conference on it which officials had tried to stop. On pay beds they once again confirmed their support for my policy of licensing; despite David's secret doubts about my proposals, he had to listen to their enthusiastic adoption of the idea. I seized the opportunity to sound them out about their attitude to the junior doctors' pay. What worried me, I said, was that my officials and the juniors' representatives had got themselves into the situation in which they were going to make one-third of the juniors worse off under the new contract. It was ridiculous not to expect the juniors to fight for the sacred principle of 'no detriment'. On the other hand, we could only ensure no one was worse off under the new contract if we made some extra money available. And this would contravene pay policy. Would the unions stand by us if it came to a strike over this? Alan went into one of his excited spins, saying that of course we must ensure 'no detriment', but Peter Jacques shook his head. He thought the one thing the TUC would demand was that there must be no breach of the pay policy. After all, lots of people had had to postpone restructuring agreements. The juniors ought to postpone their new contract till next April, when more money would be available. I asked him to contact Len Murray and let us know his views.

Wednesday, 15 October. Jack told me Peter Jacques had phoned to say that Len's deputy, whom he had consulted in Len's absence, had said, 'No extra money for the juniors. The TUC would consider this a breach of pay policy.' I told my chaps that it was essential that this should be seen to have been imposed on me by the Department of Employment, so we sent off the letter to Mike, warning him that industrial action was likely on a large scale and asking him to agree to a compromise. The press is continuing its hysterical campaign against me. Never have they carried so many stories about 'crisis' in the NHS and everything is grist to their mill. David is more convinced than ever that we have got to lie low about cuts for a bit.

Thursday, 16 October. Mike has sent me one of his charming letters, saying he's awfully sorry but he can't budge over the juniors' pay. In view of the TUC line I must accept that this is right, but I am furious that we (and the juniors' representatives) have allowed ourselves to drift into the position where we are nailing our colours to fighting for the impossible principle of making some people worse off. This is what comes of delegating detailed negotiations to officials – as pressure of work compels one to do. They just are not trained to foresee political storms. I keep telling them they must find a way of providing 'no detriment' within the available money, while not abandoning the introduction of the new contract for the rest. They keep saying it is impossible, but I refuse to believe it is.

[At Cabinet] Harold called on me to report on the position in the NHS. He has been nibbling at the idea of an independent inquiry for some days and had asked me to circulate a paper setting out the pros and cons. I have come increasingly to the conclusion that we shall never get any sense out of the medical profession until we get this obsession of theirs about an inquiry out of the way, though I am fully alive to the danger that the consultants will try to get the pay beds issue referred to it and *that* I am determined to prevent. So I had set out a purely neutral paper, but at an office meeting yesterday my lads and I agreed that the balance of advantage lay in setting up an inquiry. Not the least of our reasons was that the juniors who are now taking industrial action are giving this as one of their aims. Even David, who has been against an inquiry up to now, said he had reluctantly come to accept that it was unavoidable. 'Your political judgment, Barbara, led you always to keep this option open and you have been proved right.'

I told Cabinet that we faced a major industrial dispute with the juniors over pay policy and I wasn't going to oppose Mike on his interpretation of it. An inquiry might help marginally to improve their mood – at the very least it would take away an alibi. But we must stand firm against referring pay beds to it. And one thing I did ask: that it should be made quite clear to the juniors that I was merely operating Government pay policy and I hoped other Ministers would associate themselves with me over this. Of course, Denis was very nervous about the whole idea of an inquiry, seeing it as a potential pressure group for a bigger share of resources of the NHS (which is just what I hope it will become: this is my main reason for wanting it). Tony [Crosland] inevitably opposed the whole idea, while Harold Lever typically wanted to refer the pay beds issue to it – or, at the very least, my proposals for licensing, which clearly terrify him. (He is terrified of every socialist bit of our policy, from getting rid of direct grant schools to the Community Land Bill.) But the PM successfully steered the decision the way he wanted, overcoming all the doubts by saying that a small group of us (including himself, Denis, Mike and me) should meet immediately after lunch to agree the terms of reference, the ones I proposed having been roundly denounced by Denis as holding out the prospect of pressure for more money. The reason for the rush was that I had told Cabinet I was meeting the juniors that afternoon at their request and Harold wanted me to tell them about the inquiry in confidence before he announced it later that day. In this way he hoped my meeting would be easier.

Cabinet over, I grabbed coffee and biscuits before summoning my officials to my room in the House. We agreed that at the coming meeting on the terms of reference I should stick as closely as possible to those I had already worked out: 'To examine the financial and manpower resources of the NHS, their use and management.' But when the small Cabinet group met in Harold's room at 2 pm Denis was obdurate. He wasn't going to have anyone looking into the 'resources' of the NHS. That was entirely a matter for the Government. We had a tough battle and eventually I emerged with a forms of words which David agreed was not too bad. It means that the inquiry can look at almost anything except pay beds. I had made it clear to Harold I wouldn't stand for that and he agreed to say in his statement that we should proceed to implement our Manifesto commitment on pay beds as soon as parliamentary time was available. (The battle over parliamentary time has still to come.)

Back for the juniors' meeting at 4 pm. There were three representatives of the junior doctors – Dr Bell, Dr Ford and Dr Mander – but they were firmly led by Grabham, as Chairman of the BMA Central Committee for Hospital Medical Services, the tough egg I have had trouble with before. And, of course, there was the ubiquitous Stevenson. We met in the little ministerial conference room at the House. Grabham was succinct: the BMA, he said, backed the juniors in their claim for extra money to enable us to operate the principle of 'no detriment'. The situation was so serious they thought they should see me and find out what the Government was prepared to do to resolve the dispute. I spoke gravely, firmly. Any extra money would mean a breach of the pay policy. It wasn't Barbara Castle picking on the juniors. Cabinet had felt obliged to reaffirm that view, whatever the consequences. Grabham, who manages to make all his remarks sound politely insolent, said that they were not surprised.

It really hadn't required the Secretary of State's 'eloquence'. I kept my temper and turned to the juniors (who had sat in respectful silence while their masters spoke), deliberately bringing them in. Dr Ford, who is clearly desperately anxious for a settlement, merely said that, though he himself could accept my arguments, I had to realize they couldn't carry their grassroots with them. 'We shall be repudiated,' he said. Bell echoed this: 'This will be the end of us.' 'Well, then,' I said, 'if you are going to be finished anyway, why not go down fighting?' Grabham intervened, obviously annoyed at the rapport which was building up between me and the juniors. They would like the opportunity of discussing what I had said among themselves. I agreed at once. He then added, as insolently as ever, that he must ask that no press statement or comment should be made by me pending their decision on what I had said. Again, I agreed, despite Peter Brown's signals of alarm. As we broke up and they prepared to return to BMA House to report back, Dr Bell turned and said to me, 'Here's one who will go down fighting.'

But I wasn't out of the rough. True to Harold's instructions that I could – and should – give the juniors advance notice of the statement he was preparing to make on the independent inquiry that night, I had thrown this into the discussion. In the event, the juniors did not seem interested, but Grabham and Stevenson had pricked up their ears immediately. 'May I ask', said Grabham, 'whether the inquiry will deal with the issue of pay beds?' I had to think quickly. Realizing that, if I hesitated on this at all, the hounds would move in, I said 'No', firmly. No reaction from Grabham at that stage, but, as we broke up, he and Stevenson asked if they could have a few moments with me privately. Grabham at once proceeded to warn me that, if the Government were to go ahead with setting up the inquiry without agreeing to refer the issue of pay beds to it, there would be 'confrontation'. That was the last thing they wanted. Indeed, they would be prepared to co-operate fully with the Government if I would be prepared to do something which he knew would be difficult for me. He was asking a sacrifice: that I should agree to postpone the phasing out of pay beds for two years while the Royal Commission looked at it. (And until, hopefully from his point of view, there would be a Tory Government, I thought to myself.) I told him he really was asking the impossible, whereupon he demanded to see the PM before any announcement was made, while Derek Stevenson started squeaking his indignation. I said that of course I would convey their request to the PM at once and let them know. At last they agreed to take the juniors away and discuss what I had thought was the key issue of the moment, the juniors' dispute.

Back in my room, I had the job of trying to contact the PM. When Harold came to the phone I was relieved to find he was quite relaxed. I hardly had to do any stiffening. It would, he said, be quite wrong for him to consult anyone about the setting up of a Royal Commission, which was entirely within the Queen's prerogative. But I kicked myself for having mentioned the Royal Commission to the BMA at all. Next, Norman, David and I worked on the wording of the PM's announcement, which was eventually got out at 6.30 pm. Norman waited till it was safely out before phoning Stevenson with the PM's reply. Apparently he took it fairly calmly. The bit about the Queen's prerogative had done the trick. But when Norman went on to ask him where was the statement on the juniors' dispute which we had been promised and were waiting to see, Stevenson coolly informed him that they were just about to issue it! Norman's icy anger was a joy to listen to. He said he found it 'incredible' that, when we were holding up a statement of our own at their request in order to hear their decision, the BMA should proceed to issue its own statement without even informing us. ('Typical,' Peter Brown would say.) Apparently Stevenson blustered a bit and finally read the juniors' statement to Norman over the phone. It ran as follows:

'The leaders of the Hospital Junior Staff have considered the proposal of Mrs Castle on recent unrest over the junior contract. While they do not accept the Government's interpretation of the pay policy as applied to this new contract, they accept that there are overriding national issues at stake. They have decided therefore that the opinion of the juniors should be obtained by ballot. This will be done as quickly as possible. There will be a meeting of the Hospital Junior Staffs Committee to consider the results as soon as they are available.'

Not too bad at all. Ford and Bell are clearly doing their best for us, though we learned that Mander had walked out and resigned. David and I then had to work on my own statement and rush it out.

Sunday, 19 October. Ted Short has done his stuff wonderfully on my behalf. He was particularly nice to me at Thursday's Cabinet, saying I was having a rotten time over the doctors and a shocking deal from the press, but adding affectionately, 'You are at your best when you are under attack.' Then on Friday his office phoned to say he wanted to make a speech in my support over the weekend and sent round the draft of a searing attack on my critics. Norman said he thought it was a splendid draft and we ought to encourage it. It has come over very well in the press.

There was not much rest this weekend. This morning I had to go up to London to appear on Peter Jay's programme, *Weekend World*, the office having advised that I must not miss this opportunity to counter the hysteria about the NHS which has been built up.

Monday, 20 October. The PM's statement on the Royal Commission on the Health Service. I had spent a lot of time making sure Harold didn't give anything away. In the end, typically, he leaned over backwards to stress the 'importance' of private practice. It is the classic mistake he makes of being unable to distinguish between the need to yield on points of material interest to his critics without throwing the philosophical baby out with the practical bathwater. So we had to have a great piece in the statement about the Royal Commission being able to discuss the 'borderline' between private practice and the NHS (whatever that may mean). However, it might have been much worse and I have drilled into Harold that he mustn't yield an inch on the need to legislate on pay beds concurrently with the setting up of the Royal Commission. The BMA are still fighting back and insisting on their right to see the PM. So this has been fixed for tomorrow. But I am delighted to see that NUPE, without any prompting from me, has written to the PM to stiffen him. They have asked for the right to see him too. And why not? But I doubt Harold will agree.

Tuesday, 21 October. Meeting with the regional health authorities chairmen, who are panicking at all the talk of reorganizing the NHS. They tell me that morale is so low at the prospect of our getting rid of the regional (or some other) tier that the health authorities just can't recruit key staff. It is obvious that I shall have to reassure them, otherwise the work of the NHS threatens to snarl up: the way of the reformer is hard! So I promised I would try to include a form of words in my speech in the NHS debate next Monday that would allay the sense of uncertainty (though I am still determined to keep open my options for evolutionary reform). The debate is the latest expression of the 'crisis in the NHS' hysteria the Tories are building up. They have tabled a Motion to reduce my salary and excelled themselves by asking, not just for the token cut that convention requires, but for a cut of 50 per cent. I am honoured by this precedent!

But the highlight of the day was the PM's meeting with the BMA on the Royal Commission. As there was a running three-line whip the meeting had to be in the PM's room in the House, which meant we sat intimately close to our adversaries. Harold had summoned all the Secretaries of State concerned: Scotland, Wales and Northern Ireland as well as me. It proved the best break I've had for a long time. Grabham led the comparatively small but stern-looking contingent from the BMA and proceeded to lecture us severely. He told us the CCHMS had met yesterday. 'Attitudes are hardening.' They deplored the Government's decision to act on part of the remit of the Royal Commission before it had reported. If the Government phased out pay beds it would be breaking the undertaking on the basis of which many medical men had entered the service of the NHS. Successive governments had been paying less and less attention to the views of the medical profession: Sir Keith Joseph on reorganization, for instance. The result was a fall in morale and goodwill. The timetable of the Royal Commission should be adapted to enable it to discuss pay beds; it could always produce an interim report. 'We will resist actively any unfair legislation. The profession is absolutely determined to resist what they see as an attack on their independence.'

After this tirade my ministerial colleagues could hardly contain themselves. John Morris leaned forward and said sweetly, 'I must say I am very puzzled. There are only a handful of pay beds in Wales and I have never heard the profession say they felt they had lost their independence.' Merlyn [Rees] echoed this for Northern Ireland, while Willie [Ross] gave one of his rather opaque pontifications out of which it emerged that the medical profession in Scotland had the highest standards of them all and Scotland had only a couple of hundred pay beds. Grabham looked a bit discomfited, but at that moment the division bell rang. As we went through the lobbies my three colleagues were whistling their astonishment. What an appalling man! They couldn't believe their ears. Now they realized what I was up against. As for Joel, who had also been there, he put his arm round me commiseratingly. 'Having heard that, I must say to you, "All is forgiven." Now I understand.' I suddenly realized, to my relief, that their having been there that day meant that the atmosphere in Cabinet on the pay beds issue would be transformed.

Back in Harold's crowded room, Grabham was sitting in ramrod righteousness; Stevenson was scowling. Harold had been stiffened by their attacks rather than intimidated. He told them dismissively that our policy had been set out in the statement he had made to the House. He was not intending to put the matter of pay beds into the hands of the Royal Commission, or hold up legislation. 'Our freedom to legislate remains absolute. This is our policy and I have not heard anything that will cause us to change it.' I could not have put it better myself. After a rather terse agreement to exchange letters, they left. I only hope my colleagues will stand firm when the row breaks – as it will.

During the questioning I extracted one important admission from Grabham. I asked him, 'If, hypothetically, I were to drop the licensing of the private sector, would you drop your objection to our proposals?' 'No,' he replied emphatically.

Thursday, 23 October. I went along to Cabinet determined to get pay beds into the Queen's Speech if it killed me. For some inexplicable reason, Ted Short, Elwyn and the other pundits of the Legislation Committee have refused to move my Bill (the only Bill from my Department for the forthcoming session) up from the Reserve list. All sorts of non-politically urgent Bills (like race relations, police discipline *et al.*) have been given priority over it. They must have gone mad. Of course, I had put in amendments to Short's draft of the Queen's Speech and I geared myself up for a tough fight. Ted was at his most headmasterly, saying he wouldn't put the PLP through the sort of late night misery of the past session again. There were heaven knew how many days to be devoted to the discussion of devolution and there simply would not be time for a major controversial Bill like mine. Even Bob Mellish was unsympathetic, asking at one point what Bill from my Department I would be willing to drop to make way for this. 'This is the only Bill I have got this session,' I retorted. But I only got cheers for that. What saved me was Harold. If Grabham could only have seen how counter-productive his tirades on Tuesday had been! He twisted and turned with the tactical skill he always shows when he is determined to get his own way. This certainly was rather an urgent matter, he said. The unions were holding their people back with difficulty. On the other hand, he realized that Legislation Committee had not been able to give this priority over other Bills. However, there might be a way out. Could we find a form of words that would indicate that the Bill would be *introduced* in this session, but not necessarily passed? For example, could we say that legislation would be introduced 'in the course of the session', which wouldn't commit us to exactly when? I saw at once that this was a gimmick that would play into my hands and accepted it with a show of reluctance. There were more rumblings of protest from Ted and others, but finally Harold summed up that this had been accepted.

I had to hurry back to the office for a meeting of the nursing organizations on the consultative document on pay beds. The best of them were the nurse administrators, who said they were in favour of pay beds being phased out, though they wanted it done in an 'orderly way'. Miss Bidulph even admitted they were in favour of licensing: she merely wanted it to be done by the AHAS, rather than by the Secretary of State, saying that Manchester AHA, of which she is a member, had just refused planning permission for a large proposed private development in Manchester. My eyebrows shot up at this, because, as I told her, they really hadn't power under present legislation to refuse planning permission on any but environmental grounds. Afterwards Raymond told me that the refusal was being challenged in the courts as *ultra vires*. That just proves my point!

This is Philip Rogers's last week. I told Norman I wanted to give him farewell drinks and a present. Tonight all we Ministers assembled in my room, together with a few officials and Norman had thoughtfully invited Philip's wife. I handed Philip a very nice briefcase on our behalf, telling how much we appreciated the way he had loyally backed our policies, even when we knew he thoroughly disagreed with them. 'You have been a fine civil servant,' I told him. I then called on all the Ministers in turn and every one of them spoke warmly and genuinely. Philip was clearly deeply touched, saying, 'I doubt whether, as a good civil servant, I ought to approve of this precedent, but I do.' (Apparently they had never heard of Ministers making a presentation to their Permanent Secretary before.) The other civil servants were tickled pink at our gesture, telling me what a nice chap Philip had been to work for. A very happy and satisfying little interlude.

The IRA bombers have struck again, trying to blow up Hugh Fraser and killing Professor Fairley, the cancer expert, who was passing by. Ted is abroad at his European Parliament again. I've kept the *Evening Standard* cutting to show him, in the hope that at last it will persuade him to lock the boot of the car. With our car having to stand outside in the road at both our homes, we are a sitting target.

Friday, 24 October. David is getting cold feet over pay beds. He came into my room in one of his menacing moods to say he had just sent me a Minute which was for my eyes alone, as he didn't want officials to get any inkling of it. He gave me a great doom-laden warning about the unholy row he thought we were going to face with the medical profession. As I knew, he said, he had never agreed with me over licensing, though he did over phasing out, and he believed my licensing proposals would be the last straw. The only hope was for us to rush a simple short Bill onto the statute book as quickly as possible to do three things: legalize phasing out, fix a date (though he thought we should have to make it 1979), and take a power to control private hospital developments above a certain size. As I replied calmly that of course I would consider this, he began to relax. But the conversation didn't exactly cheer me up: bombers without, tunnellers within and a major censure Motion awaiting me on Monday. It would be lovely to have some allies for a change. But Jack and Norman remain devotees of my policy and my determination not to flinch.

Sunday, 26 October. Before I got down to my NHS speech I typed a reply to David's Minute, determined to get it on the record that I wasn't running amok. I was determined too to emphasize the points on which David had agreed with me, otherwise I could see a great 'split' story leaking into the press. What we must do, I stressed, was to have another private dinner with our TUC friends as quickly as possible and put our problem to them, pointing out that we might lose the legislation altogether for next session if we insisted on the more complicated Bill.

By midnight I was only half-way through preparing my speech, but I felt so wonky I just went to bed. 'To hell with it,' I thought. 'I'll just ad lib.'

Monday, 27 October. In the event I didn't ad lib, but scribbled away at my speech in the car at terrific speed. The words flowed and I got the last bit finished at about 2.45 pm. We raced to the House, picking up sheets of typed speech as we fled, only to find two pages missing when we arrived. They were handed to me in manuscript as I was on my feet! I didn't mind. I knew it was a good, meaty speech and I delivered it with great aplomb, despite my cold. I was enormously helped by a crowded House. Even Harold turned up to support me, which he did vocally. Our lads were there in force, cheering me to the echo. I suddenly realized that the press attacks on me had made me a Party heroine. They *trust* me again. If David thinks he is going to get me to betray that trust, he is wrong. Norman Fowler's opening attack was feeble: he didn't even mention the juniors! I drove him into a corner, to the delight of our own side. As for the Liberals, I slaughtered them. The contemptible Jeremy had joined the pack at the weekend, howling for my blood. Although the Liberals officially support the phasing out of pay beds, he had found an excuse for voting with the Tories by saying I had 'mismanaged' things. I had got Jack to turn me up a reference to Lloyd George's battle with the doctors, and, armed with this, I turned on Jeremy: 'Lloyd George would be ashamed of you!' Delirious applause from our side. I got innumerable congratulations afterwards. I was glad that Harold had heard it. I'm not going to have him thinking he is carrying an embarrassing passenger.

The depths to which the press are sinking was again illustrated by today's *Daily Mail*, which carries a front-page story with banner headline: 'New Health Service Row Breaks: Barbara's Top Men Revolt', which claims that my Permanent Secretary and other top officials are threatening to resign over my pay beds policy. Norman told me Philip was furious and, although on leave, rushed out a scathing denial. Of course that won't stop the *Daily Mail*. But I don't care. Our lads in the House are with me to a man, led by – of all people – Ian Wrigglesworth. He may be Roy Jenkins's PPS, but he is with me all the way on this. He has collected 170 signatures to his Early Day Motion backing me and calling for legislation on pay beds to be included in the Queen's Speech. Of course, we can barely get a mention of this in the press, but I hope it will stiffen David's nerve.

It was a sign of my resilience that I forgot all about Norman's rather worried warning to me earlier today. Just when I was in the middle of checking bits of my speech this morning he came in to me, looking grave. The police had just been on the phone to say that they had received a card saying that I was on the IRA list of Ministers for extermination. Only a few Ministers, the report ran, had received this. Would I take care? For a moment my heart sank; a few minutes later I had forgotten it. Norman Fowler was a far more important enemy. I went to bed happy because I had demolished him and because, despite the defection of the Liberals, the censure Motion was defeated by a majority of twenty.

Tuesday, 28 October. On the whole a very good press. Even Andrew Alexander had ignored the *Mail*'s policy to the extent of saying I had made an 'impressive' speech. But the juniors' dispute continues to be very worrying. The one ray of hope is that the BMA have asked to see me to discuss it. Of course, I have agreed.

Wednesday, 29 October. When the BMA brought the juniors along for the meeting they had requested, it was soon obvious that Lewin and Grabham saw it largely as a formality. Lewin said that they had merely come to discuss principles, not to negotiate details: that was a matter for the Joint Negotiating Committee [JNC]. But under continued pressure from me (and, I suspect, the juniors), he and Grabham reluctantly agreed to bring the JNC along the following day. Tim Nodder had produced a new formula as a result of my insistence that there must be *some* way of redistributing the available money without making anyone worse off. It now appears there is, by phasing the new contract in as juniors change jobs. The new money available next April under pay policy would enable us to complete the process without detriment.

Thursday, 30 October. The main agony in Cabinet was over dental and optical charges. My luck was out because two of my strongest allies, Peter and Shirley, were missing. Harold summed up. 'I very much regret this, but I have no doubt the majority of Cabinet think it must be done.' Ted Short just sat silent. So did Eric and John Silkin. So much for one's allies.

At the resumed meeting with the juniors it was as clear as ever that Grabham was trying to prevent an agreement. *He* doesn't want a settlement while the pay beds row is still in the air. But it was equally clear that Ford and Bell are angry and impatient with the interference of the BMA and are perfectly aware that they are being used for other people's ends. And so they began by admitting that our new proposals were 'an important advance', adding that they would put them to ballot, but that the proposals would not be enough by themselves to swing support. There were all sorts of safeguards in, and interpretations of, the new contract they would want to work out with us. So we settled down for another long session. It was nearly midnight before the principles were agreed. We gave hurried and cagey press conferences at which Ford and Bell played it extremely fair, but at which we all refused to release details, having agreed to finalize the wording of them next day.

All this over, with Stevenson out of the way, David, Jack and I had a relaxed chat with the juniors' representatives which would have astonished the press if they could have listened in at it. These were not the wild, hostile men the newspapers have been trying to make out, full of hatred and resentment of me. These were nice, worried lads who felt their chaps had a grievance, but who hated the industrial action in which they were engaged and wanted a settlement if at all possible. In fact, they even sat plotting with us as to how they could speed up the return of the ballot papers, so that they could be counted and the result announced before the Queen's Speech on 19 November! The last thing they want is to get their dispute mixed up with the consultants' row over pay beds, an issue on which they do not feel strongly. Indeed, one of the healthy things about the juniors' revolt is that they want to break with the system whereby they are exploited as 'juniors' in the hope and expectation that they will be able to exploit others when their turn comes to be consultants. I am more than ever convinced that we must get a better deal for the juniors on the foundation of which we can build a consultants' role which is less high-handed and less exploitatory. The trouble, of course, is that the consultants stand in the way of this just as much as pay policy does.

Monday, 3 November. David Owen is going about glowering these days. I feel he is brewing up some more of his 'I must warn you' private diatribes to me. I find these moods of his very oppressive when, above all else, I am longing for some moral support against the ceaseless attacks made on me in the press.

Wednesday, 5 November. Because of the three-line whip on the Lords' amendments to the Petroleum and Submarine Pipelines Bill (damn the Lords!), we had to have our dinner with the unions on the bell. Since Lockets' private room was engaged, we tried Old Russia, which is very pleasant except for the gloomy lighting. In the sepulchral shades of a quiet corner of the room we had one of our relaxed but frank talks. My insistence on these private meetings has paid enormous dividends because we have built up confidence in each other and can genuinely reveal how far each of us can go. Peter Jacques, Audrey Prime, Geoffrey Drain and Alan were all there – and, of course, Brian A–S., David and Jack. Peter began by telling us that he had been putting the Social Insurance Committee of the TUC in the picture on our pay beds problems and they fully realized our difficulties. They would therefore reluctantly accept the shorter Bill, much as they would have preferred the whole consultative document. But they insisted that all pay beds must be phased out within a year and that the licensing should include an overall limit on the size of the private sector as a whole. David took all this very meekly.

Over drinks before the meal I had casually raised the question of the chairmanship of the Royal Commission on the Health Service. Had they any suggestions? To my surprise, Audrey said enthusiastically, 'Yes, Merrison.' [Dr Alexander Merrison, Vice-Chancellor of Bristol University.] David and I were rather taken aback, but as she had served with him on the Merrison Committee,[1] she was in a better position than any of us to judge his attitude to the NHS and the things in which we believe. She was emphatic that he was a dedicated supporter of the NHS and she was sure he would have no truck with private financing and all that nonsense. David and I agreed afterwards that this made Merrison a very serious contender for the job.

Monday, 10 November. Wasily Sakalo, the wild Australian who is stirring it up among junior doctors in the North-West, has excelled himself. The papers are full of his weekend declaration: 'Blame Castle if Patients Die.' I think this beats anything they said about Nye. The juniors are all set to step up their industrial action. The tragedy is that waiting lists grow longer and the level of

[1] Dr A. W. Merrison was appointed by Sir Keith Joseph in 1973 to chair the Committee of Inquiry into the Regulation of the Medical Profession, following a dispute between doctors and the General Medical Council over the introduction of an annual registration fee. The Committee reported in April 1975. (Cmnd 6018.) Dr Merrison was knighted in 1976.

service in the NHS declines, just as the shortage of money makes it imperative that we use every penny we've got to best effect. One consolation: David is in one of his sunny moods again. Perhaps that dinner with the trade union boys last week had its effect. Anyway, it is a great relief. David's alternations of gloom and charm can be a strain.

Tuesday, 11 November. An office discussion on PESC. This is now shaping up to its familiar misery. Only this time it is even worse. Denis has circulated a memo setting out what he claims is the economic case for the biggest cuts he has yet asked for. My trouble is that I am determined to defend the NHS at all costs, but under the PESC formula that is being considered under the Chancellor's initiative all the normal programmes would have 'formula cuts' allocated to them, *i.e.* an across-the-board cut of 10 per cent in current and 15 per cent in capital expenditure by 1978–79. This would be disastrous for the NHS. Yet the formula cuts would only produce a saving of £2 billion and Denis wants a lot, lot more. His memo includes an 'illustrative list' of extra cuts necessary to give him the total figure he says he needs beyond 1976 and in it he calls for savings of over £600 million in social security, some £500 million of which he suggests should come from abandoning the 'historical' method of uprating pensions. He justifies this on the grounds that such a method, reflecting past inflation, would be too generous to pensioners 'at a time of *declining* inflation'. If I resist this he will be down on the NHS like a ton of Irish bricks. I realize that.

The only way to save the NHS from this disaster (if Cabinet agrees the Chancellor's cuts, as they will) is for me to accept the £500 million saving on the social security side by switching from the historical to the forecasting method at the next uprating. All this I had to spell out at the office meeting without exactly advocating it, while Brian O'Malley sat tense, suddenly bursting out and saying that as far as he was concerned that was totally unacceptable. 'I'm not prepared to do the pensioners out of another pound a week, to which they are entitled under the method the Treasury has always insisted on. Someone else can do that: I won't.' I listened sympathetically and handled him gently, thinking to myself that we could leave the Jack Joneses of the trade union movement to battle for the pensioners. My problem is that there is no one battling for the NHS. After an hour of this I sent Brian A–S. away to prepare all sorts of defensive briefing for the PESC row. We can make a strong case for the NHS on the basis of demographic factors, the exceptional age of so many NHS buildings, the fact that it has never had its fair share of resources, and so on. But I know perfectly well that all this finessing is wasted when the public expenditure chips are down. It is only political muscle that counts. My one weapon is that I am totally determined not to accept absolute cuts in the NHS – and it is hardly an issue on which the Government could survive my resignation.

Thursday, 13 November. The opening round of the real PESC agony in Cabinet: the first trial of strength with the Chancellor in his bid for the global sum of £3¾ billion. Denis opened with his now familiar analysis. We *must* achieve a balance in our payments by 1978, otherwise the burden of debt interest would wipe out the gains from North Sea oil and gas. It would be a 'recipe for disaster' to accept Tony C.'s proposal for cuts of only £2 billion, with another £500 million of cuts 'kept on the shelf'. Harold summed up that there was a 'very slight' majority in favour of the £3¾ billion. Eric kept whispering to me that he thought Denis would have resigned if he had been beaten. What interested me was how close a thing it had been. 'My guess is that in the end the Chancellor will settle for £3 billion,' said Tony C. contentedly to me afterwards. I left Cabinet, feeling like a wet rag, to prepare for my meeting with the BMA on pay beds.

The deputation from the BMA was led by Walpole Lewin and Rodney Smith. The only basis on which they had agreed to come was that there should be 'no preconditions' and, in welcoming them, I repeated this and invited them to give me their uninhibited views on the consultative document. A united hostile chorus then assailed me. Lewin declared that the phasing out of pay beds was not in the interests of the NHS and was a breach of the understanding the profession had had with successive governments. The licensing proposals threatened their independence. In certain areas it would be impossible to put in private specialized equipment. Private practice kept consultants working in ordinary District General Hospitals. 'We still hope you will reappraise your document,' he concluded. Sir Rodney, in that unctuous way of his, said that the Royal Colleges 'should not take part in detailed negotiations'. They were only concerned with standards of patient care, which they believed would suffer if pay beds went. Bolt, another surgeon, put his case more reasonably than most of them. He was concerned with the nitty gritty of the consultants' interests. If pay beds went, many consultants would not be able to do any private practice at all and would simply emigrate. All this was echoed by Simmons of the HCSA, Allen of the dentists, Gilmore of the juniors and Damerell of the Independent Hospitals Group. It was unanimous and I realized what a united front I was up against.

In reply, I nailed the canard that phasing out was a breach of the understanding on which they had agreed to co-operate with Nye's NHS. I reminded them gently that the profession had continued to oppose Nye long after this concession had been made by him and that they had only been won over to accepting Nye's plans (and then only grudgingly) by his legislative undertaking that doctors would be able to combine private practice with work for the NHS. That I was prepared to reaffirm in my Bill. I also told them that my proposals on licensing had been intended to safeguard the right to private practice by ensuring that private facilities would have an even geographical spread. They were merely put forward as a basis for discussion. If they preferred it, I would be prepared to consider a free-for-all, with total separation of all private facilities from the NHS and no licensing of the private sector. Stevenson bridled at this and said they were not prepared to discuss licensing at all, because they were opposed to the whole principle of phasing out. Was I in effect saying that this was not negotiable? In fact, of course, I was, but I merely said that I could not anticipate the Queen's Speech. I would report to my colleagues what they had said. Could we not meet again when the contents of the Queen's Speech were known? They agreed to that, but obviously had second thoughts afterwards, because Stevenson rushed me a letter saying that their acceptance of another meeting must be dependent on the contents of the Queen's Speech.

An epoch of total non-cooperation lies ahead.

The juniors' industrial action, though still unofficial, is becoming more widespread and more dangerous. Ironically, it is led by the lads in the North-West where that wild Australian, Wasily Sakalo, is waving his bush hat about and denouncing me as the villain of the piece. I have had a visit from the panic-stricken Regional Medical Officer of the North-West, who begged to see me to warn me he faced the closure of the NHS in certain areas. The juniors' action, he said, was being fuelled by the consultants, who would 'go to any lengths' in opposing the phasing out of pay beds. Although I discounted some of this, his picture was sufficiently gloomy to be very worrying. Some days ago I had suggested to my officials that I ought to go to Blackburn to see the juniors there, as my constituents. I ought to be able to dispel *some* of the myths that were circulating. Henry looked a bit dubious at first, but the regional chap jumped at it. And so it has been arranged.

Friday, 14 November. My meeting with the Blackburn juniors has escalated into a major meeting with all the leaders in the North-West. So Blackburn Royal Infirmary was seething with excitement when I arrived. First, I went into a cosy confab with the leaders, all of us crowded together in a small room. Dr Torry and the Blackburn lads turned out to be courteous and a little abashed, but Sakalo was there in full voice, interrupting, refusing to listen and only interested in denouncing me. With all the persuasiveness at my command, I explained why the Government could not breach the pay policy: we were not just picking on the juniors. I think I was having some effect on them, so Sakalo jumped up shouting and stalked out. But he bobbed up again at the larger meeting we had arranged with all the juniors at the hospital who could get to it. It was a rowdy affair; Sakalo kept up a running hostile commentary. 'When are you going to stop exploiting the juniors?' he shouted, and at last I told him to shut up.

Then into a press conference, where I was asked whether the whole visit had not been, in Sakalo's words, a 'waste of time'. I rejected this and went through the whole argument again gently and patiently. Just as we were getting ready to leave for our plane we heard that Heathrow had been shut down by fog. So we faced another long, weary trek home by train and it was late when I got back to HCF. But I was not dispirited. I remain firmly convinced that the only answer to these situations is to try by every means at one's disposal to get through to the grassroots and I was sure that some of the things I said would stick. Dr Torry's moderate comment to the press afterwards confirmed this view.

The search for a chairman of the Royal Commission on the NHS continues fruitlessly. Harold is playing with the idea of a judge. He would. The BMA is pressing this too. The office has put up some names. David and Jack have been checking them and they are all terrible. It is essential I get this right, for the Royal Commission will be my last legacy to the NHS.

Saturday, 15 November. My 'weekend off', which Norman had carefully arranged for me so that I could enjoy a 'prorogation break', continues to be punctuated by Departmental interruptions – and by rain. Impossible to go out and plant any bulbs. And the breakaway Junior Hospital Doctors Association has given a press conference, issuing an ultimatum to me demanding that I see them and negotiate premium overtime rates for everything over forty hours, or else they will move on to a forty-hour week, whatever happened to patients. And they claim that is within the pay policy! (Incidentally, they say the BMA ballot is 'rigged', so they will ignore the results.)

Monday, 17 November. Jack phoned with bad news about the BMA juniors' ballot. Of the 14,000 juniors (out of 20,000) who have answered the questionnaire, 7,000 have voted for industrial action and 5,000 against. Still only a third of all the juniors, but, nonetheless, a majority of those voting on this point. He read over a draft of a statement he had prepared for me and I told him it was too panicky. He said, 'Hell Corner Farm must be doing you good.' I groaned, thinking of the mud and the still unplanted bulbs. Anyway, I stiffened his statement a bit.

Tuesday, 18 November. Up to London again to face the blitz from the juniors. I had told Norman on the phone that I thought I ought to try and see them (through the BMA) today, before the pay beds decision is announced in the Queen's Speech. I want to get the BMA committed on the juniors before the consultants can use pay beds to confuse the issue. But the earliest the BMA are prepared to meet me is Thursday. Well, that lets me off the hook on the question of whether I am treating this as a matter of urgency. Norman and I also agreed that we had better ask Mike himself to come along. After all, the juniors keep challenging me on our interpretation of the pay policy and he is interpreter-in-chief of that policy.

No time to eat any lunch before I go to the 2.30 pm Cabinet. Why we should have one at this odd hour is due to the fact that Harold has been away at Rambouillet, taking part in a summit conference, and has only just got back. He reported with relish on the ensuing Declaration,[1] which he claimed as a success for us because we had encouraged the Americans to be expansionist. But the price has obviously been that we have committed ourselves against 'general' import controls, merely reserving our position on 'selective' ones – under what will clearly be highly restrictive criteria.

Hurried back to the office to plot the meeting with the BMA. What is interesting is that the juniors are beginning to lose the sympathy of the press. The decision taken yesterday by the breakaway Junior Hospital Doctors Association to start industrial action in ten days' time, unless I come up with a better overtime offer, has clearly shocked the press into examining the whole position more carefully. The *Evening Standard*'s leader tonight opens with the following significant words: 'The junior hospital doctors are now overstepping the limits of public sympathy' – though, of course, it goes on to say that the phasing out of pay beds would make matters worse. Typically, the *Evening News* manages to blame it all on me: 'There is a growing impression that Mrs

[1] The leaders of Britain, France, Germany, Italy, Japan and the United States had been meeting at Rambouillet to discuss ways of reviving the world economy without rekindling inflation. The meeting ended on Monday 17 November with a public statement promising joint action to lead the world out of recession. The section on import controls said: 'In a period when pressures are developing for a return to protectionism, it is essential for the main trading nations . . . to avoid resorting to measures by which they could try to solve their problems at the expense of others.'

Castle's obstinate posture may be based on faulty arithmetic.' Mike's readiness to come openly into the fray will be a great help, bless him.

At last, very late, I got to No. 10 for the eve-of-Queen's Speech reception. Most people there seemed to be fairly pleased with [the speech]. David, in sunny mood again, seemed almost to be congratulating me on having succeeded in getting pay beds included. 'It would never have been done without you,' he said approvingly. This is all the more strange, because he continues to bombard me with Minutes seeking to water down the pay beds policy. He has just done this over my paper to the Social Services Committee of Cabinet seeking agreement to a short, quick Bill giving legislative authority to phase out pay beds, coupled with a simple size control over private hospitals. It is he who originally suggested this as the best and easiest way to hold the line, pending fuller consultations on licensing. Now he has got cold feet over it. He is also urging that I extend my discretionary power to delay phasing out in certain cases from two years to three, arguing that consultants in certain areas and in certain specialities just won't be able to practise privately outside the NHS. So it is certainly true that, if anything *is* done over phasing out, it will be due to me.

Wednesday, 19 November. The more serious press continues its criticism of the juniors. *The Times* has a useful leader: 'But the Patients Have a Case as Well.' The *Financial Times* has an even better one, saying I have no choice but to stand firm on pay policy. This morning I put on my new dress for the State Opening and stood smiling at the Bar of the Lords as the Queen read out the bit about pay beds. Everyone glanced my way.

Thursday, 20 November. Howls from the consultants about the Queen's Speech. But that was only to be expected. Our own people are delighted. 'Government bites bullet on pay beds,' said John Cunningham in the *Guardian*. What mattered to me was that I got my paper on the pay beds Bill through the Social Services Committee of Cabinet: one hurdle crossed, though Ted Short said that, as it involved earlier legislation than visualized in our decisions on the Queen's Speech and contained the power to control private developments above a certain size, he would have to refer it to Cabinet. Despite David's pressures, I have stuck to a final date for phasing out of one year, plus a discretionary power for the Secretary of State to allow an extension of a further two years in exceptional circumstances. No one raised any difficulties, so I am pleased with what I have got through as I can return to the attack for a more comprehensive licensing system later in a separate Bill.

But the main business of the day was, of course, with the juniors, in another effort to convince them that their demands were contrary to pay policy. Mike came along to the meeting, looking a bit nervous, but he did his stuff splendidly. Lewin led the juniors into battle, but all he did was to say the BMA were not trying to breach the pay policy and then handed over to Dr Zacharias, the new leader of the militants, a thin, tight-lipped young man, clearly determined to prove he was going to deliver the goods better than his [dethroned] predecessors, Ford and Bell, had done. Zacharias began with an attack on the Department, which, he said, had been 'dragging its feet' over the juniors' claim, and he went into a long history of our misdemeanours, designed to show that we had broken faith. He warned that he and the new executive were 'truly representative of grassroots opinion'. They accepted the principle of the new contract, but were convinced there was more money available. The pay policy could be interpreted in a way that gave them all they asked. All this in an icy manner bordering on insolence.

I replied, setting the record straight and then called on Mike, who began, as usual, rather tentatively. But his very lack of glibness began to have its effect on them in spite of themselves. He stressed that no one else had been allowed to claim that they were a 'special case' and spelt out how strictly the pay policy had been observed. The argument then went round and round. After two hours of this we adjourned to take stock and to have a cup of tea. Over tea in my room I said to Mike, David and my officials that we ought to spike the juniors' guns by offering an independent audit of our figures, to scotch their suggestion that somehow we had cooked up the returns. But when, at the resumed meeting, I offered this, Zacharias rejected it. I also offered to set up a joint examination immediately on the way to reduce the juniors' excessive hours. But Zacharias would have none of this. He said rudely that he saw no point in continuing the discussion and that they had better go. Lewin, knowing I was going to make a statement in the House tomorrow, did not want to be quite so precipitate. It was not that our figures had been 'cooked'. Nonetheless, the figure of £12 million was 'clearly wrong'. I said that in that case the BMA had better submit its evidence of this to us so that we could examine it. Reluctantly he said he would.

As we left the meeting news was brought to me that the consultants have declared war over pay beds. At a meeting of the CCHMS leaders they had decided to recommend the full meeting on Tuesday to join the juniors in working 'emergencies only' from 1 December, and to start collecting undated resignations from the NHS. When the press asked me for a comment I said like a flash, 'This is a strike against the House of Commons. I find it unique in the history of strikes in Britain that we should be threatened with action about a piece of legislation before Parliament has even seen it.' Personally, I think the consultants have played into our hands.

Harold phoned me to say Arnold Goodman had been onto him.[1] Arnold had, he said, been retained by the Independent Hospitals Group [IHG] to fight the pay beds legislation and was anxious to see if an accommodation of any kind could be reached. Would I be interested in meeting him for a private talk, Harold asked casually? I jumped at it. I have been very anxious to have a talk with the professions about the timing of phasing out and what I have in mind about licensing. If Arnold was prepared to act as a go-between, he might help me to get them to see sense. (The IHG, for one thing, is far less hung up about licensing and can even see some value in it as helping to secure a better

[1] Arnold Goodman, senior partner of Goodman, Derrick & Co., solicitors, had been a close friend of Harold Wilson's for years and had been given a peerage by him in 1965. Lord Goodman had always been very generous with his legal advice to Labour MPs, including me, and Harold Wilson had used him for a number of assignments, including an exploratory visit with Sir Max Aitken to Ian Smith in August 1968 on the possibilities of a settlement. But Lord Goodman never took the Labour Whip and was ready to use his remarkable abilities under any government for any cause which aroused his interest, notably the arts. He was chairman of the Newspaper Proprietors' Association from 1970–75, in which role he clashed with Michael Foot over the issue of the closed shop for newspaper journalists.

distribution of private facilities.) So I told Harold I would contact Arnold right away and that I assumed the talks would be very hush-hush. Harold confirmed that Arnold wanted to keep them very private too. I then called in Norman, whom I swore to secrecy. I wouldn't tell anyone about this – not even David. One thing intrigued me about Arnold's approach. I am sure it has been inspired by the appalling press the consultants are getting. They may well be anxious to get themselves off the hook.

Friday, 21 November. The press is full of the consultants' threat of industrial action. The *FT* reported gravely, 'If both groups of doctors carry out their threats, then day-to-day work in the hospitals could come virtually to a standstill.' The *Telegraph* continues its almost daily attacks on me. 'In none of these areas', it said yesterday, 'is there the shambles comparable with the service presided over by the increasingly shrill and vengeful Mrs Castle.'

I phoned Arnold. We had an amicable talk and agreed to meet on Monday evening, deciding that his flat would be the safest rendezvous.

Saturday, 22 November. Denis has joined in the fray over the juniors' dispute in a weekend speech. I think Cabinet is now suddenly alive to what I am up against. At Cabinet last week, when I reported on the juniors, I urged every member of the Cabinet to back me up publicly, so that the profession could see that it wasn't my own personal pay policy I was following, but the Government's. Ted Short endorsed this warmly, saying that 'the attacks that are being made on Barbara are quite intolerable'. Denis's speech is the first fruit.

Monday, 24 November. Wedgie is in the news again with a great attack on spending cuts he made to a young workers' conference at the weekend. I am doing my propaganda more subtly. I have told Brian A-S. to draft an attack on the new philosophy which is now spreading, not only in the *Financial Times* but among right-wing members of the Cabinet, to the effect that cuts in public expenditure are positively socially desirable. This is for a speech I am to make to a local government conference on Friday on the social services. Brian A-S. has produced some wonderful stuff, which I polished up and added to at the weekend. Meanwhile the lobby against defence cuts is getting itself mobilized, and, of course, the press is lending a hand. The *Mail* carries front-page banner headlines today: 'Revolt of the Generals.' This campaign, I suspect, is being organized, not merely by Roy Mason, but by No. 10.

This suspicion was confirmed at the 'bilateral' discussion I had this afternoon with Joel on public expenditure. I went along in grim mood. The 'formula cuts' set out by the Treasury would mean an absolute cut in expenditure on the NHS and I told Joel flatly that I would never agree to this. I was prepared to accept a standstill, but, because of demographic changes, this meant I needed an increase of 1½ per cent a year. The poor lad was looking harassed, and no wonder. He just said he would have to report to Cabinet my failure to agree to what had been proposed. Peter Baldwin, coming to his aid in his quietly deadly way as usual, queried whether the demographic argument justified an increase of 1½ per cent for the NHS, but I stood my ground, while David Owen pointed out that the formula cuts for education allowed standards in primary and secondary schools to be maintained, while for us they meant that standards would go down. It was agreed that Joel's officials should look into this.

We then turned to social security and the Treasury's proposal that we should switch from the historical to the forecasting method at the next uprating. Brian O'M. predictably resisted this savagely, but I sensed that he was weakening in his resistance, since, bless him, he realizes that otherwise the Health Service will be decimated. We then went through the list of all the other optional cuts in the social security field and I said no to all of them, including the postponement of child benefit. I got the impression that Joel is not expecting to get away with anything on this side but the change in the uprating method, which will give him £500 million towards his £3¾ billion. Joel hissed to me afterwards, confirming my worst fears, 'You must support us on getting more out of Defence.'

It was against this background that Norman and I raced to Portland Place for our rendezvous with Arnold. We need not have worried: he arrived late. We were greeted at the door by Arnold's housekeeper, Mrs Roberts. She ushered us (it is the only word) into the sort of room I hadn't expected: rather dark and made darker by heavy period furniture and subdued lighting. Superb pictures everywhere, deep armchairs and sofa and a large colour TV. But the whole effect was oppressive. 'I am afraid Lord Goodman has been detained,' said Mrs Roberts, 'but please let me get you some tea.' She did so in a silver teapot and brought in a plate of cucumber sandwiches of such delicate thinness that the Ritz would have been envious.

After we had waited some twenty minutes Arnold breezed in with perfunctory apologies. I had arrived full of affectionate memories of Arnold's kindliness, but his lateness irritated me. However, we chatted amiably. He is a disarming man, always ready to acclaim one's reasonableness and to criticize his own clients' weaknesses. The important thing, he said, was to avoid a collision course and if he could make any modest contribution to this he would be glad. What he needed to do was to get the moderates in the profession to stand up and be counted. 'Mr Grabham must be bypassed.' What his clients wanted, he said, was to get the whole matter of pay beds referred to the Royal Commission. He accepted that that was out, but it might be possible to satisfy them if we could refer the *timing* of phasing out to the Royal Commission, while proceeding to legislate on the general principle. They were also terrified of my licensing proposals, which they considered, no doubt without any serious grounds, to be a threat to the practice of private medicine. He did not share my horror of pay beds, but he was sure I was not proposing to threaten private medicine. However, we had to accept that we were not dealing with people who were entirely rational. If we could refer the whole licensing proposals to the Royal Commission, that would greatly help.

I told him that he must not entertain any false hopes of being able to exclude Mr Grabham, who was the best – and toughest – negotiator of the lot of them. No deal done behind Mr Grabham's back would be worth anything. But I was sure that he, Arnold, could play an invaluable role in helping to clear away some of the more hysterical fears of the professions. As to timing, I had always intended to have a reasonable phasing-out period. What I had in mind was to include in the legislation a final date for phasing out, but to give myself, as Secretary of State, power to make exemptions to this date of up to two years or more in order to take account of the difficulties of consultants in the provinces, who supplemented their income in a modest way from a few pay beds and who would never get fat pickings from private practice as consultants in the South-East did. It would be fatal to refer the date to the Royal Commission because this would naturally provoke the unions. 'Don't forget there are two parties to peace in the NHS and one is the unions.' If only he could get the professions to sit down and discuss the problem with the unions, a solution might be reached.

Arnold said he found this 'eminently reasonable'. Unfortunately, the people he was working for considered it anathema that in any of their actions they should be responsible to the unions. What about a quadripartite meeting between the professions, the unions, the chairman of the Royal Commission and me to work out a solution? I said that I didn't think that was on (I am not prepared to have the Royal Commission brought into this at any price), but on licensing the situation could be very different. (I know I have no mandate from Cabinet – or the Manifesto – for licensing.) I was sure I could make a concession here. I was not against referring this matter to the RC, but there had to be an interim control, pending the RC's report, in order to prevent private developments from injuring the NHS. I also told him that none of this problem over pay beds need have arisen if only the profession had been willing to take up our idea of common waiting lists. Arnold pricked up his ears at this, said he liked the idea and asked me to send him further details of what we had in mind. This I agreed to do. If only we could get Arnold really committed!

Tuesday, 25 November. The more responsible press continues to be helpful. Today the *Guardian* has a leader saying, 'Undoubtedly this is the most serious crisis the NHS has faced in twenty-seven years,' but arguing that it is the consultants, not the Government, who must back down. On Sunday the *Sunday Times* had the best leader yet. It opened with the sentence, 'In its present militant posture the medical profession has lost a lot of respect.' It concluded on pay beds that 'the case for separate systems, private and public, has wide ideological support . . . To withdraw labour now, before the Minister's legislative and administrative intentions are tested, and before Parliament has voted, is, again, conduct unbecoming to a responsible profession.' Strong words. Of course, this does not deter a few of the popular papers from continuing their personal vendetta against me.

Norman has sent Arnold full details of common waiting lists. I await Arnold's conversion.

Wednesday, 26 November. The cameras were there in force outside Transport House for the NEC meeting. Reason? We are to consider Reg Prentice's appeal against his local Party's decision not to reselect him as its candidate.[1] The press

[1] At its special meeting in July the Newham North East Party had carried by twenty-nine votes to nineteen the Motion calling on him to retire at the next Election. Reg Prentice had appealed to the NEC, arguing that the complaints against him were due to Trotskyite infiltration of his local Party. The inquiry committee set up by the NEC found unanimously that the local Party was within its constitutional rights, but Reg Prentice's friends, led by Mrs Shirley Williams, continued to try to find ways to help him. They were later embarrassed when, in 1977, he joined the Conservative Party, crossed the floor of the House and started voting against the Government. Following the Conservative victory in the General Election of 1979, he was given a job in Mrs Thatcher's Government.

has been building this up wonderfully. Reg Prentice has circulated a long document, which has been given considerable publicity: any stick will do to beat the Labour Party with. But one begins to suspect that Reg is seriously embarrassing his own friends. The Inquiry Committee, consisting of Tom Bradley, John Chalmers, Alex Kitson and Reg Underhill,[1] reported that it had found no constitutional irregularities in the [local party] meeting which had decided to get rid of Reg and therefore dismissed his appeal. But it urged that attempts at reconciliation should be made. Reg Prentice's only response had been to denounce the inquiry publicly and to demand that he be allowed to address the NEC personally. To everyone's surprise it was Fred Mulley who moved that his request be not granted and it was clearly carried overwhelmingly. Not even Reg's supporters pretended to fight for him very hard.

While all this was going on Harold suddenly surprised everyone by proceeding to make a long and involved statement which we soon realized he was reading. After he had been going on for some time, Eric Heffer challenged him. What was this all in aid of? (He might had asked what did it mean? It was one of Harold's convoluted 'a plague on both your houses' pieces, including his favourite line, 'I have spent thirteen years so far trying to keep this Party together and I do not like what is going on.') Harold then said with injured dignity that he was doing what he always did: reading a prepared text which he had issued to the press. 'I'm sick of having what I say here distorted by leaks.' Eric exploded in righteous indignation. Was it in order? Could we all do the same, etc., etc.? I must say that, while I can sympathize with Harold's desire to be reported accurately, the content and tone of what he was saying was gratuitously provocative. It contained an absurd bit accusing the NEC of ignoring the constitutional role of the PLP, constantly attacking the Government and alienating the moderates. He ever threatened there might be a split between the NEC and the PLP, leading to the latter putting up their own candidates against the official Labour ones. While the rest of us sat stunned, Eric grew increasingly vociferous, while Judith said that Harold had widened the discussion so much that other people must be allowed to widen the discussion too. After a bit more of this Bryan Stanley moved next business and the row died down. But Harold has only stirred things up.

Meanwhile Geoff Bish had been up to me to say we ought to pass a Motion of support for me on my disputes with the doctors and he had put a draft in front of me. This not only backed me on pay beds but also on the juniors, putting on record our support for the £6 policy and for the 'Government's position on the junior hospital doctors' pay dispute'. Of course, I could see nothing wrong with this, but I had temporarily forgoten the ASTMS line on pay policy, and of course Mik, Eric and co. objected to this part of it. There was a great hoo-ha, with some people insisting that the £6 limit was the policy of conference, others saying there would be a disastrous leak if we tried to amend the Motion anyway. Tom Bradley, from the chair, cut through all this confusion by saying he was going to put the Motion. This was then carried by sixteen votes to nil, Mik, Eric and a few more sitting on their hands.

[1] Tom Bradley, Labour MP for Leicester East and President of the Transport Salaried Staffs Association, and John Chalmers, General Secretary of the Boilermakers' Union, were like Alex Kitson members of the trade union section of the NEC; Reg Underhill was National Agent of the Labour Party.

Boxes waiting for me when I got home, including a Minute from Henry reporting on the meeting of the Central Committee for Hospital Medical Services held today, which confirmed the decision to take industrial action over pay beds from 1 December by thirty-seven votes to three and called on consultants to hand in undated resignations from the NHS. The action is to continue until the Government agrees to hand the pay beds issue over to the Royal Commission. There had also been a meeting of the Conference of Presidents of the Royal Colleges, which decided unanimously that they could not support any action that might harm patients (and about time too). Apparently the Presidents had been to see the BMA, the HCSA and the juniors to put their feelings about the threatened industrial action 'in the strongest possible terms', but they hadn't got anywhere. With typical gloom Henry concluded, 'The outlook is not good.' For myself I don't think things are going too badly at all.

Thursday, 27 November. Arnold has replied to Norman, thanking him for the information on common waiting lists and adding, 'I will not comment on this except to say that it appears to me the information may well be very helpful to me.' Excellent! I have told Norman, however, that I had better see the PM to put him in the picture before my paper on pay beds, supplementing Ted Short's from the Social Services Committee, comes before Cabinet today. Harold agreed to see me in his study in his best conspiratorial mood. In the few moments I had with him before we had to go down to join the rest I told him that I had met Arnold, who was anxious to mediate. With regard to the reference of the pay beds issue to the Royal Commission, for which the profession is hankering, Arnold accepted that this was out, but he had been very pleased when I told him that a reference of the licensing issue might be possible. He could see my point that, when the legislation on phasing out was announced, there could be a rush of private developments to forestall any possible control system and that we needed a minimum holding power, such as a simple size control. He was 'not unhopeful' that we might reach agreement on these lines. The solution, as I saw it, was therefore that we should introduce a size control of limited duration in the legislation, pending the reference of this question to the Royal Commission. In the meantime I should try to negotiate a voluntary agreement on these lines with the Independent Hospitals Group through Arnold. We could then go ahead with my phasing-out proposals on the basis agreed with Social Services Committee. Two things, however, were essential. I must have the power to bargain with the profession through Arnold, who must appear to have wrung something from me. This meant that the negotiations must be dealt with on a 'need to know' basis and I could not tell Cabinet what I had in mind. For that I needed his help. Harold responded to all this very happily and, with a friendly 'leave it to me', he hurried me downstairs.

In Cabinet Ted Short introduced his memo on the conclusions of the Social Services Committee very fairly and helpfully, setting out the arguments for early legislation on the basis of my Bill as well as I could have done myself. I backed up his presentation with dire warnings about the risk of industrial action if we did not act legislatively. Stevenson and Grabham had both made it clear that, once Parliament legislated, they would accept it, and Norman Fowler was saying that this issue must be a matter for Parliament. So the best way to reduce the temperature was to get the Bill on the statute book. As for the control over the size of developments in the private sector, this was a holding operation pending further consultations over detailed licensing. All I wanted was authorization to go and consult on this particular package.

As I looked down the table at my colleagues I realized that this Cabinet had no fire in its belly for this particular fight. Without the PM's backing I would have been lost. Harold tossed me a note: 'If necessary I'll say that I'm setting up a small committee under my chairmanship to supervise negotiations. I always control membership and I *won't* tell them the committee will consist of two members only.' (How I blessed myself for having taken the precaution of seeing him earlier!) H.W. then proceeded to employ his familiar technique of getting his own way by obfuscating the atmosphere. He said smoothly, 'What I suggest is that we take no final decision this morning, certainly on timing, but that we should authorize Barbara in contact with me to consult on this; perhaps to set up a small commitee under my chairmanship.' One can hardly insult a Prime Minister by saying one does not trust him to negotiate, so the rest thankfully sank back into acquiescence.

Friday, 28 November. The juniors' dispute continues to gather pace. Alarmist reports about its escalating effects continue to come in to me. We continue unmoved to develop our strategy for dealing with it. Derek Stevenson has duly let me have the BMA's 'evidence' that there is more money available and I sent it at once to the Review Body for comment. Sir Ernest Woodroofe, the new chairman, has replied helpfully, from our point of view, pointing out that the Review Body 'took account of the kind of factors that Dr Stevenson referred to in his letter and made due allowance for them within the limits of the evidence available to us'. In the meantime Elinor Kapp and her militant men of the JHDA have continued to let off fireworks from the fringe of all this, furious because the BMA won't agree to include them in the negotiations with me. She has written, jumping at my offer of an independent audit, which the BMA refused. The main argument therefore now lies between her and the BMA, and between the BMA and the board, while I continue to sit tight.

The *Daily Telegraph* continues its attacks on me, saying the time has come to 'relieve' me of my ministerial duties, as my 'personality has become an obstacle to a reasonable solution of the pay beds dispute'. The *Mail* has resurrected the old story about my sojourn in a private ward way back in 1965, plus a picture of me with my sinuses strapped up, and Mr Leonard Kingdom has violated his professional obligation to keep his patients' affairs to himself by making a public attack on me about the time he treated me.

Monday, 1 December. At the office we agreed we ought to advise the PM to see Sir Rodney Smith, as the Royal Colleges are taking a correct line against industrial action. It might also be a good way of bringing pressure to bear on the BMA through the Colleges: perhaps they have plucked up their courage again! We all agreed it would be disastrous for the PM to see the BMA: a very different kettle of fish from the Colleges, who keep protesting that they are only interested in 'patient care'. Norman and I then decided we had better keep on Arnold's tail to see how he was getting on with his side of the talks. On the phone Arnold told Norman that he was seeing the BMA at 6.30 that evening. Yes, it might be a good idea if he and I were to meet before he went along to the BMA. So at 5 pm Norman and I repaired once again to Portland Place and once again awaited Arnold's dilatory pleasure.

When he arrived he was as amiable and amusing as ever, his thoughts and ideas darting about all over the place. He then flew a new kite: could there not be some kind of review body to pronounce on what rate of phasing out would be reasonable in different areas, in the light of the build-up of private facilities in those areas? He knew what a reasonable person I was, but regrettably the profession did not have the same confidence in me as he had himself, etc., etc. I probed a bit. If, I said, what he had in mind was some kind of committee containing professional representatives to advise me on what was a fair and reasonable timing in particular areas, I would be glad to consider this, but obviously the final responsibility must rest with the Secretary of State, who was answerable to Parliament. Arnold queried this: were there not statutory bodies, like National Insurance tribunals, which acted independently of the Secretary of State? I said that their role was very different. They merely adjudicated on whether the policy defined by Parliament was being correctly applied in individual cases. Arnold let it go at that.

Once again, when I asked him about licensing of the private sector, he saw no great difficulty in a simple interim control over private developments, pending the reference of the issue to the Royal Commission, to which I have agreed. He then told us that Sir Rodney Smith will be going alone to see the PM on Wednesday. He didn't want to take any of the other Royal College presidents because he apparently had some ideas he wanted to put to the PM: Arnold had no idea what they could be. As for the BMA, Arnold accepted that the PM might well be unwilling to meet them while they were taking industrial action. But he was interested in my idea of an advisory committee. He would try it on the professions and report back.

It was late before I was able to contact Arnold again by telephone. He seemed to have his tail up. The 'dreaded Grabham' had not been at the meeting. Instead, he had been represented by his number two: 'a nice little man with glasses' (presumably Mr Bolt). At the end of the meeting Arnold had told them he did not wish to be retained, as he disapproved of their action. But, I thought to myself, it can't have been much of a rebuke, because he said he went on to tell them he was 'available to act as an intermediary' without a fee. If I would meet him after lunch tomorrow he was confident we could settle it in forty-eight hours. Of course, I said I would, though there are a lot of fuzzy edges to his proposals which will have to be explored.

Tuesday, 2 December. When Norman came to call for me at the House late this afternoon to take me to Arnold's flat, his face was grim. No. 10, he said, had been on to him to say that the PM had agreed to meet the whole BMA tomorrow with Sir Rodney Smith. I was flabbergasted: meet them while industrial action was going on and when it was clear that the feeling in the country against the consultants was growing? It was impossible. I would have to speak to Harold. Norman shook his head. He had been on to Ken Stowe [the Prime Minister's Principal Private Secretary] personally; the PM was in Rome, but No. 10 had been in touch with him on the phone. He had agreed the meeting and the invitations had already gone out. Moreover, the press had been informed. Norman was as shocked as I was: the insult to me was obvious. Here was I, in charge of the negotiations, and Harold had not even consulted me about this key move. 'Arnold is behind this,' I said bitterly. I could see what was happening: Arnold did not think I was sufficiently pliable and was appealing to Harold over my head with the idea that Harold should take charge of the talks. I could just imagine what would happen them.

I went along to keep my rendezvous with Arnold in one of the intensest furies I have ever felt. Whatever happened to me, I wasn't going to be outmanœuvred in this way. As usual, Arold was late and the refined Mrs Roberts served us her now regular routine of tea and thin cucumber sandwiches. The gloom of the flat weighed on us oppressively, but couldn't dampen the anger which was smouldering in me. When Arnold at last appeared, as perfunctorily apologetic as ever, it burst into flames. He soon saw something was wrong and cut short the pleasantries. I let fly at him. Did he know the PM had invited the BMA to a meeting tomorrow? 'Of course.' Would he be attending himself? He believed so; it would be up to the Prime Minister. So he knew the invitation was going? 'Yes.' 'Then', I said angrily, 'you have wrecked the negotiations.' He was taken aback. Surely not. I told him this step had been taken without consulting me. What he had done was to go to the PM over my head without informing me, while we were still in the middle of our discussions. 'I have never been so insulted in my whole life.' I was the custodian of this Manifesto policy and I was answerable to the Party for it. I wasn't going to have the talks taken out of my hands in this way. It was clear I had shaken him and he spent the rest of the time assuring me that the last thing he wanted was to offend me and that he certainly didn't want to take the negotiations out of my hands. I said it was extremely bad for the PM's image to be seen receiving the profession's representatives when they were taking industrial action against the Government. He wouldn't accept this, but did accept my suggestion that all that ought to happen tomorrow was for the PM to listen to what the delegation had to say and then hand them over to me. So we left it at that, though I certainly wasn't pacified, particularly as Arnold is harking back to his idea of an independent review body.

Back at the House, Norman and I had a council of war. We both took the gloomiest view of the situation and I got him to tell No. 10 that I wanted to see Harold before the meeting in the morning. No. 10 replied that the PM would not be back till very late tonight or early tomorrow, but they would phone me in the morning to let me know what they had fixed. Next, I decided I had better send Harold a Minute to await him on his return and I had to sit down and draft it so that Norman could take it back and get it typed. In I stressed the political dangers that we faced if we were to accept Arnold's package. I added this: 'I would urge you should refuse to discuss any proposals for negotiation at all as this would lead to the suggestion that any eventual settlement had only been reached because you had overruled me and this makes my position untenable.'

It was a strong Minute and I was rather pleased with it. I concluded by urging that I should have a talk with him before the meeting.

Wednesday, 3 December. As the PM's meeting with the profession was not until 11.30 I had time to work a bit. Norman phoned to say No. 10 had promised to contact me direct as to when I could have my talk with the PM. At 10.30 I had still heard nothing and decided, with mounting anger, to go down there anyway. I arrived at No. 10 at 11.15. An embarrassed Private Secretary said the PM was busy, but he would tell him I was there. (No explanation as to why they had not phoned me.) I began to realize that, if I had not marched in, they would not have phoned at all. As it was, Harold bowed to the inevitable and, with five minutes to spare, I was ushered into the study upstairs.

Harold was pacing up and down, clearly irritable. He started on a long diatribe as to how he had only got back at 3 am and how tired he was – what a time he had had in Rome. Firmly I directed the conversation to my Minute and then he suddenly snapped at me. He wasn't going to be told he couldn't negotiate. 'What am I supposed to be? A cypher?' He had told Cabinet that he and I were going to do the negotiating and he wasn't going to be told now that he had got to leave it all to me. I held my ground, equally angrily. If he took over the talks now my position would be intolerable. Hadn't he seen John Cunningham's piece in the *Guardian* today? ('The PM's ingenuity in conjuring compromise out of deadlock could produce the basis for a settlement. . . .') 'You pay too much attention to the press,' Harold snapped. That from *him*! I was unmoved by his anger. I don't care a damn what he thinks of me. 'You will be playing into the hands of the Opposition,' I continued. 'Their whole line has been that you should be brought in because it is my "personality" that is preventing a settlement. They said that about Nye too, when he was fighting to create the NHS. Do you think Clem Attlee would have intervened to take the negotiations out of Nye's hands at a crucial stage?' At this tense moment a Private Secretary put his head round the door nervously.

'Lord Goodman is waiting downstairs,' he said. So that was it: Harold was prepared to see Arnold and not me! My worst fears were confirmed. 'We'd better go,' said Harold and marched downstairs. Arnold was waiting outside the Cabinet room. I stuck firmly to Harold's heels. They had a few moments of embarrassed conversation, with me standing sternly by. Arnold asked if Harold wanted him to attend the meeting. 'I should think so, ' said Harold, elaborately casual. He didn't think they should go into details that morning. Of course, if anyone wanted to put forward proposals, we could agree to consider them. But the detailed negotiations would be for me. 'Of course,' said Arnold placatingly. I trailed after Harold into the Cabinet room, more angry than ever, and stood back ostentatiously while the delegation trooped in and he shook hands.

There they were in force: Sir Rodney Smith (no more above the battle than Grabham himself), Simmons of HCSA (with an icy glare on his face), Lewin, Stevenson, Bolt, the dentists' chap, Wardle of the juniors and some secretaries. As I had told Harold, every one of them a surgeon (except the dentist and the junior), and so hardly representative of the medical profession as a whole. With me sitting rigid beside him, Harold started very tentatively, but nonetheless unctuously. Not a word of reprimand about their industrial action! Instead, he pleased them by opening with the remark that 'we are all at one in wanting to see this dispute honourably solved'. Portentous nods. 'I don't want to get into negotiations,' he continued. 'It's not my job.' Stares at that. He then asked Sir Rodney if he would like to speak. Sir R. did so with his usual unctuousness. The Royal Colleges, he said, 'must speak for the interests of patients'. It was the unanimous view of the Royal Colleges that pay beds should not disappear from the NHS, because it would be 'bad for patients'. (You would never have guessed that he is a surgeon with an extensive private practice.) The Colleges would want to put this view to the Royal Commission, he continued. (Not a word about the Colleges deploring industrial action.)

Lewin then took up the tale. The BMA, he said, would wish the dispute solved as soon as possible. 'If this great profession has been brought to this stage there must be something radically wrong,' he prosed. They believed the Government's policy on pay beds would mean loss of individual choice, loss of independence and a loss to the NHS. 'If you refer this matter to the Royal Commission, we will ask doctors to resume normal working.' Far from resenting the BMA laying down its terms for behaving properly, Harold was at his most mollifying. 'We have fully discussed that,' was all he said. 'There is no point in going over the ground again. I want to get to a situation where negotiations can be resumed with some hope.' And he continued, 'I understand Lord Goodman has been applying his mind to this. Healing is his great profession.' But he added hastily, 'We are not negotiating this morning.' Arnold took up his prearranged cue. He must first make clear, he said, that he had 'ceased to be retained' by the Independent Hospitals Group.

He has made a great virtue of this to me, saying that he had done so because he thoroughly disapproved of doctors taking industrial action; but not a word of this escaped him now. He had a proposal to make that might save the positions of both sides. 'If I may say so, Prime Minister, the tone you have set has been impeccable.' He knew we couldn't reach agreement on the principle, but we might reach agreement on the following. (1) If the Government proceeds with the legislation, doctors do not regard this as grounds for continuing industrial action. (2) There must be consultations about timing. 'Doctors find it difficult to understand the imperative haste to phase out on the basis that some other part of the community has to be satisfied.' (3) The Government has declared its intention to maintain private practice. The manifestation of this would be that phasing out of pay beds should be related in some way to the availability of private practice. 'Some method should be devised – some tribunal – to say there are ample facilities.' This body might say that three pay beds here or there might have to stay for some time – 'even for ever'. The criterion would have to be that there was a call for private medicine. The whole matter would be regulated by a governing body. 'It may not be a proposal that has the formal acceptance of doctors, but can a proposal on these lines be put to them?'

Harold, clearly bog-eyed from lack of sleep, began by saying he was not 'commenting' and then proceeded to ramble on in a 'tone' which delighted them. I was in despair as we drifted towards an implied acceptance of the Goodman plan.

We turned to the question of a press statement. To my relief, Harold agreed that it would not be right to give an outline of the proposals to the press. Arnold suggested that all we need say was that we had had a valuable talk, 'and each side wants time to consider with a view to resumption of negotiations'. Grabham got in a parting shot. He was, he said, 'most anxious' to get the situation 'absolutely clear'. And he went on offensively, 'I personally would have to say that any such discussions with the Secretary of State would not be likely to be helpful, unless it was along the lines of Lord Goodman's proposals. That is, pay beds are to be maintained by one means or another.' 'I note that,' was all Harold said. They filed out, relieved but still puzzled men. As for myself, I was in a turmoil. Harold had set the scene just as Arnold wanted it. On the other hand, he had at least accepted that he must hand the negotiations to me, so I had won that point. (After this morning's performance I began to suspect he knew he was out of his depth and would make a mess of it.) A treacherous road lay ahead of me but I was determined to try and walk it. The alternative was to resign, ostensibly because I wouldn't even try to find a solution. And I knew how little support I would get for that: none from our wretched cowardly Cabinet, a little from the PLP, some from some unions – and a trouncing from the press. I was in a trap and had to spring it as best I could, even if it entailed the loss of a limb or two.

This time Harold invited me upstairs for a drink with him and Arnold, who was very pleased with himself and full of amity towards me, stressing time and again that of course the negotiations must be with me. He also said he would let me have a copy of his formula. I groaned as I saw it was turned 1 pm. 'And I've a Nye Bevan memorial speech to finish writing for tonight,' I said. 'I've got to make a memorial speech too,' said Harold cheerfully. 'Perhaps I ought to cancel it,' I continued hopefully. Both Arnold and Harold waved the idea aside. 'So long', said Harold, 'as you don't refer to this morning's talk.' He thought a review of what Nye had been through wouldn't be at all a bad thing at the present time, while Arnold positively welcomed it.

The cinema at the Union was crowded for my lecture, a number of doctors from the Radcliffe Infirmary forming a band across the back of the hall. I had to read the speech, for safety's sake, which is always a nuisance, and I was hoarse with fatigue, but they listened carefully and applauded warmly. One of the doctors was the first of my questioners and he began by congratulating me on a 'brilliant reśumé' of the NHS's difficulties. It all went swimmingly and I had to tear myself away. Brian Abel-Smith beamed at me: 'That went very well.' 'Did I say anything I shouldn't in reply to questions?' I asked nervously. 'Not a bit of it,' Brian replied.

Thursday, 4 December. The newspapers have done just what I thought they would do with my speech last night. My enemies (the *Mail*, *Telegraph* and *Express*), who were obviously covering it with their own special reporters, have picked isolated bits out of it to headline 'Barbara rocking the boat' sensation stories. 'Castle Rocks Peace Talks', ran the banner front-page headline in the *Mail*, while the *Express* carried a story about 'Dr Harold's Dilemma' (*i.e.* me) in his noble attempt to get peace in the NHS. Even the BBC picked out one simple sentence about the 'almost reckless disregard of the needs of patients' to spotlight on the eight o'clock news. 'They're after you again,' said Edna, worriedly clutching her *Mail*. What a beginning to the day! My conscience about last night is completely clear and I don't intend to apologize to anyone about it, but this morning's press is hardly likely to help me in my determination not to let Harold do a sell-out. If he decided to bypass me now the right-wing press will say he is justified. I wish now I had followed my hunch and cancelled the lecture. And yet, I don't know: I think it was quite a distinguished speech, considering how hurriedly I had to throw it together, and I am glad to have this testimony to my beliefs placed so firmly on the record before I go – if go I have to.

When I arrived at Cabinet Norman was waiting worriedly in the foyer of No. 10 with a message from Ken Stowe: 'The PM is very disturbed at reports in the *Mail* and *Telegraph* this morning. Were you correctly reported?' I told Norman I would draft a reply.

[After Cabinet] I hurried over to the House for a bite of food. As I sat in the dining room of the Commons, chatting to Brian O'Malley and others over lunch, Harold joined us. I was completely relaxed. I now realize that the contempt I feel for his behaviour is pretty widespread among the PLP. A number of people have stopped me to ask what the hell is going on. Said Dennis Skinner to me, almost in despair, 'We're not selling out on pay beds, are we, Barbara? For God's sake, that is all this Government has got left.' I could only wring my hands in silent agony, muttering something like, 'You know I wouldn't let you down.' At table, before Harold arrived, Joel had been whispering to me to ask how things were going. 'I'm worried,' I whispered back. 'Harold's attitude worries me.' He replied, 'It's terrible.' Joel also revealed that he wasn't going to stay in the House that night and vote on the Civil List.[1] 'I signed the minority report, saying the Queen should not get a penny unless she revealed her sources of private income, or had them taxed. Harold refused even to go and discuss it with her,' he said contemptuously. (I don't remember this being raised in Cabinet.)

When Harold arrived we chatted generally for a bit. But when I asked casually, 'How did *your* memorial lecture go?' he went sour. 'Very well,' he snapped back. 'But then I didn't answer any questions.' When I replied that I had answered my questions very well, he snapped again, 'I think you have wrecked the talks.' When I replied coolly that I didn't think I had done any such thing he snarled, 'I don't want to discuss it.' As I left Brian O'Malley came with me, saying, as we walked down the corridor, 'The old man was pretty tetchy today', to which I replied that I was desperately worried. I was in a trap.

I [returned] to the office for the meeting which Norman had arranged since we agreed I ought now to put people like David Owen, Pat Nairne, Henry Yellowlees and Jack in the picture about exactly what was going on. To surprise and relief no one complained about my earlier secrecy, and neither David nor Jack seemed to find the proposed package too dreadful. David began to bubble up with ideas. Patrick Nairne assured me that I must go and see Goodman again tonight, however disinclined I might feel.

[Back to the flat and] once again Arnold kept us waiting for ten minutes or

[1] See footnote to p. 562.

so. I suspect that gives him a kick: the man who can keep Cabinet Ministers waiting and who knows he has direct access to Prime Ministers. (At least, to *our* Prime Minister.)

I was conscientiously relaxed and reasonable, determined to escape one jaw of the trap: 'She was an impossible woman with whom to negotiate.' But I found Arnold was anxious too. My attack on him on Tuesday had obviously hit home and he spent a lot of time making clear that the last thing he wanted was to bypass me and therefore make my position impossible. So that made progress easier. We went through the formula he had produced for Harold following Wednesday morning's meeting. 'Harold asked me if I could remember what we had offered, so I tried to set something down,' he said casually. The only sticky point was item three; the great concession Harold has allowed Arnold to exact from us, *i.e.* that the phasing out of pay beds should be subject to the 'solitary safeguard' of the setting up of an 'independent commission'. This, said Arnold's draft, would be composed of three persons appointed by the Government 'after consultations with the professions' (no mention of the trade unions with which this Government is supposed to have a special relationship!). It was this commission (not the Secretary of State) which would certify 'from time to time' that pay beds could be dispensed with in any particular district, because 'sufficient accommodation and facilities for the reasonable operation of private medicine' were available in that particular district. Here was the threat to our whole policy which I had to defuse as much as possible.

I began by saying that I didn't like the word 'commission', for obvious reasons and preferred a board. 'Eminently reasonable,' was Arnold's comment. Secondly, I thought there was a flaw in the logic of the profession's argument: if they said that their aim was to ensure the continuance of private practice *either* in the form of pay beds *or* of private facilities outside the NHS, they ought to be ready to allow us to dispense immediately with all those pay beds in areas where private facilities clearly existed (*e.g.* inner London). As a show of their good faith, and in order to make the compromise more acceptable to our own side, could we not insert the first list of pay beds to be phased out as a Schedule to the Bill? Arnold clearly thought this was a very fair suggestion and said that he would put it to the profession's representatives, even suggesting that as many as 2,500 beds might come into this category, though he amended this rather hastily later to 1,000 beds. We could then, I suggested, have three categories of beds for phasing out [according to the availability locally of private facilities]. It might be that one or two pay beds would continue for a considerable time; but there must not at any price be the implication that some pay beds would continue in perpetuity. Again, Arnold said he thought all this was 'eminently reasonable' and that he had always visualized a provision that, when pay beds in any area sank to a derisory level, the discretion to phase out could be switched back to me.

[Next], I said that where we retained pay beds for phasing out by the tribunal, common waiting lists should operate. Arnold said at once that the profession would accept this for urgent cases. I said this was 'no go', because there were no waiting lists for urgent cases in the NHS. It was the non-urgent cases that caused the queue jumping – *i.e.* cold surgery, like hernias. He said he would put it to his side, but he saw difficulty. I [then] asked if the profession would accept a ban on private development while the consultations went on about licensing and he said he saw no difficulty in this.

Finally, I insisted that I must carry the unions with me at every stage; otherwise we should only exchange one form of industrial action for another. Arnold was shrewd enough to see the force of this and said he was constantly impressing on his chaps that they must take the unions into account: a concept, he implied, that was contrary to their whole instincts. Summing up, Arnold said he was meeting them all at lunch tomorrow; he would put all this to them and if their reaction was reasonable, the next stage should be for me to meet them all at his place tomorrow night with a view to clinching things. Once that was done he would tell the PM that they should go into formal negotiations with me on Monday. Speed was essential. In this way my position would be safeguarded: the unwitting offence he had caused me would be expunged (and, by inference, Harold would be kept out of it). I agreed this readily, on one proviso: that I would need to put all this to my union contacts at lunch tomorrow – if I could assemble them in time. And if Arnold ran into any difficulties on any item in the proposals I had made, he could ring me at the Gay Hussar, so that I could put it to the unions over lunch. Arnold thought this was excellent and told Norman they must swap telephone numbers of our respective lunching places. My spirits began to rise.

Friday, 5 December. I picked up David for our lunch and told him, to his delight, that I'd like him and Patrick to come along to the talks with Arnold this evening. 'I'll cancel my meeting at Chichester tonight,' he said eagerly. The lunch with our union friends was, as usual, in Victor's cosy little private room at the Gay Hussar, of which we are rapidly becoming the most devoted customers. We had managed to rustle up Alan Fisher, Audrey Prime and Peter Jacques and I outlined the rough and ready deal I had struck with Arnold last night. They took it far better than I had dared to hope. Alan admitted that, if we got a Schedule in the Bill getting rid of a considerable number of pay beds at one stroke, his members would feel they were getting somewhere. 'You've done marvellously, Barbara,' said Audrey warmly.

But the promised call from Goodman reporting progress with his own side never came through. Jack reported that Norman had not even been able to find out where Arnold was lunching! He had gone to ground, leaving no trace. So we went back to the office more irritated with Lord G. than ever.

Back at the office I called an urgent meeting on the juniors. They have never been mentioned at the Goodman or No. 10 talks and yet their action is doing far more damage than the consultants' is. The break-away JHDA is trying to horn in on the act by publicly taking up my offer to the BMA of an independent audit of the money we say is available for the juniors, and Dr Kapp, their militant chairman, has had letters in the press attacking me for not responding. We therefore decided to allow the Association to put their 'evidence' on the amount available to officials. This was promptly misrepresented in the press as an agreement to meet the Association myself and equally promptly Derek Stevenson rushed to attack me publicly as 'adding confusion upon confusion'. The BMA is clearly worried at the way the JHDA is taking the initiative and has written to me saying the BMA, too, have got evidence that the latest figures of

EDA claims show a big increase and agreeing to my offer of an audit, provided we take the figures up to 5 October. We agreed that we should respond positively to the BMA, while insisting on meeting them to discuss the whole matter next week.

While we were in the middle of this meeting, the phone call came from Arnold at last. Norman reported that Arnold was clearly far from 'clinching things' but nonetheless wanted me to meet them at his place that evening. Arnold suggested that I and my chaps might come along first so that he could put us in the picture over what he saw as the difficulties. Norman had thereupon fixed for us to go along at 6 pm.

Since Patrick had a funeral to attend and could only join us later, David, Jack, Norman and I made our way to Portland Place alone. The tea tray was waiting and we gathered that the profession's representatives had been herded into the dining room so that Arnold could report to us how things were going. [Then] we decided to call the others in. They were there in force: from the BMA, effectively led by Grabham, to Simmons of the HCSA (so the BMA is still looking over its shoulder at the breakaway union!), and the gentle Allen of the dentists. And there among this partisan group was (surprise, surprise!) Sir Rodney Smith of the 'above the battle' Royal Colleges. They trooped into Arnold's sitting room in a kind of defensive tension. Arnold, presiding from a deep armchair, was at his most genial. He didn't think, he said, that we could reach agreement that evening, but we could clarify a number of points. The starting point was that an independent body must be set up to control the phasing out of pay beds, as suggested in the proposals he had put to the PM. (I recognized that I had no choice but to accept this, while Arnold had obviously convinced the other side that they had to accept that legislation would be introduced.)

In the discussion which followed Grabham made all the running. It was soon clear there were two main points. The first was my idea of a Schedule of beds to be phased out immediately, drawn up by me and included in the Bill. Here again Arnold had obviously convinced them that this was my sticking point, but Grabham was tenacious in his attempt to limit the effect of this, saying that the profession would not be willing to help draw up the Schedule in advance of legislation and trying to get the selection of the beds – and even the number – left open till after the Bill was passed, possibly being referred to the independent board. I wasn't having that.

The second main point was on specialized facilities. It suddenly became clear that this was Rodney Smith's one real concern and he was strongly backed by that other surgeon, Mr Bolt. The point that emerged was this: the right to do private practice for top surgeons like them depended on their having access to the specialized facilities in NHS hospitals because, with very few exceptions, the private sector could not afford to provide them. As David Owen pointed out, even the Wellington Hospital has no heart or lung facilities. And there were certain other highly specialized fields – such as radiotherapy and neurosurgery – where it would be extremely expensive, and often impossible, for the private sector to duplicate these facilities. Could not, said Mr Bolt almost pleadingly, the surgeon or doctor who did very specialized work continue to have access to the NHS facilities on an occasional basis? Grabham insisted that every doctor or patient ought to have access to NHS facilities as of right and pointed out that the private use of these facilities would be very limited. I said that, if I were to consider it, I should want agreement on the Schedule and on the criteria the independent board was to follow in phasing out the remaining beds.

By this time it was 11 pm and, despite the coffee, sandwiches and drinks Arnold had provided, we were all feeling a bit jaded by the intensity of the discussion and the oppressiveness of that sombre room. Arnold said we should all go away and try to draft a document and he suggested we should meet again on Sunday evening to finalize it.

We broke up, but I couldn't help feeling we'd done pretty well. I am beginning to see the shape of an agreement which will safeguard the things which are most important to me and which the unions and our own people will find tolerable. I arranged to meet David and officials at the Department on Sunday afternoon so that we could draft a document. At least, I thought as I was driven down to HCF, I shall have a peaceful Saturday.

Saturday, 6 December. It was not to be. I was just going through my boxes when a special messenger arrived, bringing an envelope. It was from David at his most typical. In a covering Minute he said he had cancelled his engagements in Plymouth that night in order to send me a draft statement to put to the consultants which he thought that, even if they rejected it, would strike 'reasonable opinion in the country' as a peace formula. What he himself called the 'key proposal' of his draft was the suggestion that instead of the Schedule to the Bill being drawn up by me, the independent board should be set up immediately to examine which pay beds could go quickly and publish its first report in time for its findings to be incorporated as a Schedule to the Bill. I got on the phone to him immediately to tell him this just wasn't on. I liked certain points in his draft, but on the crucial issue of the Schedule I was not prepared to budge. It was a clear *quid pro quo* for the other concessions I was being asked to make, particularly in the field of specialized facilities.

Sunday, 14 December. The end of one of the most intensive weeks of my ministerial life, during which I have battled with Arnold Goodman and the consultants to an uneasy compromise over the pay beds issue, had an all-night session with the junior doctors to reach a settlement of their dispute and fought a great battle in Cabinet over public expenditure. There has been no time to do a daily diary or even to eat or sleep properly. This weekend has been an almost farcical climax during which I have scarcely been off the phone as I have concluded quadripartite negotiations with Arnold, David, Patrick Nairne and Norman to try to tie up a pay beds agreement in time for my statement in the House tomorrow.

The week started last Sunday when David, Patrick, Jack, Norman, Gedling and I assembled at the department at 2.30 pm to prepare for our further meeting with Goodman's men. I found that the irrepressible David had come in early and redictated his draft statement to take account of the points I had raised with him. His second draft was a great improvement. Once again I was conscious of how well David and I complement each other: he bubbles with ideas and has a far greater knowledge of the medical scene than I have; I stubbornly defend the main political principles involved and keep a wary eye on every line of the text to make sure they are not being eroded. We make a good pair.

We went through David's draft line by line and word by word for nearly three hours. I insisted on the need to keep referring to private 'facilities' and not just 'beds', as I was determined to end private out-patient facilities as well as pay beds – a point on which I have had some argument with David. Patrick was magnificent, throwing himself wholeheartedly into the job of helping me to carry out my policy.

At Portland Place we found that Arnold had obviously been having trouble with his principals. He ushered us into the dining room, saying apologetically that his disucssions were still going on in the other room. There then ensued one of those French farce situations with Arnold going backwards and forwards between the two groups. We outlined our proposals to Arnold verbally. He indicated that he personally thought they were reasonable, but every time he reported to the other room he came back with new queries and difficulties. We then gathered that some drafting was going on and that someone had been sent off to get a document typed at BDA House. Eventually Arnold brought copies to us, rough-typed on sheets of paper torn out of an exercise book. After we had groaned over it for some time, we suggested to Arnold we should take it away and let him have our comments the following day. It had been a tiring day and we were all thankful to get to bed.

There were, of course, a pile of things for me to do when I got into the office on Monday morning. First and foremost I had to have an office meeting on the juniors at which we agreed the letter I should send to Stevenson. I pointed out that, while we should agree to the independent audit covering the extra duty allowance figures up to the latest available date, it could well be Christmas or later before we had the figures up to 5 October for which they asked. So I stressed in the letter that it would be intolerable if industrial action by the juniors were to continue till the October figures were available. I wanted us to discuss all this at our meeting with them the next day. I made the tone of the letter reasonable but tough.

At last I was able to turn to the extraordinary document Goodman had handed us the previous night. It was obvious that we ourselves would now have to put in an alternative one and I had spent part of the morning scribbling out the draft for which Arnold had asked. In it I placed the Schedule firmly in the centre of the stage. I also insisted that consultations on the composition of the independent board must not only be with the medical profession, but with 'other NHS staff'. We finally produced a document which covered all our points on the Schedule, common waiting lists and reserve licensing powers, though we decided not to make any reference at this stage to the number of pay beds to be included in the Schedule or the exact period within which they would have to go. We rushed the document to the profession's negotiators.

Tuesday morning was, of course, the PESC Cabinet. I got up early to refresh my memory on the key points I had to make in defence of my beloved NHS. I was glad I did, because I needed every one of them. Harold opened by saying that, as a result of the bilateral talks Joel has been having with us all, £2,600 million cuts had already been agreed towards the required £3¾ billion. He praised us all for being so co-operative. However, continued Harold, we were still £1,150 million short of the figure the Chancellor needed and we had to decide how the money should be found in the light of the list of options the Treasury had circulated. Denis's *coup de grâce* was that the biggest contributions would have to come from the big spenders: Health and Social Security, Environment and Defence. I was at bay.

Harold then called on me and, though I say it as shouldn't, I made the best speech I have ever made in Cabinet. [Then] I sat back breathlessly, knowing I had shaken them. But Joel still tried to do his worst. There was, he said ruthlessly, a shortfall of £296 million in the cuts needed from the health and personal social services. He accepted that the personal social services required a growth of 2 per cent. But, he continued, the same arguments didn't apply to the health side. There a standstill should mean no growth at all and that would give us a saving of £219 million.

But I had clearly impressed Cabinet and Harold jumped in in his deft way to try to help. Of course he did it circuitously. We all knew, he said, that there were too many chiefs to Indians in the NHS and that in the social services it was even worse. He would take a lot of convincing that there wasn't a lot of fat in these services. Surely we could cut administrative costs without damaging the services? (I groaned inwardly.) Of course, continued Harold, we must take account of any demographic changes. Barbara had made a great point of them. But her figures were challenged by Treasury. So she had better try to clear up this point in bilateral talks. Joel nodded approvingly at this, but before he could draw breath Harold slipped in: 'And she should discuss with the Chief Secretary what would be the least damaging way of saving £100 million.' While Joel gasped I protested vigorously, whereat Harold said disapprovingly that the purpose of the talks would be to set before Cabinet a statement showing the consequences that would flow from a cut of £100 million, so that it could consider this against its priorities generally. Eric gave me a congratulatory nudge and I subsided, realizing that, thanks to Harold, I had already saved £119 million and might yet save the rest.

After the morning's trauma my Questions in the House seemed a non-event. After Questions, Arnold smuggled himself into my room bearing the negotiators' comments on the document I had sent them last night. The comments had been drawn up by his assistant, Montgomerie, who pointed out that a number of them were trivial drafting points. I said I would consider all this and let him have my reply.

Back to the office to deal with the BMA and the juniors. I was determined to reach agreement if at all possible, as a settlement with the juniors would strengthen my hand in the pay beds row. That morning *The Times* carried an optimistic leader: 'There is no great distance now between Mrs Castle and the junior hospital doctors . . . the parties are separated essentially on a question of fact alone.' The leader-writer little knew the juniors! When I went down to the ministerial conference room to be faced by another of those mass meetings, I soon found I was in for a long haul. Zacharias was sitting as tight-lipped as usual. We cleared the details of the audit out of the way without too much difficulty. Faced with my determination to be reasonable, their accusations that we had been out to diddle them began to look pretty thin.

Seizing my advantage I turned the discussion to the need to reduce juniors' excessive hours. The stories of juniors working 120 hours a week or more, which appear regularly in the press, always arouse sympathy in the House of Commons. Every time I tell my officials we've got to do something about it they always reply that the responsibility lies with the consultants, who like to have juniors at their beck and call. And so it proved. Stevenson was lukewarm about my offer of an urgent inquiry as to how we could reduce working hours, saying it was a matter for the consultants through the Joint Negotiating Committee.

I was just about to say: 'So we are agreed' . . . when all Zacharias's pent-up fury came pouring out. There could be no agreement, he said, until their grievances about the new contract had been dealt with. He then proceeded to list their demands. The spirit of the new contract which we had agreed last January had been that their basic salary related to a forty-hour week. He accepted that the juniors had an ethical obligation to work above that in 'emergencies and unforeseen circumstances', but health authorities – abetted by the Department – had been exploiting this. Some health authorities had been saving money by refusing to fill vacancies in junior staff, or to appoint locums when colleagues went sick. And the Department had compounded this exploitation by refusing to give evidence to the DDRB that their basic salary should be related to a forty-hour week, thus leaving them with an open-ended commitment. As I listened to him I recognized the juniors' sense of injustice was very real.

But I could see the pitfalls, too. The trouble is that we and the doctors have got ourselves into an almost metaphysical dispute. The juniors clearly want an industrial type contract, with overtime being paid for eventually by premium rates, but they know they can't have it yet under pay policy and they also accept an 'ethical' commitment to fill in without pay in 'emergencies and unforeseen circumstances'. We started a long, circuitous argument. I again pointed out that there was no extra money available under the pay policy. They said that what they were interested in was the principle. I insisted that the Government couldn't just override the profession's own independent pay body by accepting the forty-hour week principle off its own bat, particularly as that body had just reported *against* such a proposition. By now it was late, so I summed up that there should be a joint meeting with officials the next day to agree the details of the audit and that I myself would meet them again on Thursday. At this we broke up exhausted and I told Norman that we must get Michael along to Thursday's meeting. I wasn't going to get myself into any situation where I was blamed for breaching pay policy. Any settlement must have his blessing.

Wednesday brought another succession of battles. It also brought a spate of hostile press comment. George Fitch excelled himself with a foul piece in the *Express* headed: 'As Barbara Castle finally back-tracked on the junior doctors' pay row, The Lady *is* for Burning.' It included such choice comments as: 'The tears and tantrums which got her her way most of the time in the last Labour Government now seem to do no more than demean every issue she touches.' It was not only accompanied by a photograph which made me look twice my age, but it was topped by an equally foul cartoon by Cummings which made me look like a haggard harridan. Not to be outdone, the *Sun* carried a sneering cartoon by Franklin. I tried not to mind and turned to the pay beds issue again.

At an early office meeting on pay beds we went through Montgomerie's comments on our last draft. There were certain minor points of redrafting which we agreed easily and I said I was willing to include a commitment not to use my discretionary power to phase out pay beds pending the legislation. I also agreed to make it clear that two of the four members of the independent board (apart from the chairman) would be members of the medical profession and approved by them. But for the rest I rejected Montgomerie's appendix outright; reiterated my determination to consult with the unions as well as the medical profession; refused to give a guaranteed life to the existence of the board (certainly not ten years!); repeated that pay beds should be dispensed with where all reasonable steps to provide alternative private facilities had not been taken; reiterated the para on common waiting lists and actually strengthened the reference to licensing by providing that, if a voluntary agreement with the private sector could not be reached, 'the Government . . . would take reserve licensing powers in the legislation'. And for the first time I added the suggestion that the reserve powers might be exercised by the independent board.

There remained the vexed question of the Schedule. I could see that the only way out was for us to go boldly for the inclusion in the Bill from the outset of a firm number of beds in the Schedule and had decided to go nap on phasing out 1,000 beds in six months. So we decided to send a 'side letter' to this effect with our main draft.

Thursday proved to be the longest and toughest day of the whole week – and that was saying something! It started with the misery and tension of another PESC Cabinet. This, I knew, was my last chance to save the NHS from another large cut. Joel opened by admitting that Treasury now accepted my figures of the demographic trends but he still thought I could save another £100 million by restricting growth on the health side to 1 per cent a year instead of the 1½ per cent for which I asked and by accepting the formula cuts on capital in both cases. I fought back desperately. I couldn't accept that we could afford to cut back capital on the social services any more than current expenditure, but if I did concede this, it would save £22 million and that would leave £78 million to come out of the NHS. That would effectively mean a moratorium on new hospital building schemes. It wouldn't be any good any of my colleagues round that table coming to me with pleas for a new hospital in their constituencies. Grimsby's new hospital, for instance, would go for a burton. So would the one at Leeds. (I'd carefully checked up which members of the Cabinet had pet hospital schemes in their constituencies.) I dilated on the backlog we already had in hospital maintenance work and fire precautions. It was a strong case, but I faced a Cabinet of desperate men. They seized my £22 million but wanted more. I volunteered to revoke the next increase in the earnings rule, due in April 1977, saying I was ready to fight *that* one through Parliament as I had never thought it was a priority. That would save another £18 million. Tony C. got nasty, saying everyone else had had to make far worse cuts than I was offering.

Harold came to my help again by going off at a tangent about how much money was being wasted by over-elaborate administration. Did we really have to be so cautious and perfectionist in the running of social security? He was always getting constituency cases where Mrs Bloggs had some small claim or a pensions query and a vast administrative effort was mounted to ascertain whether she was entitled to it. 'That is where the money is going now.' Wouldn't it be better to have rougher justice – or even to have someone getting a few pence more than they were entitled to – than carry these enormous overheads? He was convinced we could get a saving of 5 per cent in the forecast number of civil servants in 1978–79 by relaxing some of our practices and by increased efficiency. This would save £140 million. Once again I doubted whether Harold's proposition was more than a face-saver, but I jumped at it. So did everyone else, only Denis looked doubtful. The spotlight then switched back to me and Harold said smartly that I had offered £40 million, including the saving on the earnings rule, but Cabinet thought I ought to go up to £60 million, though it was recognized that £18 million of this saving was dependent on our amending the legislation on the earnings rule. I slumped back with relief. What Harold's skilful summing up meant was that I had effectively given up only £42 million, instead of the £100 million Joel was demanding.

Back at the office I found a Minute from Jack on the pay beds saga, reporting a phone call he had had from Arnold last night on the latest draft I had handed him. Arnold said, 'This is a great advance . . . if it is not accepted by them they will be extremely ill-advised.' However I had no time to bother about pay beds as I got ready for the marathon with the juniors that Michael and I faced. But I hadn't anticipated it would be quite such a marathon! We met after lunch; we finished almost at breakfast time.

We opened with both sides deploying familiar arguments. The arrangements for the audit presented no difficulty. I reported that Sir Ernest Woodroofe, redoubtable chairman of the Review Body, had agreed to look at the new contract again in the light of the latest figures the audit revealed of the money available. For their part the juniors agreed to accept the outcome of the audit, whether it produced additional money for distribution or not.

But it was soon clear that the acceptance by us of the principle of the forty-hour week contract was their sticking point. After we had talked round this for some time, and Michael had shaken his head over the implications of this for future pay policy, I suggested we had a break. Michael, our officials and I repaired upstairs to my room for a cup of tea. I told Michael firmly that I could not see how we could justify breaking on this point, when we had already – with his agreement – accepted the principle in January. The real safeguard, from the Government's point of view, was that the whole business had to be priced by the Review Body in the light of pay policy. Mike had clearly been shaken by the juniors' insistence on the principle. We sat scribbling away at a form of words. Time passed and the resourceful Norman wheeled in coffee and sandwiches. We gathered that the BMA and the juniors, similarly refreshed, were scribbling away downstairs.

Eventually, the bargain was struck word by word and line by line. The reference to the forty-hour week was a semantic masterpiece. We agreed to give joint evidence with them to the Review Body arguing that the basic salary 'should represent' only payment for forty hours, but insisted on defining the basic salary 'as determined by the Review Body from time to time'. The juniors pledged themselves not to use the forty-hour week as an argument to try to get overtime rates for their extra hours. In return we agreed that, where a junior was expected to provide cover outside his basic contract, he should be paid at the standard rate. The fine metaphysical balance had been struck again. Only time would show what its practical effects would be.

Friday morning saw us back at the office early. My statement [to the House] had to be made at 11 am and we barely got it drafted before I was on my way. Of course, with a settlement in the bag which was firmly rooted in pay policy, it was a walk-over. I even got some congratulations in that almost empty House.

It was time to turn my attention to pay beds again. Arnold had sent me a letter setting out the profession's comments on our latest draft. He hoped that I would not be 'unduly impatient that I have not been able to come back with an unqualified acceptance of the document'. There were 'certain further variations' to be recorded. First as to the Schedule: 1,000 beds was the maximum which Mr Damerell – 'our own independent expert' – could assess as available for phasing out over some period of time 'such as eighteen months'. Even that was more than he could safely estimate, but the profession was reluctantly ready to accept it. I promptly said to David I would go nap on 1,000 beds within six months. The remaining changes, wrote Arnold, were not substantial 'although the protracted debate which took place today might have led you to think otherwise'. The doctors wanted a reference to the 'right' to private practice. We agreed we weren't having that. They wanted the criterion for phasing out to be 'the availability of reasonable alternative facilities', instead of our phrase 'the reasonable availability of alternative facilities'. We decided to solve that one by having both 'reasonables' in. They wanted us to specify that the chairman of the independent board should be a legal chap, but I thought that too dangerous. It all depended on what type of fellow we could get. The profession wanted to weaken the safeguards we had built in on the use of specialized facilities for private patients by taking out the proviso that the Secretary of State had to be satisfied before authorizing this use that there would be no detriment to NHS patients. They didn't like the word 'detriment' anyway and thought it ought to be 'injustice'. I said emphatically that I wouldn't take out the proviso, though to soften this blow we decided to suggest the word 'disadvantage' instead of 'detriment'.

On licensing Arnold recognized that this 'is a fundamental matter from your point of view' and had managed to secure their agreement to wording 'which I hope will satisfy you'. This provided first that the Government needed to be satisfied that private developments did not 'significantly' endanger the NHS. Secondly, that the Government would seek 'voluntary assurances to that end'. We decided that the acceptance of the word 'significantly' would do no harm, but that we wanted more than voluntary 'assurances'. We therefore substituted the words 'and will enter into consultation with the medical profession as to how this can be achieved by voluntary means'. The important thing was that the reference to the fact that reserve powers would be taken if necessary remained in.

Last, but by no means least, Arnold turned to the paragraph on common waiting lists. It is significant that our insistence on examining the possibility of common waiting lists terrifies them more than anything. As Arnold put it, this paragraph was 'particularly troublesome'. Some of the doctors felt strongly that it should be taken out, but were prepared to accept it on the basis of amendments suggested by Arnold himself. Yes, there it was: our old friend:

'The professions maintain that if any such scheme is a possibility it can only operate for urgent cases in view of the varied nature of the waiting lists and facilities available at different hospitals.' Well, we decided, they are entitled to their view as long as the Government's contrary view is expressed in the paragraph and that the instruction to the independent board to make recommendations on this matter to the Secretary of State remains. So we accepted this.

It then remained to discuss the heading of the document. We had drafted the following: 'The following statement has been agreed by representatives of the BMA, BDA, HCSA and the Royal Colleges and the Secretary of State for Social Services on the Government's proposals for phasing private practice out of NHS hospitals.' When I gave Arnold the document he once again expressed his appreciation of the changes I had made. He was sure we could now clinch the deal with a view to my making a statement in the House on Monday. I said that it was clearly an essential part of the deal that the industrial action should be called off and that the professions must recommend this to their own people at the same time as they recommended the document. He seemed to feel that that was fair.

Afterwards Patrick said to me: 'You really have done very well, Secretary of State. This really is a remarkable achievement.' I was not so jubilant. I have had to make concessions I would not have made if Harold had not intervened and upset the applecart. Nonetheless I believe I have saved the maximum from the situation in which I was placed and safeguarded the major principles of our policy. Given the right kind of board the phasing out cannot be long delayed and at least the existence of the board means that a Tory successor could not reverse the process by an administrative act. David believes we have got an agreement that will now stick, whatever the change of government. I went down thankfully to HCF, relieved to think that the whole messy business was now sewn up.

Disillusionment came rapidly. By Saturday morning Arnold was on the phone full of apologies. First, there were some textual details to wrangle about and I then had to conduct consultations of dizzying circularity: with me ringing Norman, Norman ringing David Owen and Patrick Nairne, David and Patrick ringing me and me ringing Arnold back again. It went on for hours. Every word seemed to terrify Arnold's men. They weighed them up carefully, suspecting traps. As for me, I wasn't prepared to budge on any of my central points. Eventually some minor drafting changes were agreed.

But the main argument raged over the status of the document. Arnold reported that the professions were not prepared to say they had 'agreed' anything. He admitted that this was cowardly, but said that they went further: they were not prepared to admit that they had ever negotiated with me. They actually wanted me to write to them putting these proposals to them as my own! I was furious. I said (after more circular consultations) that I was prepared to leave out the word 'agreed' but I certainly wasn't going to have it appear that I had taken the initiative in working out this compromise. And there must be some commitment on their part to recommend the document and get industrial action stopped, or the deal was off. What about using the words 'joint statement', instead? It certainly wasn't a unilateral one.

Once again Arnold agreed that all this was 'eminently reasonable' and disappeared off the phone to try and sell it to his chaps. And once again he came back to press me to accept some 'modifications'. The professions now wanted a letter, not from me, but from the Prime Minister, following up the meeting they had had with him, with the PM putting the proposals to them as the outcome of the 'clarification' that had taken place. On the basis of this they would be willing to call an early meeting of their constituent bodies to consider them. I said this proposal was even worse: I wasn't going to have the PM humiliated by proposing the compromise, any more than I was prepared to be humiliated myself. These men must really stand up and be counted. Once again Arnold heartily agreed and disappeared off the telephone.

By this time we were into Sunday morning. Back came Arnold, full of apologies for the obstacles being put up by his side. What they now proposed, as a device for disguising that they had ever been negotiating with me, was that we should all meet in my office the following day, that he should then produce the proposals out of a hat, we should examine them as though we had never seen them before and simultaneously adopt them. They would then agree to put the proposals to early meetings of their people on the basis that the final decision must rest with them. For its part the Government could make clear that it reserved the right to withdraw the proposals if the full meeting of the professions turned them down or if industrial action was not called off. But they considered a letter from the PM to them to be a crucial element in maintaining the fiction that they hadn't been negotiating. I groaned but promptly started drafting a letter from the PM to them which would preserve the Government's – and the Prime Minister's – dignity. More circular consultations by telephone with David and Patrick to get the wording right. The crucial paragraph, we all agreed, was the following:

I understand from the Secretary of State that clarification has taken place through Lord Goodman and that, as a result, detailed proposals have evolved[!] which you are prepared to commend for approval by an early meeting of the CCHMS and the Council of the BMA. I am writing to inform you that, if the proposals are accepted by the professions as a whole and normal working is resumed, the Government would embody these proposals in its legislation.

Arnold thought this was excellent. By now, over the two days, I must have been on the telephone on and off for at least ten hours. Norman contacted No. 10 to tell them the draft letter was on its way to Chequers by special messenger. I sat down to type out the draft, together with a covering Minute from me to the PM. In it I told him that through the protracted discussions I had had on the letter, 'I have been anxious to preserve your dignity and that of the Government and, I might add, Arnold Goodman is as anxious to ensure this as I am.' And I went on: 'I think that during these difficult talks he has grown increasingly aware of the difficulties of negotiating with the medical profession and increasingly irritated with their lack of courage and leadership.'

The special messenger having arrived and my stuff having been dispatched to the PM, I relaxed. Peace at last! But not for long. Arnold rang again to say the professions had changed their minds about one phrase in the PM's letter. They were not prepared to 'commend' the document 'for approval', merely to place the proposals before the professions' committees and councils. We didn't know whether to groan or laugh. But I was angry at the professions' assumption that they could dictate to a Prime Minister in this way. I said it was up to Harold whether he would swallow it. Privately I had no doubt that he would.

At last I turned to my boxes and a long evening's belated work.

Monday, 15 December. Got to the office exhausted, completely drained by the weekend's activities. We went through the draft I had done of my statement for the House, which everybody liked. But the BMA contingent, who had assembled according to plan in another room, were still making trouble over the PM's letter which Arnold and I had agreed yesterday. They simply were not going to say they were commending the proposals for 'approval'. They were quibbling too over one or two points in the proposals, notably my insertion of the words that consultation over the contents of the Schedule would take place, not merely with them. but also with 'other NHS staff and other interested parties'. Arnold, as usual, was late. When he arrived at nearly noon he was closeted with them for some time, finally coming up to me with a form of words for the PM's letter which said they would put the proposals to their council for 'urgent consideration', plus allowing the PM to add that he understood the proposals would gain acceptance! The arrogance of [this] never occurred to them.

Out of courtesy I showed Stevenson my statement. He said it was impeccable and thanked me for its fairness. Then we brought the rest of them upstairs into my room for the pantomime of 'discovering' the proposals at Arnold's hands. Those who had turned up trooped in [and] I gave them a drink. We all looked sheepish – and felt it. Grabham had a last fling. He couldn't accept the words about consultation with other NHS staff. 'I can't agree not to consult the unions,' I replied with spirit. 'And we cannot agree to include these words,' he replied with icy obstinacy. It looked like deadlock. Arnold said mildly that I could not be stopped from consulting anyone I liked. I replied that, on that understanding, I did not mind whether the words were in the document or not, 'but I shall certainly consult the unions and I want that minuted'. 'Perfectly reasonable,' said Arnold. And so we skated to safety over thin ice. We all breathed a sigh of relief when they had left. 'I believe I actually saw a faint smile on Grabham's face at one point,' Norman recorded. 'A smile like a silver plate on a coffin,' Gedling quoted.

I was worried as to how our chaps would take my statement in the House. David reported that people like Ian Wrigglesworth thought it was an acceptable deal. It didn't go too badly, though the only people called from our side were the Bob Cryers and Dennis Skinners, who were mildly critical. 'It's better that way,' said David. 'Too much support from our side would have frightened off the consultants.' My greatest joy was to see Norman Fowler and Gerry Vaughan puzzling over their copy of the statement on their front bench before I spoke – obviously puzzled how to play it. All I want now is to get the industrial action called off; the drafting of the Bill, after all, remains in my hands.

It fascinates me to watch how Pat Nairne is settling himself into his new job. I like him enormously. I don't know whether it has anything to do with his long stint at Defence, but he clearly sees his job as to carry out orders: not to query the strategy, but to make sure it works – a welcome change from Philip's and Henry's soul-searchings.

One bright note: the press comment on my statement yesterday is not too bad, only the *Morning Star* denouncing it as a 'climb-down'. My long telephone conversation with John Cunningham [of the *Guardian*] seems to have borne fruit.

Tuesday, 16 December. A long schedule of meetings over, I found it was 7 pm and I was already late for the Transport House Christmas party, at which I try very hard to look in each year. 'This year,' I told Norman, 'there are three Christmas parties, which, our travails being temporarily over, it looks as though I should be able to attend. Why not have some belated fun?' He was only too ready to enter into the conspiracy. I arrived at Transport House at 7.15 pm. There was a light-hearted crowd there, including a number of journalists, as well as members of the NEC. The journalists, such as Ian Aitken and Matt Coady, had contributed to the political cabaret and were very anxious to watch their own handiwork. 'Come up to the gallery,' said Ron Hayward to me, 'it is the best place to watch the show.' So, with a drink in hand, and a paper plate full of salami snacks in the other, I did so, seating myself happily and affectionately between Coady and Eric Heffer. But, typically, the cabaret was late starting. By 8 pm, as the lights dimmed and the curtain went up, I had begun to worry about Edna who, I knew, had a dinner date she hoped to keep. Finally, at 8.30, I got up in despair. 'I must let Edna go,' I whispered to Eric and pushed past him to the stairs, empty glass in one hand, empty paper plate in the other, forgetting that I had my bi-focals still on my nose. As I tried to negotiate the curving fan-shaped steps in the half-dark I suddenly felt a violent shock. I was flat on my face, hands down, shin-bone in agony, my spectacles spread-eagled in front of me. 'My specs,' was all I moaned. Mercifully they were not broken, but everything else in me seemed to be. I noted in a detached way that my fall had made hardly a stir. Eric helped to haul me up, but the only person who really identified with me in that half-dark was Shirley Williams, who was herself on the way out. It was she and some unknown gentleman from Transport House who dragged me to the car. They got me back to the House and somehow up to my room. Shirley took charge of me. She was everything one would expect of her: kind, gentle and competent as she fed me hot drinks and found blankets. 'I'll get the Whips to find a doctor,' she said. 'Who would you prefer?' 'David,' I said, 'or Maurice Miller.'

It seemed ages afterwards, as I lay with my throbbing leg, that there was a stir at the door. 'I couldn't find the others, but here is a doctor,' said a Whip. I then found, to my horror, that the one they had produced was my political 'shadow', that smiling sepulchre, Gerry Vaughan [Conservative MP for Reading South and a consultant at Guy's Hospital]. 'I'm sorry it's me, Barbara,' he said. 'I'll go and wash my hands.' I almost clutched Shirley in despair. 'Anyone but him.' But of course, I had to submit. Gerry examined my leg with intense anxiety, finally pronouncing that it was a very bad fall indeed, adding something which I found profoundly contemptible: 'If it were anyone but you, Barbara, I would have sent you for an immediate x-ray.' I knew what he meant: that, with emergency departments shut down by industrial action in a number of hospitals, his wretched profession was waiting to play medical politics with my personal pain. I hissed at him, 'I would not go for an x-ray if I were dying.' Then David, Jack Ashley and a number of them came in, clucking their sympathy. David was very worried that I had to return to an empty flat, Ted being in Brussels, and wondered how I would get upstairs. It ended with him insisting on driving home with me, where he and his driver carried me upstairs. Edna put me to bed.

Wednesday, 17 December. A day of pandemonium, with the press shattering any hope of rest I might have cherished. Our GP, Dr Colin-Russ, was round early and he too said he would like to have my leg x-rayed, as I might well have chipped or cracked the shin-bone. I told him I wouldn't hear of it. Jack came in to help me fend off an *Express* reporter and cameraman who were camped outside the front door, insisting they wanted to take a picture of me in bed. Jack and I worked out a formula for answering press queries about my injuries and why I wasn't having an x-ray. I knew I would be in trouble, whatever I said: if I *did* have an x-ray I should be accused of preferential treatment in an 'emergencies only' situation. If I did not have one, the doctors would complain I was unnecessarily libelling their profession. Indeed, Norman told me that Stevenson had already started murmurings to that effect: 'There is no reason at all why the Secretary of State should not have an x-ray,' Stevenson had told him. As I was trying to rest, the phone never stopped. First, John Stevenson of the *Mail*, as nauseatingly unctuous as ever. 'This isn't a call to get a news story or anything, Barbara, just to let you know how genuinely sorry we all are,' etc. (I later learned he was immediately on to Colin-Russ, pumping him about the x-ray.) Some time later he phoned again. 'Sorry to disturb you again, Barbara, but one thing frankly puzzles me: just why aren't you having an x-ray?' 'That is a matter between my doctor and me,' I replied and hung up. Next came Norman, gently worried. 'Look, it really is wrong that you should not have an x-ray. I know Colin-Russ would be much happier if you had one and you owe it to yourself. Won't you let me ring round some hospitals in your area to see which are working normally, so that you could attend an out-patient clinic in the normal way?' [I agreed] reluctantly.

When Colin-Russ arrived later he was very amused at the antics of the press, who had been besieging his flat, interrogating his wife and following him when he left. 'They won't get anything out of me.' He told me that Norman had discovered that Whittington Hospital was operating normally and had an out-patient clinic in the morning. 'If you attend at 11 am you won't have too long to wait.' He wanted to ring up the consultant, Peyton, to tell him I was coming, but I forbade him to. 'Just write me a doctor's letter in the usual way. I will slip along without anyone knowing I am coming.' And so it was agreed. I was immensely touched to receive a beautiful bouquet of flowers from David. He is a nice lad.

Thursday, 18 December. I dressed with some difficulty and emerged timorously into the light of day, Edna having assured me that there were no pressmen lurking outside. As she humped me downstairs and packed me into the car we congratulated ourselves on our skill in evading them. (Apparently two turned up at the flat shortly after we had left.) At the hospital we followed Ernest Colin-Russ's instructions and as we turned into the yard outside Casualty Edna said, 'Someone is expecting us.' A uniformed figure waved us on. As the car stopped a man converged on us. 'Welcome, Minister. I am the Area Administrator.' The Nursing Officer emerged and introduced herself next, signalling a porter to bring a chair. Within seconds I was being wheeled smartly up the slope into the hospital. I kept bleating in bewilderment, 'But how did you know I was coming? I didn't want anyone to know.' No reply: they just wheeled me on relentlessly towards their planned destination, a well furnished little consulting room, set apart from the out-patients. A sister and nurse sprang to attention, the door opened and in marched the consultant, Mr Peyton, prim and correct. I felt like a prisoner in a Soviet psychiatric gaol, trapped by their air of medical authority and insistence on what was the 'right' treatment for me. (I'm willing to bet that the consulting room was a private one.) It was all done so swiftly and with such a sense of the proprieties that I felt helpless against it.

What saved me was a sudden onset of delayed shock: I burst into tears and howled my heart out. 'I particularly said I did not want anyone to know I was coming. I want to be treated like anyone else. Look, I've brought my doctor's letter,' I sobbed, pushing it at Mr Peyton. 'I just want to go into the out-patients' department and queue. I don't care how long I wait: one hour, two hours. I've brought my newspapers.' (*The Times* and the *Guardian* were clutched in my bruised hand.) Nurse and sister made soothing noises. 'I'll get you a coffee,' said nurse. 'And some tissues,' I begged, my eyes streaming. Mr Peyton was clearly embarrassed: 'We merely thought, Minister, that a busy person like you would not want to be held up in out-patients, though I can assure you you won't have to wait very long anyway, as clinic is nearly over. We were not trying to give you special treatment, merely to be helpful.' If he had been more human-looking I would have clutched his arm. 'I know you meant it for the best,' I said, 'but none of you have any idea how I am persecuted by the press. They have been trying to break into my flat to photograph me in bed; they never stop ringing up, so I can't get any rest; they watch the flat door day and night and follow my doctor over on his visits to me.' 'I can assure you that the press will not learn of this visit,' Mr Peyton replied rather stiffly. 'Mr Peyton,' I pleaded, 'you don't know the press. They would bribe every patient in the building to find if I had been here.' Mr Peyton succumbed. 'I think you had better register Mrs Castle at the out-patients in the normal way,' he told sister.

So sister, a very charming woman with a detached kind of gaiety, whirled me along the corridors to registry, everyone gawping as we swept by. By this time I was near to giggles: I expect this is the first time any of them have seen a Secretary of State in floods of tears. They all carried it off with great aplomb from then on. Sister dutifully deposited me in the corridor outside Mr Peyton's room. Slamming on my brakes, she said, 'I don't think you will have to wait very long.' Nor did I. The room was much barer than the earlier one, but perfectly adequate. Mr Peyton examined my leg gravely: it certainly did look a mess. He said, 'I think it is unlikely that you have broken anything, but I want to have an x-ray to make sure,' adding, with a rather wintry smile, 'I would do the same for anyone else.' So x-rayed I was and all was well, though as he bandaged my leg (very competently), Peyton told me there was always a danger of ulceration in a case like this and I must take that very seriously, resting the leg as much as possible. I thanked him – and sister – warmly and was on my way. Back in the flat without mishap, I fell into an exhausted sleep.

Later Norman phoned to suggest that we ought to forestall press inquiries by putting out a statement about my x-ray. One paper was already asking, 'Did she have to wait or did she walk straight in?' (So all my instincts were right.) Norman more or less confessed that he was responsible for tipping them off that I was coming and when I rebuked him he said, 'Well, people want to be helpful. As the Area Administrator put it to me, "She'll never believe this, but we really are quite fond of her." ' He also said John Stevenson had been trying to get in touch with me. 'Tell him from me', I said, 'that after his poisonous piece today I intend never to speak to him on a personal basis again.' 'Delighted,' drawled Norman. 'The piece really is abominable.' For, of course, John Stevenson had managed to imply that I was tight when I fell. So it gave me great satisfaction to read in my *Standard* that Harold has taken a writ out against the *Mail* for a piece suggesting that he is 'tired' (*i.e.* brandy-soaked) and wants to quit. It might frighten them off some of their poison-pen work about other people.

I have had to leave David to handle the further 'clarification' meeting for which the juniors have asked. It is clear from what Jack tells me that at the meeting with their members on Tuesday Wardle and Zacharias played it pretty straight and genuinely tried to sell the agreement. He thought the decision to ask for further clarification was as much as anything else presentational. No doubt, too, it reflects the years of mistrust and a genuine desire for reassurance on certain points. The consultants' reaction to the pay beds settlement is far more contemptible. Norman phoned to report that their Central Committee decided today to continue its industrial action while it takes a leisurely month to ballot its rank and file on the Goodman proposals. Apparently Arnold is pretty furious, because his little group have so obviously abdicated all leadership, while Grabham positively led a revolt against the proposals he himself had agreed. What is more, they have treated Arnold more cavalierly than usual, failing to tell him what line they were taking or what was going on. Personally, I think this is all to the good: the more badly the professions behave, the more they let me off the hook – and the more they alienate that powerful objective witness, Arnold Goodman, the man they themselves retained. I decided to sleep on it. My plans to go down to HCF tomorrow remain unchanged. Apart from anything else, that fall has shaken me up more than I would have believed and my leg hurts like hell.

Friday, 19 December. Our statement on my x-ray has managed to stall off most of the papers, but the *Express* carries the headline, 'Emergency my foot!' and the *Telegraph* has sunk to its usual depths, saying that, even though I went as an out-patient under the NHS, 'she was seen by a consultant surgeon, a privilege for which many NHS patients have to wait months'. Ernest Colin-Russ was so furious at this blatant lie that he swore he'd cancel his order for the paper. I never thought to suggest he should write a letter, as my GP, to repudiate it.

I found the last remnants of my Christmas shopping a great strain and it was late afternoon before Edna and I got down to HCF. Arnold was on the phone to me, full of the poltroonery of his clients. He said he found their intention to carry on their industrial action totally unforgivable. As chairman of the Newspaper Proprietors' Association, he had offered them facilities for printing their ballot papers more quickly, but, when I snorted at this, he hastily agreed it really didn't go to the heart of their iniquity. So he was proposing to write a letter to *The Times*, saying how inexcusable it was to continue industrial action in this situation, particularly as it had been highly unconstitutional in the first place. Might he respectfully suggest that I should hold up any press comment I was considering making until he had drafted his letter and read it over to me? Of course, I agreed. No thunderings by me will have half the impact of a caustic letter by the 'independent' Arnold. He told me he had offered to go and speak to today's meeting of the consultants and describe the proposals, but they had not even done him the courtesy of informing him whether his offer was accepted. He was left to gather that it wasn't. It may prove, after all, not to have been a bad thing for this peculiar chap – half high principle and half unashamed pragmatism – to have been brought into personal dealings with this autocratic profession and to experience at first hand the kind of behaviour that has been driving Ministers of Health to despair for years. As he put it to me once during our long negotiations, 'I said to them that, when it comes to compromise in the most honourable sense of the word, she is a professional and you are a bunch of amateurs.' If he really produces this letter to *The Times* I shall begin to have some faith in him.[1]

As we talked I mentioned Harold's libel writ against the *Mail*. 'Will he win?' Arnold was unhesitant. Of course. Harold could not lose. Although as chairman of the Newspaper Proprietors' Association, Arnold couldn't act for him, he had advised Harold that he had a watertight case. The *Mail*, for all its bravado, would be bound to climb down. Said Arnold, 'I have been a friend – I might say a close friend – of Harold's for many years now.' (My ears pricked up at this.) 'I have talked with him late into the night, during which he has sipped his brandy and water. At no time in our late-night talks was his judgment ever impaired. You just can't get away with suggesting that Harold Wilson, Winston Churchill or anyone else was incapable of governing the country because they sipped brandy.' I found his ringing faith very touching, but what struck me once again was the danger I had been in when Harold first tried to cook up the deal with Arnold on pay beds behind my back. It says a great deal for Arnold's judgment that he realized my anger that night was for real, and that, if I had been double-crossed, I could have destroyed his 'close friend' by resigning.

Saturday, 20 December. Tony Keable-Elliott came in, all warm and friendly, to commiserate about my leg, offer any help he could and, above all, to cope with the cholera injection that my wretched Private Office had belatedly realized I will need for my Middle East trip[2] in a few days' time. This is going to be some Christmas!

[1] His letter, condemning industrial action by the consultants, duly appeared in *The Times* on 22 December.

[2] I had arranged to visit Saudi Arabia, Kuwait and Iran to do what I could to promote the export of medical equipment, drugs and NHS know-how generally.

Monday, 22 December. Ted has come back from Brussels well below par. He has obviously caught some kind of flu bug. He is not ill enough to give in, so droops round the house, trying to put up his traditional decorations, complaining they are no good and refusing to go to bed. I manage to pack him off there each night at 6 pm, but he leaves a trail of half-finished decorations behind him which he refuses to allow me to complete. I begin not to believe in this Christmas.

Wednesday, 24 December. Ted carried on nobly till the end of the evening's proceedings and then gave in and went to bed, not to emerge for two days.

Friday, 26 December. I carried on till the end of Boxing Day and then more or less collapsed with flu, not to emerge for a week. Not one of my happiest Christmases. All that food for Sunday's party wasted! Fortunately, the children had a whale of a time, despite the maladies of the adults. But an accumulation of overwork, that horrible fall, the cholera injection and virulent flu proved too much for me. I was so weak, I even had to cancel our visit to Phil and Colin for New Year's Eve! 'You'll never get to Kuwait unless you go back to bed,' Tony Keable-Elliott had warned me. I sent Ted off to Southampton on his own while the devoted Eileen nursed me splendidly.

One bright note in the darkness: the juniors on Tuesday accepted the results of the 'clarification' talks and are going back to work. Wasily Sakalo has sent me an unctuous series of letters, Christmas cards and calendars, declaring that there had never been anything 'personal' in our dispute. (I am getting a bit bored with these retrospective confessions of amity; they remind me of the succession of acts of contrition over nurses' pay I had from the unions.) One genuine comfort is the flood of Christmas cards I have had from total strangers this year, saying they believe I have been appallingly denigrated and unfairly abused and wanting me to know how much they admire me. That sort of thing counts, because, unlike Sakalo, these senders do not release them to the press for self-glorification. Another comfort is a glorious letter to *The Times* from George Godber,[1] following up Arnold's. I wish now I hadn't hung fire on the Department's proposals to put Godber in the Lords. A few voices like his in that ghastly place and it might begin to mean something.

Finally there has been a belated letter from Harold. I know we have all been preoccupied, and no one more than he, but I did feel I deserved a mention in Cabinet, or a message of congratulations, for having settled the juniors and brought off this deal with the consultants. But not a word from No. 10. As far as the consultants were concerned, I was quite reconciled to the fact that Harold was probably nursing a grievance over the brutal way I had pushed him out of the picture – something in which I have been strongly backed by his pal, Arnold. But I did feel the triumph with the juniors deserved a nod. Now, unexpectedly, I have received a letter of 'appreciation' from Harold for the 'hard work and long hours' I have put in over the consultants' 'package'. I found it a bit stilted, but Ted thought it warm. 'You know who has inspired that, don't you? Arnold,' he said.

[1] The letter criticized industrial action by doctors. Its most telling sentence was: 'If the present course is continued I believe that many who, like myself, have been members of the BMA since qualifying will be forced to decide whether we can remain members of a body which is prepared to pursue its objects by methods harmful to patients.' (*The Times*, 31 December 1975.)

1976

Friday, 2 January. Box-loads of work have arrived for me to do before I go [to the Middle East]. Norman reports that Goodman has been on to him about the covering document on pay beds the BMA are to send out with the ballot form. Arnold says it amounts to encouraging rejection and regards this as 'complete treachery'. However, since he is no longer sufficiently trusted by the BMA to be fully consulted about this, there is little he can do about it, he says.

Monday, 5 January. Into the office for a mad last-minute rush of meetings. A highlight was the meeting with Merrison, to invite him to chair the Royal Commission on the NHS. When at last I manœuvred my way round to this point he said bluntly that he had rather guessed I was going to offer it to him. No false modesty about that man! He asked some searching questions, saying that he needed to be reassured that the Commission would be completely free and independent. Take the terms of reference, for instance: Mrs Thatcher had pointed out to the PM in the House that they did not preclude the discussion of pay beds. They were indeed very wide. For himself, as a product of a left-wing family, he was instinctively against pay beds (so Audrey Prime was right about that!), but he thought there was a case to be examined and he could not see that the Royal Commission under its terms of reference could be excluded from examining it. Some people would say that the issue was intrinsic to the future of the NHS. My heart sank and I decided to be as blunt back – so blunt as to be almost discouraging. I began to wonder whether David had not been right after all in resisting the setting up of the Royal Commission. (The decision to do so has not, in the event, had any influence on the junior doctors' dispute at all.) I told him that the Royal Commission would be free to discuss anything it liked relating to the NHS, but the Government too had its right to freedom and independence and the Government had decided that this was an issue of principle that ought to be decided by Parliament. He kept on quibbling about this, but I stood my ground, stressing that the Government intended to go ahead with its legislation in parallel with the Royal Commission's work. I was quite relieved when he indicated that the Commission might involve him in too much work and I sent him away to think about it. The worrying thing is that Derek Stevenson has indicated to Patrick Nairne that the BMA would welcome Merrison; but Audrey Prime insists he is first-class from our point of view.

My export promotion tour of the Middle East started in Saudi Arabia. Our Embassy people there advised me to wear a long dress all the time and cover my arms in order not to offend the Saudis' susceptibilities. Apparently the Duchess of Kent on a visit there had insisted on wearing normal clothes and had got away with it, but her security guards had

had an anxious time. Apparently, too, I was the first woman Minister ever to visit Saudi Arabia, so I thought I had better not expect them to make too many adjustments at the same time. I found in my wardrobe a long cotton summer evening dress with high neck and long sleeves which did perfectly, though after I had lived in it for two-and-a-half days I began to look rather creased.

To my surprise my opposite number as Minister of Health, Dr Al Jazairy, treated me perfectly naturally. This young and highly intelligent surgeon knew his country and his job and was soon grilling me about some of the more ambitious plans for health care development put forward by British consultants and British firms. He knew, as they did not seem to have grasped, that health care planning for five million people scattered over 920,000 square miles of mainly desert, served only by primitive roads, required improvization of the simplest kind.

At the end of my talks I offered to send out a group of my officials to study Saudi problems and advise on hospital design, costs of construction, health clinics and other medical services. The Minister accepted gratefully. 'One great thing in my favour', I wrote in my diary, 'was the respect in which they all hold the NHS.'

On to Kuwait across desert wastes where the gas flares from the oil fields stood out in the darkening night. My Westernized reception at the airport made me feel an anachronism in my long, crumpled dress. Greeted by TV lights, cameras and flowers, the women all in short dresses, I was in a different world. I was soon engulfed in the warm welcome of Dr Awadhi, as enthusiastically pro-British as most of the Kuwaitis are. And I was sustained throughout my visit by the export-promotion enthusiasm of Britain's remarkable ambassador, Mr Archie Lamb. But here again I found that oil-rich Kuwait, in which every other person seemed to be a millionaire, suspected Western businessmen of trying to rob this tiny state of its sudden wealth. Dr Awadhi soon made it clear that, although his Government was prepared to spend millions on a national health service, it was not going to throw its money away. Cabinet, he assured me, had insisted on competitive tendering for all hospitals. He was ready with a long shopping list of requests for Britain's technical help: the specialists, nurses and other experts he wanted me to send out to them to train their personnel. In reply I gave him a long list of what Britain had already done in this field and was prepared to do, adding that in return I would expect British firms to get their fair share of that 'competitive tendering.' Enjoying each other's frankness, we parted in the greatest amity.

In Iran another contrast awaited me. In this huge country, the size of Western Europe, most of the population of thirty-two million live in the few towns. Teheran, I noted, was one of the dirtiest and most disappointing capital cities I had ever seen. 'Iran has a Parliament,' I wrote, 'but it is clear the Shah is boss. His picture and Farah's are everywhere.' One of my main reasons for going was to clear up problems that had arisen over a British tender for a big hospital and I soon found I was up against the familiar oil states phenomenon: a deep suspicion of foreign firms. The Minister of Social Affairs, Dr Shaikh, another surgeon, was an aggressive ball of energy who knew his facts and clearly was not going to be a pushover for anyone. So there ensued some days of hard bargaining, with Dr Shaikh insisting that the British tender was preposterously high. Our wrangle was only resolved during my visit to the Prime Minister, Mr Hoveyda. I had been warned he was a tough customer, with a remarkable survival record of ten years, but we found ourselves in unexpected harmony as a result of his obvious fascination with the NHS. He congratulated me on my fight with the British doctors, declaring that doctors had become 'the bandits of society'. I seized my advantage, pointing out that the British firms whose tender had been so much criticized had built an exactly similar hospital for the NHS. This gave him an idea. Why didn't Shaikh send someone to look at it? If the hospital was okay and the firm's price was fair, they would build one in Iran and, if all went well, would standardize on it. Dr Shaikh and I responded enthusiastically and so it was arranged.

Friday, 16 January. I told Norman in strict confidence on the plane that I intend to retire this autumn, as soon as the pay beds legislation is through. 'I want to go out of government at my peak,' I said. He said he thought I was wise. 'We are in for a nasty few months,' I told him. 'I don't suppose it will be easy to get the Bill through and no doubt my departure will be a messy business.' But I am undismayed: full of the knowledge that I have done a good job in the Middle East.

I did not allow anything to spoil my homecoming. I distributed the presents I had brought back, like an oil sheikh distributing largesse. Everyone said how blooming I looked. As for the photos Shaikh had given me of his reception for me at the mountain club, Ted said he had never seen better ones of me. 'It is a fraud to pretend the woman in those pictures is about to become an old age pensioner,' he declared. The glow continued unabated, even while I waded through three red boxes. Among the papers was the Radcliffe Report by the group of Privy Councillors Harold had set up to consider the rules for ministerial memoirs. 'The attached was discussed at Cabinet today,' minuted Gerald. 'I think you have an interest!' I have indeed – and read it at once. I have never read anything more pompously written, but it did at least say that confidentiality between colleagues was a matter of honour and not for the courts, and recommend that the period of confidentiality be reduced to fifteen years. I see from Thursday's Cabinet Minutes that, though Harold wanted to publish and accept the report at once, some members of Cabinet wanted to go further towards open government. So Harold had to allow Cabinet more time to make up its mind.

I also see that Roy Mason has, as I anticipated, got away with it on public expenditure. He had only to find defence cuts of £193 million, compared with the £400 million Denis originally asked of him. So Denis's total saving is down.

Jack has sent me a copy of the *British Medical Journal*, reporting the special meeting of Council in December on the Goodman proposals. Of course, Lewin and Grabham gave distorted reports, implying that the initiative in pressing the Goodman proposals on them had come from the PM, who had urged that they should be agreed. But, they said, they had resisted this. What cowards they are! And how essential it is that I should have kept a detailed record of what actually took place.

Monday, 19 January. Spent the day working myself in at the office pretty peacefully. I doubt if it will be as relaxed as this much longer! Norman tells me he keeps being peppered with messages from No. 10 to the effect that Ministers must not retain expensive gifts they acquire on their foreign travels: anything worth more than £30 must become the property of the Department. 'I'm afraid we'll have to hang the Persian picture Shaikh gave you in the office,' he said, 'for a time, at any rate!'

Tuesday, 20 January. Office meeting on the Royal Commission. Merrison has accepted the chairmanship, with no serious further demur about the right to deal with the pay beds issue. Indeed, he has been exchanging confidential letters with Patrick Nairne, in which, while reiterating again the need for the Royal Commission to be, and be seen to be, completely independent, he has said he wouldn't like the issue of pay beds to be referred to them for an interim report.

Wednesday, 21 January. To my fury, tomorrow's Cabinet has been switched to this morning, which means I shall have to miss the first of the series of informal meetings with chairmen of local authority social service committees that I have arranged with such difficulty. Just my luck, to launch an important new initiative and then not be able to be there! It is all the more irritating because the only item for Cabinet, apart from parliamentary business, is the Radcliffe Report. Harold agreed with me that press leaks were the biggest example of the breaches of confidentiality we were supposed to deplore. Nonetheless, he had little difficulty in getting acceptance of the report through that supine Cabinet. So I face having to sign a bit of paper saying I won't do anything in breach of the report, while my colleagues – including Harold – will go on merrily briefing the press. As I told them, 'I am constitutionally incapable of leaking to the press.' And I don't intend to sign anything which prevents me putting distorted records straight.

I am also in the middle of a major row on abortion. The Labour women MPS have secured a discussion in Party meeting tomorrow on whether the Select Committee should be re-established.[1] They have been begging me to say, in replying to the discussion, that I am against it being set up again. David has told them he is sure I will and he and I have been working on a draft speech giving the reasons why I think the Select Committee has finished its useful work. I have made up my mind that the time has come for me to stand up and be counted on this and I have arranged for my speech to be released to the press in full. Somehow all this has leaked and in the lobbies this evening I have been besieged by irate Catholics.

Finally Harold waylaid me and took me to his room. His eyes were baggy and I noted that he was in one of his 'I'll get the hell out of it' moods. (I personally think he is getting ready to chuck things up.) Pouring me a brandy he said he had given up brandy himself in order to lose weight, arguing that for some unknown reason he had actually lost weight since switching to beer. 'I drink five pints a day,' he boasted, but proceeded to pour himself some Madeira. The pleasantries over, we proceeded to have a major row. He told me categorically that he wasn't going to have me splitting the Party. 'I'm sick of pulling this Party back from the brink. If this goes on I shall throw in my hand – and then see how some of you will get along.' 'Like who?' I replied, at which he gave me

[1] For some time there had been determined attempts in certain quarters of the House to limit, or even reverse, the provisions of the 1967 Abortion Act which legalized abortion in certain circumstances. One of these efforts, a Private Member's Bill introduced in November 1964, by James White, Labour MP for the highly Catholic constituency of Glasgow (Pollok), had aroused intense controversy and led to the setting up of a Select Committee to examine it. By the time the previous session had ended the Committee had only been able to make some relatively uncontroversial recommendations for strengthening the safeguards against abuse, on which David Owen and I were already acting, but the anti-abortionists were demanding that the Committee be reconstituted in order to consider more fundamental changes. It was this that David and I were resisting because we believed that the Act was basically sound, but the Government had agreed to put the matter to the House.

a hostile look, as if to say, 'You'd go, for one.' Does he realize how little his threats worry me? Harold then laid down the law: I could say how I was going to vote personally, but I must not give any reasons. If I did I must give both sides of the issue, or another Minister would have to put the reasons the other way. I quite liked this latter idea, but he did not. 'Perhaps someone else had better speak tomorrow. John Silkin, for instance,' Harold went on. I told him John was as much against re-establishing the Select Committee as I was. 'And imagine what will be said if I do not speak now,' I continued. He went on menacing me about how neutral I must be in my arguments, ending nastily, 'Think about it.' I did, going to bed wondering how I could salvage something from this wreck. Clearly the speech David and I have drafted will not do.

Thursday, 22 January. Got up early to rewrite my abortion speech. I was rather pleased with it, having, I thought, rather skilfully implied the case for not reappointing the Select Committee without defying Harold's fiat or putting backs up. And, of course, I stated that I would be voting against. Jack and David thought it was excellent, though David looked grim at Harold's ruling. 'It is going to make our position very difficult in the debate,' he said.

The meeting of the PLP was exceptionally well attended, for a Thursday night. All the abortion antagonists were there. As Shirley slipped into a seat next to me on the platform she whispered, 'I've come to the conclusion that your job is even worse than mine.' In the debate Kevin McNamara demanded that I should not disclose my own views, as this would inevitably carry the weight of a Secretary of State. Brian Walden, on the other hand, made a passionately eloquent speech, demanding that the Party should have the courage of its convictions and I of mine. I sat there calmly, convinced that the speech I had prepared would strike exactly the right note between the two. And so it proved. It was temperate, cunning and firm and it did the trick. 'Ten out of ten,' said Bob Mellish loudly afterwards.

Sunday, 25 January. My constituency conscience is at rest after a two-day visit to Blackburn. Ted is at home for the weekend, his hospital tests having so far proved negative.[1] But he has to go back for more tonight. Going through my boxes I find the *British Medical Journal*, with its report of the BMA Council meeting on 7 January. Once again, I note how Lewin and co. are wriggling over their responsibility for the Goodman proposals. Lewin was reported as repeating that the PM had asked Goodman to prepare the proposals. 'The meetings which were held over the next few days with Lord Goodman were simply to enable the profession's representatives to act as technical advisers,' he declared. Really!

Monday, 26 January. The cameras were outside Transport House as I arrived for the anticipated row over unemployment at the TUC Liaison Committee. Harold and Jim were missing, but the trade unions were there in force – even Hughie Scanlon. The original purpose of the meeting was to discuss the Devolution White Paper, but Tom Bradley, in the chair, suggested we took

[1] My husband had been losing weight and appetite and his consultant had sent him to the London Hospital for blood tests.

unemployment first. Jack Jones said grimly he would walk out unless we did. Len led off for the TUC, saying there was 'great concern' for the effect that unemployment could have on relations between the TUC and the Government. 'There is scope for selective action.' Jack Jones came in to support that. Hughie Scanlon was almost desperate. 'Whatever we do, we have missed the bus and it is going to be calamitous. Do you ever listen to us?' Alf Allen was sombre: 'The issue of credibility is crucial. I hope we are not all going to lose our nerve and indulge in virtuoso solos. Any criticism of each other in public does irreparable harm to what we are trying to do.' I found it all desperately moving, like a Greek drama. We all feel caught in a web and are fighting to keep our human identity. Denis welcomed the 'tone' of the discussion and promised to consult the TUC about the rate of reflation and to consider the particular suggestions. In the end the trade union boys were somewhat mollified – and obviously deeply anxious to preserve our unity and the Government.

A long meeting back at the office on Instructions to Parliamentary Counsel for the Private Practice Bill. I began by saying that that title (which the office had cooked up) would not do. This wasn't a Bill to safeguard private practice, but to phase out pay beds. So we agreed on the title of the 'NHS (Miscellaneous Provisions) Bill'.[1] (We are hoping to include in it mandatory vocational training for GPs, anyway.) We then went through it line by line, with me examining every dot and comma to ensure that we were not entering any trap. I noted with relief that most of the text covered the phasing out of private out-patient facilities from NHS hospitals as well.

Tuesday, 27 January. Our Parliamentary Questions went smoothly, not to say boringly. The Opposition is so muted these days it is hardly fun. Patrick Jenkin, making his first appearance on the front bench against me, didn't take me on. It was left to Gerry Vaughan to make some snide remarks about my Middle Eastern trip. I was sorry that my PQ on this was not reached. I sat in a glow of secret virtue over what I had done and a sense of satisfaction that Margaret Thatcher has ditched that posturing emptiness, Norman Fowler, and moved him to Transport. After his fiasco in trying to bring me down, it is hardly surprising, but I take it unto myself as a compliment. It is I, not he, who has drawn blood.

Wednesday, 28 January. At the office I turned the tables on David by saying to him: 'I warn you that, if the BMA ballot is unfavourable, it will be impossible for us to go ahead with the Goodman proposals. The Party and the unions will demand that we go ahead with our legislation as originally planned.' And I added, 'If Harold and Cabinet try to force me to overrule the Party on this, I shall resign. I do not intend to end my ministerial days with another *In Place of Strife*.' I think David saw the force of this. When I said, 'We shouldn't be in this mess if Harold had not cooked up that meeting with Goodman and the profession behind my back', he nodded vigorous agreement. 'That Rome business was outrageous,' he said.

[1] We later changed it again to the Health Services Bill, which became the Health Services Act in November 1976.

Friday, 30 January. [Off to Newcastle.] A dreadful journey in a freezing sleeper. The winter has taken an icy turn. Even young Gerald said to me that he had slept 'dreadfully'. There was a howling nor' easter waiting for us at Newcastle, but a warm breakfast in the hotel suite soon revived my spirits, which weren't even dampened when the Controller, Whitaker, told me that the CPSA had called on its members at our Newcastle office to demonstrate in their thousands against the proposed manpower cuts when I did my tour. Apparently this had been sparked off partly by an article in *Labour Weekly*, saying that the cuts must inevitably concentrate on places like Newcastle. My trouble was that I had a great deal of sympathy with the CPSA over this. Reading my briefs for the visit last night, I was shocked to discover how officials have interpreted the implications of the manpower cuts in their 'confidential' preliminary talks with the staff sides. They take them to imply an actual reduction in the manpower figures for 1978–79 *below* those operating last year. This isn't at all what I – and I am sure other members of Cabinet – had in mind when agreeing to Harold's rather hazy proposals for £140 million cuts on administrative costs. I certainly do not intend to accept the postponement of any of my new policies: the new pensions scheme, child benefit, etc. This would be merely to impose on me by a side wind the sort of PESC cuts I have successfully resisted – at a time, too, when Roy Mason has been allowed to include manpower cuts in his castrated contribution to PESC.

So I felt inhibited in dealing with the demonstration which faced me. I told Whitaker that I wanted above all not to seem to be running away from the demo. I wanted the car to stop short of it, so that I could be seen to be walking voluntarily towards the crowd, not bulldozing my way through it. And so it was arranged. A mass of people was awaiting me as the car drew up. I got out and walked towards my excited staff, with hand outstretched. The women at the front seized my hand eagerly; the rest crowded round in good-humoured curiosity. Only a few shouted hostilities.

Later I met the staff representatives. I told them it *was* true that the Government was considering manpower economies as part of its overall public expenditure cuts, but that it was *not* true that any detailed decisions had yet been made. As we broke up the meeting the one woman among them insisted on saying a word: 'I wanted you to know that we think the way you behaved with the crowd was magnificent.'

Monday, 2 February. My life is temporarily becalmed. Not only are there two days running with only one-line whips, but the office pressure has died down. I merely enjoyed my lull before the storm. Hopefully, pressures will be less intense during my final months in this job. A Minister really ought to have three years in a Department. The third year, by definition, is more relaxed and one can read oneself into much greater depth on one's subject instead of carrying on a hand-to-mouth guerrilla warfare with one's colleagues, with the medical profession, etc.

Jack has sent me a memo on NUPE's new line on pay beds, vigorously attacking my compromise. Well, it won't do any harm for the profession to be made aware of NUPE's militancy. The juniors, led once again by the North-West, are beginning to stir things up about pay beds. Sakalo, foiled of his great triumph over the juniors' contract, is turning his attention to this issue to disguise his failure, and David tells me he himself had a rough time with juniors from the South-West last week.

Tuesday, 3 February. I popped into the House to see the tail-end of the 'retirement of a Speaker, election of a new one' ceremony. The House was packed: it really does love the oozy unctuousness of consensus politics. Every modest little joke raised an enthusiastic laugh. Half an hour of it was enough for me.

Wednesday, 4 February. I am angry with Harold for another typical piece of cowardice. My officials, working with their usual scrupulous correctitude, have been busy trying to see that we achieve our target of getting the Second Reading of the pay beds Bill before Easter. Bob Mellish has warned us all that any Bills coming up later than that won't have a cat in hell's chance of reaching the statute book. So, in addition to beavering away at Instructions to Parliamentary Counsel, officials have been planning to get ahead with provisional consultations with health authorities on the contents of the Schedule, and have prepared a document warning the authorities they will have to go into a quick huddle with the medical profession on this as soon as the results of the BMA ballot are known. No. 10 has now vetoed this, saying we must await the outcome of the ballot. This is to play straight into the hands of the BMA, which hasn't exactly been hustling. Indeed, Arnold has complained to me more than once about their leisureliness. So I wrote to Harold pointing this out – and the fact that it is in the interests of the BMA to delay things until it is too late to legislate. (They have now announced that they have messed up the ballot. Some consultants never got their papers, so a supplementary ballot has got to be held!) Harold has replied through Ken Stowe to the effect that he still does not want me to proceed. If he sells me out over this I shall resign and denounce him publicly. My request to have a word with him has been turned down on the grounds that he has two speeches to prepare.

Harold has also got cold feet over the political advisers. He has ruled that Denis Healey's chap, Adrian Mann, may not attend the Finance and Economic Committee of the NEC and has done it in such a way that the position of other advisers on other NEC committees is uncertain. Jack and Brian A-S. are utterly dismayed. They cannot, apparently, continue to service the Social Policy Sub-Committee. The sheer short-sightedness of Harold's attitude alarms me as much as his trimming over the role of the very political advisers he agreed to create. I rang Denis to get his support in resisting this, but all he said was that he had told Harold he wasn't prepared to have his chap treated any differently from other special advisers, adding, 'I don't feel quite the same way as you do over this.' I finally decided in despair that I must take this up with Harold myself, which I did in another Minute. Fortunately, he replied that Jack and co. could continue to serve, pending a discussion of the whole matter in Cabinet. I cannot believe that Harold's trimming to hostile prejudice does him any good with anyone.

Yet, combined with this deep instinct for conventionality, Harold has a wild streak of recklessness running through him. He has got all steamed up about the Jeremy affair,[1] telling some of us at lunch in the House that he believed that it was all a plot to discredit Jeremy, set up by agents of the South African Government because the Liberal Party had opposed South African policies. He hinted darkly that he knew all about that sort of thing and had his spies working on it, because he had been the victim of it: the theft of his own confidential papers. Well, he may well be right, but I wish he would deal with it coolly, discreetly and silently, as a calculated expression of political principle, instead of in this erratic and dramatic Goldfinger way.

Thursday, 5 February. Cabinet has finally cleared the White Paper on Public Expenditure [Cmnd 6393]. I was rather pleased with the draft, because it demonstrated vividly how much more successful I have been than some of my colleagues in defending my programmes. In fact, the section on social security listed all my Department's policy initiatives on the disabled, child benefit, the new pensions scheme and so on as established fact, actually giving the dates for their implementation. Poor Fred Mulley, goaded by the summary at the end of his section (which showed a list of nothing but reductions), protested against the draft. 'You are just handing our critics their speeches in the House, ready written,' he moaned. Denis, relieved no doubt at having got a total of £3 billion reductions on expenditure in 1978–79 out of us, was in a generous mood. 'I will accept Cabinet's view on this.' So, with Bob backing Fred, it was agreed that the summaries at the end of each section, pointing out the changes from the previous PESC White Paper, should be deleted. Fortunately, I discovered before it was too late that this would eliminate all the list of Treasury's commitments to me. So the decision was amended to say that, although the separate heading on changes in expenditure should be omitted, Ministers should have the discretion to incorporate what parts of the substance they wanted in the main draft. I made a mental note that I would include most of the bits of mine. I intend to tie Treasury down in print.

Denis prefaced all this by saying that we should be attacked for not doing enough to reduce public expenditure. There would be big increases this year (5 per cent instead of the estimated $2\frac{1}{2}$ per cent), and next year as well, when there would be an increase of $1\frac{1}{2}$ per cent instead of an anticipated fall. The reason for the 1978–79 cut-backs in programmes was the big increase in expenditure on industry, so we should have to emphasize how much we had tightened control through such things as cash limits. History had shown that control by Cabinet was very weak – particularly under the Tories.

At lunch in the House Harold came over to me to say he wanted a private word with me. He has got a new idea for his plot to expose the anti-Jeremy machinations, on which he said Albert Murray was already working and 'in

[1] On 29 January Mr Norman Scott had been charged in a Barnstaple court with dishonestly obtaining £14.60 in supplementary benefits, and alleged that he was being hounded because of a sexual relationship he had had with Jeremy Thorpe. Jeremy had immediately denied the allegations, but the press had been full of revelations about the payment of money to Scott by Peter Bessell, former Liberal MP, and others. Thorpe's position as Liberal Leader had already been weakened by the publication on 29 January of a critical Department of Trade report on the collapse of a fringe bank, London and County Securities, of which he had been a non-executive director. On 5 February he survived a grilling by his fellow Liberal MPs, but Scott's allegations continued to multiply and in May Thorpe resigned as Party leader, claiming that a 'sustained witch hunt' by the press had made his and the Party's

which the Lady Falkender is naturally taking a great interest'. He believes that the Tories, or someone even more sinister, put Scott up to announcing his alleged association with Jeremy. 'The Tories had this information as long ago as 1972. Why didn't they use it then? My theory is that they thought it would rebound on Heath. But now they see their opportunity to destroy the Liberal Party. They wouldn't be beyond paying Scott to make his allegations now. And what better way of getting maximum publicity than to do it in a court case? So I want you to make some discreet inquiries about the prosecution your Department brought against Scott for fraud. How did it originate? How was he discovered? Did he even volunteer the information on which he was prosecuted?' I said I would put Jack on to it as, apart from anything else, he was a barrister. Harold thought this was a good idea and wanted the information by Monday. So, back at the office, I passed the message on to Jack and Norman in confidence. Norman spoke to the Permanent Secretary and Jack went off to do some ferreting.

Saturday, 7 February. At HCF two crammed boxes awaited me. I fear I am going to have trouble with David again over pay beds – but that's for Monday. There is a nice telegram in my box from Kuwait: from Marshall, the Commercial Counsellor, to Laurie Walker, saying that they have had a visit from Gavin Ellis, marketing director of Cementation, who was 'unreserved in his praise of Mrs Castle, whose recent meeting in London with contractors he had attended, for the work she is doing to assist British exporters'. Well, that makes a welcome change from Patrick Jenkin and the *Telegraph*, who are jointly pursuing me over the export deals I am trying to pull off. I would love British firms to pull off big contracts in Iran, thank me publicly and show up the critics.

The personal venom in the right-wing press against me and Ted shows no bounds. Poor old Ted has just had a taste of it. When he went into the London Hospital three weeks ago for the tests his excellent consultant, Brigden, has been planning for some time – they are worried about his traces of diabetes and his loss of weight – he found, to his poor dear innocent delight, that, unbeknown to him, Brigden had put him in a side room of the ward. Then, a few days later, the secretariat of the hospital rang Ted up to say the press were trying to see him and Ted told them to tell the press to get stuffed. Suddenly a charming young lass from the *Mail* walked into Ted's room brandishing a notebook and he saw her to the door. The poor innocent still didn't know what was going to hit him, but there it all was the next day in the *Mail* – 'The privacy of a single room for battling Barbara's Ted' – plus a picture of the two of us at his inauguration into the Lords, ermine and all. Ted was furious – he even toyed with the idea of taking it up with the Press Council – but I headed him off. I told him that you just have to accept that you can't win with the press and the next instalment of this thrilling drama proved it. When Ted returned to the hospital to continue his tests he was told that his single room had been needed for a man in a violent state (which the man certainly was), so he had been put in the general ward. Ted went into the ward perfectly happily, because he is a

position impossible. In December 1978 he was committed for trial at the Old Bailey with others for conspiracy and incitement to murder Scott. After a sensational trial he was acquitted the following year.

naturally gregarious chap anyway. However, the press hadn't finished with him. The next day the *Telegraph* and *Mail* carried stories to the effect that Lord Castle had been moved as a result of their revelations. This time Ted only shrugged. He is learning to take it. But the drama wasn't over. I was thankful Ted was in Brussels, his tests having proved negative, when the *Mail* delivered its final (?) shaft. There was a prominent piece in Nigel Dempster's diary on Monday to the effect that the whole ward had been thankful when Lord Castle left, because he had thrown his weight about and had obviously resented not being treated as a VIP. This brought savage rage rising into my gorge. I repeated something I often say bitterly to Ted, 'The press does not report news; it invents it.' Ted used to have great rows with me about this attitude and – to do him credit – he probably still would.

Monday, 9 February. Office meeting on the juniors to tidy up some last points on their new contract. Also a discussion on exports policy, with which Collier, catching my enthusiasm, is faithfully pressing ahead. His procurement policy working group is just about ready to submit its report to me on how we can rationalize the procurement of supplies in the NHS.

Tuesday, 10 February. I had insisted on accepting the *Financial Times* invitation to address their conference on pensions, even though it meant mugging up a lot of up-to-date technical details. In doing so I discovered that we are about to make a number of regulations on such important matters as equal access for women to firms' pensions schemes, so I told the office to hold them up till I could announce them in my speech. So it became quite a major one, Brian O'Malley co-operating willingly in my hogging the announcements in this way. There is a very real comradeship and loyalty between us. His trouble now is that he hasn't got enough to do and is bored. He would love a change of job.

Wednesday, 11 February. Long office meeting on the pay beds Bill, now renamed on my insistence the NHS (Miscellaneous Provisions) Bill. One of the problems over the Schedule is that if we attempt to give too much detail we shall run into hybridity.[1] So we must give merely an aggregate figure for the pay beds to be abolished in each area, making it clear that the figure has been based on a formula. I insisted that the Bill must allow the withdrawal of *all* pay beds in a hospital where this met the formula and suited our book. David was very restive about this. However, I stood firm. On licensing, I said we should try and get the profession to take the initiative in indicating the lines a voluntary system might take and that, for a start, officials should approach the IHG. I also told the office to prepare a Minute to the PM, asking for permission to go ahead with consultations, now that the outcome of the ballot is imminent. The biggest worry is the provision in Goodman allowing part-time consultants to continue to use specialized facilities in the NHS. We have strengthened the safeguards against abuse of this as much as possible, but I suggested an additional one: an

[1] A Public Bill may be declared hybrid, or semi-private, if it affects in part only a small, identifiable group of persons. In addition to the stages of a Public Bill, hybrid Bills are subject to lengthy Select Committee examination.

obligation on the Secretary of State to make an annual report to Parliament on the use of these powers. I think it will provide a useful check.

In the morning I had had an amusing time addressing the annual conference of Local Optical Committee representatives. Once again, it meant reading up all sorts of technical details ready for the question time I had agreed to take, but I volunteered to go because officials are so full of dire anxieties about my proposals to improve NHS spectacle frames. They have hinted at incipient revolt among opticians and had studded my brief with cautions about the need to play this down, say as little as possible, etc. This is, of course, because they don't want to try to do anything seriously on this anyway. But my tactic is always to face up to trouble as the only way to get something done. In the event, the occasion turned out to be surprisingly amicable. First, they were delighted I had volunteered to come; secondly, they were naturally courteous; thirdly, I teased them and made them laugh; fourthly, I presented my proposals as the reasonable development of the NHS, which they are. It went swimmingly and my relieved officials could not believe their ears. 'This will prove very helpful in our discussions,' said the one of them who had been foremost in advising me to play my proposals down.

One unexpected snag nearly floored me: most of my notes for questions were, as usual, prepared for me in dim and almost illegible type, which I can't read without my glasses. Yet the frames of my glasses were obviously private ones and, although I have never hidden the fact that I do wear private frames, and indeed make a point of the fact that the unattractiveness of NHS frames forces most women to do so, I knew the press photographers would be there and that the only thing the press would report of my speech would be my private frames: plus a large photo. So I decided to manage without my glasses somehow, which I did by dodging the illegible statistics and quipping my way through the answers, to the audience's delight. But it was a near thing.

Thursday, 12 February. I hurried into Cabinet early to give Harold the résumé Jack has done of the Scott file. Harold's face dropped a bit when I told him it seemed to show Jeremy's relationship with Scott had been longer and more domesticated than he had so far admitted. My aim is to warn Harold against going overboard for Jeremy too recklessly. He has already made a rather hysterical attack on the press for 'hounding' Jeremy and has exposed himself to an attack in a *Mirror* leader today. He really is an incredible mixture of caution and recklessness. Anyway, Harold thanked me for the work Jack had done, so perhaps it will do the political advisers a bit of good.

At Cabinet the two questions in which I was particularly interested were Denis's anti-unemployment package and the White Paper on direct elections to the European Parliament. On the first, I was very angry because there was no paper in front of us. Indeed, I have found it very difficult to find out what is going on, because no letters or Minutes have been circulated. Instead, we had an oral report by Denis on what he is proposing to announce this afternoon. Since his package will contain a not inconsiderable commitment of public expenditure (£220 million gross: £137 million in 1976–77), including £50 million on the construction industry, it is extremely relevant to the expansionist activities of our different Departments. I cornered Mike in the House a few days ago and gathered, from his rather evasive response, that all the money was going to go on housing improvements – I suspected with his approval. And so it proved.

Denis began by telling us that the package had been approved in detail by the MES [Ministerial Economic Strategy] committee of Cabinet and he kept a wary eye on me while he spelt it out: all £220 million of it. As soon as he had finished I leapt in with my complaint: why had we not had a paper? Why should all this be drawn up by an 'inner Cabinet deciding a mini-PESC'? I had a lot of old people at risk in old people's homes with inadequate fire precautions, and a terrifying backlog of hospital maintenance work; why could this not have been included in the construction package? Housing old people was 'housing' as much as anything else. Mike came in at once to say, 'I must say Barbara has a case.' But his remedy was to increase the amount Denis was making available. Denis, of course, was not willing to do this. Harold made soothing noises to the effect that the Chancellor had said he might need another package. The claims of the rest of us might be considered then. I persisted. 'I hope it will be minuted that there has been an additional allocation of £50 million to housing under PESC, and that, when the Chancellor has another round, it will be the turn of the rest of us.' 'I have no doubt that those who are responsible for drawing up the Minutes have already noted your points,' Harold drawled.

But my major concern was over the White Paper on direct elections, which we turned to at the derisory hour of 12.15 pm. Once again, this was typical of how to lead a Cabinet by the nose. Jim introduced the draft White Paper complacently. 'The Prime Minister and I have both given undertakings to the Community to support direct elections,' he said. We should therefore publish the White Paper, have a debate in the PLP, then a debate in the House, and it would then go to the European Council. Roy J. and Ted Short said they had nothing to add to what Jim had said. I'm not surprised!

Peter opened for the Dissenting Ministers by demanding that the paper should be labelled Green. Among other defects, 'the question of the relation of the European Parliament to the British Parliament is not looked at at all'. I then became airborne. The implications of the White Paper, I said, would have far-reaching consequences, yet it was suggested that the matter should be 'finalized' at the European Council in April. It was outrageous to rush this vital discussion through so quickly. We had never discussed this matter fully in Cabinet. Jim kept interrupting me to say that all the White Paper was doing was to quote the Assembly's suggestions, not to recommend them. I retorted by quoting paragraphs which showed that was not true. And I ended by pointing out that Article 138 of the Treaty of Rome expressed the intention to move to direct elections by a 'uniform procedure'. Now the European Council said it was too soon for that. Okay, then if it was too soon for uniformity, there was no commitment to rush the decision on direct elections either. Harold tried to dismiss my fears by insisting that there was 'not a cat in hell's chance of getting this settled in April'. This was a White Paper 'with very green edges'. Denis backed him heartily.

All this only justified everything I had said, as Mike hastened to point out. In his view it ought to be a Grey paper (*i.e.* one which made it clear no one was committed to it at all). 'A bargaining position in April commits us all.' The best proposal was to refer the matter to a Speaker's Conference and not take any decisions till then. Wedgie capped it all with one of his witty cracks. He thought we needed a new type of classification: this should be a Blue Paper, like a firework. 'One lights it, stands back and waits for it to explode.' We all laughed, but there were some sly grimaces at the aptness of the description. Haven't we drifted into this constitutional dilemma as a result of Harold's and Jim's ad hoc-ery: pretending the problems wouldn't be there until they were on top of us? And Wedgie went on devastatingly to describe how relentlessly we were confusing the channels of democratic decision-making. The British people had been trained to look to their Parliament as the repository of democratic power. Now we were busy fragmenting this: there was to be a Scottish Assembly, a British Parliament and then a European one as well. Where would power really lie? I thought his case was unanswerable and Harold bowed to it to the extent of hastily agreeing that the paper should be labelled Green and that it should make clear that no final decisions would be reached in April. So our row did some good.

But all this time I had been getting restive. It was by now 1.15 pm and I had been supposed to be at a lunch at the *Mirror* at 1 pm. I was furious when Harold said we must now turn to the text of the ['green'] White Paper, on which I had a lot of points I wanted to make. It really was intolerable for Harold to put this vital item last on the agenda, so that there was not proper time to consider it. People were already beginning to drift out and I had to go. The *Mirror* lunch was very important to me and I was already going to be half an hour late for it. Harold's behaviour was typical of the tactics of the pro-Europeans: refusing to take the future of the British House of Commons seriously. There is a story in today's *Times* to the effect that John Roper [Labour and Co-op MP for Farnworth] has written to Jim, on behalf of the Labour Committee for Europe, sending him a long memorandum on how direct elections should be organized. It even hints at the necessity for us to accept PR! That would put paid to any hope of a Labour majority: either here or in Europe. But I have always believed that the aim of the Jenkinsites is coalition government.

The *Mirror* lunch was a little private one with Tony Miles, editorial director, Mike Molloy, the new editor, and Terry Lancaster. I took Jack Straw along with me. It arose from a leader on the junior doctors the *Mirror* did some days ago which was so unexpectedly unfair and untrue it took my breath away. True to my new determination not to take these misrepresentations lying down, I got on to Tony Miles, who promptly invited me to have lunch with the three of them. It was a very pleasant affair. Tony admitted that the leader had been a bit much; we explained the facts. Great camaraderie. Just as we were finishing Jack was called to the phone. It was the result of the BMA ballot on the Goodman proposals. Fifty-three per cent poll. Good: it shows that pay beds is not the burning issue the BMA makes it out to be. Only two thousand odd (15 per cent of all consultants) were for handing in undated resignations. Again, good. But alas, a two to one majority (of those voting) for accepting the Goodman proposals. My face dropped. 'Bad,' I said to Jack. This means I am saddled with the Goodman proposals and my hopes of modifying them are gone. Yet I am saddled with them in a situation in which it is clear that we need never have accepted this fudged and dangerous compromise, if only Harold hadn't panicked and played into Goodman's hands. I face a terribly difficult bit of tightrope walking now.

My realization of this was strengthened when, back at the office, I met a deputation from NUPE to discuss the pay beds issue, at their request. The union's Executive had come out firmly against the compromise. Alan Fisher was obviously a bit embarrassed and put their case against the Goodman proposals moderately. I put a good face on it, while David made a telling plea for us to go for a solution that would 'stick' and that a successor government would not feel able to undo. I could see that Alan and the union President were impressed with this, but David was followed by an Executive member who clearly was *not*. A quiet, elderly man, he dismissed what we had said with contempt. 'We have a great admiration and respect for you, Mrs Castle. Nonetheless, we will not accept what you propose.' Bernard Dix[1] went even further, hinting that if the legislation did not fix a terminal date for phasing out pay beds, not only would the union mobilize the whole Labour movement against us, but take industrial action. Well, I'm not sorry to see that the trade unions have some life in them. This strengthens my hand in that craven Cabinet. But it is going to make great difficulties for me politically. I longed to go out with a pay beds triumph to my credit as the last achievement of my career. Now the last image of me will be smeared.

One thing I am determined: I am not going to let the BMA delay the legislation as it clearly intends to try to do. News has come in that the consultants' Central Committee has had a hurried meeting on the ballot result and passed two resolutions: one saying they will continue their out-and-out opposition to the legislation (fine: that helps me); two, that they will seek further 'exploration' of the Goodman proposals. If anyone thinks I am getting into a huddle with Goodman again, they are wrong. Typically, I heard David and Patrick agreeing that the result was 'good'. Patrick even told me it was a great success for me and the Government. We just don't begin to see eye to eye on this! It made me all the more determined to rush a Minute to Harold, setting out the position to date and saying we must go ahead with the legislation immediately. I must say that David was all in favour of our going ahead and publishing our Bill without further consultations with the BMA, except on the two points on which we are committed to consult by the Goodman proposals: the contents of the Schedule and the prospects of a voluntary agreement on licensing. We don't expect to reach agreement on the latter by any stretch of the imaginaton, and agreed that we should include the reserve powers in the Bill. After all, they are *reserve* powers. If Harold has any guts at all he will give me my head from now on.

Friday, 13 February. Peter Jenkins has got a piece in the *Guardian* urging Roy Jenkins to put his head above his parapet and go for a meaningful job like Northern Ireland. It is obvious that Roy's friends are shaping up for the succession to Harold and haven't given up the intention of pressing Roy for the leadership.

Monday, 16 February. Peter Brown has laid on the most intensive pre-briefing

[1] Alan Fisher's Assistant General Secretary for Research in NUPE.

of journalists on the PESC White Paper I have ever undertaken. It arises from a decision we DHSS Ministers reached last week that we would make a great 'interpretative' effort on the White Paper in order to boost morale in the NHS and prevent the press talking about 'crisis cuts'. Peter has thrown himself into it with gusto and I found myself in the deep end today with the *Guardian* first (Malcolm Dean and John Cunningham), next Joe Rogaly, and finally dinner with Tony Shrimsley of the *Mail*! Peter assured me that if I made it clear my comments were unattributable, and that any use of the material I gave them was embargoed till Thursday, they would play the game. So I found myself in the unusual situation of 'leaking' like mad in the knowledge nothing would be used. All the journalists were immensely grateful for this chance to digest one aspect of what is going to be a very detailed White Paper well in advance of the publication rush and I developed quite an effective line of patter, spelling out how much better the NHS had done than we dared to hope. And I could not resist pointing out that my cut was the smallest of all (essential to the NHS morale-boosting process). God knows what will come out of it, but they seemed impressed. Tony Shrimsley, over an excellent meal at Overtons, got so carried away he asked me if he might do an advance story about how Barbara Castle had saved the National Health Service in the PESC battle, swearing that he wouldn't put in any figures or details. I'm afraid I fell. It would be such a remarkable change to have the *Mail* reporting anything to my credit that I don't suppose the story will be used.

Tuesday, 17 February. Harold has replied to my long Minute on the meaning of the consultants' ballot by saying I must bring the matter before Cabinet and not enter into any consultations meanwhile. I exploded to Patrick that if this was not put on Cabinet agenda this week, we should lose the legislation. 'And then', I warned him, 'I will resign, the unions will go on strike and the PLP will go through the roof.' He said anxiously that he would get on to Ken Stowe in the Cabinet office. Whether that did the trick, or whether Harold would have done it anyway, the item is coming up this Thursday. If Cabinet delays the legislation, I shall walk out without a moment's regret.

Wednesday, 18 February. To my horror, I found that Shrimsley had got his story into the *Mail*: 'Barbara's Threats Halt Health Service Cuts.' How my colleagues will hate my guts! I steeled my courage for tomorrow's attacks in Cabinet. Anyway, my colleagues do this kind of thing to me every day of the week and I have at least offset the headlines which would otherwise inevitably have flowed in, like the one in last night's *Evening News*: 'London Faces Savage Cuts in Health Service.' (In quotation marks: but the origin of the quote was not identified.)

Peter Jenkins has gone up in my estimation by writing a piece in the *Guardian* attacking, by inference, the Roy Jenkins line that public expenditure is becoming a threat to democracy. Some sense at last!

Thursday, 19 February. I don't know why I've worried about my 'briefing' of the press. The papers yesterday were full of a real leak on the civil service manpower cuts, particularly as they affect Mike and me. I think this *must* have been a civil servant: there is no political axe-grinding involved here. Cabinet was reduced by flu: Jim and Roy J. being smitten, while Wedgie was in the US talking energy policy. That meant I had one less ally, but two less enemies, for my two major items: pay beds and fuel bonus. Harold has obviously felt compelled to bring my Minute on pay beds to Cabinet and looking back at the 27 November Cabinet Minutes, I can see why. He only got away with his ploy then by promising we would report the outcome of our 'consultations' to Cabinet. But I was far from sure to what extent he was now ready to back me up. I introduced my paper with a carefully prepared résumé of the state of play, stressing the fact that the BMA ballot had been a 'flop' and that only 2,048 consultants out of 13,000 had voted to hand in undated resignations – only slightly more than the 1,834 who had voted *in favour* of the separation of pay beds. So the anger against our proposals was not as profound as some had made out. Nonetheless, we were stuck with the Goodman proposals, since a two-to-one majority of those voting was in favour of them. But the proposals were a total package and we had to go ahead explicitly on that package, though personally I would much have preferred not to have compromised at all. But if we were now to delay legislation, while the profession 'explored' matters still further, we should be giving them an effective veto over our policy and would face an unholy row from the NEC, the PLP and the health unions, who were already unhappy about the compromise.

Harold cut me off at this point. It is no part of his tactical instinct to win a political argument. He chipped in impatiently to say the question before us was the extent to which I should be allowed to proceed with the publication of my Bill, since consultations on the two points I had mentioned in my paper had not been completed. And, typically, he managed to sound as though he was against the whole idea. A long wrangle then ensued. Ted Short said primly that Cabinet had never agreed that the Bill should be passed this session, only introduced, though he admitted that Social Services Committee of Cabinet agreed with me that for political reasons we should now lift it into the essential list. Harold Lever, of course, fought me with all his strength. It would be absurd to ruin the effect of the Goodman proposals, he urged, by proceeding to publish the Bill before I had held more talks on the Schedule (he seems very well informed about all this), or by including any reserve powers of control in the legislation. Mike did his valiant best to help me and the PM seized the opportunity to sum up far more favourably than I had dared to hope. First, he said that Cabinet 'agreed' I should introduce my Bill with a view to Second Reading before Easter (though I cannot say I noticed it!). Secondly, he suggested that I shouldn't include powers on licensing in the Bill at the outset, but publish a White Paper setting out my proposals, on which consultations with the profession could continue. In the light of those consultations a reserve power could be added at the Report stage of the Bill, if Cabinet agreed, and the long title should be framed to allow this. Finally, he ruled that I could send out my consultation letter on the Schedule to AHAs without further delay. As I hesitated, Mike nodded at me to accept this formula, so accept I did, though it has only postponed the day of battle over licensing.

Monday, 23 February. This is the day when, all the press tells us, we shall have a major row at the TUC Liaison Committee over the Healey cuts. 'Jones signals Pay Policy Dangers' runs the *Guardian* headline and, of course, Joan Lestor's resignation from the Government[1] on the public expenditure cuts has been given great prominence over the weekend. So the press was massed expectantly outside Congress House, hopeful of blood. In fact, as I had anticipated, the union attack was far more muted than the ragings of the Tribune group might have led one to expect. There is no doubt that they are worried men – and angry at not having been consulted beforehand about the cuts (why didn't Denis listen to Mike and me when we urged they should be?). But they have no patience with irresponsible talk about bringing the Government down.

The Reg Prentice issue came up again. Mik asked why we had not had a report from Ron on the progress of his 'conciliation' mission between Reg and his local party. Ron then burst out into a thinly disguised diatribe against Reg. 'Mik says he wishes we'd never suggested this mission. Let me tell the NEC no one wishes that more than I do. I went to the GMC [General Management Committee] meeting, as I was asked to do by the NEC, and I must tell the committee this: a nicer bunch of people I would never hope to meet in the Party. I have been invited to the Annual General Meeting tonight and Reg Prentice is going as well. If you tell me not to go, I shall be delighted. I remain convinced of one thing: this matter need never have arisen, with a little give and take. The bone of contention between Reg Prentice and me is that I regard the Newham Party business as family business and he regards it as public business.' This reference to Reg's recent public outbursts kept his pals on the NEC mum, while Mik expressed himself satisfied, as well he might.

Lunch at No. 10, where Harold was entertaining the Prime Minister of Luxembourg, Gaston Thorn. These occasions are always fun, because Harold invites a very catholic collection of guests and today was no exception. I was glad to meet Henry Moore [the sculptor], a small, pleasant, unassuming man with whom I swopped Yorkshire anecdotes. To balance him was Don Revie from the football world, the writer Margaret Drabble, Nancy Banks-Smith of the *Guardian* and Alan Howard, currently playing the lead in *Henry V*. And, of course, politicians and trade unionists. Jeremy Thorpe insisted on kissing me on the cheek. I found Jeremy's gesture rather distasteful in view of the barrage of personal attacks he has kept up against me, from the Oxford Union debate onwards. Perhaps he feels in need of friends, or perhaps he really did think I looked nice, because he said to me over lunch, 'I can't get over it. You look ten years younger than at any time I have seen you in the last ten years.'

The horseshoe table in the panelled dining room was ablaze with daffodils. It was a good meal and the wine was excellent. Afterwards Harold made a little speech and read every word of it, hunched over his pieces of paper as if he had never made a speech in his life before. I am at a loss to understand why he doesn't ad lib more, because his impromptu asides are usually very witty. At the very least, I can't understand why he reads his speeches in such a flat way, as though it was all a bore. He kills even the most dramatic occasion – in the

[1] Joan Lestor had resigned the previous Saturday from her post as Under-Secretary of State for Education. In her letter of resignation she particularly criticized the cuts in education.

House as well – in this way. Ted's contemptuous comment on his style afterwards was 'careless'.

Thursday, 26 February. The pay beds question is now coming to the crunch. Yesterday the BMA Council met to consider the two resolutions passed by the consultants' Central Committee. Apparently they took all day over it and ended by agreeing a resolution which was remarkably evasive. After reiterating the council's 'total opposition' to my consultative document and the legislation, it went on, 'The Council has however agreed to take part in exploratory discussions with the Government in the light of the PM's stated guarantee to the House of Commons on October 20th, 1975: "I have made it clear in my statement that the Government are committed to the continuation of private practice. We expect to see it continue and we shall guarantee it in our legislation." To this end the Council has agreed to suspend sanctions and to recommend normal working of consultants.'

Once again, I am left fuming at the consequences of Harold's unnecessary and embarrassing embroidery of my undertaking to repeat Nye's guarantee in our new legislation,[1] and the way he has hoisted me with his wretched 'compromise'. Suspend sanctions, indeed! Even David keeps agreeing that they were never operative anyway. (Jack has sent me a Minute saying that, according to Laurie Pavitt, the junior doctors' great lobby against our legislation last Tuesday was 'the biggest non-lobby fiasco of the year', with only forty juniors turning up.) But I was determined on one thing: I am not going to let these boys delay things any more.

At the office meeting I called to discuss our next steps Henry Yellowlees reported that he had had a phone call from Stevenson in which Stevenson had almost pleaded that I should issue an invitation to them to come and talk. The reason, Henry insisted, was that Stevenson was worried about the wording of the BMA Council resolution, which elaborately avoided any direct reference to Goodman. Stevenson wanted me to make it clear to them all that 'Goodman' was still on and that we were going ahead. I said that we had got to get our letter on the contents of the Schedule out to the AHAS immediately; otherwise I should not be able to show I had left enough time for the promised consultation and that would give Harold Lever another opening in Cabinet. If Stevenson and Lewin would come and see me that very day, I would agree, but I wouldn't tolerate any further delay. Henry went off, with his usual hang-dog air, to phone Stevenson and came back to say that Stevenson was sorry, but Lewin, who had been in London for three days, had left for Cambridge and that he couldn't get him back before Monday or even Tuesday of next week. I said that wasn't good enough. Why didn't they bring Lewin back this evening and I would give them both a nice meal at the Gay Hussar? My officials all laughed and Henry looked rather shocked. But I insisted that this was only a civilized thing to do and a nice meal would make us all relax anyway. Back went Henry and came back yet again with the news that Stevenson appreciated my problem, but that unfortunately it was impossible for Lewin to come back again today. Would I see him and Dr Gullick? I agreed at once, with the proviso that we must get a letter round to them from me by hand, setting out the purpose of

[1] See footnote to p. 499.

the meeting. No illusions about having 'exploratory' talks about the Goodman proposals! Norman went off to draft this: I can rely on him to get it right.

We then turned to the other area of Cabinet sensitivity: reserve control powers. Tim Nodder had put up a first shot at the White Paper for which the PM had called. But, as so often happens with legislation, the Parliamentary draftsmen reported another snag: we could not (they said) just tack reserve powers on at committee stage unless there were a far more direct reference to them in the Bill than we proposed. We spent some time discussing how this could be done within the PM's remit and decided that it was impossible. I would have to take a regulatory power unto myself in the Bill at the outset. That means I shall have to minute Harold – and heaven knows what will happen then.

Stevenson and Gullick, when they arrived at my room at the House, could not have been more conciliatory. I spelt out to them that, as the ballot had shown a majority in favour of the Goodman proposals and sanctions had been lifted, the Government would stand by its side of the agreement and was proceeding to draft the Bill strictly on the basis of those proposals, with a view to introducing the Bill before Easter. (They did not bat an eyelid at this.) I then spelt out the way we proposed to proceed with the drawing up of the Schedule. No problem there. Next I turned to licensing, read out the relevant section of the Goodman proposals to them and proceeded to extract the last ounce of advantage from it. I reported that all sorts of queries were coming in to us from private developers, asking if it would be okay for them to go ahead. Of course, we had had to keep to a completely neutral line (Gullick nodded at this), saying we could neither refuse the applications nor give them any assurances. The effect of this was to 'blight' all private developments. We needed to know what the profession hoped to deliver in its 'voluntary' agreement with us to check undesirable developments. (They looked anxious at this.) If we arrived at no satisfactory 'voluntary' arrangements, the Government was free under the proposals to introduce 'reserve' powers. What would they feel about the independent board exercising them? They seemed most impressed. Gullick, in particular, seemed attracted to the idea of using the independent board. All Stevenson asked was that I should explain this to Mr Lewin and to perhaps one or two more, as he was sure they would like to hear these explanations from me personally. Would I meet Lewin on Thursday of next week? I said firmly that I really couldn't hold up my preparations for yet another week. I wanted to be helpful, but the meeting must be on Monday at the latest. Stevenson took it meekly enough.

Monday, 1 March. [David] Loshak in the *Telegraph* is stirring it up again over pay beds, saying doctors have had an urgent meeting with Goodman, having 'suddenly' learned that legislation is 'imminent'. And, indeed, when I faced Lewin and representatives from every group except the Royal Colleges across my table today, it was soon clear that Lewin was set on drawing the battle lines again. In my opening remarks I plunged straight in, telling them exactly what I had said to Stevenson and taking it for granted that we must now go ahead on Goodman, no more and no less. I concluded by saying we must get clear what was the status of the meeting: whether it was private or public and whether we were going to issue a joint statement at the end of it.

Lewin bridled immediately and said they must be free to make a public protest at the unrealistically short time I was allowing for consultations and on their desire for further 'explorations' of Goodman. I came back at once, politely but firmly. It was quite untrue that we were foreshortening consultations. It was part of Goodman that the Government should now proceed to legislate as announced in the Queen's Speech and that meant that the Bill must be introduced before Easter. Even so, we were able to allow them six weeks to give their first comments on the Schedule. And, of course, consultations would go on through all stages of the Bill and afterwards. That shook them a bit. Wouldn't I agree to let them consult Goodman on the interpretation of his proposals, asked Grabham? I emphatically rejected this. After about an hour and a half they simmered down, Lewin even agreeing that we didn't want to rush into an open war in the press. In the end the press statement they agreed could not have been better from our point of view.

The next step was to see Arnold Goodman to find out how he saw things developing. He came to my room at the House – late, of course. I didn't think he was looking too well after his spell in hospital and, indeed, it soon became clear that he wanted to disembroil himself from the whole business. He even told me he wouldn't speak in the Lords on the pay beds Bill. However, he toyed with some ideas for licensing. What about a control through manpower numbers, rather than buildings? I said I didn't think that would work and told him how interested Gullick had seemed to be about the possibility of bringing in the independent board. He agreed to talk to the profession again. Yes, he would let me know the outcome privately before anything was put to me officially.

Wednesday, 3 March. George Brown has resigned from the Labour Party. Last night on TV he was clearly incapable. Today the *Guardian* and *Mail* honourably carry pictures of him, prostrate in the gutter after his broadcast. If it had been anyone on the Left they would certainly have printed the pictures, and the sight of George Brown whole-seas-over did something to offset the myth hastily being manufactured that he alone is a man of principle and that his resignation is proof of the further collapse of the Labour Party into the hands of the 'Marxists'. *The Times* excelled itself in the worst leader I have ever read, which included the incredible phrase, 'George Brown drunk is a better man than the Prime Minister sober.' I should think even Harold's enemies would be ashamed of it. When I remember what Harold put up with from George all those years . . .

Harold, however, has obviously got cold feet over my suggestion that I should put a reserve licensing power in the Bill. No. 10 has replied to my Minute asking me to put a paper to Cabinet.

Thursday, 4 March. In the evening I went to No. 10 for my private meeting with Harold.[1] Tony C. had had an audience too, and, as he came down from the

[1] Having made up my mind to resign in the autumn when my pay beds legislation was through, I decided to see Harold and tell him in confidence so that, if he were preparing a Cabinet reshuffle, I could time my own resignation to precede it.

upstairs study, he quipped at me that he had told Harold I was no doubt going to ask him for more money. 'I told him I didn't believe him,' said Harold amicably as he poured me a drink. He was relaxed and talkative, full of his ploy on privacy and the press, which he told me with great satisfaction he was going to develop in a speech that weekend, and I sank back in the sofa cushions to wait my time. 'Well?' he said at last. 'I'm going to ask you a very peculiar question,' I replied. 'When are you going to have your next Cabinet reshuffle?' He jumped up and started pacing up and down. 'I'm in no hurry,' he said; paused and added, 'I don't intend to be in this job much longer.' 'That's funny,' I replied. 'I came to tell you I want to get out too.' He raised his eyebrows in surprise, then settled down in his chair and swore me to secrecy.

'I want to talk to you as an old friend who has always been loyal to me,' he said. 'You are the only person I know who never leaks. I am getting tired of this job. I've spent thirteen years trying to keep this Party together and it's been a pretty thankless task. Do you know I've only been to the theatre about twenty times in all those years? Because I have had to keep on top of everything that is happening. Every weekend I have about ten one-hundred page documents to read – and I read them all. It's the only way. I have to think of everything. When I became PM this time I told the Queen the date on which I would retire from this job. She's got the record of it, so no one will be able to say afterwards that I was pushed out.' 'You work too hard,' I agreed, thinking how yellow and lined he looked. 'I hope you are taking Paddy [his dog] for those walks now.' (It is my panacea for everything.)

He obviously longed to talk. 'Tell me,' he said, 'who do you think will succeed me when I go?' When I said Denis Healey he shook his head. 'The Left hate him.' 'But they would never have Jim, and Roy ditched himself years ago,' I replied. 'There are three groups in the Left,' he continued. 'There is what is now called the "soft" Left, to which you and I and Michael always belonged. There is a middle group and then there are the really vicious group.' He thought they'd go for Wedgie first and let someone other than Denis in. 'But it has got to be someone who is willing to work at it, not going out to dinner all the time, like Roy. Eric is too young, though he's very good and his turn may come. I'll tell you who I think has developed remarkably: Peter Shore. He's really become very impressive.' (I agreed with that, remembering the air of authority he developed during the referendum campaign. But whether he has an emollient enough temperament to lead our stormy party, I very much doubt.)

'What are you going to do when you give this up?' I asked. 'Go into academic life?' 'Heavens, no. I shall just retire to the back-benches and enjoy myself. I've told my local Party I will fight another Election and have one more Parliament. Then I'll retire.' I could see time slipping away and managed to inject my own problem into the conversation. 'Harold, I want to get the pay beds Bill through Parliament, then give up my job.' 'Why?' he asked, puzzled. 'Because I've had a good run for my money and it's time I made room for one of the younger ones. There are a lot of able young MPs pressing up from below. For your own sake, Harold, you ought to make room for them.' He shook his head. 'It's very difficult.' 'I shall give up my seat: I'm not running again,' I continued. That really surprised him. 'So there'll be two Castles in the Lords,' he grinned. I ignored that. 'But', I persisted, 'I want to go with dignity. I don't want the press to be able to say that I've been pushed out.' 'This conversation is proof that you haven't been. We'll minute it if you like,' he replied. 'Heavens, no,' I cried. 'It would be round Whitehall in a flash. These civil servants leak like mad.' 'Not the No. 10 ones,' he said rather grandly. 'I want to go by the end of the summer recess,' I continued. 'That is why it is so essential that the pay beds Bill isn't dropped.' 'It won't be,' he assured me. 'What I think we should drop is Weights and Measures: horribly boring anyway.'

He thought a moment, then said, 'Your timetable ought to fit into mine all right.' 'What *is* the date you told the Queen?' I asked. He shook his head. 'I told it her on Privy Council terms.' 'Well, I'm a Privy Councillor,' I replied. He still shook his head, adding, 'I may be forced to stay another six months or so.' I began to suspect that his date wasn't as firm as he had implied. At that moment a secretary put his head round the door. 'Lord Goodman is waiting.' I nearly laughed outright. What are those two up to *now*? We parted amicably and I was glad I had spoken to him. After all these years I would hate to resign on him and I know he will play it so as to help me to achieve my ends, complete the jobs I've got on hand and retire with my tail up.

In the hall I spoke to Arnold, who told me he had had a meeting with the medicos and got them thinking out a scheme for controlling the private sector. He promised he would let me have details. I doubt whether it will amount to very much, with the professions sounding off already about the phasing out of the thousand beds.

Sunday, 7 March. Home for Sunday breakfast: tired but still happy. I even did some digging in the bitter wind. Alan Watkins, in the *Observer*, has a piece about Harold's imminent retirement: 'Harold: This Year, Next Year, Sometime——' I hope Harold doesn't think I have been talking to him! Alan advances one interesting theory: that Harold is planning to leave in 1977, after he has helped to celebrate the Queen's Jubilee year. Well, now I come to think of it, I can't see him missing that. If so, I have plenty of time to work out my own ploy.

Monday, 8 March. Ted had to get up at 6.30 am to catch his plane to Brussels, so it hasn't been a particularly restful weekend. Nonetheless, I feel relaxed – almost euphoric, now I have settled things with Harold. At the office I told Norman what had transpired and agreed to see Patrick at his request that afternoon. 'Is he going to suggest the right person to succeed you?' I asked Norman, who has been warning me that Establishment Division is preparing to move him. Norman assured me that the chap to be offered to me was the 'best buy'. (I suspect Graham will have had a hand in choosing him, so that will be okay by me. After all, he chose Norman for me.) When Patrick started to outline why it was necessary to start thinking about a successor for Norman, whose stint in Private Office has run its normal course, I chipped in, swore him to secrecy, and told him what I had told the PM. He was his usual charming self about it, thanked me for taking him into my confidence, said how much they would all miss me. 'You get younger all the time. I have never worked for a Minister who had so much vitality,' he said and promised to gear Norman's departure to suit my convenience. Private Office have overwhelmed me by depositing a sheaf of spring flowers on my desk, accompanied by an anniversary card. I had forgotten that this was two years to the day since I came to DHSS. 'We couldn't let your second birthday go uncelebrated,' they said. So I invited them in to a drink, bless them. After all they have suffered!

Tuesday, 9 March. I was just finishing my lunch in the House when Harold joined the communal table in the Members' dining room. He was so carried away by his compulsive need for conversation that he launched on a not very clear but very protracted revelation about what he was going to say at his Question time that afternoon. He had, he said, turning to me, established that BOSS [the South African Bureau of State Security] had been involved in the Thorpe affair. 'It's been a great detective exercise, I can tell you. Detective Inspector Falkender has been up to her eyes in it. I've got conclusive evidence that South African money has been involved. After all, she's been through the same thing. So have I. No Minister or political party is safe unless we expose this. Of course, I can't reveal my sources but, then, neither could Macmillan when he invited me to come and talk to him. If the Right Hon. Lady, the Leader of the Opposition, likes to challenge me to reveal them, I'll invite her to come and talk to me.' Those of us who were left were by this time completely mystified, but Harold was like a Boy Scout playing cops and robbers. He was chuckling at the way he had arranged to make his great announcement that afternoon through the medium of a Question that was only remotely to do with it. 'I have got one of my most vociferous critics to ask a supplementary. I'm rather good at drafting questions.' 'Not Willie Hamilton,' I pleaded, appalled. 'No,' he replied: 'Jim Wellbeloved [Labour MP for Bexley, Erith and Crayford].' I was astonished at his recklessness. If he *was* fixing Question time in this way, one would have thought he would have kept mum about it. But not our Harold. 'What number Question is it?' I asked. 'Number 4.' 'But how can you be sure it will be reached?' 'It will be,' he replied knowingly. 'Of course,' he added, 'I shall have to say the South African Government isn't involved, because we need their help over Rhodesia.' I almost despaired of him. I can see him getting involved again in a complicated manœuvre which will merely make him look devious rather than a Sir Galahad. He has been obsessed with this defence of Jeremy for weeks and I have no doubt he is right that the South African security forces are active in this country and are capable of anything. But I couldn't see quite why they should pick on the Liberals, a spent force, rather than us. 'They have already picked on me,' Harold explained. 'But they believe it was the Liberal intervention that let us into office and the first thing we did was to stop arms for South Africa.' 'Are you saying that there was nothing in the Jeremy–Scott affair and they have been inventing it, or that there *was* something and they are exploiting it?' I asked. 'I dare say there may have been something at some time,' said Harold indifferently, 'but they are out to destroy the Liberal leader and they would destroy any successor to him. There is big money involved in this'. I decided I had better rearrange my afternoon engagements so that I could be present at the unveiling of this mystery.

When I slipped into the chamber for Harold's Questions Jeremy rushed in just ahead of me. He clearly knew what was coming. It was fascinating to watch the plot unfold. Question Number 4, asked by a Tory, seemed a most unlikely vehicle: something about Harold's next visit to the UN, which enabled the Tories to keep up their barrage about Russian intervention in Angola. Then George Thomas dutifully called Jim Wellbeloved, who, without looking at a note, carefully rolled out his prepared supplementary: 'Has my Right Honourable Friend received any evidence about the involvement of South African agents in the framing of leading Liberal Party members?' Harold took up his cue in an opaque reply which began crisply: 'I have no doubt at all that there is strong South African participation in recent activities relating to the Right Honourable Gentleman the Leader of the Liberal Party.' He then tailed off into an apologia for the South African Government: he had 'no evidence at all' that it had any connection 'with these unsavoury activities'. I thought he had succeeded in destroying the whole impact. Most people in the House looked puzzled. Jeremy sat with his ear glued to the amplifier. Chattering among the Liberal ranks. Jeremy was nodding to John Pardoe [Liberal MP for Cornwall North] and Pardoe got up. But George Thomas was playing his part to perfection. He called Tory after Tory, who kept up the anti-Russian refrain. I thought George had lost his cue, but, in contrast to the speed with which he had raced through earlier questions, he was timing this perfectly. After the Tories had had their run he called Pardoe, who rose to ask, in view of the 'extremely serious and important statement' the Prime Minister had made, what action he proposed to take. Harold came back ponderously, egging the pudding of his exoneration of the South African Government. 'I said there is no evidence of South African Government participation in this matter.' He then went off at a tangent. Jim Callaghan was sitting next to me. 'Did you know about this?' I asked. He shook his head. 'What is it all about?' I went on. 'I haven't a clue,' he replied. Question Number 4, having taken as much time as the first three put together, had exhausted the PM's Question time.

I waited for the nine o'clock news, fascinated. Harold's instinct hadn't deserted him. The news led on this incident and included an interview with Pardoe, who exactly echoed Harold's line about the reasons why South African 'business interests' should be interested in destroying the Liberal Party. I don't suppose Harold will worry if the 'police inquiries' don't lead anywhere. But the significant thing was the way Margaret Thatcher had been caught unawares. She was not prepared for anything like this, with one of her carefully worked out and stylized interventions and she wasn't politician enough to react instinctively. If she could only have improvised, she could have driven Harold into a corner. He really is an incredibly rash and romantic man. Why go overboard for Jeremy, for heaven's sake? For the political moral Harold was hinting at was so set about with equivocations that it could not really get home.

The publication of the White Paper on Public Expenditure on 19 February (Cmnd 6393), providing for cuts of £3 billion in 1978–79, had widened the rift between the left wing and the Government. Despairing of the direction which the Government was taking, thirty Tribune MPS *abstained in the vote on the White Paper on 10 March, thus ensuring the Government's defeat. Two days later left-wing union leaders, Jack Jones and Hugh Scanlon, combined with moderate David Basnett to issue a call for unity behind the*

Government and an end to the 'splits and divisions which have recently emerged'.

Nonetheless doubts were deepening as to whether the growth visualized in the 'central case' of economic projections in the White Paper could be achieved. This central projection was based on a growth in GDP *of just under 3·5 per cent per annum between 1974 and 1979, and the White Paper proposed a flattening out of public expenditure after 1976–77 to make way for it. The cutback was to be underpinned by the widespread introduction of cash limits and by pressure on the local authorities through the Consultative Council and the rate support grant to achieve a similar standstill in their current expenditure. But after two years of a slump in growth and investment, this central case called for a far higher rate of recovery than from past performance seemed possible. True, there were some encouraging signs. In March unemployment fell slightly for the first time in two years, though still over one million. The pay policy was holding – so was industrial peace, the number of working days lost through strikes in 1975 having been the lowest for seven years. Export volume was up. But there were as yet no signs of world recovery on the scale required. Nor was it likely that Britain, with her chronic tendency to import, would be in a position to take advantage of it. At the end of March Mr Wynne Godley and his Cambridge colleagues reiterated their warning that unemployment would rise to between one-and-a-half million and two million by the end of the decade unless imports were controlled. The* NEC *continued to urge a modified version of the Cambridge policy on the Government.*

The pleas fell on deaf ears. At the end of 1975 Denis Healey had negotiated with the IMF *a drawing of £1,000 million special drawing rights under the oil facility and a further stand-by credit of £700 million. In this letter of application he had not only reiterated his intention to continue with his present policies, but undertook not to impose new restrictions on payments or trade without prior consultation with the Fund. On the industrial front the Government was spending more on industrial promotion and its job protection schemes, but it remained adamant about the need to pursue consensus policies. In February Denis Healey flatly told a deputation from the* NEC *that he was not going to shift from the tripartite approach to industrial strategy.*

Meanwhile he was preparing a Budget designed to persuade unions and workers to accept another round of wage restraint. The present pay limit, he argued, should cut the inflation rate by well over half by the end of the year, but, if we were to keep in line with our competitors, inflation must be halved yet again by the end of 1977. That meant that the pay limit in the coming year must be halved as well. To secure this he proposed to bribe the unions with tax concessions, offering to increase income tax reliefs by about £1,300 million in two stages: the first £370 million increase being unconditional, the second £1,000 million being dependent on the unions agreeing to a pay limit of around 3 per cent. The majority of workers, he told the House of Commons on 6 April, would be better off with a lower pay limit and the extra tax reliefs than with a higher limit and lower reliefs, adding that the package would slightly boost demand and would increase confidence. He looked forward optimistically to the recovery gathering speed over the next twelve months, with growth reaching 4 per cent per year, investment reviving, unemployment beginning to fall and inflation down to less than 10 per cent.

In my Department we were enjoying a temporary lull. Morale in the Health Service had been improved by our success in coming out of the public expenditure exercise relatively well. At the end of March David Owen and I published a consultative document setting out our priorities for the health and personal social services in the new situation, one of the first attempts at planning in this field. My pay beds legislation inched its way slowly but surely through Cabinet. On 16 March Harold Wilson astonished all of us by announcing his decision to resign the premiership and my own fortunes took a dramatic turn.

Wednesday, 10 March. The press and the BBC are extracting the last ounce of excitement out of Harold's statement [in the House] – but it isn't helping Jeremy. Cyril Smith is busy rocking Jeremy's boat from his hospital bed and the *Mail* carries a centre spread on Cyril and his Ma which reduces the whole business to a roaring farce. The *Mirror* has taken up Harold's cue on its front page (all prearranged by Harold, I suspect), but even the *Mirror* hasn't been able to resist a centre spread on 'Thorpe's Follies'. So Harold has thrown away his great revelation in the wrong cause.

As I went down to the House in the evening the air was electric with the message: 'We are going to be defeated tonight.' Despite all Bob's ingenuity in trying to head off a Tribunite revolt on the White Paper on Public Expenditure, (a) by drafting the Government Motion in the most emollient form possible[1] and (b) by provoking the Opposition to put down the sort of amendment on which we could all unite,[2] it had become apparent that massive abstentions by our 'Left' were planned.

The vote on the Tory amendment presented no problems: a majority of thirty. In the division lobby on the Government Motion rumour was running wild. 'We're defeated. It looks as though thirty have abstained.' When the tellers came to the table before a crowded House a great cheer went up from the Tories as the Opposition Whips took their place on the right-hand side. We had been defeated by thirty-seven votes. Of course, Margaret was on her feet in a flash: tense and rather attractive in a vivid green. Poor Ted Short, ramrod and colourless at the best of times, was no match for her. And suddenly the rumble went round the House: where was Harold? Ted promised a statement somewhen. The Tories fed their anger on this evasiveness. George Thomas was disastrously weak in the chair and even the most faithful of us began to mutter at Harold's absence. Half an hour of farce ensued, during which I once again regretted that the sobering effect of TV was missing. Eventually Ted Short was forced to offer a statement tomorrow. Somehow, eventually, the hubbub died down and the House adjourned, the rest of the night's business having been sacrificed. As we streamed out I asked Bob why Harold hadn't been there. 'You know him as well as I do, duckie. He just said he would keep out of this.' A great mistake in my view. 'I wonder if there will be any sterling left tomorrow,' a Tory MP said to me.

Thursday, 11 March. 'I don't think there will be any normal business discussed at tomorrow's Cabinet,' Roy Jenkins said to me last night. In the event, the atmosphere in Cabinet was remarkably calm. Harold looked refreshed and disposed of the 'confidence' matter quite briskly for him. One would never have thought he had been 'humiliated'. Having thought things over during the night, he had concluded that the best thing was for us to take the vote right

[1] The Government Motion read: 'That this House, in rejecting the demand for massive and immediate cuts in public expenditure which would increase both unemployment and the cost of living, recognizes the need to ensure that manufacturing industry can take full advantage of the upturn in world trade by levelling off total public expenditure from April 1977 while keeping under continuous review the priority between programmes.'

[2] The Tory amendment deleted all after 'That this House' and substituted: 'declines to approve a White Paper which will lead only to lower living standards, fewer jobs and higher taxes.'

away today on the Motion for the Adjournment, which he would then make a question of confidence.

Of course, there were office meetings conflicting with the start of the great debate on the vote of confidence so Harold was nearing the end of his speech when at last I got into the crowded chamber. 'How's he doing?' I whispered to Shirley. 'Very well,' she replied. 'He's been laying into the abstainers and they have just been sitting mum. I don't think they are too happy.' Certainly Harold seemed to be in confident form and sat down to great cheers, though, having told us this morning he was only going to make a 'very short' speech, he had gone on for nearly three-quarters of an hour. Margaret was shorter and, I thought, effective, because she just harped on one simple theme: that Harold could no longer command his own side's loyalty. She sat down to ecstatic cheers from her own side.

Back into the chamber in time for Denis's winding-up. He was almost bellowing and, as I sat crammed among his pals like Edmund Dell, both they and I became increasingly embarrassed. It was an appalling speech: arrogant, offensive and near-hysterical. 'He must have gone off his rocker,' I muttered. 'If he hasn't lost us this vote, he ought to have done.' But of course he hadn't, and the emptiness of the abstainers' gesture was shown when they meekly filed into the Government lobby after a speech which deserved to provoke a revolt. So this was Harold and Denis making up for the fact that we couldn't have a substantive Motion! However angry I may have been about the abstainers' folly, I would never accept Denis's right to insult them in that frenetic way. We won the division by a majority of seventeen. Enoch Powell, the master maverick, persuaded most of his fellow Unionists to sit on their hands.

Monday, 15 March. Great activity on the pay beds front. Norman reports that Goodman would like to see me today; Patrick has been having off-the-record talks with Stevenson. Patrick tells me that Stevenson talked frankly to him, admitting that the profession would never volunteer any proposals for a voluntary system of licensing, but would acquiesce in any reasonable proposals put forward by us, even though screaming aloud about them publicly. It appears that the fight has gone out of the consultants and the only question mark now is about the attitude of the juniors and Keable-Elliott. Apparently also the BMA is pretty well in the know about the divisions in the Cabinet over licensing.

I arranged to see Arnold in my room at 3.45 pm. He arrived at 4.15 pm, saying something about having been detained by Harold. What about I can only guess. Arnold was in amusing and expansive mood. After he had wandered round the scene for some time I proceeded to tie him down. Did he accept that paragraph 3(f) of the Goodman proposals meant that, if a voluntary agreement was not reached, the Government had the right to legislate unilaterally on controls? 'Of course,' he replied. Secondly, did he realize that our information was that the profession would never volunteer any proposals of its own? His answer to that was that he would have to talk to them and make them take a line. Perhaps I could just put in the Bill some general vague right to make regulations on this in order to give more time for discussions? I said that would be fine by me, but that the profession would have to suggest it: if it came from me it would be regarded as sinister. He saw this at once, saying, 'They must start by putting proposals to you, otherwise you are walking into a trap.' Finally, I stressed the urgency of the timetable: could he let me have a report on his talks by Thursday? He said he would try. I left him with the idea that the best way out was to put something firm in the Bill along the lines of giving the independent board licensing powers for all developments over a certain size.

The real trouble is that the profession and I will never agree over the size of private hospital developments which would escape control. They are talking of exempting all hospitals with less than two hundred beds and I won't go further than seventy-five beds at any cost. I only know that if I get any control mechanism at all into the legislation it will be a miracle, given the opposition I've got in Cabinet. I then sat down to an office meeting, at which we agreed it was premature for me to put any paper to Cabinet and that it would be better for me to send an explanatory letter to Harold at this stage.

Tuesday, 16 March. I arrived at Cabinet, all unsuspecting that Harold's time-bomb was about to go off. As we settled down in our seats Harold said calmly that he had just come from the Palace and had a statement to make to us. He then read a lengthy statement announcing his 'irrevocable' decision to give up office. As he went through it, personal copies were circulated to each one of us, which he had signed individually. He certainly has developed a flair for drama. The statement was very movingly worded – and included typical Harold statistical touches about how he had presided over 472 Cabinets and answered more than 12,000 Parliamentary Questions. It included some propaganda for the achievements of Labour Governments and he informed us that he was releasing the statement (indeed, had already released it) to the press. It also very skilfully set out the identikit for his successor: he must be loyal to the counter-inflationary policy and to Nato, be ready to work himself to death ('these are not the easy, spacious, socially-orientated days of some of my predecessors') and make a point of getting out into the country and meeting the people. 'Above all remember the Party is the Party in the country – not the Palace of Westminster, not Smith Square.'

We listened in stunned silence. Eric passed me a note: 'Were you aware he was going to do this?' I hesitated, then scribbled back: 'I can't answer that question.' Harold then embroidered his statement with a few casual and almost inaudible explanations. He had made up his mind to do this when he won the Election two years ago, he told us. There was never a 'right time' to carry out such an intention, but he thought he had chosen the best possible.

The silence which followed this was, I thought, the most moving tribute we could have paid to him. There was no rush of ready falsities. Ted Short blurted out something almost incoherent about what an appalling shock and blow this was. Another silence, then Jim hesitatingly took up the theme. He didn't, he said, want to 'pre-empt' what anybody else might want to say. There would be other occasions to pay proper tributes. But he couldn't let this pass without expressing his thanks to Harold for all the generosities he had always showed to him. He remembered, for instance, how, when Harold had won the leadership thirteen years ago, he had at once turned to him and said: 'Of course you'll carry on, Jim, as shadow Foreign Secretary.' Jim concluded haltingly, 'Thank you, Harold, for all you have done for us.' More silence. I felt near to tears, I don't quite know why. Tears of farewell to the friendly familiar? Eric passed me another note: 'It's a very emotional moment.' To which I replied: 'What's your reaction?' Eric: 'I think he's wrong.' Me: 'I think it will prove how difficult it is to replace him.' Harold then asked us to excuse him, as he had various people to talk to, including the chairman of the PLP with whom he had to discuss the quick holding of an election for his successor. He told Ted Short to take the chair and disappeared just as, once again, the waiters filed in with those welcome cups of coffee.

When he had gone we fumbled for the right procedure. I think it was Shirley who said we should minute a tribute to Harold right away and I said we ought to issue something to the press. Anyway, we both found ourselves sent away to draft something, which we did, short and sweet but making it quite clear that the Cabinet had been taken by surprise. After some amending by Jim and Roy it was agreed and issued, John Hunt adding the discreet prefix that the statement had been agreed 'in the Prime Minister's temporary absence'. These civil servants think of everything.

While Shirley and I were drafting upstairs I asked her what she thought. 'Very sad,' she said and I think she meant it, though I don't think she was heart-broken. Impulsively I said, 'There is only one compromise candidate: Michael.' She didn't protest, but she didn't exactly endorse it either.

Some irreverent questions about Harold's whole manœuvre began to creep into my mind. Okay, so a man has the right to decide he will give up office, and whatever date he chooses will have its snags, but for Harold to do this so gratuitously and so apparently senselessly, in the middle of a perfectly reasonably successful term of office, almost looks like frivolity. Has one the *right* to throw one's Party into turmoil for no apparent cause, to face them with a *fait accompli* because one knows they would plead with one to stay if they knew in time? What exactly *was* Harold up to? More than had met the eye, I had no doubt. And he certainly hadn't bothered a whit about the effect of the timing of his retirement on my own. That cosy conversation had not amounted to a row of beans.

As Cabinet broke up I grabbed Michael. 'You've got to stand for the leadership,' I said. Peter endorsed this warmly. 'Perhaps. We must discuss it,' said Mike and I realized he had made up his mind to fight. In his new tough mood I wouldn't be surprised if he fought hard.

I rang up Norman and found him in a tizzy about the news. (Of course, it was all round Whitehall before we'd left Cabinet.) When I said I wanted to go into the House for the PM's Questions he replied, 'Of course. Don't you want to cancel all your office meetings this afternoon?' I told him not a bit of it: it was business as usual. Everybody I met in the House over lunch seemed shell-shocked. As I walked into the crowded chamber behind Jim the Opposition put up a great ironical cheer (for Jim, not me). The front bench was squashed almost unbearably. As we sat chattering like sparrows I said to Jim, 'Did you know?' He tried to pretend he didn't, failed, and, when I challenged him, just smiled deprecatingly. (So there may be something in the rumour already circulating that Harold has set the whole thing up for Jim.) Bob Mellish has told me he didn't know and that Ted Short had been told ten minutes before

Cabinet. As for Denis, 'Harold told him in the lavatory.' We consulted anxiously on the front bench as to whether we should stand up for Harold when he came in for his Questions. Jim thought we should; then decided we had better wait and see what the back benches did. In the event, the back benches cheered heartily enough, but had no truck with standing ovations. Some people waved Order Papers. The gallery was crammed.

Harold was obviously enjoying himself. He was on form. He just played with Margaret Thatcher, who sat, as she usually does before a parliamentary effort, head down and lips pursed, as if summoning up some superior wisdom of which we ordinary mortals do not know. Her intervention, when it came, was not in my view exactly masterly. 'She can't rise to an occasion,' an impatient back bencher behind me said. Jeremy spoiled a good intervention by long-windedness. Not for the first time it was left to Ted Heath to dominate the House from the Opposition side. His tribute to Harold was unrestrainedly generous and Harold replied in like form. 'The House of Commons at its best,' I could imagine those people saying who love the glutinous.

George Thomas achieved his best moment yet in the chair when Harold said that he had informed Mr Speaker of his intentions only last week. 'That's correct,' George boomed. The tension dissolved in laughter. 'It *is* the end of an era,' Harold Lever whispered to me. The nagging query grew in my mind: 'What is the old maestro up to?'

The orgy over, Brian O'Malley came into my room for a drink, obviously worrying where *he* stands now. I told him we'd got to root for Mike and he agreed. Mike called in too, to tell me he would stand. I asked him if Wedgie was standing and he havered a bit. Obviously, he said, it would be better if Wedgie didn't stand, but he wanted to talk to him and tell him he didn't want to get in his way. 'I'll talk to Wedgie myself,' I replied and went at once to Wedgie's room. I found him closeted with Joe Ashton and Joe's wife. 'I thought you'd been sacked,' I said jocularly to Joe.[1] 'Technically, I have been,' he replied, but it was clear he was still spiritually and practically Wedgie's PPS, only just this side of idolatry. I felt a bit constrained, but said bravely to Wedgie, 'The future is with you, but not this moment. This election is a forceps delivery.' Looking a bit haggard, he seemed to agree. Joe was passionate: this election was not about personalities, but about policies. Dennis Skinner was right, he insisted: every candidate for the leadership should be made to set out the policies for which he stood. The important thing, I suggested, was to stop Jim. 'Don't worry,' said Joe grimly. 'The "Stop Jim" movement is already under way: from the Right as well as from the Left.' Both he and Wedgie agreed that they would rather have Denis than Jim, just as Mike had done earlier. My Ted came in hotfoot from Brussels, for once cursing the European Parliament that had kept him away from a great occasion in the Parliament he really loved. Wedgie, the teetotaller, gave us drinks from his cabinet. At last I was able to get home to bed.

Wednesday, 17 March. Woke with eyes streaming and feeling wretched. Somehow I got through a lunch with the General Medical Council.

[1] Joe Ashton had abstained in the vote on the public expenditure cuts the previous week and Harold Wilson had demanded that he be sacked as Parliamentary Private Secretary to Tony Benn.

Thursday, 18 March. Woke in a sad state. I just couldn't see to read. I hoped that a day in bed would do the trick. With streaming eyes I got through my boxes as best I could. I have amused myself reading all the press comments on Harold's dramatic move. It must give him great satisfaction to read the belated tributes to him while he is still alive. Even Bernard Levin writes a friendly piece on him today ('Making my peace, finally, with Mr Wilson'), while the *Sun*, of all papers, carried a leader yesterday headed: 'Thank you from all of us.' So much for the venom that has been poured on Harold all these years. We shall have the doctors canonizing me yet! (In fact, George Godber has written a very balanced article in the *British Medical Journal*, in which he says they ought to be grateful to me for getting more resources for the NHS.)

The press is laying heavy odds on Jim winning the leadership. He is the favourite with them, though some papers plump for Roy. Denis has not put his name forward yet and there is talk that he may stay out of the contest. This thought worried me no end. To be left with Jim would be too terrible! So on an impulse I got the office to get Denis to ring me, which he did as soon as he emerged from Cabinet. I told him frankly I was rooting for Mike, but that I thought he, Denis, ought to stand as he would certainly be my – and a lot of other people's – second choice. He was equally frank back. He had given a lot of thought to it, but the advice from his friends was that he shouldn't. And the statistics were against him. He calculated that on the first ballot Jim would get a hundred votes, Mike ninety and Roy about seventy, which would leave about forty votes to divide between Wedgie, Tony and him. So he would be eliminated humiliatingly. I replied that it was true he ran the risk of humiliation on the first ballot, but if he could only survive into the second his chances would improve enormously. He must realize that there were a lot of people – more than he probably guessed – who, next to wanting to see their own man in, were leading a 'Stop Jim' campaign. They wanted somebody else than Jim to vote for in the last resort. He agreed, adding, 'I think I am the only person who could defeat Jim: Mike couldn't.' I also told him that a very telling campaigning line would be to say that what the Party needed above all things was to keep the Foot/Healey axis round which the Government revolved. It was a winning combination. He liked that. Finally I told him that Alf Bates[1] had been doing a head-count for Brian O'Malley. Would he like Brian to have a word with him at the division that night? Denis thanked me and said he would.

Next I rang Michael to make sure that he agreed it would be helpful to him if Denis ran. He said, 'Of course.' Finally I rang Brian to put him in the picture. 'Denis won't run,' he told me firmly. 'Both Joel and Denis's own PPS, Mark Hughes, have been urging him not to.' I said that it was worth a try anyway and he agreed to see Denis as I had arranged. Later, on the nine o'clock news, I heard that Denis had decided to run after all and let out a hoarse 'Whoopee!' Who knows, I may have secured Mike's victory by that timely phone call.

Saturday, 20 March. The press seems to think that Healey's intervention changes the odds on Jim markedly. Hurray! As my eyes were still streaming I

[1] Alf Bates, Labour MP for Bebington and Ellesmere Port, was Brian O'Malley's Parliamentary Private Secretary from 1974 to 1976; he became an assistant Government Whip in 1976.

called in the doctor, who put me on antibiotics. I wrapped up warmly and Edna drove me to HCF and bed.

Sunday, 21 March. With my sinusitis somewhat abated, I did a spell in the garden, took the dogs for a walk and then got down to work. Raymond Gedling has put up a draft of the paper on pay beds I am to put to Cabinet next week and has reported on the consultations officials had with the professions last Thursday. Deadlock has been reached with Grabham and co., but the men from the Independent Hospitals Group seem ready to vest control powers in the independent board, though they want 'smaller' hospital developments exempted from control – *i.e.* those involving fewer than 200–250 beds. 'Smaller', indeed! There would be only a handful left. The worrying thing was, Raymond said, the growing resistance by the GPS to any form of control – even though I have met the GPS on all their points about health centres, etc. On the phone Raymond told me that he feared we were in for a 'major row' if we went ahead.

I brooded on all this for a while, then went and phoned Jack to find out what he really thought. He was heartening. He might be wrong, he said, but he thought that, if we did press ahead with licensing, it would be very difficult for the consultants to get the GPS and juniors out on strike. 'My feeling is that there isn't a head of steam about this,' he said. One junior, for instance, had told him, 'We've had our orgasm over our pay.' Moreover, if I didn't get some kind of licensing into the Bill this year, it 'wouldn't happen at all'. Just imagine what another Minister would do in a year's time – perhaps under J.C.'s premiership!

Next I decided to ring Arnold. We began chattily. 'When did Harold tell you he was going to resign?' I asked boldly. 'Well before Christmas,' he replied, 'but he never indicated a precise date, except to say he didn't want to stay after Easter.' We discussed the mystery and Arnold agreed he couldn't understand why Harold should do it, 'except that he was absolutely tired and fed up'. Arnold also believed that Mary [Wilson] had had a great deal to do with it. I then turned to licensing, telling him that tomorrow I had to finalize a paper for Cabinet and we were getting nowhere in our discussions with the professions. He rejected this as too gloomy, said that, although he was no longer 'the blue-eyed boy of the situation', he was in close touch with Robb [of BUPA] and Gullick and believed from what they told him that an agreement with the IHG was possible. And if we got that, the consultants would have to fall into line. From what he said it would appear that I could accept their ideas, except that they want to exempt from controls all developments of under 250 beds, which even Arnold said was 'too high'. I told him that my limit was seventy-five beds. He did not quail, but promised to chase Robb tomorrow urgently.

Monday, 22 March. At the office I had a meeting on private practice. We discussed the latest print of the Health Services Bill (as the pay beds Bill is now called), with which I was far from satisfied, and went through my draft paper for Cabinet.

I then went to the House to await the arrival of Lord Goodman in my room. He was late as usual, which gave me the chance to slip into a campaign meeting in Mike's room just down the corridor. I was very pleased to see lively youngsters like Neil Kinnock [Labour MP for Bedwellty] (and of course Brian O'M.) taking such an active part. John Silkin, as Mike's campaign manager, had his tail up, but then I don't trust his euphoria. When Arnold eventually arrived he said he had had a hopeful talk with Mr Robb of the Independent Hospitals Group, who seemed willing to reach a voluntary agreement along the lines I have always been prepared to visualize, *i.e.* licensing to operate above a certain size of development and to be run by the independent board. The figure at which licensing should start to operate, continued Arnold, would be 250 beds. Of course I told him that was impossible and he agreed it was 'ridiculous'. I stressed that the figure of seventy-five beds was not negotiable. I had already given away too much. Arnold said he was due to see the whole bunch of representatives the next day. If they were not prepared to endorse this compromise, he would be prepared to float it publicly himself.

Tonight was the great farewell dinner Harold had promised us. I found time to make up my face and put on my long black velvet dress. Marcia was there, as elegantly groomed as always. She was in a huddle with Eric Varley and we teased them: 'What is going on between you two?' Harold wandered around with a rather detached air. I suspect that levitation has begun. After we had chatted for about twenty minutes or so over champagne the news went round that we were waiting for Shirley – late as usual. She blew in at last, in the same rather crumpled white frock that she had been wearing all day, her hair uncombed. An ironical cheer went up. Harold then asked us all to come into the main reception room, where TV and other cameras had been set up. I realized for the first time that this was the time we were to have an official valedictory Cabinet photo taken with him. Shirley and I both protested when we found that, once again, we had each been posted on the far outside of the front row: typical of the way the Party treated women, we said. With a lot of laughter and quipping we all at last settled ourselves down and smiled.

When we moved into the dining room I found to my annoyance that Harold had played safe with the seating arrangements and exactly reproduced the order of sitting in Cabinet. 'This is just like a Cabinet meeting with food,' I said disgustedly. Harold's promised menu turned out to be lavish, but not particularly imaginative. The wines, as usual with government catering, were superb. But as the evening went on I felt there was something artificial about it. It did not come alight. This was a real event, Harold's abrupt and unnecessary departure, and I felt that this ought to be expressed spontaneously in some way. Coffee was served and Ted Short, on Harold's left, stood up to make a speech. It was of almost painful banality. Harold followed him. He talked in that curiously toneless and emotionless way he has almost made a virtue of, so that his natural wit and liveliness were tossed away. 'Ted said I didn't bear grudges,' he began, promisingly. 'If I had, I would have had the smallest Cabinet in history.' He then went on to tell us that 'even on placement tonight I have been vigilant to the end'. That was why he had reproduced a replica of the Cabinet seating, so that no one could read anything into anything. He went on: 'The time to go is while they are saying why do you go, not why do you stay.' What was he most proud of? The Open University. As for his obituary, he was 'amazed to be canonized so quickly'.

After Harold had finished there was a flat pause. I felt desperately that we should all have been asked to say something, however impromptu, going round the table. Wedgie jumped in with some of his witticisms. He told us a funny story about how he had been asked in 1965 to contribute to a TV programme on Harold's obituary. And he repeated the crack: 'If Harold falls under a bus, find out who is driving the bus.' For a moment I thought he had brought the evening to life. Roy followed him with a few polished sentences of tribute. I hoped others would follow, but the life soon fizzled out of the occasion. We broke up raggedly and I went home feeling dispirited.

Tuesday, 23 March. As we DHSS Ministers assembled on the front bench for Questions Brian O'Malley said to me, 'I don't feel like Questions today. Come to think of it, I don't feel like work at all.' That was so unlike him I was rather surprised. He answered Question No. 4 with his usual fluency. I was just in the middle of answering Queston No. 5 when I heard him say rather thickly, 'Take Question No. 6,' which he was due to answer. I thought it was some kind of silly joke and waved him aside impatiently as I tried to catch the supplementary question that was being addressed at me. The next thing I knew was a flurry on the bench, Brian hurrying out and David saying to me, 'Brian's not well. I'll take Question No. 6.' Questions over, I hurried to Brian's room, to find him white and drawn. He had been vomiting and was complaining about his head. As they wheeled him off to the ambulance he muttered to me, 'Anyway, I've voted.' (It would be for Mike, of course.) Next he said, 'Don't tell my wife.' Of course, we took no notice of that and someone went off to telephone Kathleen. We all hung around anxiously, trying to find out what was wrong. Later Maurice Miller told me it was a 'subarachnoid' haemorrhage – not a cerebral one – and everything should be all right. But we were all deeply disturbed. I told Janet to send lots of flowers and find out when I could visit him.

Wednesday, 24 March. Next I had to prepare for my meeting at the Treasury with Denis on the next uprating of pensions and benefits. As I walked into the room I said to Denis and Joel: 'There's no fight in me today. I'm too sick at heart about Brian. You will be able to walk all over me.' Brian has had a brain operation and has not yet come round. The unhappy Kate is by his bedside. We are all suspended in misery and uncertainty. I thought of how Brian and I would have come into that meeting with Denis together, ready to do battle for the earlier uprating on which we have set our hearts. We would have passed the ball backwards and forwards to each other in a piece of high-speed play as we always did. Worrying about him, the heart has gone out of me. Joel shared my wretchedness. He is as fond of Brian as I am. In the event, Denis took the wind out of my sails by saying he knew he had to do something to meet the TUC policy on pensions: so what he proposed was to pay the TUC's suggested rate of £13.50 for a married couple in November instead of the £13 that would be due under a straight interpretation of the forecasting method. I pointed out that the TUC had been asking for this rate to be paid in *July* not November and that payment in November would mean he would only be giving back £45 million of the £500 million he had saved by switching from the historical method and urged him at the very least to advance the uprating by three weeks. An October uprating would make all the psychological difference. He said he would look into it.

Still no news from the ever-effervescent Lord G. so I spoke to him on the phone. He told me he had met the Independent Hospitals Group, the BMA *et al.* yesterday. Incidentally, Gerry Vaughan was there! There had been a 'slightly acrimonious discussion'. The consultants and juniors were very 'bolshie' and wouldn't accept anything he proposed. He had to accept, said Arnold, that they were 'highly political'. The scheme I had suggested was acceptable to IHG apart from the question of numbers of beds. They had decided to adjourn the meeting. Robb was coming in at noon tomorrow to tell him what the figure of beds should be.

Thursday, 25 March. At Cabinet I was all keyed up for my paper on pay beds in which I reported my discussions with Goodman so far, asked for permission to embody control powers in the Bill from the outset along the lines I had spelt out to the IHG and plumped for seventy-five beds firmly as the starting point of licensing. I introduced it by supplementing it with a report on my phone conversation with Arnold yesterday. Harold seized on this to railroad my proposals through. Once again he faced a determined opposition from Harold Lever, backed this time by Shirley. Harold Lever was all for consultations continuing, however much more time they took. (Of course he would be only too pleased if we lost the Bill through the delay.) The PM swept that aside by saying that of course talks could go on, but, if there was a change in the situation, the Bill could be altered during its passage in the House. Shirley then said we would be 'attacked' for the licensing proposals. The form of control by the independent board was okay, but she was worried about the figure of seventy-five beds. If we discouraged the building of private hospitals, we should lose a lot of foreign exchange from rich overseas patients. Denis backed her pontifically. Despite all this the PM nobly discharged his last obligation to me and got all my proposals through. On the figure of beds, however, I suppose it was inevitable he should show his 'neutrality' by yielding a bit. Unfortunately I played into his hands by saying I would be prepared, if it would get agreement, to agree to one hundred beds in London and fifty in the provinces. Harold seized on this to say: 'I suggest one hundred in London and seventy-five in the provinces.' The rest looked at me as if to say, 'That's reasonable: accept it, Barbara.' 'But Arnold may actually get agreement on a lower figure than that for all I know,' I moaned. 'Then let's say seventy-five and one hundred unless a lower figure is agreed,' said Denis cheerfully. I jumped at that, repeating after him: 'All right then, unless a *lower* figure is agreed.' And so it was clinched. The most important thing from my point of view is that, whatever Arnold comes up with now, I can't be forced higher. Not too bad at all.

In the evening I had the first of my 'export' parties: an informal gathering over drinks for medical equipment manufacturers to tell them what I had been up to in the Middle East. As usual the office had been a bit diffident about my intention to make this a relaxed social occasion. They can't get used to my passion for doing business over food and drink. Anyway, Norman had entered into the spirit of the thing as usual and the caterers had turned my room into an attractive buffet. All the invitees streamed in dead on time and I was astonished to find some of them had come from as far afield as Glasgow and Devon. We all got on famously. They were extrovert types with whom I found it easy to get on to familiar terms. Eventually I called them to order, perched on the edge of the table and talked to them rousingly about the export possibilities in the Middle East. I ended up with some frank comments about where they were going wrong: notably their failure to organize proper servicing. Their response was remarkable. They frankly admitted I was right; exchanged ideas audibly among themselves about what they could do to remedy this; agreed there ought to be collective action among the smaller firms and promised me, hand on heart, to organize all this through the BHEC. When at last they left, lining up to offer their profuse thanks, James Collier looked dazed at the success.

I had been surprised that David Owen was missing. The explanation came when he turned up at the end, admitting that he had been at a meeting of Jenkinsites, discussing with their leader what he should do as a result of the vote he has got in the first ballot for the leadership: only fifty-six votes to Jim's eighty-four while Michael tops the poll with ninety. David was clearly pretty worked up: 'We decided he should withdraw,' he told me pugnaciously. I was staggered and told him so. This further display of political daintiness proves conclusively what I have always known: that Jenkins will never lead the Labour Party. I bet Denis stays in the ring, despite his derisory thirty votes. But then, he's a pugilist, not a patrician. Wedgie's withdrawal in Mike's favour was a foregone conclusion. His thirty-seven votes will now almost certainly switch to Mike. I was not surprised by Crosland's dismissal with a mere seventeen votes. Despite the endless build-up he gets in the press, he isn't a serious contender at all.

Friday, 26 March. This was to have been our all-day meeting at Chequers to dicuss EEC policy. In view of Harold's imminent departure, it got itself downgraded rapidly. First it was transferred to No. 10; then Harold opened by saying he gathered a number of people wanted to get away. Could we finish at 1 pm? In fact, if it weren't for the fact that we had been promised the right to brief the PM and Foreign Secretary on the question of direct elections, I think Harold would have cancelled it altogether. As it was he said that Cabinet would no doubt like the opportunity to comment on the line the Government should take in next week's debate. I myself had got up early to wade through a mass of documents, including a 'draft Convention' on direct elections which the President of the Commission has circulated [and] on which Jack had done me a first-class, thorough briefing, raising all sorts of alarm calls on various points. Above all, he pressed me to insist on the Select Committee being set up for which over 100 Labour MPs are now calling in an Early Day Motion. So I was ready to do battle all on my own, if necessary, but I soon found that the majority of Cabinet was ready to do battle too. Faced with the implications of that draft Convention, everyone had clearly had second thoughts and we ended the morning's discussion by reversing nearly everything we had been saying as a government previously.

Harold summed up reassuringly. It was agreed, he said, that in the Commons we should give the Select Committee a fair wind but see that it was chaired by a Minister. We would make it clear that the Government will make no firm commitments at this stage and Cabinet itself would reach no final decision until after the Select Committee had reported.

Monday, 29 March. The Cambridge Economic Policy Group has come out with dire forecasts about our prospects for 1980 if we continue to manage our economic affairs as we do now. Their remedy: a protectionist policy. Denis, of course, rejects their forecasting as unreliable. I am not expert enough to judge. In this leadership election atmosphere we are all poised on the edge of uncertainty. Jack and Brian Abel-Smith, for instance, tell me that they have been served with the sack. The PM has circulated a Minute saying that their appointments 'cease automatically with the end of the Administration in which they were appointed'. So at the moment of the PM's resignation (*i.e.* the end of the leadership election) they will go. Hopefully they will be immediately reappointed, but that will depend on my being confirmed in office. Jack has told me that, if I go, he would like to stay on as political adviser to someone else, provided another Minister he is in sympathy with offers him a job. Apparently the attractions of the Bar are no substitute for politics! Norman is organizing office meetings on this and that because I want to get my potential successor committed on as many things as possible. (We are hurrying out the circular on joint financing this week.)

An essential part of all this is to get Lord Goodman sewn up before it is too late. On Friday we at last received a letter from him setting out in rather obscure terms his draft of a possible agreement with the Independent Hospitals Group over licensing and I arranged to see him this evening. This morning we had an office meeting to discuss our line. The outstanding snag is over the number of beds at which licensing would start. Goodman says the IHG is still standing by 250, which he knows is unacceptable to me, and adds in his letter that he himself has an idea of the figure he would suggest but 'I am hesitant to put it on paper lest it gives you apoplexy'. My guess is that he has a figure of 150 in mind: double what I have told him is my maximum.

In our office discussion we agreed to try to detach the question of the figure from the structure, get an agreement on the latter and agree to differ on the former. I also said that I didn't want any agreement which emerges to be labelled a 'Goodman' one: after all, it is I who have had to fight single-handed to get any licensing provisions included at all (they were never in the Manifesto or the Queen's Speech). So I want to be able to claim this unto myself for righteousness in the eyes of our own side. I suggested we tell Arnold that the IHG must write me a letter putting these proposals to me and I asked officials to draft a form of words which would broadly cover the points Arnold has sketched out, but more lucidly and leaving out the figure of beds. Our problem is that, if we are to keep to our publication timetable, the print of the Bill must be settled by Wednesday of this week. If necessary we shall just have to undertake to introduce Government amendments at the committee stage.

Brian Abel-Smith and officials have produced an excellent briefing showing that the rate of benefit at which no one will be worse off, including one-parent families and larger families, is about £2.60 a week. When we arrived at the Treasury Joel embraced me with his usual affection, asking anxiously after Brian O'Malley. I told him he was expected to make a full recovery, but it would be slow: he had still not come round from the six-hour brain operation at the weekend. Joel then asked me to suggest my figure for child benefit. Quietly I spelt out my analysis of the minimum need for family support, particularly in view of the continuing price increases under CAP and the fact that we should have added 50 pence per week per child to the cost of school meals by November 1977. I would not, I said, be unrealistic but it did seem to me reasonable that, in launching this major aspect of our social policy, we should get back to 1971, i.e., a rate worth £7 for three children. They watched me avidly as I said slowly: 'And that gives us a rate of £2.85 a week.' Joel exploded with laughter at his officials' dismay. 'I told you,' he spluttered, clutching Pliatzky's[1] arm, 'you don't know her as well as I do. And what would this sumptuous figure cost?' 'We don't know,' said Pliatzky, tearing his hair, 'the Secretary of State has gone right through the top of our table.' 'It would cost £217 million,' I said sweetly, 'only slightly above the £200 million which is the top end of the amount earmarked in the Contingency Fund for this purpose.' 'Nothing is "earmarked",' said Joel desperately. 'Don't you realize that the claims on the Contingency Fund already exceed it several times?' He then tried to assert some kind of control over the situation by spelling out the figure *he* had in mind: £2.40 plus a premium of 22 pence a week for one-parent and large families to ensure they did not actually lose. It was my turn to give an incredulous laugh. The Treasury wasn't actually suggesting, was it, I asked, that we should spend Civil Service manpower on paying out little extra driblets of money to a few families because we were in the process of making them poorer?

Joel then went into one of the now fashionable diatribes against universal benefits. Here we were with our backs to the wall and I was proposing an across-the-board increase in family support which would give help to families who did not need it. It is at moments like this that I despair of this Government, dominated as it is by people who don't believe in the policy on which they fought the election. Denis can say till he is blue in the face that the public expenditure cuts don't reflect any abandonment of Labour's philosophy, but here was his right-hand man talking exactly like Roy Jenkins – or, worse still, like Margaret Thatcher. 'I really don't know why you don't join the Tory Party,' I told Joel coldly. 'Because the policy of *our* party is to extend the payment of benefits as of right on the basis of functional need and then to take back from those who don't need them the value of those benefits in taxation.' Joel merely said testily that I was talking sentimental nonsense. It is this kind of attitude that makes me fight for my own departmental corner absolutely ruthlessly. I am expected to accept meekly the reinterpretations of party doctrine which the Treasury (ably aided by right-wingers like Roy Jenkins) just imposes on us. Not on me, they're not going to, as long as my talons remain long and sharp.

The atmosphere was beginning to get quite nasty, but once again I was saved by the Treasury overreaching itself. Miss Jennifer Forsyth[2] started asserting that there would be no administrative difficulties at all about operating a selective premium. I thereupon brought in Tony Crocker who wiped the floor with her. Lance Errington, of all people, clinched it by pointing out that every one-parent or large family would have to have *two* books in order to get

[1] Leo Pliatzky was Permanent Secretary for Public Expenditure in the Treasury.

[2] Miss Jennifer Forsyth was the Under-Secretary in the Treasury who headed the division scrutinizing social service expenditure.

another miserly 22 pence per week. Collapse of Treasury party. 'The line at which we break even,' I pointed out, 'is £2.60 per week.' Joel pounced: 'Does that mean that you'll accept £2.60?' 'Not at all,' I replied smoothly, 'my minimum is £2.70.' Joel said that was impossible and the matter would have to go to Cabinet. So we broke up, Joel and I embracing affectionately again to the bewilderment of his officials. (Mine are used to my histrionics by now and they know they pay dividends.)

We gathered in my room at the House at about 6 pm to approve the draft officials had been drawing up to present to Arnold as the basis of the letter the Independent Hospitals Group was to send to me and eventually were on our way to Portland Place.

Arnold was full of apologies for having dragged me there. I went through the routine I had agreed at my meeting with officials. We could broadly agree with the points in the draft he had sent us, but what was the figure of pay beds which he had said would give me 'apoplexy'? As we had guessed he said '150'. I shook my head and said we had really better agree to disagree on the figure. After all, the profession could always continue its battle to get it amended in the House. He thought that there was probably sense in that and said that he would submit my draft to the IHG. We then sped home, his promise to let us have an answer the next day ringing in our ears.

While we were talking in Arnold's study, I kept glancing over my shoulder at the Graham Sutherland life-size portrait of him which was propped against the wall behind me. 'I keep thinking there are two of you in the room,' I said. 'That must be very unnerving,' Arnold replied. 'It is,' said I. But we both agreed it was a superb portrait: 'The best he's ever done,' said Arnold complacently.

Tuesday, 30 March. Of course there is no news from Arnold. In the meantime we went ahead with an office meeting on finalizing the text of the Bill. I said we would go ahead and put Cabinet's figures in the Bill, whatever the figure Arnold came up with (as it certainly wouldn't be lower). But when I asked Norman to turn up the Cabinet Minutes of last Thursday, I was furious. Despite all Norman's efforts the PM was reported as summing up that the figures would be one hundred and seventy-five 'unless the outcome of Lord Goodman's latest consultations *suggested otherwise*'. 'That's not what we agreed at all,' I exploded. 'I distinctly remember repeating that we had decided firmly on the figures *unless Goodman's figure was lower* and everyone agreed. I'm sick of fighting and winning major battles in Cabinet only to have all my work undermined by inaccurate Minute-taking.' They tried to soothe me down, saying they didn't think the wording would make much difference, but it was the principle of the thing that angered me.

However, I was pleased by my success in strengthening the clause in the Bill which contains the 'broad declaration' in Goodman that private beds and facilities shall be phased out of the NHS. The draftsman, even in the second print, had produced a wishy-washy phrase to the effect that the provisions of this part of the Bill 'shall have a view to' separating private facilities and 'to that end securing the progressive *reduction* of the extent to which accommodation and services are available' for private practice in the NHS, etc. I could not imagine anything more likely to rouse the suspicions of our side that the

Goodman proposals were a device for keeping pay beds indefinitely. Anyway I've now got it changed to 'shall have effect for the purpose of securing the separation of facilities' and 'to that end securing the progressive *withdrawal* of accommodation and services'. That is a fair interpretation of Goodman, to which I am sticking rigidly.

The declaration of the result of the second ballot for the Party leadership was a bit of an anti-climax. The excitement went out of the contest when Mike dropped to second place, with 133 votes to Jim's 141, with Denis collecting a mere 38. At our campaign meeting in Mike's room afterwards John Silkin was as blandly optimistic as ever, but I think the rest of us knew it was all over bar the shouting. Mike would need to get 24 of the Healey votes to win. I said I would make myself responsible for trying to get two of those votes: Joel Barnett's and David Owen's. Mike remained clearly determined to fight to the end. I have been very interested to note how firmly and unequivocally he is going for the leadership. There is a hidden toughness in Mike and it is showing now.

Wednesday, 31 March. Another long office meeting on private practice. First, the BMA have written to Gedling trying to suggest that I have refused to allow them to discuss any parts of the Bill at all, except the Schedule and licensing, and I know this will be used against me by Gerry Vaughan and co. as proof of my 'arrogance'. (In fact it was David who advised that I should refuse to consult them over the details of the Bill as, if I did, we should be enmeshed in wrangles for months, and he was quite right.) I said that I ought to sign the reply to the BMA and give them an indication of the scope of the Bill, without going into details. This was agreed and we eventually finalized a draft between us which Norman said ought to stand us in very good stead in the battles ahead. We rushed it round to the BMA by hand so that they could have it for their council meeting.

A phone call has come from Arnold: the talks with IHG are going well, but he must have more time. He thought he could get them to write to me next Monday. The trouble about this, of course, is that the Bill must go to the printers today if it is to appear before Legislation Committee of Cabinet next Tuesday. Gedling then reported that the Legislation Committee meeting had been postponed because of the change of 'administration' due to take place on Tuesday. Apparently all government goes into limbo until Harold's successor has announced his dispositions! This worried me, because I am anxious to get the print of the Bill circulated before Jim takes over, in case he sacks me. It will be invaluable for me to have that on the record, because I shall keep up the battle on pay beds from the back benches. I therefore said we should go ahead and circulate the Bill on Friday: together with my Minute to the PM, reporting on the outcome of my talks with Arnold. I decided I wouldn't send it till the last minute as I don't want to give Harold Lever and co. the chance to try and reopen the Cabinet decisions.

Later I managed to get a word with David about the party leadership, or rather several words, when I saw him privately. 'Have you voted yet?' I asked him. He laughed and said: 'I rather thought you wanted to talk to me about that.' We then talked for three-quarters of an hour very matily. I developed a new tack: Mike had no chance of winning now, but if the final ballot revealed that practically all the Healey votes had switched to Jim, I believed the Healey/Foot axis on which the Government was founded might well collapse. There would be an immense sourness among the Left, many of whom would have been willing to vote for Healey to stop Jim, but who would discover that, when the chips were down, all the Healeyites wanted to do was to stop the Left. He said he hadn't finally made up his mind and would consider what I had said. We then had a discursive chat about what would happen if Jim won. 'Don't worry,' David said. 'They'll keep you on. They'd be mad not to. No one else could get the pay beds thing through. And we *will* get it through: I think we are out of the wood now.' 'I'd like to see the Bill through and then go,' I told him. He was sure that I would be able to do that. As for himself, he wanted a move. Where to? Either Chief Secretary at the Treasury ('we really have to be tougher over public expenditure') or Minister of Defence ('I'd get some real cuts'.) And we must safeguard Brian's position, he added affectionately. I couldn't help thinking what a camaraderie we have forged. I told David we couldn't spare him yet. We still had policy initiatives to finish on the health side. 'Looking back, you know,' I said, 'we really have some remarkable achievements to our credit in the past two years. We've transformed this department – and I couldn't have begun to do it without Brian and you. We've been a magnificent trinity.' He agreed, saying he had enjoyed every minute of it. 'You really are remarkable in the way you delegate,' he told me. 'And you have had the sense to concentrate on general policy and not just departmental policies as so many Ministers do.' Altogether it was a very pleasant talk which warmed my heart.

Thursday, 1 April. No Cabinet! Whether it is that Harold's sense of emancipation has gone to his head, or what, I don't know.

Another office meeting on private practice. We approved the Minute to go to the PM tomorrow. We also discussed Arnold's suggestion that it would help very much towards an agreement, not only if we would say the chair of the independent board would be legally qualified, but actually gave his name. I have had Jack ferreting away to clear certain names with Bill Wedderburn[1] and others and was all for submitting them to the PM so that, once again, it would be on the record what I had proposed and what Harold's successor had run away from (if he did). However, Patrick raised some very powerful objections to our including this in the Minute, *e.g.* we were committed to consulting on the appointment, not only the professions, but the trade unions. I then came clean and said my problem was that, at my coming press conference on the Bill, I was not prepared to say we had agreed that the chairman should be legally qualified unless and until I knew that the sort of names I had in mind were likely to be accepted by the PM. Patrick, who is a completely honourable man, who considers his overriding duty is to his own Secretary of State and who never tries to twist things to meet his own personal views, immediately saw the strength of this. We thereupon decided to send a separate letter to the PM on this point, setting out the three top names on Jack's list. Hopefully, even the new PM will be able to give me a reply on this point before the Bill is introduced.

[1] K. W. Wedderburn, a barrister and Cassel Professor of Commercial Law at the London School of Economics. He became a Labour Peer in 1977.

With the prospect that I may be out of a job by Monday I decided I would take Friday off. (In any case I want to catch up with my diary.) As I worked late at the office clearing things up, Raymond came in to report the result of his meeting that afternoon with the Joint Consultative Committee on the Schedule to the Bill. It was obvious, he said, that they were completely divided, some of them trying to make an issue of how little time I had allowed for consultation, others admitting they would never have agreed anyway on what the Schedule should contain. In the end they were ready to leave the real negotiating to the IHG, who were at the meeting. The professions just wiped their hands of the whole thing. But what Raymond has divined from his chats with IHG is that they are going to suggest a compromise on the number of beds to be subject to licensing. This fits in with a telephone conversation we have had from Arnold's secretary. 'So, if I may say so, Secretary of State,' said Raymond, 'it would be advisable to get your Minute off to the PM without delay, before the IHG letter arrives.' He's a good chap, is Raymond and has entered marvellously into the spirit of my tussle with the consultants.

Sunday, 4 April. The Sunday papers are full of the inevitability of Jim's victory and how he is spending the weekend preparing a major reshuffle of the Cabinet. So tomorrow evening I may be out of a job. I am quite indifferent. The advantages of being asked to carry on for a while would be that the press would be made to look silly again and it would be quite clear that I hadn't just been Harold's old retainer. Also I would have the fun of fighting my Bill through the House. The disadvantages would be that I would face a hectic week in the House: a late debate on Tuesday on occupational pensions; a statement on the pensions uprating on Wednesday following the Chancellor's Budget statement and a major speech in the Budget debate (since I gather that the Opposition is likely to choose this as one of their subjects during the week). Lance Errington and co. are fighting magnificently on my behalf to get the Chancellor to spell out in his Budget statement the fact that we have switched from the historical to the forecasting method instead of leaving the dirty work to me. I can leave it to them to do the in-fighting.

I have at least got the Chancellor to agree that I shall announce the details of the improvements we have obtained from him in short-term benefits. I feel a deep obligation to my poor Brian in all this. He is still unconscious after his operation. David tells me that this is not unusual after major brain surgery, but none of us will be at peace until he comes round and we know that the prognosis is okay. Until that happens he is obviously critically ill. I am still not allowed to see him. I talk on the phone to Kate from time to time but she won't leave his bedside and come and have a meal with me, though I am sure it would do her good to pour out her heart to someone at greater length than she can do on the phone. Joel and I do a piece of joint mourning every time we meet. I miss Brian so: keep looking towards the corner table in the Members' dining room where he and I used to have so many good plotting meals – either alone or with Joel and Bob. 'I've never known a more popular person in this House,' Joel keeps saying to me, shaking his head. I only know that I have fought Brian over a number of issues. He is instinctively a bit of a male chauvinist pig. But I love him dearly and have a natural chemical affinity with him over so many aspects of social and economic policy. He has been the real architect of the new pensions scheme. All I have done is to inject certain refinements into it and have defended and fought it through Cabinet. I cannot bear the thought that, in my retirement, I shall not be able to watch his progress and do anything I can to promote it.

This morbid train of thought has been fed by my streaming cold. I felt so ill I just had to go to bed, where I slept hour upon hour. Ted got quite worried at my low state and I made up my mind to grab some more antibiotics the moment I got back to London. I can't get through this heavy week until at least my streaming eyes clear up. Things aren't made any better by the fact that Denis has turned me down over my plea that he should advance the next uprating date. Moreover he is wriggling about our demand that in his Budget speech he ought to make it clear that we are switching methods of calculating the pension – and why. He clearly intends to leave that to me. Trust a man to pass the buck to a woman!

Monday, 5 April. With my sinusitis slightly more under control I was able to face the Budget Cabinet, despite the crowds and cameras outside No. 10. It was embarrassing to know how to greet Jim C., who we all know will soon be PM. How to avoid being ingratiating without actually seeming rude? Well, Mike managed it successfully when we came to comment on Denis's Budget proposals, which Denis took nearly fifty minutes to spell out to us. He told us he had to have a neutral Budget which put all the emphasis on the need to improve industrial performance. So that meant balancing tax concessions with tax increases. He had a dig at Harold (Wilson) when he said that he was going to exclude pipe tobacco from the tobacco price increases: 'Retired people smoke pipes and may find themselves in reduced circumstances. So, as a farewell present to you, Harold, I am not increasing pipe tobacco.' We all laughed and Harold chuckled through a wreath of pipe smoke: 'You're not going to say *that* in your speech.' 'I certainly am,' retorted Denis.

There is no doubt that a victory by Jim will strengthen and embolden the Right in the Cabinet and I foresee trouble ahead as soon as the courtesies of the contest are over. My heart is low in my boots, partly because I don't like the feel of a government led by J.C. and fear the worst for the Party. But my greatest sadness is over Brian O'Malley, about whom the news is now pretty disastrous. John Silkin passed me a note saying that his condition was deteriorating rapidly. This whole sudden tragedy is too horrible to believe. I was near to tears.

Back at the office we went through the routine of work, though everyone is obviously wondering whether we will all be there tomorrow, while Brian's condition cast a deep gloom. David was obviously as deeply moved as I was. Somehow I managed to polish up my putative statement on the benefits uprating and my notes for tomorrow night's speech on occupational pensions. By 4 pm sharp we Labour MPS were all crowded into No. 14 committee room for the leadership election result, with the press massed outside. There it was at last: the predicted victory for Jim, only sadly Mike had done slightly less well than we had hoped: 139 votes to Jim's 176. There then followed an orgy of speeches. Jim's was quite fluent (though he had prepared it, he admitted, over the weekend and he read it out). Significantly Jim remarked: 'I shall be making changes and asking some of my colleagues who are doing a competent job to make way for younger ones.' 'He can't mean you, Barbara,' audibly remarked Dennis Skinner, who has become quite a fan of mine. Harold's speech was almost a casual throwaway. Then came Mike's turn. He stood up without a note, soon had everyone laughing and yet injected a note of political seriousness without a cliché or a touch of pretentiousness. I thought as I listened what a joy it was to have a touch of quality brought back into our political dialogue. Mike is the only one to give it to us since Nye died. I believe this country is hungry for a bit of political spontaneity. Anyway Mike got even warmer applause than Jim. Harold got the biggest reception of all, with a standing ovation. I think everyone in the room realized that in his own funny way he had been a big man.

As we broke up to leave the room, Mike whispered to me: 'I want a word with you.' When I went to his room I found about a dozen of us there. Mike was quietly and authoritatively in command. He told us he had been to see Jim that morning and said to him that he thought he, Jim, would win. But he wanted to warn him that he should be very careful in the changes he made. ('Mike won't let Jim be nasty to you,' whispered Jill [Foot], who was sitting on the sofa next to me.) I felt warmed and comforted by the comradeship of that room after the cold winds of exclusion that had been blowing around me. Suddenly I realized I desperately wanted to stay in the Government: that my elaborate assumption of indifference was merely my rationalization of what I felt inside me was necessity – like steeling myself to face the hostility of the doctors. As we broke up to go Mike said to me: 'I must make a phone call. Then I want to talk to you. I'll come to your room.' I sat waiting with a new hope that I might be safe.

Mike came in with a slightly harassed air. He had talked to Jim about me that morning, saying I mustn't be moved, and Jim had said he had been told I wanted to go anyway. Was that true? So Harold had betrayed my confidence! I explained to Mike what I had said to Harold about a month ago, but stressed that I had always made it clear that I wanted to stay until I had got my Bill through and that I wanted to go with dignity, not just be sloughed off in a mass reshuffle. 'They owe me that.' Mike said he was having another talk with Jim tomorrow and would rub this in. I wasn't to worry: Jim hadn't indicated that he was going to drop me. 'Did you try to stop Jenkins becoming Foreign Secretary?' I asked. 'Yes,' said Mike, 'I told Jim it wouldn't be received at all well.' I settled down to a night's work on my boxes, took my penicillin and went to bed, gloomy at heart about the political future that faces the Party now.

Tuesday, 6 April. I had a long exhausted sleep and woke up feeling rather ill. Obviously penicillin doesn't suit me after all. I dare not take any more. As I was finishing my bath the phone bell rang. It was the Press Association. Was I aware that Mr O'Malley had died at 6 am that morning? 'Oh, no . . .' Would I care to dictate a tribute to him? 'Oh, yes . . .' The words poured out of me: his brilliance, the memorial to him in the new pensions scheme and, not least, his personality. 'He was one of the nicest people I have ever met.' I had to go to an early meeting of Legislation Committee to get my pay beds Bill cleared but I was haunted by the need to see Kate

[O'Malley]. I rang Norman and asked him to try to find out where she was.

At Legislation Committee there were a few snags on the text of the Bill itself, but there came a nasty moment when Bob tried to create difficulties. 'The Secretary of State had to report to Cabinet on the result of her latest talks with the profession on licensing,' he insisted. I blessed Ted Short for one of his bursts of no-nonsense radicalism. 'Barbara circulated a letter at the weekend and any member of Cabinet had the right to comment if they wished to,' he said. 'No one did.' Bob subsided, obviously having failed to read his documents. So everything went through. I then passed Ted a note saying that I hoped he would excuse me if I did not stay for the Devolution Committee meeting as I wanted to try and contact Brian's widow. Ted interrupted the proceedings at once to say that he was sure they would all excuse me and ask me to pass their condolences to Mrs O'Malley. There were murmurs of approval and I slipped out thankfully.

My faithful Edna was waiting and rushed me to the House. Norman, bless him, had tracked down Kate at the hospital, where I gathered she would be glad to see me, and said he was coming over to accompany me. That lad has a genius for knowing the moment to bring me the sustenance of his company. We sped to the Nervous Diseases Hospital in Bloomsbury – no time to warn anybody, thank God, that the Secretary of State was on her way. I am not normally morbid about hospitals, but as we walked through the corridors and up the lift to Brian's floor I said to myself: 'There is a smell of death in the air.' My own head was muzzy; there seemed to be intolerable pressures on my brain. Why shouldn't my membrane split suddenly, too, or anyone else's for that matter? I was haunted by man's physical frailty – the thin line that stands between him and death, the line that should have held for Brian and which proved too thin. 'I'll wait outside till you need me,' murmured Norman as we knocked on Kate's door. She stood there, thin and distraught after nine days of hell, then fell on to my shoulder and sobbed bitterly. The young Elizabeth stood there, prettier than I remembered her, so like Brian it was almost unbearable.

Eventually we got down to discussing the funeral. Kate said it would be next Tuesday in Rotherham. 'May I come?' I asked hesitantly. Her face lit up. 'Oh, would you?' It was clear that the one thing she wanted for Brian was full parliamentary honours, because she knew that Parliament had been his life. Elizabeth comforted her with that uncanny maturity which had struck me when last year I attended Brian's Party's annual dinner and visited their home. 'You must make your mother eat,' I admonished her. 'Brian loved good food. He has stood me more good dinners than I can count. He would want you to eat something good now. What about smoked salmon?' Elizabeth wriggled with delight at the very thought. 'The hospital food hasn't been very nice,' she said.

So when at last we left the hospital, I told Norman we must find some smoked salmon at any cost. He rang up Pat [Folger, of my Private Office] on the car telephone to ask her if she knew anywhere we could get it in Bloomsbury. She was a broken reed. 'Things aren't what they were in the civil service,' said Norman, putting down the phone. 'Civil servants don't lunch off smoked salmon any more.' 'Right,' I said, 'then it's Fortnum and Mason's.' At the delicatessen counter I filled a basket of goodies. Edna said she would be only too delighted to take them to the hospital. It was for all three of us as though a member of our own family had died.

After such an emotional morning the Budget speech, over two hours long, seemed an anti-climax. I certainly wasn't going to sit through all of it and went up to my room to work through the first hour. Wedgie also absented himself, saying audibly that the first hour of any Chancellor's economic analysis ought to be written into the record as they do in America. I slipped back on to the front bench in time to hear Denis deal with social security. All my officials' valiant efforts to make him stand up and be counted on the change from the historical to the forecasting method for the pensions uprating have failed. He skimmed over it and so got a cheer from our side for the amount of the increase, whose relevance they did not understand.

Ran into Dennis Skinner who said to me: 'If they sack you, it won't be because of your age, but because of your pay beds policy.' Nice to have the backing of the Left again.

I dodged the PLP meeting on the Budget in order to prepare for the debate on the occupational pensions schemes regulations for which the Opposition have asked. I wanted to take this anyway, once Brian fell ill, in order to dispel any suggestion that I can't handle the technical intricacies of the pensions scheme. But as things have turned out I was very glad to have the opportunity of dealing with this tonight, so as to pay my first parliamentary tribute to Brian. The pensions officials from the Department turned up for a briefing meeting and, emotionally drained as I was, I had to force myself to master all the esoteric details of the regulations. Eventually I was satisfied and Gerald [Johnson, of my Private Office] and I sat down to wait for 10 pm. I say 'sat', but all I wanted to do was to wander restlessly about the room, trying to come to terms with the horror of Brian's death. 'What I need', I said to Gerald, who watched sympathetically, 'is a good howl, but I haven't got a shoulder to howl on when I get home.' Ted *would* be in Brussels this week of all weeks.

I got through the debate pretty well, all things considered, though my voice nearly broke when I paid my tribute to Brian. The Tories were obviously as shocked as we were and their tributes came pouring out of them. By 11 pm it was all over. My officials were very pleased with me and it gave me a bit of inner warmth with which to return to our empty flat and my sad thoughts. For myself, I felt I had proved myself to be a real old trouper: the show had gone on under impossible circumstances.

Wednesday, 7 April. Up early for a hair-do. I have to make my uprating statement today and hold a press conference and I don't intend to *look* ill at this particular moment, however ill I feel. My stomach has gone back on me and I am fighting a wretched sense of nausea. I cannot shake off my feeling of shellshock: in the literal sense the end of an era, with Harold suddenly pulling the rug from under everyone's feet; the election of an alien right-winger as leader of a Party that I was beginning to think might go somewhere exciting; then Brian's death. At the office David was as downcast as I was. He said he wanted to come to Brian's funeral but, as parliamentary business stood next week, he would be tied to the House by a debate on the Children's and Young Persons Act. Would I write to the Chief Whip and try and get it postponed? Of course I agreed. He was also gloomy about the outcome of the leadership election, though he kept repeating 'They won't move you,' whether to reassure himself or me I was not clear.

I held an office meeting on the child benefit rate: officials reported that the Treasury might try to lure us to accept the low rate of £2.50 with the bait of a 50 pence premium for one-parent and larger families. After discussion I agreed with Brian Abel-Smith, despite Tony Lynes's pleas for a special rate for large families, that we should resist this and go for the highest possible rate for everyone as the base on which we could build other things eventually. Brian's steady, informed and perceptive help is a tower of strength. I then struggled through my nausea to master the intricacies of the detail of the uprating, conscious that I faced a difficult time in the House over the switch to the forecasting method, on which there has already been considerable comment in the press.

As I stood up to make my statement I noticed that Jim had slipped into his place next to me and wondered vaguely why. But I wasn't concerned about him, but once again about Brian, to whom I was determined to pay an official tribute in a full House. The words I had drafted were received with great murmurs of approval. I then read the rest of the statement in a firm voice. Patrick Jenkin moved in at once to attack Denis for not having had the courage yesterday to accept responsibility for the change to forecasting: I handled him easily. It was more difficult dealing with our own side, but when I answered one question from George Cunningham rather well, Jim murmured, 'A very good answer.' Afterwards, he said to me: 'Well done, Barbara. There are an enormous number of figures to remember, aren't there?' If, I thought to myself, he came along to see whether I can still perform effectively in the House, I have nothing to fear.

My press conference also went swimmingly. I took the issue of the change of method head-on in my opening remarks and didn't get a murmur from anyone. In the TV interviews afterwards I got the inevitable question: did I think I would survive? 'I never answer hypothetical questions,' I replied loftily, which tickled Peter pink. 'I've never heard a less hypothetical question in my whole life,' he said. 'Anyway, it nonplussed them,' I replied, unabashed. The result of this successful warding off was, of course, that not a word of my interviews was used.

The Tories are genuinely shocked at Brian's death. Paul Dean [Conservative MP for Somerset North] came up to me to plead that there should be a memorial service – so many of them wanted to come.

Norman and I have taken another precautionary step. In case the worst happens I want, if I can, to sew up the chairmanship of the independent board which will phase out pay beds. So I've sent Jim Callaghan a letter suggesting three names of legal luminaries Jack has drawn up for me and who, he assures me, could be relied on to interpret the legislation progressively. We don't want any High Court judge!

Thursday, 8 April. I woke slightly refreshed. The nausea had abated a bit and with my greater clarity of mind I began to wonder just what Jim was up to. The Cabinet agenda this morning consists merely of parliamentary business and foreign affairs so Cabinet isn't till 11 am. That should at least give me a bit of time to fill some gaps in my diary. (Must continue to do some contingency planning!) Jim having shown no signs of a reshuffle, I said to myself that I am going to participate in a Callaghan Cabinet meeting after all and shall be able to compare his and Harold's style. But the papers still continue to refer to coming changes: the eight o'clock news and *Today* talk of Jim wanting his changes completed by Friday, when he is due in Cardiff. So where do we all stand?

I suddenly decide to ring Mike and I catch him just as he is going out. 'What the hell does Jim think he is playing at?' I ask. 'Some of us have policy matters to settle urgently and don't know where we are. I, for instance, have to introduce the pay beds Bill on Monday. Or have I?' Mike was as earnestly reasonable as always. He thought it was only right that Jim should have time to consult people and he himself was going to see him again at 10 am that morning. He would tell him again that it was wrong to say I wanted to retire now and that I ought to be given time to complete my pay beds legislation. I told Mike I didn't want him to just fight *my* battles. What mattered was the political balance in Cabinet. 'Look,' said Mike, 'Cabinet shouldn't last very long. Let's meet in your room in the House afterwards.' So I bathed, climbed into a dressing gown and sat down in our cramped little dining room, swamped with papers, to type my diary.

Nine-thirty am Pat phoned from the office to say Cabinet was cancelled. Good, I thought at first, more time to do diary. Then I realized the significance of that remark and typed all the more frantically. Ten am Pat phoned again. The PM wanted to see me at 10.30 am. 'But Edna hasn't arrived yet,' I wailed. 'Tell him I'll be late.' There ensued one of my frantic attempts to get myself dressed and made up to the degree necessary to face what I knew would be a battery of cameras. But I was still calm. I did not believe Jim would sack me. I didn't deserve that.

Edna and I tore out of the flat with me having to put my lipstick on in the car. (It reminded me of the real wartime blitz when I always used to put on lipstick every time the sirens went.) Yes, there were the cameras outside No. 10 in a solid phalanx and a small crowd of onlookers. I was thankful I had had my hair done yesterday and waved jauntily as I got out of the car. The press, hemmed in behind crash barriers, called out: 'Look this way, Mrs Castle.' I sailed into No. 10. Inside I got a curious message from the policemen. 'The duty secretary has told us to tell him when Mrs Castle has arrived and not to let her past here till he knows.' I paused a moment, puzzled, then walked defiantly through to the outer lobby of the Cabinet room, with them bleating ineffectually behind me. The appropriate Private Secretary rushed out and said: 'Please come upstairs, Mrs Castle.' (Not Secretary of State, I noted.) Out of the corner of my eye I saw Shirley perched on the window-sill near the lobby telephone from which I have so often phoned my office. She just looked at me blankly. I was hurried upstairs to the lobby outside the PM's study. One thing struck me as curious: the display cabinets which surround the walls and which are normally filled with the treasures of a Prime Minister's period of office were all empty. It looked as though the bailiffs had moved in. When I got upstairs I was, to my surprise, guided into one of the drawing rooms: the very one in which I had worked out the minutiae of the *In Place of Strife* argument – and many other industrial battles of the 1966–70 Wilson era. Nigel Wicks [assistant Private Secretary at No. 10] appeared, solicitous. 'I'm afraid we are running late, Secretary of State. Would you like some coffee?' I said indeed I would. He disappeared to get some. As I sat in the drawing room I noticed that it was rather bare of ornaments, too. I feared the worst and said to myself wryly as I sat on the lavishly covered sofa and looked round at the damask-covered chairs and at the other elaborations of décor for which Ted Heath was responsible: 'They are burying me with satin.' But I still didn't believe that a Prime Minister could cut across a legislative programme in mid-session so crudely, so indifferently. If government is not about policies, what is it about?

A quarter of an hour later Nigel Wicks arrived to fetch me. 'Haven't you had your coffee yet?' he asked me anxiously. 'Don't worry,' I said lightly, 'I'll get it afterwards.' I swept into Jim's study, my head in the air. As I went I said to Wicks: 'What has happened to everything in the display cabinets?' 'Oh,' he replied, 'they were Harold's and he has taken them with him.' 'I bet they cost more than £30 each,' I said sweetly and he grinned. He knew the Prime Ministerial Minute I was referring to! Jim was sitting tense in the study, which struck me as being pretty bare of bric-à-brac, too. He waved me to a seat and said quickly: 'I don't want to soft soap you, Barbara. I must reduce the average age of Cabinet and I want to ask you for your portfolio.' I felt detached. 'Did someone tell you that I wanted to retire at Easter?' I asked. He shrugged. 'It was Harold,' I went on. He replied: 'Whoever it was, this isn't the reason.' I paused and then said: 'I never intended to hang on indefinitely. But I did see Harold about a month ago to tell him I wanted to see my pay beds Bill through Parliament. Then I would wish to retire – with dignity. You do realize that I am due to introduce that Bill on Monday?' He shrugged again and looked miserable. I continued: 'It is, of course, your right to ask for my portfolio. In fact, as I understand it, you have got it already. I received, as we all did, a letter from Harold saying that our portfolios were at the disposal of the incoming Prime Minister and that we should carry on meanwhile. So there is nothing I can do.' 'Do you want to go into the Lords?' said Jim. 'Good God, no,' I replied. 'Thank heavens,' said Jim (it would have meant a by-election), 'though I can't refuse it to you any time you ask for it.'

Another pause and I added: 'Who else is going?' 'Ted Short, Willie Ross and Bob Mellish,' said Jim. 'Not Fred?' I said ironically. 'Not yet,' said Jim. 'There will be other changes later.' 'May I ask who is to succeed me?' 'I can't say that,' said Jim wretchedly, 'because there are two people in it and I don't know yet which it will turn out to be.' Another pause, then Jim burst out: 'Harold said to me that the worst thing about this job would be the Parliamentary Questions. It isn't that: it is this.' 'Harold thought that, too,' I replied sweetly, 'that's why he didn't do it.' Another pause and Jim said with a semblance of briskness: 'So you will let me have a letter saying that you are putting your job at my disposal in order to make way for someone younger.' 'Oh, no,' I replied even more briskly. 'So you are going back on what you have just said,' replied Jim with a show of nastiness. 'Not at all,' I replied. 'What I have said is that I have no choice. But I am not doing this voluntarily. I want to stay to finish my legislation. And that is what I shall say in my letter to you. And I shall hold a press conference to spell this out. I shall go on to the Standing Committee on the Bill and shall defend it line by line.' 'Heaven help your successor,' he replied mournfully. 'Don't worry, Jim,' I said cheerfully, 'I shan't attack you personally, I shall just tell the truth. When will it be known?' 'The announcement will be made at 5 pm and I must ask you not to tell anyone else meanwhile.' I told him that was nonsense: I was due back at my office to clear a paper on the rate of child benefit for Tuesday's Cabinet. He himself had commissioned it and it had to be cleared before noon. If I stopped that now, the cat would be out of the bag. After hesitating he said I had better go ahead with the paper and I could tell my Private Secretary, if he was reliable.

I got up to go and Jim held out his hand: 'Wish me well, Barbara.' I shook his hand and said: 'Good luck.' He said almost desperately: 'You should know that Mike has fought for you very hard. I had to tell him this was one thing I could not give him. Perhaps this is the first mistake I have made but, as Harold said to me, I must make my own mistakes.' I said nothing and Jim said to me impulsively: 'Will you let me do this?' and kissed me on the cheek. I said 'Cheerio' and walked out of the room. Outside the waiter was waiting with my tray of coffee. 'How kind of you,' I said, drank it and walked outside to the waiting cameras. 'Have you anything to say to us, Barbara?' asked one journalist pleadingly over the crash barrier. I waved airily and walked to my car. The crowd put up a cheer as I left and I waved to them. I couldn't even tell Edna, who was as anxious as I was to learn my, and therefore her, fate. I asked her to drive me to the House.[1]

In my room I rang Mike. He was just hurrying into the Standing Committee on the Dock Work Regulation Bill and I could forgive him for being *distrait*. He merely made clucking noises when I told him what had happened and we arranged to meet in my room at 3.30 pm that afternoon. I couldn't help thinking of that night when Mike, Wedgie and I and all of us had moved in on Harold to tell him that if he sacked Judith he sacked us all. I suppose solidarity gets watered down a bit when one of the victims is sixty-five. Yet the thought stubbornly persists in me that this argument wears a bit thin when the new PM himself is sixty-four – and Mike is nearly sixty-three.

I then faced a dilemma: how to prepare my day's activities when I was not allowed to share my news? I was determined to have a farewell party at the office. I also had a letter to prepare to send to Jim. I scribbled a draft and hurried to the office to find a strained atmosphere of uncertainty and Jack and Brian Abel-Smith waiting nervously outside my room. I discovered that my devoted Norman, on whom I was relying to see me through this mess, had taken the day off to help his wife move house! Jack assured me that Norman had asked I should phone him if necessary, which I did. When I told him, 'I'm leaving,' Norman's voice almost broke. 'I really am terribly, terribly sorry.' He would hurry back to the office immediately and meet me at my room at the House. I gave Jack and Brian my draft reply to brood over and arranged to meet them all later, telling them that what really worried me was what would happen to them. Their treatment is even more brutal than mine. I then went into the Members' dining room for lunch (not that I felt like any) and sat

[1] Some months later I was chatting in the Commons to Merlyn Rees, one of Jim Callaghan's strongest backers, and he recalled how much Jim had hated dismissing me. 'He told me it spoilt his day,' he remarked apologetically. 'It spoilt my session,' I retorted.

deliberately at my usual place at the collective table. I found Mervyn, Joel, Jimmy Dunn, Bob and others discussing Brian O'Malley's funeral. They wanted to attend it and I had to sit coolly play-acting while Joel pleaded with me to try and postpone our joint paper on child benefit which is due to come before Cabinet on Tuesday. I solemnly said I would try to see if it could be done. Joel clearly had no idea that he and I would not ever again be presenting joint papers to Cabinet.

I found a saddened Norman waiting for me when I got up to my room. Yet it isn't my room any more: within a few hours' time it will be my successor's. I shall be as homeless and powerless as the next. What interests me is the stubbornness of my sense of power and authority. When we lost the last Election I never had this rooted belief that I was part of government. I lapsed into obscurity, almost with a sense of thankfulness. Now I find it inconceivable that I shall not be at Tuesday's Cabinet; not fighting for a proper rate of child benefit; not introducing the pay beds Bill on Monday; not coping with the new problem of the juniors; not conducting our discussions on the consultative document on health priorities; not fighting for the proper treatment of pensions in the next round of pay policy. Authority is ingrained in me in a new way and I just don't believe anyone can discharge it better in DHSS. An unaccustomed self-assurance. And a deep sense of nostalgia. As I paced round the room I said to Norman wryly: 'I always knew I should not live to see the redecoration of this room complete.' (I had been planning it for some time.) I looked out of the window at the still half-finished landscaping of New Palace Yard. 'This view will be worth having soon.' Norman said stoutly: 'Think of all you have achieved. You have crammed five years' work into two.' But I wasn't comforted. My own governmental death stirred up again my deep sense of tragedy over Brian: how ironical that it should be I who had lost my job and he who had died before he could inherit it! Yet I wondered very much whether Jim would have had the generosity and political flair to put Brian in the Cabinet. (Jim had refused to pay the tribute to Brian in the House: something I would have done if I had been PM.) I thanked Norman for all he had done for me and said I'd told Patrick Nairne he was outstandingly the best Private Secretary I had ever had.

Jack and Brian arrived with some emollient additions to my letter to the PM. Norman hurried off to get it typed and to arrange a farewell drinks party at the office for 5 pm. I sat down in some confusion, wondering where I should put all my papers: I haven't even a desk allocated to me as a back bencher and I am under instructions from Jim not to breathe a word to anyone before 5 pm. Just before that hour I broke the news to Edna and Janet. They had sensed something and were deep in gloom. Jack phoned to say that Mike was to become Leader of the House. He would like to work for him. Could I put in a word for him? I said of course. He also said my successor was to be David Ennals. I was shocked. None of us trust him since his Common Market switch. But I scribbled a note of congratulations to him in order to put in a word for my special advisers, suggesting he might consider keeping them on. Jack's desire not to go back to the Bar is interesting: it shows that, like me, he is a politician to his finger tips. He is a great lad. He has been invaluable.

Mike came into my room, sorry but not desolate. He said he had tried very hard to get Jim to change his mind about me, but without success. There was nothing more he could have done, short of threatening to resign. 'Perhaps I should have done that.' I didn't reproach him, but I had a profound sense that the Left has been weakened in this new Cabinet. We wouldn't have let Harold get away with this! Clearly Mike had been preoccupied with three things: first to get the leadership of the House himself; secondly, to stop Jenkins getting the Foreign Secretaryship; thirdly, to get Albert Booth as his own successor at Employment. He obviously thought that a score of three out of four was satisfactory. Perhaps he felt that the falling off in his vote in the last ballot had weakened his position. And he said worriedly that Tony Benn was furious with him, because he thought, if Mike was going to move, *he* should have been given Employment (which he obviously thinks is a much better political base than Energy). I told Mike about Jack's wish to become his political adviser. Had he got one? He said no, looking apprehensive at the whole idea. I told him Jack had specialized on the devolution issue for me and knew all the details. Moreover as a barrister he would be of particular use on constitutional and legal matters. Mike pricked up his ears on this: I can't see him enjoying the details of the devolution side of his remit! He said he would think about it and hurried off like the White Rabbit, nervously looking at his watch.

Ted phoned from Brussels to commiserate with me about Brian's death. I broke my own shock news to him. He burst out with violent expletives about 'that . . . Jim Callaghan'. He told me not to worry about transport at the weekend. We'd cope somehow. He wished more than ever that he was at home with me. So did I.

Although a number of civil servants were at Sunningdale for a conference, they all hurried back for my farewell party: except Henry, from whom not a peep. First into my room was David Owen, who was visibly moved. He kissed me affectionately and sadly on the cheek. I have never felt closer to him. Michael Meacher was outraged. My officials filed in to tell me how much they would miss me, even Charles Regan [Under-Secretary at the Department] assuring me it had been 'very stimulating'. As for my dear old Tony Crocker he said: 'I can tell you now what I have always said about you: "She's not only a very good Minister, she's a honey." ' (I wish civil servants could talk to the press!) Patrick Nairne was, I think, genuinely sad. I took him aside to thank him for the unswerving loyalty he had always shown to me, at which he protested that it was he who should thank me. 'You are so young,' he said. Brian Abel-Smith said it had been such 'fun' – I gathered he had himself already written to David offering his services. Jack was utterly dejected. I had insisted on the entire Private Office being invited, as well as Stan, the messenger, and Edna. The youngsters from the outer office were inconsolable. They produced a bunch of flowers ('all we could get in the time') and a good luck card and said that life would never be the same again: 'even tho' there will be less work to do'. I began to feel near to tears.

David then interrupted the proceedings to give us the latest list of appointments which he had had monitored on his office radio. Stan Orme to be the new Minister of State at DHSS; Peter to Environment, etc. And he then went straight on to make a little speech about what a remarkable Minister I had been; what I had achieved; how good I was to work with; how well I had delegated, etc., concluding with his conviction that, on the pay beds issue, we had produced a solution that would stick. I was so moved by his warmth I thought I was going to blub.

Swallowing hard I made my valedictory speech, warning David that he had dangerously softened my stiff upper lip. I then thanked each group in turn: my remarkable Ministerial team, my political advisers ('I think you know you could not manage without them now'), Patrick Nairne, my officials, my Private Office. 'What I shall miss most is the comradeship – and I am not talking in some sinister Marxist sense.' It was the comradeship of battle in which we all pulled and plotted together for victory. I told them I had never accepted the conventional criticisms of civil servants. It was their duty to tell the Minister frankly the dangers and snags they saw in her policy: 'It is far better that they should be voiced and faced in this room than for the Minister to encounter them for the first time at the dispatch box or in the press.' We needed strong civil servants and a strong Minister to digest their advice and make what use of it she thought fit. The words poured out of me though I hadn't prepared anything. Patrick then insisted on saying a few words. 'The sight of you sitting at the top of that table and pulling out your pen to draft something before our eyes is an object lesson none of us will forget.' At last we broke up. David was in a savagely depressed mood. 'I don't want to stay here. I want to get out. This has been a marvellous two years. I don't suppose I shall ever again be so happy in a ministerial job.'

Earlier Norman had said to me unhappily: 'I do hope you will forgive me if I slip away from the party: David Ennals wants to see me.' I said of course. His new master must come first. But I realized later amid the confusion that Norman had come back again. He was quietly organizing the collection of all my personal papers and anything else he could do to help. He whipped my Persian picture off the wall, saying firmly: 'You're taking *that*.' 'Well,' I replied, 'if the PM can take his treasures, so can I.' I recorded an interview for the *Today* programme, turned down requests for TV (I must have been looking pretty tear-stained by now), and got Norman to cancel my dinner with Geoffrey Smith of *The Times*. All I wanted to do was to go to cover till I had collected myself but, alas, I was due to catch the night sleeper to Blackburn. Suddenly I realized that technically I had no transport any more. Edna ceased to be mine from that moment on. But Norman wasn't having any of that nonsense. He said he would square it with the government garage that she was to take me to the train (just as, on Tuesday, he had fought and won a battle with them to get Brian's driver to drive Mrs O'Malley and Elizabeth back to Rotherham). I shook hands with Gerald and Pat. Then Norman escorted me to the car for the last time. As he helped me in he leant forward impulsively and kissed me on the cheek. At that I really did nearly howl! A downcast Edna drove me to the flat and cooked us bacon and egg while I tried to collect my wits and my things.

The phone went endlessly: the press wanting interviews; family and friends who had just heard the news. All of this took so much time, and I was so *distrait*, that I nearly missed my train. Then I read for a long time before I tried to sleep.

Friday, 9 April. It was a hectic day I faced in Blackburn and it would have been a strain at the best of times. As it was, I knew it would require all my famous reserves of energy to get through the pressures and press queries. One lass from the *Evening Standard* even booked herself into the sleeper next to mine in the hope of getting an interview. I gave it her in the morning in the car from the station, out of compassion and because she was very sweet. My reward was that she left all the morning papers with me; no great comfort for me in any of them and a typically nasty piece in the *Daily Mail*.

Breakfast over, my first concern was to go and have a comb-out. (The Castle motto throughout the ages: 'When the sirens sound, make sure you look your best.') I could then face with aplomb the cameras that materialized from nowhere. Finally I had to succumb to insistent requests and agree to interrupt my lunch with the North-West Tourist Board to give interviews on Granada and BBC. (Mercifully I managed not to look as exhausted as I felt.) Once again I realized that perhaps my greatest asset in life has been my stamina: I ought to have been dead! It was curiously natural and comforting to slip back into ordinary constituency work: to talk to the shop stewards of the British Aircraft Corporation at Samlesbury and have them say worriedly that they didn't like my being sacked but hoped I would be active on the back benches; to go and see old people about their electricity bills and to promise to take up their problem with the chairman of the SBC [Supplementary Benefits Commission](!); to have my local Party at our evening meeting express their anger at my treatment and their delight that I had said I wanted to remain a commoner.

The most unnerving moment of the whole day came when I returned to the Party offices after lunch for constituency interviews and found waiting for me in the hall Mrs Green, General Secretary of the National Federation of Old Age Pensioners' Associations, and her deputy, holding a magnificent bouquet. They thrust it into my hands saying that it was an expression of gratitude for all I had done for the pensioners – and they are a couple of Tories too! That really undid me: the ice melted and the tears came. To hell with Jim Callaghan's ingratitude. 'That is quite the nicest thing that has happened to me,' I told them through my tears. 'We hoped you'd feel that,' they beamed and hurried away.

Sunday, 11 April. Back to the consolations of HCF and Ted's company. The *Sunday Mirror* has been nice to me this morning: it makes a change. I remain strangely stirred to my very depths by a sense of finality and nostalgia. And I am deeply hurt by Jim's cavalier discarding of me like so much old junk. I know – and have always known – that I am one of the best Ministers in this Government: and certainly the toughest fighter for our Party's policies. And I am at the peak of my powers. To turn me out for *Ennals* – really! I wouldn't have minded if my going had led to some real rejuvenation of the Government – if, for instance, Jim had brought Judith Hart back. (Incidentally it shows how superficial is our Party's devotion to the cause of promoting women that Jim could so complacently reduce the number of women in his Cabinet.) If Shirley had gone to my job, I could have understood it, too – though on second thoughts I realize she couldn't have taken it, because she disagrees with my policy on pay beds.

One of Norman's last little pieces of mischief just before I left had been to suggest to me that I ask Harold Lever and Shirley Williams to be among the sponsors of my pay beds Bill. I duly did so. They both refused, Harold in a letter of nauseating hypocrisy. Ted is still rumbling with anger over Jim's action. It is a great comfort to have him back and we talk long and tenderly. He tells me that Bob Mitchell was boasting at Strasbourg when the news of the changes came through that 'we' (i.e. the Right) had told Jim Callaghan that they would not tolerate any attempt to get rid of Reg Prentice. So the Right was strong enough to save that anti-party man while the Left was not strong enough to save me. It is this wider significance of my going that is so disturbing.

Phone call from Eric Heffer to say how outraged he was at my sacking. We had had our disagreements, but no one doubted I had more socialism in my little finger than the rest of the Cabinet put together. 'Thank God you are still on the NEC.' I hadn't intended to run again but this made me wonder whether I should. Another heart-warming surprise was a note from Tony Keable-Elliott, which he pushed through the door. It said that, despite our disagreements over pay beds, he wanted to thank me for all I had done for the primary care teams and the NHS. I hadn't expected that!

In the evening Jack phoned to tell me that DHSS was 'like a morgue' and he doubted that he could stay, though David Ennals had asked them all to stay on. David had come in on Friday for a general talk and Lord Goodman had been in to see him. It was fascinating to see the difference in Arnold's manner towards David. 'None of the amusing *bonhomie* he showed with you,' said Jack. 'He blatantly tried to bully him, actually making out that it had been agreed that no pay beds were to be phased out unless and until an equivalent amount of private beds had been provided in their place. I just couldn't keep quiet and told him he was talking nonsense. It was a good job I was there.'

One of my major problems now is transport. With Ted so much in Europe he isn't available to do his old job of chauffeuring me. I can use public transport, up to a point, but I can't carry around with me the masses of food and other things we ferry down to the cottage every weekend. We shall have to make some uncomfortable adjustments, starting with tomorrow morning when Ted is off to Brussels again. We shall have to get up at an early hour so that he can drop me at High Wycombe station on his way to his plane.

Monday, 12 April. Climb into the train at High Wycombe. I wish I weren't so recognizable. One can never be a purely private person again: everyone nudges his neighbour and points me out. It is like asking Harold Wilson to travel incognito. Catch a bus to the flat, clutching my piles of parcels. Change into a pretty dress, because this is my day to say goodbye to the Queen. The office rings: David Ennals would like to talk to me. David comes on thanking me effusively for my note of congratulations and saying of course he would be delighted to keep on my advisers. He knew and respected Brian Abel-Smith from the old days. As for Jack Straw, he had checked up with people at the office and they all spoke highly of him. (If he checked up with Norman he would get a panegyric – those two are close buddies.) Yes, he was going ahead with the press conference introducing the Bill that afternoon. But he first had to see the BMA: they had asked for it and he couldn't refuse. I wished him well and thanked him for letting me continue to use his ministerial room until he needed it.

Caught the underground to the House and then realized I was not coming in by ministerial car and I hadn't got my security pass with me. The policeman in New Palace Yard just smiled at me and waved me on. It was as natural as breathing to go up to my old room. There I found Janet waiting for me and a magnificent bowl of roses on my desk: it was from her and Vince. Once again I felt my eyes dampening, particularly when I read the note which accompanied it: 'To those of us who grew up with the names of Nye Bevan and Barbara Castle it is the end of an era – and we are sorry!' I rebuked her: 'You'll make me cry.' 'Then read those,' she replied, pushing a pile of letters under my nose. As I read them I was engulfed in a warm tide of affection, regret, anger and gratitude. They were letters from unknown old age pensioners, from Tory chairmen of AHAS, from Party workers, from nurses, from trade unions, from MPS (including some Tory ones like Teddy Taylor) all saying that they were sorry and/or it was a scandal I was going; all thanking me for what I had done. Among the ones which pleased me most were those from Peter Jacques and Liz Arnott [of Labour Party HQ]; the most surprising included letters from Merrison, Philip Allen of the Occupational Pensions Board and Derek Stevenson, who actually thanked me for 'the time and trouble you always took over your negotiations and discussion with the BMA'. The two most perfunctory were from Elwyn and Wedgie Benn. I could read their minds: 'Hard cheese, but she can't really complain.' Oddly enough there was only one abusive letter in the whole pile: from a consultant in Sutton Coldfield who wrote: 'I thank God you have been sacked.' I think, however, that the most moving letter of them all was from young Michael Meacher. He is no time-server. He is extremely able and a genuine radical. It was a matter of pride to me that he should write about my 'patent burning sense of socialist purpose and drive', and my 'capacity to inspire'. The ice began to melt around my heart, but my anger against Jim Callaghan's petty 'reconstruction' of his Government grew. Every newspaper has commented on the swing to the Right in the new Cabinet.

It was the last day of the Budget debate and I saw Mike's name go up on the indicator. I went down to hear him and had to stop myself at the door of the Chamber from walking onto the front bench. I crept instead onto the third bench above the gangway and sank thankfully next to nice Tam Dalyell, feeling the eyes of the whole House and the press gallery were on me in my reduction to the ranks. I listened to Mike rather distractedly. No doubt it was my fault that I found his rhetoric a little unreal. Then it was time to go and see the Queen. Once again I wondered how I was supposed to get there. Janet asked me if she should order a taxi, but I didn't like the idea of its clock ticking up endlessly in the courtyard of Buckingham Palace. I felt there ought to be a way of going with slightly more dignity. So I rang up Ted Short who was due to go at the same time and asked if I could cadge a lift, expecting he would have his own car. I went down to Speaker's Court to wait for him. The drivers were there, coping in their usual friendly way with ex-Ministers. Winnie, Mike's driver, took pity on me and insisted on my sheltering in Mike's car from the cold wind. 'You know you could have had a ministerial car to go to the Palace,' she said to me. 'It is absurd the way no one explains this to you.' And sure enough Ted Short arrived in a ministerial car. Anyway it was nice to have his company. He had been at his office clearing out his things. He didn't attempt to hide his bitterness. 'You and I backed a loser, Barbara, and we are paying for it.' 'So you didn't vote for Jim?' 'I voted for Denis, then switched to Mike. This fellow we've got is no good.' 'Are you going into the Lords?' 'Not yet, anyway.' He brooded a bit, then said: 'The irony is that I feel at the top of my powers. I don't feel tired or stale. I expect you are the same. You ought to have been allowed to finish your pay beds legislation. I would have liked to finish my work on devolution. I have spent months on it.' More brooding, then: 'You and I, Barbara, are going to have difficulty in filling our time.' It was the only thing on which I disagreed with him.

At the Palace the staff greeted us courteously. 'The audience is upstairs.' We traversed the long carpeted corridors and climbed the stairs to a small boudoir. Martin Charteris, the Queen's secretary, greeted the former Lord President affectionately. 'How are you, Ted.' 'Fine, Martin.' 'I'm afraid we're running late,' said Charteris. 'It's been a busy day. We had a Privy Council this morning at Windsor.' (I knew that – I had been supposed to attend it.) 'Then there were the new Ministers to receive. Now this. These farewell occasions are always very sad.' 'Was Michael Foot there this morning?' I asked. 'Because he was on his feet in the House at 3.30 pm.' 'We had to give him a hurried lunch,' said Charteris. 'He only had one course.'

We looked out on the garden, which Charteris remarked was looking very beautiful. 'Not as beautiful as ours at Hell Corner Farm,' I replied truthfully. 'You drew me a picture of your cottage once in Cabinet,' said Ted with his rather wintry but honest smile. 'Those were the days when you were Chief Whip,' I replied, 'and we sat together at the bottom of the Cabinet table.' I noticed idly that the polyanthus in the floral decoration on the table were wilting. The tiny room was crowded with bric-à-brac. Still we waited. Willie Ross joined us. I was interested by the order of precedence: first the Lord President, then me, then the Secretary of State for Scotland. What *would* the Nationalists say? We were joined by Charteris's deputy, Philip Moore, recently recruited from the civil service. He asked about Patrick Nairne: 'We always used to say he was the best of the whole bunch of us.' I agreed he was an excellent civil servant indeed. Norman Crowther-Hunt drifted in last, red-faced and cherubic. He explained that this was the right time for him to go because his period of leave from his academic job was nearly up, but he had enjoyed every minute in government. (I am always intrigued by the fascination which public life has for academics.) Willie chatted knowledgeably to Charteris about Scottish nationalism. No doubt the Queen's secretary must keep in touch. I couldn't help thinking that we 'golden oldies', as Ted put it, weren't feeling like has-beens at all. In fact we were feeling rather superior and arrogant.

At last the message came: the Queen was ready. Charteris jumped to attention and Ted was out through the door in one minute flat, calling over his shoulder to me: 'I'll wait for you.' As we sat there someone asked where Bob Mellish was. 'He asked to be excused because he wasn't feeling well,' said Charteris. This amused me because earlier I had heard Bob declaring over lunch in the House that he was blowed if he was going to say goodbye to the Queen: 'During the whole time we have been in government she has never once asked my wife and me to any function, so she can keep her thanks.' Ted came out and I was whisked in to the Queen. She was sitting on an elegant sofa in a larger room. I noted with approval how nice she looked: hair well groomed, a charming simple woollen dress, blue which she seems to prefer, with a bow at the neck. I noted for future non-action how well a circle of real pearls looks on a round neckline. She chatted easily and informally, talking about how difficult my job had been, remembering her visit to the new Southampton hospital and what we had talked about, quoting Dick Crossman (not for the first time). I admired her as a fellow professional. After ten minutes she said: 'I want to thank you, Mrs Castle, for all you have done.' I bowed and thanked her for receiving me. I was out and collecting Ted Short. We were escorted courteously to our car. Back to the House.

Thuesday, 13 April. Tuesday, the thirteenth: an appropriate date for Brian's funeral. Jack, all consideration, had insisted on collecting me and being responsible for my rail ticket. I wondered distractedly what to wear. The sun shone and the flat was warm. It was to be a formal funeral at Rotherham's Roman Catholic church. So I supposed I must wear black – and a hat. I have no Private Secretary to advise me now. Jack had borrowed Anthea's best black hat for me but it was straw. I teetered between my dress with Anthea's hat or my black coat with fur collar and no hat. I ended in my confused state by emerging with neither hat nor coat. Outside the wind was icy. Jack wanted me to go back for my coat but I was afraid of missing the train. I soldiered on. We strap-hung on the Victoria line to King's Cross with me worrying about my clothes and then deciding that the best tribute I could pay to Brian was to be wrongly dressed: the accolade of sincerity.

In the train I was soon engulfed in the warmth of comradeship. Our compartment began to fill up with an impressive parliamentary array. We crowded into the dining car for breakfast. There was Walter Harrison[1] and Stan Orme, me and Jack and Brian Abel-Smith, Alf Bates and Michael Meacher. At the last minute David Owen arrived. 'I thought you had a debate on the Children and Young Persons Act,' I said to him (my efforts with the Chief Whip to get it postponed at David's request having failed). 'I told them to stuff it,' he replied valiantly. 'I have got Alex Lyon[2] to deal with it. One has to get one's priorities right.' I have never liked David more. Then I noticed Margaret Jackson,[3] as inadequately and thinly clothed as I was. I thought to myself that Brian could not have had a more eloquent testimony. I discovered that we were all to walk behind the coffin to the church. 'You'll all be back shortly for my funeral,' I warned them. 'But, when I die of pneumonia, I shall instruct Ted that the ceremony will be at Hell Corner Farm and you will have the biggest booze-up you have ever had.' There was an extraordinary feeling of closeness among us in that dining car. Jack told me that the BMA's meeting with David [Ennals] yesterday had been a scream. The BMA boys had been at their worst, Grabham telling David that he was behaving abominably. So the target has changed with dramatic speed! Jack also told me my officials were still subdued.

[1] Labour MP for Wakefield and Deputy Chief Whip.

[2] Labour MP for York and Minister of State at the Home Office. Jim Callaghan was to remove him from his job.

[3] Labour MP for Lincoln and Under-Secretary of State for Education.

Tim Nodder, particularly. He had told Jack how illuminating the past two years had been to him. For the first time in his life he had learned the value of words. 'We were rather good at drafting,' I replied complacently.

At Doncaster station a fleet of ministerial and mayoral cars were waiting to take us to Rotherham. There were refreshments waiting for us in the mayor's parlour. I was astonished how many of Brian's colleagues came crowding in: Joe Harper,[1], Merlyn Rees, John Silkin, Alf Morris, Alice Bacon,[2] Dennis Skinner, Guy Barnett,[3] Joel Barnett. It was a long way for them all to come. From the office had come Alice Perkins, Brian's devoted Private Secretary, and the gentle Alec Atkinson, who Brian always said was the best civil servant on the pensions side. They grieved openly. Alec took me aside to say what a 'remarkable' farewell speech I had made to them. That pleased me a lot. Then came the order to fall into line behind the coffin. Despite the cold wind the streets were lined with onlookers. We shivered under the grey skies.

At the church Merlyn was shocked when the usher directed me into the second row, Cabinet Ministers and the mayoral party sitting in state in front. I didn't give a damn, thankful to rest my head against the wall, drained of all vitality. The rather homely service left me unmoved. I watched Kate as she stood there dry-eyed and dignified, doing what she thought Brian would want her to do. As we left the pews Merlyn, typically nice, insisted on standing back and making me walk out first with John Silkin. It was as though they were burying me with honours, too! As we stood outside in the biting wind, waiting for our cars to come, a woman in the crowd recognized me: 'It's Barbara.' Within minutes I was surrounded by a crowd of women wanting to shake my hand. My colleagues looked on in amusement as I was lost in a sea of excited women. 'That's star quality,' said David. 'Her successor won't have it.'

Back in the town hall there were coffee and buns for the horde of mourners. 'I thought you had child benefit at Cabinet this morning?' I said to Joel. 'I got them to postpone it,' he said. 'I was determined to come here.' We chi-iked about the rate of benefit that should be fixed. 'I'm ready to settle at the figure I know you would have accepted,' said Joel. 'What's that?' I replied. '£2.65?' 'You know you would have settled below that,' he said. 'I know nothing of the kind,' I retorted. It was quite like old times. Suddenly Joel burst out: 'It is absurd that he should have sacked you.' 'It's not absurd, it's bloody wicked,' snarled Dennis Skinner. 'God knows what's going to happen under this man,' gloomed Joel. 'I told you not to vote for him,' I quipped. 'I myself would have voted for Denis if Mike had been knocked out.' 'I know, I know,' he murmured uneasily.

John Silkin, who had come in his ministerial car, insisted on my driving back with him. He said he wanted to talk to me. It turned out that he wanted to theorize about the reasons for Harold's resignation. He didn't think we had got to the bottom of it yet and was sure Harold was planning to come back in some way. But not, he thought, a coalition. It was all very inconclusive. What he was obviously more preoccupied with was his own fate. He was sure he would be sacked on the next round. Mike had tried to get him the job of Environment,

[1] Labour MP for Pontefract.
[2] Former Labour MP for Leeds, now Baroness Bacon.
[3] Labour MP for Greenwich and Under-Secretary of State at the Department of the Environment.

but Jim had said he 'hadn't a very high opinion of my capabilities'. John was all very relaxed about it, as he is about everything. He is the kindest chap, but has not yet proved himself a political heavyweight. I snuggled down between him and Guy Barnett in the back seat and fell sound asleep.

Epilogue

The Pay Beds Bill duly received its Second Reading on 27 April, David Ennals being anxious to show that he was not reversing my policy. After an argument with the Chief Whip I managed to get myself on to the Standing Committee on the Bill, ready to pounce if the Government looked like giving way to the medical profession on any important point. The Bill became law, substantially unchanged, in November 1976. Some 1,000 pay beds were abolished at once and the Health Services Board was set up to deal with the rest. Thanks to the vigilance of its two trade union members, Bernard Dix of NUPE and Ray Buckton of ASLEF, and to the fairness of its independent chairman Lord Wigoder, it proceeded to apply the Act scrupulously. I was particularly glad of the provision under which the Board had to produce a report on common waiting lists within six months. This it did in May 1977 (Cmnd 6828), recommending that private and NHS patients should be placed on the same waiting list and move up it on the basis of the same criteria. Consultations over the report dragged on endlessly and no action had been taken by the time the Government fell two years later. The Board also ran into difficulties over the criteria for phasing out pay beds, partly because of the failure of the medical profession and the DHSS to provide the information it required. It was clear that the Act needed strengthening, but my attempt as a member of the NEC to get a passage promising this into the Manifesto for the 1979 General Election failed.

There were even greater setbacks over child benefit. When I left the Government, Cabinet had been about to agree the rate at which it would be introduced in 1977 but silence fell until 25 May when David Ennals announced that the scheme had been postponed indefinitely. Instead, family allowance of £1 a week would be introduced for the first child. The excuse given was that the trade unions had shied away from the cut in their members' take-home pay which the loss of child tax allowances would mean, even though the family as a whole would benefit. Labour back benchers, particularly women MPS, were furious and I persuaded the Liaison committee to set up a working party to argue things out. The trade union members of the working party – Alf Allen of USDAW and Terry Parry of the Fire Brigades Union – proved devoted allies of child benefit and, faced with their determination, the Government was forced to accept a compromise under which the scheme was phased in over three years. By the time of the General Election, child benefit had been fully introduced at a rate of £4 a week, with the promise of more to come, and the Government was glad to claim it as the cornerstone of its policy for the family.

Despite these hard-won victories, the social contract was being steadily breached by the Government. The summer of 1976 marked the political turning point. Pay policy had been holding well, public spending on industry had been increased, confidence was being restored and the pound strengthened. This immediately raised the spectre of Britain's deep-seated uncompetitiveness, which a strong pound made even worse. Two options were open to the Government: either to rebuild our manufacturing strength behind temporary protective walls (which was contrary to our commitments to the IMF, to say nothing of the EEC) or to weaken sterling deliberately. The Treasury preferred the latter. In March 1976, almost unnoticed, the Bank of England began to sell sterling. The pound fell sharply and the 'crisis' atmosphere returned. In July, Denis Healey used it to get an emergency package through Cabinet, consisting of a £1,000 million more cuts in public expenditure and a £1,000 million increase in employers' national insurance contributions. The package did not do the trick. In October the minimum lending rate was raised to 15 per cent and in December Denis Healey accepted a further package of public expenditure cuts as the price of an IMF loan of some £3 billion.

The deflationary moves had their predictable effect. The balance of payments deficit was reduced and so was inflation. Callaghan's target of bringing it down to single figures by 1979 began to seem feasible. But output was stagnant, investment low and already by mid-1978 unemployment had risen to a post-war record of 1·3 million. For the Government, Michael Foot rushed through some job creation schemes which provided or saved some 275,000 jobs, but it was clear that orthodox policies had not solved the classic dilemma of how to stimulate growth while keeping inflation down. The deeper the Government sank into the mire, the more stubbornly it resisted the demands of the Left for an alternative economic strategy and the pleas of the TUC for some modest reflation. The breach with the unions was widening. They had kept their side of the social contract by acquiescing, however reluctantly, in the Government's pay and anti-inflation policies, but their patience was wearing thin. In the summer of 1978 the Government, which had been seeking to enforce a pay increase limit of 10 per cent, announced that this must be halved to 5 per cent in the coming year. With inflation still in double figures, this effectively meant a pay cut and the dam burst. In the Liaison Committee union leaders privately warned the Government that they could not hold their members, but their warnings were ignored. Within a few months the country was plunged into a rash of strikes in the 'winter of discontent'.

In the Commons the Government had been kept alive by a pact with the Liberals and the cynical tolerance of the Ulster Unionists, but support from the Labour benches was waning. Splits over devolution brought matters to a head and in May 1979 the Government fell. Margaret Thatcher, the voice of the new Right, was returned, committed to uncompromising monetarist policies.

I had decided some time earlier that I would not stand again for Parliament. This was partly due to my disillusionment with the Callaghan Government, but mainly to my belief that I should make way for younger aspirants. Against my vote, the Commons had agreed to direct elections to the European Parliament and it was suggested to me that my ministerial experience would be valuable to the new Labour MEPs, most of whom had never been in any Parliament. I could see that more and more decisions would pass to Brussels and Strasbourg and that it was imperative we should monitor, and try to control, what was happening there. I became an MEP in my beloved North-West, first for Greater Manchester East and then again in 1984 for Greater Manchester West.

My ten years in the European Parliament have covered a period in which, as I had anticipated, power has moved increasingly from national Parliaments to the European Commission and Council of Ministers. But this has not prevented Mrs Thatcher from applying her own brand of government ruthlessly at home. After ten years in office she has not yet succeeded, any more than her predecessors, in reconciling the main indicators of economic success: growth, employment, low inflation and a healthy balance of payments. After her initial success in bringing inflation down, it is now rising again; our growth rate is faltering; unemployment is still well above the level she inherited and the balance of payments deficit has risen to record heights. In 1989 I retired from the European Parliament in order to have more time to study and analyse the lessons of the last twenty-five years: where governments have succeeded and where they have failed.

List of Abbreviations

AAM	Anti-Apartheid Movement
ACAS	Advisory Conciliation and Arbitration Service
AEF	Amalgamated Union of Engineering and Foundry Workers
AEU	Amalgamated Engineering Union
AFTA	Atlantic Free Trade Area
AHA	Area Health Authority
ANF	Atlantic Nuclear Force
APEX	Association of Professional, Executive, Clerical and Computer Staff
ASLEF	Amalgamated Society of Locomotive Engineers and Firemen
ASSET	Association of Supervisory Staffs, Executives and Technicians
ASTMS	Association of Scientific, Technical and Managerial Staffs
ATS	Auxiliary Territorial Service
AUEW	Amalgamated Union of Engineering Workers
BAA	British Airports Authority
BART	Bay Area Rapid Transport District
BBC	British Broadcasting Corporation
BDA	British Dental Association
BEA	British European Airways
BET	British Electric Traction
BIS	Bank for International Settlements
BISAKTA	British Iron and Steel and Kindred Trades Association
BMA	British Medical Association
BOAC	British Overseas Airways Corporation
BOSS	South African Bureau of State Security
BR	British Railways
BRB	British Railways Board
BRS	British Road Services
BSC	British Steel Corporation
BTC	British Transport Commission
BUA	British United Airways
BUPA	British United Provident Association
CAP	Common Agricultural Policy
CAWU	Clerical and Administrative Workers Union
CBI	Confederation of British Industry
CCHMS	Central Committee for Hospital Medical Services

CDS	Campaign for Democratic Socialism
CIM	Commission for Industry and Manpower
CIR	Commission for Industrial Relations
CLP	Constituency Labour Party
Cmnd	Command paper
COHSE	Confederation of Health Service Employees
CPRS	Central Policy Review Staff
CPSA	Civil and Public Services Association
CRO	Commonwealth Relations Office
CSD	Civil Service Department
CSEU	Confederation of Shipbuilding and Engineering Unions
CTA	Conurbation Transport Association
DAC	Development Assistance Committee
DATA	Draughtsman's and Allied Technical Association
DDRB	Doctors' and Dentists' Review Body
DEA	Department of Economic Affairs
DEP	Department of Employment and Productivity
DHSS	Department of Health and Social Security
DIG	Disablement Income Group
DTC	Department of Technical Co-operation
DVO	Development Committee
EC	Executive Committee
EC(P)	Economic Policy Committee (1974–76)
ECMT	European Conference of Ministers of Transport
ECOSOC	The Economic and Social Council of the UN
EDC	Economic Development Committee
EEC	European Economic Community
EETPU	Electrical, Electronic, Telecommunications and Plumbing Union
EFTA	European Free Trade Area
EN	Economic Committee
EPC	Economic Policy Committee (1964–70)
ETU	Electrical Trades Union
FAM	Family Allowance
FAO	Food and Agriculture Organization
FBI	Federation of British Industry
FCO	Foreign and Commonwealth Office
FIC	Freight Integration Council
FO	Foreign Office
GAS	General Aviation Services
GATT	General Agreement on Tariffs and Trade
GEC	General Electric Council
GITA	Go it Alone
GLC	Greater London Council

GMC	General Medical Council
GMWU	General and Municipal Workers Union
GNP	Gross National Product
GNR	Great Northern Railway
HAC	Home Affairs Committee
HCF	Hell Corner Farm
HCSA	Hospital Consultants and Specialists Association
HMG	Her Majesty's Government
IDC	Industrial Development Certificate
IHG	Independent Hospitals Group
ILO	International Labour Organization
ILP	Independent Labour Party
IMF	International Monetary Fund
IP	Industrial Policy
IPC	International Publishing Corporation
IR	Industrial Relations
IRC	Industrial Relations Committee; Industrial Reorganization Corporation
ISTC	Iron and Steel Trades Confederation
IWA	Inland Waterways Authority
JASP	Joint Approach to Social Policy Committee of Cabinet
JHDA	Junior Hospital Doctors' Association
JSG	Joint Steering Group
LTB	London Transport Board
MEDD	Middle East Development Division
MES	Ministerial Economic Strategy Committee of Cabinet
MIRA	Motor Industry Research Association
MISC	Miscellaneous Committee of Cabinet
MLF	Multilateral Fleet
MOD	Ministry of Defence
MOT	Ministry of Transport
MTA	Medium-term assessment
NAB	National Assistance Board
NALGO	National Association of Local Government Officers
NATO	North Atlantic Treaty Organization
NEB	National Enterprise Board
NEC	National Executive Committee
NEDC (Neddy)	National Economic Development Council
NFA	National Freight Authority
NFC	National Freight Corporation
NFU	National Farmers Union
NHS	National Health Service

NIBMR	No Independence Before Majority Rule
NIESR	National Institute for Economic and Social Research
NJAC	National Joint Advisory Council
NJC	National Joint Council
NJNC	National Joint Negotiating Committee
NPA	National Ports Authority
NPO	National Ports Organization
NRC	National Referendum Campaign
NUM	National Union of Mineworkers
NUPE	National Union of Public Employees
NUR	National Union of Railwaymen
NUS	National Union of Seamen
NUVB	National Union of Vehicle Builders
OAU	Organization for African Unity
ODM	Overseas Development Ministry
OECD	Organization for Economic Co-operation and Development
OMO	One-man bus operation
OPD	Overseas and Defence Policy
OTO	Overseas Telegraph Operators
OTRU	Overseas tape unity relay
P and I	Prices and Incomes
PEP	Political and Economic Planning
PESC	Public Expenditure Scrutiny Committee
PIB	Prices and Incomes Board
PIF	Prices and Incomes Committee
PLP	Parliamentary Labour Party
PNQ	Private Notice Question
POEU	Post Office Engineering Union
PPS	Parliamentary or principal private secretary
PQ	Parliamentary Question
PRU	Pay Research Unit
PSM	Profession Supplementary to Medicine
PTA	Passenger Transport Authority
RAWP	Resources Allocation Working Party
RC	Royal Commission
RCU	Road Construction Unit
RHA	Regional Health Authority, Road Haulage Association
RIBA	Royal Institute of British Architects
SBC	Supplementary Benefits Commission
SCS	Society of Civil Servants
SEP	Economic Strategy Committee
SET	Selective Employment Tax
SMMT	Society of Motor Manufacturers and Traders

TA Tartan Arrow
TAB Technical Assistance Board
TCPA Town and Country Planning Association
TGWU Transport and General Workers Union
THC Transport Holding Company
TSSA Transport and Salaried Staffs Association
TUC Trades Union Congress

UCATT Union of Construction, Allied Trades and Technicians
UCH University College Hospital
UDI Unilateral Declaration of Independence
UNESCO United Nations Educational, Scientific and Cultural Organization
UNO United Nations Organization
UPW Union of Post Office Workers
USDAW Union of Shop, Distributive and Allied Workers

VAT Value Added Tax

WP White Paper

Index